Oracle®8i and Java™

THE PRENTICE HALL PTR ORACLE® SERIES

The Independent Voice on Oracle

ORACLE8™ AND UNIX® PERFORMANCE TUNING
Alomari

ORACLE8*i*™ AND UNIX® PERFORMANCE TUNING
Alomari

SOFTWARE ENGINEERING WITH ORACLE: BEST PRACTICES FOR MISSION-CRITICAL SYSTEMS
Bonazzi

ORACLE8*i*™ AND JAVA™: FROM CLIENT/SERVER TO E-COMMERCE
Bonazzi/Stokol

ORACLE8™ DATABASE ADMINISTRATION FOR WINDOWS NT®
Brown

WEB DEVELOPMENT WITH ORACLE PORTAL
El-Mallah

ORACLE DESK REFERENCE
Harrison

ORACLE SQL® HIGH PERFORMANCE TUNING, SECOND EDITION
Harrison

ORACLE DESIGNER: A TEMPLATE FOR DEVELOPING AN ENTERPRISE STANDARDS DOCUMENT
Kramm/Graziano

ORACLE DEVELOPER/2000 FORMS
Lulushi

ORACLE FORMS DEVELOPER'S HANDBOOK
Lulushi

ORACLE SQL® INTERACTIVE WORKBOOK
Morrison/Rischert

ORACLE FORMS INTERACTIVE WORKBOOK
Motivala

ORACLE PL/SQL™ INTERACTIVE WORKBOOK
Rosenzweig/Silvestrova

ORACLE DBA INTERACTIVE WORKBOOK
Scherer/Caffrey

ORACLE DEVELOPER 2000 HANDBOOK, SECOND EDITION
Stowe

DATA WAREHOUSING WITH ORACLE
Yazdani/Wong

ORACLE CERTIFIED DBA EXAM QUESTION AND ANSWER BOOK
Yazdani/Wong/Tong

Oracle8i and Java
From Client/Server to e-Commerce

Elio Bonazzi

Glenn Stokol

Prentice Hall PTR
Upper Saddle River, New Jersey 07458

Library of Congress Cataloging-in-Publication Data

Bonazzi, Elio
Oracle8i and Java : from client/server to E-commerce / Elio Bonazzi, Glenn Stokol.
p. cm.
ISBN 0-13-017613-3
1. Oracle (Computer file) 2. Java (Computer program language) 3. Client/server computing. 4. E-commerce. I. Stokol, Glenn. II. Title.

QA76.9.D3 B655 2001
005.75'85--dc21

2001021849

Acquisitions editor: *Tim Moore*
Cover designer: *Nina Scuderi*
Cover design director: *Jerry Votta*
Manufacturing manager: *Maura Zaldivar*
Editorial Assistant: *Allyson Kloss*
Marketing manager: *Debby van Dijk*
Project coordinator: *Anne Trowbridge*
Compositor/Production services: *Pine Tree Composition, Inc.*

Prentice-Hall, Inc.
Upper Saddle River, New Jersey 07458

Prentice Hall books are widely used by corporations and government agencies for training, marketing, and resale.

The publisher offers discounts on this book when ordered in bulk quantities. For more information contact:

Corporate Sales Department
Phone: 800-382-3419
Fax: 201-236-7141
E-mail: corpsales@prenhall.com

Or write:

Prentice Hall PTR
Corp. Sales Dept.
One Lake Street
Upper Saddle River, New Jersey 07458

Printed in the United States of America
10 9 8 7 6 5 4 3 2 1

ISBN 0-13-017613-3

Pearson Education Ltd.
Pearson Education Australia PTY, Ltd.
Pearson Education Singapore, Pte. Ltd.
Pearson Education North Asia Ltd.
Pearson Education Canada, Ltd.
Pearson Educación de Mexico, S.A. de C.V.
Pearson Education—Japan
Pearson Education Malaysia, Pte. Ltd.
Pearson Education, Upper Saddle River, New Jersey

To Professor Ian Angell, the author of "The New Barbarian Manifesto," who introduced me to techno-libertarianism and made me aware of "The Global Consequences of Information Technology."

Elio Bonazzi

To my loves and joy, my wife Sharon and son Michael.

Glenn Stokol

CONTENTS

INTRODUCTION AND OVERVIEW

This book is about software development using Oracle and Java, two of the most powerful and robust platforms available for building Internet-enabled applications. Since there are many books about Oracle, and even more about Java, we embarked on this project to bring these two worlds together, firm in our belief that there are few books that give a detailed perspective by combining the strengths of Oracle and Java in one book. We see this book as a valuable friend, learning aid, and reference for any Java developer building web-enabled applications accessing an Oracle database.

This is a book written for developers by seasoned professionals who have been actively using and teaching Oracle and Java technology for some years. The focus of *Oracle8i and Java: From Client/Server to E-Commerce* is primarily from a software developer's perspective. However, application designers and system architects will also find this book valuable because they will gain a broad and solid understanding of combining the object oriented world of Java with the object-relational world of Oracle technology. With this in mind, we have assumed that:

- You already know how to develop basic Java code and understand the fundamental object-oriented features of the Java language.
- You may have used SQL and relational databases, possibly even Oracle, but do not know much detail about Oracle databases.

Therefore, a portion of this book is devoted to Oracle database fundamentals and object-relational features found in SQL and PL/SQL. The first chapter provides a discussion of the database model and tables used for most of the examples found in the book. When coupled with the SQL and PL/SQL chapters, it provides a foundation on which to build Java code that capitalizes on the best features of an Oracle database.

If you are already experienced with Oracle SQL and PL/SQL, you may find that you can skip the first six chapters of the book. However, we recommend that you read the first chapter, and encourage you to look at the early chapters, as we believe you are likely to find valuable information on the Oracle database architecture, SQL and PL/SQL functionality, and, particularly, information on using object-relational structures.

Many organizations are now building web-enabled applications, most likely for electronic commerce. Thus, the contents of this book place an emphasis on Java development using technology in the middle-tier such as Oracle Application Server or equivalent web servers, and, in the backend, using an Oracle8i database. During this project there were rapid changes in the Java and Oracle software platforms, making the task of keeping up with these moving targets impossible, and we were in danger of being caught in a never-ending documentation cycle. Like all projects, there had to be an end, and despite the fact that Oracle released a successor to Oracle Application Server, i.e. Oracle9i Application Server, and announced that Oracle9i was around the corner, we felt this book had a great deal to offer and know that its contents, for the most part, will be applicable in the context of future releases of Java and Oracle software.

The code examples were developed using either Oracle8i Release 1 (8.1.5) and/or Release 2 (8.1.6) using the JDK 1.1.8 and, in some cases, JDK 1.2 with JDeveloper 3.0 and JDeveloper 3.1. The platforms used for code development included Microsoft Windows, Solaris, and Linux. Historically, the original title of the book was *Oracle for Java Programmers,* which was replaced by its published title *Oracle8i and Java: From Client/Server to E-Commerce.* For this reason, you will find our source code examples use Java package names like `com.prenhall.OFJP.*`, where the `OFJP` acronym was derived from the first letters of the original book title.

THE STRUCTURE OF THE BOOK CONTENTS

The first chapter provides unique coverage of using an object-oriented database design approach and transformation into a relational, or object-relational implementation, by using an object-oriented style of persistence that closely fits the world of Java application development. In addition, there is coverage of Oracle8 SQL Object types and SQL collections that are not widely used, and, therefore, not widely written about in the context of Java and SQLJ applications. Information on SQL Objects, provided here, will provide a basic understanding enabling you to leap into the promising future releases of the Oracle database with impending changes to the object-relational functionality that cannot be covered in this book due to time constraints.

Although this book has no physical indication of major parts, the twenty-four chapters are logically arranged into four parts:

- **Part I: Oracle Object-Relational Databases and the SQL Language** introduces you to some object and relational database analysis and design principles, and mapping an object design to a relational implementation. You are provided with a basic introduction to Oracle SQL and PL/SQL, and discussions highlighting new features found in Oracle8i syntax. The SQL and PL/SQL chapters provide less comprehensive examples to cover syntax, avoid creating a huge book, and cover subject matter well covered elsewhere. The chapters included in this part are:
  - Chapter 1: Introduction to Oracle Object-Relational Database Design and Architecture
  - Chapter 2: Data Definition Language (DDL) Statements
  - Chapter 3: Query Processing
  - Chapter 4: Data Manipulation Language (DML) Statements and Transactions
  - Chapter 5: Oracle Architecture and Performance Considerations
  - Chapter 6: Internet Security and Oracle Security
- **Part II: Oracle PL/SQL and Java Stored Procedures, Business Components and XML** discusses programmatic functionality within the database in the form of PL/SQL and Java Stored procedures, and outside the database using Java with comprehensive coverage of JDBC 1.0 and some JDBC 2.0 features, and a chapter devoted to SQLJ technology. A special highlight in this group of chapters is the introduction to Oracle Business Components for Java—a framework of generated Java classes and XML files used to manage your database data independent of the user presentation layer. Oracle Business Components for Java is a technology yet to be discovered and can change the way your Java applications manage database data in any relational database. The chapters applicable to this part are:
  - Chapter 7: Introduction to PL/SQL
  - Chapter 8: PL/SQL Procedures, Functions, Packages, and Exceptions
  - Chapter 9: Data Access with JDBC–Java Database Connectivity
  - Chapter 10: Enhanced Database Access with JDBC
  - Chapter 11: Data Access with SQLJ–Embedding SQL in Java
  - Chapter 12: Java Stored Procedures in Oracle
  - Chapter 13: Business Components for Java and XML
- **Part III: Middleware: Servlets, Java Server Pages and Application Servers** devotes itself to developing Java code in the middle-tier. Therefore, as the

title states, you read about Java Servlets and JavaServer Pages using the Oracle platform, while non-Oracle environments are discussed for contrast. This section is also about scalability, and covers connection pooling, advanced queuing, distributing, and replicating the Oracle database data. Integration techniques are covered for web-enabling legacy systems through the use of Java Native Interface (JNI) API, and Java network sockets. The chapters that cover these topics include:
  - Chapter 14: Data Access Using Java Servlets and Connection Pooling
  - Chapter 15: Java Server Pages and Active Server Pages
  - Chapter 16: Using Java in Oracle Application Server
  - Chapter 17: Web-Enabling Legacy Applications Using Network Sockets
  - Chapter 18: Web-Enabling Legacy Applications Using JNI
  - Chapter 19: Accessing Oracle Advanced Queuing Through Java
  - Chapter 20: Using Oracle Replication to Build Distributed Systems
- **Part IV: Oracle8i: The Internet Database (The Engine Room)** covers Java components in the database. The chapters in this section guide you through development and deployment of Session Enterprise JavaBean in the Oracle8i database, use of security, and transaction management services provided by the Oracle8i Enterprise JavaBean container. Two chapters are devoted to developing Java application code to be deployed as CORBA objects inside the Oracle8i database engine. The chapter titles are:
  - Chapter 21: The Enterprise JavaBean: An Introduction
  - Chapter 22: Deploying and Using an Enterprise JavaBean
  - Chapter 23: CORBA and its Implementation in Oracle8i: An Overview
  - Chapter 24: Advanced CORBA Topics

From this structure it should be evident there is much breadth and depth in the material. Therefore, we trust you will find this book a valuable resource for your work using Java and Oracle technology.

DOWNLOADING ORACLE SOFTWARE

The Oracle Technology Network (OTN) is an industry-first Developer Service Provider (DSP) that offers a broad set of services for developing, testing, and deploying Oracle-based solutions and applications. These include a supporting workplace environment for online collaborative development, online support with access to Oracle and industry experts, as well as free software downloads, technical libraries, and a job marketplace for Oracle-related positions. Membership is FREE, and so is the latest development software. Join OTN today at http://www.oracle.com/books/.

You can also join and visit Oracle Technology network at http://technet.oracle.com.

AUTHOR NOTES

Before we embarked on the project resulting in this book, Elio had seen his first efforts as an author come to fruition with release of his book *Software Engineering with Oracle,* published by Prentice Hall. Elio was actively involved in several projects as an architect for Java-based systems, and had run out of time and space to include Java material in a book devoted to designing and developing C/C++ based applications with Oracle. In my case, I had been actively teaching Java courses and providing consulting services for Java and database related projects.

Elio had indicated a crazy desire (in his own terms, and with hindsight I agree) to write about Java and Oracle, which had become a passion for him as it was for me. My involvement in this book began with an idle suggestion that Elio should consider writing a book about Java and Oracle with a coauthor (i.e., me), saving him the monstrous effort of writing yet another book by himself. We both laughed off the suggestion and I thought it was dropped, until two weeks later Elio called me and said I was employed as a coauthor and that Prentice Hall jumped at the suggestion.

We soon embarked on a six-month plan to write an advanced book on Java and Oracle, assuming that our audience would already know the basics of using Oracle SQL and PL/SQL, and had core Java programming skills under their belt.

After some initial reviews it became evident that our plan was perceived to be too complex. After all, that's what we embarked on and that was our initial intent. Elio and I relented to suggestions to simplify the content and ease the reader into the more complex topics. This involved a redesign of a book, which started out with 5 huge chapters broken into lots of smaller digestible pieces, twenty-four chapters organized into 4 logical parts to be exact. This resulted in more manageable pieces of information for you as the reader, but it took much longer to complete, eighteen instead of the original six months. The time to complete this book increased for several reasons:

- Elio and I were writing in our spare time. This generally amounted to 3 or 4 hours a night and, in some cases, all nighters resulting in sandy eyes and short tempers.
- The work load in our respective jobs increased due to the changes in software versions hitting the market.
- With the new versions of software available, we endeavored to update our code and commentary, but had to stop to avoid the never ending catch up trap that one can fall into in these circumstances.
- My wife Sharon was pregnant with our first child, who was born in the latter stages of writing this book. My best intention was to have finished this book before my son Michael was born, but life circumstances were getting in the way, making the task of completing the project even more of a challenge. My focus in spare hours was joyfully with my family, and the late nights got later and longer.

I share this information with you as a way of documenting the journey that I took to complete the creation of this book, not as a list of excuses. Now I am the proud father of two: Michael and this book. The more important one arrived first!

ACKNOWLEDGMENTS

The creation of this book was with the assistance, support, encouragement, and professionalism of many individuals. Without the labor and commitment of our team, this book would not have been a great reference your bookshelf. A special, huge amount of thanks must go to Bryan Higgs our technical reviewer who we chose as a replacement for the initial reviewers employed for the book. For you budding authors, I strongly advise that you employ a good reviewer who will be constructively critical and has an eye for detail. Bryan Higgs provided even more than those two important services, and also spent his valuable spare time reviewing this book causing me to choose to rewrite at least two chapters, but definitely for the better. I had to learn to swallow my pride, and learn that it was acceptable to scrap some work to start again in order to provide you with some more clarity and a better reading experience. Bryan's professionalism and work was above and beyond the call of duty.

Additional special thanks must go to the Prentice Hall team, Tim Moore, Mike Meehan, Anne Trowbridge, Patty Donovan, Dana Smith, of Pine Tree Composition, and particularly to Russ Hall, our developmental editor, who probably thought that this project would be completed in the blink of an eye, but found that it was like running a marathon. Russ, thanks for your encouragement, for cracking the whip, and for your support for the duration of this project. I hope the two Tooheys (Australia beer) that I sent eased the process a bit. I would be happy to send you more. At least, I now have the leisure time to indulge myself in purchasing and reading the books that you have written.

Indebted thanks must go to my wife Sharon, who exercised an enormous amount of patience with me, particularly in light of the long duration of this project. Sharon had promised to be the project manager to keep me on target, but taking care of herself and the growing baby inside was much higher on the agenda. Had Sharon acted on her suggestion, I would have been finished months ago. I also thank my son Michael for being an incredible being and a joy in this world, particularly for being a fantastic sleeper at such a young age. Thanks to Brett Hannath, before he left Oracle, for his support and contacts. Thank you to Frank Cselko, Director, Oracle Education Australia, for his support, interest, and encouragement in my efforts and always asking how it was going, and often wondering if it was ever going to end. Thanks, Andrew Killen and John Hall for granting approval to publish this work. Special acknowledgement to all my colleagues for their assistance, and for being additional resources for me. To Kishore Bhamidipati for his friendship and suggestions. Thanks to Cecelia Glover and Alex Weisiger for guiding me through my legal obligations with Oracle, and the process of trying to obtain Oracle software that unfortunately could not be included with this book for various reasons. Thanks to Tony Obermeit for always asking the real hard questions and pushing my boundaries, and particularly for the humorous email messages that kept my perspective about this world balanced and sane, or should that be insane! Thanks to my students for asking many difficult questions in class and driving me to find answers for the harder questions. There are numerous others who have been involved and I apologize for not mentioning you all, but thanks for being there!

Finally, thank you Elio for being a great friend, resource, technical guru, and so easy going! It has been a pleasure to work with you on another project! To Marcia and George, I am sorry you had to go through a repeat episode of book writing; I will not embark on a project like this, and the way we did it, again.

Glenn Stokol

I would like to thank several people who helped me write this book. Vadim Leovski, from Quest Software Melbourne, a true PL/SQL guru, accomplished the difficult task of setting me straight in my Java enthusiasm by showing me that PL/SQL is not an obsolete piece of archeology, but still a very useful component of the Oracle platform, which can achieve its peak when properly used in conjunction with Java. Section 12.4, "PL/SQL versus Java: Choosing the Right Tool for your Task" is the direct result of our discussions (somebody could say arguments. . .).

Every day we learn something new, by sharing ideas and exchanging experiences with our colleagues and friends. I feel I have to quote as "indirect" contributors to this book my friends Gerard Hocks, Peter Maher, Julian and Gerard Neil (Gid), and Daniel Parnell; we often discuss computers, and share the same passion for leading-edge electronic toys and new technologies. The constant interaction with these people gave me the necessary incentive to research and deepen my knowledge about Java and Oracle. Rob Griffin and Julian Salerno are by no means Oracle experts, but I learned a lot of Java re-use from them. They showed me how to design components that work in different and varied scenarios, and taught me never to be happy with something that merely satisfies the immediate needs, but is too specific to be reused in the future in a slightly different context. I hope I have been able to transmit most of the knowledge acquired from my interactions with all the talented IT professionals I have been lucky to work with throughout this book.

Bryan Higgs directly contributed to improve the overall quality of "Oracle and Java: From Client/Server to E-Commerce." While Glenn and I are fully responsible for any inaccuracy or mistake contained in the book, Bryan performed an outstanding task, often within a very tight schedule, to pinpoint potential issues and problems, and to correct technical mistakes. We owe Bryan a lot for his efforts; I hope to return the favor to him one day.

This book would not have seen the light without the hard work of several staff members at Prentice Hall. I would like to thank Tim Moore, the initial acquisition editor, who effectively started this project. Tim has been replaced by Mike

Meehan, who caught up quickly and competently. Anne Trowbridge, the production coordinator, managed the difficult task of putting up with my sarcasm, my way of reacting to the little glitches that inevitably affect projects of this size and length.

Russ Hall, our developmental editor, himself an author, is a guy who writes "real" books, like fiction and action thrillers. He has been involved in the project to help us write proper English. I hope he didn't get too bored by the dry content of the chapters he had to revise with an eye to grammar, punctuation, etc. If you are not into Oracle or Java, it must be terrible to read more than one thousand pages of source code, acronyms, technical terms, and the like. Thanks, Russ. With your help, this book is definitely more readable.

Lastly I would like to thank Patty Donovan, our project editor, who gave the final touch to the aesthetics of this book.

Elio Bonazzi

ABOUT THE AUTHORS

Elio Bonazzi (left) and Glenn Stokol

Glenn Stokol was born in Johannesburg, South Africa, in 1960, and became an Australian citizen after migrating to Australia in 1981. After graduating from Monash University in 1983, Glenn began working in the computer industry as a software developer for a company providing hardware and software to the world of typography for high-end publishing. Since then, Glenn's career evolved into a technical consulting role, encompassing a broader set of experiences as a software architect and designer of myriads of applications ranging from business systems to distributed network applications covering the full life cycle of software development, from design through implementation and support. Glenn worked on many programming assignments with a wide range of languages including PDP-11 Macro, Pascal, Algol, Fortran, mostly C, Oracle databases Pro*C, SQL, and PL/SQL. It was during one of these projects that Glenn and Elio worked together on using Oracle technology for a large retail organization. Their friendship grew though mutual professional and external interests yet both took different paths into the exciting world of Java.

Glenn currently works for Oracle Corporation Australia as a Java Specialist, teaching a range of Oracle training courses to customers. Training and ad-hoc consulting assignments keep Glenn abreast of the real issues that customers face in building industry strength Internet applications. Prior to writing this book, Glenn cut his teeth writing several articles for Oracle Australian User group newsletters, and delivering presentations, tutorials, and hands on sessions at various events in Australia, such as Oracle Openworld, iDevelop, ObjectWorld, and JavaAus conferences.

Glenn is not only a new author, but also the father of an eight month old, helping his young son work though a period of cutting his real teeth. Besides working with technology, Glenn is passionate about music, and is an accomplished percussionist, having played drums in reception bands, rock bands, a big band, Jazz ensembles, and musical theatre, to tympani in an orchestra. Glenn continues to expand his musical skills by studying piano.

Elio Bonazzi was born in Calais, France, in 1960. He started his IT career in Italy, initially as a DEC employee, and later as a free-lance consultant for VMS/RdB projects. At the beginning of the '90s Elio made his transition from OpenVMS/RdB to Unix and Oracle. After an initial cultural shock, Elio started loving Unix more than OpenVMS. This passion is still alive today: Elio's laptop runs Linux, and his desktop system at home is a Sun workstation.

In November 1992, Elio migrated to Australia, where he continued to work as a consultant in the field of mission-critical, Oracle-based IT projects. He has been providing his consulting services to telecommunication companies, large retail organizations, and governmental utilities. The two common threads in all projects where Elio worked have been the Oracle database and the criticality to the business of the application being developed. In 1997, Elio started falling in love with Java. Since 1999 Elio has been working as a system architect on projects that use Java technologies to access relational databases. In most cases this means Oracle, but Elio has also worked with IBM DB2 and, more recently, Postgresql. Occasionally, Elio works as an instructor for Oracle Corporation, teaching a range of Oracle training courses, mainly in the Java stream.

Elio is currently working for Quest Software Australia, leading a project in the field of performance monitoring of Java application servers.

Apart from technology and Computer Science, which take most of his time, Elio enjoys practicing scuba diving, skiing, and skydiving. He doesn't share Glenn's great musical talent, but he likes listening to classical music and Opera.

Chapter 1

Introduction to Oracle Object-Relational Database Design and Architecture

- Relational Model and Design for the Bookstore
- Importance of the Database Model and Design
- Transforming an ERD into a Table Design
- Transforming Supertype and Subtype Entities
- Generic Subtype Design
- Table or System Design
- Object Model and Design for the Bookstore
- Mapping the Class Model to an Oracle Database
- Object to Relational Mapping Rules
- Summary

This chapter provides a basic introduction to the Oracle Object-Relational Database architecture. You will learn about the design and structure of the bookstore database and some of the associated functionality. The database is first documented using an entity relationship diagram (ERD) to represent the business information requirements. The ERD is transformed into a database design to give a system/technical view of the data needs. The Oracle database structure is represented as a basic ERD model, and you are shown logically where the data for tables or indexes are stored.

In subsequent chapters, you will learn how to use the SQL language to implement the database structures specified by the models and design decisions you make. Your Java applications use the SQL language through JDBC or SQLJ technology to process the database data.

1.1 RELATIONAL MODEL AND DESIGN FOR THE BOOKSTORE

The bookstore has a simple database that holds the records of book products available for purchase. Each customer must register with the bookstore before purchases can be made. The customer can browse the products and search for them using the criteria available. It is not mandatory for a customer to place an order for a product.

Once having decided to purchase products, the customer adds items to a shopping basket. The shopping basket is created when the first item is selected. A cumulative total is built as items are added to the basket, and this total is visible when the contents of the basket are viewed. The contents of the basket are only transferred to the official order entry tables in the database when the customer submits the order with the payment details.

The contents of the shopping basket are copied to the order items when the order is created and the basket contents are deleted. A courier is immediately associated with the order and is selected by the customer when he or she accepts the purchases made.

The summary of the business rules presented here has been simplified to keep examples focused and unencumbered by too much detail. As you read this book, additional detail will be revealed about some of the business rules governing design decisions for the bookstore database, and about the implications of the changes needed to modify the structures to build a real-life implementation for the bookstore system.

The entity relationship diagram representing the bookstore's information requirements is shown in Figure 1.1.

The ERD represents the key business rules that govern the way data are stored and related in the database. The ERD is a *conceptual model* of information needs, although it is often called a *logical model*. The ERD model was created using Custom Development Method (CDM) diagramming conventions and nota-

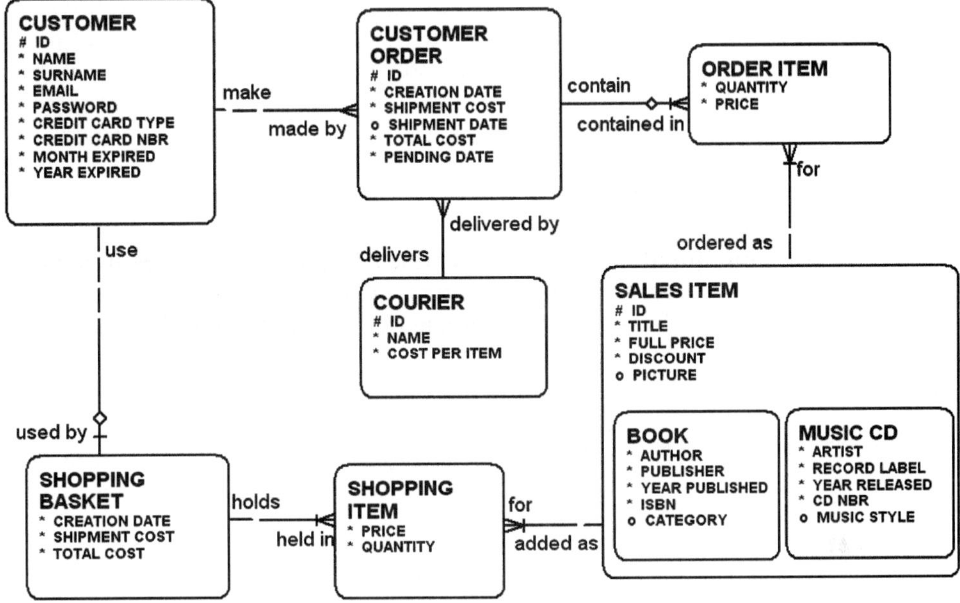

FIGURE 1.1 ERD of the bookstore

tion.[1] Depending on your education, and the tools available, the diagram conventions are different but intrinsically similar. The meaning of the CDM notation in used in the ERD is explained in subsequent sections of this chapter.

1.1.1 ENTITY NOTATION

Each entity is represented as a round-cornered box, with its name is written in uppercase and singular form. For example: CUSTOMER.

1.1.2 ATTRIBUTE NOTATION

Each attribute is written in lowercase text in singular form and is marked with one of the following characters:

- # indicates that the attribute is part of the unique identifier; it must be mandatory if it is part of the primary key, but it can be optional as a unique key.
- * indicates that the attribute value is mandatory, i.e., its value must be known (a null value is not allowed).

[1]CDM is a modeling convention developed by Richard Barker who was an employee of Oracle Corporation. The diagrams created by the Oracle Designer tool are based on CDM conventions.

- **o** means that the attribute value is optional, i.e., it can be unknown (a null value is allowed). Names are in singular form and written in lowercase. Attributes with more than one word are listed in full with spaces, as shown in Figure 1.1.

1.1.3 RELATIONSHIP NOTATION

Lines are drawn to link entities in a relationship. Each relationship line has an *optionality* (minimum cardinality), a *degree* (maximum cardinality), and a *name.* The optionality indicates a mandatory (*must be*) or an optional (*may be*) relationship.

- A solid line indicates a mandatory relationship. For example, each ORDER ITEM *must be* contained in a CUSTOMER ORDER.
- A dotted line indicates an optional relationship. For example, each SALES ITEM *may be* ordered as an ORDER ITEM, which implies that some sale items may not be ordered at all.

A relationship line can be entirely mandatory, completely optional, or half one and half the other. The degree indicates the maximum cardinality that can be related to one record of the related entity. There are two ways of representing the degree:

- A single line, meaning *one and only one.*
- Three lines, called a *crow's foot*, meaning *one or more.*

The relationship names at each end of a relationship complete the business rules defining the relationship between entities. Relationship names are highly recommended to give clarity and completeness to the conceptual model.

A small single bar line, called a *UID bar,* can be drawn across one end of a relationship line. The UID bar is typically found the on the same side as a crow's foot. It indicates that each instance of the entity nearest the UID bar is uniquely identified by the combination of primary unique attributes from the two entities involved in the marked relationship. An example in the Figure 1.1 ERD diagram is the ORDER ITEM entity. To uniquely identify a specific instance (row) of an order item, you must know the order number and item number.

A diamond shape on a line represents a non-transferable relationship. For example, the shopping basket for one customer cannot be associated with another customer, and therefore, by definition, is nontransferable.

The relationship is read from both directions, resulting in basic rules. When reading the relationship, you start at one entity, which is called the *source entity*, the other one being the *related entity*. The following rule can be used to complete the meaning of each relationship:

Each **{source entity}** *{optionality}* *{<u>relationship-name</u>}* *{degree}* *{***related entity***}*

This forms a statement about each relationship to validate the model. The following notational conventions assist in understanding the syntax for reading ERD relationships:

- Entity names are in bold normal text.
- Relationship optionality is in italic text before the relationship name.
- Relationship names are in underlined italic text.
- Degree is in italic text after the relationship name.

For example, take the relationship represented in Figure 1.2, which was extracted from the ERD model in Figure 1.1.

Reading the relationship using the specified syntax and starting with the CUSTOMER entity, the relationship means:

Each **CUSTOMER** *may* *<u>make</u>* *one or more* **CUSTOMER ORDER***s*

Since relationships are bidirectional, you need to create a relationship rule starting with the CUSTOMER ORDER entity, and the relationship now reads:

Each **CUSTOMER ORDER** *must be* *<u>made by</u>* *one and only one* **CUSTOMER.**

In the resulting relationship business rule or statement, the word *each* indicates that the relationship is read out as it would apply for *one instance* of the source entity (e.g., CUSTOMER) associated to the instances of the related entity (e.g., CUSTOMER ORDER). The optional relationship (dotted line), at the customer end, indicates that a customer may exist but does not have to make an

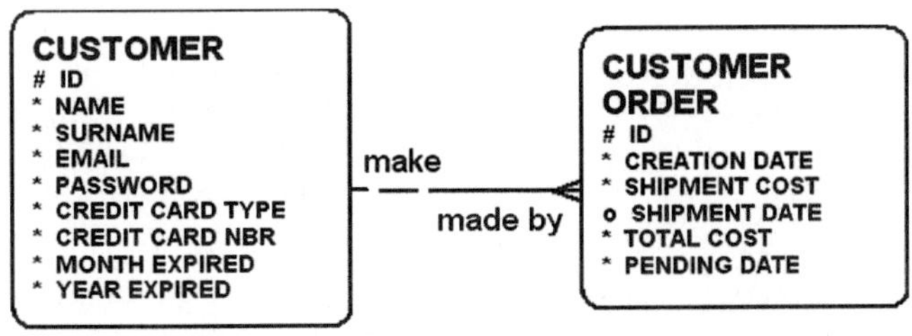

FIGURE 1.2 Customer and order relationship

order, known as a *zero-to-many* relationship. Note that there are other ERD diagramming conventions that follow similar semantics but are visually different.

To validate the model, you ask whether two statements derived from a relationship between entities are true for the business. If the business analyst or owner ratifies the statements, the model is an accurate representation of the information required; if not, modifications to the model are necessary.

Once all the relationships have been validated, the ERD model is developed into a system representation, also called a *logical model.*[2] The logical model, which is the system's view of the data, typically goes through changes and refinements to create a physical database. The primary goal of an ERD design is to visually represent a relationship between entities, and also to normalize the data. Normalization is part of the ERD design process, and often an independent process, to remove redundant (duplicate) storage of data items. When the ERD is converted into the physical database table design, the changes or refinements that can be made involve:

- ❑ Physical organization of the database files that store the data.
- ❑ Using database views for ease of access or security reasons.
- ❑ Applying table partitioning for performance.
- ❑ Adding, removing, or disabling indexes and integrity rules.
- ❑ Denormalization and data summarization, which are both forms of adding redundant information to the data storage. Denormalized and summarized data do not usually appear in an ERD model unless you are modeling a data warehouse, but they do usually appear in the logical or physical database design.
- ❑ Adding historical data.

These issues are common to all relational database designs, and are done to address issues of performance and security. For simplicity and clarity, the bookstore schema shows some redundancy in the ERD model to avoid lengthy discussions about transformation and philosophical design issues that are always associated with a tradeoff between performance, code simplicity, and data storage requirements.

An ERD model is considered to be independent of the choice of physical database implemented. However, the ERD model is typically converted into a re-

---

[2]The terms "conceptual model" and "logical model" are often used interchangeably for both the ERD and the table model of the database. The term "data model" makes things even more confusing, because it encompasses the logical and physical data models The terminology in this book defines a conceptual model as an abstract representation of real-world information, and a logical model as a representation of the conceptual model using a specific type of technology for implementation; for example, using a relational logical model, which in many cases may as well be the physical model.

lational database implementation. From the availability of Oracle8, an object-based relational implementation is also possible.

1.2 IMPORTANCE OF THE DATABASE MODEL AND DESIGN

The data model is important for a high-level understanding of the business rules, and makes it easy to change and convey the business information requirements in a simple way. The model is primarily used for:

- Communication with all of the stakeholders in the system.
- Communication with the system designers as the starting point for the database design and implementation.
- Design documentation purposes.

Using a tool like Oracle Designer makes it easy to build a model, maintain changes to it, and generate an initial design from the model using standard transformation rules.

The database table design is important for developers to know because it facilitates the understanding of the data values, relationships, and validation rules that must be followed to meet the business needs identified by the model. Developers writing code to access a database must have an understanding of the data model in order to write the SQL statements that produce the correct results.

As a Java developer, you can create an object representation of a data row in a table by defining a class containing attributes with compatible data types for each column. The class definition may be created with or without methods. Alternatively, if the database table is created as an Oracle object table of a user-defined *object type*, then your Java class is typically created to mirror the structure of the object type.

The goal of creating Java classes to represent data stored in a row or an object table is to enable developers to work with database data in a way natural to Java. The Java classes create a layer of abstraction on top of the data-access mechanisms, and shield the Java programmer from the specific data-access logic used to access the database.

The task of creating Java classes and methods to encapsulate and implement business logic and validation rules for each table can be time-consuming. Oracle creates a Java framework of classes, called Business Components for Java that encapsulates the database data, business, and validation rules. JDeveloper, an Oracle Java development tool, has built-in functionality to generate a Business Components for Java framework for any relational database. Not surprisingly, the set of classes created in each framework are called entity and view objects. *Entity objects* encapsulate the database tables, and implement business and validation rules to ensure data integrity. *View objects* allow the developer to gather data from entity objects suited to the specific needs of some application. View and entity objects are collectively used to build an application or reusable application component to manage data access and manipulation.

1.3 TRANSFORMING AN ERD INTO A TABLE DESIGN

The bookstore model, used as the basis for various code examples in this book, is transformed into a relational table design by applying a simple one-to-one mapping from the ERD model that converts most of the entities shown in Figure 1.1 into its corresponding database table. Here are the rules that govern mapping an ERD to a table design:

1. *Each entity becomes a table.* The name of the table is typically the same as the name of the entity. In accordance with the naming rules for structures in the database entity, names are often abbreviated or given an alias.[3] The CDM school of thought makes the table name the plural form of the entity name. In this book, the table names are kept singular, as in the ERD model. The only exception is the CUSTOMER ORDER entity, in which the word CUSTOMER is abbreviated to CUST.
2. *Each attribute becomes a column in the owning table.* The column name derived from the attribute name replaces spaces with underscored characters.
3. *Each relationship is converted into a foreign key column.* The foreign key column is added to the table, which is at the many or mandatory end of a relationship line.[4] A relationship is formed between rows when a value in a foreign key column has the same value as a primary or unique key column in a related table. The foreign key is a *logical* association rather than a physical association, because the database does not store pointers from one column to the other. The ERD model does not show the foreign key columns as an attribute in each entity, because the ERD is a conceptual view of information requirements, and foreign keys are meaningful in the table design. Therefore, the relationship lines in the ERD imply the need for a foreign key.
4. The *unique identifiers*, attributes marked with the hash character (#), *are converted either to a primary or a unique key.* If an entity has more than one unique

[3]When using abbreviations, it is important to be consistent. To ensure consistent names and abbreviations, designers should construct domain-specific naming and abbreviation standards for each project.

[4]If the relationship is a one-to-one relationship, then the foreign key is placed in the table at the mandatory end of the relationship. If the relationship is fully optional one-to-one, the foreign key can go to either table, but typically to the one that contains more records.

identifier, each of them is numbered to identify that there is more than one way to determine uniqueness for each instance of the entity. One of the unique identifiers is selected to be the primary key, and the others become unique keys.

1.4 TRANSFORMING SUPERTYPE AND SUBTYPE ENTITIES

The SALES ITEM entity is designed as a *supertype*. In relational terms, a supertype contains one or more subtypes.[5] All subtypes must be mutually exclusive from one another. For example, a sales item record representing a book cannot also be a music CD. Additionally, all attributes and relationships defined in the supertype apply to each subtype. A subtype may also have its own relationships and attributes.

> The supertype/subtype concept is analogous to an object hierarchy. The supertype is the generalization holding common attributes and relationships, and the subtype is the specialization that holds attributes and relationships unique to the subtype.

In the bookstore data model, each subtype is "a *kind*" of sales item. Although the model shows books and music CD's, the initial design caters only to books.

The supertype and subtype components of the ERD model provide a way for analysts to indicate that new and different types of sales items may be added to the system. Depending on the implementation, changes to the model and design can minimize the impact of changes on applications. With this design, it becomes even more important to separate the application business logic from the data-access logic by employing encapsulation techniques for data-access code. The supertype and subtype entities can be implemented as one or more tables. The choices for implementing a supertype and subtype design, as modeled by the SALES ITEM entity, are:

- *A single table for supertype and subtypes.* This implementation implies that an extra column is added as an indicator column to identify the subtype instance represented by each data row in the table (see the PRD_TYPE column in the SALES_ITEM table in Figure 1.3). The supertype may also need to be

[5]A supertype and subtype design can be cleanly mapped into an object-oriented world with the supertype represented as a superclass and the subtype as a subclass.

identified as a subtype, but in the bookstore model the supertype is not meaningful as a subtype.

- *A distinct table for each subtype* with its own copy of the supertype attributes and relationships (foreign key columns). A table is not created for the supertype.
- *Separate tables for the supertype and each subtype,* with a one-to-one mandatory relationship between the supertype table and each subtype table.

For each choice there is a tradeoff to consider involving decisions about:

- Simplicity of data access and integrity rules.
- Performance, such as, minimizing join operations.
- Adding or minimizing duplicate data storage.

A single table for the supertype and subtype is the easiest to implement, but comes with an overhead of wasted space for unused columns. In a single-table implementation, the subtype attributes must be null-valued when the row instance represents a different subtype, thereby adding to the wasted storage space.[6] It is easier to implement referential and data integrity through declarative rules or logic in the database. Oracle provides declarative constraints and database triggers that can be applied to tables to enforce integrity (Declarative constraints are covered in Chapter 2).

Implementing a design with a distinct table for each subtype is appropriate if there are more differences between the subtypes in terms of number and type of attributes, and if there are fewer attributes in the supertype. In addition, referential integrity is harder to implement, for example, to ensure that supertype attributes are not duplicated in different subtype instances. Whenever you add a new subtype, you must create a new table and add node code to the application. Application coding is more work, since the developer must know which table to access for the required data, and more joins are required to access more than one subtype's data at the same time. In addition, storage space is better used; and attribute definitions can be kept in line with the model specification.

An implementation that uses separate tables for the supertype and the subtypes is closest to an object-oriented approach. In this approach, the supertype and subtype tables each hold only the information relevant to their type. A relationship must be formed between the supertype and its subtype tables to keep the appropriate data related, and this adds extra data storage for the foreign key values stored in the subtype. Performance may be an issue if there is a serious need to access all the details of a subtype in addition to the supertype.

---

[6]In an Oracle database, null storage does not have too dramatic an effect, as a null has minimal overhead due to the variable-length record structure.

The physical table implementation can be changed at will, minimizing the impact on applications, if you employ techniques to abstract the way the data are physically stored and accessed by creating a layered application design.[7]

Having covered the design choices and implications for a supertype and subtype scenario, the transformation chosen for the SALES ITEM table is a single-table design, minus the music CD's attributes. If the music CD columns are added to the implementation, then access to the different subtype data can be simplified through the use of database views.[8] Each view can query the data in the SALES_ITEM table using a filter that compares a known value for each subtype against the actual value stored in the PRD_TYPE column. Views can be added and removed without sacrificing the simplicity of data management inherited by a single-table design, thereby providing application developers with more flexible ways of accessing the data.

1.5 GENERIC SUBTYPE DESIGN

A consideration to keep in mind for the addition of the MUSIC CD entity data is that the MUSIC CD subtype is structurally very similar to the BOOK subtype. The number and types of attributes, in this case, are the same, but the interpretations of the attributes are different. The implication is that, instead of adding attributes to the SALES_ITEM table for the music CD attributes, the music CD attributes can overlap the columns already provided by the attributes of the BOOK subtype. This is known as a *generic data design*, and is usually avoided because of the ambiguity in the meaning of the design. The column names need to be altered to be more generic, with the danger of a loss of clarity in the design. Loss of clarity can be addressed by providing adequate documentation. A generic design has considerable advantages for application developers because the code only has to be written once, and adding additional subtypes is as simple as adding new data rows with a different value for the subtype indicator column, thus making the application highly data-driven. A disadvantage arises when the number and data types of the attributes of the subtypes differ. This can be solved using a character data type for the subtype attributes sharing a column definition. Generic design often requires additional code in the application or in SQL statements to perform data conversion, adding a performance overhead, and is considered a bad idea by some data managers and developers. A generic design also adds complexity to the way data integrity rules are managed.

---

[7]The topic of layered application design is thoroughly covered in a Prentice-Hall book called *Software Engineering with Oracle* by Elio Bonazzi.

[8]Database views are queries stored in the database that provide access to the data in one or more tables. The mode of presentation of the views makes them resemble a table.

1.6 TABLE OR SYSTEM DESIGN

The diagram shown in Figure 1.3 is a logical model, or database system design, representing the tables and columns, including the data types required by each column. A design should also include such information as the size of each column. The example diagram was created using Oracle Designer,[9] which does contain column-size information, but it is not visually presented in the figure.

In Figure 1.3, each entity is now shown as a database table with all of its columns including the foreign keys. Although the foreign keys are not visually represented, they can be determined by the column name, which uses as a prefix an abbreviation of the related entity (at the end of a single line entering the entity) to the letter "_ID." For example, the CUST_ID column in the CUST_ORDER table

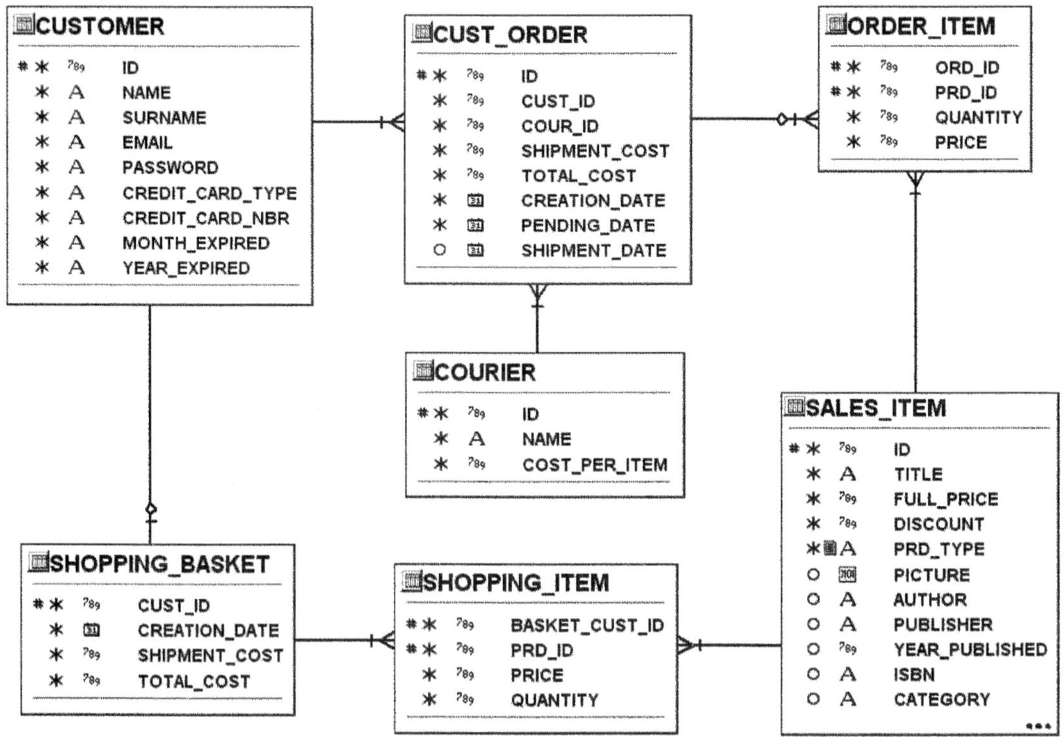

FIGURE 1.3 Server model/table model of bookstore database

[9]Oracle Designer keeps track of the attribute details internally in a repository that is used to build the visual-design representation. This information is used to generate an SQL data-definition language statement required to build the database schema represented in the diagram.

is the foreign key column linking the CUST_ORDER rows to an instance of a CUSTOMER identified by the value in the CUST_ID column.

The diagram in Figure 1.3 is often called a *logical model* because it is still considered to be independent of the physical relational database product. Choosing a physical database can require additional changes to the design. The diagram in Figure 1.3 can now be used to create the SQL data-definition language (DDL) statements to build the physical table structures. One way to implement the logical system model into a physical database is to manually write the SQL statements. Another way is to use a design tool to generate the SQL statements.

1.7 OBJECT MODEL AND DESIGN FOR THE BOOKSTORE

An object-oriented modeling and design approach may also be used for database structures. The "impedance mismatch" between the object-oriented world and a relational database world requires a discussion of mapping options from an object-oriented model to a relational design. Using an Oracle database, the mapping can be done to standard relational tables or to object tables based on Oracle object types.

When you model in an object-oriented way and then wish to transform the model into a relational database, one of the key decisions you need to make is whether to:

- Preserve the object-oriented structure as closely as possible, or
- Dilute the object model to gain the extra benefits that relational technology provides.

There is a tradeoff with each approach, and the following issues will influence your decision:

- Ease of coding.
- Efficiency of data storage.
- Performance.

Using an object-oriented approach to design databases, you typically use a class or object instance diagram (the term *class model*, from this point on in this section, can mean either a class model or an object instance model). The simplest mapping rule is a one-to-one approach that transforms each class in the model into a table. Due to performance considerations, a one-to-one mapping is not always practical, and thus the resulting transformation yields a combination of the following cases:

- A class maps to a single table.
- A class maps to more than one table.
- Multiple classes map to a single table.

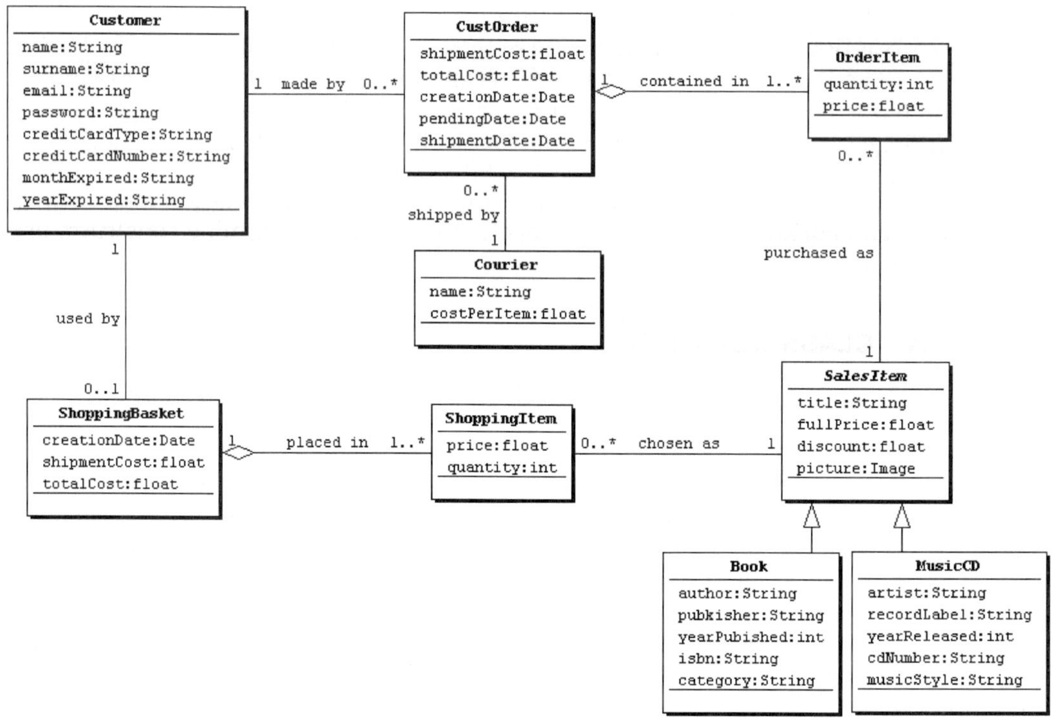

FIGURE 1.4 Bookstore database object-oriented class model

Like an ERD, a class model is constructed to be independent of the technology chosen for implementation. Where no transformation is required, object models are a better choice for pure object-oriented applications and object-oriented databases. As more designers versed in traditional relational design become conversant with object modeling techniques, object modeling will be more widely used even for database design.

The object-oriented model uses class diagram conventions based on the Unified Modeling Language (UML).[10] A class diagram alone is not enough for a complete picture of an object-oriented system, which typically includes developing *state-transition, Interaction (use case/collaboration and sequence)* diagrams. However, a class diagram is sufficient for representing a database design in an object-oriented way. Figure 1.4 is a class diagram that models the bookstore database.

[10]UML was a collaborative development by Grady Booch, Ivar Jacobson, and James Rumbaugh at Rational Software Corporation.

Figure 1.4 is an object-oriented model of the bookstore you have already seen represented using an ERD model. Note that the classes do not all specify a unique identifier as an attribute. The lack of a unique identifier for an attribute is due to the understanding that when an object instance is created from a class, it is automatically assigned a unique object identifier. The mapping of this into a relational table or object table is covered later in this section, where you will see how to transform the class diagram into a relational database representation. First, look at an abridged description of each of the UML diagramming constructs used in Figure 1.4.

1.7.1 CLASS NOTATION

A class is represented, as in Figure 1.5, by a box containing the class name and zero or more attributes and operations.

Attribute names can be shown with or without their data type and an initial value. If a class contains operations (methods),[11] they can specify arguments and a return type. If the class name is italicized, it represents an abstract class. Depending on the tool used, all these details and the scope of attributes and methods may be visible in the diagram. Figure 1.5 does not show method arguments or attribute and method visibility (scope).

Since the diagram in Figure 1.4 is a model that is transformed into a relational database, the methods have not been specified. Methods should be added to the class diagram for the following reasons:

- Your Java application requires class definitions, from which object instances are created for each data row and table.
- The methods specified provide interfaces through which the business rules are implemented and are applied to the associated object attributes. Operations can be as simple as a get or set method, or can involve simple to complex validation rules.

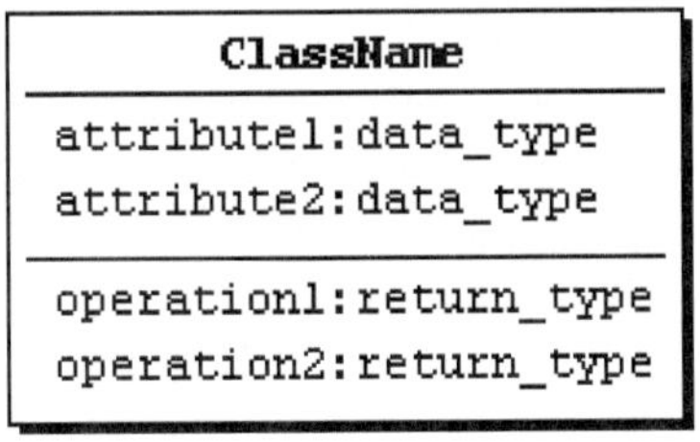

```
ClassName
-----------------------------
attribute1:data_type
attribute2:data_type
-----------------------------
operation1:return_type
operation2:return_type
```

FIGURE 1.5 A UML class

[11]Methods are often omitted when a class is a representation of a database structure.

1.7.2 LINK NOTATION: ASSOCIATIONS AND AGGREGATIONS

In an object-oriented world, a *link* is a physical or conceptual connection between object instances, whereas a relationship in an ERD is a conceptual and logical connection, not a physical one. However, references between Oracle object instances in object tables are physical links.

Relationships in an ERD model are implemented through a foreign key reference. In object types and object-oriented environments, links connecting object instances are implemented through a reference or pointer mechanism.

In UML diagramming, objects are linked by the convention of drawing a line between the objects involved in a relationship. A link line has numbers at each end to indicate the cardinality of the association. Links are represented graphically in one of two ways:

- An *association,* also called a *collaboration* (see Figure 1.6).
- An *aggregation* of objects or a composite object (see Figure 1.7). A composite object has one or more attributes that are themselves object structures.

1.7.2.1 Association Links. Associations, also known as *binary associations* because they are bi-directional, identify a group of links having a common structure and meaning. Figure 1.6 represents an association link between two classes. The association has a name that defines the link direction and meaning of the association. Associations can also define roles and cardinality at each end.

The association name is read from the supplier of the link to the client; that is, Class2 has an association named with Class1. Role names are displayed under the association line, and cardinality is shown above the line. Cardinality, better known as *multiplicity,* is expressed as either

- A single digit *n*, or
- A range *n..m*, where, if *n* is 0, then *m* can be 1, or *, otherwise if *n* is 1, then *m* must be a *.

  Here are some typical multiplicity values:
- 1, as used in Figure 1.6, indicates that a Class2 object holds *exactly one* Class1 object.
- 0 .1, indicates a class object that *may* hold a zero or other class object.
- 0..*, used in Figure 1.6, indicates that a Class1 object *may* hold either a collection of Class2 objects or none at all.

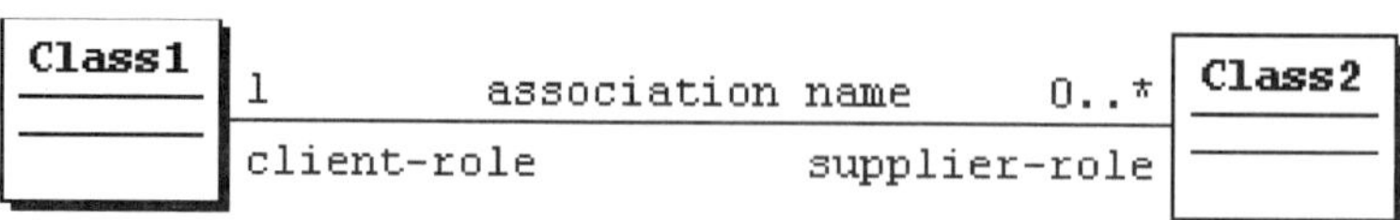

FIGURE 1.6 UML association link

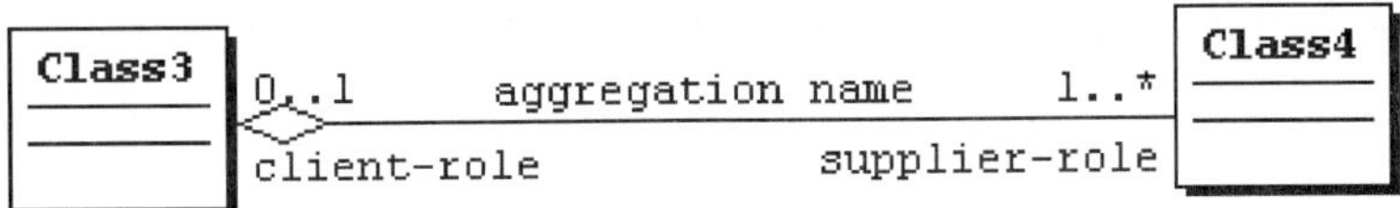

FIGURE 1.7 UML aggregation link

- 1..*, indicates a class object that holds a collection of one or more of the other class objects.

The asterisk (*) indicates an unlimited or unknown amount.

An association link itself may have attributes that are meaningful on the line and yet not with either of the associated classes. Link attributes are drawn as a class connected by a dotted line to the middle of the association link.

1.7.2.2 Aggregation Links. Aggregation links are visually similar to association links, with the addition of a diamond shape at one end of the line, as shown in Figure 1.7. As with associations, roles appear below the line, and multiplicity above the line.

The example in Figure 1.7 shows the Class3 object as an aggregate object consisting of a collection of one or more Class4 objects. In other words, the Class3 object assembles the collection of Class2 objects. For example, an order is made up of one or more order items. Class3 would represent the order, and Class4 the order items.

1.7.3 INHERITANCE HIERARCHY NOTATION

The class diagram in Figure 1.8 shows the notation for inheritance. The arrow points to the superclass and originates at the subclass.

The example shows Class5 as the superclass, and Class6 as the subclass. The diagram shows concrete classes, but an abstract class or method is indicated with names displayed in italic text.

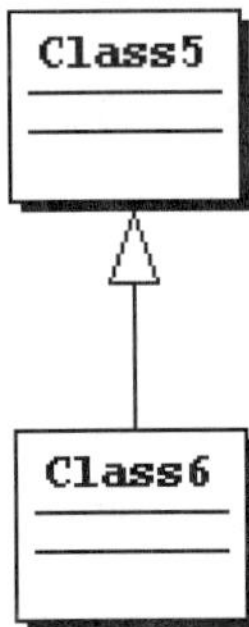

FIGURE 1.8 UML inheritance hierarchy (superclass and subclass)

1.8 MAPPING THE CLASS MODEL TO AN ORACLE DATABASE

Now that you have an understanding of the class model representation, you can transform the classes, associations, aggregations, and inheritance into appropriate database structures. The class model can be implemented in two ways:

1. A relational table design that uses relational structures only.
2. An object-relational design that uses object types and relational structures.

The relational table implementation is possible with any RDBMS, whereas the object-relational implementation is only possible with an Oracle8 database or with RDBMS products that support SQL object types. The object-relational implementation can be based purely on Oracle8 object types or on a combination of relational and object type database structures. To begin, you will need an introduction to Oracle8 object types and object tables.

1.8.1 ORACLE OBJECT TYPES, OBJECT TABLES, AND OBJECT VIEWS

The first version of Oracle8 took the initial steps toward a hybrid object-relational database product with the introduction of object types and object tables.

An *object type* can be defined as a user-defined data type or an abstract data type. It is more than data, however, because its methods, like its attributes, are similar in structure to most of the objects in an object-oriented world. On the other hand, it is *not* a purely object-oriented structure because:

- Its attributes cannot be fully encapsulated. This is because its attributes are public; they cannot be made private.
- Inheritance is not directly supported because one object type cannot extend another. An object type can be nested within another, but this is aggregation, not inheritance.
- Polymorphism is not supported, due to the strong type-checking mechanisms on relational and object types in the database. The type-checking mechanism on relational and object types prevents the assignment of incompatible types. Object types can be modeled in a superclass/ subclass relationship, but without a built-in inheritance mechanism in the implementation environment to support an "is kind of" relationship in the database. The general rule is that *an object type cannot be assigned to any other object type or object reference.*

Based on the above points, the Oracle8 object type is considered to be "object-like" in structure, because it supports the grouping of attributes and methods.

In a more direct comparison with Java, the object type is analogous to creating a final Java class containing:

- All public instance variables.
- A combination of public and/or private instance or static methods.

On the surface, object types may not seem to be a useful asset. Their advantages become apparent when you realize that an object-oriented application can store object states persistently in database data in structures that more closely resemble their structure in the application.

An Oracle8 object type defined in the database can be used as:

- The data type definition attribute in another object type.
- The data type definition of a column in a relational table.
- The structure for a table of objects
- The data type for a PL/SQL variable

These are the reasons why the object type is also referred to as a *user-defined data type*. This gives a greater deal of flexibility to the way you can manage and store data in a relational database. Oracle provides a tool called JPublisher that automatically generates the source for a Java class for an Oracle SQL object type definition.[12] Oracle JPublisher is discussed below in Chapter 10 and 11.

Be cautious in choosing a pure Oracle object table using object types as the basis for your design implementation.

The reason is that the entire set of object instances will have to be reloaded into the table if any change is made in the structure of an object type after the object instances have been added to the table. In short, the object table must be recreated. An added complication arises if there are any object instances in other object tables that have associations (references) with existing object instances before the change is made to the original object table. This is because the designer must provide a column in the associated object instance's type to store the unique object identifier of the referenced object to maintain the association, and also because each instance of an Oracle object type is given a globally unique object identifier. Reloading data assigns a new object identifier for each object instance and is effectively the same as creating a new object, even if the object is created with its original attribute values. Therefore, when object references are stored in object tables other than the original object instances, they are invalidated (they become *dangling references* in Oracle RDBMS terms). Object instances in other ta-

---

[12]JPublisher comes with Oracle JDeveloper, and can be obtained separately for Java developers using other Java development tools.

bles containing dangling references must be updated so that their association link contains the object identifier of the appropriate newly created object instance in the reloaded table.

The general rule that governs the choice of design implementation is determined by the answer to the question: Is it likely that any object type structure may need to be changed in the lifetime of the system, to meet changing business requirements?

If the answer is no, then a pure object table and object type implementation can be chosen. If the answer is yes (i.e., changes to a data structure are likely to occur), then you are advised to implement the design using standard relational tables and not use object types and object tables.

If you do not use object tables, you can still use Oracle object types with the data stored in relational tables by emulating object tables through the use of an object view.

An *object view* is a query on a relational table that presents the data to the user as if each row were an instance of an object type. Creating object types, object tables, and object views are covered in Chapter 2, and using them in SQL are covered in chapters 3 and 4. Using object views gives you more flexibility when the design may need to be changed, and avoids the complexity of rebuilding the data in object tables. For example, adding a column to a relational table does not require the data in the table to be reloaded.

1.9 OBJECT TO RELATIONAL MAPPING RULES

The process of mapping the object class model into a relational implementation needs careful consideration. The mapping is not as straightforward as with the ERD model, but it is not complex either. Design decisions similar to those made when implementing the ERD as a set of relational tables must be made to address performance issues and redundancy of data storage. During the design process, you need to decide how closely you want to stick to the class model and preserve the object structure defined by each class.

1.9.1 OBJECT IDENTIFIERS VERSUS UNIQUE IDENTIFIERS

Before beginning, some words need to be said about object identifiers (OIDs). In an object-oriented environment like the Java Virtual Machine, the OID is inherently a part of an object when an instance is created and is mostly invisible to the application code. The OID has no business meaning, nor should it. Since the OID is a unique identifier for the object instance, the class definitions need to show a unique identifier in the model.

However, a well-designed relational database guarantees a way to uniquely identify each row in each table. Therefore, when creating a table to represent persistent storage for an object of a class, you need to explicitly create a unique identifier for the attributes of each object instance stored as a row in the table.

The unique identifier for each table typically becomes the primary key for the row instances in the table, and the related table holds this primary key value in the foreign key column for each related object row instance. The primary key values created for OID's are usually system- or application-generated values. In the case of an Oracle database, using a sequence generates primary key values. You may have to build your own OID number-generation mechanism if you do not want gaps in the number sequence or if you want to ensure that the OID value is unique for all the rows in all the tables in order to emulate an object world.

If you map the class model to Oracle object tables based on object types, the OID value for each object instance is created and maintained as a globally unique value by the Oracle engine, since Object tables contain object instances with the structure defined by an object type. The OID is intrinsically a part of an object instance, without needing a column to be created for its value, analogous to the way the Java Virtual Machine manages Java object instances.

Object types, in object tables that have an association to other objects, must provide an attribute containing an object reference to maintain the link with the referenced object-type instance. The attribute containing the object stores the global unique identifier of the referenced object. This is similar in concept to when a variable in a Java object is assigned an object reference value to build an association with another object instance.

19.2 MAPPING ATTRIBUTES TO COLUMNS

In general, an attribute in a class maps to a column in a table. However, you may decide that attributes representing derived or calculated values should not be stored in a table because they add redundancy to the data and extra coding overhead to keep them synchronized with changes. If the attributes are complex or represent a collection, they cannot be mapped to a single column. Complex and collection-based attributes are likely to be mapped into tables. Collections are a special case to consider, because an Oracle8i database provides several collection data types for use in relational tables. You may wish to consider using collection types as an alternative to creating additional tables, which is discussed in the section about mapping aggregations.

Columns may also appear that are not mapped directly from modeled attributes. The additional columns can be derived from:

- Storage for the OID or primary key for each object instance (this applies when you are mapping to a relational table rather than an object table).
- Foreign keys or OID references instance data stored in rows in other tables for the implementation of associations or aggregations.

1.9.3 MAPPING CLASSES TO TABLES

You might think that one class maps to one table, and you would be correct for simple databases. Quite often, however, a class maps to more than one table, and sometimes classes are merged into a single table. When implementing a relational database, it helps to have a good understanding of both the object world and the relational environment in order to make appropriate design decisions. The scenarios that follow should help you with these decisions.

The concept of *horizontal and vertical partitioning* of objects in a class may need to be considered when mapping classes to tables. *Partitioning* is the way to map attributes or instances of an object into separate tables.

Horizontal partitioning is the process of mapping attributes into different tables based on access patterns. In this case, you are deciding to store different attributes from the same class in more than one table, and also to have a copy of the OID in each table to keep the information related.

Vertical partitioning is the process of storing more frequently accessed object instances in one table, and less frequently accessed instances in another, where both tables have the same physical structure. An example of vertical partitioning is when historical data need to be kept online but not all of them are required for the most common access patterns. This situation can lead to performance problems. To improve performance, the most recent history records are stored in one table, and the remaining, older historical records in one or more other tables. In relational terms, vertical partitioning can be thought of as *table partitioning,* which is a common practice for large-volume tables. Typically, a database view called a *partitioned view*[13] is built on top of data partitioned into more than one table, and the view provides access to all the data for query processing, but an application must access the correct table for insert, update, and delete operations. The Oracle8 database version added partitioning features allowing a database administrator to physically partition the data in a way transparent to the table structure, that is, without the need to create more than one physical table. Partitioning in this form provides enormous performance gains when you access the data, without the penalty of more complex code.

Relational table designs always go through an optimization and denormalization process to address performance issues as such. Horizontal and vertical partitioning may be an automatic outcome of the implementation decisions made.

1.9.3.1 Mapping One Class to One Table. Due to the relative simplicity of the class model in Figure 1.4, this rule is most commonly used in transformations to a relational design, and in some cases with some additional optimizations for a relational implementation.

Figure 1.9 is a pictorial example of a one-to-one mapping using the `Customer` class on the left and the corresponding `CUSTOMER` table on the right.

---

[13]A partitioned view is a query based on UNION or UNION ALL set operations across more than one table with the same structure (the number of columns and data type of each column are the same).

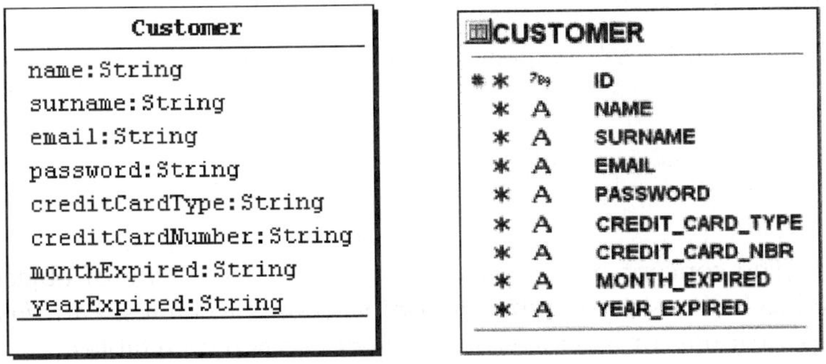

Customer

name:String
surname:String
email:String
password:String
creditCardType:String
creditCardNumber:String
monthExpired:String
yearExpired:String

CUSTOMER

ID
NAME
SURNAME
EMAIL
PASSWORD
CREDIT_CARD_TYPE
CREDIT_CARD_NBR
MONTH_EXPIRED
YEAR_EXPIRED

FIGURE 1.9 Customer class and corresponding table

This mapping illustrates that the relational table must acquire a unique identifier (the `id` column) for the persistent storage of object instances in the relational table. The object identifier is not shown in the class diagram because it is implied by the fact that each object instance is unique, and by definition it has an internal unique identifier.

1.9.3.2 Mapping One Class to More Than One Table. Mapping a single class to more than one table is the same as vertical partitioning. You may apply this mapping process if different access patterns are required on the attributes of objects. Your decision may depend on the complexity of the attribute structures in the class.

A simple attribute is based on a primitive data type or on a simple object structure like a Java String.

A complex attribute can be:

- A collection of objects.
- A nested object or a reference to another object that may also be composed of nested objects.

If you are mapping to relational tables, use the following guidelines:

- Simple attributes should not be partitioned into another table unless they are seldom accessed and clutter the table definition. Partitioning simple attributes into another table creates a one-to-one mapping between relational tables, which is generally not good practice because it promotes less efficient SQL and more work for the application.
- A collection attribute is better partitioned into a separate table. The collection maps to its own table, and contains a foreign key column to link the collection object instances to its appropriate instance in the related table. The result is a simple one-to-many relationship between the original object and its collection.
- An attribute that is a nested object or a reference to an object may be created in its own table if its component parts are not frequently accessed or its structure

is too complex to flatten into a single table. A reference to an object can be handled in the same way as a one-to-one association. A collection can be added to the same table, but how you do this depends on the implementation model.

If mapping to object tables, use the following guidelines in addition to those covered in the section on mapping aggregations (see Section 1.9.6):

- ❑ Simple attributes should be kept in the same object table.
- ❑ A collection attribute can be implemented as a nested table or as a varying array in the same object table. Alternatively, create an attribute as an object reference to a collection implemented in its own object table.
- ❑ A nested object type can remain in the same object table, because an object type encapsulates complexity, providing a simple way to manage the data contained in its structure.

1.9.3.3 Mapping More Than One Class to One Table. Mapping more than one class to a single relational table may be considered for:

- ❑ Classes in the same inheritance hierarchy.
- ❑ Two classes related in a one-to-one association.
- ❑ Aggregated classes. Smaller, simpler classes can be collapsed into the class that groups them together.
- ❑ Fixed collections, such as an array with a known upper limit.

1.9.4 MAPPING INHERITANCE HIERARCHIES

The mapping choices for classes in an inheritance tree are similar to those discussed for relational supertypes and subtypes. The choices are:

1. Use one table for the entire class hierarchy, where all attributes for all classes in the hierarchy are stored in a single table.
2. Use one table per concrete class, where each table contains its own attributes and those inherited from the abstract superclasses.
3. Use one table per class in the hierarchy, where each table holds the attributes contained in each class

1.9.4.1 Map All Classes to One Table. The first choice is the simplest to implement. The table must provide a column to hold a unique identifier for each object in addition to a column for all the attributes defined for classes in the hierarchy. The SalesItem, Book, and MusicCD classes are shown with their corresponding table mapping in the SALES_ITEM table in Figure 1.10.

This is the same result that was achieved earlier in this chapter using the ERD-to-relational design. In this mapping scenario, a form of polymorphism is also possible, where a single row instance can be represented in one of two ways:

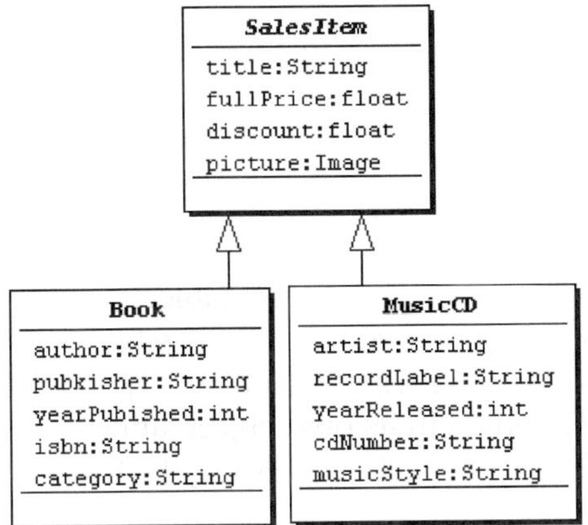

SALES_ITEM

# *	789	ID
*	A	TITLE
*	789	FULL_PRICE
*	789	DISCOUNT
*	A	PRD_TYPE
o	0101	PICTURE
o	A	AUTHOR
o	A	PUBLISHER
o	789	YEAR_PUBLISHED
o	A	ISBN
o	A	CATEGORY
o	A	ARTIST
o	A	RECORD_LABEL
o	789	YEAR_RELEASED
o	A	CD_NBR
o	A	MUSIC_STYLE

FIGURE 1.10 Mapping the SalesItem class hierarchy to a single table

- As a superclass, where only the superclass attributes are relevant.
- As a subclass in the hierarchy, where all the attributes and inherited ones relevant to that class are relevant.

In the bookstore model, the SalesItem superclass, with its attributes alone, is unlikely to be processed meaningfully because it is an abstract class in the model. This form of polymorphism, which could be labeled *pseudo-polymorphism*, should not be confused with the true polymorphism implemented in the Java Virtual Machine or the supertype and subtype concepts in the ERD model.[14] However, similar to the mapping supertypes and its subtype to a single table, an indicator column is added to the table created by flattening the class hierarchy. The indicator column enables an application to identify the attributes relevant for an object instance being accessed.

1.9.4.2 Map Only Concrete Classes to Their Own Table. This case is easier to understand using the SalesItem class hierarchy as an example. The SalesItem class is abstract, and the Book and MusicCD classes are concrete. Only the Book and MusicCD classes are mapped to their own tables, shown in Figure 1.11, where each table acquires all the attributes defined in their abstract superclasses, and each must be given its own object identifier column.

[14]The principle embodied by the supertype and subtype entities in the ERD model states that the same row instance cannot be different types at the same time; therefore, the form of polymorphism discussed violates this principle. Supertype and subtypes do not imply that polymorphism is possible.

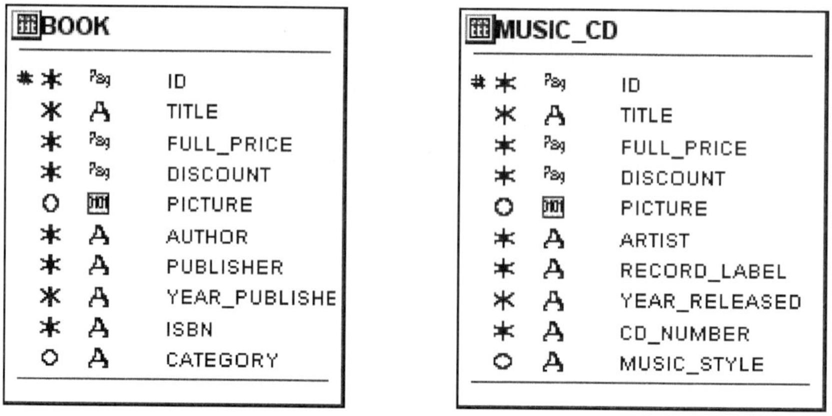

BOOK	
# *	ID
*	TITLE
*	FULL_PRICE
*	DISCOUNT
o	PICTURE
*	AUTHOR
*	PUBLISHER
*	YEAR_PUBLISHE
*	ISBN
o	CATEGORY

MUSIC_CD	
# *	ID
*	TITLE
*	FULL_PRICE
*	DISCOUNT
o	PICTURE
*	ARTIST
*	RECORD_LABEL
*	YEAR_RELEASED
*	CD_NUMBER
o	MUSIC_STYLE

FIGURE 1.11 Mapping concrete subclasses in the SalesItem hierarchy

There is no need for a type indicator, since the existence of the two tables is itself an indicator that they contain different objects. Figures 1.11 and 1.12 only show the resulting relational tables after mapping the class hierarchy presented in Figure 1.10.

1.9.4.3 Map All Classes to Their Own Tables. Mapping each class in the hierarchy to its own table covers the case when a superclass or all the ancestor classes in the hierarchy are also concrete. This scenario can be illustrated if you assume for the moment that the SalesItem class is also a concrete class and not abstract, although you can still choose to map an abstract class to a table. The mapping results in the three tables shown in Figure 1.12, one for each class in the hierarchy.

Each table in the figure has a column added for the unique object identifier, where the value stored in the superclass table's unique identifier column is duplicated in the corresponding subclass tables to link the subclass attributes with their superclass attributes.

In addition, the SALES_ITEM table has acquired a type indicator column (PRD_TYPE) that identifies each object instance in the superclass table as an instance either of:

- The superclass instance, or
- One of the subclasses, requiring a join between the two tables to access all the inherited and subclass attributes.

Your decision to map a superclass to its own table may be influenced by the number of attributes defined in the superclass. Creating a table for the superclass can minimize storage if it has many attributes. Otherwise, if the superclass has fewer attributes, merging the superattributes into each of the subclass tables, as shown in Figure 1.11, yields a less complex design.

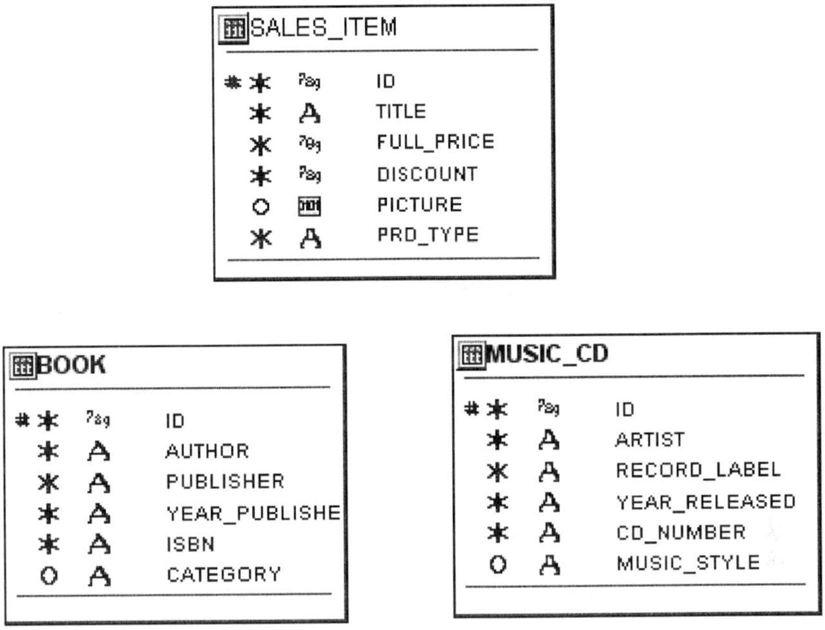

SALES_ITEM

# *	789	ID
*	A	TITLE
*	789	FULL_PRICE
*	789	DISCOUNT
o		PICTURE
*	A	PRD_TYPE

BOOK

# *	789	ID
*	A	AUTHOR
*	A	PUBLISHER
*	A	YEAR_PUBLISHE
*	A	ISBN
o	A	CATEGORY

MUSIC_CD

# *	789	ID
*	A	ARTIST
*	A	RECORD_LABEL
*	A	YEAR_RELEASED
*	A	CD_NUMBER
o	A	MUSIC_STYLE

FIGURE 1.12 Mapping if all classes in the hierarchy are concrete

1.9.5 MAPPING ASSOCIATIONS

The rules that govern the transformation of an association link depend largely on the multiplicity of the associations and also, to an extent, upon the direction implied by the association name.

1.9.5.1 Many-to-Many Associations. Implementing a many-to-many association is relatively simple, because the association is represented in its own table. The bookstore model does not have a many-to-many association, so the diagram in Figure 1.13 has been created as an example to show a CustOrder class having one-to-many SalesItems, and one or more SalesItems can be purchased in a CustOrder.

The resulting relational table structures are shown in Figure 1.14. They show that each class has been mapped to its own tables. In addition, the relational table representation has a unique identifier column, the ORD_ID and ITEM_ID for CUST_ORDER and SALES_ITEM tables respectively. The association link has been transformed into the ORDER_ITEM table, with two columns that act as links between instances in the other tables. In other words, ORDER_ITEM is an association table (or cross-reference table).

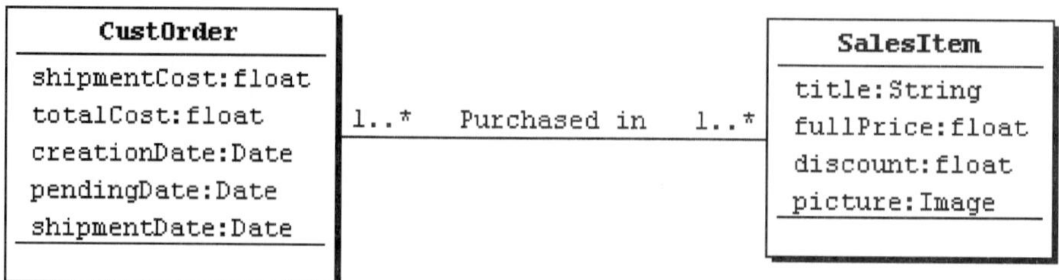

FIGURE 1.13 Many-to-many associations

In the ORDER_ITEM table, CUST_ORDER_ID is a foreign key column referring to ORD_ID column in the CUST_ORDER table, and SALESITEM_ID is a foreign key that references the ITEM_ID in the SALES_ITEM table. The combination of CUST_ORDER_ID and SALESITEM_ID column values is the composite primary key for the ORDER_ITEM table, and forms a link between instances in the related tables.

Attributes assigned to the association link appear as additional columns in the association table.[15]

1.9.5.2 Many-to-Many as an Object-relational Design. An object-relational design is made up of object tables whose structure is based on Oracle object types. The object table implementation is derived from the object type design shown in Figure 1.15.

The diagram in the figure, drawn using Oracle Designer, shows the object type structure upon which the object tables are defined.

The lines with an *open diamond* (an association line) at one end and an arrow (◇——→) at the other represent object references where the attribute that holds the

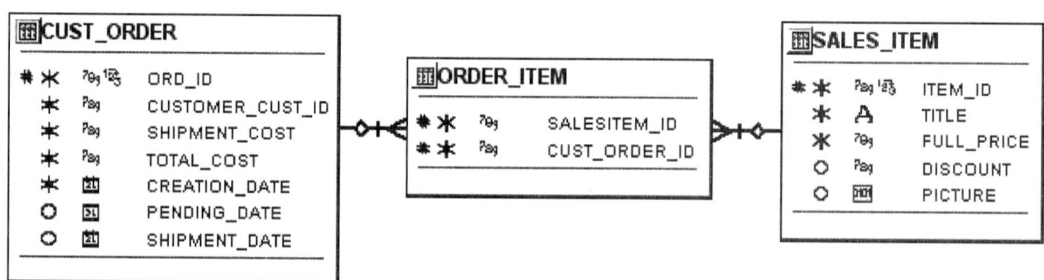

FIGURE 1.14 Results of mapping many-to-many associations

[15]An association with attributes is visually represented as a class connected by a dotted line to the middle of the association link. The tools used by the author do not support the creation of UML link attributes.

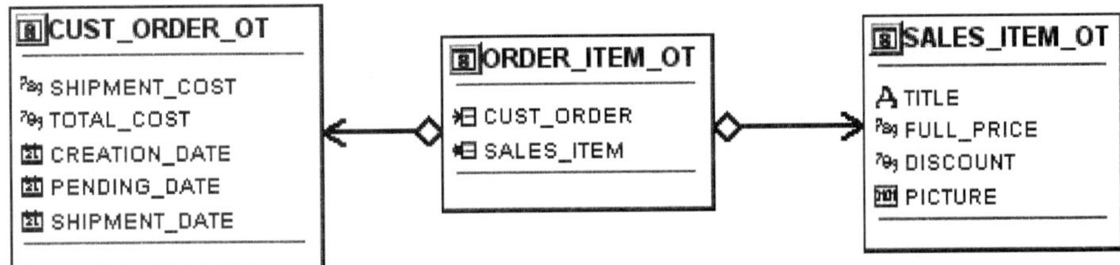

FIGURE 1.15 Object table mapping of many-to-many associations

object reference is defined in the object type at the diamond end of the link. A line without an arrow and a solid (or closed) diamond at one end of the arrow represents an aggregation.

In the example in Figure 1.15, the attribute SALES_ITEM holds a reference to an object instance of the object type SALES_ITEM_OT. An object table called SALES_ITEM (not shown in the diagram) is defined to hold object instances, of the user-defined type, called SALES_ITEM_OT. Note that the object type definitions, which are pointed to by the association links, do not contain any attributes for a unique object identifier. This is because the object instances of each object type are internally assigned a globally unique object identifier, much as a relational database gets an internal row identifier.

From this object type design, you can see a direct correlation to a relational design. The key implementation differences can be summarized as structure, identification unique instances, and link representation.

Structure

- Object tables are composed of object instances based on object types (user defined types).
- Relational tables are composed of row instances based on a grouping of columns with standard data types.

Identification unique instances

- An internally allocated global object identifier uniquely identifies object instances in object tables.
- One or more columns designated as a primary key uniquely identify each row in a relational table.

Link Implementation

- Links between objects are implemented through object references stored in REF columns.

- Links between rows are implemented through a foreign key column value referencing a primary key in another row.

1.9.5.3 One-to-Many Associations. The bookstore model consists mainly of one-to-many associations. There are two options available:

1. *Mapping the association to its own table* produces the same result as the resolution for a many-to-many association. In a relational table implementation, additional rules may need to be built into the database or application to ensure that the instance data in the association table enforces a single occurrence of the object instance at the "one" end of the relationship. This is accomplished by applying a unique index, or an Oracle unique key constraint, on the appropriate column. This approach preserves the object structures represented in the model.
2. *Mapping the association as an attribute reference* in the table at the "many" end of the link. This is the most common mapping approach for relational implementations and has the advantage that only two tables are created instead of three. As a result, SQL statements perform better, because the number of table joins required to access related data is minimized.

The diagram in Figure 1.16 shows the one-to-many association between the Customer and CustOrder classes. The diagram in Figure 1.17 is the result of mapping the one-to-many association between the Customer and the CustOrder classes into tables by applying the second option discussed.

The main point is that the association becomes embedded as a foreign key column (CUST_ID) in the CUST_ORDER table at the many end of the relationship. In a Java class, the direction indicated by the association name labeled *made by* means that a reference attribute to the Customer needs to be added to the

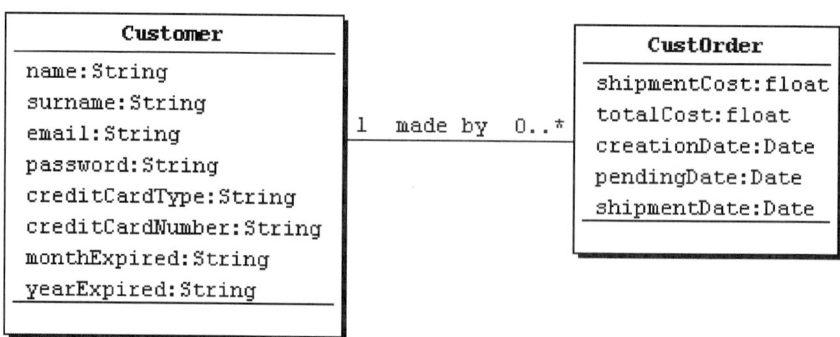

FIGURE 1.16 Customer and CustOrder one-to-many association

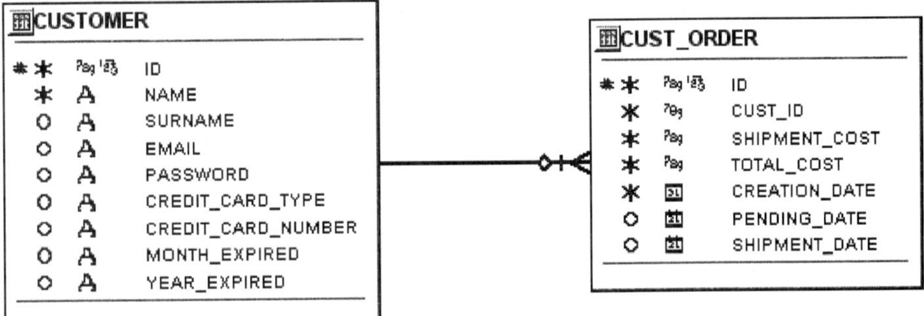

FIGURE 1.17 Relational table mapping for one-to-many association

CustOrder object. This is a hint to the designer that the object reference column should be placed in the table mapped for the CustOrder class.

The advantage of this implementation is that fewer tables are produced when compared to the first option, at the cost of losing the object-oriented model structure and having encapsulation principles violated. This is a good example of the impedance mismatch between the object-oriented and relational worlds. The object world prefers an undiluted object structure, meaning that one object has a lack of knowledge about the components or structure of other objects. In this case, the CUST_ORDER table is diluted with some of the CUSTOMER details because it stores the customer identification value in the foreign key column to preserve the relationship.

1.9.5.4 One-to-Many as an Object-relational Design. Figure 1.18 represents the one possible object type structure that can resolve the one-to-many mapping for the classes in Figure 1.16.

The association is implemented in the CUST_ORDER_OT object type definition, which embeds the CUST_ID attributed as an object reference to an object in-

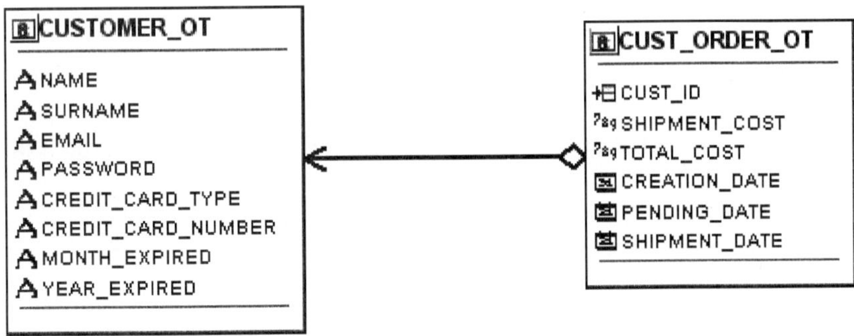

FIGURE 1.18 One-to-many as an object-relational implementation

stance of the CUSTOMER_OT object type. The arrow in Figure 1.18 represents the traversal direction from the CUST_ORDER_OT to the CUSTOMER_OT object type.

In a Java application, the problem with this design is that you must traverse the order objects in order to find the associated customer, because the object reference attribute (CUST_ID) is located in the object instance of the CUST_ORDER_OT object type. However, in an object-relational design, the object reference behaves more like a foreign key, and does not exhibit the same behavior as a Java object reference. This difference can be summarized as follows:

- Java object references allow object instances to collaborate or communicate, and are also used to traverse through object networks.
- Oracle object references allow object instances to form a relationship with another object, and can be operated on using relational operators, such as a join.

Depending on your application's access patterns, you can modify the design. For example, if you want to start with the customer and find the orders made by the customer, possible solutions are:

- Add a collection as an attribute to the CUSTOMER_OT object type. The collection can consist either of object instances of, or object references to, the CUST_ORDER_OT object type.
- Add an object reference attribute to the CUSTOMER_OT object type, which references a collection of CUST_ORDER_OT object instances.

An object table design still requires that associations between objects be preserved.

1.9.5.5 One-to-One Associations. Mapping one-to-one associations is similar to the many-to-many case. If you wish to preserve the object model structure, the idea is to convert the one-to-one association to a table. The steps involved are:

1. Create an association table to cross-reference instances from the associated tables.
2. Add two foreign key columns into the association table, each to reference one of the two associated classes.
3. In addition, create a unique key on each foreign key column. This step enforces the one-to-one association by eliminating the presence of a duplicate value in the foreign key column.

If you think this is overkill for a mapping a one-to-one association to a relational environment, you are correct. In a relational database, eliminating the association table and embedding a unique foreign key column in the table for the associated class optimizes the design. Alternatively, the two associated classes are merged into the same physical table.

1.9.5.6 Ternary or n-ary (Higher-Order) Associations. A *ternary association* is when three classes are associated by a common link. An *n-ary association,* termed a higher-order association, is when *n (many)* classes are involved in the association.[16]

In both cases, the association is mapped to its own association table, which has *n* columns for a reference to each class involved in the link to maintain the simultaneous relationships. Link attributes are then mapped into the association table as additional columns.

1.9.6 MAPPING AGGREGATIONS

The rules for aggregations follow those described in association mappings. Since many-to-many aggregations do not occur, you only need to consider the association mapping rules discussed for one-to-one and one-to-many aggregations.

The key point here is that in an object environment like Java, an aggregation is often implemented as an attribute representing a collection of the aggregated objects. Using Oracle8 collection data types, you can mirror what is done in Java in your database table implementation. The diagram in Figure 1.19 represents an aggregation.

It is visually represented by the solid diamond at one end of the association link, with no arrow at the other end. The icon -⊟ preceding the

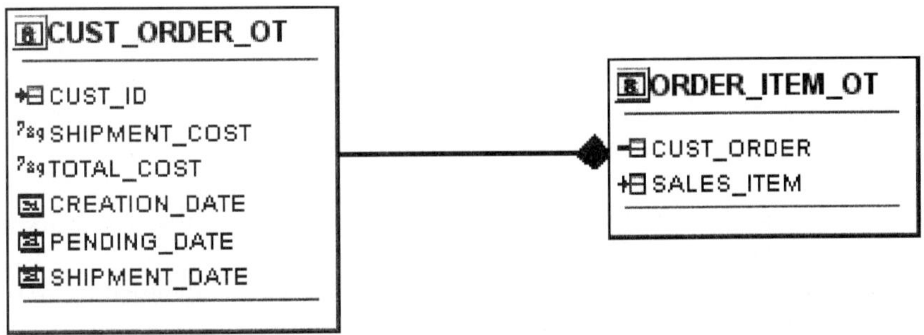

FIGURE 1.19 An aggregation object type implementation

[16]The UML documentation, which can be obtained from Rational Corporation Web site at *http://www.rational.com,* has some examples of *n*-ary associations

CUST_ORDER attribute indicates that it is an embedded object type. This implies that the ORDER_ITEM_OT is an embedded collection, either a nested table or a varying array in the physical definition of the CUST_ORDER_OT. This is similar to defining an attribute in a Java class that is either an object reference to vector of objects or an array of some object. The +⊟ icon represents an attribute as an object reference.

The use of these Oracle8 features means that the aggregated class can be mapped to a compatible collection type embedded in the table representing the class that is aggregating other objects. Oracle8 collection data types include the use of either of the following:

- A *varying array* (VARRAY), which has a fixed upper limit to the number of instances in the collection.
- A *nested table*, with no upper limit to the number of instances in the collection.

The use of a collection embedded in a relational table can reduce the number of physical tables created for the design.

1.9.7 THE CLASS MODEL MAPPED AS ORACLE RELATIONAL TABLES

Now that you are aware of some of the design issues and decisions, you can understand the relational table design represented in Figure 1.20. In Chapter 2 on SQL, you will learn how to create object views based on this model.

If you compare the design in Figure 1.20 to the ERD-to-relational design in Figure 1.3, you will find them *almost* identical. The similarities you will notice in the class-to-relational design in Figure 1.20 are:

- Each table has its own unique identifier column
- Each table at the crow's foot end of a one-to-many relationship has a foreign key column that refers to the primary key at the other end of the relationship.
- The SALES_ITEM table shows a column for each attribute in the superclass and all the subclasses in the inheritance hierarchy (as in Figure 1.3, the MusicCD columns are removed from the initial design to satisfy the business requirements). The SALES_ITEM shows the case of mapping all the classes in the inheritance hierarchy to one table, which includes the addition of the PRD_TYPE column to enable each row instance to be designated as a book or a music CD.

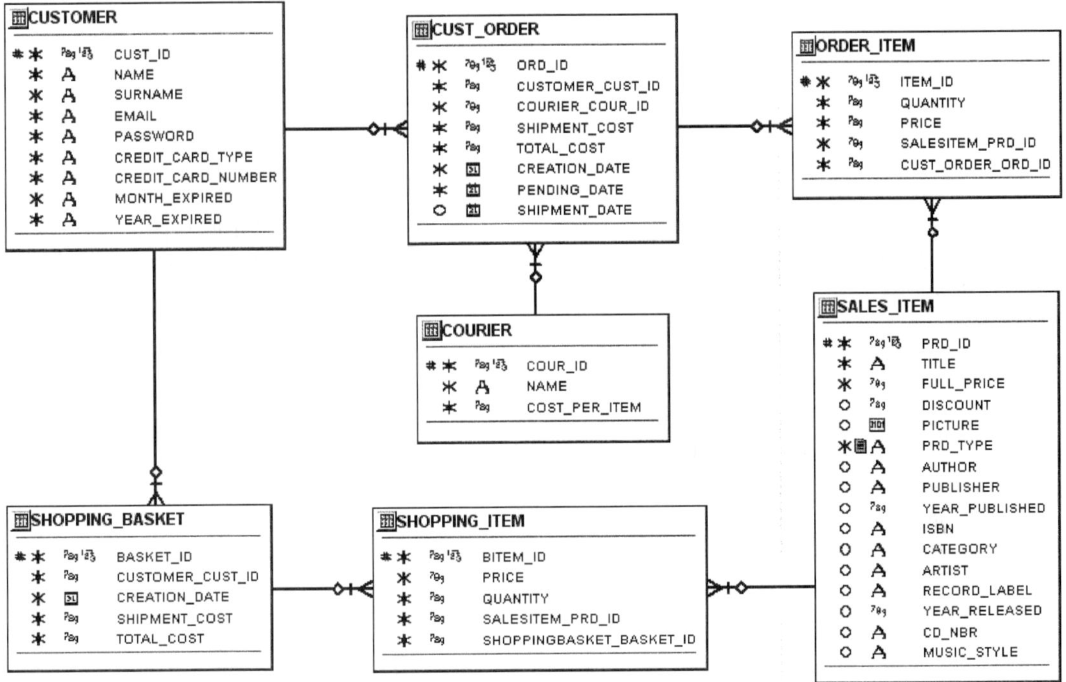

FIGURE 1.20 Relational table design mapped from the class diagram

The bookstore is a simple enough example to use either of the following two methods and their associated mapping rules:

- ❑ An ERD model mapped to a relational design.
- ❑ A class model mapped to a relational design.
  The two methods result in designs that are *almost* identical.

1.9.8 THE CLASS MODEL MAPPED AS ORACLE OBJECT TABLES

Figure 1.21 is a representation of an Oracle object-relational object-type design. An object-type design is not a diagram of tables and closely resembles the class diagram, with exception of the SalesItem inheritance hierarchy.

The mapping rules for this design result in the creation of an object table for each object type, except for the SalesItem class because it is an abstract class. For clarity, Listing 1.1 is an example of using Oracle SQL statements to create an object table for the Courier class.

The structure of the object table in Listing 1.1 is derived from the object type on which it is defined. The contents of the object table are object instances.

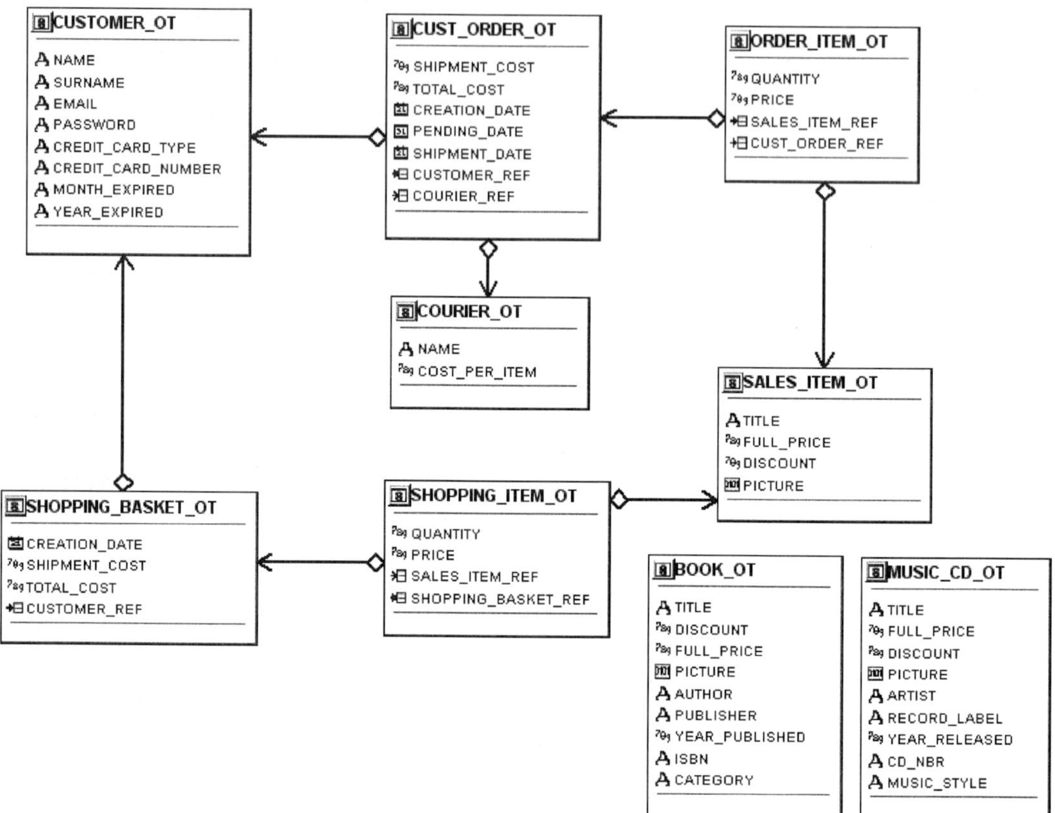

FIGURE 1.21 Object-relational design mapped from the class diagram

Oracle tools can present these object instances because they are rows in a table. This is one of the mechanisms in the Oracle database that you can use to achieve object persistence, as well as to take full advantage of its powerful search and data manipulation feature. In a relational database, the foreign key columns are used to form a relationship between rows in tables. In the Oracle RDBMS, an object table contains one or more object instances with a structure defined by an object type, as shown in Listing 1.1. The object type definition forms a relationship with another object by defining an attribute to be a reference to another object type, called an *object reference* or *REF*. In the Oracle database object-relational environment, the object reference is conceptually equivalent to a foreign key. Hence, the similarity to relational relationships between columns; the object-relational relationship is between object instances, not between tables.

1) First create the object type called COURIER_OT:

```
CREATE OR REPLACE TYPE COURIER_OT AS OBJECT (
  NAME VARCHAR2(30),
  COST_PER_ITEM NUMBER(6)
);
```

2) Now create the object table called COURIER:

```
CREATE TABLE COURIER OF COURIER_OT (
  NAME NOT NULL,
  COST_PER_ITEM NOT NULL
);
```

LISTING 1.1 Example of creating an object type and object table

The design in Figure 1.21 could not be implemented directly as shown without some modification to the object type and table representation of the SALES_ITEM_OT inheritance hierarchy. The diagram shows inheritance of the SALES_ITEM_OT attributes in the BOOK_OT and the MUSIC_CD_OT. However, the BOOK_OT and MUSIC_CD_OT are not associated with any other object type. This is a problem, because the business sells books, not sales items. Since the sales item is abstract, its structure is too generic for persistent storage, because the book and/or CD details must be saved, and must also be associated to the appropriate order items. The choices for modification can be one of the following, and you can think of others too:

- Replace the SALES_ITEM_OT with the BOOK_OT. This would work, but only if the business sells books, as the BOOT_OT has physically inherited all the attributes defined in the SALES_ITEM_OT.
- Add a discriminator attribute, as well as the attributes of BOOK_OT and the MUSIC_CD_OT, into the SALES_ITEM_OT (see Figure 1.22). This design is similar to mapping all classes into one table. In this case, you are mapping the attributes of all classes into one object type. The discriminator columns are required for applications to determine the type of sales item being represented. This dilutes the object-oriented model by creating a structure that no longer resembles the classes in the class model. No dilution would occur if you used an object-oriented database where the classes in the model are implemented in the database without changes to their structural definition.
- Add a discriminator attribute to SALES_ITEM_OT, and two attributes, one that references BOOK_OT, and one referencing MUSIC_CD_OT. You do not need to remove all the attributes inherited from SALES_ITEM_OT, from BOOK_OT and MUSIC_CD_OT to eliminate the duplicate storage of infor-

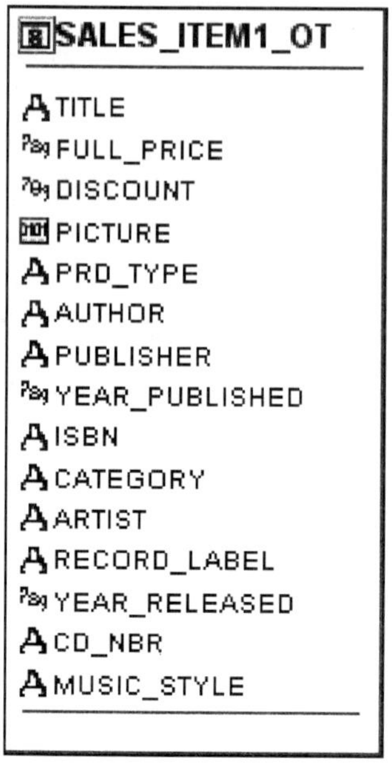

SALES_ITEM1_OT

TITLE
FULL_PRICE
DISCOUNT
PICTURE
PRD_TYPE
AUTHOR
PUBLISHER
YEAR_PUBLISHED
ISBN
CATEGORY
ARTIST
RECORD_LABEL
YEAR_RELEASED
CD_NBR
MUSIC_STYLE

FIGURE 1.22 Adding subclass attributes to SALES_ITEM_OT

mation (see Figure 1.23). In this case, all the superclass information is held in an object instance of the superclass object type, and the discriminator column, by referring to one of the other objects, indicates that the instance is a book or a music CD.

- Add a discriminator attribute to SALES_ITEM_OT, and two attributes, one *embedding* BOOK_OT, and the other *embedding* MUSIC_CD_OT (see Figure 1.24). This is a variation of the preceding point, and, thus, you still need to remove all the attributes inherited from SALES_ITEM_OT, from BOOK_OT, and from MUSIC_CD_OT to eliminate duplicate storage of information.
- Create an object view for the SALES_ITEM rather than an object table. The object view can present a SALES_ITEM_OT in any of the ways described in the preceding points, thereby abstracting the physical database structure and preserving the object design.

Any of these design modifications can lead to a workable implementation. The object views can be used with relational and/or object-relational structures to give your applications access to the SQL object features, while the data are stored in relational table structures.

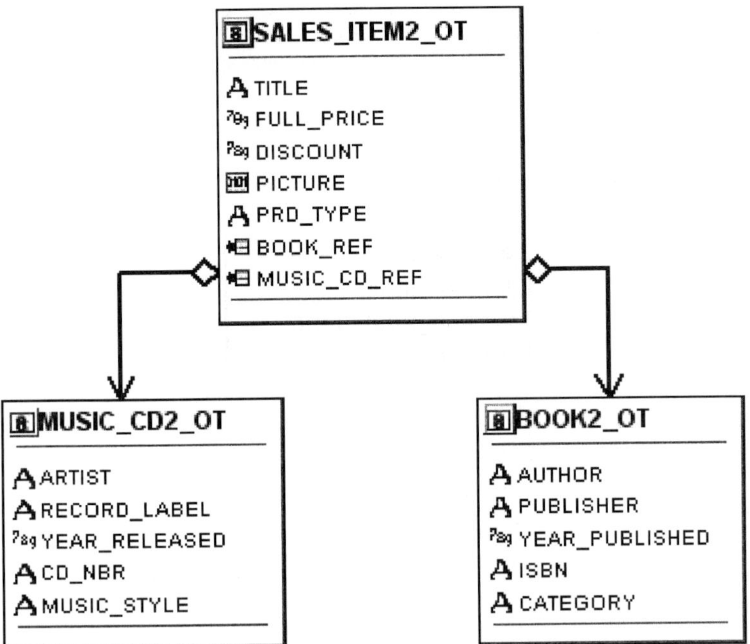

FIGURE 1.23 Adding subclass references SALES_ITEM_OT

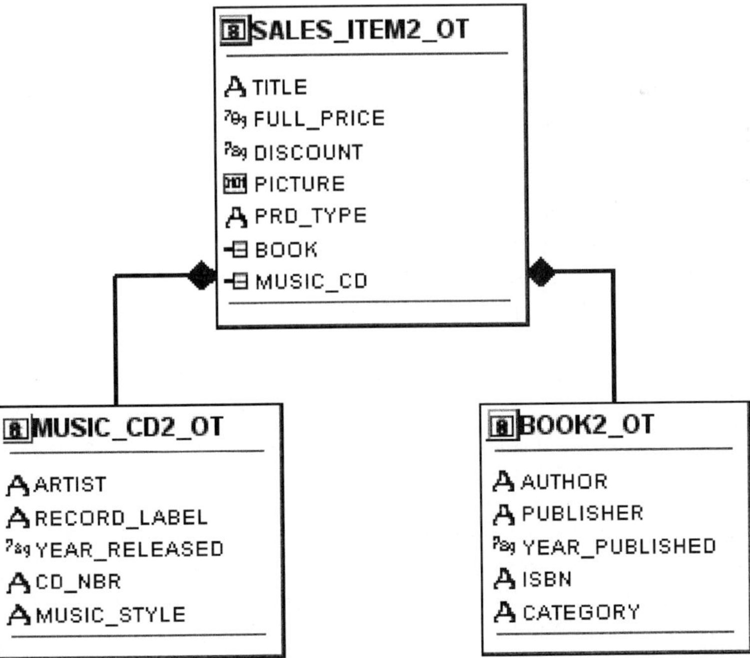

FIGURE 1.24 Embedding/nesting the subclass in SALES_ITEM_OT

SUMMARY

This chapter introduced the principles of database models and showed how to implement the models into workable database design architecture. It also explored ways to compare ERD modeling, using the CDM conventions and principles, with a taste of object-modeling techniques, based on UML conventions, and transforming the class model into a relational or an object-relational database. Hopefully, you are now inspired to use object-modeling techniques for your databases, having gained valuable insight into some of the fundamental transformation rules that can immediately be applied to any project.

Chapter 2

DATA DEFINITION LANGUAGE (DDL) STATEMENTS

- Overview of SQL Statements
- A Brief Introduction to Oracle SQL*Plus
- Generic DDL Syntax
- Oracle Naming Rules for Database Structures
- Oracle8 Built-in Data Types
- Relational Tables
- Alternative Create Tables Syntax
- Relational Views
- Oracle Sequences
- Oracle Synonyms
- Oracle Object Types
- Oracle Object Tables
- Oracle Object Views
- Security: Access-Control Statements
- Summary

This chapter introduces some of the features of Structured Query Language (SQL). The description of these features is not intended to be a comprehensive guide to the SQL language, since there are many books that do a superb job on that subject. The aim of this chapter is to look at the SQL syntax as supported by the Oracle database and to provide the basic understanding you need to interact with relational and object-relational database constructs using JDBC or SQLJ from a Java application.

DDL statements are discussed before the SQL query syntax, so that you can create database structures and populate them with data before you start querying the data.

2.1 OVERVIEW OF SQL STATEMENTS

SQL statements are designed to be English-like in structure. They are nonprocedural, meaning that they are executed as they are entered, and they lack procedural constructs, such as conditional statements and loops. A programming language like Java, C, or PL/SQL must be used to embed, or encapsulate, SQL statements in procedural logic.

The SQL language is made up of one or more statements, which are categorized in Table 2.1.

This chapter focuses on the syntax of the SQL category of Data Definition Language (DDL) statements, as implemented in Oracle. DDL statements are used to create database structures, such as tables, indexes, views, object types, object tables, and object views.

The conventions used in this chapter for the SQL statement syntax are as follows:

- Text in capitals are reserved words, such as CREATE, SELECT, INSERT.
- Text in italics indicates a placeholder for user-supplied information; normal text shows examples of what could be provided as values.
- Text enclosed in square brackets indicates optional syntax elements.
- Text separated by a vertical bar (|) consists of alternate (mutually exclusive) choices.

This chapter provides examples of the use of the basic language syntax for each of the DDL commands listed in Table 2.1 for the following *database structures:*[1]

- Relational tables
- Relational views

[1]The term "database structures" is used here to avoid confusion with the term "objects," which is used in object-oriented languages. Oracle database structures are normally termed "database objects."

TABLE 2.1 SQL statement categories

QUERY LANGUAGE	
SELECT	Queries data in one or more tables and/or views
DATA DEFINITION LANGUAGE (DDL) STATEMENTS	
CREATE	Creates definitions of database structures
ALTER	Alters definitions of database structures
DROP	Deletes database structures
DATA MANIPULATION LANGUAGE (DML) STATEMENTS	
INSERT	Adds records or objects to tables
UPDATE	Changes existing records or objects in tables
DELETE	Deletes existing records or objects from tables
TRANSACTION CONTROL LANGUAGE STATEMENTS	
COMMIT	Makes one or more DML changes permanent
ROLLBACK	Undoes one or more DML changes
SAVEPOINT	Adds marker between DML statements
ACCESS CONTROL LANGUAGE STATEMENTS	
GRANT	Assigns privileges to registered user
REVOKE	Removes privileges from registered user

- ❑ Oracle sequences
- ❑ Oracle synonyms
- ❑ Oracle object types
- ❑ Oracle object tables
- ❑ Oracle object views

An important point you must be aware of is that all Oracle DDL commands are transactions in their own right; that is, when you execute a DDL command, the following steps occur in sequence:

I. Outstanding changes made using DML statements are committed.
II. The DDL command is executed.

Therefore, any changes made by DML statements prior to the DDL statement will be saved regardless of the success or failure of the DDL statement.

2.2 A BRIEF INTRODUCTION TO ORACLE SQL*PLUS

SQL*Plus is an Oracle tool that can be used to execute SQL statements in an Oracle database. All of the SQL statements discussed in this book can be executed in SQL*Plus. The SQL*Plus tool provides an environment in which you can interactively execute SQL statements. On starting the SQL*Plus tool, you are prompted to log in to the database as a registered user before you can execute SQL statements. The command-line syntax[2] for SQL*Plus is:

```
sqlplus [user][/password][@connect-string] [{@ | start}
filename ]
```

All command-line arguments are optional, but if command-line arguments are provided, then:

- *User* is a registered database user name.
- *Password* is the password for the registered database user. A forward slash (/) must precede the password.
- *Connect-string* is the SQL*Net or Net8 name used to connect to a specific database in the network.
- *Filename* is a text file containing SQL*Plus commands, SQL statements, or PL/SQL blocks of code. The at-sign (@) or the keyword *start* must appear before the name of the file on the command line. The file named after the @ symbol is executed immediately after SQL*Plus has successfully connected to the database as the specified user.

SQL*Plus is an excellent tool for testing SQL statements, and you benefit from knowing that your SQL statements are valid before placing them into your JDBC-enabled application. The reason is that SQL statements executed using JDBC calls are only checked for syntax errors at application run-time.

Using SQL*Plus, you can edit, compile, load, and execute Oracle PL/SQL code and stored procedures. You can also load Java stored procedures into the database using the CREATE JAVA command, which is discussed in Chapter 12.

SQL*Plus has a command language of its own, in addition to supporting the SQL commands listed in Table 2.1. Using the SQL*Plus commands, you can:

---

[2]The sqlplus command works on Unix and with some versions of Oracle software under Windows NT. In Windows NT, SQL*Plus can be run in a DOS-mode window or as a Windows application. Invoking sqlplus will start the DOS-mode version, and in some cases the Windows version. In Windows, SQL*plus can be started by executing the plusXXw.exe application where XX is a version number for the product.

- Control the output format of query results.
- Provide parameters for SQL statements and PL/SQL code.
- Change its own environmental settings, such as page and line size.
- Connect to and disconnect from a database.

SQL*Plus can do a whole lot more. Examples of SQL*Plus commands, appearing after the SQL*Plus prompt (SQL>) are:

- PROMPT, which echoes text arguments to the screen, as follows:

```
SQL> prompt Echo this line of text
Echo this line of text
```

- SET command, to set the number of characters per line or lines per page.

```
SQL> set linesize 100
SQL> set pagesize 24
```

Many other settings can be controlled with the set command.

SQL*Plus can read its commands and SQL statements from text entered on the command line or from a file on disk. One or more SQL*Plus and SQL statements can be saved in a file called an *SQL script* file. To execute an SQL script file, use the at-sign (@) or the START keyword followed by the name of the file. For example:

```
SQL> start myscript.sql

SQL> @myscript
```

In the example shown, the file name after the at-sign does not specify a file extension. By default, SQL*Plus assumes that script files have a file name extension of ".sql" unless you explicitly enter the file name with an extension."[3] All lines in the script file are executed in sequential order. Erroneous commands, by default, cause errors to be displayed, but processing of the SQL script will continue unless you use an SQL*Plus command to alter the behavior of your SQL*Plus session in the event of an error. You can use the SQL*Plus WHENEVER SQLERROR command to continue processing the SQL script or you can terminate when the error occurs. For example:

```
SQL> WHENEVER SQLERROR EXIT FAILURE ROLLBACK
```

This WHENEVER command tells SQL*Plus to terminate with a failure condition and perform a rollback on uncommitted changes when an SQL error occurs. There are many variations to the WHENEVER command. Finally, a few more useful SQL*Plus commands include, the `PAUSE` and `SPOOL` commands.

---

[3]The extension is created in lowercase text in case sensitive operating systems, like Unix.

The PAUSE command pauses before each page of output from an SQL query until you type the enter key. For example:

```
SQL> SET PAUSE ON PAUSE "More..."
```

The example also shows how to use a single SET command with more than one *option value* pair. In the example, the first option value pair is PAUSE ON, the second pair is PAUSE "More..." The second option ensures that the string "More..." is displayed after each page of output as a prompt indicating that there is another page of data to be viewed. Use the command SET PAUSE OFF to turn off this feature.

The SPOOL command saves all SQL*Plus input and output into the text file named after the SPOOL keyword. For example:

```
SQL> SPOOL filename
```

The SPOOL OFF command turns the feature off and closes the file. This is useful for saving, emailing, or printing ad-hoc reports. Printing such reports is no better than printing a plain ASCII text file without formatting commands.

2.3 GENERIC DDL SYNTAX

Most DDL statements share a common syntactic structure, as follows:

```
DDL-KEYWORD DB-STRUCTURE-TYPE db-structure-name
 [structure-options]
```

Where

- DDL-KEYWORD is the word CREATE, ALTER, or DROP.
- DB-STRUCTURE-TYPE will be, for example, TABLE, VIEW, SEQUENCE, SYNONYM, etc.
- *Db-structure-name* is a user-provided name.
- [*Structure-options*] depends on the type of structure created.

The structure names chosen must be unique to the database schema within which they are created.

2.4 ORACLE NAMING RULES FOR DATABASE STRUCTURES

Oracle data structure names must begin with an alphabetic character, but the rest of the name may consist of alphanumeric characters and the dollar, pound (#), and underscore characters. Using the dollar and pound characters is discouraged.

Relational database structure names have a maximum length of thirty characters. By default, all names are case-insensitive when accessed by application code using the SQL language. Internally, by default, the names are stored in the data dictionary in uppercase text.

However, if you enclose database structure names in double quotes, the name is saved as entered and becomes case-sensitive. A name in double quotes can contain any printable character, including a space. Avoid the practice of enclosing database structure names in double quotes. Doing this leads to ugly SQL code that may be prone to unintended syntax errors, because you will have to remember to always enclose the names in double quotes in every SQL statement used.

2.5 ORACLE8 BUILT-IN DATA TYPES

Creating a database table requires knowledge of Oracle data types. The data types specify the kind and amount of data stored in a column. Table 2.2 provides a list of Oracle data types.

Object-relational data types are called User Defined Types (UDTs) and are covered later in this chapter.

2.6 RELATIONAL TABLES

A relational database table is two-dimensional and is made up of rows and columns. Creating a table defines the row structure by one or more columns with a name and data type. The table structure, once created, can be altered or deleted. Deleting a table will also delete the data.

There are two ways to create a table using SQL:

1. Using a CREATE TABLE statement that explicitly defines each column name and data type.
2. Using a CREATE TABLE statement that uses an SQL query to define the column names and derives the data types.

While creating a table, or after it is created, you may want to implement referential integrity to ensure that valid relationships are formed or to add simple data-validation rules. The referential-integrity rule ensures that a column value exists, in a row of the related table, for a relationship to be valid. You can implement referential-integrity rules by using *database constraints*. The types of database constraints you can create are:

- ❑ Primary keys
- ❑ Unique keys
- ❑ Foreign keys

TABLE 2.2 Basic data types in Oracle8

DATA TYPE	DESCRIPTION
VARCHAR2(n)	Variable-length character data with maximum length specified by 'n'. The upper limit is a maximum of 2000 for 4000.
CHAR(n)	Fix length character data, n <= 2 56 prior to Oracle8 and n 000
NUMBER, NUMBER(p) NUMBER(p,s)	Numeric data type for floating point values. The 'p' represents a precision, and the 's' a scale. If the precision and scale are not specified, the number has a 38-digit precision, by default.
DATE	Stores date and time information in a 7-byte value containing the day, month, year, century, hour, minute, and second. The valid date range is 4712BC to 4712AD. Oracle databases do not have a time data type.
LONG	Variable-length character data up to a maximum of 2 gigabytes. Only one LONG column is allowed per table, and length is not specified. A LONG must be managed as one chunk of data.
RAW(n)	Variable binary data up to a maximum of 4000 bytes
LONG RAW	Variable-length binary data up to a maximum of 2 gigabytes. Only one LONG RAW column is allowed per table, and data must be inserted, updated, or retrieved as one chunk.
CLOB	A locator reference to a character large object, storing up to 4 gigabytes of data. Contents can be modified or retrieved in chunk sizes specified by a programmer. More than one CLOB is allowed per table.
BLOB	A locator reference to a binary large object, storing up to 4 gigabytes of data. BLOB contents can be modified or retrieved in chunk sizes specified by a programmer. More than one BLOB column is allowed per table.
BFILE	Reference to an external binary file that is accessed via a "logical" directory. The logical directory is a database structure name linked to a physical directory, containing the files, in the host operating system.

These integrity constraints are discussed in more detail below in Section 2.6.2 .

2.6.1 CREATING A TABLE

The following DDL syntax is used to create a relational table:

```
CREATE TABLE table-name (
  column-definition [column-constraint-options, ...], ...
  [table-constraint-options, ...]
);
```

The CREATE TABLE statement contains one or more column definitions, separated by commas. The column definitions are all enclosed in parentheses, and a semicolon terminates the statement. A column definition has several parts:

1. A column name.
2. A data type identifying the format and precision of the value stored.
3. An optional constraint applied to the column.

A comma is placed at the end of a column definition only if it precedes another column definition or a table constraint. One or more spaces or a new line may separate each part. The example in Listing 2.1 is used to create the CUSTOMER table in the bookstore schema.

```
CREATE TABLE customer (
  id                NUMBER(6),
  name              VARCHAR2(30),
  surname           VARCHAR2(30),
  email             VARCHAR2(50),
  password          VARCHAR2(10),
  credit_card_type  VARCHAR2(10),
  credit_card_nbr   VARCHAR2(20),
  month_expired     VARCHAR2(2),
  year_expired      VARCHAR2(2)
);
```

LISTING 2.1 DDL statement to create the CUSTOMER table

The CREATE TABLE statement can be executed, as shown, in SQL*Plus, or programmatically, using JDBC code in a Java application.

2.6.2 DATABASE CONSTRAINTS/DATA INTEGRITY RULES

The database can be used to centralize the checking of referential integrity or validation rules. These rules can be added in a declarative way by using *constraints*, which function to preserve the integrity and accuracy of the data and relationships. A constraint can be declared in the CREATE TABLE statement, or can be added to the table using the ALTER TABLE statement.

A *column constraint* applies to one column and is embedded in the column definition. A *table constraint* applies to two or more columns, and must be embedded *after* all the column definitions in the CREATE TABLE statement.

The syntax for a column constraint is entered after the column data type and has the following structure:

```
[CONSTRAINT constraint-name] constraint-type
```

The constraint is made up of two parts:

1. The constraint name
2. The constraint type

Although the constraint name is optional, it should be specified to assist with quick diagnosis of integrity problems should any arise; otherwise you are left to deal with ugly constraint names generated by the Oracle database.

The types of constraints that can be defined in the column definition are shown in Table 2.3.

All the constraint types listed in Table 2.3, except the NOT NULL constraint, may be embedded in a CREATE TABLE statement as a column or table constraint. The NOT NULL constraint can only apply to a single column and must entered as a column constraint.

The syntax for declaring a table constraint is a little different from the column constraint, as shown below:

```
[CONSTRAINT constraint-name] constraint-type(col[,…])
```

The table constraint has two key points that distinguish it from a column constraint.

1. It identifies the column(s) to which it applies
2. One or more columns may be identified.

The following example shows the creation of the COURIER table, with a primary key and two NOT NULL column constraints defined:

TABLE 2.3 Oracle constraint types

CONSTRAINT TYPE	DESCRIPTION
NOT NULL	Designates the column as mandatory. The value must be known, nulls are not allowed.
PRIMARY KEY	Identifies the column as the primary key, which by definition must have a unique value across all rows. This column is also automatically defined as a not null column. Only one primary key can be defined per table.
UNIQUE KEY	Identifies the column as a unique key and ensures that the values in the column are unique across all rows. More than one unique key is allowed.
FOREIGN KEY	Identifies the column as the foreign key, meaning that the value contained in the column is a "logical" reference to a row in a related table based on its value.
CHECK	Defines a condition to be evaluated on the data in the column.

```
CREATE TABLE courier(
  id             NUMBER(2) CONSTRAINT cour_pk PRIMARY KEY,
  name           VARCHAR2(30) NOT NULL,
  cost_per_item  NUMBER(6,2) NOT NULL
);
```

The primary key constraint is named COUR_PK. Each constraint name must be unique in the schema owning the table.[4] Each NOT NULL constraint is automatically assigned a name like SYS_Cn, where n is a uniquely generated number.

The next example shows a combination of column and table constraint definitions for the CREATE TABLE statement for the ORDER_ITEM table:

```
CREATE TABLE order_item (
  ord_id   NUMBER(6),
  prd_id   NUMBER(6),
  quantity NUMBER(4) NOT NULL,
  price    NUMBER(6,2) NOT NULL,
  CONSTRAINT order_item_pk PRIMARY KEY (ord_id, prd_id),
  CONSTRAINT order_item_fk1 FOREIGN KEY (prd_id)
                            REFERENCES sales_item(id)
);
```

The ORDER_ITEM_PK primary key is a composite or concatenated key because it is formed by the combination of the ORD_ID and PRD_ID columns.

> The SELECT statement can specify conditions to restrict the amount of data queried. If a column defined in a composite primary or unique key constraint is frequently used in the conditions of a query, it should be declared as the first in the list of composite key columns. This is because the index key is created from the concatenated values of the columns. The Oracle RDBMS can do a range search on a part of the key, but only if that part appears first.

The second table constraint is an example of a foreign key constraint. The PRD_ID column entered in brackets after the keywords FOREIGN KEY is the foreign key column. Values in the PRD_ID column must be the same as any value stored in the ID column of the SALES_ITEM. The REFERENCES keyword in the foreign key constraint forms the logical relationship between columns, based on the equality of the values stored in related columns.

---

[4]The owner of a collection of database structures is known as a schema. A schema is defined as a grouping of related database structures.

2.7 ALTERNATIVE CREATE TABLE SYNTAX

The second form of the CREATE TABLE statement allows the designer to copy the definition of another table and at the same time populates the new table with data from the source. The syntax is:

```
CREATE TABLE table-name [(column-name-list)]
 AS subquery;
```

The data type and precision for columns in the new table are derived from the columns in the originating table or from the expressions used in the select clause subquery.[5] For example, copy the CUSTOMER table and all its data:

```
CREATE TABLE cust_copy
 AS SELECT * FROM customer;
```

The names of columns are implicitly determined either by the column names listed after the new table name or by alias names used in the select clause of the subquery. If you use alias names for columns in the subquery, do not place the alias inside double quotes, otherwise it will be stored in case-sensitive format. To copy a table structure without the data, the subquery may use a condition that evaluates to a false result. The subquery can also sort the rows to create a new table populated with an ordered set of rows.

Using the second form of the CREATE TABLE statement is very useful for creating data summarization, as needed, or for making copies of the original data. An important point, however, is that the data integrity rules defined in the original table, with exception of the NOT NULL constraint, are *not* copied to the new table.

2.7.1 MODIFYING THE TABLE STRUCTURE

The ALTER TABLE command allows the designer to change the structure of a table as the requirements for business information changes. Naturally, changes to structure should be minimized to avoid overhead necessitated by changing the code using the database structure. The syntax is:

```
ALTER TABLE table-name
  alteration-clause[, …];
```

Using the ALTER TABLE statement, you can modify the table structure in the following ways:

---

[5]The chapter on the SQL query discusses subqueries.

- Columns can be added (appended) to the table definition.
- The data type and precision of a column can be changed, but only if there are no data in the table. However, if data exist in the table, the data type cannot be changed (unless the types are compatible; i.e., changing type from CHAR to VARCHAR2 is permissible), and the size can only be increased.
- Columns or table constraints can be added or removed.
- Columns can be dropped/removed from a table.

2.7.1.1 Adding a Column. To add a column, use the following syntax of the ALTER TABLE statement:

```
ALTER TABLE table-name
  ADD (column-name datatype [, …]);
```

Assume, for example, that you want to record more detail about a customer, such as a zip code. To add a zip code column to the database, you would execute the following SQL statement:

```
ALTER TABLE customer
  ADD (zip_code varchar2(4));
```

2.7.1.2 Modifying a Column. To modify the data type or precision of a column, use the following syntax:

```
ALTER TABLE table-name
  MODIFY (column-name new-datatype [, …]);
```

For example, to increase the precision of the customer's name, you would enter the following statement:

```
ALTER TABLE customer
  MODIFY (name varchar2(40));
```

Increasing the precision of a column is a valid modification whether data exist in the column or not. However, column size can be decreased if and only if every row in the table contains a NULL in the column.

2.7.1.3 Adding a Constraint. To add a constraint to a table, use:

```
ALTER TABLE table-name
  ADD (CONSTRAINT constraint-name
    constraint-type(column-name[,…]);
```

You can create the table definitions without embedding constraints in the CREATE TABLE statement. For example, to enforce an integrity check to ensure that a valid customer is associated with CUST_ORDER record, you create a primary key on the ID column in the CUSTOMER table, and a foreign key on the CUST_ID column in the CUST_ORDER table:

```
ALTER TABLE customer
  ADD PRIMARY KEY (id);

ALTER TABLE cust_order
  ADD FOREIGN KEY (cust_id)
      REFERENCES customer(id)
```

The command must be done in the order shown. Note that the syntax used to add these constraints is the same as for the table constraints embedded in a CREATE TABLE statement. With the exception of NOT NULL, the constraints cannot be modified, and therefore must be dropped and re-created.

2.7.1.4 Removing a Constraint. To remove a constraint, either to delete the integrity rule it enforces or to change the constraint definition by re-creating it, use the following SQL command:

```
ALTER TABLE table-name
  DROP ({CONSTRAINT constraint-name | PRIMARY KEY}
        [CASCADE]);
```

Assume that the designer erroneously placed a unique constraint on the customer NAME column. You decide it is inappropriate and need to remove the unique key constraint. The following command would achieve the desired goal:

```
ALTER TABLE customer
  DROP (CONSTRAINT cust_name_uk);
```

In order to drop a constraint, you need to know its name. This is a very good reason for always supplying a name for a constraint when it is created, rather than letting Oracle generate one for you. The only exception is the primary key constraint. Since there is only one primary key per table, you can drop the primary key constraint using the keywords PRIMARY KEY, as follows:

```
ALTER TABLE customer
  DROP PRIMARY KEY CASCADE;
```

The optional keyword CASCADE is required when a foreign key constraint refers to the primary key being dropped, otherwise the operation will fail. Using the CASCADE keyword drops all foreign key constraints referring to the primary key, and then the primary key is dropped. Dropping a constraint does not affect data stored in the constrained columns.

It is good idea to keep track of all related constraints, in case you ever need to reinstate them. The Oracle data dictionary provides the information needed to identify constraint definitions.

The Oracle data dictionary comprises several tables and views that you can query using a SELECT statement. For example, you can determine the names and structure of database tables, views, and objects from the database dictionary tables. Names of dictionary tables begin with ALL_, USER_, or DBA_. The DBA tables are only visible to a database user who has been granted DBA privileges.

2.7.1.5 Disabling and enabling a constraint. A constraint can be disabled rather than removed. If you are doing bulk data loads, you may want to disable constraint checks to get better load performance. To disable a constraint, use:

```
ALTER TABLE table-name
  DISABLE { constraint-name | PRIMARY KEY } [CASCADE];
```

To enable the constraint, enter the following statement:

```
ALTER TABLE table-name
  ENABLE { constraint-name | PRIMARY KEY };
```

The CASCADE keywords can be added to simultaneously disable related constraints, but cannot be used when you enable constraints.

2.7.1.6 Adding or removing the NOT NULL constraint. The MODIFY clause of the ALTER TABLE statement is used to change a column that allows a NULL value into a column that disallows a NULL value. An example is shown on the `SHIPMENT_DATE` of the `CUST_ORDER`:

```
ALTER TABLE cust_order
  MODIFY shipment_date NOT NULL;

ALTER TABLE cust_order
  MODIFY shipment_date NULL;
```

The first statement adds a NOT NULL constraint to the `SHIPMENT_DATE` column of the `CUST_ORDER` table, and the second removes the constraint. The NOT NULL constraint cannot be applied if any row for the specified column contains a null value.

2.7.1.7 Removing Columns. Prior to Oracle8i, dropping a column from a table was not easy and required several steps. Here are the steps in one technique for removing a column:

1. Create a new table that does not include the column to be removed from the original table, using the CREATE TABLE with the subquery format. In this case, all integrity constraints must be added except for the NOT NULL constraints, which are copied with the data.
2. Drop the original table.
3. Rename the new table to the original table name.
4. Add any missing integrity constraints to the new table.

Oracle8i eliminated the four steps. It is now possible to drop a column and its data using the ALTER TABLE command, as follows:

```
ALTER TABLE table-name
  DROP COLUMN column-name;
```

Dropping a column should not be done very often. Applications have to be changed, and for performance reasons, because of the way data are stored in an Oracle database, physically removing a column has an overhead needed by the RDBMS to reorganize the data stored in the table. You can defer physical removal of a column and its data by marking the column deleted, but not issuing the command to physically remove the data until the system resources are available. To mark a column for deletion, use the statement:

```
ALTER TABLE table-name
  SET UNUSED COLUMN column-name;
```

A column marked as unused is no longer accessible to SQL statements. At a later stage, when the system workload is low, you can physically remove the unused columns and their data with the statement:

```
ALTER TABLE table-name
  DROP UNUSED COLUMNS;
```

The table data are reorganized and the unused disk space is only reclaimed when the column and its data are physically removed.

2.7.2 REMOVING A TABLE AND ITS DATA

Using the DROP TABLE statement, as shown below, removes a database table and its data, subject to integrity rules:

```
DROP TABLE table-name [CASCADE CONSTRAINTS];
```

The CASCADE CONSTRAINTS first remove the integrity rules that prevent the table from being removed, then the data and the table structure are permanently removed.

If you only want to delete the data and not the table structure, and you do not need to undo the delete operation, use a TRUNCATE TABLE statement. This statement removes all the data without using rollback segment storage, making the operation more efficient than a DELETE statement (The DELETE statement is a DML command. As with the DROP TABLE command, the data deleted with the TRUNCATE statement are permanently removed and cannot be recovered unless there is a backup of the data.

2.8 RELATIONAL VIEWS

Database views can be used for a variety of purposes. Among other things, they can:

- Simplify access to data stored in one or more tables.
- Hide data from unauthorized access.
- Provide summary calculations.
- Abstract the physical table structure from an application. This technique is often used to allow a database administrator to change to the underlying physical table structure with minimal (possibly no) impact on the source code in the application accessing the data through a view, as long as the view query is not violated and the original view structure is preserved.

Depending on the complexity of the view definition, the data in the underlying tables may not always be modified using data manipulation statements. Oracle8i provides a database trigger called the INSTEAD OF trigger for use with views. This allows you to implement correct data manipulation functionality for DML operations performed on any view.

2.8.1 CREATING A VIEW

The syntax for creating a view is:

```
CREATE VIEW view-name [(column-name-list)]
  AS subquery
  [WITH CHECK [constraint-name] | WITH READ ONLY ];
```

A subquery is a SELECT statement used to retrieve column data from one or more tables.[6] An optional list of names can be specified, after the view name, to give the queried data specific column names. The number of names listed must match the number of columns selected in the subquery part of the statement. Creating a view does not create any data. In fact, the Oracle database stores the subquery and view definition in its data dictionary tables. The view appears to applications or users as if it were a database table, and, subject to some restrictions, can be accessed with most of the operations that can be applied to a table.

Since DML operations may be performed through a view, the WITH CHECK option may be added at the end of the view definition to ensure that changes made with DML statements are consistent with the view definition. In short, the WHERE clause defined in the view query governs the rules that determine the type of DML operation that can be performed through the view. Alternatively, a view definition can prohibit DML operations by adding the keywords WITH READ ONLY at the end of the view definition.

The next example creates a view that summarizes the customer order information by listing some customer identification details and the total amount of expenditure for the items ordered:

```
CREATE VIEW cust_expenditure
  (cust_id, cust_name, total_spent)
AS SELECT c.id, c.name, sum(o.total_cost)
   FROM customer c, cust_order o
   WHERE c.id = o.cust_id
   GROUP BY c.id, c.name;
```

To use this view, just write another query as shown, which lists all customer order numbers and totals where the order total is greater than 1000.

```
SELECT *
FROM cust_expenditure
WHERE total_spent > 1000;
```

The query executed on `CUST_EXPENDITURE` is combined with the view subquery to form the final query, which is optimized and executed by the Oracle engine.

---

[6]A subquery is a SQL SELECT statement. You may need to read details about the select statement in Chapter 6 to give the information presented about views more clarity.

2.8.2 MODIFYING A VIEW

You can modify a view by dropping and re-creating it, or by using the following syntax:

```
CREATE OR REPLACE VIEW view-name [(column-name-list)]
AS subquery;
```

The keywords "OR REPLACE" inserted between CREATE and VIEW create a new view if it does not already exist; otherwise, the statement overwrites the original view definition in the data dictionary.

2.8.3 DELETING A VIEW

To delete a view, use the DROP VIEW statement, as follows:

```
DROP VIEW view-name;
```

Sensitive data can be protected from nonprivileged users by excluding sensitive column names from the query defined in the view. The owner of the view and table only needs to grant SELECT (read) access to users of the view. Privileged users may be granted SELECT access directly on the table.

2.9 ORACLE SEQUENCES

Oracle sequence structures are very useful for generating numbers. The sequence starting number and increment can be chosen, but must be integer-based. A positive increment creates an ascending sequence up to a specified MAXVALUE, or internal maximum. A negative increment creates a descending sequence.

Sequences are typically used for generating the unique numbers required for primary key column values. The syntax for creating a sequence is:

```
CREATE SEQUENCE sequence-name
 [ STARTS WITH n ]
 [ INCREMENT BY n ]
 [ MAXVALUE n | MINVALUE n ]
 [ CACHE n | NOCACHE ]
 [ CYCLE | NOCYCLE ];
```

A cyclic sequence is not well suited for primary key values, because when the sequence reaches the maximum value, it recycles through the numbers. By default, a sequence is not cyclic, and when it reaches the specified maximum or built-in maximum, no more numbers will be allocated.

2.9.1 CREATING A SEQUENCE

Here is how to create a sequence without additional options:

```
CREATE SEQUENCE custid_seq;
```

In this case, the starting number is set to one, the increment is by one, and the maximum value can be the largest 28-digit number, that is, 10^{27}. The default cache size is twenty, and when the sequence is used the first time, the next nineteen numbers are stored in a cache, and subsequently retrieved from the cache until it is emptied. Requesting the twenty-first sequence number causes the next nineteen to be loaded into the cache, and so on.

Since a sequence number cannot be put back once it has been allocated, it should be used if possible. Gaps can occur when a sequence number is not saved. For example, if you allocate a sequence number and use it in an insert or update statement, but for some reason the DML changes must be undone, you lose the numbers already allocated. Oracle RDBMS sequences are not subject to transaction-control mechanisms. This feature is intended to eliminate the potential for locking problems when requesting a new sequence number.

2.9.2 MODIFYING A SEQUENCE

Modifying a sequence is accomplished with the ALTER SEQUENCE statement. The syntax is shown here:

```
ALTER SEQUENCE sequence-name
 [ INCREMENT BY n ]
 [ MAXVALUE n | MINVALUE n ]
 [ CACHE n | NOCACHE ]
 [ CYCLE | NOCYCLE ];
```

Alterations to the sequence definition are validated to ensure that the current state of the sequence is preserved. For example:

- ❑ The maximum value of the sequence cannot be made smaller than the last number used.
- ❑ To change the starting point, the sequence must be dropped and then re-created.

2.9.3 DELETING A SEQUENCE

To permanently remove a sequence definition, use the following SQL statement:

```
DROP SEQUENCE sequence-name
```

2.10 ORACLE SYNONYMS

A synonym is used to create an alternative name, or alias, for a structure in the same or a different schema[7] in the same database instance.[8] Prior to Oracle8i Release 2, every registered database user was associated with a database schema identified by the user name. A synonym can be created for the following structures:

- Tables or object tables
- Views or object views
- Sequences
- Stored procedures, functions, or packages
- Materialized views
- Java class schema objects
- Synonyms

A synonym is usually created for one of the listed items owned by another schema. The syntax for creating a synonym is:

```
CREATE SYNONYM synonym-name FOR db-structure-name;
```

You may wish to deal with sales items as if they were only books. To create an alternative name—for example, `BOOKS`—for the `SALES_ITEM` table, the follow statement applies:

```
CREATE SYNONYM book FOR SALES_ITEM;
```

Assume that the SALES_ITEM table is located in another schema, called MAINSTORE. You must place the schema name in front of the referenced structure name, using a dot notation. For example:

---

[7]In an Oracle database, a schema includes all the database tables and structures created and owned by a particular user. In Oracle8i Release 2, scheme and user are separated.

[8]A database instance includes all the control files, data files, processes, and System Global Area (SGA) required to start a specific Oracle database.

```
CREATE SYNONYM book FOR mainstore.sales_item;
```

The synonym name created can be used in any SQL statement that performs a valid operation on the structure to which the synonym refers. For example, to display all the SALES_ITEM records, using the BOOK synonym, you execute the following query, irrespective of the schema location of the SALES_ITEM:

```
SELECT *
FROM   book;
```

Instead of:

```
SELECT *
FROM   mainstore.sales_item;
```

The physical location of the structure referenced by a synonym is transparent to the user of the synonym. A synonym cannot be altered; you must first drop it and then re-create it.

A synonym is removed using the following statement:

```
DROP SYNONYM sequence-name;
```

A database administrator may create or drop a public synonym. A public synonym creates a database-wide name for a database structure. The public synonym is visible to all users registered in the database, but the user must be granted access to the structure the synonym describes. A user-defined synonym or user database structure with the same name as a public synonym will override that public synonym.

2.11 ORACLE OBJECT TYPES

Oracle8 introduced object-oriented-like features into the database by allowing developers to define object types. An *object type* is a user-defined type (UDT), and can contain attributes and methods.

The four pillars of object-oriented systems are:

- Abstraction
- Inheritance
- Encapsulation
- Polymorphism

Of these four, only abstraction is naturally inherent in object types. Abstraction is a process of classifying common attributes and behavior (methods) in an object type. There are two reasons why object types are not purely object-oriented in nature:

- Encapsulation is not complete.
- Inheritance is not supported, and without it polymorphism is not possible.

Keep in mind that a database provides a way for you to make application object instances persistent, and Oracle object types and tables bring the object-oriented and relational environments closer together.

Java serialization is a way to make objects persistent without a database. The object structure and attribute data are consistently stored to a file on a permanent storage device. An object instance and its state can be re-created from its persistent form. Using Oracle relational or object tables is another way to make object instance data persistent. To a Java application, using relational or object tables is less transparent than standard Java serialization, due to the impedance mismatch between the two paradigms. As long as the impedance mismatch exists, you cannot avoid the mapping process required when using a relational database for object persistence.

2.11.1 CREATING AN OBJECT TYPE

Creating an object type creates both a storage place for object instances and a definition of an object structure: attributes and behavior. Conceptually, it is similar to creating a Java class. In Java, object instances are created in memory, and in Oracle, object instances are inserted into object tables. However, transient object instances can created in a PL/SQL execution environment, without saving the instances into database tables.

Object types are created using the CREATE TYPE statement in the Oracle SQL language. Object types have two parts:

- The specification holds the attribute and method declarations.
- The body holds the method implementations.

The specification part is created using the following command syntax:

```
CREATE TYPE object-type-name AS OBJECT (
  attribute-name attribute-data-type
  [, ...]
  {STATIC|MEMBER} method-type method-name[(args)][RETURN
  data-type]
  [,..]
);
```

Attributes are declared before the method signatures, are always public instance variables, and cannot be defined as private or static.

The method signature consists of:

- The keyword STATIC for defining a type method, or the keyword MEMBER for defining an instance method.
- The method type, either the keyword PROCEDURE or the keyword FUNCTION. A procedure does not return a value, like a void method in Java. A function returns a value, as indicated by the return data type.
- The method name, which can be overloaded but cannot be the same as the name of one of the type attributes.
- Optional arguments, and a return data type indicator for functions

The syntax for an instance method, defined as a procedure or function, is:

```
MEMBER PROCEDURE method-name[(args[,..])]

MEMBER FUNCTION method-name[(args[,..])] RETURN data-type
```

All method definitions appearing in the object type specification must be defined and implemented in the type body. A type specification does not declare methods the body does not require. The syntax for the type body is:

```
CREATE TYPE BODY object-type-name AS OBJECT (
 [{STATIC|MEMBER}] method-type method-
 name[(args)][RETURN data-type]
 IS
 BEGIN
   :
   [RETURN value;]
 END;
 :
 :
);
```

Attributes cannot be created in the type body; only method implementations can be added. Every method in the type body that is also declared in the type specification is a *public* method; all other methods are *private.*

The syntax method in the type body shows a *PL/SQL block* structure.[9] However, if the method body is implemented in Java or C, the type specification

---

[9]Chapter 9 discusses the PL/SQL Language and block structure.

identifies that the code is implemented in Java or C. Thus, the same object type definition may include methods implemented in different languages.

The syntax for object type method specification does not change when you create a method specification written in Java, but the syntax in the type body will identify that the method implementation is Java language, and not PL/SQL, as shown in bold text:

```
CREATE TYPE BODY object-type-name AS OBJECT (
  attribute-name attribute-data-type
  [, ...]
  MEMBER method-type method-name[(args)] [RETURN method-type]
     AS LANGUAGE JAVA NAME 'java-stored-procedure-signature'
 [,..]
);
```

The method for the object-relational environment retains its PL/SQL signature in the form of a procedure or function declaration. However, the body part is constructed of a call specification, which identifies a Java Stored Procedure. The keywords `AS LANGUAGE JAVA NAME`, followed by a case-sensitive string between the single quotes, provides a mapping from the PL/SQL declaration to the method signature of a Java Stored Procedure. Each of the PL/SQL data types used in the method arguments, or as the return type for a function, must be mapped to its corresponding Java type in the specified Java Stored Procedure signature.

2.11.1.1 Incomplete Object Types. Oracle8i allows you to create an incomplete object type definition. To create an incomplete object type, you enter the CREATE TYPE command with the name of the type, and nothing more. The syntax is:

```
CREATE TYPE object-type-name;
```

Creating an incomplete object type is similar to creating a forward declaration. The incomplete type definition caters for the situation when two object types have a reference to each other. In this case, called a *cyclic reference*, one of the object types cannot be completely defined until the other one is complete, but a name must exist for it to be completed. The steps required to accomplish a cyclic reference are:

- ❑ Create an incomplete object type of the first object.
- ❑ Create a definition of the second object type that refers to the first.
- ❑ Complete the definition of the first object type.

2.11.1.2 Bookstore Object Type Definitions. Some of the object type definitions for the bookstore design are presented in Listing 2.2. No methods are defined in any of the object types in the examples.

A new data type, called the REF, is introduced in Listing 2.2. The `CUSTOMER_REF`, and `COURIER_REF` columns are declared as references to object type definitions. The object instance, to which a REF column refers, must reside in an object table or collection of a compatible data type. Listing 2.2 also shows an incomplete object type definition, for the `COURIER_OT`,

```
-- Object type for Customer
--
CREATE TYPE customer_ot AS OBJECT (
  name                    VARCHAR2(30),
  surname                 VARCHAR2(30),
  email                   VARCHAR2(50),
  password                VARCHAR2(10),
  credit_card_type        VARCHAR2(10),
  credit_card_number      VARCHAR2(20),
  month_expired           VARCHAR2(2),
  year_expired            VARCHAR2(2)
);

-- Incomplete type for Courier, because the CustOrder
-- needs to reference Courier before it is created.
--
CREATE TYPE courier_ot;

-- Object type for CustOrder
--
CREATE TYPE cust_order_ot AS OBJECT (
  shipment_cost     NUMBER(5),
  total_cost        NUMBER(6)
  creation_date     DATE
  pending_date      DATE
  shipment_date     DATE
  customer_ref      REF customer_ot
  courier_ref       REF courier_ot
);
```

LISTING 2.2 Bookstore object type examples

which allows completion of CUST_ORDER_OT with the reference column to COURIER_OT.

Listing 2.3 completes the definition of the COURIER_OT, and shows the SALES_ITEM_OT and BOOK_OT structures. You can make design changes to both the SALES_ITEM_OT and the BOOK_OT. For example, since the first four attributes in the BOOK_OT and the SALES_OT are the same, you may want to consider redefining the BOOK_OT to make use of the overlap of attribute definitions. There are several options:

- ❑ Create a nested object type in BOOK_OT based on the SALES_ITEM_OT.
- ❑ Create a reference to a SALES_ITEM_OT in the BOOK_OT.

```
-- Complete the Object type definition for Courier
--
CREATE OR REPLACE TYPE courier_ot AS OBJECT (
  name             VARCHAR2(30),
  cost_per_item    NUMBER(6)
);

-- Create Object type for SalesItem and Book
--
CREATE TYPE sales_item_ot AS OBJECT (
  title            VARCHAR2(80),
  full_price       NUMBER(6),
  discount         NUMBER(6),
  picture          BLOB
);

CREATE TYPE book_ot AS OBJECT(
  title            VARCHAR2(80),
  discount         NUMBER(6),
  full_price       NUMBER(6),
  picture          BLOB,
  author           VARCHAR2(80),
  publisher        VARCHAR2(40),
  year_published   NUMBER(4),
  isbn             VARCHAR2(30),
  category         VARCHAR2(40)
);
```

LISTING 2.3 More bookstore object type examples

- ❑ Create a reference to the BOOK_OT from the SALES_ITEM_OT, and delete attributes from BOOK_OT that are already defined in the SALES_ITEM_OT.

Creating a Nested Object Type

Refine BOOK_OT to use the SALES_ITEM_OT definition. Listing 2.4 shows the outcome of this design change.

In Listing 2.4, you are storing an object instance in the SALES_ITEM attribute for each object instance of BOOK_OT.

Creating a REF to an Object Type

You have seen examples of a reference to another object. Listing 2.5 is a variation on the example shown in Listing 2.4, where the object instance for the SALES_ITEM attribute stores a reference to an object instance of the BOOK_OT.

The design change in Listing 2.5 implies that each instance of the book holds a reference to its superclass attributes in an instance of SALES_ITEM_OT stored in another object table, column, or collection. This example can be modified, such that the SALES_ITEM_OT stores a nested object or a reference to a BOOK_OT. Listing 2.6 shows the transformation.

```
-- Create Object type for SalesItem and Book
--
CREATE TYPE sales_item_ot AS OBJECT (
  title              VARCHAR2(80),
  full_price         NUMBER(6),
  discount           NUMBER(6),
  picture            BLOB
);

CREATE TYPE book_ot AS OBJECT(
  sales_item         sales_item_ot,
  author             VARCHAR2(80),
  publisher          VARCHAR2(40),
  year_published     NUMBER(4),
  isbn               VARCHAR2(30),
  category           VARCHAR2(40)
);
```

LISTING 2.4 Merged with a nested object type

```
-- Create Object type for SalesItem and Book
--
CREATE TYPE sales_item_ot AS OBJECT (
  title             VARCHAR2(80),
  full_price        NUMBER(6),
  discount          NUMBER(6),
  picture           BLOB
);

CREATE TYPE book_ot AS OBJECT(
  sales_item        ref sales_item_ot,
  author            VARCHAR2(80),
  publisher         VARCHAR2(40),
  year_published    NUMBER(4),
  isbn              VARCHAR2(30),
  category          VARCHAR2(40)
);
```

LISTING 2.5 Merged with a reference to object type

Due to strong type checking on database data types, you cannot create an attribute to reference an arbitrary object type in place of the book attribute. Thus, if you need to extend the design to support music CD's, you must add an attribute to the sales item object type structure, in order to access a new sales item based on a `MUSIC_CD_OT`. The impact on the database is enormous if object instances based the sales item object type are already stored in object tables and object columns. Oracle8i does not allow you to add or remove attributes from an object type structure once it is in use. You have to drop the object type definition and re-create it, and thus you have to rebuild the data in the database.

2.11.1.3 Object Type Constructors. Oracle automatically assigns an implicit constructor method to every object type created. The general syntax for constructors is:

```
Object-type(attribute-values, ...)
```

The constructor has the same name as the object type, and must have one value for each attribute defined in the object type structure. The constructor cannot be overloaded. Using the book object type as an example:

```
-- Redesigned Book object type
--
CREATE TYPE book_ot AS OBJECT(
  author            VARCHAR2(80),
  publisher         VARCHAR2(40),
  year_published    NUMBER(4),
  isbn              VARCHAR2(30),
  category          VARCHAR2(40)
);

-- Create Object type for SalesItem and
-- a nested attribute for Book
--
CREATE TYPE sales_item_ot AS OBJECT (
  title             VARCHAR2(80),
  full_price        NUMBER(6),
  discount          NUMBER(6),
  picture           BLOB,
  book              book_ot
);

-- Alternatively, SalesItem can reference a Book
--
CREATE TYPE sales_item_ot AS OBJECT (
  title             VARCHAR2(80),
  full_price        NUMBER(6),
  discount          NUMBER(6),
  picture           BLOB,
  book              ref book_ot
);
```

LISTING 2.6 Superclass with nested/referenced object type

```
-- Book object type
--
CREATE TYPE book_ot AS OBJECT(
  author            VARCHAR2(80),
  publisher         VARCHAR2(40),
  year_published    NUMBER(4),
  isbn              VARCHAR2(30),
  category          VARCHAR2(40)
);
```

The constructor used to create an instance of a BOOK_OT looks like:

```
-- Constructor for Book object instance
--
book_ot('Elio Bonazzi',          -- value for attr: author
        'Prentice-Hall',         -- value for attr: publisher
        1999,                    -- value for attr: year_published
        'ISBN 0-13-020091-3',-- value for attr: isbn
        'COMPUTER');             -- value for attr: category
```

The example shows a constructor based on an object type name in bold, with comments at the end of each line identifying which values match their corresponding attributes. Values are provided in the sequence in which the attributes are defined in the object type definition.

The object type constructor is used to insert object instances into an object table, and may also be used for other DML operations, as well as for queries in an object view definition. Oracle SQL*Plus uses the constructor syntax to display the value of an object instance when requested to do so using an SQL query.

2.11.1.4 Creating an Object Type with Methods. The object types in the bookstore example do not have methods; so assume that sales items are subject to a value-added or general sales tax (VAT/GST). The SALES_ITEM_OT can be altered by add methods, without the need to unload and reload the data in object tables, because you would not be changing the attribute structure of the object type. A simple calculation has been chosen for the tax calculation. Listing 2.7 shows an example of creating the SALES_ITEM_OT for the first time, with a nested attribute for the book. Read the section on "Modifying an object type" for an example of how to add additional functions to an existing object type, with the new code shown in bold text.

An object type body can be added, removed, or replaced without affecting the data stored in object instances based on the object type undergoing change.

The keyword SELF is also new in Listing 2.7. SELF provides a way for an object instance method to refer to the current object instance variables. The keyword SELF is implicitly available to member functions, as if it were declared as a parameter to each member method. The reasons for using SELF are analogous to those for using the keyword *this* in Java methods. Each member method may explicitly declare SELF as a parameter, but it must always be the first parameter listed. A static method cannot use the keyword SELF at all.

```
-- Create Object type for SalesItem and
-- A nested attribute for Book, and a get_tax() method
--
CREATE TYPE sales_item_ot AS OBJECT (
  title              VARCHAR2(80),
  full_price         NUMBER(6),
  discount           NUMBER(6),
  picture            BLOB,
  book               book_ot,
  member function get_tax(tax_rate number) return number
);


-- The SalesItem body/implementation for the member function
--
CREATE TYPE BODY sales_item_ot AS
  member function get_tax(tax_rate number) return number
  is
  begin
     return (self.full_price - self.discount) * tax_rate;
 end;
END;
```

LISTING 2.7 Creating an object type with a method

2.11.2 MAP AND ORDER MEMBER METHODS

Scalar data types, such as VARCHAR2 or NUMBER, are easily sorted by their intrinsic values, which also allow them to be compared. However, instances of an object type are compound data types and have no predefined values by which they can be ordered or compared. Therefore, an object type declares two special kinds of member methods:

- A MAP method, which converts the object into a scalar representation.
- An ORDER method, which allows an object to compare itself to another of the same type.

Only one map or order method at a time can be declared in an object type, but not both at the same time.

2.11.2.1 The MAP Method. A MAP member method has no parameters and must return a value based on a scalar data type. The syntax for a MAP method is:

```
MAP MEMBER FUNCTION method-name RETURN data-type;
```

The MAP member function converts the object into a scalar value representation. This enables an SQL statement to perform comparisons on object columns or to sort a row based on a column containing object instances. Listing 2.8, with `CUSTOMER_OT` as an example, shows how you can use the surname attribute as a way to represent the object as a string. Since character values are case-sensitive, the `value_of()` method, in the example, maps the object instance into the surname in uppercase text, to ensure that comparisons or sorts are case-insensitive.

In reality, using a surname by itself may be insufficient for sorting or comparison rules. If you want to display all customers in alphabetic sequence, using the surname as the primary sort and the first name as a secondary sort, you cannot do this using a MAP function. The solution is to use an ORDER member function, which can compare itself to another object instance of the same type.

```
-- Customer Specification
CREATE TYPE customer_ot AS OBJECT (
  name                    VARCHAR2(30),
  surname                 VARCHAR2(30),
  email                   VARCHAR2(50),
  password                VARCHAR2(10),
  credit_card_type        VARCHAR2(10),
  credit_card_number      VARCHAR2(20),
  month_expired           VARCHAR2(2),
  year_expired            VARCHAR2(2),
  MAP MEMBER FUNCTION value_of RETURN VARCHAR2
);

-- Customer Body/Implementation
CREATE TYPE BODY customer_ot AS
  MAP MEMBER FUNCTION value_of RETURN VARCHAR2 IS
  BEGIN
    return UPPER(surname);
  END;
END;
```

LISTING 2.8 Object type with a MAP method

2.11.2.2 The ORDER Method. The ORDER method is primarily used to perform a comparison of itself to another object, and it must return a result to indicate the outcome of the comparison. The integer result value returned is one of three values:

- A negative value indicates that the current object is lexically less than the other object.
- A zero value indicates that the current object is lexically equal to the other object.
- A positive value indicates that the current object is lexically greater than the other object.

A sort process can use these results to order the object instances when requested by a query. The syntax for an ORDER member method is:

```
ORDER MEMBER FUNCTION method-name(arg object-type)
RETURN integer;
```

The customer object instances can be compared to each other based on the surname and also the first name. The example in Listing 2.9 implements an order method called compare_to(), which accepts another object instance of the same type as a parameter in order to perform the required comparison.

The ORDER method uses one argument that always has the current object type as its data type. This allows the current object to compare itself with another object instance of the same type. An ORDER method may have an additional argument that must be for the current object instance itself, which is declared as SELF. You explicitly declare SELF as the first parameter of the ORDER method as follows:

```
CREATE TYPE customer_ot AS OBJECT (
  ORDER MEMBER
    FUNCTION compare_to(self customer_ot, cust customer_ot)
    RETURN INTEGER;
);
```

The examples in Listings 2.8 and 2.9 should give you a good appreciation of the difference between the MAP and ORDER methods.

2.11.3 USING OBJECT TYPES

To sum up, Oracle8 allows object type definitions to be used in the following ways:

```
CREATE TYPE customer_ot AS OBJECT (
  name                      VARCHAR2(30),
  surname                   VARCHAR2(30),
  email                     VARCHAR2(50),
  password                  VARCHAR2(10),
  credit_card_type          VARCHAR2(10),
  credit_card_number        VARCHAR2(20),
  month_expired             VARCHAR2(2),
  year_expired              VARCHAR2(2),
  ORDER MEMBER FUNCTION compare_to(cust customer_ot)
  RETURN INTEGER
);


CREATE TYPE BODY customer_ot AS
  ORDER MEMBER FUNCTION compare_to(cust customer_ot)
  RETURN INTEGER
  IS
   result  pls_integer := 0;
  BEGIN
    IF upper(self.surname) < upper(cust.surname) THEN
      result := -1;
    ELSIF upper(self.surname) > upper(cust.surname) THEN
      result := 1;
    ELSE
      /*
      ** The customer name needs to be checked now
      because the
      ** surnames are equal
      */
    IF upper(self.name) < upper(cust.name) THEN
      result := -1;
    ELSIF upper(self.name) > upper(cust.name) THEN
      result := 1;
    ELSE
      result := 0;
     END IF;
    END IF;
    RETURN (result);
   END;
END;
```

LISTING 2.9 Object type with an ORDER method

- As the data type for a relational database column. A column may hold an object instance (a nested object instance) or the reference of an object instance.
- As the data type for an attribute in object type, creating a nested object.
- To create a table of objects, called an *object table*, where each row in the table is an instance of the object type.

You can only reference an object type in an object table. Object types nested in a relational column or another object type are not given unique object identifiers. This means that a reference to a nested object instance cannot be stored in a column of a relational table or an attribute of another object type.

2.11.4 MODIFYING OBJECT TYPES

There are two ways to modify an object type without causing the data in tables to be reloaded:

- Add additional methods to extend the object type functionality.
- Change the implementation of the method functionality in the type body.

The example in Listing 2.10 shows how to replace an existing object type with a new definition to add an additional method.

In Listing 2.10, the keywords OR REPLACE have been added after the word CREATE. The syntax for CREATE OR REPLACE enables you to alter the definition of an existing object type without removing its definition. Note that the full object type definition, including the additional method, is specified in the CREATE OR REPLACE statement for an existing object type.

To add or remove an attribute from an object type definition, you must first delete the existing object type and re-create it.

2.11.5 DELETING OBJECT TYPES

The DROP statement is used to remove object type specifications and/or type bodies from a schema. The first command syntax is:

```
DROP TYPE type-name;
```

The drop type statement removes both the type specification and body. The second command syntax is:

```
DROP TYPE BODY type-name;
```

```
-- Replace SaleItem to add new method
CREATE OR REPLACE TYPE sales_item_ot AS OBJECT (
  title             VARCHAR2(80),
  full_price        NUMBER(6),
  discount          NUMBER(6),
  picture           BLOB,
  book              book_ot,
  member function get_tax(tax_rate number) return number,
  member function get_bulk_discount(qty number) return number
);

-- The SalesItem body with new member function
--
CREATE OR REPLACE TYPE BODY sales_item_ot AS
  member function get_tax(tax_rate number) return number is
  begin
     return (self.full_price - self.discount) * tax_rate;
  end;

 -- The CustOrder could call this method and provide the
 -- quantity ordered a the parameter value
 member function get_bulk_discount(qty number) return number is
    -- Initialize discount rate to the current object value
    -- and return this value for quantities less than 10
    discount_rate number := self.discount;
  begin
    if (qty >= 10) and (qty < 20) then
       discount_rate := 10; – give 10% discount
    elsif (qty >= 20)
       discount_rate := 20; – give 20% discount
    end if;
    return discount_rate;
 end;

END;
```

LISTING 2.10 Replacing an existing object type to add a method

The drop type body statement removes the type body but not the specification. An object type cannot be dropped if it is being used in the definition of another database structure.

2.12 ORACLE OBJECT TABLES

In a relational database, the table is the basic unit of storage for information. Therefore, to make object instances created from object type definitions persistent, you must create object tables, or relational tables with nested object type columns. Object tables are created using the CREATE TABLE SQL statement. The same statement is also used for creating relational tables, but with some differences.

2.12.1 CREATING OBJECT TABLES

The syntax is different for object tables because they are containers for object instances, whereas relational tables are rows composed of columns. The syntax to create an object table is:

```
CREATE TABLE table-name OF object-type-name
 [(object-properties, ...) ]
 [OBJECT IDENTIFIER IS {SYSTEM GENERATED|PRIMARY KEY}];
```

The object type defines the structure of objects stored in an object table; the object table defines object properties that affect the process of inserting, updating, and deleting object instances. Listing 2.11 shows an example of creating an object table from the CUSTOMER_OT object type, and describing the object table.

Describing the object type, using SQL*Plus, reveals the object type attributes and methods. When the CUSTOMER table is created, object properties have been applied to attributes using NOT NULL constraints. The object properties, which can be applied to attributes, can be:

- Column constraints, such as PRIMARY KEY, UNIQUE KEY, CHECK, or NOT NULL. These constraints follow the same syntax as is used in relational tables.
- SCOPE constraints. These are used on a REF column/attribute to restrict references values to objects in the named table. A REF column/attribute can reference any object instance in different object tables, provided the instances are of the same object type.
- WITH ROWID constraints. These are used to make Oracle store the ROWID of the reference object with the REF attribute/column. If the REF is scoped, then you cannot use the WITH ROWID option. Using the ROWID with the reference improves performance at the cost of the extra storage space required for the ROWID value.
- Referential integrity constraints. The REFERENCES keyword forces the

```
SQL> describe customer_ot
 Name                           Null?    Type
 ------------------------------ -------- ------------
 NAME                                    VARCHAR2(30)
 SURNAME                                 VARCHAR2(30)
 EMAIL                                   VARCHAR2(50)
 PASSWORD                                VARCHAR2(10)
 CREDIT_CARD_TYPE                        VARCHAR2(10)
 CREDIT_CARD_NUMBER                      VARCHAR2(20)
 MONTH_EXPIRED                           VARCHAR2(2)
 YEAR_EXPIRED                            VARCHAR2(2)

METHOD
------
 MEMBER FUNCTION FULL_NAME RETURNS VARCHAR2

METHOD
------
 ORDER MEMBER FUNCTION COMPARE_TO RETURNS NUMBER
 Argument Name    Type
 --------------   ---------
 CUST             CUST_OT

-- Create the table based on the object type
--
CREATE TABLE customer OF customer_ot (
  name                      NOT NULL,
  surname                   NOT NULL,
  email                     NOT NULL,
  password                  NOT NULL,
  credit_card_type          NOT NULL,
  credit_card_number        NOT NULL,
  month_expired             NOT NULL,
  year_expired              NOT NULL
  );
```

LISTING 2.11 Creating and describing an object table

association of REF to object instances a specific object table. This is similar to using the SCOPE constraint.

Listing 2.12 shows the creation of the COURIER table and three different ways to create the CUST_ORDER object table, which is based on the CUST_ORDER_OT:

```
CREATE TABLE courier OF courier_ot (
  name              NOT NULL,
  cost_per_item     NOT NULL
);

-- Example 1: Unconstrained REF, using WITH ROWID
--
CREATE TABLE cust_order OF cust_order_ot (
  shipment_cost                 NOT NULL,
  total_cost                    NOT NULL,
  creation_date                 NOT NULL,
  pending_date                  NOT NULL,
  customer_ref     WITH ROWID   NOT NULL,
  courier_ref      WITH ROWID   NOT NULL
);

-- Example 2: Constrained REF, using SCOPE IS
--
CREATE TABLE cust_order OF cust_order_ot (
  shipment_cost                          NOT NULL,
  total_cost                             NOT NULL,
  creation_date                          NOT NULL,
  pending_date                           NOT NULL,
  customer_ref     SCOPE IS customer     NOT NULL,
  courier_ref      SCOPE IS courier      NOT NULL
);

-- Example 3: Constrained REF, using REFERENCES
--
CREATE TABLE cust_order OF cust_order_ot (
  shipment_cost                               NOT NULL,
  total_cost                                  NOT NULL,
  creation_date                               NOT NULL,
  pending_date                                NOT NULL,
  customer_ref     REFERENCES customer        NOT NULL,
  courier_ref      REFERENCES courier         NOT NULL
);
```

LISTING 2.12 CUST_ORDER with unconstrained or constrained REF

- An object table with an unconstrained REF attribute, with stored ROWID to object types in the customer table.
- An object table with a constrained REF, with the SCOPE keyword.
- An object table with a constrained REF, with the REFERENCES keyword.

The SCOPE IS and REFERENCES constraint specifies the constraining object table. Therefore, the CUSTOMER_REF attribute must reference an object instance in the CUSTOMER table, and an attribute in the CUST_ORDER table based on the COURIER_REF must reference an object instance in the COURIER table.

2.12.2 MODIFYING OBJECT TABLES

You cannot change the structure of the object types upon which object tables are defined. However, by dropping and adding columns in a way similar to relational tables, you can modify tables with a column based on an object type. Some of the object properties applied to object type attributes could be added, modified, or removed, using the ALTER TABLE statement. Properties that can be added are:

- PRIMARY KEY, UNIQUE KEY, CHECK, SCOPE, FOREIGN KEY
  Properties that can be modified:

- NULL to NOT NULL, and vice versa.
  Properties that can be removed:

- All of the above with exception of the SCOPE property.

An example of adding object properties is shown in Listing 2.13, using the ALTER TABLE statement.

```
ALTER TABLE cust_order
  ADD (SCOPE FOR (customer_ref) IS customer);
```

LISTING 2.13 Adding object properties for attributes

Modifying an object property for an attribute that allows nulls or to disallow nulls is shown in Listing 2.14.

```
ALTER TABLE customer
  MODIFY (credit_card_type  NULL);      -- allow null values

ALTER TABLE customer
  MODIFY (credit_card_type  NOT NULL); -- disallows null values
```

LISTING 2.14 Adding or removing the NOT NULL property

Properties can be removed by using the DROP option in the ALTER TABLE statement, as in Listing 2.15.

```
ALTER TABLE table-name
  DROP CONSTRAINT constraint-name;
```

LISTING 2.15 Adding or removing constraint properties

The syntax for dropping a constraint on an object table is the same as for dropping a constraint from a relational table. Therefore, it is important to apply sensible names to the constraint properties you add to an object table.

2.12.2.1 Adding or Removing Attributes from an Object Type. An object type must be dropped and re-created to add or remove attributes. This is restrictive and relies on the designer to provide a thorough object design before placing the definition in production. However, if you need to add or remove attributes to an object type in use, the workaround is:

- Copy the object instances from the object table into a temporary table, or export the table data.
- Drop the object table.
- Create the new object type definition.
- Re-create the object table.
- Reload the relevant object instance data from the temporary table, or import the object instance data.

If it is likely that an object type will evolve in the lifetime of the system, and the suggested workaround is unacceptable, consider using object views defined over relational tables. Changing the definitions of object types and the object views based on them does not affect the structure of the relational table or the data stored in it.

2.12.3 DROPPING OBJECT TABLES

The DROP statement is used to delete an object table and all the instances in the table. The syntax is:

```
DROP TABLE table-name;
```

A table will not be deleted if there are foreign key column values that depend on data in the table being dropped. There are three ways to delete a table that has data dependencies:

- Remove or disable the foreign key constraint preventing table deletion.
- Delete or alter the related data dependencies.
- Use the drop table statement with the CASCADE keyword.

The third option is achieved by adding the CASCADE keyword to the end of the DROP table statement. For example:

```
DROP TABLE table-name CASCADE;
```

The CASCADE keyword removes the foreign key constraint but does not remove the data rows in the related table. This can lead to data integrity problems if you do not modify the related data.

2.13 ORACLE OBJECT VIEWS

An *object view* is a query based on row objects that is created to present relational data as if they were instances of an object type. Since a view is a way to abstract data in relational tables, an object view is a way to abstract relational structures into objects. Doing this simplifies the mapping of relational data into the object-oriented world of Java.

Creating an object view is a three-step process:

1. Create the object types that will be used to superimpose the relational table columns. This only works well if the columns in the relational tables are sensibly organized.
2. Create the object view based on a query on the relational tables, using the object type definitions created in step 1 to present relational data in object form.
3. If the object view is based on a relational table, choose an attribute with a unique value as the object identifier. For relational tables, the object identifiers are based on the primary key.

2.13.1 CHOOSING OBJECT IDENTIFIERS

Creating an object view may require that you choose an object identifier for each row queried by the view. If the table queried by the object view is a relational table, then the unique object identifier is the primary key column(s).

An object view does not accept an object type attribute as the basis for an object identifier; it accepts only a simple column from the base table. Therefore, it is important to keep the unique identifier columns out of the object type definitions that used to overlay the relational table structure. Oracle object views cannot use a primary key column that is embedded as an attribute inside an object type.

The problem with unique identifiers does not exist when the object view is based on object tables, which already have unique object identifier values.

2.13.2 CREATING OBJECT VIEWS

To create an object view, you must first identify the common structures for which you will create object type definitions. The syntax for creating an object view is:

```
CREATE VIEW view-name OF object-type
  WITH OBJECT OID (simple-column-name) AS
  select-statement;
```

The object type that view is defined on must exist, and must include as a simple attribute the values to be used for the unique object identifier. The keywords WITH OBJECT OID (simple-column-name) mark the attribute name, as it is defined in the object type, as the unique identifier. The select statement is any SQL SELECT statement used to query the relational tables. The query must provide the correct number of columns, and the corresponding column data types, for the object type attribute structure used by the view. The select statement can use a combination of column names and/or embedded object type constructors to provide the values for the view structure.

2.13.3 AN EXAMPLE OF AN OBJECT VIEW

The next example, which illustrates creating an object view, is based on using the `SALES_ITEM` table. The sales item table was initially designed with columns to hold the details for books, but with a `PRD_TYPE` column added in anticipation of adding music CD's to the type of products to be offered. Using object views, you can quickly synthesize book and music CD object types and views to give the impression that the business is selling more than one type of product without changing the relational table structure. The structure of the `SALES_ITEM` relational table is:

```
CREATE TABLE SALES_ITEM (
  ID NUMBER(6)                NOT NULL,
 ------------------------------------
  TITLE VARCHAR2(100)         NOT NULL,
  FULL_PRICE NUMBER(6,2)      NOT NULL,
  DISCOUNT NUMBER(5,2)        NOT NULL,
  PRD_TYPE VARCHAR2(10)       NOT NULL,
  PICTURE                     BLOB,          -- Music CD attribute
  -----------------------------------
  AUTHOR                      VARCHAR2(80),  -- ARTIST
  PUBLISHER                   VARCHAR2(40),  -- RECORD_LABEL
  YEAR_PUBLISHED              NUMBER(4),     -- YEAR_RELEASED
```

```
  ISBN                          VARCHAR2(30),  -- CD_NBR
  CATEGORY                      VARCHAR2(40)   -- MUSIC_STYLE
);
```

The table structure shows where the music CD attributes overlap the corresponding book columns, which is a simple one-to-one match. The sales Item table structure is used as the basis for designing object types that are applied to object views for books and music CD's. In this example, the music CD object view is easy to add without changing the relational table structure, thereby enabling the business to provide information about new music products with little impact on the code managing book data. The sales item table definition has dash characters surrounding the attributes that are common to the book and music CD. These attributes are captured in a sales item object type that is used in the definition of a book and a music CD.

The first step is to create the object type definitions for:

- The sales item attributes common to books and CD's: TITLE, FULL_PRICE, and DISCOUNT. The PRD_TYPE and PICTURE attributes have been excluded from this example to simplify the SQL statements used to build the views. You can add in the PICTURE type, but the idea is to exclude the PRD_TYPE and let the database engine manage the PRD_TYPE column value through the use of default values and database triggers.
- The book attributes, which include the ID, a nested sales item object type, AUTHOR, PUBLISHER, YEAR_PUBLISHED, ISBN, and CATEGORY.
- The music CD attributes, which include the ID, a nested sales item object type, ARTIST, RECORD_LABEL, YEAR_RELEASED, CD_NBR, and MUSIC_STYLE. In the case of the music CD type, the additional attribute names overlay and rename the AUTHOR, PUBLISHER, YEAR_PUBLISHED, ISBN, and CATEGORY attributes, respectively.

The ID attribute has been excluded from the sales item object type definition because each object view uses the ID column as the unique object identifier for book and music CD object instances.

```
CREATE TYPE sales_item_vt AS OBJECT (
  Title              varchar2(100),
  full_price         number(6,2),
  discount           number(5,2)
  -- ,prd_type       varchar2(10),
  -- picture         blob
);

CREATE TYPE book_vt AS OBJECT (
  id                 NUMBER(6),
  item               SALES_ITEM_VT,
  author             VARCHAR2(80),
  publisher          VARCHAR2(40),
  yearPublished      NUMBER(4),
  isbn               VARCHAR2(30),
  category           VARCHAR2(40)
);

CREATE TYPE music_cd_vt AS OBJECT (
  id                 NUMBER(6),
  item               SALES_ITEM_VT,
  artist             VARCHAR2(80),
  recordLabel        VARCHAR2(40),
  yearReleased       NUMBER(4),
  CdNbr              VARCHAR2(30),
  musicStyle         VARCHAR2(40)
);
```

The example about Oracle object types uses a naming convention that appends the letters _VT to indicate that the structures are object view types, so that they do not conflict with the object types defined using the _OT suffix for the object type used by object tables.

The next step is to create object views for books and music CD's that use the object types created. The query used in each object view maps the relational table columns to the corresponding attributes defined by object type applied to the view.

```
-- Create the object view for books
--
CREATE VIEW book_ov OF book_vt
       WITH OBJECT OID (id) AS
       SELECT  id, sales_item_vt(title, full_price,
               discount) item,
```

```
              author, publisher, year_published, isbn,
              category
        FROM    sales_item a
        WHERE   prd_type = 'BK';

-- Create the object view for music CD's
--
CREATE VIEW music_cd_ov OF music_cd_vt
      WITH OBJECT OID (id) AS
        SELECT  id, sales_item_vt(title, full_price,
                discount) item, author, publisher,
                year_published, isbn, category
        FROM    sales_item
        WHERE   prd_type = 'CD';
```

The example views can now be used as if they were object tables. The bold text in the example highlights:

- The create view definition, using the object type to control the structure of the query used in the view.
- The use of the SALES_ITEM_VT() constructor to provide the view with common attributes in a nested object structure.
- A WHERE clause using the PRD_TYPE to filter out unwanted data and show either the books or the music CD's.

The SELECT statement must use all the correct column names found in the SALES_ITEM table. The SALES_ITEM_VT() constructor parameter values are supplied by the related columns in the SALES_ITEM table. One feature of using views is that you have the flexibility of presenting information in a way that is meaningful to the users of the data. This flexibility is reflected in Listing 2.16, which shows that the book and music CD object views have different names for their attributes, even though the data come from the same columns in the SALES_ITEM table.

2.13.4 MODIFYING OBJECT VIEWS

Modification of an object view is simply the process of redefining the view query and/or the object type structures. You have the freedom and flexibility to change these object types and views without needing to reorganize your data.

If you must change the object type structure, the view must first be dropped. You can re-create the view after modifying the object type. The changes are simple if the object type is not used for anything other than the

```
SQL> describe book_ov
 Name                       Null?    Type
 ------------------         -------  ------------
 ID                                  NUMBER(6)
 ITEM                                SALES_ITEM_T
 AUTHOR                              VARCHAR2(80)
 PUBLISHER                           VARCHAR2(40)
 YEARPUBLISHED                       NUMBER(4)
 ISBN                                VARCHAR2(30)
 CATEGORY                            VARCHAR2(40)

SQL> describe music_cd_ov
 Name                       Null?    Type
 -------------------        -------  ------------
 ID                                  NUMBER(6)
 ITEM                                SALES_ITEM_T
 ARTIST                              VARCHAR2(80)
 RECORDLABEL                         VARCHAR2(40)
 YEARRELEASED                        NUMBER(4)
 CDNBR                               VARCHAR2(30)
 MUSICSTYLE                          VARCHAR2(40)
```

LISTING 2.16 SQL*Plus description of object views

object views, because the relational data do not have to be unloaded and then reloaded.

2.13.5 DELETING OBJECT VIEWS

Deleting an object view is the simple process of dropping its definition from the database. The syntax is:

```
DROP VIEW object-view-name;
```

2.13.6 CREATING COLLECTIONS

Collection data types were added in Oracle version 8.0. There are two types of collection structures available:

- Nested tables
- Varying arrays

The collection type must be defined before it is used as a user-defined data type for a column in a relational table or as an attribute in an object type. Each collection is made up of one or more elements; and each element defines the data type for the data stored in the collection.

Nested tables are unconstrained collections, analogous to a Java vector, where the number of elements is unknown, and elements can be dynamically added or removed.

Varying arrays are constrained to a specified size, analogous to a Java array, where the number of elements is set at creation time, and elements cannot be added or removed. The size of a varying array cannot change.

2.13.6.1 Creating a Nested Table Collection. Creating and using a nested table is a two-step process:

- Define the nested table data type using the CREATE TYPE statement.
- Use the nested table data type for defining a column or an attribute.

The syntax to create a nested table data type is:

```
CREATE TYPE type-name IS TABLE OF element-type
```

The nested table *element-type* can be:

- A scalar data type, like VARCHAR, NUMBER, etc.
- A user-defined data type.
- A REF to a user-defined data type.

Listing 2.17 is an example of creating a nested table collection of shopping-item objects. Each shopping item in the collection holds the price, quantity, and reference to sales item purchased.

Listing 2.18 shows the creation of the shopping-basket object table, which is based on the shopping-basket object type. The shopping-basket object type has the `ITEMS` attribute defined as the nested table, or collection, of shopping items. The creation of the object table for the sales items is also shown.

In Listing 2.18, the second CREATE TABLE statement creates the shopping-basket table, and makes its `ID` attribute the primary key. All the nested table attributes, such as `ITEMS`, must be associated with a named storage area. The nested table is associated with a storage area when the table is created by adding the keywords:

```
NESTED TABLE attribute-name STORE AS storage-area-name
```

The NESTED TABLE specifies the attribute-name associated with the named storage area after the STORE AS keywords.

```
-- Create the SalesItem object type definition
--
CREATE TYPE sales_item_ot AS OBJECT (
  title             VARCHAR2(100),
  full_price        NUMBER(6,2),
  discount          NUMBER(5,2),
  picture           BLOB);

-- Create the ShoppingItem object type definition
--
CREATE TYPE shopping_item_ot AS OBJECT (
  quantity          NUMBER(4),
  price             NUMBER(6,2),
  sales_item_ref    REF SALES_ITEM_OT);

-- Create the Nested Table of ShoppingItem objects
--
CREATE TYPE nt_shopping_item_ot AS TABLE OF shopping_item_ot;
```

LISTING 2.17 Shopping basket with items as a nested table

```
-- Create the ShoppingBasket object type
-- The items attribute is defined as a nested table of
-- shopping item objects
--
CREATE TYPE shopping_basket_ot AS OBJECT (
  id                NUMBER(6),
  creation_date     DATE,
  shipment_cost     NUMBER(5,2),
  total_cost        NUMBER(6,2),
  items             NT_SHOPPING_ITEM_OT); -- the collection

-- Create the object table of SalesItem instances
--
CREATE TABLE sales_items OF sales_item_ot;

-- Create the object table of ShoppingBasket instances
--
CREATE TABLE shopping_basket OF shopping_basket_ot (
  id PRIMARY KEY)
  NESTED TABLE items STORE AS SHOPPING_ITEMS;
```

LISTING 2.18 Shopping basket with collection of shopping items

2.13.6.2 Creating a Varying-array Collection. Creating varying arrays also requires two steps:

- Define a VARRAY data type in a CREATE TYPE statement.
- Use the varying-array data type to define a column or an attribute.

Unlike nested tables, varying arrays do not need to be associated with a named storage area, although it is possible to do so. The syntax required to create a user-defined data type to represent a varying array is:

```
CREATE TYPE type-name IS VARRAY(max-entries)
  OF element-type
```

Or,

```
CREATE TYPE type-name IS VARYING ARRAY(max-entries)
  OF element-type
```

Listing 2.19 is an example of creating a varying-array collection type of shopping items, which is assigned as the data type to the `ITEMS` attribute in the shopping basket.

```
-- Create the Varying Array of ShoppingItem objects
--
CREATE TYPE shopping_item_va_ot AS VARRAY(20) OF shopping_item_ot;

-- Create the ShoppingBasket object type
-- The items attribute is defined to be a varying array
--
CREATE TYPE shopping_basket_ot AS OBJECT (
  id                          NUMBER(6),
  creation_date               DATE,
  shipment_cost               NUMBER(5,2),
  total_cost                  NUMBER(6,2),
  items                       SHOPPING_ITEM_VA_OT);

-- Create the object table of ShoppingBasket instances
--
CREATE TABLE shopping_basket OF shopping_basket_ot (
  id PRIMARY KEY);
```

LISTING 2.19 Shopping basket with a varying-array collection

The shopping basket cannot have more items than specified in the maximum number of elements in the varying array. A varying-array implementation can be useful to limit consumption of resources but should be avoided if the number of elements may grow beyond the maximum specified.

2.14 SECURITY: ACCESS-CONTROL STATEMENTS

The GRANT and REVOKE statements are access-control statements that alter information stored in the Oracle data dictionary and allow a suitably privileged user to grant or revoke access register users, perform database commands, or access database structure in another schema.

Oracle databases control the types of SQL commands a user can perform by granting appropriate system privileges. System privileges control what a user can do if allowed to connect to the database. A registered user must be given the CREATE SESSION privilege in order to log in to the database.

Object privileges control the type of SQL operation that can be performed on a database structure, such as allowing a user to query, or to modify data in a table. An object privilege can grant a user the right to execute SQL statements that alter the database structure or definition.

2.14.1 GRANT STATEMENT FOR SYSTEM PRIVILEGES

The GRANT statement is used to assign one or more privileges to another user in the database. The REVOKE statement is used to remove privileges assigned to a user by the GRANT statement. The GRANT statement syntax for assigning system privileges to one or more users is:

```
GRANT system-privilege [, system-privilege]
TO user [, …];
```

The syntax shows that one or more system privileges can be assigned to one or more users in the same command. Examples of some system privileges are:

- CREATE SESSION allows a user to connect to and log in to a database.
- CREATE TABLE allows a user to create a table.
- ALTER TABLE allows the user to change the table structure.
- DROP TABLE allows the user to remove the table.

If a database ROLE is created, the role name to which the privileges are assigned is specified in the location of the user list. For example:

```
CREATE ROLE sql_user;

GRANT CREATE SESSION TO sql_user;

GRANT sql_user TO bhannath;
```

The database administrator executes the first line of the example to create the role, unless the user executing the command has the CREATE ROLE system privilege. The second command, the GRANT statement, assigns the system privilege CREATE SESSION to the role named `SQL_USER`. The last GRANT statement associates the `SQL_USER` role with a registered database user called `bhannath`. As more privileges are assigned to the `SQL_USER` role, any users who are associated with that role will automatically acquire the new privileges added to it.

A database role represents a collection of privileges that can be granted to or revoked from a user or another role.

2.14.2 REVOKE STATEMENTS FOR SYSTEM PRIVILEGES

The revoke statement is used to remove privileges from a user or a database role. The REVOKE statement syntax required to remove system privileges from a user or role is:

```
REVOKE system-privilege [, system-privilege …]
FROM {user | role} [, …];
```

2.14.3 DATABASE OBJECT PRIVILEGES

Object privileges control how other users can work with database structures.

2.14.3.1 Granting Object Privileges. Only the user who owns the schema structures can grant or revoke object privileges unless the grantor uses the WITH GRANT OPTION in the following statement:

```
GRANT object-privilege [, object-privilege…]
TO {user | role} [, …]
[WITH GRANT OPTION];
```

The object privilege `ALL` can be used to give all applicable privileges on the database object based on the type of object involved. Object privileges have names that correspond to the types of actions that can be performed on the type of database structure used. For example, you can select, insert, update, or delete data from a table. Some of the common database structures you will use, and the privileges that may be granted or revoked on them, are shown in Table 2.4.

The next examples grant read, insert, and update access on the SALES_ITEM table to a role called PURCHASING_OFFICER, and the next grant command gives read access to all users (public) on the same table.

```
GRANT SELECT, INSERT, UPDATE
ON    SALES_ITEM
TO    PURCHASING_OFFICER

GRANT SELECT
ON    SALES_ITEM
TO    PUBLIC
```

Any user who is assigned the PURCHASING_OFFICER role is allowed to query, insert, and update data in the SALES_ITEM table. The PUBLIC keyword means that the privilege is granted to all users registered in the database.

TABLE 2.4

STRUCTURE /OBJECT	APPLICABLE PRIVILEGES
TABLE	ALTER to allow altering the table structure SELECT to allow reading data in the table INSERT to insert data into the table UPDATE to update data in the table DELETE to delete rows from the table INDEX to create indexes on columns in the table REFERENCE to create foreign key references to columns in the table
VIEW	SELECT to read data through the view INSERT to insert data through the view UPDATE to update data through the view DELETE to delete data through the view ALTER to alter the definition of the view query
SEQUENCE	SELECT to allocate sequence numbers ALTER to change the definition of the sequence
OBJECT TYPES	EXECUTE to share the definition and allow execution of object methods. EXECUTE access is required by other users, because the default constructor is needed to create instances of the object type.

2.14.3.2 Revoking Object Privileges. Revoking an object privilege is done using the REVOKE statement, as follows:

```
REVOKE object-privilege [, object-privilege …]
ON     database-object
FROM {user | role} [, …];
```

If a privilege given with the WITH GRANT OPTION feature is revoked from a user or role, then it is revoked both from the user and from any others to whom the user granted the privilege. The keyword ALL may be used to revoke all privileges granted on a database structure. If a privilege is granted to a specific user and to PUBLIC, then revoking the privilege from PUBLIC does not revoke it from a user to which it was explicitly granted. Here is an example:

```
GRANT SELECT
ON    CUST_ORDER
TO    ORDER_ENTRY_CLERK, PUBLIC;


REVOKE SELECT
ON     CUST_ORDER
FROM   PUBLIC;
```

The GRANT statement allows users associated with the ORDER_ENTRY_CLERK role, and all registered databases users (PUBLIC), SELECT access to the CUST_ORDER table. The REVOKE statement removes the SELECT access on the CUST_ORDER table from all registered users except those granted the ORDER_ENTRY_CLERK role.

If you intend to remove SELECT access for every database user, an additional REVOKE statement is needed to explicitly remove SELECT access on CUST_ORDER from the ORDER_ENTRY_CLERK role.

SUMMARY

This chapter covered the basics of using Oracle DDL statements to create, modify, and delete the following database structures:

- ❑ Tables
- ❑ Sequences

- Relational views
- Object types
- Object tables
- Object views
- Nested tables and varying-array collections

Oracle object types are "object–like" in structure and behavior, and provide a way to store relational data in an object-relational environment. Object types can be a powerful bridge between the relational database world of persistent data storage and the object-oriented world of Java, made up of transient instances of these objects.

Chapter 3

QUERY PROCESSING

- SELECT Statements
- Single Row Functions
- *WHERE* Clause to Restrict Rows Retrieved
- Table Join Operations
- ORDER BY
- Aggregate Functions
- GROUP BY Clauses
- HAVING Clauses
- Subqueries
- Querying Object Structures
- Summary

The SELECT keyword begins the SQL statement used to retrieve data from one or more tables in a relational database. In the discussion of DDL statements in the preceding chapter, you learned how to create database tables to store data. The present chapter focuses on querying the data with which the tables were populated. The subjects it treats include:

- The clauses of the select statement.
- Single row and group functions.
- Joining data in more than one table.
- Subquery processing.
- Querying data structured using Oracle Object types and collections.

The next chapter covers DML statements that can be used to populate the tables with data and modify the data.

3.1 SELECT STATEMENTS

A SQL SELECT statement is made of one or more clauses, each of which begins with an SQL keyword. All of the common clauses in the SELECT statement are shown here:

```
SELECT column-specification(s)
FROM   table-specification(s)
WHERE  condition(s)
GROUP BY group-criteria
HAVING condition(s)
ORDER BY order-criteria;
```

Depending on the tool you use to execute the SQL statement, the statement terminator commonly used is a semicolon.[1] An easy to read formatting convention is to place each clause in the statement on its own line, as shown in the sample syntax. All the keywords in the select statement, with the exception of the SELECT and FROM keywords, are optional, so the minimum requirements for a SELECT statement are:

```
SELECT column-specification(s)
FROM   table-specification(s);
```

The SELECT clause identifies *what* data is to be retrieved i.e. what columns, and the FROM clause identifies *where* the data comes from, that is, which table contains the data.

---

[1]SQL statements processed using JDBC do not require the semicolon in the query string. SQL*Plus requires either the semicolon or its own statement terminator, a slash (/) on a line by itself.

The operation of selecting columns from a table is called *projection*. The data returned by a query, if any, are a set of rows commonly known in Java JDBC as a *result set*. The SQL language has many "set-like" operations that can be used on the data, such as joins, outer joins, unions, intersections, and minuses. Some of these terms may conjure up memories of set algebra learned in school. An example of a simple SELECT statement is:

```
SELECT *
FROM customer;
```

The asterisk character (*) represents a request for data in *all columns* from the specified table. In the example, the query retrieves the data in all columns and all rows from the `CUSTOMER` table.

The `column_specification` part of the query can be entered as follows:

```
* | {column-expression [AS] [alias]}
```

Where the `column_expression` is a

- Column name
- SQL single row or aggregate (group) function
- Literal value, or a
- Combination of the above three to form either an arithmetic, string, or date expression (calculation), an alias name can be supplied after the column expression.

3.1.1 COLUMN ALIASES

The optional keyword AS introduces a column *alias,* which is used to give the `column_expression` a meaningful name that can be used by application environments executing the SQL statement. JDBC code uses the alias to retrieve the value for the expression by the alias name. Oracle SQL*Plus uses the alias for applying data-output formatting rules. An alias is useful in providing a meaningful name for an expression. Assume, for example, that the column expression is calculation, such as determining the price for a quantity of products ordered:

```
SELECT price * quantity
FROM   cust_order
WHERE  id = 1;
```

The expression is made more readable, meaningful, and useful by adding a column alias, for example, `ITEM_TOTAL`, with the resulting column expression being written as:

```
SELECT price * quantity as item_total
FROM   cust_order
WHERE  id = 1;
```

Remember, the AS keyword is optional, but at least one space is required after the end of the column expression and before the first letter of the alias, as shown in this alternative syntax:

```
SELECT price * quantity item_total
FROM   cust_order
WHERE  id = 1;
```

3.1.1.1 A Word on Aliases. An alias may be enclosed in double-quote characters. If it is enclosed in double quotes, then it can contain any printable character and becomes case-sensitive. If the alias is *not* enclosed in double quotes, then it can only be made up of alphanumeric and underscore characters. As a rule, it is best to use avoid placing double quotes around the alias name, so as to simplify the resulting SQL or code embedding the SQL statement.

3.1.2 CALCULATIONS IN SQL EXPRESSIONS

Calculations like the ones in the preceding examples, where the derived item cost is based on the quantity multiplied by the unit price, are often necessary. Using a SQL statement to perform these calculations is a powerful way to derive meaningful data from one or more columns. Using calculations in SQL can simplify the code in the application and eliminate the need for extra lines of code to perform the calculation. SQL expressions include arithmetic, character, and date calculations, using a combination of data in columns and literals.

3.1.2.1 Literal Values. *Literal values* are hard-coded values in a specific data type.

Literal Numbers

A *numeric literal* is a positive or negative number, typed as an integer, a decimal, or in scientific notation. For example:

- Integer: 10 – 20 1001
- Decimal: 24.50 – 40.59 0.011
- Scientific: 2E-3 (same as $2.0 * 10^{-3}$) – 4.512E10 (meaning – $4.512 * 10^{10}$)

Literal Strings

A *string literal*, also known as a *character literal*, is a combination of one or more characters enclosed in single quotes. All character literal values are case-sensitive. Some examples of character literals are:

```
'Here is the world of SQL', 'A', 'b', '1001 ways to
  write SQL'
```

If your string literal must contain a single quote as part of the text, the rule is: Place one additional single-quote character next to each single quote that must appear in the string, excluding the single quotes that enclose the literal text. The following steps show a foolproof way of building an SQL string literal with embedded single quotes:

1. Write the text string, as you would like it to be stored or appear. For example: **`Here's an example, it's quite easy`**
2. Next, add one single quote immediately next to the single quotes in the text, either before or after the existing single quotes, resulting in a text string like: **`Here''s an example, it''s quite easy`**
3. Finally, convert the text into a literal string by adding the enclosing single quotes, one at the beginning of the text, and one at the end. The final result is: **`'Here''s an example, it''s quite easy'`**

Literal Dates

In Oracle SQL syntax, in order to simplify date data entry for application users, a literal date value is entered as a quoted string in a specific format. The default date format for an Oracle database is 'DD-MON-YY'. The "DD" characters represent the day of the month, "MON" is the abbreviated month name, "YY" the last two digits of the year, and the minus characters are required as delimiters. The default date format had all sorts of implications for developing an application that was Y2K-compliant. Therefore, you could change the default date format for all database users by specifying the desired default date format in the database initialization file,[2] or you could use the following SQL statement to change the default date format for your session:

```
ALTER SESSION SET NLS_DATE_FORMAT='date-format';
```

[2]The database initialization file is called initXXX.ora, where XXX is your database name called an SID. The initialization parameter used to specify the default date format is called NLS_DATE_FORMAT. NLS means National Language Support, indicating that you could specify a date format in a language-specific way.

Several valid date format characters are listed in Table 3.4. A date string is implicitly converted into the Oracle RDBMS internal date format.[3] The default date format assumes the current century of the system clock. However, since Oracle RDBMS version 8.0, the default data entry format for a date literal has become more flexible, so that you can now enter the year as one, two, three, or four digits, without having to alter the date format for the database or session. Table 3.1 shows different valid date literal values and the results they represent if stored in the database using an Oracle SQL environment. The example assumes that the current century is 2000.

Oracle date values also have a time component that includes the hours, minutes, and seconds. The resulting date created internally for a date literal value entered without a time component, as shown in any of the forms listed in Table 3.1, has the hour, minute, and second of the time set to a default value of zero. In these cases, the date literal becomes a date with a time representing the start of the day, that is, at the zero hour.

All date literal values are implicitly converted into a 7-byte value internally. The internal date value is used for date operations or comparisons. You can perform an explicit conversion of a date string literal into an internal date format by using the TO_DATE function conversion provided as a built-in operation in the Oracle SQL processing environment. A list of conversion functions is provided below in the discussion of single row functions in section 3.2 of this chapter.

3.1.2.2 Basic Arithmetic Operators. Table 3.2 shows the basic arithmetic operators that can be used in SQL language expressions.

Other operators, such as modulus operations, are implemented through SQL functions. For example, `MOD(value,modulus)`, which returns the remainder after dividing the modulus parameter into the value parameter. A subset of Oracle SQL functions is discussed later in this chapter.

3.1.2.3 String Concatenation Operators. Only one string operator is used to concatenate string values. All other string operations are performed using functions. The string concatenation operator is two vertical bars, next to each other, and placed between two character values. For example:

TABLE 3.1 Oracle date literal values

LITERAL DATE ENTERED	ACTUAL VALUE REPRESENTED
01-JAN-9	January 1, 2009
01-JAN-99	January 1, 2099
01-JAN-999	January 1, 0999 (yes, year 999)
01-JAN-1999	January 1,1999

[3]Oracle stores dates and time internally as a series of 7 bytes.

TABLE 3.2 SQL arithmetic operators

OPERATOR	DESCRIPTION
*	Multiplication
/	Division
+	Addition
-	Subtraction

- column1 || column2
- `'literal value ' || column || ' other literal'`

If you concatenate a text string with a numeric literal, the numeric literal is first implicitly converted into its string representation, and then concatenated with the string. For example:

- The expression: `'The value is: ' || 20.22`
- Is first converted into: `'The value is: ' || '20.22'`
- The result of which is: `'The value is: 20.22'`

A string literal containing no characters, that is, two single quotes with nothing in between, is implicitly converted into a NULL value. For reasons of readability, a NULL value is best represented by the keyword NULL.

An important point is that any arithmetic expression involving a NULL value always computes to a NULL result.

For example, to calculate the product selling-price, you may subtract the discount from the full price:

```
SELECT full_price - discount AS selling_price
FROM   sales_item;
```

If the price, or the discount column, holds a NULL value, the result for the selling-price calculation is NULL. For reliable calculation results, Oracle SQL provides a function called `NVL()`, which can be used to convert a NULL value into a suitable alternative to be used in an SQL expression.

3.1.2.4 Date Operators. Date operators are the plus and minus signs. Oracle SQL allows you to subtract one date value from another, resulting in the number of days between dates. The resulting number of days may be a decimal value, if the dates subtracted have a non-zero time component. For example, assume that the order-creation date is January 1, 2000, and the date of shipment is

January 3, 2000, with both dates having a zero value for all parts of the time. Then the following SQL statement results in a value of two days for the number of days to deliver an order based on its creation date:

```
SELECT shipment_date - creation_date AS days_to_deliver
FROM cust_order
WHERE id = 1;
```

You can add or subtract a decimal value from a date to alter the date or time. For example, if the creation date and time value are '1-JAN-2000 00:00:00', then:

- creation_date + 1, results in '2-JAN-2000 00:00:00'
- creation_date + 0.5, results in '1-JAN-2000 12:00:00'. Here you are adding 12 hours (0.5 represents half a day)
- creation_date - 1, results in '31-DEC-1999 00:00:00'. Oracle date arithmetic handles changes of year, month, days accordingly, including leap years.
- creation_date - 0.25, results in '31-DEC-1999 18:00:00'

These examples can be tested in Oracle SQL*Plus, using the following SQL statement:

```
SELECT to_char(to_date('01-JAN-2000')-0.25,
               'DD-MON-YYYY HH24:MI:SS') as new_date
FROM dual;
```

The following points explain the various parts of this example:

- `to_date('01-JAN-2000')`, converts the date string literal into an internal date data type.
- `to_date('01-JAN-2000')-0.25`, subtracts six hours from the internal date to result in a new internal date, which is nested to provide the value for the first parameter in the to_char() function.
- `to_char(date, 'DD-MON-YYYY HH24:MI:SS')`, converts the `date` value, from an internal DATE data type, to a character string. The format of the character string is controlled by the string literal in the second parameter of the `to_char()` function. Refer to the notes on the `to_char()` function later in this chapter for more detail on the meaning of the date format characters.

3.1.2.5 DUAL Tables. The DUAL table is actually a database synonym name that references the real table called DUAL, which is found in the SYS schema in an Oracle database.[4] The single row content of the DUAL table is used

---

[4]The SYS schema contains all the Oracle data dictionary tables, some of which are read-only to all register users, through database views.

only in executing a query that returns a single row as a result, with one or more column values. The DUAL table is used to perform calculations that are not related to the data in a particular table.

3.2 SINGLE ROW FUNCTIONS

Oracle SQL provides an enormous range of functions to assist with all sorts of calculations and data transformations. Some functions are known as *single row functions,* because they *execute and return a value for each row* retrieved. If you cannot find the calculation you desire, then you can create your own in the form of a stored function using PL/SQL, Java, or C. Table 3.3 is an abridged list of the SQL functions that are built into the Oracle database and can be used in your SQL statements:

The select statement, in the next example, uses the `LOWER()` and `UPPER()` case conversion string functions on text columns in the `SALES_ITEM` table:

```
SELECT lower(title), upper(publisher)
FROM sales_item
where full_price > 50;
```

Some sample output would appear as follows:

```
LOWER(TITLE)            UPPER(PUBLISHER)      FULL_PRICE
----------------------- --------------------- ----------
oracle pl/sql built-ins O'REILLY & ASSOCIATES       6.95
pocket reference

oracle pl/sql language  O'REILLY & ASSOCIATES       7.95
pocket reference
```

3.2.1 THE TO_CHAR CONVERSION FUNCTION

The TO_CHAR function is an interesting example of an overloaded function in the Oracle SQL environment. The TO_CHAR function can accept a date or a number data type as its first argument, and then the meaning of the string value in the second argument is interpreted differently. The second argument is a string of format-control characters. When using the TO_CHAR function to convert dates to a string, the format-control characters are also case-sensitive. Table 3.4 shows the most commonly used subset of valid format-control characters and their meanings.

TABLE 3.3 Abridged list of Oracle single row SQL functions

STRING FUNCTIONS	DESCRIPTION
UPPER(value)	Returns alphabetic characters in upper case
LOWER(value)	Returns alphabetic characters in lower case
INITCAP(value)	Returns first letter of each word capitalized, the rest in lower case
LENGTH(value)	Returns the number of characters in a string
SUBSTR(value, start [, len])	Extracts a substring beginning at the start position for a specified length
NUMBER FUNCTIONS	
ROUND(value [, precision])	Rounds numbers to nearest-decimal precision
TRUNC(value [, precision])	Truncates numbers to nearest-decimal precision
MOD(value, divisor)	Returns the remainder of a value divided by the divisor, works on decimals
SIGN(value)	Returns −1 for negative values; 0 when zero, and +1 for positive values
DATE FUNCTIONS	
MONTHS_BETWEEN(d1,d2)	Returns the number of months between two dates
NEXT_DAY(date,[day])	Returns the date of the nearest 'day of week' relative to the specified date
ROUND(date [,string])	Rounds a date to the nearest day (default), month, or year
TRUNC(date [, string])	Truncates the date to the nearest day (default), month, or year. Since Oracle dates contain time component, this function sets time to 0 hours, 0 minutes, and 0 seconds
CONVERSION FUNCTIONS	
TO_CHAR(date [, 'format'])	Returns a formatted string representation of a date value
TO_CHAR(nbr [, 'format'])	Returns a formatted string representation of a numeric value
TO_DATE('date' [,'format'])	Returns a date value for a formatted date string
TO_NUMBER(string)	Returns a numeric value for a string of digits in decimal or scientific format
DECODE(value, cmp1, result1 [, cmp2, result2 …] [, default])	Returns the result corresponding to the comparison value that is equal to the value in the first argument. This decode function is Oracle's equivalent of a switch/case statement in the SQL language It is a form of an if then else if otherwise sequence. If the default is returned if the value in the first argument does not match any comparison value, and if the default is omitted, then a NULL value is returned (see the example in UPDATE statement discussion)
NVL(value1, value2)	Returns the value2 if value1 is NULL, otherwise value1 is returned.

TABLE 3.4 Date conversion format characters

FORMAT	DESCRIPTION
DD	Represents the day of the month
D	Day of the week, where 1 = Sunday, 2 = Monday, etc.
MON	Represents the three-letter abbreviation of the month name
MONTH	Represents the full word of the month name, which is blank- padded to fill nine characters by default (the blank padding can be suppressed by using the format characters FM as a prefix before the blank-padded words. The FM prefix also suppresses leading zeros in number strings.
MM	Represents the numeric value of the month, i.e., 01 for January up to 12 for December
YYYY	Represents the year and century. If you omit any Y's from this format, the left-most digits in the year are removed. For example, for the year 1989: ❑ Using format YYY results in 989 being produced ❑ Using format YY results in 89 being produced.
HH24	Produces two digits for the hour component of the time in twenty-four-hour format
HH or HH12	Produces two digits for the hour component of the time in twelve-hour format
MI	Represents two digits for the minute component of time
SS	Represents two digits for the second component of time
AM or PM	Represents the text AM or PM depending on the actual time of the day. If the actual time is 13:40:15, using a format of: HH:MI:SSam would product a value of '01:40:15pm'.
Colon, comma	General punctuation characters that are represented in the specified location without transformation

There are many more choices and options available than are represented in the table, and the *Oracle SQL Reference Manual* should be consulted as a more comprehensive reference.

An important fact to remember is that an Oracle DATE column holds the century, day, month, year, hour, minute, and second.

Here is an example:

```
SELECT
  'Today is '|| TO_CHAR(SYSDATE,'DD-MON-YYYY
   HH24:MI:SS') DATE_TIME
FROM DUAL;
```

results in the following output:

```
DATE_TIME
-----------------------------
Today is 29-AUG-1999 23:41:10
```

The TO_CHAR function converts the current date and time, returned by the SYSDATE function, into a string representation defined by the data format control characters, listed in the second parameter of the TO_CHAR function. The DATE_TIME text is the column alias name.

3.3 *WHERE* CLAUSE TO RESTRICT ROWS RETRIEVED

If a database table contains thousands or millions of rows, it is impractical to retrieve them all at once, unless it is for batch-processing requirements. To restrict the number of rows in a result set returned from select statement, you can add a WHERE clause to the select statement, as shown in the following syntax:

```
SELECT column_expression(s)
FROM  table_expression(s)
WHERE condition(s);
```

The WHERE clause, evaluates one or more logical conditions for *each row* in the specified table. If the outcome of the conditional expression is true for a given row, then the row is added to the result set; otherwise, the row is excluded from the results.

3.3.1 QUERY CONDITIONAL EXPRESSIONS

The basic structure of the conditional expression used in the WHERE clause is:

```
left-hand-side operator right-hand-side
```

The left-hand or the right-hand-side of the condition can be specified as a:

- Literal value
- Column name
- SQL function
- SQL expression

The comparison operator can be one of those listed in the Table 3.5.

3.3.2 NEGATING CONDITIONS

In the additional forms of conditional expressions to be discussed, the NOT keyword, shown in square brackets, is optional. Adding the NOT keyword in the location shown converts the value of the conditional expression to its negative

TABLE 3.5 Logical comparison operators

OPERATOR	DESCRIPTION
=	For an equality comparison
>	For greater than, or
>=	greater than or equal to comparisons
<	For less than, or
<=	less than or equal to comparisons
<>	For nonequality comparisons (!=, and, ^= also represent a not equal operator)

meaning. Alternatively, the NOT keyword can be placed before the condition. For example:

```
NOT condition
```

The NOT operator appears before the condition when the comparison operator is one listed in Table 3.5.

3.3.3 THE LIST COMPARISON OPERATOR

The IN condition operator is called the *list* operator:

```
column [NOT] IN (value1, value2, …, valueN)
```

The IN operator compares the specified column to any of the values in the comma-separated list for equality. Using an IN operator is a simplified form of multiple conditions that compare the same column with different values, and each condition is bound together using an OR operator. The following query:

```
SELECT *
FROM   customer
WHERE credit_card_type = 'AMEX'
   OR credit_card_type = 'MASTERCARD'
   OR credit_card_type = 'VISA';
```

could be rewritten as:

```
SELECT *
FROM   customer
WHERE credit_card_type IN ('AMEX', 'MASTERCARD', 'VISA');
```

The Oracle RDBMS optimizer may rewrite the second query as if you had entered the first, even though the first example is more verbose.

3.3.4 THE RANGE COMPARISON OPERATOR

The BETWEEN operator is known as the *range* operator:

```
column [NOT] BETWEEN low_value AND high_value
```

The BETWEEN operator compares the specified column to a range of values inclusive of the low and high values. The low and high values can be entered as literal values or column names, and applied to the following data types:

- NUMBER
- CHAR or VARCHAR2
- DATE

The data type of the column must be consistent with those used for the low and high values. For example:

```
SELECT *
FROM   cust_order
WHERE total_cost BETWEEN 120.0 AND 250.0;
```

3.3.5 THE PATTERN MATCH COMPARISON OPERATOR

The LIKE operator is known as the *pattern match* operator and only applies to string or textual comparisons:

```
column [NOT] LIKE 'pattern' [ ESCAPE 'char' ]
```

The LIKE operator compares the column specified as a text string to a text pattern. The text pattern is any combination of characters. However, two characters, shown in Table 3.6, are reserved as special characters in the context of the pattern.

TABLE 3.6 Wildcard characters for use with LIKE operator

SPECIAL CHARACTER	MEANING
% (percent)	Matches zero or more characters at its location in the pattern
_ (underscore)	Matches exactly one character at its location in the pattern

This operator is very useful for providing Web-based customers with a flexible way to search for products by title. Be aware that the pattern match string is case-sensitive. For example:

```
SELECT title, full_price
FROM  sales_item
WHERE title like '%Performance%'
```

With results like:

```
TITLE                                        FULL_PRICE
-------------------------------------------- ----------
High Performance Oracle8 Tuning                   49.99
Oracle SQL High Performance Tuning                49.95
Oracle Performance Tuning Tips & Techniques       49.99
Oracle Performance Tuning, 2nd Edition            47.95
```

The query results list all books with a title containing the word "Performance" surrounded by zero or more characters. The next example shows a query for books with an author name starting with a capital *E*.

```
SELECT title, author, full_price
FROM   sales_item
WHERE  title like 'E%'
```

With the following results:

```
TITLE                                  AUTHOR
------------------------------------ ------------------
Teach Yourself Oracle8 in 21 Days    Edward Whalen et al.
Software Engineering With Oracle     Elio Bonazzi
```

If you enter a search request that must find one of the special characters in the text column, then the ESCAPE keyword identifies another character used immediately before the special character, to suppress the meaning of the special character. For example, locate all books containing a percent character in the title:

```
SELECT title, author, full_price
FROM   sales_item
WHERE  title like '%\%%' ESCAPE '\';
```

The interpretation of the pattern text in the example is:

- The first percent character retains its special meaning to match zero or more characters.
- The second percent is preceded by the escape character; therefore, its special meaning is suppressed, and the combination of "\%" characters represent the percent character itself.
- The third percent also retains its special meaning to match zero or more characters.

3.3.6 HANDLING NULL VALUES

Columns in a relational database may hold a NULL value. The NULL is not the same as a zero literal value or a zero-length string,[5] but represents either the absence of a value or an unknown value. To select rows with a column containing a NULL value, use the IS operator in the condition:

```
column IS NULL
```

To select rows with columns that do not contain a NULL value, use:

```
column IS NOT NULL
```

Alternatively, you may use the NVL() conversion function. The NVL() first converts a NULL value, if present, into an alternative quantifiable value that can be successfully used in a logical comparison. For example, a condition to test for a NULL value a column could be written as follows:

```
NVL(column, -1) = -1
```

However, this is not a particularly good way to do the test, because the condition is true for a –1 value stored in the column.

The NVL() function accepts two parameters that must be the same data types. The preceding example implies that "column" is numeric, because the second argument is a numeric literal. If the column data type is a string, you could write the condition as:

```
NVL(column, '?') = '?'
```

The value you choose for second parameter will be dependent on the type of data and the valid values stored in the column.

---

[5]An empty or zero-length string cannot be stored as a value for a character column in an Oracle relational database.

3.3.6.1 Conditions Involving NULL Values.

As warning to you, if you enter a condition comparing a column with the NULL value, using any logical operator (shown in Table 3.5), the condition yields a NULL (unknown) result. Any condition with an unknown result is treated as if the condition returned a false result. For example:

```
SELECT title
FROM sales_item
WHERE author = NULL
```

The condition `author = NULL` is always false, independent of the data in the author column. Therefore, no rows are returned by the query, because the comparison yields an unknown results, that is, a NULL result. Logically speaking, a known value can never equal (=) an unknown value. The remedy used the techniques discussed in the section called "Handling NULL values" previously mentioned in this chapter.

3.3.7 COMBINING MULTIPLE CONDITIONS

Multiple conditions can be used to further restrict the set of rows that satisfy a query. A WHERE clause can be made up of additional conditions separated by a logical AND or a logical OR operator. Each condition may also be negated with a NOT operator.

For example, to find all books published only by Prentice-Hall and in the year 1999, you can execute the query:

```
SELECT title, author, publisher
FROM   sales_item
WHERE  publisher = 'Prentice Hall'
  AND  year_published = 1999;
```

If you execute the same query using an OR operator instead of the AND operator, the meaning of the statement changes and the result set returned is different:

```
SEECT title, author, publisher
FROM  sales_item
WHERE publisher = 'Prentice Hall'
  OR  year_published = 1999;
```

The results would show all books published in the year 1999 independently of the publisher, and also all books published by Prentice-Hall independently of the year published.

3.4 TABLE JOIN OPERATIONS

To form a join operation, more than one table name must appear in the FROM clause in a query, and the WHERE clause requires a join condition to link the data from the related tables. Remember that the WHERE clause is not mandatory and you can forget to include the join condition. For example:

```
SELECT name, surname, email, total_cost
FROM customer, cust_order;
```

The problem with this statement is that there is no join condition to link a row in the customer table with the corresponding row in the customer order table. The result of this query is that all the records in the customer table are joined with all the records in the `CUST_ORDER` table, forming what is known as a *Cartesian product*. The results of a Cartesian product are often meaningless, cause performance problems, and are not very useful.

To correct the problem and avoid the Cartesian product, you must provide a join condition in the WHERE clause of the query. The required join condition for the sample query should compare a column value in the customer table with a related value in a column from the `CUST_ORDER` table. For example:

```
SELECT name, surname, email, total_cost
FROM customer, cust_order
WHERE customer.id = cust_order.cust_id; – row join condition
```

LISTING 3.1 Query with join condition

A foreign key column, like `CUST_ORDER.CUST_ID`, is usually involved in a join condition, because the foreign key value represents a relationship to another row. As a summary of what you have learned here, a condition that is used to compare values between two different rows in the same or different tables is known as a *join condition*.

The rule of thumb is that for each "*additional*" table name listed in the FROM clause, the statement requires a join condition, and this prevents a Cartesian product from occurring. Table 3.7 summarizes the rule.

In short, the equation to represent the rule of thumb is (number_of_tables –1) join conditions are required.

Listing 3.1 shows that the column names listed in the join condition are prefixed, using a dot notation, by the table name in which the column is declared. Column names that are unique across all tables used in the query do not require the table name as a prefix. If the table name is too long, using it as a prefix for all the columns in a query can be tedious. Therefore, all the table names used in the

TABLE 3.7 Rules for Joining tables

NUMBER OF TABLES IN FROM CLAUSE	NUMBER OF JOIN CONDITIONS
1	0
2	1
3	2
:	:
N	N-1

FROM clause can be given an alias called a *table alias*. The table alias appears immediately after each table name in the FROM clause. For example:

```
SELECT cus.name, cus.surname, cus.email, ord.total_cost
FROM customer cus, cust_order ord
WHERE cus.id = ord.cust_id;
```

The table aliases, shown in bold text, are declared after the table names, and are separated from the table name by at least one space.

3.4.1 OUTER JOIN OPERATIONS

The outer join operation is an extension of the join that retrieves rows satisfying the join condition. It also returns any orphan rows from one of the tables that would not normally be in a join due to the absence of information in the related table. This scenario occurs in a design that permits rows to exist in one table without a direct match to a row in another table. The scenario also occurs when the database implementation does not enforce the use of data-integrity rules.

To explain the concept of the outer join, recall the entity relationship model developed in Chapter 1, which has a relationship between the ORDER_ITEM and SALES_ITEM entities, as shown in Figure 3.1.

The basic business rules defining the relationship between these two entities are:

- Each SALES ITEM ***may be*** purchased as one or more ORDER ITEMs.
- Each ORDER ITEM must be for one and only one SALES ITEM.

From the first rule you can also state that a sales item may *not* be the subject of a purchase at all. If a sales item has not been ordered, then a row for the product exists in the SALES_ITEM table, but the ORDER_ITEM table has no records that reference the SALES_ITEM.

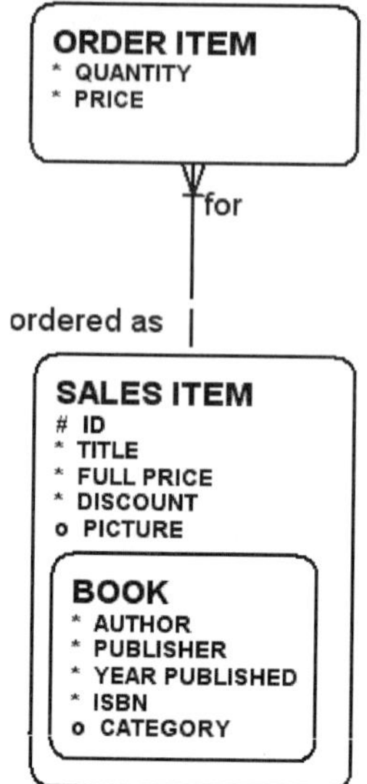

FIGURE 3.1 ORDER ITEM and SALES ITEM entity relationship model

The business wants to know which products are not selling, in order to take some action, such as additional discounting or promotions. The JOIN operation cannot be used to identify products not ordered, because of the absence of a row in the ORDER_ITEM table for a join condition to occur. If a query is written as a simple join:

```
SELECT orditm.ord_id, orditm.price, sitm.title
FROM order_item orditm, sales_item sitm
WHERE orditm.prd_id = sitm.id;
```

LISTING 3.2 Joining **SALES_ITEM** with **ORDER_ITEM** table

The results produced from this query show all the records in the SALES_ITEM that have already been ordered. What about the records that have not been ordered? The solution is to use the outer join operator, which lists all the sales items that have not been ordered, in addition to all the sales items that have been ordered.

The syntax for the Oracle SQL outer join operator is a plus sign enclosed in parentheses (+). The outer join operator can only be placed on one side of a join condition, after the name of a column in the condition. For example:

```
WHERE table1.column1 (+) = table2.column2
```

or

```
WHERE table1.column1 = table2.column2 (+)
```

Where do you place the outer join operator? Place it after the column belonging to the table with unknown information.

The SQL statement in Listing 3.2 will only display all the sales items that have been placed in an existing order item. If you also want to display the sales items that have not been ordered, you would add the outer join operator to the condition where the column belongs to the ORDER_ITEM table, because the order item information may be unknown for some sales items. The query in Listing 3.2 is rewritten as:

```
SELECT orditm.ord_id, orditm.price, sitm.title
FROM   order_item orditm, sales_item sitm
WHERE  orditm.prd_id (+) = sitm.id
ORDER BY orditm.ord_id;
```

Sample results would produce something similar to the following fragment of output:

```
ORD_ID   PRICE TITLE
------ ------- --------------------------------
    51   37.49 Software Engineering With Oracle
   101   37.49 Oracle Database Construction Kit
<null> <null>  Oracle Design
<null> <null>  Oracle JDeveloper
```

The two rows shown in bold are examples of two products that have never been ordered. The outer join operator causes these records to appear, and the SQL engine assigns NULL values to the columns that are normally filled with data from the related table, that is, the ORDER_ITEM table. In this case, item column values for the two rows, shown in bold text, are NULL because there is no item record for these products. The last two rows in the output would not be displayed for the query in Listing 3.2.

The NULL values from the results produced for the unknown data are used, in additional conditions to keep only the rows that do have NULL values. The displayed result set would show the sales items that have not been ordered, and not sales items that have been ordered. For example:

```
SELECT orditm.ord_id, orditm.price, sitm.title
FROM   order_item orditm, sales_item sitm
WHERE  orditm.prd_id (+) = sitm.id
AND    orditm.ord_id is NULL
ORDER BY orditm.ord_id;
```

This output result set only includes sales items that are not ordered. For example:

```
ORD_ID  PRICE  TITLE
------ ------ -------------------------
<null> <null> Oracle Design
<null> <null> Oracle JDeveloper
```

The ANSI-92 SQL syntax discusses left and right outer joins, which are supported by the Oracle SQL outer join syntax.

3.5 ORDER BY

The examples illustrating the discussion of joins and outer join operations made use of the ORDER BY clause. Simply put, the ORDER BY clause allows you to specify how to sort the records returned by a query. Its general syntax is shown below:

```
ORDER BY order_criteria
```

Where the syntax of the order criteria is

```
column_expression [ASC | DESC] [, … ]
```

The order_criteria can be a comma-separated list of column expressions, and each column expression can be:

- A column name.
- An expression or calculation.
- A column alias defined in a column expression in the SELECT clause.
- A number identifying a column expression by position in the SELECT clause (this feature is deprecated in the SQL standards, but is commonly used in UNION, INTERSECT, or MINUS operations).

The keyword ASC or DESC appears after each column expression to control the direction of the sort.

```
SELECT orditm.ord_id, orditm.price, sitm.title
FROM   order_item orditm, sales_item sitm
WHERE orditm.prd_id = sitm.id
ORDER BY orditm.ord_id, orditm.price;
```

The preceding example shows a simple sort using two columns in the sort criteria:

- The first column in the order by clause, called `ORDITM.ORD_ID`, is used for the primary sort in ascending sequence.
- The second sort column, `ORDITM.PRICE`, is a secondary sort, or sub-sort, relative to the primary sort.

The ascending-sequence sort order is implied by the absence of explicitly adding the keyword ASC or DESC after each of the sort column names. To explicitly specify the sort sequence used for each column, after each column in the order by clause add:

- ASC for an ascending sort.
- DESC for a descending sort.

For example:

```
ORDER BY orditm.ord_id ASC, orditm.price DESC
```

If a sorted column contains null values, by default:

- Null values appear *last* in an ascending sort.
- Null values appear *first* in a descending sort.

If you need more control over the sort order of null values, then you can convert the null values into something meaningful. The NVL() or DECODE() functions can be used to convert a NULL into a meaningful value. The NVL() function syntax is:

```
NVL(arg1, arg2)
```

If the value of arg1 is a null, then the function returns arg2; otherwise it returns arg1. The following pseudo code illustrates the conceptual internal behavior of the NVL function:

```
FUNCTION NVL(arg1, arg2) RETURN val
BEGIN
  IF (arg1 is null) THEN
    return arg2
  ELSE
    return arg1
  END IF
END NVL
```

The NVL() is overloaded to support different database data types in its arguments; and the data types of both arguments must be the same. There are performance ramifications when functions are used in the order by clause.

The next example uses the NVL() function in the selected list of columns and the order by clause:

```
SELECT NVL(orditm.ord_id-1), orditm.price, sitm.title
FROM  sales_item sitm, order_item orditm
WHERE orditm.prd_id (+) = sitm.id
ORDER BY NVL(orditm.ord_id,-1), orditm.price DESC;
```

The following result set is returned:

```
ORD_ID   PRICE TITLE
------ ------- ---------------------------------
    -1 <null>  Oracle Design
    -1 <null>  Oracle JDeveloper
    51   37.49  Software Engineering With Oracle
         37.49  Oracle Database Construction Kit
```

Example notes:

- The value for `ORD_ID` columns displays a `-1` because the NULL have been converted by using the NVL() function.
- The <null> text can be added by entering following SQL*Plus command before the SQL statement: `SQL>` **`set null "<null>"`**

3.6 AGGREGATE FUNCTIONS

Aggregate, or group, functions operate on one or more rows, and by default they *ignore NULL values* in specified columns. Table 3.8 contain a list of group functions and their meanings.

The group functions are used to perform data summarization and calculation operations. They can be used in the query SELECT, HAVING, and ORDER BY clauses. An aggregate function cannot be directly used in the condition of a WHERE clause.

The shopping item table has a quantity and price for each item, and the shopping basket holds the summary value for the total cost of goods added to the basket. You can use a sum function to determine the total cost of items in the basket, using the query:

```
SELECT SUM(item.quantity * item.price) AS total_cost
FROM  shopping_item item
WHERE item.basket_cust_id = :some_customer_id;
```

TABLE 3.8 Oracle group functions

GROUP FUNCTION	DESCRIPTION
COUNT(arg)	Counts the number of rows in the query group for the specified argument, which could be a column or an expression. The argument may be specified as the asterisk (*) character to count all rows independent of specific values. Works for columns with any data type.
SUM(arg)	Calculates the summation of the specified column or expression argument for rows in the query group. Only works for number data types.
MAX(arg)	Returns the maximum value from the rows in the query group for the specified columns or expression in the argument. Works with number, character, and date data types.
MIN(arg)	Returns the minimum value from the rows in the query group for the specified columns or expression in the argument. Works with number, character, and date data types.
AVG(arg)	Returns the average value from the rows in the query group for the specified columns or expression in the argument. Works with number data types. If NULL values occur in the group of records for the argument, they are not included, resulting in a non-true average. Apply the NVL function around to the argument to convert NULL before the average is calculated for a true average value.
VARIANCE(arg)	Returns the variance of number data types in the query group.
STDDEV(arg)	Returns the standard deviation of number data types in the query group.

The SUM() operation in the query always returns a single row value as the result, which may include a null result when no rows satisfy the query. Group functions typically process more than one row of data, and return a single result for the set of rows processed. In the example, the shopping basket number was known, so there was no requirement to qualify the shopping items with the basket number to which they belong.

If you wanted to calculate the total cost for shopping items in more than one shopping basket, you would need to know which basket the total cost is associated with. The GROUP BY clause helps to provide the answer.

3.7 GROUP BY CLAUSES

The GROUP BY clause sorts records into groups ordered by a specified grouping criterion. It is used when aggregate functions must be applied to more than one group of rows at the same time. To utilize the grouping functionality provided by the SQL language, use the GROUP BY keywords after the conditions listed in the WHERE clause of a query:

```
SELECT [column, ...] group-function(column) [ ,... ]
FROM   table-list
[ WHERE condition(s) ]
GROUP BY group-criteria-list
```

The group criterion is a comma-separated list of one or more column names that may, or may not, appear in the displayed column list.

> Any column listed in the SELECT clause that is not the subject of a group function must be listed in the group criteria.

The query clauses are processed in the following sequence:

1. The WHERE clause, if present, is applied first.
2. Rows still available are then sorted according to the GROUP BY criteria.
3. Group functions appearing in the select list are calculated once for each group of sorted rows.

Suppose you want to find out the total number of items in a specific order, assuming that the following data exist in the order item table:

```
  ORD_ID   PRD_ID  QUANTITY   PRICE
-------- -------- --------- -------
      51       10         1   37.49
      51       69         1   37.49
      51        3         1   33.74

     101       69         1   37.49
     101       68         1   31.46
     101       17         1   14.96
     101       45         1   48.74
     101       42         1   37.49

     102        1         1   44.99

     103        1         1   44.99
     103       20         1   29.99
```

You determine the total number of items in an order with the following statement:

```
SELECT sum(i.quantity) num_items
FROM   order_item i
WHERE i.ord_id = 51
```

```
--The result may be, for example:

 NUM_ITEMS
----------
         3
```

Perhaps you now wish to find out the total number of items for all orders. The query is changed by simply removing the WHERE clause and adding a GROUP BY ORD_ID:

```
SELECT sum(i.quantity) num_items
FROM  order_item i
GROUP BY i.ord_id

-- There is one value returned for each unique ord_id value

 NUM_ITEMS
----------
         3
         5
         1
         2
```

The GROUP BY on the ORD_ID column is required; otherwise the SUM() function would add all item quantities for all order rows, giving a single value of 11 as the result. However, the result set returned with the GROUP BY on ORD_ID is a list of values with no indication of their order. To qualify the order to which each result value belongs, the query is modified to include the ORD_ID column in the select list:

```
SELECT i.ord_id, sum(i.quantity) num_items
FROM  order_item i
GROUP BY i.ord_id

-- Each value returned is qualified by their unique ord_id

  ORD_ID NUM_ITEMS
-------- ---------
      51         3
     101         5
     102         1
     103         2
```

Note that the result set is sorted in ascending sequence based on the group criteria column value. Now, suppose you also want to know the customer name details for each order. Then you modify the query as follows:

```
SELECT c.name, i.ord_id, sum(i.quantity) num_items
FROM   order_item i, cust_order o, customer c
WHERE i.ord_id = o.id
AND    o.cust_id = c.id
GROUP BY i.ord_id
```

The statement select list now includes the customer name, which requires the two tables CUST_ORDER and customer to be added to the FROM clause. The three-table join is needed to link the customer with the item details through the order table, and thus the two conditions in the WHERE clause are needed to ensure that the relationships between the rows in each column are preserved. However, the statement fails, with the following Oracle error message:

```
ORA-00979: not a GROUP BY expression
```

The error indicates that the customer name column must be included in the GROUP BY clause, because it is in a group expression. The statement is corrected by adding the customer name column into the GROUP BY list:

```
SELECT c.name, i.ord_id, sum(i.quantity) num_items
FROM   order_item i, cust_order o, customer c
WHERE i.ord_id = o.id
AND    o.cust_id = c.id
GROUP BY c.name, i.ord_id
```

The sample results produced are:

```
NAME         ORD_ID NUM_ITEMS
---------- ------- ---------
Elio             51         3
Elio            101         5
Ilaria          103         2
Mailliw         102         1
```

One person here is obviously a good customer. The business may use this information to determine who its loyal customers are, and to offer rewards for their loyalty on future purchases.

The example shows that more than one column can participate in the group criterion. The resultant data are sorted using the first column in the group criterion. Subsequent columns named in the group criteria cause an additional sorting of the data relative to the sorted valued of the preceding group column.

> It is important to understand that the *last* column in the group by list defines the level at which group functions are calculated. In the example the SUM is executed once for each unique combination of values for the list of group columns named in the GROUP BY clause.

Since the example has a one-to-many mapping between the customer and the order, the summed quantity is for the number of items in a specific customer order, as reflected by the order of the column names `C.NAME, I.ORD_ID` in the GROUP BY clause.

If you were to modify the query by replacing the `ORD_ID` column in the select list, and the group criterion, with the unique identifier of the customer, then you would determine the total quantity of products purchased by each customer. For example:

```
SELECT c.id, c.name, sum(i.quantity) num_items
FROM order_item i, cust_order o, customer c
WHERE i.ord_id = o.id
AND   o.cust_id = c.id
GROUP BY c.id, c.name;

-- Result is:

    ID NAME         NUM_ITEMS
------ ----------- ----------
    23 Ilaria               2
    41 Elio                 8
    51 Mailliw              1
```

Keeping performance in mind, you may want to minimize the use of GROUP BY functionality because of its sort-processing overhead.

3.8 HAVING CLAUSES

A HAVING clause can only be used when a GROUP BY clause exists in a query. HAVING clauses can be used for either of two purposes:

- To include a group from the result set.
- To exclude a group from the result set.

Therefore, the HAVING clause applies to the results for each group. Here is the syntax for the HAVING clause shown in the context of a generic query:

```
SELECT column(s)
FROM table(s)
WHERE conditions(s)
GROUP BY group-criterion
HAVING condition(s)
[ORDER BY columns(s) ]
```

There are several differences between the WHERE clause and the HAVING clause:

- The WHERE clause applies to each row, and cannot use group functions in conditions unless the group functions are nested in a subquery or encapsulated in user-defined functions.
- The HAVING clause applies to each group, and permits the use of group functions in its conditions.

The sequence in which the clauses are applied is:

1. The WHERE clause is applied.
2. GROUP BY sorting is performed.
3. Group function expressions are evaluated for each group result.
4. The HAVING clause is applied as filter on the group results.
5. The ORDER BY clause sorts the final set of rows, if any.

Do not use the GROUP BY and ORDER BY clauses in the same query, because of the overhead of two sort operations.

As an example, here is how to prepare a list of all customers who have purchased more than five products. The query to solve this question is:

```
SELECT c.id, c.name, sum(i.quantity) num_items
FROM order_item i, cust_order o, customer c
WHERE i.ord_id = o.id
AND   o.cust_id = c.id
GROUP BY c.id, c.name
HAVING sum(i.quantity) > 5;

-- Based on the data produced by last example
-- presented in the GROUP BY section, the result is:
```

```
    ID NAME       NUM_ITEMS
------ --------- ----------
    41 Elio               8
```

The query must use the expression `SUM(i.quantity)` and not the column alias `num_items` in the condition. Only column names are permitted in the HAVING clause, but no aliases at the same query level.[6] Note that the condition in the HAVING clause excludes the following data from the result set:

```
    ID NAME       NUM_ITEMS
------ --------- ----------
    23 Ilaria             2
    51 Mailliw            1
```

3.9 SUBQUERIES

A subquery is a SELECT statement nested in the context of another SQL statement. The nested subquery is termed the *child query*, and the part of the query that contains the nested subquery is called the *main* or *parent query*. The SELECT, INSERT, UPDATE, and DELETE statements all support the use of nested subqueries. The generic SQL statement syntax for subqueries is:

```
SELECT column(s), (single-value sub-query) [col-alias]
FROM table(s) | (multi-value sub-query) table-alias
WHERE (single-value sub-query) OP (single/multiple-value
sub-query)
GROUP BY group-criteria
HAVING expression OP (single/multiple-value sub-query)
ORDER BY order-criteria;
```

The subquery is another SELECT statement embedded inside the parentheses.

3.9.1 RULES ON USING SUBQUERIES

Here are some rules on the use of subqueries in a SELECT statement:

- In a SELECT clause, the subquery must return only one row with a single column value. Therefore, it is called a *single-value* subquery, in the syntax above.

---

[6]Alias names for columns in a nested subquery can be used as if they were column names in the context of their parent query.

- In a FROM clause, the subquery may return one or more rows and columns. Therefore, it is as if the subquery were returning a table of data.
- In a WHERE clause, the subquery on the left side of the comparison operator (OP) must return a single row and a single column value. The subquery on the right side may return a single value from one or more rows depending on the type of comparison operator used.[7] There are variant subqueries in the WHERE clause that allow multiple columns to be present on both the left and right sides of the comparison operator.
- In a HAVING clause, the subquery may return one column from one or more rows depending on the comparison operator used.

A subquery itself is created from a SELECT statement, which in turn can have nested subqueries in the same locations already identified. Additional points to be aware of are:

- A subquery must be enclosed in parentheses.
- A subquery in a FROM clause should be given a table alias to distinguish the column name retrieved from those in the outer query if there is any element of ambiguity.
- An ORDER BY clause is not permitted in a nested subquery statement. The outermost query is the only part of the statement that uses an ORDER BY clause.
- Subqueries may be nested to a level of 255 deep. The number of levels used in a subquery can result in a very complex statement, and could lead to poor performance. You can simplify the SQL statements by using PL/SQL or Java stored functions to replace the functionality of the subquery. If well done, this could lead to more modular, reusable code and some performance gains.

When a subquery is used in a WHERE or HAVING clause, it is necessary to choose an appropriate comparison operator to compare column values to the subquery results. There are two types of comparison operators:

- Single-value comparison operators.
- Multi-value comparison operators.

The single-value comparison operators can be either: =, <, >, >=, <=, or <>. If you are using single-value comparison operators, the subquery must return a single row. However, if the subquery returns multiple rows, then the comparison operator must be one of the multi-value comparison operators, such as IN, > ANY,

---

[7]Comparison operators are classified as single-value comparison operators, such as the equality operator, or multi-value comparison operators, such as the IN operator.

< ANY, =ANY. A runtime error will occur if you use a single-value comparison operator when the subquery returns multiple rows.

3.9.1.1 Example: Subquery in the SELECT clause.

```
SELECT c.id, c.name,
 (select sum(quantity) from order_item where ord_id = o.id)
num_items
FROM  cust_order o, customer c
WHERE c.id = o.cust_id;

-- Results:
    ID NAME        NUM_ITEMS
------ --------- ----------
    23 Ilaria             2
    41 Elio               3
    41 Elio               5
    51 Mailliw            1
```

This example is similar in result to the statements shown in the discussion of GROUP BY functionality. In this case, a join is eliminated by using the subquery to derive the value for the quantity of items ordered by each customer. Join operations can often be rewritten using a subquery. Performance must be measured to find which is better, because a variety of factors affect query performance. Using a subquery in a SELECT clause is supported in Oracle8i Version 8.1.x.

3.9.1.2 Example: Subquery in the FROM clause.

```
SELECT c.id, c.name, sum(itm.total)
FROM customer c, (SELECT o.cust_id, i.price*i.quantity total
                  FROM  cust_order o, order_item i
                  WHERE o.id = i.ord_id) itm
WHERE c.id = itm.cust_id
GROUP BY c.id, c.name;

-- Results of query:

    ID NAME              SUM(ITM.TOTAL)
------ ----------------- --------------
    23 Ilaria                     74.98
    41 Elio                      278.86
    51 Mailliw                    44.99
```

The subquery in the FROM clause returns a set of rows containing the customer id from the customer order table. The subquery also calculates a value for the item price multiplied by the quantity ordered, and assigns the value an alias name of `TOTAL`. The column and alias names in the subquery are visible to the parent query when they are qualified by the name `ITM.`, which in this case is a required table alias assigned to the subquery.

The subquery in this example forms a virtual table that can be thought of as an inline view. If you execute the subquery on its own, you get the following information, for the related data:

```
SELECT o.cust_id, i.price*i.quantity total
FROM   cust_order o, order_item i
WHERE o.id = i.ord_id;

  CUST_ID      TOTAL
--------- ---------
       41      37.49
       41      37.49
       41      33.74
       41      37.49
       41      31.46
       41      14.96
       41      48.74
       41      37.49
       51      44.99
       23      44.99
       23      29.99
```

This information is joined to the customer table, using the customer `ID` and subquery `CUST_ID` values to form a relationship, and then the total is summed.

3.9.1.3 Example: Subquery in the WHERE clause.

```
SELECT c.id, c.name, c.surname, o.id
FROM   customer c, cust_order o
WHERE c.id = o.cust_id
AND    o.total_cost < (SELECT avg(total_cost) FROM cust_order);

    ID NAME       SURNAME          ID
------ ---------- --------- --------
    51 Mailliw    Rekir          102
    23 Ilaria     Ilaria         103
```

The subquery in this example calculates the average TOTAL_COST for all the orders in the system. The subquery is executed alone, and the result is:

```
SELECT avg(total_cost)
FROM cust_order;

-- Result:

AVG(TOTAL_COST)
---------------
       117.5825
```

The parent query then uses the average result value of 117.5825, returned by the subquery, in the comparison to the TOTAL_COST of each order. The parent query displays the customer details and the associated order number for all orders that have a total cost less than the average total cost for all orders.

Subqueries are often the result of breaking a problem into multiple parts and solving each part using a query. The queries can be combined to form a subquery or, sometimes, a join operation.

3.9.2 TYPES OF SUBQUERIES

Subqueries are classified into two types:

1. Nested subqueries
2. Correlated subqueries

3.9.2.1 Nested Subqueries. Nested subqueries are independent of their parent query data, and are executed once before their parent query. A nested subquery executes first, returning a result that can be used by the parent query. All the subqueries shown in the preceding sections were nested subqueries. However, the example of a subquery in the FROM clause is a special case, because the parent query was dependent on the names as well as the values of the subquery.

3.9.2.2 Correlated Subqueries. A correlated subquery has a dependency on information from its parent query. The data value from each parent row is used to evaluate the correlated child subquery, which then returns a result that can be used in the parent query. The correlated subquery must execute once for each row processed by its parent query. To demonstrate correlated subquery processing, here is some pseudo code that illustrates the behavior:

```
Parent query fetches first record
WHILE (Row exists in Parent query)
LOOP
  Execute correlated subquery with data from a parent query row
  Correlated query returns results to parent query
  Parent query applies a comparison operator on child query result
  IF comparison result is true for the current row THEN
     include the parent row in the result set
  ELSE
    exclude the parent row from the result set
  END IF
  fetch the next parent query row
END LOOP
```

The following example is a query to list all customers who have placed more than one order. The query is:

```
SELECT c.id, c.name, c.surname
FROM   customer c
WHERE (SELECT count(o.*)
       FROM cust_order o
       WHERE o.cust_id = c.id) > 1;

-- Result:

    ID NAME    SURNAME
------ ------- ---------
    41 Elio    Izzanob
```

The subquery has a dependency on the value of customer id `C.ID` in order to calculate the number of orders made by a specific customer. The bold text marks the dependent data value. The dependency exists because the inner/subquery requires a value from the parent query in order to complete. Note that the query applies a feature of Oracle8i that permits a subquery to be placed on the left side of a conditional operator. In earlier versions of the Oracle database, using the subquery on the right-hand side of the conditional operator yields the same result:

```
SELECT c.id, c.name, c.surname
FROM   customer c
WHERE 1 < (SELECT count(o.*)
           FROM cust_order o
           WHERE o.cust_id = c.id);

-- Result:
```

```
    ID NAME    SURNAME
------ ------- ---------
    41 Elio    Izzanob
```

3.10 QUERYING OBJECT STRUCTURES

Object instances and their attribute values may also be queried from object tables or nested in columns. Object instances can be queried in such a way that the attribute data appear as column values in rows or object instance structures.

3.10.1 QUERIES ON OBJECT TABLES AND COLUMNS

An object table contains one or more object instances, and each object instance comprises one or more attributes. When you write a select statement based on an object table, the Oracle database engine allows you to treat each instance as if it were a row in a relational table, and each attribute in each object instance as if it were a column in a row.

The query syntax is:

```
SELECT column-list
FROM table-list
WHERE condition(s)
GROUP BY group-criteria
HAVING condition(s)
ORDER BY columns(s)
```

You can specify attribute names in the column list, and object table names in the table list. Attribute names can be used anywhere a column can appear.

Suppose you create the courier object `COURIER_T`, and courier object table as follows:

```
CREATE TYPE courier_t AS OBJECT (
  id                NUMBER(4),
  name              VARCHAR2(30),
  cost_per_item     NUMBER(6,2)
);

CREATE TABLE courier OF courier_t(
  id CONSTRAINT courier_pk PRIMARY KEY,
  name NOT NULL,
 cost_per_item NOT NULL
);
```

For convenience, the ID attribute has been added to the courier table[8] to simplify the process of uniquely identifying each courier object instance. The simplest query is to select all attributes and all object instances from the courier table:

```
SELECT *
FROM courier;

-- With sample result values as:

      ID NAME                    COST_PER_ITEM
-------- --------------------- -------------
       1 Federal Impress                 6.5
       2 GKL International                 6
       3 Snail Mail Inc                  1.7
       4 Universal Post                  4.5
```

The query is exactly the same statement that is used on a COURIER relational table. In this case, the object instance and its attribute values are displayed as if they are column values in a row of a relational table. The simplified presentation of object data allows you to display user objects without writing proprietary SQL statements in your Java JDBC programs.

If you wanted to display each instance in the object table as an object instance, the query would be modified as follows:

```
SELECT VALUE(c)
FROM courier c;

-- With sample result values as:

VALUE(C)(ID, NAME, COST_PER_ITEM)
----------------------------------------
COURIER_T(1, 'Federal Impress', 6.50)
COURIER_T(2, 'GKL International', 6.00)
COURIER_T(3, 'Snail Mail Inc', 1.70)
COURIER_T(4, 'Universal Post', 4.50)
```

The results show each attribute value encapsulated in the COURIER_T object type constructor for each instance, as represented when using Oracle

[8]The courier table holds information about shipping companies.

SQL*Plus to execute the SQL statement. The table alias `c`, used after the courier table name, must be provided in order for the `VALUE()` function to return a row as an object instance.

3.10.2 USEFUL FUNCTIONS FOR OBJECT INSTANCES IN OBJECT TABLES

If you are using object types and reference columns to objects, the following functions become valuable tools in your toolbox:

- The VALUE() function.
- The REF() function.
- The DEREF() function.

3.10.2.1 The VALUE Function. The VALUE(alias) function is designed to return an object instance, where:

- The parameter to the VALUE() function, when used in a SQL statement, is table alias providing the association to an object instance (or row) in an object table.
- The return value of the VALUE() function is an object instance whose object type is the type used for the definition of the object table.

3.10.2.2 The REF Function. The REF(alias) function is used to return a reference to an object instance. This is similar to retrieving the internal object identifier for, or pointer to, the object instance.

```
SELECT REF(c)
FROM courier c;

-- Result values:

REF(C)
--------------------------------------------------------------------------------------
000028020980799146E20311D3BCF6000000000000807990FEE20311D3BCF60000000000000080325F0000
000028020980799147E20311D3BCF6000000000000807990FEE20311D3BCF60000000000000080325F0001
000028020980799148E20311D3BCF6000000000000807990FEE20311D3BCF60000000000000080325F0002
000028020980799149E20311D3BCF6000000000000807990FEE20311D3BCF60000000000000080325F0003
```

The object identifier values are not visually useful, but are globally unique. They are used to form an association between a REF column and the object instance referenced. In an INSERT or UPDATE statement, the REF() function is used to populate REF columns with a reference to an object instance. The REF() function can also be used in comparison operations to form a link with an associated object instance in another table.

To demonstrate how a reference column can be used, consider the customer object type and table, with the customer shopping basket object type and table:

```
CREATE TYPE customer_t AS OBJECT(
  id                      NUMBER(6),
  name                    VARCHAR2(30),
  surname                 VARCHAR2(30),
  email                   VARCHAR2(50),
  password                VARCHAR2(10),
  credit_card_type        VARCHAR2(10),
  credit_card_number      VARCHAR2(20),
  month_expired           VARCHAR2(2),
  year_expired            VARCHAR2(2)
);

CREATE TYPE shopping_basket_t AS OBJECT (
  creation_date     DATE,
  shipment_cost     NUMBER(5),
  total_cost        NUMBER(6),
  customer_ref      REF customer_t,
  items             SHOPPING_ITEM_NT_T
 );

CREATE TABLE customer OF customer_t;
CREATE TABLE shopping_basket OF shopping_basket_t;
```

The shopping basket type definition highlights, in bold text, the CUSTOMER_REF attribute, which is a reference to an object type of CUSTOMER_T. A query showing the shopping basket for a specific customer, using the REF() function in a condition to match a particular customer, is:

```
SELECT *
FROM shopping_basket
WHERE customer_ref = (SELECT REF(c) FROM customer c WHERE id = 50)
```

The example uses REF() function in the subquery to get a unique global object identifier for customer whose id is 50. The REF() function value retrieved is compared to the value in the CUSTOMER_REF column. The query shows all the shopping basket details for the specified customer.

Another way to get the same results is to perform a comparison by object value. For example:

```
SELECT *
FROM shopping_basket
WHERE DEREF(customer_ref) = (SELECT VALUE(c)
                             FROM customer c WHERE id = 50)
```

The DEREF() function results in an object instance value that is compared to the object instance value returned by the subquery using the VALUE() function.

If your object instance contains an object reference column/attribute, you can directly access the attributes of the referenced object using a dot notation to qualify the referenced object attribute, via a table alias. The syntax to access a referenced attribute value is:

table-alias.reference-col-name.attribute-name

For example:

```
SELECT b.customer_ref.id, b.customer_ref.name, creation_date
FROM   shopping_basket b;

-- Results are:

CUSTOMER_REF.ID CUSTOMER_REF.NAME        CREATION_
--------------- ------------------------ ---------
             20 Elio                     13.FEB-00
             50 Glenn                    15-FEB-00
```

The example requires the table alias "b" for the basket in order to use the dot notation to directly access the attribute of an instance located through an object reference value. If you do not use the table alias, the query shows the error message that ensues:

```
SELECT customer_ref.id, customer_ref.name, creation_date
FROM   shopping_basket b;

-- Error results is:

SELECT customer_ref.id, customer_ref.name, creation_date
                                           *
ERROR at line 1:
ORA-00904: invalid column name
```

Oracle SQL cannot resolve the attributes name id and name via the object reference attribute alone. Therefore, the alias for the object table is required as a qualifier to the reference attribute.

3.10.2.3 The DEREF Function. The DEREF() function returns the object instance value via a reference argument. The argument must be a REF to the object instance.

Here is the query used to display the shopping basket and its referenced customer object value:[9]

```
SELECT creation_date, DEREF(customer_ref)
FROM   shopping_basket;
```

```
CREATION_  DEREF(CUSTOMER_REF)(ID, NAME, SURNAME, EMAIL, PASSWORD, CREDIT_CARD_TYPE,
                 CREDIT_CARD_NUMBER, MONTH_ ...)
---------  ------------------------------------------------------------------------
13.FEB-00  CUSTOMER_T(20, 'Elio', 'Izzanob', 'ebonazzi@one.net.au', 'ultrix', 'AMEX',
                 '2734527345234', '07', '00')

15-FEB-00  CUSTOMER_T(50, 'Glenn', 'Lokots', 'G.Lokots@vic.net', 'orajava', 'VISA',
                 '2333 4343 3432 2323', '11', '00')
```

In this example, the CUSTOMER_REF value is de-referenced, using the DEREF() function, to obtain the customer object instance value.

3.10.3 QUERYING NESTED OBJECT INSTANCE VALUES

To study an example of a nested object instance value, consider the sales item type:

```
CREATE TYPE sales_item_t AS OBJECT (
  id               NUMBER(6),
  title            VARCHAR2(100),
  full_price       NUMBER(6,2),
  discount         NUMBER(5,2),
  picture          BLOB,
  prd_type         VARCHAR2(2),
  book             BOOK_T,        -- nested object type
  cd               MUSIC_CD_T     -- nested object type
);
```

[9]The object value combines the object's attribute values; the object identifier value is a reference to the object value.

The attribute BOOK is defined as nested object of type BOOK_T, and the attribute CD is also based on nested type called MUSIC_CD_T. The type definitions of the BOOK_T, and MUSIC_CD_T, are:

```
CREATE TYPE book_t AS OBJECT (
  Author          VARCHAR2(80),
  publisher       VARCHAR2(40),
  year_published  NUMBER(4),
  isbn            VARCHAR2(30),
  category        VARCHAR2(40)
);

CREATE TYPE music_cd_t AS OBJECT (
  artist          VARCHAR2(80),
  record_label    VARCHAR2(50),
  year_released   NUMBER(4),
  cd_nbr          VARCHAR2(30),
  music_style     VARCHAR2(30)
);

-- Type definition of SALES_ITEM_T

CREATE TYPE sales_item_t AS OBJECT (
  id              NUMBER(6),
  title           VARCHAR2(100),
  full_price      NUMBER(6,2),
  discount        NUMBER(5,2),
  picture         BLOB,
  prd_type        VARCHAR2(2),
  book            BOOK_T,      – nested object type
  cd              MUSIC_CD_T   – nested object type
);

/
```

The query used to display a sales item object instance and the values for the nested object instance in the BOOK attribute is:

```
SELECT id, title, book
FROM   sales_item
WHERE  id = 20
AND   prd_type = 'BK';

-- Results are
```

```
        ID TITLE            BOOK(AUTHOR, PUBLISHER, YEAR_P
-------- --------------- ------------------------------
        20 Oracle8 Data     BOOK_T('Gary Dodge, et al',
           Warehousing      'John Wiley', 1998, NULL, NULL)
```

The results display the nested object value; its constructor and its parameters are the actual attribute values for the nested object instance. The attributes, in the nested book object instance, can be displayed as if they were column values in the sales item table, by using a dot notation to qualify the BOOK attributes:

```
SELECT id, title, i.book.author author
FROM   sales_item i
WHERE id BETWEEN 20 AND 25
AND    prd_type = 'BK';

-- Results are:

   ID TITLE                          AUTHOR
----- --------------------------- -------------------
   20 Oracle8 Data Warehousing    Gary Dodge, et al.

   21 Oracle Dba Exam Cram, Test Michael R. Ault et al.
      3 and Test 4: Whether
      You're Certifying

   22 Oracle8 Architecture        Steve Bobrowski

   23 Oracle NT Handbook: A       Rama Velpuri et al.
      Practical Guide to Managing
      Oracle8 onWindows NT

   24 Oracle Financials Handbook    David James
```

The AUTHOR attribute, as defined in the book type, can only be accessed if you qualify the BOOK attribute in sales item type, with the table alias name (the underlined text) as a prefix.

3.10.4 QUERYING COLLECTIONS

If your object table is based on a type that contains a collection, such as a nested table, you can used the TABLE() function to flatten the nested table into a set of rows and columns. The flattened structure can then be treated as if it were a standard relational table that can be operated on using standard SQL statements. The TABLE() can be used in the FROM clause in two forms:

1. TABLE(subquery on collection attribute name)
2. TABLE(collection attribute name) table-alias

Consider the shopping basket containing the "items" attribute as a nested table of shopping items:

```
CREATE TYPE shopping_item_t AS OBJECT (
  quantity         NUMBER(4),
  price            NUMBER(6,2),
  sales_item_ref   REF sales_item_t
);

-- Create the Nested Table collection of shopping items

CREATE TYPE shopping_item_nt_t AS TABLE OF
shopping_item_t;

CREATE TYPE shopping_basket_t AS OBJECT (
  creation_date          DATE,
  shipment_cost          NUMBER(5),
  total_cost             NUMBER(6),
  customer_ref           REF customer_t,
  items                  shopping_item_nt_t
);
```

To query the contents of the items collection as a nested table, you can write a query with a TABLE() function using a subquery, as follows:

```
SELECT i.quantity, i.price, i.sales_item_ref.title title
FROM TABLE(SELECT items
           FROM shopping_basket
           WHERE customer_ref = (SELECT ref(c)
                                 FROM  customer c
                                 WHERE id = 50)) i

-- With the following results

  QUANTITY    PRICE TITLE
---------- -------- ------------------------------
        10    29.99 Oracle8 Data Warehousing
         1    22.49 Oracle Dba Exam Cram, Test 3 and
                    Test 4: Whether You're Certifying
```

The TABLE() function used with a subquery, in bold text, restricts the selection of a nested table to a specific row instance of a shopping basket; otherwise you receive an Oracle SQL error of "too many rows." The TABLE() function flattens the "items" attributes so that you can access each of the values of a shopping item element in the collection just as you would access columns in a standard relational table. The alias, i, simplifies directly accessing the nested sales item attributes through its object reference value.

Alternatively, you can use the TABLE() function to create a join table out of the collection attribute:

```
SELECT b.customer_ref.name name,
       i.quantity, i.price, i.sales_item_ref.title title
FROM shopping_basket b, TABLE(items) i

Results in:

NAME      QUANTITY  PRICE TITLE
------- --------- ------ ------------------------------
Glenn           10  29.99 Oracle8 Data Warehousing
Glenn            1  22.49 Oracle Dba Exam Cram, Test 3
                          and Test 4: Whether You're
                          Certifying

Elio            10  29.99 The Developer's Guide to Oracle
                          Web Application Server
```

The TABLE() function in this latter example fabricates set of rows and column values for the object instances in the nested table. In addition, the query implicitly performs a join condition between the shopping basket instance and the associated object instance in the items collection.[10] The form of the TABLE() function gives you a lot more query flexibility. These examples also work for collections of the varying-array type.

In a final example, the CURSOR() function is combined with a subquery based on the TABLE(collection-attribute-name). The results are similar:

```
SELECT b.customer_ref.name name,
  CURSOR(SELECT i.quantity, i.price, i.sales_item_ref.title title
         FROM TABLE(items) i)
FROM shopping_basket b;
```

[10]Note the absence of a WHERE clause with a join condition. Oracle knows that the items in the nested table belong to the shopping basket though an internal foreign key mechanism linking each instance in the collection to the parent instance of the shopping basket.

```
-- Outputs results as follows in SQL*Plus

NAME       CURSOR(SELECTI.QUANT
---------- --------------------
Elio       CURSOR STATEMENT : 2

CURSOR STATEMENT : 2

  QUANTITY      PRICE TITLE
---------- --------- -----------------------------------
        10      29.99 The Developer's Guide to Oracle Web
                      Application Server

Glenn      CURSOR STATEMENT : 2

CURSOR STATEMENT : 2

  QUANTITY     PRICE TITLE
---------- -------- --------------------------------
        10    29.99 Oracle8 Data Warehousing
         1    22.49 Oracle Dba Exam Cram, Test 3 and
                    Test 4: Whether You're Certifying
```

The CURSOR() function in this example opens a inner/nested cursor for processing one or more collection elements as if they were rows in a table. The parent/outer query defines the execution context for the inner cursor to process related collection elements. In a closer look at the output generated by the CURSOR() function, the bold text is a parent row. For example:

```
Glenn    CURSOR STATEMENT : 2
```

The text represents a row instance fetched in the outer cursor loop, and the text that follows is:

```
CURSOR STATEMENT : 2

  QUANTITY     PRICE TITLE
---------- -------- --------------------------------
        10    29.99 Oracle8 Data Warehousing
         1    22.49 Oracle Dba Exam Cram, Test 3 and
                    Test 4: Whether You're Certifying
```

The output represents each element value in the collection related to the parent row instance in bold text above it.

SUMMARY

This chapter has provided a comprehensive but not exhaustive introduction to the powerful functionality afforded by Oracle SQL statements. If you use query processing in the database to perform all the data transformations and conversions prior to receiving the values in your Java code, you may get some gains in performance and simplify the Java program. This chapter discussed how to retrieve data using simple SQL queries, joins, and subqueries. Oracle database single row and group functions were covered. You were shown how to query tables containing Oracle Object types and collections.

In the Java language, when using a JDBC driver compatible with the Oracle database, you can execute all the types of statements covered in this chapter. To query Oracle object instances in Java code may require the creation of a Java class structure compatible with the object definition. The Java class can be created manually, or Oracle JPublisher can be used to facilitate the creation of Java classes based on an object type structure defined in your database. Querying Oracle objects and collections in Java is discussed in Chapters 10 and 11, which also discuss using Oracle JPublisher.

In this chapter, the object type definitions had to be created with identifier columns because this simplifies the query statements used to retrieve a unique object instance. Without a unique identifier, queries for retrieving unique object instances would contain complex conditions. Because of their complex structure, object identifiers created for each structure are not practical for use in queries. Global object identifiers are better suited to linking object instances together through the reference attribute/column data types, thereby minimizing redundant data storage. The bottom line is that each object type acquires an attribute for unique identification of each instance to simplify the SQL statement used to query and manipulate the data in the object table.

Chapter 4

Data Manipulation Language (DML) Statements and Transactions

- DML on Relational Tables
- DML on Object Tables
- DML on Collection Objects
- Getting More Performance with DML
- Transactions in Oracle SQL
- Summary

This chapter focuses on statements in the SQL data manipulation language (DML) group. DML statements are used to add, modify, or remove data in relational or object tables. The initial part of this chapter looks at the use of DML on relational tables, followed by examples of DML applied to object tables, and collections.

The concept of database transactions is included because it cannot be separated from the process of applying changes to the data.

4.1 DML ON RELATIONAL TABLES

The three SQL statements that allow changes to be applied to data in tables are:

- INSERT—to add one or more rows.
- UPDATE—to modify one or more rows.
- DELETE—to remove one or more rows.

The effects of all of these commands can be undone by using a ROLLBACK statement. A COMMIT statement will permanently save the changes.

4.1.1 INSERT STATEMENTS

INSERT statements are used to add rows into relational tables or object instances into object tables. The INSERT statement has two forms:

- The first allows the insertion of one data row, or object instance, at a time.
- The second allows the insertion more than one row, or object instance, copied from another table.

4.1.1.1 Inserting One Row at a Time.

The syntax of the INSERT statement for adding one row at a time row is:

```
INSERT INTO table_name [ (column(s) [, …] ]
VALUES (value(s) [, …]);
```

The list of column names appearing after the table name is optional, and, if provided, is a comma-separated list of column names defined in the table. If the list of column names is omitted, then a value is required in the VALUES clause for every column defined in the table. The order of the values must match, in data type and sequence, the columns as defined in the table.

It is recommended that the list of column names after the table name are included, for reading clarity and to minimize effects of modifications made to the table definition, provided the table structure alterations do not invalidate the statement. If the data type of the value is incompatible with its corresponding column, then you can use the Oracle RDBMS single row conversion functions, such as TO_CHAR(), TO_DATE(), TO_NUMBER(), NVL(), or user-defined functions to assist with the required explicit transformations.[1] The following example shows an insert statement adding a new record into the `CUSTOMER` table:

```
INSERT INTO customer
  (id, name, surname, email, password,
   credit_card_type, credit_card_nbr, month_expired, year_expired)
VALUES
  (50, 'Glenn', 'Stokol', 'g.stokol@vic.net.au', 'orajava',
   'VISA', '2333 4343 3432 2323', '11', '00');
```

The record inserted is saved when you issue a COMMIT statement; otherwise the operation can be undone by using the ROLLBACK statement. All SQL statements can use bind/host variables to supply the values for each column. For performance reasons, it is better to provide values from variables in the application hosting execution of the SQL statement. In Oracle SQL*Plus you can create host variables using the VARIABLE command, as follows:

```
SQL> VARIABLE variable-name data-type
```

The VARIABLE command is part of the SQL*Plus tool, and is not an SQL statement. Some of the data types that can be used for SQL*Plus variables are:

- NUMBER
- CHAR(n)
- VARCHAR2(n)
- DATE
- REF CURSOR

Using bind variables is analogous to using placeholders in SQL requests executed in Java via JDBC `PreparedStatement` or CallableStatement classes. Listing 4.1 shows an example of creating three host/bind variables in SQL*Plus, for obtaining data values to be inserted into the `COURIER` table.

[1]To achieve better query parse time and performance, it is recommended that you use explicit data type conversion functions, rather than rely on the Oracle optimizer to do the work for you.

```
SQL> -- Declare the bind/host variables
SQL>
SQL> variable id number
SQL> variable name varchar2(30)
SQL> variable item_cost number
SQL>
SQL>   BEGIN
  2     :id := 4;
  •     :name := 'Universal Post';
  •     :item_cost := 4.5;
  •    END;
  •    /

Procedure successfully completed.

SQL> INSERT INTO courier (id, name, cost_per_item)
  2 VALUES (:id, :name, :item_cost);

SQL> -- Change the variable values and insert another record
SQL>
SQL>  BEGIN
  2    :id := 5;
  •    :name := 'Quantum Service';
  •    :item_cost := 3.75;
  •   END;
  •   /

Procedure successfully completed.

SQL> INSERT INTO courier (id, name, cost_per_item)
  2 VALUES (:id, :name, :item_cost);
```

LISTING 4.1 Using host/bind variables to insert records

The INSERT statement is unchanged; only the data values stored in the host/bind variable are changed. In SQL*Plus, the bind/host variable values are assigned by using a PL/SQL anonymous block. Host/bind variables are prefixed with the colon (:) character when they are referred to in the context of an SQL statement or a PL/SQL block.

In Java, using JDBC, the bind variables that hold data values can be class, instance, or method variables bound to placeholders in the `PreparedStatement` object instance. For example:

```
void addCourier
      (Connection conn, int id, String name, double itemCost)
{
  PreparedStatement ps;

  ps = conn.prepareStatement("INSERT INTO courier " +
                             "(id, name, cost_per_item) " +
                             "VALUES (?, ?, ?)");
  ps.setInt(1, id);
  ps.setString(2, name);
  ps.setDouble(3, itemCost);
}
```

In Java JDBC, bind variables are known as *placeholders*. They identify a location where values must be provided. The question mark character is the JDBC placeholder marker. The value associated with each placeholder is achieved by calling a `set<datatype>()` method, from the JDBC `PreparedStatement` class. The `set<datatype>()` method:

- Binds a value contained in the Java variable to a placeholder associated with a column in the SQL statement.
- Performs conversion or mapping between compatible Java and SQL data types. The Java data type forms part of the SET method name used to store the Java value into the database column.

In SQLJ, the SQL statement uses the bind variable syntax shown in Listing 4.1. The host variables in an SQLJ program can be Java class variables, instance variables, or method variables. For example, in SQLJ, the `addCourier` method is written as follows:

```
void addCourier (int id, String name, double itemCost)
{
  #sql { INSERT INTO courier (id, name, cost_per_item)
         VALUES (:id, :name, :itemCost) };
}
```

The SQLJ source code contains SQL statements embedded in Java code. The `#sql` marker precedes an SQL statement enclosed in braces. The SQLJ source is translated into a pure Java source, containing a JDBC class, by using an SQLJ translator utility provided by a vendor supporting the SQLJ standard.

The benefit of using host/bind variables is that the Oracle server can reuse SQL statements in a memory caches, called *shared cursors,* and thereby improve subsequent statement execution time. Improvements made to the Oracle8i query optimization, enable an SQL statement containing literal values to be rewritten to use host/bind variables to maximize shared SQL statement reuse in the server. Regardless, the use of bind/host variables explicitly is recommended to reduce the amount of statement optimization activity required.

4.1.1.2 Inserting One or More Rows at a Time: Copying Rows. The insert statement can be used with a query, instead of a list of values for each column. The syntax for copying rows from one table into another is:

```
INSERT INTO target-table-name [(column(s) [, …]]
SELECT column-specification(s)
FROM source-table-name(s)
[WHERE condition(s)]
[GROUP BY group-criteria [HAVING condition(s)]];
```

In this syntax, the VALUES clause is replaced with a SELECT statement called a subquery. The column specifications listed in the subquery provide the rows and column values to be copied, or inserted, into the target table. This is similar to the CREATE TABLE statement using a subquery. All parts of a SELECT statement can be used except for the ORDER BY clause, which is not allowed or very useful in the subquery. This type of insert statement can replace several lines of procedural code that do the same thing.

The example in Listing 4.2 shows how to copy the details for a shopping basket to the customer order, assuming that the customer has accepted the purchase for the items in the shopping basket:

```
INSERT INTO cust_order
  (id, cust_id, cour_id, shipment_cost, total_cost,
   creation_date, pending_date)
SELECT :order_id, cust_id, :courier, shipment_cost,
   total_cost, trunc(sysdate), trunc(sysdate)+1)
FROM  shopping_basket
WHERE cust_id = :cust_basket_id
```

LISTING 4.2 Copying a shopping basket to the customer order

Listing 4.2 illustrates that each column name after the `CUST_ORDER` table must be provided with a value in the select statement. The shipment date column is not included in the statement because it is unknown until the shipment occurs. If the column name list is not included in the statement, then the select statement must provide values for all the columns in the target table structure in the same sequence in which they are defined in the data dictionary.

The example makes use of bind/host variables to provide the values for the new order number (in `:order_id`), and the courier (in `:courier`), associated with the order for the shopping basket owned by a specific customer (in :cust_basket_id). The values for the host/bind variable can be provided from the HTML form used to submit the purchase order.

Column expressions can be used in the query portion of the statement; the expression: "trunc(sysdate)+1",[2] for example, adds one day to the creation date of the today to be stored in the pending-shipment date column. The database transaction completes with an additional insert statement that copies the items from the shopping basket into the order item table:

```
INSERT INTO order_item (order_id, prd_id, quantity, price)
SELECT :order_id, prd_id, quantity, price
FROM   shopping_item
WHERE basket_cust_id = :cust_basket_id
```

To complete the transaction, the bind variables :order_id, and :cust_basket_id, should contain the same values used in Listing 4.2, to ensure that the items in the order remain associated with the appropriate order.

New rows are subject to integrity rules defined in the tables being modified.

4.1.2 UPDATE STATEMENTS

The UPDATE statement is used to modify the data in the specified columns of a table. The syntax of the update statement is:

```
UPDATE table-name
  SET column-name = expression
   [, column-name = expression ... ]
[WHERE condition(s)];
```

The keyword SET introduces a column name whose value is to be modified to equal the expression, or calculation, listed after the assignment (=) operator. The value in the column is changed for all rows if the WHERE clause is omitted. The expression on the right side of the assignment operator includes:

- A column name from the same table to provide a new value.
- A column expression or calculation.
- A subquery returning a single value from the same or another table.

The sequence in which you want to reduce prices by ten percent for all items ordered in bulk quantities can be done with the following update statement on the customer order item records:

---

[2]The trunc() function sets the hour, minute, and second components of a date value to zero.

```
UPDATE order_item
  SET price = price - (price * 0.1)
WHERE quantity > 10
AND   ord_id = :cust_order_nbr;
```

The expression on the right side of the equal sign in the SET clause takes ten percent of the price using the expression, `price*0.1`, which is subtracted from the original price. The resultant price is used to update the price column for records for items with an ordered quantity greater than ten units. The condition `quantity>10` in the WHERE clause ensures that the price change applies to item records with ordered quantities in excess of ten units.

Updating more than one column in the same table is done by including additional expressions assigning new values to other columns in the SET portion of the statement. Commas are used to separate the additional columns and their update expressions.

Assume that a customer submits data entered in HTML form to modify the quantity ordered for an item in the shopping basket, and your business rules apply a price discount based on the quantity ordered. In the update action, both the price and the quantity will be modified at the same time. Assume that the following bind variables hold their associated value:

- `:qty` holds the new quantity for the item.
- `:prd_id` holds the item product number.
- `:cust_id` holds the shopping basket number, which is derived from the customer number.

The update statement changes the quantity and price at the same time:

```
UPDATE shopping_item
SET
 quantity = :qty,          -- comma separates each column
 modified
 price = (select
            full_price * decode(sign(:qty-5), -1, 1, 0,
            .95, 1, 0.9)
          from sales_item
          where id = :prd_id)
where prd_id = :prd_id
and   basket_cust_id = :cust_id;
```

- Taking a closer look at the example, you can see the following:
- The quantity is set to the new value in the :qty variable.

- The price is a calculation based on the results of the nested select statement, also known as a nested subquery.
- The nested subquery multiplies the full_price of the product, in the sales item table, by the value returned by the DECODE() expression.
- The WHERE clause has two conditions that will restrict the change made to specified item in the customer's shopping basket.

Examining the expression:

```
DECODE(SIGN(:qty-5), -1, 1, 0, .95, 1, 0.9)
```

the first argument is a nested function expression: `sign(:qty-5)`, which returns:

- A negative value (–1) if `:qty-5` is less than zero.
- A zero (0) if `:qty-5` is equal to zero.
- A positive value (+1) is `:qty-5` is greater than zero.

The DECODE statement compares the result returned by the first argument for equality to each of the bold parameters in the decode expression, and returns the underlined result value next to the bold value that is equal to the first parameter.

The Oracle RDBMS DECODE() function is like having a Java switch statement implemented in SQL. The equivalent Java code, written in a method, to implement the logic provided by the DECODE expression is:

```
double newPrice(double fullPrice, int qty) {
  double result;
  int    sign = (qty-5) < 0 ? -1 : ((qty-5) == 0 ? 0 : 1);
  :
  switch (sign) {
    case -1:
      result = 1.0;
      break;
    case 0:
      result = 0.95;
      break;
    case 1:
      result = 0.9;
      break;
  }
  return (fullPrice * result);
}
```

The result returned by the DECODE expression is multiplied by the full_price of the sales item to yield a new price value used to modify the price in the shopping basket.

Changed rows are also subject to integrity rules defined in the tables being modified.

4.1.3 DELETE STATEMENTS

The DELETE statement is used to remove rows from a table. The syntax is:

```
DELETE [FROM] table-name
 [ WHERE condition(s) ];
```

All the rows are deleted from a table if a WHERE condition is omitted, subject to any integrity constraints defined on the table data. The FROM keyword is optional and is supported for ANSI SQL compliance. Adding the WHERE clause to the DELETE statement, restricts the operation to a specific row or set of rows in a table.

Suppose that the customer issues a request to empty the shopping basket. Here is an example of a delete statement used to empty a specific shopping basket:

```
DELETE FROM shopping_item WHERE basket_cust_id = :basket_nbr
```

If, however, the customer issues a request to remove one item from the basket, you combine the product number with the customer basket number to restrict the delete operation to a specific row, as follows:

```
DELETE  FROM shopping_item
  WHERE prd_id = :item_nbr
  AND   basket_cust_id = :cust_id;
```

The example assumes that the :item_nbr and :cust_id bind variables are populated with the correct values for the item number and customer's basket number. The conditions in the WHERE clause ensure that one record is deleted, because the combination of basket_cust_id and prd_id columns forms the primary key of a shopping item in the basket.

4.1.4 SUBQUERIES IN DML STATEMENTS

Subqueries may also be used in data manipulation statements. Oracle8i allows subqueries in a variety of places, thereby providing powerful and rich ways to manipulate data. The INSERT, UPDATE, and DELETE statements can make use of subqueries to assist with data management.

4.1.4.1 Subqueries in INSERT Statements. A subquery can be used in the value list of an INSERT statement. The general syntax is:

```
INSERT INTO table-name [ ( column-name(s) , …) ]
VALUES (value1, (single-value subquery), …);
```

Support for using a subquery in the values list of an insert statement was added in Oracle8i.

4.1.4.2 Subqueries in Update Statements. The syntax for using subqueries in an UPDATE statement is:

```
UPDATE table-name
   SET column-name = (single-value subquery)
    [, column-name = (single-value subquery) …]
[WHERE expression OP (single/multiple-value subquery) ];
```

The expression in the WHERE clause may also be a single-value subquery, as discussed in relation to select statements. You can use the UPDATE statement with a multiple value subquery in the SET clause. For example:

```
UPDATE table-name
   SET (column1, column2) = (SELECT value1, value2 FROM …)
 [WHERE expression OP (single/multiple-value subquery) ];
```

When updating more than one column with a subquery, the subquery must return a single row but multiple columns. For example:

```
UPDATE cust_order ord
  SET (shipment_cost, total_cost) =
    (SELECT sum(i.quantity * c.cost_per_item),
            sum(i.quantity * (i.price + c.cost_per_item))
     FROM   order_item i, courier c
     WHERE  i.ord_id = ord.id
     AND    ord.cour_id = c.id)
WHERE ord.cust_id = 51;
```

In this example, the subquery calculates the shipment cost and the total cost of each order for customer 51. The values returned by the subquery update the relevant order details, because the subquery depends on the order id being provided by the parent update statement. Therefore, the subquery is a correlated subquery.

The first underlined, expression in the subquery SELECT clause provides the value for the first underlined, column in the SET clause of the update statement. The second expression in the subquery provides the value for the second column in the SET clause of the update statement.

4.1.4.3 Subqueries in DELETE Statements. In a DELETE statement, a subquery is typically found in the WHERE clause. The syntax is:

```
DELETE FROM table-name
 [ WHERE expression operator (single/multi-value subquery) ];
```

If the business rules state that orders must have at least one item, you may wish to remove all customer orders that have no associated items. The DELETE statement to accomplish this is:

```
DELETE FROM cust_order o
 WHERE 0 = (SELECT count(i.*)
             FROM order_item i
             WHERE i.ord_id = o.id);
```

The value on the left-hand side of the comparison is a zero. The subquery is a correlated subquery, which returns a zero value if an order has no associated items. The rows deleted are the ones that have no order items rows with the value of an order id for a given customer order.

A subquery, particularly a correlated subquery, may get a performance benefit from an alternative form of the condition structure, using the EXISTS or NOT EXISTS conditional operator. These operators are very useful when the subquery is testing the existence or absence of a row. The DELETE example can be rewritten as follows:

```
DELETE FROM cust_order o
 WHERE NOT EXISTS (SELECT 'X'
                   FROM order_item i
                   WHERE i.ord_id = o.id);
```

Applying the NOT EXISTS operator to the subquery makes it possible for the subquery to an index on the `ord_id` column to resolve the answer, without any need to access the data in the `ORDER_ITEM` table. There is no need to access the data in the `ORDER_ITEM` table, because the query is not retrieving data, since the selected column value is a literal. The queries enclosed in an EXISTS or NOT EXISTS comparison operator terminate as soon as one row satisfies the subquery, which also reduces unnecessary disk I/O activity.

4.2 DML ON OBJECT TABLES

The three DML statements, INSERT, UPDATE, and DELETE, are also used to create, manipulate, and remove object instances from object tables. Oracle SQL allows the data held in object instance attributes to be manipulated, using DML, as if the attributes were columns belonging to a relational table. The SQL code has syntax consistent with the traditional DML statements used on relational tables. Oracle SQL also provides DML syntax extensions to work with object instances in an object-like manner. Object type methods defined in object types can be used to encapsulate the data manipulation logic, and these methods are invoked from a Java or PL/SQL application to call the DML.

4.2.1 INSERTING OBJECT INSTANCES

The INSERT statement can be used in two ways to insert object instances into an object table. The first method treats the object table instances as rows and columns:

```
INSERT INTO customer (name, surname, email, password,
                      credit_card_type, credit_card_ number,
                      month_expired, year_expired)
VALUES ('James', 'Museo', 'James.Museo@javinst.au', 'wiggle',
       'VISA', '1112 3232 4344 3233',
       '12', '01');
```

This first insert statement has the same structure as a relational table. The examples assume the following object type and table definitions:

```
CREATE OR REPLACE TYPE customer_ot AS OBJECT (
  NAME                  VARCHAR2(30),
  SURNAME               VARCHAR2(30),
  EMAIL                 VARCHAR2(50),
  PASSWORD              VARCHAR2(10),
  CREDIT_CARD_TYPE      VARCHAR2(10),
  CREDIT_CARD_NUMBER    VARCHAR2(20),
  MONTH_EXPIRED         VARCHAR2(2),
  YEAR_EXPIRED          VARCHAR2(2)
 );
```

```
CREATE TABLE customer OF customer_ot (
  NAME                     NOT NULL,
  SURNAME                  NOT NULL,
  EMAIL                    NOT NULL,
  PASSWORD                 NOT NULL,
  CREDIT_CARD_TYPE         NOT NULL,
  CREDIT_CARD_NUMBER       NOT NULL,
  MONTH_EXPIRED            NOT NULL,
  YEAR_EXPIRED             NOT NULL
);
```

The alternative is that you insert instances into the object table using the constructor of the object type. For example:

```
INSERT INTO customer
VALUES (
  customer_ot('Nel', 'Lokots', 'N.Lokots@yahoo.com', 'nibble',
            'MASTERCARD', '9222 1333 2444 4333',
            '11', '02'));
```

LISTING 4.3 Inserting an object instance into an object table

Listing 4.3 uses the customer object type constructor to create an instance that is inserted into the table. An object type has one constructor, to create object instances, and the constructor must provide a parameter for each attribute defined in the object type. The parameter values are provided according to the definition order of the attributes in the object type. The insert statement in Listing 4.3 does not allow a list of column/attribute names to be provided after the table name, and this is a subtle difference in the insert syntax.

It is easy to copy relational column data into an object instance, using an insert statement based on a query. For example:

```
INSERT INTO customer
SELECT customer_ot(name, surname, email, password,
              credit_card_type, credit_card_nbr,
              month_expired, year_expired)
FROM new_customer
WHERE id = 50;
```

LISTING 4.4 Copying data from a relational table to an object table

In Listing 4.4, the select statement acquires its values from a new customer relational table, by supplying the column names as the parameter values in the object type constructor.

4.2.1.1 Inserting When Attributes are Objects.

If the object type definition contains an attribute based on a user-defined data type, the insert statement must use the constructor method of the embedded object type.

The example in Listing 4.5 creates two object types:

- The book_ot, which hold attribute details for a book.
- The sales_item_ot, which holds the attributes for a sales item and a book attribute nesting the book details in an object type.
- The SALES_ITEM object table containing object instances of sales_item_ot.

```
-- Create the object types
--
CREATE TYPE book_ot AS OBJECT (
  author            VARCHAR2(80),
  publisher         VARCHAR2(40),
  yearPublished     NUMBER(4),
  isbn              VARCHAR2(30),
  category          VARCHAR2(40)
);

CREATE TYPE sales_item_ot AS OBJECT (
  id                NUMBER(6),
  title             varchar2(100),
  full_price        number(6,2),
  discount          number(5,2)
  prd_type          varchar2(10),
  picture           blob,
  book              book_vt; -- attribute as nested object
);

-- Create the object table
CREATE TABLE sales_item of sales_item_ot;

-- Insert a new sales item
--
INSERT INTO sales_item
VALUES (1, 'Oracle for Java Programmers', 90.0, 10, 'BK', null,
        book_ot('Elio Bonazzi & Glenn Stokol', 'Prentice Hall',
                2000, null, 'Computers'));
```

LISTING 4.5 Inserting values into nested object attributes

The book_ot() constructor must be used to provide an object instance value for the book attribute. The same INSERT statement syntax applies if SALES_ITEM was defined as a relational table, with an object column called book based on the book_ot data type.

4.2.2 UPDATING OBJECT INSTANCE ATTRIBUTES

The SQL update statement is also used to modify object instances held in:

- A column in a relational database
- An attribute in another object type
- An object table

The object type constructor is used to replace an object instance with a new value. However, if it is only an attribute value of an object instance that needs to be changed, and not the entire object, the SQL syntax uses a dot notation to refer to an object instance attribute. For example:

```
object-identifier-name.attribute-name
```

In addition, to set or get an attribute value the context of an SQL statement, you are required to use a table alias to qualify references to object methods or attributes. This particularly applies when referencing attributes involving a REF to an object type. For example, look at a sales item type, which contains the book attribute based on the book_ot() type:

```
UPDATE sales_item s
   SET s.book.publisher = 'Prentice Hall'
WHERE id = 40;
```

The table alias s is used to qualify the object identifier name book, which is the formal name of the object type attribute in the definition of the sales_item_ot. The table alias must be used before the identifier name of the object containing the attribute of interest. The table alias avoids ambiguity in the statement if it is executed in a schema that also has a table called BOOK with a column called publisher. For example:

```
CREATE TABLE book (
   Author          varchar2(30),
   Publisher varchar2(30));

UPDATE sales_item
   SET book.publisher = 'Prentice Hall'
WHERE id = 40;
```

The dot notation is also used to refer to column names in a relational table, and by default the SQL processor would assume it is looking for a column name called `publisher` in a table called `BOOK`. This would cause a statement error, because the `BOOK` table is not included in the query or the column does not exist in the `SALES_ITEM` table.

In order to replace an object instance with a new value, the constructor of the object type to used to create the new value, as follows:

```
UPDATE sales_item s
  SET s.book = book_ot('Elio Bonazzi & Glenn Stokol',
                       'Prentice Hall', 2000, null, 'Computers')
WHERE id = 40;
```

Assume that all books more than one year old must be sold at a discount price. The following updating modifies the discount attribute for all sales item objects whose year published antedates the current year by one:

```
UPDATE sales_item s
  SET discount = 20
WHERE s.book.yearPublished = to_number(to_char(sysdate,'YYYY'))-1
```

The example WHERE clause shows how you can reference an object column/attribute value. In the WHERE clause:

- `to_char(sysdate, 'YYYY')` converts the year from the current date and time from a date to a string value.
- `to_number(year)-1` first converts the year string into its numeric value and then subtracts one from the current year. The year value is derived from the value returned by the function `to_char(sysdate, 'YYYY')`, which is nested as the parameter of the `to_number()` function.

The dot notation, on object type attributes, is used wherever you reference the attribute.

4.2.3 DELETING OBJECT INSTANCES

The DELETE statement in the SQL language is used to remove object instances from an object table. Using the WHERE clause allows you to restrict the delete operation to a specific object instance, by applying a comparison to an object type attribute value. The next example deletes all sales items where the year published is more than five years ago.

```
DELETE FROM sales_item s
WHERE s.book.yearPublished < to_number(to_char (sysdate,'YYYY'))-5
```

To delete an object instance contained in a column, or an attribute of an object type, you would update the attribute value to be NULL, which is only possible if a null value is permitted in the column. For example:

```
UPDATE sales_item s
  SET s.book = NULL
WHERE s.book.yearPublished = to_number(to_char
  (sysdate,'YYYY'))-1
```

There is no way to apply a DELETE statement to an object type nested as an attribute or column.

4.2.4 DML WITH OBJECT REFERENCES

A relational table may contain a column, or an object table may hold an attribute, which is based on a reference (REF) to another object instance. To work with referenced objects, additional operators or functions are provided. These are:

- The REF() function – used to obtain a reference to the object instance.
- The DEREF() function – used to deference the referenced object instance.
- The VALUE() function – used to obtain an object instance value through a reference.

Working with reference columns or attributes requires:

- First, that you obtain the reference to the appropriate object instance.
- Second, that you store the object reference value in an object reference column or attribute.

These two steps can easily be done in a programming language like PL/SQL or Java, or nested subqueries can be used to return a value for the object instance reference. The examples that follow show how to use SQL with stored object reference values using the REF(), DEREF(), and VALUE() functions.

The examples are based on the association between a customer and his or her order.

```
CREATE TYPE customer_ot AS OBJECT (
  id                    NUMBER(8),
  name                VARCHAR2(30),
```

```
  surname               VARCHAR2(30),
  email                 VARCHAR2(50),
  password              VARCHAR2(10),
  credit_card_type      VARCHAR2(10),
  credit_card_nbr       VARCHAR2(20),
  month_expired         VARCHAR2(2),
  year_expired          VARCHAR2(2));

CREATE TYPE cust_order_ot AS OBJECT (
  id                  NUMBER(8),
  shipment_cost       NUMBER(5),
  total_cost          NUMBER(6),
  creation_date       DATE,
  pending_date        DATE,
  shipment_date       DATE,
  customer_ref        REF customer_ot);

CREATE TABLE customer OF customer_ot;

CREATE TABLE cust_order OF cust_order_ot;
```

The customer order holds the reference to the customer who owns the order. The object type definitions for the customer and the customer order have both been given an extra unique identifier column, which will be used as a primary key. As will soon become apparent, using SQL statements to work with object-relational database structures can be difficult without a useful and efficient means of locating a specific object instance, hence the addition of the id columns. Unfortunately, the addition of these unique identifiers dilutes the object model and design, but it is a practical transformation in an impure object world. In an object-oriented world, an object, by definition, is unique regardless of its state.[3] Therefore a unique identifier is redundant in an object application. However, when you save the state of an object in to a database, you need some reliable way to retrieve the state to re-create the object. In consequence, the addition of unique identifiers becomes mandatory in your object type definition, and from an object-oriented perspective, this dilutes the structure of the object.

4.2.4.1 Inserting an Object Reference. Assuming that customer object instances have already been inserted, you can focus on the specific DML techniques used to populate a column or attribute that holds a reference to another object.

[3]The state of an object is the set of values of its attributes at a specific point in time.

```
1: INSERT INTO cust_order
2: SELECT cust_order_ot(:id, :shipment_cost, :total_cost,
3:                    :creation_date, :pending_date,
                      :shipment_date,
4:                     REF(cust))
5: FROM customer cust
6: WHERE cust.id = 10;
```

The example uses a SELECT statement to retrieve the reference to the customer, and at the same time gets the values for other columns from bind variables. The combination of values is supplied to the INSERT statement to create a record that contains the object reference.

- Lines 2–4 make use of the `cust_order_ot()` constructor to create an object instance for the customer order. The constructor's parameters, each of which is preceded by a colon, represent single values to be inserted as the attribute values of the object instance. The bind variables substitute for literal values.
- Line 4 is the only value not provided directly from a program or user, but supplied from the subquery. The function `REF(cust)` returns value an object reference to the customer object whose `id` attribute is a value of 10. Without the unique id value in the customer object, the task of locating a specific customer would require the use of more than one attribute and conditions.
- In line 4, the REF() function requires the alias name in its parameter, as a correlation name, to be a reference to the `CUSTOMER` object table; otherwise executing the statement returns an error.
- Line 5 declares the table alias name `cust` for the `CUSTOMER` table.
- In line 6, the condition locates a specific customer instance by using the dot notation with the cust alias and the id attribute belonging to the `CUSTOMER` table.

This single SQL statement can be issued as two separate SQL statements in a Java or PL/SQL context to achieve the same results. The select statement would get the reference to the customer instance, store it in an object reference variable, and then execute an insert statement to store the result. For example, using PL/SQL:

```
DECLARE
  v_cust_ref REF customer_ot; – a REF variable of a
  customer
BEGIN
  /*
```

```
    ** Get the reference of the customer instance into a
    local
    ** variable
    */
    SELECT REF(cust) INTO :v_cust_ref
    FROM customer cust
    WHERE cust.id = 10;

    /*
    ** Insert a new customer order for the referenced
    customer
    */
    INSERT INTO cust_order
    VALUES (cust_order_ot(:id, :shipment_cost, :total_cost,
                          :creation_date, :pending_date,
                          :shipment_date,
                          REF(cust)));
END;
/
```

The example is a PL/SQL anonymous block, which uses embedded SQL statements as a subset of its language syntax. Chapter 7 discusses PL/SQL anonymous blocks in more detail. The select statement receives the customer object reference into a local variable, and stores the result in the customer order instance.

Another way to obtain a reference value is to use a nested subquery in the values list of the insert statement. The REF(cust) expression in the values clause is effectively replaced by a SELECT statement, yielding the following SQL statement:

```
INSERT INTO cust_order
VALUES (cust_order_ot(:id, :shipment_cost, :total_cost,
        :creation_date, :pending_date, :shipment_date,
        (SELECT REF(cust) FROM customer cust WHERE
           cust.id = 10));
```

4.2.4.2 Updating or Deleting an Object Reference. Updating the value of a reference column or attribute entails no more than changing the referenced object to another referenced object. This is accomplished by using the REF() function in a subquery. The update statement allows a subquery to be used on the right-hand side of an assignment to a column in the SET part of the statement:

```
UPDATE TABLE table-name
SET   column-name =  (SELECT statement subquery);
```

In the update syntax, the SELECT statement used as the subquery must return exactly one row for the single column named on the left side of the assignment operator.

If the column name being updated is defined as an object REF type, then the SELECT statement should only retrieve a REF value for an object instance of a compatible type.

To delete a reference value, you execute an UPDATE statement to set the object reference column to a null value, subject to integrity constraints.

4.3 DML ON COLLECTION OBJECTS

If your relational table contains an object column, or your object type contains an attribute, based on a nested table or a varying array, then you can use some additional extensions to DML statements that support collection data types.

When inserting values into to nested tables or varying arrays, you must write a query that targets one row or object instance that represents the owner or container of the collection.

Oracle SQL provides a TABLE()operator that effectively flattens the object instances or rows in collection. The effect of flattening the collection allows the data to presented and managed as a set of rows and columns.[4] A query is placed inside the braces of the TABLE operator, which returns a result set of data to be manipulated. The general syntax for the TABLE operator is

```
TABLE (query)
```

Listing 4.6 presents the object-relational table design for a shopping basket. It contains a collection in the form of a nested table of shopping items. Each shopping item holds a reference to a sales item object instance.

The sample tables in Listing 4.6 illustrate how Oracle SQL works with collection objects and with object reference variables.

- Lines 1–5 create an object type definition for the `SALES_ITEM` object table, which is created in line 22.
- Lines 7–10 create the object type definition for the shopping item. Line 10 defines the `SALES_ITEM_REF` attribute as a reference to an object type of `SALES_ITEM_OT`.

---

[4]The TABLE() operator replaces the THE() operator introduced in earlier versions of Oracle8. The operator THE() has been deprecated.

```
 1: CREATE TYPE sales_item_ot AS OBJECT (
 2:   title          VARCHAR2(100),
 3:   full_price     NUMBER(6,2),
 4:   discount       NUMBER(5,2),
 5:   picture        BLOB);
 6:
 7: CREATE TYPE shopping_item_ot AS OBJECT (
 8:   quantity             NUMBER(4),
 9:   price                NUMBER(6,2),
10:   sales_item_ref       REF sales_item_ot);
11:
12: CREATE TYPE nt_shopping_item_ot
13:   AS TABLE OF shopping_item_ot;
14:
15: CREATE TYPE shopping_basket_ot AS OBJECT (
16:   id                   NUMBER(6),
17:   creation_date        DATE,
18:   shipment_cost        NUMBER(5,2),
19:   total_cost           NUMBER(6,2),
20:   items                nt_shopping_item_ot)
21:
22: CREATE TABLE sales_item OF sales_item_ot;
23:
24: CREATE TABLE shopping_basket OF shopping_basket_ot (
25:   id                         PRIMARY KEY,
26:   NESTED TABLE items  STORE AS SHOPPING_ITEMS);
```

LISTING 4.6 Shopping basket with a collection of shopping items

- Lines 12–13 create a collection called `NT_SHOPPING_ITEM_OT`, which is defined as a TABLE of shopping items. This type is used to create a nested table in the definition of the `items` attribute, in line 20 of the shopping basket type.
- Lines 15–20 create the shopping basket object type definition. Most noteworthy is line 20, which declares a column, called `items`, as a nested table of shopping items.
- Lines 24–26 create the `SHOPPING_BASKET` table, declaring the `id` attribute as the primary key, and `items` as a nested table whose storage space is named: `SHOPPING_ITEMS`.

4.3.1 INSERTING INTO A COLLECTION

The collection object type name forms a no-argument constructor that is used to initialize an empty collection. The first example creates a new shopping basket by inserting a new record into the shopping basket object table. The item collection in the shopping basket is initialized using the collection constructor, called *nt_shopping_item_ot()*.

```
INSERT INTO shopping_basket (id, creation_date, shipment_cost,
                             total_cost, items)
VALUES (:id, TRUNC(SYSDATE), :ship_cost, :total_cost,
        nt_shopping_item_ot())
```

The first example uses bind variables to supply the values for the shopping basket record. TRUNC(sysdate) stores the current date and time as the creation date. The TRUNC() function applied to its parameter ensures that the hours, minutes, and seconds are zero.

The next example shows how to use the TABLE() operation to flatten the collection into a set of rows and columns. The flattened result set forms a table-like structure into which additional elements are inserted, and therefore, adds new elements into the collection.

```
1: INSERT INTO TABLE(SELECT items FROM shopping_basket
2:                   WHERE id = :basket_id
3:                   AND   creation_date = trunc (sysdate))
4: VALUES (shopping_item_ot(:quantity, : price, :item_ref)
```

Example notes:

- Lines 1–3 highlights the TABLE(subquery), which is used to flatten the nested table collection. The WHERE clause in the subquery is required to ensure that the collection being operated on belongs to only one owner record.
- Line 4 uses the `shopping_item_ot()` constructor to create an instance of a shopping item, which is inserted into the collection. The shopping item attribute values are supplied by bind variables.

The examples presented above are consistent in syntax for nested table collections. Inserting elements into a varying-array collection requires a constructor for the varying array and a value for the element being added to the array, up to the maximum number of entries specified by the varying array. For example:

```
 1: CREATE TYPE va_shopping_item_ot
 2:        AS VARRAY(10) OF shopping_item_ot;
 3:
 4: CREATE TYPE shopping_basket_ot AS OBJECT (
 5:   id                  NUMBER(6),
 6:   creation_date       DATE,
 7:   shipment_cost       NUMBER(5,2),
 8:   total_cost          NUMBER(6,2),
 9:   items               va_shopping_item_ot)
10:
11: CREATE TABLE shopping_basket OF shopping_basket_ot (
12:   id                  PRIMARY KEY);
13:
14: INSERT INTO shopping_basket
15: VALUES (:id, trunc(sysdate), :ship_cost, :total-cost,
16:   va_shopping_item_ot(shopping_item_ot(3, 30, :item_ref1),
17:                       shopping_item_ot(2, 45, :item_ref4),
18:                       shopping_item_ot(1, 40, :item_ref3)))
```

The varying array is treated differently in the insert operation. Example notes:

- Lines 1–2 create the varying-array structure.
- Line 9 creates the `items` collection as a varying array up to a maximum of ten items.
- Line 16 uses the varying-array constructor to build the collection.
- Lines 16–18 use the `shopping_item_ot` constructor to create three elements to be added into the varying-array collection.

All the varying-array elements must be added at the same time, making this type of collection a little difficult to work with. It is not possible to add another element to a varying-array collection unless you query all the existing elements and append the new element in an update operation. This type of work is best done programmatically with PL/SQL or Java.

4.3.2 UPDATING A COLLECTION

The process of updating a collection is simple enough if you use the TABLE() operations to flatten the collection into a relational structure. The easiest way to update a collection element is to:

- Flatten the collection for a specific parent row that owns the collection.

- ❑ Update the column/attribute value in the flattened collection, using a WHERE clause to target a specific element by a unique column/attribute.

For example, update the price of a specific item in a shopping basket:

```
1: UPDATE TABLE(SELECT items FROM shopping_basket)
2:    SET price = price * 0.9
3:  WHERE quantity > 10;
```

- ❑ Line 1 uses the TABLE() operator to flatten the items nested table into rows made up of three columns: quantity, price, and sales_item_ref.
- ❑ Lines 2 and 3 uses the simple attribute names as columns in the statement for the shopping items contained in the shopping basket.

If the collection is a varying array, the above syntax does not work, and the Oracle SQL engine returns the following, not very meaningful, error:

```
ORA-25015: cannot perform DML on this nested view column
```

To update a collection based on a varying array, you must replace the entire contents of the varying array, even when adding new elements to the existing element values. The existing elements in a varying array can be replaced with new values by a simple update statement that assigns a new collection of values to the collection instance. For example, removing all the items in a basket and replacing them with another single item can be done as follows:

```
UPDATE shopping_basket
SET items = va_shopping_items_t(shopping_item_t(10, 10,
:ref_item))
WHERE id = :basket_id
```

The update assigns a new collection containing one element to the items for a basket specified by the value contained in the `:basket_id` bind variable.

Adding new elements to an existing set of varying-array values with a single SQL statement is more difficult. The steps for adding elements to the varying array are:

- ❑ Read the existing elements and save them.
- ❑ Append the new elements to the saved elements.
- ❑ Store the new set of elements in the varying array.

However, if the new set of elements to be added can be queried as a group of rows and columns, then Oracle SQL syntax provides a way to cast the result set into a matching collection type. In order to cast rows and columns into a collection, the number and data type of the columns in each row must match the attributes defined in the collection. For example, assume that create a temporary relational table, called SPECIAL_ITEMS, which is populated with one or more rows. The table definition is:

```
CREATE TABLE special_items (
  quantity          NUMBER(4),
  price             NUMBER(6,2),
  sales_item_ref    REF sales_item_ot);
```

Suppose you want to replace the contents of your shopping basket with special items. This is done using the following update statement:

```
UPDATE shopping_basket
SET items =
  CAST(MULTISET(SELECT * FROM special_items) as
  va_shopping_item_ot)
WHERE id = :basket_id
```

In this example, the CAST operator is wrapped around a set of multiple rows returned by a query.[5] The query is nested inside a MULTISET operator, which informs the cast operator that more than one element exists. The MULTISET keyword is required for a data type compatibility check that the result set returned can be mapped to the specified collection. Taking a closer look:

- Query = (`SELECT * FROM special_items`) – returns one or more relational table rows, with a structure compatible to the `shopping_item_ot`.
- Collection = `MULTISET(Query)` – identifies the set of rows as a multiple instances of a structure.
- `CAST(Collection AS va_shopping_item_ot)` – performs the final data type check and conversion from a result set of rows into a varying-array collection of shopping items.

Casting a result set with more rows than the maximum number of elements allowed in the varying array will cause an error. The CAST mechanism can be used to cast a set of relational rows into a nested table collection. Object views can make use of the CAST operation to present rows of relational data as if they were a collection belonging to another object. The CAST operation relies on having an existing definition for the target data type.

---

[5]The CAST operator also allows Oracle scalar data types to be converted from one type to another compatible type. For example: SELECT CAST('10-01-2000' as DATE) FROM DUAL, is a statement showing that a value '10-01-2000' in a varchar2 format can be cast into a date type.

4.3.3 DELETING FROM A COLLECTION

An element can be deleted from a nested table by using the TABLE() operation to flatten the collection, and then targeting a specific element or set of elements in the collection through the use of a condition in the query's WHERE clause. For example, you may want to delete all the items (in a nested table) from the basket where the quantity is greater than ten:

```
DELETE FROM
  TABLE(SELECT items FROM shopping_basket where id = :basket_id)
WHERE quantity > 10;
```

The TABLE() operation ensures that the items from a specific basket are flattened, so that the condition (quantity>10) is only applied to the set of elements in the nested table for the basket identified by the value contained in the bind-variable :basket_id.

Deleting an element from a varying array is subject to the same rules as updating a collection. You must replace the entire set of elements with the original values, minus the one to be removed. This entails:

- ❑ Copying the elements to a temporary location.
- ❑ Deleting the unwanted element from the temporary location.
- ❑ Updating the varying array with the remaining elements from the temporary location.

The three steps can be simplified into a single query if a view is created on the varying array to represent it as a table of rows, which can be subject to a filtering condition to eliminate unwanted rows. The resulting rows can then be cast back into the varying-array structure to update the collection.

4.4 GETTING MORE PERFORMANCE WITH DML

Oracle SQL dialect provides a pseudo column called a ROWID that returns a value that physically locates the start of a record in the database. The ROWID also uniquely identifies a row in the database. You can query the ROWID and use its value in the condition of the WHERE clauses for UPDATE and DELETE statements. Using the ROWID is the fastest way to access the data for a specific row or instance.

Accessing rows using a ROWID is faster than using a primary key or unique key index. To use a ROWID, you just use the keyword ROWID anywhere a column name can appear in an SQL statement. For example:

```
-- Get the row ID for the current customer
SELECT ROWID FROM shopping_basket INTO :row_id
  WHERE id = :current_cust_id;

DELETE FROM
  TABLE(SELECT items FROM shopping_basket WHERE ROWID = :row_id)
WHERE quantity > 10;
```

The SELECT statement queries the ROWID for a shopping basket of the customer identified by bind-variable `:current_cust_id`, and stores the ROWID value into the bind-variable `:row_id`, as a character string. The DELETE statement is used to delete a collection of items contained in the shopping basket with a ROWID equal to the value in the `:row_id` bind variable.

The Oracle RDBMS ROWID values are called a physical or logical ROWID. A physical ROWID is either an extended ROWID or a restricted ROWID. The extended ROWID was introduced in Oracle8 and stores the physical address for:

- A row in a relational table.
- An object instance in an object table.
- An object instance in a nested table collection.

However, a ROWID is not maintained for:

- Items in a varying array.
- Index-organized tables.[6]

In Oracle8 databases and later versions, the extended ROWID is internally stored as a binary value, but it can be retrieved as an eighteen-character string in a base 64 encoding. The format of the eighteen-character ROWID, when displayed, is:

`OOOOOO`*`FFF`*`BBBBBB`*`RRR`*

Where:

- `OOOOOO` identifies the database segment where the data is stored.
- *`FFF`* is a data file number, within a table space, that contains the row.
- `BBBBBB` locates the data block that contains the row. Block numbers are relative to their data file, not their table space.

---

[6]An index-organized table (IOT) is a very efficient way to store data in Oracle. If all the values of a table can be contained in an index, then the index contains the actual values and no rows exist. An IOT is useful for intersection tables, which do not contain additional columns, but only the columns used to form relationships between row instances in related tables.

- *RRR* locates the start of the row in the block.

The restricted ROWID format is used for backward compatibility with Oracle databases earlier than version 8. The restricted ROWID is a binary value, displayed as sixteen hexadecimal characters in the following format:

```
BBBBBBBB.RRRR.FFFF
```

Where

- `BBBBBBBB` is an eight-digit hexadecimal value for the block contained within a file.
- `RRRR` is a four-digit hexadecimal value representing the row within the block.
- `FFF` is a four-digit hexadecimal value representing the file within a database instance.

Logical ROWIDs are used to access data in index-organized tables. An index-organized tables sorts the data for rows in the index, therefore there is no need for the extra physical storage of data rows. In this case, a logical ROWID is created by the Oracle database for you to access a row in the index-organized table.

Oracle8i has introduced a new data type, called a Universal ROWID or UROWID. The universal ROWID can store all the different types of ROWIDs discussed above, including access to foreign data in non-Oracle databases, by using an Oracle database gateway product.

The Oracle database uses an optimistic locking model, such that, a row is implicitly locked when you modify it, and is cannot be altered by application in a different session. You can implement a pessimistic locking model by explicitly requesting a lock on the record. You can explicitly cause rows to be locked with a SELECT statement by adding the keywords `FOR UPDATE` at the end of query. If you use `FOR UPDATE NOWAIT` with the SELECT statement and the records are locked by another session, the SELECT statement fails. This technique is useful because you have control over your SQL logic; otherwise, attempting to lock or modify a record locked by another session places your application in a wait state.

4.5 TRANSACTIONS IN ORACLE SQL

In the Oracle RDBMS environment, by default, changes made by data manipulation statements are not visible to sessions other than the session initiating the changes. It is only when the changes made by one session are committed that the other sessions see them. This satisfies the principle of isolation to which all transactions should conform. Isolation and the other principles governing transactions in Oracle SQL are laid out in an easy-to-remember acronym, ACID:

Atomicity—all operations are completed as a whole, or all are undone.

Consistency—the data are left in a consistent state after all changes have been made.

Isolation—transactions do not interfere with one another.

Durability—once committed, changes are persistent even if the system fails.

The type of isolation mechanism used defines the level concurrency. The Oracle engine, by default, will perform a row or instance level lock on data that have changed. The original state of a row or instance under change is still accessible to other sessions. The Oracle database implements transaction control through the use of buffering mechanisms called *rollback segments*.

In Oracle SQL, the first DML statement executed implicitly starts a transaction, and the transaction explicitly ends when either of the following two transaction control commands is executed:

- COMMIT—to permanently save change made with DML operations.
- ROLLBACK—to undo changes made with DML operations.

This type of transaction, in which the changes affect only one database, is termed a *local transaction*. A *global* or *distributed transaction* occurs when changes are made to more than one database in a single session. Ending the transaction makes use of a two-phase commit protocol to ensure that all the changes to all the databases involved are constantly performed or none at all, thereby satisfying the ACID principles.

In relational databases it not sufficient to just save or undo work done at any time, without considering the consistency and accuracy of the changes made. For example, when a customer submits a request to purchase the items in the shopping basket, a customer order record must be created and all related items added to the order. If the order record is saved before all its items are properly added, then the state of order will be inconsistent with the customer request. Creating the order record and all its item records must be considered a logical unit of work.

A database transaction is often defined as "a logical unit of work resulting in a consistent set of changes to the data." If any part of a logical unit of work is incorrect, or fails, the whole set of changes must be undone. This satisfies the principle of consistency. The ERD, or class, models and additional business rules will define the boundaries that constitute a logical unit of work.

4.5.1 TRANSACTION CONTROL AND BOUNDARIES

Transaction boundaries are defined by business rules that specify "logical units" of work to guarantee integrity of the data after the transaction is complete. A transaction has a logical start and end point. Each database connection, or session, has its own transaction context that is isolated from others session. The Oracle database engine can perform implicit and explicit transactions, and Oracle8i or higher provides for autonomous transactions. Insert, update, and delete operations always implicitly lock the records changed until the transaction is ended. The Oracle SQL engine will detect deadlock situations and informs an application creating the deadlock with an error condition.

4.5.1.1 Implicit Transactions. An implicit transaction begins when the first DML statement is executed.

Any DDL statement executed will implicitly commit an open transaction. Examples of DDL include statements that begin with keywords such as CREATE, ALTER, or DROP, which are treated as a transaction in their own right.

4.5.1.2 Explicit Transactions. Executing the SET TRANSACTION statement, using one of the following, explicitly starts a transaction:

```
1: SET TRANSACTION READ ONLY;
2: SET TRANSACTION READ WRITE
3:
4: SET TRANSACTION ISOLATION LEVEL SERIALIZABLE;
5: SET TRANSACTION ISOLATION LEVEL READ COMMITTED;
6:
7: SET TRANSACTION ISOLATION USE ROLLBACK SEGMENT segment-name;
```

- ❑ Line 1 is used to establish read consistency for the entire transaction, to ensure that all reads see only the changes made before the transaction begins. Changes made by another session during the transaction are not visible.
- ❑ Line 2, the default, establishes read consistency for the current statement, so that changes made by another session to the same data being read for the current statement are not visible.
- ❑ Lines 4 and 5 set the isolation level to serializable, which prevents modifying data that were already changed prior to the serializable transaction. The alternative, and the default, is a read committed transaction allowing the current session to modify any rows not locked by another session's transaction, and those the current session has previously changed.
- ❑ Line 7 allows the developer to request a specific rollback segment, or undo buffer space, used by the database engine. This is typically used when applications have very different transaction patterns. For example, a batch load program may require a large rollback segment to manage bulk changes

efficiently, while smaller rollback segments are more suitable for normal online transaction processing (OLTP) programs.

All SET TRANSACTION statement settings are cleared when the transaction is committed or rolled back. Executing either the COMMIT or ROLLBACK statement explicitly ends a transaction.

4.5.1.3 Commit to Save Changes. The syntax for the COMMIT statement is:

```
COMMIT [WORK];
```

All changes since the start of the transaction are saved. The database locks and rollback segment space is released. The example that follows creates a customer order and inserts an item into it. To complete the transaction, additional statements not included in the example are required to compute derived total fields in the order row.

```
SET TRANSACTION READ WRITE;

-- Create the order record
INSERT INTO cust_order
  (id, cust_id, cour_id, shipment_cost, total_cost,
   creation_date, pending_date)
SELECT :order_id, cust_id, :courier, shipment_cost, total_cost,
   trunc(sysdate), trunc(sysdate)+1)
FROM shopping_basket
WHERE cust_id = :cust_basket_id;

-- Create the item records
INSERT INTO order_item (order_id, prd_id, quantity, price)
SELECT :order_id, prd_id, quantity, price
FROM shopping_item
WHERE basket_cust_id = :cust_basket_id

COMMIT;
```

The default read-consistent isolation level allows the derived total in the order to be updated, if needed. However, the shopping basket has already computed the total cost, which is copied to the order record. In addition, the bind variables used for `:cust_basket_id` and `:order_id` help to keep the order and item data consistently related.

4.5.1.4 Rollback to Undo Changes. The syntax for the ROLLBACK command is:

```
ROLLBACK [WORK];
```

All changes since the start of the transaction are undone, the database locks, and rollback segment space is released.

The keyword WORK appearing after the COMMIT or ROLLBACK statement is optional, and is provided for ISO/ANSI standard SQL compliance. Consider the same example as shown for the commit, but assume there was an error in copying the items from the shopping basket to the order items table. A rollback could be executed before the whole operation is repeated:

```
SET TRANSACTION READ WRITE;

-- Create the order record
INSERT INTO cust_order
  (id, cust_id, cour_id, shipment_cost, total_cost,
   creation_date, pending_date)
SELECT :order_id, cust_id, :courier, shipment_cost, total_cost,
   trunc(sysdate), trunc(sysdate)+1)
FROM shopping_basket
WHERE cust_id = :cust_basket_id;

-- Create the item records
INSERT INTO order_item (order_id, prd_id, quantity, price)
SELECT :order_id, prd_id, quantity, price
FROM shopping_item
WHERE basket_cust_id = :cust_basket_id

-- Assume some error occurs ...

ROLLBACK;
```

If you issue the rollback statement, changes made by *both* insert operations are undone. The rollback is not required, because in the event of an error, the database engine performs an implicit statement-level rollback for each DML statement. Therefore, the item record insert operation can be repeated without having to redo the insert operation for the order record.

Consider the case when a customer adds more than one item to the shopping basket. The application inserts the item into the table, but does not commit the change. The customer then decides to remove the last item added from the basket, either because of a mistake or because it is no longer wanted.

If the application executes a ROLLBACK command, to remove the last item, then the last item and all the items inserted before it will be removed. This undesirable result would be the equivalent of having to tear up a paper order only to rewrite the entire order.

The Oracle SQL SAVEPOINT statement can be used to overcome this problem.

4.5.1.5 Transactions and Savepoints. Oracle SQL allows one or more savepoint statements to be executed as part of a transaction. The savepoint serves as a serial named marker. The program or session executing the transaction can issue a rollback statement to a named savepoint. This is like rolling back to a point in time and undoing all the work done after the savepoint was executed to the time the rollback statement is made. The syntax to create a savepoint is:

```
SAVEPOINT savepoint-name;
```

The savepoint name must start with an alphabetic character, and follows the same naming rules as tables and columns. More than one savepoint can be created during the life of a transaction to subdivide the entire transaction into smaller units of work. However, you can only commit full changes, not individual parts. A savepoint exists for the life of the transaction or if a rollback statement undoes any work to a prior savepoint.

The syntax used to rollback to a savepoint is:

```
ROLLBACK TO [SAVEPOINT] savepoint-name;
```

The keyword SAVEPOINT is optional. The next example creates some items in a shopping basket, and then removes the last item added in the operation:

```
SET TRANSACTION READ WRITE;

-- Create the shopping basket
INSERT INTO shopping_basket
VALUES

-- Add a new item

INSERT INTO shopping_item (basket_cust_id, prd_id,
price, quantity)
VALUES (:basket_id, :prd_id, :price, :qty);

-- Mark the place before the next item with a save
-- point called before_new_item
```

```
SAVEPOINT before_new_item;

-- Add another item to the shopping basket

INSERT INTO shopping_item (basket_cust_id, prd_id,
price, quantity)
VALUES (:basket_id, :prd_id, :price, :qty);

-- The customer wants to remove the latest addition to
the basket

ROLLBACK TO SAVEPOINT before_new_item;
```

Only the effects of the last insert statement are undone in the above example.

If you are creating additional savepoints, each of them should have a different name. However, you may want to create a savepoint with the same name as an earlier one. This effectively moves the earlier savepoint forward in time, eliminating the possibility of undoing work to the point in time marked by the original savepoint, unless you rollback the entire transaction. A rollback to a savepoint sequential undoes changes back to the named savepoint, but does not remove the savepoint.

4.5.1.6 Autonomous Transactions. Oracle8i introduced autonomous transactions. An *autonomous transaction* allows another completely independent transaction to be performed during a transaction already in progress. The Oracle PL/SQL environment is used to implement autonomous transactions.

An autonomous transaction executes in a different context than the calling transaction. Changes made by the calling transaction are not visible to the autonomous transaction. In the context of the autonomous transaction, the commit or rollback operation does not affect the state of the calling transaction, which can be continued as normal.

An example where this may be of use is when you want to guarantee audit or error log information saved in a database independent of the main transaction sequence that caused an error or audit event to occur. Perhaps the transaction fails when you are copying the order and items from the shopping basket to the customer order and order items tables. The autonomous transaction can log the error in the database without being affected by the rollback necessary to undo the order. Without autonomous transactions, you would have to create a separate database session to receive and store the log messages on behalf of the session doing the actual work.

SUMMARY

This chapter has explained SQL data manipulation statements and shown you how to manage changes to data stored in object instances based on object type structures. You have seen the rich mechanisms that can be used to manipulate data in:

- Rows or columns in relational tables.
- Object instances in object tables.
- Object instances nested in object columns or attributes of another object type.
- Collection objects, including nested tables and varying arrays.

The concept of a database transaction has highlighted the importance of maintaining data consistency by designing DML changes into a logical unit of work to ensure accuracy of data.

Chapter 5

Oracle Architecture and Performance Considerations

- Architectural Elements
- Performance Tuning
- Summary

In this chapter you will explore the complex Oracle RDBMS architecture in an effort to demystify its most difficult aspects. A basic understanding of the architectural components of Oracle is important in order to make sound design decisions that have a significant impact on the overall performance of your applications. The preceding chapters illustrate how to interact with an Oracle system from a very practical point of view. You have seen *how* things work in an Oracle server; it is now time to understand *why* they work that way.

Oracle can accomplish certain tasks in several different ways. For instance, here are the different mechanisms that can be used for one of the simplest operations, fetching data from an Oracle table or object type:

- SQL statements directly submitted to the engine through JDBC.
- SQL statements formulated in SQLJ.
- Result set obtained by a call to a stored procedure coded in PL/SQL, with a Java wrapper.
- Result set obtained by a call to a stored procedure coded in Java.

The "correct" mechanism is chosen based on such parameters as scalability, portability, verbosity, and compatibility.

Knowing what happens "behind the scenes" when you submit a SQL statement (or invoke a Java stored procedure) is crucial if you want to deploy scalable applications that don't suffer from performance problems.

Knowing the Oracle architecture is a good starting point, but alone is not enough to fine-tune the performance of the SQL statements submitted to the engine. You will learn below how to use the tools provided by Oracle to perform SQL analysis. The chapter ends by illustrating the use of a freeware utility found in the companion CD-ROM; it helps in browsing the Oracle shared pool in order to pinpoint poorly formulated SQL statements.

5.1 ARCHITECTURAL ELEMENTS

An Oracle server consists of an Oracle *database* and an Oracle server *instance* (background processes/threads and shared memory described in a few pages). The database consists of a physical structure, based upon file system entities as defined by the hosting operating system, and a logical structure, based upon the concept of *tablespace*. A tablespace organizes the Oracle schema objects listed in Table 5.1.

Typically, a tablespace consists of one or more *data files*. Adding more data files to a tablespace can extend the physical disk space allocated to it. The important concept here is that the physical space taken by Oracle objects does not grow steadily as new objects are inserted into the database.

The database administrator (DBA) usually allocates entire disks to Oracle tablespaces at the moment of database creation. System administrators soon learn that there is no need to panic if disks allocated to Oracle are 98 percent or even

TABLE 5.1 Oracle Objects

ORACLE OBJECT	MEANING
Tables	The basic unit of data storage in an Oracle database.
Views	Tailored presentations of the data contained in one or more tables (or other views).
Synonyms	Aliases for tables, views, or other Oracle objects (e.g., sequences, functions, packages).
Stored Procedures	Procedures and functions are schema objects that logically group a set of SQL and other PL/SQL programming language statements together to perform a specific task.
Sequence	Sequential series of numbers generated by the Oracle sequence generator. Sequence numbers are Oracle integers defined in the database of up to 38 digits. A sequence definition indicates general information: the name of the sequence, whether it ascends or descends, the interval between numbers, etc.
Database Link	Defines a one-way communication path from an Oracle database to another database.
Index	Optional structure associated with tables and clusters. Indexes can be created ion one or more columns of a table to speed SQL statement execution on that table.
Cluster	Optional method of storing table data. A cluster is a group of tables that share the same data blocks because they share common columns and are often used together.
Object Type	Abstraction of the real-world entities that an application program deals with. An object type is a schema object with three kinds of components: • A name that identifies the object type uniquely within the schema. • Attributes that model the structure and state of the real-world entity. Attributes are built-in types or other user-defined types. • Methods, i.e., functions or procedures written in PL/SQL or Java and stored in the database, or written in a language like C and stored externally. Methods implement operations the application can perform on the real world entity.
Trigger	Procedure that executes implicitly when an INSERT, UPDATE, or DELETE statement is issued against the associated table (or, in some cases, against a view) or when database system actions occur. Triggers can be written in PL/SQL or Java and stored in the database, or can be written as C callouts.
Java Object	Starting with release 8.1.5 Oracle has included a Java Virtual Machine in its kernel. The database thus contains a complete Java infrastructure. Users can load their own Java classes using the loadjava utility.

100 percent full, since the space allocated to the disks is not going to grow any further. Note, too, that the data files comprising one tablespace can reside on different disks, thereby allowing one tablespace to span several or many disks.

Data files are one of the three types of files managed by an Oracle system. As stated earlier, they contain all the relational and object type objects used by custom applications. The data file format is identical for all the data files of a specific Oracle release for a specific operating system, irrespective of the type of objects stored. In other words, the internal format of two data files does not change if one contains indexes and the other contains tables.

The other two types of file used by Oracle are redo log files and control files. *Redo log files* contain details of transactions that may not as yet have been written to the data files. The main purpose of redo log files is to allow for the recovery of the database should a system or database failure occur.

Control files contain information about the physical and logical structure of the database and about database checkpoints. They are constantly updated by the Oracle engine, which stores internal counters in them, such as the transaction counters, or System Change Number (SCN). Control files are generally small, just a handful of megabytes, but they are essential to the running of Oracle. If you lose them, you have lost the entire database, with very little chance of recovery. For this reason, Oracle can be configured to automatically mirror the information stored in the control files in multiple locations, which should, for obvious reasons, reside on different physical disks.

5.1.1 ORACLE SGA AND BACKGROUND PROCESSES/THREADS

An Oracle system also includes several background processes (under operating systems such as Unix) or threads (under MS Windows NT), and memory buffers shared among all database users.

Background processes/threads and shared memory under Oracle control are called an *Oracle instance.* The central element of an Oracle instance is the System Global Area (SGA), a shared area of memory that Oracle allocates when it starts up. The SGA comprises five main objects, as shown in Table 5.2.

As important as the SGA for the functioning of an Oracle system are the background processes or threads that comprise, with the SGA, the Oracle instance. These processes or threads are shown in Table 5.3.

The discussion so far has examined the components of the Oracle architecture: that is, the *anatomy* of Oracle. To understand how it really works, you need to explore its *physiology*. First, look at the pictorial representation of the Oracle architecture displayed in Figure 5.1, which illustrates the interactions between the components of an Oracle instance.

Then Next, examine a transaction lifecycle, identifying the relevant steps and relating them to specific marks shown in Figure 5.1. This exercise should help you see how the Oracle components cooperate to provide fast access to data in a secure and recoverable manner.

Figure 5.1 shows what happens when a SQL statement is submitted to the Oracle engine. The same sequence of events occurs irrespective of the means used to submit SQL statements. In other words, whether you are using an Oracle-provided tool, such as SQL*Plus, or are connecting through a JDBC driver, your requests are served in the same manner. There are two different types of connections to an Oracle instance:

TABLE 5.2 SGA Objects

SGA OBJECT	PURPOSE
Shared Pool	Contains cached SQL and PL/SQL statements, data dictionary information, and private session information when the Oracle multi-threaded server configuration is used.
Buffer Cache	An area of the SGA that contains copies of data blocks from database files. Its purpose is to reduce disk I/O by allowing sessions to access frequently or recently accessed data directly in memory.
Large Pool	Issued for large memory allocation that would normally be made from the shared pool.
Java Pool	Contains shared memory required by the Oracle 8i Java Virtual Machine.
Redo Buffer	Contains redo log entries not yet written into the redo log files. It is flushed periodically, and is always flushed when a COMMIT occurs.

1. Connection through a dedicated server.
2. Connection through a dispatcher served by a shared server.

Using a dedicated server connection requires the creation of one process per connected user. The memory requirements are on the order of a few megabytes (typically at least two) per process. In order to lower the memory requirement of servers hosting large populations of Oracle users, the Multi-Threaded Server (MTS) configuration is provided by Oracle. In an MTS configuration, multiple client (or application) processes are connected to a limited number of dispatchers, which in turn allows a dialog exchange between shared servers through the Oracle SGA. Not all applications are suitable for a multi-threaded server configuration; in fact, multiplexing is made possible by using the idle time of a client process for the benefit of the other processes. The basic assumption here, is that an application user spends 80 percent of the time looking at the screen, assimilating the information just displayed, deciding on the next course of action, and perhaps questioning a customer over the phone. Only 20 percent of the time is the user process busy, actively fetching data from the database server. If an application is not substantially interactive, and of the type just described, the adoption of an MTS architecture is not likely to increase the number of potential users.

Figure 5.1 shows both types of connections. The bottom-left section of the figure shows step 1, Request Connection, and step 2, Dedicated Server Connection. The dedicated client requests a connection from the SQL*Net/Net8 listener,[1] which forks a process (the dedicated server process) that establishes a network connection with the dedicated client. The latter can then submit SQL statements, which will be executed by the dedicated server on its behalf.

[1]SQL*Net/Net8 is a SQL-oriented network protocol developed by Oracle to allow client processes to connect to the Oracle instance. It is included in every Oracle distribution kit. Net8, the release of SQL*Net shipped with Oracle 8, introduced features that allow for great scalability (up to thousands of users).

TABLE 5.3 Oracle Background Processes

BACKGROUND PROCESS	FUNCTION
Database Writer (DBWn)	Writes modified database blocks to the data files. An Oracle instance can have more than one database writer; in this case the last character of the process name is a number that identifies each process.
Log Writer (LGWR)	Responsible for redo log entries, generated by database transactions, to the online redo log files.
System Monitor (SMON)	Responsible for instance recovery during startup, for temporary segment cleaning and for coalescing of the free space in the tablespaces.
Process Monitor (PMON)	Cleans up the allocated memory structures for processes that have abruptly terminated.
Archiver (ARCn)	Archives completed redo logs to a backup location.
Checkpoint (CKPT)	Updates data file headers during checkpoint operations.
Recoverer (RECO)	Resolves inconsistencies in distributed operations that have not committed normally.
Lock (LCKn)	Performs cross-instance locking when the Oracle Parallel Server configuration is enabled.
Queue Monitor Process (QMNn)	Monitors application queues created using the Oracle Advanced Queuing facility.
Job Queue (SNPn)	Process requests placed in the job queue. The latter is a cron[1]-like facility administered internally by Oracle.
Parallel Query Slave (Pnnn)	Supports parallel SQL queries.
Shared Server (Snnn)	Performs database operations on behalf of multiple connected clients, when the Multi-Threaded Server option is enabled.
Dispatcher (Dnnn)	Mediates connections between Oracle sessions and their shared servers. A session will be assigned a specific dispatcher process that will forwards SQL requests to the least-busy shared server.
Dedicated Server	Performs database operations on behalf of a single client that can be accessing Oracle services through Oracle Pro*C, SQL*Plus, Java, etc.

[1]For readers unfamiliar with Unix: cron is a system utility that allows tasks to be executed at regularly scheduled intervals.

The top-left section of Figure 5.1 shows a shared connection, where the SQL*Net/Net8 listener "connects" a client program requesting a connection to a dispatcher. The dispatcher in turn sends SQL statements to the shared server, which returns the result sets fetched from the database to the shared client. This exchange of data is shown in Figure 5.1, steps 3, 4, and 5.

5.1.2 THE TRANSACTION LIFECYCLE

The Oracle transaction lifecycle is summarized in Table 5.4.

The Oracle architecture depicted in Figure 5.1 is characterized by several well-integrated components, each highly optimized and highly specialized to

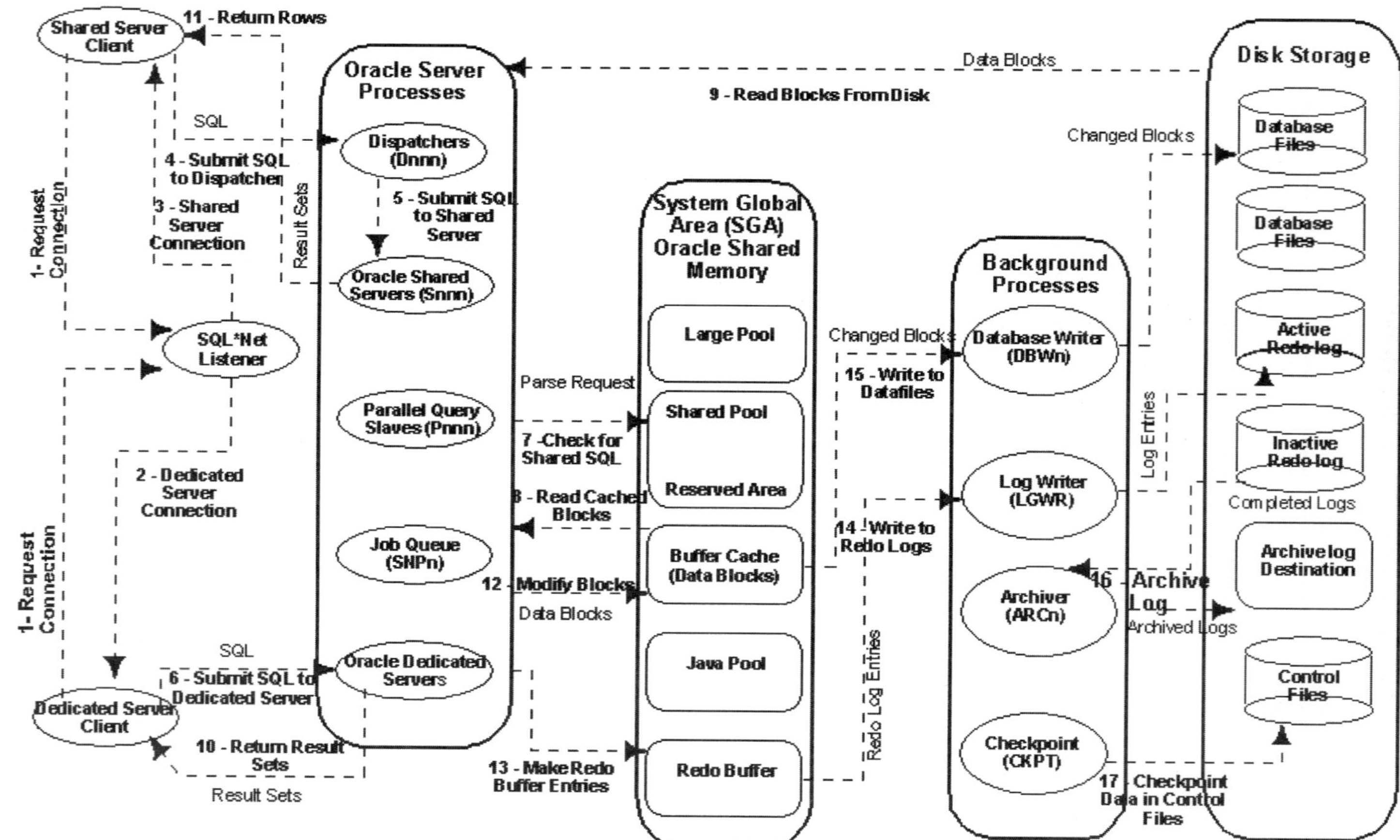

Figure 5.1 Oracle 8i Architecture. (Courtesy by Quest Software, www.quest.com)

TABLE 5.4 The Oracle transaction lifecycle

STEP	ACTION	EXPLANATION
1	**Request Connection**	A client application connects to the SQL*Net/Net8 listener and requests a connection.
2	**Dedicated Server Connection**	If the requested connection is a dedicated connection, a dedicated server is created and allocated to the client session.
3	**Shared Server Connection**	If a shared connection is to be established, one of the available dispatchers is assigned to the client session.
4	**Submit SQL to Dispatcher**	The client session sends SQL requests to the dispatcher.
5	**Submit SQL to Shared Server**	The dispatcher transmits the SQL requests to the first available shared server.
6	**Submit SQL to Dedicated Server**	The dedicated client submits SQL requests to the dedicated server process.
7	**Check for Shared SQL**	The server process checks the shared pool looking for an identical statement. If no statement is found, the server process parses the SQL statement, storing it in the library cache.
8	**Read Cached Blocks**	The server process accesses the buffer cache, looking for the data blocks identified by the SQL statement.
9	**Read Blocks from Disk**	If the preceding step cannot entirely satisfy the SQL query, the server process fetches the requested data from the database files.
10	**Return Result Sets**	The dedicated server process returns the data retrieved by the preceding steps to the client process.
11	**Return Rows**	The shared server process returns the rows retrieved by the preceding steps to the client process.
12	**Modify Blocks**	If the submitted SQL is a DML statement, the data blocks affected by the statement are modified in the buffer cache.
13	**Make Redo Buffer Entries**	Details of any modification to data blocks are concurrently written to the redo buffer.
14	**Write to Redo Logs**	When a COMMIT statement is issued, the log writer process copies the content of the redo log buffer into the redo log file.
15	**Write to Data Files**	The database writer background process periodically copies modified data blocks from the buffer cache to the database files.
16	**Archive Redo Logs**	When the redo log files become full, they are copied to the archived redo log directory by the archiver background process.
17	**Checkpoint**	At a regular intervals, or when a redo log switch occurs, Oracle performs a checkpoint that causes the control files to be updated and all data blocks to be check pointed to disk.

(Adapted from the "Instance Monitor Poster," courtesy of Quest Software, www.quest.com)

perform one and only one task (or set of tasks). The database writer (DBWR), for example, scans at regular intervals the *buffer cache*, an area of the SGA that temporarily stores data blocks, looking for "dirty" blocks to be checkpointed to disk. A dedicated server is a highly optimized object that browses the shared pool looking for an identical SQL statement, parsing the statement if one is not found. It "knows" how to browse the buffer cache looking for database blocks identified by the query being processed, and also knows how to access the database files if the required blocks are not already cached. If the statement being processed modified data blocks, the changes are propagated to the redo buffer. But what happens next falls outside the jurisdiction of the dedicated server process. The transaction recovery subsystem takes over. The log writer (LGWR) background process supervises all transaction-based operations, and is responsible for checkpointing the changes recorded in the redo buffer to the redo log file as soon as a COMMIT statement is issued. Note that modified data blocks are not written to the database files as soon as the change occurs. After the changes have been written to the redo log files, Oracle can rebuild the transaction in case of system failure. When an Oracle engine boots up, it verifies that the transaction log is consistent with the data stored in the database files. If a discrepancy is detected, an automatic recovery process will synchronize the content of the database files with the data stored in the transaction log.

The various subsystems comprising an Oracle engine are designed to work asynchronously, but they cannot work in absolute isolation from each other. Mechanisms called *latches,* based on semaphores, signals, queues, and memory locks, are in place to ensure coordination and synchronization among the processes and memory structures belonging to the various subsystems. Operations that should naturally occur in one of the subsystems are sometimes delayed because of the need for synchronization with other subsystems.

For example, consider a dedicated server that must change data blocks, as instructed by a DML statement. In order to do this, it must obtain a latch to prevent other sessions from changing the same blocks. If no latches are currently available, the process must wait. The process also requires one or more latches to be able to store an entry in the redo log buffer. If the redo log buffer is currently full, the session will wait until the log writer process has made more space available in the redo log buffer, by checkpointing its entries into the redo log file.

Given all the dependencies that govern the various components of an Oracle engine, a small number of wait events is unavoidable. Sometimes, however, wait events assume pathological proportions. Performance tuners have to intervene to investigate the causes of the engine malfunctioning. While such a topic is very advanced, and definitely outside the scope of this book, a few basic performance-boosting techniques must be known by all developers involved with Oracle technologies at any level of competence, including beginners.

5.1.3 ORACLE SGA COMPONENTS

The system global area includes the *buffer cache*, where data blocks are temporarily stored and either kept, if frequently accessed, or thrown away, if less frequently accessed, and the *shared pool*, where SQL statements receive the same treatment. If an SQL statement is frequently used by the application, its place in the shared pool will be almost guaranteed. Statements that are rarely executed will be discarded from the shared pool on the basis of an LRU (least recently used) type of algorithm.[2]

It is up to the DBA to size the buffer cache to maximize the likelihood of user sessions to find the required data blocks in the SGA, rather than fetching them from disk. Further increasing the size of an already large buffer cache does not really increase the chance of finding all required data blocks in the SGA, but it subtracts precious memory from the system hosting the Oracle instance, as the SGA runs in real, rather than virtual, memory

Conversely, making the buffer cache too small forces disk I/O much more often, adversely affecting the overall system performance. While proper buffer cache sizing is in the realm of the database administrators, developers can definitely influence what happens in the shared pool. Consider step 7 in the transaction lifecycle, which reads: "The server process checks the shared pool looking for an identical statement. If no statement is found, the server process parses the SQL statement, storing it into the library cache."

5.1.4 SQL STATEMENTS AND BIND VARIABLES

The concept of identical SQL statement deserves your attention. Consider an e-commerce application, deployed by a car dealer that allows customers to look for second-hand cars based on brand, model, and price range. Potential buyers use an HTML interface to fill in the request form. Information regarding brand name, model, and price range is entered in a controlled manner; that is, the values are chosen from list boxes. Car data reside in an Oracle database, and the HTML forms posted from the client browsers are interpreted by Java code run by a servlet. The latter connects to Oracle using a JDBC driver. User requests are reformulated in SQL terms by the servlet. Thus, a request from a user who is looking for a '96 Ford Taurus in the $8,000–$10,000 range can be formulated in SQL as:

```
SELECT car, description from second_hand_car where
maker='Ford' and model = 'Taurus' and year_made=1996 and
price between 8000 and 10000;
```

Similarly, a request from a customer looking for a '97 Mazda 626, and prepared to spend between 12,000 and $14,000 to buy it, generates the following SQL statement:

---

[2]A statement, function, or procedure can be forced to remain in the shared pool irrespective of the frequency of its use by the system. The keep function that allows developers to "pin" specific objects in the shared pool in provided as a PL/SQL built-in package (DBMS_SHARED_POOL).

```
SELECT car, description from second_hand_car where
maker='Mazda' and model = '626' and year_made=1997 and
price between 12000 and 14000;
```

The two statements are obviously not identical. If the Java code submits them in succession to Oracle through the JDBC driver, the dedicated server will not find an identical statement already stored in the shared pool, and will parse both statements. Parsing is an expensive operation because the SQL syntax must be checked for validity, and Oracle must make sure that the database objects referred to by the query actually exist and are accessible by the user submitting the query. In many cases, parsing accounts for more than 50 half of the time required by Oracle to return the rows identified by the query. In addition, parsing a statement and storing it into the shared pool require the server process to acquire one or more latches. This operation cannot be executed in parallel by two or more processes. Parsing can only occur sequentially, one statement after the other. As you can see, this operation is potentially a bottleneck.

Clearly, there is an incentive for developers to try to avoid parsing SQL statements. How can this be achieved? How can the two SQL statements shown above be made to look identical?

The SQL standard supports parameterized queries; that is, the operands of the WHERE clause can be placeholders, which are replaced by real values just before each execution of the statement. If you reformulate the above SQL statements as:

```
SELECT car, description from second_hand_car where
maker=? and model = ? and year_made=? and
price between ? and ?;
```

you achieve your goal, since the same statement can be used to satisfy both queries. Using JDBC terminology, an application programmer will "prepare" the statement, that is, will cause the statement to be parsed and stored in the shared pool. Each query parameter, identified by a question mark, must be replaced by a value before the statement is executed.

Note

Oracle 8i Release 2 (otherwise known as 8.1.6) introduces a new performance-boosting feature: the engine now has the ability to automatically substitute bind variables *en lieu* of literal values. Even if sloppy or inexperienced programmers submit SQL queries that contain literal values in the where clause, internally Oracle will silently operate a replacement, which translates into a drastic reduction of statement parsing.

While this new feature is more than welcome, developers should perform explicit binding anyway, rather than relying on the automatic substitution operated by Oracle.

Experience shows that even applications concurrently accessed by a large user population send a limited number of SQL statements to the Oracle engine, perhaps as few as twenty or thirty different statements. This is the *core* SQL, used and reused by the application clients several or many times per session. Particular care must be given to the proper formulation of the core SQL queries.

5.2 PERFORMANCE TUNING

If you have access to the dynamic tables, the ones characterized by the V$ prefix, you can compute the number of parameters used to customize the behavior of an Oracle engine. The SQL statement

```
select count(*) from V$PARAMETER;
```

returns the number of parameters available to your Oracle engine. While this number varies with the specific OS platforms that host the Oracle system, and also with the different releases of Oracle, it is close to 200. Not all parameters have a direct influence on the overall performance delivered by the engine. Many of them specify the location of the various files and directories needed by Oracle to work, other deal with particular Oracle configurations, such as Parallel Server and MTS, or with the size of the engine's components. A considerable number of database parameters, however, can be used to fine-tune the engine's behavior.

This topic is definitely advanced, and of interest mainly to DBAs rather than developers. The specifics of engine parameters are outside the scope of this book. But note the following consideration: Striving to achieve the best-possible performance from an Oracle engine by tuning the engine parameters is useful and beneficial when it is done just before going live with a production system. If your application is poorly designed, and you have not given enough care to the construction of SQL statements or Java stored procedures, then you face certain failure even if you assemble a "dream team" of world-renowned Oracle performance experts to help just before going to production. By then it is far too late for useful intervention. The irreparable damage has already been done.

As a developer or designer of an application that uses Oracle as the back-end database, you can make an impact on the overall performance of the final product by designing intelligent, efficient data-retrieval paths that minimize convoluted table joins while providing an acceptable average response time under most circumstances. The recipe for success in an Oracle environment calls for a performance-driven data model and careful revision of every SQL statement submitted to the engine. This sounds like a daunting task, but Oracle, as you will see in the next paragraphs, provides powerful means to assess the efficiency of the SQL statements parsed by the engine.

5.2.1 PERFORMANCE-CONSCIOUS SQL STATEMENTS

Developers with a background in PC-based databases, such as Borland dBASE, and Microsoft FoxPro or Access, usually tend to apply functions to the columns appearing in the WHERE clause. This is done to force exact comparisons between the operands of the WHERE clause. For example, if you want to avoid confusion with strings that contain both lowercase and uppercase characters, you could use the SQL UPPER function in both sides of the WHERE clause, as in

```
where upper(surname) = upper(:my_surname);
```

Oracle also allows programmers to apply functions to columns appearing as operands of the WHERE clause. Unfortunately, there is a major side effect associated with this technique. If the column in question is indexed, the function coercing the column prevents the index from being used. This applies only to the columns appearing in the WHERE clause, and not to the values they are compared against. An SQL function can be used to coerce the value appearing on the right side of the comparison operator, as in

```
where surname = UPPER(:var_surname);
```

In this case, Oracle can use the index on the surname column to retrieve the rows.

Oracle 8i introduced a new feature that improves index creation. It is, in fact, possible to create indexes with embedded functions, as in:

```
create index upp_surname on customer  (UPPER(surname));
```

This *function-based index* allows SQL queries to use indexes even if a function is used in the WHERE clause. For example, the statement:

```
select * from customer where upper(surname) = upper('ellison');
```

uses the index previously created.

There are occasions when calculations are needed to identify the value that must be used to select the wanted rows. In the following example, you want to select all employees who are older than thirty-five. The date of birth of each employee is stored in the employee table. Your query could be as follows:

```
select surname from employee where DOB +(365 * 35) > SYSDATE;
```

The query shown above is syntactically correct, but unfortunately an index on the DOB column cannot be used. Functions and calculations performed against the column appearing in the WHERE clause disable the associated index, unless a function-based index has been created using the same function.

You can obtain the same result, but this time allowing Oracle to use the index on the date-of-birth column, by rewording the SQL statement in this way:

```
select surname from employee where DOB > SYSDATE - (365 * 35);
```

Oracle cannot use indexes when looking for rows using NULL keys. The SQL statement

```
select surname from employee where dob is null;
```

always uses a full table scan to return the requested rows.

5.2.2 ORACLE QUERY OPTIMIZERS

In order to retrieve the rows requested by the user in the most efficient way, recent Oracle releases use the services of a cost-based query optimizer; unlike older releases, which used a rule-based optimizer. This ranks every possible access path for each table. The access path with the lowest ranking is preferred and chosen because it is supposedly the most efficient. The ranking of the access paths follows mechanical rules that are applied without taking the size of each table into consideration.

According to the rule-based optimizer:

- Indexes are preferred to table scans.
- Unique indexes are preferred to non-unique indexes.
- Concatenated indexes are preferred to single-column indexes (if the entire concatenated index is used).
- Single values are preferred to ranges.
- Bounded ranges (e.g., BETWEEN) are preferred to unbounded ranges (e.g., GREATER THAN).

If access path rankings are equal, the order in which the tables are listed determines the access path. The table specified last in the FROM clause becomes the first table in the JOIN order. In other words, the right-most table in the FROM clause is the *driving table* of the join operation. In the old days of Oracle SQL optimization, determining the driving table was very important. The *position* of the table in the wording of the SQL statement made a significant difference. The driving table was chosen based on its size. The smallest table should have been the last in the FROM clause.

The problem of the rule-based optimizer is that its analysis is hopelessly static. It repeatedly chooses the same optimization pattern for the lifetime of the application, without taking the size of the tables into consideration. The smallest table at the moment of the initial optimization, the one chosen to be the driving table for the core joins performed by the application, might grow faster than the other tables. After a while, it may not be the best candidate for the driving table. Yet, unless the application maintainers rework the SQL statements, it continues to stand in the position of driving table, causing performance to degrade and to worsen over time.

In addition, the Oracle rule-based optimizer requires human intervention, at least initially, to study and determine the best combinations and the best wording of the SQL statements. A rule-based optimizer can be used successfully when an application consists of a few well-known data access paths, as in the case of OLTP applications. In decision-support environments, such as data warehousing, the designers are not in a position to predetermine all the potential data access paths that will eventually be required by the users.

In these contexts, a rule-based optimizer is definitely not a viable solution. For this reason, starting with release 7.0 of the database server, Oracle Corporation introduced the cost-based optimizer. The cost-based optimizer performs better than the rule-based optimizer in most cases. The two optimizers now coexist in the database server, but Oracle Corporation warns that the rule-based optimizer will eventually be phased out. In addition, while the cost-based optimizer is continually being improved, the rule-based technology is no longer being developed. The cost-based optimizer is today the only reasonable option.

What is a cost-based optimizer, and why it is better than the rule-based alternative? A cost-based optimizer compares possible execution plans by estimating the amount of I/O they require. This estimate is based on statistics periodically generated on the database. The execution plan for the queries is *dynamically adjusted,* taking table size into account. The position where the tables appear in the SQL statement is irrelevant. The driving table automatically chosen by the cost-based optimizer is guaranteed to always be the one that generates the most efficient data retrieval and incurs the least cost.

Thanks to the cost-based optimizer, SQL queries are, to a certain degree, self-tuning. The cost-based optimizer receives its input from the statistics on the database objects stored in the data dictionary. The gathering database object statistics does not happen magically, but has to be arranged by the database administrator. Most sites run the statistics generation as a batch job that is performed overnight, together with other housekeeping tasks. Up-to-date statistics on the database objects accessed by the SQL queries are crucial for the correct functioning of the cost-based optimizer.

Which optimizer the engine will use is decided at startup time. An engine parameter, OPTIMIZER_MODE, can assume a few values, such as RULE, which selects an engine-wide rule-based optimizer, CHOOSE, which selects cost-based optimization if statistics have been gathered into the data dictionary tables, FIRST_ROWS, which selects a cost-based optimizer that minimizes response time, and ALL_ROWS, which selects a cost-based optimizer that minimizes the total execution time.

The optimization policy selected when the engine boots up can be changed at a session by issuing an ALTER SESSION command. For example, the engine-wide OPTIMIZER_MODE parameter is set to CHOOSE, and you know that statistics have been gathered for the tables you want to analyze. This makes the optimizer use the cost-based policy while choosing the most efficient execution plan.

If you want to override the default behavior, using, for instance, a rule-based policy, you can issue the following command:

```
ALTER SESSION set OPTIMIZER_MODE=RULE;
```

From this point onward, the optimizer changes its initial policy, switching to the policy specified at a session level.

5.2.3 SQL STATEMENT ANALYSIS

How do programmers know when an SQL statement is likely to perform satisfactorily? Oracle provides two methods that facilitate the optimization of SQL statements. The first relies on DML's EXPLAIN PLAN command, is simpler to use, and can easily be operated by client-server programmers who do not have an account on the back-end computer. A client workstation equipped with SQL*Plus is sufficient to perform SQL analysis based on EXPLAIN PLAN.

The second method forces Oracle to trace the execution of the SQL statements into a file that is saved in the file system of the host machine. The file produced by the internal Oracle trace facility is difficult to interpret unless it is filtered through a utility called TKPROF to produce a human-readable output. In order to proficiently use the Oracle trace facility and TKPROF, a programmer must be granted access to the host computer, that is, must have a host account and appropriate privileges.

The EXPLAIN PLAN and AUTOTRACE facilities will be explored in the next few paragraphs because of their accessibility and ease of use. If you are interested in performing advanced SQL analysis using Oracle trace and TKPROF, begin by reading about these tools in Chapter 14 of the standard Oracle manual, "Oracle 8i Tuning." Additional literature on the topic is available from Prentice-Hall and O'Reilly and Associates.[3]

Java developers who want to ensure the efficiency of the SQL statements they submit to the Oracle engine should use SQL*Plus to perform the initial SQL analysis. When satisfied with the results, they should cut the statements from SQL*Plus and paste them into their Java code.

---

[3] "Oracle SQL: High Performance Tuning," by Guy Harrison, Prentice Hall, 1997 and "Oracle Performance Tuning," by M. Gurry and P. Corrigan, O'Reilly and Associates, 1996 are the current best references in this field.

> **Tip**
>
> While operating in SQL*Plus, statements entered interactively can contain either literals or bind variables; SQL*Plus is able to show the execution plan for both types of statement. When the SQL analysis session is finished and the optimized statement are pasted into the Java code, developers should make sure that all literals are replaced with bind variables. If JDBC is used all parameters appearing in SQL statements should be expressed using question marks (?). If the interface of choice is SQLJ, instead of JDBC, each query parameter is prefixed by a colon (:).

5.2.3.1 Explain Plan. The EXPLAIN PLAN command instructs Oracle to place the execution plan for a SQL statement into a table in the schema of the user who requested it. By default, EXPLAIN PLAN looks for a table called PLAN_TABLE, but it is possible to explicitly name a table other than PLAN_TABLE. The PLAN_TABLE, or the user-defined alternative, has a specific structure. If you try to explain a command without having the PLAN_TABLE in your schema, Oracle complains by issuing the following message:

```
SQL> explain plan for
  2  select table_name from user_tables;
select table_name from user_tables
                       *
ERROR at line 2:
ORA-02402: PLAN_TABLE not found
```

Oracle provides a PLAN_TABLE creation script that is installed by default. This script is called UTLXPLAN.SQL. In a Unix environment, it can be found in $ORACLE_HOME/rdbms/admin. In MS Windows NT, it is found in <ORACLE_DIR>\ORA81\RDBMS\ADMIN. All users should have read-only access to the file, so that they can run the script to create the PLAN_TABLE in their own schemas.

EXPLAIN PLAN also allows you the option of explicitly naming the statement to be explained. This is useful if you want to explain multiple statements in your session. You can extract the SQL statistics from the PLAN_TABLE by referring to each statement's statement id. There is also another alternative whereby you do not name the statement, but invoke EXPLAIN PLAN and truncate the PLAN TABLE right after the SQL statistics are extracted.

Warning

A common mistake is to run the same statement twice without truncating the PLAN_TABLE between the two runs, or to run EXPLAIN PLAN twice forgetting to name the two statements differently. Oracle appends the statistics of the two runs without complaining, but you will encounter problems when extracting the SQL statistics.

In order to interpret the statistics stored by Oracle in the PLAN_TABLE, you have to issue a hierarchical query against the table. That is, an Oracle-specific SQL extension must be used in order to recursively fetch rows that are in a hierarchical relationship of the parent-child type.

A commonly used SQL script for extracting SQL statistics from the PLAN_TABLE follows:

```
select lpad(' ',2*level)||rtrim(operation)||' '||
      rtrim(options)||'        '||object_name query_plan
from plan_table
connect by prior id=parent_id
start with id=0;
```

It is now time to put all this into practice. Save the above script into a file called explain.sql, so that you can execute it repeatedly from your SQL*Plus session. Launch SQL*Plus, either from the command line or from Windows, and after having connected to your default schema, make sure that you have the table required by the EXPLAIN PLAN facility:

```
SQL> describe plan_table;
```

If PLAN_TABLE has already been created, SQL*Plus will display its structure. Otherwise it will complain with the following message:

```
SQL> describe plan_table;
ERROR:
ORA-04043: object plan_table does not exist
```

In this case you have to create the required table, running the UTLXPLAN script. If you are operating under Unix, you can use the ORACLE_HOME environment variable to identify the path to the script, as in:

```
SQL> @ORACLE_HOME/rdbms/admin/utlxplan

Table created.
```

If you are an MS Windows user, you will have to provide the absolute path to the UTLXPLAN file, as the ORACLE_HOME variable only works under Unix/OpenVMS.

Note that to invoke the execution of the script you used the at (@) sign. You can now proceed to create a table, issuing the following command:

```
SQL> create table employee
  2  (
  3     emp_id number primary key,
  4     surname varchar2(30),
  5     name varchar2(30),
  6     address varchar2(50));

Table created.
```

Now submit a query that uses the primary key to select a given employee. Oracle enforces primary keys by silently creating a unique index on the column (or columns) comprising the primary key. Expect to be very efficient if you select a row using the primary key column as a selection criterion.

```
SQL> explain plan for
  2  select * from
  3  employee where emp_id=30;
Explained.
```

To show the execution plan chosen by Oracle to fetch the required data, you invoke the explain script that you have already saved (see above).

```
SQL> @explain

QUERY_PLAN
---------------------------------------------------------------
  SELECT STATEMENT
    TABLE ACCESS BY INDEX ROWID              EMPLOYEE
      INDEX UNIQUE SCAN                      SYS_C001734
```

To interpret the output produced by the script, which interprets the statistics generated by EXPLAIN PLAN, start from the most indented line, which contains the first step taken by the optimizer to fetch the required data, and proceed toward the less-indented steps. In your case, the optimizer scans the index SYS_C001734 to retrieve the ROWID that points to the required row in the EMPLOYEE table. SYS_C001734 is the name arbitrarily chosen by Oracle for the hidden index associated to the primary key created on the CUST_ID column.

The INDEX UNIQUE RANGE execution step is the most efficient way to retrieve a row in Oracle. You now want to exclude the index when you perform your lookup, to see if and how the execution plan chosen by the optimizer varies. In Section 5.2.1 you learned that Oracle cannot use an index if you use a function on a column with an associated index. If you use a function that does not change the EMP_ID value, you can still fetch the required row, but Oracle will not use the SYS_C001734 index. One of the functions you can use is ABS, which returns the absolute value of the given number.

First, clear any residual analysis from PLAN_TABLE by using the truncate command, and then reissue your query, modified to include the ABS function.

```
SQL> truncate table plan_table;

Table truncated.

SQL> explain plan for
  2  select * from employee where
  3  abs(emp_id) = 45;

Explained.

SQL> @explain

QUERY_PLAN
-------------------------------------------
  SELECT STATEMENT
    TABLE ACCESS FULL   EMPLOYEE
```

The execution plan shows that Oracle performs a full table scan to fetch the requested row, excluding the SYS_C001734 index from the execution plan. The ABS function does not do much, because the number stored in EMP_ID is a positive number by default. The net effect of applying the ABS function to the EMP_ID column is the exclusion of the index.

Unfortunately, it is not always that simple to interpret the output of a hierarchical query performed on the PLAN_TABLE.

The queries issued against Oracle data dictionary views are generally more complex, because of their deeply nested structure. Observe the execution plan of a query that lists all the tables owned by the user's schema:

```
SQL> explain plan for
  2  select table_name from user_tables;
```

```
Explained.
SQL> @explain

QUERY_PLAN
--------------------------------------------------------
  SELECT STATEMENT
    NESTED LOOPS
      NESTED LOOPS OUTER
        NESTED LOOPS OUTER
          NESTED LOOPS
            TABLE ACCESS BY INDEX ROWID  OBJ$
              INDEX RANGE SCAN           I_OBJ2
            TABLE ACCESS CLUSTER         TAB$
              INDEX UNIQUE SCAN          I_OBJ#
          INDEX UNIQUE SCAN              I_OBJ1
        TABLE ACCESS CLUSTER             SEG$
          INDEX UNIQUE SCAN              I_FILE#_BLOCK#
      TABLE ACCESS CLUSTER               TS$
        INDEX UNIQUE SCAN                I_TS#
```

The first rule is trying not to be overwhelmed by the output. Proceed sequentially, and identify the most indented part of the statement. In this case, you should start by the unique index scan of the I_OBJ# index and progress toward the less-indented parts of the plan. To interpret an execution plan, you should be familiar with the common execution steps performed by Oracle when processing an SQL statement.

The execution steps in the preceding query plan are explained below:

INDEX UNIQUE SCAN is an index lookup that returns the ROWID of only one row.

INDEX RANGE SCAN is an index lookup that returns the ROWID of multiple rows. This can happen either because the index is non-unique or because the query contains a range operator (BETWEEN, GREATER THAN, etc).

NESTED LOOPS are being performed on the preceding step. For each row in the parent result set, the child set is scanned to find a matching value.

NESTED LOOPS OUTER are an outer join imposed upon a nested loop join.

TABLE ACCESS CLUSTER is an index cluster key is used to access data in the table in question.

TABLE ACCESS BY ROWID the ROWID of a row is used to access data in a table. This is the fastest way to retrieve data in Oracle. Usually the ROWID is found by using an index lookup in a preceding step.

TABLE ACCESS FULL is the full table scan. Oracle reads every block containing data associated to the table being accessed.

The access steps listed above are only a subset of the access paths supported by Oracle. The best way to get acquainted with SQL optimization is by experience. Everything will begin to make sense once you have explained the execution plan of a few dozen queries and understand each access step performed by Oracle. There is no substitute for experience. Every programmer working with Oracle should become familiar with SQL optimization through the standard Oracle tools.

5.2.3.2 Full Table Scans Can Be Efficient. As stressed here several times, under certain circumstances Oracle is unable to use an index associated with a column or set of columns in a table. Programmers should be aware when they are excluding an index from the query. It is now time to rectify this position a little, in order not to generate the false impression that the infamous full table scan is the worst enemy of an SQL developer. Sometimes you intentionally force Oracle not to use the index associated to a column, to *increase* the efficiency of a query.

The idea that it is more efficient to perform a sequential scan of a table than to use an index seems counterintuitive. This is due to the strategy used by Oracle to retrieve the data blocks that contain the data selected by the query. Index traversal in Oracle begins with the index root node access, and reads the subsequent nodes via direct I/O to fetch the wanted block. Each block read requires a single read call.

When Oracle is requested to perform a full table scan, it uses a smart lookahead algorithm that fetches multiple blocks at once, up to the number defined by the DB_FILE_MULTI_BLOCK_READ_COUNT instance parameter. This is a database parameter read by the engine at boot time. A single block usually contains multiple rows, which are all read in one I/O call.

To understand why a full table scan can be more efficient than an index lookup, consider the following example. A table contains 1,000 rows, and each block contains, on average, 10 rows. If DB_FILE_MULTI_BLOCK_READ_COUNT is set to 8 (the default), in one read Oracle will fetch (10 * 8) = 80 rows from disk to the SGA. It would take Oracle approximately thirteen I/O operations to fetch the entire table into the SGA.

Now consider an index lookup that fetches six rows. It takes twelve I/O calls, one to read the index, and one to fetch the block, multiplied by the number of rows. If the query selects seven rows, a full table scan becomes more efficient.

This example is very "experimental" and oversimplifies the way Oracle works, since reality is more complex than the situation presented here. It is likely that the index lookup would not perform exactly twelve I/O calls, because the probability of finding the required data block already in the SGA grows with the number of I/O calls. Nevertheless, it should be clear now why the selectivity of an index must be considered before opting for index creation.

5.2.3.3 The AUTOTRACE Facility. The most recent releases of SQL*Plus offer the AUTOTRACE system variable to simplify the process of explaining the SQL statements submitted to the engine. To analyze the SQL statements, the AUTOTRACE variable can be set to OFF (the default), which means no execution statistics, or ON, which produces a report on the execution plan.

When AUTOTRACE is set to ON, there are further available parameters:

ON STATISTICS The AUTOTRACE report shows only the SQL statement execution statistics.

ON EXPLAIN The AUTOTRACE report shows only the optimizer execution path.

AUTOTRACE can be enabled with the TRACEONLY parameter, which suppresses the output of the query.

By default, the AUTOTRACE facility displays execution statistics after the output produced by the query. For this reason, you populate one table with data, so that you can see the statistics computed by AUTOTRACE when you submit a query that actually retrieves rows.

The data dictionary view ALL_TABLES contains all the tables created in the database that are visible from our schema. ALL_TABLES is a view owned by SYS and available to all schemas; it selects from data dictionary tables such as sys.user$, sys.ts$, sys.seg$, and sys.obj$. Use the statement given below to rapidly create a table populated with data, so that you can test the AUTOTRACE facility without manually inserting data in a table created ad hoc.

```
create table db_table as select * from all_tables;
```

DB_TABLE is now a real table, created from the all_tables view in your default schema. You can build indexes and alter them at will. To test AUTOTRACE, create one composite index on the OWNER and TABLE_NAME columns:

```
create index db_ndx1 on db_table (owner,table_name);
```

Now enable AUTOTRACE and issue a query to see the facility in action:

```
SQL> SET AUTOTRACE ON
SQL> select owner,table_name,blocks,empty_blocks
from db_table where owner='EBONAZZI';

EBONAZZI           COURIER                    1       0
EBONAZZI           CUSTOMER                   1      63
EBONAZZI           CUST_ORDER                 1      63
EBONAZZI           LOCAL_PLAN_TABLE           1       3
EBONAZZI           ORDER_ITEM                 1     128
EBONAZZI           PLAN_TABLE                 1       3
EBONAZZI           SALES_ITEM               133       0

Execution Plan
----------------------------------------------------------
   0      SELECT STATEMENT Optimizer=CHOOSE
   1    0   TABLE ACCESS (BY INDEX ROWID) OF 'DB_TABLE'
   2    1     INDEX (RANGE SCAN) OF 'DB_NDX1' (NON-
UNIQUE)


Statistics
----------------------------------------------------------
          0  recursive calls
          0  db block gets
          9  consistent gets
          0  physical reads
          0  redo size
       1607  bytes sent via SQL*Net to client
        716  bytes received via SQL*Net from client
          4  SQL*Net roundtrips to/from client
          1  sorts (memory)
          0  sorts (disk)
          7  rows processed
```

SQL*Plus has executed the query and displayed the results. After the query output, AUTOTRACE prints the execution plan for the query, which tells you that the optimizer has performed an index range scan on DB_NDX1 to fetch the ROWID for the required entries stored in DB_TABLE. The query statistics follow.

The AUTOTRACE facility simplifies SQL performance analysis, but has a major drawback. In order to display statistics and execution plan, SQL*Plus performs the query. Enabling the TRACEONLY parameter suppresses the query output, but Oracle still processes the statement. When the EXPLAIN PLAN command is executed, instead of using the AUTOTRACE facility, no rows are fetched, but the execution plan is stored in the PLAN_TABLE. If you are unsure whether a statement will produce a full table scan of a large table, use EXPLAIN PLAN. You will know the answer in no time. If you are sharing your development instance of Oracle with other developers, they will complain if the engine slows down because you are playing with AUTOTRACE, performing resource hungry full table scans while optimizing your queries.

5.2.3.4 Influencing the Optimizer Through Query Hints. When you used the ABS function to exclude the index automatically created by Oracle to enforce the primary key built on the EMP_ID column in a preceding example, you actually influenced the optimizer. In a way, you tricked it, forcing Oracle out of its "natural" behavior.

Does this mean that it is possible to influence the Oracle optimizer using the same technique? The answer is yes. Not only can the execution plans produced by the optimizer be influenced, but Oracle provides the means to do so, without using artificial tricks like the one shown in the preceding example. The mechanism that allows programmers to change the behavior of the optimizer is based on a series of *hints*, or keywords, that appear in the SQL statements as comments. Here is an example of a statement containing a hint:

```
select  /*+FIRST_ROWS */ customer_name from customer
where customer_id > 16;
```

A few things are worthy of mention. First, the syntax to enable the hint. The plus sign after the comment symbol is mandatory. A hint must follow the SQL Data Manipulation Language statement. If the comment containing the hint is not placed right after the DML statement, Oracle ignores it.

Oracle allows one only hint per statement block. A statement block is a parent statement or a subquery of a composite statement, a SELECT, UPDATE, or DELETE statement, or an element of a compound query. For instance, a compound query composed of two query elements connected by a UNION includes two statement blocks. Each of the two can be influenced by a hint.

If hints are incorrectly specified, or conflict with each other, Oracle simply ignores them.

If you want to instruct the optimizer to perform a full table scan, even if an index is available, use the /*+FULL(<table_name>) */ hint.

The most commonly used hints, with a brief explanation, are listed below.

ALL_ROWS requests the use of the cost-based optimizer with the goal of best throughput. That is, the statement will be performed consuming the least-possible amount of resources.

FIRST_ROWS	indicates that the optimizer will seek to achieve the best response time to retrieve the first rows.
RULE	request the rule-based optimizer.
ORDERED	instructs the optimizer to join the tables in the order they appear in the SQL statement.
INDEX(table_name, [index_name])	instructs the optimizer to use the specified index to retrieve rows from the table. If no index is specified, use any available index.
FULL(table_name)	forces the optimizer to perform a full table scan for the specified table.
CACHE	requests the optimizer to keep the rows fetched through a full table scan in the SGA, to optimize further reuse.
STAR	asks the optimizer to privilege the STAR methodology over other methods of table join.

Warning

Before using hints in your SQL code, you should consult the Database Administrator and/or the application's designers and architects. If you are integrating Java code and technologies into legacy applications, sharing the same Oracle database, using hints could have unwanted side effects, for example forcing Oracle to use the cost based optimizer. If the legacy application had been optimized using the rule based optimizer, the overall performance of the system could suffer.

5.2.4 BROWSING THE ORACLE SHARED POOL

EXPLAIN PLAN and AUTOTRACE can be very helpful in the initial crafting of SQL statements. Java developers who use SQLJ or JDBC to interface to Oracle should use SQL*Plus to test the efficiency and quality of their SQL statements. When satisfied with the results, you cut the statements from SQL*Plus and paste them into the Java IDE of your choice.

This is fine during the development phase, when you are coding one or a few SQL statements in one session and want to test them on the fly. Sometimes, however, you like to have a broader picture of your SQL statements and how they perform in the overall context of the application.

Oracle makes accessible to database users all the parsed SQL statements stored in the shared pool, through a few dynamic performance views (yet again the famous V$ views!). The V$SQLAREA and V$SQLTEXT views are commonly used to take a snapshot of all SQL statements currently parsed in the shared pool. V$SQLAREA contains a great many statistics on the statement that are very useful in pinpointing performance problems.

The information stored in V$SQLAREA proves invaluable in the classical scenario wherein a particular query is very efficient in the development environment, but performs poorly in the production environment. Sometimes this is due to a "forgotten" index that was created in the development database but overlooked in production. In another common scenario, an apparently tuned statement does not perform well in production because it was optimized against a limited data sample; the scaled-up version of the same tables, found in the production instance, uncover the weakness of the SQL statement.

The V$SQLAREA dynamic performance view contains the first eighty characters of each parsed SQL statement, together with several useful statistics. In order to fetch the complete text of the SQL statements, V$SQLTEXT must also be accessed. A composite key, based on two columns, is used to relate each child entry into V$SQLTEXT to a parent entry in V$SQLAREA. The two columns are ADDRESS and HASH_VALUE. Table 5.5 lists the most important columns that appear in V$SQLAREA.

V$SQLTEXT contains only five columns, two of which are the composite key used to join V$SQLTEXT with V$SQLAREA. The structure of V$SQLTEXT is shown in Table 5.6.

TABLE 5.5 Relevant columns of V$SQLAREA

COLUMN NAME	DATATYPE	EXPLANATION
SQL_TEXT	VARCHAR2	The first eighty characters of the SQL text for the current cursor.
SHARABLE_MEM	NUMBER	The sum of all sharable memory, in bytes, of all the child cursors under this parent.
PERSISTENT_MEM	NUMBER	The sum of all persistent memory, in bytes, of all the child cursors under this parent.
SORTS	NUMBER	The sum of the number of sorts done for all the children.
EXECUTIONS	NUMBER	The total number of executions, totaled over all the children.
PARSE_CALLS	NUMBER	The sum of all parse calls to all the child cursors under this parent.
DISK_READS	NUMBER	The sum of the number of disk reads over all child cursors.
BUFFER_GETS	NUMBER	The sum of buffer gets over all child cursors.
ROWS_PROCESSED	NUMBER	The total number of rows processed on behalf of this SQL statement.
EXECUTIONS	NUMBER	The total number of executions, totaled over all the children.
ADDRESS	RAW(4)	The address of the handle to the parent for this cursor.
HASH_VALUE	NUMBER	The hash value of the parent statement in the library cache.

(The grayed columns are the composite key to V$SQLTEXT)

TABLE 5.6 Columns displayed by V$SQLTEXT

COLUMN NAME	DATATYPE	EXPLANATION
ADDRESS	RAW(4)	The address of the handle to the parent for this cursor.
HASH_VALUE	NUMBER	The hash value of the parent statement in the library cache.
PIECE	NUMBER	Number used to order the pieces of SQL text.
SQL_TEXT	VARCHAR2	A column containing one piece of the SQL text.
COMMAND_TYPE	NUMBER	Code for the type of SQL statement (SELECT, INSERT, etc.).

The complete text of a long SQL statement is stored in multiple rows of V$SQLTEXT. Each row (or SQL piece) is sequentially numbered, so that the statement can be reassembled correctly.

Tip

The dynamic performance views, characterized by the V$ prefix, are not available by default to all Oracle users. If your Oracle database is looked after by a DBA, speak to him or her to obtain the privileges required to access the dynamic views. If you are using your own Oracle database, connect as SYS (the default password is change_on_install) and grant the select privilege on V$SQLAREA and V$SQLTEXT to the user/schema that you use to access the database. For example, John Smith uses the jsmith user account/schema to connect to his personal Oracle instance running on his or her workstation. In order to "see" the V$ views, John connects as sys and grants select on jsmith:

```
SQL > connect sys/change_on_install
Connected.
SQL > grant select on V_$SQLAREA to jsmith;
Grant succeeded.
SQL > grant select on V_$SQLTEXT to jsmith;
Grant succeeded.
```

"change_on_install" is the default password for the SYS account, automatically set by Oracle at the moment of database creation, which can optionally occur when you install Oracle. Since SYS is a privileged account, the default password should be changed immediately after the database has been created. If the SYS password is still set to the default value, take this chance and change it using this syntax:

```
alter user sys identified by <new password>;
```

You must be connected as SYS to change the password.

> Also, note that the underscore between V and $ in V_$SQLAREA is not a typo. The real view defined in the SYS schema is V_$SQLAREA, but a public synonym exists that redefines that name as V$SQLAREA. This is valid for all dynamic views.

To identify the most expensive SQL statement currently parsed in the Oracle shared pool, enter this query:

```
SELECT SQL_TEXT, BUFFER_GETS, EXECUTIONS,
RAWTOHEX(ADDRESS),HASH_VALUE FROM V$SQLAREA
ORDER BY BUFFER_GETS DESC;
```

The statements displayed first are the ones you have to further optimize. In some situations, however, the SQL_TEXT column included in V$SQLAREA does not contain enough characters to uniquely identify an offensive statement. Remember, SQL_TEXT only stores the first eighty characters of a statement. If you have submitted long, complex SQL statements that share a very similar initial part, you need to access V$SQLTEXT to assemble the entire statement by concatenating the various pieces together. The following query fetches all the SQL statement pieces for a specific statement, given its address and hash value:

```
select sql_text from v$sqltext
where address = '<address>' and
hash_value = <hash value>
order by piece;
```

Since it is quite tedious to manually enter the required SQL statement to retrieve performance information interactively, several commercial and freeware utilities are available to facilitate instance-wide SQL analysis. One of these freeware utilities, called ShrPool, can be found in the companion CD, under the *chapter05/ShrPool* directory. ShrPool is a Win32 application, which requires Oracle SQL*Net/Net8 client installed on the PC used to browse the Oracle shared pool. Since ShrPool connects through SQL*Net/Net, it can be used to analyze remote Oracle instances running, for instance, on Unix.

The source code of ShrPool is also available in the *src* subdirectory of *chapter05/ShrPool*. ShrPool is written in "C", and interacts with Oracle using the Oracle Call Interface (OCI). ShrPool is not the best utility in its field, as commercial tools provide more functionality and a more sophisticated user interface, but it is freely modifiable and customizable by anybody who can use a "C" compiler in a Windows environment.

A tool like ShrPool offers a twofold advantage. Not only does it relieve developers from manually entering SQL queries against V$SQLAREA and V$SQL-

TEXT to identify problematic statements, but it is also able to explain the execution path of selected statements interactively.

Before using ShrPool or any other similar tool, you should run your Java application for a few minutes to exercise most of its parts, or at least those parts that access Oracle most intensely, in order to populate the Oracle shared pool with the largest possible number of parsed SQL statements.

Assuming that you have successfully installed ShrPool on your PC, you should launch it and connect to Oracle using the same account accessed by your application. After a successful connection to Oracle, ask ShrPool to display the SQL statement selection criteria window by clicking on the "File" menu and selecting the "Shared Pool" entry. The SQL statement fetch options window is shown in Figure 5.2.

The fetch options window allows for the retrieval of parsed SQL statements from the shared pool according to several criteria that act as a filter for the statements being fetched. You can influence the sort order of the fetched statements, and can exclude statements that do not match predefined selections criteria—for instance, statements that have not been executed at least a specific number of times. If the requested sort order is based on disk reads, ShrPool lists the statements that are most expensive in terms of I/O first. If the sort order is based on buffer gets, ShrPool lists the most expensive statements in terms of CPU time first. It is also possible to fetch only those statements that affect a specific table or any other database object by specifying the wanted object in the text box labeled "Only show statements containing this string."

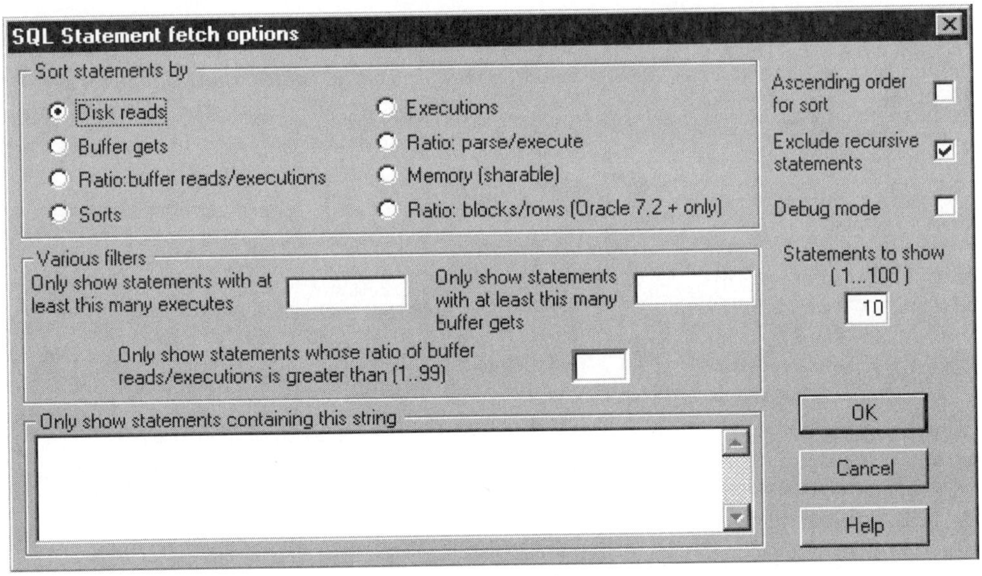

FIGURE 5.2 The SQL statement fetch options window

Once the selection criteria have been entered, click on the OK button. This forces ShrPool to retrieve the parsed SQL statements from V$SQLAREA. They are displayed in the window shown in Figure 5.3.

You can visually select a specific statement from the ones displayed in the main list box of the window. If you tick the "Explain Plan for statement(s)" check box and you have the right privileges, ShrPool shows the execution plan for the required statement. Alternatively, if you don't have the privileges to explain the statement, you can always look at the statistics for the required statement gathered from V$SQLAREA. If you are connected to an Oracle schema, and know that you don't have the privileges to explain a specific statement using it, ShrPool allows you to enter a username and password to connect "on the fly" to the schema that owns the objects accessed by the statement, so that an execution plan can be generated. If you are allowed to generate an execution plan for a particular statement, ShrPool displays statistics and execution plan in a window. An example is shown in Figure 5.4.

The requested SQL statement is displayed at the top of the window. Since the statement is assembled from V$SQLTEXT, even long and complex SQL syntax is entirely displayed in the text box.

The middle part of the window shows the execution plan for the statement. The bottom part of the window displays the statement statistics.

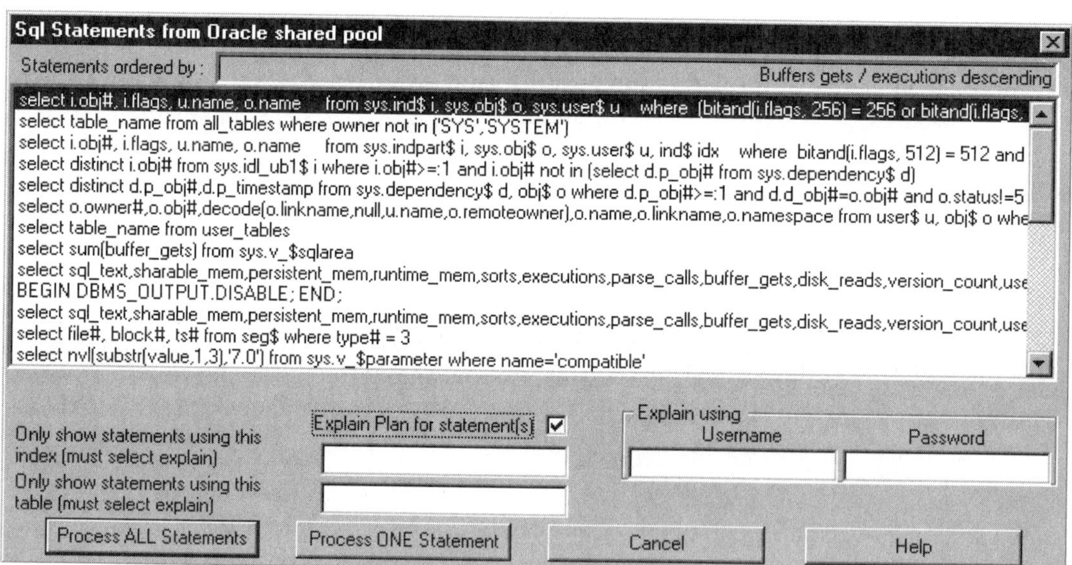

FIGURE 5.3 SQL Statements from Oracle Shared Pool Window

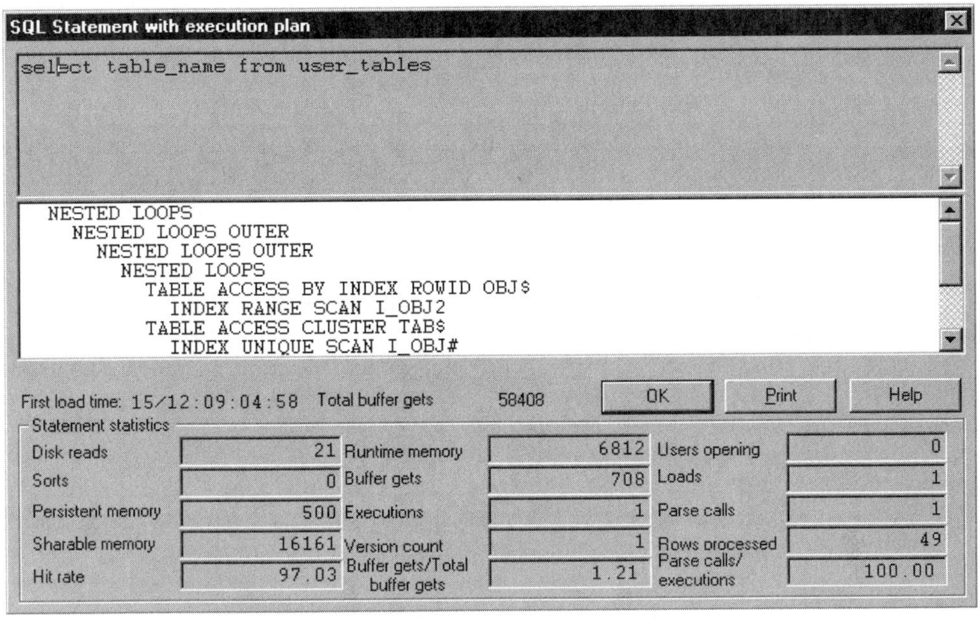

SQL Statement with execution plan

```
select table_name from user_tables
```

```
NESTED LOOPS
  NESTED LOOPS OUTER
    NESTED LOOPS OUTER
      NESTED LOOPS
        TABLE ACCESS BY INDEX ROWID OBJ$
          INDEX RANGE SCAN I_OBJ2
        TABLE ACCESS CLUSTER TAB$
          INDEX UNIQUE SCAN I_OBJ#
```

First load time: 15/12:09:04:58 Total buffer gets 58408 OK Print Help

Statement statistics

Disk reads	21	Runtime memory	6812	Users opening	0
Sorts	0	Buffer gets	708	Loads	1
Persistent memory	500	Executions	1	Parse calls	1
Sharable memory	16161	Version count	1	Rows processed	49
Hit rate	97.03	Buffer gets/Total buffer gets	1.21	Parse calls/ executions	100.00

FIGURE 5.4 SQL statement with execution plan window

ShrPool facilitates SQL analysis, and can be very helpful in pinpointing problematic statements. The market offers several similar utilities, and you are encouraged to explore the various alternatives. No matter what tool you select, be sure to analyze the SQL statements you have produced before releasing your code. This will help you to avoid the panic situation that invariably occurs when a new release of a software product is shipped to production and the system does not perform as expected.

SUMMARY

In this chapter you explored the various elements of the Oracle architecture, analyzing its most significant components, such as tablespaces, datafiles, background processes, and the System Global Area (SGA). You have also briefly seen how the various components of Oracle interact and cooperate to provide efficient, recoverable data insertion and retrieval. Examining the transaction lifecycle helped you to understand the interdependencies between the major subsystems that constitute an Oracle engine.

Although we only scratched the surface of a complex subject, getting an overview of the Oracle architecture was a crucial step leading to the chapter's main topic: how to improve the performance of the SQL statements submitted by your Java programs to the Oracle engine.

You have learned how to use basic techniques that facilitate SQL analysis, using SQL*Plus, the standard Oracle tool shipped with every distribution of the Oracle software, and therefore accessible to everyone. The standard Oracle tools can be complemented with ShrPool, a freeware utility found in the companion CD, which simplifies the task of analyzing the performance of the SQL statements parsed by the Oracle engine and stored in the shared pool.

Chapter 6

INTERNET SECURITY AND ORACLE SECURITY

- Network Firewalls
- Oracle Security
- The Demilitarized Zone
- Using Oracle Security and Synonyms to Implement a Development Environment
- New Oracle Security Features
- Summary

In this chapter, you will become acquainted with some security issues related to the deployment of Web-enabled applications. While Oracle provides a great many security-oriented features, companies that embrace e-commerce cannot rely solely on Oracle to guarantee an adequate level of security for application components that are implemented outside the realm of the database. Network firewalls are commonly used to prevent unauthorized access to corporate resources. The most sophisticated security requirements can be satisfied by implementing demilitarized zones (DMZs), network environments delimited by at least two firewalls, where network packets are scrutinized and filtered by a combination of dedicated software and hardware. Only selected network traffic that complies with strict policies is granted access through the firewalls.

The required security level of the environment where your application will be deployed determines the architecture options that you have to consider while designing the application. This chapter introduces you to the security-driven constraints that you have to take into account in designing the operating environment of the delivered application.

The chapter will also teach you how to benefit from the Oracle-provided security subsystem during the development phase, to establish a sound development environment where developers cooperate without overriding one other's files and objects.

6.1 NETWORK FIREWALLS

An ever increasing number of companies require Internet-provided services, such as the World Wide Web (WWW), Internet mail, Telnet, and File Transfer Protocol (FTP). The same companies also want to offer their customers WWW pages and possibly FTP access, so that they can download information stored in files. Obviously, there are security issues that must be addressed in order to regulate the network traffic from the company to the Internet, and from the Internet to the company. Almost all companies implement one or more Internet firewalls—systems that enforce a security policy between an organization's network and the Internet.

The security policy enforced by a firewall creates a sort of perimeter defense around the boundaries of the company's network. For a firewall to be effective, all traffic to and from the Internet must go through it, so that each network packet can be scrutinized and verified. A firewall is not, or not only, a combination of hardware and software that oversees the network packets transiting through the company's network. It must be part of a comprehensive security policy that includes users' awareness of the duties and responsibilities associated with the ownership of computer accounts, such as password management.

Many IT professionals mistakenly equate security with encryption. The crude reality is that hackers rarely use brute-force methods to crack passwords. More often, they gain access to a company's network by finding obvious weak points in the security policy of the company under attack. As a defense against such intrusion, network administrators can periodically use SATAN (Security

Analysis Tool for Auditing Networks) and other freely available tools to probe their systems and check the security state of health of their networks.

If you are wondering why firewalls and security are discussed in a book about Java and Oracle, rest assured that this is not a useless digression. The presence or absence of a firewall at the company expected to use your software will have a major impact on your design decisions, as will the security policies the company enforces. It makes a considerable difference whether your application runs within the firewall perimeter or through it. In the first case, your range of options for client-to-server communication extends from RMI to sockets. In the second case, you will probably be forced into an HTTP solution, such as the TCP/IP traffic going through port 80, the port traditionally dedicated to HTTP, and one that is generally allowed by firewalls.

Two diametrically opposed security philosophies govern the deployment of Internet firewalls:

- Everything not specifically permitted is denied.
- Everything not specifically denied is permitted.

According to the first philosophy, all traffic should be blocked by the firewall, and only a few selected services should be allowed to progress through the secured network. The degree of security is very high, but ease of use is compromised.

The opposite philosophy allows user freedom and ease of use, but it jeopardizes security. It is likely that commercial organizations will implement security philosophies of the first kind, while academic and research institutions will implement security philosophies of the second kind.

You may be tempted to presume that your application is so important that the network administrators will open a hole in the firewall to allow, for instance, a socket port to be accessed. This is a dangerous assumption that may severely limit your potential customer base. Large corporations tend to be inflexible as far as their policies are concerned, and when a security policy states that no socket ports can be accessible through the firewall, even the most useful and powerful software product will not persuade the IT managers to relax security.

Forbidding socket access also affects RMI, since it uses TCP/IP sockets as the low-level network layer. The use of RMI through firewalls requires direct intervention by the network administrators, who must explicitly allow for specific known ports to be accessible, that is, not stopped by the firewall.

RMI has built-in mechanisms that attempt an alternative connection to the default direct socket connection to the required host if the default method fails. The implementation of sockets in the standard JDK can use a SOCKS server, if one is found, after the direct socket connection fails. SOCKS is a networking protocol that enables hosts on one side of the SOCKS server to gain full access to hosts on the other side of the SOCKS server without requiring direct IP accessibility.

SOCKS is normally implemented to allow users within a firewall perimeter to use Internet services, such as HTTP, and prevent Internet users from accessing the hosts protected by the firewall. SOCKS was born as an internal project at NEC, and is freely downloadable from www.socks.nec.com. Commercial implementations of SOCKS are also available from leading vendors, including SUN Microsystems.

While the SOCKS protocol is becoming increasingly popular, it does not provide a full solution for the "RMI through firewalls" problem. In fact, it only allows outgoing RMI calls from hosts protected by the firewall to hosts residing outside the firewall, but not vice versa. This means that RMI callbacks are not supported, nor are incoming RMI calls.

A few methods of allowing a bi-directional RMI flow are available, but they all require either specific settings that relax firewall security or the presence of application-level proxy servers, which translates into an increased administrative burden and a more complex development environment. The "graceful degradation" algorithm used by RMI to establish a connection does not stop after the initial attempts through a direct socket port and SOCKS. If an HTTP proxy server is available and configured, RMI attempts two types of HTTP tunneling, http-to-port and http-to-cgi. This kind of HTTP tunneling introduces performance and security issues, and heavily affects the overall scalability of the application.

Given the security issues associated with RMI, application architects tend to limit its use to Intranet-based environments that run Java applications, rather than applets within the company's firewall. Alternatively, RMI can be used together with Http tunneling to serve requests coming from clients residing outside the firewall.

While security is a crucial consideration likely to influence your design decisions, other factors will play an equally important role in the decision process that shapes the architecture of your application. Consider the following scenario: You are called in on a project that has been set up with the goal of replacing and enhancing a traditional client/server application initially developed using a Win32 RAD tool, say MS Visual Basic. The application will be exclusively used by the company's workforce operating from PCs and workstations located in its headquarters.

You are in control because you can dictate the application environment. You can standardize on a specific browser, or you can develop for the Java plug-in, rather than rely on a browser vendor implementation of the Java Virtual Machine. In other words, you agree on a specific hardware and software configuration, which becomes the standard configuration that PCs and workstations must support in order to run the application.

If the business rules governing the application are likely to change often, it makes sense to develop applets, which are downloaded on the fly at each client connection. This arrangement avoids the deployment issues that heavily affected the first wave of client/server computing.

Alternatively, you can opt for a Java application, which will provide a more robust environment for both development and deployment at the expense of flexibility. The downside of this option is that you have to deploy new releases of the software when database fields are added or dropped, exactly as in the old days, when Visual Basic, Delphi, and Powerbuilder were the environments of choice.

Another option is to use only plain HTML on the client, letting the server format dynamically created Web pages that display information fetched from the back-end database. All user input happens through HTML forms, using POST or GET methods. If the degree of user interactivity is not very high, this solution has its advantages.

Now consider a different scenario. A large car dealer that wants a Web presence has hired you. The e-commerce site being built will promote the sale of a large stock of second-hand cars. Potential customers are both end-users and other car dealers. As the application architect, you are not in control, since users can access the site using all kinds of browsing devices, ranging from very old releases of Netscape to HTML rendering components embedded into Windows applications. Java on the client is definitely not an option, because users can either access your site from within firewalls that prevent the use of Java or through browsers that are not Java-enabled.

Java on the server, however, would be a very effective solution; for instance, Java Server Pages or servlets that fetch data from Oracle and create HTML pages dynamically. From a client perspective, the minimal requirements are easily matched even by older browser configurations, but the application allows a satisfactory level of interactivity.

6.2 ORACLE SECURITY

Oracle implements a complex and powerful security system to regulate access to every object defined in the database. It resembles the security subsystem of an operating system like Unix or OpenVMS. Two classes of privileges exist in Oracle, object level and system level. A *system-level* privilege always overrides an *object-level* privilege.

To understand how security is implemented in Oracle, the concept of schema must be introduced. A *schema* is a collection of objects, such as tables, indexes, or views. Every Oracle database implements a list of users allowed to access the data it contains. Associated with each database user is a schema by the same name.

For example, a developer by the name of John Taylor is authorized to access a specific database, and the database administrator creates the *jtaylor* account. When Taylor logs in the database, he has access to his schema, jtaylor. Database objects created by Taylor in his own schema are accessible from other schemas using dot notation (i.e., jtaylor.customer, jtaylor.sales, etc.).

A second developer, Sally Green, has been granted access to the same database under the username *sgreen*, but she cannot access objects defined in other schemas unless she is granted privileges to do so.

Object-level privileges allow a schema owner to control access to the schema objects from other accounts. Both object-level and system-level privileges are granted through the GRANT command, which is a Data Definition Language (DDL) command. For instance, Taylor wants to allow Green to fetch data from the customer table defined in his schema. Using an interactive environment such as SQL*Plus, provided by Oracle, he issues the following command:

```
GRANT select on customer to sgreen;
```

Green, connected to the database and operating under her default schema, can now perform a select query from the customer table owned by the jtaylor schema:

```
SELECT * from jtaylor.customer where area_code ='NY';
```

Note that the sgreen schema can perform a select operation, but cannot change or modify data in the table unless specific privileges are granted. The Oracle security system offers fine-grained options for data protection. It provides, among others, the following commonly used object-level privileges:

- SELECT
- ALTER
- UPDATE
- DELETE
- INDEX
- INSERT
- EXECUTE

Many of the privileges are self-explanatory. The ALTER privilege allows the external schema to alter the object definition, DELETE allows external schemas to delete the object, INDEX allows external schemas to create indexes against tables that have been granted this privilege, and so forth.

The EXECUTE privilege is worthy of special attention, because it allows for the implementation of a very secure environment, where users connected to the database interact with data indirectly, and do not need specific privileges to access application objects. This is an important concept, which needs to be explained in depth, given its relevance in the present context.

Stored procedures or stored functions are modules that perform database actions, such as accessing or modifying data. They can be written in either Java or PL/SQL, and, most important, they can return result sets. Instead of using JDBC or SQLJ calls to submit SQL statements to the database engine, developers can obtain results sets from stored procedures. To be able to call a stored procedure, users must be granted the EXECUTE privilege for the required stored procedure. This arrangement provides a security advantage, as shown in the next example. Consider the following scenario:

> A client application written in Java connects directly to an Oracle database. The user types in username, password, and connection string at the moment of the initial log-in. If the same user installs SQL*Plus or a similar interactive tool on the client and uses the same log-in parameters, then it is possible for him or her to insert and potentially delete data with no control whatsoever. All built-in data-consistency checks in the application would be completely by-passed. The user in question could update or delete access to database objects, but his or her ability to inadvertently perform dangerous or destructive actions would be constrained programmatically by the application. This kind of control cannot be enforced if the user gains access to the database in an uncontrolled manner.
>
> If, on the other hand, all data is fetched through stored procedures, the user who logs-in from the client side only needs to be granted an execute privilege on all stored procedures used by the application. The application administrator can safely revoke from all users the privileges to select, insert, update, and delete data from/to the application tables. The stored procedures still work, but users are prevented from accessing the tables stored in the application schema directly, using an interactive tool.

System privileges are granted to schemas rather than to objects. In other words, a system privilege is not linked to a schema object; it allows a foreign schema to perform specific operations on objects in all schemas. If the DBA grants the system privilege SELECT ANY TABLE to sgreen, that database account can then perform SELECT statements against all tables defined in all schemas, even if the other schemas did not specifically grant the SELECT object-level privilege to sgreen.

Every Oracle account/schema is given some system-level privileges. An account used for a connection to an Oracle instance must have the CREATE SESSION privilege. An account must have the CREATE TABLE system privilege to create a table. System-level privileges regulate all activities and operations allowed in Oracle. They give the DBA a powerful management tool for both security and resource-allocation control.

There are many system-level privileges; several exist in a dual-form, single-schema level and all-schema level. For instance the CREATE TABLE privilege allows the grantee to create a table in his or her own schema. The CREATE ANY TABLE privilege allows the grantee to create tables in any schema. System-level privileges are characterized by the word ANY, as in create ANY index or drop ANY table.

An exhaustive treatment of all Oracle-provided system-level and object-level privileges is beyond the scope of this book, and possibly more relevant to database administrators than to developers. However, designers and programmers involved with Oracle technologies at all levels should be aware of the Oracle security model, at least in its basic terms. If database security is properly implemented, Oracle can become a sort of "Fort Alamo" for corporate data, or the ultimate line of defense against a hacker attack. Although malicious users could, in fact, penetrate the firewall perimeter and gain access to the host computers, doing this would not be enough to steal valuable data from the company, since they would have to break through one more barrier. By the time they were able to do so, the intrusion-detection mechanisms commonly provided by commercial firewall systems would, in all probability, have alerted network administrators of the ongoing attack.

6.3 THE DEMILITARIZED ZONE

The demilitarized zone, or DMZ, is an isolated environment in a company's network that does not contain confidential information. A DMZ is usually protected by at least two firewalls, one between the Internet, or the external users, and the company, and the other between the DMZ and the servers where confidential data resides. Even if an intruder succeeds in bypassing the first firewall, the corporate data are still protected behind the second firewall.

To understand why such an arrangement is called a DMZ, think about the function of a true demilitarized zone, like the one in Korea. The Korean peninsula is divided by a 155-mile-long demilitarized zone that separates North and South Korea from east to west, along the 38th Parallel. The DMZ is approximately three miles wide, and was established in July, 1953 at the end of the Korean War. Since no peace treaty has ever been signed between South and North Korea, technically a state of war still exists. This is more commonly called a state of armistice. The DMZ is constantly kept under strict surveillance by sophisticated equipment, and is patrolled day and night by patrols on both sides. Stern regulations, agreed upon by both sides, dictate allowed patrol paths and schedules, authorized weapons, and territorial off-limits.

Bearing the foregoing explanation in mind, you can see how suitable the DMZ metaphor is in the context of Web security. The characteristics of constant surveillance and prompt reaction in case of protocol violations apply perfectly to the narrow "network corridor" where data coming from outside the company boundaries are allowed to transit both in and out. In a network context, a DMZ is delimited by at least two firewalls. The firewall erected between the external world and the DMZ usually allows traffic on port 80 Software residing in the DMZ receives and interprets Http packets, and re-routes them to other software components, which commonly use different protocols and different ports to access the company's data through the second firewall, the one erected between the DMZ and corporate data.

For example, consider an application that allows external users to interact via HTML forms with a corporate database. The HTML traffic over the Http port is allowed to transit through the external firewall. A Web server and a servlet engine run in the DMZ. The application servlet intercepts the user requests and uses RMI to communicate with a server that accesses the corporate database. The servlet running in the DMZ does not access the database directly; instead, it remotely invokes methods that run on a different host computer, located behind the second firewall, which has been configured to allow RMI traffic through a specific predefined port. In this example the protocol of choice is RMI, but nothing would prevent designers from opting for other vendor-provided protocols, such as Oracle SQL*Net/Net8, or a custom-written protocol, implemented using network sockets.

Figure 6.1 shows a pictorial representation of the DMZ implementation discussed above. Note that a hole has been made in the second firewall to allow traffic through port 1099, which is the standard RMI port. It is probably better to use a different port in real-life implementations, to make things more difficult for potential hackers. This principle is termed *security through obscurity.*

In Figure 6.1, the first firewall only allows traffic through port 80, while the second firewall only allows traffic through port 1099. No other traffic is permitted to transit across the two firewalls.

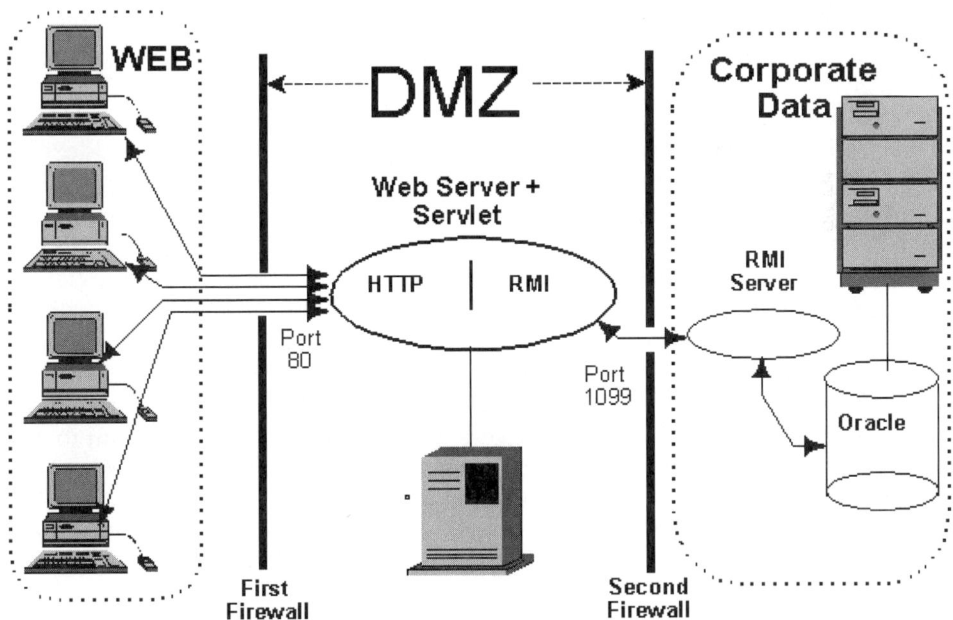

FIGURE 6.1 Implementation of a DMZ that uses two firewalls

6.4 USING ORACLE SECURITY AND SYNONYMS TO IMPLEMENT A DEVELOPMENT ENVIRONMENT

Several application environments are usually required to support the development and testing of a complex database-centric application. Multiple development and testing environments are used to avoid interference between developers and testers, and to isolate the production environment from indiscriminate and uncontrolled changes.

The number of application environments depends on the size of the project, the number of developers involved, and the nature of the application. Large, complex projects usually have three or four separate physical environments, each with its own computer or cluster. Less-critical projects combine the development and test environments in one machine.

Environments can be created within the same Oracle instance by using the Oracle schema structure. Alternatively, a separate Oracle instance can be created for each environment. In practice, many projects combine these by providing one instance for development and one for testing. The instances are then subdivided into several schemas, usually one per developer and one per testing environment.

When many schemas are created, it is important to minimize the space each requires. The arrangement that works best is to have one schema containing all the application objects and use public synonyms to access the application objects from the developer schemas. The following example clarifies the concept.

Assume that you are building a system called "newgen." The main application schema is named after the project, so you name it "newgen." The newgen schema is the owner of all application objects, such as tables, indexes, packages, sequences, Java classes, Java stored procedures, and so on. The tables are loaded with sufficient test data to support development and unit testing of the code modules. Each developer is assigned a database schema, usually named after the developer's username. Instead of re-creating an entire set of tables and objects per developer, synonyms are created to refer to all of the application's objects.

Oracle supports two types of synonyms, public and private. A *public synonym* is accessible to all users, while a *private synonym* is associated with the schema where it is created. The dot notation, as in <schema>**.**<synonym name>, can be used from other accounts to access private synonyms. If you want to create a public synonym for the table "customer" stored in the newgen schema, the syntax is:

```
create public synonym customer for newgen.customer;
```

All the schemas are able to access the customer table defined in the newgen schema through this synonym.

To create a public synonym, an account must be granted the CREATE PUBLIC SYNONYMS privilege. To create a private synonym, the CREATE SYNONYM privilege is needed.

Synonyms are invaluable for creating and setting up development environments based on strict change-management procedures. You must be able to change the structure of database objects, develop code that accesses and manipulates them, and test your modules without affecting the environments of other developers. This is reciprocal in the sense that other developers don't want to see their code broken by your changes. Developers can be prevented from interfering with each other through the synonym mechanism, used in conjunction with object-level security on shared objects.

This is how it works. No objects are locally defined in a schema assigned to a developer. The code that accesses the database can still run within the developer's schema by accessing objects through public synonyms, which point to the objects owned by the application schema (in your example, the newgen schema). Oracle security is used to prevent developers from changing the structure of the objects defined in the application schema. For example, object-level security allows developers to select, insert, and update rows in tables owned by the application schema, in order to allow them to perform unit testing of their modules. Other privileges, such as the object-level *alter* and the system-level *drop*, are revoked from all developers, so that objects defined in the application schema cannot be modified in any way, even accidentally, by developers. When objects must be changed, developers use their own accounts to perform the changes, and unit testing is conducted on the modified objects stored in the developer's schemas, and on the unmodified objects stored in the application schema.

An example will clarify the concept. Imagine that developer ebonazzi is given the task of modifying the customer table. An additional column is required to support financial calculations. The developer codes and tests it, but coding the table modification and new calculations could take several days, possibly a few weeks. The newgen customer table must maintain its integrity during this period, to ensure that other developers are not disrupted. This is achieved by defining the table locally in the ebonazzi schema. An example of an SQL*Plus session that accomplishes this is shown below.

```
$ sqlplus ebonazzi/supersecret

SQL*Plus: Release 8.1.5.0 -Production on Wed Mar 1 21:38:59 2000
(c) Copyright 1999 Oracle Corporation.  All rights reserved.

Connected to:
Oracle8i Enterprise Edition Release 8.1.6.0.0 - Production
With the Partitioning option
JServer Release 8.1.6.0.0 - Production

SQL> show user
user is "EBONAZZI"
```

The default schema is *ebonazzi*. The developer now "describes" the customer table, accessing the customer object, as defined in the newgen schema, through a publicly defined synonym:

```
SQL> desc customer
 Name                              Null?    Type
 --------------------------------- -------- ------------
 NAME                                       VARCHAR2(30)
 ADDRESS                                    VARCHAR2(50)
 COMPANY_NAME                               VARCHAR2(40)

SQL>
```

A local copy of the customer table is now defined.

```
SQL> create table customer as select * from newgen.customer;

Table created.

SQL>
```

All the rows the customer table defined in the newgen schema have been copied locally to a new table in the ebonazzi schema. This is useful for unit testing. The local copy of the table can now be modified.

```
SQL> alter table customer add discount_pct number (6,2);

Table altered.

SQL>
```

The local table is now different from the same table defined in the newgen schema. The new version of the table is only visible from the ebonazzi account. Oracle first tries to resolve object names at a local level. If a name does not correspond to an object defined locally, that is, within the user's own schema, Oracle searches through the publicly defined synonyms. This is why all other developers see the customer table defined in the newgen schema and their code is not affected by the changes made to the table locally defined in ebonazzi. What goes for tables (data) is also valid for procedures and functions (code). The newgen schema owns a Java procedure that displays the entire content of the customer table. The source code of the Java procedure is shown below.[1]

```
import java.sql.*;
import java.io.*;
import oracle.jdbc.driver.*;
public class StoredProc
{
  public static void DisplayCustomer() throws SQLException
  {
    String sql =
      "select name,address,company_name from customer";
    try
    {
      Connection conn =
       DriverManager.getConnection("jdbc:default :connection:");
      PreparedStatement pstmt = conn.prepareStatement (sql);
      ResultSet rs = pstmt.executeQuery();
      while (rs.next())
      {
        System.out.println(rs.getString(1)+" "+
                           rs.getString(2)+" "+
                         rs.getString(3));
      }
      pstmt.close();
    }
    catch (SQLException e)
    {
        System.err.println(e.getMessage());
    }
  }
}
```

In order for this procedure to run inside the database, it must be loaded using *loadjava*.

```
$ loadjava -user newgen/newgen@echidna:1521:sun816 -resolve
   -thin StoredProc.class
```

[1]You might want to revisit this example after you have read Chapters 11 through 13. For the time being, just take for granted that it is possible to load Java classes into an Oracle instance and to call Java methods from SQL or PL/SQL

To make the Java procedure accessible to database users, a PL/SQL wrapper must be defined.

```
create or replace procedure display_data
AS LANGUAGE JAVA
NAME 'StoredProc.DisplayCustomer()';
SQL> /
SQL> Procedure created.
```

A public synonym is also defined, so that users different from newgen can launch the display_data procedure from any schema. The following CREATE SYNONYM command does the trick:

```
SQL> CREATE SYNONYM DISPLAY_DATA for newgen.display_data;
Synonym created.
```

All the developers on the team can now access the display_data procedure, which in turn calls the Java stored procedure. The following SQL*Plus session shows the procedure called from the sgreen account.

```
$ sqlplus sgreen/sgreen@sun816
SQL*Plus: Release 8.1.5.0.0 - Production on Fri Mar 3
(c) Copyright 1999 Oracle Corporation. All rights reserved.
Connected to:
Oracle8i Enterprise Edition Release 8.1.6.0.0 - Production
With the Partitioning option
JServer Release 8.1.6.0.0 - Production
SQL> set serveroutput on
SQL> call dbms_java.set_output(4000);
Call completed.
SQL> execute display_data();
John Smith 3, Felix Drive Richmond California Federal Impress
Mike Taylor 17, Tree Ave, Brighton, Montana Rabbit Couriers
PL/SQL procedure successfully completed.
```

Developer ebonazzi has modified the customer table. Consequently, the display_data procedure must be modified to print the additional field. The Java source code is checked out from the source control system into ebonazzi's working directory, and two lines of code are modified. The following listing shows the modifications in bold.

```
import java.sql.*;
import java.io.*;
import oracle.jdbc.driver.*;
public class StoredProc
{
  public static void DisplayCustomer() throws SQLException
  {
    String sql = "select name,address,company_name, "+
                 "discount_pct from customer";
    try
    {
      Connection conn =
      DriverManager.getConnection("jdbc:default :connection:");
      PreparedStatement pstmt = conn.prepareStatement (sql);
      ResultSet rs = pstmt.executeQuery();
      while (rs.next())
      {
        System.out.println(rs.getString(1)+" "+
         rs.getString(2)+" "+
         rs.getString(3) +" " +
                          Float.toString(rs.getFloat(4)));
      }

      pstmt.close();
    }
    catch (SQLException e)
    {
          System.err.println(e.getMessage());
    }
  }
}
```

The Java source is recompiled, and the class produced by the compilation pass is loaded into the database, using the ebonazzi account. If display_data is launched from the ebonazzi schema, the Java stored procedure that is executed is the one defined in newgen, because the public synonym display_data would invoke the version of the display_data PL/SQL wrapper stored in newgen. But if a new PL/SQL wrapper is defined in the ebonazzi schema, the new version of the Java method will be invoked the next time display_data is invoked from ebonazzi.

In the next SQL session, the "central" version of display_data is initially called. The new PL/SQL wrapper is subsequently defined, and display_data is called again. This time, the discount_pct field is also displayed.

```
$ sqlplus ebonazzi/supersecret@sun816
SQL*Plus: Release 8.1.5.0.0 - Production on Fri Mar 3
(c) Copyright 1999 Oracle Corporation. All rights reserved.
Connected to:
Oracle8i Enterprise Edition Release 8.1.6.0.0 - Production
With the Partitioning option
JServer Release 8.1.6.0.0 - Production
SQL> execute display_data();
John Smith 3, Felix Drive Richmond California Federal Impress
Mike Taylor 17, Tree Ave, Brighton, Montana Rabbit Couriers
PL/SQL procedure successfully completed.
SQL> create procedure display_data AS LANGUAGE JAVA
     NAME 'StoredProc.DisplayCustomer()';
     /
Procedure created.
SQL> execute display_data();
John Smith 3, Felix Drive Richmond California Federal Impress 23.5
Mike Taylor 17, Tree Ave, Brighton, Montana Rabbit Couriers 23.5
PL/SQL procedure successfully completed.
```

The output from the second running of display_data shows one more field, discount_pct, printed at the end of the line. Developer ebonazzi can now work on a new branch of the source, without interfering with other developers, who continue to "see" the previous release of the customer table and the previous release of the display_data PL/SQL wrapper. After all the modifications are finished, and unit testing has been performed satisfactorily, the new customer table and the new Java method/PL/SQL wrapper are loaded in the newgen schema. From that moment on, all developers start using the new release. The usefulness of synonyms, coupled with the power of Oracle security, helps in establishing a development environment where change is controlled and managed, and discipline is enforced over developers working together.

6.5 NEW ORACLE SECURITY FEATURES

Until the release of Oracle 8.1.6, the concept of user and the concept of schema were closely related. Oracle never provided a CREATE SCHEMA command. A schema was created by default when a new user account was created by the DBA using the CREATE USER command. Each user was assigned a default schema in the database, or an object container where objects could have been created and owned by the user.

While this arrangement worked well for developers and power users, it showed its limits when Oracle databases began to grow and reached enterprise-level size and complexity. There are a few major drawbacks associated with the user/schema coupling. Users who only access an application using a graphical front-end do not really need a schema, because they never create or own any database object.

If an application has thousands of concurrent users, several policies can be adopted, and have been adopted in the past, to authenticate such a large user population. The easiest—and least recommendable—policy is to allow all users to share one single account and its password. With this policy, security is virtually nonexistent, and administrators find it difficult to identify problematic sessions.

While data dictionary tables and dynamic performance views make it possible to associate an Oracle session with the operating system account/process of the user accessing Oracle, so that the user can be alerted before the session is killed, this procedure is not simple and sometimes not accurate. It is much better if each user uses an individual account to connect to Oracle, so that a one-to-one correspondence between user and Oracle session can be easily established.

Another common arrangement is to create an authentication subsystem in the application that uses an Oracle table to store usernames and passwords. While this system is better because it forces users not to share their passwords, it still uses only one schema to initially authenticate the users of the application.

Oracle 8.0.x introduced the password aging facility, which improves the security system, since it forces users to regularly change their passwords after a predetermined expire time. Possibly the best authentication policy is to use one account per user. This does not force Oracle out of its natural behavior and provides a reasonable compromise between security and administrative burden. If you adopt this policy, and Oracle is in widespread use in your enterprise, it is likely that each user will require access to more than one database. If password aging is enforced across all Oracle instances, it is possible that users will not be able to use the same password to connect to multiple databases, because of the difficulty of maintaining absolute synchronization between the expiration dates of all the Oracle instances.

In the worst possible scenario, user X has to remember that to connect to database A the required password is "alpha," to connect to database B the password is "beta," and so on and so forth. The normal human response to such a password nightmare is to write all the passwords down on a piece of paper, usually kept in the first drawer of the work desk, if not on a sticky yellow note attached to the terminal. Security is obviously compromised. If a user leaves the organization, the DBAs should track all the databases he or she used and remove all the accounts with their associated schemas.

Furthermore, consider an e-commerce application where customers are requested to open an account to store their personal and financial details and to keep track of their purchases. It would be good to use the Oracle built-in facility to create a database account and to authenticate the users, forcing them to regularly change their passwords. Again, this would mean creating possibly hundreds of thousands of accounts/schemas, an unnecessary burden for DBAs and application administrators.

Luckily, Oracle Corporation has responded to the challenge outlined above by providing the Enterprise User Security feature, available through the Advanced Security Option of Oracle Server 8.1.6. The new feature allows for user/schema separation. Oracle Internet Directory, a Lightweight Directory Access Protocol (LDAP) directory service, implemented as an application running in an Oracle8i database, provides the management of information about distributed users acting within a corporate environment, and their authentication across multiple Oracle databases.

All the resources managed through the Oracle Internet Directory, including users, are assigned a Distinguished Name (DN) that is unique across the enterprise. Once configured in the Oracle LDAP environment, a user can be assigned enterprise roles (which are containers of database-specific *global roles*) that determine the user's access privileges in databases. Moreover, using this facility, multiple users can access a single application schema, defined as an enterprise user in the directory. Instead of creating one account (or schema) in each database that individual users need to access, the security administrator configures the users in the central directory, and assigns them the shared application schema.

Since all the information required to authenticate users is kept in a single central point (the Oracle Internet Directory, or OID), making changes and modifications to user profiles, and revoking user access when they leave the company, becomes much simpler if all the databases accessed by the users share the same OID.

Oracle provides GUI and command-line tools to administer advanced security. Setting up an LDAP-enforced security environment is a sophisticated task that requires advanced DBA skills, so you won't find an example here. Even if the how-to is beyond the scope of this book, in your capacity of designer/architect of Java/Oracle applications you should know about this new and important feature introduced with Oracle 8i release 2.

SUMMARY

This chapter initially discussed security issues commonly faced by applications that must be deployed over the Web. It then shifted the focus to Oracle security, explaining how to benefit from the Oracle security subsystem to both increase data security for the deployed application and provide a development environment where changes and modifications are strictly controlled, and developers are prevented from stepping on each other's toes.

The chapter concluded by examining some of the new security features introduced with the release 2 of Oracle 8i (8.1.6).

Chapter 7

INTRODUCTION TO PL/SQL

- Anonymous Blocks
- PL/SQL Variables and Data Types
- Conditional and Sequential Controls
- Using SQL Statements in PL/SQL
- Cursors
- PL/SQL Tables and Varying Arrays
- User-Defined/Object Types in PL/SQL
- Summary

PL/SQL is Oracle's procedural language for SQL. It is a portable high-level language that provides the programmer with seamless integration of SQL statements with procedural statement constructs, such as flow control, procedures, and functions. PL/SQL is compiled into a processor independent binary format known as "p-code." A PL/SQL interpreter or PL/SQL runtime engine executes the p-code generated by the compiler. Executing PL/SQL code in an Oracle PL/SQL executable environment is conceptually analogous to executing a Java class in a Java Virtual Machine.

SQL is nonprocedural, and thus PL/SQL, with the ability to wrap procedural logical around SQL, provides the database programmer with enormous flexibility and control over data management. PL/SQL is a third-generation language that became available for use as database stored procedure logic when Oracle7 arrived.[1] In versions prior to Oracle7, PL/SQL was used for processing database trigger code in the server. Database triggers allow developers to centralize the logic used to supplement DML operations, and to enforce business data and integrity rules. The Oracle8i database release added support for the Java Virtual Machine to the database server to allow the Java language to be used as an alternative to the PL/SQL language for execution of stored procedural code in server. The Oracle8i database provides the mechanisms for PL/SQL code to call Java Stored Procedures, and for Java Stored Procedures to call PL/SQL code (Java Stored Procedures are covered below in Chapter 12).

The PL/SQL language compiler, whose roots are derived from an early version of an Ada compiler, has inherited some object-oriented like capabilities, in the form of function (method) overloading and encapsulating techniques with PL/SQL packages.

The introduction of SQL procedures executing in the database enabled a client application to tap into the power and capabilities of a data server environment, and allowed developers to partition their logic between the client application and the database server, a process known as *application partitioning*. The benefit of application partitioning, having control to decide where to execute your logic, can ultimately lead to better performance for applications. Since SQL must be executed in the server, why not do it in a Stored Procedure?

7.1 ANONYMOUS BLOCKS

PL/SQL is a block-structured language, and identifier names for constants, variables, procedures, or function declarations must be declared before they are referenced. Like Java, PL/SQL is a strongly typed language, but it is not object-

[1]PL/SQL is also used in Oracle application-development tools, such as Oracle Forms and Oracle Reports.

oriented; however, it does have some of the features found in object-oriented environments.

7.1.1 PL/SQL BLOCK STRUCTURE

A basic PL/SQL block has the following structure:

```
BEGIN
  -- executable section
  executable statements;
[EXCEPTION]
  -- exception section
  [ exception handlers ]
END;
```

This block structure is known as an *anonymous block*, because the block of code is not identified by a name. A PL/SQL anonymous block is generally used to initiate procedural processing from its host application. An anonymous block can be thought of as the main line code of a PL/SQL program.

7.1.1.1 The Executable Section. Code placed between the BEGIN and END keywords is called the *executable section*. The BEGIN and END keywords form the block basic PL/SQL block structure and are mandatory for all PL/SQL blocks. At least one executable statement is required between the BEGIN and END keywords. The semicolon after the END keyword is a required part of the PL/SQL block syntax.

7.1.1.2 The Exception Section. The *exception section*, which is optional, is introduced by the keyword EXCEPTION placed within the PL/SQL block, and is used to trap errors raised in the executable section. The exception section, when present, ends the executable section, and must appear at the end of the block. The exception section contains one or more exception handlers. Each exception handler traps a specified error raised within the block, or the error is propagated from within the block to the calling environment.

The PL/SQL anonymous block structure is also treated as a compound statement, and can be placed inside another PL/SQL block. Using the anonymous block as a compound statement is known as *nesting*. For example:

```
BEGIN
  statement;
  :
  BEGIN   -- start of nested block
     statement;
     :
  [EXCEPTION]
```

```
        [exception handler …]
    END;     -- end of nested block
    :
    statement;
    :
  [EXCEPTION]
    -- exception section
    [ exception handler … ]
  END;
```

7.1.1.3 The Declaration Section. Variables are declared in the *declaration section* before they are used in the executable section. The declaration section of an anonymous block starts with the keyword DECLARE, followed by one or more variable declarations entered before the BEGIN keyword. For example:

```
DECLARE
  -- This is the declaration section
  variable_name1  data_type;
  variable_name2  data_type;
BEGIN
  -- executable section
  one or more executable statements;
[EXCEPTION]
  -- exception section
  [ exception handlers ]
END;
```

The semicolon is a terminator for each variable declaration and PL/SQL statement. You can only declare one variable name before its data type. A comma-separated list of variable declarations is not supported syntax. For example:

```
DECLARE
  x1, y1  pls_integer;    -- this causes a compilation error
  x2 pls_integer;
  y2 pls_integer;
BEGIN
  x1 := 1;
  y1 := x1 * 10;
  :
END;
```

The correction to this example would be to declare the variables x and y separately, with each declaration typically placed on its own line. The following example shows some possible corrections:

```
DECLARE
  x pls_integer; y pls_integer;
  x1 pls_integer;
  y1 pls_integer;
  :
BEGIN
  x1 := 1;
  x1 := x1  * 10;
END;
```

The semicolon completes each variable declaration; otherwise PL/SQL text is entered in a free format, that is, one or more spaces, tabs, or new line characters can be entered between names, keywords, and delimiters.

Variables in the declaration section have a scope, also known as *visibility*, which is checked at compile time. The visibility of a variable determines where you can access or use the variable in a block of code. The rule is: A variable can be used within the block in which it is declared, and within any nested block. For example:

```
DECLARE -- outer block
  X  pls_integer;
BEGIN
  X := 10;
  :
  DECLARE  -- nested inner block
    Y pls_integer;
  BEGIN
    Y := X * 10;
    X := Y;
  [ EXCEPTION -- section optional]
     :
  END; -- inner block
  -- Y does not exist when inner block terminates
  X := X + 1;
  :
  [ EXCEPTION -- section optional ]
END; -- outer block
```

In the example, the variable X is accessible/usable in the outer and inner blocks, but the variable Y is only accessible in the inner block.

7.1.2 EXECUTING PL/SQL BLOCKS

PL/SQL can be executed in:

- The database server PL/SQL engine, or
- A client side PL/SQL engine.

Only Oracle developer tools (specifically, Oracle Forms and Oracle Reports) have a client-side executable engine. Although a PL/SQL anonymous block can execute in the database server, it cannot by itself be stored in the database as a unit of code. To store PL/SQL in the database, you need to use named PL/SQL blocks, in the form of procedures, functions, or packages.

To run PL/SQL code from the SQL*Plus command line:

- Enter your code for the anonymous block.
- After typing the closing END for your PL/SQL block, enter a carriage return.
- In the first character on the blank line, enter a forward slash (/) followed by a carriage return.

The forward slash character must be the first character on the last line in the SQL*Plus statement buffer; otherwise, it does not act as a PL/SQL code entry terminator. For example:

```
SQL> set serveroutput on
SQL> BEGIN
   2     DBMS_OUTPUT.PUT_LINE('Welcome to PL/SQL');
   3 END;
   4 /
```

LISTING 7.1 Executing a PL/SQL anonymous block

Notes for Listing 7.1:

- Line 1 in Listing 7.1 is an SQL*Plus command used to prepare SQL*Plus to receive output data from PL/SQL blocks running on the server.
- Line 2 calls a built-in PL/SQL procedure called PUT_LINE in database server package called DBMS_OUTPUT. The DBMS_OUTPUT is a PL/SQL package[2] that is typically used for printing text and data to the SQL*Plus output screen/window. Before sophisticated PL/SQL debugging tools became available, the DBMS_OUTPUT.PUT_LINE procedure was used to debug PL/SQL code executing in the database, when invoked from the SQL*Plus application.

When SQL*Plus sends the PL/SQL block to the server, two steps take place:

- The PL/SQL code block is compiled.
- If the compilation is successful, then the PL/SQL code executes; otherwise an error message is displayed indicating the compilation errors that occurred.

---

[2]A stored PL/SQL package is a named database object treated as one logical unit, just like a stored procedure or function. A PL/SQL package is typically used to encapsulate the data and implementation logic of one or more functionally related procedures and/or functions.

The remaining examples in this chapter present the PL/SQL code without showing the terminating slash character.

7.2 PL/SQL VARIABLES AND DATA TYPES

PL/SQL data types constitute a superset, or extension, of the database data types. Some PL/SQL data types are the same as their database counterparts, differing only in their maximum storage capacity. The advantages of PL/SQL data types and the database types being the same are:

- Simplicity of code interacting with the database data.
- Seamless data type matching, therefore, data type mapping is not required, compared to using JDBC code in Java to access SQL data.

The syntax used to declare a PL/SQL variable is:

```
Variable_name data-type [ := initial_value ];
```

PL/SQL variable names start with an alphabetic character; the remaining characters are made up of:

- Alphabetic characters
- Numeric digits (0–9)
- Underscores
- The # and $ signs, which are considered reserved by Oracle.[3]

You can initialize variables in the declaration by using the assignment operator followed by an initial value, after the data type. The PL/SQL assignment operator is a colon followed by an equals sign with no space between them (:=). For example:

```
DECLARE
  tax_rate number := 8.25;
BEGIN
  dbms_output.put_line(The tax rate is: '||tax_rate);
END;
```

[3]It is quite possible to create a variable name with a dollar or hash sign in the name. Although their use in variable, table, or database construct names is discouraged, preventing the use of these characters is not enforced.

The keyword DEFAULT can be used instead of the assignment operator, as follows:

```
DECLARE
  tax_rate number DEFAULT 8.25;
BEGIN
  dbms_output.put_line(The tax rate is: '||tax_rate);
END;
```

Declaring a constant requires the addition of the keyword CONSTANT after the variable name and before the data type:

```
variable_name CONSTANT data_type := initial-value;
```

A constant, by definition, must be given an initial value.

7.2.1 SUBTYPE DEFINITIONS

The PL/SQL language allows user-defined subtypes. Creating and using a subtype is done in the PL/SQL declaration section using the following syntax:

```
SUBTYPE subtype_name IS base_type_name[(length [,scale])];
```

The subtype name can then be used as a data type for other variables in the declaration section. The base type is derived from a list of valid PL/SQL scalar data types (see Table 7.1) or user-defined PL/SQL types. The length and scale values optionally entered after the base type name control the range of values represented by the subtype.

```
-- Example 1:
--
DECLARE
   SUBTYPE money IS number;     -- declare an unconstrained subtype
   tax  money(8,2);           -- use sub type and constrain variable
BEGIN
   tax := 999999.99;          -- max value for this variable
   dbms_output.put_line('Tax is: ' || tax);
END;


-- Example 2:
--
DECLARE
   SUBTYPE money IS number(8,2);      -- declare constrained subtype
```

```
      tax   money;                    -- use sub type for
                                         variable
   BEGIN
      tax := 999999.99;
      dbms_output.put_line('Tax is: ' || tax);
   END;
```

In example 1, the precision and scale of (8,2) for the tax variable overrides the base definition of the money subtype, which defaults to a 38-digit number.

In example 2, the tax variable takes the same precision and scale (8,2) as specified in the subtype declaration for money.

7.2.2 SCALAR DATA TYPES

A PL/SQL scalar data type holds a single value at any given time, and is similar in concept to a Java primitive data type. The PL/SQL scalar data types are designed to map as seamlessly as possible with the database column data types. However, since PL/SQL is a programming environment, additional scalar types have been added for efficient storage and calculations. Table 7.1 is an abbreviated list and description of PL/SQL scalar data types.

7.2.3 LARGE-OBJECT DATA TYPES

Large-object database types were introduced in Oracle8 to overcome the limitations of working with LONG or LONG RAW data types. The limitations of LONG data are:

- You can have only one LONG or LONG RAW column per table, to store up to two gigabytes of information.
- You have to read or write all the data in a LONG or LONG RAW as one chunk. This limitation is imposed on PL/SQL, which cannot read or write data larger than the maximum length of a LONG data type. The maximum length for a PL/SQL LONG variable is 32,760 bytes, and cannot be used to read a LONG database column containing more data than 32,760 bytes.

The Oracle8i RDBMS version provides a TO_LOB(long-column) function that converts its parameter from a LONG column into a LOB data type. For example:

```
CREATE TABLE resume (
  id        NUMBER(4),
  name      VARCHAR2(30),
  text      LONG);

INSERT INTO resume
VALUES (1, 'Glenn', 'This is the value of the long column');
COMMIT;
```

TABLE 7.1 PL/SQL scalar data types

DATA TYPE	DESCRIPTION
CHAR[(n)], NCHAR(n)	Represents fixed-length character data from 1 up to a maximum of 32767 bytes. NCHAR is for multi-byte national language character sets, and will be changed to be for UNICODE characters.
VARCHAR2(n) NVARCHAR2(n)[1]	For variable-length character data up to 32727 bytes, VARCHAR and STRING are subtypes of VARCHAR2.
NUMBER[(p,s)]	For integer, real, or floating point decimal numbers of up to 38 digits of precision. The precision (p) and scale (s) are optional, but should be used to constrain the range of values stored and the size allocated for the values.
DATE	Stores date and time internally in binary format values ranging from January 1, 4712 BC to December 31, 4712 AD. A Julian date is the number of days since January 1, 4712 BC.
BINARY_INTEGER, PLS_INTEGER	Signed integers in the range of -2147483647 to 2147483647. Both of these require less storage than NUMBER data types, but PLS_INTEGER operations are faster than BINARY_INTEGER.
FLOAT, REAL	Subtypes of the NUMBER data type for ANSI/ISO compatibility. FLOAT allows up to 38 decimal digits in precision, and REAL allows up to 18 digits in precision. PL/SQL allows developers to define subtypes as a subset of another base type.
BOOLEAN	The truth value of TRUE or FALSE, but can be NULL for an undefined state of the variable.
LONG	Variable-length data up to 32760 characters.
RAW	Variable-length data up to 2000 binary characters not interpreted. Converting RAW to VARCHAR2 results in raw data expanded into the textual equivalent value in hexadecimal characters.
LONG RAW	Up to 32760 characters of binary data that are not interpreted.
ROWID	Contains information needed to locate a row. In particular, a data object number, data file number (1 for the first file) , a data block in the data file, and a row in the data block (the first row is 0). This rates a mention because the ROWID is the fastest means of accessing a data row.

[1]For CHAR and VARCHAR types, the length specifies the maximum number of bytes, but for NCHAR and NVARCHAR data types should be interpreted as the maximum number of characters.

```
-- Now create a table with a LOB column
CREATE TABLE resume_lob (
  resume_id        NUMBER(4),
  name             VARCHAR2(30),
  contents         CLOB);

-- Copy and Convert the row with the LONG into a row with a CLOB
INSERT INTO resume_lob
```

TABLE 7.2 Large-object data types

DATA TYPE	DESCRIPTION
CLOB	Locator (pointer) to a character large object data type inline or out of line from the row data.
BLOB	Locator (pointer) to a binary large object data type of noninterpreted data.
BFILE	Locator or handle to a binary file stored external to the database data, i.e., in the file system of the host operating system.
NCLOB	Multi-byte variable-length character data.

```
SELECT id, name, TO_LOB(text)
FROM resume;
COMMIT;
```

7.2.4 COMPOSITE DATA TYPES

Composite data types are user-defined types that contain one or more components (see Table 7.3).

Listing 7.2 show examples of declaring variables using scalar and composite data types.

TABLE 7.3 Composite user-defined data types

DATA TYPE	DESCRIPTION
RECORD	Records are made up of one or more related member variables. A member variable may be also be a record structure. This is similar to a third-generation language record structure, such as a "struct" definition in C, or like creating a Java class without any methods.
PL/SQL tables Index-By, or Nested Tables	Dynamic collection structures that can store values in scalar, LOB, or composite data types. The size of index-By tables is constrained by the BINARY_INTEGER type (see Table 7.1), and a nested table is unconstrained in number.
VARRAY(n)	A collection of a variable number of array elements up to the specified maximum value of "n". All entries in the array have the same data type.
Object Types	Strictly speaking, these belong in a category by themselves, but object types are also composite data types that have members (attributes) and methods.

```
 1: -- Scalar examples
 2: salary          NUMBER(9,2);
 3: minutes         PLS_INTEGER;
 4: birth_date      DATE;
 5:
 6: -- PL/SQL record example
 7: TYPE prod_rec_type IS RECORD (
 8:  barcode        VARCHAR2(6),
 9:  description    VARCHAR2(40)
10: );
11: product_rec     prod_rec_type;
12:
13: -- PL/SQL Table example
14: TYPE int_array_type IS TABLE OF PLS_INTEGER
15:    INDEX BY BINARY_INTEGER;
16: my_int_array  int_array_type; -- This is an index-By table
17:
18: TYPE char_collection_type IS TABLE OF VARCHAR2(20);
19: name_list  char_collection_type; -- This is a nested table
20:
21: -- Large-Object examples
22: image_date     BLOB;
23: resume         CLOB;
23: infile         BFILE;
```

LISTING 7.2 Variable and data type declaration examples

Notes for Listing 7.2:

- Lines 7–10 show a user-defined type for a PL/SQL record structure, which is assign a type name of `prod_rec_type`. The type name is used for the variable declaration in line 11.
- Lines 14–15 show another user-defined type for an index-by table named `int_array_type` is used as the data type for the declaration of the variable `my_int_array` in line 16. Index-by tables are discussed in more detail later in this chapter.
- Line 18 is a user-defined type for a nested table, used in line 19. User-defined types and nested tables are also discussed later in this chapter.

The TYPE keyword is used to create a user-defined PL/SQL type in the declaration section of a PL/SQL block. The SQL statement CREATE TYPE, discussed in Chapter 2, is used to create a user-defined SQL object type, which can also be used as a data type for a PL/SQL variable. The main difference is that one is created in the context of PL/SQL, and the other (CREATE TYPE) is defined outside the context of PL/SQL.

7.2.5 DERIVING PL/SQL DATA TYPES FROM THE DATABASE

The data types for PL/SQL scalar and record variables can be derived at compile time from a column in a table defined in the Oracle database. This data type derivation is implemented by the PL/SQL compiler, which looks up the data type for a column or row from the Oracle data dictionary.

7.2.5.1 Deriving a PL/SQL Scalar Data Type from a Column. The declaration syntax used to define a variable data type based on a column is:

```
variable_name        table_name.column_name%TYPE;
```

For example:

```
v_title     sales_item.title%TYPE;
```

%TYPE is appended to the table and column name. In the example, the PL/SQL compiler determines the data type and precision of the variable, `v_title`, from the `TITLE` column in the `SALES_ITEM` table. Using %TYPE to declare data types for variables that are used to interact with database data is highly recommended. Declaring variables with %TYPE can minimize the need for you to alter your PL/SQL source code if the definition of the referenced column changes. Depending on the type of change made to the column definition, you may only need to recompile the PL/SQL code.

7.2.5.2 Deriving a PL/SQL Record from a Table. A PL/SQL variable may also be declared as a record structure derived from a database table definition. The record structure contains one member variable for each column defined in the table. The data type of each member is based on the data type of its corresponding column.

The syntax required when declaring a PL/SQL record variable is to append the %ROWTYPE suffix after the table name in the data type:

```
record_variable_name       table_name%ROWTYPE;
```

For example:

```
courier_rec          courier%ROWTYPE;
```

You can create a record without using the %ROWTYPE mechanism. Using %ROWTYPE simplifies the creation of record structures based on the complete definition of a table. However, you can explicitly create a record structure based on a table (e.g., the `COURIER` table) as follows:

```
-- The table definition
CREATE TABLE courier (
```

```
    Id                  NUMBER(2),
    Name                VARCHAR2(30),
    cost_per_item       NUMBER(6,2)
);

-- PL/SQL block
DECLARE
  -- Create the record type definition
  TYPE courier_rectype IS RECORD (
    Id                    courier.id%TYPE,
    name                  courier.name%TYPE,
    cost_per_item         courier.cost_per_item%TYPE
  );

  -- Create the record variable
  courier_rec             product_rectype;
BEGIN
  . . .
END;
```

In this example, if the table structure changes, then the source code using the explicitly defined record structure must be altered to accommodate the changes. The benefit of using the %TYPE or %ROWTYPE mechanism is that your source code may not need to be altered if a column or table definition is changed. The change is automatic when you recompile your PL/SQL code.

7.2.6 REFERENCE DATA TYPES

Reference types are useful for a minimizing the effects of changes. There are two reference types in an Oracle database (see Table 7.4):

- The REF CURSOR type is a pointer to a result set, and has been available since Oracle7.2. It is used to create cursor variables to hold the pointer to a row in a result set.
- The REF type is a pointer to an SQL object created by PL/SQL code, and was introduced as part of the Oracle8 object relational features.

TABLE 7.4 Reference data types

DATA TYPE	DESCRIPTION
REF CURSOR	A REF CURSOR is effectively a pointer to a result set cursor. A cursor is a reference to a row in a result set.
REF object-type	The REF is a pointer to an SQL object created by PL/SQL code.

7.2.6.1 Reference Cursors. There are two kinds of reference cursors:

1. A *strongly-typed reference cursor,* where the result set structure is predefined at compilation time.
2. A *weakly-typed reference cursor,* where the result set is unknown at compilation time.

Creating a cursor variable requires that you first define the reference cursor (data) type and use the type for the variable. For example:

```
DECLARE
  TYPE sales_item_refcsr AS
     REF CURSOR RETURN SALES_ITEM%ROWTYPE;
  product_resultset       sales_item_refcsr;
BEGIN
  OPEN product_resultset FOR SELECT * FROM SALES_ITEM;
  :
  -- process the result set
  :
END;
```

The sales_item_refcsr type defines a strongly-typed reference cursor type, and the product_resultset variable is defined as the reference cursor. The OPEN statement associates a query whose select list must match the structure required by the product_resultset variable (otherwise an incompatible data type compilation error occurs).

The next example shows the use of a weakly-typed reference cursor:

```
DECLARE
  TYPE any_refcsr AS REF CURSOR;   -- no return type
  any_resultset    any_refcsr;
BEGIN
  OPEN any_resultset FOR SELECT * FROM SALES_ITEM;
-- process the product result set
:
  OPEN any_resultset FOR
      SELECT ORD_ID, SUM(PRICE) FROM ORDER_ITEM
      GROUP BY ORD_ID;
  -- process result set rows for
  -- total sales by product barcode
  :
END;
```

The `any_refcsr` type is a weakly-typed cursor reference that can be associated with any query, to return any number of columns. However, in order to process the data returned from a weakly-typed ref-cursor the PL/SQL code must know ahead of time what the result set structure will be. When using PL/SQL cursors, unlike Java, the query metadata information is not available to PL/SQL code for processing at runtime, unless you resort to using Oracle's built-in DBMS_SQL package to perform dynamic SQL processing.

An Example of Using the REF to an Object

To use SQL objects in PL/SQL, the CREATE TYPE command in SQL must be used to create the type. Assume that the object type `courier_t` has been created in the database, as follows:

```
CREATE TYPE courier_t AS OBJECT (
  id                NUMBER(4),
  name              VARCHAR2(30),
  cost_per_item     NUMBER(6,2)
);
```

Remember that the SQL object type definition is stored in the database data dictionary, and not defined as a PL/SQL type in the declaration section. SQL object variables can be declared in PL/SQL by using the object type name in the variable data type. You can declare a PL/SQL variable as a reference to an SQL object type by prefixing the keyword REF before the object type name. For example:

```
DECLARE
  v_courier            courier_t;
  v_courier_ref        REF courier_t;
BEGIN
  v_courier := courier_t(3, 'Fast As a Rocket', 4.5);
  ...
  SELECT REF(c) INTO v_courier_ref
  FROM courier c
  WHERE c.id = 1;
  ...
  SELECT DEREF(v_courier_ref) INTO v_courier FROM DUAL;
  v_courier.name := 'UltraFast Courier';
  ...
END;
```

LISTING 7.3 Using objects and object references in PL/SQL

Notes for Listing 7.3:

- Line 2 declares a variable to hold an instance of object type `courier_t`.
- Line 3 declares a variable to hold the reference of an SQL object type `courier_t`.
- Line 5 creates an instance of `courier_t` and stores the object in `v_courier`.
- Line 7 selects a reference of an object instance into a REF variable. The REF() function can only be used in an SQL statement, and returns a value that represents the pointer to the SQL object. Note: you cannot access the SQL object attributes or methods via the reference variable value in PL/SQL. If you need to work with the object contents or functionality, you must obtain the SQL object itself.
- Line 11 obtains a copy of the SQL object, via the reference, into the object variable. The DEREF() function must also be used in the context of an SQL statement, and is responsible for converting the SQL object reference value stored in the REF column into the SQL object being referenced.
- Line 12 accesses an attribute of the object via the object variable `v_courier`, and changes the value of the name attribute in memory.
- Using SQL statements in PL/SQL, such as those used in the preceding example to execute the REF() or DEREF() functions, is covered in more detail later in this chapter.

7.2.7 LITERAL VALUES

Numeric literal values consist of digits, with decimal points for fixed-point for floating-point (approximate numeric) numbers. Numbers can be made negative or positive by prefixing the value with a + or – sign. A literal number can also be entered using "E" or "e" notation for exponential format, with or without a + or – sign following the E character. For example:

```
DECLARE
  Age        pls_integer := 21;
  price      number(6,2) := 10500.95;
  large_val  number(20,10);
BEGIN
  large_val := 2.12E10;   -- scientific/exponential notation
  ...
END;
```

Character and string literal values always use single quotes, as in the SQL language:

```
DECLARE
  cust_name   varchar2(40)  := 'Analeb Serrot';
  gender      varchar2(1)   := 'M';
```

TABLE 7.5 String to Date Conversion results

DATE FORMAT	RESULT
DD-MON-Y, or DD-MON-YY	If using one or two digits for the year, the current century is used. The result would always be in year 2000 if the current century is 2000.
DD-MON-YYY	The year is always the value specified; for example, YYY=999 convert to the year 0999.
DD-MON-YYYY	The year specified as a four-digit value; it is converted as the four-digit year specified.

```
BEGIN
  ...
END;
```

Dates can be entered as string literal, and in the correct context quote date strings are implicitly converted to an internal date formats. Table 7.5 summarizes the results of a string-to-date conversion when using the format shown in column 1.

If you want to control the conversion of date strings into internal date format, then you must use the TO_DATE() SQL function with an explicit date format. A database administrator (DBA) can control the default format for implicit date conversion. In the database initialization file, the DBA can set the NLS_DATE_FORMAT initialization parameter to a specific date string. For example:

```
NLS_DATE_FORMAT = DD-MON-YYYY
```

The date format of YYYY allows a user to enter a date with a year made up of one, two, three, or four digits. Therefore, if you want to force data entry users to enter the date with exactly four digits for the year, add the FX[4] prefix to the NLS_DATE_FORMAT string as follows:

```
NLS_DATE_FORMAT = FXDD-MON-YYYY
```

The default date format settings applied by the DBA for the database instance can be explicitly overridden by any session that has different requirements, and if the user executing the statement also has the ALTER SESSION privilege. This can be done with the ALTER SESSION statement:

```
ALTER SESSION SET NLS_DATE_FORMAT = 'FXDD-MON-YYYY';
```

SQL statements that are executed in SQL*Plus and return date values, display the dates with the default format set in the NLS_DATE_FORMAT variable.

---

[4]In Oracle8i databases the FX format has been relaxed and appears redundant because it does not enforce the fix format.

If the database initialization file does not specify a value for NLS_DATE_FORMAT, then the default display date format is: 'DD-MON-YY'.

```
DECLARE
  the_date   DATE:= '10-JAN-1999';
BEGIN
  -- Use explicit date to string conversion for output
  dbms_output.put_line(
     'Date:'||to_char(the_date, 'DD-MON-YYYY HH24:MI:SS'));

  -- Use implicit conversion via default NLS_DATE_FORMAT
  dbms_output.put_line('Date: '|| the_date);
END;

-- Results on output are:
Date: 10-JAN-1999 00:00:00
Date: 10-JAN-99
```

Before Oracle8, Oracle input date formats that did not match the default date format for the session required the explicit conversion of date strings into internal date format. Explicit conversion of date strings into a data date type is achieved by using the TO_DATE conversion function with a user-defined input date format mask. Here is an example of an explicit date conversion:

```
DECLARE
  birth_date date;
BEGIN
  birth_date := to_date('21-12-1970', 'DD-MM-YYYY');
END;
```

The TO_DATE function uses its second argument to apply the conversion format used on the date string in the first argument. Table 7.6 is an abbreviated list of valid characters for use in date format masks.

Remember that an Oracle date also contains the time. Punctuation marks, such as commas, dots, slashes, and dashes, are also valid date format characters representing themselves.

7.3 CONDITIONAL AND SEQUENTIAL CONTROLS

Flow-control statements are similar to those in many other computer languages. Processing flows in a sequential manner from one statement to the next unless conditional statements alter the flow. We will now cover the syntax of PL/SQL conditional statements.

TABLE 7.6 Valid characters for date format conversion

CHARACTER MASK	MEANING
D	Day of the week where 1 = Sun, 2 = Mon, … 7 = Sat
DD	Day of the month
DDD	Day of the year since January 1
J	Julian date since January 1, 1970
MM	Two-digit- month value, 01 through 12
MON	Three-letter abbreviation of the month name
MONTH	Full-month name blank padded to nine characters wide
Y	Last digit of the year, century is not visible
YY	Last two digits of the year
YYY	Last three digits of the year
YYYY	All four digits of the year
HH, HH12	Hours in twelve-hour clock format
HH24	Hours in twenty-four-hour clock format
MI	Minutes
SS	Seconds
SSSS	Seconds past midnight
AM, PM	AM or PM indicator

7.3.1 IF STATEMENTS

The IF statement has several forms depending on the logic required. The first basic form of an IF statement is:

```
IF condition THEN
  Statement;
  :
END IF;
```

In the IF statement syntax, the final keywords END IF are separated by at least one white space character. Each statement, contained between the IF and END IF, is terminated by a semicolon. An IF statement may have an ELSE part, as shown here:

```
IF condition THEN
  Statement;
  :
ELSE
  Statement;
  :
END IF;
```

Only one ELSE keyword is allowed for an IF statement. You may find yourself writing nested IF statements, as shown in Listing 7.4.[5]

```
IF condition THEN
  Statement;
  :
ELSE
  IF condition THEN   -- if nested in 1st else
    Statement;
    :
  ELSE
    IF condition THEN - if nested in 2nd else
      Statement;
      :
    ELSE
      Statement;
      :
    END IF;    /* "end if" required for each "if" */
  END IF;
END IF;
```

LISTING 7.4 Nested IF statements

Care must be taken with the structure of your nested IF statements. Listing 7.4 can be simplified using an alternate form of the IF statement, as shown in Listing 7.5.

```
IF condition THEN
  Statement;
  :
ELSIF condition THEN   -- ELSIF is one keyword
  Statement;
  :
ELSIF condition THEN
  Statement;
  :
ELSE   -- this ELSE is optional
  Statement;
  :
END IF;   -- only one END IF is required here
```

LISTING 7.5 Composite IF-THEN-ELSIF statement

---

[5]Single-line comments appear after two dashes, and multiple-line comments appear between /* and */ exactly like Java multiple-line comments.

Notes for Listing 7.5:

- The underlined keyword ELSIF is entered as one word.
- You can have more than one ELSIF part to the same IF statement.
- There is only one ELSE part to the IF statement.
- There is only one END IF needed to end the IF statement.

You may nest any of the IF statements discussed above within any other IF statement construct.

7.3.1.1 Conditions. Conditions, as in Java, must be boolean expressions. A boolean expression evaluates to a boolean value. Comparison, or relational, operators compare two operands and return a boolean result. Comparison operators are shown below in bold:

```
value1 = value2    -- equals (note: only one equals
                      sign)
value1 < value2    -- less than
value1 > value2    -- greater than
value1 <= value2   -- less than or equal to
value1 >= value2   -- greater than or equal to

value1 <> value2   -- Not equal
value1 != value2   -- Also not equal
```

Conditions with SQL comparison operators are also allowed. For example:

```
variable [NOT] IN (value1, value2, .. ,valueN)
variable [NOT] BETWEEN low_value AND high_value
variable [NOT] LIKE 'character_pattern'
variable IS [NOT] NULL
```

The SQL comparison operators give the PL/SQL language power and flexibility, especially when the LIKE pattern-matching mechanism is used to compare character data.

The NOT keyword negates the meaning of the condition, and can be used before the condition. For example:

```
NOT condition
```

Multiple conditions can be combined using the following logical operators:

- AND, which has higher precedence than
- OR

Parentheses are used to override the order of evaluation of conditions implied by the default precedence of the operators used in conditions. Be aware that the result of a condition can be a NULL value. A NULL result is interpreted as if a FALSE value occurred. For example:

```
DECLARE
  age   pls_integer := null;
  b     boolean := false;
BEGIN
  b := age < 10;   -- b is assigned a NULL value
  IF b THEN
    -- never executed
  ELSE
    -- false condition is executed
  END IF;
END;
```

As with SQL statement comparison operations, PL/SQL cannot compare a quantifiable value with an unknown quantity like the NULL value. The result of any comparison with an unknown quantity, a NULL, results in a NULL value. The avoid this problem, use the IS NULL or IS NOT NULL comparison operators, or perform explicit conversion of NULL values by using the NVL() function before a comparison takes place. The code extract that follows shows the use of the IS NULL comparison in a conditional expression:

```
DECLARE
  age   pls_integer := null;
  b     boolean := false;
BEGIN
  b := age IS NULL;   -- b is assigned a NULL value
  IF b THEN
    -- this is now executed
    age := 10;
  END IF;
  IF age < 10 THEN
    :
  END IF;
END;
```

The condition in the preceding example can be better written as follows:

```
IF age is NULL THEN
```

This eliminates the need for the boolean variable b, but the point about testing NULL correctly should now be clear.

7.3.2 LOOP CONSTRUCTS

For iteration, PL/SQL has three loop constructs:

- The basic loop
- The WHILE loop
- The FOR loop

7.3.2.1 The Basic Loop.

The basic loop construct is:

```
LOOP
  :
  statement;
  :
  EXIT [WHEN condition];
  :
  statement;
  :
END LOOP;
```

The EXIT statement causes the enclosing loop to terminate, and can be used to terminate WHILE or FOR loops, which are discussed next. You may have more than one EXIT statement within a loop, each specified with a different condition.

The keyword WHEN and its associated condition are optional. Alternatively, you can place an EXIT statement in an IF statement inside the loop. If an EXIT statement is not present in the loop, or the EXIT condition never becomes true, then the loop is infinite.

7.3.2.2 The WHILE Loop.

The WHILE loop allows a condition to be tested prior to starting iteration, and as long as the condition evaluates to true the loop continues.

```
WHILE condition
LOOP
  :
  statements;
  :
END LOOP;
```

7.3.2.3 The FOR Loop. The FOR loop iteration is controlled in the following way:

- A loop counter variable is initialized to an integer-valued lower bound.
- If the counter is less than or equal to the upper bound, the body of the loop is executed.
- The counter is incremented by one.

For example:

```
FOR loop_counter IN low_value .. high_value
LOOP
  :
  statements;
  :
END LOOP;
```

The double dot operator (..) is called the range operator, which specifies the low and high values for the loop iteration. The loop counter is a name of a variable that is implicitly declared as an integer with its scope limited to the body of the FOR loop. The loop counter variable cannot be modified; it is read-only.

The FOR loop iteration can be done in reverse, in which case the higher bound is used as to initialize the loop counter. The counter is decremented by one until its value is equal to the lower bound.

```
FOR loop_counter IN REVERSE low_value .. high_value
LOOP
  :
  statements;
  :
END LOOP;
```

7.3.2.4 Nested Loops. You can place a loop within another loop known as a *nested loop*. For example:

```
LOOP
  :
  statements;
  :
  LOOP  -- nested loop
     :
     statements;
```

```
        :
        EXIT WHEN condition;   -- only ends the nested loop
        :
    END LOOP;
    :
END LOOP;
```

In this pseudo-code example, the EXIT statement only ends the nested loop, because an EXIT statement will only end its enclosing loop. Therefore, the outer loop is not explicitly terminated. You can structure your logic to use additional EXIT statements in the outer loop, or you can use a labeled EXIT statement to terminate the nested and its outer loop in one step.

7.3.2.5 PL/SQL Labels. The PL/SQL language allows you to put a label before a statement. A PL/SQL label is an identifier name enclosed between two less-than signs and two greater-than signs, as follows:

```
<<loop_label_name>>
```

When a PL/SQL label appears immediately before a PL/SQL block or loop, the label name becomes associated with the block or loop. The label can then be used in an EXIT statement to terminate the labeled loop by its associated name. The following example shows how you can use a labeled EXIT statement:

```
<<outer_loop>> LOOP
  :
  statements;
  :
  <<inner_loop>> LOOP
     :
     statements;
     :
     EXIT WHEN condition1;
     EXIT inner_loop WHEN condition2;
     EXIT outer_loop WHEN condition3;
     :
  END LOOP;
  :
END LOOP;
```

In this example, when `condition1` one is true, the inner loop is terminated (an unlabeled EXIT always terminates the immediately enclosing loop). When condition2 is true, the inner loop is also terminated. When condition3 is true, the outer loop is terminated.

GOTO Statements

The GOTO statement is supported in PL/SQL for unconditional jumps to code in the same block. A label name is required for a GOTO statement, and the syntax is:

```
<<label>>
  :
GOTO label;
```

In various schools of computer science, the use of a GOTO is generally discouraged. However, here is simple example showing the use of a GOTO statement in a PL/SQL block:

```
DECLARE
  val   PLS_INTEGER := 2;
BEGIN
  dbms_output.put_line('Val='|| val);
  IF val = 1 THEN
     GOTO one;
  ELSIF val = 2 THEN
     GOTO two;
  ELSIF val = 3 THEN
     GOTO three;
  ELSE
     GOTO end_of_block;
  END IF:
  dbms_output.put_line('No match for val='|| val);

<<one>>
  dbms_output.put_line('one');
  GOTO end_of_block;

<<two>>
  dbms_output.put_line('two');
  GOTO end_of_block;

<<three>>
  dbms_output.put_line('three');

<<end_of_block>> -- not legal unless followed by a statement
```

```
  dbms_output.put_line('end');
END;
```

This style of coding is tedious, and hard to maintain. The results for this example would be displayed as:

```
Val=2
two
end
```

7.4 USING SQL STATEMENTS IN PL/SQL

The only SQL statements directly supported in PL/SQL are the ones used for data retrieval and manipulation and for supporting transaction control. These statements are:

- SELECT
- INSERT
- UPDATE
- DELETE
- COMMIT
- ROLLBACK
- SAVEPOINT
- ROLLBACK TO SAVEPOINT

Using any other SQL statement syntax in PL/SQL requires the Oracle RDBMS built-in package called DBMS_SQL, which makes it possible for you to dynamically execute any SQL statement, including DDL statements like CREATE, ALTER, and DROP.

7.4.1 USING SELECT STATEMENTS IN PL/SQL

The SELECT statement when used in PL/SQL is limited to fetching a single row at a time, called a singleton SELECT. PL/SQL provides cursors for processing more than one row. The syntax of the singleton SELECT statement in PL/SQL is:

```
SELECT column(s)
INTO   variable(s) | record
FROM   table(s)
WHERE  condition(s)
GROUP BY group_criteria
HAVING condition(s);
```

The INTO clause defines the variable names to receive the values from the SELECT statement by matching positions with the columns listed in the SELECT clause. A PL/SQL record structure can be substituted for multiple variable names to reduce the number of variables required, but the record structure must be consistent in the number of members and data types matching the columns requested. Here is an example:

```
DECLARE
  v_name        courier.name%TYPE;
  v_id          courier.id%TYPE := 1;
BEGIN
  :
  SELECT name INTO v_name
  FROM   courier
  WHERE  id = v_id;
  :
END;
```

This code extract introduces a few noteworthy concepts:

1. PL/SQL variables are used to provide values to control the query or receive values from the query.
2. At least one row should be retrieved; otherwise a NO_DATA_FOUND exception is raised ("thrown," in Java terminology).[6]
3. If the query returns more than one row, a TOO_MANY_ROWS exception is raised.

Exceptions generated by executing a SQL statement can be handled ("caught," in Java terminology) in the exception section of a PL/SQL block.

7.4.2 DML STATEMENTS IN PL/SQL

The syntax of other DML statement syntax remains unchanged; however, there have been some enhancements in Oracle8i. The major difference between the DML statements used in PL/SQL and the DML statements used in SQL outside of a PL/SQL block is that the values in the DML statements are supplied by PL/SQL variables, or bind variables,[7] for data held outside a PL/SQL block. As a result, you can avoid hard-coded values when using DML operations in PL/SQL programs. The syntax of the INSERT statement is:

---

[6]The NO_DATA_FOUND exception is a predefined exception in PL/SQL. In Java, Exception objects are thrown, whereas in PL/SQL, exceptions (which are numbers) are raised. Some PL/SQL exceptions have predefined names called exception identifiers.

[7]Bind variables are discussed in Chapter 4 in the section on the INSERT statement.

```
INSERT INTO table_name [ (column(s) [, …] ]
VALUES (literal|variable[, …]);
```

The number of values must match the number of columns specified in the insert clause; otherwise one literal or variable value is required per column in the table definition, if the list of columns is not specified after the table name.

The syntax of the UPDATE statement is:

```
UPDATE table_name
  SET column_name = variable_name|expression
   [, column_name = variable_name|expression … ]
[WHERE condition(s)];
```

You can use a PL/SQL variable name[8] on the right-hand side of the equal sign in the SET clause, to provide the values for a column.

The DELETE statement syntax is:

```
DELETE FROM table_name
 [WHERE condition(s)];
```

The conditions in the WHERE clause of the UPDATE and DELETE statements can be evaluated using PL/SQL variable values.

Transactional commands, such as COMMIT and ROLLBACK, remain unchanged and appear in PL/SQL as they would in native SQL environments.

7.4.2.1 Using DML Statements to Return Values. One enhancement made to DML statements is the addition of the RETURNING INTO keywords as part of the syntax:

```
RETURNING column(s) INTO variable(s)
```

The RETURNING keyword is added after the DML statement, and eliminates the need to explicitly write a SELECT statement to query the changes made. The benefits are:

- Fewer network round trips.
- Fewer cursors are used.
- Less need for server CPU time and memory.

In Oracle8i PL/SQL the INSERT, UPDATE, and DELETE statements support the addition of a RETURNING INTO clause. The RETURNING INTO feature allows

[8]The variable names used in the SQL statements of a PL/SQL are subject to scooping rules.

the PL/SQL application to receive values modified by the DML statement. The syntax for using RETURNING INTO in a DML statement is:

```
INSERT INTO table_name [ (column(s) [, …] ]
VALUES (variable(s) [, …]);
RETURNING column(s) INTO variable(s)


UPDATE table-name
  SET column_name = variable_name|expression
   [, column_name = variable_name|expression … ]
[WHERE condition(s)];
RETURNING column(s) INTO variable(s)


DELETE FROM table_name
 [WHERE condition(s)];
RETURNING column(s) INTO variable(s)
```

Assuming that you have the following data in a courier table:

```
        ID NAME                           COST_PER_ITEM
---------- ------------------------------ -------------
         1 Federal Impress                          6.5
         2 GKL International                          6
         3 Snail Mail Inc                           1.7
         4 Universal Post                           4.5
```

Listing 7.6 shows the use DML statements to returning values modified by the statement into your PL/SQL variables. The example prints the variable values before and after the DML statement is executed.
The results of executing the code in Listing 7.6 are:

```
BEFORE INSERT:
AFTER INSERT: 6 Jack Rabbit Couriers 5.25
------------
BEFORE UPDATE: 6 Jack Rabbit Couriers 5.25
AFTER UPDATE: 1 FEDERAL IMPRESS 6.5
------------
BEFORE DELETE: 1 FEDERAL IMPRESS 6.5
AFTER DELETE: 4 Universal Post 4.5

-- Data in the table after modification is:
```

```
DECLARE
  v_id          courier.id%type;
  v_name        courier.name%type;
  v_item_cost      courier.cost_per_item%type;
BEGIN
  DBMS_OUTPUT.PUT_LINE('BEFORE INSERT: ' ||
    v_id ||' '||v_name||' '|| v_item_cost);
  INSERT INTO courier c
  VALUES (courier_t(6, 'Jack Rabbit Couriers', 5.25))
  RETURNING id, name, cost_per_item INTO v_id, v_name,
v_item_cost;
  DBMS_OUTPUT.PUT_LINE('AFTER INSERT: ' ||
    v_id ||' '||v_name||' '|| v_item_cost);
  DBMS_OUTPUT.PUT_LINE('------------');
  DBMS_OUTPUT.PUT_LINE('BEFORE UPDATE: ' ||
    v_id ||' '||v_name||' '|| v_item_cost);
  UPDATE courier
    SET name = upper(name)
  WHERE id = 1
  RETURNING id, name, cost_per_item INTO v_id, v_name,
v_item_cost;
  DBMS_OUTPUT.PUT_LINE('AFTER UPDATE: ' ||
    v_id ||' '||v_name||' '|| v_item_cost);
  DBMS_OUTPUT.PUT_LINE('------------');
  DBMS_OUTPUT.PUT_LINE('BEFORE DELETE: ' ||
    v_id ||' '||v_name||' '|| v_item_cost);
  DELETE FROM courier
    WHERE id = 4
  RETURNING id, name, cost_per_item INTO v_id, v_name,
v_item_cost;
  DBMS_OUTPUT.PUT_LINE('AFTER DELETE: ' ||
   v_id ||' '||v_name||' '|| v_item_cost);
END;
```

LISTING 7.6 Using RETURNING INTO with DML in PL/SQL

```
        ID NAME                           COST_PER_ITEM
---------- ------------------------------ -------------
         1 FEDERAL IMPRESS                          6.5
         2 GKL International                        6
         3 Snail Mail Inc                           1.7
         6 Jack Rabbit Couriers                     5.25
```

TABLE 7.7 Summary of using RETURNING clause in DML statement

DML	RESULTS OF RETURNING COLUMN(S) INTO VARIABLE(S)
INSERT	The new values inserted into the row/instance are returned in the PL/SQL variables
UPDATE	The new values in the row/instance AFTER the update occurs
DELETE	The values in the row/instance BEFORE the delete occurs.

The results of the DML statements using the RETURNING option are summarized in Table 7.7.

The use of the RETURNING option with DML is a powerful performance-enhancing feature that is extremely useful when you are working with a REF to an SQL Object data type. For example, you can create a new object instance and return a REF to that object in one INSERT statement. Then store the Object REF value for updating a table that needs to store the object REF value.

```
DECLARE
  v_courier_ref    REF courier_t;
  v_order_id       cust_order.id%TYPE := . . .;
  v_cust_id        cust_order.cust_id%TYPE := . . .;
BEGIN
  INSERT INTO courier c
  VALUES (courier_t(5, 'Speedy Shipments', 3.35))
  RETURNING REF(c) INTO v_courier_ref;

  UPDATE cust_order
     SET courier_ref = v_courier_ref
     WHERE id = v_order_id AND cust_id = v_cust_id;
END;
```

The example uses one INSERT statement to create the object instance in the courier table, and return its reference to the `v_courier_ref` variable. The update statement then stores the reference to the courier for customer order record. Without the RETURNING feature, the equivalent PL/SQL code is:

```
DECLARE
  v_courier_ref REF courier_t;
  v_order_id       cust_order.id%TYPE := . . .;
  v_cust_id        cust_order.cust_id%TYPE := . . .;
BEGIN
  INSERT INTO courier c
  VALUES (courier_t(5, 'Speedy Shipments', 3.35));
```

```
    SELECT REF(c) INTO v_courier_ref
    FROM courier c
    WHERE id = 5;

    UPDATE cust_order
       SET courier_ref = v_courier_ref
       WHERE id = v_order_id AND cust_id = v_cust_id;
END;
```

The second example shows, in bold, the extra SQL SELECT statement needed to obtain the REF of the courier object to be used in the UPDATE statement.

It should be clear that the RETURNING feature of DML reduces the number of SQL statements needed to obtain the same results, and, as already stated, minimizes network and server overhead.

7.5 CURSORS

A cursor is a private SQL work area in memory. In PL/SQL you can explicitly assign a name to the SQL area for a query. Oracle RDBMS uses the work area for the SELECT and DML statements to parse, optimize, and execute the SQL statement, as well as to maintain attributes about it.[9]

In PL/SQL you can explicitly declare a name for a cursor and associate the name to a SELECT statement. The SELECT statement that defines a named cursor is used to process one or more rows in a table. The cursor name acts like a handle to the work area, and you control cursor processing through the handle name. This section discusses the two types of PL/SQL cursors:

- Implicit cursors
- Explicit cursors

7.5.1 IMPLICIT CURSORS

In PL/SQL the SELECT, INSERT, UPDATE, and DELETE statements use an implicit cursor work area. You need to declare the implicit cursor; it has a predefined name of SQL.

PL/SQL cursors have four attributes, listed in Table 7.8, that can be checked to determine the outcome of an SQL operation.

---

[9]An SQL statement submitted for execute is identical to a statement already in the work area; the SQL area is transparently reused by the server. This is a performance feature you can take advantage of by being consistent in your naming and case conventions, and your use of bind variables.

TABLE 7.8 Implicit SQL cursor attributes

ATTRIBUTE	RETURN TYPE	VALUE WITH IMPLICIT CURSOR	VALUE WITH EXPLICIT CURSOR
%FOUND	BOOLEAN	TRUE if one or more rows is affected by statement, otherwise value is FALSE	TRUE is one or more rows is affected by statement, otherwise value is FALSE
%NOTFOUND	BOOLEAN	Opposite of %FOUND	Opposite of %FOUND
%ROWCOUNT	INTEGER	Number of rows affected by statement	Current number of rows processed in a cursor loop
%ISOPEN	BOOLEAN	Always FALSE at time of checking the value	TRUE if the cursor is still open, otherwise FALSE

You read the value of a cursor attribute after executing a statement. The cursor attribute value is obtained from a name constructed from the cursor name concatenated with the cursor attribute name. For example, using the implicit cursor name "SQL", you can check the value of the %NOTFOUND attribute by using "SQL%NOTFOUND". For example:

```
DECLARE
  nbr_rows_updated       pls_integer;
BEGIN
  UPDATE courier
    SET cost_per_item = cost_per_item * 1.1
  WHERE id = 1;
  IF SQL%FOUND THEN
    nbr_rows_updated := SQL%ROWCOUNT;
  ELSE
    nbr_rows_updated := 0;
  END IF;
END;
```

Cursor attributes values should be tested and used immediately after executing the SQL statement.

7.5.2 EXPLICIT CURSORS

In PL/SQL explicit cursors are used to write queries for processing data in result sets. You assign a name to the explicit cursor and the associated SELECT statement. It is much better to use an explicit cursor to retrieve data from a database table, even for one row, than to use a standalone SELECT statement. This is because you have more control over the record processing with an explicit cursor.

When a singleton SELECT statement was used in versions of the database prior to Oracle8, the PL/SQL engine needed an additional fetch to determine whether you in fact got only one row, or whether the query returned more than one row. The extra fetch determined whether it was necessary to raise a TOO_MANY_ROWS exception. If you only want one row from a query, and you know that there are no data integrity problems, then using an explicit cursor means that you can ensure that only one fetch is performed. The syntax used to declare an explicit cursor in PL/SQL is:

```
CURSOR cursor_type_name IS
  Select_statement;
```

For example:

```
CURSOR sales_item_csr IS
  SELECT id, title, full_price
  FROM sales_item;
```

The example defines the cursor name and query, but does not execute the query. Explicit cursors are controlled using the following steps:

- Open the cursor.
- Fetch a row from the cursor result set, and loop until complete.
- Close the cursor.

7.5.2.1 Opening a Cursor. To open a cursor, use the OPEN statement. For example:

```
OPEN sales_item_csr;
IF sales_item_csr%ISOPEN THEN
  -- start processing the result set
END IF;
```

As shown in the example, you can test whether the cursor was successfully opened with the %ISOPEN attribute. You may want to test the %ISOPEN state before opening a cursor; otherwise an exception is raised if you attempt to open a cursor that is already opened.

7.5.2.2 Fetch and Test the Cursor. The fetch operation is performed to get the next row from the cursor result set. You must test whether the fetch operation received any row before attempting to process data. The fetch and test operations are typically defined in a loop using the FETCH statement to get a row, and the cursor attribute to test whether a row was found. The syntax for a FETCH loop is:

```
-- cursor is open so process the result set data
LOOP
  FETCH sales_item_csr INTO sales_rec;
  EXIT WHEN sales_item_csr%NOTFOUND;
  -- do record data processing here
END LOOP;
```

The FETCH statement has a INTO clause that identifies the PL/SQL variables that acquire the values for each column defined in the cursor SELECT list. You need one variable per column in the query or use a record structure with the correct number of fields. In the preceding example, the column values are read into a PL/SQL record whose structure should be compatible with the SELECT statement defined in the cursor. After each FETCH, you should test for the end of the result set by using the explicit cursor attributes, such as %NOTFOUND.

7.5.2.3 Closing the Cursor. When you finish processing the result set rows, close the cursor to release resource held by executing the CLOSE statement. For example:

```
CLOSE sales_item_csr;
```

Here is a complete example of using an explicit cursor:

```
DECLARE
  CURSOR sales_item_csr IS
    SELECT id, title, full_price FROM sales_item;
  v_id      sales_item.id%TYPE;
  v_title   sales_item.title%TYPE;
  v_price   sales_item.full_price%TYPE;
BEGIN
  OPEN sales_item_csr;
  LOOP
    FETCH sales_item_csr INTO v_id, v_title, v_price;
    EXIT WHEN sales_item_csr%NOTFOUND;
    -- Process the data row
    DBMS_OUTPUT.PUT_LINE(v_id || ' ' ||
                         v_title || ' ' ||
                         v_price);
  END LOOP;
  CLOSE sales_item_csr;
END;
```

7.5.2.4 Using a Cursor to Declare a PL/SQL Record Variable. A PL/SQL record is your saving grace when using cursors, because it saves you having to declare many variables to receive the results for each row the cursor processes. The record structure must be compatible with the number, data type, and order of the columns listed in the cursor SELECT statement. To save you the hassle of explicitly declaring your own record structures for each cursor, PL/SQL allows you to use the cursor name concatenated with the %ROWTYPE attribute as a data type for a record variable. For example:

```
DECLARE
  CURSOR sales_item_csr IS
    SELECT id, title, full_price FROM sales_item;

-- Create the record variable
  sales_rec          sales_item_csr%ROWTYPE;
BEGIN
...
END;
```

The advantage of this feature is that it minimizes the need to edit your code if the column list in cursor query is changed. The compiler automatically determines the number and data types of record member variables from the number and data types of the columns selected in the cursor query definition. Record member variable names are derived from the column or alias names used in the query.

7.5.2.5 Cursor FOR Loops. Another way of working with explicit cursors in PL/SQL is to use the cursor FOR loop. The syntax for the PL/SQL cursor FOR loop is:

```
FOR record_variable_name IN cursor_type_name
LOOP
  /* Process the data here accessing the record
  ** member values with a dot notation after the
  ** record_variable_name
  **    record_variable_name.member_variable_name
  */
END LOOP;
```

In the cursor FOR loop, the record variable name is implicitly declared to be the `cursor-type-name%ROWTYPE`. The record variable visibility is local to the cursor FOR loop. The main advantages of using a cursor FOR loop are:

- The cursor is automatically opened, eliminating the need for an explicit OPEN statement.
- The FETCH operation is done, and the test for the end of result set is automatically performed.
- The cursor is automatically closed when exiting the cursor FOR loop independently of how the loop is terminated.

The explicit cursor processing steps previously discussed can be written as follows:

```
DECLARE
  CURSOR sales_item_csr IS
    SELECT id, title, full_price FROM sales_item;
BEGIN
  FOR sales_rec IN sales_item_csr
  LOOP
    DBMS_OUTPUT.PUT_LINE(sales_rec.id || ' ' ||
                         sales_rec.title || ' ' ||
                         sale_rec.full_price);
END LOOP;
```

7.6 PL/SQL TABLES AND VARYING ARRAYS

PL/SQL tables are dynamic collections of the same data or record type. Each table element can be a scalar data type to hold a single value, or a composite data type, such as a record, to hold multiple related values. In Oracle8, there are two types of PL/SQL tables:

1. Nested tables (available in Oracle8 and above)
2. Index-by tables

7.6.1 NESTED TABLES

Nested tables are a collection of data used to keep data for sorting, manipulation, or searching operations in memory. Performing work in memory can minimize disk I/O and improve performance. Creating a nested table in PL/SQL is done in two steps:

1. Declare a nested table type.
2. Define a nested table variable based on the type.

The syntax for these steps is:

```
01: DECLARE
02:  TYPE nested_type_name IS TABLE OF element_type [NOT NULL];
03:  nested_table_name      table_type_name;
04:
05: BEGIN
06:   -- Create an empty collection using its constructor
07:   nested_table_name := nested_type_name();
08:   nested_table_name.extend();    -- add one element
09:  ...
10: END;
```

The element-type defines the data type structure contained in each element of the table. Before you can use a nested table, you must first explicitly create it by calling its constructor method, as shown in line 7. The value of a nested table variable is atomically NULL until it is explicitly constructed. Nested tables are treated as a collection, similar to using a Java vector, where new elements are allocated and added in sequential order. A nested table can only be indexed by a positive integer in the range 1 through 2147483647. Nested table entries must be created before a value can be assigned to any entry.

Changing the size and number of entries in a nested table can be achieved using the following methods:

- EXTEND to extend the table by one null element at the end of the table.
- EXTEND(n) to extend the table by `n` null valued elements at the end of the table.
- EXTEND(n, v) to extend the table by `n` elements at the end of the table, each with an initial value of `v`.
- TRIM to remove the last element from the table.
- TRIM(n) to remove the last `n` elements from the table.

7.6.2 INDEX-BY TABLES

Index-by tables first appeared in PL/SQL Version 2.0 with Oracle7, to provide a way to keep data values queried from a database table in a memory data structure, for quicker access and to minimize disk I/O.

As with the nested table, there are two steps in creating an index-by table:

- Create the index-by table type, which must include the text INDEX BY BINARY_INTEGER, which identifies the table as an index-by table.
- Create the table variable based on the index-by table type.

The syntax for defining an index-by table is:

```
DECLARE
  TYPE index_by_type_name IS TABLE OF element-type
    INDEX BY BINARY_INTEGER;
  Index_by_table_name   index_by_type_name;

BEGIN
  -- Add an element at index value idx to the table
  index_by_table_name(idx) :=  element_value;
  ...
END;
```

Elements in the index-by table are also indexed by an integer, but within the range of –2147483647 to 2147483647, as constrained by the BINARY_INTEGER type.

Elements in an index-by table do not exist, that is, do not take up memory, until a value is explicitly assigned to an element in the table. Assigning a value to an element implicitly creates the space/memory for it. This is different to the nested table, which required the space/memory to be allocated before assigning the value to the element. Therefore, index-baby tables only consume memory for allocated entries that have been assigned a value.

Unlike the nested table, the index-by table variable cannot be NULL. However, an element *value* in an index-by table can be NULL.

By default, the index-by table is implicitly empty, and elements are added by simply assigning a value to any index in the table. For example:

```
DECLARE
  TYPE number_tabtype IS TABLE OF NUMBER(4)
    INDEX BY BINARY_INTEGER;
  number_table    number_tabtype;

BEGIN
  -- Create element 10 with a value of 42
  number_table(10) := 42;
END;
```

Thus, to reference or assign a value to an entry in a PL/SQL table holding a single scalar value, use the following syntax:

```
Plsql_table_var_name(entry_index)
```

If the PL/SQL table element holds a record structure, use the following syntax to store a record value:

```
Plsql_var_table_name(entry_index) := some-record
```

The PL/SQL table name and the index value represent a record. Therefore, use the following syntax to read or write record member value at a specific element index:

```
Plsql_var_table_name(entry_index).record_member_name
```

PL/SQL tables are similar to objects in that they have methods that can be used to operate on the specific elements or the entire table structure. The methods are invoked as shown in the following syntax:

```
Plsql_table_variable_name.method_name[(arguments)]
```

Some methods have arguments, and others do not. Table 7.9 lists some of the methods that are common to nested and index-by PL/SQL tables.

The example in Listing 7.7 demonstrates some features of an index-by PL/SQL table and its methods.

The first loop in Listing 7.7 adds elements for each even-numbered element, while the second loop steps through each value in the array to display the values

TABLE 7.9 Methods Common to Index-By and Nested PL/SQL tables

PL/SQL TABLE METHOD NAME	DESCRIPTION
COUNT	Returns the number of entries allocated with values in the array.
NEXT(idx)	Returns the binary index value of the next allocated array entry relative to the specified idx parameter.
PRIOR(idx)	Returns the binary index value of the previously allocated array entry relative to the specified idx parameter. This can be null if the specified idx value represents the smallest indexed entry in the table.
DELETE(idx)	
DELETE	Removes the entry for the specified index, memory is deallocated, and the entry does not exist any more. Delete used without an argument deletes all entries. A delete operation used on a nested table marks the entries as an empty placeholder, but the memory remains allocated until removed with a TRIM method.
EXISTS(idx)	A test that returns a true value if an entry at the index is allocated a value, otherwise it returns a false result.
FIRST	Returns the smallest integer index with an assigned value.
LAST	Returns the largest integer index with an assigned value.

```
DECLARE
  TYPE num_table_type AS TABLE OF number(6)
     INDEX BY BINARY_INTEGER;
  num_array                        num_table_type;
  idx        pls_integer := 0;
  entry_idx pls_integer;
  entry_val    number(6);
  MAX_ENTRIES     constant pls_integer := 10;
BEGIN
  /*
  ** populate the even entries in the array
  */
  WHILE idx <= MAX_ENTRIES
  LOOP
    num_arry(idx) := idx * 10;  -- creates an entry
    idx := idx + 2;  -- only even numbers
  END LOOP;

  DBMS_OUTPUT.PUT_LINE('Number of entries: '||
                        num_arry.COUNT);  -- prints 6
  /*
  ** Loop through array displaying
  ** the entries in even locations
  */
  entry_idx := num_arry.FIRST;
  entry_val := num_arry(entry_idx);
  FOR i IN 1 .. num_arry.COUNT
  LOOP
    DBMS_OUTPUT.PUT_LINE(entry_idx||' '||entry_val);
    entry_idx := num_arry.NEXT(entry_idx);
    EXIT WHEN NOT num_arry.EXISTS(entry_idx);
    entry_val := num_arry(entry_idx);
  END LOOP;
END;
```

LISTING 7.7 Using an Index-by table collection in PL/SQL

in allocated index entries, skipping unallocated odd entries by using the `next()` method of the PL/SQL table variable.

Listing 7.8 show the creation and use of a nested PL/SQL table. The key difference in the declaration of the nested table is that the INDEX BY BINARY_INTEGER is omitted from the type definition.

```
DECLARE
  TYPE num_array_table AS TABLE OF number(6);
  num_array           num_array_table;
  other_arry    num_arry_table;
BEGIN
  /*
  ** Call the nested table constructor.
  ** The constructor name is the type name
  ** Creates an empty table
  */
  IF num_array is NULL THEN
    num_array := num_arry_table();
  END IF;
  /*
  ** Extend the table with 10 null valued elements
  */
  num_arry.EXTEND(10);
  /*
  ** Initialize each entry in the table
  */
  FOR idx IN 1 .. num_arry.COUNT
  LOOP
    num_arry(idx) := idx;
  END LOOP;
  --delete all entries in the table
  num_arry.TRIM(num_arry.COUNT);

  /*
  ** Create and initialize other_arry
  ** using a constructor, creating
  ** 5 elements with even numbers
  */
  other_array := num_arry_table(2,4,6,8,10);

  /*
  ** Display element values in array
  */
  FOR idx IN 1 .. num_arry.COUNT
  LOOP
    DBMS_OUTPUT.PUT_LINE(other_arry(idx));
  END LOOP;

END;
```

LISTING 7.8 Using a nested table collection in PL/SQL

7.6.3 VARYING ARRAYS

A *varying array* is a collection of elements that can be accessed individually or manipulated as a complete unit of information. Varying-array elements retain their order when stored in the database. A varying array has a fixed upper limit that cannot be changed. If you need the number of elements to grow dynamically, then use a nested table or an index-by table. To create a varying array in PL/SQL:

- ❑ First define the array type name, maximum size, and data type for each element.
- ❑ Then define a variable identifier using the varying-array type name.

The syntax required to defined a varying-array variable is:

```
DECLARE
  TYPE varray_type_name IS VARRAY (size_limit)
     OF element_type [NOT NULL];

  -- Or

  TYPE varray_type_name IS VARYING ARRAY (size_limit)
     OF element_type [NOT NULL];

  varray_name       varray_type_name | db_varray_type;
BEGIN
  -- Create an empty collection using its constructor
  varray_name := varray_type_name();
  varray_name.extend();    -- add one element to the
table
  :
  varray(1) := element_type;   -- initialize the element
END;
```

The declaration of the variable varray_name shows that you can use the PL/SQL varray_type_name as the data type, or from an object type in the database created as a varray collection using the SQL statement:

```
CREATE TYPE db_varray_type AS VARRAY(size_limit) OF element_type;
```

There is no need to create a varying-array type in PL/SQL if a varying-array object type exists in the database. There are some restrictions on the element types used for varying arrays: you cannot define an array based on the following element types:

- Booleans
- Object types with BLOB or CLOB attributes
- Object types with TABLE or VARRAY attributes
- Ref cursors
- Varying arrays or tables
- For a list of other types not allowed as element types, refer to the Oracle PL/SQL documentation on collections.

If the element type is a record structure, then record fields should be scalar variable types. If the element type is an object type, the object type should only contain scalar members.

Varying arrays have a maximum size, specified in their definition, and each element of a varying array is always occupied. You cannot delete individual elements from a varying array; and, when stored in the database, elements in varying arrays retain their order and subscript value. Varying arrays are best used for obtaining an entire collection as a whole, but are only used for smaller collections to reduce the impact on I/O activity.

7.6.4 ADVANTAGES OF NESTED TABLES AND VARYING ARRAYS

The main advantage of using nested table or varying-array collections is that they can be used in SQL statements to query and manipulate compatible collection structures in database tables. However, a PL/SQL variable declared as a nested table or a varying array must have the same data type as defined in the associated column or attribute.

Listing 7.9 shows the creation of a varying array of five elements for items in a shopping cart.

```
CREATE OR REPLACE TYPE shopping_item_va_t AS
    VARRAY(5) OF shopping_item_t;

CREATE OR REPLACE TYPE shopping_cart_t AS OBJECT (
  id     number(6),
  creation_date  date,
  shipment_cost  number(5),
  total_cost     number(6),
  customer_ref   ref customer_t,
  items          shopping_item_va_t);

CREATE TABLE shopping_cart OF shopping_cart_t;
```

LISTING 7.9 Declaring a varying array of items in a shopping cart

Listing 7.10 shows adding items into a memory-based varying-array structure used to store the items in a newly created shopping cart entry in the shopping cart table.

The example in Listing 7.10 has no exception-handling code. It was omitted to keep the example simple.

```
DECLARE
 item_List              shopping_item_va_t;
 the_Price              sales_item.full_price%type;
 the_Total_Cost         number(6,2) := 0.0;
 the_Ship_Cost          number(6,2) := 0.0;
 item_Ref               REF sales_item_t;
 cust_Ref               REF customer_t;
BEGIN
 /*
 ** Create the varying array in memory and
 ** allocate and assign values for for 5 item entries
 */
 item_List := shopping_item_va_t();
 item_List.extend(5);
 FOR itm_nbr IN 1 .. 5
 LOOP
   /*
   ** Lookup the price and reference of a sales item
   */
   SELECT si.full_price, ref(si) into the_Price, item_Ref
   FROM SALES_ITEM si
   WHERE si.id = itm_nbr;
   /*
   ** Store item details, and a quantity of 1, in the item list.
   */
   item_List(itm_nbr) := shopping_item_t(1, the_Price, item_Ref);
   the_Total_Cost := the_Total_Cost  + the_Price;
 END LOOP;
 /*
 ** Assume the Courier id is 1, to get the shipment cost
 */
 SELECT cost_per_item INTO the_Ship_Cost
 FROM courier
 WHERE id = 1;
 the_Ship_Cost := the_Ship_Cost * item_List.count;
```

LISTING 7.10 Using PL/SQL to populate a varying array of items

```
36:
37:   /*
38:   ** Add a new shopping cart with zero items, Use the
39:   ** empty constructor for the varying array of items
40:   */
41:   SELECT ref(c) INTO cust_Ref
42:   FROM customer c
43:   WHERE id = 51;
44:   INSERT INTO shopping_cart (id, creation_date,
45:          shipment_cost, total_cost, customer_ref, items)
46:   VALUES (51, trunc(sysdate), the_Ship_Cost, the_Total_Cost,
47:            cust_Ref, item_List);
48:   COMMIT;
49: END;
50: /
```

LISTING 7.10 *Continued*

Notes for Listing 7.10:

- In line 2, the `item_List` variable is declared as a varying array based on the database type created in Listing 7.9.
- Line 13 creates an empty varying array without entries using the object type constructor, which has zero arguments.
- Line 14 allocates space for five entries in the varying array, the maximum size allowed for this example.
- The loop in lines 15–28 accesses data from the `SALES_ITEM` table to provide the price and the reference to the item. The example is somewhat contrived; it locates only the first five sales items, but serves to illustrate how to populate each varying array element.
- Line 26 populates the varying element with a value by using the shopping-item object type constructor, which must provide three arguments for the quantity (always set to one in this example), price, and reference to the sales item. The latter two values are obtained from the SELECT statement in lines 20–22, which shows how to access object reference values.
- In lines 44–47, the INSERT statement is used to create a new shopping cart for the customer. In particular, the `item_List` variable on line 47 is highlighted to shown how simple it is to store a value in a varying-array column in a database table, from the PL/SQL varying-array variable whose data type is compatible with the items attribute in the `SHOPPING_CART` table.

Another advantage of using a PL/SQL nested table is that you can cast the memory structure into a virtual database table in memory, and perform SQL statements on data in memory. The example in Listing 7.11 shows how to use an SQL SELECT statement on a local nested table in memory. The following object type definitions are used for the example:

```
CREATE TYPE person_t AS OBJECT (
  id      number(4),
  name    varchar2(20),
  surname varchar2(20)
);

CREATE TYPE person_nt_t AS TABLE OF person_t;
```

The example using the person nested table, and person object type is:

```
DECLARE
    v_people  person_nt_t;
    v_person  person_t;
BEGIN
   v_people := person_nt_t();
   v_people.extend(4);
   v_people(1) := person_t(1, 'Sam', 'Malone');
   v_people(2) := person_t(2, 'Dianne', 'Chambers');
   v_people(3) := person_t(3, 'Darrel', 'Sommers');
   v_people(4) := person_t(4, 'Jackie', 'McLean');
   --
   -- Retrieve an object value from the Nest tabled in memory
   --
   SELECT value(p) INTO v_person
   FROM TABLE(CAST(v_people AS person_nt_t)) p
   WHERE p.id = 1;
   --
   -- Output the resultant object contents
   --
   dbms_output.put_line(v_person.id || ' ' ||
                        v_person.name || ' '||
                        v_person.surname);
END;
/

-- The output result is:

1 Sam Malone

PL/SQL procedure successfully completed.
```

LISTING 7.11 Accessing a nested table in memory using SQL

Notes for Listing 7.11:

- Line 2 creates the nested table variable for the memory cache of data.
- Line 3 creates a variable to obtain the resultant object from the select statement in lines 14–16.
- Lines 4–10 set up cache size and the contents of the cache in the nested table.
- Lines 14–16, show the SELECT statement that obtains the first object element from the nested table and saves it in the `v_person` variable. The important work is performed in the FROM clause, where a "local" in memory table is created by the TABLE and CAST operations:[10] `TABLE(CAST (v_people AS person_nt_t))`. Here, you see the use of the CAST operator forces the SQL statement to view data in the v_people as a nested table. The nested table is then wrapped in a TABLE() operator, which creates an in memory table structure that can be queried or manipulated as if the table were a normal relation table on disk. This technique is a very powerful way to get performance by executing SQL operations on data in memory, instead of writing a loop to perform the appropriate in-memory operations, or SQL on data files.
- Lines 20–22 output the resultant object instance attribute values.

The ability to perform SQL on memory data structures provides a significant performance benefit when you use the nested table as a cache of information.

7.7 USER-DEFINED/OBJECT TYPES IN PL/SQL

Once an object type definition exists in the database, you can use the object type name as the data type for a PL/SQL variable. A PL/SQL variable based on an object type defines a transient representation of an object instance. The syntax is:

In SQL:

```
CREATE TYPE object_type AS OBJECT (...);
```

In PL/SQL:

```
DECLARE
  variable_name         object_type;  -- declare using object type
  ref_variable          REF object_type;
```

[10]The TABLE and CAST operators are discussed in Chapter 4.

```
BEGIN
  /*
  ** Create the PL/SQL object instance by initializing
  ** the PL/SQL variable using the object type constructor
  */
  variable_name := object_type_name(…);
  :
END;
```

You can use a PL/SQL variable to retrieve an object instance from an object table or object column. You can also use DML statements to write a PL/SQL object instance to a database object table or object column.

To obtain a reference to an object instance and store it in a reference variable, you must use SELECT statement. The REF(), DEREF(), and VALUE() functions used on object types can only be used in SQL statements embedded in PL/SQL code blocks.[11] The code in Listing 7.9 shows examples of using object type definitions directly in PL/SQL for variable data type declaration, as well as the use of REF() in the context of an SQL statement.

It is unfortunate that the PL/SQL developer must resort to using SQL to obtain a reference, but this is because the reference value is the globally unique object identifier (OID), which Oracle only allocates to stored object instance data, not to transient objects created in PL/SQL. A transient object, instantiated in PL/SQL code, must first be written to an object table before the OID is allocated. Using a RETURNING, you can perform the operation in one SQL statement.

SUMMARY

This chapter has provided an introduction to the basic features of Oracle PL/SQL, including language syntax and the declaration of variables, data types, and SQL object constructs. You have learned how to use SQL statements in PL/SQL to read data from tables, and to add, modify, or delete database data. The chapter included a discussion of using SQL collection data types, such as index-by tables, nested tables, and varying arrays.

Writing robust code requires that you create manageable modular code and deal with exceptions in a graceful manner. Modularizing your code through the use of PL/SQL procedures, functions, packages, and exception handling is discussed in the next chapter.

---

[11]The functionality for the REF(), DEREF(), and VALUE() functions is discussed in Chapter 3.

Chapter 8

PL/SQL Procedures, Functions, Packages, and Exceptions

This chapter discusses stored subprograms that use PL/SQL as the language and introduces Java Stored procedures. You will learn about:

- ❏ Stored procedures
- ❏ Stored functions
- ❏ Stored packages

There is also a brief introductory discussion of PL/SQL packages in the Oracle server available to PL/SQL and Java developers. The benefits and performance considerations of using stored code in the database are covered. A robust program should deal with errors in a practical manner, so exception handling is also treated in this chapter.

8.1 STORED PROCEDURES AND FUNCTIONS

Stored procedures and functions are major features of the PL/SQL language. They provide developers with the means to create and store highly structured modular code that can be reused and executed in the database server. Procedures and functions are created as database constructs in their own right, and are termed *standalone procedures* or *functions*. All PL/SQL code stored in one schema can be made available to registered database users by granting them the EXECUTE privilege on the stored PL/SQL code.

In Oracle8i, PL/SQL procedures can be executed with definer rights or invoker rights. In earlier versions of the database, PL/SQL code could only execute with the privileges associated with the owner/creator of the code. *Definer rights* means that the PL/SQL code executes with privileges associated with the creator of the stored code. *Invoker rights* means that it executes with privileges associated with the user calling the stored code.

PL/SQL procedures, functions, and packages are called *named blocks* because they are identified by a name. In Java terms, a procedure is roughly equivalent to a void method, and a function is like a method that returns a specific data type.

In SQL*Plus, the CREATE PROCEDURE and CREATE FUNCTION statements are used, respectively, to create stored procedures and functions.

8.1.1 CREATING A PROCEDURE

A procedure is a block of code or functionality that performs a set task. The syntax to create a procedure is:

```
CREATE PROCEDURE procedure_name[(arguments)]
IS
  -- Declare local variables here, if needed
BEGIN
  executable-statements;
[EXCEPTION -- section optional
  exception-handlers ]
END [procedure_name];
/
```

LISTING 8.1 Syntax for creating a stored procedure

In Listing 8.1, you can see the basic PL/SQL BEGIN-END block structure is preserved. The PL/SQL block heading is required for procedures and functions, and forms the signature, or *formal declaration*, of the procedure. The *signature* of a PL/SQL procedure declaration is a combination of the procedure name, and the order, number, and types of parameters.

Procedures may have zero, one, or more arguments, also called *formal parameters*. If the procedure has no arguments, you must omit the parentheses from the declaration. PL/SQL provides for input only, output only, and input/output arguments (see the discussion of parameter modes in Section 8.1.7 of this chapter).

8.1.2 INVOKING A PROCEDURE

To invoke a procedure, the name of the procedure must be entered, with actual values for required arguments. A call to invoke a procedure is done inside the BEGIN-END section of any PL/SQL block. For example:

```
CREATE PROCEDURE hello IS
BEGIN
  DBMS_OUTPUT.PUT_LINE('Hello Java World');
END;
/

CREATE PROCEDURE motd(message VARCHAR2) IS
BEGIN
  DBMS_OUTPUT.PUT_LINE('The message of the day is: ');
  DBMS_OUTPUT.PUT_LINE(message);
END;
/
```

```
/*
** Using an anonymous block to invoke procedure hello, and
** a procedure called motd with a VARCHAR2 argument.
*/
BEGIN
  hello;
  motd('PL/SQL is easy to master');
END;
/
```

The example calls the hello procedure, which has no formal arguments. Note that, unlike Java, parentheses are not required when calling a procedure without arguments. However, since Oracle8 (8.0.x), you can optionally include the parentheses in the call when no argument values are needed.[1] For example:

```
-- Invoke procedure hello, with new supported
-- syntax in Oracle8 or higher.

BEGIN
  hello();   -- parentheses are optional without
arguments
END;
/
```

8.1.3 CREATING A FUNCTION

A function is a block of code that performs a task and always returns a single value of a specified data type. The syntax to create a PL/SQL function is:

```
CREATE FUNCTION function_name[(arguments)] RETURN data_type
IS
  -- Declare local variables here, if needed
BEGIN
  executable-statements;
  RETURN return-value;    -- a return is required
[EXCEPTION -- section optional
  exception-handlers ]
END [function_name];
/
```

LISTING 8.2 Syntax for creating a stored function

[1]In Oracle7 databases, calling a procedure with no parameters between parentheses is treated as syntax error.

In Listing 8.2, a function, like a procedure, has a name and optional arguments. The function requires a RETURN statement in its implementation to ensure that a value is returned to the calling environment. Multiple return statements are permitted. Functions allow input only arguments, and can also return values to the caller through output arguments.

8.1.4 CALLING A FUNCTION

You call a function by specifying the name of the function followed by its required parameters enclosed in parentheses. However, as you already know, functions return a value that must either be stored in another variable or used as a parameter to another procedure or function. For example:

```
CREATE FUNCTION show_time(fmt VARCHAR2) RETURN VARCHAR2
IS
BEGIN
  RETURN TO_CHAR(sysdate, fmt);
END show_time;

/*
** Call the show_time function with a format argument
** that shows the hours, minutes and seconds in twenty four hour
** format
*/

DECLARE
  curr_time   VARCHAR2(40);
BEGIN
  /*
  ** Save the function return value in local variable curr_time.
  */
  curr_time := show_time('HH24:MI:SS');
  DBMS_OUTPUT.PUT_LINE('The time is: ' || curr_time);

  /*
  ** Use the return value of the function for the input value
  ** of the parameter in the motd() procedure.
  */
  motd('The current time is: ' || show_time('HH:MI:SSam'));

END;
```

The example uses the return value from both invocations of the `show_time` function. Unlike Java, PL/SQL function return values cannot be ignored. For example, in Java you do not have to use the return value:

```
public class MethodCall {

  static int addInt(int val1, int val2) {
    return (val1 + val2);
  }

  public static void main(String[] args) {
    addInt(10, 20);
}
```

The Java compiler accepts the add call in the main() method; and it also runs successfully, but the return is not used and lost. The equivalent in PL/SQL is:

```
CREATE FUNCTION addint(val1 NUMBER, val2 NUMBER) RETURN NUMBER IS
BEGIN
  RETURN (val1 + val2);
END;
/

Function created.

-- The above function is compiled successfully, but
--
-- The call to the function does not compile, with the error shown
--
BEGIN                        -- line 1
  addint(10, 20);            -- line 2
END;                         -- line 3
/
BEGIN
*
ERROR at line 1:
ORA-06550: line 2, column 3:
PLS-00221: 'ADDINT' is not a procedure or is undefined
ORA-06550: line 2, column 3:
PL/SQL: Statement ignored
```

The PL/SQL compiler does not allow you to call a function and ignore the return value.

8.1.5 EXECUTING PL/SQL CODE WITH DEFINER OR INVOKER RIGHTS

In Oracle8i, the AUTHID clause can be used in the definition of PL/SQL procedures, functions, packages, and object type method bodies to control whether the PL/SQL code is executed in the context of the definer or the invoker. The following syntax examples show where to specify the AUTHID clause for each of the PL/SQL constructs:

```
-- In a stand-alone function
CREATE FUNCTION function_name[(parameters)] RETURN
data_type
[AUTHID {CURRENT_USER | DEFINER}] IS
BEGIN
 :
END;

-- In a stand-alone procedure
CREATE PROCEDURE procedure_name[(parameters)]
[AUTHID {CURRENT_USER | DEFINER}] IS
BEGIN
 :
END;

-- In a package specification
CREATE PACKAGE package_name [AUTHID {CURRENT_USER |
   DEFINER}] IS
 :
END;

-- In an object type specification
CREATE TYPE object_type_name
[AUTHID {CURRENT_USER | DEFINER}] IS OBJECT (
 :
);
```

Note that the AUTHID clause can only be used in stand-alone procedure and function headings, and in the specification part of a package or object type definition. If the AUTHID clause is omitted, then the PL/SQL code, by default, runs as the definer of the PL/SQL code. This default setting is indicated in the preceding syntax by the underlining of the keyword DEFINER. PL/SQL executing under definer's rights means that the PL/SQL code has all the privileges associated with the owner/creator of the procedural code. Executing the PL/SQL code under invoker's rights means that the code runs with the privileges associated with the user calling it.

In Oracle RDBMS environments prior to Oracle8i, stored subprograms always execute with definer rights.

8.1.6 REPLACING A PROCEDURE OR FUNCTION

If a PL/SQL procedure or function already exists, it can be modified using the following syntax:

```
CREATE OR REPLACE PROCEDURE procedure_name[(arguments)] ...
CREATE OR REPLACE FUNCTION function_name[(arguments)] ...
```

The CREATE OR REPLACE statement creates the PL/SQL code if it does not exist, and overwrites existing code.

8.1.7 SPECIFYING ARGUMENTS

A PL/SQL procedure or function may specify zero, one, or more arguments.[2] Parameters are declared as a comma-separated list of argument name and data type pairs. The data type is specified without a precision.

```
CREATE PROCEDURE proc(param1 boolean, param2 varchar2)
IS
BEGIN
  :
END;
```

LISTING 8.3 Specifying procedure arguments

The parameter declarations declared in the procedure heading, such as param1 and param2, are called *formal parameters*.

In Listing 8.3, the procedure has two parameters:

- Param1 is the name for an argument that accepts a boolean value as input.
- Param2 is the name for an argument that accepts a variable-length character string as input, up to a maximum length of 32,676 characters.

Listing 8.4 shows a function accepting two input parameters, the first a boolean value, the second a variable-length character string. The function returns a number value.

```
CREATE FUNCTION func(param1 boolean, param2 varchar2)
RETURN number
IS
  result  number;
BEGIN
 :
 RETURN result;
END;
```

LISTING 8.4 Specifying function arguments and return type

[2]Since Oracle8 Version 8.0, the parentheses are optional when calling a no argument procedure. However, you must omit the parentheses if the PL/SQL code is being called in an Oracle7 database.

8.1.7.1 Parameter Modes. By default, if not explicitly specified, PL/SQL parameters are read-only input parameters. The parameter mode can be explicitly specified between the parameter name and its data type as one of the following:

- `IN` for a read-only input argument.
- `OUT` for a write-only output argument.
- `IN OUT` for an input/output argument.

Unlike many traditional third-generation languages, an IN parameter is passed by reference, where a pointer to the actual parameter is given to the corresponding formal parameter. However, the PL/SQL compiler does not allow you to modify the value of an input parameter.

Parameters declared as an OUT or an IN OUT variable are passed by value. Output parameters are passed as a copy in order to avoid the data inconsistencies that can arise under exception conditions during subprogram execution. If the subprogram exits normally, the result values from the formal parameters are copied into their corresponding actual parameters.

For Web-based applications, performance is a primary goal of any application design. So, if parameters hold large amounts of data, such as collections, records, and instances of object types, the copying that occurs with output arguments can incur the overhead of slower execution, and the consumption of additional memory. You can use the NOCOPY hint, which is placed after the parameter mode, to request that the PL/SQL compiler pass OUT and IN OUT parameters by reference, and thus provide performance gains.[3] The NOCOPY option is merely a hint, and the compiler may choose to ignore it under special circumstances; for example, when implicit data type conversion is required between the actual and formal parameters.

Listing 8.5 shows examples of declaring and using the various parameter-passing modes.

```
CREATE PROCEDURE proc(param1 IN boolean,
                      param2 OUT varchar2,
                      param3 IN OUT number)
IS
BEGIN
  :
END;
```

LISTING 8.5 Specifying arguments modes

[3]The NOCOPY feature has been added to Oracle8i versions.

Parameters declared as IN cannot be modified in the body of the PL/SQL block. The PL/SQL compiler generates an error if you attempt to assign a value to an input-only argument. The compiler also flags an error if the code attempts to read the contents of an output-only parameter before it is assigned a value. All SQL and PL/SQL data types, predefined and user-defined types, can be used in the definition of an argument.

8.1.7.2 Using the NOCOPY Hint. The NOCOPY hint is best used when passing large-volume structures like collections in the form of index-by tables, nested tables, or varying arrays. Listing 8.6 shows a PL/SQL block calling two different but functionally equivalent procedures to demonstrate the performance gains of using the NOCOPY hint with a collection parameter type.

The first of the two procedures, `set_discount1`, accepts an IN OUT nested table parameter, called `tab`, *without* using the NOCOPY hint. The procedure loops through the table, modifying the discount field of object instances in each element.

```
PROCEDURE set_discount1 (tab IN OUT sales_item_nt_t) IS
BEGIN
  FOR i IN 1..tab.count
  LOOP
    tab(i).discount := 5;
  END LOOP;
END;
```

The second of the two procedures, `set_discount2`, accepts an IN OUT parameter that *uses* the NOCOPY hint.

```
PROCEDURE set_discount2 (tab IN OUT NOCOPY sales_item_nt_t) IS
BEGIN
  FOR i IN 1..tab.count
  LOOP
    tab(i).discount := 6;
  END LOOP;
END;
```

The PL/SQL block used to invoke the above procedures is:

```
01: DECLARE
02:   t1 number;
03:   t2 number;
04:   t3 number;
05:   products  sales_item_nt_t;
06: BEGIN
07:    products := sales_item_nt_t(
08:            sales_item_t(1, 'Java Patterns',
09:                         49.90, 10, null,
10:                         'BK', null, null)); -- initialize
11:    products.EXTEND(9999, 1);
12:    DBMS_OUTPUT.PUT_LINE('Array has '||products.count||
       'entries');
13:    --
14:    t1 := dbms_utility.get_time;
15:    set_discount1(products);  -- pass as IN OUT parameter
16:    t2 := dbms_utility.get_time;
17:    set_discount2(products);  -- pass as IN OUT NOCOPY parameter
18:    t3 := dbms_utility.get_time;
19:    --
20:    DBMS_OUTPUT.PUT_LINE('Call Duration (100th of a secs)');
21:    DBMS_OUTPUT.PUT_LINE('-------------------------------');
22:    DBMS_OUTPUT.PUT_LINE('Just IN OUT: ' || TO_CHAR(t2 - t1));
23:    DBMS_OUTPUT.PUT_LINE('With NOCOPY: ' || TO_CHAR(t3 - t2));
24: END;
```

LISTING 8.6 Performance passing parameters with/without NOCOPY

Notes on Listing 8.6:

- Line 5 declares the `products` variable as a nested table collection.
- Lines 7–10 initializes the `products` nested table with one entry.
- Line 11 extends the `products` table to have 10,000 entries; 9,999 entries are a duplicate of the first entry.
- Line 14 gets the current time in hundredths of a second (using a server-supplied PL/SQL function called `DBMS_UTILITY.GET_TIME`)[4] before calling the `set_discount1` procedure.
- Line 15 executes the `set_discount1` procedure, passing in the products collection *using a copy operation*.

---

[4] The `DBMS_UTILITY.GET_TIME` function returns the current time in hundredths of a second, and is used in this example to determine elapsed time.

- Line 16 gets the current time in hundredths of a second, after calling the `set_discount1` procedure, but before calling the `set_discount2` procedure.
- Line 17 executes the `set_discount2` procedure passing in the products collection *using a NOCOPY operation.*
- Line 18 gets the current time in hundredths of a second after calling the `set_discount2` procedure.
- Line 22 prints the duration, in hundredths of a second, to process an array passed in as a copy.
- Line 23 prints the duration, in hundredths of a second, to process an array passed in as by reference using NOCOPY.

If you were to execute the code example in Listing 8.6, the performance gains would be obvious. Running Oracle8i (8.1.5) on a 366MHz Windows NT platform with 256Mb of RAM, Listing 8.6 produced the following results:

```
-- NOTE: Sample output (will vary on different systems)

Array has 10000 entries
Call Duration (100th of a secs)
-------------------------------
Just IN OUT: 302
With NOCOPY: 4
```

8.1.7.3 Using Default Parameter Values. In the declaration of a PL/SQL procedure or function, an input-only and input/output argument may be assigned a default value. This feature allows you to call the procedure without specifying values for parameters with default values, if the parameter default values are desired. If you provide a value for a procedure parameter with a default value, the value provided is used and the default is ignored.

To give a default value to a declared parameter, you use the assignment operator := (or the keyword DEFAULT) after the parameter data type name, fol-

```
CREATE PROCEDURE proc(param1 IN boolean := true,
                      param2 OUT varchar2,
                      param3 IN OUT number DEFAULT 10)
IS
BEGIN
  :
END;
```

LISTING 8.7 Assigning default values to Pl/SQL parameters

lowed by the default value. The default value must be a literal value[5] or an expression involving only literal values and constant identifiers. For example:

In Listing 8.7, param1 is assigned a default value of true, using the assignment operator. The caller must specify the value for param2, it is a required parameter; and param3 has been assigned a default value of 10, using the keyword DEFAULT as an alternative to the assignment operator, as used in the declaration of param3.

8.1.8 PASSING PARAMETERS TO PROCEDURES AND FUNCTIONS

As already stated, a procedure is called using its name followed by values for each of the arguments. Any tool or third-generation language can use an anonymous block to call a stored procedure.[6] The anonymous block acts like a main method in the context of a PL/SQL environment.

```
01: DECLARE
02:    v_in1      boolean := true; -- initialized
03:    v_out2     varchar2(30);
04:    v_inout3   number := 10;
05: BEGIN
06:    proc(false, v_out2, v_inout3);
07:    proc(v_in1, v_out2, v_inout3);
08: END;
```

LISTING 8.8 Calling a procedure from an anonymous block

Listing 8.8 illustrates some important points:

- In lines 6 and 7, when calling the proc procedure, the target for the OUT parameter (param2 in Listing 8.7) and the IN OUT parameter (param3 in Listing 8.7) must be variable for the values returned.
- In line 6, the first call to proc provides a literal value for the first argument.
- In line 7, the second call to proc provides an input value for the first argument whose value comes from the local variable called v_in1.
- All argument values in a call are supplied using a positional notation.

Arguments with default values are optional, and do not have to be provided with a value when a procedure is called, when the default values are desired. If parameters with default values are commonly used, it is better to declare them last in

---

[5]Default parameter values can be assigned a value of NULL.

[6]Java would typically use a CallableStatement to invoke stored procedures. The Oracle JDBC drivers provide support for calling a PL/SQL anonymous block through a CallableStatement object. The CallableStatement is discussed in Chapter 10.

the formal procedure declaration so as to simplify the call syntax. The example in Listing 8.9 shows a procedure that provides default values for parameters.

```
CREATE PROCEDURE mycode(p1 in number,
                        p2 in number := 20,
                        p3 in number := 30)
IS
BEGIN
  DBMS_OUTPUT.PUT_LINE('p1 = ' || p1);
  DBMS_OUTPUT.PUT_LINE('p2 = ' || p2);
  DBMS_OUTPUT.PUT_LINE('p3 = ' || p3);
END;
```

LISTING 8.9 Procedure with default values

The call syntax for PL/SQL subprograms supports two styles of parameter passing notation:

- Positional notation
- Named notation

You can combine positional and named notation syntax. Listing 8.10 shows several calls to the procedure `mycode`, declared in Listing 8.9, using the different notational styles to provided parameter values.

```
01: CREATE PROCEDURE main IS   -- no arguments
02: BEGIN
03:    mycode(1);   -- 1st argument is required
04:    mycode(1, 2);
05:    mycode(1, 2, 3);
06:    mycode(100, p3 => 300); -- named notation
07: END;
```

LISTING 8.10 Parameter passing mechanisms in PL/SQL

Notes on Listing 8.10:

- In Line 3, the code provides a value for the first parameter, as required. Values for parameters 2 and 3 are omitted in the actual call, causing default values in the procedure definition to be assigned to them. The resulting output from the procedure is:

```
p1 = 1
p2 = 20
p3 = 30
```

- Line 4 passes values to parameters 1 and 2, using positional notation. Parameters are passed by position as a comma-separated list of values. The output results show that the third parameter retains its default value:

```
p1 = 1
p2 = 2
p3 = 30
```

- Line 5 also passes parameters by position, for all three values. The output results shows the corresponding input values:

```
p1 = 1
p2 = 2
p3 = 3
```

- The call in line 6 shows how to pass a value to the third argument, bypassing the need to specify a value for the second, which is assigned its default value.
- Line 6 uses a mix of values passed by position for argument 1, and by named notation for argument 3. The results show that parameter 2 maintains its default value:

```
p1 = 100
p2 = 20
p3 = 300
```

Using named notation requires that the caller know the name of the formal parameter and use the PL/SQL *association* operator (=>) to link the argument value with its parameter by name.

8.1.8.1 Example of using a PL/SQL Function in PL/SQL. In Australia, the population voted for a government that promised tax reform. The tax reform introduced a new Goods and Services Tax, called the GST. The GST is similar to the sales tax in the United States, or the value-added tax (VAT) in the United Kingdom. Listing 8.11 shows an example of a function used to calculate the GST to return 10 percent of the input argument.

```
CREATE OR REPLACE FUNCTION gst(p_val NUMBER) RETURN
NUMBER
IS
BEGIN
  RETURN p_val * 0.10;
END;
```

LISTING 8.11 User-defined tax function

```
 1: CREATE PROCEDURE calc_tax(p_cust_id number) IS
 2:    tax_Rate number;
 3:    CURSOR order_csr IS
 4:       SELECT id, total_cost
 5:       FROM cust_order
 6:       WHERE cust_id = p_cust_id;
 7: BEGIN
 8:    tax_Rate := gst(100);
 9:    FOR rec IN order_csr
10:    LOOP
11:       DBMS_OUTPUT.PUT_LINE(rec.id || ' ' ||
          gst(rec.total_cost));
12:    END LOOP;
13: END;
```

LISTING 8.12 Using the GST() tax function

The code used to invoke the tax function is shown in Listing 8.12.
Notes for Listing 8.12:

- Line 1 declares the input parameter `p_ord_id` to provide the search context for the cursor WHERE clause in line 6.
- Line 8 calls the `GST` function, passing in a literal value of 100. The return result of 10.0 is stored in the variable called `tax_Rate`.
- Lines 9–12 create a cursor FOR loop, implicitly defining the variable `rec` as `order_csr%rowtype`. It processes all order records for a given customer.
- Line 11 prints the order number concatenated with the return value from the `GST` function representing the tax on the `total_cost` of the order.

8.1.8.2 Example of using a PL/SQL Function in SQL. The code in Listing 8.12 can be further simplified by using the user-defined function in the SQL statement. This is one of the most exciting and powerful features of PL/SQL, and it enables you to extend the capabilities of an SQL environment. For example, the `GST` function can now be used in a SELECT, INSERT, UPDATE, or DELETE statement wherever a standard single-row function can be called. This capability is even more powerful when you realize that you can call a stored procedure written in Java that returns the calculated result.

Calling user-defined functions from an SQL statement is subject to some restrictions. The two simplest restrictions on functions called from SQL statements are:

- Arguments and return values must be valid database column data types.
- The function must not use an INSERT, UPDATE, DELETE, COMMIT, or ROLLBACK statement. However, you can use a SELECT statement within the function.

The SELECT statement example shows how to use the GST function to add the tax to the total cost column for all order records in the customer order table:

```
SELECT ID, CUST_ID, TOTAL_COST + GST(TOTAL_COST) PRICE_WITH_TAX
FROM CUST_ORDER;
```

The next example uses an INSERT statement in a PL/SQL block to add a new order item record to an order, using the GST function to add the tax to the item price.DECLARE.

```
DECLARE
  price    number := 100.00;
  qty      pls_integer := 1;
BEGIN
  INSERT INTO ORDER_ITEM (ORD_ID, PRD_ID, QUANTITY, PRICE)
  VALUES (100, 5, qty, qty*(price + GST(price)));
  COMMIT;
END;
```

The UPDATE example modifies the prices of all the items in all orders to include the tax value, by applying the GST function to each record in the order item table.

```
UPDATE ORDER_ITEM
   SET PRICE = PRICE + GST(PRICE));
```

The DELETE example removes all records where the GST function result on the price of an ORDER_ITEM record is less than $4.

```
DELETE FROM ORDER_ITEM
  WHERE GST(PRICE) < 4;
```

Each of the DML examples presented above shows how easy it is to put your own functions to work in the context of SQL statements. This technique can greatly simplify SQL statements, and provides significant improvements in query performance.

8.2 PL/SQL PACKAGES

A PL/SQL package is a way to group a collection of related procedures and/or functions.[7] A PL/SQL package is made up of one or both of the following:

- A specification part
- An optional body part

The PL/SQL specification must be created before the body, and contains public declarations and subprogram signatures only. The body contains the implementation of the methods declared in the specification, and may have private components that are not accessible outside the package body.

Oracle supplies many PL/SQL packages that are built into the database server, such as the DBMS_OUTPUT package used in various PL/SQL examples throughout this chapter. The DBMS_OUTPUT package contains many procedures and functions, of which only the PUT_LINE procedure has been used in examples in this book.

8.2.1 THE PACKAGE SPECIFICATION

The *package specification* contains all the public components, which include:

- Type declarations
- Variable or constant definitions
- Procedure or function definitions (signatures only)

The syntax of a package specification is:

```
CREATE OR REPLACE PACKAGE package_name IS
  [TYPE declarations ]
  [variable declarations;    -- public variables]
  PROCEDURE procedure_name[(args)];
  FUNCTION function_name[(args)] RETURN data_type;
  :
END [package_name];
```

[7]Do not confuse PL/SQL packages with Java packages. In Java, the class files are separate files that are logically grouped according to the package name. In PL/SQL, procedures and functions are embedded in a package to form a one physical unit of code, which is stored in the database. The PL/SQL package name has only one level, and must be used to qualify the name of the procedure or function invoked.

The procedure and function definitions found in the package specification define the functionality that must be implemented in the package body. This is similar to defining an interface in Java, in that the PL/SQL specification forces the implementation of the subprograms to be defined, but the implementation and rules for building a PL/SQL package are quite different from the implementation and rules associated with a Java interface. Type declarations, variables, and constants declared in the specification part are available to the body part as if they were declared the local body. A package specification can exist without a package body if the specification contains only type, variable, and constant declarations but no procedures or functions.

> To loosely compare PL/SQL with Java,[8] a package specification is comparable to a Java abstract class, although PL/SQL does not support inheritance. In the PL/SQL package specification:
>
> I. PL/SQL variables are analogous to Java public static variables.
> II. PL/SQL constants are analogous to public static final variables.
> III. Procedures are analogous to public abstract static void methods.
> IV. Functions are analogous to public abstract static methods that return a value of some type.
>
> The PL/SQL package body is conceptually similar to creating a subclass of an abstract class that must implement all the abstract methods defined in the specification.
>
> Conversely, a PL/SQL package is a cross between a Java package for explicit name resolution and a Java class for the implementation of the functionality.[9]

8.2.2 THE PACKAGE BODY

The package body name must be the same as the package specification name, and the body provides the implementation of the procedures and functions defined in the package specification. Therefore, a package body *must* contain:

- ❑ The implementations of all procedures and functions declared in the package specification.

The body may have optional private constructs, such as:

- ❑ Additional procedures and functions not listed in the specification part.
- ❑ Variables, constants, and type definitions local to the body.

---

[8]The comparison can only be a loose one, because PL/SQL, unlike Java, is not object-oriented.

[9]To call a PL/SQL packaged procedure or function, the package name must be specified. In Java you need to explicitly use the package name before a class if the package path has not been imported and the class is not in the `java.lang` package. PL/SQL has a package called `STANDARD` in which the functions and procedures do not need to be qualified.

The SQL syntax for creating a PL/SQL package body is:

```
CREATE OR REPLACE PACKAGE BODY package_name IS
  [TYPE declarations - private ones]
  [variable declarations; -- private ones]

  PROCEDURE procedure_name[(args)] IS
  BEGIN
    statements;
    :
  [EXCEPTION
     exception-handlers; ]
  END [procedure_name];

  :

  FUNCTION function_name[(args)] RETURN data_type IS
  BEGIN
    statements;
    :
    RETURN data_value;
  [EXCEPTION
     exception-handlers; ]
  END [function_name];

[BEGIN  -- optional package initialization section
   initialization-statements;
   :
 ]
END [package_name];
```

All PL/SQL constructs defined in the package body but not listed in the specification part are private to the package, and, therefore, can only be referenced from within the package body in which they are defined. The combination of public and private components gives the PL/SQL developer a way to encapsulate data and implementation details. In this way, the benefits of information hiding can be seen, and internal complexity can be managed.

Keep in mind that PL/SQL is a strictly block-structured language; so all constructs must be declared before they are referenced. In situations when two procedures are co-dependent, and one procedure must call another that in turn needs to call the first procedure, PL/SQL also provides a mechanism for a private *forward declaration*,[10] which is a declaration of the procedure or function signature only. Forward declarations of package subprograms must be defined in the pack-

[10]Procedures and function declarations in the package specification are effectively public forward declarations.

age body before the formal implementation of the subprogram, allowing the subprogram to be referenced before it is formally defined.

The package procedure and function code is contained within the package body. A package body may also have an initialization section, which appears at the end of the package body, after the procedures and functions. The package initialization section is executed once (and only once) for each session, when any public package construct is referenced for the first time.

The state, or value, of package variables is maintained for the duration of each database session, or connection. Although sessions and connections are related, a *connection* is a communication path between a user or application process and an Oracle database instance. A *session* is a specific connection of a user or application to an Oracle database. Each database session has its own copy of the package state, but the code for a package is shared. Data are shared among sessions by using database tables, inter-process messaging, database signals, or advanced queuing.

8.2.3 CALLING A PACKAGED PROCEDURE OR FUNCTION

To call a PL/SQL procedure or function, or reference a PL/SQL type definition or variable declared in a package specification, you must use the package name followed by a dot and then the name of the construct being used. The syntax elements for referencing package constructs are shown in Listing 8.13.

```
DECLARE
  -- declare a variable based on a public package type definition
  variable1    plsql_package_name.type_name;
  variable2    plql_data_type;
BEGIN

 -- read a public package variable (variable in the specification)
 variable2 := plsql_package_name.public_variable;

 -- set a public package variable (declared in the specification)
 plsql_package_name.public_variable := value;

 -- call a public package procedure defined in the specification
 plsql_package_name.procedure_name[(args)];

 -- call a public package function defined in the specification
 variable1 := plsql_package_name.func_name[(args)];

END;
```

LISTING 8.13 Using PL/SQL constructs

Notes on Listing 8.13:

- Line 3 declares a variable, based on a used-defined type defined in the package specification.
- Line 8 copies the contents of a PL/SQL variable, declared in the package specification, into `variable2`.
- Line 11 sets the PL/SQL variable, declared in a package specification, to the value.
- Line 14 is an example of calling a PL/SQL procedure declared in the package specification.
- Line 17 is an example of calling a PL/SQL function, declared in the package specification, whose return result is stored in `variable1`.

8.2.4 PROCEDURE AND FUNCTION OVERLOADING

PL/SQL supports the concept of procedure or function *overloading* by providing the ability to declare more than one procedure or function with the same name. The rules of overloading in PL/SQL are similar to those in Java, in that there must be at least one difference in the subprogram signature.

As was briefly stated earlier in this chapter, the *signature* of a subprogram is made up of:

- The subprogram name.
- The number, order, and type of parameters in the subprogram declaration.

The parameter types in PL/SQL signatures must belong to different families in order for the parameter to be of the overloaded procedure or function in the number, order, or data type of argument. Overloading can only be achieved if the procedure or function is declared in:

- A PL/SQL package specification or body.
- A declaration section of an anonymous block.
- A declaration section of a procedure or function.

A standalone procedure or function cannot be overloaded. As a simple demonstration of PL/SQL procedure overloading, the next example creates a package called `outp` which has several `println` procedures to emulate some of the features provided by the DBMS_OUTPUT.PRINT_LINE procedure, to support display of the values for different data types. The package specification is:

```
CREATE OR REPLACE PACKAGE outp IS
  PROCEDURE println(p1 varchar2);
  PROCEDURE println(p1 date);
  PROCEDURE println(p1 date, fmt varchar2);
  PROCEDURE println(p1 number, fmt varchar2);
END;
```

The package body is:

```
CREATE OR REPLACE PACKAGE BODY outp IS
  PROCEDURE println(p1 varchar2) IS
  BEGIN
    dbms_output.put_line(p1);
  END;

  PROCEDURE println(p1 date) IS
  BEGIN
    dbms_output.put_line(to_char(p1));
  END;

  PROCEDURE println(p1 date, fmt varchar2) IS
  BEGIN
    dbms_output.put_line(to_char(p1, fmt));
  END;

  PROCEDURE println(p1 number, fmt varchar2) IS
  BEGIN
    dbms_output.put_line(to_char(p1, fmt));
  END;
END;
```

Using the package is demonstrated in the following anonymous block:

```
BEGIN
  outp.println('This overloading really works');
  outp.println(sysdate);
  outp.println(10200.34);
  outp.println(to_date('10-JAN-99'), 'DD-MON-YYYY');
  outp.println(3450, '09,999.00');
END;
```

The output generated by the anonymous block calling the outp package procedure is:

```
This overloading really works
23-JUN-00
10200.34
10-JAN-2099
03,450.00
```

The next example shows the specification, body, and an anonymous block with the results to demonstrate calling an overloaded GST function, in a tax package. The tax package code example makes use of the outp package in the preceding example.

```
-- The specification: public declarations
---------------------------------------------------
CREATE OR REPLACE PACKAGE tax IS
  FUNCTION gst(p1 number) RETURN number;
  FUNCTION gst(p1 number, rate number) RETURN number;
END;

-- The body: implementation for public components
---------------------------------------------------
CREATE OR REPLACE PACKAGE BODY tax IS
  FUNCTION gst(p1 number) RETURN number IS
  BEGIN
    RETURN p1 * 0.10;
  END;

  FUNCTION gst(p1 number, rate number) RETURN number IS
  BEGIN
    RETURN p1 * rate;
  END;
END;

-- Testing the overloaded function
---------------------------------------------------

DECLARE
  price number := 222.00;
BEGIN
  outp.println('10% Tax of '|| price ||' = '|| tax.gst(price));
  outp.println('20% Tax of '|| price ||' = '|| tax.gst(price,
0.2));
END;
```

```
-- The results of the text
--------------------------------------------------
10% Tax of 222 = 22.2
20% Tax of 222 = 44.4
```

Overloading does not work if parameters in different procedure declarations are from the same data type family; for example, if you added the new tax function shown in bold.

```
CREATE OR REPLACE PACKAGE tax IS
  FUNCTION gst(p1 number) RETURN number;
  FUNCTION gst(p1 real) RETURN integer;
  FUNCTION gst(p1 number, rate number) RETURN number;
END;

CREATE OR REPLACE PACKAGE BODY tax IS
  FUNCTION gst(p1 number) RETURN number IS
  BEGIN
    RETURN p1 * 0.10;
  END;

  FUNCTION gst(p1 real) RETURN integer IS
  BEGIN
    RETURN round(p1 * 0.15, 0);
  END;

  FUNCTION gst(p1 number, rate number) RETURN number IS
  BEGIN
    RETURN p1 * rate;
  END;
END;
```

The compiler will readily create these package components without error, but the PL/SQL REAL and NUMBER data types are from the same family—the numeric family of data types. However, when you attempt to compile some PL/SQL that references one of the `GST` functions with a single numeric argument, the compiler detects the ambiguity. For example:

```
DECLARE
  price number := 222.00;
BEGIN
```

```
  outp.println('10% Tax of '|| price || ' = ' ||
tax.gst(price));
END;

-- The PL/SQL Compiler error message generated is:
--------------------------------------------------
DECLARE
*
ERROR at line 1:
ORA-06550: line 4, column 50:
PLS-00307: too many declarations of 'GST' match this call
ORA-06550: line 4, column 3:
PL/SQL: Statement ignored
```

Similarly, an overloaded function that differs only in the return type will also not work. For example:

```
DECLARE
   /*
   ** Local variables
   */
   date_of_birth   DATE := to_date('01-JAN-1982');
   years_old               NUMBER;
   months_old              VARCHAR2(100);
   /*
   ** Local Overloaded functions
   */
   FUNCTION age(birth_date date) RETURN number IS
     years number;
   BEGIN
      years := round(months_between(sysdate,
      birth_date)/12, 0);
       --
       -- Returns whole age in years as a number
      RETURN years;
   END;
   --
   FUNCTION age(birth_date date) RETURN varchar2 IS
     months number;
   BEGIN
     months := round(months_between(sysdate,
     birth_date), 0);
```

```
24:        --
25:        -- Returns whole age in months as a varchar2
26:        RETURN to_char(months);
27:      END;
28:      --
29:   BEGIN
30:      years_old := age(date_of_birth);
31:      months_old := age(date_of_birth);
32:      outp.println('Date in years: '||years_old);
33:      outp.println('Date in : '|| months_old);
34: END;
```

The PL/SQL compiler generates the error message shown below when it encounters the second declaration of the age function on line 20, indicating that the previous declaration of the age function on line 11 conflicts with the function declaration on line 20.

```
DECLARE
*
ERROR at line 1:
ORA-06550: line 20, column 4:
PLS-00305: previous use of 'AGE' (at line 11) conflicts
with this use
ORA-06550: line 20, column 4:
PL/SQL: Item ignored
```

8.2.4.1 Using Overloading in a PL/SQL Anonymous Block. The preceding example used local function overloading in an anonymous block. Listing 8.14 shows the use of procedure overloading in the declaration section of a PL/SQL anonymous block, known as overloading in a local block.

Here are the output results for the sample code presented in Listing 8.14:

```
str = Use the string overloaded procedure
d = 01-OCT-1999
money =  $10,982.78
```

8.2.4.2 Using Overloading in a PL/SQL Package. Listing 8.15 declares a PL/SQL package specification used to process items for a given order number that uses function overloading mechanisms. The package declares a private cursor in the body, in Listing 8.16, that is opened, processed, and closed using public procedures. The example employs encapsulation techniques by declaring the cursor in the body, making it private, which means that it is only possible to access

```
DECLARE
  PROCEDURE print(money number) IS
  BEGIN
    DBMS_OUTPUT.PUT_LINE('money = '||to_char(money, '$999,999.99'));
  END;

  PROCEDURE print(str varchar2) IS
  BEGIN
    DBMS_OUTPUT.PUT_LINE('str = ' || str);
  END;

  PROCEDURE print(d date, fmt varchar2 := 'DD-MON-YYYY') IS
  BEGIN
    DBMS_OUTPUT.PUT_LINE('d = ' || to_char(d, fmt));
  END;

BEGIN
  print('Use the string overloaded procedure');
  print(to_date('10/01/1999','MM/DD/YYYY'));
  print(10982.78);
END;
```

LISTING 8.14 PL/SQL procedure overloading in an anonymous block

```
CREATE OR REPLACE PACKAGE ord_item IS
 DEFAULT_BATCH_SIZE  constant pls_integer := 10;
 MAX_BATCH_SIZE      constant pls_integer := 100;

 TYPE item_rec_table IS TABLE OF order_item%rowtype
   INDEX BY BINARY_INTEGER;

 PROCEDURE set_batch_size(p_size pls_integer);
 FUNCTION  get_batch_size RETURN pls_integer;

 PROCEDURE open(p_order items.order_id%type);

 FUNCTION next(p_item_list items_rec_table) RETURN boolean;
 FUNCTION next(p_item_rec order_item%rowtype) RETURN boolean;

 PROCEDURE close;
END ord_item;
```

LISTING 8.15 Using overloading in a PL/SQL package specification

the cursor result data via calls to public functions or procedures declared in the package specification.

The code for the package body is shown in Listings 8.16a and 8.16b.

After you have created the package and stored it in the database, you can use the public package it constructs in the context of any PL/SQL block, such as the anonymous block shown in Listing 8.17. The example is annotated with arrows before the text to indicate the public package constructs referenced from the `ord_item` package specification in Listing 8.15.

Prior to Oracle8i, there was a limitation of 64K bytes on the total number of characters in a package body, but this restriction has been lifted. However, in

```
CREATE OR REPLACE PACKAGE BODY ord_item IS
  /* Local private variables */
  batch_size  pls_integer;

  CURSOR item_csr(p_order order_item.ord_id%type) IS
    SELECT * FROM ORDER_ITEM WHERE ord_id = p_order
      ORDER by ord_id;

  PROCEDURE set_batch_size(p_size pls_integer) IS
  BEGIN
    IF p_size <= MAX_BATCH_SIZE THEN
      batch_size := p_size;
    END IF;
  END;

  FUNCTION get_batch_size RETURN pls_integer IS
  BEGIN
    RETURN batch_size;
  END;

  PROCEDURE open(p_order order_item.ord_id%type) IS
  BEGIN
    IF item_csr%ISOPEN THEN
       CLOSE item_csr;
    END IF;
    OPEN item_csr(p_order);
  END;
```

LISTING 8.16A Using overloading in a PL/SQL package body

```
FUNCTION next(p_item_list items_rec_table) RETURN boolean IS
    more_rows boolean := true;
  BEGIN
     IF NOT item_csr%ISOPEN THEN
       more_rows := false;
     ELSE
       p_item_rec.delete;   -- empty the table
       FOR idx IN 1 .. batch_size
       LOOP
         FETCH item_csr INTO p_item_rec(idx);
         IF item_csr%NOTFOUND THEN
           more_rows := false;  -- set end condition
           EXIT;   -- terminate loop
         END IF;
       END LOOP;
     END IF;
     RETURN more_rows;
  END;

  /*
  ** The next() function is overloaded to allow for a single
  ** record fetch or an array table fetch
  */
  FUNCTION next(p_item_rec order_item%rowtype) RETURN boolean IS
    more_rows boolean := true;
  BEGIN
    IF NOT item_csr%ISOPEN THEN
       more_rows := false;
     ELSE
       FETCH item_csr INTO p_item_rec(idx);
       more_rows := item_csr%FOUND;
     END IF;
     RETURN more_rows;
  END;

  PROCEDURE close IS
  BEGIN
    IF item_csr%ISOPEN THEN
      CLOSE item_csr;
    END IF;
  END;
BEGIN
   /* initialize the batch size */
   batch_size := DEFAULT_BATCH_SIZE
END ord_itm;
```

LISTING 8.16B *Continued*

```
DECLARE
  -- used package data type for PL/SQL table
  item_list         ord_item.item_rec_table; → line 5 in
listing 8.15
  item_rec           order_item%rowtype;
  batch_count        pls_integer;
  v_order_id        order_item.ord_id%type;
  more          boolean;
BEGIN
  -- demo set the default batch size
  batch_count:=ord_item.DEFAULT_BATCH_SIZE; → line 2 in
listing 8.15


  -- but call get_batch_size function anyway
  batch_count := ord_item.get_batch_size; → line 9 in
listing 8.15

  IF batch_count < 15 THEN
     batch_count := 15;
     ord_item.set_batch_size(batch_count); → line 8 in
listing 8.15
  END IF;

  v_order_id := 100;
  ord_item.open(v_order_id); → line 11 in listing 8.15

  -- process records in batches
  more : = true;   -- ensure we loop once
  WHILE more
  LOOP
     more := ord_item.next(item_list); → line 13 in listing 8.15
     /*
     ** if more is false there may still be
     ** records to process in the PL/SQL table.
     ** Thus the loop is still attempted, and
     ** if there are no records the item_list.count
     ** will be zero, so the loop will not process
     ** any rows.
     */
     FOR idx IN 1 .. item_list.count
     LOOP
```

LISTING 8.17 Using PL/SQL overloaded package functions

```
        DBMS_OUTPUT.PUT_LINE(item_list(idx).id ||
            ' $' || item_list(idx).total);
      END LOOP;
   END LOOP;
   ord_item.close; → line 16 in listing 8.15

   -- process records a row at a time
   -- A cursor can be reopened
   v_order_id := 200;
   item_csr.open(v_order_id); → line 11 in listing 8.15
   /*
   ** In this case we can terminate the
   ** loop if the call to next is false
   ** because we get one row or no rows
   */
   WHILE ord_item.next(item_rec) → line 14 in listing 8.15
   LOOP
     DBMS_OUTPUT.PUT_LINE(item_rec.id ||
            ' $' || item_rec.total);
   END LOOP;
   ord_item.close; → line 16 in listing 8.15
END;
```

LISTING 8.17 *Continued*

general, it is a good idea to keep packages small, thus saving on the memory needed to keep the package available for sessions accessing its features.

8.2.5 EXTENDING SQL USING PACKAGE FUNCTIONS

A package function, like a stand-alone function, may also be used in an SQL statement, subject to the same restrictions that apply to stand-alone functions, such as the `GST` function example presented earlier in this chapter. Prior to Oracle8i (8.1.5), if you placed a GST function in a PL/SQL package, you were required to indicate the *purity level* of the GST function to the environment if you intended to use the packaged function in an SQL statement. Since Oracle8i, the PRAGMA is optional and the purity is checked at runtime, not compile time.

Using a compiler directive, a PRAGMA called RESTRICT_REFERENCES, after the function declaration in the package specification, indicates the purity level for the package function. The syntax of the PRAGMA statement is:

```
PRAGMA RESTRICT_REFERENCES(func_name, WNDS [,RNDS][,WNPS][, RNPS]);
```

The parameters to the PRAGMA are:

- The name for the function to which the PRAGMA is applied.
- A comma-separated list of one or more of the four-letter purity-level indicators listed after the function name. The four-letter indicators define the purity level of the package function.

The WNDS setting is the only indicator required in the PRAGMA; the remaining ones are optional.

The purpose of using these purity-level indicators is to perform a compile-time check that you have not violated the restrictions enforced when using a packaged function in an SQL statement. In Oracle8i, the PRAGMA is optional, but the runtime engine will perform the purity-level check for you, and will raise an exception for an SQL statement using the function that violates the restriction. In earlier releases of the Oracle database, the compilation process required the PRAGMA to be present for functions to be considered for use in an SQL statement, because the database SQL execution process would immediately fail any SQL statement using a package function without an appropriate PRAGMA. Table 8.1 explains the meaning of the PRAGMA purity-level indicators.

The compiler flags an error if a function violates any of the PRAGMA settings. The example in Listing 8.18 places the GST function in a package with an associated PRAGMA statement.

The `GST` function in the `UTILS` package can now be used in an SQL statement, as follows:

```
SELECT ord_id, total_price, utils.gst(total_price, 0.0825) gst
FROM  order_item
WHERE ord_id IN (100, 200);
```

TABLE 8.1 PRAGMA RESTRICT_REFERENCE purity-level indicators

PURITY LEVEL	EXPLANATION
WNDS	**W**rites **N**o **D**atabase **S**tate; i.e., the function does not execute DML or COMMIT and ROLLBACK statements.
RNDS	**R**eads **N**o **D**atabase **S**tate; i.e., the function does not execute a SELECT statement.
WNPS	**W**rites **N**o **P**ackage **S**tate; i.e., the function does not modify package variables.
RNPS	**R**eads **N**o **P**ackage **S**tate; i.e., the function does not read any package variables.

```
CREATE OR REPLACE PACKAGE utils IS
  FUNCTION gst(p_value number, p_rate number) RETURN number;
  PRAGMA RESTRICT_REFERENCES(gst, WNDS);
END;

CREATE OR REPLACE PACKAGE BODY utils IS
  FUNCTION gst(p_value number, p_rate number)
    RETURN number IS
  BEGIN
    return p_value * p_rate;
  END;
END;
```

LISTING 8.18 Package function using RESTRICT_REFERENCES

8.3 PL/SQL AND OBJECT TYPES

The discussion of DDL statements in Chapter 2 introduced PL/SQL creating Oracle object types. Object types are database structures used to store rich and complex data in the database. In addition to data, object types allow methods to be defined to perform operations on the data. In this part of the chapter, you will see how to create objects in PL/SQL memory by:

- Declaring variables whose data type is an object type
- Instantiating an object

To work with variables and methods in SQL object types, you use a dot notation in which the object type variable is followed by a dot and the name of variable or method. This is similar to the way you would access Java public variables and methods.

8.3.1 DECLARING PL/SQL OBJECT VARIABLES

Before you can create an object variable in PL/SQL, the object type definition must exist in the database. Executing the CREATE TYPE statement, as discussed in detail in Chapter 2, creates the object type definition. For example:

```
CREATE TYPE person_t IS OBJECT (
  ID              NUMBER(4),
  FIRST_NAME      VARCHAR2(30),
  LAST_NAME       VARCHAR2(30));
```

Once the object type definition exists, you can use the object name in the type of a variable declaration for:

- Variables
- Procedure and function arguments
- Function return types

You can also create an object reference variable where the variable is declared as a REF the object type name. The following simple example illustrates how to declare object variables using the PERSON_T object type:

```
DECLARE
  person          person_t;
  person_ref      REF person_t;

  FUNCTION get_person(v_id number) RETURN person_t IS
    a_person    person_t;
  BEGIN
    :
    -- query a person object into a_person
    :
    RETURN a_person
  END;

  PROCEDURE set_person(the_person person_t) IS
  BEGIN
    :
    person1 := the_person;
  END;

BEGIN
  person1 := get_person(10);
  set_person(person1);
END;
```

Here is the general syntax for declaring object variables, with additional complete examples shown in the next section:

```
01 CREATE TYPE object_type AS OBJECT ( … );
02
03 CREATE PROCEDURE procedure_name(param_name [REF]
   object_type) IS
04   local-var-name          [REF] object_type;
05 BEGIN … END;
06
07 CREATE FUNCTION function_name(param_name [REF]
   object_type)
08   RETURN [REF] object_type IS
09  local-var-name          [REF] object_type;
10 BEGIN … END;
11
12 CREATE PACKAGE package-name IS
13  package_var_name[REF] object_type; …
14 END;
```

LISTING 8.19 Declaring PL/SQL objects

Listing 8.19 shows that variables, procedure or function parameters, and return values can hold object instances or references to object instances.

- Line 1 is an SQL statement that creates the object type structure.
- Lines 3 and 7 indicate that the type for a subprogram parameter can be an SQL object or a REF to an SQL object. The REF keyword is indicated as optional by being placed within square brackets in the above syntax.
- Lines 4 and 9 are the syntax for declaring a local variable as an SQL object or a REF to an SQL object.
- Line 8 indicates that an SQL object, or a REF to an SQL object, can be returned from a function.
- Line 13 is the syntax used to declare a package variable as an SQL object or an SQL object reference.

PL/SQL does not let you access object attributes or methods via an object reference variable. The PL/SQL object reference variable is mostly useful for retrieving or storing the reference value in a REF column in the database.

8.3.2 INSTANTIATING OBJECT INSTANCES IN PL/SQL

You create an instance of an object variable by calling the SQL object type constructor as if it were a function and assigning the return result to the object variable. The SQL object constructor comprises the name of the SQL type and a comma-separated list of values for each attribute enclosed in parentheses. The code to create an SQL object for the `PERSON_T` SQL type is:

```
DECLARE
  person_obj              person_t;
BEGIN
  person_obj := person_t(007, 'James', 'Bond');
END;
```

The SQL object instances you create reside in the PL/SQL application memory until written to an object column or table in the database. The SQL object type constructor for <<**word missing?**>> must always be an argument value for each attribute in the object type definition.

```
CREATE OR REPLACE TYPE book_t AS OBJECT (
  author          VARCHAR2(80),
  publisher       VARCHAR2(40),
  year_published  NUMBER(4),
  isbn            VARCHAR2(30),
  category        VARCHAR2(40));

CREATE OR REPLACE TYPE music_cd_t AS OBJECT (
  artist          VARCHAR2(80),
  record_label    VARCHAR2(50),
  year_released   NUMBER(4),
  cd_nbr          VARCHAR2(30),
  music_style     VARCHAR2(30));

CREATE OR REPLACE TYPE sales_item_t AS OBJECT (
  id              NUMBER(6),
  title           VARCHAR2(100),
  full_price      NUMBER(6,2),
  discount        NUMBER(5,2),
  picture         BLOB,
  prd_type        VARCHAR2(2),
  book            BOOK_T,       -- nested BOOK_T type
  cd              MUSIC_CD_T, -- nested MUSIC_CD_T type
  MEMBER FUNCTION get_Discount_Price RETURN number,
  MEMBER FUNCTION calc_Discounted_Price RETURN number
);
```

LISTING 8.20 Object types created in SQL for use in PL/SQL

Listing 8.20 shows the declaration of three object types:

- The `book_t` – for keeping specific details of a book type.
- The `music_cd_t` – for keeping specific details of a CD type.
- The `sales_item_t` – representing a sales item, which can be either a book or a CD. The `sales_item_t` type uses the `book_t` and `music_cd_t`

types for two of its attributes. This is an example of nesting an SQL object within another.

Methods `get_Discount_Price` and `calc_Discounted_Price` are added to the object type later in this chapter. The key point discussed here is how to create an SQL object and operate on its variables, called *attributes*.

Listings 8.21a and 8.21b show the PL/SQL code using the SQL object type definitions created in Listing 8.20, by invoking the appropriate constructors to create each object.

```
-- Constructing a sales item containing a book

DECLARE
  sales_item1      sales_item_t;
  book             book_t;
BEGIN
  -- Create a Book object and embed in the book in a Sales Item

  book := BOOK_T('Bruce Eckel',      -- Author
                 'Prentice Hall',    -- Publisher
                 1998,               -- year published
                 '0-13-659723-8',    -- Isbn
                 'JAVA');            -- Category

  sales_item1 := SALES_ITEM_T(
                  75,                         -- id
                  'Thinking In Java',         -- title
                  45.95,                      -- price
                  20,                         -- discount
                  null,                       -- image
                  book,                       -- book object variable
                  null);                      -- this is not a CD

END;
```

LISTING 8.21A Creating an SQL object in PL/SQL: A book sales item

The example in Listing 8.21a is quite straightforward, in that the `sales_item1` and book object variable are based on their respective SQL object type definitions. The `book_t` constructor is used to assign a book object to the book variable. The `sales_item_t` constructor is used to create a new sales item.

The bold text in listing 8.21a indicates that the book object variable provides the value for the book object attribute nested in the sales item object. Alternatively, you could nest the `book_t` constructor inside the `sales_item_t` constructor, as follows:

```
DECLARE
  sales_item1       sales_item_t;
BEGIN
  sales_item1 := SALES_ITEM_T(75, 'Thinking In Java', 45.95,
  20,
         null, BOOK_T('Bruce Eckel', 'Prentice Hall', 1998,
                  '0-13-659723-8', 'JAVA'),
         null);
 END;
```

The next example is similar to listing 8.21a, but uses the MUSIC_CD_T object type.

Now that you know how to create an SQL object, you will want to know how you can manipulate the object attributes and invoke their methods.

```
-- Constructing a sales item containing a CD

DECLARE
  sales_item2     sales_item_t;
  cd              music_cd_t;
BEGIN
  -- Create a CD object and embed in the CD in a Sales Item

  cd := MUSIC_CD_T('Emma Pask',            -- Artist
                  'Morrison Records',      -- Record label
                  1999,                    -- Year released
                  'MR007',                 -- CD number
                  'JAZZ');                 -- Music style

  sales_item2 := SALES_ITEM_T(
                  76,                      -- id
                  'Emma',                  -- title
                  21.50,                   -- price
                  10,                      -- discount
                  null,                    -- image
                  null,                    -- this is not a
                                              BOOK
                  cd);                     -- CD object
                                              variable
END;
```

LISTING 8.21B Creating an SQL Object in PL/SQL: A CD sales item

8.3.3 USING SQL OBJECT ATTRIBUTES AND METHODS IN PL/SQL

Having created an SQL object and assigned it to a PL/SQL object variable, you can use the object variable like a handle (or link) to read or change its attributes or invoke the object methods.

8.3.3.1 Referencing the SQL Object Attributes. To reference the contents of an SQL object attribute, or invoke one of its methods, you use a dot notation similar to the way the one in Java. Here is an example of referencing an object's attributes based on the `PERSON_T` object type seen earlier in this section:

```
DECLARE
  person_a   person_t := person_t(10, 'Jackie', 'Chan');
  person_b       person_t;
BEGIN
  person_b.id := 20;
  person_b.first_name := 'Sue';
  person_b.last_name := person_a.last_name;
END;
```

8.3.3.2 Creating and Calling SQL Object Methods. A more comprehensive example is shown in Listing 8.22, based on the definition of a sales item object type and the body of the object type, which implements the two methods declared in the object type specification. The two methods are shown below:

1. `get_Discount_Price` returns the value of the full price multiplied by the discount percentage, rounded to the nearest two decimal points.
2. `calc_Discounted_Price` returns the value of the full price of the book minus the discount price returned by the `get_Discount_Price` method, which determines the effective selling price.

The function `calc_Discounted_Price` in Listing 8.22 calls the `get_Discount_Price` method.

> When you call an SQL object method without arguments, such as `get_Discount_ Price`, the parentheses are required.

To call one of the object methods using an object variable, you use the same dot notation as is used in accessing attributes. In this case, the information entered after the object variable name and the dot is the method signature. For example:

```
CREATE OR REPLACE TYPE sales_item_t AS OBJECT (
  id                NUMBER(6),
  title             VARCHAR2(100),
  full_price        NUMBER(6,2),
  discount          NUMBER(5,2),
  picture           BLOB,
  prd_type          VARCHAR2(2),
  book              BOOK_T,
  cd                MUSIC_CD_T,
  MEMBER FUNCTION get_Discount_Price RETURN number,
  MEMBER FUNCTION calc_Discounted_Price RETURN number
);

CREATE OR REPLACE TYPE BODY sales_item_t IS
  MEMBER FUNCTION get_Discount_Price RETURN number IS
  BEGIN
    RETURN ROUND(self.full_price * self.discount / 100,2);
  END;

  MEMBER FUNCTION calc_Discounted_Price RETURN number IS
  BEGIN
    RETURN ROUND(self.full_price - self.get_Discount_price(),2);
  END;
END;
```

LISTING 8.22 `SALES_ITEM_T` object type specification and body

```
DECLARE
  sales_item1 sales_item_t;
BEGIN
  sales_item1 := SALES_ITEM_T(75, 'Thinking In Java', 45.95, 20,
         null, BOOK_T('Bruce Eckel', 'Prentice Hall', 1998,
                   '0-13-659723-8', 'JAVA'),
         null);

  dbms_output.put_line('The discount for book: ' ||
                       sales_item1.title || ' is ' ||
                       sales_item1.get_Discount_Price());
END;
```

8.3.3.3 Saving SQL Objects in the Database. The next example creates a PL/SQL package called PROD, which will be used to demonstrate how to use SQL object types in PL/SQL and save them in the database.

Building the PROD Package

The `PROD` package is shown a series of code fragment listings:

- ❑ Listing 8.23a shows the PL/SQL package specification.
- ❑ Listing 8.23b is split into several sections for discussion purposes.

The PROD package body defines several methods for operating on the sales item table, and demonstrates using SQL objects in PL/SQL and how to make them persistent as object instances in the database, using SQL statements. It is a good example of how the bridge between the relational and object worlds occurs. The `PROD` package is quite complex, as it also illustrates:

- ❑ Additional examples of method overloading.
- ❑ Using SQL objects for subprogram parameters, and function return values.
- ❑ Using a REF CURSOR to retrieve a result set of object instances.

```
CREATE OR REPLACE PACKAGE prod IS
  TYPE sales_item_ResultSet IS REF CURSOR;
  PROCEDURE add_Book(p_Title varchar2, p_Price number,
                     p_Disc number, p_Book book_t);
  PROCEDURE add_CD(p_Title varchar2, p_Price number,
                   p_Disc number, p_Cd music_cd_t);
  FUNCTION get_Item(p_Id number) RETURN sales_item_t;
  FUNCTION get_Item(p_Title varchar2) RETURN sales_item_t;
  FUNCTION get_ItemRef(p_Id number) RETURN REF sales_item_t;
  FUNCTION get_Items(p_Title varchar2) RETURN
  sales_item_ResultSet;
  FUNCTION get_Books(p_Title varchar2) RETURN
  sales_item_ResultSet;
  FUNCTION get_Cds(p_Title varchar2) RETURN
  sales_item_ResultSet;
END;
```

LISTING 8.23A PL/SQL package specification

In Listing 8.23a, the declaration of the `sales_item_ResultSet` is a public type. All users granted execute privilege on this package can use the public type as the data type for any PL/SQL variable, by prefixing the type name with the name of the package in which it is declared. Also note that:

- The sales_item_ResultSet is also the return type of the functions get_Items, get_Books, and get_Cds, but because these functions are declared in the same PL/SQL package, the package name prefix before the return type of sales_item_ResultSet type is optional in this context.
- Function get_Item is overloaded. The first declaration accepts an input parameter type of number, while the second declaration accepts a variable-length character string.
- Both functions get_Item return a sales_item_t object, and get_Item-Ref returns a REF to the object.

```
CREATE OR REPLACE PACKAGE BODY prod IS
  PROCEDURE add_Book(p_Title varchar2, p_Price number,
                     p_Disc number, p_Book book_t) IS
  BEGIN
    INSERT INTO sales_item
           (ID, TITLE, FULL_PRICE, DISCOUNT,
            PICTURE, PRD_TYPE, BOOK, CD)
    VALUES (prod_Seq.nextval, p_Title, p_Price, p_Disc,
            null, 'BK', p_Book, null);
  END;

  PROCEDURE add_CD(p_Title varchar2, p_Price number,
            p_Disc number, p_Cd music_cd_t) IS
  BEGIN
    INSERT INTO sales_item
    VALUES (sales_item_t(prod_Seq.nextval, p_Title, p_Price, p_Disc,
                         null, 'CD', null, p_Cd));
  END;

  :
END;
```

LISTING 8.23B1 PROD package add_Book and add_Cd

Notes for Listing 8.23b1:

- The procedures add_Book and add_Cd show how you can receive an SQL object as an input parameter.
- The add_Book procedure inserts data into the sales_item object table using normal SQL INSERT statement syntax. The prd_type field is set to

the value BK, to indicate that the SQL object in the p_Book input parameter is meaningful when stored in the new sales item object.

- The add_Cd procedure uses the sales_item_t constructor to insert an sales item SQL object into the object table, setting the prd_type to a value of CD, and stores the SQL object held in the p_Cd parameter into the object column of the sales_item_t object.

The add_Cd and add_Book procedures use an Oracle sequence called PROD_SEQ to allocate the next unique number for the newly created sales item.[11]

Listing 8.23b2 shows an overloaded function called get_Item. The input argument for each function is used to form a different search condition in the query's WHERE clause. These functions allow the caller to look up the first sales item by an id or a title. The search by title could potentially retrieve more than one row. To keep the discussion simple, the functions use an explicit cursor to ensure that one row is returned.

Listing 8.23b3 shows the get_ItemRef function, a variation of the get_Item function, which retrieves an SQL object REF value for an object stored in an object table. The bold text shows the statements used:

- To read the object REF value in the select statement.
- The declaration of the sales_ItemRef object REF variable.
- The data type indicating that an object REF is returned.

The underlined text highlights the usage of the PL/SQL object REF variable to receive the object REF value for return to the calling environment.

Listing 8.23b4 demonstrates how you can use a REF cursor variable in PL/SQL to return a pointer to a result set. In Listing 8.23a, the sales_item_ResultSet type was declared as a REF cursor, as shown:

```
TYPE sales_item_ResultSet IS REF CURSOR;
```

Oracle PL/SQL provides the syntax shown immediately below to obtain a pointer to a work area, describing a result set, into a PL/SQL variable called a reference *cursor variable*.[12]

```
OPEN reference_cursor_variable FOR query;
```

The query defines the active set of rows,[13] and returns to the reference cursor variable a pointer to the first row of a result set in the cursor work area.

---

[11]Oracle sequences are discussed in Chapter 2.

[12]Cursors are discussed in more detail in Section 7.2.6 of Chapter 7.

[13]The active set is a set of rows that satisfy the query criteria, which constitute the result set.

```
CREATE OR REPLACE PACKAGE BODY prod IS
  :
  FUNCTION get_Item(p_Id number) RETURN sales_item_t IS
    CURSOR sales_Item_Csr IS
      SELECT value(i)
      FROM sales_item i
      WHERE i.id = p_id;
    sales_Item    sales_item_t := null;
  BEGIN
    OPEN  sales_Item_Csr;
    FETCH sales_Item_Csr INTO sales_Item;
    IF sales_Item_Csr%NOTFOUND THEN
      sales_Item := null;
    END IF;
    CLOSE sales_Item_Csr;
    RETURN sales_Item;
  END;

  FUNCTION get_Item(p_Title varchar2) RETURN sales_item_t IS
    CURSOR sales_Item_Csr IS
      SELECT value(i)
      FROM   sales_item i
      WHERE upper(i.title) like upper('%'||p_Title||'%');
    sales_Item    sales_item_t := null;
  BEGIN
    OPEN  sales_Item_Csr;
    FETCH sales_Item_Csr INTO sales_Item;
    IF sales_Item_Csr%NOTFOUND THEN
      sales_Item := null;
    END IF;
    CLOSE sales_Item_Csr;
    RETURN sales_Item;
  END;
  :
END;
```

LISTING 8.23B2 PROD package get_Item overloaded function

In particular, the reference cursor variable sales_Item_Csr is a weakly-typed REF cursor, because the definition of the sales_item_ResultSet type does not return a specific row structure. If you need to get a reference cursor to a result set containing SQL objects, then you must use a weakly-typed REF cursor. PL/SQL does not support the use of strongly-typed reference cursors of SQL objects. A strongly-typed reference cursor constrains the return type of the query to

```
CREATE OR REPLACE PACKAGE BODY prod IS
  :
  FUNCTION get_ItemRef(p_Id number) RETURN REF sales_item_t IS
    CURSOR sales_Item_Csr IS
      SELECT REF(i)
      FROM sales_item i
      WHERE i.id = p_id;
    sales_ItemRef REF sales_item_t := null;
  BEGIN
    OPEN  sales_Item_Csr;
    FETCH sales_Item_Csr INTO sales_ItemRef;
    IF sales_Item_Csr%NOTFOUND THEN
      sales_ItemRef := null;
    END IF;
    CLOSE sales_Item_Csr;
    RETURN sales_ItemRef;
  END;
  :
END;
```

LISTING 8.23B3 `PROD` package `get_ItemRef` function

match a specific record structure, and PL/SQL does not allow you to use an object type as the return type for a reference cursor.[14]

These examples are shown primarily as a reminder that you can use reference cursors in stored procedures to achieve better query performance by centralizing the query execution in the server.

Note that although the `get_Items`, `get_Books`, and `get_Cds` functions are all functionally equivalent, different result sets are returned. More specifically:

- The `get_Items` function returns a result set of all the items in the sales item table, books, and CDs.
- The `get_Books` function returns a result set of books only by restricting the object instances queried by the select statement to the prd_type of `BK`.
- The `get_Cds` restricts the query to return sales items where the `prd_type` is a `CD`.

There are many ways to implement this kind of functionality: all three functions could have been combined into a single parameterized function that accepts the type of product desired as a parameter value.

[14]Strongly-typed and weakly-typed reference cursors are discussed in Chapter 7.

```
CREATE OR REPLACE PACKAGE BODY prod IS
  :
  FUNCTION get_Items(p_Title varchar2) RETURN
sales_item_ResultSet IS
    sales_item_Csr  sales_item_ResultSet;
  BEGIN
    OPEN sales_item_Csr
    FOR SELECT value(i)
      FROM   sales_item i
      WHERE upper(i.title) like upper('%'||p_Title||'%')
      ORDER by i.id;
    RETURN sales_item_Csr;
  END;

  FUNCTION get_Books(p_Title varchar2) RETURN
sales_item_ResultSet IS
    sales_item_Csr  sales_item_ResultSet;
  BEGIN
    OPEN sales_item_Csr
    FOR SELECT value(i)
      FROM   sales_item i
      WHERE upper(i.title) like upper('%'||p_Title||'%')
      AND   prd_type = 'BK'
      ORDER by i.id;
    RETURN sales_item_Csr;
  END;

  FUNCTION get_Cds(p_Title varchar2) RETURN
sales_item_ResultSet IS
    sales_item_Csr  sales_item_ResultSet;
  BEGIN
    OPEN sales_item_Csr
    FOR SELECT value(i)
      FROM   sales_item i
      WHERE upper(i.title) like upper('%'||p_Title||'%')
      AND   prd_type = 'CD'
      ORDER by i.id;
    RETURN sales_item_Csr;
  END;
  :
END;
```

LISTING 8.23B4 PROD function returning result sets

Using the PROD package functionality

Listing 8.24 shows some PL/SQL code that invokes the PROD package to perform certain operations on the data in the sales item table.

```
01: DECLARE
02:   rSet              prod.sales_item_ResultSet;
03:   sales_item              sales_item_t;
04: BEGIN
05:   rSet := prod.get_items(:title);
06:   LOOP
07:     FETCH rSet INTO sales_item;
08:     EXIT WHEN rSet%notfound;
09:     dbms_output.put_line('Product Details: ');
10:     dbms_output.put_line('Id:          ' ||sales_item.id);
11:     dbms_output.put_line('Title:       '
                                ||sales_item.title);
12:     dbms_output.put_line('Author:      '
                                ||sales_item.book.author);
13:     dbms_output.put_line('Publisher: ' ||
14:                             sales_item.book.publisher);
15:     dbms_output.put_line('Full Price:             '||
16:          rpad(to_char(sales_item.full_price,
                             '$99,999.00'),11));
17:     dbms_output.put_line('Discount:               '||
18:          rpad(to_char(sales_item.get_Discount_Price(),
19:                         '$99,999.00'), 11)||
20:                         ' (@'||sales_item.discount||
                              '%)');
21:     dbms_output.put_line('Price (with Discount): '||
22:          rpad(to_char(sales_item.calc_Discounted_Price(),
23:                         '$99,999.00'),11));
24:   END LOOP;
25:   CLOSE rSet;
26: END;
```

LISTING 8.24 Example of PL/SQL using PROD package

The code in Listing 8.24 shows the use of the PROD package to access a result set of SQL objects. Notes:

- Line 2 declares a reference cursor variable based on the PROD package sales_item_ResultSet type. This returns a REF cursor to a result set of sales item objects.

- Line 5 calls the `prod.get_Items` function. The function call accepts a search value as input from the bind variable title (created externally to the PL/SQL block). The value in the title bind variable specifies the name of the product to be queried by the `prod.get_Items` function. If successful, `prod.get_Items` returns a reference to the result set of objects satisfying the request.
- Lines 6–24 show a loop to process the set of object returned by subsequent fetch calls to the REF cursor variable.
- Line 7 retrieves the next sales item object from the REF cursor.
- Line 8 exits the loop if the fetch operation in line 7 reaches the end of the result set.
- Lines 9–23 process the object retrieves by the last fetch operation. The code simply prints the state of the object using the DBMS_OUTPUT .PUT_LINE package procedure.

From the perspective of using an SQL Object in PL/SQL, several lines of the code should be noted:

- Line 11 shows how to reference the title attribute in the `sales_item` object.
- Line 12 is more interesting because it shows how to reference an attribute of an attribute that is also an object. The attribute of a nested object is referenced using a cascading dot notation. This is similar to forming a path to the innermost attribute where the dot is the path separator.
- Lines 18 and 22 are object method calls invoked by using the dot notation previously discussed. Keep in mind that an object method, when called, will always require parentheses after its name regardless of the number of parameters required.

8.4 EXCEPTION HANDLING IN PL/SQL

PL/SQL has a robust exception-handling mechanism that is somewhat similar to the Java exception-handling mechanism. In PL/SQL, exceptions are numbers, whereas Java exceptions are Exception objects. In PL/SQL, exceptions are *raised* and then *handled* in an exception section. (In Java, exceptions are *thrown* and then *caught* in a catch block.) Any exception, raised in a PL/SQL block but not explicitly handled is implicitly propagated to the calling environment, as is also true for Java. Unlike Java, which requires a throws specification on any method that could throw an exception, PL/SQL does not require any explicit declaration that a PL/SQL block raises an exception. PL/SQL exceptions can be raised in the following ways:

- By explicitly using the RAISE statement
- Implicitly, by the PL/SQL engine, if it detects a PL/SQL or SQL runtime error

The exception can be trapped using:

- A predefined name
- A user-defined name
- A specification that all exceptions be handled (WHEN OTHERS)

8.4.1 TRAPPING EXCEPTIONS

Exceptions are trapped and acted on within an EXCEPTION section that can be added to any PL/SQL code block. The syntax of the EXCEPTION section, in the context of an anonymous PL/SQL block, is:

```
BEGIN   -- some block
 :
 /* exception is raised somewhere here */
 :
EXCEPTION
  WHEN exception-name1 [ OR exception-name2 …] THEN
    action-handler-statements;
    :

 [WHEN exception-name3 [ OR exception-name4 …] THEN
    action-handler-statements;
    :
 …]

 [WHEN OTHERS THEN
    action-handler-statements;
    :
 …]

END;  -- some block
```

The EXCEPTION section, when added to a PL/SQL block, should contain at least one *exception handler*. The syntax structure for a PL/SQL exception handler is:

```
WHEN exception-name1 [ OR exception-name2 …] THEN
    action-handler-statements;
```

An exception handler consists of the following element:

- A heading that includes the keyword WHEN followed by the exception identifier name and the keyword THEN.

- One or more PL/SQL statements, called *action handler statements*, to perform the required error-handling logic in the syntax shown.

Here is some pseudo-code showing how to declare a user-defined exception identifier (discussed in the next section) called `some_error`. The code raises, traps, and handles the exception.

```
DECLARE
  some_error  exception;
BEGIN
  IF the error occurred THEN
     RAISE some_error;
  END IF;
  :
EXCEPTION
  WHEN some_error THEN
    DBMS_OUTPUT.PUT_LINE('An error occurred');
END;
```

Additional exception handlers are added by repeating the exception handler code structure after the action statements of the previous exception handler. For example:

```
DECLARE
  some_error          exception;
  some_other_error          exception;
BEGIN
  IF the error occurred THEN
     RAISE some_error;
  END IF;
  :
  IF another error occurred THEN
     RAISE some_other_error;
  END IF;
  :
EXCEPTION
  WHEN some_error THEN
    DBMS_OUTPUT.PUT_LINE('Some error occurred');

  WHEN some_other_error THEN
    DBMS_OUTPUT.PUT_LINE('Some other error occurred');

END;
```

If you want more one exception to be handled in the same way, you can use a single exception handler to trap more than one exception. You achieve this by including a list of exception identifier names separated by the keyword OR in the exception handler heading. For example:

```
DECLARE
  some_error              exception;
  some_other_error        exception;
BEGIN
  IF the error occurred THEN
     RAISE some_error;
  END IF;
  :
  IF another error occurred THEN
     RAISE some_other_error;
  END IF;
  :
EXCEPTION
  WHEN some_error OR some_other_error THEN
    DBMS_OUTPUT.PUT_LINE('Some OR Some other error
occurred');

END;
```

At runtime, when an exception is raised within the PL/SQL block, the exception handler with the matching exception identifier name found in its WHEN clause is executed. After the exception handler executes, the PL/SQL block is exited.

8.4.2 PREDEFINED EXCEPTIONS

A *predefined exception* is an exception whose name is implicitly defined by the PL/SQL compiler and automatically associated with a common PL/SQL or SQL statement error code. For example:

- NO_DATA_FOUND is the exception identifier for the condition arising from executing a SELECT statement that does not fetch any rows, or that has come to the end of its result set.
- TOO_MANY_ROWS is a predefined exception identifier for the condition that a single-row SELECT statement returns more than one record.

The example shows how to trap predefined exceptions using more than one exception handler section, each with its own actions.

```
DECLARE
  product_title          sales_item.title%type;
BEGIN
  /*
  ** Get the title for product 1002
  */
  SELECT title INTO product_title
  FROM SALES_ITEM
  WHERE id = 1002;  -- generated NO_DATA_FOUND when
executed

  /*
  ** Next line is not executed as control
  ** passes to exception section when an
  ** exception occurs
  */
  DBMS_OUTPUT.PUT_LINE(product_title);

EXCEPTION
  WHEN no_data_found THEN  -- predefined exception
    DBMS_OUTPUT.PUT_LINE('Product does not exist');
  WHEN too_many_rows THEN
    DBMS_OUTPUT.PUT_LINE('Duplicate product record');
END;
```

8.4.3 USER-DEFINED EXCEPTIONS

A *user-defined* exception is an identifier name that is declared by the developer. User-defined identifiers may optionally be associated with any specific Oracle database error number. Associating a user-defined exception with an Oracle error number allows the PL/SQL code to process non-predefined errors by a named association rather than by an error code. The following example illustrates the use of a user-defined exception based on a business rule requiring that sales item discounts not exceed a specific threshold of 30 percent.

The example in Listing 8.25 declares a user-defined exception called `invalid_discount` in line 3. The data type for the user-defined exception is the keyword EXCEPTION.

Additional notes:

- Line 9 checks whether the discount for sales item record is in a valid range of values.
- Line 10 raises an `invalid_discount` exception if the discount is not valid.

```
01: DECLARE
02:   max_discount              CONSTANT PLS_INTEGER := 30;
03:   invalid_discount   EXCEPTION; -- user defined
04:   item_id            sales_item.id%type;
05: BEGIN
06:   FOR rec IN (SELECT id, discount FROM SALES_ITEM)
07:   LOOP
08:     item_id := rec.id;   -- copy for exception report
09:     IF rec.discount NOT BETWEEN 0 AND max_discount THEN
10:       RAISE invalid_discount;   -- throw exception
11:     END IF;
12:     DBMS_OUTPUT.PUT_LINE('Item Id: '||rec.id||' discount OK');
13:  END LOOP;
14:
15: EXCEPTION
16:  WHEN invalid_discount THEN  -- trap user exception
17:    DBMS_OUTPUT.PUT_LINE('Sales Item ID: ' || item_id ||
18:                          ' has an invalid discount');
19: END;
```

LISTING 8.25 Trapping a user-defined exception

When the exception is raised, control is passed to the exception section in line 15. The only exception handler found advertises that it has trapped the `invalid_discount` exception, and so the exception handler executes the action to inform the user that a sales item has an invalid discount value.

In this example, if an exception occurs, the loop is also terminated. If you wanted the loop to continue processing additional records, and to print a report for each record whose discount is not valid, the code would need to be modified to localize exception handling in an anonymous block within the loop, as follows:

```
DECLARE
  max_discount              CONSTANT PLS_INTEGER := 30;
  invalid_discount          EXCEPTION; -- user defined
  item_id            sales_item.id%type;
BEGIN
  FOR rec IN (SELECT id, discount FROM SALES_ITEM)
  LOOP
    item_id := rec.id;  -- copy for exception report
     BEGIN
```

```
          IF rec.discount NOT BETWEEN 0 AND max_discount THEN
            RAISE invalid_discount;    -- throw exception
          END IF;
        EXCEPTION
          WHEN invalid_discount THEN   -- trap user exception
            DBMS_OUTPUT.PUT_LINE('Sales Item ID: ' || item_id ||
                                 ' has an invalid discount');
        END;
        DBMS_OUTPUT.PUT_LINE('Item Id: '||rec.id||' discount OK');
      END LOOP;
    END;
```

Although this latter example is not a very practical one, it serves to show that you can control the flow of code using nested anonymous blocks to localize exception handling around one or more statements. In this case, the loop continues to process the records in the sales item table even when the `invalid_discount` exception, if any, occurs.

8.4.3.1 Associating a User-Defined Exception with an Oracle Error.

A user-defined exception name can be associated with any Oracle error number. The Oracle error number may or may not already be associated with a predefined exception name. To associate a user-defined exception name with an Oracle RDBMS error, you do the following:

1. Declare the exception identifier name.
2. Associate the exception identifier name with an Oracle RDBMS error number. This association is formed using a complier directive called PRAGMA EXCEPTION_INIT.

These two steps can be done in the declaration section of a PL/SQL block or a package specification. The syntax for these two steps is:

```
user_defined_name             exception;
PRAGMA EXCEPTION_INIT(user_defined_name, error_number);
```

The first argument in the EXCEPTION_INIT pragma is the user-defined exception identifier name; and the second argument is an Oracle RDBMS error number to be associated with the name. When the Oracle RDBMS raises the error with the number listed in the PRAGMA, the exception can be trapped using an exception handler advertising that it will trap the associated exception name. For example:

```
DECLARE
  invalid_product_type  exception;
  PRAGMA EXCEPTION_INIT (invalid_product_type, -2290);
BEGIN
   UPDATE sales_item
     SET prd_type = 'XX'
   WHERE id = 75;
EXCEPTION
   /*
   ** Trap check constraint error by user-defined name
   ** not by error number
   */
   WHEN invalid_product_type THEN
      dbms_output.put_line('Error: The product type is not valid');
END;
```

This example traps an integrity error generated when the Oracle RDBMS detects that a check constraint has been violated. The generic Oracle RDBMS error number raised when a check constraint is violated is –2290.[15] This can be checked by executing the update statement in SQL*Plus as follows:

```
SQL> UPDATE sales_item
   2  SET prd_type = 'XX'
   3 WHERE id = 75;
UPDATE sales_item
*
ERROR at line 1:
ORA-02290: check constraint
(BOOKSTORE.AVCON_2449_PRD_T_000) violated
```

The Oracle RDBMS generates the following error message:

```
UPDATE sales_item
*
ERROR at line 1:
ORA-02290: check constraint (BOOKSTORE.PRD_TYPE_CK) violated
```

[15]You can check the generic error message for an Oracle RDBMS error by calling the SQLERRM function with the error number as its parameter. The following PL/SQL anonymous block shows an example:

BEGIN DBMS_OUTPUT.PUT_LINE(SQLERRM(-2290)); END;

This prints the following message: "ORA-02290: check constraint (.) violated."

The name BOOKSTORE.PRD_TYPE_CK is the fully qualified name for the check constraint defined in the SALES_ITEM table to ensure that the PRD_TYPE column must have a value of BK (for a book item), or CD (for a CD item). The PL/SQL code hides this error message by trapping the check generic constraint error, and replaces the Oracle RDBMS–generated error with a more meaningful message in the context of the business operation performed.

Using an exception name makes the code more readable. The alternative is to determine the error number in the exception handler and use an IF statement to take specific action. An example of this is shown in the next section, which discusses generic exception handling.

8.4.4 GENERIC EXCEPTION HANDLING TO TRAP ANY EXCEPTION

Trapping any error and determining its cause is possible using a generic error handler. A catch-all exception handler uses a reserved exception identifier named OTHERS. An exception handler that uses the OTHERS identifier to trap any exception must be declared as the last handler in the EXCEPTION section.

The next example demonstrates how to trap an Oracle data integrity error without creating a user-defined exception.

```
DECLARE -- nested block in exception handler
  product_idsales_item.id%type := 21;
  err_message     varchar2(100);
BEGIN
  DELETE FROM SALES_ITEM
    WHERE id = product_id;
  IF SQL%ROWCOUNT > 0 THEN
    DBMS_OUTPUT.PUT_LINE(product_id || ' sales item deleted');
  END IF;
  -- end of normal block
EXCEPTION
  /* catch an unexpected Oracle exception */
  WHEN OTHERS THEN
    IF SQLCODE = -2291 THEN   -- error code for integrity error
      DBMS_OUTPUT.PUT_LINE('Product with id: ' || product_id ||
             ' is referenced by another record');
    ELSE
      /* print out any other error message */
       err_message := SQLERRM;
       DBMS_OUTPUT.PUT_LINE(err_message);
    END IF;
END; -- nested block in exception handler
```

This example also introduces two Oracle RDBMS built-in functions that you can use to determine the error number and error message for the exception that occurred.

- The SQLCODE function returns the error number as an integer.
- The SQLERRM function returns the message as a string.

An alternative way to create and generate a user-defined exception is to use Oracle's RAISE_APPLICATION_ERROR procedure. The raise application error procedure has the following syntax:

```
RAISE_APPLICATION_ERROR(errno, err_msg [, trace]);
```

where:

- **errno** is a user-selected error number in the range of -20000 to -20999. The SQLCODE function returns this number if the exception is trapped in an exception handler.
- **err_msg** is a user-specified error message associated with the chosen error number. The SQLERRM function returns this message when trapping the RAISE_APPLICATION_ERROR in an exception section.
- **trace** is an optional boolean value of TRUE or FALSE, where FALSE is the default value if the parameter is omitted. Setting trace to TRUE causes Oracle to keep each message in an internal buffer. In this way, an error message stack trace can be created by appending more messages to the stack trace buffer. If the trace parameter is used, it must be consistently set to the TRUE for each call to RAISE_APPLICATION_ERROR in each PL/SQL block in the call stack. Using the RAISE_APPLICATION_ERROR procedure with the trace parameter set to FALSE clears the message buffer before new messages are added, and previous messages in the buffer are lost.

Here is a simple example:

```
BEGIN
   dbms_output.put_line('Started');
   raise_application_error(-20000, 'This is a forced error');
   dbms_output.put_line('Ended');
END;
```

The output results for the example, when executed in SQL*Plus, are:

```
Started
BEGIN
*
```

```
ERROR at line 1:
ORA-20000: This is a forced error
ORA-06512: at line 3
```

The output for line 2 is printed, but the statement on line 4 is not executed, because line 3 calls the RAISE_APPLICATION_ERROR built-in procedure to force the raising of an exception. The exception number chosen is –20000.

The trace parameter in RAISE_APPLICATION_ERROR is optional; since the example did not explicitly specify a value for the trace parameter, it was set to its default value of FALSE. Using the trace parameter with a value of TRUE is only meaningful if your code executes more than one call to RAISE_APPLICATION_ERROR. This is only possible if you do the following steps:

1. Call RAISE_APPLICATION_ERROR with trace = TRUE.
2. Trap the exception generated by the RAISE_APPLICATION_ERROR call.
3. In the exception section, call RAISE_APPLICATION_ERROR again, with `trace` = TRUE.

Here is an example that demonstrates these steps:

```
BEGIN
  dbms_output.put_line('Started');
  raise_application_error(-20001,
      'First error by RAISE_APPLICATION_ERROR', TRUE); -
- trace on
  dbms_output.put_line('Ended');

EXCEPTION
  /*
  ** Trap the error generated by first raise application
error
  */
  WHEN OTHERS THEN
     raise_application_error(-20002,
      'Second error by RAISE_APPLICATION_ERROR', TRUE);
-- keep trace
END;
```

The output generated for the example is:

```
Started
BEGIN
*
ERROR at line 1:
```

```
ORA-20002: Second error by RAISE_APPLICATION_ERROR
ORA-06512: at line 7
ORA-20001: First error by RAISE_APPLICATION_ERROR
```

The error messages are displayed in reverse sequence of occurrence. Stated another way, the most recent error message is listed first.

In effect, what you are doing is building an error trace back message list. You can use this technique to replace a previously generated error, calling another RAISE_APPLICATION_ERROR with a more meaningful error and setting the trace parameter to a value of FALSE.

8.5 TRANSACTIONS IN PL/SQL

Transaction management in PL/SQL is quite similar to the way you manage transactions in the SQL environment. The same rules apply as in SQL, where a transaction is started with the execution of the first DML statement and completes when a COMMIT or ROLLBACK statement is issued.

If you are using SQL statements, and PL/SQL procedure calls for making changes in the same application, a database transaction will span the procedure boundary. In other words, if you start a transaction with an SQL statement that is not invoked in a PL/SQL procedure, and then execute a PL/SQL procedure that also changes the data, then all changes made to the data by the SQL statement and the procedure call are considered part of the same transaction. In this scenario, any COMMIT statement executed by the stored procedure will saves all the changes made by the SQL statements and the procedure, and a ROLLBACK undoes the change made by the SQL statement and the procedure prior to the ROLLBACK being executed. The same rules apply if the COMMIT or ROLLBACK statement is executed after the procedure is called.

In another scenario, if a PL/SQL procedure is called before a transaction is ended, and the procedure fails with an unhandled exception, then only the changes made since the start of the procedure are implicitly rolled back. Any changes made with SQL statements prior to calling the failed procedure remain unaffected.

8.5.1 AUTONOMOUS TRANSACTIONS

Autonomous transactions are self-contained transactions that can be called during the progress of an existing transaction. The autonomous transaction feature is only accessible through PL/SQL by using a compiler directive called PRAGMA AUTONOMOUS_TRANSACTION in the declaration section of a PL/SQL block.[16]

---

[16]Autonomous transactions cannot be created in nested anonymous blocks.

Autonomous transactions execute in their own context, and if one is called while an existing transaction is in progress, the existing transaction is suspended for the duration of the autonomous transaction. An autonomous transaction must be terminated with a COMMIT or ROLLBACK statement; otherwise an Oracle RDBMS exception with the following error number and message occurs:

```
ORA-06519: active autonomous transaction detected and rolled back
```

An autonomous transaction is not the same as a nested transaction, which executes in the same context as an existing transaction.

The uses of autonomous transaction include:

- Auditing data changes and operations
- Logging events or errors
- Shadow copying of data
- Event notification

The boundaries of an autonomous transaction are determined by the beginning and end of the PL/SQL block in which it is declared. To declare a PL/SQL block as an autonomous transaction, you add the AUTONOMOUS transaction PRAGMA to the PL/SQL block declaration.

```
PROCEDURE message_logger(msg varchar2) is
  PRAGMA AUTONOMOUS_TRANSACTION;
BEGIN
  INSERT INTO message_log (time_stamp, text)
  VALUES (sysdate, msg);
  COMMIT;  -- This must be present, or an exception is raised
END;
```

If the PL/SQL procedure or function is contained in a PL/SQL package, each program unit that uses autonomous transactions must be individually identified. Although the example is shown in a procedure, the same syntax applies for a top-level anonymous block, procedures, and functions declared in a PL/SQL package body.

Here is an anonymous block that demonstrates the behavior of an autonomous transaction:

```
01: BEGIN  -- the main transaction
02:   INSERT INTO message_log values (sysdate-1, 'Started
        yesterday');
```

```
03:   message_logger('A procedure was called');
04:   ROLLBACK;
05: END;
```

Assuming that the MESSAGE_LOG table was empty, the INSERT statement on line 2 would insert the first row. A call is made to the message_logger procedure, which begins an independent autonomous transaction. The original transaction, or main transaction, started in line 2 is suspended.

The message_logger procedure inserts a row to the log table and commits the record. Line 4 resumes the main transaction, but performs a rollback. The data from the INSERT statement on line 2 are removed, but the row inserted by the message_logger procedure will be found in the message_log table.

However, since the main transaction is suspended to allow the autonomous transaction to execute, changes made by the main transaction, except for INSERT operations, may be affected by the operation of autonomous transactions. You can prevent the autonomous transaction from affecting a main transaction in progress by starting the main transaction as *serialized*. If you execute the following SQL statement as the first statement of the transaction, a serialized transaction begins:

```
SET TRANSACTION ISOLATION LEVEL SERIALIZABLE;
```

Thereafter, any changes made by autonomous transactions are not visible to any main transaction that may already be in progress. New rows inserted by the main transaction are not visible to the autonomous transaction even if the main transaction is not serialized.

However, you still need to take care that the autonomous transaction does not attempt to access any row modified by the main transaction (which cannot resume until the autonomous routine completes); otherwise a deadlock may occur. This can happen if you attempt to modify a record already changed by the main transaction (which has been suspended). The deadlock is detected by the Oracle database and the autonomous transaction is aborted.

In addition, you should take to care not to exceed the maximum number of concurrent transactions per database session. The maximum number of concurrent transactions per session is set using the TRANSACTIONS database initialization parameter.

8.6 JAVA AND PL/SQL: A COMPARISON

Many comparisons between Java and PL/SQL have already been made throughout this chapter. This section summarizes and highlights some of the more important comparisons, excluding flow control and basic variable declaration data types.

- Java and PL/SQL are interpreted and run in a portable execution environment. Java is an open standard, while PL/SQL is proprietary.
- PL/SQL is not object-oriented, but has some object-like features. Java is object-oriented.
- PL/SQL and Java share similar exception-processing models, where PL/SQL exceptions are numbers and Java exceptions are Exception objects.
- PL/SQL treats SQL statements as if they were native to the language. Java must use JDBC or SQLJ (or some other proprietary) technology to execute SQL statements. The tight integration of PL/SQL with SQL makes it a very efficient environment for processing SQL statements.
- PL/SQL is excellent at the procedural processing of data-manipulation operations performed on database tables. Java is superior at data manipulation stored in memory and number-crunching operations.

8.6.1 HOW PL/SQL AND JAVA INTERACT

Java uses the JDBC class library to interact with relational database constructs. To invoke a database-stored procedure or function, whether stand-alone or in a PL/SQL package, a Java program must use a `CallableStatement` object. Chapter 10 covers the use of the JDBC `CallableStatement` object in detail.

SQL and PL/SQL can call Java code stored in the database, if the Java code is saved as a Java stored procedure in Oracle8i. Oracle has tools that load the Java class into the database and provide a way to publish a call specification for each Java method or entry point stored in the database. The published call specification for a Java method resembles a PL/SQL procedure, function, or packaged procedure or function specification. The published specification provides an interface compatible with a relational SQL environment and Oracle's PL/SQL language. Thus, SQL or PL/SQL code can call stored Java methods in the same way as they would call a PL/SQL procedure or function. Java stored procedures greatly extend the capabilities of what can be done in the database.

8.7 PERFORMANCE CONSIDERATIONS

Application and data-access performance must be addressed when building enterprise applications, particularly Internet-enabled applications. Enhancements to PL/SQL have given it the edge over Java when executing SQL intensive operations in the database. In earlier implementations of Oracle8i, Java performed better.

The general rule is: Use PL/SQL for code that is predominantly SQL intensive, and use Java for computationally intensive activities. Keep in mind that with a lot of tweaking and good programming style, Java could well outperform PL/SQL is some circumstances.

8.7.1 CLIENT/SERVER APPLICATION PARTITIONING

Application partitioning is the process of dividing the application logic processing among several computers. *Distributed processing* is a more generalized abstraction of application partitioning. A major reason for using application partitioning is to introduce performance gains by loading processing tasks into an environment more suited to the task at hand.

Application partitioning can still be considered a way to improve application performance, even in a distributed application environment. Traditionally, application partitioning arose around client/server systems, but the concept can be broadened to be more abstract, and is generally applied to multi-tier application environments.

Stored procedures are a boon to database developers, because all the SQL processing can be handled in the database where processing is done best. As an additional gain, stored procedures minimize network traffic by eliminating the transfer of SQL statements, in addition to the data, between the client and server systems.

Application partitioning has also introduced new problems; developers have to be multi-skilled if more than one language and platform are used to develop an enterprise system.

Application partitioning with PL/SQL has traditionally only been possible in two tiers: the client and the database server. Oracle8i is designed to serve as an application server, and this gives the developer an environment that makes PL/SQL look like it can run on all tiers. Client-side PL/SQL is not suited to a thin-client architecture. However, Java is well suited for all tiers of an Internet architecture, which means that a developer can now choose one language, Java, for all the software written in the enterprise.

The main advantages of a pure Java solution for a development project are:

- Most of the Java code can potentially be executed anywhere in the network, except in the GUI presentation code, which must reside in a client.
- Developers need to learn only two languages: Java for all the processing, and SQL for data access.
- Properly designed Java class libraries can maximize reuse of development effort, reducing time to market, or implementation of new systems.

8.7.2 MINIMIZING NETWORK ROUND-TRIPS

Minimization of network round-trips is another goal for well-designed application code developed for Internet environments, and is part of the process of applying the principles of application partitioning. The use of Java gives you far more choice over where the code can be executed, while PL/SQL is primarily executed in the database. A thin client/browser does not support PL/SQL.

You can minimize the number of SQL statements a client application sends to a server if the SQL code can be packaged into a PL/SQL procedure. Then the client makes a single request to invoke the stored procedure, and only receives the result set data after the SQL code has been executed in the server. This technique is a simple yet excellent way to minimize network traffic and boost application performance.

8.7.3 TUNING DATA-ACCESS CODE

A developer who does not understand the database features available to write fast data-processing logic will find it all too easy to create poorly written data-access code using SQL. Writing SQL statements to achieve better performance varies widely from one database vendor environment to another. This is another reason to use more stored logic: Let the database expert write the database-access code in the vendor database environment, and use Java to interface with the procedures via JDBC. SQL performance must also be addressed, and is affected by the logical and physical design of the database. A bad design can get in the way of improving SQL processing, and thus can mean complete failure for a project.

Oracle has made significant enhancements to PL/SQL to help developers achieve maximum performance when using SQL in procedures. Here are some features you may want to explore further and take advantage of:

- ❑ Bulk binding for DML or bulk collecting for queries can be used for efficient data exchange between PL/SQL collection variables and related database tables.
- ❑ Array processing for DML statements.
- ❑ NOCOPY hint on parameters.

Many of these feature were introduced in Oracle8i, and do not exist in earlier releases of the product.

8.7.3.1 Bulk Binding. Bulk binding can be done for the INSERT, UPDATE, DELETE, and SELECT statements. The bulk binding features of PL/SQL give the language the performance enhancements needed for processing multiple rows in the context of any application environment, particularly the Internet. Listing 8.24 has been rewritten as Listing 8.26 to show how to use bulk collection, fetching, of data from the object table into a PL/SQL nested table collection.

```
DECLARE
   rSet              prod.sales_item_ResultSet;
   TYPE sales_item_list IS TABLE OF sales_item_t1;
   sales_items       sales_item_list;
   discount          number(5,2);
   sale_price        number(6,2);
   PROCEDURE print(s varchar2) IS
   BEGIN
     dbms_output.put_line(s);
   END;
   FUNCTION to_String(val number, fmt varchar2 :=
   '$99,999.00')
      RETURN varchar2 IS
   BEGIN
     return (rpad( to_char(val, fmt), length(fmt)+1
     ) );
   END;
BEGIN
  rSet := refc.get_items(:title);
  FETCH rSet BULK COLLECT INTO sales_items;
  CLOSE rSet;
  dbms_output.put_line(sales_items.count ||'
  Products read');
  FOR i IN 1 .. sales_items.count
  LOOP
    print('***************************');
    print('Id:         ' || sales_items(i).id);
    print('Title:      ' || sales_items(i).title);
    print('Author:     ' ||
    sales_items(i).book.author);
    print('Publisher: ' ||
    sales_items(i).book.publisher);
    print('Price:      ' ||
    to_String(sales_items(i).full_price));
    discount := sales_items(i).get_Discount_Price();
    print('Discount:  ' || to_String(discount) ||
                  ' (@' || sales_items(i).discount
                     || '%)');
    sale_price := sales_items(i).calc_Discounted_
    Price();
    print('SalePrice: ' || to_String(sale_price));
 END LOOP;
END;
```

LISTING 8.26 Using bulk collect features of PL/SQL

The example in Listing 8.26 does not explicitly initialize the collection size or elements prior to executing the fetch logic. The bulk collection operation of the FETCH statement dynamically performs initialization, and assignment of element values, for the collection object.

Notes for Listing 8.26:

- Line 17 is the same as in Listing 8.24, where the `:title` bind variable defines the data used by the query search. The result set is returned into the `rSet` variable.
- Line 18 replaces the loop in Listing 8.24 by using a FETCH statement with the keywords BULK COLLECT INTO followed by the name of the collection variable.
- Line 19 closes the result set.
- Lines 20–34 loop through the collection data, printing out the details of each object instance saved in the collection structure in memory.
- The `print` procedure is an example of using a PL/SQL procedure, local to the block in which it is declared, in the declaration section. It is a convenient procedure for this example.
- The `to_String` function is also a convenient function local to this block of code that simplifies the management of converting the number to a string and right-padding the number to the length of the format string value plus one.

If you wish to take advantage of the bulk bind features, you may also want to combine this with the NOCOPY option to minimize the overhead of copying collection data in memory from the calling code to the called code. The syntax for bulk collection can be used with a FETCH statement or a SELECT statement:

```
FETCH cursor-var-name BULK COLLECT INTO collection_var-name;
```

Or

```
SELECT column-name1, column-name2, …
  BULK COLLECT INTO collection_var-name1, collection_var-name2, …
  FROM table-name;
```

The following syntax shows how you can use bulk bind syntax to process rows in DML statements and return arrays without using loop flow control statements in PL/SQL:

```
FORALL index IN lower-bound .. upper-bound
   sql-statement;
```

Although the FORALL has an index, and upper and lower bounds, note that it is *not* the same as a loop in PL/SQL. Here is a possible example:

```
DECLARE
   TYPE sales_item_Ids IS TABLE OF number;
   sales_Items  sales_item_Ids := sales_item_Ids(1, 4,
10, 20, ...);
BEGIN
  :
  FORALL i IN sales_Items.FIRST .. sales_Items.LAST
    UPDATE sales_item si
      SET si.full_price = si.full_price * 1.1
    WHERE si.id = sales_Items(i);
END;
```

The example here increments the price by 10 percent for all the sales item instances identified by an id value appearing in the list of collection elements. The index variable i is used by the FORALL construct to index the collection for values to target each appropriate object instance or row in the sales item table. The underlined text shows that the FORALL statement uses the collection methods FIRST and LAST, respectively, to control accessing the range of values in the collection used by the update statement.

Using the syntax shown below, you can combine the FORALL statement with a DML statement that uses the RETURNING clause to get the values before or after the changes made by the DML statement.

```
FORALL index IN lower-bound .. upper-bound
   dml-statement
   RETURNING values BULK COLLECT INTO plsql-collection-variable;
```

This is a very powerful extension to the PL/SQL language, and if used properly, it can give PL/SQL a performance edge when using SQL for data processing, compared to Java using JDBC and SQL to process data stored in an Oracle relational database.

Be aware that there are several restrictions on the use of bulk binding and bulk collections, and therefore you are urged to consult the Oracle PL/SQL reference manuals for information about the restrictions that apply.

SUMMARY

This chapter completes the discussion of the rich potential of using Oracle PL/SQL in the database. It explained, with examples, how to create and use:

- PL/SQL stored procedures
- PL/SQL stored functions
- PL/SQL stored packages

You were shown how to use SQL object types with methods in your PL/SQL applications, and some performance features and considerations when using PL/SQL were discussed.

The section on PL/SQL exception handling should provide you with the understanding needed to build robust PL/SQL procedures. Oracle has provided a powerful vehicle for procedural SQL data processing through PL/SQL and has taken major steps to ensure seamless operation between PL/SQL and Java, and Java calling PL/SQL.

Chapter 9

Data Access with JDBC–Java Database Connectivity

This chapter introduces the JDBC class library and its use in the Oracle environment.[1] JDBC defines a standard API with which you can write Java applications to access any database in a consistent way.

JDBC is modeled around two key concepts:

- You load a vendor-specific JDBC driver to allow a Java application to connect to and interact with the vendor's database.[2]
- You write code using the JDBC API. Because the JDBC API is defined in a vendor-independent way, you are able to write highly portable applications.

This chapter covers how to:

- Load and use Oracle JDBC drivers
- Connect to and disconnect from a database
- Execute queries and process result sets
- Execute DDL, INSERT, UPDATE, and DELETE statements
- Manage database transactions
- Call stored procedures, functions, and PL/SQL packages

JDBC can be used in applications executing anywhere in your network. For example, you can use JDBC on:

- The client, in an applet or in a standalone application
- The Web server, in a servlet, Java server page, Enterprise JavaBean, or CORBA component
- The Oracle8i server, in a Java stored procedure, Enterprise JavaBean, or CORBA object

Java developers will find that Oracle's Java runtime environment conforms with the Java standards set by Sun Microsystems. Therefore, you only need to learn the programming techniques once, and you can apply them to any Java context. JDBC allows for extensions provided by vendor-specific drivers to allow access to features unique to each vendor's environment. Oracle extensions to JDBC are discussed in Chapter 10, "Oracle JDBC Extensions and JDBC 2.0."

---

[1]JDBC is a trademark name, not an acronym, but it is often used as if it meant "Java Database Connectivity."

[2]By comparison, an ODBC driver must be installed on a client, while some JDBC drivers can be downloaded from the network, which eliminates the need to install software in the client.

9.1 INTRODUCING THE JDBC ARCHITECTURE

JDBC technology, as depicted in Figure 9.1, provides a layer of abstraction for accessing relational databases. The abstraction is implemented using Java interfaces and classes.[3]

The Java application communicates with the database using JDBC calls that encapsulate the details of DBMS-specific access protocols implemented by each JDBC driver. The relationship of a JDBC driver to the Java JDBC application is shown in Figure 9.3. The driver consists of a set of classes that implement the interfaces defined in the JDBC specification. The JDBC API provides interfaces, such as DatabaseMetaData and ResultSetMetaData, which allow the Java code to query the capabilities supported by a JDBC driver, and allow you to build applications that can dynamically adapt to the features supported by the JDBC driver implementation.

The architecture in Figure 9.1 is suitable for a traditional client-server application running in your Intranet, where the client code for this two-tier architecture can be a Java application or a Java applet that connects directly to the database. The DBMS-specific protocol, such as the Oracle Two Task Common (TTC) protocol, is layered on top of other network protocols, such as TCP/IP, that facilitate establishing a connection between a client application and a specific server. However, the architecture is not suitable for an Internet application unless the DBMS-specific protocols are supported by the firewall.[4] A *firewall* is a server that acts as a gateway for network traffic that is placed in the communication path between the client and server. Acting like a traffic cop, the firewall may or may not permit a connection to be established between a client and server, based on a set of configuration rules. However, you may wish to deploy the application in a thin-client multi-tier Intranet or Internet architecture, as represented in Figure 9.2.

The architecture represented in Figure 9.2 is a typical three-tier arrangement in which a client application communicates with a Java servlet or Java server page (JSP) application running in a Web server using the HTTP protocol. The Java code in the Web server uses JDBC calls to access the database. The client could be HTML-based, a Java application, or an applet.

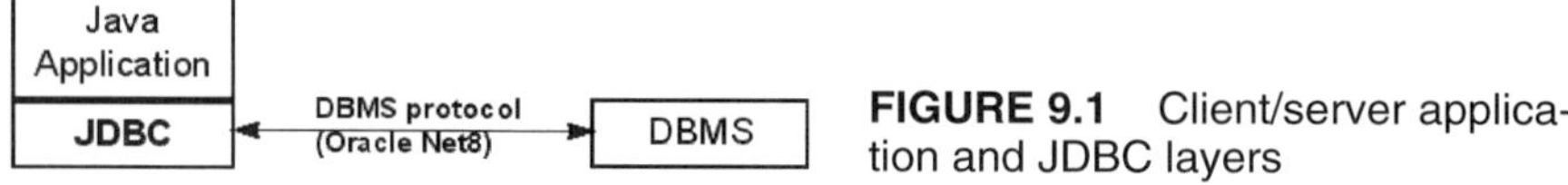

FIGURE 9.1 Client/server application and JDBC layers

---

[3]Java interfaces are a clean way to provide, and enforce, a consistently reliable call interface.

[4]Firewalls and their security implications are covered in Chapter 6.

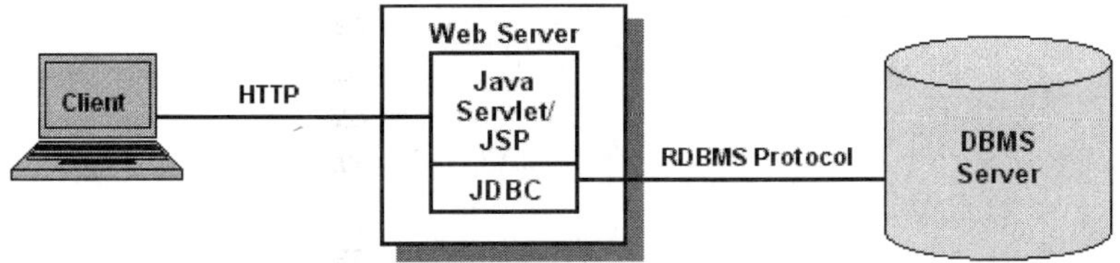

FIGURE 9.2 Typical Internet application architecture using JDBC

The Java servlet, or JSP, may also make use of other server-based technologies, such as an Enterprise JavaBean, CORBA, or operating system services, to access the database.

The JDBC API calls in the application architectures represented by Figures 9.1 and 9.2 require a vendor-specific JDBC driver to be loaded into the application and registered with the JDBC driver manager.

9.2 THE DRIVER MANAGER AND JDBC DRIVERS

A Java database application typically makes use of the following JDBC components:

1. The JDBC class library found in the `java.sql` package that has been part of the Java Development Kits (JDK 1.1).
2. The JDBC DriverManager class, which can be thought of as an object factory that creates JDBC objects to implement the interfaces found in the JDBC API. The driver manager interacts with the JDBC driver code.
3. Vendor-specific JDBC drivers, which provide the required classes to implement the JDBC API.

These three components are shown in Figure 9.3.

The DriverManager is a class defined in the JDBC API, and the JDBC drivers must implement appropriate interfaces in the JDBC API to conform to the JDBC standard. Figure 9.3 shows that the same Java application can load more than one JDBC driver to access different vendor databases. Each JDBC driver must be loaded and registered with the driver manager. The JDBC application can then request a connection via the driver manager.

9.2.1 JDBC DRIVER TYPES

JDBC drivers are classified into four types:

- Type 1 is the JDBC-ODBC bridge driver.
- Type 2 is the Java to native-API driver.

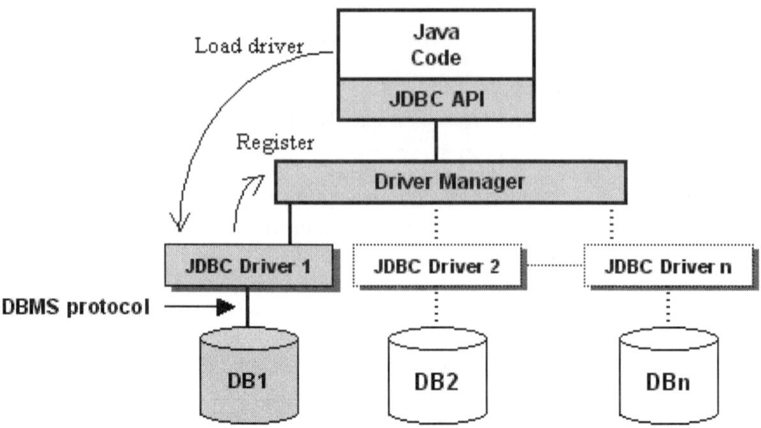

FIGURE 9.3 The relationship between JDBC API, driver manager, and JDBC driver relationship

- Type 3 is the JDBC-Net pure Java driver.
- Type 4 is the native-protocol pure Java driver.

The Type 3 and Type 4 JDBC drivers are more desirable for an Internet application because the JDBC driver code is written entirely in Java. Drivers written entirely in Java can be downloaded to the client without any need to install additional software on the client machine. Table 9.1 lists the four different driver types defined in the JDBC specification.

9.2.2 ORACLE JDBC DRIVERS

Oracle provides four different JDBC drivers, two for JDBC in client or middle-tier applications, and two for use when executing JDBC in the database Java Virtual Machine. Although this chapter focuses primarily on the JDBC drivers used by applications executing outside the database, here is a list of the four Oracle JDBC drivers:

- Two Type 2 drivers
  a) Client-side Oracle JDBC OCI[5] driver
  b) Server-side Oracle JDBC KPRB driver[6]
- Two Type 4 drivers
  c) Client-side Oracle JDBC thin driver
  d) Server-side Oracle JDBC thin driver[7]

---

[5]OCI stands for Oracle Call Interface, the standard Oracle C library code used by applications to access the database.

[6]This driver is used in the Oracle database server.

[7]This driver is used in the Oracle database server.

TABLE 9.1 JDBC driver types

DRIVER	CATEGORY	DESCRIPTION
Type 1	Driver	The ***JDBC-ODBC bridge driver*** translates JDBC calls into ODBC calls, which in turn use vendor-specific ODBC drivers to access the database. Using this driver, both ODBC binary code and database vendor ODBC drivers must be loaded into the host environment. This driver is considered beta quality and inappropriate for work in a corporate application, but it is provided in the java.sql package in the core JDK class library.
Type 2	Driver	The ***Java to Native-API driver*** converts JDBC calls into vendor-specific database API requests. For example, in Oracle the JDBC calls would make calls to SQL*net or Net8 libraries via Java Native Interface (JNI) calls, because core Oracle APIs are written in C. Like the Type 1 driver, this requires that vendor-specific API binary code be loaded into the application environment.
Type 3	Driver	The ***JDBC-Net pure Java driver*** translates JDBC calls into a DBMS-independent net protocol. A form of middleware in the server translates the DBMS-independent protocol into a DBMS-specific protocol, which is then able to connect pure Java clients to different databases. This is the most flexible driver, but is dependent on vendors implementing DBMS-independent protocols.
Type 4	Driver	The ***native-protocol pure Java driver*** is written in Java, with no reliance on vendor API code, and converts JDBC directly into a DBMS-specific vendor network protocol. Type 4 drivers can be used in any Java application or applet, and were intended to be downloaded into the client, such as a Java applet, to eliminate the need to manually install additional DBMS software in the client.

Although the term "client-side" is used to describe some of these drivers, they can be used by any client application, applet, or middle-tier logic, such as a servlet, JSP, or Enterprise JavaBean. The server-side JDBC drivers use Java code running in the Oracle8i Java Virtual Machine. The server-side drivers are mentioned in this chapter, but their use is discussed in detail in Chapter 12. Table 9.2 summarizes the four drivers and the differences between them.

The JDBC OCI drivers are typically used by standalone applications with access to the Oracle OCI library, which must be installed in the same environment as the application.

The thin JDBC driver was intended for use in Java applets because it can be downloaded from a middle-tier server and used without installing additional software in the applet environment. However, it is not limited to use in applets, and can be used by any Java application.

JDBC drivers come in different versions and provide support for either JDBC 1.0 or the JDBC 2.0 standard. The JDBC 1.0 API provides the basic functionality for data access, and the JDBC 2.0 API supplements the basic API with

TABLE 9.2 Summary of Oracle JDBC drivers

DRIVER	NOTES	REASONS FOR USE
OCI driver (client-side) **Type 2**	Uses JNI to call Oracle OCI libraries, making it require platform-dependent code (Oracle SQL*net/Net8) that needs to be installed.	Two- or three-tier standalone applications, not applets unless they are signed.
Thin driver (client-side) **Type 4**	100% pure Java code can be downloaded. Platform-independent; no additional software needed in the client.	Suitable for all code, particularly signed applets.
KPRB driver (server-side) In the DBMS **Type 2**	Uses JNI to call a C library that directly interacts with the internal SQL engine. It requires platform-dependent code.	Used by Java code in the database to access data in the local database.
Thin driver (server-side) In the DBMS **Type 4**	100% pure Java code, platform-independent, same functionality as thin client driver.	Used by Java code in database to access data in a local or remote database.

more advanced features, such as SQL object types. The JDBC 1.0 standard is part of the JDK 1.1.x class library, and the JDBC 2.0 standard is part of the JDK 1.2.x class library. Oracle JDBC drivers are provided for both JDBC 1.0 and JDBC 2.0. These are:

- Drivers compatible with JDK 1.1.x and the JDBC 1.0 standard. They include Oracle JDBC extensions, some of which are part of the JDBC 2.0 standard.
- Drivers compatible with JDK 1.2.x and the JDBC 2.0 standard.

There are JDBC drivers for the different versions of Oracle databases, ranging from Oracle7 (7.3.4) to the latest version of Oracle8i. The most current JDBC driver can be used with the earlier versions of the database. For example, the Oracle 8.1.5 JDBC driver can be used to connect to all the databases from Oracle7 (version 7.3.4) through Oracle8i (version 8.1.5).

9.2.3 THE JDBC DRIVER MANAGER

The JDBC API specifies a class called the DriverManager, used to manage one or more JDBC drivers that can be loaded by an application. The drivers loaded can be from the same or different vendors. Figure 9.3 shows a more detailed view of the model in Figure 9.1, to depict how the driver manager and a JDBC driver interact.

A Java application using the JDBC API must first load the vendor-specific JDBC drivers in order to access the databases. The JDBC driver, when loaded, is registered as available for use with the driver manager. After the driver is loaded and registered with the driver manager, the application can request a database connection using a URL[8] string identifying the driver and the target RDBMS. Refer to section 9.4.1 for a detailed discussion of the URL format.

9.2.4 LOADING A JDBC DRIVER

Remember that a Java application can load one or more JDBC drivers at the same time, from any number of different vendors, as depicted in Figure 9.3. There are several ways to explicitly load a JDBC driver into your Java application:

- ❑ Use the Class.forName() method.
- ❑ Use the DriverManager.registerDriver() method.
- ❑ Create a JDBC driver object using the vendor Driver class constructor.
- ❑ Use the `jdbc.drivers` system property.

In all cases, when the driver is loaded it always registers itself with the driver manager.

1. The first way of loading the JDBC driver is to use the method Class.forName():

```
Class.forName("oracle.jdbc.driver.OracleDriver");
```

Using the Class.forName() method dynamically locates, and loads the driver into the Java application.

2. Another way to load the JDBC driver is to use the method DriverManager.registerDriver():

```
DriverManager.registerDriver(new
oracle.jdbc.driver.OracleDriver());
```

3. You can also load the JDBC driver by creating an object using the Driver class representing the vendor JDBC driver. The Oracle JDBC driver class is called "OracleDriver":

```
import oracle.jdbc.driver.OracleDriver;

class JdbcExampleClass {
  OracleDriver driver = new OracleDriver();
  :
}
```

[8]URL means Uniform Resource Locator. The JDBC connection string specifies a "jdbc:" protocol, just as an HTTP URL specifies an "http:" protocol.

4. There is one more way to load a JDBC driver: Provide a system property, `jdbc.drivers`, whose value is a list of driver class names, separated by colons. For example, you can specify the property when running your Java program, as follows:

```
java -Djdbc.drivers=oracle.jdbc.driver.OracleDriver:
jdbc.odbc.JdbcOdbcDriver
...
```

As long as the specified classes can be found in the classpath, the driver manager automatically loads them into your program.

Regardless of which technique you use to load it, the driver is added to the list of available drivers known to the driver manager at runtime.

In all cases, the vendor's JDBC driver must be in the CLASSPATH at runtime.

The Oracle JDBC driver class library is found in the `oracle.jdbc.driver` package, which is located in a ZIP file called classes<n>.zip. The value for <n> represents the version of the JDK for which the Oracle JDBC driver classes are compatible. Oracle ships JDBC drivers in files called:

- classes111.zip—This contains JDBC drivers for JDK 1.1.x that provide JDBC 1.0 features and Oracle extensions. The classes111.zip file provided with Oracle8i also contains a package called oracle.jdbc2, which implements JDBC 2.0 functionality.
- classes12.zip—This contains JDBC drivers for JDK 1.2.x with JDBC 2.0 support.

Oracle JDBC class libraries are shipped with Oracle8i and JDeveloper, and can be downloaded from the Oracle Technology Network Web site (http://technet.oracle.com/).

9.3 OVERVIEW OF JDBC INTERFACES AND CLASSES

The JDBC 1.x API was first introduced in the JDK 1.1 release. The classes and interfaces in the JDBC API are grouped into the `java.sql` Java package.

The JDBC 2.x API is part of the JDK 1.2 (Java 2) platform, and beyond, has upward compatibility with the JDBC 1.x API, but added new features to the JDBC functionality.

The key JDBC classes, and interfaces, you are likely to use are:

- DriverManager—used to access the specific JDBC driver
- Connection—used to represent a database connection
- Statement—used to execute SQL statements

- PreparedStatement—used to execute pre-parsed and parameterized SQL statements
- CallableStatement—used to call stored procedures and functions
- ResultSet—used to process the results of a query

And optionally,

- DatabaseMetaData—used to determine supported database functionality
- ResultSetMetaData—used to determine row structure, column names, and data types for a result set returned by an SQL query

Most vendors provide extensions to these core classes through additional classes, or methods added to the driver classes, beyond those specified in the JDBC specification. The main purpose of the JDBC interfaces is to guarantee that the Java developer can consistently write the same code to work with any vendor database.

9.4 USING JDBC OBJECTS

Using JDBC classes follows a common pattern. The flow diagram in Figure 9.4 depicts the typical sequence and options.

The steps shown in Figure 9.4 provide a high-level representation of the JDBC objects used to access a database. After obtaining a Connection object, you can use it to obtain one of the following objects:

- A **Statement** object to execute SQL statements.
- A **PreparedStatement** to execute pre-parsed SQL statements that obtain values from, or return results to, application variables.
- A **CallableStatement** to execute code stored in the database, such as PL/SQL procedures, functions, packages, or object type methods, and Java stored procedures.

A **ResultSet** object is created if the Statement, PreparedStatement, or CallableStatement returns a set of rows because of executing a query.

9.4.1 CONNECTING TO THE DATABASE

You use the driver manager to obtain a database connection via the JDBC driver. The driver manager requires a URL string to make a connection via a registered JDBC driver. The URL string used to request a connection from the driver manager has the following generic format:

```
jdbc:<sub-protocol>:subname
```

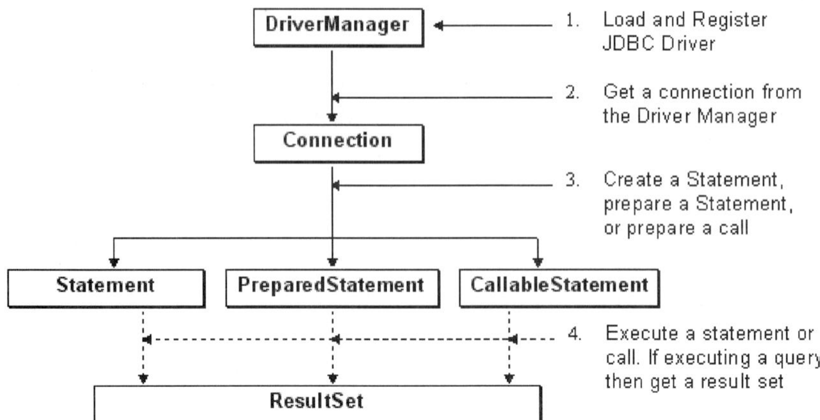

FIGURE 9.4 Diagram of Core JDBC classes

For example a URL used with the Oracle Thin JDBC driver is:

```
jdbc:oracle:thin:@host:port:SID
```

The `<sub-protocol>:subname` portions of the URL string are usually vendor-dependent names used to identify the vendor and vendor database protocol. As in the example above, subprotocol is `oracle`, the vendor name, and subname identifies the type of JDBC driver to be used. For example:

- **thin**—for the client-side/server-side JDBC thin driver.
- **oci8**—for the client/server-side JDBC OCI driver for Oracle8 databases or earlier.
- **oci7**—for the client/server-side JDBC OCI driver for Oracle7 databases.

The JDBC driver manager uses the URL subprotocol to find the appropriate JDBC driver, and the driver then uses the URL subprotocol and subname (and login credentials, if required) to create a connection to a database when requested by the application code.

9.4.1.1 Connecting with the Thin JDBC Driver. The URL connection details are arguments to the getConnection() method in the DriverManager class. There are several overloaded getConnection() methods in the DriverManager class which give you alternative ways to obtain a connection. For example, here is one way to obtain a connection (see Listing 9.1).

```
public class DBConnectExample1 {
  private static final
     String url = "jdbc:oracle:thin:@localhost:1521:ORA815"
  private static final String theUser = "bookstore";
  private static final String thePassword = "bookstore";
  private Connection conn = null;

  public void makeConnection() throws SQLException,
                                    ClassNotFoundException {
    Class.forName("oracle.jdbc.driver.OracleDriver");

    conn = DriverManager.getConnection(url, user, password);
  }
  :
}
```

LISTING 9.1 Get a connection using DriverManager.getConnection()

The DBConnectExample1 class uses the getConnection() method with a URL string, username, and password arguments. If the method succeeds, it returns a Connection object. The connection details appearing after the subname "thin" in the URL differ depending on the driver type specified. As in the example, when using the Oracle thin JDBC driver, the syntax for the connection detail is:

```
jdbc:oracle:thin:[username/password]@<hostname>:<port>:<dbsid>
```

After the driver type name **"thin,"** the fields separated by a colon, from left to right, are:

- An optional username and password separated by a forward slash.
- <hostname>—The @-sign followed by the DNS host name or IP address, identifying the server running the Oracle database instance, is required.
- <port>—The TCP/IP port used by the database instance to listen for connection requests.
- <sid>—The Oracle database service name (for Oracle8i databases) or system identifier (for pre-Oracle8i databases). The Oracle system identifier is known as a SID,[9] which represents a unique name for a database instance.[10]

[9]An SID actually uniquely identifies shared memory of an instance on a host.

[10]An Oracle instance is the combination of an allocated system global area (SGA) and the Oracle background processes that are created when a database is started. The system global area is an area of shared memory used for database information. These concepts are covered in detail in Chapter 5.

If the username and password values are provided in the URL, they override any login credentials supplied in a java.util.Properties object, or any String values provided in parameters of the overloaded getConnection() methods found in the DriverManager class.

The DBConnectExample2 uses the getConnection() method with a URL string and a java.util.Properties object containing the login details. The property object is required to be populated with the user name and password if needed for a connect request. For example:

```
import java.sql.*;
import java.util.Properties;    // this is a subclass of Hashtable

public class DBConnectExample2 {
  private static final
       String url = "jdbc:oracle:thin:@localhost:1521:ORA815";
  private static final String theUser = "bookstore";
  private static final String thePassword = "bookstore";

  public Connection makeConnection() throws SQLException,
                                  ClassNotFoundException {
    Connection conn = null;

    Class.forName("oracle.jdbc.driver.OracleDriver");

    Properties connProperties = new Properties();
    connProperties.put("user", theUser);
    connProperties.put("password", thePassword);

    conn = DriverManager.getConnection(url, properties);
    return conn;
  }
  :
}
```

9.4.1.2 Connecting with an OCI JDBC Driver. If the driver type is oci8 or oci7, in the JDBC URL you can specify an Oracle connect string that specifies a *network service name* (or *TNS name*).[11] From here on, the book will use the term "network service name" to represent the TNS name as well. The network service name is a logical name mapped to a listener process that services connection requests for one or more database instances.[12] The OCI driver requires Oracle SQL*Net/Net8

[11]The network service name is often called a TNS name. The acronym TNS stands for "Transparent Network Substrate." TNS provides a protocol-independent network layer for Oracle applications.

[12]See above, Chapter 5.

software to be installed and configured on the system executing the Java application. Before looking at an example of an OCI JDBC connection URL string, a bit of background is needed about Oracle SQL*net/Net8 configuration files.

Oracle SQL*Net/Net8 configuration tools, or a text editor, can be used to create the network service name, which is saved in a configuration file called TNSNAMES.ORA. The SQL*net Configuration files are typically located in the subdirectory related to the root directory chosen for installing the Oracle database software, know as the Oracle home directory (ORACLE_HOME). By default, the subdirectory that contains the SQL*net/Net8 configuration files for all releases of the Oracle database since Oracle7, except for Oracle8 (8.0.x versions), is:

`ORACLE_HOME/`**`network`**`/admin`

For Oracle8 (8.0.x) databases, the SQL*net configuration files are stored in:

`ORACLE_HOME/`**`net8`**`/admin`

On Unix platforms you can define the TNS_ADMIN environment variable set to the directory path containing the SQL*net/Net8 configuration files. In Windows NT, TNS_ADMIN is created as registry value in the HKEY_LOCAL_MACHINE\SOFTWARE\ORACLE tree. The Oracle Database Listener will use the value of TNS_ADMIN, if defined, to locate the SQL*Net/Net8 configuration files to resolve the service names.

If you use the Oracle JDBC OCI driver—the oci8 driver, for example— the URL string used to establish a connection is:

`jdbc:oracle:`**`oci8`**`:`*`[username/password]`***`@network-service-name`**

The JDBC driver passes the network service name, entered after the @ sign in the URL string, to the SQL*net/Net8 OCI software to obtain the connection. The SQL*net/Net8 OCI software looks up the network-service-name in the configuration files to obtain the host, network protocol, socket number, etc., used to establish a connection with a database listener process.[13] A typical example of a network service name entry, as found in a TNSNAME.ORA file, is shown below (the line numbers are not part of the contents of the file):

```
network-service-name =
(DESCRIPTION =
  (ADDRESS_LIST =
    (ADDRESS =(PROTOCOL = TCP)(HOST = hostname)(PORT = 1521))
  )
  (CONNECT_DATA = (SERVICE_NAME = db-service-name))
)
```

[13]An Oracle database listener process receives connection requests on a known socket/port number.

Example:

```
ORA815_DB =
 (DESCRIPTION =
   (ADDRESS_LIST =
     (ADDRESS =(PROTOCOL = TCP)(HOST = myhost)(PORT = 1521)))
   (CONNECT_DATA = (SERVICE_NAME = ORA815))
 )
```

Notes on the network service name:

- Line 4 defines how the client SQL*Net/Net8 software routes the connect request to a TNS listener servicing a database instance. It specifies the network protocol, such as TCP, the domain name or IP address for a server, and the network protocol port used by the database listener.
- Line 6 uses the CONNECT_DATA option to specify the service name used to identify the database instance name for the connection, or a system identifier (SID).[14]

When using the OCI JDBC driver with SQL*Net/Nte8 software, and if the TNSNAMES.ORA file does not exist in the client environment, the JDBC URL can specify the entire string, normally found in the TNSNAME.ORA file, that represents the listener service for a network service name. For example:

```
import java.sql.*;

public class OCIConnectExample {
  private static final String url =
     "jdbc:oracle:oci8:bookstore/bookstore" +
        "@(description=(address_list=" +

"(address=(protocol=tcp)(port=1521)(host=gstokol)))" +
           "(connect_data=(sid=ORA815)))";

  public Connection makeConnection() throws SQLException,
                                  ClassNotFoundException {
    Connection conn = null;

    Class.forName("oracle.jdbc.driver.OracleDriver");
    conn = DriverManager.getConnection(url);
    return conn;
  }
  :
}
```

[14]Database instance name and SID are defined earlier in this section.

Placing the mapped network service name details inside the JDBC URL eliminates the need to maintain the TNSNAMES.ORA configuration file on the client, but the SQL*net/Net8 software must still be present. To eliminate the need to install SQL*net/Net8 software in the client, you can use the thin JDBC driver by substituting the text **thin** for **oci8** in the URL. The Oracle Thin JDBC driver also accepts the fully mapped network service name in the JDBC URL. However, using the thin JDBC driver the CONNECT_DATA option shown in the OCIConnectExample class can be specified as:

```
CONNECT_DATA=(SID=ORA815))
```

Where ORA815 is the SID name, the OCI8 driver accepts either of the following details in the connect string:

- (CONNECT_DATA=(SID=ORA815)), or
- (CONNECT_DATE=(SERVICE_NAME=db-service-name))

9.4.1.3 Connecting from the Client Applet or Application. If the client is an applet, you can connect to the database using the thin JDBC driver. The connection request is made in the applet's init() method, or when a login request is made by a user. The getConnection() request shown in the DBConnectExample1 class or the DBConnectExample2 class can be used to create a connection from an applet. Java applications on the client (non-applets) or on the middle tier can use either the thin or the OCI JDBC driver.

9.4.1.4 Disconnecting from the Database. You disconnect from the database by calling the close() method on the Connection object, which also releases resources allocated for the connection. For example:

```
Connection conn = null;

try {
  conn= DriverManager.getConnection(url);
  :
}
catch (SQLException e) {
 . . .
}
finally {
  try {
    conn.close();    // close the connection
    conn = null;
  } catch (Exception e) { }
}
```

The close() method is called in the finally block to ensure that the connection resource is released, independent of success or failure in the first try-catch block.

9.4.2 EXECUTING SQL STATEMENTS

After creating a connection, you are ready to execute SQL statements. The Connection object provides one of three object types that can be used to execute SQL statements:

- The Statement
- The PreparedStatement
- The CallableStatement

Calls to methods in JDBC classes should be enclosed in a Java exception-handling block, since they can throw an SQLException.[15] The SQLException is classified as a "checked exception"[16] in Java. Subsequent examples in this chapter make use of Java exception-handling blocks with no further comment.

9.4.2.1 Using a Statement Object. The Statement class is used to execute SQL statements that do not have parameters. However, the JDBC methods accept SQL statements as a string argument; thus, SQL statements can be constructed dynamically. After loading the JDBC driver and obtaining a Connection object, you create a Statement object as follows:

- Declare a Statement variable.
- Call the Connection createStatement() method, and assign the return value to the Statement variable.

Listing 9.2 shows the creation of a Statement object, with the two key statements in bold. Once you have created a Statement object, you can execute any SQL statement, including DDL and SELECT, INSERT, UPDATE, and DELETE statements. The Statement object has the following methods that can be used to execute SQL operations:

---

[15]Calls to the DriverManager.getConnection() method and Connection.close() method can also throw an SQLException.

[16]The java.lang.Exception class and its subclasses, excluding the RuntimeException, are classified as checked exceptions. The Java compiler checks whether your code catches or propagates a checked exception; and if not, a compilation error occurs.

```
import java.sql.*;

public class MakeJDBCStatement {

  public static void main(String[] args) {
    private Connection  conn = null;
    private static final String url =
             "jdbc:oracle:thin:@localhost:1521:ORA815";
    try {
      Class.forName("oracle.jdbc.driver.OracleDriver");
      conn = DriverManager.getConnection(url, "book", "book");
      conn.setAutoCommit(false);

      Statement stmt = null;
        stmt = conn.createStatement();
      :
    }
    catch (Exception e) {
      e.printStackTrace();
    }
  }
}
```

LISTING 9.2 Creating a Statement object

- The executeQuery() method to execute queries that return a result set.
- The executeUpdate() method to execute INSERT, UPDATE, DELETE, or DDL statements that do not return a result set.
- The execute() method for any of the above SQL statements if you are not sure which type of SQL statement has been entered.

Using the executeQuery() Method

The executeQuery() method in the Statement class is designed to return a ResultSet after executing a SELECT statement. The executeQuery method always returns a ResultSet object. Note that the method can throw an SQLException. Here is a snippet of code showing the use of executeQuery(), after creating a statement:

```
import java.sql.*;

public class MakeJDBCStatement {
```

```
    public static void main(String[] args) {
      private Connection  conn = null;
      private static final String url =
                "jdbc:oracle:thin:@localhost:1521:ORA815";
      try {
        Class.forName("oracle.jdbc.driver.OracleDriver");
        conn =
        DriverManager.getConnection(
        url, "book", "book");
        conn.setAutoCommit(false);

        Statement stmt = null;
        stmt = conn.createStatement();
        ResultSet rset = stmt.executeQuery("select * from
        customer");
        . . .
      }
      catch (Exception e) {
        e.printStackTrace();
      }
    }
}
```

The executeQuery() method takes a query string as its argument, and returns a JDBC ResultSet object.

Using the JDBC ResultSet

A ResultSet, returned from the executeQuery() method, represents the set of rows returned by the query, and provides methods to sequentially access each row and the data items in each row. The commonly used methods in the ResultSet object are:

- A next() method used to step to the next rows.
- Various getXXX() methods used to access the data values of individual items in a row, and to convert the values from the SQL data type format into a Java data type.[17] The XXX portion in the name of the getXXX() method identifies the target Java data type name for the conversion.

A ResultSet effectively maintains a cursor to the current row in the set, and initially points before the first row, if it exists. The ResultSet next() method must be called at least once to determine whether any rows have been returned. The

---

[17]The getXXX() methods are discussed in more detail in the following section.

next() method returns a boolean result of true if a row is in the next position in the result set; if not, a result of false is returned to indicate that there are no more rows.

The typical code sequence used to process one or more rows using a ResultSet is:

- Call the ResultSet method next() to retrieve a row.
- If next() returns a true result, then access the data by calling the getXXX() methods. The data items can be accessed in any order, but for portability, it is best to read them once in a left-to-right sequence.
- If next() returns a false value, terminate processing the result data.
- Repeat from step 1.

For example, print the first column of each row found in a result set:

```
ResultSet rset = stmt.executeQuery(
                    "select name, surname from customer");

ResultSet rset =  stmt.getResultSet();
while (rset.next()) {   // if a row exists then process data
   /*
   ** Use getString(1) to read data for the first column in each row
   */
   System.out.println("Name:      " + rset.getString(1));
   System.out.println("Surname:   " + rset.getString(2));
   . . .
}
```

The getString(1) and getString(2) methods are used to convert the first and second column data items, respectively, into their Java String representations, showing an example of using ResultSet getXXX() methods to access a data item in a two column position in the query.

There is one getXXX() method for each JDBC data type declared in the java.sql.Types class. Table 9.3 provides a matrix of SQL types and the corresponding getXXX() methods that can be used to retrieve the SQL value into your Java application.

The getXXX() methods are overloaded so that you can access a column value in a row by specifying the first parameter of the getXXX() method as:

- A non-zero index integer identifying the column position in the query. Column positions begin with an index of 1.
- A string identifying the column or alias name used in the query.

TABLE 9.3 Converting SQL to Java type using ResultSet get methods[18]

		SMALLINT	INTEGER	BIGINT	REAL	FLOAT	DOUBLE	DECIMAL	NUMERIC	BIT	CHAR	VARCHAR	LONGVARCHAR	BINARY	VARBINARY	LONGVARBINARY	DATE	TIME	TIMESTAMP
getByte	**X**	x	x	x	x	x	x	x	x	x	x	x	x						
getShort	x	**X**	x	x	x	x	x	x	x	x	x	x	x						
getInt	x	x	**X**	x	x	x	x	x	x	x	x	x	x						
getLong	x	x	x	**X**	x	x	x	x	x	x	x	x	x						
getFloat	x	x	x	x	**X**	x	x	x	x	x	x	x	x						
getDouble	x	x	x	x	x	**X**	**X**	x	x	x	x	x	x						
getBigDecimal	x	x	x	x	x	x	x	**X**	**X**	x	x	x	x						
getBoolean	x	x	x	x	x	x	x	x	x	**X**	x	x	x						
getString	x	x	x	x	x	x	x	x	x	x	**X**	**X**	x	x	x	x	x	x	x
getBytes														**X**	**X**	x			
getDate											x	x	x				**X**		x
getTime											x	x	x					**X**	x
getTimestamp											x	x	x				x		**X**
getAsciiStream											x	x	**X**	x	x	x			
getUnicodeStream											x	x	**X**	x	x	x			
getBinaryStream														x	x	**X**			
getObject	x	x	x	x	x	x	x	x	x	x	x	x	x	x	x	x	x	x	x

Use of ResultSet.getXXX methods to retrieve common SQL data types.
An "x" means that the given getXXX method can be used to retrieve the given SQL type.
An "x" means that the given getXXX method is recommended for retrieving the given SQL type.

For example:

```
Statement stmt = stmt.executeQuery(
                    "select id, surname from customer");
ResultSet rset =  stmt.getResultSet();
while (rset.next()) {  // if a row exists then process data
```

[18]The matrix is used here with the permission of Sun Microsystems.

```
        /*
        ** Get first column value by index
        */
        System.out.println(rset.getString(1));
        /*
        ** Get second column by its name
        */
        System.out.println(rset.getString("surname"));
    }
```

Accessing a column value using an index is generally more efficient than accessing the column by its name. If the query has a column expression without an alias, you need to access its value using an integer index.

You can use the getString() method to convert any column data type into a Java string. SQL numeric types for a database column can be converted into a byte, short, int, long, or java.math.BigDecimal in the Java application, depending on the precision of the actual value stored in the column. However, you should use a Java data type that provides for a maximum precision compatible with the data type declared for the SQL column.

```
import java.sql.*;

public class ExecuteSQL {

  private static final
      String url = "jdbc:oracle:thin:@localhost:1521:ORA815";
  private static final String usr = "bookstore";
  private static final String psw = "bookstore";
  private static Connection conn;

  public static void defaultConnection() {…}
  public static void closeConnection() {…}
  private static String fillColumn(String text, int maxSize) {…}
  public static void printResults(ResultSet rset)
      throws SQLException {…}

  public static void executeQuery(String sqlQuery) {
    Statement stmt = null;
    ResultSet rset = null;
    try {
      stmt = conn.createStatement();
      rset = stmt.executeQuery(sqlQuery);
      printResults(rset);
    }
```

LISTING 9.3 Executing a query and printing the result set.

```
25:      catch (Exception e) { e.printStackTrace(); }
26:      finally {
27:        try {
28:          if (rset != null) { rset.close(); rset = null; }
29:          if (stmt != null) { stmt.close(); stmt = null; }
30:        }
31:        catch (Exception e) {}
32:      }
33:    }
34:
35:    public static void main(String[] args) {
36:      String query = "select id, name, cost_per_item cost" +
37:                     " from courier";
38:      defaultConnection();
39:      executeQuery(query);
40:      closeConnection();
41:    }
42: }
```

LISTING 9.3 *Continued*

Notes on Listing 9.3:

- Lines 5–8 define constant values for a default database connection.
- Lines 11, 12, 13, and 14 show method declarations for supporting code to set the default connection, close the connection, and fill a column for formatting result values in the printResultSet method. These methods are discussed later in this chapter, but for now the focus is the JDBC executeQuery() method.
- Line 17 declares the executeQuery() method for the ExecuteSQL class. The parameter is the string to be executed.
- Line 21 creates the statement object.
- Line 22 executes the query in the sqlQuery parameter by invoking the JDBC executeQuery() method. If there is no SQLException executing the query, a ResultSet object is returned.
- Line 23 calls the printResults() method to display the result set data. The printResults() method has been written to generically handle a result set for any query.
- Lines 26–30 show the final block used to ensure that the result set and statement objects are closed and marked for garbage collection, independent of the success or failure of the query execution.
- Lines 36 and 37 define the query string.
- Line 38 sets the default database connection for the query.
- Line 39 initiates the query execution.
- Line 40 closes the database connection.

The results for Listing 9.3 are:

```
ID      NAME                COST
1       Federal Impress     6.50
2       GKL International   6
3       Snail Mail Inc      1.70
4       Universal Post      4.50
```

The executeQuery() example of Listing 9.3 shows how you can process the results for any SELECT statement passed in as a parameter string. Next you will see how to execute non-query SQL statements using the Statement.executeUpdate() method.

Using the executeUpdate() method

The Statement.executeUpdate() method is used to execute a INSERT, UPDATE, DELETE, or DDL statement string passed in as its argument and return an update count. The update count indicates the number of rows affected by the statement, such that it is,

- Always zero for DDL statements.
- Greater than or equal to zero for INSERT, UPDATE, or DELETE statements.

The JDBC executeUpdate() method may throw an SQLException. Listing 9.4 shows an example of how to execute any INSERT, UPDATE, DELETE, or DDL statement. The main method tests the code with an UPDATE statement.

```
import java.sql.*;

public class ExecuteSQL {

  private static final
      String url = "jdbc:oracle:thin:@localhost:1521:ORA815";
  private static final String usr = "bookstore";
  private static final String psw = "bookstore";
  private static Connection conn;

  public static void defaultConnection() {...}
  public static void closeConnection() {...}
  private static String fillColumn(String text, int maxSize) {...}
  public static void printResults(ResultSet rset)
```

LISTING 9.4 Executing an UPDATE statement

```
15:       throws SQLException {…}
16:   public static void executeQuery(String sqlQuery) {…}
17:
18:   public static void executeUpdate(String dmlStatement) {
19:     Statement stmt = null;
20:     try {
21:       stmt = conn.createStatement();
22:       int rowCount = stmt.executeUpdate(dmlStatement);
23:       System.out.println(rowCount + " rows(s) modified");
24:     }
25:     catch (Exception e) { e.printStackTrace(); }
26:     finally {
27:       try {
28:         if (stmt != null) { stmt.close(); stmt = null; }
29:       }
30:       catch (Exception e) {}
31:     }
32:   }
33:
34:   public static void main(String[] args) {
35:     String query = "select id, name, cost_per_item cost" +
36:                    " from courier";
37:     defaultConnection();
38:     executeQuery(query);
39:     executeUpdate("update courier" +
40:                   " set cost_per_item = cost_per_item * 1.1");
41:     executeQuery(query);
42:     closeConnection();
43:   }
44: }
```

LISTING 9.4 Executing an UPDATE statement (continued)

Notes on Listing 9.4:

- Lines 1–16 are the same code as found in Listing 9.3, with the body of the executeQuery() method excluded.
- Lines 18–32 show the executeUpdate() method that executes any DDL, INSERT, UPDATE, or DELETE operation supplied in the dmlStatement parameter.
- Line 22 is the actual JDBC executeUpdate() method to execute the SQL operation and return the row count.

- Lines 35 and 36 define a query used in line 38 for a list of data rows before the update is processed, and used again in line 41 to print the result set for rows after the update has occurred.
- Lines 39 and 40 initiate the SQL update statement to increase the cost per item by 10 percent for each courier row in the table.

Here is some sample output for the rows in the courier table, before and after the update statement is executed in Listing 9.4:

```
Data Before the Update

ID   NAME               COST
1    Federal Impress    6.50
2    GKL International 6
3    Snail Mail Inc     1.70
4    Universal Post     4.50

4 rows(s) modified

Data After the Update

ID   NAME               COST
1    Federal Impress    7.15
2    GKL International 6.60
3    Snail Mail Inc     1.87
4    Universal Post     4.95
```

The next code example demonstrates using the same executUpdate() method to execute a DROP TABLE statement:

```
public static void main(String[] args) {
  defaultConnection();
  executeUpdate("drop table test");
  closeConnection();
}
```

```
Result is:

0 rows(s) modified
```

The row count value returned by the JDBC executeUpdate() method after executing the DROP statement is a value of zero. If you attempt to delete/drop a nonexistent TEST, then an SQLException is thrown and the program displays the following error message:

```
public static void main(String[] args) {
  defaultConnection();
  executeUpdate("drop table test");   // table does not
exist
  closeConnection();
}
```

```
Result is:

java.sql.SQLException: ORA-00942: table or view does not
exist
. . .followed by the usual stack trace information . . .
```

Using the ResultSetMetaData

You can request a ResultSetMetaData object from a new ResultSet. The ResultSetMetaData object provides some details about the result set for a query. For example, the ResultSetMetaData provides methods to determine:

- The number of column values queried, using the getColumnCount() method.
- The name of each column, using the getColumnName(position) method
- The maximum display size for each column, using the getColumnDisplaySize(position) method.

The position parameter in some of the ResultSetMetaData methods is an integer used to specify the column position in the query list. Column positions start with a value of 1, and end with a value returned by the getColumnCount() method. Other details about a result set can be obtained dynamically through the remaining methods available in the ResultSetMetaData class. The ResultSetMetaData object is created by calling the getMetaData() method of a ResultSet. For example:

```
ResultSet rset = stmt.executeQuery(someQueryString);
ResultSetMetaData metaData = rset.getMetaData();
```

Displaying Query Results

Listing 9.5 shows the printResults() method used to display the results of a query for the code in Listings 9.3 and 9.4. The printResults() method uses the JDBC ResultSetMetaData object to provide a generic way of printing the results

```
private static String fillColumn(String text, int maxSize) {
  if (text.length() < maxSize) {
    // Pad remaining column width with spaces
    for (int j = text.length(); j < maxSize; j++) {
      text += ' ';
    }
  }
  // Ensure return string <= maximum column width
  return text.substring(0, maxSize);
}

public static void printResults(ResultSet rset)
 throws SQLException {
  StringBuffer rowInfo = new StringBuffer();
  ResultSetMetaData metaData = rset.getMetaData();
  int nbrColumns = metaData.getColumnCount();
  int colSize[] = new int[nbrColumns];
  /*
  ** Display Column headings
  */
  for (int i = 0; i < nbrColumns; i++) {
      String colName = metaData.getColumnName(i+1);
      colSize[i] = metaData.getColumnDisplaySize(i+1);

      rowInfo.append(fillColumn(colName, colSize[i]));
      rowInfo.append(' ');
  }
  System.out.println(rowInfo.toString());
  /*
  ** Display Column Data
  */
  while (rset.next()) {
    rowInfo.setLength(0);
    for (int i = 0; i < nbrColumns; i++) {
      String colValue = rset.getString(i+1);
      if (rset.wasNull()) colValue = "null";
      rowInfo.append(fillColumn(colValue, colSize[i]));
      rowInfo.append(' ');
    }
    System.out.println(rowInfo.toString());
  }
  rset.close();
}
```

LISTING 9.5 Displaying result set data for any query

from any query. The printResults() method applies some basic formatting of the data, using the column maximum width determined from the ResultSetMetaData information.

The printResults() method highlights interesting features found in the JDBC class library, enabling you to develop code that can adapt dynamically to the results generated in the execution environment.

Notes on Listing 9.5:

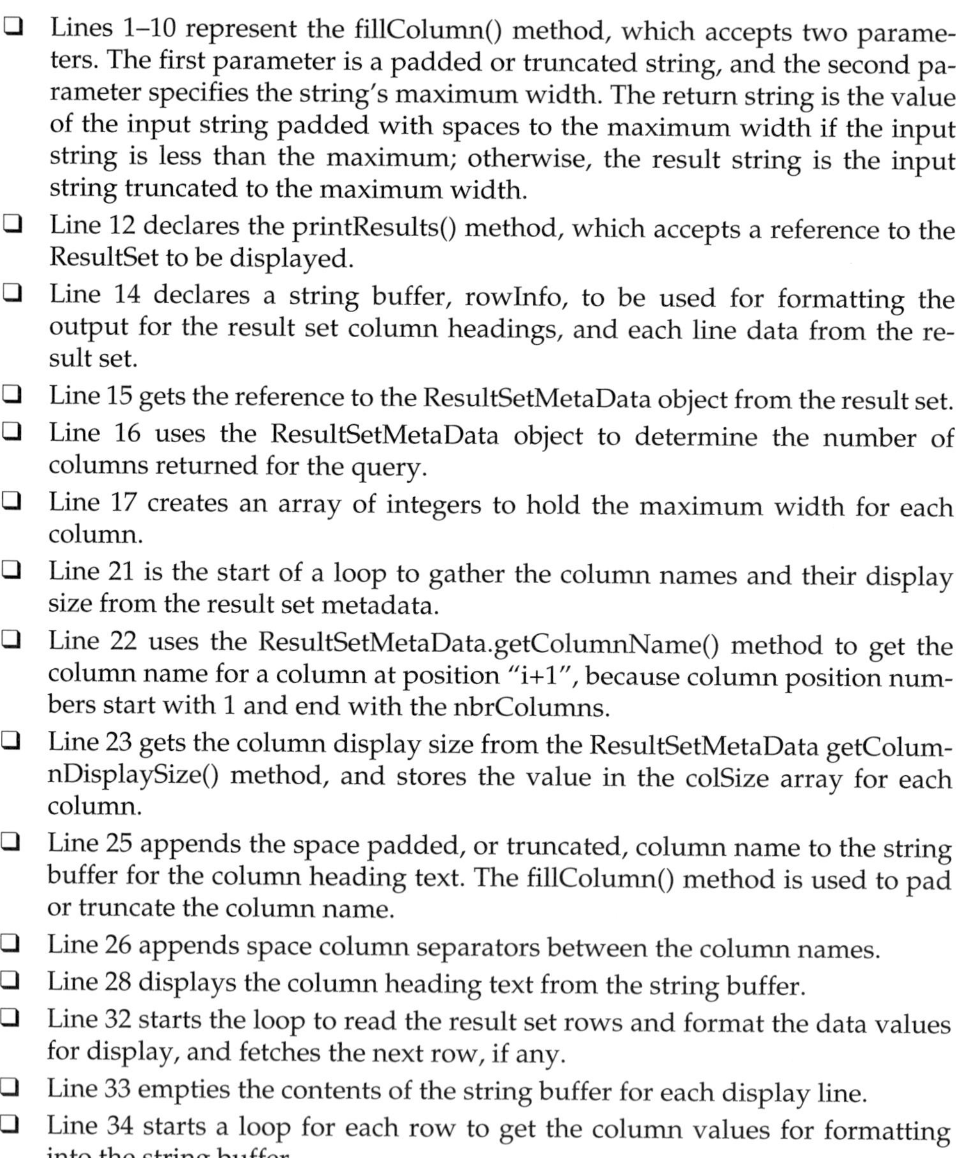

- Lines 1–10 represent the fillColumn() method, which accepts two parameters. The first parameter is a padded or truncated string, and the second parameter specifies the string's maximum width. The return string is the value of the input string padded with spaces to the maximum width if the input string is less than the maximum; otherwise, the result string is the input string truncated to the maximum width.
- Line 12 declares the printResults() method, which accepts a reference to the ResultSet to be displayed.
- Line 14 declares a string buffer, rowInfo, to be used for formatting the output for the result set column headings, and each line data from the result set.
- Line 15 gets the reference to the ResultSetMetaData object from the result set.
- Line 16 uses the ResultSetMetaData object to determine the number of columns returned for the query.
- Line 17 creates an array of integers to hold the maximum width for each column.
- Line 21 is the start of a loop to gather the column names and their display size from the result set metadata.
- Line 22 uses the ResultSetMetaData.getColumnName() method to get the column name for a column at position "i+1", because column position numbers start with 1 and end with the nbrColumns.
- Line 23 gets the column display size from the ResultSetMetaData getColumnDisplaySize() method, and stores the value in the colSize array for each column.
- Line 25 appends the space padded, or truncated, column name to the string buffer for the column heading text. The fillColumn() method is used to pad or truncate the column name.
- Line 26 appends space column separators between the column names.
- Line 28 displays the column heading text from the string buffer.
- Line 32 starts the loop to read the result set rows and format the data values for display, and fetches the next row, if any.
- Line 33 empties the contents of the string buffer for each display line.
- Line 34 starts a loop for each row to get the column values for formatting into the string buffer.

- Line 35 reads a column value at position "i+1" as a string because the loop is zero based, but a column value position starts at 1.
- Line 36 replaces the colValue with the null string literal if the column value returned was an SQL NULL value.
- Line 37 formats a space padded or truncated column value into the string buffer, based on the column size stored in the colSize array.
- Line 38 appends a space as the column separator.
- Line 40 displays the column data values formatted in the string buffer.
- Line 42 closes the result set to release resources.

The code example in Listing 9.6 demonstrates the flexibility gained by using the code from the executeQuery(), executeUpdate(), and printResults() methods discussed in Listings 9.3, 9.4, and 9.5.

In Listing 9.6, every statement is a hard-code SQL string, but could be dynamically constructed from a user interface or read from an input file. The output results from the code in Listing 9.6, using some sample data, are:

```
public static void main(String[] args) {
  defaultConnection();
  executeQuery("select * from courier");
  executeUpdate("drop table test");
  executeUpdate(
     "create table test (id number(3), text varchar2(20))");
  executeUpdate(
     "insert into test (id , text) values (1, 'demo 1')");
  executeUpdate(
   "insert into test (id , text) values (2, 'demo 2')");
  executeQuery("select * from test");
  executeQuery("select id, title, full_price " +
    "from sales_item where title like '%Oracle8i%'");
  executeUpdate("update sales_item " +
    "set full_price = full_price * 0.9 " +
    "where title like '%Oracle8i%'");
  executeQuery("select id, title, full_price " +
               "from sales_item where title like '%Oracle8i%'");
  closeConnection();
}
```

LISTING 9.6 Executing Dynamic SQL statements

```
SQL> select * from courier
ID  NAME                    COST_PER_ITEM
1   Federal Impress        6.50
2   GKL International      6
3   Snail Mail Inc         1.70
4   Universal Post         4.50
SQL> drop table test
0 rows(s) modified
SQL> create table test (id number(3), text varchar2(20))
0 rows(s) modified
SQL> insert into test (id , text) values (1, 'demo 1')
1 rows(s) modified
SQL> insert into test (id , text) values (2, 'demo 2')
1 rows(s) modified
SQL> select * from test
ID                  TEXT
1                   demo 1
2                   demo 2
SQL> select id, title, full_price from sales_item where
title like '%Oracle8i%'
ID   TITLE
FULL_PRICE
10   Oracle8i DBA Handbook
40.09
12   Oracle8i: A Beginner's Guide
36.08
17   Oracle8i Internal Services for Waits, Latches,
Locks, and Memory  16
SQL> update sales_item set full_price = full_price * 0.9
     where title like '%Oracle8i%'
3 rows(s) modified
SQL> select id, title, full_price from sales_item where
title like '%Oracle8i%'
ID   TITLE
FULL_PRICE
10   Oracle8i DBA Handbook
36.08
12   Oracle8i: A Beginner's Guide
32.47
17   Oracle8i Internal Services for Waits, Latches,
Locks, and Memory  14.40
```

LISTING 9.6 *Continued*

The SQL statements used in Listing 9.6 could be modified to accept user-provided search criteria. Look at the following example, showing how you can construct SQL statements with user input added to form the resulting SQL string.

```
import java.sql.*;

public class ExecuteSQL {
  :
  public static void main(String[] args) {
    String searchText = null;
    if (arg.length == 1) {
      searchText = arg[0];
    }
    defaultConnection();
    executeQuery(
        "select id, title, full_price from sales_item" +
         (searchText != null ?
            " where title like '%" + searchText + "%'" : ""));
    executeUpdate("update sales_item " +
        "set full_price = full_price * 0.9" +
         (searchText != null ?
            " where title like '%" + searchText + "%'" : ""));

    closeConnection();
  }
}
```

The main method gets search criteria from the command-line argument, args[0], and saves the text in the searchText string. The SQL statement in the call to executeQuery() uses string concatenation to add a query condition using the searchText if the searchText is not null reference; otherwise, the query executes without a query condition. The SQL statement used in the executeUpdate() method applies the same principle used with the executeQuery() example.

The technique of building SQL statement strings by concatenating variable values into the strings is widely accepted, but it is recommended here that you use a PreparedStatement object to parameterize your SQL statements. Using a PreparedStatement provides a more efficient way of processing parameterized SQL statements, particularly if the statement is executed repeatedly, and each time the statement is executed different values are used for the parameters. Refer to the section of this chapter on using the PreparedStatement for more detail.

Using the Statement execute() Method

The execute() method can be used to process any SQL statement, and is particularly useful if you do not know what kind of SQL statement has been entered. The definition of execute() method in the JDBC Statement class is:

```
public boolean execute(String sql) throws SQLException
```

The execute() method returns a boolean value that is:

- **True** if the statement executed returns a result set; i.e., a query was processed.
- **False** if the statement returns an update count; i.e., a DDL or non-SELECT DML statement was processed.

As stated, the execute() method is useful for executing any SQL statement entered by a user. Listing 9.7 shows a method designed to handle any kind of SQL statement and provide some feedback. If a query is executed, the result set is displayed, and if a non-query is executed, a row count is displayed.

```
01:   public static void executeSQL(String sqlText) {
02:     Statement stmt = null;
03:     try {
04:       System.out.println("SQL> " + sqlText);
05:       stmt = conn.createStatement();
06:       if (stmt.execute(sqlText))  {
07:         printResults(stmt.getResultSet());
08:       }
09:       else {
10:         System.out.println(""
11:                             " row(s) altered");
12:       }
13:     }
14:     catch (Exception e) { e.printStackTrace(); }
15:     finally {
16:       try { stmt.close(); stmt = null; }
          catch (Exception e) {}
17:     }
18:   }
```

LISTING 9.7 Handling any SQL statement in JDBC

Notes on Listing 9.7:

- Line 6 uses the execute() method in the JDBC Statement object to process a statement in the sqlText parameter.
- Line 7 passes the result set obtained from the Statement object getResult-Set() method to printResults() method, which displays the data.

- ❑ Line 10 deals with the non-query statements and calls the Statement object getUpdateCount() method, which returns a row count value.

The main() method in Listing 9.6 can now be modified to call the executeSQL() to process all the SQL statements. For example:

```
public static void main(String[] args) {
  defaultConnection();
  executeSQL("select * from courier");
  executeSQL("drop table test");
  executeSQL(
     "create table test (id number(3), text varchar2(20))");
  executeSQL(
     "insert into test (id , text) values (1, 'demo 1')");
  executeSQL(
   "insert into test (id , text) values (2, 'demo 2')");
  executeSQL("select * from test");
  executeSQL("select id, title, full_price " +
    "from sales_item where title like '%Oracle8i%'");
  executeSQL("update sales_item " +
    "set full_price = full_price * 0.9 " +
    "where title like '%Oracle8i%'");
  executeSQL("select id, title, full_price " +
            "from sales_item where title like '%Oracle8i%'");
  closeConnection();
}
```

The resulting output is the same as that shown for Listing 9.6.

Additional Comments on Using Statement.execute()

The JDBC documentation states that multiple result sets can be returned by executing an SQL statement processed by the execute() method. This may be true when using other JDBC drivers, but Oracle JDBC drivers only return one result set per call.

9.4.2.2 Using a PreparedStatement Object. A PreparedStatement object is best used when you wish to execute the same SQL statement repeatedly in the same application, and each time the statement is executed optionally provide different search criteria or values. The advantage of using PreparedStatement over Statement object is that your program requests the database to pre-parse the statement. Although some JDBC drives may not support PreparedStatements, the Oracle JDBC drivers do support them.

You create an instance of a PreparedStatement using the Connection class method prepareStatement():

```
public PreparedStatement prepareStatement(String sql)
  throws SQLException
```

The prepareStatement() method accepts an SQL statement string as a parameter.

Using PreparedStatement with Parameters

An important feature of the SQL statement string passed into the prepareStatement() method is that you can specify query parameters, called placeholders. A *placeholder* is a question-mark character included in the text of an SQL statement; it represents a part of the query where an *input value* is substituted, or bound, at runtime from a Java variable.

To associate a variable value with each placeholder included in a statement, you must call the PreparedStatement setXXX() methods. For example:

```
PreparedStatement pstmt;
pstmt = conn.prepareStatement(
            "select * from customer where name = ?");
pstmt.setString(1 , "Glenn");
```

The placeholder characters are referred to in the same sequence in which they occur relative to the start of the statement, starting with number 1. A PreparedStatement object is used to efficiently execute such a statement multiple times, providing a different value for each placeholder for each separate execution. There are many setXXX() methods defined in PreparedStatement to convert Java data type into the appropriate SQL type. Table 9.4 shows the compatible choices for mapping Java types to JDBC SQL types.

Table 9.4 shows the default mappings used by JDBC drivers when using the setObject() method without specifying the SQL data type. The table is presented here so that you can choose a setXXX() method compatible with an SQL data type in the table. An "x" in the matrix cells indicates compatible conversions.

Listing 9.8 shows another example of using PreparedStatement with a query.

TABLE 9.4 Java to SQL types using PreparedStatement set methods[19]

	TINYINT	SMALLINT	INTEGER	BIGINT	REAL	FLOAT	DOUBLE	DECIMAL	NUMERIC	BIT	CHAR	VARCHAR	LONGVARCHAR	BINARY	VARBINARY	LONGVARBINARY	DATE	TIME	TIMESTAMP	ARRAY	BLOB	CLOB	STRUCT	REF	JAVA OBJECT
String	x	x	x	x	x	x	x	x	x	x	x	x	x	x	x	x	x	x	x						
java.math. BigDecimal	x	x	x	x	x	x	x	x	x	x	x	x	x												
Boolean	x	x	x	x	x	x	x	x	x	x	x	x	x												
Integer	x	x	x	x	x	x	x	x	x	x	x	x	x												
Long	x	x	x	x	x	x	x	x	x	x	x	x	x												
Float	x	x	x	x	x	x	x	x	x	x	x	x	x												
Double	x	x	x	x	x	x	x	x	x	x	x	x	x												
byte[]														x	x	x									
java.sql. Date											x	x	x				x		x						
java.sql. Time											x	x	x					x							
java.sql. Timestamp											x	x	x				x	x	x						
Array																				x					
Blob																					x				
Clob																						x			
Struct																							x		
Ref																								x	
Java class																									x

An "x" means that the given Java type can be stored as the SQL type using a setXXX() method, where XXX is the Java type

[19]The matrix is used here with the permission of Sun Microsystems.

```
01: import java.sql.*;
02:
03: public class PreparedSQL {
04:   :
05:   private PreparedStatement pQuery = null;
06:
07:   public void getSalesItem(int id) {
08:      try {
09:       if (pQuery == null) {
10:         String sqlQuery = "select id, title, full_price " +
11:                           "from sales_item " +
12:                           "where id = ?";
13:         pQuery = conn.prepareStatement(sqlQuery);
14:       }
15:       pQuery.setInt(1, id);
16:       ResultSet rset = pQuery.executeQuery();
17:       this.printResults(rset);
18:     }
19:     catch (SQLException e) {
20:       System.out.println("SQL error: " + e.getMessage());
21:     }
22:   }
23:
24:   public static void main(String[] args) {
25:
26:     PreparedSQL pSql = new PreparedSQL();
27:
28:     pSql.getSalesItem(1);
29:     pSql.getSalesItem(2);
30:     pSql.getSalesItem(3);
31:
32:     pSql.close();
33:   }
34: }
```

LISTING 9.8 Using a PreparedStatement with a query

Notes on Listing 9.8:

- In line 5 the PreparedStatement object variable is declared, and is initialized the first time the getSalesItem(int) method is called.
- In line 9 of getSalesItem(), the method checks whether the PreparedStatement object is initialized; if not, a SELECT statement is created on lines 10–12 with a single placeholder character.
- In line 13, the SQL statement is given to the prepareStatement() method, which causes the JDBC driver to ask the database to parse the statement.

Note that the statement is only prepared once, and the method can be called with a different value for the id parameter each time.

- Line 15 is where the value held in the id parameter is associated with the placeholder. The call to setInt(1, id) specifies that the first placeholder should have its value set to the value in id.
- Line 16 finally executes the query, and returns a result set for processing.

The getSalesItem() method does not close the PreparedStatement object as it is used repeatedly. The main() method in Listing 9.8 creates a PreparedSQL object and then calls the getSalesItem() method a few times with different values for the id parameter. The results are:

```
ID  TITLE
FULL_PRICE
1   Oracle8: The Complete Reference                         59.99
ID  TITLE
FULL_PRICE
2   Oracle PL/SQL Programming                               46.95
ID  TITLE
FULL_PRICE
3   Oracle8 PL/SQL Programming: The Essential Guide for Ever   4
```

Listing 9.9 shows the code for a preparing an update statement that is also defined in the PrepareSQL class. The updatePrice(int id, double newPrice) method updates the full_price column to the value in newPrice for a sales item uniquely identified by the value of the id parameter.

```
01: import java.sql.*;
02:
03: public class PreparedSQL {
04:   :
05:   private PreparedStatement pDml = null;
06:
07:   public void updatePrice(int id, double newPrice) {
08:     try {
09:       if (pDml == null) {
10:         String dmlStmt = "update sales_item " +
11:                          "set full_price = ? where id = ?";
12:         pDml = conn.prepareStatement(dmlStmt);
13:       }
14:       pDml.setDouble(1, newPrice);
15:       pDml.setInt(2, id);
16:       int rowCount = pDml.executeUpdate();
17:       conn.commit();
```

LISTING 9.9 Using a PreparedStatement with an UPDATE statement

```
18:         System.out.println(
19:            pDml.getUpdateCount() + " row(s) altered");
20:         }
21:         catch (SQLException e) {
22:           System.out.println("SQL error: " + e.getMessage());
23:         }
24:     }
25:
26:     public static void main(String[] args) {
27:       PreparedSQL pSql = new PreparedSQL();
28:
29:       pSql.getSalesItem(1);
30:       pSql.updatePrice(1, 35.95);
31:       pSql.getSalesItem(1);
32:
33:       pSql.getSalesItem(2);
34:       pSql.updatePrice(2, 45.95);
35:       pSql.getSalesItem(2);
36:
37:       pSql.close();
38:     }
39: }
```

LISTING 9.9 *Continued*

Notes on Listing 9.9:

- In line 5, the PreparedStatement variable is declared and initialized to the null reference.
- Lines 10 and 11 create the UPDATE statement string with two placeholders the first time the method is called. The first placeholder marks the place for the new full_price, and the second placeholder marks the place for the id of the sales item row to be modified.
- Line 14 associates the newPrice value with the first placeholder by calling the setDouble() method. The first argument, of the setDouble() method identifies the first placeholder in the statement, and the second argument sets the first placeholder value to newPrice.
- Line 15 associates the second placeholder with the value in variable "id" by calling the setInt() method of the prepared statement.
- Line 16 executes the prepared DML statement to update the nominated sales item record. The executeUpdate() method returns a value indicating the number of rows updated.

After setting the values for each placeholder, you can also use the execute() method to process any PreparedStatement, and to process the results in the same way as with the Statement object (see Listing 9.6). The results of executing the main() method shown in Listing 9.9 are:

```
ID     TITLE                                            FULL_PRICE
1      Oracle8: The Complete Reference                  44.50
1 row(s) altered
ID     TITLE                                            FULL_PRICE
1      Oracle8: The Complete Reference                  35.95

ID     TITLE                                            FULL_PRICE
2      Oracle PL/SQL Programming                        50
1 row(s) altered
ID     TITLE                                            FULL_PRICE
2      Oracle PL/SQL Programming                        45.95
```

To summarize, the key processing steps when using a PreparedStatement are:

- Obtain a PreparedStatement object using the prepareStatement(stmt) method from the Connection object.
- For each placeholder in the statement, call an appropriate setXXX() method to associate a variable value with that placeholder.
- Execute the statement using the executeQuery() method for queries, executeUpdate() for DDL or non-SELECT DML statements, or the execute() method for all types of statements.
- If a query was executed using executeQuery(), you can process the result set it returns. If the PreparedStatement was processed with the execute() method, you can call its getResultSet() method.

The PreparedStatement class has many setXXX() methods where XXX is a Java data type name type to specify how the Java value will be mapped to an SQL data type.

9.4.2.3 Using a CallableStatement Object. A CallableStatement object is used to execute stored procedures in the database, independent of the language used to implement the functionality.[20] The prepareCall() method, defined in the Connection interface, returns a CallableStatement based on a call string specification provided as a parameter. The JDBC signature for prepareCall() is:

---

[20]The term "stored procedure" is used in this text to refer to any type of code stored and executed in the database, such as procedures, functions, packages, or object type methods, unless explicitly stated otherwise.

```
public CallableStatement prepareCall(String sql) throws
SQLException
```

The string argument in the prepareCall() method specifies how to invoke a procedure by specifying:

- The name of the procedure to be called.
- Optional placeholders for input and output parameters, or the function return value.

Calling a Procedure

The database-independent argument syntax for the prepareCall() to call a procedure is:

"**{ call** *procedure-name [(?,…)]* **}**"

The braces at the start and end of the string are required, and the keyword CALL precedes the name of the stored procedure. Placeholders for procedure parameters, if required, are specified after the procedure name inside parentheses as a comma-separated list. Parameter values can be literals, and the parentheses can be omitted if there are no parameters.

Calling a Function

The prepareCall() string argument syntax to call a function is:

"**{ ? = call** *function-name [(?,…)]* **}**"

The function call string requires the placeholder and the equals sign to be entered before the keyword CALL in order to receive the function return value.

Calling a Packaged Procedure or Function

If you are calling a procedure or function from a PL/SQL package, the PL/SQL package name must be used to qualify the name of the procedure or function, as follows:

<u>Calling a procedure in a PL/SQL package</u>

```
conn.prepareCall("{ call package-name.procedure-name[…]}")
```

<u>Calling a function in a PL/SQL package</u>

```
conn.prepareCall("{ ? = call package-name.function-name[…]}")
```

Before you execute the prepared CallableStatement, you must provide values for all the input parameters, using the various setXXX() methods available in the CallableStatement, and you must also register the output values expected from the procedure output parameters, or a function return value.

The CallableStatement execute() method calls the procedure and always returns a boolean result of false. Thus, the execute() method of a CallableStatement is commonly used without testing the return value.

Handling Procedure or Function Parameters and Return Values

The Java code calling the procedure must provide a value for each input parameter, using the setXXX() methods provided by the CallableStatement class. In addition, the Java code must register, with the JDBC driver, the data type of each parameter for each output parameter, using the registerOutParameter() method of the CallableStatement class.

The registerOutParameter() method has two arguments:

- The first parameter identifies the placeholder position in the procedure call string.
- The second parameter specifies the return value Java data type for the output result. The JDBC driver uses the registered data type to convert the underlining SQL data type into the Java data type, if compatible.

The procedure can be executed after the input values are supplied and the output data types are registered. After executing a procedure, you can use the various getXXX() methods to obtain the values for the registered return values.

Example of Calling a Simple Procedure or Function

Here is a simple PL/SQL procedure definition that accepts two arguments:

- The customer id as an input value.
- The full customer name as the output value.

Since the procedure does not handle exceptions, the caller would be required to manage them.

```
PROCEDURE get_customer_name(custid IN number, full_name
OUT varchar2)
IS
BEGIN
  SELECT name||' '||surname INTO full_name
  FROM customer
  WHERE id = custid;
END;
```

The SELECT statement sets the value of the output parameter to the concatenated result of the name and surname of a customer, if the row exists; otherwise an exception occurs and full_name is undefined. The JDBC code used to call this get_customer_name procedure is:

Lines 18–22 embody the key steps required to execute a procedure with parameters.

```
01: import java.sql.*;
02:
03: public class CallProc {
04:
05:   private final static
06:       String url = "jdbc:oracle:thin:@localhost: 1521:ORA815";
07:   private final static String usr = "bookstore";
08:   private final static String psw = "bookstore";
09:   private static Connection conn = null;
10:
11:   public static void main(String[] args) {
12:     CallableStatement pCall = null;
13:     String fullName;
14:     try {
15:       Class.forName("oracle.jdbc.driver. OracleDriver");
16:       conn = DriverManager.getConnection(url, usr, psw);
17:
18:       pCall = conn.prepareCall("{call get_customer_name(?,?)}");
19:       pCall.setInt(1, 20);
20:       pCall.registerOutParameter(2, Types.VARCHAR);
21:       pCall.execute();
22:       fullName = pCall.getString(2);
23:       System.out.println("Customer 20 name is: " + fullName);
24:     }
25:     catch (Exception e) {
26:       e.printStackTrace();
27:     }
28:     finally {
29:       try {
30:         if (pCall != null) pCall.close();
31:         if (conn != null) conn.close();
32:       }
33:       catch (Exception e) {}
34:     }
35:   }
36: }
```

LISTING 9.10 Calling a PL/SQL procedure with Java JDBC

Notes on Listing 9.10:

- Line 18 prepares the call string for the procedure with two placeholders. The first placeholder is for the input value, the second, for the output result.
- Line 19 sets the input value to a value of 20.
- Line 20 registers the output parameter for placeholder two as a Java string. The java.sql.Types package defines several static final int variables, such as Types.VARCHAR.
- Line 21 executes the procedure.
- Line 22 is executed if the procedure completes successfully, and obtains the value returned, via the second placeholder, as a Java string.

The get_customer_name procedure could be rewritten as a function accepting a single input value, and returning the result. For example:

```
FUNCTION get_cust_name(custid IN NUMBER) RETURN VARCHAR2
IS
  full_name  VARCHAR2(61);
BEGIN
  SELECT name||' '||surname INTO full_name
  FROM customer
  WHERE id = custid;
  RETURN full_name;
END;
```

The Java code snippet that can be used to call the function is:

```
pCall = conn.prepareCall(
              "{ ? = call get_cust_name(?) }");
pCall.setInt(2, 20);
pCall.registerOutParameter(1, Types.VARCHAR);
pCall.execute();
fullName = pCall.getString(1);
```

The five lines of Java code used to call the function can replace lines 18–22 in Listing 9.10, instead of calling the procedure. To set up the function call, you register the first placeholder as the output parameter, and set the second placeholder with the input value. After executing the statement, you get the value returned by the function from the first placeholder.

The principles of calling a procedure or function are the same:

- Prepare the procedure or function call string.
- Set values for placeholder identifying input values.

- Register Java data types for placeholders identifying output results.
- Execute the procedure or function call.
- Get output values from registered output placeholders.

9.4.2.4 Example: Calling PL/SQL Packaged Procedures and Functions. The next example is a more comprehensive one that uses a PL/SQL package provided in an e-commerce shopping cart implementation. The "cart" package contains:

- A procedure, called add_item, to add items to the cart.
- A function, called get_basket, to locate an existing cart or to create one if it does not exist.
- A function, called get_items, to return the items in the shopping cart as a result set, and the total price for all items.

The example is designed to demonstrate how to call PL/SQL package procedures and functions, and how to retrieve a PL/SQL reference cursor as a JDBC result set.

The Cart PL/SQL Package Specification

```
CREATE OR REPLACE PACKAGE cart IS – specification
   TYPE item_refcsr IS REF CURSOR;

   PROCEDURE add_item(p_basket_id shopping_item.basket_cust_id%type,
                      p_prd_id    shopping_item.prd_id%type,
                      p_qty       shopping_item.quantity%type);

   FUNCTION get_basket(p_basket_id shopping_basket.cust_id%type)
        RETURN shopping_basket.cust_id%type;

   FUNCTION get_items(p_basket_id shopping_item.basket_cust_id%type,
                      p_price out shopping_item.price%type)
        RETURN item_refcsr;
END;
```

LISTING 9.11 CART PL/SQL package specification

Note on Listing 9.11:

- Line 2 in the specification declares a reference cursor data type that can be used by PL/SQL variable declarations to return a result set to a calling program.

The Cart PL/SQL Package Body

Listing 9.14 contains part of the cart package body implementation for the add_item procedure and the get_basket function. The rest of the package code for the get_items is shown later in Listing 9.14.

```
create or replace package body cart is

  cursor bcsr(p_id number) is
    select * from shopping_basket
    where cust_id = p_id;

  cursor itmcsr(p_id number) is
    select * from shopping_item
    where basket_cust_id = p_id;

  procedure add_item(p_basket_id shopping_item.basket_
  cust_id%type,
                     p_prd_id    shopping_item.prd_id%type,
                     p_qty       shopping_item.
                     quantity%type) is
    v_basket_id  shopping_item.basket_cust_id%type;
    v_price      shopping_item.price%type;
  begin
    v_basket_id := get_basket(p_basket_id);
    /*
    ** Insert the item
    */
    v_price := sales.get_discount_price(p_prd_id);
    insert into shopping_item
           (basket_cust_id, prd_id, price, quantity)
    values (v_basket_id, p_prd_id, v_price, p_qty);
    /*
    ** Update the shopping basket total count
    */
    update shopping_basket
```

LISTING 9.12 Shopping CART.ADD_ITEM procedure in PL/SQL

```
29:       set total_cost = total_cost + (v_price * p_qty)
30:     where cust_id = v_basket_id;
31:   end;
32:
33:   function get_basket(p_basket_id shopping_basket.cust_
      id%type)
34:        return shopping_basket.cust_id%type is
35:     brec shopping_basket%rowtype;
36:   begin
37:      brec.cust_id := p_basket_id;
38:      open bcsr(p_basket_id);
39:      fetch bcsr into brec;
40:      if bcsr%notfound then
41:        insert into shopping_basket
42:               (cust_id, creation_date, shipment_cost,
                   total_cost)
43:        values (p_basket_id, trunc(sysdate), 0.0, 0.0);
44:      end if;
45:      close bcsr;
46:      return brec.cust_id;
47:   end;
48:   . . . // rest of package body
```

LISTING 9.12 *Continued*

Notes on Listing 9.12:
The add item procedure receives three input parameters:

- The id of the shopping basket into which the item is added.
- The product id for the item to be added.
- The quantity of the product to be added.

The add_item procedure adds items, and maintains the basket total price as each new item is added

- In line 17, a calls the get_basket function in the same package, which returns the id of the shopping basket. In the get_basket function, in lines 33–47, an attempt to retrieve the basket record is made, and if it fails, then a new shopping basket entry is created.
- Line 21 calls the SALES.GET_DISCOUNT_PRICE function (shown after these notes) for the specified product id.
- In lines 22–24, a new item record is added to the shopping basket.
- Lines 28–30 update the shopping basket total cost by multiplying the product discount price by the quantity, which is added to the cumulative total of the shopping basket.

The function to get the discount price for the product is located in another package, called sales, and the PL/SQL code is:

```
CREATE OR REPLACE PACKAGE BODY sales IS
   :
   FUNCTION get_discount_price(p_id sales_item.id%type)
RETURN NUMBER IS
     v_discount_price
sales_item.full_price%type;
   BEGIN
     SELECT round(full_price-(full_price *
discount/100), 2)
     INTO v_discount_price
     FROM sales_item
     WHERE id = p_id;
     RETURN v_discount_price;
   END;
   :
END:
```

Creating a Cart and Adding Items from Java using the Cart Package

The Java code example for the ShoppingBasket class, in Listing 9.13, makes use of the PL/SQL functionality built into the cart package by calling its add_item procedure. The cart examples demonstrate how you can group your SQL statements into a stored-procedure environment, and invoke the functionality from your Java applications using JDBC calls.

```
import java.sql.*;

public class ShoppingBasket {
  private int basketId;
  private Connection conn;
  private static final
         String url = "jdbc:oracle:thin:
         @localhost:1521:ORA815";
  private static final String usr = "bookstore";
  private static final String psw = "bookstore";
  private CallableStatement callStmt;

  public ShoppingBasket(int id) {
    if (conn == null) {
      try {
```

LISTING 9.13 Calling a PL/SQL Package procedure from JDBC

```
        Class.forName("oracle.jdbc.driver.
        OracleDriver");
        conn = DriverManager.getConnection(url, usr,
        psw);
        conn.setAutoCommit(false);
        basketId = id;
      }
      catch (Exception e) {
        e.printStackTrace();
      }
    }
  }

  public void addItem(int itemId, int quantity) {
    try {
      callStmt=conn.prepareCall("{ call
      cart.add_item(?,?,?) }");
      callStmt.setInt(1, basketId);
      callStmt.setInt(2, itemId);
      callStmt.setInt(3, quantity);
      callStmt.execute();
      System.out.println("Item Added");
    }
    catch (SQLException e) {
      e.printStackTrace();
    }
    finally {
      try {
        callStmt.close();
      }
      catch (Exception e) {}
    }
  }

  public void saveItems() {
    try {
      conn.commit();
    }
    catch (SQLException e) {
      e.printStackTrace();
    }
  }
```

LISTING 9.13 *Continued*

```
54:
55:   public static void main(String[] args) {
56:     ShoppingBasket cart = new ShoppingBasket(22);
57:     cart.addItem(41, 1);
58:     cart.addItem(20, 1);
59:     cart.saveItems();
60:     cart.close();
61:   }
62: }
```

LISTING 9.13 *Continued*

Notes on listing 9.13:

- Lines 12–24 are the ShoppingBasket constructor, which establishes the JDBC connection, and initializes the basketId instance variable.
- Lines 26–44 show a Java addItem() wrapper method to call the PL/SQL cart.add_item() procedure. The addItem() method requires two arguments: the sales item id, and the quantity ordered.
  a) Line 28 prepares the call to the cart.add_item procedure, with a placeholder for the three input parameters.
  b) Line 29 assigns the value in basketId to the first placeholder.
  c) Line 30 assigns the value in itemId to the second placeholder.
  d) Line 31 sets the value in the quantity for the third placeholder.
  e) Line 32 executes the call, and if it fails, an SQLException is thrown and the catch block manages the error.
  f) Lines 38–42 are the final block used to ensure that the callStmt object is closed before exiting the method.
- Lines 55–61 show the main method used to test the ShoppingBasket class functionality.
  a) Line 56 creates a new shopping basket with a basket id of 22.
  b) Lines 57 and 58, respectively add one item 41 and item 20 into the basket.
  c) Line 59 calls the saveItems() method to commit the SQL changes made to the database.
  d) Line 60 closes the database connection.

This example shows how seamless the integration is between Java and database-stored procedures, independent of the language used in the database procedures. PL/SQL is very efficient at SQL operations; Java is very efficient with computations.

PL/SQL and Java Code for Reading Items in a Cart

Listing 9.16 demonstrates calling the get_items function in the cart package, and shows how to use an Oracle PL/SQL REF CURSOR to obtain a pointer to a result set/cursor of records. The get_item function has two arguments:

- The shopping basket number as an input parameter.
- The total cost for items in the shopping basket as an output parameter.

The function returns a reference cursor to items in the cart.

To receive a result set from PL/SQL into your Java application, the return value from the function of item_refcsr must be converted into a JDBC ResultSet. The item_refcsr type is declared as a REF CURSOR in the PL/SQL package specification (see Listing 9.11, line 2). The REF CURSOR is weakly typed; that is, it is not restricted to return a specific number of columns, and the data type of the columns is not predefined for each query used with the cursor.

```
FUNCTION get_items(p_basket_id shopping_item.basket_cust_id%type,
  p_price out shopping_item.price%type) RETURN item_refcsr IS
    item_csr item_refcsr;
    brec  bcsr%rowtype;  -- bcsr is declared line 3 Listing 9.14
BEGIN
  open bcsr(p_basket_id);
  fetch bcsr into brec;
  if bcsr%found then
    p_price := brec.total_cost;
  else
    p_price := -1;
  end if;
  close bcsr;
  open item_csr for
     select * from shopping_item
     where basket_cust_id = p_basket_id;

   return item_csr;
END;
```

LISTING: 9.14 PL/SQL package function returning a REF CURSOR

Notes on listing 9.14:

- ❑ Line 2 identifies the REF CURSOR type as the return value.
- ❑ Line 3 declares a local variable for the reference cursor value when it is associated with the result set for a query.
- ❑ Line 4 declares a record for the reading shopping basket record (see Listing 9.14, line 3 for the declaration of the bcsr type).
- ❑ Line 6 opens the cursor for shopping basket. The cursor "bcsr" is parameterized with the basket identification to ensure that you get the total cost for the specified shopping basket id.
- ❑ Lines 14–16 initialize the REF cursor variable, item_csr, to point to a set of item rows for the specified basket id. The rows from the REF cursor variable are not fetched.
- ❑ Line 18 returns the REF cursor variable value to the caller.

Listing 9.17 shows a code extract for the showBasket() method, in the ShoppingBasket class. The showBasket() method calls the PL/SQL cart.get_items function, and prints each item record returned from the function. The REF cursor returned by the function is converted into a JDBC ResultSet, whose contents are displayed by calling the printResults() method presented in Listing 9.5.

```
import java.sql.*;
import oracle.jdbc.driver.*;

public class ShoppingBasket {
  private int basketId;
  :
  private CallableStatement callStmt;

  public void showBasket() {
    try {
      System.out.println("Getting Items and Total");
      callStmt=conn.prepareCall("{?=call
      cart.get_items(?,?)}");
      callStmt.registerOutParameter(1,
      OracleTypes.CURSOR);
      callStmt.setInt(2, basketId);
      callStmt.registerOutParameter(3,
      OracleTypes.FLOAT);
      callStmt.execute();

```

LISTING 9.15 Converting a PL/SQL REF Cursor into a Java ResultSet

```
18:       System.out.println("Basket Id: " + basketId);
19:       this.printResults((ResultSet)
          callStmt.getObject(1));
20:       System.out.println("Total Cost: " +
          callStmt.getFloat(3));
21:     }
22:     catch (SQLException e) {
23:       e.printStackTrace();
24:     }
25:
26:   }
27:
28:   :
29:   public static void main(String[] args) {
30:     ShoppingBasket cart = new ShoppingBasket(22);
31:     cart.addItem(41, 1);
32:     cart.addItem(20, 1);
33:     cart.showBasket();
34:     cart.saveItems();
35:     cart.close();
36:   }
37: }
```

LISTING 9.15 *Continued*

Notes on Listing 9.15:

- Line 2 imports the oracle.jdbc.driver packages for using the OracleTypes class final variables to register the REF Cursor as an output return type in line 13.
- Lines 12–16 prepare and execute the get_items function.
  a) Line 12 prepares the function call, with a placeholder for the return value, and two placeholders for the function parameters.
  b) Line 13 registers the first placeholder as an output type of OracleTypes.CURSOR, which is found in the oracle.jdbc.driver package.
  c) Line 14 assigns the basketId value to the second placeholder.
  d) Line 15 registers the third placeholder output type to return an OracleTypes.FLOAT type.
  e) Line 16 executes the PL/SQL function call.
  f) Line 19 calls the getObject() method to convert the REC Cursor returned by the function into a ResultSet. The getObject() method returns a reference to a Java Object type, requiring the cast to a "ResultSet". The Re-

sultSet object returned is passed as a parameter to the printResults() method (see Listing 9.5).

g) Line 20 displays the total cost for items, whose value is returned via the third placeholder in the function call.

- Line 30 creates the cart.
- Lines 31 and 32 each add an item to the cart.
- Line 33 calls the showBasket() method to display the basket contents.

This function call example shows a more complex case of mixing Java with Oracle PL/SQL. It uses a proprietary feature provided as a JDBC extension in the Oracle JDBC drivers. Once again, the database code is responsible for the SQL activity, and the Java code manages the presentation of the data.

9.4.3 JDBC AND TRANSACTIONS

If you are using any JDBC driver in a JVM *outside* the Oracle8i database, then each connection has the auto-commit state set to true. This means that each SQL statement used to modify the database data is automatically committed after successful execution. If you want to control transactional boundaries in your application, set the auto-commit state to false immediately after getting the connection object. The JDBC Connection class has a setAutoCommit() method that is used to change the auto-commit state for a connection, as shown in the following example:

After you have set the auto-commit state to false, you can control when a COMMIT or ROLLBACK operation is performed by calling either the commit() or the rollback() method on the Connection object.

The saveWork() and undoWork() methods in the ExplicitTxControl class of Listing 9.18 show how to use the commit() and rollback() methods.

However, if you have obtained a connection in the JVM *inside* the Oracle8i database, then the auto-commit state is set to false. You must then explicitly issue commit() or rollback() calls, as required.

9.4.4 USING JDBC IN APPLETS

If you are building a Java applet to access the database directly, the issues you must consider are:

- The time it takes to start an applet for the first time, when the JDBC driver classes are required.
- Java applet security constraints and the implications on connecting to your database.

```
import java.sql.*;

public class ExplicitTxControl {
  private Connection  conn;

  public void setConnection (String url, String usr,
String psw) {
    try {
      // load driver
      Class.forName("oracle.jdbc.driver.OracleDriver");

      conn = DriverManager.getConnection(url, usr, psw);
      conn.setAutoCommit(false);  // disable auto commit

    }
    catch (Exception e) {
      e.printStackTrace();
    }
  }

  :

  public void saveWork() {
     conn.commit();            // use commit method
  }

  public void undoWork() {
     conn.rollback();          // use rollback method
  }
  :
}
```

LISTING 9.16 Transaction control in JDBC

9.4.4.1 Java Applet Start-up Time. When downloading an applet requiring a database connection, the thin-client JDBC driver classes must also be pulled into the browser, unless you install the JDBC driver classes default classpath for your browser. Depending on the version of the JDBC driver used, anything between 300K to 550K of additional code has to be pulled across the network.

The overhead of downloading the JDBC classes is a done the first time an applet in a browser needs to use the JDBC driver. Usually, a browser will keep the classes in a disk cache until they are removed to make space for other files in the cache, and in some cases when you end the browser session. The limited lifetime of classes held in the default browser cache can be overcome by using alternative Java Virtual Machine plugins for your Web browser, such as:

- Oracle Jinitiator.
- Sun's Java Plugin.

Fortunately, the default JVM installed with Web browsers can coexist with the alternative Java plug-in options. Oracle Jinitiator and the Sun Java Plugin both provide a Java class cache that is persistent across browser sessions, such that classes are only downloaded when:

- The server classes are newer than versions held in the client cache.
- The client classes have been expired from the cache.

In addition, Oracle Jinitiator and Sun's Java Plugin are available in versions that support up-to-date JDK class libraries, such as JDK 1.2. The disadvantages of using a Java plug-in in the Web browser are:

1. The software for the Java Plugin must be installed in the client.
2. You must modify your HTML file tags to direct the applet to run in the correct JVM in the browser.
3. The Java plug-in is available only on a subset of platforms.

Since not all Web browsers are equal, you need to write the HTML code, or use the Sun Java HTML Converter tool, to support the required syntax for each browser to run your applet in a Java plug-in, and support the default JVM using:

- The <APPLET> tag, to run the applet in browser's default JVM.
- The <EMBED> tag, to direct your applet to use a Java plug-in when using Netscape Navigator.
- The <OBJECT> tag, to direct your applet to use a Java plug-in when using Microsoft Internet Explorer.

Oracle provides sample HTML files showing how to use direct an applet to use Oracle Jinitiator in a browser.

9.4.4.2 Java Applet Security and Database Connections. The default applet security restrictions (known as the *sandbox*) prevent the applet from connecting to another server other than the web server from which it originated. An applet is considered untrusted under the default security settings. Therefore, if your applet requires a database connection, the database must be running on the same host as the Web server used to send the applet to the browser. One solution to this problem is to use a DBMS proxy listener in the Web server, such as the

Oracle8 Connection manager. If you use an RDBMS proxy service, you are required to modify the JDBC connection request in your Java code to identify the host and the RDBMS proxy service listener, in addition to the target database connection.

Another solution is to sign the applet so that it becomes trusted, and the security restrictions are relaxed, eliminating the need to deploy connection proxy software. Signing an applet requires additional coding and managing the client-browser environment; the latter can be logistically unmanageable if your client is located anywhere in the world.

To complicate matters, if your database is kept behind a firewall, the vendor's DBMS protocol would need to support HTTP tunneling techniques, or your firewall would need to provide support for the DBMS vendor protocol; and the network administrator would need to open the appropriate port on the firewall to allow a connection to the database. One solution is for the applet to communicate with a Java Servlet in the Web server, using HTTP tunneling techniques; and the Java servlet running inside the firewall can mediate requests to the database in a uncomplicated and secure manner.

The reason for this digression about JDBC-enabled applets is to point out some of the complex issues that can affect your design and deployment decisions. The solutions to these problem are numerous, and some of the techniques you can employ you are discussed in this book, such as HTTP tunneling, and using servlets, Java server pages, Enterprise JavaBeans, or CORBA objects in the middle tier, or in the Oracle8i database server, to perform the data access on behalf of the applet.

CHAPTER SUMMARY

This chapter covered the basics of JDBC programming in an RDBMS environment. The examples throughout the chapter show how all the SQL statements in JDBC are dynamically constructed as Java strings, and are supplied for processing to various JDBC classes and methods.

You examined examples using the JDBC Statement and PreparedStatement classes for executing SQL statements to query or modify data, and for processing DDL to create database objects. The JDBC CallableStatement was covered to show how to make calls to stored procedures or functions in the database.

The techniques covered in this chapter are the standard low-level calls that a Java application needs to access data in a relational database. The next chapter examines some features of JDBC 2.0, and Oracle Extensions to JDBC 1.0, some of which are part of the JDBC 2.0 standard.

Chapter 10

ENHANCED DATABASE ACCESS WITH JDBC

This chapter extends the work of the preceding chapter, "Data Access with JDBC—Java Database Connectivity." It focuses on two main subjects:

1. Extensions added to the Oracle JDBC 1.0 drivers, and equivalent features now included in JDBC 2.0 core API.
2. Support for certain JDBC 2.0 Optional Package features.[1]

Extensions are supplied with the Oracle JDBC drivers to assist in developing applications that execute with reduced network activity and use extended data types. The features discussed include:

- Row prefetching for processing query result sets
- Batch execution of non-query operations
- Using streaming data types
    - Oracle LONG and LONG RAW columns
    - Oracle CLOB, BLOB, and BFILE columns
- Oracle SQL object types
- Varying-array and nested-table collections.

The JDBC 2.0 Optional Package features covered include:

- Scrollable cursors
- Using the JDBC DataSource for connections
- Using Java Naming and Directory Interface (JNDI) to obtain JDBC Connections
- Connection pooling

10.1 EXTENSIONS TO ORACLE JDBC DRIVERS

This section begins by covering techniques that minimize network traffic by using row prefetching and batch updates. It then explores examples demonstrating how to use extended JDBC driver features to work with more complex data types.

10.1.1 USING JDBC DRIVER EXTENSIONS

When you use the standard JDBC call to obtain a connection from the driver manager, the vendor JDBC driver specified in the connection URL creates the Connection object. The Connection object typically contains all the standard JDBC functionality plus vendor-specific extensions. Subsequently, when you create a Statement, PreparedStatement, and CallableStatement object from a Connec-

[1]The JDBC 2.0 Optional Package was formerly known as the JDBC 2.0 Standard Extension API.

tion, a vendor-specific object is created. For highly portable code, you write code using the standard JDBC classes and methods available.

However, there are times when you need to invoke the vendor-specific extensions, as when you wish to take advantage of performance enhancements or to use features only available in vendor-specific data source, for example, the BFILE data type in an Oracle database.[2] You can write your Java code to use vendor extensions in one of two ways:

1. Instantiate standard JDBC objects, and then cast them to the vendor-specific objects as needed. For example:

```
package com.prenhall.OFJP.jdbc;

import java.sql.*;
import oracle.jdbc.driver.*;

public class MyClass {
  public static void main(String[] args) throws Exception {
    Connection conn = DriverManager.getConnection("url...", ...);
    ((OracleConnection) conn).setDefaultExecuteBatch(2); // CAST!!
    :
  }
}
```

2. Cast the JDBC object when obtained and then directly use the vendor-specific functionality. For example:

```
package com.prenhall.OFJP.jdbc;

import java.sql.*;
import oracle.jdbc.driver.*;

public class MyClass {
  public static void main(String[] args) throws Exception {
    OracleConnection conn =  // cast
       (OracleConnection) DriverManager.getConnection("url...");
    conn.setDefaultExecuteBatch(2);   //use
    :
  }
}
```

[2]BFILE represents a locator to a file stored in a directory of the operating system. The BFILE type was introduced in Chapters 2 and 7, but is covered in more detail in this chapter.

In either case, you need to use the vendor-specific classes, and, as shown in the preceding examples, the Oracle JDBC driver classes are located in the `oracle.jdbc.driver` package. It is a good idea to include this package in an import statement before your class definition. The examples in this book use the first technique where possible.

10.1.2 ROW PREFETCHING

Calling the ResultSet next() JDBC method typically fetches one row at a time, and a row fetch operation, depending on your JDBC driver, may require a single-network roundtrip to the database. With Oracle JDBC drivers, you can set the number of rows to prefetch when requesting a result set that is populated during a query. This has the benefit of reducing the number of network round trips to the server. You can set the number of rows to prefetch for either of the two following possibilities:

- Queries for all Statement and PreparedStatement objects used with Connection.
- Queries executed with a particular Statement or PreparedStatement object.

Assume that the prefetch size is 10. In that case, when you execute a query, the JDBC driver prefetches ten rows before you process the first row with a call to the ResultSet next() method. The next() method fetches the first row from the JDBC driver buffers, until the tenth row has been read by the application. When the eleventh fetch operation is initiated, the JDBC driver buffers the next ten rows.

10.1.2.1 Setting the Default Row Prefetch. Calling a method on a Connection object sets the default row prefetch for all queries executed with Statement or PreparedStatement objects derived from the connection.

The technique used to alter the default row prefetch size is to cast the Connection object reference to an OracleConnection in order to call the setDefaultPrefetch() method. For example:

```
package com.prenhall.OFJP.jdbc;

import java.sql.*;
import oracle.jdbc.driver.*;

public class RowPrefetch {

```

LISTING 10.1 Setting or getting the default row prefetch size

```
08:   private static final String url = "jdbc:oracle:thin:" +
09:                 "bookstore/bookstore@localhost:1521:ORA815";
10:   private static Connection conn = null;
11:   private static Statement stmt = null;
12:
13:   public static void main(String[] args) {
14:     try {
15:       DriverManager.registerDriver(new OracleDriver());
16:       conn = DriverManager.getConnection(url);
17:       conn.setAuto-commit(false);
18:
19:       System.out.println("Default conn prefetch: " +
20:         ((OracleConnection) conn).getDefaultRowPrefetch());
21:
22:       ((OracleConnection) conn).setDefaultRowPrefetch(5);
23:
24:       System.out.println("Default conn prefetch: " +
25:         ((OracleConnection) conn).getDefaultRowPrefetch());
26:
  :
39:     }
40:     catch (Exception e) {
41:       e.printStackTrace();
42:     }
43:     finally {
44:       try {if (stmt != null) stmt.close();} catch(Exception e) {}
45:       try {if (conn != null) conn.close();} catch(Exception e) {}
46:     }
47:   }
48: }
```

Resulting output is:

```
Default conn prefetch: 10
Default conn prefetch: 5
```

LISTING 10.1 *Continued*

Notes on Listing 10.1:

- Line 4 is the import of the package for the Oracle JDBC driver classes.
- Line 20 casts the Connection object into an OracleConnection to call the getDefaultRowPrefetch() method.
- Line 22 casts the Connection into an OracleConnection to call the setDefaultRowPrefetch() method, which changes the default row prefetch size for all subsequent queries executed with this Connection.
- Lines 27–38 are omitted from this listing because they are shown in Listing 10.2.

The output results of Listing 10.1 reveal that the default row prefetch size for Oracle JDBC Drivers has a value of ten.

10.1.2.2 Setting the Row Prefetch for a Statement. There may be times when you find that the default row prefetch size applied to a Statement or PreparedStatement object derived from a Connection is not suitable for some scenarios. For example, the Oracle JDBC drivers automatically set the row prefetch size to one if a query is processing a streaming data type, such as LONG or LOB types. Therefore, if you have a requirement to execute a query with a row prefetch size different from the default, you call the setRowPrefetch() method when you cast:

- ❑ A Statement object to an OracleStatement
- ❑ A PreparedStatement to an OraclePreparedStatement
- ❑ A CallableStatement to a OracleCallableStatement

In each case, a call to the setRowPrefetch() method changes the row prefetch setting for the queries executed with the specific statement object. For example:

```
package com.prenhall.OFJP.jdbc;

import java.sql.*;
import oracle.jdbc.driver.*;

public class RowPrefetch {

  private static final String url = "jdbc:oracle:thin:" +
            "bookstore/bookstore@localhost:1521:ORA815";
  private static Connection conn = null;
  private static Statement stmt = null;

  public static void main(String[] args) {
    try {
      DriverManager.registerDriver(new OracleDriver());
      conn = DriverManager.getConnection(url);
      conn.setAuto-commit(false);
      // Default Row fetch set to five.
 :
      stmt = conn.createStatement();
      System.out.println("Connection row prefetch: " +
```

LISTING 10.2 Setting and getting a Statement row Prefetch size

```
29:          ((OracleConnection) conn).getDefaultRowPrefetch() + "\n"+
30:          "Statement row prefetch: " +
31:          ((OracleStatement) stmt).getRowPrefetch());
32:
33:        ((OracleStatement) stmt).setRowPrefetch(2);
34:
35:        System.out.println("Connection row prefetch: " +
36:          ((OracleConnection) conn).getDefaultRowPrefetch() + "\n"+
37:          "Statement row prefetch: " +
38:          ((OracleStatement) stmt).getRowPrefetch());
39:      }
40:      catch (Exception e) {
41:        e.printStackTrace();
42:      }
43:      finally {
44:        try {if (stmt != null) stmt.close();} catch(Exception e) {}
45:        try {if (conn != null) conn.close();} catch(Exception e) {}
46:      }
47:    }
48: }
```

LISTING 10.2 *Continued*

Listing 10.2 is the same class as Listing 10.1, but lines 19–26 are excluded in this example to focus on the calls to the OracleStatement getRowFetch() and setRowFetch() methods.

Notes on Listing 10.2:

- ❑ Lines 29–31 print the row prefetch setting for the Connection and for the Statement, which are initially the same.
- ❑ Line 33 sets the row prefetch on Statement object, which is first cast to an OracleStatement to call the setRowPrefetch() method.
- ❑ Line 38 uses the getRowPrefetch() method on the OracleStatement object to confirm the new row prefetch size of two. The same print statement should show that the default row prefetch size for the Connection is still five.

The row prefetch extension affects data retrieval through queries. Batch updates are supported for insert, update, and delete operations.

10.1.3 USING BATCH UPDATES

Like the row prefetch extension, the purpose of using batch updates is to minimize network traffic for non-query operations. By default, the Oracle JDBC driver has an execute batch size of one. Therefore, the Oracle JDBC driver executes an

INSERT, UPDATE, or DELETE statement immediately upon request in one network roundtrip,[3] via the execute() or executeUpdate() method. If you want to reduce the amount of network traffic that can result from executing a large number of statements, then you can set the execute batch size to a specified number appropriate for your application.[4] The Oracle JDBC driver uses the specified batch size to control the maximum number of statements sent to the database for execution in a single network roundtrip.

The JDBC driver automatically sends batched updates to the server for execution when the number of updates executed equals the execute batch size. If the number of updates executed is less than the execute batch size, then you have to call a method to force the JDBC driver to send the batched operations to the database server for execution.

To use the Oracle JDBC Driver batch update facility, you can call the following methods in the OracleConnection class:

- The setDefaultExecuteBatch(int) method to set the batch size for all update operations.
- The getDefaultExecuteBatch() method to determine the default execute batch size.

You can also use the JDBC driver batch features with the following methods in the OraclePreparedStatement class:

- The setExecuteBatch() method to set the execute batch size for operations executed using the specific PreparedStatement object. This overrides the default execute batch size set for the connection object.
- The getExecuteBatch() method to determine the batch size for the PreparedStatement.
- The sendBatch() method to force the JDBC driver to send a partially filled batch for execution.

An incomplete batch is also sent to the database for execution when any of the following conditions occur:

- A commit() operation is performed.
- The statement is closed.
- The connection is closed.

---

[3]In a network roundtrip, a request is sent to the server, the server executes the request, and the result is returned to the application initiating the request.

[4]There is no documented limit to the execute batch size used by the Oracle JDBC driver.

If automatic commit mode is enabled in the Oracle JDBC driver, then batch operations are committed immediately after they are sent to the database for execution; otherwise the operations sent to the database are executed but are not saved until the application explicitly performs a commit operation. The example in Listing 10.3 illustrates the behavior of batched updates.

```
package com.prenhall.OFJP.jdbc;
import java.sql.*;
import oracle.jdbc.driver.*;

public class BatchUpdate {
  private static final String url =
    "jdbc:oracle:thin:bookstore/bookstore@localhost:1521:ORA815";
  private static Connection conn = null;
  private static Statement stmt = null;
  private static ResultSet rset = null;
  private static PreparedStatement pstmt = null;

  public static void main(String[] args) {
    try {
      DriverManager.registerDriver(new OracleDriver());
      conn = DriverManager.getConnection(url);
      conn.setAuto-commit(false);

      stmt = conn.createStatement();
      try { stmt.execute("drop table demo_upd"); }
      catch (SQLException e) {}
      stmt.execute("create table demo_upd (col1  number(4))");

      pstmt = conn.prepareStatement(
                    "insert into demo_upd (col1) values (?)");
      System.out.println("Default batch size: " +
        ((OracleConnection) conn).getDefaultExecuteBatch());
      System.out.println("Prepared Statement batch size: " +
        ((OraclePreparedStatement) pstmt).getExecuteBatch());

      ((OracleConnection) conn).setDefaultExecuteBatch(5);
      ((OraclePreparedStatement) pstmt).setExecuteBatch(2);

      System.out.println("Default batch size: " +
        ((OracleConnection) conn).getDefaultExecuteBatch());
      System.out.println("Prepared Statement batch size: " +
        ((OraclePreparedStatement) pstmt).getExecuteBatch());
```

LISTING 10.3 Using batch updates with Oracle JDBC driver

```
38:       for (int i = 1; i <= 5; i++) {
39:         pstmt.setInt(1, i);
40:         pstmt.executeUpdate();
41:         rset = stmt.executeQuery(
42:                  "select count(*) from demo_upd");
43:         if (rset.next()) {
44:           System.out.println("Batch Update count: " + i +
45:              " -> Table row count: " + rset.getInt(1));
46:         }
47:       }
48:       ((OraclePreparedStatement) pstmt).sendBatch();
49:       rset = stmt.executeQuery("select count(*) from demo_upd");
50:       if (rset.next()) {
51:         System.out.println("Final row count: " + rset.getInt(1));
52:       }
53:     }
54:     catch (Exception e) { e.printStackTrace(); }
55:     finally {
56:       try {if (rset != null) rset.close();}catch(Exception e){}
57:       try {if (stmt != null) stmt.close();}catch(Exception e){}
58:       try {if (pstmt != null) pstmt.close();}catch(Exception e){}
59:       try {if (conn != null) conn.close();}catch(Exception e){}
60:     }
61:   }
62: }
```

LISTING 10.3 *Continued*

Notes on Listing 10.3:

- Lines 15–17 create the database connection.
- Lines 19–22 are to first drop the demo_upd table and then to re-create it. If the drop table fails, it is ignored because the table does not exist.
- Lines 24 and 25 prepare a statement to test the batch updates with an insert statement on the demo_upd table.
- Lines 26–29 print the update batch size for the Connection and the PreparedStatement. At this point, the batch size is the same for both objects.
- Line 31 sets the default batch size for all PreparedStatements to five. The setDefaultExecuteBatch() method of OracleConnection object is called to set the default batch size.
- Line 32 overrides the default batch size of five, and sets the batch size to two for the PreparedStatement. The OraclePreparedStatement setExecuteBatch() method is called to set the batch size for the statement.

- Lines 34–37 confirm the default and the PreparedStatement executes batch settings.
- Lines 38–47 show a loop that executes the PreparedStatement five times. After each call to execute the PreparedStatement, a query is performed to determine how many rows are physically in the database table (see the resulting output after these notes)
- Line 48 makes a call to the PreparedStatement sendBatch() method to flush the fifth and last record to the database.
- Lines 49–52 confirm that the last update is flushed to the table.

The result, excluding the line numbers, produced by the method represented in Listing 10.3 is:

```
01: Default batch size: 1
02: Prepared Statement batch size: 1
03: Default batch size: 5
04: Prepared Statement batch size: 2
05: Batch Update count: 1  -> Table row count: 0
06: Batch Update count: 2  -> Table row count: 2
07: Batch Update count: 3  -> Table row count: 2
08: Batch Update count: 4  -> Table row count: 4
09: Batch Update count: 5  -> Table row count: 4
10: Final row count: 5
```

Notes on Listing 10.3 results:

- In lines 1 and 2, the default batch size is one, immediately after obtaining a connection.
- Line 4 highlights that the PreparedStatement will batch two rows at a time.
- Line 5 shows that one update has been performed, but that there are no rows in the table. The JDBC driver has cached the update request.
- Line 6 shows that the second update is done. The JDBC driver detects that the batch update row size has been reached, and sends the two cached update statements to the database to be executed. Therefore, the number of rows in the table is now also shown as two.
- Line 7 shows that another update is cached, with two rows still in the database table.
- Line 8 causes both cached statements to be executed on the table, resulting in four rows being added to the table.
- Line 9 indicates that a fifth update has been made but not yet added to the table.
- Line 10 shows that the final update has been added to the table, after the sendBatch() method was called.

Although batching your updates reduces network traffic and improves performance, it comes at the cost of extra memory usage in your application environment. Batch operations are temporarily disabled when an SQL operation involves streaming data types for SQL large object types. The next part of this section covers data management of streaming data types.

10.1.4 STREAMING DATA TYPES

Streaming data types refer to columns designed to hold unstructured data, such as images, video, or music. This type of information is often too large to query or change using simple SET and GET methods. The column data types that are classified as streaming data types are the SQL large object types, which include:

- LONG and LONG RAW
- CLOB, BLOB, and BFILE

In order to read data from, or write data to, columns based on these types, you have to use Java stream classes.

10.1.4.1 LONG, LONG RAW, and LOBs. Oracle database tables allow storage of up to two gigabytes of data in a LONG or LONG RAW column. A LONG column stores character data, and a LONG RAW stores binary data. Oracle databases only allow one LONG or LONG RAW column to be present in a table. In Oracle8, large object data types (LOBs) were added to extend storage management of large unstructured data, and you can have more than one LOB column per table. Three LOB types are available in Oracle8 and above:

- The Character Large Object (CLOB) type allows up to four gigabytes of character data to be stored.[5]
- The Binary Large Object (BLOB) type allows up to four gigabytes of binary data to be stored.[6]
- The BFILE type is used for read-only access of files physically located in the operating system directories.[7]

10.1.4.2 Creating CLOBs, BLOBs, and BFILEs. CLOBs and BLOBs are made up of two parts, as pictured in Figure 10.1.

---

[5]The CLOB is referred to as an internal LOB because the data are stored in the database.

[6]The BLOB is referred to as an internal LOB because the data are stored in the database.

[7]The BFILE type is referred to as an external LOB because the data are stored external to the database.

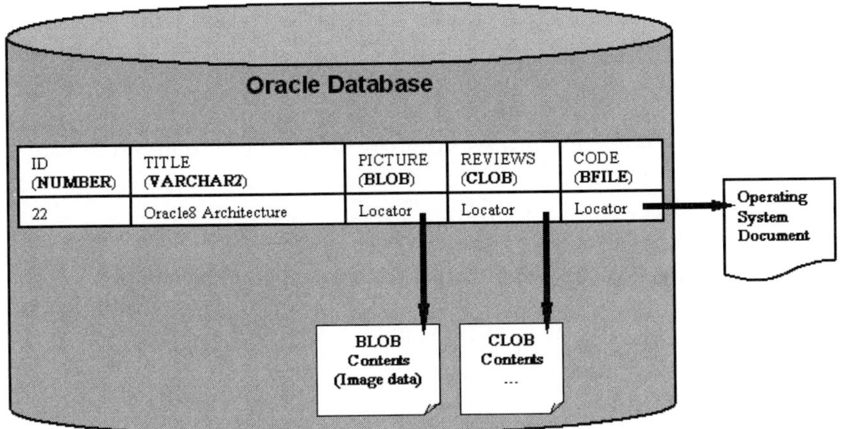

FIGURE 10.1 CLOB, BLOB, and BFILE storage

- A *locator* is a pointer to the location where the LOB contents are stored. The locator value is stored in the row of a table containing the large object column.
- The contents of the large object data stored in the database are physically separate from the data row holding the LOB locator.

Figure 10.1 shows a table with one CLOB, BLOB, and BFILE column with sample data for one row depicting the storage of large object data.

You can use the Oracle SQL functions EMPTY_CLOB() and EMPTY_BLOB(), respectively, to create and initialize CLOBs and BLOBs. For example:

```
CREATE TABLE sales_item (
  id          NUMBER(6) PRIMARY KEY,
  title       VARCHAR2(40) NOT NULL,
  picture     BLOB,
  reviews     CLOB,
  code        BFILE);

INSERT INTO sales_item (id, title, picture)
VALUES (1, 'Oracle, Java and E-Commerce', EMPTY_BLOB());

UPDATE sales_item
  SET reviews = EMPTY_CLOB()
WHERE id = 1;
```

LISTING 10.4 Creating an empty CLOB and BLOB using SQL

Listing 10.4 creates the table, pictured in Figure 10.1, and then populates one row with an empty BLOB to initialize the locator. The CLOB column, which is set to NULL with the INSERT statement, is initialized to be an empty CLOB locator during the UPDATE statement. The BFILE column is left NULL for the moment. Listing 10.4 demonstrates how to use SQL to create an empty LOB to initialize the LOB locator to point to an empty content area. The locator is created before the LOB contents are added. These statements are executed using a JDBC Statement or a PreparedStatement.

To populate the LOB contents, you must first read the LOB locator value stored in a row using a SELECT statement, and then use the LOB locator like a file handle:

- ❑ In the Oracle PL/SQL DBMS_LOB package supplied with Oracle8 databases and higher, to read or write the LOB contents.
- ❑ Converted into a Java stream object, and then use the Java I/O stream API to read and write the LOB contents (this section shows how to work with LOB data types using Java streams).

Write operations performed on the LOB locator and contents are subject to database transaction control, such that a COMMIT will save changes made to a LOB, and a ROLLBACK will discard any changes made to the LOB.

A BFILE data type is a locator pointing to a physical file in the directory of the operating system executing the Oracle RDBMS software. Before you create a BFILE locator, you should create a directory alias that identifies the path to where the files will be stored in the file system. The BFILE locator is then created using the Oracle SQL function called BFILENAME() with the following two required arguments:

1. The directory alias, or logical name, identifying a path to a physical directory in the file system that contains the files.
2. The filename of the physical file located in the directory pointed to by the alias.

Listing 10.5 shows how you can create a BFILE locator, using the SQL language, that can be executed from your Java code using JDBC calls.

```
CREATE DIRECTORY sales_item_docs AS 'D:\sales_item\images';

UPDATE sales_item
  SET code = BFILENAME('SALES_ITEM_DOCS', 'supplier_ref.doc')
WHERE id = 1;
```

LISTING 10.5 Creating a BFILE locator using SQL

Notes on Listing 10.5:

- The name appearing after the CREATE DIRECTORY keywords is the directory alias, or logical name. The path of the directory is enclosed in single quotes after the keyword AS, and case-sensitivity is dependent on the underlying operating system. If you enclose the alias in double quotes, it is stored in the Oracle data dictionary with the case preserved; otherwise it is stored in uppercase text by default.
- The CREATE DIRECTORY statement requires you to have the CREATE ANY DIRECTORY system privilege. Database users who have the DBA role have this right by default.
- The first parameter to the BFILENAME function is a case-sensitive directory alias name, which must be entered in uppercase letters if the alias was not enclosed in double quotes when created.
- The second parameter to the BFILENAME function is the file name to be located in the directory identified by the alias. The case-sensitivity of the file name is dependent on the underlying operating system.

The physical directory and the file do not need to exist in order for you to create the directory alias or the BFILE locator. However, the physical directory and file must exist before you attempt to access the contents of the file using Java streams or the PL/SQL DBMS_LOB package functionality.

10.1.4.3 A Note on Code Examples. The stream code examples are shown in the context of a class shown in Listing 10.6.

```
package com.prenhall.OFJP.jdbc;

import java.io.*;
import java.sql.*;
import oracle.jdbc.driver.*;

public class LongsLobsBfile {
  private static Connection conn;

  public static void executeSql(String sql) {
    Statement stmt = null;
    System.out.println("Execute: " + sql);
    try {
      stmt = conn.createStatement();
      if (stmt.execute(sql))  {
```

LISTING 10.6 Class structure for streams

```
16:         ExecuteQuery.printResults(stmt.getResultSet());
17:       }
18:       else {
19:         System.out.println(stmt.getUpdateCount() +
20:            " row(s) altered");
21:       }
22:     }
23:     catch (Exception e) { e.printStackTrace(); }
24:     finally {
25:       try { if (stmt != null) stmt.close(); }
26:       catch (Exception e){}
27:     }
28:   }
29:
30:   public static void main(String[] args) {
31:     String url = "jdbc:oracle:thin:" +
32:        "bookstore/bookstore@localhost:1521:ORA815";
33:     try {
34:       if (args.length == 1) url = args[0];
35:       DriverManager.registerDriver(
36:          new oracle.jdbc.driver.OracleDriver());
37:       conn = DriverManager.getConnection(url);
38:       // do some work
39:     }
40:     catch (Exception e) { e.printStackTrace(); }
41:     finally {
42:       try { if (conn != null) conn.close(); }
43:       catch (Exception e) {}
44:       conn = null;
45:     }
46:   } // end of main()
47: }
```

LISTING 10.6 *Continued*

Notes on Listing 10.6:

- In line 38, the comment "do some work" is replaced with calls to the executeSql() method, shown in lines 10–28, and calls to the method demonstrating the use of a stream type.
- Lines 10–28 reveal the executeSql() code fragment and are not shown in subsequent examples.

However, the main() method in the examples shows the relevant calls. It is time now to look at some Java code that uses LONGs, LOBs, and BFILEs.

10.1.4.4 Reading from a LONG Column. A LONG column can be used to store character data, such as unformatted resume information, reviews, and commentaries. The following steps are necessary to read data from a LONG or LONG RAW column:[8]

1. Use a JDBC statement to query the table with a LONG or LONG RAW column.
2. Get the column as a stream object using either:
   - ❑ The getAsciiStream() method for a LONG.[9]
   - ❑ The getBinaryStream() for a LONG RAW.
3. Use the stream read methods to copy the data from the column into application buffers.
4. Close the stream.

The method in Listing 10.7 shows how to read data from a LONG column.

```
package com.prenhall.OFJP.jdbc;

import java.io.*;
import java.sql.*;
import oracle.jdbc.driver.*;

public class LongsLobsBfile {
  private static Connection conn;

  public static void readLong(int id) {
    PreparedStatement ps = null;
    ResultSet r = null;
    InputStream in = null;

    try {
      ps = conn.prepareStatement(
             "select len, data from demo_long where id = ?");
      ps.setInt(1, id);
```

LISTING 10.7 Reading a LONG column

[8]The JDBC driver temporarily sets the row prefetch to one for queries fetching data from a LONG or LONG RAW column.

[9]The getAsciiStream() method is part of the JDBC 1.0 specification. However, the getCharacterStream() method has been added to JDBC 2.0 and is recommended because it provides support for internationalization.

```
      r = ps.executeQuery();
      if (r.next()) {
        int length = r.getInt(1);
        in = r.getAsciiStream(2);
        System.out.println("Long has " + length + " characters");
        byte[] data = new byte[length];
        in.read(data);
        System.out.println(new String(data));
      }
      else {
         System.out.println("No record with id = " + id);
      }
    }
    catch (Exception e) { e.printStackTrace(); }
    finally {
      try { if (in != null) in.close(); } catch (Exception e) {}
      try { if (r != null) r.close(); } catch (Exception e) {}
      try { if (ps != null) ps.close(); } catch (Exception e) {}
    }
  }
  public static void main(String[] args) {
    String url = "jdbc:oracle:thin:" +
                 "bookstore/bookstore@localhost:1521:ORA815";
    try {
      if (args.length == 1) url = args[0];
      DriverManager.registerDriver(
         new oracle.jdbc.driver.OracleDriver());
      conn = DriverManager.getConnection(url);

      executeSql("drop table demo_long");
      executeSql("create table demo_long " +
              "(id number(4), len number(6), data long)");
      writeLong(1, "long0.txt");
      readLong(1);
    }
    catch (Exception e) { e.printStackTrace(); }
    finally {
      try { if (conn != null) conn.close(); }
      catch (Exception e) {}
      conn = null;
    }
  }
}
```

LISTING 10.7 *Continued*

Notes for Listing 10.7:

- Line 10 defines the start of the readLong method, which accepts a single parameter for a query to read a row with a long column.
- Lines 16 and 17 create a query to read two columns for a row with a value specified in the id parameter. The first column (len) holds the length of the data stored in the second LONG column (data).[10]
- Line 19 executes the query.
- Line 20 fetches the row.
- Line 21 gets the length of the data in column two.
- Line 22 calls the result set getAsciiStream() method, which returns an InputStream object for the LONG column.
- Line 24 creates a byte array buffer large enough to hold the data, based on the length of the LONG column.
- Line 25 reads the data into the byte array.
- Line 26 prints the array contents.
- Line 48 drops a table called demo_long if it exists.
- Lines 49 and 59 create the table demo_long.
- Line 51 inserts a record with long column value set to the contents of a file called "long0.txt". The writeLong() method is covered later in this chapter.
- Line 52 calls the readLong() method to read the contents of a long column created by line 51.

If you wish to ignore the stream data for the LONG column, you can immediately close the input stream.

10.1.4.5 Reading from a LONG RAW Column. In an Oracle7 or higher database, LONG RAW columns can be used to store binary data, such as images,[11] and formatted data, such as Microsoft Word or Excel documents. This section shows the code to read data a LONG RAW column that contains image data. The data is read into a byte buffer, which is given to a PictureFrame object. The code for the PictureFrame object is shown after the code for reading the LONG RAW data.

---

[10]It is a good idea to have a column to hold the length of the data in a LONG column to help process the data. SQL's LENGTH() function does not work with LONG columns.

[11]In an Oracle8 or higher database, the BLOB or BFILE is recommended for binary data storage.

```
package com.prenhall.OFJP.jdbc;
import java.io.*;
import java.sql.*;
import oracle.jdbc.driver.*;

public class LongsLobsBfile {
  private static Connection conn;

  public static void readLongRaw(int id) {
    PreparedStatement ps = null;
    PictureFrame window = null;
    ResultSet r = null;
    InputStream in = null;

    try {
      ps = conn.prepareStatement(
            "select id, len, data " +
            "from demo_longraw where id = ?");
      ps.setInt(1, id);
      r = ps.executeQuery();
      if (r.next()) {
        id = r.getInt(1);
        int length = r.getInt(2);
        in = r.getBinaryStream(3);
        byte[] buf = new byte[length];
        in.read(buf);
        System.out.println("Long has " + length + " characters");
        window = new PictureFrame(buf);
        window.setVisible(true);
      }
    }
    catch (Exception e) { e.printStackTrace(); }
    finally {
      window = null;
      try { if (r != null) r.close(); } catch (Exception e) {}
      try { if (in != null) in.close(); } catch (Exception e) {}
      try { if (ps != null) ps.close(); } catch (Exception e) {}
    }
  }

  public static void main(String[] args) {
    String url = "jdbc:oracle:thin:" +
                 "bookstore/bookstore@localhost:1521:ORA815";
    try {
```

LISTING 10.8 Reading a LONG RAW column

```
45:         if (args.length == 1) url = args[0];
46:         DriverManager.registerDriver(
47:            new oracle.jdbc.driver.OracleDriver());
48:         conn = DriverManager.getConnection(url);
49:         executeSql("drop table demo_longraw");
50:         executeSql("create table demo_longraw " +
51:               "(id number(4), len number(6), data long raw)");
52:         writeLongRaw(1, "jdev1.jpg");
53:         readLongRaw(1);
54:      }
55:      catch (Exception e) { e.printStackTrace(); }
56:      finally {
57:        try { if (conn != null) conn.close(); }
58:        catch (Exception e) {}
59:        conn = null;
60:      }
61:    }
62: }
```

LISTING 10.8 *Continued*

Notes on Listing 10.8:

- Lines 16–18 prepare and execute a query to read in the image data, including the length of the binary data.
- Line 19 sets the image row primary key value for the query.
- Line 23 gets the length of the image data.
- Line 24 creates an InputStream to the LONG RAW column using the getBinaryStream() method.
- Line 25 creates an array of bytes large enough to hold all the image data in the long raw column.
- Line 26 reads all the image data into the byte buffer.
- Lines 28 and 29 create a PictureFrame object to display the image in a Java frame. The code for the PictureFrame class is shown in Listing 10.9.

The PictureFrame Class

The PictureFrame class presented in Listing 10.9 is a utility class that you can use to display an image read from any source. To use the PictureFrame class, you need to:

1. Read the image data into an array of bytes.
2. Create the PictureFrame object passing the array of bytes as an argument to the PictureFrame constructor.

   For example:

```
int imageDataLen = . . .;
byte[] imageArray = new byte[imageDataLen]; // set array size
//1. Read image data into the array
. . .
//2. Create the PictureFrame with the array
PictureFrame frame = new PictureFrame(imageArray);
```

```
package com.prenhall.OFJP.jdbc;

import java.awt.*;
import java.awt.event.*;
import javax.swing.*;

public class PictureFrame extends Frame {
  public static final int MAX_WIDTH = 500;
  public static final int MAX_HEIGHT = 600;
  private Image imageData;

  private class MyCanvas extends Canvas {
    public void paint(Graphics p0) {
      super.paint(p0);
      p0.drawImage(imageData, 0, 0,
           this.getSize().width, this.getSize().height, this);
    }
  }

  public PictureFrame(byte[] theImage) {
    try {
      ImageIcon imageIcon = new ImageIcon(theImage);
      int width = imageIcon.getIconWidth();
      int height = imageIcon.getIconHeight();
      if (height > MAX_HEIGHT) height = MAX_HEIGHT;
      if (width > MAX_WIDTH) width = MAX_WIDTH;

      imageData = imageIcon.getImage();
```

LISTING 10.9 PictureFrame source code

```
29:       this.setSize(width, height);
30:       this.addWindowListener(new WindowAdapter() {
31:         public void windowClosing(WindowEvent e) {
32:           System.exit(0);
33:         }
34:       });
35:       this.add(new MyCanvas());
36:     }
37:     catch (Exception e) {
38:       e.printStackTrace();
39:     }
40:   }
41: }
```

LISTING 10.9 *Continued*

Notes on Listing 10.9:

- On line 7, the PictureFrame class is defined as a subclass of the Java AWT Frame class. This class is designed to display an image within the Frame, based on the size of the image.
- The width and height of an image are constrained to a maximum size specified by the values of the MAX_WIDTH and MAX_HEIGHT constants.
- Lines 12–18 are the lines for an inner class called MyCanvas that extends the Java AWT Canvas class. This inner class is used to paint the image into the frame.
- Lines 20–40 contain the code for the constructor of the PictureFrame class. The constructor receives a byte array as an argument.
- Line 22 creates a Java ImageIcon object using the data in the byte array parameter.
- Lines 23–26 constrain the image size, if required.
- Line 28 initializes the imageData instance variable of the PictureFrame class. The imageData instance references the Java AWT image object.
- Line 29 sets the frame dimensions based on the actual or adjusted width and height of the image.
- Lines 30–34 are the lines of code for the event handler of the window-closing event on the frame.
- Line 35 adds a MyCanvas object into the Frame image object rendered to the frame, by the MyCanvas, whose contents are the image. The image is painted to the frame when the frame becomes visible.

The PictureFrame class is a basic utility that can be used to display the image data read from a database column. Subsequent examples in this chapter that read binary images from the database use the PictureFrame class to display the image.

10.1.4.6 Writing to a LONG Column. In an Oracle7 or higher database, if you want to write a large amount of character data into a column—i.e., more than 2,000 characters (4,000 for Oracle8)—then the LONG column could be used. The steps to write data to a LONG (or a LONG RAW) column are:[12]

1. Create an InputStream for the source of the data to be written to the column.
2. Create the SQL statement to insert data into the table containing the LONG (or LONG RAW) column.
3. Use the setAsciiStream()method for a LONG, and the setBinaryStream() for a LONG RAW, to associate the InputStream with the column in the table. [13]
4. Execute the SQL statement, which automatically writes the InputStream data to the long column.

Listing 10.10 is an example of writing a text file to a long column.

```
package com.prenhall.OFJP.jdbc;
import java.io.*;
import java.sql.*;
import oracle.jdbc.driver.*;

public class LongsLobsBfile {
  private static Connection conn;

  public static void writeLong(int id, String filename) {
    PreparedStatement ps = null;
    BufferedInputStream in = null;
    File f = null;

    try {
```

LISTING 10.10 Writing to a LONG column

[12]In Oracle8 and higher, the recommended column type for large amounts of character data is the CLOB, and for binary data the BLOB.

[13]The code example is tested with a JDBC 1.0 driver; if you are using a JDBC 2.0 driver, use the setCharacterStream() method to write correctly internationalized applications.

```
      ps = conn.prepareStatement(
            "insert into demo_long (id, len, data) " +
            "values (?,?,?)");
      f = new File(filename);
      System.out.println("File: " + f.getAbsolutePath());
      in = new BufferedInputStream(new FileInputStream(f));
      ps.setInt(1, id);
      ps.setInt(2, (int) f.length());
      ps.setAsciiStream(3, in, (int) f.length());
      ps.execute();
      System.out.println("Inserted " + ps.getUpdateCount());
    }
    catch (Exception e) {e.printStackTrace(); }
    finally {
      f = null;
      try { if (in != null) in.close(); } catch (Exception e) {}
      try { if (ps != null) ps.close(); } catch (Exception e) {}
    }
  }

  public static void main(String[] args) {
    String url = "jdbc:oracle:thin:" +
        "bookstore/bookstore@localhost:1521:ORA815";
    try {
      if (args.length == 1) url = args[0];
      DriverManager.registerDriver(
         new oracle.jdbc.driver.OracleDriver());
      conn = DriverManager.getConnection(url);
      executeSql("drop table demo_long");
      executeSql("create table demo_long " +
          "(id number(4), len number(6), data long)");
      writeLong(1, "long0.txt");
      writeLong(2, "long1.txt");
    }
    catch (Exception e) { e.printStackTrace(); }
    finally {
      try { if (conn != null) conn.close(); }
      catch (Exception e) {}
      conn = null;
    }
  }
}
```

LISTING 10.10 *Continued*

Notes on Listing 10.10:

- Line 9 is the declaration of the writeLong() method, which accepts an id and a filename. The id is a unique number for a new row to be added to the demo_long table, which contains a LONG column to hold the contents of the file named in the second parameter.
- Lines 15–17 create a prepared statement to insert the data.
- Line 20 creates a BufferedInputStream for a file input stream for the file on disk.
- Line 22 gets the length of the file from the File object, and sets the length value for the second column in the SQL INSERT operation.
- Line 23 sets the InputStream and length for an AsciiStream for the LONG in the third column of the INSERT operation.
- Line 24 executes the INSERT operation and stores the row data with the file contents in the LONG column. The inserted row is automatically saved, because the default auto-commit state is true for the connection.

10.1.4.7 Writing to a LONG RAW Column. LONG RAW columns are typically used to store amounts of large binary data up to two gigabytes. Although the recommended approach for an Oracle8 or higher database is to use a BLOB, the example in Listing 10.11 shows how you can write data to a LONG RAW column. The example uses a FileInputStream() object as the source for the binary data, which could be any binary information, such as an image, video clip, or some digital music.

```
package com.prenhall.OFJP.jdbc;
import java.io.*;
import java.sql.*;
import oracle.jdbc.driver.*;

public class LongsLobsBfile {
  private static Connection conn;

  public static void writeLongRaw(int id, String filename) {
    PreparedStatement ps = null;
    InputStream in = null;
    File f= null;

    try {
      ps = conn.prepareStatement(
        "insert into demo_longraw (id, len, data) " +
```

LISTING 10.11 Writing to a LONG RAW column

```
        "values (?,?,?)");
      f = new File(filename);
      System.out.println("File: " + f.getAbsolutePath());
      in = new FileInputStream(f);

      ps.setInt(1, id);
      ps.setInt(2, (int) f.length());
      ps.setBinaryStream(3, in, (int) f.length());
      ps.execute();
      System.out.println("Inserted " + ps.getUpdateCount());
    }
    catch (Exception e) { e.printStackTrace(); }
    finally {
      f = null;
      try { if (in != null) in.close(); } catch (Exception e) {}
      try { if (ps != null) ps.close(); } catch (Exception e) {}
    }
  }

  public static void main(String[] args) {
    String url = "jdbc:oracle:thin:" +
        "bookstore/bookstore@localhost:1521:ORA815";
    try {
      if (args.length == 1) url = args[0];
      DriverManager.registerDriver(
         new oracle.jdbc.driver.OracleDriver());
      conn = DriverManager.getConnection(url);
      executeSql("drop table demo_longraw");
      executeSql("create table demo_longraw " +
         "(id number(4), len number(6), data long raw)");
      writeLongRaw(1, "jdev1.jpg");
      writeLongRaw(2, "javamap1.gif");
      writeLongRaw(3, "panpac.jpg");
    }
    catch (Exception e) { e.printStackTrace(); }
    finally {
      try { if (conn != null) conn.close(); }
      catch (Exception e) {}
      conn = null;
    }
  }
}
```

LISTING 10.11 *Continued*

Notes on Listing 10.11:

- Line 15–17 prepares an INSERT statement to add a row to the `demo_longraw` table.
- Line 23 sets the second column value to the length of the binary data to be stored in the LONG RAW column. The length of the data is determined from the file object created on line 18.
- Line 24 associates the InputStream with a binary stream to the third column in the INSERT statement.
- Line 25 performs the INSERT operation, which also writes the binary data from the FileInputStream to the column. The insert operation is committed because auto-commit mode is on.

In JDBC terms, reading from or writing to a LONG or LONG RAW column, where the data are stored in line with other column data, is similar to reading or writing standard column data types. The key is to associate the correct Java object type with the corresponding column data type.

10.1.4.8 Reading from a LOB Column. The process of reading or writing large object types is a little different from working with LONG and LONG RAW types. As stated in the section on creating LOBs earlier in this chapter, when you use a large object type, a LOB locator is stored in the LOB column with each data row, but the LOB data are stored in a location physically separate from the row inside the database.

The following steps are required when reading a LOB and its contents in Java:

1. Query the result set, and fetch the row.
2. Get the LOB locator as a Java stream object.
3. Call the getCharacterStream() method for a CLOB, and the getBinaryStream() for a BLOB.
4. Process the data via the stream object before processing any other data. If you wish to skip processing the LOB data, you can call the stream close() method immediately after getting the stream object.

Reading from a CLOB

Listing 10.12 shows an example of reading data from a CLOB column by first reading the LOB locator and then getting a stream to the LOB data via the LOB locator.

```
package com.prenhall.OFJP.jdbc;
import java.io.*;
import java.sql.*;
import oracle.jdbc.driver.*;

public class LongsLobsBfile {
  private static Connection conn;

  public static void readClob(int id) {
    PreparedStatement ps = null;
    BufferedReader br = null;
    ResultSet r = null;

    try {
      ps = conn.prepareStatement(
         "select id, cdata from demo_clob where id = ?");
      ps.setInt(1, id);
      r = ps.executeQuery();
      if (r.next()) {
        System.out.println("Clob id: " + r.getInt(1));
        oracle.sql.CLOB clob = ((OracleResultSet)r).getCLOB(2);
        br = new BufferedReader(clob.getCharacterStream());
        String s;
        System.out.println("Clob Data");
        System.out.println("———-");
        while ((s = br.readLine()) != null) {
          System.out.println(s);
        }
      }
      else {
        System.out.println("No CLOB with id = " + id);
      }
    }
    catch (Exception e) { e.printStackTrace(); }
    finally {
      try { if (r != null) r.close(); } catch (Exception e) {}
      try { if (br != null) br.close(); } catch (Exception e) {}
      try { if (ps != null) ps.close(); } catch (Exception e) {}
    }
  }

  public static void main(String[] args) {
    String url = "jdbc:oracle:thin:" +
```

LISTING 10.12 Reading data from a CLOB column

```
44:         "bookstore/bookstore@localhost:1521:ORA815";
45:     try {
46:       if (args.length == 1) url = args[0];
47:       DriverManager.registerDriver(
48:          new oracle.jdbc.driver.OracleDriver());
49:       conn = DriverManager.getConnection(url);
50:       executeSql("drop table demo_clob");
51:       executeSql("create table demo_clob " +
52:          "(id number(4) primary key, cdata clob)");
53:       writeClob(1, "clob1.txt");
54:       readClob(1);
55:     }
56:     catch (Exception e) { e.printStackTrace(); }
57:     finally {
58:       try { if (conn != null) conn.close(); }
59:       catch (Exception e) {}
60:       conn = null;
61:     }
62:   }
63: }
```

LISTING 10.12 *Continued*

Notes for Listing 10.12:

- Line 9 declares the readClob() method, which receives an integer parameter specifying the id of a row containing the CLOB data to be read.
- Line 10 declares a PreparedStatement variable for executing the query to read the CLOB locator.
- Line 11 declares a BufferedReader variable for reading the CLOB data.
- Lines 15 and 16 prepare the query to read the `cdata` column containing the CLOB locator for a specified id.
- Line 17 associates the input parameter value with the placeholder in the WHERE clause of the query, and line 18 executes the query.
- Line 21 casts the ResultSet variable `r` to an OracleResultSet reference in order to call the getCLOB() method for the CLOB column in the query. The OracleResultSet.getCLOB() method returns a reference to an oracle.sql.CLOB object which is a Java class representing the CLOB locator.
- Line 22 uses the CLOB object getCharacterStream() method to return an input stream, which is wrapped into a BufferedReader object.
- Lines 26–28 use the BufferedReader object to read the contents of the CLOB and print the result.

- Line 51 uses the executeSql() method, discussed in Listing 10.6, to create the `demo_clob` table with the CLOB column `cdata`.
- Line 53 uses a writeClob() method to populate the CLOB column with data. The writeClob() method is discussed in the next section, "Writing to a LOB Column."
- Line 54 invokes the readClob() method.

The example code, in line 21 uses the oracle.sql.CLOB object to read the CLOB locator from a database column. The oracle.sql.CLOB class was added to the Oracle JDBC driver class library, as an extension to the JDBC 1.0 standard,[14] in order to handle CLOB data in an Oracle-specific way.

With a JDBC 2.0–capable JDBC driver, you can use the java.sql.Clob class, instead of the oracle.sql.CLOB class, for handling CLOB data types. To use the JDBC 2.0 java.sql.Clob class, the following code changes are made in lines 21 and 22 in Listing 10.12:

```
21:         java.sql.Clob clob = r.getClob(2);
22:         br = new BufferedReader(clob.getCharacterStream());
```

So why use the java.sql.Clob or the oracle.sql.CLOB class? Use the java.sql.Clob class if you must develop JDBC-compliant code without vendor extensions. However, using java.sql.Clob, you can only write data from one CLOB column to another. This leaves you with the problem of populating the first CLOB with data using vendor-specific commands.

The oracle.sql.CLOB class is an extension in the Oracle JDBC driver that allows you to write the CLOB data from an OutputStream or a Writer as the source of the data.

The writeClob() method, in the section called "Writing to a LOB," shows how you can use the oracle.sql.CLOB class to write the CLOB data from a Java OutputStream or Writer.

Reading from a BLOB

Reading a BLOB column is similar to reading a CLOB, except that a binary stream object is used instead of an ASCII or Unicode stream. If you obtain a binary stream object from a BLOB, you can work with the binary data using JDK binary stream classes, if appropriate.

If the data are a stream of bytes, such as the data for an image, use the getBytes() method from the oracle.sql.BLOB or java.sql.Blob class. The oracle.sql.BLOB is an Oracle JDBC driver extension to JDBC. The java.sql.Blob

---

[14]The JDBC 2.0 specification added functionality for the CLOB and BLOB data types.

class is part of the JDBC 2.0 standard and is equivalent to using the oracle.sql.BLOB, but without the capability to write to the BLOB using a stream.

The oracle.sql.BLOB and the java.sql.Blob have getBytes() method signatures that specify two arguments:

1. The first is a long value for the byte position to starting reading the data.
2. The second is an integer (int) value for the number bytes or length of data to be read.

The getBytes()returns a byte array object.[15] Listing 10.13 is an example of reading from a BLOB column as a stream of bytes into a byte array. The byte array is then given to a new PictureFrame object (see Listing 10.9) to display the image.

```
package com.prenhall.OFJP.jdbc;
import java.io.*;
import java.sql.*;
import oracle.jdbc.driver.*;

public class LongsLobsBfile {
  private static Connection conn;

  public static void readBlob(int id) {
    PreparedStatement ps = null;
    ResultSet r = null;
    PictureFrame window = null;

    try {
      ps = conn.prepareStatement(
          "select id, bdata from demo_blob where id = ?");
      ps.setInt(1, id);
      r = ps.executeQuery();
      if (r.next()) {
        System.out.println("Blob id: " + r.getInt(1));
        oracle.sql.BLOB blob =  ((OracleResultSet) r).getBLOB(2);
        byte[] buf = blob.getBytes(1L, (int)blob.length());
        System.out.println("Blob: " + blob.length() + " bytes");
```

LISTING 10.13 Reading data from a BLOB column

[15]The oracle.sql.BLOB class has an overloaded version of the getBytes() method:
byteCount = blob.getBytes(1L, buf.length, buf)
The method returns the number of bytes actually read, and the third argument is a byte array object that must be created before the call. Using this method signature is less portable than the two-argument getByte() method shown in the example.

```
24:         window = new PictureFrame(buf);
25:         window.setVisible(true);
26:       }
27:       else {
28:         System.out.println("No BLOB record with id = " + id);
29:       }
30:     }
31:     catch (Exception e) { e.printStackTrace(); }
32:     finally {
33:       window = null;
34:       try { if (r != null)  r.close(); } catch (Exception e) {}
35:       try { if (ps != null) ps.close(); } catch (Exception e) {}
36:     }
37:   }
38:
39:   public static void main(String[] args) {
40:     String url = "jdbc:oracle:thin:" +
41:         "bookstore/bookstore@localhost:1521:ORA815";
42:     try {
43:       if (args.length == 1) url = args[0];
44:       DriverManager.registerDriver(
45:          new oracle.jdbc.driver.OracleDriver());
46:       conn = DriverManager.getConnection(url);
47:       executeSql("drop table demo_blob");
48:       executeSql("create table demo_blob " +
49:           "(id number(4) primary key, bdata blob)");
50:       writeBlob(1, "jdev2.gif");
51:       readBlob(1);
52:     }
53:     catch (Exception e) { e.printStackTrace(); }
54:     finally {
55:       try { if (conn != null) conn.close(); }
56:       catch (Exception e) {}
57:       conn = null;
58:     }
59:   }
60: }
```

LISTING 10.13 *Continued*

Notes for Listing 10.13:

- Line 16 creates a prepared statement to read the row containing the specified id and BLOB locator.

- ❑ Line 18 executes the query, and line 19 fetches the row; if one exists, lines 20–26 read and display the image contained in the BLOB.
- ❑ Line 21 reads the BLOB locator using the getBLOB() method from the JDBC ResultSet when it is cast to OracleResultSet.
- ❑ Line 22 calls the BLOB object getBytes() method to read the binary image data into a byte array.
- ❑ Line 24 passes the image byte array as an argument to the PictureFrame constructor, to create a Frame that displays the image.
- ❑ Lines 48 and 49 create the table to hold the BLOB data.
- ❑ Line 50 stores an image from a file in the database table using the writeBlob() method, which is covered in the next section, "Writing to a LOB Column."
- ❑ Line 51 uses the readLob() method to read the image from the database column, and displays the image in a Java frame.

If you want to use JDBC 2.0 classes, you can replace lines 21 and 22 with the following code:

```
21:   java.sql.Blob blob =  r.getBlob(2);
22:   byte[] buf = blob.getBytes(1L, (int)blob.length());
```

10.1.4.9 Writing to a LOB Column. Writing to a LOB column can be done using the oracle.sql.CLOB or oracle.sql.BLOB class, if the source of your data is outside the database. To write to an LOB using the oracle.sql classes, you perform the following steps:

1. Turn auto-commit off to enable starting a transaction.
2. If a LOB does not exist, first create a LOB locator using an SQL insert statement (refer to the section called "Creating CLOBs, BLOBs, and BFILEs"), and query the LOB locator. Alternatively, you can execute a PL/SQL block, procedure, or function with an INSERT statement, using the RETURNING clause to create and retrieve the BLOB locator in a single SQL call.
3. If you are using a CLOB locator, then get its AsciiOutputStream or CharacterOutputStream object for writing character data. If you are using a BLOB locator, get the BinaryOutputStream for writing binary data.
4. Use the stream write/output methods to store data in the LOB contents.
5. Always flush, or close, the LOB output stream before you perform a commit. A part of your LOB data will not be saved if you perform a commit before flushing the LOB stream.
6. Call the commit() method to complete the transaction.

The example in Listing 10.14 shows how to write to a new CLOB column, and the example in Listing 10.15 demonstrates how to store data in a BLOB column. Changes to the contents of a CLOB or a BLOB are part of a transaction and are saved using a COMMIT statement, or discarded using a ROLLBACK statement. Therefore, it is important to turn auto-commit off when inserting a new LOB, because you want the LOB locator and the LOB contents to be part of the same transaction to be saved or discarded as a logical unit of work.

Writing to a CLOB

```
package com.prenhall.OFJP.jdbc;
import java.io.*;
import java.sql.*;
import oracle.jdbc.driver.*;

public class LongsLobsBfile {
  private static Connection conn;

  public static void writeClob(int id, String filename) {
    PreparedStatement ps = null;
    ResultSet r = null;
    PrintWriter cw = null;
    BufferedReader in = null;
    File f= null;

    try {
      conn.setAuto-commit(false);
      ps = conn.prepareStatement(
              "insert into demo_clob (id, cdata) " +
              "values (?, EMPTY_CLOB())");
      ps.setInt(1, id);
      ps.executeUpdate();
      System.out.println("Inserted clob: "+ ps.getUpdateCount());

      // query the clob locator
      ps = conn.prepareStatement(
          "select cdata from demo_clob " +
          "where id = ? for update");
      ps.setInt(1, id);
      r = ps.executeQuery();
      if (r.next()) {
        oracle.sql.CLOB clob =  ((OracleResultSet) r).getCLOB(1);
        f = new File(filename);
        System.out.println("File: " + f.getAbsolutePath());
        cw = new PrintWriter(clob.getCharacterOutputStream());
        in = new BufferedReader(new InputStreamReader(
                                  new FileInputStream(f)));
```

LISTING 10.14 Writing to a CLOB column

```
        String line;
        while ((line = in.readLine()) != null) {
          cw.println(line);
        }
        cw.flush();
        conn.commit();
        System.out.println("File copied to Clob");
      }
    }
    catch (Exception e) {
       try { conn.rollback(); } catch (Exception e1) {}
       e.printStackTrace();
    }
    finally {
      f = null;
      try { conn.setAuto-commit(true); } catch (Exception e) {}
      try { if (cw != null) cw.close(); } catch (Exception e) {}
      try { if (in != null) in.close(); } catch (Exception e) {}
      try { if (r != null)  r.close(); } catch (Exception e) {}
      try { if (ps != null) ps.close(); } catch (Exception e) {}
    }
  }

  public static void main(String[] args) {
    String url = "jdbc:oracle:thin:" +
        "bookstore/bookstore@localhost:1521:ORA815";
    try {
      if (args.length == 1) url = args[0];
      DriverManager.registerDriver(
         new oracle.jdbc.driver.OracleDriver());
      conn = DriverManager.getConnection(url);
      executeSql("drop table demo_clob");
      executeSql("create table demo_clob " +
         "(id number(4) primary key, cdata clob)");
      writeClob(1, "clob1.txt");
      writeClob(2, "clob2.txt");
    }
    catch (Exception e) { e.printStackTrace(); }
    finally {
      try { if (conn != null) conn.close(); }
      catch (Exception e) {}
      conn = null;
    }
  }
}
```

LISTING 10.14 *Continued*

Notes on Listing 10.14:

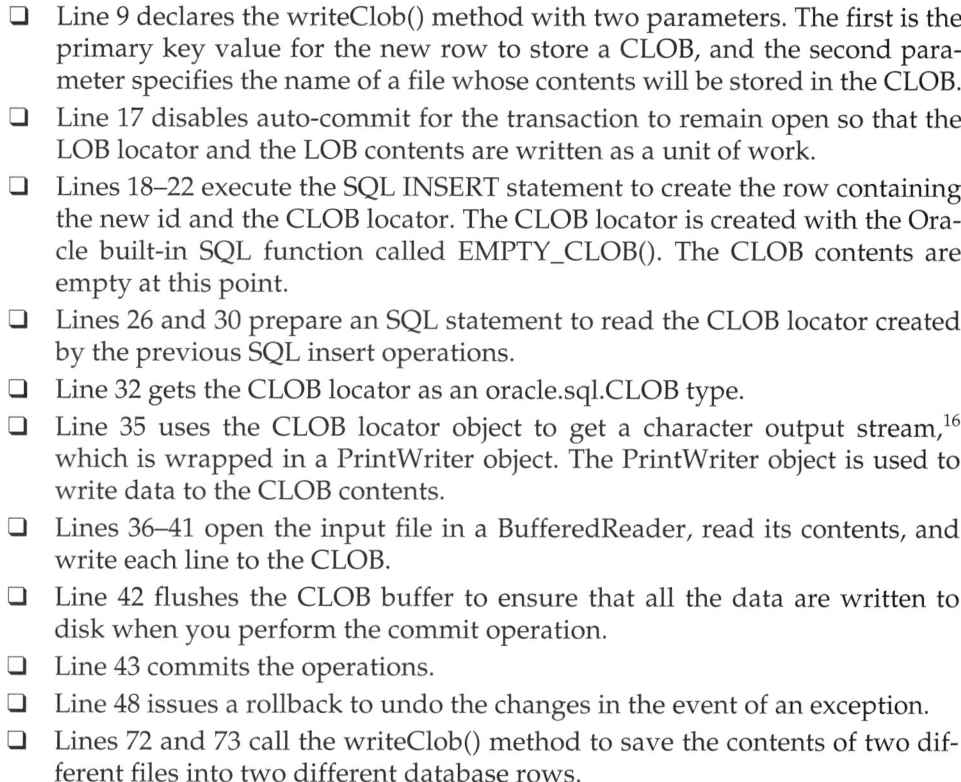

- Line 9 declares the writeClob() method with two parameters. The first is the primary key value for the new row to store a CLOB, and the second parameter specifies the name of a file whose contents will be stored in the CLOB.
- Line 17 disables auto-commit for the transaction to remain open so that the LOB locator and the LOB contents are written as a unit of work.
- Lines 18–22 execute the SQL INSERT statement to create the row containing the new id and the CLOB locator. The CLOB locator is created with the Oracle built-in SQL function called EMPTY_CLOB(). The CLOB contents are empty at this point.
- Lines 26 and 30 prepare an SQL statement to read the CLOB locator created by the previous SQL insert operations.
- Line 32 gets the CLOB locator as an oracle.sql.CLOB type.
- Line 35 uses the CLOB locator object to get a character output stream,[16] which is wrapped in a PrintWriter object. The PrintWriter object is used to write data to the CLOB contents.
- Lines 36–41 open the input file in a BufferedReader, read its contents, and write each line to the CLOB.
- Line 42 flushes the CLOB buffer to ensure that all the data are written to disk when you perform the commit operation.
- Line 43 commits the operations.
- Line 48 issues a rollback to undo the changes in the event of an exception.
- Lines 72 and 73 call the writeClob() method to save the contents of two different files into two different database rows.

Managing Output with Oracle LOB Classes

When using the oracle.sql.CLOB class or oracle.sql.BLOB class, you may wish to manage the amount of disk output performed to write the data to the LOB contents. Instead of writing your data one character at a time, you may want to write it in chunks (i.e., more than one character at a time). To assist in minimizing I/O activity, you can call the CLOB or BLOB getChunkSize() method to determine the LOB storage chunk size in bytes. Each chunk represents part of the total data contents. Listing 10.15 shows how you can make use of the chunk size to minimize I/O operations when writing a BLOB column.

---

[16]The CharacterOutputStream was used here instead of the AsciiOutputStream because it is easier to internationalize an application with a character output stream. The example was developed using an Oracle JDBC 1.x compliant driver that provides both types of streams.

Writing to a BLOB

```
package com.prenhall.OFJP.jdbc;
import java.io.*;
import java.sql.*;
import oracle.jdbc.driver.*;

public class LongsLobsBfile {
  private static Connection conn;

  public static void writeBlob(int id, String filename) {
    PreparedStatement ps = null;
    ResultSet r = null;
    File f = null;
    OutputStream out = null;
    InputStream in = null;
    byte[] buf = null;
    int len;

    try {
      conn.setAuto-commit(false);
      ps = conn.prepareStatement(
         "insert into demo_blob (id, bdata) " +
         "values (?, EMPTY_BLOB())");
      ps.setInt(1, id);
      ps.execute();
      System.out.println("Inserted: " + ps.getUpdateCount());

      // query the blob locator
      ps = conn.prepareStatement(
          "select bdata from demo_blob " +
          "where id = ? for update");
      ps.setInt(1, id);
      r = ps.executeQuery();
      if (r.next()) {
        oracle.sql.BLOB blob =  ((OracleResultSet) r).getBLOB(1);
        f = new File(filename);
        System.out.println("File: " + f.getAbsolutePath());
        out = blob.getBinaryOutputStream();
        in = new FileInputStream(f);
        buf = new byte[blob.getChunkSize()];

        while ((len = in.read(buf)) != -1) {
          out.write(buf, 0, len);
```

LISTING 10.15 Writing to a BLOB column

```
        }
        out.flush();
        conn.commit();
        System.out.println("File copied to Blob");
      }
    }
    catch (Exception e) {
      try { conn.rollback(); } catch (Exception e1) {}
      e.printStackTrace();
    }
    finally {
      f = null;
      buf = null;
      try { conn.setAuto-commit(true); } catch (Exception e) {}
      try { if (out != null)  out.close();} catch(Exception e) {}
      try { if (in != null)  in.close(); } catch (Exception e) {}
      try { if (r != null)  r.close(); } catch (Exception e) {}
      try { if (ps != null) ps.close(); } catch (Exception e) {}
    }
  }

  public static void main(String[] args) {
    String url = "jdbc:oracle:thin:" +
        "bookstore/bookstore@localhost:1521:ORA815";
    try {
      if (args.length == 1) url = args[0];
      DriverManager.registerDriver(
         new oracle.jdbc.driver.OracleDriver());
      conn = DriverManager.getConnection(url);
      executeSql("drop table demo_blob");
      executeSql("create table demo_blob " +
         "(id number(4) primary key, bdata blob)");
      writeBlob(1, "jdeveloper.gif");
      writeBlob(2, "jdevlogo.jpg");
    }
    catch (Exception e) { e.printStackTrace(); }
    finally {
      try { if (conn != null) conn.close(); }
      catch (Exception e) {}
      conn = null;
    }
  }
}
```

LISTING 10.15 *Continued*

Notes on Listing 10.15:

- ❑ Line 19 turns auto-commit off to give you control over the transaction boundary so that you can insert the BLOB locator and write the BLOB contents before the COMMIT.
- ❑ Lines 20–24 create a PreparedStatement to insert an new row with an empty BLOB, initializing the BLOB locator with the Oracle built-in SQL function called EMPTY_BLOB().
- ❑ Lines 28–32 prepare and execute a query to read the BLOB locator.
- ❑ Line 34 obtains the BLOB locator into a Java oracle.sql.BLOB. The oracle.sql.BLOB type is used because you can obtain an OutputStream, or Writer, object for adding the LOB contents. The java.sql.Blob class does not provide output streams, only inputs streams. The ResultSet object variable `r` is cast to an OracleResultSet to call the extended functionality to get the first column as a BLOB.
- ❑ Line 37 gets the BinaryOutputStream object from the BLOB locator. The stream is used to write the contents of the BLOB to the database.
- ❑ Line 38 creates an input stream to a file for the source of the image data.
- ❑ Line 39 creates a byte array based with a size of the BLOB getChunkSize() value.
- ❑ Lines 41–43 use the `buf` byte array to read bytes from the input stream in chunk-size blocks, and write each block of data to the BLOB contents.
- ❑ Line 44 calls the flush() method of the BLOB output stream to ensure that all data are saved in the BLOB contents.
- ❑ Line 45 completes the transaction, saving the LOB locator and its associated LOB contents.

10.1.4.10 An ImageLoader Application. Using the knowledge gained about BLOB data types, you can examine an example of using a BLOB to store images. The example is called the ImageLoader application. The ImageLoader application requires a file name in its first command-line argument. The file name can include wildcard characters. The optional second, third, and fourth command-line arguments are for the user name, password, and JDBC URL, respectively.

The ImageLoader utility uses the file name argument to construct a list of files, each of which is read as image data and inserted in a BLOB column for a new row in a table.

The LoadImage class constructor, dbInitialize(), and dbClose() methods are shown in Listing 10.16.

```
package com.prenhall.OFJP.jdbc;
import java.sql.*;
import java.io.*;
import oracle.jdbc.driver.*;
```

LISTING 10.16 The ImageLoader Class constructor and initialization

```
public class LoadImage {
  private static String user = "bookstore";
  private static String pswd = "bookstore";
  private static
     String url = "jdbc:oracle:thin:@localhost:1521:ORA815";
  private static String file = "*.*";
  private File fileList = null;
  private Connection conn;
  private PreparedStatement pstmt1, pstmt2;
  private String[] fileNames;

  public LoadImage() {
    dbInitialize();
    if (fileNames != null) {
      loadImages();
    }
    dbClose();
  }

  private void dbInitialize() {
    try {
      Class.forName("oracle.jdbc.driver.OracleDriver");
      conn = DriverManager.getConnection(url, user, pswd);
      conn.setAuto-commit(false);
      pstmt1 = conn.prepareStatement(
         "insert into images (filename, picture) " +
         "values (?, EMPTY_BLOB())");
      pstmt2 = conn.prepareStatement(
         "select picture from images where filename = ?");
      fileList = new File(file);
      fileNames = fileList.list(new ImageFilter());
      System.out.println("File path: " + fileList.getPath() +
                         fileList.separator);
    }
    catch (Exception e) {
      e.printStackTrace();
    }
  }

  private void dbClose() {
    try {
      pstmt1.close();
      pstmt2.close();
```

LISTING 10.16 *Continued*

```
48:         conn.close();
49:       }
50:       catch (SQLException e) {
51:         e.printStackTrace();
52:       }
53:     }
54:     :
55: }
```

LISTING 10.16 *Continued*

Notes on Listing 10.16:

- Lines 16–22 are for the LoadImage() constructor, which calls the dbInitialize() method, checks whether there are file names in the list to be processed, and then calls the loadImages() method to process the files in the file name list. The dbClose() method is used to close the connection with the database and to release other resources.
- Lines 24–42 show the dbInitialize() method, which performs the following tasks:
  - Line 26 loads the JDBC driver.
  - Line 27 connects to the database.
  - Line 28 sets auto-commit to false, required when creating LOB locators and writing data to the LOB.
  - Lines 29–31 create a PreparedStatement that populates a specific image table record with an image id and a BLOB locator to LOB with empty contents. The PreparedStatement is reused for each LOB added to the image table.
  - Lines 32–33 show the PreparedStatement used to get the LOB locator into the Java application. It is assumed that the file name is unique.
  - Line 34 creates a new java.io.File object using the string value in the `file` variable.
  - Line 35 calls the list() method of the File object to return an array of image files. The list() method uses the ImageFilter class (see Listing 10.17) to apply a file name filter to ensure that files with valid extensions are processed by the application.
- Lines 44–53 show the dbClose() method that disconnects from the database after releasing resources used by the PreparedStatement objects.

The code for the ImageLoader file-name filter class is shown in Listing 10.17.

```
package com.prenhall.OFJP.jdbc;
import java.io.*;
class ImageFilter implements FilenameFilter {
  public boolean accept(File dir, String name) {
    return (name.toLowerCase().endsWith(".gif") ||
            name.toLowerCase().endsWith(".jpeg") ||
            name.toLowerCase().endsWith(".jpg"));
  }
}
```

LISTING 10.17 ImageFilter class used to create a file-name filter

Notes on Listing 10.17:

- The ImageFilter class implements the FilenameFilter interface defined in the java.io package. This is the implementation of the FilenameFilter interface `accept()` method that checks the file type (or extension) for one of the listed extensions.

This class and method can be extended to support additional image file extensions without changing the code that uses the ImageFilter class.

The main() method of the ImageLoader class is shown in Listing 10.18.

```
public class LoadImage {
  :

  public static void main(String[] args) {
    switch (args.length) {
      case 4:
        url = args[3];
      case 3:
        pswd = args[2];
      case 2:
        user = args[1];
      case 1:
        files = args[0];
        break;
      default:
        if (args.length > 0) {
          System.out.println(
```

LISTING 10.18 ImageLoader main() method

```
18:               "Usage: LoadImage [file] [user] [pswd] [url]");
19:           System.exit(1);
20:         }
21:         break;
22:     }
24:
25:     new LoadImage();
26:     System.out.println("Done");
27:   }
28:
29: }
```

LISTING 10.18 *Continued*

Notes on Listing 10.18:

- The main method accepts several command-line arguments:
  1. A file name, with or without wildcards.
  2. A valid database username.
  3. A valid database password for the specified user.
  4. The JDBC URL for the database to store the image data.
- The switch statement starting at line 5 stores the command-line argument values into the appropriate static variables.
- Line 25 creates a new LoadImage() object which processes the data. Note that the code must be modified to write data to different database columns and tables.

The code in Listing 10.19 shows the methods that process each file in the file name list by opening each image file and storing its contents in the appropriate BLOB column.

```
public class LoadImage {
  :
  private void loadImageData(String fileName,
                             oracle.sql.BLOB blob) {
    try {
      File binaryFile = new File(fileList.getPath() +
                                 fileList.separator+fileName);
      FileInputStream instream = new FileInputStream(binaryFile);
      OutputStream outstream = blob.getBinaryOutputStream();

```

LISTING 10.19 ImageLoader JDBC code

```
      int chunk = blob.getChunkSize();
      byte[] buffer = new byte[chunk];
      int length = -1;

      while ((length = instream.read(buffer)) != -1) {
        outstream.write(buffer, 0, length);
      }
      outstream.close();
      instream.close();
    }
    catch (Exception e) {
      e.printStackTrace();
    }
  }

  private void loadImages() {
    int rows = 0;
    ResultSet rset = null;
    try {
       for (int i = 0; i < fileNames.length; i++) {
          System.out.println("Process image: " + fileNames[i]);
          pstmt1.setString(1, fileNames[i]);
          pstmt2.setString(1, fileNames[i]);
          rows += pstmt1.executeUpdate();
          rset = pstmt2.executeQuery();
          if (rset.next()) {
            loadImageData(fileNames[i],
            ((OracleResultSet)rset).getBLOB(1)); }
          conn.commit();
          System.out.println(rows + " rows(s) processed");
       }
    }
    catch (Exception e) {
      try { conn.rollback(); } catch (Exception e1) {}
      e.printStackTrace();
    }
    finally {
      try {if (rset != null) rset.close();}catch(Exception e){}
    }
  }
  :
}
```

LISTING 10.19 *Continued*

Notes for Listing 10.19:

- Lines 3–23 are the code used to open and read contents of the file represented by the `fileName` argument. The file contents are written to the BLOB contents associated with the BLOB locator passed in the second argument. This code uses the same technique discussed in "Writing to a BLOB" earlier in this chapter.
- Lines 26–50 show the code that loops through the array of file names, and for each file name inserts a record containing the file name and a BLOB locator pointing to empty BLOB contents. The SQL statements used are found in Listing 10.16.
- Lines 32 and 34, respectively, prepare and execute the INSERT statement to create the BLOB locator for the image.
- Lines 33 and 35 execute the query to get the BLOB locator for the new row inserted in line 34.
- Line 36 fetches the row containing the BLOB locator.
- Line 37 passes the file name and the BLOB locator to the loadImageData() method.

An alternative to storing a file's contents in a database LOB column is to use a BFILE column (refer to "Creating CLOBs, BLOBs, and BFILEs").

10.1.4.11 Reading Data from a BFILE. Using a BFILE is useful for accessing read-only data stored in files that are seldom changed, such as image files. As stated in "Creating CLOBs, BLOBs, and BFILEs," two steps are required before a file can be accessed via a BFILE column:

1. A database directory alias must be created for the physical directory on the platform containing the files. The alias is created with the Oracle SQL CREATE DIRECTORY statement. Only users with the CREATE ANY DIRECTORY privilege (e.g., users with DBA roles) can execute the CREATE DIRECTORY statement.
2. An INSERT or UPDATE statement must be executed with the BFILENAME() function to set the value for the BFILE column. The BFILENAME() function creates a BFILE locator, a logical pointer to the physical file.

Since BFILE columns are read-only LOBs, you cannot modify the contents of the file pointed to by the BFILE locator. The BFILE locator value can be changed to point to a different physical file or set to a NULL value breaking the link with its associated physical file. Listing 10.20 shows a Java method that creates a BFILE locator to point to a physical file.

```
01: public void writeBFile(int id, String filename) {
02:   if (conn != null) {
03:     try {
04:       PreparedStatement ps = conn.prepareStatement(
05:          "insert into demo_bfile (id, fileptr) " +
06:          "values (?, BFILENAME('BFILE_DIR', ?))");
07:       ps.setInt(1, id);
08:       ps.setString(2, filename);
09:       ps.execute();
10:       System.out.println("Initialized: "+id+" file: "+filename);
11:       ps.close();
12:     }
13:     catch (Exception e) {
14:       e.printStackTrace();
15:     }
16:   }
17:   else {
18:     System.out.println("Connection required");
19:   }
20: }
```

LISTING 10.20 Creating BFILE links

Notes on Listing 10.20:

- Lines 4– 6 create a PreparedStatement to insert a new BFILE locator. The BFILENAME() function uses the value for the directory alias as 'BFILE_DIR'. In this example, it is assumed that the directory alias BFILE_DIR has been created using an appropriate CREATE DIRECTORY statement (refer to "Creating CLOBs, BLOBs, and BFILEs").
- Line 7 uses the `id` variable value to set the primary key column for the new record.
- Line 8 uses the `filename` variable for the BFILE physical file.
- Line 9 executes the INSERT statement.

Having created a logical link to the physical file using the BFILE column, you can read the contents of the file with Java streams.

The key steps required to read the BFILE contents are:

1. Obtain the BFILE locator.

2. Use the BFILE locator to test whether the physical file exists. If the file exists, open it and continue with the remaining steps; otherwise, raise an exception and terminate.
3. Open an InputStream or Reader for the file.
4. Close the InputStream or Reader.
5. Close the file.

Listing 10.21 uses a BFILE to read and display the contents of a file. The example uses the file extension to determine how to display its contents, and shows the use of a few of the methods in the BFILE class. If the file name ends with an "html" or "htm" extension, the contents are printed to standard output; otherwise, the file is assumed to be an image and displayed in a Java Frame using the PictureFrame class discussed earlier in this chapter.

```
package com.prenhall.OFJP.jdbc;
import java.io.*;
import java.sql.*;
import oracle.jdbc.driver.*;

public class LongsLobsBfile {
  private static Connection conn;

  public static void readBFile(int id) {
    PreparedStatement ps = null;
    ResultSet r = null;
    byte[] buf = null;
    InputStream in = null;
    try {
      ps = conn.prepareStatement(
          "select id, fileptr from demo_bfile where id = ?");
      ps.setInt(1, id);  r = ps.executeQuery();
      if (r.next()) {
        oracle.sql.BFILE bfile = null;
        System.out.println("BFILE id: " + r.getInt(1));
        bfile = ((OracleResultSet) r).getBFILE(2);
        String fileName = bfile.getName().trim();
        System.out.println("Dir Alias: " + bfile.getDirAlias() +
                           " Filename: " + fileName);
        if (bfile.fileExists() & (!bfile.isFileOpen())) {
          try {
            bfile.openFile();
            System.out.println("File length: " + bfile.length());
```

LISTING 10.21 Reading BFILE contents

```
       // —— Read the file
       buf = new byte[(int)bfile.length()];
       in = bfile.getBinaryStream();
       in.read(buf);
       // —— Display contents
       if (fileName.toLowerCase().endsWith("html") ||
           fileName.toLowerCase().endsWith("htm")) {
         for (int i = 0; i < buf.length; i++) {
           System.out.print((char) buf[i]);
         }
         System.out.println();
       }
       else {
          new PictureFrame(buf).setVisible(true);
       }
      }
      catch (SQLException sqle) { sqle.printStackTrace(); }
      finally {
       if (bfile != null) bfile.closeFile();
       if (in != null) in.close();
      }
     }
    }
   }
   catch (Exception e) { e.printStackTrace(); }
   finally {
    buf = null;
    try { if (r != null)  r.close(); } catch (Exception e) {}
    try { if (ps != null) ps.close(); } catch (Exception e) {}
   }
  }

  public static void main(String[] args) {
   String url = "jdbc:oracle:thin:" +
      "bookstore/bookstore@localhost:1521:ORA815";
   try {
    if (args.length == 1) url = args[0];
    DriverManager.registerDriver(
       new oracle.jdbc.driver.OracleDriver());
    conn = DriverManager.getConnection(url);

    executeSql("DROP DIRECTORY bfile_dir");
    executeSql("CREATE DIRECTORY bfile_dir AS 'D:\\bfiles'");
    executeSql("drop table demo_bfile");
```

LISTING 10.21 *Continued*

```
73:       executeSql("CREATE TABLE demo_bfile " +
74:                  "(id NUMBER(4) PRIMARY KEY, fileptr BFILE)");
75:       writeBFile(1, "jdev1.jpg");
76:       writeBFile(2, "oraedu.html");
77:       readBFile(1);
78:       readBFile(2);
79:     }
80:     catch (Exception e) { e.printStackTrace(); }
81:     finally {
82:       try {if (conn != null) conn.close();} catch(Exception e){}
83:       conn = null;
84:     }
85:   }
86: }
```

LISTING 10.21 *Continued*

Notes on Listing 10.21:

- Lines 15–17 execute the query to read the primary key (id) and BFILE locator (fileptr) from the DEMO_BFILE table.
- Line 18 declares the `bfile` variable as an oracle.sql.BFILE object reference.
- Line 21 sets the `bfile` variable to the return value of the getBFILE() method. The ResultSet variable `r` is cast to an OracleResultSet to invoke this Oracle extension.
- Line 22 stores the file name of the BFILE in a local filename variable, after removing leading and trailing spaces.
- Line 23 displays the file name and the directory alias name given to the physical directory containing the file.
- Line 25 tests whether the BFILE exists and is not already open before the contents are processed. Since the BFILE locator is a logical link to the physical file, it is possible that the physical file does not exist or was removed before it was accessed. Attempting to access a physical directory or file that does not exist will throw the following exception: `java.sql.SQLException:ORA-22288: file or LOB operation FILEOPEN failed`
- Line 27 opens the BFILE for processing, and must be done before you open a stream to read the file contents.
- Lines 28 displays the file length in bytes by calling BFILE length() method.
- Line 30 creates a byte array for the length of the BFILE, to hold its contents.
- Line 31 opens a BinaryStream to the BFILE contents.
- Line 32 reads the entire contents into the byte array.
- Lines 34–43 are used to display the contents of the array as either a character data or an image, depending on the file extension.

- Line 47 closes the BFILE, and line 48 closes in BinaryStream.
- Line 71 executes the SQL statement to create the directory alias.
- Line 73 creates a table called `demo_bfile` containing a BFILE column.
- Line 75 executes a call to writeBFile() to copy the contents of the jdev1.jpg image to the BFILE column in the first row in the table.
- Line 76 calls writeBFile() to copy the contents of the oraedu.html file to the BFILE column of the second row in the table.
- Lines 77 and 78 read the contents of the BFILE column from the first and second rows, respectively.

In line 21 the BFILE locator is obtained by casting the ResulSet to an OracleResultSet to call the getBFILE() method. An alternative way to obtain a BFILE object is to use the ResultSet getObject() method, and cast the return result to the oracle.sql.BFILE, as follows:

```
21:          bfile = (oracle.sql.BFILE) r.getObject(2);
```

Using the getObject() method eliminates the need to cast the ResultSet.

10.1.5 USING THE ORACLE ROWID

Using the ROWID pseudo-column value is the fastest way to access any row in an Oracle database. The ROWID is called a pseudo-column because it is not specified when creating a table. The Oracle database associates the ROWID value with a value to directly access the physical location of the row. The physical location of a row is identified by the combination of:

- The row in a data block
- The data block in data file
- The data file of an Oracle database instance

The ROWID value for a row can be accessed as a string value in your Java application, and then used in the condition or WHERE clause in any SELECT, UPDATE, or DELETE statement. When you pass the ROWID value to a condition in a WHERE clause, it must be entered as single-quoted string or you must use the setString() method of the PreparedStatement class. Using the ROWID to access a row is faster than using a primary or unique key column.

10.1.6 CALLING PL/SQL ANONYMOUS BLOCKS

The OracleCallableStatement class allows an SQL statement in a prepareCall() method to be an anonymous PL/SQL block. This is a very useful feature, particularly to produce performance gains in creating or managing LOB and BFILE locator values. Using PL/SQL code, you can issue INSERT, UPDATE, or DELETE statements with the RETURNING clause to create or update a record and return the new or changed values in one I/O or network roundtrip. This saves you from executing several SQL statements to do the same thing.

You can also use PL/SQL blocks to return a ResultSet object from PL/SQL into your Java application. For example:

```
01: CallableStatement cs = null;
02: ResultSet cursor = null;
03: try {
04:   cs = conn.prepareCall
05:       ("begin open ? for select name from customer; end;");
06:   cs.registerOutParameter(1,
07:                           oracle.jdbc.driver.OracleTypes.CURSOR);
08:   cs.execute();
09:   cursor = ((OracleCallableStatement)cs).getCursor(1);
10:   while (cursor.next()) {
11:     System.out.println(cursor.getString(1));
12:   }
13:    }
14:    catch (SQLException e) { e.printStackTrace(); }
15: finally {
16:   try {if (cursor != null) cursor.close();} catch(Exception e){}
17:   try {if (cs != null) cs.close();} catch(Exception e){}
18: }
```

LISTING 10.22 Using a PL/SQL anonymous block to return a result set

Notes on Listing 10.22:

- Lines 4 and 5 prepare a call to a PL/SQL anonymous block. This is a feature supported by the Oracle JDBC drivers. The PL/SQL block uses a cursor OPEN statement followed by a JDBC placeholder. The JDBC placeholder represents the output value from the PL/SQL block,[17] and the output value in PL/SQL is a REFCURSOR data type.
- Lines 6 and 7 register the output result from the PL/SQL block as an OracleTypes.CURSOR,[18] which enables the Oracle JDBC driver to map the PL/SQL REFCURSOR into a Java ResultSet object.

---

[17]A result set can also be the return value from a PL/SQL function or an output argument from a procedure or function.

[18]The OracleTypes class is located in the oracle.jdbc.driver package.

- Line 9 casts the CallableStatement object reference to an OracleCallableStatement to call the getCursor() method. The getCursor() method returns a Java ResultSet.
- Lines 10–12 processes the ResultSet object in the standard way.

10.1.7 READING AND WRITING JAVA OBJECTS

Instead of mapping each object attribute to its own database column, you can achieve object persistence by saving serialized Java objects (or a serialized Java object network) and writing them to an Oracle LONG RAW or BLOB column. The steps in writing a serialized Java object to a LONG RAW database column are:

1. Create a ByteArrayOutputStream for the serialized objects.
2. Open an ObjectOutputStream to the ByteArrayOutputStream.
3. Serialize your Java objects to the ByteArrayOutputStream.
4. Write the contents of the ByteArrayOutputStream to the database column.

If the column is a BLOB, the steps are:

1. Insert a BLOB locator to the BLOB column (refer to "Writing to a BLOB").
2. Create a ByteArrayOutputStream for the serialized objects.
3. Wrap the ByteArrayOutputStream in an ObjectOutputStream.
4. Serialize the objects to the ObjectOutputStream.
5. Write the contents of the ByteArrayOutputStream to the BLOB contents.

When working with a BLOB you can replace steps 2 and 3 by wrapping the BinaryOutputStream obtained from the BLOB locator in an ObjectOutputStream (see Listing 10.27) and write the serialized objects directly to the BLOB contents. For example:

```
oracle.sql.BLOB blob = null;
ObjectOutputStream out = null;

// Query the BLOB locator column

if (r.next()) {
  blob =  ((OracleResultSet) r).getBLOB(1);
  out = new ObjectOutputStream(blob.getBinaryOutputStream());
  :
  // Write objects to the output stream
}
```

Listing 10.23 shows the structure of a Customer class used to create customer object instances. Each customer instance is a Java representation of a customer row in the database. The SQL CREATE statement used to create the table to store the customer object instances is:

```
CREATE TABLE client (
  id  NUMBER(4) PRIMARY KEY,
  obj LONG RAW
);
```

The Customer Java class is:

```
package com.prenhall.OFJP.jdbc;
import java.io.Serializable;

public class Customer extends Object implements Serializable {
  static final long serialVersionUID = -7967938230152106576L;
  private static int nextId = 0;
  private int id;
  private String name;
  private String surname;
  private String password;
  private String creditCardType;
  private String creditCardNbr;
  private String monthExpired;
  private String yearExpired;

  public Customer(String newName, String newSurname) {
    id = ++nextId;
    name = newName;
    surname = newSurname;
    System.out.println("Created: " + this);
  }

  public String toString() {
    return id + " " + name + " " + surname;
  }

  public int getId() { return id; }
  public void setId(int i) { id = i; }
```

LISTING 10.23 Serializable customer class

```
  public String getName() { return name; }
  public void setName(String newName) { name = newName; }

  public String getSurname() { return surname; }
  public void setSurname(String newSurname) { surname = newSurname; }

  public String getPassword() { return password; }
  public void setPassword(String newPassword) {
     password = newPassword; }

  public String getCreditCardType() {return creditCardType; }
  public void setCreditCardType(String newCreditCardType) {
    creditCardType = newCreditCardType; }

  public String getCreditCardNbr() { return creditCardNbr; }
  public void setCreditCardNbr(String newCreditCardNbr) {
    creditCardNbr = newCreditCardNbr; }

  public String getMonthExpired() { return monthExpired; }
  public void setMonthExpired(String newMonthExpired) {
    monthExpired = newMonthExpired; }

  public String getYearExpired() { return yearExpired; }
  public void setYearExpired(String newYearExpired) {
    yearExpired = newYearExpired; }
}
```

LISTING 10.23 *Continued*

The steps in writing a customer object instance to a relational database column are demonstrated by the writeCustomer() method shown in Listing 10.24.

```
package com.prenhall.OFJP.jdbc;
import java.sql.*;
import java.io.*;

public class ReadWriteObject {
  private Connection conn;
  private PreparedStatement pstmt;
```

LISTING 10.24 Writing a Java serialized object to a LONG RAW column

```
08:    private PreparedStatement pqstmt;
09:
10:    public ReadWriteObject(String url) {
11:       try {
12:         Class.forName("oracle.jdbc.driver.OracleDriver");
13:         conn = DriverManager.getConnection(url);
14:       }
15:       catch (Exception e) {
16:         e.printStackTrace();
17:       }
18:    }
19:
20:    public void writeCustomer(int idx, Customer cust) {
21:      try {
22:        if (pstmt == null) {
23:          pstmt = conn.prepareStatement(
24:             "insert into client (id, obj) values (?, ?)");
25:        }
26:
27:        ByteArrayOutputStream bAry = new ByteArrayOutputStream();
28:        ObjectOutputStream objout = new ObjectOutputStream(bAry);
29:        objout.writeObject(cust);
30:        ByteArrayInputStream bin = new ByteArrayInputStream(
31:                                            bAry.toByteArray());
32:
33:        pstmt.setInt(1, cust.getId());
34:        pstmt.setBinaryStream(2, bin, bAry.size());
35:        if (pstmt.execute()) {
36:          System.out.println(
37:            pstmt.getUpdateCount() + " row(s) inserted");
38:        }
39:      }
40:      catch (Exception e) {
41:         e.printStackTrace();
42:      }
43:    }
44:  :
45: }
```

LISTING 10.24 *Continued*

Notes on Listing 10.24:

- Lines 6– 8 declare instance variables in the ReadWriteObject class.
- Lines 10–18 are the constructor for the class that loads the JDBC driver and creates a Connection.

- Line 20 is the writeCustomer() method, which accepts two parameters: a unique id and the customer object.
- Lines 22–25 prepare the INSERT statement for storing a serialized customer object instance. The first placeholder is for the unique id, which is provided for querying a unique customer object instance, and the second placeholder is for the serialized object itself.
- Line 27 creates a ByteArrayOutputStream to store the serialized object in memory.
- Line 28 creates an ObjectOutputStream object, which directs its output to the byte array created in line 27.
- Line 29 calls the object serialization method writeObject() on the object output stream to serialize a Customer object, which is stored in the byte array.
- Line 30 creates a ByteArrayInputStream from the byte array contents to be the source of the data that will be stored in a LONG RAW column in the database.
- Line 34 uses the setBinaryStream() method of the PreparedStatement to ensure that the serialized object is written to the LONG RAW column when the statement is executed on line 35. The second argument to the setBinaryStream() method is ByteArrayInputStream, and the third argument is the length in bytes of the serialized data in the byte array.

Now that you can write a Java object to a column, you will want to read it to create an instance from its saved state, by reversing the process. The steps in reading serialized data from a database column are:

1. If the column that contains the Java serialized object is a BLOB, then query the BLOB locator, and get a binary stream from the BLOB locator object. If the column is a LONG RAW column, then get a binary stream object for the column.
2. Wrap the binary object stream in a ObjectInputStream.
3. Using the ObjectInputStream, call the readObject() method to read the serialized object into its associated object reference variable.

The readCustomer() method in Listing 10.15 is an example of how to read a serialized object stored in a database column.

```
package com.prenhall.OFJP.jdbc;
import java.sql.*;
import java.io.*;
public class ReadWriteObject {   :

  public Customer readCustomer(int theId) {
    Customer c = null;
```

LISTING 10.25 Instantiating a serialized object from a database column

```
08:
09:     try {
10:       if (pqstmt == null) {
11:         pqstmt = conn.prepareStatement(
12:                    "select obj from client where id = ?");
13:       }
14:       pqstmt.setInt(1, theId);
15:       ResultSet r = pqstmt.executeQuery();
16:       if (r.next()) {
17:         System.out.println("Got one row");
18:         ObjectInputStream objin = new ObjectInputStream(
19:                                        r.getBinaryStream(1));
20:         c = (Customer) objin.readObject();
21:       }
22:       else {
23:         System.out.println("Customer "+theId+" does not exist");
24:       }
25:     }
26:     catch (Exception e) {
27:       e.printStackTrace();
28:     }
29:     return c;
30:   }
31:   :
32: }
```

LISTING 10.25 *Continued*

Notes on Listing 10.25:

- Lines 10–13 prepare the query to read the column containing the serialized customer object from the database.
- Lines 14 and 15 set the query search criteria to locate a row by customer id and execute the statement.
- Lines 18 and 19 map the saved object column to a binary stream and wrap the binary stream object in an ObjectInputStream.
- Line 20 calls the readObject() method to read the serialized data, and returns the customer object as a Java object, which is cast into a Customer object.

A test harness program to test writing and reading customer objects is shown in Listing 10.26.

```
package com.prenhall.OFJP.jdbc;
import java.sql.*;
import java.io.*;
public class ReadWriteObject {
  :
  public void doSql(String sql) {
    try {
      Statement s = conn.createStatement();
      s.execute(sql);
    }
    catch (Exception e) {
      e.printStackTrace();
    }
  }

  public void close() {
     try {
        if (pstmt != null) pstmt.close();
        if (pqstmt != null) pqstmt.close();
        if (conn != null) conn.close();
     }
     catch (Exception e) {
       e.printStackTrace();
     }
  }

  public static void main(String[] args) {
    String url = "jdbc:oracle:thin:bookstore/bookstore" +
                 "@localhost:1521:ORA815";
    ReadWriteObject rw = new ReadWriteObject(url);

    rw.doSql("drop table client");
    rw.doSql("create table client (id number(4) primary key," +
             "obj long raw)");
    Customer person1 = new Customer("Ziggy", "Mooch");
    Customer person2 = new Customer("Simple", "Simon");
    rw.writeCustomer(person1.getId(), person1);
    rw.writeCustomer(person2.getId(), person2);

    Customer c1 = rw.readCustomer(person1.getId());
    Customer c2 = rw.readCustomer(person2.getId());
    System.out.println(c1);
```

LISTING 10.26 Testing writing and reading objects to LONG RAW

```
    System.out.println(c2);

    rw.close();
  }
}
```

LISTING 10.26 *Continued*

10.1.7.1 Reading and Writing Java Objects from a BLOB. Using a BLOB column to write and read Java objects is sometimes more elegant than using a LONG RAW column. You can extend the customer example to write any serializable object to a BLOB column, and read the object into your application. The sample code is as follows:

- Listing 10.27 shows a writeObject() method to write any Java object to a BLOB column.
- Listing 10.28 shows a readObject() method to read any Java object from a BLOB column.
- Listing 10.29 shows a main() method to test the writeObject() and readObject() methods.

The examples presented assume that the following database table structure has been provided for the Java objects:

```
CREATE TABLE java_objects (
  id  NUMBER(4) PRIMARY KEY,
  ser BLOB
);
```

The code for the writeObject() method to write the object is:

```
public void writeObject(int objId, Object o) {
  try {
    CallableStatement cs = conn.prepareCall(
          "begin insert into java_objects (id, ser) " +
          "values (?, empty_blob()) " +
          "returning ser into ?; end;");
    cs.setInt(1, objId);
    cs.registerOutParameter(2, OracleTypes.BLOB);
    cs.execute();
    BLOB blob = ((OracleCallableStatement) cs).getBLOB(2);
```

LISTING 10.27 Writing a Java object to a BLOB column

```
11:     ObjectOutputStream out = new ObjectOutputStream(
12:        blob.getBinaryOutputStream());
13:     out.writeObject(o);
14:
15:     out.close();
16:     cs.close();
17:     conn.commit();
18:   }
19:   catch (Exception e) {
20:     e.printStackTrace();
21:   }
22: }
```

LISTING 10.27 *Continued*

Notes for Listing 10.27:

- Lines 3–6 prepare a call to a PL/SQL block that creates the row for the serialized Java object, with an empty BLOB. The PL/SQL block is used in order to execute the INSERT statement with the RETURNING feature to create and retrieve the BLOB locator in one statement.
- Line 11 wraps the BLOB binary output stream object in an ObjectOutputStream that can be used to write the object directly to the BLOB column contents.
- Line 13 serializes and writes the object passed as the second argument to the writeObject() method.
- Line 17 commits the data for persistent storage.

The code for the readObject() method to read the object is:

```
public Object readObject(int objId) {
  Object o = null;
  try {
    PreparedStatement ps = conn.prepareStatement(
         "select id, ser from java_objects where id =?");
    ps.setInt(1, objId);
    ResultSet r = ps.executeQuery();
    if (r.next()) {
      int id = r.getInt(1);
      BLOB blob = ((OracleResultSet) r).getBLOB(2);
      ObjectInputStream in = new ObjectInputStream(
```

LISTING 10.28 Reading a Java object from a BLOB column

```
12:           blob.getBinaryStream());
13:       o = in.readObject();
14:       in.close();
15:       ps.close();
16:     }
17:   }
18:   catch (Exception e) {
19:     e.printStackTrace();
20:   }
21:   return o;
22: }
```

LISTING 10.28 *Continued*

Notes for Listing 10.28:

- Lines 4 and 5 prepare a query to read the BLOB locator.
- Line 6 sets the search criteria for the query.
- Line 10 gets the BLOB locator after the query is executed and the row fetched.
- Lines 11 and 12 wrap the binary InputStream object for the BLOB contents into an ObjectInputStream.
- Line 13 uses the readObject() method of the ObjectInputStream to read the object, which is assigned to the local object reference variable returned as the result.

The code for the main() method to test the writeObject() and readObject() methods is:

```
public static void main(String[] args) {
  RWObject rwo = new RWObject();

  Customer c = new Customer("Sam", "Theman");

  // write some objects
  rwo.writeObject(1, c);
  rwo.writeObject(2, "This is a serialized Java string");
  rwo.writeObject(3, new Float(3.412));

  Frame f = new Frame("Demo Serialize");
  f.setLayout(new BorderLayout());
```

LISTING 10.29 Test writing and reading objects with a BLOB column

```
13:    f.setSize(100, 200);
14:    Label n = new Label("North");
15:    Button b = new Button("Exit");
16:    n.setBackground(Color.cyan);
17:    f.add(n, BorderLayout.NORTH);
18:    f.add(b, BorderLayout.CENTER);
19:
20:    rwo.writeObject(4, f);
21:
22:    // read the objects
23:    for (int i = 1; i < 4; i++) {
24:      Object o = rwo.readObject(i);
25:      System.out.println("Object class: "+o.getClass().getName());
26:      System.out.println("Object value: "+o.toString());
27:    }
28:
29:    Frame newFrame = (Frame) rwo.readObject(4);
30:
31:    newFrame.addWindowListener(new WindowAdapter() {
32:        public void windowClosing(WindowEvent e) {
33:          System.exit(0);
34:        }
35:      });
36:    Button b1 = (Button) newFrame.getComponent(1);
37:    b1.addActionListener(new ActionListener() {
38:                   private int count = 0;
39:                   public void actionPerformed(ActionEvent ae) {
40:                     Button b1 = (Button) ae.getSource();
41:                     count++;
42:                     b1.setLabel("Clicked " + count +" times");
43:                   }
44:                 });
45:    rwo.close();
46:    newFrame.setVisible(true);
47:  }
```

LISTING 10.29 *Continued*

Notes for Listing 10.29:

- Line 4 creates a Customer object.
- Lines 7, 8, and 9, respectively, write Customer, String, and Float objects to the database BLOB column.
- Lines 11–18 create a Java AWT Frame object with a label in the north part of the Frame, and a Button in the center of the Frame. This is an example of an

object network, where the Frame is a composition of one or more objects such as the BorderLayout, the Label, and the Button.

- Line 20 writes the Frame object to the BLOB column as the fourth row.
- Lines 23–27 execute a loop to read the first three objects from the BLOB column in their respective rows. The loop statement prints the object class name and the string representation of the object by calling its toString() method.
- Line 29 reads the fourth object from the BLOB column of its row and assigns the object to a Java Frame object reference variable.
- Lines 31–44 add event handlers to the Frame to terminate the application when the window-closing event occurs. The event handler code is added to the Frame after the object has been deserialized, because the class code is saved with the object state during the Java serialization process.

Saving serialized objects into a database has some ramifications over time, particularly if the object structure or interface changes. Some changes can make the old version of the class invalid, so you must carefully manage object serialization and object version control. Serializing object in the way shown in this section can be useful if the serialized object does not change over time.

10.1.8 READING AND WRITING ORACLE OBJECT TYPES

Instead of serializing your Java objects, you may find it appropriate to map the Java class to a database object type. The object type represents the persistent state of an object, with the additional benefit that the object state may be easily modified or searched using SQL statements. This section examines how to read and write Oracle object types using JDBC. You need to use a custom-built Java class that is designed to map to an associated Oracle object type. The key steps are:

1. Create the Java class structures.
2. Populate an instance of the Java class from the database object type, or write the database object type from the Java object instance.

10.1.8.1 Creating a Java Class for an Object Type. You must create a Java class with a structure that is compatible with an Oracle database object type. There are several options for creating the Java class for the associated object type:

- Create it manually, using default JDBC mapping where the JDBC driver materializes an object type as an oracle.sql.STRUCT when using a JDBC 1.0 compliant JDBC driver, or use the java.sql.Struct type when using a JDBC 2.0 compliant JDBC driver. [19]

---

[19] The java.sql.Struct class is part of the core JDBC 2.0 class library.

- Create it manually, using an OracleConnection type map to associate a specific Java class with the Oracle object type, in addition to implementing a specific Java interface. The materialization of the Java class for the associated Oracle object type is controlled by the interface implemented. If you want your code to use standard JDBC API calls, use the SQLData interface, or use the CustomDatum interface if you want to use the Oracle JDBC extensions. Both interfaces provide the hooks for the JDBC driver to convert a Java class to its associated Oracle object type, and vice versa, and give you control of the data type used for attributes.
- Generate it automatically, using Oracle JPublisher. Oracle JPublisher only generates a Java class that uses the CustomDatum interface technique.

10.1.8.2 Using Default JDBC Mapping for Object Types. When converting a Java class, implementing either the SQLData or the CustomDatum interface into its SQL Object type, a default mapping process occurs between Java and the SQL data types for each of the attributes. The JDBC driver applies the default mapping by utilizing a default type map. The default type map specifies the Java to SQL, and the SQL Java data type conversion that should take place.

If you use the oracle.sql.STRUCT object, the data values are presented to the Java code in Oracle SQL data type format. This means that the JDBC driver does not do extract work to convert the STRUCT attributes from an Oracle format into their Java form. However, if you use the java.sql.Struct type, the JDBC driver must convert each of the attributes in the SQL object type from their SQL data type into compatible Java types. To use the STRUCT/Struct types you need to:

- Create a standard Java class with an instance variable for each attribute defined in the SQL Object Type.
- Read the SQL object instance using the appropriate JDBC Resultset method calls.
  - Use the ResultSet getSTRUCT() method to create an oracle.sql.STRUCT object.
  - Use the ResultSet getObject() method to create a java.sql.Struct object. If using the java.sqlStruct class, you can call the getAttributes() method to retrieve values for the Oracle object type into a array of objects for processing.

The manual mapping process and JDBC code to read an Oracle object type into a Java class are demonstrated with an Oracle Object type called PERSON_T and the Java Person class, as shown in Listing 10.30.

Oracle Object Type: PERSON_T

```
CREATE OR REPLACE TYPE person_t AS OBJECT (
  id          NUMBER(6),
  firstname   VARCHAR2(20),
  lastname    VARCHAR2(20),
  birthdate   DATE
);
/
```

Java Class: Person

```
package com.prenhall.OFJP.jdbc;
import java.sql.*;
import java.text.*;

public class Person {

  private int id;
  private String name;
  private String surname;
  private Date birthDate;

  public Person() {
  }

  public String toString() {
    return id + " " + name + " " +
           surname + " " + dateFormat(birthDate);
  }

  public Date getBirthDate() {
    return birthDate;
  }

  public void setBirthDate(Date newBirthDate) {
    birthDate = newBirthDate;
  }

  public int getId() { return id; }
  public void setId(int newId) { id = newId; }

  public String getName() { return name;}
```

LISTING 10.30 PERSON_T object type and Java Person class

```
  public void setName(String newName) { name = newName; }

  public String getSurname() { return surname; }
  public void setSurname(String newSurname) { surname = newSurname; }

  public String dateFormat(Date d) {
    SimpleDateFormat df = new SimpleDateFormat("d-MMM-yyyy");
    return df.format(d);
  }
}
```

LISTING 10.30 *Continued*

The Java class, Person, is constructed as a mirror of the Oracle object type, `person_t`, in respect to number of attributes and compatible data types.

The example code in Listings 10.31a, 10.31b, and 10.31c shows how to use the java.sql.Struct object to read a `person_t` oracle object from a column in a relational table, and to manually copy the attribute data into Java class instance variables. The code also shows how to construct a Struct object to insert a new Person Java object into the column as an Oracle `person_t` object. To create the table using JDBC code:

```
public void createRelationalTable() {
  try {
    s = conn.createStatement();
    s.execute("drop table employee");
    s.execute("create table employee (" +
              "person person_t, primary key (person.id))");
    s.execute("insert into employee values ("+
        "person_t(1, 'James', 'Bland', '01-APR-1945'))");
    s.execute("insert into employee values ("+
        "person_t(2, 'Susan', 'Juggler', '01-APR-1980'))");
    conn.commit();
  }
  catch (SQLException e) {
    e.printStackTrace();
  }
}
```

LISTING 10.31a Creating the table with an object column

The code in Listing 10.31a creates a table called EMPLOYEE with a column called PERSON of the `person_t` type. Two records are inserted into the table to populate the person column in each row, using SQL INSERT statements with hard-coded values to create the object type instances. Listing 10.31b shows how to use JDBC to insert a value into an object column by using a Java object as the source for the values.

```
public Date getDate(int day, int month, int year) {
  GregorianCalendar gc = new GregorianCalendar(year, month, day);
  return new Date(gc.getTime().getTime());
}

public void writeAsStruct() {
  Person p = new Person();
  p.setId(3);
  p.setName("Jasmine");
  p.setSurname("Zegna");
  p.setBirthDate(getDate(3, Calendar.OCTOBER, 1960));

  try {
    PreparedStatement ps = conn.prepareStatement(
        "insert into employee values (?)");

    Object[] attr = { new Integer(p.getId()),
                      p.getName(),
                      p.getSurname(),
                      p.getBirthDate() };
    STRUCT struct = new STRUCT(
         new StructDescriptor("BOOKSTORE.PERSON_T", conn),
         conn, attr);

    ((OraclePreparedStatement)ps).setOracleObject(1, struct);
    ps.execute();
    ps.close();
    conn.commit();
  }
  catch (Exception e) {
    e.printStackTrace();
  }
}
```

LISTING 10.31b Write a Java object into an object column

Notes on Listing 10.31b:

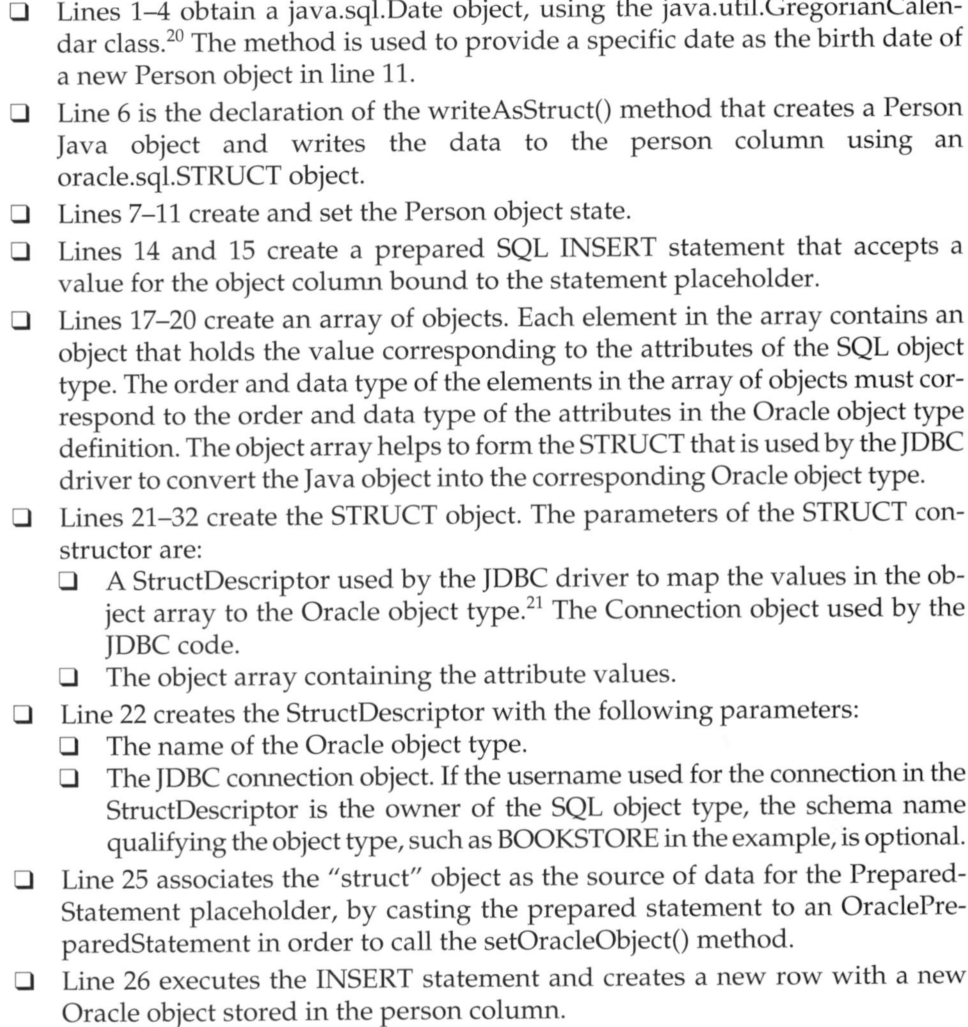

- Lines 1–4 obtain a java.sql.Date object, using the java.util.GregorianCalendar class.[20] The method is used to provide a specific date as the birth date of a new Person object in line 11.
- Line 6 is the declaration of the writeAsStruct() method that creates a Person Java object and writes the data to the person column using an oracle.sql.STRUCT object.
- Lines 7–11 create and set the Person object state.
- Lines 14 and 15 create a prepared SQL INSERT statement that accepts a value for the object column bound to the statement placeholder.
- Lines 17–20 create an array of objects. Each element in the array contains an object that holds the value corresponding to the attributes of the SQL object type. The order and data type of the elements in the array of objects must correspond to the order and data type of the attributes in the Oracle object type definition. The object array helps to form the STRUCT that is used by the JDBC driver to convert the Java object into the corresponding Oracle object type.
- Lines 21–32 create the STRUCT object. The parameters of the STRUCT constructor are:
  - A StructDescriptor used by the JDBC driver to map the values in the object array to the Oracle object type.[21] The Connection object used by the JDBC code.
  - The object array containing the attribute values.
- Line 22 creates the StructDescriptor with the following parameters:
  - The name of the Oracle object type.
  - The JDBC connection object. If the username used for the connection in the StructDescriptor is the owner of the SQL object type, the schema name qualifying the object type, such as BOOKSTORE in the example, is optional.
- Line 25 associates the "struct" object as the source of data for the PreparedStatement placeholder, by casting the prepared statement to an OraclePreparedStatement in order to call the setOracleObject() method.
- Line 26 executes the INSERT statement and creates a new row with a new Oracle object stored in the person column.

The technique shown in Listing 10.31b works well, but requires knowledge of the order and correct Java data type to be used for each of the database object

---

[20]The GregorianDate class was used because the java.util.Date(year, month, day) and java.sql.Date(year, month, day) constructors have been deprecated in JDK.

[21]The Oracle Documentation on the StructDescriptor is not comprehensive, and you are left to guess the rest.

attributes. Reading the objects reverses the process, but without the need to use the StructDescriptor.

```
01: public void readAsStruct() {
02:   try {
03:     java.sql.Struct struct;   // if using a JDBC 2.0 driver
04:
05:     ps = conn.prepareStatement("select person from employee");
06:     ResultSet r = ps.executeQuery();
07:     while (r.next()) {
08:       struct = (java.sql.Struct) r.getObject(1);
09:       Object[] a = struct.getAttributes();
10:
11:       Person p = new Person();
12:       p.setId(((BigDecimal) a[0]).intValue());
13:       p.setName((String) a[1]);
14:       p.setSurname((String) a[2]);
15:       p.setBirthDate(new Date(((Timestamp) a[3]).getTime()));
16:       System.out.println("Person: " + p.toString());
17:     }
18:     r.close();
19:     ps.close();
20:   }
21:   catch (SQLException e) {
22:     e.printStackTrace();
23:   }
24: }
```

LISTING 10.31c Reading an object column into a Java object

The readAsStruct() method demonstrates the process of reading an SQL object type using the JDBC 2.0 java.sql.Struct class.

Notes on Listing 10.31c:

- Line 3 declares the Struct object variable
- Lines 5, 6, and 7, create the SQL query, execute the query to return the ResultSet, and fetch the next row.
- Line 8 retrieves the Oracle SQL object type into an oracle.jdbc2.Struct variable by calling the getObject() method of the ResultSet.
- Line 9 uses the getAttributes() method of the Struct object to return the SQL object attribute values into an array of Objects. Here is an abbreviated list of

the default mapping from the database attribute/column type to the Java object:[22]

- NUMBER creates a java.math.BigDecimal object.
- VARCHAR2 creates a java.lang.String object.
- DATE creates a java.sql.Timestamp object.

- Line 11 creates the Person object.
- Lines 12–15 copy the SQL object attribute values into their respective Java object instance variables by using the various setXXX() methods defined in the Person class.
  - The first SQL attribute is returned as a BigDecimal, which is copied as an int as the person id.
  - The second and third attributes are copied as a String.
  - The forth attribute is received as a java.sql.Timestamp, which is converted into a java.sql.Date.

10.1.8.3 Using Explicit Mapping of Object Types. The explicit mapping technique still requires you to write code to map and convert SQL attribute values into their Java attributes. The code to perform the mapping is encapsulated in the Java class that implements the java.sql.SQLData interface. When implementing the SQLData interface, you must also create a type map in which you associate the Java class implementing the SQLData interface with the SQL object type. The type map is required so that the JDBC driver will call the methods implemented for the SQLData interface.

The SQLData Interface defines the following three methods that must be implemented:

- `String getSQLTypeName()`, which returns a fully qualified SQL object type name, such as, BOOKSTORE.PERSON_T.
- `void readSQL(SQLInput stream, String typeName)`, which is used to populate your Java object instance variable with SQL object type attribute values.
- `void writeSQL(SQLOutput stream)`, which you use to populate the SQL object with data from your Java object instance variables.

The Person class shown in Listing 10.30 is now modified to implement the SQLData interface. Listing 10.32a shows a modified Person class, with additional components added to it to support the implementation of the SQLData interface. The additions to the Person class are highlighted in bold text.

---

[22]After obtaining the array of objects using the getAttributes() method type structure, you can determine the object types in the array of objects by printing the results of: array-variable-name[array-index].getClass().getName(). This helps to determine the Java class mapped for each attribute by the JDBC driver.

The SQLData, SQLInput, and SQLOutput classes are all defined in the java.sql package in the JDBC 2.0 core API. The SQLInput interface defines various readXXX() methods to read structured data types from a stream, and SQLOutput has various writeXXX() methods for writing structured data to a stream.

```
package com.prenhall.OFJP.jdbc;
import java.sql.*;
import java.text.*;

public class Person implements java.sql.SQLData {

  private String sqlType;
  private int id;
  private String name;
  private String surname;
  private Date birthDate;

  public Person() {
  }

  public Person(String typeName, int newId, String newName,
                String newSurname, Date newBirthDate) {
    sqlType = typeName;
    id = newId;
    name = newName;
    surname = newSurname;
    birthDate = newBirthDate;
  }

  public String getSQLTypeName() throws SQLException {
    return sqlType;
  }

  public void readSQL(SQLInput stream, String sqlType)
   throws SQLException {
    this.sqlType = sqlType;
    id = stream.readInt();
    name = stream.readString();
    surname = stream.readString();
    birthDate = stream.readDate();
  }
```

LISTING 10.32a Person class implementing SQLData interface

```
37:
38:    public void writeSQL(SQLOutput stream) throws SQLException {
39:       stream.writeInt(id);
40:       stream.writeString(name);
41:       stream.writeString(surname);
42:       stream.writeDate(new Date(birthDate.getTime()));
43:    }
44:    :
45:    // other get and set methods …
46: }
```

LISTING 10.32a *Continued*

Notes for Listing 10.32a:

- Line 5 specifies the Person class that implements the SQLData interface.
- Line 7 adds a String instance variable to hold the fully qualified type name for the SQL object to which this Java class will be mapped. This instance variable is required as the return value from the getSQLTypeName() method, which is called by the JDBC driver to assist with the mapping and conversion process. The type name is set when the Person class is constructed.
- Lines 13 and 14 define a no-argument constructor. This is required. Otherwise the JDBC driver throws an SQLException when trying to create an instance of a Person object when reading the SQL Object value into the Java class.
- Lines 16–23 establish a Person constructor that sets each of its instance variables from parameter values, where the first parameter must be for the fully qualified SQL object type name.
- Lines 25–27 show the implementation of the getSQLTypeName() method that returns the SQL object type name.
- Lines 29–36 show the implementation of the readSQL() method, which calls readXXX() methods to retrieve the Oracle SQL object values into the Java class instance variable. The order of the calls to readXXX() methods must correspond to the order of attributes defined in the object type. You can call any readXXX() method compatible with the database data type of corresponding SQL attribute.
- Lines 38–42 display the implementation of the writeSQL() method, which writes the Java instance variable values into the Oracle SQL object attributes. The order of the calls to writeXXX() methods must correspond to the order of attributes defined in the object type.

The code to write the Java class is now greatly simplified because the Java class that implements the SQLData interface encapsulates the functionality for the mapping and conversion process. The writeSQL() method is called automatically by the JDBC driver, but only if you have modified the data type conversion map, called a *type map*, for the connection.

```
01: public void writeAsObject() {
02:   PreparedStatement ps = null;
03:   try {
04:     Person p = new Person("BOOKSTORE.PERSON_T", 5,
05:                           "Mandy", "Disney",
06:                           getDate(10, Calendar.JANUARY, 1982));
07:     ps = conn.prepareStatement(
08:              "insert into employee values (?)");
09:     ps.setObject(1, p, OracleTypes.STRUCT);
10:     ps.execute();
11:     conn.commit();
12:   }
13:   catch (SQLException e) {
14:     e.printStackTrace();
15:   }
16: }
```

LISTING 10.32b Writing an SQL object from a Java class with SQLData

Notes on Listing 10.32b:

- Lines 4–6 create a Person Java object with the first argument identifying the fully qualified Oracle SQL object type name. The type name should be in uppercase, because the Oracle data dictionary stores the type name in uppercase by default.
- Lines 7 and 8 prepare the INSERT statement to write the object. This INSERT statement can be used to insert an SQL object instance into an object table, or into an object column of a relation table.
- Line 9 binds the Java Person object instance to PreparedStatement placeholder. The third argument to the setObject() method must be the value OracleTypes.STRUCT.[23]

[23]The OracleTypes class is located in the oracle.jdbc.driver package in Oracle's JDBC driver class library.

- ❑ Line 10 performs the INSERT operation, and the JDBC driver calls the writeSQL() method implemented in the Person class to do the work.

```
01: public void readAsObject() {
02:   PreparedStatement ps = null;
03:   try {
04:     Person p;
05:
06:     ps = conn.prepareStatement(
07:            "select person from employee");
08:     ResultSet r = ps.executeQuery();
09:     while (r.next()) {
10:       p =  (Person) r.getObject(1);
11:       System.out.println("Person:  " + p);
12:     }
13:     r.close();
14:     ps.close();
15:   }
16:   catch (SQLException e) {
17:     e.printStackTrace();
18:   }
19: }
```

LISTING 10.32c Reading an SQL Object from Java class with SQLData

Notes on Listing 10.32c:

- ❑ Line 4 defines a person object variable.
- ❑ Lines 6 and 7 create an SQL query to read an object instance value from an object column in a relational table. If you want to read an SQL object instance from an object table, change the SQL statement to "`select value(e) from employee e`" without any need to change the rest of the method code.
- ❑ Line 10 retrieves the SQL object instance into the Java class as an object, and the cast converts it to the Person class to assign the value to the Person object variable. At this point, the readSQL() method, implemented in the Person class, is automatically called by the JDBC driver to assist with the creation of the Person object.

You can see how much more succinct the code is compared with the STRUCT technique. Before you can use the readAsObject() and writeAsObject() methods, as shown, a very important sequence of statements must be executed:

1. Obtain the type map from the JDBC driver for the connection. The type map is used for the default data type conversion between the Java and SQL data types.
2. Modify the type map to associate the Oracle SQL object type with the Java class that implements the SQLData interface.

These steps are best done after creating the Connection. The code in Listing 10.33 demonstrates an example of modifying a type map.

```
01: private java.util.Dictionary map;
02:
03: public OraObject(String url) {
04:   try {
05:     Class.forName("oracle.jdbc.driver.OracleDriver");
06:     conn = (OracleConnection) DriverManager.getConnection(url);
07:     conn.setAuto-commit(false);
08:     /*
09:     ** Modify the Type map if using SQL objects
10:     */
11:     map = conn.getTypeMap();
12:     map.put("BOOKSTORE.PERSON_T", Class.forName("Person"));
13:     this.writeAsObject();
14:     this.readAsObject();
15:   }
16:   catch (ClassNotFoundException e) {
17:     e.printStackTrace();
18:   }
19: }
```

LISTING 10.33 Obtaining and modifying a JDBC type map

Notes on Listing 10.33:

- Line 1 declares an instance variable based on the java.util.Dictionary abstract class.
- Line 11 the getTypeMap() method, of the connection object, returns a type map object, which is a subclass of the Dictionary class.
- Line 12 calls the put() method of the type map object, to add an entry for associating the fully qualified SQL Object type name in the first parameter with the Java class loaded in the second parameter. The Java class specified in the second parameter must be fully qualified if you are using the Class.forName() method, as shown.

- Lines 13 and 14 call the methods to read and write the SQL object type with its associated Java object type.

10.1.8.4 Reading and Writing SQL Objects Using the CustomDatum Technique. The Oracle JDBC class library also provides another way to read and write SQL objects. You can use the oracle.sql.CustomDatum interface and the oracle.sql.CustomDatumFactory interface. Since manually constructing classes to implement these interfaces is error-prone and tedious, it is better to use the Oracle JPublisher tool to create the Java class from the Oracle SQL object type definition. This section briefly introduces how to use JPublisher to create a Java class from an Oracle SQL object type. JPublisher is discussed in more detail in Chapter 11.

The main advantage of the SQLData interface is that it is part of the JDBC 2.0 standard, and is more a more portable way of using SQL object types. The advantages of the CustomDatum interface are:

- It provides a more efficient way of reading and writing Oracle SQL objects, because the data can be maintained in Oracle JDBC format.
- Mapping between Oracle database types and Java types is eliminated, which gives you some performance benefit.
- You have complete control over data type mappings at the attribute level.
- You can read and write Java objects serialized to or from RAW columns.

The disadvantage of the CustomDatum interface technique is that it is not portable and is only available as an Oracle extension to the JDBC standards.

The code example presented with the Person class implementing the SQLData interface can be used in the same way for a Java class generated by Oracle JPublisher.

To enable JDBC code to read an Oracle SQL object into a Java object, and to write a Java object into an Oracle SQL object, you would perform the following steps:

1. Generate the source for a Java class from the Oracle SQL object type definition in the database, using JPublisher.
2. In your Java program use either of the following techniques:
   a. Cast the object returned by the getObject(idx) method, which retrieves the SQL object, to the Java class. Use the setObject(idx, obj, OracleTypes.STRUCT) method to write the Java object to the SQL object. *Note:* This technique still requires that you modify the connection type map to associate the Oracle SQL object type with the Java class generated by JPublisher.
   b. Use the OracleResultSet.getCustomDatum() method, and the getFactory() class method, of the generated Java class to materialize an Oracle SQL object, and cast it to the Java class generated by JPublisher. Call the

setCustomDatum() method of the OraclePreparedStatement to write the Java class into the Oracle SQL object. *Note:* This technique does not require you to modify the type map.

The CustomDatum interface defines the following method that must be implemented:

```
public oracle.sql.Datum toDatum(OracleConnection c)
```

The Datum object type returned is how the Oracle JDBC driver internally manages Oracle SQL data types and their values. It is not well documented.

The CustomDatumFactory interface defines the following method:

```
public java.sql.CustomDatum create(
                                        oracle.sql.Datum d, int sqlType)
```

The CustomDatum object returned by the `create` method can be cast to the appropriate Java class. The Datum argument holds the data for the object, the sqlType parameter is an identifier for the SQL Object.

10.1.8.5 Using JPublisher to Generate a Java Class. Oracle JPublisher is a command-line utility shipped with Oracle8i software, and is found in the bin subdirectory of your Oracle8i installation home. JPublisher allows you to create a Java class from an Oracle SQL object type. You provide command-line options to control the generation of source for the Java classes. The generated Java classes implement the CustomDatum and the CustomDatumFactory interfaces. JPublisher does not support the generation of a Java class that implements the SQLData interface.

Running JPublisher to generate the Java class requires the following steps:

1. Add the following class libraries to your class path:
   ORAHOME/jdbc/lib/classes111.zip—for Oracle JDBC driver
   ORAHOME/sqlj/lib/translator.zip—for the JPublisher utility,where ORAHOME is the Oracle home for your installation. Path names need a backslash character for the Windows NT platform.
2. Optionally modify or customize the generated sources for the Java classes. JPublisher generates two Java source files, one for the SQL object value, and one for the SQL object REF.
3. Write the JDBC code for the Java class

Listing 10.34 is an example of using JPublisher to generate the Person.java and PersonRef.java Java class source files from the PERSON_T Oracle SQL object type. The example is for the Windows NT platform:

```
01: set CLASSPATH= D:\orant8i\jdbc\lib\classes111.zip;
02:               D:\orant8i\sqlj\lib\translator.zip;%CLASSPATH%
03:
04: jpub -user=bookstore/bookstore
05:     -mapping=jdbc
06:     -sql=person_t:Person
07:     -url=jdbc:oracle:oci8:@ORA815
```

LISTING 10.34 Using JPublisher to generate Java classes

Listing 10.34 shows the commands split over more than one line for clarity. Lines 1 and 2 form the "set" commands, and lines 4–7 form the "jpub" command, where each command should be on one line. Notes on the JPublisher command:

- The –user option is required; it identifies the database and user that own the SQL object type definition. JPublisher uses this option to login to the database.
- The –url option specifies the database to which JPublisher connects. (JPublisher is a Java application.)
- The –mapping option indicates that JPublisher should generate JDBC-compatible data types for SQL object attributes.
- The –sql option identifies the SQL object type name before the colon, and the based name of the Java class generated after the colon.

The example shown generates two files:

1. Person.java, which contains the source for the SQL object as a Java Person object.
2. PersonRef.java, which contains the Java source for an SQL object REF as Java PersonRef object.

Listing 10.35 shows some of the key methods generated by JPublisher for the Person class implementing the CustomDatum interfaces.

```
package com.prenhall.OFJP.jdbc;
import java.sql.SQLException;
import oracle.jdbc.driver.OracleConnection;
import oracle.jdbc.driver.OracleTypes;
import oracle.sql.CustomDatum;
import oracle.sql.CustomDatumFactory;
import oracle.sql.Datum;
import oracle.sql.STRUCT;
```

LISTING 10.35 Part of Person class generated by JPublisher

```
import oracle.jpub.runtime.MutableStruct;
public class Person implements CustomDatum, CustomDatumFactory
{
  public static final String _SQL_NAME = "BOOKSTORE.PERSON_T";
  public static final int _SQL_TYPECODE = OracleTypes.STRUCT;

  private static int[] _sqlType =
  {
    2, 12, 12, 91
  };

  private static CustomDatumFactory[] _factory =
                  new CustomDatumFactory[4];
  private MutableStruct _struct;

  private static final Person _PersonFactory = new Person();
  public static CustomDatumFactory getFactory()
  {
    return _PersonFactory;
  }

  /* constructor */
  public Person()
  {
    _struct = new MutableStruct(new Object[4],
                                  _sqlType, _factory);
  }
  /* CustomDatum interface */
  public Datum toDatum(OracleConnection c) throws SQLException
  {
    return _struct.toDatum(c, _SQL_NAME);
  }

  /* CustomDatumFactory interface */
  public CustomDatum create(Datum d, int sqlType)
  throws SQLException  {
    if (d == null) return null;
    Person o = new Person();
    o._struct =
         new MutableStruct((STRUCT) d, _sqlType, _factory);
    return o;
  }
  :
}
```

LISTING 10.35 *Continued*

Notes on Listing 10.35:

- ❑ Lines 15–18 define the data types for each attribute value stored in the STRUCT created for a Person object.
- ❑ Lines 31–35 are the statements for the constructor of the Person object called by the create() method. The constructor makes an Oracle JDBC STRUCT object a MutableStruct, which contains each attribute value for the SQL object in an object array.
- ❑ Lines 37–40 represent the method implemented for the CustomDatum interface. They return a Datum object created from a STRUCT object. The STRUCT object contains the values for each of the Oracle object type attributes. The JDBC driver does the work of building STRUCT and mapping the data, based on the SQL object type identified in the _SQL_NAME class variable.
- ❑ Lines 42–50 show the Java method, implemented for the CustomDatumFactory interface, that returns a CustomDatum object. The CustomDatum object returned is, in fact, the Person object itself, which is a type of CustomDatum object because it implements the CustomDatum interface. The create() method is called by the JDBC driver to make a Person object when you read a PERSON_T Oracle SQL object value.

The Java code that reads a PERSON_T object into a Person object is:

```
01: public void readAsDatum() throw SQLException {
02:    Person p = null;
03:    PreparedStatment ps = null;
04:
05:    ps = conn.prepareStatement("select person from employee");
06:    ResultSet r = ps.executeQuery();
07:    while (r.next()) {
08:      p = (Person) ((OracleResultSet)r).getCustomDatum(
09:                                    1, Person.getFactory());
10:      System.out.println("Person: " + p);
11:    }
12:    r.close();
13:    ps.close();
14: }
```

Notes:

- ❑ Lines 8 and 9 create the Person object by casting the ResultSet object to an OracleResultSet, so that you can call the getCustomDatum() method. The arguments for getCustomDatum() method are:

    - The Index of the column value retrieved; in this case the PERSON_T SQL object.
    - The Person object instance, which is populated by the JDBC driver from the attribute values of the SQL object type, and created by the Person.getFactory() method.
- If you modify the type map for connection prior to fetching the object, you can replace lines 8 and 9 with the following code: `p = (Person) r.getObject(1);`

The Java code that writes a Person object into a PERSON_T object is:

```
01: public void writeAsDatum() throws SQLException {
02:   PreparedStatement ps = null;
03:   Person p = new Person();
04:
05:   p.setId(new BigDecimal(4));
06:   p.setFirstname("Jose");
07:   p.setLastname("Demarco");
08:   p.setBirthdate(new java.sql.Timestamp(86, 11, 1, 0, 0, 0, 0));
09:
10:   ps = conn.prepareStatement("insert into employee values (?)");
11:   ((OraclePreparedStatement)ps).setCustomDatum(1, p);
12:   ps.execute();
13: }
```

Notes:

- Line 3 creates a Person object.
- Lines 5–8 set the Person state. The setXXX() methods used are generated by JPublisher. By default, JPublisher generates a setXXX() and getXXX() method for each attribute defined in the Oracle SQL Object type. You can customize the code after it has been generated.
- Line 11 uses the OraclePreparedStatement to call the setCustomDatum() method to bind the Person object value to the INSERT statement placeholder.
- If you have set the type map for the connection to associate the SQL object type with the Java class, then the code in line 11 can be replaced with: `ps.setObject(1,p,OracleTypes.STRUCT);`

These examples show how you can use the CustomDatum technique to read or write object values, with or without modifying the type map on the JDBC connection.

10.1.8.6 Reading and Writing Oracle SQL Object REFs. The Oracle JDBC driver supports reading and writing Oracle object type REF values as Java objects. You can use the OracleResultSet.getREF() method to read an REF to an SQL object. Once the SQL object REF is obtained, you can call the getValue() method to convert the REF into its Java class representing the object instance value. To write an SQL object REF, use the OraclePreparedStatement.setREF() method.

10.1.9 READING AND WRITING COLLECTIONS

If you decide to use Oracle database collection types, such as varying arrays and nested tables, you can use Oracle extensions to JDBC to process data in your Oracle SQL collections. The extensions for ARRAY data types are also supported in JDBC 2.0–enabled JDBC drivers.

10.1.9.1 Writing To Varying Arrays. This section shows an example of writing to an Oracle SQL varying-array column. The SQL structures used for this example are:

```
CREATE OR REPLACE TYPE person_t AS OBJECT (
  id           number(6),
  firstName    varchar2(20),
  lastName     varchar2(20),
  birthDate    date);

CREATE TYPE person_va_t AS varray(5) OF person_t;

CREATE TABLE family (
  id      number(4) primary key,
  members person_va_t);
```

The Person object type is used for the example:

```
void writeArray() throws SQLException {
  // create a new ARRAY of Person objects
  Person members[] = {
    new Person("BOOKSTORE.PERSON_T", 2,
               "Zilbert", "Magnus",
               getDate(10, Calendar.JANUARY, 1982)),
    new Person("BOOKSTORE.PERSON_T", 3,
               "Jenna", "Magnus",
               getDate(10, Calendar.FEBRUARY, 1982)),
    };

```

```
12:   ArrayDescriptor desc = ArrayDescriptor.createDescriptor(
13:                              "BOOKSTORE.PERSON_VA_T", conn);
14:   ARRAY newArray = new ARRAY(desc, conn, members);
15:
16:   PreparedStatement ps =
17:     conn.prepareStatement ("insert into family values (?, ?)");
18:   ps.setInt(1, 2);
19:   ((OraclePreparedStatement)ps).setARRAY (2, newArray);
20:   ps.execute ();
21:   conn.commit();
22: }
```

Notes:

- Lines 3–10 create a Java array of Person objects. The example assumes that the Person class is implementing the SQLData interface. Therefore, the object type name appears in the first argument of the constructor for each Person object.
- Lines 12 and 13 declare the ArrayDescriptor class, defined in the oracle.sql package, which instantiates an array descriptor used to build the definition of the array structure used by the JDBC driver to map and write the contents to the SQL varying-array column.
- Line 14 builds the array object from the descriptor and the Java person object array.
- Line 19 uses the OraclePreparedStatement setARRAY() method to associate the ARRAY object instance with the second placeholder in the INSERT statement.

The example also assumes that the type map for the connection has associated the PERSON_T Oracle SQL object with the Person Java class.

10.1.9.2 Reading from Varying Arrays. The SQL structures used for the example here are the same ones that were used in the section of this chapter on writing varying arrays. This section shows an example of reading an Oracle SQL varying-array column of Person objects.

```
public void readArray() throws SQLException {
  Statement stmt = conn.createStatement ();
  ResultSet rs = stmt.executeQuery("SELECT * FROM family");
  int line = 0;
  while (rs.next())
  {
```

```
07:     int id = rs.getInt(1);
08: //  oracle.sql.ARRAY array = ((OracleResultSet)rs).getARRAY(2);
09:     oracle.jdbc2.Array array = ((OracleResultSet)rs).getArray(2);
10:
11:     // get Array elements
12:     Object[] values = (Object[]) array.getArray();
13:
14:     for (int i=0; i<values.length; i++)
15:     {
16:       Person value = (Person) values[i];
17:       System.out.println(">> " + i + " = " + value);
18:     }
19:
20:     /*
21:     ** Or process array elements as a ResultSet
22:     *
23:     ResultSet ars = array.getResultSet();
24:     while (ars.next()) {
25:       System.out.println("Index: " + ars.getInt(1));
26:       System.out.println("Value: " + (Person) ars.getObject(2));
27:     }
28:     */
29:   }
30: }
```

Notes:

- Line 8 uses the JDBC 2.0 Array object to read in a varying array. Line 7 shows the equivalent Oracle extension to JDBC 1.x that achieves the same result. In both cases, you cast the ResultSet object to an OracleResultSet to call the getArray() (or getARRAY()) method. The casting is not required if you use a standard JDBC 2.0 driver.
- Line 12 uses the Array object getArray() method to return an array of objects, where each element in the array contains a Person object. This technique can be used for any data type stored in the varying array.
- Lines 14–18 set a loop that casts each object reference in the object array to a Person object in order to process the data as a Person object.
- Lines 20–28 are commented out, and show an alternative way of processing varying-array values. You can use the getResultSet() method of the array to process the array elements as rows in result set. The result set contains two columns; the first is the index of the array element, and the second is the actual element value. Line 26 uses a technique that relies on the PERSON_T object type being mapped in a type map to the Person class.

10.1.9.3 Writing to Oracle Nested Tables. The examples here are based on an SQL table and nested table defined in the database as:

```
CREATE TYPE person_nt_t AS TABLE OF person_t;

CREATE TABLE team (
  id number(4) primary key,
  members person_nt_t)
  nested table members store as team_members;
```

Here is how to write to a column defined as a nested table of Person objects:

```
01: public void writeNestedTable() throws SQLException {
02:   // create a new ARRAY object
03:   Person members[] = {
04:     new Person("BOOKSTORE.PERSON_T", 10,
05:             "Nambert", "Rollus",
06:             getDate(10, Calendar.JANUARY, 1982)),
07:     new Person("BOOKSTORE.PERSON_T", 20,
08:             "Zubenal", "Ganubee",
09:             getDate(10, Calendar.FEBRUARY, 1982)),
10:     };
11:
12:   PreparedStatement ps = conn.prepareStatement ("insert into " +
13:     "table (select members from team where id = ?) values (?)");
14:   ps.setInt(1, 1);
15:   for (int i = 0; i < members.length; i++) {
16:     ps.setObject(2, members[i], OracleTypes.STRUCT);
17:     ps.execute();
18:   }
19:   conn.commit();
20: }
```

Notes:

- Lines 4–10 create a Person object array.
- Lines 12 and 13 create the statement that uses the TABLE operator, in the Oracle SQL syntax, to make the nested-table column appear as if it is a table on its own.
- Line 14 binds the first placeholder in the INSERT statement to ensure that the nested table for one row is processed.
- Lines 15–17 are loop statements that execute the prepared INSERT statement once for each Person object in the object array.

10.1.9.4 Reading from Nested Tables.

The example here is based the same SQL structures that were used for the writing example. Here you learn how to read a column defined as a nested table:

```
01: public void readNestedTable() throws SQLException {
02:   Statement stmt = conn.createStatement ();
03:   ResultSet rs = stmt.executeQuery("SELECT * FROM team");
04:
05:   while (rs.next()) {
06:     int id = rs.getInt(1);
07:     oracle.jdbc2.Array array = ((OracleResultSet)rs).getArray(2);
08:
09:     ResultSet ars = array.getResultSet();
10:     while (ars.next()) {
11:       System.out.println("Index: " + ars.getInt(1));
12:       System.out.println("Value: " + (Person) ars.getObject(2));
13:     }
14:   }
15: }
```

Notes:

- Line 7 creates a JDBC 2.0–compliant object by casting the ResultSet to an OracleResultSet, in order to call the getArray() method for the nested table in the second column of the query.
- Line 9 creates a ResultSet from the array for each row in the nested table. The ResultSet is processed as if it were a varying array, where the first column is the index into the array, and the second column is the Person object value. You can also retrieve and process the rows in the nested table as an array of Java objects.

10.2 SUPPORT FOR THE JDBC 2.0 OPTIONAL PACKAGE

The Oracle JDBC drivers found in the classes12.zip file, shipped with Oracle 8.1.6 or higher, natively support JDBC 2.0 standards. Examples showing the use of the following subset of features are discussed:

- Scrollable cursors.
- Connection pooling. You will want to take advantage of connection pooling for Internet-enabled applications to share the available database connections across many clients, and to maximize your site scalability requirements.
- Connecting to the database using JNDI connection string.

10.2.1 USING SCROLLABLE RESULTSET

Scrollable resultset provide the ability to process previously fetched result set data without your having to cache the results. The JDBC driver will cache the results for you. In JDBC 2.0, methods have been added to the ResultSet interface that fetch previous rows. The additional methods added to the ResultSet class include:

- boolean previous()—to go back one row.
- void beforeFirst()—position before the first row, to process results in a forward direction.
- void afterLast()—position after the last row, for processing results in a backward direction.
- boolean first()—position in the first row in the result set.
- boolean last()—position in the last row in the result set.
- boolean absolute(int row)—position in the specified row in the result set, relative to the beginning of the result set if the argument is positive, at the end of the result set if the row is negative.
- boolean relative(int row)—position in the next row relative to the current row.

There are several methods to support testing the current position, and to set or change the state of the scrollable ResultSet.

Scrollable ResultSets can also be updatable to allow the execution of DML operations on row data as you step through the result set. Thus, there are many updateXXX() methods to facilitate updating the fields of a row, where XXX is represents a suitable Java type compatible with the underlying SQL type for the column modified.

In general, a scrollable ResultSet is not recommended for processing large amounts of data, due to the memory consumed by the JDBC driver in holding data for result set rows already processed. The JDBC driver caches rows to allow your application to step to previous rows without requiring additional I/O to fetch the rows.

10.2.2 THE JDBC 2.0 DATASOURCE

The JDBC 2.0 specification provides an interface called javax.sql.DataSource that is an encapsulation of a vendor-independent representation for a data source (e.g., a database). DataSource has become the preferred alternative technique for obtaining a database connection, as compared to using java.sql.DriverManager class from the JDBC 1.0 class library. The advantage of using a DataSource object is that it does not require vendor-dependent code, such as vendor-specific code to load JDBC drivers, and the use of URLs to get connections.

Oracle implements the javax.sql.DataSource interface in a class called OracleDataSource that provides overloaded getConnection() methods. The OracleDataSource class provides methods to explicitly set vendor-specific properties, such as user name, or JDBC drivers, should you need to do so.

The code example in Listing 10.36 shows how to:

- Create a data source object with a default username and password.
- Request a database connection using the default username and password.
- Request a database connection using an alternative username and password from the default values.

```
package com.prenhall.OFJP.jdbc;
import java.sql.*;
import javax.sql.*;
import oracle.jdbc.pool.OracleDataSource;
public class JDBCDataSource {
  private DataSource dataSrc = null;
  private Connection conn = null;
  private Statement stmt = null;
  private ResultSet rset = null;

:
  public JDBCDataSource(String host, String dbName)
    throws SQLException {
    // Create a vendor data source
    OracleDataSource ods = new OracleDataSource();
    ods.setUser("scott");
    ods.setPassword("tiger");
    ods.setDriverType("thin");
    ods.setNetworkProtocol("tcp");
    ods.setPortNumber(1521);
    ods.setServerName(host);
    ods.setDatabaseName(dbName);

    // assign to javax.sql.DataSource object reference
    dataSrc = ods;

    // Get a connect with the default user
    String query = "SELECT user, " +
                   "sysdate " +
                   "FROM dual";
```

LISTING 10.36 Creating a DataSource to obtain a JDBC connection

```
43:
44:       conn = dataSrc.getConnection();
45:       this.executeQuery(conn, query);
46:       conn.close();
47:
48:        // Get a connection with a specified user
49:       conn = dataSrc.getConnection("bookstore", "bookstore");
50:       this.executeQuery(conn, query);
51:       conn.close();
52:       conn = null;
53:     }
54:
55:     public static void main(String[] args) {
56:       try {
57:         new JDBCDataSource("localhost", "ORA815");
58:       }
59:       catch (SQLException e) {
60:         e.printStackTrace();
61:       }
62:     }
63: }
```

LISTING 10.36 *Continued*

Notes for Listing 10.36:

- Lines 1–3 are the import statements showing that you need to reference the oracle.jdbc.pool package to resolve the OracleDataSource object. Note that there is no requirement in this code to load the JDBC driver or to use the DriverManager to obtain the connection.
- Line 6 declares a javax.sql.DataSource object reference, followed by the code to create the OracleDataSource object.
- Lines 27–34 instantiate the OracleDataSource object and set the properties for the associated physical data source. You must use the OracleDataSource object to do this, because the javax.sql.DataSource interface does not contain any of the setXXX methods. This is where the intended vendor-independence is lost. However, you can write an application that uses vendor-specific code to register/bind a DataSource object to a name in a JNDI-enabled service, and then write a vendor-independent application to use JNDI lookup calls to obtain the DataSource object (how to locate a DataSource stored in a JNDI-enabled service is discussed below in section 10.2.3).

- Line 37 assigns the OracleDataSource to a javax.sql.DataSource reference, so that the rest of the code can be vendor-independent.
- Line 44 requests a JDBC Connection object from the data source using the getConnection() method without arguments. The data source must have been created with a user name and password for this to work. The Connection is used to execute a query, which confirms from the Oracle database the name of the connected user and the time of the query.
- Line 45 requests a JDBC connection and specifies a user name and password. The user name and password provided in the getConnection() method override any default values assigned to the data source.

The code for lines 11–23, missing from Listing 10.36, executes a query using standard JDBC calls.

```
11:   public void executeQuery(Connection conn, String theQuery)
12:     throws SQLException {
13:     stmt = conn.createStatement ();
14:     rset = stmt.executeQuery (theQuery);
15:     while (rset.next ()) {
16:       System.out.println (
17:           "Executing as User name: " + rset.getString (1) +
18:           " at " + rset.getString(2));
19:     }
20:     rset.close();
21:     stmt.close();
22:   }
```

Here the query is supplied as a string parameter. In the query shown in Listing 10.36 on lines 40–42, the SELECT statement uses the Oracle database built-in function USER to return the database user name, and uses the SYSDATE function to return the date and time of the query.

10.2.3 OBTAINING CONNECTIONS USING JNDI

The Java Naming and Directory Interface (JNDI) technology is a set of Java classes that provide methods to access naming and directory services. The JNDI API provides a layer of abstraction for your Java application in the way it accesses directory services, with the goal of enabling you to write vendor-independent code.

10.2.3.1 Basic JNDI Architecture. The diagram in Figure 10.2 depicts the JNDI architecture, showing the relationship between your Java code and the naming and directory service, and identifying the following components:

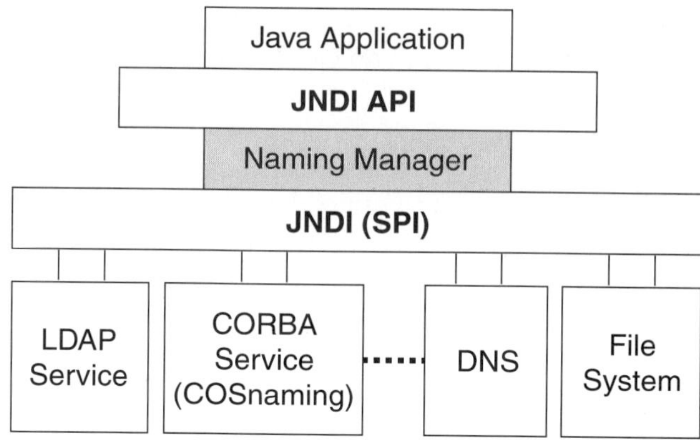

FIGURE 10.2 JNDI application architecture

- The application creating or requesting a resource/object by name.
- The JNDI API library.[24]
- The JNDI Service Provider Interface (SPI) library.
- A set of classes for a vendor-specific directory service that provides the name registry and directory lookup services.

Figure 10.2 represents the JNDI application architecture where the Java application accesses a naming and directory service via the JNDI API class.[25] JNDI calls are managed by the Naming Manager layer, which uses semantics and rules to direct JNDI requests to the appropriate service using JNDI SPI. The JNDI SPI is an API specification that developers of a naming and directory service must use to ensure that their implementation is compatible with and can be plugged into the JNDI architecture. The net result is that your Java code is shielded from the specific API calls to interact with the different vendor services.

10.2.3.2 Naming Rules. Each naming service defines rules for the format of names. For example, to access an HTTP server you are required to use the Universal Resource Locator (URL) http://host:port in order to establish a connection with the HTTP server. This naming convention combines rules from the Domain Name System (DNS) for the host/ip address, embedded in the URL. The

---

[24]The JNDI API classes were released as part of the Java 2 SDK, Enterprise Edition, v1.2.1 or higher. To use JNDI classes with earlier versions of the JDK, you can download the jndi.jar file with the relevant classes. You may also need to download a service-provider implementation, such as the Sun Microsystems File System Implementation.

[25]For more detail on JNDI, refer to the Web site at http://java.sun.com/products/jndi/.

URL structure is required to satisfy the rules of the HTTP protocol. In the URL, you can optionally specify a path/directory and/or a target file after the host and/or port. For example: http://www.javasoft.com/jndi/index.html.

The path is `jndi/`, relative to the HTTP server document root,[26] and the target `index.html` is the end-point. The path `/jndi/index.html` can be compared directly to a file system, where `jndi/` represents a directory, and index.html is a file in that directory. In JNDI terminology, the equivalent of an HTTP document root is known as an *initial context*. The initial context is the point from which you would start searching for, or looking up, an object via its *bind name*. The bind name refers to the name of the object as registered in the JNDI-enabled directory service.

In JNDI terms, a directory would be called a *context*, and index.html would represent an *atomic name*. The name should be unique within the context and represents the link to an object; that is, the index.html file name is the link to the contents of the file in the file system directory. In JNDI terms, from the perspective of the directory service, the association of the name to the actual file on disk is called a *binding*.

To access the file contents, you first look up the directory to locate the file name, and then request the file contents (i.e., the object itself). The binding is then resolved to locate the contents of the file via the directory service, and return a handle/reference to the file object so that the application can read the file contents. This is analogous to how your Java application uses objects in a JNDI-enabled directory service.

By convention, a bind name, relative to the directory service root, has the following syntax for JDBC-based resources, such as a DataSource:

```
jdbc/<your-unique-name>
```

The context name "jdbc" is a convention, and was not enforced at the time of writing this book. The text <your-unique-name> is to be replaced with a unique identifying name for your JDBC-based resource.

10.2.3.3 Using JNDI with a DataSource Object. This section does not attempt to fully describe the terms, interfaces, and classes of JNDI API, but does explain some concepts that will enable you to see JNDI API can be used to:

- ❑ Register a JDBC DataSource in a directory service and bind it to a logical name.
- ❑ Look up a DataSource object using the JNDI-registered name, and create the DataSource object with the same state it was registered in the JNDI directory service.

---

[26]The HTTP document root is represented by be the path "/", which is implied after the host/port in the URL if not explicitly entered. The document root is translated to a physical directory path in the file system of the Web server, which represents the top-level or root directory for static content for a Web listener.

At the time of writing this book, the Oracle8i database provided an implementation of a CORBA-based naming and directory service. This service supports JNDI access to Enterprise JavaBeans, or CORBA objects stored in the database, but it does not support the use of JNDI binding techniques to associate a name with a DataSource object. Therefore, the examples shown store JDBC DataSource objects in a naming and directory service in the local file system of the Java application, using the file system–based reference implementation of a JNDI SPI driver from JavaSoft.

To use the file system as a naming and directory service, you must perform the following actions:

1. Download fscontext1_*.zip from the Service Provider link at the JavaSoft JNDI products Web site (at http://www.javasoft.com/jndi/). Where "*" is a part of the name that changes with new versions of the library code.
2. Include in your CLASSPATH the providerutil.jar and fscontext.jar files extracted from the above ZIP.

Figure 10.3 is a pictorial representation of the Java application code with respect to JNDI naming and directory service.

The code for Java Application 1 (AddJndiDataSource.java) in Figure 10.3 is shown in Listing 10.37, which shows how to create a DataSource object and register with the JNDI file system service.

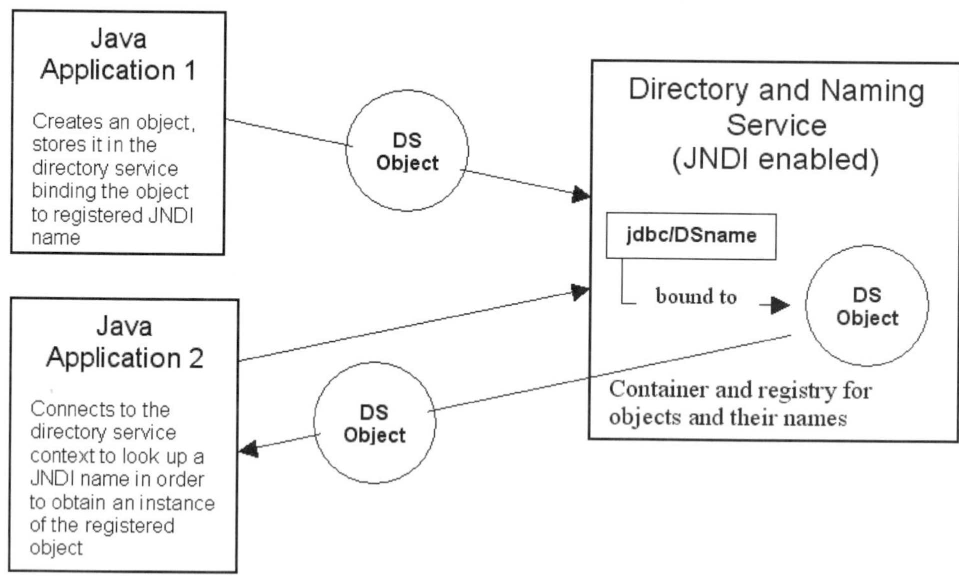

FIGURE 10.3 Java code using JNDI naming and directory service

The code for Java Application 2 (JdbcJndiConnection.java), represented in Listing 10.38, shows how to connect to a JNDI service provider (the file system in this case), look up a JDBC DataSource by its bind name, and then obtain a JDBC connection from the DataSource object.

The code for both applications can be in one source, but the example separates functionality to show how the second application, the user looking up the JNDI service, can be written in a highly portable way, independent of vendor-specifics. The same independence cannot be applied to the first application type, which loads the object, binds and publishes the name of the object.

```
package com.prenhall.OFJP.jdbc;
import java.sql.*;
import javax.sql.*;
import javax.naming.*;
import java.util.Hashtable;
import oracle.jdbc.pool.OracleDataSource;
public class AddJndiDataSource {

  private Context initCtx;

  public AddJndiDataSource() {
    this("jdbc/demo_ds", "localhost", 1521, "ORA815");
  }

  public AddJndiDataSource(String jndiName, String serverName,
                           int port, String database) {
    DataSource dataSource;
    try {
      this.setInitCtx();
      dataSource = newJdbcDataSource(serverName, port, database);
      initCtx.bind(jndiName, dataSource);
    }
    catch (Exception e) {
      e.printStackTrace();
    }
  }

  public DataSource newJdbcDataSource(
       String serverName, int port, String database)
       throws SQLException {
    OracleDataSource ods = new OracleDataSource();
    ods.setDriverType("thin");
    ods.setNetworkProtocol("tcp");
    ods.setServerName(serverName);
```

LISTING 10.37 Registering a DataSource in a JNDI-enabled service

```
35:     ods.setPortNumber(port);
36:     ods.setDatabaseName(database);
37:     return ods;
38:   }
39:
40:   public void setInitCtx() throws NamingException {
41:     Hashtable env = new Hashtable ();
42:     env.put (Context.INITIAL_CONTEXT_FACTORY,
43:              "com.sun.jndi.fscontext.RefFSContextFactory");
44:     env.put (Context.PROVIDER_URL, "file:/jndi");
45:     initCtx = new InitialContext(env);
46:   }
47:
48:   public static void main(String[] args) {
        // Method to invoke the application
76:   }
77: }
```

LISTING 10.37 *Continued*

Notes for Listing 10.37:

- Line 2 is the required import for the DataSource interface.
- Line 3 is for the JNDI naming classes, such as InitialContext and Context.
- Line 5 is for using the OracleDataSource class, which must be used to create an appropriate object for storing in the JNDI-based service. In fact, OracleDataSource implements the javax.naming.Referenceable interface. The Referenceable interface allows the JNDI service to store sufficient information to reconstruct the state on an object, without the need to serialize the instance. Support for serialized objects and/or referenced objects in a JNDI service-provider implementation is dependent on the capabilities of the JNDI-enabled product supplied by the vendor.
- Line 9 declares the initial context variable, to hold the starting point for adding named items into the directory service. All JNDI operations are relative to the root defined by the initial context.
- Lines 11–13 show a default constructor that sets a default value for creating a JNDI name, and values to store in an instance of its associated OracleDataSource.
- Lines 15–26 are the main constructor code, which calls the setInitCtx() method to establish a link with the JNDI naming and directory service.

- Line 20 calls the new JdbcDataSource() method to return an instance of an OracleDataSource.
- Line 21 performs the binding operation to associate the jndiName with the data source in the JNDI-based service. This line of code is the registration operation, and can generate a javax.naming.NamingException if the JNDI name supplied is already registered in the directory. You can replace the call to the InitialContext bind() with the rebind() method, which creates the binding if it does not exist, or overwrites an existing binding. The rebind() method accepts the same parameters as the bind() method. This operation completes the task of the application.
- Lines 28–38 create the OracleDataSource object calling the appropriate set methods to define its state with the values of its parameters and some default values.
- Lines 40–46 create the initial context for JNDI operations. The Hashtable is used to define properties needed for constructing the initial context. The first property added, in lines 42 and 43, is called Context.INITIAL_CONTEXT_FACTORY, and its value, "com.sun.jndi.fscontext.RefFSContextFactory," defines the class used to set up the initial context for naming operations.
- In Line 44, the second parameter, Context.PROVIDER_URL, is used for the File System JNDI implementation to set the root directory for the initial context based on the URL value of "file:/jndi," which requires that the "jndi" directory exist on the current disk drive or volume from which the application is launched.

The example sets JNDI properties values in a way that is dependent on the File System JNDI service-provider implementation. If you change your JNDI service provider, then you also have to change your code. You can overcome this by getting the JNDI properties from a Java Properties file or System Properties. Replace lines 41–44 with the following line of code:

```
Properties env = System.getProperties();
```

Invoke the application using a Java command line with the following defines:

```
java -Djava.naming.factory.initial=com.sun.jndi.fscontext.RefFSContextFactory
     -Djava.naming.provider.url=file:/jndi
  com.prenhall.OFJP.jdbc.AddJndiDataSource jdbc/ds1 ...
```

If you change the service provider, then you only need to change the java command line used to invoke the JNDI application, not your source code. For the sample code in Listing 10.37, the command line to invoke the AddJndiDataSource application is:

```
java com.prenhall.OFJP.jdbc.AddJndiDataSource jdbc/ds1 localhost 1521 ORA815
```

The first parameter is the bind name for the data source, and the remaining three parameters are values used to set the state of the data source object.

- The second parameter is the server name hosting the database.
- The third parameter is the Oracle database connection listener port number.
- The fourth parameter is the database system identification, known as the SID.

The main method of the AddJndiDataSource code reads these arguments and calls the constructor of the class. Here is the code for the AddJndiDataSource.main() method:

```
public static void main(String[] args) {
  private String jndiName = "jdbc/demo_ds";      // args 0
  private String database = "ORA815";            // args 1
  private String serverName = "localhost";       // args 2
  private int port = 1521;                       // args 3

  switch (args.length) {
    case 4:
      database = args[3];
    case 3:
      try {
        port = Integer.parseInt(args[3]);
      }
      catch (NumberFormatException e) {
        port = 1521;
      }
    case 2:
      serverName = args[1];
    case 1:
      jndiName = args[0];
  }

  System.out.println("Add JDNI name: " + jndiName);
  System.out.println("ServerName: " + serverName);
  System.out.println("Port: " + port);
  System.out.println("Database: " + database);
```

```
      new AddJndiDataSource(jndiName, serverName, port, database);
      System.out.println("Done!");
  }
```

When using the File System JNDI reference implementation, a file called `.bindings` is created in the file system root directory of the initial context. The bindings file contains the values needed to reconstruct the DataSource object when an application requests it by its JNDI bind name.

Now you will look at the code required to look up the DataSource bind name in the JNDI naming service to construct a DataSource so as to obtain the JDBC connection for your database-enabled application.

```
package com.prenhall.OFJP.jdbc;
import java.sql.*;
import javax.sql.*;
import javax.naming.*;
import java.util.Hashtable;
public class JdbcJndiConnection {

  public JdbcJndiConnection(String jndiName) {
    try {
      Context iCtx;
      Hashtable env = new Hashtable ();

      System.out.println(
         "Connect to File System naming and directory service");
      env.put (Context.INITIAL_CONTEXT_FACTORY,
             "com.sun.jndi.fscontext.RefFSContextFactory");
      env.put (Context.PROVIDER_URL, "file:/jndi");

      iCtx = new InitialContext(env);

      System.out.println("Lookup JNDI name=" + jndiName);
      DataSource ds = (DataSource) iCtx.lookup(jndiName);

      Connection conn;
      PreparedStatement pstmt;

      System.out.println("get JDBC connection from datasource");
      conn = ds.getConnection("bookstore", "bookstore");

      pstmt = conn.prepareStatement(
        "SELECT id, name, surname FROM customer " +
        "WHERE upper(credit_card_type) = ?");
```

LISTING 10.38 Looking up a DataSource from a JNDI-enabled service

```
33:         pstmt.setString(1, "VISA");
34:
35:         System.out.println("List of Visa Customers");
36:         ResultSet rset = pstmt.executeQuery();
37:         while (rset.next()) {
38:           System.out.println(rset.getString(1) + " " +
39:                              rset.getString(2) + " " +
40:                              rset.getString(3));
41:         }
42:         rset.close();
43:         pstmt.close();
44:         conn.close();
45:         System.out.println("Done!");
46:       }
47:       catch (Exception e) {
48:         e.printStackTrace();
49:       }
50:     }
51:
52:     public static void main(String[] args) {
53:       String jndiName = "jdbc/demo_ds";
54:
55:       if (args.length > 0) {
56:         jndiName = args[0];
57:       }
58:       new JdbcJndiConnection(jndiName);
59:     }
60: }
```

LISTING 10.38 *Continued*

Notes for Listing 10.38:

- Line 10 creates the object reference variable for the JNDI initial context object.
- Lines 15–19 create the initial context object, defining the starting point for name-lookup requests.
- Line 22 performs the lookup request by calling the lookup() method of the initial context. The parameter supplied to the lookup() method is the JNDI bind name given to the DataSource object saved in the directory (in this case the binding file). The lookup() method always returns a reference to the object class. You need to cast the returned value to the appropriate object type and variable. In this example, the JNDI object is a DataSource. Note that this code uses the javax.sql.DataSource interface, and not the OracleDataSource class, which makes the code more portable.

- ❑ Line 28 requests a JDBC connection, with the supplied user name and password, from the DataSource object. The rest of the code is just standard JDBC calls.

This introduction to JNDI provides a basic understanding of how you can use JNDI services. In later chapters, discussing the use of Oracle8i Enterprise JavaBeans and CORBA services, you will encounter the need to use JNDI to access Oracle8i CORBA and EJB objects via the naming and directory services provided by the CORBA services inside the Oracle Aurora engine.

10.2.4 USING JDBC 2.0 CONNECTION POOLING

In this section, you will look at the concepts of using a JDBC 2.0 PooledConnection and ConnectionPoolDataSource interfaces.

The reason for using connection pooling is to enable application threads to share database connections in order to minimize the performance overhead of constantly opening and closing connections. In a Web-enabled application, such as a Java servlet, if each thread opened its own database connection, you would quickly exceed the capacity of data server resources or reach the limits imposed by licensing agreements. By using a pooled connection, you can work around these limits to provide scalable applications. Sharing a resource brings with it a need to synchronize access to the resource, and this, too, can lead to performance problems if not managed carefully.

In the JDBC 1.0 specification, each Connection object represents a physical connection with a database. The same applies to acquiring a Connection from a DataSource.

However, in JDBC 2.0, you can create an object that implements the javax.sql.PooledConnection interface, such as the OraclePooledConnection. A PooledConnection object is manufactured through a class that implements ConnectionPoolDataSource, such as OracleConnectionPoolDataSource.

The ConnectionPoolDataSource implementation class acts as a factory for PooledConnection objects.

In this case, the PooledConnection establishes and maintains the physical database link, but provides the application with a getConnection() method to return a JDBC 1.0 style connection, which is logically linked to the active physical connection. The pooled connection can be reassigned to different logical connection objects in the same application, but only one logical connection can be associated with a single pooled connection at a time. This is depicted in Figure 10.4.

The solid line in Figure 10.4 represents an active logical JDBC connection, and the dotted lines represent additional JDBC connections that share the same physical connection held by the pooled connection. When you close a logical connection, it severs the link with the pooled connection, but the pooled connection keeps the physical connection open until the close() method of the pooled connection is invoked. If you associate the pooled connection object with another logical

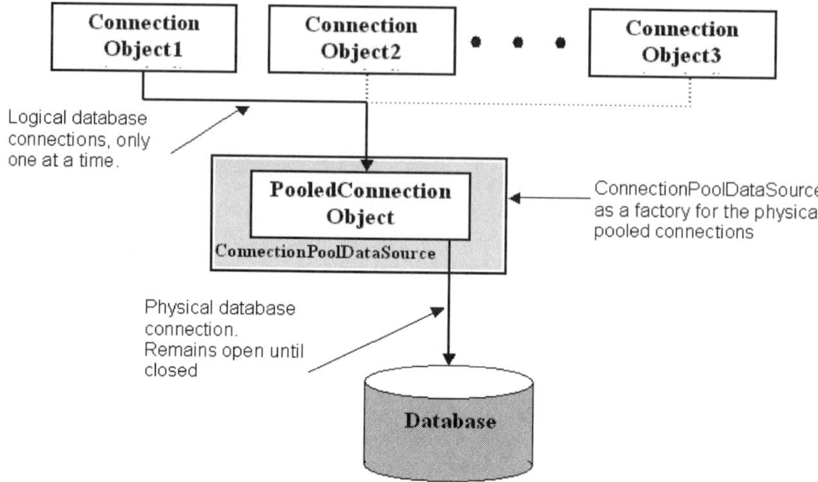

FIGURE 10.4 Reusing a PooledConnection object

Connection object, an active logical Connection is automatically closed. The code that follows demonstrates how to establish a pooled connection object and the principle of automatic closure of a logical connection.

```
package com.prenhall.OFJP.jdbc;
import java.sql.*;
import javax.sql.*;
import oracle.jdbc.pool.*;
public class PooledExample {

  public PooledExample() {
    try {
      Connection conn1;
      Connection conn2;
      SysConnection sysConn = new SysConnection();

      OracleConnectionPoolDataSource poolDataSrc =
                 new OracleConnectionPoolDataSource();
      poolDataSrc.setDriverType("thin");
      poolDataSrc.setServerName("localhost");
      poolDataSrc.setPortNumber(1521);
      poolDataSrc.setDatabaseName("ORA815");

      System.out.println("Count before pooled: " +
```

LISTING 10.39 Creating and using a JDBC 2.0 pooled connection

```
21:           sysConn.getSessionCount());
22:       // Get a physical pooled connection
23:       PooledConnection pooledConn =
24:        poolDataSrc.getPooledConnection("bookstore", "bookstore");
25:       System.out.println(
26:           "Count after pooled Before 1st logical: " +
27:            sysConn.getSessionCount());
28:       // Open a JDBC 1.0 Connection as a logical connection
29:       conn1 = pooledConn.getConnection();
30:
31:       System.out.println("Count after 1st logical : " +
32:           sysConn.getSessionCount());
33:
34:       // Open logical connection 2 close conn1
35:
36:       conn2 = pooledConn.getConnection();
37:
38:       System.out.println("Count after 2nd logical : " +
39:           sysConn.getSessionCount());
40:
41:       sysConn.close();
42:     }
43:     catch (Exception e) {
44:       e.printStackTrace();
45:     }
46:   }
47:
48:   public static void main(String[] args) {
49:     new PooledExample();
50:   }
51: }
```

LISTING 10.39 *Continued*

The steps in creating and using a pooled connection are enumerated below and shown in Listing 10.39. They are:

1. Create a ConnectionPoolDataSource—the factory for PooledConnections.
2. Obtain a PooledConnection from the ConnectionPoolDataSource.
3. Obtain a Connection from the PooledConnection.

Notes for Listing 10.39:

- Line 11 creates a SysConnection object to log in as a DBA user to monitor the number of database connections used in the application, by calling the getSessionCount() method, in lines 21, 27, 32, and 39. The count is determined before and after the pooled connection and connection objects are instantiated. The SysConnection class code is listed at the end of these notes.

- Lines 13–18 create and initialize the ConnectionPoolDataSource,[27] the PooledConnection factory.
- Lines 23 and 24 obtain the pooled connection from the connection pool data source object, establishing the physical database connection. The subsequent call to the sysConn.getSessionCount() should return a value incremented by one relative to the previous invocation of the same method.
- Line 29 creates a JDBC 1.0–style connection that is logically associated with the physical connection maintained by the PooledConnection object. You then execute your JDBC calls with the conn1 object. The session count should not be increased in the printed output for the next call to sysConn.getSessionCount().
- Line 36 automatically closes conn1, severing its logical association with the pooled connection, and logically assigns pooled connection to the conn2 object. The sysConn.getSessionCount() should remain unchanged; that is, no additional physical connections are used. If you now attempt to use conn1, you will receive an SQLException.

The output generated by the code in Listing 10.39 might be similar to the following:

Sample Output

```
Count before pooled: 9
Count after pooled Before 1st logical: 10
Count after 1st logical: 10
Count after 2nd logical: 10
```

Note that the initial session count before the pooled connection is established is nine. The session count is only incremented by one after the pooled connection is established, and not after each logical connection is obtained. Finally, the code used to count the number of sessions (physical connections) established in the database is:

```
package com.prenhall.OFJP.jdbc;
import java.sql.*;
import java.util.Properties;
public class SysConnection {
```

[27]The ConnectionPoolDataSource object can be used with JNDI in the same way as previously shown with the DataSource objects.

```
  private Connection sysConn;
  private Properties prop = new Properties();
  private PreparedStatement sysStmt;

  public SysConnection() throws Exception {
    prop.put ("internal_logon","test");
    Class.forName("oracle.jdbc.driver.OracleDriver");
    sysConn = DriverManager.getConnection(
        "jdbc:oracle:thin:@localhost:1521:ORA815",
        "system", "manager");
    sysStmt = sysConn.prepareStatement(
                        "select count(*) from V$SESSION");
  }

  public int getSessionCount () throws SQLException {
    ResultSet rset = sysStmt.executeQuery();
    rset.next();
    int cnt = rset.getInt(1);
    rset.close();
    rset = null;
    return cnt;
  }

  public void close() throws SQLException {
    sysStmt.close();
    sysStmt = null;
    sysConn.close();
    sysConn = null;
  }
}
```

The SysConnection code must execute the query with a database user who has read access to the V$ tables in the Oracle data dictionary.

In order for the PooledConnection to be of value in a multithreaded application environment, you need to create a cache of PooledConnection objects from the ConnectionPooledDataSource. Your code has to synchronize obtaining a pooled connection from the cache and returning a pooled connection from the cache. Oracle provides a reference implementation of a connection pool cache that can be used. For more information on Oracle's implementation of a connection pool cache, refer to the documentation in the Oracle JDBC Developers Guide and Reference for Oracle 8.1.6 or higher.

SUMMARY

This chapter covered extended and advanced features of using JDBC programming in an Oracle environment as well as techniques used to read and write:

- ❑ LONG, LONG RAW, CLOB, or BLOB data types, including image data
- ❑ Oracle SQL object types
- ❑ Serialized Java object

As JDBC 2.0 features are more widely supported, you can use them to improve application performance and scalability, such as batch processing for data query and update operations, scrollable cursors, and connection pooling.

Writing JDBC code can be an onerous task, requiring a lot of code to manage data in the database. The number of lines of JDBC code needed increases proportionally to the number of columns and tables needed by the application. The potential for typographical or logical errors also increases. Errors in SQL statements executed via JDBC can only be determined at runtime, which can slow down the development life cycle.

Oracle has collaborated with other vendors, including IBM, Tandem, and Sun, to develop SQLI, a standard way of embedding SQL statements in Java source. By using SQLJ, which is covered in the next chapter, the JDBC code explored in this chapter can be greatly simplified, with the advantages of doing syntactic checks on SQL statements at compile time, thereby improving code accuracy before runtime and speeding up the application development process.

Chapter 11

DATA ACCESS WITH SQLJ—EMBEDDING SQL IN JAVA

- An Overview of SQLJ
- Connecting to a Database in SQLJ
- Executing SQL Statements Using SQLJ
- Processing Oracle SQL Object Types
- Processing SQL Collections
- Managing Large Data Types
- Executing Stored Procedures and Functions
- Summary

This chapter covers the use of embedded SQL in Java, known as SQLJ technology. The focus of the chapter is on how to use SQLJ rather than JDBC to perform database operations from a Java application. The topics covered include:

- Connecting to the database
- Executing SQL statements
- Processing SQL object types
- Processing SQL collections

The chapter also discusses Oracle JPublisher in more detail and shows how you can use the Java classes generated by JPublisher when processing object types or collections in SQLJ.

> **Note**
>
> In order to focus on the key functionality discussed, and to minimize the amount of extra code written and documented, the examples shown in this chapter do not use proper code-management techniques for closing connections and error handling. For example, the code listings close database connections in the try section of a try-catch block. This does not cater for the case when an error occurs. It is better practice to close a database connection in the final section of a try-catch-finally block to ensure that the connection is closed for the success and failure conditions in your code.

11.1 AN OVERVIEW OF SQLJ

For years, vendors have provided a way for third-generation languages to execute SQL, in order to access data in relational databases. It was only natural that the same would happen with Java. The major benefits to developers are:

- Faster development because SQLJ typically requires fewer lines of code when compared to using JDBC.
- Early validation of SQL syntax at compile time, leading to more robust code.

SQLJ allows you to embed static SQL statements in Java code in a way that is compatible with the Java design principles. Static SQL statements specify predefined operations that do not change at runtime. Dynamic SQL statements specify SQL operations that are not predefined at compile time, where as a Java program can construct the SQL statement on the fly at runtime.

SQLJ and JDBC code can be mixed in the same program, and, as well, can share connections and structures.

11.1.1 SQLJ COMPONENTS

SQLJ consists of two primary components:

1. An SQLJ translator
2. An SQLJ runtime

One other component is a customizer that can be used to tailor SQLJ profiles for a specific database.[1] Since Oracle SQLJ Translator uses an Oracle-supplied customizer, you can access the extended features of an Oracle RDBMS environment.

11.1.1.1 The SQLJ Translator. The SQLJ translator is a preprocessor that reads SQLJ source code from a file with an `.sqlj` extension,[2] and produces a Java source in a `.java` file and one or more SQLJ profile files.[3] The SQLJ translator automatically compiles the Java source to produce the class file.

The Oracle SQLJ translator is available as a command-line utility for manually translating an SQLJ file into the Java source and class. Oracle JDeveloper automatically invokes the SQLJ translator when you build an SQLJ file. During the translation of the SQLJ source to the Java source, you can add an SQLJ translator command-line option to perform syntax checking of embedded SQL statements.

The SQLJ Translator class library is located in a file called translator.zip, which can be found in the `ORACLE_HOME/sqlj/lib` sub-directory of your Oracle8i installation. The `translator.zip` file and the SQLJ runtime classes must be in the class path at development time.

11.1.1.2 The SQLJ Runtime. SQLJ Runtime is automatically invoked when a Java program containing SQLJ code is executed. The SQLJ Runtime component implements the SQL operations embedded in the SQLJ code. Oracle SQLJ runtime requires the use of an Oracle JDBC driver to access the database, even though the SQLJ standard does not require the SQLJ runtime to use a JDBC driver to access a database. The SQLJ Runtime component class library is found in the file `ORACLE_HOME/sqlj/lib/runtime.zip`. This file must be in the class

---

[1] An SQLJ profile is a class, usually in serialized form, used by the SQLJ runtime to invoke SQL operations.

[2] The Oracle SQLJ Translator is written in pure Java.

[3] An SQLJ profile file contains serialized Java objects in a file with a `.ser` extension. Alternatively, a SQLJ profile can be created in a `.class` file. The serialized Java objects contain details about the embedded SQL operations in your SQLJ source code.

path when you are executing an SQLJ application. Note that the SQLJ Translator is not required at runtime.

11.1.2 CREATING AN SQLJ FILE

Any text editor or development environment with an editor can be used to create an SQLJ file. Oracle JDeveloper is a development environment that provides support for creating SQLJ files. The key features of an SQLJ file are:

- The file must have an extension named **sqlj.**
- The file must contain Java code for a Java class definition, with or without embedded SQLJ statements. The file name must be the same as the name of the public Java class contained in the file.
- The file must import the following two packages for compilation of SQLJ runtime classes that are generated or used:
  - sqlj.runtime.*
  - sqlj.runtime.ref.*

Listing 11.1 shows the basic structure of an SQLJ source, and the general syntax used to embed an SQL statement in the Java code.

```
File name: RegisterCustomer.sqlj

01: import sqlj.runtime.*;
02: import sqlj.runtime.ref.*;
03:
04: public class RegisterCustomer {
05:
06:   public static void main(String[] args) {
07:     #sql { sql-statement };
08:   }
09: }
```

LISTING 11.1 SQLJ source with generic embedded SQL statement

Listing 11.1 notes:

- Lines 1 and 2 are the import statements for the required classes found in SQLJ packages.
- Line 4 is the Java class name, which is the same as the file name and contains the methods that executes SQLJ statements.

- Line 7 is an example of the generic syntax for an SQL statement when it is embedded in your Java source code.
  - The text **#sql** must precede all SQLJ statements.
  - All SQL statements are placed between braces with no semicolon terminator inside the braces. A semicolon is placed outside the closing brace of the SQLJ statement.

Additional imports may be required, depending on the Java class used by the SQLJ source code. The SQLJ code is still primarily a Java source file.

11.1.3 TRANSLATING THE SQLJ FILE

The SQLJ translator converts the SQLJ source into a Java source that is automatically compiled into a class file.

11.1.3.1 Running the SQLJ Translator. The steps in running the SQLJ translator from the command line are:

1. Add the file ORACLE_HOME/sqlj/lib/translator.zip to your class path.
2. Run the **sqlj** command-line utility. The SQLJ translator executable is located in your ORACLE_HOME/bin directory.[4]

The steps are shown in Listing 11.2.

```
Step 1: Set the Classpath
For Windows NT:
  set CLASSPATH=D:\orant8i\sqlj\lib\translator.zip;%CLASSPATH%

For Unix Bourne or Korn Shell:
  CLASSPATH=$ORACLE_HOME/sqlj/lib/translator.zip:$CLASSPATH
  export CLASSPATH

For Unix C-Shell:
  setenv CLASSPATH $ORACLE_HOME/sqlj/lib/translator.zip:$CLASSPATH

Step 2: Run the SQLJ Translator
sqlj [options] file.sqlj
```

LISTING 11.2 Using the SQLJ translator

[4]If you are using Oracle JDeveloper, the SQLJ Translator command-line utility is found in the `bin` subdirectory, relative to your base directory for the JDeveloper installation. This will typically be `<drive>:\Program Files\Oracle JDeveloper 3.0\bin`, if you are using JDeveloper 3.0.

If you enter the SQLJ command by itself, the application prints a brief listing showing some help text for the command-line syntax and options.

The SQLJ translator has several command-line options. The command options are entered as:

```
-name
```

or,

```
-name=value
```

The hyphen, as shown, must immediately precede the option name. The option's value is either true or false. Turn on the option by entering the option as-name or –name=true, otherwise you must enter –name=false to turn the option off. Table 11.1 is a brief list of SQLJ translator command-line options.

TABLE 11.1 SQLJ translator command-line options

OPTION	DESCRIPTION AND VALUES
-user=*user/password*	The username and password used by the SQLJ translator to log into a database specified by the *url* option. The `user` option is only used if you want the SQLJ translator to perform syntax checking of embedded SQL statements.
-url=*jdbc-url*	The JDBC URL that identifies the database used for validating SQL statements and the database structures on which they operate. By default the URL is "`jdbc:oracle:oci8:@`".
-d=*directory*	Specifies the output root directory for generated binary (`ser` and `class`) files. The generated Java source file is not affected by this option.
-status	Displays status messages to the screen during the translation process.
-compile=false	Suppresses compilation of the generated Java source. No class files are created. Compilation is performed by default.
-ser2class	Creates profile files in the form of `.class` files, not `.ser` files. *Note:* This option should be used if your JVM environment does not support loading SER files.
-J-*option*	Specifies command-line options for the JVM that runs the SQLJ translator.
-classpath=*classpath*	Specifies the CLASSPATH to the JVM (java) and compiler (javac) used by the SQLJ translator.
-linemap	Causes the translator to generate SQLJ source-line numbers as comments in the Java source.

You specify command-line options separated by one or more spaces. For example:

```
sqlj -user=bookstore/bookstore -linemap
     -url=jdbc:oracle:thin:@localhost:1521:ORA815 file.sqlj
```

The example should be entered on one line. For clarity, the example is shown on more than one line with no command-line continuation characters, which are platform-dependent, if supported.

The SQLJ translator performs the following steps in sequence depending on the options used:

1. The Java Virtual Machine invokes the SQLJ Translator.
2. The translator parses the SQLJ source code, checking for proper SQLJ syntax.
3. The semantics checker is invoked to check whether the embedded SQL statements use valid database structures, such as columns, tables, procedures, data type validation, and more.
4. The SQLJ source code is converted into a Java source that makes calls to the SQLJ runtime API. One or more SQLJ profiles are also created (see below, "Profile Files," for more information). The SQLJ translator also generates a file known as the *profile-keys class*, which is the class definition file for a specialized class used in conjunction with the profiles. The profile-keys class is used to load and access serialized profiles, and contains mapping information between the SQLJ runtime calls and their SQL operations stored in a serialized profile. The SQLJ Runtime is called to implement the actions of your embedded SQL operations.
5. Normally, the SQLJ Translator invokes the Java compiler to compile the generated Java source, and, optionally, produce a class file for each of the serialized resource files (`.ser` files) if you specified the `-ser2class` option.
6. The Oracle SQLJ customizer is invoked. This step can be suppressed if you use the option: `-profile=false`.

11.1.3.2 Files Generated by the SQLJ Translator. If your SQLJ source file name is called `ShoppingCart.sqlj`, then the SQLJ Translator generates at least the following files:

1. `ShoppingCart.java`—the generated Java source, which includes calls to the SQLJ Runtime to implement the operations specified by SQLJ statements.
2. `ShoppingCart.class`—the compiled version of the generated Java source.

3. `ShoppingCart_SJProfileKeys.ser`—contains mappings for the SQLJ Runtime calls in your application and the SQL operations stored in the serialized profile.
4. `ShoppingCart_SJProfile0.ser`—is the generated profile file describing the SQL operations to be performed.

Profile Files

The generated profile files contain information about all of the embedded SQL statements in your SQLJ source code. This includes:

1. SQL operations to execute.
2. Tables to access.
3. Stored procedures and functions to call.
4. The data types being manipulated.

The SQLJ Runtime accesses the profile files (using information in the profile-key class) to retrieve the SQL operations and pass them to the JDBC driver for processing.

By default, profiles are placed in serialized resource files, each with a `.ser` extension. The SQLJ Translator command-line option `-ser2class` is used to specify that the profiles should be created as a `.class` file.

SQL operations are executed in the context of a database connection called a *connection context*. The SQLJ language provides a way to create more than one connection context in your application. This would be typical for applications needing to manage data in different databases, such as a funds-transfer application. The SQLJ Translator generates a profile file for each connection context used in your application A unique number, starting from 0 and incremented by 1 for each connection context, is appended to the file name.

11.1.4 RUNNING THE SQLJ FILE

In general, any Java program that connects to a database can be SQLJ enabled. For example, if the SQLJ file contains a `main` method, as used in a standard Java application, you can run the class generated by the SQLJ Translator using the `java` command-line tool. If you created an SQLJ source as a Java applet, you can run the Applet class generated by the SQLJ Translator in a Java-enabled Web browser.

Oracle JDeveloper has built-in support for compiling, debugging, and executing SQLJ applications. Oracle JDeveloper debugger makes it easier to debug SQLJ code by allowing you to debug from the SQLJ source rather than the generated Java source.

11.2 CONNECTING TO A DATABASE IN SQLJ

An SQLJ application always has a connection context. Normally, if your application is only using a single database connection, you use the default connection context. If you require additional database connections from the same application, you can create a named connection context.

11.2.1 SETTING THE DEFAULT CONNECTION CONTEXT

Creating a default connection does not require an explicit context name. The process has two main steps:

1. Load a database JDBC driver class or register an instance of the driver.
2. Set the default connection context by providing a connection string and optional username/password.

In order to set the default connection context, you need to create a DefaultContext object. The DefaultContext object is typically used for applications that require a single database connection.

Listing 11.3 shows two ways to create a connection using a DefaultContext object to set the default connection context for SQLJ statements in your application.

```
package com.prenhall.OFJP.sqlj;
import sqlj.runtime.*;
import sqlj.runtime.ref.*;
import java.sql.*;

public class MakeConnection {
  public MakeConnection(String url) {
    try {
      DriverManager.registerDriver(
         new oracle.jdbc.driver.OracleDriver());

      // Setting a Default Context from a JDBC connection
      Connection conn = DriverManager.getConnection(url);
      DefaultContext dctx = new DefaultContext(conn);
      DefaultContext.setDefaultContext(dctx);

      String result;
      #sql { select user||' '||to_char(sysdate)
```

LISTING 11.3 Creating a connection for the default context

```
19:                into :result
20:                from dual };
21:        System.out.println("result:  " + result);
22:
23:        dctx.close();
24:      }
25:      catch (Exception e) {
26:        e.printStackTrace();
27:      }
28:    }
29:
30:    public static void main(String[] args) {
31:      new MakeConnection("jdbc:oracle:thin:" +
32:         "bookstore/bookstore@localhost:1521:ORA815");
33:    }
34: }
```

LISTING 11.3 *Continued*

Notes for Listing 11.3:

- Lines 2 and 3 are required imports for an SQLJ application. The java.sql package is present because JDBC calls are used to load the JDBC driver and create a JDBC Connection.
- Lines 9–13 load the JDBC driver and create a JDBC connection using the DriverManager.
- Line 14 creates a DefaultContext object to be associated with the JDBC Connection created in line 13.
- Line 15 sets the default context for all unqualified SQLJ statements, which execute using the underlining JDBC connection. This example shows how you can work with SQLJ and JDBC code in the same application.
- Lines 18–20 show an SQLJ statement executing a SELECT statement to query the current database user name and the current date.
- Line 23 closes the default connection context. Note that the JDBC connection is also closed by this action. You can keep the underlying JDBC connection open by calling the DefaultContext close() method with a `false` value for the boolean argument. For example:

  `dctx.close(false)`[5]

---

[5]You can use the class constant `ConnectionContext.KEEP_CONNECTION` as the parameter value, instead of the keyword `false`.

Since all SQL code embedded as SQLJ statements can throw an SQLException, the code should either be enclosed in a try-catch-finally block or the exception must be propagated to the caller.

11.2.1.1 Alternative Ways of Setting the Default Context.

An alternative way to set the default context is:

```
01: Class.forName("oracle.jdbc.driver.OracleDriver");
02: DefaultContext.setDefaultContext(new DefaultContext(url, false));
```

Line 1 loads the JDBC driver, which is required for line 2 to work.

Line 2 sets the default connection context for SQLJ statements that have not been qualified with a connection context name. The DefaultContext object is used to create the connection context used by the setDefaultContext() method.

There are more than one DefaultContext constructors. The example uses a form of the constructor that has a URL as the first parameter, and a boolean value as the second parameter to set the auto-commit state to false for the underlying JDBC connection.

If you want control over transaction processing, set the auto-commit mode to false. Another way to set auto-commit to false is to use the connection object associated with the default context. For example:

```
// Assume you have used the DefaultContext constructor with a
// connection object
DefaultContext dctx = new DefaultContext(
                                DriverManager.getConnection(url));

// Set the connection associated with the default context to false
dctx.getConnection().setAutoCommit(false);
```

Another Oracle-specific way to create a default context is to use the static `connect()` method in the `oracle.sqlj.runtime.Oracle` class. For example:

```
DefaultContext dctx = Oracle.connect(url);
```

Using the `Oracle.connect()` method performs the following operations:

- Loads the Oracle JDBC driver.
- Connects to the database specified by the URL parameter.
- Sets the default context and returns the default context.

If you use either of the alternative techniques discussed here, then you do not need to import the java.sql package. However, if you use the `Oracle.connect()` technique, your code will only work with the Oracle SQLJ class libraries, and so is less portable.

Once you have a default context object, you can obtain the associated JDBC connection as follows:

```
Connection conn = dctx.getConnection();
```

Regardless of which method you use, you can still mix JDBC calls and SQLJ statements in the same application.

11.2.2 CREATING AND USING ADDITIONAL CONNECTION CONTEXTS

Your SQLJ application may need more than one database connection. This is achieved by creating additional connection contexts. Each connection context is associated with a new database connection, either to the same or a different database. To create an additional connection context:

- Declare a connection context class, using an SQLJ context declaration.

For example:

```
#sql context MyContext;
```

In this example, the SQLJ Translator generates a class called MyContext. The SQLJ language specification provides for declarations and statements. There are two types of declarations:

1. Context class declarations (discussed here)
2. Iterator class declarations (discussed below in section 11.3.2, subsection "Reading Multiple Rows Using Iterators")

The SQLJ Translator generates a class with a name as specified by you in the declaration. A declaration type can be preceded by Java modifiers, such as `public`, `private`, or `protected`, and followed by an `implements` clause, as follows:

```
#sql <modifiers> context ClassName implements InterfaceName, ...;
```

To use the connection context:

1. Instantiate an object for the new connection context class.

2. Qualify the SQLJ statements using the object variable name, enclosed in square brackets,[6] for the new connection context object.

   For example:

```
package com.prenhall.OFJP.sqlj;
import sqlj.runtime.*;
import sqlj.runtime.ref.*;
import oracle.sqlj.runtime.*;

#sql context MyContext;

public class NewContext {
  public NewContext(String url1, String url2) {
    String userName1, userName2;
    try {
      Class.forName("oracle.jdbc.driver.OracleDriver");
      DefaultContext.setDefaultContext(
          new DefaultContext(url1, false));
      // Execute in the default context
      #sql { select user into :userName1 from dual };
      System.out.println("User(default context): " + userName1);

      MyContext ctx = new MyContext(url2, false);
      // execute in the additional context
      #sql [ctx] { select user into :userName2 from dual };
      System.out.println("User(new context): " + userName2);

      DefaultContext.getDefaultContext().close();
      ctx.close();
    }
    catch (Exception e) {
      e.printStackTrace();
    }
  }

  public static void main(String[] args) {
    new NewContext(
      "jdbc:oracle:oci8:bookstore/bookstore@ORA815",
      "jdbc:oracle:oci8:scott/tiger@ORA815");
  }
}
```

LISTING 11.4 Using more than one connection context

[6]In the SQLJ syntax, square brackets are required around the object reference name to qualify statements executed in the specified context.

Notes for Listing 11.4:

- In line 6, the SQLJ context declaration creates the context class MyContext to be used for creating additional connection context objects.
- Lines 13 and 14 set the default context using the connection formed from the URL in url1.
- Line 16 executes a SQL SELECT statement using the default context.
- Line 19 creates a new context object using the MyContext class, for the URL in url2.
- Line 21 executes another SQL SELECT using the connection context `ctx` defined as a MyContext object. To execute the SQLJ statement in the second connection context (MyContext), you use the `ctx` reference variable in square brackets, i.e., **`[ctx]`**, and place it between the `#sql` token and the SQL statement.
- Line 24 closes the default connection.
- Line 25 closes the new connection context.

The SQLJ Translator generates a `.java` file, and a `.class` file for the `MyContext` SQLJ declaration on line 6 for the `NewContext` class.

Listing 11.5 shows some of the Java code generated for the following SQLJ declaration:

```
#sql context MyContext;
```

```
class MyContext
extends sqlj.runtime.ref.ConnectionContextImpl
implements sqlj.runtime.ConnectionContext
{
  public MyContext(Connection conn) throws SQLException {
    super(profiles, conn);
  }

  public MyContext(String url, String user,
                   String password, boolean autoCommit)
    throws SQLException {
    super(profiles, url, user, password, autoCommit);
  }
  :
  private static final sqlj.runtime.ref.ProfileGroup
              profiles = new sqlj.runtime.ref.ProfileGroup();
}
```

LISTING 11.5 Example of a generated context class

Notes for Listing 11.5:

- Line 2 shows that the connection context `MyContext` is a subclass of `ConnectionContextImpl` in the `sqlj.runtine.ref` package, and implements the `ConnectionContext` interface from the `sqlj.runtime` package.
- Lines 5–7 and 9–13 represent two of the five constructors that must be provided for a connection context class definition.
- The other methods produced by the SQLJ Translator, but not shown in the example, include:
  - The getDefaultContext() and setDefaultContext() methods for getting and setting the default context, respectively.
  - The getProfileKey() method for getting the profile key file.
  - The getProfile() method for getting a profile file used for the connection context.

It is not important to delve into the details of these classes unless you need to make customizations of your own. The rest of this chapter focuses on the usage of SQLJ technology, and occasionally shows some of the underlying code generated.

11.2.3 EXECUTION CONTEXTS

Each connection context is created with an implicit execution context object. The execution context provides the environment in which an SQL operation is executed.

The execution context class, called `sqlj.runtime.ExecutionContext`, contains accessor methods for execution control, status, and cancellation of an SQL statement. The execution control methods modify the semantics of subsequent SQL operations. The execution status methods describe the results of the last SQL operation. For example, they detect the number of rows modified by an UPDATE statement. The execution cancellation methods terminate the current SQL operation.

The code snippet that follows, in the MySQLJApp class, shows how you can obtain a reference to an `ExecutionContext` object that is implicitly created with the default connection context. The code uses the execution context to determine the number of rows affected by an SQL UPDATE statement.

```
package com.prenhall.OFJP.sqlj;
import sqlj.runtime.*;
import sqlj.runtime.ref.*;

public class MySQLJApp {
```

```
06:   public static void main(String[] args) {
07:     String url = "jdbc:oracle:thin:" +
08:                  "bookstore/bookstore@localhost:1521:ORA815";
09:     try {
10:       if (args.length == 1) {
11:         url = args[0];
12:       }
13:       Class.forName("oracle.jdbc.driver.OracleDriver");
14:
15:       DefaultContext dCtx = new DefaultContext(url, false);
16:       DefaultContext.setDefaultContext(dCtx);
17:
18:       ExecutionContext exeCtx = dCtx.getExecutionContext();
19:
20:       #sql { update courier
21:                set cost_per_item = cost_per_item * 1.1 };
22:
23:       System.out.println(exeCtx.getUpdateCount() +
24:                          " row(s) updated");
25:       dCtx.close();
26:     }
27:     catch (Exception e) {
28:       e.printStackTrace();
29:     }
30:   }
31: }
```

The bold text in line 18 shows how to obtain the implicit execution context object associated with the default connection context. In line 23, the number of rows affected by the preceding SQL UPDATE operation is determined by calling the execution context getUpdateCount() method. The getUpdateCount() accessor method is referred to as a status method.

When writing a multithreaded application, you may want each thread to manage the execution control, status, and cancellation of its own SQL operations. You can create an execution context object for each thread that uses the same connection context. To use multiple execution contexts, you explicitly create the execution context object and qualify each SQL operation with the execution context variable. The execution context variable inside square brackets is placed between the #sql token and the SQL operation.

The next two code snippets show how to explicitly associate an execution context with an SQL statement. The first example uses the default connection context, and the second uses a named connection context.

11.2.3.1 ExecutionContext with a Default Connection Context.

```
ExecutionContext exeCtx = connCtx.getExecutionContext();

#sql [exeCtx] { update courier
                set cost_per_item = cost_per_item * 1.1 };
```

The default connection context is used because it is absent from the SQLJ statement.

11.2.3.2 ExecutionContext with a Named Connection Context. If you have multiple connection contexts and want to execute an SQL operation in an explicit execution context on a specific connection, use the following syntax in the SQLJ statement:

```
DefaultContext connCtx = new DefaultContext(url, false);
DefaultContext.setDefaultContext(connCtx);
ExecutionContext exeCtx = connCtx.getExecutionContext();

#sql [connCtx, exeCtx] { update courier
                set cost_per_item = cost_per_item * 1.1 };
```

This example shows that you place the connection context variable `connCtx`, followed by the execution context variable `exeCtx`, inside the square brackets and separated by a comma. The connection context variable must appear before the execution context variable.

The ExecutionContext class has accessor methods known as *status methods*:

- ❑ getWarnings()—to get the first warning for the most recent SQL statement. Then call getNextWarning() to access chained warnings.
- ❑ getUpdateCount()—the number of rows affected by the SQL statement.

It also has accessor methods known as *control methods*:

- ❑ setBatching(boolean), isBatching()—to set set batching or determine whether batching is in operation.
- ❑ setBatchSize(), getBatchSize()—to set or get the size of batching operations.
- ❑ setMaxRows(), getMaxRows()—to set or get the number of rows that can be processed for a query operation, excess rows are silently ignored.

The accessor methods known as *cancellation methods* are:

- ❑ setQueryTimeout(), getQueryTimeout()—to manage query execution time.
- ❑ cancel()—to abort a query when executing in a multithreaded environment.

11.3 EXECUTING SQL STATEMENTS USING SQLJ

The major benefit of executing SQL statements in SQLJ is the simplicity of accessing the database from a Java program, particularly if you are already conversant with the SQL language. If the SQL statement is a complex one, requiring or returning many column values, many lines of JDBC code can be reduced to one embedded SQLJ statement, excluding the declaration of variables required to store values for the SQL statement.

Consider the following SQL statement:

```
SELECT name, surname, email FROM customer WHERE id = value
```

If you want to process this statement with JDBC calls, the following fragment of code to read a single row is required (ignoring the establishment of the database connection):

```
public void getCustomerInfo(Connection conn, int id) {
  String name;
  String surname;
  String email;

  PreparedStatement ps = conn.prepareStatement(
     "select name, surname, email from customer where id = ?");
  ps.setInt(1, id);
  ResultSet rs = ps.executeQuery();
  if (rs.next()) {
    name = rs.getString(1);
    surname = rs.getString(2);
    email = rs.getString(3);
    System.out.println(
      "Customer: " + name + " " + surname + " " + email);
  }
  rs.close();
  ps.close();
}
```

The equivalent code to read a single row in SQLJ is:

```
public void getCustomerInfo(int id)
throws SQLException {
  String name;
  String surname;
```

```
05:   String email;
06:
07:   #sql { select name, surname, email into :name, :surname, :email
08:          from customer where id = :id };
09:   System.out.println(
10:     "Customer: " + name + " " + surname + " " + email);
11: }
```

The SQLJ code requires less typing than the JDBC code, and is far easier for the programmer to read. In addition, using the SQLJ Translator command-line options, you can validate the SQL statement at compile time, which you cannot do with JDBC statements.

Line 7 of the SQLJ code example introduces some interesting syntactic elements of an SQLJ statement:

- Unlike with JDBC, no quotes are used around the SQL statement.
- In the SQL statement, you bind the values from, or into, Java host variables by using a colon immediately preceding the Java variable name.
- The SQL statement can be split over one or more lines, with no need for line-continuation characters.
- The SQL statement must be enclosed inside braces, and a semicolon is placed outside the closing brace.

The SQL SELECT statement in the SQLJ example is limited to fetching only one row, because the Java variables can only contain one variable at a time. In the SQLJ example, an SQLException is thrown if either of the following cases arise:

- No rows are returned by the query.
- More than one row is returned by the query.

Although these two conditions can occur in the JDBC code example, exceptions are not thrown. The JDBC code gives you more control over managing these error conditions.

If you wish to process more than one row in a SQLJ application, you need to use an SQLJ iterator (refer to section 11.3.2, subsection "Reading Multiple Rows Using Iterators").

11.3.1 USING HOST VARIABLES

In an SQLJ statement, you use or modify the value of a Java variable by prefixing it with a colon. A Java variable prefixed with a colon in an SQLJ statement is known as a *bind/host variable*. For example:

```
int customerId = 10;
String customerName;

#sql { SELECT name INTO :customerName
       FROM customer
       WHERE id = :customerId  };
```

The SQLJ Translator sets the mode of a host variable as *input, output,* or *input-output,* depending on the context of the variable usage in the SQL statement. By default, the mode is IN, except when the host variable is part of an INTO list in a SELECT statement, or is the target of an assignment in an SQLJ SET statement, in which case the mode is OUT. You can explicitly set the mode of the host variable by using one of the following mode specifiers:

- IN—for input only.
- OUT—for output only.
- INOUT—for input and output.

Mode names are case-insensitive. For example:

```
:mode-specifier hostVar
```

where *mode-specifier* = IN or OUT or INOUT, for example:

```
:IN hostVar
:in hostVar

:OUT hostVar
:INOUT hostVar
```

For readability, it is recommended that no spaces appear between the colon and the mode specifier. At least one space character is required between the mode specifier and the host variable name.

You can create *host expressions* for input values by enclosing an expression in parentheses after the colon or mode specifier. Examples are:

```
:(hostVar1 + hostVar2)
:IN(hostVar1 * hostVar2)
```

The parentheses, as shown, are required to enclose the expression. To set the value of a Java host variable, you can uses a host expression with the SQLJ SET statement. For example:

```
java.sql.Date hostVar1;

#sql { SET :hostVar1 = to_char(sysdate) };

// This is equivalent to:

#sql { SET :OUT hostVar1 = to_char(sysdate) };

// This equivalent to an embedded PL/SQL block:

#sql { BEGIN :OUT hostVar1 := to_char(sysdate); END; };
```

> **Note**
>
> These PL/SQL block expressions are evaluated prior to the SQLJ statement being executed.

The rule for using host variables is: Prefix the Java variable with a colon if it is inside the braces of the SQLJ statement.

11.3.2 USING DML AND DDL STATEMENTS IN SQLJ

Executing an SQL data manipulation or data definition language statement is as simple as placing the SQL statement inside braces after the #sql token. Listing 11.6 shows two methods using DDL statements:

- The createTable() method executes a CREATE TABLE statement.
- The dropTable() method executes a DROP TABLE statement.

```
public void createTable() {
  try {
    dropTable();
    #sql { create table music_cd (
             id number(4) primary key,
             title varchar2(40) not null,
             artist varchar2(40) not null,
             create_date date) };
  }
  catch (Exception e) {
    e.printStackTrace();
```

LISTING 11.6 Using DDL statements in SQLJ

```
12:     }
13: }
14:
15: public void dropTable() {
16:   int existCount;
17:   try {
18:     #sql { select count(*) into :existCount
19:            from user_tables where table_name = 'MUSIC_CD' };
20:     if (existCount > 0) {
21:       #sql { drop table music_cd };
22:     }
23:   }
24:   catch (Exception e) {
25:     e.printStackTrace();
26:   }
27: }
```

LISTING 11.6 *Continued*

Notes on Listing 11.6:

- Line 3 calls the dropTable() method before creating the table.
- Lines 15–27 show the dropTable() method, which uses a SELECT statement to read the Oracle data dictionary table USER_TABLES to determine whether the MUSIC_CD table exists. If the MUSIC_CD table does exist, the existCount is non-zero, and the table is dropped. The example shows that SQLJ statements can be placed inside flow-control statements.

The next example, in Listing 11.7, uses an INSERT statement to add a row to the MUSIC_CD table.

```
public void insertCD(int id, String title, String artist) {
  try {
    #sql { insert into music_cd (id, title, artist, create_date)
           values (:id, :title, :artist, sysdate) };
    #sql { commit };
  }
  catch (Exception e) {
    e.printStackTrace();
  }
}
```

LISTING 11.7 Using DML in SQLJ

Notes on Listing 11.7:

- Line 4 of the INSERT statement uses the Java method arguments as input host variables to supply values for the insert statement.
- Line 5 executes a COMMIT statement, assuming that auto-commit has been disabled for the default context used.

11.3.2.1 Storing NULL Values. Java primitive types, such as `byte`, `int`, `short`, `long`, `float`, `double`, and `boolean`, cannot be used to store a database NULL value in a column. To store a NULL value in a column, you must use one of the Java wrapper classes that has been set to a Java `null` reference value, and use the Java object as the host variable in an SQL operation. An example of inserting a NULL value into a numeric column is shown in Listing 11.8.

```
01: public void insertCD(int id, String title, String artist) {
02:   Integer yearReleased = null;
03:   try {
04:     #sql { insert into music_cd
05:              (id, title, artist, year_released, create_date)
06:            values
07:              (:id, :title, :artist, :yearReleased, sysdate) };
08:     #sql { commit };
09:   }
10:   catch (Exception e) {
11:     e.printStackTrace();
12:   }
13: }
```

LISTING 11.8 Inserting a NULL value

Notes on Listing 11.8:

- Line 2 declares a Java object variable yearReleased for the Integer, which is initialized to a `null` value.
- Line 7 in the INSERT statement uses the yearReleased as the input host variable for the year_released column. A NULL value is inserted into the year_released column, because the SQLJ code detects that the object reference is null and converts this into a database NULL value for the column.

The same technique can be used for changing a column value to a NULL, if appropriate, in an UPDATE statement.

To read a column containing a NULL value, you must use a Java object variable defined as an appropriate wrapper class as a host variable. Then, if and only if the Java object reference is not a `null`, you can convert the value in the Java object into its primitive value, At runtime, if you attempt to read a database NULL value into a primitive, the SQLJ statement will fail with the following exception message:

```
sqlj.runtime.SQLNullException: cannot fetch null into primitive data type
```

Reading database NULL values is discussed below in section 11.3.3.

11.3.2.2 Transactions in SQLJ. Transaction control is handled in the same way as storing NULL values, since you perform these tasks in a pure SQL environment. For manual control, you must ensure that the connection context used has auto-commit disabled. To issue a COMMIT, use the SQLJ statement:

```
#sql { COMMIT };
```

To ROLLBACK, execute the following SQLJ statement:

```
#sql { ROLLBACK };
```

You can use the auto-commit feature of the underling JDBC connection if appropriate.

11.3.3 QUERY PROCESSING

In the context of a programming language, data can be queried in two ways. You can retrieve a single row at a time or process a set of rows. Reading a single row requires that you have some way of targeting one and only one row in your query using search criteria, usually an appropriate condition in the WHERE clause of your query.

Processing multiple rows requires creating a cursor structure and stepping through each row of data. In JDBC, you use a ResultSet; in SQLJ, you create an *iterator.*

11.3.3.1 Reading a Single Row. Reading a single row is as simple as embedding a SELECT statement in the code, with the addition of an INTO clause to the query. The syntax for the general structure of a SELECT statement to retrieve a single row is:

```
#sql {  SELECT col(s) INTO variable(s)
        FROM table
        WHERE condition(s) };
```

The number of variables specified in the INTO clause must match the number of columns queried. The data type of each Java variable in the INTO clause must be type-compatible with the SQL type of its corresponding column. The SELECT statement can use any form of Oracle SQL discussed in the earlier chapters of this book. Listing 11.9 shows an example of selecting a single row from the MUSIC_CD table.

```
public void readCd(int id) {
  String title = null;
  String artist = null;
  Integer yearReleased = null;
  java.sql.Date createDate = null;

  try {
    #sql { SELECT title, artist, year_released, create_date
           INTO :title, :artist, :yearReleased, :createDate
           FROM music_cd
           WHERE id = :id };
    System.out.println("Cd: " + id + " " + title + " " +
                       artist + " " + yearReleased + " " +
                       createDate);
  }
  catch (Exception e) {
    e.printStackTrace();
  }
}
```

LISTING 11.9 Selecting a single database row

Errors can occur if the search criteria value entered causes no rows to be returned for the query. In this case, the SQLException thrown contains the following message:

```
java.sql.SQLException:
no rows found for select into statement
```

If more than one row is returned by the SELECT statement, the following exception message is generated by the SQLJ Runtime:

```
java.sql.SQLException:
multiple rows found for select into statement
```

If you want to read the Oracle ROWID pseudo-column for each row, include the ROWID in the query and read the value into a Java string variable. The ROWID value can then be used in the WHERE clause of the UPDATE or DELETE statements for fast row access.

11.3.3.2 Reading Multiple Rows Using Iterators. Reading more than one row requires the creation of an SQLJ iterator. An *iterator* is a strongly typed result set. The data types expected for each column in the query are controlled by an SQLJ iterator declaration. There are two types of SQLJ iterators:

- A named iterator declares the names and data type of each column.
- A positional iterator declares only the data type of each column.

The syntax for declaring iterators is:

```
#sql iterator CustomerIterator (int id, String name);

#sql iterator CourierIterator (int, String);
```

The SQLJ Translator creates a Java class for each SQLJ iterator where the class name is derived from the name following the iterator keyword. Each iterator is associated with a query. The number columns selected in the query must match the number of parameters defined inside the parentheses after the iterator name.

To use an iterator, you perform the following steps:

1. Declare the iterator class.
2. Define a Java variable of the iterator class type.
3. Execute a query, compatible with the iterator definition, that returns its results into the Java iterator variable.
4. Use the iterator class methods to fetch each row, and process the column data in each row. The way you process data returned from a named iterator is different from the way you use a positional iterator, but it is conceptually similar to the way you process a JDBC ResultSet.

Here is the general syntax of an iterator and a use example:

```
// 1. Declare the iterator class
#sql iterator MyIterator (int, String);

  :
// 2. Define a variable using the iterator class
MyIterator iter;
```

LISTING 11.10 Syntax and example for using an iterator

```
// 3. Execute a query compatible with the iterator definition
#sql iter = { SELECT id, name FROM table … };

// 4. process the result data using the iter object methods

For example:

#sql iterator CourierIter (int id, String name);

public class Courier {
   public CourierIter getCouriers() {
     CourierIter iter = null;
     try {
       #sql iter = { SELECT id, name FROM courier };
     }
     catch (Exception e) {
       . . .
     }
     return iter;
   }
}
```

LISTING 11.10 *Continued*

Note that the SQLJ Translator generates a Java class for each iterator declared. The methods contained in the generated iterator class enable it to:

- Step through the rows retrieved by a query returning a result set.
- Get column values.

Named and positional iterator declarations cause different method names to be generated in their respective iterator classes.

Declaring and Using a Named Iterator

To declare a named iterator, you must specify a data type and a name for each column value expected from a query that returns a result set to the iterator.

The SQLJ Translator uses the column names specified in the iterator declaration to derive the names of the column value accessor methods in the iterator class. These method names are case-sensitive, as defined by the names in the iterator declaration. The column names in the associated query must match the names defined in the iterator declaration. However, the column names in the query are treated case-insensitively. The Java data type specified for each iterator column must be type-compatible with its corresponding database column.

Listing 11.10 shows how to create a named iterator to read some of the details from the customer table.

```
#sql iterator CustomerList (int id, String name, String surname);
```

LISTING 11.10 Creating a named iterator for the CUSTOMER table

The SQLJ Translator generates a Java class for the named iterator, called CustomerList, which contains the following methods:

- boolean next()—allows you to fetch the next row of data; returns a true if a row is found, and a false if there are no more rows.
- int id()—returns the customer id as an int, for the current row.
- String name() – returns the customer name as a String.
- String surname() – returns the customer surname as a String.

These methods are used to process the query data. The next() method is common to all named iterators, and the remaining method names depend on the iterator declaration. One method is created for each column name specified in the iterator declaration, which returns a value of the data type declared before the name. The number of columns in the SQL query must be equal to or greater than the number of names listed in the iterator declaration. Additional columns in the query are ignored.

Listing 11.11 shows a method called listCustomers() which uses a modified form of the CustomerList named iterator to display the customer id, name, and email address.

```
#sql iterator CustomerList (int id, String fullName,
                            String email);
public void listCustomers() {
  CustomerList custList;

  try {
    #sql custList = { SELECT name||' '||surname AS fullname,
                             email, id
                      FROM customer };

    while (custList.next()) {
```

LISTING 11.11 Display customer details using a named iterator

```
12:       System.out.println("Customer: " + custList.id() + " " +
13:                          custList.fullName() + " " +
14:                          custList.email());
15:     }
16:     custList.close();
17:   }
18:   catch (Exception e) {
19:     e.printStackTrace();
20:   }
21: }
```

LISTING 11.11 *Continued*

The example in Listing 11.11 highlights some additional points discussed in the notes. Notes for Listing 11.11:

- Lines 1 and 2 declare a named iterator with a comma-separated list of three columns, each preceded by a Java data type.
- Line 7 executes the query that returns the columns for the iterator object. The iterator object variable appears after the #sql token, and before an assignment operator prior to the braces containing the query. The query can also be parameterized with host variables. If the query uses a column expression, then a column alias, with the same name as the corresponding name in the iterator declaration, must be used. In this example, the query uses a concatenated expression of values, the `first_name`, a space, and the `last_name`. The column alias must be specified as `fullname` to match the second iterator column name in line 1.
- Line 11 calls the next() method of the iterator class, as you would with a JDBC ResultSet to process each row of data.
- Lines 12, 13, and 14 print the values returned in each row by calling each of the named iterator methods for the column values defined.

The Java source code generated for the CustomerList class is shown in Listing 11.12.

```
class CustomerList extends sqlj.runtime.ref.ResultSetIterImpl
                   implements sqlj.runtime.NamedIterator
{
  public CustomerList(sqlj.runtime.profile.RTResultSet resultSet)
    throws java.sql.SQLException
  {
```

LISTING 11.12 Generated Java source for a named iterator

```
    super(resultSet);
    idNdx = findColumn("id");
    fullNameNdx = findColumn("fullName");
    emailNdx = findColumn("email");
  }

  public int id() throws java.sql.SQLException {
    return resultSet.getIntNoNull(idNdx);
  }
  private int idNdx;

  public String fullName() throws java.sql.SQLException {
    return resultSet.getString(fullNameNdx);
  }
  private int fullNameNdx;

  public String email() throws java.sql.SQLException {
    return resultSet.getString(emailNdx);
  }
  private int emailNdx;
}
```

LISTING 11.12 *Continued*

The source code in Listing 11.12 is added to the Java source generated for the SQLJ file containing the #sql iterator declaration. The iterator class is subject to Java scoping rules depending on where it is declared. For example, you can declare an iterator as a standalone class or an inner class. The following example illustrates this point:

```
package com.prenhall.OFJP.sqlj;

/* SQLJ iterator generated as normal class with visibility
   defined with "default" access within the package */
#sql iterator CustomerIter (…);

public class OrderEntry {
  // SQLJ iterator declared as an inner class
  #sql iterator CustOrderIter (…);
```

```
    class OrderItem {
      // SQLJ iterator declared as nested inner class
      #sql iterator CourierIter (...);
    }

    public OrderEntry(...) {   // constructor
    }

    public void addItem(...) { }   // instance method
      #sql iterator SaleItemIter (...); // generates a compile time error
}
```

An SQLJ declaration, like these iterators, is invalid inside a method, because the SQLJ Translator does not allow them to be specified in the body of a method. The SQLJ Translator generates an error.

Declaring and Using a Positional Iterator

Declaring a positional iterator is similar to declaring a named iterator, but with a comma-separated list of Java data types without the names. For example:

```
#sql iterator CustomerList (int, String, String);
```

The CustomerList iterator is still considered a strongly typed mechanism. The names of column names/aliases in a query are irrelevant to a positional iterator, as long as the column data type matches the corresponding iterator column declaration.

To process rows with a positional iterator, you first execute an SQLJ FETCH statement, followed by a call to the endFetch() method to test the outcome of the FETCH operation. The SQLJ Translator generates the following methods for a positional iterator:

- boolean endFetch()—returns true if the last SQLJ fetch statement executed returns a row; otherwise, it returns a false.
- getCol<n>() method, where <n> is a number from 1 to the number of column data types specified in the positional iterator definition. Each method returns a value of the data type corresponding to its position.

Listing 11.13 shows the code generated by the SQLJ Translator for a positional iterator:

```
class CustomerIter extends sqlj.runtime.ref.ResultSetIterImpl
                   implements sqlj.runtime.PositionedIterator
{
  public CustomerIter(sqlj.runtime.profile.RTResultSet resultSet)
    throws java.sql.SQLException
  {
    super(resultSet, 3);
  }

  public int getCol1() throws java.sql.SQLException {
    return resultSet.getIntNoNull(1);
  }

  public String getCol2() throws java.sql.SQLException {
    return resultSet.getString(2);
  }

  public String getCol3() throws java.sql.SQLException {
    return resultSet.getString(3);
  }
}
```

LISTING 11.13 Generated Java source for a positional iterator

The endFetch() method is not shown because it is inherited from the sqlj.runtime.ref.ResultSetIterImpl superclass. While you use the getCol<n>() methods to obtain the column values for each row, accessing the row data is accomplished with the SQLJ FETCH statement. An example showing the syntax for a FETCH statement is:

```
package com.prenhall.OFJP.sqlj;
#import sqlj.runtime.*;
#import sqlj.runtime.ref.*;

#sql iterator CustomerIter (int id, String name, String email);

public class RegisterCustomer {

  public void listCustomers() {
    CustomerIter custIter = null;
    int    custId;
    String custName;
    String email;
    #sql custIter = { SELECT id, name, email FROM customer };
```

```
    try {
      while (true) {
        #sql { FETCH :customerIter INTO :custId, :custName, :email };
        if (iter.endFetch()) break;
        :
        // process data here
        :
      }
    }
    catch (Exception e) { . . . }
    finally { . . . }
  }
}
```

The variable name, like `customerIter`, appearing after the FETCH keyword must be of a positional iterator class type. The iterator variable must be preceded by the colon, as is each of the variables after the INTO keyword. The Java host variables after the INTO keyword must be present for each position corresponding with the iterator column definition; and each must be of a compatible data type. Always test whether the fetch operation was successful by executing the iterator endFetch() method.

Listing 11.14 shows an example of the use of a positional iterator for receiving some of the customer details from the customer table.

```
#sql iterator CustomerIter (int, String, String);

public void getCustomerDetails() {
  try {
    CustomerIter custList = null;
    int id  = 0;
    String name = null;
    String email = null;

    #sql custList = { SELECT id, name ||' '||surname, email
                      FROM customer };

    do {
      #sql { FETCH :custList INTO :id, :name, :email };
      if (custList.endFetch()) break;
      System.out.println("Cust: " + id +" "+ name +" "+ email);
    }
```

LISTING 11.14 Using a positional iterator to read customer details

```
18:       while (true);
19:       custList.close();
20:     }
21:     catch (Exception e) {
22:       e.printStackTrace();
23:     }
24: }
```

LISTING 11.14 *Continued*

Notes for Listing 11.14:

- Line 1 declares the positional iterator class.
- Line 5 defines the iterator variable.
- Lines 6, 7, and 8 define variables for values retrieved from the query.
- Line 10 executes the query returning the result set for the positional iterator object variable custList.
- Lines 13–18 comprise the loop to process each row read in for the specified query.
- Line 14 executes the SQL FETCH statement, receiving one column value per data type position defined in the positional iterator.
- Line 15 tests whether the last FETCH operation was successful, and, if not, the loop is terminated by executing a break statement. Otherwise, the loop continues to process the data.

11.3.3.3 Closing Iterators. Iterators, like the JDBC ResultSet, consume resources, so it is important to close an iterator after processing all the data it returns. Simply call the close() method of the iterator to close it.

11.3.3.4 Reading NULL Values. If any column in the data base table can contain a NULL, then you should read the column value into a Java object reference of a compatible type. This applies specifically to values you wish to receive as a Java primitive type. Primitive types cannot store a Java null value, so you should use the appropriate Java wrapper. For example:

```
#sql iterator DemoIter (int, String);

public void insertNull() {
  try {
    #sql { DROP TABLE demonull };
  }
  catch (Exception e) {}
```

```
  try {
    DemoIter demo = null;

    #sql { CREATE TABLE demonull(id number(4), text varchar2(30)) };
    #sql { INSERT INTO demonull values (1, 'Does not have nulls') };
    #sql { INSERT INTO demonull values (null, 'Has a null') };
    #sql { COMMIT };

    #sql demo = { SELECT * FROM demonull };
    do {
      int idValue = 0;
      String textValue = null;

      #sql { FETCH :demo INTO :idValue, :textValue };
      if (demo.endFetch()) break;
      System.out.println("Row: " + idValue + " " + textValue);
    }
    while (true);
    demo.close();
  }
  catch (Exception e) {
    e.printStackTrace();
  }
}
```

The exception occurs when fetching the second row, and the message generated by SQLJ runtime when attempting to read the NULL valued column is:

```
sqlj.runtime.SQLNullException: cannot fetch null into
primitive data type
```

To avoid this problem:

- Change the iterator definition to read the NULL valued column as a corresponding Java wrapper instead of the primitive type.
- Test the object reference value used to receive the value for a null.
- If the Java object reference is null, then the value in the column was a database NULL value; otherwise, you have an object reference to the value that can be used to convert the value contained in the object into its primitive value by using the appropriate wrapper class method.

The code that shows the suggested changes in bold text is:

```
#sql iterator DemoIter (Integer, String);

public void insertNull() {
  try {
    #sql { DROP TABLE demonull };
  }
  catch (Exception e) {}

  try {
    DemoIter demo = null;

    #sql {
    CREATE TABLE demonull(
       id number(4), text varchar2(30))
    };
    #sql {
    INSERT INTO demonull
    values (1, 'Does not have nulls')
    };
    #sql {
    INSERT INTO demonull
    values (null, 'Has a null')
    };
    #sql { COMMIT };

    #sql demo = { SELECT * FROM demonull };
    do {
      Integer idValue = null;
      String textValue = null;

      #sql { FETCH :demo INTO :idValue, :textValue };
      if (demo.endFetch()) break;
      if (idValue == null) {
        System.out.println("Row: NULL " + textValue);
      }
      else {
        int idVal = idValue.intValue();
        System.out.println(
        "Row: " + idVal + " " + textValue);
      }
    }
    while (true);
    demo.close();
  }
  catch (Exception e) {
```

```
            e.printStackTrace();
        }
    }
```

Two changes were made:

1. The data type of the first column in the iterator definition was changed to an Integer type.
2. The idValue variable was changed to an Integer object.

If the id column has a non-null value, the JDBC driver creates an Integer object for the value; otherwise the object variable, idValue, is assigned a Java null value, that is, no object is created. You can simply test the object reference for `null` to detect whether you have read a NULL database value.

11.3.3.5 Advanced Iterators. In the definition of an iterator, Oracle SQLJ allows a data type for a column to be a ResultSet or another Iterator. This is useful for returning result sets from a nested query, such as when retrieving data in a nested table. In Oracle8i SQL, you can emulate a nested table for related tables by using the CURSOR operator. The following query is an example of an SQL statement that requires an iterator to be defined as a column data type for its associated iterator:

```
SELECT id, name,
       CURSOR (select id, cour_id, total_cost
               FROM cust_order WHERE cust_id = customer.id) orders
FROM customer
WHERE id = :customerId;
```

In the example, the CURSOR operator executes a correlated subquery to return all order records for a specific customer. The subquery returns more than one column value and a set of rows, as if it were a nested table.

The named iterator definition to read the customer id, name, and order rows, using a JDBC ResultSet, is:

```
// Named Iterator
#sql iterator CustOrders (int id, String name, ResultSet orders);
```

The positional iterator to achieve a similar result is:

```
// Positional Iterator
#sql iterator CustOrders (int, String, ResultSet);
```

The query column alias, `orders`, is applied to the CURSOR query so that you can use a named iterator. Without the alias applied to the nested cursor query, you would be forced to use a positional iterator.

Listing 11.15 shows how to process the data in the nested cursor result set.

```
01: #sql iterator CustOrders (int id, String name, ResultSet orders);
02:
03: public void getOrders(int customerId) {
04:   try {
05:     CustOrders custOrders = null;
06:
07:     #sql custOrders = { SELECT id, name,
08:              CURSOR ( SELECT id, cour_id, total_cost
09:                       FROM cust_order
10:                       WHERE cust_id = customer.id) orders
11:            FROM customer WHERE id = :customerId };
12:
13:     while (custOrders.next()) {
14:       int id = custOrders.id();
15:       String name = custOrders.name();
16:       System.out.println("Orders for: " + id + " " + name);
17:       ResultSet ordData = custOrders.orders();
18:       while (ordData.next()) {
19:         System.out.println("\t" +
20:           ordData.getInt(1) + " " +   // order id
21:           ordData.getInt(2) + " " +   // courier id
22:           ordData.getDouble(3));      // total cost
23:       }
24:       ordData.close();
25:     }
26:     custOrders.close();
27:   }
28:   catch (Exception e) {
29:     e.printStackTrace();
30:   }
31: }
```

LISTING 11.15 Using a JDBC ResultSet as an iterator column

Notes for Listing 11.15:

- The example assumes that you have imported the `java.sql` package in addition to the SQLJ packages.
- Line 1 declares a named iterator with the third column data type as a JDBC ResultSet.
- Line 5 creates the object variable for the iterator.
- Lines 7–11 execute the query to return the customer details and the nested result set of orders for the customer.

- Lines 13–25 are the loop to process the rows returned by the iterator, using the iterator methods created by the SQLJ Translator.
- Line 17 gets the ResultSet from the third iterator column, which returns zero or more order rows for the given customer.
- Lines 18–23 loop to read the rows from the nested result set of order data for the given customer.
- When you compile this example with Oracle JDeveloper, it issues a warning that using a ResultSet in an iterator is nonportable, because the ability to use a JDBC result set inside the definition of another iterator is a feature implemented by the Oracle SQLJ Translator.

Instead of using a JDBC ResultSet in the iterator column definition, you can use another iterator. However, to use an iterator nested as a column data type of another iterator, the following applies:

- The nested iterator must be `public` to have the SQLJ Translator create a public iterator class.
- The iterator should be in a separate SQLJ source file because it is declared as public.
- The filename containing the iterator definition must be the same name as the iterator.

For example:

```
// File name: Orders.sqlj

package com.prenhall.OFJP.sqlj;

import sqlj.runtime.*;
import sqlj.runtime.ref.*;

#sql public iterator Orders (int ordId,
                             Integer courId,
                             Double totalCost);
```

After you have run the SQLJ Translator on the public iterator `Orders`,[7] you can use the `Orders` iterator class name, qualified by its package if required, as the column type in the iterator definition. For example:

[7]If building the SQLJ class using JDeveloper, the SQLJ Translator issues a warning that the public iterator class is public and "should be declared in a file named <Iterator>.java." This cannot be done because the SQLJ Translator works on the SQLJ file. You can disable the warning message by clearing the "Show Warnings" checkbox in the JDeveloper project properties "Compiler" tab.

```
// Declare the application iterator to use a another public iterator

#sql iterator CustOrders (int id, String name,
                            com.prenhall.OFJP.sqlj.Orders orders);
```

Listing 11.16 shows the code that uses the `Orders` iterator nested inside the `CustOrders` iterator.

```
File: Orders.sqlj
package com.prenhall.OFJP.sqlj;

import sqlj.runtime.*;
import sqlj.runtime.ref.*;

#sql public iterator Orders (int ordId,
                             Integer courId,
                             Double totalCost);
```

```
File: NestedIterator.sqlj
package com.prenhall.OFJP.sqlj;

import java.sql.*;
import sqlj.runtime.*;
import sqlj.runtime.ref.*;

#sql iterator CustOrders (int id, String name, Orders orders);

public class NestedIterator {
  :
  public void getOrders(int customerId) {
    try {
      CustOrders custOrders = null;

      #sql custOrders = { SELECT id, name,
             CURSOR ( SELECT id ordid,
                             cour_id courid,
                             total_cost totalcost
                      FROM cust_order
                      WHERE cust_id = customer.id) orders
           FROM customer WHERE id = :customerId };

```

LISTING 11.16 Using a nested iterator as an iterator column

```
23:       while (custOrders.next()) {
24:         int id = custOrders.id();
25:         String name = custOrders.name();
26:
27:         System.out.println("Customer: " + id + "  " +
28:                          name + " has orders:");
29:         Orders ordData = custOrders.orders();
30:         while (ordData.next()) {
31:           System.out.println("\t" +
32:             ordData.ordId() + "  " +
33:             ordData.courId() + "  " +
34:             ordData.totalCost());
35:         }
36:         ordData.close();
37:       }
38:       custOrders.close();
39:     }
40:     catch (Exception e) {
41:       e.printStackTrace();
42:     }
43:   }
44: }
```

LISTING 11.16 *Continued*

The code to process the nested iterator data is almost identical in structure to the code in Listing 11.15. The main difference is the methods you use to extract the actual data. The methods you use depend on the type of iterator definition you used; that is, whether it was a named or a positional iterator.

Notes on Listing 11.16:

- Line 7 declares the third iterator column as an `Orders` iterator type.
- Lines 16–20 are the Oracle8i SQL CURSOR subquery providing the data for the nested iterator column. The CURSOR subquery is given an alias of `orders` to match the third iterator column in the `CustOrders` named iterator in line 7.
- Line 21 calls the `orders()` method, from the generated `CustOrders` class, which returns an `Orders` iterator.
- Lines 22–27 print the column values from each row in the `Orders` iterator using the methods generated for that iterator. The `Orders` iterator method names match the alias names for each column in the nested cursor query in lines 16–20.

11.4 PROCESSING ORACLE SQL OBJECT TYPES

In SQLJ, you can also read and write SQL object types using the host variable syntax. The Java type declared for host variables receiving an SQL object must be compatible with the SQL object definition, and is derived from a Java class that can be manually created.[8] However, it is usually more productive to use Oracle JPublisher to generate a custom class from the SQL object definition. This section discusses how to use Oracle JPublisher to generate the classes for Oracle SQL object types, and then shows how to use the generated classes in your SQLJ code to work with Oracle SQL objects.

11.4.1 USING ORACLE JPUBLISHER

Oracle JPublisher is a Java application that reads an Oracle database object and generates the source code for a Java class with the structure and functionality representing it. Oracle JPublisher can generate Java classes for:

- Oracle SQL object types and their methods.
- Oracle SQL Reference types.
- Oracle varying-array and nested-table collections.
- Oracle PL/SQL packages.
- Oracle procedures and functions not defined in a PL/SQL package.

This section explains how to work with JPublisher to generate a Java class for an SQL object type, and how to use the generated Java class either to read an SQL object into your Java application or to save a Java object into its compatible SQL object in an object table or column.

11.4.1.1 Using the Oracle JPublisher Command-Line Utility. Oracle JPublisher is provided as a command-line utility called **jpub** shipped with the Oracle8i software. You can find the utility in the ORACLE_HOME/bin directory. Oracle JPublisher is integrated into Oracle JDeveloper 3.0 or later versions, and can be invoked in a GUI environment. To use Oracle JPublisher you must include in your CLASSPATH the ORACLE_HOME/sqlj/lib/translator.zip file and the JDBC class libraries. The generic syntax of an Oracle JPublisher command line is:

```
jpub -option=value [ -option=value … ]
```

---

[8] Appropriate Java interfaces must be implemented to manually construct a class to read an SQL object. This technique was covered in the discussion of SQLData and CustomDatum interfaces in Chapter 10.

The jpub command is followed by one or more option=value pairs. Spaces are not allowed between the minus sign option name, the equals sign, and the value. The options control the rules that govern the generation of the Java class. To preserve Java naming conventions, Oracle JPublisher options let you specify the Java class name generated and its corresponding SQL object type. This is achieved by using JPublisher command-line options or via options specified in a properties file. For example:

```
jpub -user=bookstore/bookstore
     -url=jdbc:oracle:thin:@localhost:1521:ORA815
     -sql=customer_t:Customer
     -package=com.prenhall.OFJP.jpub
```

This example generates a Customer.java class file for the customer_t SQL object in a package called com.prenhall.OFJP.jpub.

If you use an input file, you can also control the names of the methods generated in the Java class for each attribute found in the SQL object definition. For example:

```
With a customer t Object type defined as:

CREATE TYPE customer_t AS OBJECT (
  id         NUMBER(6),
  name       VARCHAR2(30),
  surname    VARCHAR2(40)
);

Using a properties file called of myprops.jpub containing:
jpub.user=bookstore/bookstore
jpub.url=jdbc:oracle:thin:@localhost:1521:ORA815
jpub.sql=customer_t
jpub.package=com.prenhall.OFJP.jpub
jpub.input=translate.txt

And the file translate.txt containing:
SQL customer_t AS Customer
   TRANSLATE name AS FirstName,
             surname AS Surname

The JPublisher command is:

Jpub -props=myprops.jpub
```

The preceding example creates a `Customer.java` file with an accessor method for each attribute. The default accessor method name for the `id` attribute is called getId(). However, the accessor method generated for the `name` attribute is called getFirstName(), as controlled by the input-file commands, as is the method getSurname() for the `surname` attribute. The input option provides a file of command-to-control method name generation.

11.4.1.2 JPublisher Command-Line Options. Table 11.2 lists some of the common JPublisher command-line options and their values. It shows default values (if applicable) in bold text, and required values in italic text.

The same options can be specified more than once, with the last occurrence overriding any previous settings on the command line or in the properties file. Options in the property file are processed as if they were entered on the command line where the `props` option is used.

TABLE 11.2 Oracle JPublisher command-line options

OPTION	VALUES	DESCRIPTION
user	*<username>/password>*	Required option to select the user name and password for the database user who owns the SQL object type definitions.
url	*jdbc-url* jdbc:oracle:oci8:@	The URL can be for other JDBC drivers supported by the vendor. You can use the Oracle thin driver with JPublisher if you do not have SQL*net/Net8 client software installed on your development platform.
package	*Package-name*	The Java package name for the generated Java code. This creates a subdirectory structure based on the package name in the directory specified by the "dir" option.
sql	*sql-type-name:java-class-name*	Sets the name Java class for the corresponding SQL object type.
props	*Filename*	Specifies the name of the properties file containing additional JPublisher options.
methods	all, named, none Using an input file with the "named" value allows you to specify which SQL methods are mapped, and all others are ignored. A value of true is a synonym for all, and false is a synonym for none.	Specifies whether the generated Java class contains wrapper methods for those found in the SQL object type or PL/SQL package.
input	*Filename*	Specifies a file name that contains commands controlling how SQL object types, PL/SQL packages, and subcomponents are translated.

11.4.1.3 Files Generated by JPublisher. The files generated by Oracle JPublisher depend on how the –sql option is used. For example, if you specify:

```
jpub -sql=oracle-type:ClassName . . .
```

then JPublisher generates the following files:

- An SQLJ or Java file called `ClassName.sqlj or ClassName.java`. The SQLJ file is generated if you specify the `-methods=true` command-line option, otherwise the `.java` file is generated.
- A Java file called for a `ClassNameREF.java` to work with a database REF to an SQL object type. This file is only generated when the *oracle-type* specifies an SQL object type name.
- If the *oracle-type* is a PL/SQL package name or the keyword `TOPLEVEL`, you must also include the `-methods=true` option.

The Java data types generated for attributes, method return values, and method arguments are influenced by the `-mapping` options, or via the four options: `-builtintypes`, `-usertypes`, `-lobtypes`, and `-numbertypes`. Mapping options are mentioned to highlight that you can control the data types generated for Java variables and methods, but it would be too much of a digression to discuss them in any detail.

11.4.1.4 Using a Properties File. If you use a properties file specified in the `-props=filename` option, each line of the property file specifies a property whose name is prefixed with **`jpub.`** The option is followed by an equals sign and the value. For example:

```
jpub.user=bookstore/bookstore
jpub.sql=customer_t
jpub.mapping=jdbc
jpub.package=com.prenhall.OFJP.jpub
```

The equivalent command line is:

```
jpub -user=bookstore/bookstore -sql=customer_t -mapping=jdbc
    -package=com.prenhall.OFJP.jpub
```

Options not prefixed with `jpub` are ignored.

> **Note**
>
> The command line is continued according to the rules of the operating system or command-line handler.

11.4.1.5 Controlling the Generation of Class Names. To control the names generated in your Java class and for each accessor method created for the SQL object type attributes, use the `-input` option, which specifies a file name containing one or more *translation statements* that control the name generation.

A translation statement begins with the keyword SQL followed by the name of the database structure to be translated and additional instructions introduced with the keywords GENERATE, AS, and TRANSLATE.[9] The abbreviated syntax of a translation statement is:

```
SQL name [AS java-name-2]
  [TRANSLATE database-member-name AS simple-java-name
          [, database-member-name AS simple-java-name … ]
```

The ***name*** entered after the SQL keyword can be specified as:

- An SQL object type name or a PL/SQL package name.
- An SQL object type or a PL/SQL package prefixed with a specific database schema name.
- The keyword TOPLEVEL, which specifies that all PL/SQL procedures and functions in the current schema are to be translated as methods into the same Java class. The keyword TOPLEVEL is a reserved word, and can be prefixed with a database schema name.

For example, if the input file contains:

```
SQL customer_t AS Customer
```

`Customer` is used as the file and class name generated for the SQL object type called `customer_t`. The name after the AS keyword is case-sensitive. For example:

```
SQL customer_t AS CustoMER
```

This would generate a file called `CustoMER.java` and the class name would appear as follows:

```
public class CustoMER {
    :
  }
```

[9]The SQL keyword is the preferred command, but can be replaced with the keyword TYPE. However, the TYPE keyword may be deprecated in future versions of Oracle JPublisher.

Therefore, you must take care with the case of characters entered for the Java class name.

11.4.1.6 Controlling the Generation of Method Names. The TRANSLATE command in the input file specifies how to convert attributes in the SQL object type into Java accessor method names. Oracle JPublisher creates a get and set method for each attribute found in the SQL object type definition. The "get" and "set" keywords, in lowercase, are prefixed to a Java method name specified TRANSLATE command. For example:

```
SQL customer_ot AS Customer
  TRANSLATE name AS FirstName,
            surname AS Surname
```

The Java class file generated is called Customer.java, and contains methods with the signatures shown in the following code snippet:

```
public class Customer {
  :

  public void setFirstName(String FirstName) throws SQLException {
    :
  }

  public String getFirstName() throws SQLException {
    :
  }

  public void setSurname(String Surname) throws SQLException {
    :
  }

  public String getSurname() throws SQLException {
    :
  }
}
```

Note that the argument names preserve the case of the java attribute names specified in the TRANSLATE command option.

11.4.1.7 Using the Command Line to Control Class Name Generation. The `-sql` option is a shortcut alternative to the `-input` option for controlling the generation of a class name. The `-sql` option can be specified as:

```
-sql=type-name
```

This creates a Java class with the same name as the type name. However, underscore characters in the type-name are excluded from the resulting Java class name, and each word is capitalized. For example:

```
jpub -sql=customer_t
```

This creates two Java class files named CustomerT.java, and CustomerTRef. java.

Alternatively, you can use the `-sql` option to name the Java class as follows:

```
-sql=type-name:Javaclass
```

This creates a Java class of the name you specify. The Java class names if entered are case-sensitive, but the database type-name is not case-sensitive. More than one `type-name:java-class` combination can be entered, separated by commas and without spaces. For example:

```
jpub -sql=custorder_t:CustomerOrder,courier_t:Courier
```

This JPublisher command will generate four Java source files:

- CustomerOrder.java and CustomerOrderRef.java for the `customer_t` SQL object type.
- Courier.java file and CourierRef.java for the `courier_t` SQL object type.

11.4.2 USING THE CLASSES GENERATED BY JPUBLISHER

The SQLJ or Java class files generated by JPublisher can be used in your SQLJ or JDBC code. The examples in this chapter focus on using the generated classes in SQLJ. If you want to use them in JDBC, follow the examples in Chapter 10 2, which discusses using the SQLData and CustomDatum interfaces for object types. The examples in SQLJ are based on an SQL object type called `customer_t`. The `customer_t` object type definition is:

```
CREATE TYPE customer_t AS OBJECT (
  ID                        NUMBER(6),
  NAME                      VARCHAR2(30),
  SURNAME                   VARCHAR2(30),
  EMAIL                     VARCHAR2(50),
  PASSWORD                  VARCHAR2(10),
  CREDIT_CARD_TYPE          VARCHAR2(10),
```

```
08:   CREDIT_CARD_NUMBER        VARCHAR2(20),
09:   MONTH_EXPIRED             VARCHAR2(2),
10:   YEAR_EXPIRED              VARCHAR2(2)
11: );
12:
13: -- Create Object Table
14: create table customer of customer_t;
15:
16: // Create Relational Table with Object Column
17: create table best_cust (
18:   ID    NUMBER(4) CONSTRAINT best_cust_pk PRIMARY KEY,
19:   CUST  CUSTOMER_T
20: );
21:
22: // Create Relational Table with REF to Object
23: create table reg_cust (
24:   ID          NUMBER(4) CONSTRAINT reg_cust_pk PRIMARY KEY,
25:   CUSTREF     REF CUSTOMER_T
26: );
```

- Line 14 creates an object table of customers
- Lines 17–20 create the BEST_CUST table, which is used for reading or updating an object column.
- Lines 23–26 create the REG_CUST, which is used for inserting and reading a SQL reference to an object column.

The Oracle JPublisher command line used to generate the Customer.java and CustomerRef.java file is:

```
jpub -sql=customer_t:Customer
     -url=jdbc:oracle:thin:@localhost:1521:ORA815
     -user=obook/obook
```

The `jpub` command and options have been shown on three lines for clarity, but it should all be entered on one line. This JPublisher command creates two files:

1. Customer.java (see Listing 11.17)[10]
2. CustomerRef.java (see Listing 11.18)

[10]The file is called Customer.sqlj if you invoke JPublisher from JDeveloper.

The generated Customer.java file uses the CustomDatum and CustomDatumFactory interfaces, making the code not portable to other database environments.

```
public class Customer
  implements CustomDatum, CustomDatumFactory
{
  public static final String _SQL_NAME = "OBOOK.CUSTOMER_T";
  public static final int _SQL_TYPECODE = OracleTypes.STRUCT;

  /* constructors */
  public Customer() { ... }
  public Customer(ConnectionContext c)
    throws SQLException { ... }
  public Customer(Connection c)
    throws SQLException { ... }

  /* CustomDatum interface */
  public Datum toDatum(OracleConnection c)
     throws SQLException { ... }

  /* CustomDatumFactory interface */
  public CustomDatum create(Datum d, int sqlType)
    throws SQLException { ... }

  /* shallow copy method: give object same attributes as args */
  void shallowCopy(Customer d) throws SQLException {
    _struct = d._struct;
  }

  /* accessor methods */
  public BigDecimal getId() throws SQLException
  { return (BigDecimal) _struct.getAttribute(0); }

  public void setId(BigDecimal id) throws SQLException
  { _struct.setAttribute(0, id); }

  public String getName() throws SQLException
  { return (String) _struct.getAttribute(1); }

  public void setName(String name) throws SQLException
  { _struct.setAttribute(1, name); }

  // other accessor methods ...
}
```

LISTING 11.17 JPublisher-generated Customer.java class

For brevity, most of the generated code for the Customer.java source has been omitted, such as imports and method bodies. Some of the method signatures have been kept, to highlight the class structure.

Notes on Listing 11.17:

- Line 5 identifies the Java object as being an OracleTypes.STRUCT for the JDBC layer to manage the type mapping.
- Lines 8–12 are the constructors for the class; the no-argument constructor must be present.
- Lines 14–16 show the implementation of the CustomDatum.toDatum() method.
- Lines 18–20 implement the CustomDatumFactory.create() method to instantiate a Customer object.
- Lines 27–41 are the class getter and setter methods, which manage the state of each Customer instance.

The Customer.java class should be compiled first, because it is referenced in the CustomerRef.java class.

```
import java.sql.SQLException;
import oracle.jdbc.driver.OracleConnection;
import oracle.jdbc.driver.OracleTypes;
import oracle.sql.CustomDatum;
import oracle.sql.CustomDatumFactory;
import oracle.sql.Datum;
import oracle.sql.REF;
import oracle.sql.STRUCT;

public class CustomerRef
   implements CustomDatum, CustomDatumFactory
{
  public static final String _SQL_BASETYPE = "OBOOK.CUSTOMER_T";
  public static final int _SQL_TYPECODE = OracleTypes.REF;

  REF _ref;

  static final
     CustomerRef _CustomerRefFactory = new CustomerRef();

  public static CustomDatumFactory getFactory() {
    return _CustomerRefFactory;
  }

```

LISTING 11.18 JPublisher-generated CustomerRef.java class

```
25:   public CustomerRef() { // constructor
26:   }
27:
28:   /* CustomDatum interface */
29:   public Datum toDatum(OracleConnection c)
30:                                throws SQLException {
31:     return _ref;
32:   }
33:
34:   /* CustomDatumFactory interface */
35:   public CustomDatum create(Datum d, int sqlType)
36:                                    throws SQLException {
37:     if (d == null) return null;
38:     CustomerRef r = new CustomerRef();
39:     r._ref = (REF) d;
40:     return r;
41:   }
42:
43:   public Customer getValue() throws SQLException {
44:      return (Customer) Customer.getFactory().create(
45:        (Datum)  _ref.getValue(), OracleTypes.REF);
46:   }
47:
48:   public void setValue(Customer c) throws SQLException {
49:     _ref.setValue((STRUCT) c.toDatum(_ref.getConnection()));
50:   }
51: }
```

LISTING 11.18 *Continued*

The CustomerRef class provides Java developers with a way to work with SQL object type REF values.

Notes on Listing 11.18:

- Line 14 identifies the object instance as an OracleTypes.REF for the JDBC layer type mapping.
- Line 29 implements the toDatum() method for the CustomDatum, and line 35 implements the create() method for the CustomDatumFactory interface.
- Lines 43–46 show the getValue() method, which you can use to obtain an instance of the Customer via the CustomerRef object.
- Lines 48–50 show the setValue() method, which provides you with a means to write a reference to a Customer object previously obtained from the database.

Listings 11.17 and 11.18 provide you with a quick look under the hood at the classes generated by JPublisher. The JPublisher tools save a great deal of coding effort, and eliminate an error-prone manual process, to create custom classes for Oracle SQL object types and an object type REF.

11.4.2.1 Selecting Oracle SQL Objects in SQLJ. To select an SQL object into your Java application, you create an SQLJ SELECT statement to retrieve the data from an object table or column, and store the SQL object value in a Java variable declared with the class name generated by JPublisher for the corresponding SQL object type.

Listing 11.19 shows an example that queries all customer instances from an object table, using a named SQLJ iterator.

```
package com.prenhall.OFJP.sqlj;

import sqlj.runtime.*;
import sqlj.runtime.ref.*;
import java.math.BigDecimal;

public class ManageCustomer {

  public ManageCustomer(String url) { ... }

  #sql iterator List(Customer cust);

  public void listCustomers() {
     List     customers;

     try {
       #sql customers = { select value(c) cust from customer c };
       while (customers.next()) {
         Customer theCust = customers.cust();
         System.out.println(theCust.getId() + " " +
                            theCust.getName() + " " +
                            theCust.getSurname());
       }
       customers.close();
     }
     catch (Exception e) {
       e.printStackTrace();
     }
  }
}
```

LISTING 11.19 Selecting an SQL object from an object table

Notes for listing 11.19:

- Line 9 is the skeleton for the ManageCustomer constructor. The default connection context is initialized in the constructor.
- Line 11 defines a named iterator called `List`, which defines the column data type as `Customer` and name as `cust`.
- Line 14 declares a local iterator variable called `customers`.
- Line 17 executes the SELECT statement to read the customer object instances from the table, and returns the result set to the `customers` iterator.
- Line 19 obtains the Customer object instance from the iterator cust() method.
- Lines 20–22 call some of the getter methods generated by JPublisher to display some of the customer details.[11]

Listing 11.20 shows how to use a positional iterator to fetch a specific customer instance from the object table.

```
package com.prenhall.OFJP.sqlj;

import sqlj.runtime.*;
import sqlj.runtime.ref.*;
import java.math.BigDecimal;

public class ManageCustomer {

  public ManageCustomer(String url) { ... }

  #sql iterator PList(Customer);

  public void getCustomer(int id) {
    PList iter;
    Customer c = null;

    try {
       #sql iter = { select value(c)
                     from customer c
```

LISTING 11.20 Reading an Object Type using a positional iterator

[11]In addition to accessor methods, JPublisher can also generate Java wrapper methods for each member method in the SQL object type definition if you use the JPublisher `-methods` command-line option.

```
20:                      where c.id = :id };
21:        #sql { fetch :iter into :c };
22:        if (!iter.endFetch()) {
23:          System.out.println(c.getId() + " " +
24:                        c.getName() + " " +
25:                        c.getSurname());
26:        }
27:        else {
28:          System.out.println(
29:             "Customer with " + id + " does not exist");
30:        }
31:     }
32:     catch (Exception e) {
33:       e.printStackTrace();
34:     }
35:   }
36: }
```

LISTING 11.20 *Continued*

Notes on Listing 11.20:

- Line 11 declares the positional iterator class called PList.
- Line 18 assigns the result set from the select statement to the iterator variable, declared in line 14.
- Line 21 fetches an SQL CUSTOMER_T object into the Java object reference for a Customer.
- Lines 23–25 call the getter methods from the Customer class to display some of the attribute values.

The SQLJ code for retrieving the SQL object is quite simple, because the complexity of converting an Oracle SQL object type into a Java object is managed by the code generated by Oracle JPublisher.

11.4.2.2 Inserting, Updating, and Deleting an Oracle SQL Object. Inserting or updating an SQL object with a new Java object instance data is a three-step process:

1. Instantiate the Java object from the class generated by JPublisher.
2. Call the various set methods in the object to set the attributes.
3. Bind the object reference variable in an SQLJ insert or update statement.

Listing 11.21 is an example of creating a customer object, calling the setter methods to define the object state, and then inserting the data into an SQL object instance in an object table. The example also shows how to insert an object into an object column in a relational table.

```
package com.prenhall.OFJP.sqlj;

import sqlj.runtime.*;
import sqlj.runtime.ref.*;
import java.math.BigDecimal;

public class ManageCustomer {

  public ManageCustomer(String url) { ... }

  public  void addCustomer(int id, String name,
                            String surname, String cardNumber) {
     try {
       Customer c = new Customer();
       c.setId(new BigDecimal(id));
       c.setName(name);
       c.setSurname(surname);
       String email = name.substring(1,2).toUpperCase() +
                      "." + surname + "@ozemail.com.au";
       c.setEmail(email);
       c.setPassword("welcome");
       c.setCreditCardType("AMEX");
       c.setCreditCardNumber(cardNumber);
       c.setMonthExpired("02");
       c.setYearExpired("02");

       #sql { insert into customer values (:c) };
       #sql { insert into best_cust values (:id, :c) };

       #sql { commit };
     }
     catch (Exception e) {
       e.printStackTrace();
     }
  }
}
```

LISTING 11.21 Inserting Java objects into an object table or column

This example is somewhat contrived and explicit to show the creation of a Customer object and the operations necessary to INSERT it into an object table and an object column. The code could be written to receive a reference to Customer object, which would be created by the caller of the addCustomer() method. The addCustomer() method signature would then be:

```
public void addCustomer(Customer newCustomer) { . . . }
```

Notes on Listing 11.21:

- Line 14 instantiates the Customer object using its no-argument constructor.
- Lines 15–25 call the set accessor methods of the Customer class to set the state of the customer object.
- Line 27 inserts the object into the customer object table.
- Line 28 inserts the object into an object column of a relational table.

The INSERT statement adding the object into the object table could be written in two other ways. With one, you insert the data using standard SQL INSERT syntax:

```
#sql { insert into customer (id, name, surname, email,
          password, credit_card_type, credit_card_number,
          month_expired, year_expired)
       values (
            :(c.getId()),
            :(c.getName()),
            :(c.getSurname()),
            :(c.getEmail()),
            :(c.getPassword()),
            :(c.getCreditCardType()),
            :(c.getCreditCardNumber()),
            :(c.getMonthExpired()),
            :(c.getYearExpired())
       )
     };
```

Alternatively, you can insert the data using the SQL object type constructor:

```
#sql { insert into customer values (
    CUSTOMER_T(:(c.getId()),
               :(c.getName()),
               :(c.getSurname()),
               :(c.getEmail()),
```

```
                        :(c.getPassword()),
                        :(c.getCreditCardType()),
                        :(c.getCreditCardNumber()),
                        :(c.getMonthExpired()),
                        :(c.getYearExpired())
                        ))
        };
```

The preceding examples show that, instead of obtaining the SQL statement values from a Java variable, you can place a colon before a host expression enclosed between brackets. In these examples, each host expression calls a Java method to return a result. The result is supplied as the value for the target columns in the SQL statement. In the example, all SQL attributes values are obtained directly from the Customer object in the Java code.

Listing 11.22 provides an example of executing an SQL UPDATE statement on an object column in the SQLJ application.

```
package com.prenhall.OFJP.sqlj;

import sqlj.runtime.*;
import sqlj.runtime.ref.*;
import java.math.BigDecimal;

public class ManageCustomer {

  public ManageCustomer(String url) { ... }

  public void changeCustomer(int id) {
     try {
       Customer aCust = new Customer();
       aCust.setId(new BigDecimal(98));
       aCust.setName("Xak");
       aCust.setSurname("Idran");
       aCust.setEmail("Z.Idran@amil.com.za");
       aCust.setPassword("welkom");
       aCust.setCreditCardType("VISA");
       aCust.setCreditCardNumber("2230414134093333");
       aCust.setMonthExpired("12");
       aCust.setYearExpired("01");

       #sql { update best_cust
```

LISTING 11.22 Updating an SQL object in an object column

```
25:                  set cust = :aCust where id = :id  };
26:
27:           #sql { commit };
28:         }
29:         catch (Exception e) {
30:           e.printStackTrace();
31:         }
32:     }
33: }
```

LISTING 11.22 *Continued*

Notes on Listing 11.22:

- Lines 13–22 instantiate the object and set the state of each instance variable by calling the Customer setter methods.
- Lines 24 and 25 show the update statement used to change the object instance in the `cust` column of the `best_cust` table for a specified customer id. The original instance in the `cust` column is overwritten by the new instance.

You cannot use an UPDATE statement to replace an entire object instance in an object table. However, you can modify the attribute values of an existing object instance by using a standard SQL UPDATE statement.

You can delete an object instance by executing any DELETE statement with a condition to target the specific instance. To remove an object instance from an object column, you set the column to a NULL using an UPDATE statement, provided the object column allows a NULL value. For example:

```
package com.prenhall.OFJP.sqlj;

import sqlj.runtime.*;
import sqlj.runtime.ref.*;
import java.math.BigDecimal;

public class ManageCustomer {

public ManageCustomer(String url) { ... }

  public void removeCustomer(int id) {
    try {
      #sql { update best_cust
             set cust = NULL where id = :id  };
```

```
      #sql { commit };
    }
    catch (Exception e) {
      e.printStackTrace();
    }
  }
}
```

11.4.2.3 Extending Classes Generated by JPublisher. The best way to modify the classes generated by JPublisher is to create a subclass of the generated class, and add additional constructors, attributes, and methods to it. The less attractive alternative is to directly modify the generated class. This risks loss of code if you need to regenerate the Java class, due to changes made to the associated SQL object type.

If you create a subclass from the Java class generated by Oracle JPublisher, and subsequently modify the base object type, you must use the Oracle JPublisher input file with the GENERATE AS syntax for the translator command. For example, if the properties file myprops.jpub contains:

```
jpub.user=bookstore/bookstore
jpub.url=jdbc:oracle:thin:@localhost:1521:ORA815
```

where the translate.txt file contains:

```
SQL customer_t
   GENERATE CustomerImpl
    AS MyCustomer
```

you can use the following Oracle JPublisher command line:

```
jpub -props=myprops.jpub -input=translate.txt
```

This example creates two Java files, CustomerImpl.java and CustomerImplRef.java. However, Oracle JPublisher does not generate the file called MyCustomer.java. MyCustomer is added to the translator command after the keyword AS, when using the GENERATE keyword, to prevent JPublisher from creating MyCustomer.java file. Use this technique if you have manually created MyCustomer.java as a subclass of CustomerImpl.java and want to preserve the extension you have made. You can safely regenerate the CustomerImpl class and inherit the appropriate changes.

The shortcut Oracle JPublisher command to perform the same task, using the properties file and not the input translator file, is:

```
jpub -props=p1.jpub -sql=customer_t:CustomerImpl:MyCustomer
```

11.4.2.4 Compile and Runtime SQL Checks. It is usually a good idea to invoke translation-time SQL syntax and validity checks. The compile-time SQL checking is achieved with the SQLJ command line, by providing:

- A username and password with the `-user` option.
- A database connection string using the `-url` option.

However, testing done with the SQLJ Translator shows that if a value assigned to an instance variable in the Java object is too large for the precision of the associated attribute defined in the SQL object type, then a runtime exception would be thrown.[12] Since the SQLJ translation-syntax checking cannot detect the attribute size and bound problems that may occur at runtime, particularly with String data types, you should add the necessary data-validation code before you execute the SQL statement.

11.4.2.5 Using the Java Class for an Object Type REF. As previously stated, for each SQL object type generated by the Oracle JPublisher utility, you get a Java class representing the object REF for the object type. Listing 11.23 demonstrates how you can query and use an object REF type.

```
package com.prenhall.OFJP.sqlj;

import sqlj.runtime.*;
import sqlj.runtime.ref.*;
import java.math.BigDecimal;

public class ManageCustomer {

  public ManageCustomer(String url) { ... }

  public void getCustFromRef(int id) {
     try {
       CustomerRef aCustRef = null;
       Customer c = null;

```

LISTING 11.23 Querying an object type REF column

[12]The tests were done with the SQLJ Translator shipped with JDeveloper 3.0.

```
16:         #sql { select ref(c) into :aCustRef
17:                from customer c
18:                where "ID" = :id };
19:
20:         c = aCustRef.getValue();
21:         System.out.println(c.getId() + " " +
22:                                 c.getName() + " " +
23:                                 c.getSurname());
24:
25:         #sql { insert into reg_cust (id, cust_ref)
26:                values (:id, :aCustRef) };
27:
28:         #sql { commit };
29:       }
30:       catch (Exception e) {
31:         e.printStackTrace();
32:       }
33:   }
34: }
```

LISTING 11.23 *Continued*

Notes on Listing 11.23:

- Line 13 declares the Java variable for the REF of a Customer object.
- Line 14 creates the variable for the Customer object referenced by the CustomerRef object.
- Lines 16–18 execute the Oracle select statement to read an object type REF value into the CustomerRef object. The `id` column is quoted in uppercase to work around a problem with using JDeveloper 3.0 code editor.
- Line 20 calls the getValue() method of the Object REF component to acquire the Customer object instance referenced by the REF value.
- Lines 25 and 26 show an insert statement for storing the CustomerRef into a column `cust_ref` defined as a REF to the `customer_t` in the `reg_cust` table.

The safest way to insert an Object REF value into a REF column in the database is to:

- Select the Object REF value into the Java CustomerRef class from a valid CUSTOMER_T object instance.
- Execute an INSERT or UPDATE statement with the CustomerRef object retrieved, as shown in Listing 11.23.

You can see from the simplicity of the examples used that it is very easy to work with Oracle object types in Java code. There is a natural one-to-one match between the Java object and the SQL object, and using the JPublisher tool simplifies the process of creating the Java class for an SQL object.

11.5 PROCESSING SQL COLLECTIONS

Oracle varying-array and nested-table object types are collections that can be read into, and written from, your Java application. The Java classes compatible with the collection data type definition must first be generated using JPublisher. The following example uses:

- A PERSON_T object type, which contains PL/SQL methods.
- A varying-array collection, called PERSON_VA_T of PERSON_T objects.
- A nested-table collection, called PERSON_NT_T of PERSON_T objects.

The steps in generating and using these SQL objects in Java are shown in the following order:

1. Creating the PERSON_T Object type, Collections, and tables.
2. Generating the Java classes for PERSON_T object type and collections.
3. Using the object type and collections.

11.5.1 CREATING THE SQL COLLECTIONS AND TABLES

Listing 11.24a shows the SQL code used to create the PERSON_T object type. Listing 11.24b shows the creation of the PERSON_VA_T and PERSON_NT_T collections, as well as the following database tables:

- A TEAM table for a nested table of team members.
- A FAMILY table containing a varying array of members.

```
CREATE OR REPLACE TYPE person_t AS OBJECT (
  id          NUMBER(6),
  firstName   VARCHAR2(20),
  lastName    VARCHAR2(20),
  birthDate   date,
  MEMBER FUNCTION getAge RETURN NUMBER,
  MEMBER PROCEDURE setFirstName(newName VARCHAR2),
```

Listing 11.24a Creating PERSON_T SQL object and methods

```
  MEMBER PROCEDURE setLastName(newName VARCHAR2),
  MEMBER PROCEDURE setBirthDate(newDate DATE),
  MEMBER FUNCTION getName RETURN VARCHAR2,
  MEMBER FUNCTION toString RETURN VARCHAR2
);
/

CREATE OR REPLACE TYPE BODY person_t IS
  member function getAge return number is
  begin
    return round(months_between(trunc(sysdate),self.birthDate)/12,2);
  end;

  member procedure setFirstName(newName varchar2) is
  begin
     self.firstName := initcap(newName);
  end;

  member procedure setLastName(newName varchar2) is
  begin
     self.lastName := initcap(newName);
  end;

  member procedure setBirthDate(newDate date) is
  begin
    self.birthDate := trunc(newDate);
  end;

  member function getName return varchar2 is
  begin
    return firstName||' '||lastName;
  end;

  member function toString return varchar2 is
  begin
     return id ||': '||self.getName||' ('||self.getAge||')';
  end;

END;
/
```

Listing 11.24a *Continued*

Listing 11.24a shows a simple object type structure that contains several methods to operate on the object instance in application memory, whether a PL/SQL application or a Java application. The methods defined for the PERSON_T object are:

- Function `getAge` returns the current age of the person. The age is determined by calculating the months between the person's birth date and the current date and time,[13] and dividing the value by twelve using Oracle data arithmetic.
- Procedure `setFirstName` changes the first-name attribute of the SQL object.
- Procedure `setLastName` changes the last-name attribute of a person object.
- Procedure `setBirthDate` changes the birth date in the object.
- Function `getName` returns the concatenated result of the person's first and last names.
- Function `toString` returns a concatenated string representation of the person object attributes.

The method names have been entered using Java naming conventions, but the Oracle database treats each name in a case-insensitive way. Note that the names are stored in uppercase form in the Oracle data dictionary. The method names chosen minimized the need to specify an input file with the Oracle JPublisher command line that was used to create the corresponding Java class. The method names defined in the type body are called through wrapper methods in the Java class generated by JPublisher by specifying the `-methods` command-line option.

The SQL statements used to create the varying-array, nested-table, and database tables based on these types are shown in Listing 11.24b.

```
-- Create the nested table type definition
CREATE TYPE person_nt_t AS TABLE OF person_t;
/

-- Create the varying array type definition
CREATE TYPE person_va_t AS VARRAY(5) OF person_t;
/

-- Create the family table using the varying array for members
```

LISTING 11.24b Creating SQL collections and tables for PERSON_T

[13]The Oracle SQL date functions do not provide a function to determine the years between two dates.

```
CREATE TABLE FAMILY (
  ID         NUMBER(4) CONSTRAINT family_pk PRIMARY KEY,
  MEMBERS    PERSON_VA_T
);

-- Create the team table using the nested table for members
CREATE TABLE TEAM (
  id         NUMBER(4) CONSTRAINT team_pk PRIMARY KEY,
  members    PERSON_NT_T)
NESTED TABLE members STORE AS TEAM_MEMBERS;
```

LISTING 11.24b *Continued*

Having created the SQL types and tables using Oracle JPublisher either as a standalone command-line tool or invoked through JDeveloper, you create Java classes for the object types you wish to work with in your Java applications.

11.5.2 GENERATING JAVA CLASSES FOR SQL COLLECTIONS

Listing 11.25 shows the JPublisher command line and input file used to generate the Java classes for the PERSON_T, PERSON_VA_T object types. A Java class for PERSON_NT_T also needs to be created for manipulation of the data in a nested table. Section 11.5.3, "Accessing the SQL Collections from Java," gives an example of using the generated collection classes.

```
01: jpub -sql=person_t:Person,person_va_t:PersonArray
02:      -url=jdbc:oracle:thin:@localhost:1521:ORA815
03:      -user=bookstore/bookstore
```

LISTING 11.25 Generating the Collection Java class with JPublisher

Notes on Listing 11.25:

The entire command line is entered on one line, but is split into three lines for presentation here.

- Line 1 converts the PERSON_T into a Person.java, and PERSON_VA_T into PersonArray, which creates methods to manage a collection of Person objects.
- Lines 2 and 3 are database connection details to locate the definitions of the SQL object types.

JPublisher generates the following Java sources:

- Person.java is the Java class for the PERSON_T object.
- PersonRef.java is the Java class for a REF to a PERSON_T object.
- PersonArray.java is a collection of Person objects.

If the command line in Listing 11.25 had included the "–methods=true" option, a Person.sqlj file would be generated instead of the Person.java file. In addition, the Person.sqlj file would include Java wrapper methods for each method defined in the PERSON_T object type. The names generated for wrapper methods can be changed by using an SQLJ Translator input file with appropriate TRANSLATE commands.

The generated wrapper methods invoke the SQL object methods by executing a PL/SQL anonymous block in a SQLJ statement. However, now focus on how you can use the generated classes to perform SQLJ operations from Java on the collections. Listing 11.26 shows the resulting method signatures for the PersonArray.java source that can be used to manage a collection of objects.

```
public class PersonArray
  implements CustomDatum, CustomDatumFactory
{
  public static CustomDatumFactory getFactory();
  public PersonArray();
  public PersonArray(Person[] a);

  /* CustomDatum interface */
  public Datum toDatum(OracleConnection c) …;
  /* CustomDatumFactory interface */
  public CustomDatum create(Datum d, int sqlType) …;

  public int length();
  public int getBaseType();
  public String getBaseTypeName();
  public ArrayDescriptor getDescriptor();

  /* array accessor methods */
  public Person[] getArray();
  public void setArray(Person[] a);
  public Person[] getArray(long index, int count);
  public void setArray(Person[] a, long index);
  public Person getElement(long index);
  public void setElement(Person a, long index);
}
```

LISTING 11.26 Java object method signatures for the SQL collection

Notes on Listing 11.26:

- Lines 4– 6 are the methods used to construct the array object.
- Lines 8–11 are the methods required because of the implementing of the CustomDatum and CustomeDatumFactory interfaces.
- Lines 13–24 are methods for accessing information about the collection, including getting a specific Person element and adding new Person elements.

The collection can be read and written using SQLJ statements, and the above methods are useful for constructing and using the collection in your application.

11.5.3 ACCESSING THE SQL COLLECTIONS FROM JAVA

The example in Listing 11.27 shows how to construct a Java array of Person objects and add it to a PersonArray object, which, in turn, is inserted as a new record into the family table (see Listing 11.24b), and then shows how to read the contents of the family table.

```
import sqlj.runtime.*;
import sqlj.runtime.ref.*;

public class VarArrayExample {

  #sql iterator Families (int id, PersonArray members);

  public VarArrayExample() {
    DefaultContext ctx = null;
    Families family = null;   // declare iterator variable
    String driver = "jdbc:oracle:thin:";
    try {
      Class.forName("oracle.jdbc.driver.OracleDriver");
      ctx = new DefaultContext(
         driver + "bookstore/bookstore@localhost:1521:ORA815",
         false);
      DefaultContext.setDefaultContext(ctx);

      String[] firstNames = { "Jackie", "Larry", "Sandra" };
      String[] lastNames = { "Chandra", "Chandra", "Chandra" };
      /*
      ** Construct the array of Person objects built from
      ** the array of first and last names. Generate
```

LISTING 11.27 Accessing SQL varying-array collection in SQLJ

```
    ** a new id for each person, and a date of birth
    ** based on the loop iteration variable value
    */
    Person[] members = new Person[firstNames.length];
    for (int i = 0; i < members.length; i++) {
      members[i] = new Person();
      members[i].setId(new java.math.BigDecimal(i+20));
      members[i].setFirstname(firstNames[i]);
      members[i].setLastname(lastNames[i]);
      members[i].setBirthdate(
        new java.sql.Timestamp(72+i, 1+i, 10+i, 0, 0, 0, 0));
    }

    /*
    ** COnstruct the PersonArray collection from the
    ** array Person objects in the member variable
    */
    PersonArray aFamily = new PersonArray(members);
    /*
    ** Use an SQLJ Insert to create a new family, assigning
    ** an unique id for the family generated from an
    ** Oracle sequence called family_seq.
    */
    #sql { insert into family (id, members)
           values (family_seq.nextval, :aFamily) };

    /*
    ** Now populate the family iterator with
    ** each family record, where the members
    ** column is read as a PersonArray object
    */
    #sql family = { select id, members from family };
    while (family.next()) {
      PersonArray pa = family.members();
      System.out.println("Family: " + family.id());

      for (int j = 0; j < pa.length(); j++) {
        Person p = pa.getElement(j);
        System.out.println("\t" + p.getId() + " " +
                           p.getFirstname() + " " +
                           p.getLastname() + " " +
                           p.getBirthdate());
      }
```

LISTING 11.27 *Continued*

```
67:       }
68:       family.close();
69:       #sql { commit; };
70:       ctx.close();
71:     }
72:     catch (Exception e) {
73:       e.printStackTrace();
74:     }
75:   }
76:
77:   public static void main(String[] args) {
78:     new VarArrayExample();
79:   }
80: }
```

LISTING 11.27 *Continued*

Notes on Listing 11.27:

- Line 6 creates a named iterator class, called Families, which is used to query the SQL varying-array collection column. The second iterator data type uses the PersonArray class to receive the SQL collection for the member column in the FAMILY table.
- Line 10 declares the iterator variable called families used for querying the SQL collection data.
- Lines 27–35 create the array of Person objects to be used for the insert operation.
- Line 41 instantiates the PersonArray collection class with elements from the member array of Person objects. The PersonArray construct accepts an array of Person objects (see line 6 of Listing 11.26).
- Lines 47 and 48 show a simple SQL INSERT statement that accepts the PersonArray collection object referenced by the aFamily variable. This is all that is required to insert a new collection of varying-array objects.
- Line 55 issues the query on the family table and returns the result set to the "families" iterator variable.
- Line 56 is the start of the iterator loop mechanism that calls the next() method to step through each family record retrieved from the database table.
- Line 57 uses the named iterators members() method to return a PersonArray object reference to the SQL varying-array collection for a specific family record.

- Lines 60–66 show an inner loop using the PersonArray length() method to control the loop. It calls the getElement() method to obtain a reference to each Person object contained in the PersonArray object, and prints some of the details of each Person object in the family record.

Listing 11.27 shows how the use of SQLJ and JPublisher technology can simplify accessing and manipulating collections of SQL objects.

Using JPublisher, a class called PersonNestedTable is generated for the PERSON_NT_T nested table. Listing 11.28 shows an example using the Person and PersonNestedTable classes on data contained in the TEAM table, which contains a nested table of PERSON_T objects for the team members (see Listing 11.24b).

```
import sqlj.runtime.*;
import sqlj.runtime.ref.*;
import java.io.*;
import java.util.*;
import java.math.*;

public class NestedTableExample {

  String driver = "jdbc:oracle:thin:";
  String url = driver +
              "bookstore/bookstore@localhost:1521:ORA815";

  #sql iterator TeamMember (int id, PersonNestedTable members);

  public NestedTableExample(int teamId, String fileName) {
    DefaultContext ctx = null;
    TeamMember team = null;

    try {
      Class.forName("oracle.jdbc.driver.OracleDriver");
      ctx = new DefaultContext(url, false);
      DefaultContext.setDefaultContext(ctx);

      Vector memberList = readMembers(fileName);

      PersonNestedTable newTeam = new PersonNestedTable(
                    new Person[memberList.size()]);
      for (int i = 0; i < memberList.size(); i++) {
        newTeam.setElement((Person) memberList.elementAt(i), i);
      }
```

LISTING 11.28 Accessing a SQL nested-table collection

```
31:
32:         #sql { insert into team (id, members)
33:                values (:teamId, :newTeam) };
34:         System.out.println("New Team inserted");
35:
36:         #sql team = { select id, members from team };
37:         while (team.next()) {
38:           PersonNestedTable pa = team.members();
39:
40:           System.out.println("Team: " + team.id());
41:           for (int j = 0; j < pa.length(); j++) {
42:             Person p = pa.getElement(j);
43:             System.out.println("\t" + p.getId() + " " +
44:               p.getFirstname() + " " + p.getLastname() + " " +
45:               p.getBirthdate());
46:           }
47:         }
48:         team.close();
49:         ctx.close();
50:       }
51:       catch (Exception e) {
52:         e.printStackTrace();
53:       }
54:     }
```

LISTING 11.28 *Continued*

Notes on Listing 11.28:

- Line 13 declares a SQLJ iterator for reading the rows from the TEAM table, whose second column is a nested table.
- Line 17 declares the iterator variable for the query result set.
- Line 24 calls a readMembers() method (see Listing 11.29) to read member records from a text file to build a vector of members. This step is needed in order to find out how many elements are needed to size the array of Person objects instantiated in the argument for the PersonNestedTable constructor in lines 26 and 27.
- Lines 26 and 27 create the PersonNestedTable collection object, which must have an array argument whose size is pre-allocated before you can set each array element to contain a Person object.
- Lines 28–30 copy the Person object references from the vector into the nested-table collection used in the insert operation.

- Lines 32 and 33 execute the SQLJ INSERT statement to add a new TEAM row with a collection of members.
- Line 36 initiates a query to process the contents of the TEAM table, returning a result set to the team iterator variable (declared in line 17).
- Line 38 obtains a reference to a team row nested-collection object.
- Lines 41–46 loop through each of the nested-table elements to print the Person object contents.

It is interesting that the SQL varying-array and nested-table collections can both be read into either a PersonArray or PersonNestedTable object. This is only possible because the PersonArray and PersonNestedTable classes are structurally similar with similar method calls. However, you should use classes appropriate for the related database type.

```
public Vector readMembers (String fileName) throws Exception {
    BufferedReader br = new BufferedReader(
                              new FileReader(fileName));
    Vector memberList = new Vector();
    StringTokenizer st = null;
    Person member = null;
    int idx = 0;
    String str = null;

    while ((str = br.readLine()) != null) {
       member = new Person();
       st = new StringTokenizer(str, ":", false);
       while (st.hasMoreTokens()) {
         int id = 0;
         try { id = Integer.parseInt(st.nextToken()); }
         catch (Exception nfe) { id = 1; }
         member.setId(new BigDecimal(id));
         member.setFirstname(st.nextToken());
         member.setLastname(st.nextToken());
         member.setBirthdate(
           new java.sql.Timestamp(72+28, 03, id, 0, 0, 0, 0));
         memberList.addElement(member);
       }
       idx++;
    }
```

LISTING 11.29 Creating a collection of members from a text file

```
      br.close();
      return memberList;
  }

  public static void main(String[] args) {
    new NestedTableExample(2, "team1.txt");
  }
}
```

LISTING 11.29 *Continued*

The remaining piece of code for this example is shown in Listing 11.29. It reads a text file of tokenized member information.

The readMembers() method reads the member data on each line in the file. Each line in the file has the member id, first name, and last name separated by a colon. The java.util.StringTokenizer object is used to extract the field values for a member to build each Person object. The Person objects are added to a Java vector. The vector is returned to the caller of the readMembers() method as a collection of Person objects.

11.6 MANAGING LARGE DATA TYPES

In Chapter 10, you learned how to read LONG or large-object LOB columns. In this section you will look at similar examples using SQLJ. The SQLJ runtime class library provides three classes for working with large objects:

- AsciiStream—for processing character data in bytes.
- BinaryStream—for processing binary data in bytes.
- UnicodeStream—for processing character data in 16-bit characters.

All of these classes, which are defined in the sqlj.runtime package, are subclasses of sqlj.runtime.StreamWrapper. The StreamWrapper class is a subclass of java.io.FilterInputStream. These classes act as an input source for data inserted into large columns, or an input source when extracting data from large columns.

The key thing to remember when processing streams associated with database columns is that you must process their contents before you work with another column, and before you move to the next row. Positional iterators always declare the stream column last, and are limited to only one stream object per query. Named iterators do not have this restriction. SQLJ imposes the additional restriction that you cannot use a stream object in the INTO clause of a SELECT statement. Therefore, most of the code examples in this section make use of iterators, except for the examples that operate on the CLOB, BLOB, and BFILE locators.

The examples that follow show how to use stream classes in SQLJ to read from, and write to, a database column. The examples are presented as the method only, which you add to any class.

11.6.1 READING FROM A LONG COLUMN

```
01: #sql iterator LongAscii (int getId, int getLen,
02:                          AsciiStream getData);
03: public void readLongAscii(int idVal) {
04:   try {
05:     LongAscii iter;
06:     #sql iter = { select id getid, len getlen, data getdata
07:                   from demo_long
08:                   where id = :idVal};
09:     while (iter.next()) {
10:       System.out.println("Record id: " + iter.getId());
11:       byte[] buf = new byte[iter.getLen()];
12:       AsciiStream aStream = iter.getData();
13:       aStream.read(buf);
14:       aStream.close();
15:       StringBuffer sb = new StringBuffer(buf.length);
16:       for (int i = 0; i < buf.length; i++) {
17:          sb.append((char)buf[i]);
18:       }
19:       System.out.println(sb);
20:     }
21:     iter.close();
22:   }
23:   catch (Exception e) {
24:     e.printStackTrace();
25:   }
26: }
```

The key steps in reading text from a LONG column are:

1. Get the column as an AsciiStream object (line 12 gets the stream from the iterator column).
2. Read the data from the stream (line 13).
3. Close the stream (line 14).

The remainder of the example adds the byte array to a StringBuffer for printing on the screen.

11.6.2 WRITING TO A LONG COLUMN

```
01: public void writeLongAscii(int nextId, String filename) {
02:   try {
03:     File f = new File(filename);
04:     if (f.exists()) {
05:       int len = (int) f.length();
06:       AsciiStream inData = new AsciiStream(
07:                               new FileInputStream(f), len);
08:       #sql { insert into demo_long (id, len, data)
09:              values (:nextId, :len, :inData) };
10:       inData.close();
11:       #sql { commit };
12:     }
13:     else {
14:        System.out.println("File " + f.getAbsolutePath() +
15:                             " does not exist");
16:     }
17:   }
18:   catch (Exception e) {
19:     e.printStackTrace();
20:   }
21: }
```

Writing a LONG column requires you to associate an input stream with an AsciiStream object. The example uses a file as the input source and stores the contents of the file in the LONG column.

- Lines 6 and 7 use the AsciiStream constructor with two arguments, the input stream, and the length of the data. The length is very important for the example to work. Alternatively, you can construct the stream object using a new AsciiStream (InputStream), and call the setLength() method to ensure that the data volume is set before executing the insert statement.
- Lines 8 and 9 perform the insert, and the AsciiStream is processed as a bind variable.
- Line 10 closes the input stream.

11.6.3 READING FROM A LONG RAW COLUMN

```
#sql iterator LongRaw (int getId, int getLen,
                             BinaryStream getData);
public void readLongRaw(int idVal) {
  try {
    LongRaw iter;
    #sql iter = { select id getid, len getlen, data getdata
```

```
                    from demo_longraw
                    where id = :idVal};
    while (iter.next()) {
      int len = (int) iter.getLen();
      System.out.println("Record id: " + iter.getId());
      BinaryStream aStream = iter.getData();
      byte[] buf = new byte[len];
      aStream.read(buf);
      aStream.close();
      PictureFrame pic = new PictureFrame(buf);
      pic.setVisible(true);
    }
    iter.close();
  }
  catch (Exception e) {
    e.printStackTrace();
  }
}
```

Reading from a LONG RAW column follows the same steps as reading from a LONG column. However, in this case, a BinaryStream is used, as shown in bold. The same PictureFrame class that is described in Chapter 10 is used to display the image in a Java frame. Here is a sample of what an image would look like using the PictureFrame class:

11.6.4 WRITING TO A LONG RAW COLUMN

```
public void writeLongRaw(int nextId, String filename) {
  try {
    File f = new File(filename);
    if (f.exists()) {
      int len = (int) f.length();

      BinaryStream inData = new BinaryStream(
                              new FileInputStream(f), len);
      #sql { insert into demo_longraw (id, len, data)
             values (:nextId, :len, :inData) };
      inData.close();
      #sql { commit };
    }
    else {
      System.out.println("File " +
             f.getAbsolutePath() + " does not exist");
    }
  }
  catch (Exception e) {
    e.printStackTrace();
  }
}
```

Writing a file to a LONG RAW column is similar to writing to a LONG column, but uses a BinaryStream object, as shown in bold.

11.6.5 READING FROM A CLOB

```
public void readClob(int idVal) {
  try {
    oracle.sql.CLOB theClob = null;   // not portable
    #sql { select cdata into :theClob
           from demo_clob
           where id = :idVal};
    BufferedReader bf = new BufferedReader(
                           theClob.getCharacterStream());
    System.out.println("Length of data: " + theClob.length());
    String s;
    while ((s = bf.readLine()) != null) {
      System.out.println(s);
    }
    bf.close();
  }
  catch (Exception e) {
```

```
17:     e.printStackTrace();
18:   }
19: }
```

Reading from a CLOB column is straightforward, as seen in the preceding example. The bold text shows the declaration of the oracle.sql.CLOB object in line 3.[14] The SQLJ SELECT statement reads the CLOB locator into the CLOB object. Line 8 obtains a stream object from the CLOB locator, and the contents are accessed as you would a standard Java stream.

11.6.6 WRITING TO A CLOB

```
public void writeClob(int newId, String filename) {
  try {
    oracle.sql.CLOB theClob = null;    // not portable

    #sql { begin
             insert into demo_clob (id, cdata)
             values (:newId, empty_clob())
             returning cdata into :out theClob;
           end;
    };
    if (theClob != null) {
      PrintWriter out = new PrintWriter(
                          theClob.getCharacterOutputStream());
      BufferedReader in = new BufferedReader(
                            new FileReader(filename));
      String s;
      while ((s = in.readLine()) != null) {
        out.println(s);
      }
      in.close();
      out.close();
    }
    else {
      System.out.println("The clob is null");
    }
  }
  catch (Exception e) {
    e.printStackTrace();
  }
}
```

[14]The SQLJ Translator issues a warning to indicate that the oracle.sql.CLOB column is not portable. When the Oracle SQLJ Translator is updated to support the JDBC 2.0 CLOB class, portability will be possible.

Writing to a CLOB column requires two major steps:

1. Create the CLOB locator value using the Oracle database built-in function EMPTY_CLOB().
2. Write the CLOB contents, after getting an output stream from the CLOB locator.

In the example, lines 5–10 execute a PL/SQL anonymous block that creates the LOB locator, and returns the value to the Java application. If you are using a database prior to Oracle8i, then you have to:

- Execute the INSERT statement to create the empty LOB.
- Execute a SELECT statement to retrieve the LOB locator value.
- Write to the LOB using a stream object.

The PL/SQL anonymous block was used because it allows the use of the DML returning clause, and combines the two SQL steps of creating the LOB locator and reading it into one operation.

11.6.7 READING FROM A BLOB

```
public void readBlob(int idVal) {
  try {
    oracle.sql.BLOB theBlob = null;    // not portable
    #sql { select bdata into :theBlob
             from demo_blob
             where id = :idVal};
    InputStream in = theBlob.getBinaryStream();
    System.out.println("Length of data: " + theBlob.length());
    byte[] buf = new byte[(int)theBlob.length()];
    in.read(buf);
    in.close();
    PictureFrame pic = new PictureFrame(buf);
    pic.setVisible(true);
  }
  catch (Exception e) {
    e.printStackTrace();
  }
}
```

Reading from a BLOB column requires that you obtain the BLOB locator column and then a binary stream object. Once the binary stream object is created, you process the data using the stream methods. The example assumes that it is reading an image object, which is then passed to the PictureFrame class.

11.6.8 WRITING TO A BLOB

```
public void writeBlob(int newId, String filename) {
  try {
    oracle.sql.BLOB theBlob = null;    // not portable

    #sql { begin
             insert into demo_blob (id, bdata)
             values (:newId, empty_blob())
             returning bdata into :out theBlob;
           end;
    };
    if (theBlob != null) {
      OutputStream out = theBlob.getBinaryOutputStream();
      InputStream in = new FileInputStream(filename);
      int dataByte = 0;
      while ((dataByte = in.read()) != -1) {
        out.write(dataByte);
      }
      in.close();
      out.close();
    }
    else {
      System.out.println("The blob is null");
    }
  }
  catch (Exception e) {
    e.printStackTrace();
  }
}
```

Writing to a BLOB also requires that you first obtain the LOB locator, and then route the binary output stream to the BLOB contents. Using the write() methods of the output stream, you can modify the contents of the LOB.

11.6.9 READING FROM A LONG COLUMN WITH A UNICODESTREAM

```
#sql iterator LongUnicode (int getId, int getLen,
                           UnicodeStream getData);
public void readLongUnicode(int idVal) {
  try {
    LongUnicode iter;
    #sql iter = { select id getid, len getlen, data getdata
                  from demo_long
                  where id = :idVal};
    while (iter.next()) {
```

```
10:        int len = iter.getLen();
11:        System.out.println("Record: " + iter.getId());
12:        UnicodeStream aStream = iter.getData();
13:        StringBuffer sb = new StringBuffer(len);
14:        for (int i = 0; i < len; i++) {
15:           sb.append((char)aStream.read());
16:        }
17:        aStream.close();
18:        System.out.println(sb);
19:      }
20:      iter.close();
21:    }
22:    catch (Exception e) {
23:      e.printStackTrace();
24:    }
25: }
```

The example here uses a UnicodeStream to read 16-bit characters from a LONG column. The iterator reads the LONG column as a UnicodeStream, and the stream is accessed using the read() methods. The cast to (char), in line 15, is done to add a Unicode character to the StringBuffer.

11.6.10 WRITING TO A LONG COLUMN WITH A UNICODESTREAM

```
public void writeLongUnicode(int newId, String filename) {
  try {
    File f = new File(filename);
    if (f.exists()) {
      int len = (int) (f.length() / 2);
      UnicodeStream inData = new UnicodeStream(
                              new FileInputStream(f), len);
      #sql { insert into demo_long (id, len, data)
             values (:nextId, :len, :inData) };
      inData.close();
      #sql { commit };
    }
    else {
       System.out.println("File " +
         f.getAbsolutePath() + " does not exist");
    }
  }
  catch (Exception e) {
    e.printStackTrace();
   }
}
```

Writing a Unicode file to LONG column requires the following steps:

1. Determine the length of the file in characters by calling the length() method to obtain its length in bytes and then dividing by two, as shown in line 5.
2. Create the UnicodeStream object using the appropriate constructor, and ensure that the correct length is set, as shown in lines 6 and 7.
3. Execute the INSERT statement, passing the Unicode stream object as a bind value. The Oracle JDBC driver does the rest.

Reading or writing Unicode characters with the UnicodeStream object requires that the high byte be first and the low byte second.[15]

11.6.11 READING A BFILE

To read a BFILE, you first obtain the locator, and then use it like a file handle to open the file and read the contents.

```
public void readBFile(int idVal) {
  try {
    oracle.sql.BFILE bfile = null;

    #sql { select fileptr into :bfile
           from demo_bfile
           where id = :idVal };

    bfile.openFile();
    byte[] buf = bfile.getBytes(1L, (int)bfile. length());
    bfile.closeFile();
    PictureFrame pic = new PictureFrame(buf);
    pic.setVisible(true);
  }
  catch (Exception e) {
    e.printStackTrace();
  }
}
```

The example uses the openFile() method of the BFILE object before reading the contents. The length() method is used to get the length of the BFILE in bytes.

Alternatively, you can read the contents of the BFILE using the following code:

```
InputStream in = bfile.getBinaryStream();
byte[] buf = new byte[(int) bfile.length()];
```

[15]On the Microsoft Windows NT platform, Notepad creates Unicode files with the low byte first. Therefore, you need to byte swap each character read from the file.

```
in.read(buf);
in.close();
```

In this alternative example, you request a stream object (in this case a binary stream), and then read the contents using the stream read() method.

11.6.12 WRITING A BFILE

Writing a BFILE is simply the act of inserting a logical link from the database to the external file.

```
public void writeBfile(int newId, String filename) {
  try {
    #sql { insert into demo_bfile (id, fileptr)
      values (:newId, bfilename('BFILE_DIR', :filename)) };
  }
  catch (Exception e) {
    e.printStackTrace();
  }
}
```

The code example inserts a new record into a table that holds the BFILE locators that reference the external files. This is accomplished by calling the Oracle RDBMS built-in function called BFILENAME. The first argument to the BFILENAME is an Oracle8 DIRECTORY object, and the second parameter is the name of the file located in the directory. The directory object is created with the CREATE DIRECTORY statement, which defines a logical name and association for a physical directory in the operating system. The hard-coded directory name should be replaced with a parameterized value.

11.7 EXECUTING STORED PROCEDURES AND FUNCTIONS

As in JDBC, the SQLJ environment allows you to execute stored procedures in a vendor-independent way, regardless of the language used to write the stored procedure. In the Oracle RDBMS environment, the SQLJ Translator also allows you to invoke PL/SQL anonymous blocks, as seen in the CLOB and BLOB examples in the preceding section. Here the focus is on the syntactic aspects of calling a procedure or a function, without specific examples.

11.7.1 CALLING A STORED PROCEDURE

The syntax used to call a stored procedure is:

```
#sql { call procedure-name [(arguments, …)] };
```

The procedure name can include an Oracle database schema name and a package name, using the standard dot notation to qualify the procedure.

The arguments are optional, depending on the formal parameters declared in the procedure call. When using Oracle7 databases, you must omit the brackets if there are no arguments.

11.7.2 CALLING A STORED FUNCTION

Calling a stored function requires the following syntax:

```
type-name result;

#sql result = { values (function-name [(arguments, …)]) };
```

In the syntax shown, the type-name is the return data type expected for the function return value. The VALUES keyword is required, and the called function name is placed inside brackets. The function name can include an Oracle database schema name and/or a PL/SQL package name, and have optional arguments. The function result is stored in the Java variable whose name is listed before the assignment operator.[16]

11.7.3 STORED PROCEDURE OR FUNCTION ARGUMENTS

Stored procedures and functions accept arguments using different parameter-passing methods. In the Oracle environment, a parameter has one of the following modes:

- IN—accepts a value from an input-only argument.
- OUT—returns a value to the caller using an output-only argument.
- INOUT—accepts a value from the caller, and returns a modified value using the same argument.

When you call a stored procedure/function in SQLJ, you must explicitly identify the mode used for each bind variable used as a parameter. The syntax for specifying a parameter-passing mode is to include one of the keywords, IN, OUT, or INOUT, immediately after the colon and before the bind variable name. For example:

```
int id;
int custName;

#sql { get_customer(:in id, :out custName) };
```

[16]The function result does not need a preceding colon because it is outside the curly braces. The general rule is: if the Java variable is inside the curly braces, then it must be preceded by a colon to be treated as a bind variable.

The example calls a procedure called get_customer, passing an input integer argument as the first parameter, and receives the customer name from the second output string argument.

SUMMARY

SQLJ is a standard way to embed SQL statements in Java code in order to interact with a relational database. The simplicity of using SQLJ has been demonstrated; its coding benefits include:

- ❑ Reducing the amount of code to be written.
- ❑ Stronger type checking and validation at translation time.

You have read about using SQLJ to perform most of the same tasks you can do in JDBC, such as executing SQL statements, stored procedures, and functions, and processing large object data types and complex structures like SQL objects. You were introduced to the Oracle JPublisher utility that showed how to generate a Java class for an SQL object type that allows your SQLJ applications to work with database SQL object data in a way natural to a Java developer.

Using SQLJ, or JDBC, a set of classes can be developed that encapsulate the logic needed to access the database. An application developer can focus on building the business process logic to use the classes that provide database access. Subsequent changes to the data-access implementation classes can minimize the impact on changes made to the application business-process logic. The task of writing a class to manage the business rules that manage the data is time-consuming. SQLJ can reduce the time it takes to develop the database class library.

As an alternative, you can use Oracle JDeveloper to generate a set of classes that conform to a framework called Business Components for Java that encapsulates the data-access layer and associated data-validation rules. This is the next step toward even more rapid application development for your enterprise class applications. If you do not use Oracle JDeveloper, you have to handcraft the framework or the data access layer API yourself.

Chapter 12

Java Stored Procedures in Oracle

- Java Code Running in the Oracle Kernel
- Three Steps to Develop and Deploy Stored Procedures
- Making Java and PL/SQL Interact
- PL/SQL Versus Java: Choosing the Right Tool for Your Task
- Summary

This chapter focuses on Java methods that are uploaded to an Oracle RDBMS and run under the Java Virtual Machine (JVM) implemented in the Oracle kernel. Starting with release 8.1.5 of its flagship database, Oracle Corporation gave developers the option to use Java as a language for server-side programming, in addition to the more traditional and established PL/SQL.

Java can be used to accomplish tasks that were previously only achievable through PL/SQL, such as the implementation of database triggers. Furthermore, the inclusion of Java in the RDBMS kernel opens the doors to a completely new set of possibilities. For example, it is possible to use ZIP compression of files, using the classes implemented in the java.util.zip package, and store them in RDBMS tables.

PL/SQL and Java enjoy almost seamless integration and can be used interchangeably. Each has its own areas of strength and weakness, however, as will be elaborated in section 12.4. Java is best for numerically and computationally intensive tasks, while PL/SQL is the preferred choice when large volumes of data must be efficiently retrieved and accessed by server-side code.

12.1 JAVA CODE RUNNING IN THE ORACLE KERNEL

With release 8i of the Oracle RDBMS, Oracle Corporation demonstrated a strong commitment to Java by incorporating a Java Virtual Machine in the RDBMS kernel. Up to that time, only one language had been used by developers for server-side Oracle tasks: PL/SQL. With Oracle 8i, Java can now carry out tasks that were traditionally accomplished with PL/SQL, the Oracle proprietary extension to SQL. Java can be used not only to code server-side business logic in stored procedures but also to code database triggers, or actions that are associated with tables, objects, or views. They are automatically fired by the Oracle RDBMS when specific Data Manipulation Language (DML) operations affect the table, object, or view that has one or more associated triggers. Other events that can provoke the execution of triggers include a user logging into the database, the occurrence of specific database errors, and the creation or deletion of database objects.

The ability to use Java for coding server-side logic directly into the database has been enthusiastically welcomed by the community of Java developers who use the Oracle RDBMS to support their applications. As usually happens in the field of information technology, however, additional features do not come without limitations, and the JVM that runs in the Oracle RDBMS kernel is no exception. On the other hand, using Java to code stored procedures and functions provides a number of distinctive advantages that can be adopted by application designers and developers to improve the software development lifecycle.

12.1.1 ADVANTAGES

The JVM that shipped with Oracle 8i release 2 includes the JServer accelerator, a native-code compiler that speeds up the execution of Java programs that rely on standard core Java classes (the ones included in the JDK). JServer avoids the overhead associated with the Java interpreter, since it uses natively compiled versions of the core Java libraries. User-written Java code loaded into the database is still interpreted, but all calls to JDK classes invoke their natively compiled implementations. This ensures considerable performance gains for Java code executed inside the Oracle JVM.

If business logic that can be shared across applications is coded in Java stored procedures, a twofold benefit is achieved:

1. Applications written in other languages or environments, such as "C" or Oracle Forms, can still use the services provided by business logic components developed in Java.
2. Several complex business rules can be grouped together and executed in one single call, which minimizes network roundtrips.

The Oracle JServer complies with the Java 2 security policies implemented in the JVM. In order to access both classes and operating system resources, users need adequate permissions. Furthermore, it is possible to deny user access to Oracle data stored in tables, allowing selected access only through stored procedures that manipulate data in a strictly controlled manner.

Java stored procedures use a server-side JDBC internal driver, which is aware of the Oracle-specific data types, and is highly optimized and tuned. Developers can achieve performance gains by moving Java code that runs outside Oracle, and connects using type 2 or type 4 JDBC drivers, into the database.

12.1.2 LIMITATIONS

Developers coding business logic in stored procedures must be aware of the limitations the model imposes. Primarily, the entry point of a Java stored procedure must be a static method. All attributes and methods of classes implementing stored procedures are static; only public static methods can be published in the Oracle data dictionary.[1]

Java code that runs within the server-side Oracle JVM cannot instantiate GUI objects. It can, however, use GUI facilities provided by the AWT and by Swing to manipulate GUI objects, such as images, as long as they are not displayed.

---

[1]Only member methods of object types can be published as instance methods.

Perhaps the most annoying limitation is the one that affects multi-threading. While multi-threaded Java applications can run unmodified in the server-side Oracle JVM, the threads run sequentially rather than concurrently. Each thread spawned from a method call dies when the call terminates. Furthermore, threads running in JServer (the server-side JVM) are reminiscent of an MS Windows 3.x "feature": they are non-preemptive. In other words, if one thread "monopolizes" the CPU, no other thread can run within that session.

Keeping these limitations in mind, you can now proceed with the development of server-side stored procedures in Java.

12.2 THREE STEPS TO DEVELOP AND DEPLOY STORED PROCEDURES

In order to successfully deploy Java stored procedures, developers must follow three basic steps:

1. Write the Java code that implements the business logic.
2. Load the Java source or bytecodes into the Oracle server. An Oracle standard utility, *loadjava,* is used to upload Java classes and resources to an Oracle 8i server. Alternatively, the PL/SQL package DBMS_JAVA provides a *loadjava* method that makes it possible to load Java classes into the database programmatically.
3. Publish the Java methods that implement the entry points for the stored procedures, together with their signatures, so that other database objects can interact with Java objects through a common SQL and/or PL/SQL interface.

These three steps are explained in detail in the sections that follow.

12.2.1 DEVELOPING STORED PROCEDURES IN JAVA

The following six rules apply when developing stored procedures in Java:

1. The class that implements the stored procedures does not declare constructors.
2. All attributes and methods are static.
3. Methods that use Oracle objects, such as tables, views, and sequences, check the database connection, and establish one if necessary.
4. Method declarations include both input and output parameters.
5. Output parameters are stored in arrays, so they are passed by reference rather than by value, and thus can be modified by the stored procedure and returned to the caller.

6. All methods use the default connection provided by the server-side JDBC internal driver.

With the rules shown above firmly in mind, you are now ready to delve into Java code writing. Your first stored procedure is actually a function that returns the number of the Fibonacci series. There are several applications for this series of numbers initially discovered by an Italian mathematician, but perhaps the most popular is the rabbit-colony growth model and the demographic regulation operated by a fox colony living in the same area.[2] Each term in a Fibonacci sequence is the sum of the two terms that immediately precede it. The Java code follows:

```
public class Fibonacci
{
 public static int fibonacciNumber( int num)
 {
        if (num == 1 || num == 2)
              return 1;
        else
              return fibonacciNumber(num -1) +
                     fibonacciNumber(num - 2);
 }
}
```

Since the Fibonacci function does not access a database object, you don't need to check a database connection and create one if necessary. The real power of stored objects is in their ability to be used in SQL expressions. In other words, you can "extend" the SQL provided by Oracle with user-defined functions. For example, after loading the Fibonacci class into Oracle and publishing its method to the data dictionary, you could use the following SQL syntax to compute the Fibonacci series from numbers stored in an Oracle table:

```
select fibonacciNumber(OBS_NUMBER), ID
from LAB_SAMPLE
where OBS_DATE > TO_DATE('07/23/2000','MM/DD/YYYY);
```

---

[2]A *rabbit sequence* is a sequence that arises in the hypothetical reproduction of a population of rabbits. Let the substitution map $0 \to 1$ correspond to young rabbits growing old, and $1 \to 10$ correspond to old rabbits producing young rabbits. Starting with 0 and iterating using string rewriting gives the terms 1, 10, 101, 10110, 10110101, 1011010110110, ... Converted to binary, this sequence gives 1, 2, 5, 22, 181, ... , with the nth term given by the recurrence relation:

$$a(n) = a(n-1)2^{F_{n-1}} + a(n-2),$$

with $a(0)=0$, $a(1)=1$, and F_n the nth Fibonacci number.

All numbers identified by the WHERE clause in the OBS_NUMBER column of the LAB_SAMPLE table are passed to your Java function, which computes the Fibonacci series.

It is now time to create a stored procedure that actually interacts with Oracle objects, using the internal JDBC driver.

The EMP table in the standard SCOTT schema is used to implement a stored procedure that increments all employee salaries by a specified amount:

```
import java.sql.*;
import oracle.jdbc.driver.*;

public class FirstStoredProc
{
     public static void increaseSalary(float incr)
                        throws SQLException
     {
         Connection conn =
           DriverManager.getConnection("jdbc:default:connection:");
         String sqlStatement =
                   "update emp set sal = sal * (1 + ?)";
         PreparedStatement stmt =
            conn.prepareStatement(sqlStatement);
         stmt.setFloat(1,incr);
         stmt.executeUpdate();
         stmt.close();
     }
}
```

Pay special attention to the connection creation and the definition of the procedure, which accepts a single float as a parameter.

12.2.1.1 Parameter Passing Modes. Stored procedures and functions written in Java can be called from SQL and PL/SQL. This is only possible if a mechanism to regulate parameter passing between Java and PL/SQL is in place.

As shown in Table 12.1, PL/SQL defines three modes of parameter passing that a procedure or function can receive.

In Java, method parameters are passed by value if they are primitive data types, and by reference if they are objects. This means that if you want a primitive data type to be modified by a stored procedure, with the result available to the caller of the procedure, you must define an array of one cell containing your parameter. The array is passed by reference to the stored procedure, but the value inside the array's cell is stored by value. The caller of the stored procedure can access the modified value once the procedure returns it. For example, consider a swap procedure that swaps the values of its arguments:

TABLE 12.1 PL/SQL Parameter Passing Modes

PARAMETER	MODE	COMMENT
IN	Read-only	The value of the parameter can be referenced inside the module, but cannot be changed by the module.
OUT	Write-only	The value of the parameter can be assigned by the module, but the parameter's value cannot be referenced in the module.
IN OUT	Read-Write	The module can both reference and modify the value of the parameter it received.

```
public class Swap extends Object
{
   public static void swap (int [] a, int [] b)
   {
      int temp = a[0];
      a[0] = b[0];
      b[0] = temp;
   }
}
```

When the swap procedure is published to the Oracle database, the two parameters are both defined as IN OUT, so that PL/SQL modules calling the procedure can pass and receive them as if they were scalar values rather than arrays. Note that the parameters are published as IN OUT parameters because the swap procedure both references and modifies them. Later in this chapter you will learn how to publish Java stored procedures so as to make them visible to other Oracle objects that want to interact with them. If you cannot wait (or if curiosity is killing you!), jump to section 12.2.3, "Publishing Java Classes in the Database."

The next example shows a stored procedure that receives four parameters, two of mode IN and two of mode OUT. The procedure computes the mean and variance of a numeric column received as a parameter. The table to which the column belongs is also passed as a parameter.

```
import java.sql.*;
import oracle.jdbc.driver.*;

public class SecondStoreProc extends Object
{
    public static void computeMeanVariance(String tbl, String col,
                                           float [] mean,
                                           float [] var)
                                           throws SQLException
    {
        Connection conn =
```

```
          DriverManager.getConnection("jdbc:default:connection:");
        String sql_stmt = "select AVG("+col+"), "+
              "VARIANCE ("+col+") "+
                          "FROM "+tbl;
        Statement stmt = conn.createStatement();
        ResultSet rset = stmt.executeQuery(sql_stmt);
        rset.next();
        mean[0] = rset.getFloat(1);
        var[0] = rset.getFloat(2);
        rset.close();
    }
}
```

In the preceding example, the two first parameters (*tbl* and *col*) are IN parameters, since they are referenced by the *computeMeanVariance()* method, but are not modified by it. The next two parameters, *mean* and *var*, are OUT parameters because they are not referenced by *computeMeanVariance(),* but are modified through an assignment.

Declaring the type of parameter passed (IN, OUT, IN OUT) is just the beginning of the process of having PL/SQL and Java interact with each other. You also have to know the Java–PL/SQL data type compatibility table, so that you can pass data types that are compatible back and forth between Java and PL/SQL. For example, the Oracle data type NUMBER can be a very big number—up to 38 digits of precision. The precision of an Oracle number can be specified to be less than the maximum; it is not at all unusual to find numeric column definitions like:

```
employee#              NUMBER(6)
```

or

```
interest_rate          NUMBER(5,2)
```

In this case, the employee id number has been reduced to a decimal of six digits of precision. A Java int is, therefore, large enough to hold the contents of the employee# column without incurring overflow. Accordingly, a Java float is large enough to hold the contents of the interest_rate column without truncating any decimal digits. What happens when you cast Oracle data types into Java data types, and vice-versa? Oracle defines a list of legal data type mappings, and automatically provides the required conversions. While this arrangement is, in general, very convenient, exceptions are sometimes thrown if numeric overflows occur during the conversion. Consider the example in Table 12.2. The SQL type NUMBER can be legally mapped to the Java primitives or objects shown in the table.

If you want to store an Oracle SQL NUMBER in a Java short, you must make sure that the content of that specific number can fit. If it does not, an excep-

TABLE 12.2 Java Datatypes That Can Be Legally Mapped to the SQL Type NUMBER

java.lang.Byte	Byte
java.lang.Short	Short
java.lang.Integer	Int
java.lang.Long	long
java.lang.Float	float
java.lang.Double	double
java.math.BigDecimal	
oracle.sql.NUMBER	

tion will be thrown (SQLException, "Numeric Overflow"). To limit or eliminate such situations, map your Oracle data types into Java data types large enough to store the largest number. Very often this is done by reducing the number of significant digits allowed in an Oracle column. The largest number that can be stored in a Java int is 2,147,483,647 (a 10-digit number). Defining your Oracle column to be NUMBER(9) guarantees that a Java int will always be capable of storing that number without incurring a numeric overflow. In this case, the largest number you can store in the column is 999,999,999. If you are dealing with larger numbers, define your Oracle column as NUMBER(18), and always use a Java long to store numbers fetched from that Oracle column. Alternatively, use the type defined in the oracle.sql.NUMBER class, which is guaranteed to store any Oracle number without loss of precision. This arrangement requires you to use methods to convert the Oracle number to Java primitive data types.

Table 12.3 summarizes the legal Java to PL/SQL data type mappings for the most common data types.

TABLE 12.3 Java to PL/SQL Data Type Mappings

SQL TYPE	JAVA TYPE
CHAR, NCHAR, LONG, VARCHAR2, NVARCHAR2	oracle.sql.CHAR, java.lang.String, java.sql.Date, java.sql.Time, java.sql.Timestamp, java.lang.Byte, java.lang.Short, java.lang.Integer, java.lang.Long, java.lang.Float, java.lang.Double, java.math.BigDecimal, byte, short, int, long, float, double
DATE	oracle.sql.DATE, java.sql.Date, java.sql.Time, java.sql.Timestamp, java.lang.String,
NUMBER	oracle.sql.NUMBER, java.lang.Byte, java.lang.Short, java.lang.Integer, java.lang.Long, java.lang.Float, java.lang.Double, java.math.BigDecimal, byte, short, int, long, float, double
RAW, LONG RAW	oracle.sql.RAW, byte[ ]
ROWID	oracle.sql.CHAR, oracle.sql.ROWID, java.lang.String
BFILE	oracle.sql.BFILE
BLOB	oracle.sql.BLOB, oracle.jdbc2.Blob
OBJECT	oracle.sql.STRUCT, oracle.sqljData, oracle.jdbc2.Struct
TABLE, VARRAY	oracle.sql.ARRAY, oracle.jdbc2.Array

As you can see in the table, the content of an Oracle VARCHAR2 can be read into a Java numeric data type. Indeed, if you try to cast a VARCHAR2 that represents a number into a numeric data type, you will be pleasantly surprised to see that the conversion is automatic. Sometimes, however, this nice feature can be dangerous, and you should code defensively (always surround your conversions in *try .. catch* blocks and handle potential exceptions!). If you expect a VARCHAR2 column to contain an ASCII representation of numbers, but the column value does not obey the rules of numbers, then attempting to store such a value in a Java int or long will fail with the following exception:

```
Fail to convert to internal representation
```

12.2.1.2 Default Database Connection. Normally, JDBC connections established from external sources use the DriverManager class, which loads the required JDBC drivers. The getConnection() method returns a Connection object, which represents a database session. The connection object provides methods to instantiate SQL statements, and all database activity occurs in the context of one or more connections.

Things are different, however, when you use the internal JDBC driver. Server-side Java code runs within the Oracle server, where, in a sense, the session running the Java code is already connected. Your Java code should not register the JDBC driver, since is it already pre-registered and instantiated. In order to create your SQL statements, you still need a connection object, which is obtained using the following statement:

```
Connection conn =
      DriverManager.getConnection("jdbc:default:connection:");
```

This statement works with Oracle 8i release 2 (8.1.6). If you are coding your Java stored procedures for an 8.1.5 database, the default connection is obtained with:

```
Connection conn =
      DriverManager.getConnection("jdbc:oracle:kprb:");
```

There are a few important points to remember when using the internal JDBC driver. First of all, SQL statements and generated result sets persist across calls. This means that you must manage your cursors—that is, close them when you are finished with them. The best way to make sure that you close the cursors used during a database session is to include the close statements within a finally clause. However, remember not to close your connection when you are done with it, since you do not control the implicit connection available through the internal JDBC driver. The classical symptom indicating that something is wrong with cursor management is when your program throws an exception with the following message:

```
ORA-01000 maximum open cursors exceeded
```

Closing cursors after their use is a good programming practice under all circumstances, but in server-side Java programming it is essential.

Other important points to remember:

- The server-side JDBC driver does not support auto-commits. This means that your JDBC or SQLJ code must manage transactions explicitly.
- You cannot connect to a remote database using the server-side JDBC driver.
- You cannot physically close the database connection you obtained from the internal DriverManager. If you call the *close()* method, you only lose the reference to the connection object, and you must call the *getConnection()* method again to obtain a new reference. The physical connection, however, remains active and is not de-allocated.

12.1.2.3 Database Access through SQLJ. JServer comes equipped with a server-side SQLJ translator. You can use SQLJ instead of JDBC in your server-side Java stored procedures. There are two options for resolving the SQLJ calls into Java classes:

- You can use the client-side SQLJ translator and upload the generated .class files into JServer.
- You can upload the SQLJ source code into JServer, and compile them after they have been loaded.

Here is an example of a Java stored procedure that uses SQLJ. It prints the user name of the current user and its Oracle session id:

```
import java.sql.*;

public class GetSessionId extends Object
{
  public static void getSessionId()
  {
    try
    {
      String user,userId;
 #sql {SELECT user,userenv('SESSIONID') INTO :user, :userId FROM DUAL};
      printServerLine("You are: "+user+". Your session id is:
                           "+userId);
    }
```

```
    catch (Exception exc)
    {
      printServerLine("Exception occurred: " + exc.getMessage());
    }
  }
  private static void  printServerLine(String msg)
  {
    try
    {
      #sql {CALL DBMS_OUTPUT.PUT_LINE(:msg)};
    }
    catch (SQLException SQLExc)
    {
      System.err.println("Exception: "+SQLExc.getMessage()) ;
    }
  }
}
```

The source code shown above does not create a connection. Server-side SQLJ is assigned by default an implicit "channel" to the database, relieving developers from having to register drivers or specify connections. Note, too, that there is an important difference between client-side SQLJ and server-side SQLJ: the first must import the SQLJ runtime packages (sqlj.runtime.*; and sqlj.runtime.ref.*;), while the latter can omit them, as they are available by default.

Since SQLJ is translated to Java code that uses JDBC to access the database, the default connection used by SQLJ cannot make connections to remote databases. You can, however, access remote data through database links.[3]

12.2.2 LOADING JAVA BYTECODES INTO ORACLE

When developing server-side Java code, there are two ways to upload the code to an Oracle instance:

- You compile and test your code on the client, perhaps using a Java IDE like JDeveloper, create your .class files or a JAR archive containing the .class files and resources, and upload them to the database. In other words, you upload the finished product.
- You upload the Java source code and use the Java compiler of JServer to create the compiled Java files.

---

[3]A database link allows you to access objects stored on a remote database. A database link, say MKTG, points to a remote database owned by the marketing department. If you have the appropriate privileges, you can access the customer table stored in the remote database using the following syntax:

```
select * from customer@MKTG;
```

In both cases, however, you must physically upload files into the Oracle database. There are two ways to do this:

- You use the standard utility *loadjava*, located in $ORACLE_HOME/bin. *loadjava* requires a number of command-line parameters, including the names of the files you want to upload to Oracle, and loads the Java files and resources as Oracle schema objects.
- You use the PL/SQL overloaded procedure *loadjava()*, in the DBMS_JAVA package, to upload Java files and resources programmatically.

The discussion in this section focuses on the first method, using *loadjava* from the command line.

The syntax required for the proper use of *loadjava* follows:

```
loadjava {-user | -u} username/password[@database]
     [-option_name -option_name ... ] filename filename ...
```

The most commonly used command-line options are listed in Table 12.4.

TABLE 12.4 Commonly Used *loadjava* Command-Line Options

OPTION NAME	EFFECT
-resolve	After all files and resources specified on the command line are loaded and compiled, this option forces the resolution of all external references in those classes. It cannot be used together with –andresolve. If neither option is given, the files are loaded but not compiled and resolved.
-andresolve	Unlike –resolve, this option does not compile and resolve previously loaded classes.
-definer	Informs JServer that the methods of the uploaded classes must be executed with the privileges of the class definer rather than the invoker of the methods. The latter is the default JServer security policy.
-force	Forces the loading of classes whether or not they were previously loaded. By default, previously loaded classes are not reloaded.
-grant	Grants the listed users the EXECUTE privilege on the uploaded classes.
-oci8	Instructs loadjava to connect to the Oracle instance using the JDBC OCI driver.
-schema	Uploads the specified Java classes creating Java schema objects in the specified schema. By default, loadjava creates the objects in the logon schema. It requires the CREATE ANY PROCEDURE and CREATE ANY TABLE privileges to be granted to the logon schema, if the schema specified with the –schema option differs from the logon schema.
-synonym	Instructs Oracle to create public synonyms for the uploaded Java classes, so that they become visible to all database schemas. It requires the CREATE PUBLIC SYNONYM privilege granted to the logon schema.
-thin	Instructs loadjava to connect to the Oracle instance using the JDBC Thin driver.
-verbose	Instructs loadjava to display messages during the uploading phases.

The simplest way to use loadjava is to create a Jar file containing all the classes and resources needed and then load it into Oracle using the –resolve option. If you stored all Java executables and resources in the file MyFirstExample.jar, and your database, named ORCL, runs on the node called LYON, you can upload your Java code using this syntax:

```
loadjava -user scott/tiger@lyon:1521:ORCL -thin -resolve -verbose \
  MyFirstExample.jar
```

The loadjava utility requires a precise syntax. All names and options must be separated only by spaces, not commas, while user lists must be separated only by commas and not spaces. For instance, in the next example you upload the jar file and specify a list of database users who receive the EXECUTE privilege on the methods being uploaded:

```
loadjava -user scott/tiger@lyon:1521:ORCL -thin -resolve -verbose \
 -grant JTAYLOR,SJONES,NBRENNAN MyFirstExample.jar
```

Oracle Corporation recommends that you get rid of Java objects using the same mechanism with which they were loaded in the database. To remove Java objects from user schemas, use either the Oracle-specific SQL syntax DROP JAVA [CLASS | SOURCE | RESOURCE] or the *dropjava* utility. If you upload a class using loadjava, and subsequently delete it using the DROP JAVA command, you must use the loadjava –force option when you reload the class again. If you don't specify the –force option, the upload will fail.

It is a good practice to use dropjava to remove Java objects that were uploaded through loadjava. For example, if you uploaded MyFirstExample.jar using loadjava, use the following syntax to delete all classes and resources contained in the jar file:

```
dropjava -user scott/tiger@lyon:1521:ORCL -thin MyFirstExample.jar
```

Not only is using dropjava the preferred way to remove Java objects, it is also the most convenient. If your jar file contains a large number of classes and resources, identifying all the objects to be removed could prove difficult. By using dropjava, you only provide the jar file; the utility removes the elements in the jar file cascadingly.

The dropjava utility accepts a subset of the options recognized by loadjava. The most commonly used command-line options are:

- –oci8 and –thin direct dropjava to connect to the Oracle instance using either the thin or the thick (OCI8) JDBC driver

- –schema allows you to drop objects from another user's schema if you have the DROP ANY PROCEDURE privilege
- –synonym drops the public synonyms for all methods created by loadjava.

After you have loaded Java objects into, or dropped them from, your database schema, it is a good practice to verify the status of the loaded classes. The database exposes useful object-level information through the USER_OBJECTS table, which can be queried to determine the status of your objects. Use the following SQL script from SQL*Plus to display all Java-related objects appearing in your schema:

```
set linesize 132
set pagesize 24
column obj_name heading 'Java name'
column OBJECT_TYPE heading Type
column STATUS heading Status
select substr(object_name,1,60) obj_name, OBJECT_TYPE,STATUS
from user_objects where object_name not like 'SYS_%'
and object_name not like 'CREATE$%'
and object_name not like 'JAVA$%'
and object_name not like 'LOADLOB%'
and object_type like 'JAVA %';
```

Running the script shown above against the SCOTT schema, after you have loaded the Java examples discussed in this chapter, produces the following output:

```
Java name                                                    Type               Status
------------------------------------------------------------ ------------------ -------
/2e6b1c4a_GetSessionId_SJProfi                               JAVA RESOURCE      VALID
Fibonacci                                                    JAVA CLASS         VALID
FirstStoredProc                                              JAVA CLASS         VALID
GetSessionId                                                 JAVA CLASS         VALID
GetSessionId_SJProfile0                                      JAVA CLASS         VALID
GetSessionId_SJProfileKeys                                   JAVA CLASS         VALID
META-INF/MANIFEST.MF                                         JAVA RESOURCE      VALID
SecondStoreProc                                              JAVA CLASS         VALID
Swap                                                         JAVA CLASS         VALID
TryRemote                                                    JAVA CLASS         VALID
TryRemote_SJProfile0                                         JAVA CLASS         VALID
TryRemote_SJProfileKeys                                      JAVA CLASS         VALID
connections.properties                                       JAVA RESOURCE      VALID

13 rows selected.
```

12.2.3 PUBLISHING JAVA CLASSES IN THE DATABASE

In order to make Java procedures and functions available to other database objects, you must publish their signatures to the data dictionary; that is, you must create PL/SQL wrappers, called *Call Specs*, that map Java procedure names and parameter types to their PL/SQL counterparts.

A Java procedure or function can be defined as:

- a top-level call specification
- a member of a package
- a member of an object type

A top-level call specification maps a Java object that is available in the schema where it is defined. For example, user SCOTT creates a Java procedure called FirstProcedure and uses the following SQL statement to publish it:

```
CREATE OR REPLACE PROCEDURE FIRST_PROCEDURE ( u_name VARCHAR2)
AS LANGUAGE JAVA
NAME 'StoredProcedure.FirstProcedure(java.lang.String)';
```

The syntax shown above defines a top-level call specification, because the procedure is defined at the same hierarchical level as other objects, such as tables and views, at the top level of the SCOTT schema. In other words, other users could call FIRST_PROCEDURE using the dot notation, as in SCOTT.FIRST_PROCEDURE('Robert');.

Java procedures can also be grouped in PL/SQL packages (see Chapter 8 if you don't remember what a PL/SQL package is). A package consists of two parts, a required package specification and an optional package body. The package-specification section declares types, constants, variables, exceptions, and subprograms exported by the package. The package-body section provides the implementation for the specification. If the package is written entirely in PL/SQL, its package body is almost always present. However, if the implementation of the procedures and functions is in Java, it is required to expose the Java call specifications in the package specification, omitting the package body.

The object-relational implementation of Oracle 8i allows object types to have member functions or procedures written in Java. When the object type is defined using the CREATE OBJECT syntax, either the MEMBER FUNCTION or the MEMBER PROCEDURE verb can be used to encapsulate behavior into the object being created.

In the following sections, you will see examples of all types of call specifications, starting with top-level calls.

The syntax for publishing top-level specifications is as follows:

```
CREATE [OR REPLACE]
{ PROCEDURE proc_name [(parameter [, parameter] …)]
| FUNCTION func_name [(parameter [, parameter] …)] RETURN  sql_type }
[ AUTHID { DEFINER | CURRENT_USER } ]
```

```
[PARALLEL_ENABLE]
[DETERMINISTIC]
{ IS | AS } LANGUAGE JAVA
NAME 'method_full_name
     ( java_type_fullname [, java_type_fullname] … )
     [return ret_type]';
```

PL/SQL has been covered extensively in the preceding chapters, so most of the syntax shown above should be familiar to you. Table 12.5 provides some information about the more esoteric keywords used to define top-level call specifications.

Using the syntax introduced above, you can now publish the Java function that computes the Fibonacci series developed at the beginning of the chapter.

```
CREATE OR REPLACE
FUNCTION FIBONACCINUMBER ("num" IN NUMBER)
RETURN NUMBER
AUTHID CURRENT_USER
AS LANGUAGE JAVA
NAME 'Fibonacci.fibonacciNumber(int) return int';
```

The top-level call specifications for the other examples developed in the chapter, *increaseSalary()* and *swap()*, are shown below:

TABLE 12.5 Parameters Used to Publish Top-Level Stored Procedure Specifications in the Data Dictionary

KEYWORD	EFFECT
AUTHID	Determines whether a stored procedure is run with the privileges of the schema under which the stored procedure was created or with the privileges of the schema that invokes the stored procedure. The same applies to unqualified schema object references.[4]
PARALLEL_ENABLE	Determines whether a stored function can be safely used together with the parallel query option. If the stored function is used in a slave session of a parallel DML query, the result of the function must not depend on the state of its variables; otherwise the result could vary across sessions.
DETERMINISTIC	A stored function specified as deterministic should not depend on the state of session variables or schema objects. Deterministic functions are used by the optimizer to minimize redundant function calls. Only deterministic functions can be used in function-based indexes and in materialized views that rely on query-rewrite capabilities.

[4]If both the definer and the invoker of the procedure have the same object name defined in their respective schemas, and that object is referenced in the procedure without a fully qualified dot notation, the AUTHID clause directs Oracle to choose the object defined either in the definer's schema (DEFINER) or in the invoker's schema (CURRENT_USER).

```
CREATE OR REPLACE
PROCEDURE INCREASESALARY (incr IN NUMBER)
AUTHID CURRENT_USER
AS LANGUAGE JAVA
NAME 'FirstStoredProc.increaseSalary(float)';

CREATE OR REPLACE
PROCEDURE SWAP (p0 IN OUT NUMBER, p1 IN OUT NUMBER)
AUTHID CURRENT_USER
AS LANGUAGE JAVA
NAME 'Swap.swap(int[], int[])';
```

The preceding examples all use Java primitive data types as parameters or return values. If you want to pass or receive a Java String object, you must fully qualify the package in your call specification, as shown in the next example.

```
CREATE OR REPLACE
PROCEDURE COMPUTEMEANVARIANCE ( p0 IN VARCHAR2, p1 IN VARCHAR2,
                                p2 OUT NUMBER, p3 OUT NUMBER)
AUTHID CURRENT_USER
AS LANGUAGE JAVA
NAME 'SecondStoreProc.computeMeanVariance(java.lang.String,
     java.lang.String, float[], float[])';
```

The `java.lang` package is available by default to Java programs, but must be referred to explicitly in call specifications.

The syntax used to define package-level call specifications is shown below:

```
CREATE [OR REPLACE] PACKAGE package_name
[AUTHID {CURRENT_USER | DEFINER}]
 {IS | AS}
 [type_definition [type_definition] ...]
 [cursor_spec [cursor_spec] ...]
 [item_declaration [item_declaration] ...]
 [{subprogram_spec | call_spec} [{subprogram_spec | call_spec}]...]
END [package_name];

[CREATE [OR REPLACE] PACKAGE BODY package_name
{IS | AS}
  [type_definition [type_definition] ...]
  [cursor_body [cursor_body] ...]
  [item_declaration [item_declaration] ...]
  [{subprogram_spec | call_spec} [{subprogram_spec | call_spec}]...]
```

```
 [BEGIN
       sequence_of_statements]
 END [package_name];]
```

Suppose you change your mind and want to package together all the procedures and functions developed so far, in a package named STRPRC. The following syntax will accomplish the task:

```
CREATE OR REPLACE PACKAGE STRPRC AUTHID DEFINER AS
FUNCTION FIBONACCINUMBER ("num" IN NUMBER)
 RETURN NUMBER
AS LANGUAGE JAVA
NAME 'Fibonacci.fibonacciNumber(int) return int';
PROCEDURE INCREASESALARY ("incr" IN NUMBER)
AS LANGUAGE JAVA
NAME 'FirstStoredProc.increaseSalary(float)';
PROCEDURE GETSESSIONID AS LANGUAGE JAVA
NAME 'GetSessionId.getSessionId()';
PROCEDURE COMPUTEMEANVARIANCE (p0 IN VARCHAR2, p1 IN VARCHAR2, p2
OUT NUMBER, p3 OUT NUMBER)
AS LANGUAGE JAVA
NAME 'SecondStoreProc.computeMeanVariance( java.lang.String,
                                           java.lang.String,
                                           float[], float[])';
PROCEDURE SWAP (p0 IN OUT NUMBER, p1 IN OUT NUMBER)
AS LANGUAGE JAVA
NAME 'Swap.swap(int[], int[])';
END STRPRC;
```

To invoke the Java stored procedures contained in the STRPRC package, you must now use the dot notation, as in the following example:

```
STRPRC.INCREASESALARY(0.04);
```

Since the AUTHID clause appears at the package-specification level, and its value is DEFINER, all the methods grouped in the package run using the privileges of the schema where the package is created.

The last type of call specification is the one that allows you to encapsulate data structures with functions and procedures in an object type.

The generic syntax for writing object type call specifications follows:

```
CREATE [OR REPLACE] TYPE type_name
[AUTHID {CURRENT_USER | DEFINER}]
{IS | AS} OBJECT (
```

```
  attribute_name datatype[, attribute_name datatype]...
  [ {MAP | ORDER} MEMBER {function_spec | call_spec}, ]
  [ {MEMBER | STATIC} {subprogram_spec | call_spec}
        [, {MEMBER | STATIC} {subprogram_spec | call_spec}]... ]
);

[CREATE [OR REPLACE] TYPE BODY type_name
{IS | AS}
  { {MAP | ORDER} MEMBER function_body;
   | {MEMBER | STATIC} {subprogram_body | call_spec}; }
        [ {MAP | ORDER} MEMBER function_body;
         | {MEMBER | STATIC} {subprogram_body | call_spec}; ]...
END;]
```

Using the syntax illustrated above, you create an object type that implements a very simple Customer object. The object type defines three attributes (name, address, and discount) and one member procedure, implemented in Java:

```
CREATE TYPE Customer_t AS OBJECT
(
    NAME         VARCHAR2(40),
    ADDRESS      VARCHAR2(50),
    DISCOUNT     NUMBER,
    MEMBER PROCEDURE setDiscount( disc NUMBER)
     AS LANGUAGE JAVA
     NAME 'CustomerDiscount.setDiscount(java.math.BigDecimal)'
);
```

The *setDiscount()* procedure sets the discount policy for each instance of Customer. The Java class CustomerDiscount, which implements the setDiscount() method, implements the JDBC 2.0 standard SQLData interface. The latter defines two methods, readSQL() and writeSQL(), which are called by the JDBC driver to read a stream of values and populate the Java class with run-time data.

The source code of CustomerDiscount follows.

```
import java.sql.*;
import java.io.*;
import oracle.sql.*;
import oracle.jdbc.driver.*;
import java.math.*;

public class CustomerDiscount extends Object
      implements SQLData
{
```

```
    private String sql_type;
    private String custName;
    private String custAddress;
    private BigDecimal discount;

    public void setDiscount(BigDecimal disc)
    {
        this.discount = disc;
    }

    //The methods below implement the SQLData interface.
    public String getSQLTypeName() throws SQLException
    {
      return sql_type;
    }

    public void readSQL(SQLInput stream, String typeName)
                throws SQLException
    {
      sql_type = typeName;
      custName = stream.readString();
      custAddress = stream.readString();
      discount = stream.readBigDecimal();
    }

    public void writeSQL(SQLOutput stream)
          throws SQLException
    {
       stream.writeString(custName);
       stream.writeString(custAddress);
       stream.writeBigDecimal(discount);
    }
}
```

To test the object type call specification, you being by creating an object table based upon customer_t:

```
CREATE TABLE CUSTOMER of CUSTOMER_T;
```

You then populate the object table with test data:

```
insert into customer values (customer_t('Toys for
Everybody','1, Melrose Court Miami Florida FL',0.05))
/
```

```
insert into customer values (customer_t('Skateboards
Magic','12, Sepulveda Blvd Los Angeles CA',0.07))
/
insert into customer values (customer_t('La Bonnita','L7
235 Jefferson Place Chicago IL',0.045))
/
```

The following simple PL/SQL anonymous block loops through the rows stored in CUSTOMER and set the discount policy for each customer:

```
SQL> declare
       p1 customer_t;
     begin
       for rec in (select value(p) pobj from customer p)
       loop
         p1 := rec.pobj;
         p1.setDiscount(0.08);
       end loop;
     end;
     /
PL/SQL procedure successfully completed.
SQL> commit;
Commit complete.
```

The setDiscount() method is mapped to your Java MEMBER PROCEDURE, invoked after having obtained a reference to the object stored in the customer object table. The procedure is made available through an object-type call specification.

12.2.4 USING JDEVELOPER'S AUTOMATED DEPLOYMENT FEATURE

By using Oracle JDeveloper as your Java IDE, you can automate and simplify the task of developing a Java stored procedure. The JDeveloper deployment wizard that supervises the deployment of Java stored procedures and functions is actually quite smart. It is able to read your Java source code to determine whether a parameter of a procedure is of IN, OUT, or IN OUT type. It also generates the loadjava syntax for you, uploading your classes to the target database. In addition, it creates the SQL syntax necessary to publish your Java methods, easily creating both top-level and package-level call specifications.

After you have completed and tested your Java stored procedure in a JDeveloper session, use the deployment wizard to upload the Java classes to the target database and to publish the Java methods.

To activate the deployment wizard from within JDeveloper, click on the project node in JDeveloper's project navigator, and press the right mouse button. Choose the "New Deployment Profile" option from the pop-up menu, as shown in Figure 12.1.

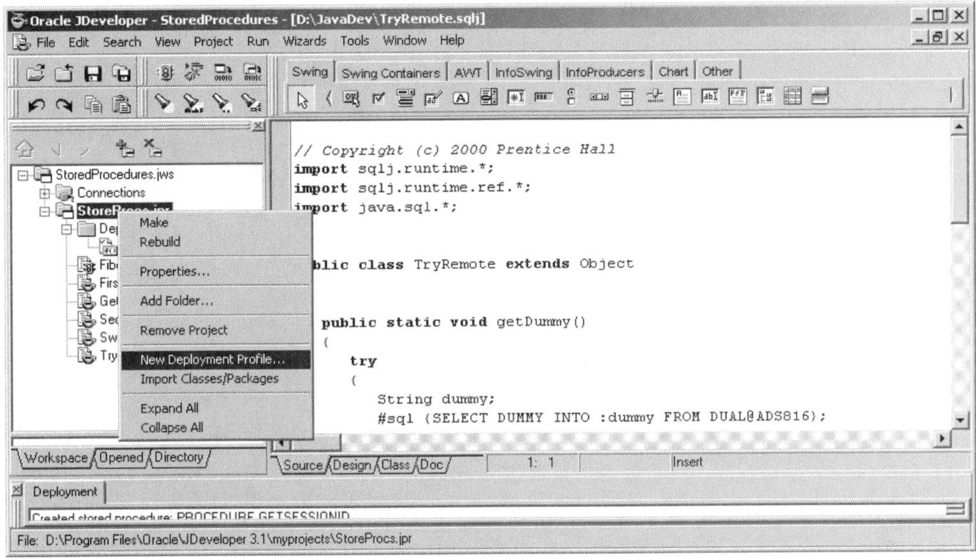

FIGURE 12.1 A pop-up window allows you to start the deployment wizard.

The deployment wizard guides you through the steps necessary to select the required methods and deployment policies. As shown in Figure 12.2, the first page of the wizard allows you to select the deployment delivery method, in your case "Classes and Java Stored procedures to Oracle 8i."[5]

The next step, illustrated in Figure 12.3, demonstrates the intelligence of the wizard. It scans all files contained within the project for which you are specifying the deployment policy, and reads and interprets the Java syntax. Each class can be selected to allow it to be included in the deployment, or deselected to prevent its deployment. From that window, you can also access the advanced deployment options by clicking on the "Advanced..." button. In the resulting advanced-deployment option window, you can modify the way class dependencies are determined by JDeveloper, or exclude/include specific libraries or packages. The advanced-deployment option is not needed in this exercise, so instead click on the "Next" button, to display the list of Java methods to be published to the data dictionary.

Step 3 of the deployment wizard, illustrated in Figure 12.4, displays all the Java methods identified by the preceding step and allows you to specify important aspects of the deployment policy. For instance, you can select/deselect each

[5]The very first time you use the wizard, the first page displayed is a welcome page. You can uncheck the checkbox marked "Display this page next time" to prevent it from appearing when you subsequently invoke the deployment wizard. From that moment on, the first page becomes the page shown in Figure 12.2.

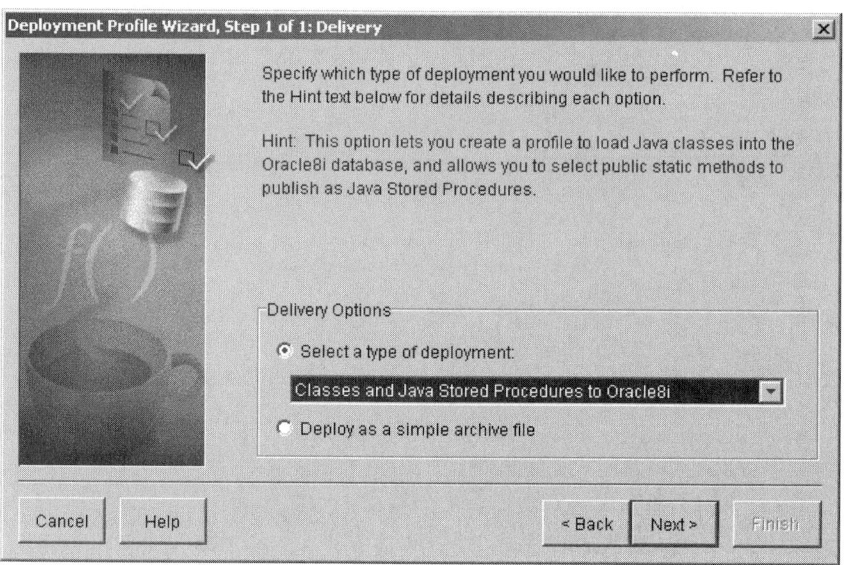

FIGURE 12.2 The deployment delivery is selected.

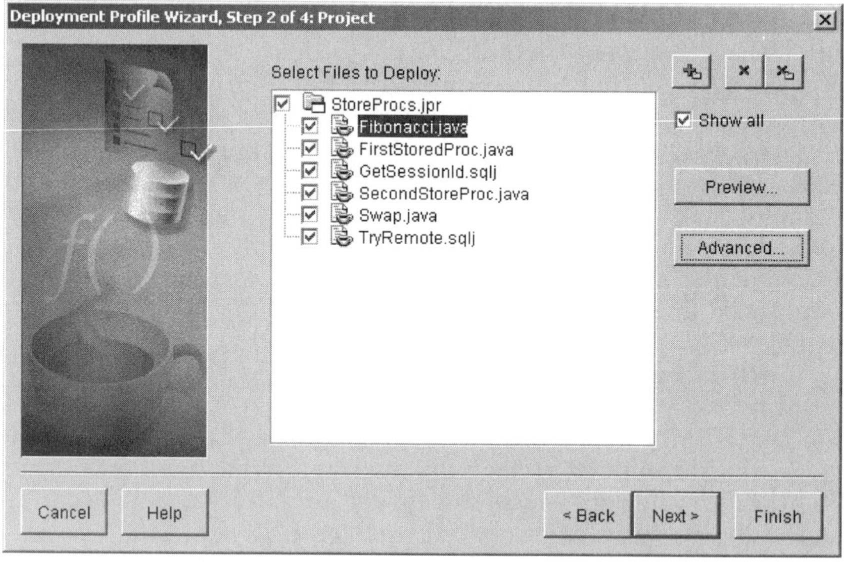

FIGURE 12.3 You can choose the Java classes to be deployed.

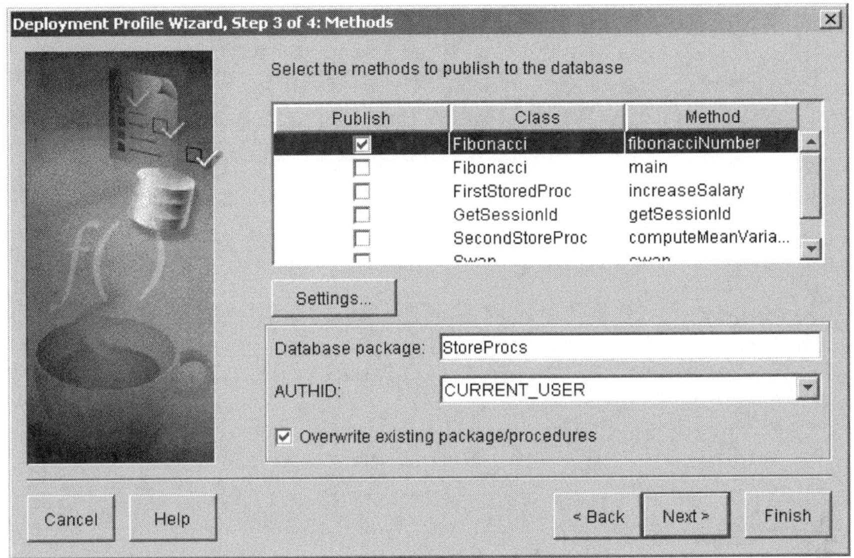

FIGURE 12.4 You can specify deployment options for each method.

method displayed in the grid, and this allows you to control the deployment of single methods defined in your classes. The same window also allows you to choose a package name if you want to publish package-level call specifications. If you leave this field blank, the deployment wizard generates top-level call specifications. Additionally, you can specify whether the Java stored procedures will run with invoker or definer privileges, and you can direct loadjava to overwrite existing packages and procedures. This is equivalent to specifying the –force option when using loadjava from the command line.

If you highlight a method and click on the "Settings …" button, the Settings window is displayed by the wizard, as shown in Figure 12.5.

Note that the wizard scanned your Java code, detecting the type of each of your parameters. The wizard does not allow you to change an IN parameter to an OUT parameter; the OUT option is not displayed in the drop-down menu if the parameter in question cannot be logically used as an OUT parameter. However, you can change the PL/SQL return type of functions by selecting an alternative type instead of the default type suggested by the wizard.

The last step of the wizard allows you to specify a connection profile that determines the schema where the Java classes are uploaded.

In the example shown in Figure 12.6, the Java classes are uploaded in the SCOTT schema, as specified by the connection profile.

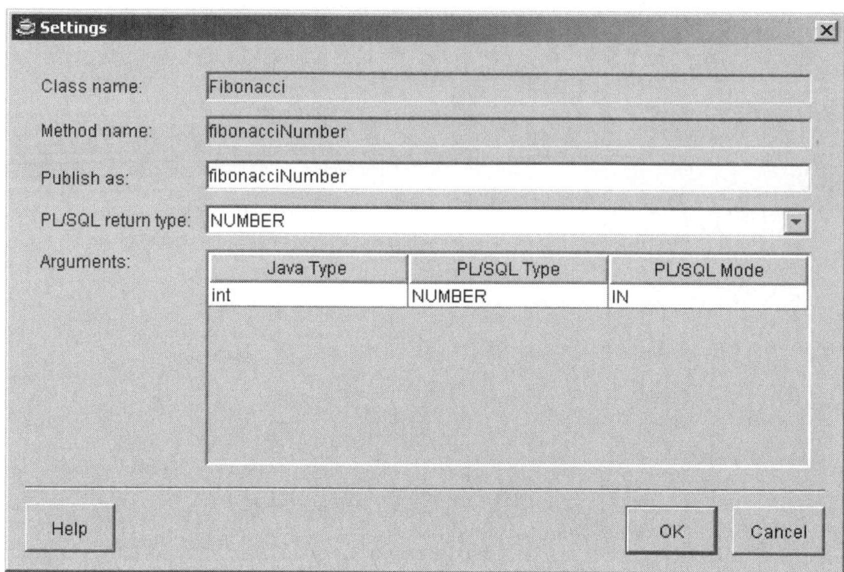

FIGURE 12.5 The wizard allows you to modify method-level settings.

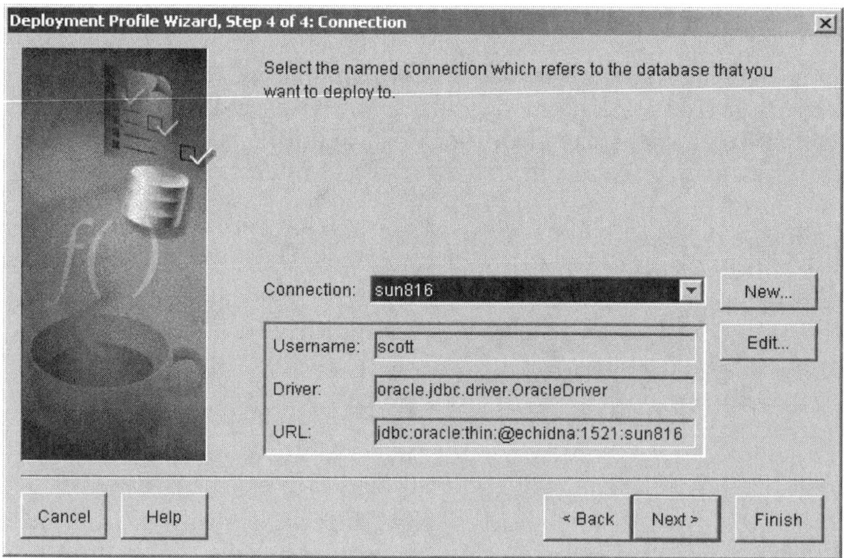

FIGURE 12.6 A connection profile specifies the schema use for class uploading.

12.3 MAKING JAVA AND PL/SQL INTERACT

Server-side programming in Oracle can be accomplished using the two supported languages, PL/SQL and Java, interchangeably. Java stored procedures can call PL/SQL procedures/functions, and vice versa. The ability to integrate the two worlds is one of the best features offered by the Oracle platform; developers can use Java for tasks best accomplished using a truly object-oriented language, and PL/SQL for low-level data access, an area in which PL/SQL shines. For a comparison of the points of strength and weakness of the two languages, see section 12.4, "PL/SQL versus Java: Choosing the Right Tool for Your Task."

12.3.1 CALLING PL/SQL FROM JAVA

Both JDBC and SQLJ allow you to call stored procedures and functions from Java. Table 12.6 illustrates the syntax required to call parameterless stored procedures, stored procedures with parameters, and stored functions from JDBC and from SQLJ.

In order to see JDBC and SQLJ at work, interacting with PL/SQL, you code three PL/SQL procedures, or, more precisely,

- ❑ one parameterless procedure
- ❑ one procedure that takes parameters
- ❑ one function

This is illustrated below:

```
CREATE OR REPLACE
FUNCTION DEPT_SAL_SUM (DEPT NUMBER) RETURN NUMBER
IS
```

TABLE 12.6 Syntax Used to Call Stored Procedures and Stored Functions

	JDBC	SQLJ
Parameterless Stored Procedure	CallableStatement cs = conn.prepareCall("{ CALL proc }");	#sql { CALL proc() };
Stored Procedure with Parameters	CallableStatement cs = conn.prepareCall("{ CALL proc(?,?) }");	#sql { CALL proc(par1,par2,...) };
Stored Function	CallableStatement cs = conn.prepareCall("{ ? = CALL func(?,?) }");	#sql result = { VALUES(func(par1,par2,...)) };

```
SUM_SAL NUMBER :=0;
BEGIN
    SELECT SUM(SAL) INTO SUM_SAL FROM EMP WHERE DEPTNO = DEPT;
    RETURN SUM_SAL;
END;
/

CREATE OR REPLACE
PROCEDURE PRINT_DATE
IS
TOD_DATE VARCHAR2(10);
BEGIN
    SELECT TO_CHAR(SYSDATE,'MM-DD-YYYY')
    INTO TOD_DATE
    FROM DUAL;
    DBMS_OUTPUT.PUT_LINE(TOD_DATE);
END;
/

CREATE OR REPLACE
PROCEDURE RAISE_SALARY (EMPID NUMBER, SAL_INCR NUMBER)
IS
BEGIN
    UPDATE EMP SET SAL = SAL * (1 + SAL_INCR)
    WHERE EMPNO = EMPID;

EXCEPTION
    WHEN OTHERS THEN
    DBMS_OUTPUT.PUT_LINE(
         'Stored proc raise_salary raised exception');
END;
/
```

You can now test calling the PL/SQL function and procedures from Java, using JDBC. The source code follows:

```
import java.sql.*;
import oracle.sql.*;
import oracle.jdbc.driver.*;

public class TestPLSQLIntegration extends Object
{
  public static void testPLSQL(int empid, int deptno,
                               float salIncr)
```

```
  {
      CallableStatement cs;
      try
      {
         Connection conn =
         DriverManager.getConnection("jdbc:default:connection:");
         cs = conn.prepareCall("{CALL PRINT_DATE}");
         cs.execute();
         cs = conn.prepareCall("{CALL RAISE_SALARY(?,?)}");
         cs.setInt(1,empid);
         cs.setFloat(2,salIncr);
         cs.executeUpdate();
         System.out.println("Salary for emp "+
                             empid + " has been raised");
         cs = conn.prepareCall("{? = call DEPT_SAL_SUM(?)}");
         cs.registerOutParameter(1,Types.BIGINT);
         cs.setInt(2,deptno);
         cs.executeUpdate();
         int sum_sal = cs.getInt(1);
         System.out.println(
                        "The sum of all salaries " +
                        "for dept" + deptno +
                        " is: " + sum_sal);
      }
      catch (SQLException exc)
      {
         System.out.println("Exception: " + exc.getMessage());
         exc.printStackTrace();
      }
   }
}
```

After you deploy the Java stored procedure to the database, you can test it from SQL*Plus:

```
SQL> call testplsql(7900,30,0.015);
07-02-2000
Salary for emp 7900 has been raised
The sum of all salaries for dept 30 is: 9414
```

The same test can be performed using SQLJ instead of JDBC. The source code that invokes the same PL/SQL function and procedures is shown below. Note its brevity, as compared to the relative wordiness of JDBC.

```
import java.sql.*;

public class TestPLSQLFromSQLJ extends Object
{
   public static void testPLSQLFromSQLJ(int empid, int deptno,
                                         float salIncr)
   {
      try
      {
        int sumSal = 0;
        #sql { CALL PRINT_DATE() };
        #sql { CALL RAISE_SALARY(:IN empid, :IN salIncr) };
        System.out.println("Salary for emp " + empid +
                           " has been raised");
        #sql sumSal = { VALUES (DEPT_SAL_SUM(:IN deptno)) };
        System.out.println("The sum of all salaries for "+
                           "dept " + deptno + " is: " + sumSal);
      }
      catch (SQLException exc)
      {
         System.out.println("Exception: " + exc.getMessage());
         exc.printStackTrace();
      }
   }
}
```

12.3.2 CALLING JAVA FROM PL/SQL

After the Java methods have been loaded and published to the database, they become visible to other database objects, and can be invoked from PL/SQL anonymous blocks, subprograms, and packages. In addition, Java methods can be called by PL/SQL when they are implemented as object type methods.

12.3.3 ACCESSING RESULT SETS

All the stored procedures and functions developed so far in this chapter have one thing in common: they do not return a result set. However, stored procedures can return result sets using the PL/SQL REF CURSOR type, which is called a weakly typed reference cursor because any query structure can be assigned to it.

The PL/SQL code shown below creates a simple package that simply defines a REF CURSOR object.

```
SQL> CREATE OR REPLACE
package csr is
 type csr is ref cursor;
end;
/
SQL> Package created.
```

A REF CURSOR object can be an OUT parameter to a function or procedure. The code below creates a PL/SQL function that returns the REF CURSOR defined in the package previously created.

```
SQL> CREATE OR REPLACE
function getemp(deptid number) return csr.csr is
empcsr csr.csr;
begin
open empcsr for select * from emp where deptno = deptid;
return empcsr; end;
/
     SQL> Function created.
```

You are now in a position to map the result set into the REF CURSOR from Java. The GetResultSet class defines the static method *getResultSet(int deptId)*, which will be uploaded to Oracle as a stored procedure. That method uses a JDBC CallableStatement object to get the REF CURSOR returned by the PL/SQL function GETEMP(). This is possible thanks to an Oracle extension to the standard JDBC CallableStatement object, the getCursor() method. By casting the CallableStatement object into an OracleCallableStatement object, the getCursor() method becomes available and can be invoked.

```
import java.sql.*;
import oracle.jdbc.driver.*;

public class GetResultSet extends Object
{
  public static void getResultSet(int deptId)
                    throws SQLException
  {
    CallableStatement cs;
    Connection conn =
      DriverManager.getConnection("jdbc:default:connection:");
    cs = conn.prepareCall("{ ? = call getemp(?) }");
    cs.registerOutParameter(1,
```

```
         oracle.jdbc.driver.OracleTypes.CURSOR);
      cs.setInt(2, deptId);
      cs.execute();
      /*
      ** The OracleCallableStatement extension has
      ** a getCursor() method, which allows a PL/SQL
      ** REF CURSOR to be returned as a ResulSet object.
      */
      ResultSet rset =
        ((oracle.jdbc.driver.OracleCallableStatement)cs).getCursor(1);
      while (rset.next())
      {
          System.out.println(
                         rset.getInt("deptno") + " " +
                         rset.getString("ename") + " " +
                         rset.getFloat("sal"));
      }
      rset.close();
      cs.close();
    }
}
```

After you compile the source code of GetResultSet, you can upload and publish it to the SCOTT schema as a Java stored procedure. You can then test it from an SQL*Plus session, as follows:

```
SQL> SET SERVEROUTPUT ON SIZE 5000
SQL> CALL dbms_java.set_output(5000);
Call completed.
SQL>  execute getresultset(10);
10 CLARK 1739.01
10 KING 3549.0
10 MILLER 922.74
PL/SQL procedure successfully completed.
```

The ability to obtain result sets from PL/SQL stored procedures provides a high degree of integration between Java and PL/SQL. Unfortunately, the opposite is not true: you cannot return a result set from a Java stored procedure because there is no mapping between a REF CURSOR and a ResultSet object. This lack of mapping prevents Java stored procedures from returning a result set to be published to the data dictionary through call-specification statements.

12.4 PL/SQL VERSUS JAVA: CHOOSING THE RIGHT TOOL FOR YOUR TASK

Since the first release of Oracle 8i, developers have been able to rely on two languages for server-side RDBMS programming. The high level of integration between the two environments, as shown in the preceding sections, allows for the combined use of PL/SQL and Java. They can indeed cooperate, giving Oracle developers an edge over competing environments, which must necessarily rely on only one server-side language to implement RDBMS processing.

PL/SQL and Java programmers often ask which tasks are best done with Java, and which with PL/SQL. There is no simple answer, because a lot depends on the background of the individual developer, but two basic rules apply:

- Use PL/SQL for the most efficient data retrieval from database tables.
- Use Java for the most demanding, computationally intensive tasks.

Even when JDBC is enhanced with Oracle's proprietary performance-boosting extensions, such as the *setDefaultRowPrefetch()* method, which allows for array fetching, PL/SQL is superior, and JDBC is *significantly* slower. You can prove this claim for yourself by using the following Java stored function that accesses the ALL_OBJECTS data dictionary table, fetching all rows into a large array, returning the number of rows fetched.

```
import java.lang.*;
import java.sql.*;
import oracle.sql.*;
import oracle.jdbc.driver.*;

public class ReadObjectsJava
{
 public static int readObjectsJava(int arraySize)
 {
  String objectName;
  int objectCount = 0;
  try
  {
    Connection conn =
     DriverManager.getConnection("jdbc:default:connection:");
    ((OracleConnection)conn).setDefaultRowPrefetch(arraySize);
    Statement sqlStmt = conn.createStatement();
    String sql = "SELECT object_name FROM all_objects";
    ResultSet dbResults = sqlStmt.executeQuery(sql);
    while (dbResults.next())
    {
      objectName = dbResults.getString(1);
      objectCount = objectCount + 1;
```

```
    }
    dbResults.close();
    sqlStmt.close();
  }
  catch (SQLException sqlError)
  {
    System.out.println("SQL Error!"+sqlError.getMessage());
  }
  return objectCount;
 }
}
```

A PL/SQL function follows. It performs the same task, using PL/SQL techniques.

```
CREATE OR REPLACE
FUNCTION ReadObjectsPLSQL (p_array_size IN NUMBER)
   RETURN NUMBER
IS
   cur            NUMBER                      := DBMS_SQL.open_cursor;
   fdbk           NUMBER;
   obj_nm_tab     DBMS_SQL.varchar2_table;
   indx           NUMBER                      := p_array_size * (-1);
   nbr_objects    NUMBER                      := 0;
BEGIN
   DBMS_SQL.parse (
      cur,
      'select object_name from all_objects',
      DBMS_SQL.native
   );
   DBMS_SQL.define_array (cur, 1, obj_nm_tab, p_array_size, indx);
   fdbk := DBMS_SQL.execute (cur);

   LOOP
      fdbk := DBMS_SQL.fetch_rows (cur);
      DBMS_SQL.column_value (cur, 1, obj_nm_tab);
      nbr_objects := nbr_objects + fdbk;
      EXIT WHEN fdbk != p_array_size;
   END LOOP;

   DBMS_SQL.close_cursor (cur);
   RETURN (nbr_objects);
EXCEPTION
   WHEN OTHERS
   THEN
      IF DBMS_SQL.is_open (cur)
      THEN
         DBMS_SQL.close_cursor (cur);
      END IF;

      RETURN (nbr_objects);
END;
/
```

You can use the timing feature provided by SQL*Plus to measure the time required by each function to perform the task. First, you must upload the Java class and publish the top-level Java stored function:

```
CREATE OR REPLACE
FUNCTION READOBJECTSJAVA ("arraySize" IN NUMBER)
 RETURN NUMBER
AUTHID CURRENT_USER
AS LANGUAGE JAVA
NAME 'ReadObjectsJava.readObjectsJava(int) return int';
```

Then you launch SQL*Plus, issue the set timing command, and test the two functions:

```
SQL> set timing on
SQL> variable n number
SQL> call readobjectsplsql(1000) into :n;
Call completed.
Elapsed: 00:00:06.59
SQL> print n
         N
----------
     19318

SQL> call readobjectsjava(1000) into :n;
Call completed.
Elapsed: 00:00:10.56
SQL> print n
         N
----------
     19318
SQL>
```

The two functions access the same table, using the same array size, and produce (as expected) the same result, but the function coded in PL/SQL is 38 percent faster than the corresponding Java function. The results shown above were obtained with a Sun Ultra5 workstation, equipped with 256 MB Ram, running Oracle 8.1.6 under Solaris 8. (Bear in mind that your mileage may vary if you attempt such comparisons, because of system and configuration differences.)

The situation radically changes, however, when computationally intensive tasks must be performed by code running within the RDBMS. At the beginning of the chapter, you developed the Java function that computes a Fibonacci series. The function was published to the SCOTT schema with the name of FIBONACCI-

NUMBER. To compare this Java implementation with PL/SQL, you must code a PL/SQL counterpart:

```
CREATE OR REPLACE
FUNCTION FibonacciPLSQL (p_in IN NUMBER)
   RETURN NUMBER
IS
BEGIN
   IF (p_in = 1) OR (p_in = 2) THEN
        RETURN 1;
   ELSE
        RETURN FibonacciPLSQL(p_in - 1) +
             FibonacciPLSQL(p_in - 2);
   END IF;
END;
/
```

We again use SQL*Plus with timing enabled to make the comparison. The result follows:

```
SQL> variable n number
SQL> call fibonacciplsql(30) into :n;
Call completed.
Elapsed: 00:00:29.83
SQL> print n
         N
----------
    832040

SQL> call fibonaccinumber(30) into :n;
Call completed.
Elapsed: 00:00:04.37
SQL> print n
         N
----------
    832040
```

The two tests performed above confirm what was stated at the beginning of this section; PL/SQL is still superior for raw data access, whereas Java performs much better for number crunching. Keep the results of this test in mind when designing your application and the structure of your stored procedures/functions.

SUMMARY

This chapter focused on Java stored procedures and functions. It examined how to code and deploy them to the RDBMS, and how to achieve interoperability between PL/SQL and Java. Throughout the chapter, PL/SQL functions and procedures were called from Java using both JDBC and SQLJ, and functions and procedures written in Java were published to a database that makes them available to other database objects through the familiar SQL and PL/SQL interfaces.

The chapter also explored the performance side of each language, concluding that PL/SQL still provides the fastest interface for data retrieval, while Java has an edge when computationally intensive tasks must be performed by methods running inside the database.

Chapter 13

BUSINESS COMPONENTS FOR JAVA AND XML

Oracle Business Components for Java is a framework of classes for multi-tier database applications constructed from reusable components. This chapter presents an introduction to the framework, with a little look under the hood, but the topic really deserves a book in its own right.

A database application typically consists of three parts:

- A client user interface or presentation layer.
- Business logic to validate and transform data, entered via the user interface into a form suitable for storage in a database table but preserving the data relationship and integrity specified by business requirements. For example, a shopping cart object ensures that one or more items are present before a purchase can be made, and creates an order record with related order items. This business logic is considered a middle-tier component because it provides the glue between the user view of the data and the physical storage format of the data in a database.
- The database tables used for data storage and retrieval.

Middle-tier logic is typically a set of business rules independent of user presentation details and data storage format. For example, a business rule may state that a client order should not remain unpaid for more than 60 days, or that an order must be shipped within three days of the purchase date. These rules must be consistently enforced, preferably in a layer of centralized reusable code for representation on any user interface or for storage in any database. Code in the middle tier can be implemented in two ways:

- Locally, using calls to business objects created in the same JVM as the client application.
- Remotely, using calls to a business objects executing in a different JVM from the client application, typically in another computer.

Creating reusable components, modules, or objects for middle-tier logic makes them easy to distribute. This is known as application partitioning. By design, the components, modules, and objects are decoupled from the specifics of user interface or database storage, and consistently provide appropriate transformations of user data into database data and back again.

The combination of the Java platform and Oracle Business Components for Java is a powerful means to execute the code of any Java context and any tier of a network architecture:

- A GUI client (e.g., a Java applet or application).
- An HTML client (e.g., a JavaServer page, or servlet).

- An Oracle business component can be wrapped up as a distributed object in the form of a CORBA object[1] or an Enterprise JavaBean (EJB).[2] CORBA and EJB components can be deployed to a suitable Web server or an Oracle8i database.

Oracle Business Components for Java is implemented through the combination of Java and XML. This chapter provides a brief description of XML and XML parsing concepts to enable you to appreciate the Oracle Business Components for Java framework. You will learn:

- How to use JDeveloper wizards to create and edit Business Components for Java.[3]
- How to manually write a command-line application that uses business components.
- How to package your business components for deployment to their runtime environments.

The chapter includes brief examples of the use of Oracle Business Components for Java in an HTML client, such as a servlet or a JavaServer page application.

13.1 THE BUSINESS COMPONENT FOR JAVA FRAMEWORK

Business Components for Java provides a framework of cooperating classes to implement database-access logic, with associated validation rules for managing data integrity, and no need to write low-level JDBC code. The framework provides a database-programming model that consistently hides the implementation details, freeing you to focus on data presentation, data management, and developing the validation rules to enforce data integrity. Although the implementation details of Oracle Business Components for Java are hidden, this chapter shows how Java and XML are used in combination to implement the functionality provided by the Oracle business component framework.

Historically, JDeveloper 2.0 was the first version to use the business component framework technology, which at the time was known as Java Business Object, called the Oracle JBO class library. The details of the Business Component

---

[1]CORBA, meaning Common Object Request Broker Architecture, is covered in Chapters 23 and 24 of this book.

[2]The Enterprise JavaBean is covered in Chapters 21 and 22 of this book.

[3]At the time of this writing, JDeveloper could only run on the Windows NT platform. A future pure Java release is planned that will run on any Java-enabled platform.

API were published with the release of JDeveloper 3.0. The JBO acronym appears in the package and class names of the Business Component API.

13.1.1 BUSINESS COMPONENT FOR JAVA APPLICATION STRUCTURE

An Oracle business components application represents a fully functional application module constructed from cooperating classes and XML files that manage data in one or more related database tables. The application module is a reusable component, which encapsulates all the logic and validation rules to coordinate data retrieval and modification operations. The application module also defines a transaction boundary, such that all changes made to one or more business component tables within the context of an application module are committed or rolled back as a transaction unit. Figure 13.1 shows an example of the architecture of an application module.

As can be seen in Figure 13.1, an application module is formed from one or more of the following components:

- *Entity objects* comprise one or more attributes. Each entity object represents a single row in a database table, and each attribute holds the value for a column in the row. In Figure 13.1, `ShoppingBasket`, `ShoppingItem`, and `SalesItem` are entity objects.

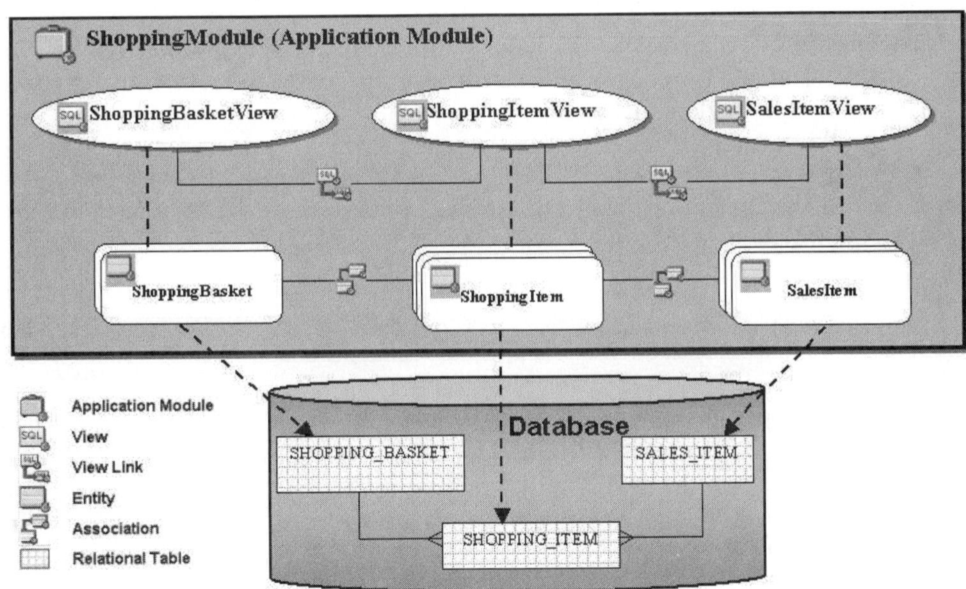

FIGURE 13.1 Business component application module architecture.

- *Association objects* form bi-directional links between entity objects. Each association object implements a relationship between two database tables.
- *View objects* define SQL queries to obtain filtered subsets of attributes from entity objects. In Figure 13.1, `ShoppingBasketView`, `ShoppingItemView`, and `SalesItemView` are view objects. Figure 13.1 shows each view obtaining data from a single source of entity objects. However, a view object can obtain data from more than one set of entity objects; this is analogous to performing a join operation between two database tables.
- *View link* objects, which form a one-way link between two view objects. A view link synchronizes data in two related view objects, thereby providing you with a way to implement a master-detail relationship in your application. A master-detail relationship requires one view object, called the master view, to provide a context for accessing data in a related view object, called the detail view. A master-detail scenario causes the detail information to be synchronized with the context provided by an active master row, such that the related detail rows are accessible when you change the master row. For example, if you only want to see the item details for a specific order, the order record is the master (or parent) for the order item records.
- Domain objects and validation rules are not represented in Figure 13.1. They can be associated with attributes in entity objects to implement business data validation rules.

The application data model (i.e., the collection of view objects defined in an application module) forms the default set of data accessible to a client application. The client application or presentation layer interacts with the view objects defined in application module.

Every entity object, view object, or other business component has a Java source and an associated XML source that together define the component's structure and behavior through a combination of declarative and programmatic constructs.

13.2 INTRODUCTION TO XML BASICS

The eXtensible Markup Language (XML) originated in Standard Generalized Markup Language (SGML), and is, in fact, a subset of SGML. The term *markup* has its roots in the world of typesetting, when hard-copy text was literally scribbled on, cut, and pasted to format a rendition of a document, the result being a newspaper, magazine, or printed document.

13.2.1 TEXT DATA AND MARKUP

An XML document consists of textual data and markup elements that describe the data. For example:

```
<AUTHOR>Glenn Stokol</AUTHOR>
```

Here `<AUTHOR>` and `</AUTHOR>` are markup elements, and the text `Glenn Stokol` is textual data. The *tag* name (e.g., `AUTHOR`) given to the markup element describes the text enclosed inside the element. Markup elements are erroneously often called tags. A tag is a descriptive case-sensitive name given to an element and the value it identifies.[4] Unlike HTML tags and other page-description languages, the XML markup elements do not describe formatting rules. The XML Stylesheet Language (XSL) provides a way to transform XML into a formatted markup like HTML.

XML markup elements are typically paired, the opening element (start-tag) beginning with a less-than symbol (<) and ending with a greater-than symbol (>).

The closing element (end-tag) is a string consisting of a less-than symbol and a forward-slash (</) and ends with a greater-than sign (>).

If the markup element does not enclose textual data, it is called an empty-element tag. Empty-element tags usually contain one or more *attributes* that give meaningful properties to the tag. An attribute is made up of a name assigned (=) to value, where the value is enclosed in quotes.[5] The empty-element tag name is enclosed by a less-than symbol (<) and a string made up of a forward-slash and greater-than symbol (/>). For example:

```
<AUTHOR NAME="Glenn Stokol" />
```

Here the markup element is not paired, but contains an attribute called `NAME` whose assigned property value is "`Glenn Stokol`".

13.2.2 ELEMENTS VS. ATTRIBUTES

There are no hard-and-fast rules about the use of paired-element tags versus empty-element tags with attributes. The rule of thumb is: "Use attributes only if they describe something about the tag itself, or when an element need not be broken into subcomponents."

---

[4]Caution, some early XML parsers do not enforce case-sensitive tag names.

[5]You can use single or double quotes, but must be consistent with the same attribute value. Double quotes are most common.

13.2.3 XML REPRESENTS HIERARCHICAL INFORMATION

XML markup elements can be nested to form hierarchical structures. For example, you may have a document that describes sales items:

```
<?xml version="1.0"?>
<saleitems>
  <book>
  <title>Oracle and Java: From client Server to e-Commerce</title>
  <publisher>Prentice Hall PTR</publisher>
  <author name="Elio Bonazzi" />
  <author name="Glenn Stokol" />
  </book>

  <book>
  <title>The XML Handbook</title>
  <publisher>Prentice Hall PTR</publisher>
  <author name="Charles F. Goldfarb" />
  <author name="Paul Prescod" />
  </book>
</saleitems>
```

LISTING 13.1 XML document describing sale items.

The <saleitems> element is called the root element because it represents the start of the hierarchical structure that follows. The <book> element is a nested element, and <title> is contained within the book.

XML documents usually begin with a prolog, or header, comprising an *XML declaration* and a *document type declaration*. Here is a minimal XML declaration describing the XML version, as seen in the <saleitems> example:

```
<?xml version="1.0"?>
```

The format of a document type declaration is:

```
<!DOCTYPE name SYSTEM "url">
```

In the <!DOCTYPE declaration, the name assigns a description of the type of document in use, and after the SYSTEM keyword an http URL to reference a file containing markup declarations expressing the document type definition (DTD). *Note:* a DTD is optional and can be embedded in its associated XML document. The DTD is used to check the structural integrity, or validity, of an XML document that enables an XML-based application to be robust and reliable.

On a Microsoft platform using Internet Explorer, which has a built-in XML parser, you can display the XML document elements in a treelike structure, and collapse or expand the tree nodes.

13.2.4 DOCUMENT TYPE DEFINITION (DTD)

The Document Type Definition describes the type of document being processed. For example, a DTD can be created for the sales items XML document, describing the structure of the document defining the allowed name for the root element, and allowed names for subelements in the document's hierarchical structure. An XML document that conforms to the named DTD is said to be *valid*. Using a DTD is like applying grammatical rules to text, and if the DTD rules are followed, the result is a valid text structure. The DTD for the `saleitems` XML file is:

```
<!ELEMENT saleitems (book+)>
<!ELEMENT book (title, publisher, author+)>
<!ELEMENT title (#PCDATA)>
<!ELEMENT publisher (#PCDATA)>
<!ELEMENT author EMPTY>
<!ATTLIST author name CDATA #REQUIRED>
```

LISTING 13.2 Document Type Definition for sale items.

Notes on Listing 13.2

- The tokens `ELEMENT`, `#PCDATA`, `EMPTY`, `CDATA`, and `#REQUIRED` must all be in uppercase text.
- The `<!ELEMENT` string declares an element type, its name, and its content enclosed in brackets. The EMPTY token indicates that the element does not contain text between the element tags (e.g., the `author` element).
- The `saleitems` element defines its content to be `book+`. The trailing plus sign (+), called an *occurrence indicator*, indicates that at least one or more books can be contained in the `saleitems` element. The DTD specification defines other occurrence indicators, such as *, meaning zero or more. The absence of an occurrence indicator means one and only one.
- The `book` element structure contains one `title`, one `publisher`, and one or more `author` elements.
- The `#PCDATA` content for `title` and `publisher` indicates that these elements can hold mixed character data, including child elements.
- The author element does not hold any content, but has an attribute list of one attribute.

- The <!ATTLIST string declares the name attribute for author. The CDATA token indicates that the attribute value is made up of character data only, and #REQUIRED indicates the value is mandatory.

Assuming that Listing 13.2 is saved in a file called saleitems.dtd, you associate the XML document with its document type using the <!DOCTYPE declaration, as follows:

```
<?xml version="1.0"?>
<!DOCTYPE saleitems SYSTEM "saleitems.dtd">
<saleitems>
  <book>
  <title>Oracle and Java: From client Server to e-Commerce</title>
  <publisher>Prentice Hall PTR</publisher>
  <author name="Elio Bonazzi" />
  <author name="Glenn Stokol" />
  </book>

  <book>
  <title>The XML Handbook</title>
  <publisher>Prentice Hall PTR</publisher>
  <author name="Charles F. Goldfarb" />
  <author name="Paul Precod" />
  </book>
</saleitems>
```

Microsoft Internet Explorer has a built-in XML parser allowing it to easily test XML and DTD documents. By default, Microsoft Internet Explorer displays the tree hierarchy represented by the XML document.

13.2.5 XML PARSERS, DOM AND SAX API'S

The XML world has many other features identified by acronyms. Of interest is the XML parser. It can be used as a standalone program to display the XML document tree and validate the document using a DTD, if present. Alternatively, the XML parser can be used programmatically to build and walk the tree of an XML document, or to perform event-based processing on elements found in the tree. Two programmatic interfaces are available:

1. The *Document Object Module* (DOM) provides a tree-based API to compile an XML document into an internal tree structure. Using the DOM API you can build and navigate a document structure by adding, modifying, or deleting elements and content.

2. The *Simple API for XML* (SAX) is an event-based API that reports parsing events to the application through callbacks. Parsing events usually occur at the start and end of elements, which are handled by an application that deals with events. The XML document tree is not constructed using SAX.

An implementation of an XML parser supports both the DOM and SAX API's.

13.2.6 STYLESHEETS (CSS AND XSL)

An XML parser can transform an XML document into another format using two forms of stylesheet:

- ❑ Cascading Stylesheets (CSS), typically used with HTML documents.
- ❑ XML Stylesheet Language (XSL).

Using CSS, you can format the XML document elements into a presentation format like HTML. You cannot format attributes contained in empty elements. The term *cascading* implies that you can combine various elements to arrive at a final resulting output format.

Using XSL, which obeys the XML document syntax, you can transform elements and attributes into a variety of formats, including: HTML, another XML document, or whatever suits your requirements.

This book does not discuss CSS and XSL syntax, because they are beyond its scope. More information about CSS and XSL can be found at the World Wide Web consortium Web site at http://www.w3c.org.

13.2.7 XML AND ORACLE BUSINESS COMPONENTS FOR JAVA

XML is an integral part of the Business Components for Java framework, which generates an XML file for every component created, and with BC4J technology utilizes an XML parser to process the information kept in the generated XML files.

For example, when you create an entity object, a Java source and associated XML file are created. Information contained in the entity object XML file describes the object structure (i.e., the attribute names) and their SQL and related Java data types. The XML file also contains references to declarative or programmatic validation rules assigned to the entity attributes.

You can customize your application by modifying the declarative rules defined in the XML file without modifying the associated Java code.

This chapter steps you through the creation of a business component application module consisting of a single entity and view object. The module can be used from any Java-client application. You will be shown how to construct a prototype GUI client and JavaServer page application to use the application module, using JDeveloper wizards to rapidly construct these prototype applications.

13.3 CREATING A BUSINESS COMPONENT APPLICATION MODULE

Oracle JDeveloper provides a Business Components for Java wizard and an editor to generate components and assemble them into an application module. The steps in building a client application that uses a business components application module are listed below.

1. Create a named connection for your business components project.
2. Create a project for your business components.
3. Generate and edit the business components.
   3.1 Generate an entity object based on a database table or view via the connection created in step 2.[6]
   3.2 Optionally, add validation rules to check the changes made to the attribute values of the entity. For example: check for accepted types of credit cards.
   3.3 Generate view objects based on the entity object.
   3.4 Build the application module comprising the view objects.
4. Test the application module's functionality and validation logic with a built-in testing tool provided by JDeveloper.
5. Create the client application providing the user interface or presentation layer for the application module.

JDeveloper provides several wizards for building GUI- and HTML-based client applications that utilize a business component application module. However, this chapter demonstrates how to use an application module from hand-coded client applications.

13.3.1 CREATING A NAMED CONNECTION FOR YOUR PROJECT

First, start JDeveloper from the Windows `Start` menu in the `Programs->Oracle JDeveloper 3.x` submenu, and create a connection. Your business component project must have a named connection because it is used to locate the database objects on which the entity objects are based. You can create a named connection in JDeveloper by right-clicking on the Connections folder to launch the connection manager wizard, as shown in Figure 13.2.

Clicking the New... button allows you to create a new named connection in the connection editor shown in Figure 13.3.

A connection required for a business component application must have a connection name, a JDBC driver, and associated driver-connection details, such

[6]Your database object can also be an Oracle synonym or snapshot.

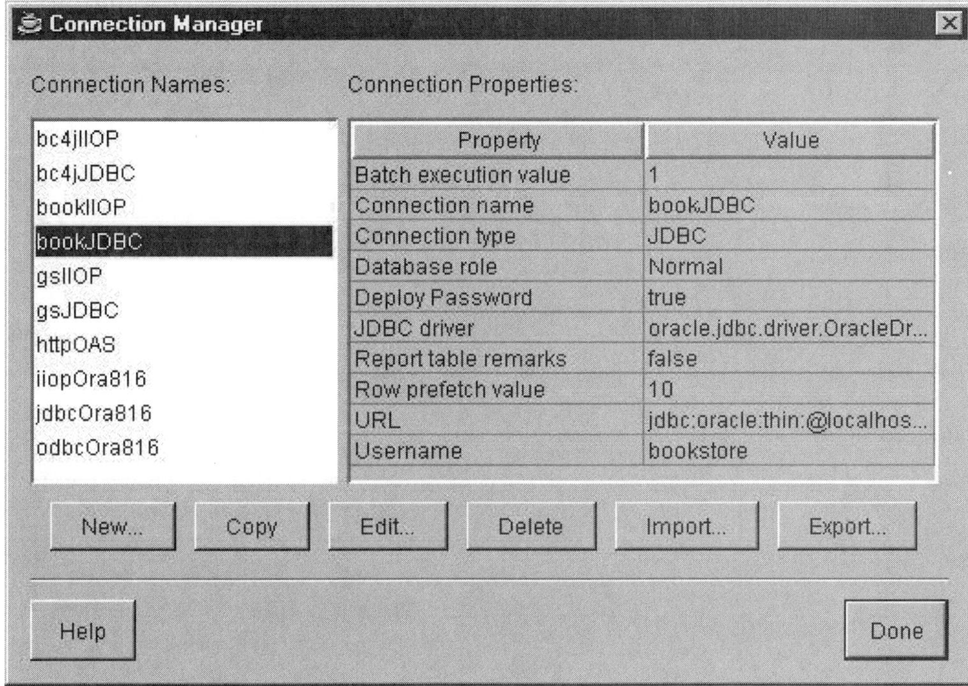

FIGURE 13.2 JDeveloper connection manager.

as the user name, password, and optional database role. The database-connection information entered depends on your choice of JDBC driver and connection method.

The connection settings chosen for the Row Prefetch, Batch Value, and Report `TABLE_REMARKS` depend on a JDBC driver supporting these features. Oracle JDBC drivers support these features for improving the execution of SQL operations performed with JDBC calls (see Chapter 10 for a discussion of these features).

It is recommended that you click the `Test Connection` button before closing the connection editor window to validate the connection details. A successful connection results in a success message next to the button:

If the connection is invalid (e.g., if you entered an incorrect user name/password combination), a failure message is displayed next to the `Test Connection` button:

Test Connection ORA-01017: invalid username/password; logon denied

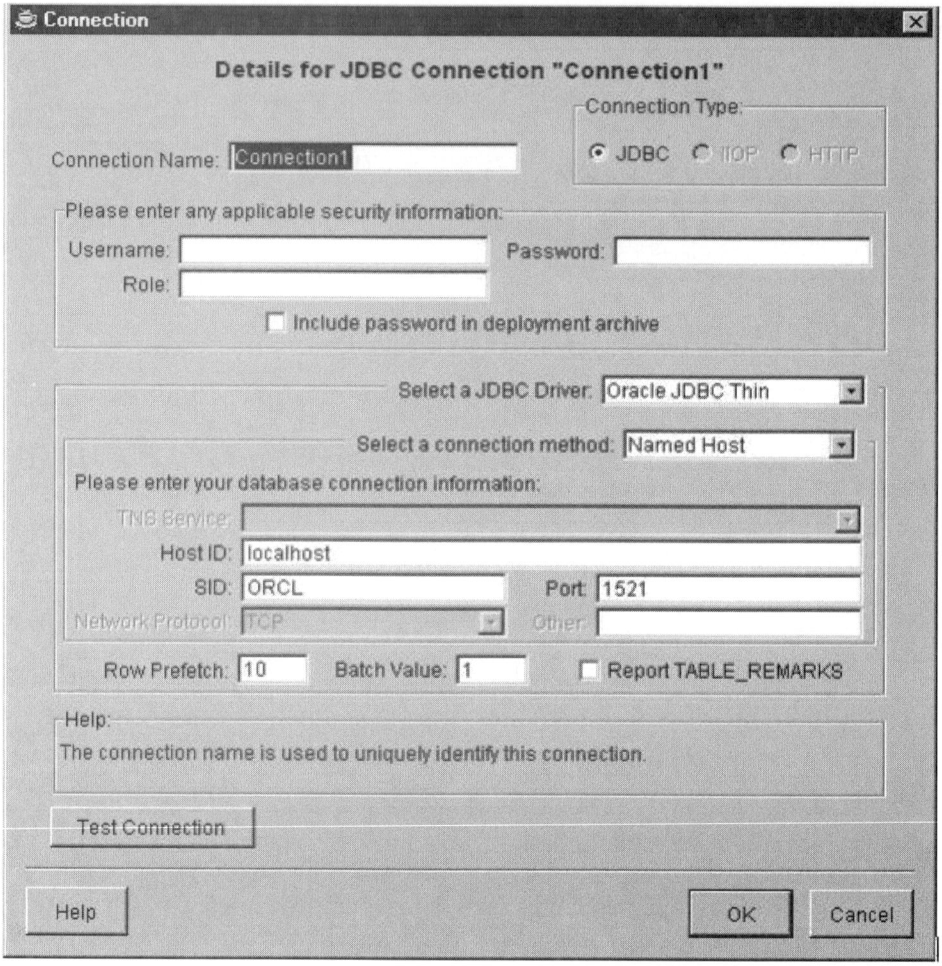

FIGURE 13.3 Creating a new database connection in JDeveloper.

At development time, the file `IDEConnections.properties`, located in the `bin` subdirectory of your JDeveloper installation directory, stores the connection details, which are available for use in all workspaces and projects. At runtime, the application module reads the connection details from a `connections.properties` file located in the project output root directory (i.e., in the project `CLASSPATH`). Therefore, the `connections.properties` file must be packaged with the business component application module at deployment time. Here is an example of a named connection in the properties file (spread over several lines to ease readability):

```
CM_Connection1=URL=jdbc:oracle:thin:@localhost:1521:ORCL,
ConnectionName=Connection1,
remarksReporting=false,
JdbcDriver=oracle.jdbc.driver.OracleDriver,
password=bookstore,
DeployPassword=true,
ConnectionType=JDBC,
defaultRowPrefetch=10,
user=bookstore,
defaultBatchValue=1
```

A connection identifier of the form `CM_Connection<n>`, where `<n>` is a numeric value starting at one, is created for each named connection. The connection details, such as connection name, username, password, and database properties, appear as a comma-separated list of `name=value` pairs.

The `ConnectionName` property value should never be changed once created, as the wizard generates code that references the connection name. Database-connection properties, such as username, password, and connection string, may be changed.

13.3.2 GENERATING BUSINESS COMPONENTS WITH JDEVELOPER

The discussion in this section will guide you through the JDeveloper project and business component wizard to build an application module that manages customer information. The customer application module contains a single view object based on one entity object. The entity object structure is derived from the `CUSTOMER` table.

13.3.2.1 Creating a Business Component Project. In JDeveloper, select the `File->New Workspace` menu item to create a new workspace, which is shown as a folder that will contain one or more project folders. Select the `File->Save` menu option to name the workspace file, such as `Customer.wks`. Create a project in the workspace by selecting the `File->Create Project...` menu. A project folder contains one or more source files created for the project application. JDeveloper displays the project wizard welcome page and then guides you through a three-step process.

1. Choose the project file name and type of project (see Figure 13.4).
2. Select the project options and properties (see Figure 13.5).
3. Provide documentation about the project (see Figure 13.6).

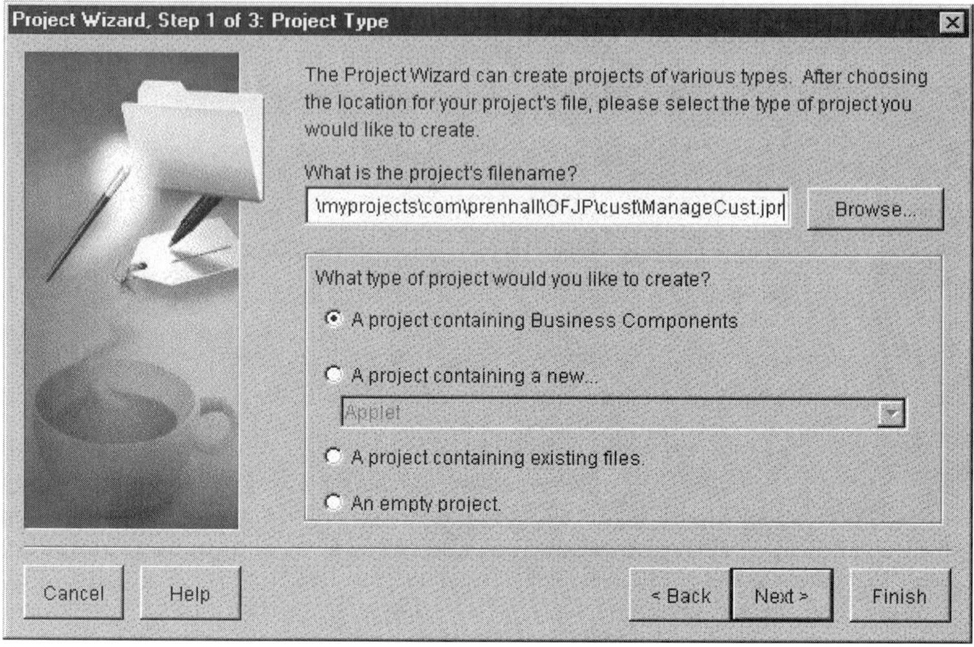

FIGURE 13.4 JDeveloper project wizard, step 1.

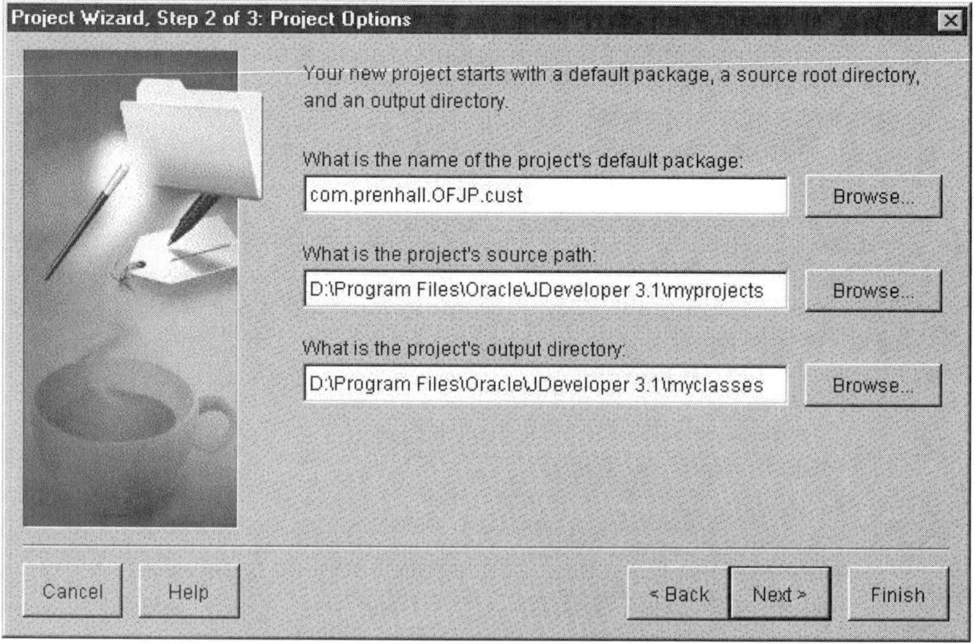

FIGURE 13.5 JDeveloper project wizard, step 2.

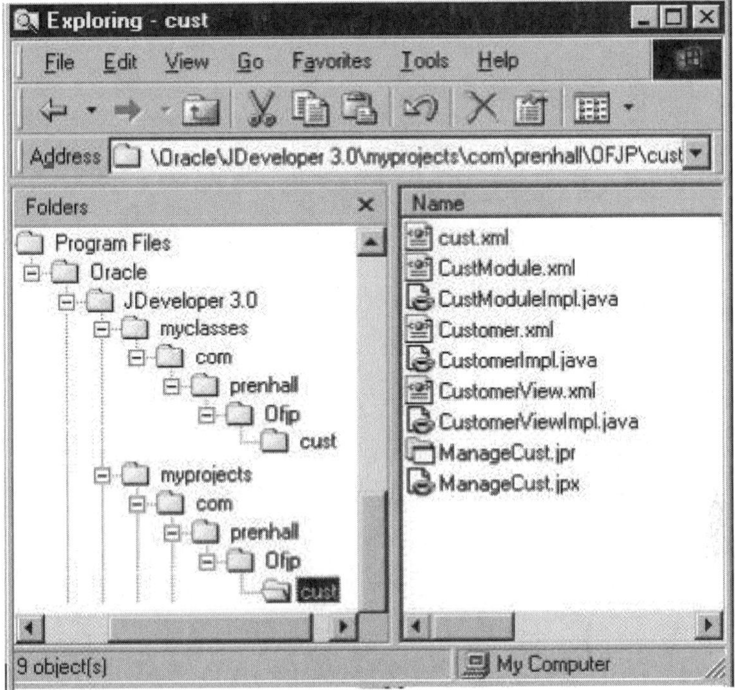

FIGURE 13.6 Project source and class directory structure.

In step 1 of the wizard, select the radio button to build "A Project containing Business Components" for JDeveloper to add the necessary class libraries to your project's CLASSPATH.

The default Java package name entered is assigned to all the classes created in the project. In Figure 13.5 the package name is `com.prenhall.OFJP.cust`. The `Project's source path` sets the root directory path for the Java source files in the project.[7] The `Project's output directory` is part of the project `CLASSPATH` containing compiled Java class files for the project. After the files in the project are created, and the classes compiled, the resulting directory structure for the project, if using the `com.prenhall.OFJP.cust` package, is shown in Figure 13.6.

The source files are saved in a subdirectory whose name is derived from the package name appended to the source path; the compiled class files are saved in a mirrored subdirectory structure below the output directory.

Selecting the checkbox labeled "Generate Project HTML File" in Figure 13.7 causes the text entered in this page to be saved in a project HTML file. The text

[7]Clicking the browse button allows you to add additional directories to the source path.

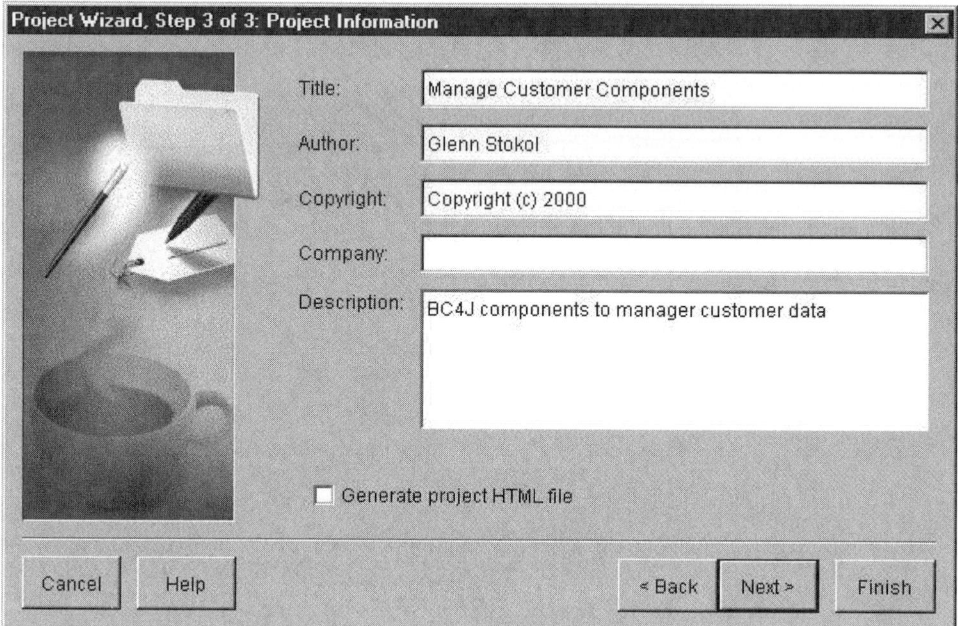

FIGURE 13.7 JDeveloper project wizard, step 3.

entered can be optionally used to generate header comments at the top of each Java source file created in the project. Clicking the `Finish` button creates the project file with a `.jpr` extension, after which JDeveloper starts the business component wizard.

13.3.2.2 Creating an Entity Object. Using the business component wizard is the quickest way to start generating business components and an associated application module. The business component wizard connects to a specified database connection, allowing you to choose the database object used to create entity objects. One entity object is created for each table or view selected from the database.

An entity object is an encapsulation of database data, storage details, and associated business logic. Structurally, an entity object resembles the database table, view, or snapshot upon which it is based. If an entity object is based on a table, for example, it has one attribute for each column in the table.

Using the Business Component Wizard

After the business component wizard is started, it shows the welcome page that describes the three major steps to be performed.

1. Select a database connection for your project. Create a database connection if none are available.
2. Create an initial Java package name for your project.
3. Add business components to the project.

Step 1: Select a Database Connection

Figure 13.8 shows the page for selecting the database connection.

Clicking the `New...` button next to the Connection pop list allows you to create a new database connection. Alternatively, you can click the `Edit...` button to change the attributes of the existing connection.

Step 2: Setting the Java Package Name

Figure 13.9 shows the page for the second step, where you enter the Java package name that will be assigned to all the component classes created in the project.

The name following the last period in the package is the name of the default application module. A default application module comprises all the view objects in the project. The application module name for the example in Figure 13.9 would be `CustModule`.

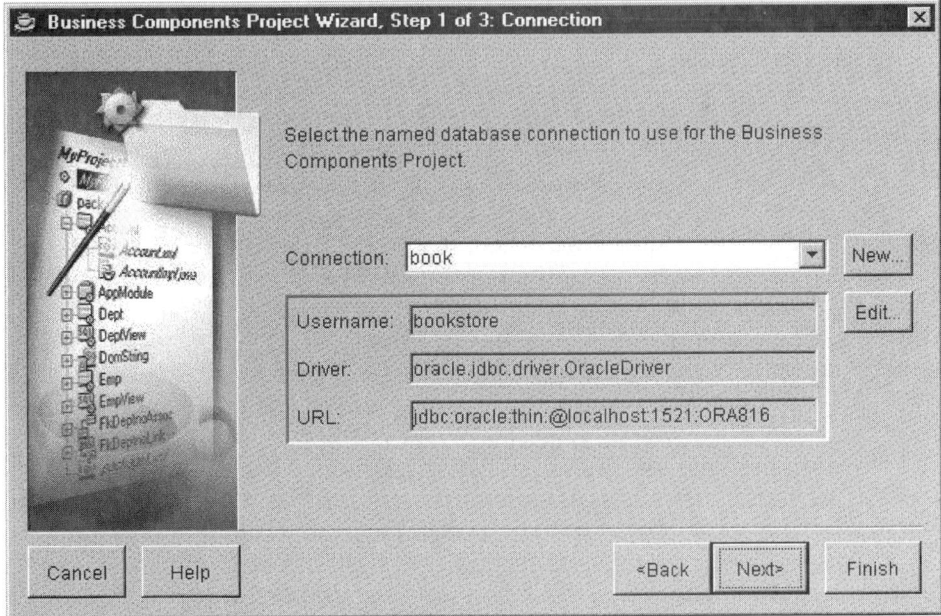

FIGURE 13.8 Select a connection for Business Components.

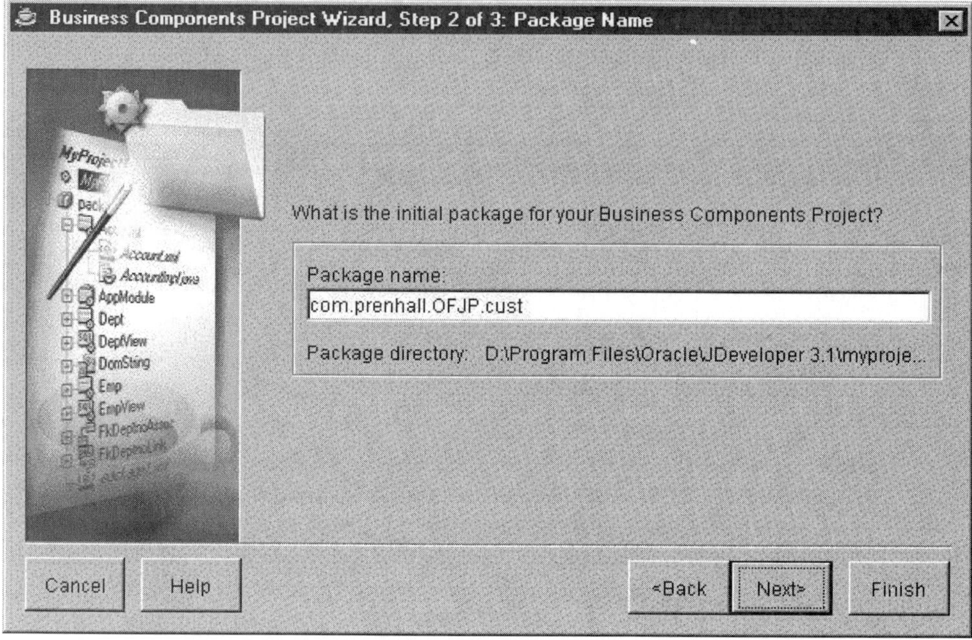

FIGURE 13.9 Select a package name for business components.

Step 3: Selecting tables for business components.

Figure 13.10 shows the page where you select a database table, view, synonym, or snapshot to provide the structure of an entity object.

Select `Tables`, `Views`, `Synonyms`, or `Snapshot` checkboxes to view the names of those types of objects in the `Available` list. In Figure 13.10, only the database table names are listed, and the `CUSTOMER` table has been copied to the `Selected:` list. A business component entity object is created for each database object copied to the selected list.

Selecting the `View objects and View links` checkbox generates a default view object for each entity table; view links are created for each pair of related tables if two or more tables are selected. The application module checkbox also becomes active if you select `View objects and View links`, allowing you to generate a default application module that comprises all the default view objects and view links generated by the wizard. In this example, you are only creating the entity object; you will create a view object and application module later. After selecting the tables and checkboxes, click the `Finish` button to generate the selected components.

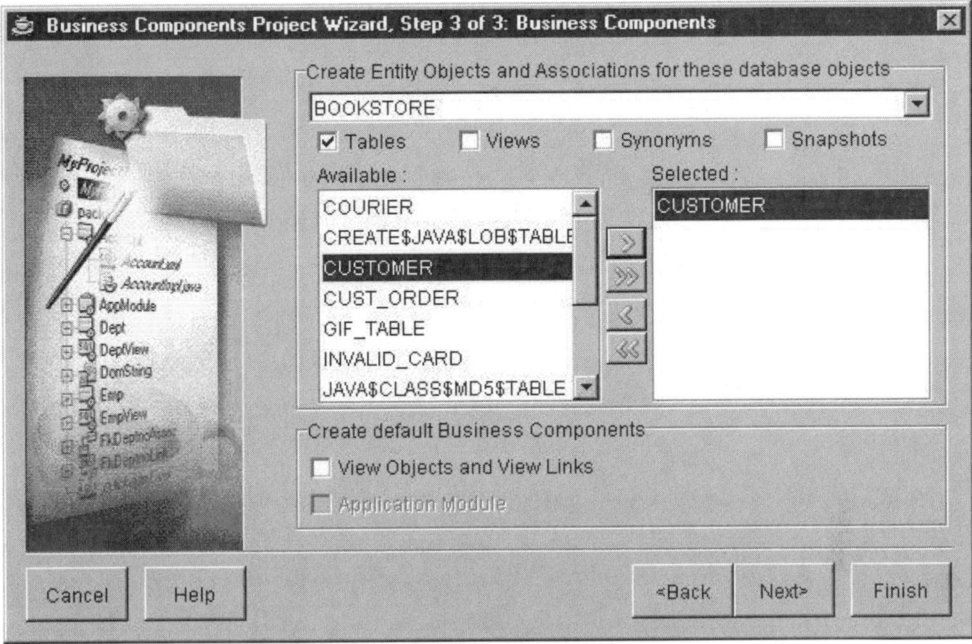

FIGURE 13.10 Select a database table for an entity object.

Business Component Files Generated

You can view the generated files in the JDeveloper navigator panel after the entity component is generated. Figure 13.11 shows the files generated in the project for the previous sequence of tasks.

The generated files created by the business component wizard are:

- A folder for the business component, named using the package name `com.prenhall.OFJP.cust`. This folder contains the following generated components for the `Customer` entity object:
    - The `cust.xml` file - used by JDeveloper to identify the business components that belong to the package.
    - The Customer folder, containing the files for the customer entity object:
        - Customer.xml describes the entity object structure (i.e., the attributes and keys).
        - CustomerImpl.java is a Java source implementing the structure and associated functionality defined by the Customer.xml file.
- The `ManageCust.jpx` file is used by JDeveloper to track the business component package name and the associated named connections used by the components in the project.

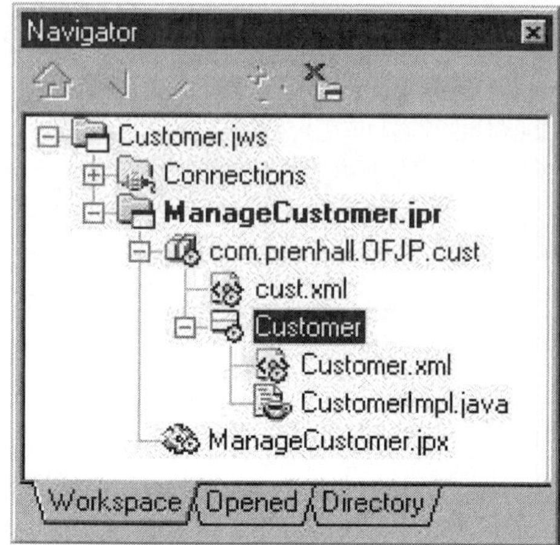

FIGURE 13.11 Generated entity object in JDeveloper navigator.

Two files represent each business component, like the entity object:

1. An XML file whose name is <component-name>`.xml`.
2. A Java file whose name is <component-name>`Impl.java`.

The XML file defines the structure of the component and any associations, while the Java file provides the implementation of the component object. The Java implementation class uses an XML parser to parse its associated XML file to extract the information it contains. In JDeveloper 3.1 or earlier, you can only view the XML file, and can only modify the XML file using the business component wizards or an editor external to the JDeveloper tool, such as Notepad or your favorite text or XML editor. The Java file can be viewed or modified using the JDeveloper source viewer/editor window.

The Entity Object XML File

The entity XML file describes the structure of an entity object. Attributes and keys (e.g., a primary key) form the structure of an entity object. Listing 13.3 shows some of the lines from the `Customer.xml` file for the `Customer` entity object.

```
<?xml version="1.0" encoding='WINDOWS-1252'?>
<!DOCTYPE Entity SYSTEM "jbo_02_01.dtd">

<Entity
   Name="Customer"
   DBObjectType="table"
   DBObjectName="CUSTOMER"
```

LISITING 13.3 Entity XML file – `Customer.xml.`

```
AliasName="Customer"
CodeGenFlag="4"
RowClass="com.prenhall.OFJP.cust.CustomerImpl" >
<DesignTime>
   <Attr Name="_isCodegen" Value="true" />
   <AttrArray Name="_publishEvents">
   </AttrArray>
</DesignTime>
<Attribute
   Name="Id"
   Type="oracle.jbo.domain.Number"
   ColumnName="ID"
   ColumnType="NUMBER"
   SQLType="NUMERIC"
   IsNotNull="true"
   TableName="CUSTOMER"
   PrimaryKey="true"
   Precision="6"
   Scale="0" >
   <DesignTime>
      <Attr Name="_DisplaySize" Value="0" />
   </DesignTime>
</Attribute>
<Attribute
   Name="Name"
   Type="java.lang.String"
   ColumnName="NAME"
   ColumnType="VARCHAR2"
   SQLType="VARCHAR"
   IsNotNull="true"
   TableName="CUSTOMER"
   Precision="30" >
   <DesignTime>
      <Attr Name="_DisplaySize" Value="30" />
   </DesignTime>
</Attribute>
 :
<Key
   Name="CustPk" >
   <DesignTime>
    <Attr Name="_DBObjectName" Value="CUST_PK" />
    <Attr Name="_isPrimary" Value="true" />
    <Attr Name="_isNotNull" Value="false" />
    <Attr Name="_isUnique" Value="false" />
```

LISITING 13.3 *Continued*

```
        <Attr Name="_isCheck" Value="false" />
        <Attr Name="_isCascadeDelete" Value="false" />
        <Attr Name="_isDeferrableConstraint" Value="true" />
        <Attr Name="_isValidateConstraint" Value="false" />
        <Attr Name="_isInitiallyDeferredConstraint" Value="true" />
        <Attr Name="_isDisabledConstraint" Value="false" />
        <AttrArray Name="_attributes">
           <Item Value="com.prenhall.OFJP.cust.Customer.Id" />
        </AttrArray>
      </DesignTime>
   </Key>
   :
</Entity>
```

LISITING 13.3 *Continued*

Notes on Listing 13.3:

- The `<Entity>` element is the root for this XML document, which conforms to the `Entity` document type defined by `jbo_02_01.dtd`, located in the JDeveloper `jbomt.zip` class library that should be in application `CLASSPATH` (see subsection 13.7.2).
- The `<Entity>` element has attributes that associate the entity with the `CUSTOMER` table.
- There is one `<Attribute>` element for each column in the `CUSTOMER` database table. Each `<Attribute>` element defines characteristics for a data item held in the entity object. The characteristics stored for each attribute include:
  - The Java data type.
  - A generic and specific database SQL type.
  - The precision and/or scale of the attribute.
  - A `PrimaryKey` boolean value indicating that the attribute belongs to the primary key for the entity object.
  - A `isNotNull` boolean indicator identifying whether the attribute allows a database NULL value.
- The `<Key>` tag describes details of the database integrity rules, such as the primary key.

The framework uses the entity XML file to construct a runtime instance of the entity object that will contain the column values from a row in the associated database table.

The Entity Object Java Implementation File

The generated entity object Java implementation file contains the code to construct, initialize, and destroy an entity object. It also contains set and get methods that can be called to modify attribute values in the object.

Listing 13.4 shows part of the `CustomerImpl.java` file that accompanies the `Customer.xml` file.

```
package com.prenhall.OFJP.cust;

// ---------------------------------------------------------------
// ---    File generated by Oracle Business Components for Java.
// ---------------------------------------------------------------

import oracle.jbo.server.*;
import oracle.jbo.RowIterator;
import oracle.jbo.domain.Number;

public class CustomerImpl extends oracle.jbo.server.EntityImpl {
  /**
    * Attribute accessor Indices
    */
  protected static final int ID = 0;
  protected static final int NAME = 1;
  protected static final int SURNAME = 2;
  protected static final int EMAIL = 3;
  protected static final int PASSWORD = 4;
  protected static final int CREDITCARDTYPE = 5;
  protected static final int CREDITCARDNBR = 6;
  protected static final int MONTHEXPIRED = 7;
  protected static final int YEAREXPIRED = 8;

  private static EntityDefImpl mDefinitionObject;
  /**
    * This is the default constructor (do not remove)
    */

  public CustomerImpl() {
  }

  /**
    * Retrieves the definition object for this instance class.
    */
```

LISTING 13.4 Entity Object Java Implementation File: `CustomerImpl.java`.

```
  public static synchronized EntityDefImpl getDefinitionObject() {
    if (mDefinitionObject == null) {
      mDefinitionObject = (EntityDefImpl)EntityDefImpl.
              findDefObject("com.prenhall.OFJP.cust.Customer");
    }
    return mDefinitionObject;
  }

  /**
    * Gets the attribute value for Id, using the alias name Id
    */

  public Number getId() {
    return (Number)getAttributeInternal(ID);
  }

  /**
    * Sets <code>value</code> as the attribute value for Id
    */

  public void setId(Number value) {
    setAttributeInternal(ID, value);
  }
  /**
    * Gets the attribute value for Name, using the alias name Name
    */
  public String getName() {
    return (String)getAttributeInternal(NAME);
  }

  /**
    * Sets <code>value</code> as the attribute value for Name
    */
  public void setName(String value) {
    setAttributeInternal(NAME, value);
  }

  :
}
```

LISTING 13.4 *Continued*

Notes on Listing 13.4:

- The example `CustomerImpl` class is a subclass of the `oracle.jbo.server.EntityImpl`[8] from which a great deal of functionality is inherited.
- The code for `CustomerImpl` contains a get and set method for each attribute defined in the entity object. The get and set methods follow the standard Java naming convention where the attribute name is preceded by the word `get` or `set`.
- A closer look at each of the get and set methods reveals that the get methods call an inherited method called `getAttributeInternal()`, and the set methods call `setAttributeInternal()`. The methods `getAttributeInternal()` and `setAttributeInternal()` use the protected class constants (final variables) to access the attribute value held within the entity object. Using the JDeveloper debugger reveals that attribute values are held in an array of Java objects. The integer constants are used to index the object array to access the attribute values. The `<Attribute>` element in the `Customer.xml` file defines the Java object type used to hold the attribute value.
- You can override inherited methods, and add code to the entity object Java implementation class to implement customizations and validation rules.

The Java and/or XML file can be modified to customize the entity object functionality or structure. Examples of customizing the entity object are shown later in this chapter. Using the default entity object, you need to build a view object and then the application module. The next section explains how to build a view object.

13.3.2.3 Creating a View Object. A view object represents a query used to access the data held in the database. The view object provides SQL operations to join, filter, and sort business data, and to prepare the data for client application consumption or manipulation. A client application uses a view object as an updateable scrollable row set.

After the view object query is executed, each database row retrieved from the view object is created in application memory as an entity object. The entity objects created for each row form a data cache of the database data. Attribute values updated using the view object get and set methods are delegated to the appropriate entity object, where the changes are applied to values in memory until the application issues a request to save them. The changes to each attribute are subject to the validation logic and rules implemented in the entity object, which can veto any change.

[8]The `oracle.jbo.server` package contains the core classes for the BC4J framework.

Using the JDeveloper business component wizard, you can create a default view object whose query contains all the attributes from a single entity object. Figure 13.12 illustrates how to create a default view object for the `Customer` entity object.

Right-clicking on the entity object, as shown in Figure 3.12, gives you the option of creating a default view object.[9] Note that you can also use this menu to:

- Edit or delete the selected entity object, so as to customize the component functionality. Later in this chapter you will learn about editing the entity object.
- Create an association object to link the entity object to a related entity object.
- Create an entity constraint, such as a primary key, foreign key, or unique key. This option is used to add the constraints if they are not present in the database table structure.

The resulting component generated by JDeveloper is shown in Figure 13.13.

An XML file and a Java source are generated, in a view object folder, to represent the view object. In addition, the package XML file (e.g., `cust.xml`) is modified with a new `<Containee>` element indicating that the view component has been added to the package, shown as bold text in the following example:

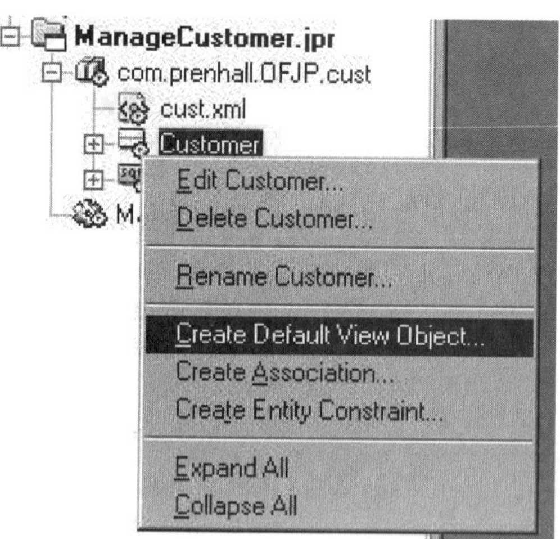

FIGURE 13.12 Creating a default view object with JDeveloper.

[9]Another way to create the default view object is to select the `View object and View link` checkbox when selecting the table for the entity object, as shown in Figure 13.8.

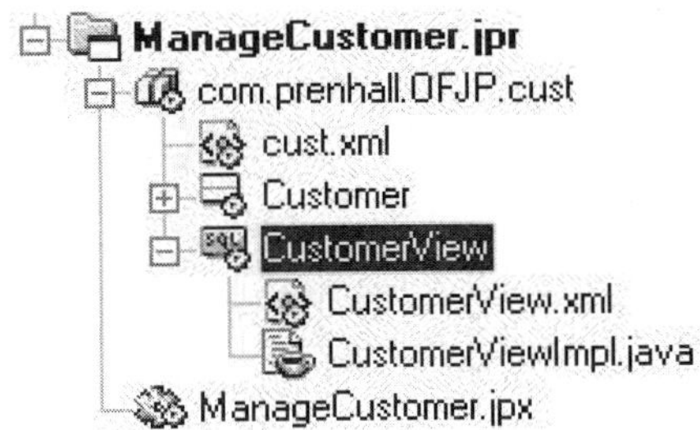

FIGURE 13.13 Default view object files in JDeveloper.

```
<?xml version="1.0" encoding='WINDOWS-1252'?>
<!DOCTYPE JboPackage SYSTEM "jbo_03_01.dtd">
<JboPackage
   Name="cust"    ...
   :
   <Containee
      Name="CustomerView"
      FullName="com.prenhall.OFJP.cust.CustomerView"
      ObjectType="ViewObject" >
   </Containee>
</JboPackage>
```

The View Object XML File

Listing 13.4 shows part of the view object XML file.

```
<?xml version="1.0" encoding='WINDOWS-1252'?>
<!DOCTYPE ViewObject SYSTEM "jbo_03_01.dtd">
<ViewObject
   Name="CustomerView"
   SelectList="Customer.ID, Customer.NAME, Customer.SURNAME,
Customer.EMAIL, Customer.PASSWORD, Customer.CREDIT_CARD_TYPE,
Customer.CREDIT_CARD_NBR, Customer.MONTH_EXPIRED,
Customer.YEAR_EXPIRED"
   FromList="CUSTOMER Customer"
   BindingStyle="Oracle"
   CustomQuery="false"
   ComponentClass="com.prenhall.OFJP.cust.CustomerViewImpl" >
   <DesignTime>
      <Attr Name="_codeGenFlag" Value="20" />
   </DesignTime>
```

LISTING 13.4 A view object XML source.

```
    <EntityUsage
       Name="Customer"
       Entity="com.prenhall.OFJP.cust.Customer" >
       <DesignTime>
          <Attr Name="_ReadOnly" Value="false" />
          <Attr Name="_EntireObjectTable" Value="false" />
          <Attr Name="_queryClause" Value="false" />
       </DesignTime>
    </EntityUsage>
    <ViewAttribute
       Name="Id"
       EntityAttrName="Id"
       EntityUsage="Customer"
       AliasName="ID" >
       <DesignTime>
          <Attr Name="_DisplaySize" Value="0" />
       </DesignTime>
    </ViewAttribute>
    <ViewAttribute
       Name="Name"
       EntityAttrName="Name"
       EntityUsage="Customer"
       AliasName="NAME" >
       <DesignTime>
          <Attr Name="_DisplaySize" Value="0" />
       </DesignTime>
    </ViewAttribute>
:
</ViewObject>
```

LISTING 13.4 *Continued*

Notes on Listing 14.3:

- The `<ViewObject>` element contains the information in the `SelectList` and `FromList` XML attributes used to form the SQL query.
- The `<Entity Usage>` element associates the customer entity object with the view object. The view object uses this information to read the database column value for a row and store it in an instance of an entity object.
- For a default view object, one `<ViewAttribute>` element is created for each attribute in the associated entity object. A non-default view object can be created with a subset of attributes from the entity object, or a query-only view object based on a query and not an entity object. View objects can also

contain a ViewAttribute representing derived data, such as a calculated or summarized field.

The View Object Java File

Listing 13.5 shows the contents of the ViewObject Java file. The amount of Java code is minimal, but most of the functionality is inherited.

```
package com.prenhall.OFJP.cust;
// ----------------------------------------------------------------
// ---    File generated by Oracle Business Components for Java.
// ----------------------------------------------------------------
import oracle.jbo.server.*;
import oracle.jbo.RowIterator;

public class CustomerViewImpl
               extends oracle.jbo.server.ViewObjectImpl {
  /**
    * This is the default constructor (do not remove)
    */
  public CustomerViewImpl() {  }

}
```

LISTING 13.5 View Object Java Source.

Notes on Listing 13.5

- Most of the view object functionality is inherited from the `oracle.jbo.server.ViewObjectImpl` class. The methods inherited by the View object include:
  - `addOrderbyClause()` to programmatically influence the sort order of the rows returned by the query.
  - `addWhereClause()` to programmatically add search criteria to the ViewObject query and restrict the number of rows processed.
  - `first()` and `last()` to position the view object iterator at the first or last row of the result set.
  - `hasNext()` method to determine whether a row object exists in the view before accessing its contents.
  - `next()` method to fetch a result set row, during forward iteration, as an `oracle.job.Row` object. The oracle.jbo.Row is an interface inherited by the entity object. Obtaining a Row reference from a view object gives you a handle to a specific instance of an entity object.

Many other methods are also inherited. After getting a row object from the view object you can use the row's get and set accessor methods to read or update attribute values in the associated entity object.

13.3.2.4 Creating an Application Module. A Business Component Application module is a reusable component encapsulating the logic that a client application needs in order to interact with database data. The application module provides the client application with access to one or more view objects and view links if required. The view objects are used by a client application to query and modify data in the database. If the view objects are associated with an entity object, the entity objects are cached in the application module instance. An application module provides a database connection and the session context for executing transactions. It also provides:

- Concurrency control when accessing the data. By default the application module uses a pessimistic locking mechanism. Pessimistic locking occurs when a database row is locked prior to performing an SQL `UPDATE` or `DELETE` operation. When you modify data in the BC4J framework, the changes are made to the copy of the row data in memory (i.e., the attribute values in the entity object representing the row). When the changes to an entity object are made, the BC4J framework issues an Oracle `SELECT` statement with the `FOR UPDATE` clause to lock the associated database row to implement pessimistic locking (see Chapter 4 for a discussion of the use of the `SELECT` statement with the `FOR UPDATE` clause). You can modify the locking mode of the application module to use optimistic locking[10] or disabling locking.
- Performance gains by using a collection of view objects with their cache of entity objects to reduce network round-trips when retrieving and updating the data.
- Ability to distribute an application module into the middle tier as an Enterprise JavaBean (see Chapters 21 and 22).

Using JDeveloper, an application module can be created in three ways.

1. When creating the entity object, by selecting the `View object and View link` checkbox, and the `Application module` checkbox (see Figure 13.10). This creates an application module with the default view object.
2. Selecting the `Create Application module` ... menu item from the popup menu when right-clicking the mouse on the BC4J package name.
3. Selecting JDeveloper `File->New` menu, clicking the `Business Component` tag page, and double-clicking on the `Application module` icon (see Figure 13.14).

---

[10]Optimistic locking assumes that the database row is free for modification at the time when the SQL DML operation is executed.

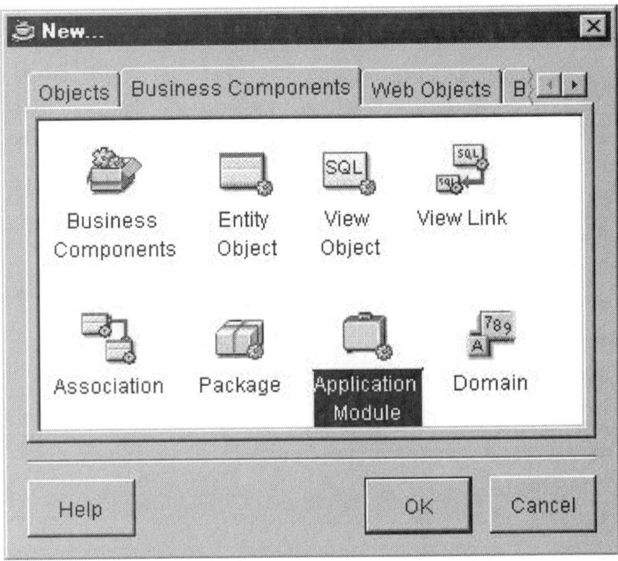

FIGURE 13.14 Launching the application module wizard.

The discussion in this section uses the last approach to launch the application module wizard, to allow you to select the view object to be used.

Only two of the four pages in the application module wizard are relevant for the simple example created in this chapter. In the first page of interest (Figure 13.15), you provide the name for your application module.

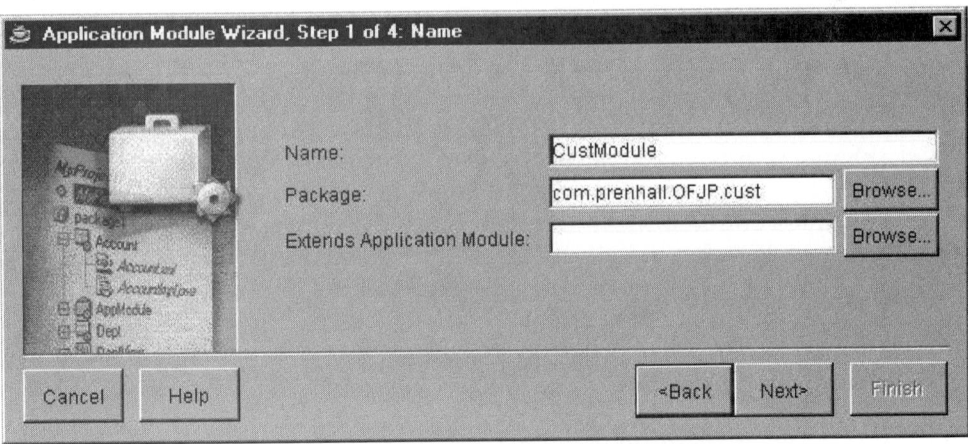

FIGURE 13.15 Choosing a name for the application module.

In the second page (Figure 13.16), you select the view objects to be added to the application module.

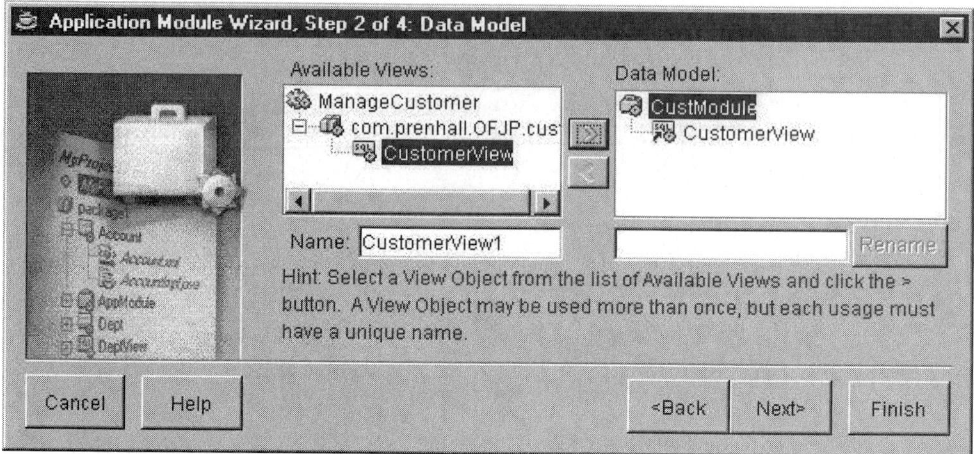

FIGURE 13.16 Adding a view object to the application module.

The collection of view objects and view links (if any) that are added to the application module are called a *data model*. Figure 13.16 shows the `CustomerView` View object added to the `CustModule`.

To summarize the process of creating an application module:

1. Create the entity objects.
2. Create the view objects derived from the entity objects.
3. Create an application module containing the view objects.

The application module should be designed around a set of operations representing a consistent set of changes to related data. For example, a shopping cart application module provides access to sales items, which can be added to a shopping basket/cart owned by a customer. When the items in the shopping cart are purchased, there may be a requirement for the customer to designate a courier (or shipping company). To provide the functionality to manipulate the data for the business entities, the application module requires access to the customer, shopping basket, shopping items, sales items, and courier.

When a customer makes a purchase, the data can be passed to a separate order-processing application module. The order application module copies items from the shopping basket into the order-entry system, and notifies the designated courier of the pending order.

13.3.2.5 Summary of How Business Components Interact. Figure 13.17 is a pictorial representation of how components interact in a business component application module. To keep the diagram and discussion simple, the scenario is based on an application module using a single view and a single entity to read and modify data in a single database table.

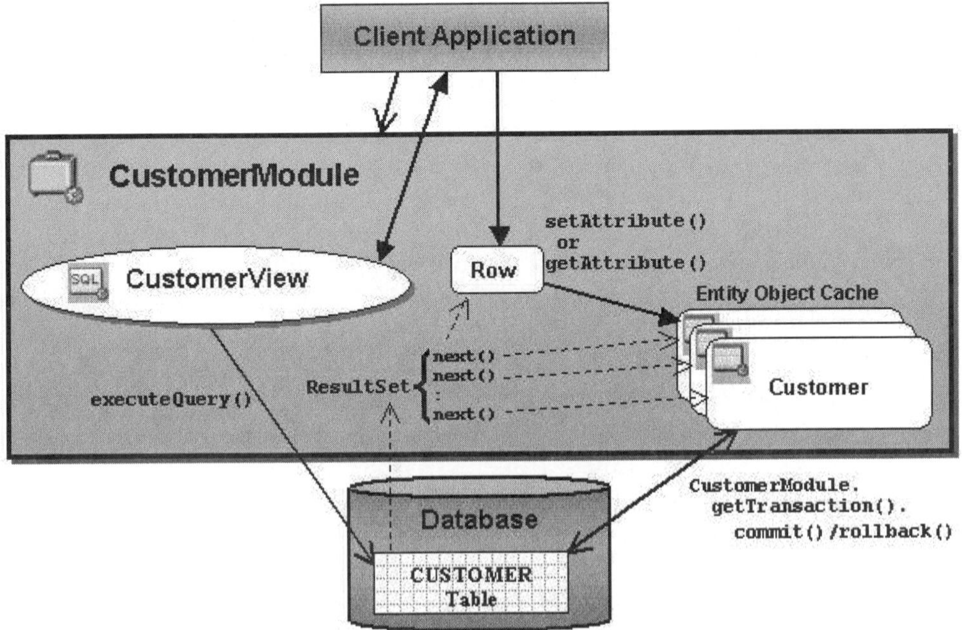

FIGURE 13.17 How business components interact.

A client creates an instance of an application module and a view object provided by the application module. The view object executes a query defined in its associated XML file, using a JDBC call that returns a result set.[11] The client application fetches a row from the view object result set, where the row is received as an object reference to an entity object. An entity object is created for each row to store the column data in memory.[12] The client application uses the `getAttribute()` method to read the attribute data in the entity object, and the `setAttribute()` method to update the data. If the application module is using a pessimistic locking mode, the database row associated with the modified entity object is locked.

Using the application module transaction context, the client request changes to the entity object to be saved. This involves to steps:

- A *posting phase* where the database `INSERT`, `UPDATE`, or `DELETE` operation is performed for each entity based a state indicating the type of change made to the entity object.
- A *commit phase* where the `INSERT`, `UPDATE`, or `DELETE` done in the posting-phase is committed.

---

[11]The Business Components for Java framework can fetch a single row, a batch of rows, or entire set of rows from the database table.

[12]The entity object stores column data values in an internal object array of attributes.

13.4 TESTING COMPONENTS AND THE APPLICATION MODULE

Components can be tested using the JDeveloper test tool built into the integrated development environment (IDE). The test tool allows you to exercise each component through the view objects or view links available in an application module. The test tool is a prototype GUI application with which you can thoroughly test the business and validation rules implemented by each component.

The testing process has the following advantages:

- It helps to detect logic errors rapidly before you build your user interface or presentation logic.
- It provides you with a feel for how application components function.
- You can iterate through view object result sets or test-coordinated result sets via their view link.
- The testing tool can test application modules deployed locally with or remotely from the client application.

The test tool can be invoked via the package or application module icons next to their names in the JDeveloper navigator pane. Figure 13.18 shows the test menu item in the menu displayed when right-clicking on the application module.

Select the `Test`... menu item from the menu to invoke the test tool. If the tool is launched via the application module icon, an instance of the application module is automatically created, with the view objects and view links defined in the data model.

When invoking the test tool via the package name, you must use the tool menus to explicitly create an application module instance, view objects, or view links. In either case, you can dynamically create additional copies of each component to be tested.

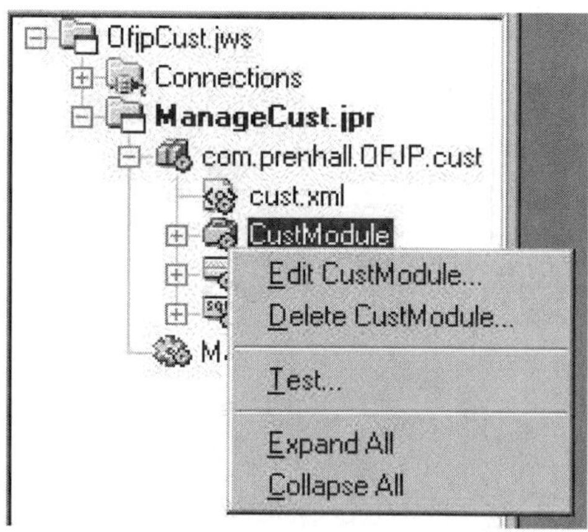

FIGURE 13.18 Invoking the test tool via the application module.

The example walk-through presented in this section shows how the test tool can be invoked and used via the application module icon. Figure 13.19 is displayed when you select the `Test...` menu item.

The middle-tier server type dropdown box allows you test an application module deployed in a local mode (in the same JVM as the client application) or in a remote environment. To test a remote-application module, you must first deploy the application module and related components into the remote environment. This chapter demonstrates how to test the application module locally. To proceed you must select a named JDBC connection and the application module name before clicking the `Connect` button shown in Figure 13.19. After you have successfully connected to the database and created the application module instance, JDeveloper shows the dialog depicted in Figure 13.20.

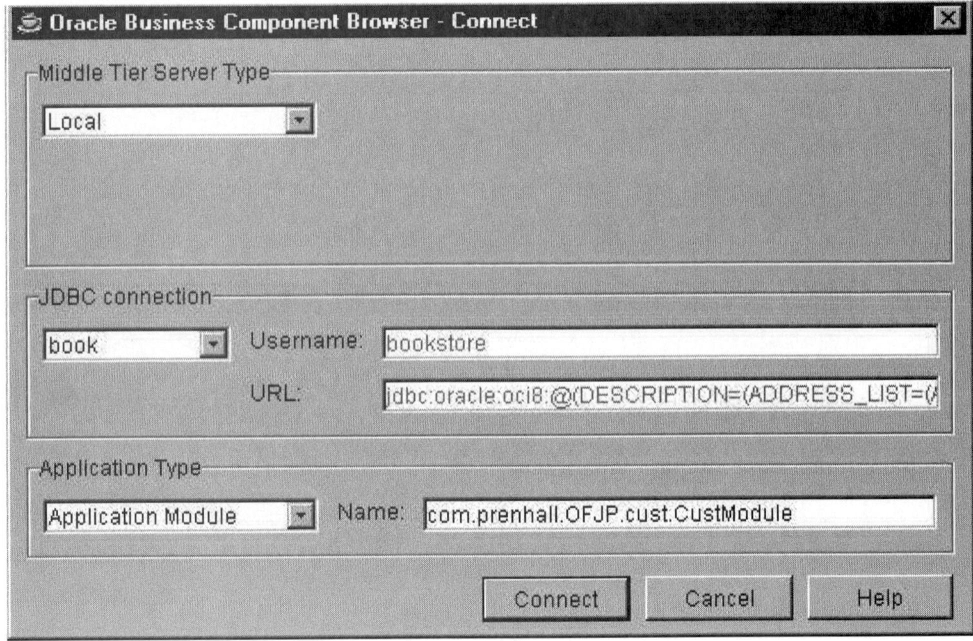

FIGURE 13.19 JDeveloper business component test tool.

The left-hand windowpane in Figure 13.20 shows the `CustModule` instance containing the `CustomerView object`. Double-click on the `CustomerView` icon to display, in the right-hand pane, a GUI form providing text fields for each attribute defined in the view object. Figure 13.21 shows how the data appear for the first row of `CustomerView`.

A tab is created for each view object tested so that you can exercise multiple view objects (or view links) during the same test session. Each tab is accompanied by a navigation toolbar, as shown in Figure 13.22.

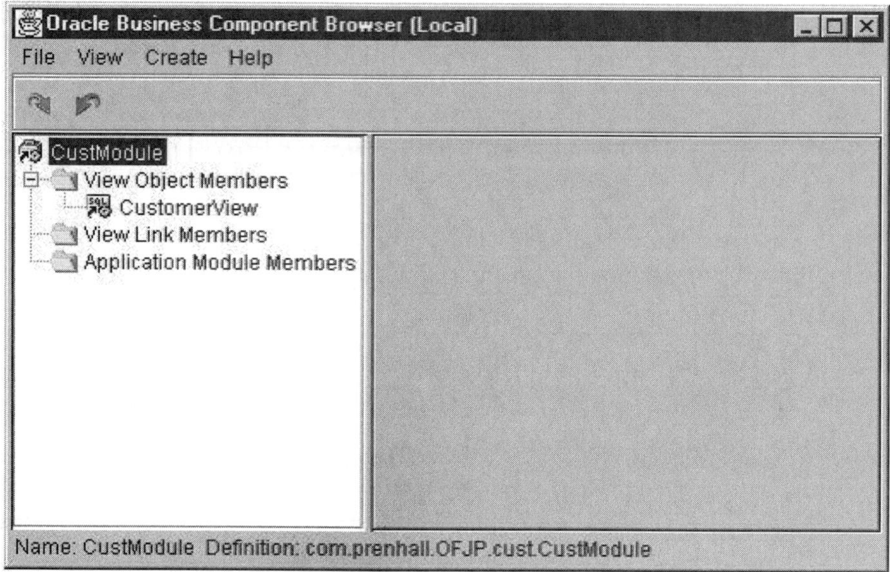

FIGURE 13.20 Testing the `CustModule` application module.

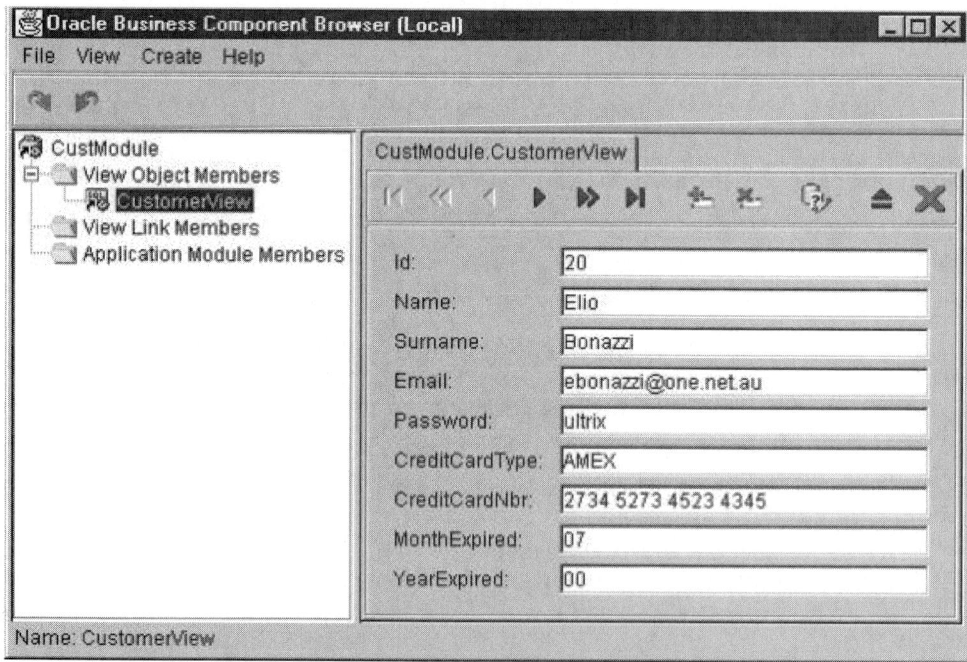

FIGURE 13.21 Display data for the `CustomerView` view object.

FIGURE 13.22 View object test navigation toolbar.

The navigation toolbar provides the following functions for each icon:

- first record, last record.
- previous record, next record.
- next page, previous page. A page represents a set of rows, when more than one row is displayed at a time. Since the CustomerView shows only one row at a time, the previous page action has the same result as the previous record.
- create/add new record, delete record.
- find/query dialog, display as separate window.
- close/delete test object window.

Modifying a text field for any attribute value updates the row. Changes made to the attributes are buffered in memory (i.e., in the entity object cache). Changes can be saved using the commit icon, and discarded with the rollback icon. The test tool provides the commit icon ( ) and the rollback icon ( ) in a toolbar under the main menu (see Figure 13.21). Using the test tool is a fantastic enhancement of productivity in rapidly building robust applications.

13.5 CREATING BC4J CLIENT APPLICATIONS

The customer application module created in the first part of the chapter will now be used to build a simple GUI client/server application. The GUI application provides functionality similar to the test tool discussed earlier above.

You will then create a JavaServer page user interface using the same business component application module to give the data a Web/HTML user interface.

You will also learn more about the business component class library through manually coded client applications. A manually coded client application can be deployed into any client in the form of:

- A command-line application.
- A standard Java Swing/AWT client application or applet.

- A hand-crafted Java servlet or JavaServer page application.
- A distributed Java component, such as an Enterprise JavaBean.[13]

13.5.1 CREATING A SIMPLE GUI CLIENT

Using the Data-Aware Controls provided with JDeveloper, you can quickly build a prototype client application and customize the interface to build a fully functional application. The Data-Aware Controls (DAC) provided by JDeveloper are a subset of their Swing counterparts. The controls are called data-aware because they obtain data from an object producing the data, called a data producer. Setting a bean property in the DAC forms its association with its data producer. Data that become available from the data producer are displayed in the GUI environment by the data-aware control.

For example, the Java Swing `JTextField` component does not know how to obtain data directly from any data source, and must be set using its `setText()` method. The data-aware control and data-producer exchange information through an event-driven interface defined by the Sun Microsystems Java extension, infoBus API.[14]

Here is a brief overview of the infoBus architecture and how data-aware controls interact with business component view objects via data-producer controls.

13.5.1.1 Data-Aware Control Architecture. JDeveloper provides several Swing-based visual components, and some non-visual data-producing controls that cooperate using the infoBus architecture. The infoBus architecture is shown in Figure 13.23.

A data consumer and data producer both subscribe to the same data channel. The data consumer generates an event on the infoBus to request data. The data producer receives the event and provides the data. The data producer can drive the operation by generating events to notify data consumers that information has been supplied on the infoBus.

The infoBus standard does not specify the kind of data-consumer or data-producer components. Data consumers are typically visual, such as a text field control. Data producers are typically non-visual, such as a row set class.

JDeveloper data-aware controls follow the infoBus model, as shown in Figure 13.24. In JDeveloper data producers are called *infoProducers*, and data consumers are called *infoSwing* controls.

Figure 13.24 shows infoProducer components obtaining data directly from view objects in the business component application module. The business com-

---

[13]See Chapters 21 and 22 for a full discussion of Enterprise JavaBeans.

[14]For information on Sun's infoBus technology, visit the URL http://java.sun.com/beans/infobus/.

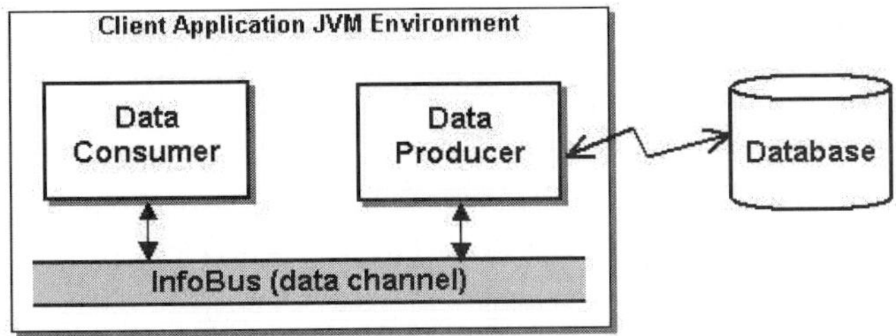

FIGURE 13.23 The infoBus architecture.

ponent application module can run in the same JVM as the infoProducer control or can execute in a remote JVM.

13.5.1.2 Building a GUI Client Application. In JDeveloper select the `File->New` menu to display the JDeveloper Object Gallery in Figure 13.25.

There are two ways to create a client using a business components data form in a Java frame from the object gallery:

1. Select the application icon, and, in the application wizard, add a default frame type as a new Business Components for Java Data form. This creates the Java source application with the standard `main(String[] args)` method, and then starts the business components data form wizard to create the frame used by the application.
2. Select the Business Components Data Form icon. Using this approach you can choose the kind of Swing container for the business component form from a JFrame, JPanel, or JApplet (see Figure 13.24). The application to use the frame must be created separately.

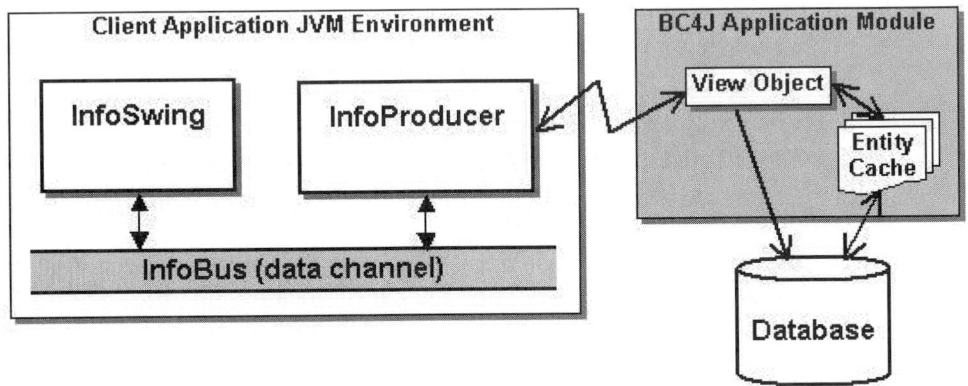

FIGURE 13.24 Oracle data-aware control architecture with BC4J.

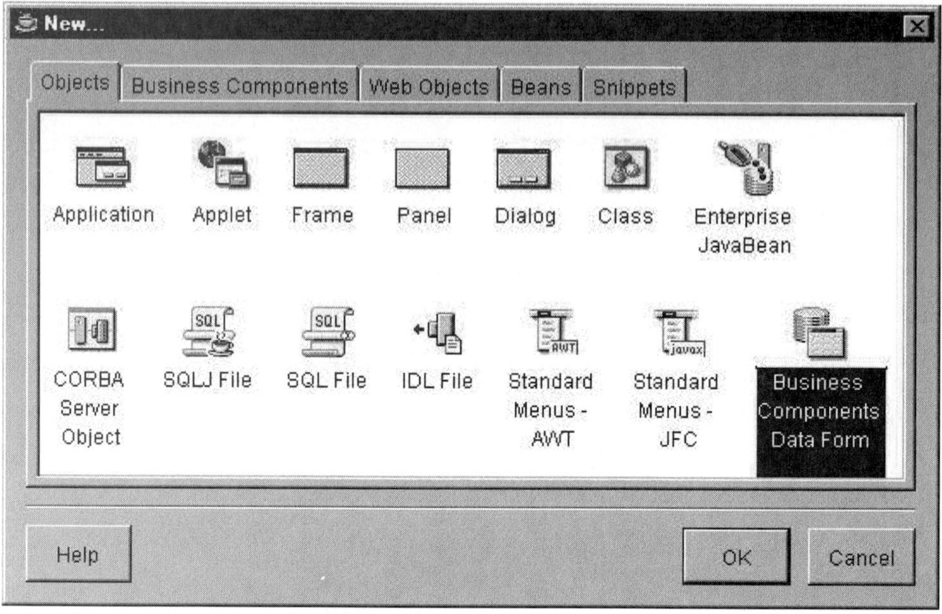

FIGURE 13.25 Oracle JDeveloper object gallery.

When using the business component data form wizard you are guided through several pages that ask you to make choices about your frame contents and enter the following pieces of information:

- Choose a single or master-detail table form type (see Figure 13.26).
- Select the business component application module (see Figure 13. 27).
- Choose the Java package name, class name, and title (see Figure 13.28).
- Select a database connection and deployment mode (see Figure 13.29).
- Choose a view object for a single table form, or two view objects for a master-detail form (see Figure 13.30).
- Choose the attributes/fields to be displayed in the form (see Figure 13.31).
- Choose a default layout and presentation template (see Figure 13.32).

The frame is created as a subclass of the `InfoFrame` class in the `oracle.dacf.control.swing` package, located in the `jdev_home\lib\dacf.zip` file provided with JDeveloper (where `jdev_home` represents the installation home directory for JDeveloper).

The page shown in Figure 13.27 also lets you can start the business component wizard to create an application module by choosing the `Current Project` radio button.

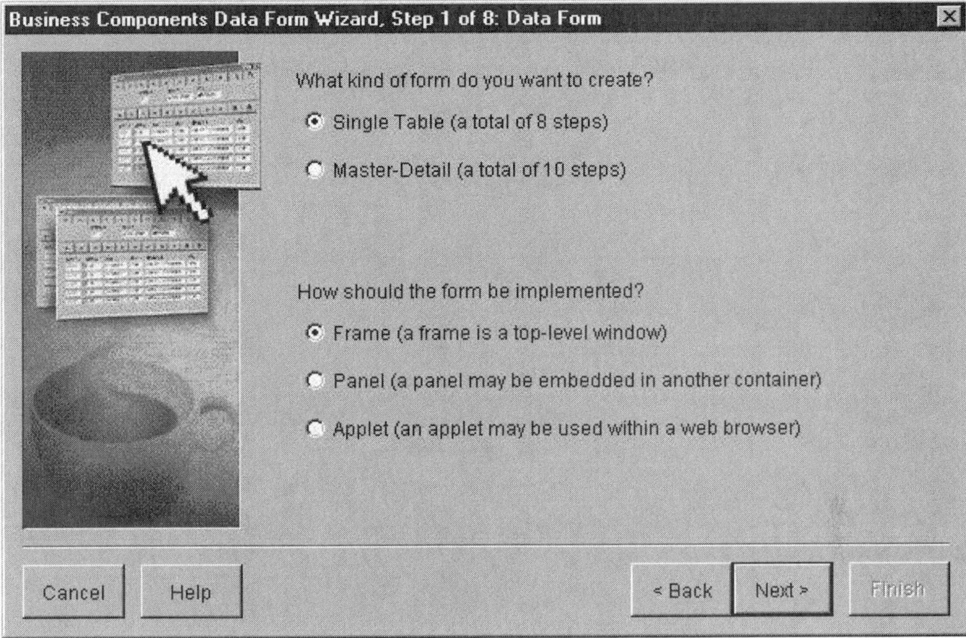

FIGURE 13.26 Choose form type and Java container.

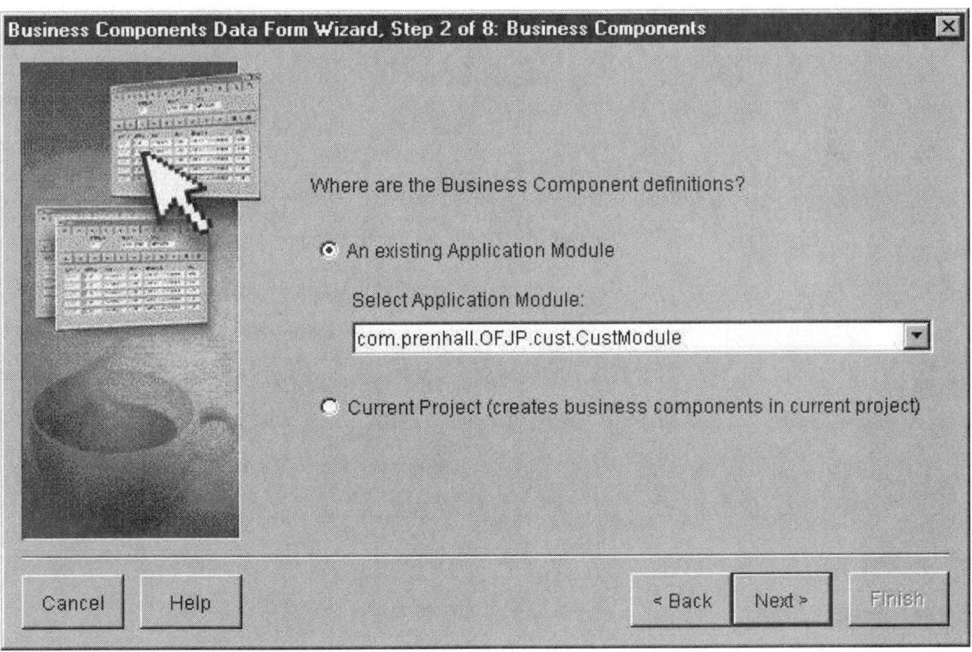

FIGURE 13.27 Select the business component application module.

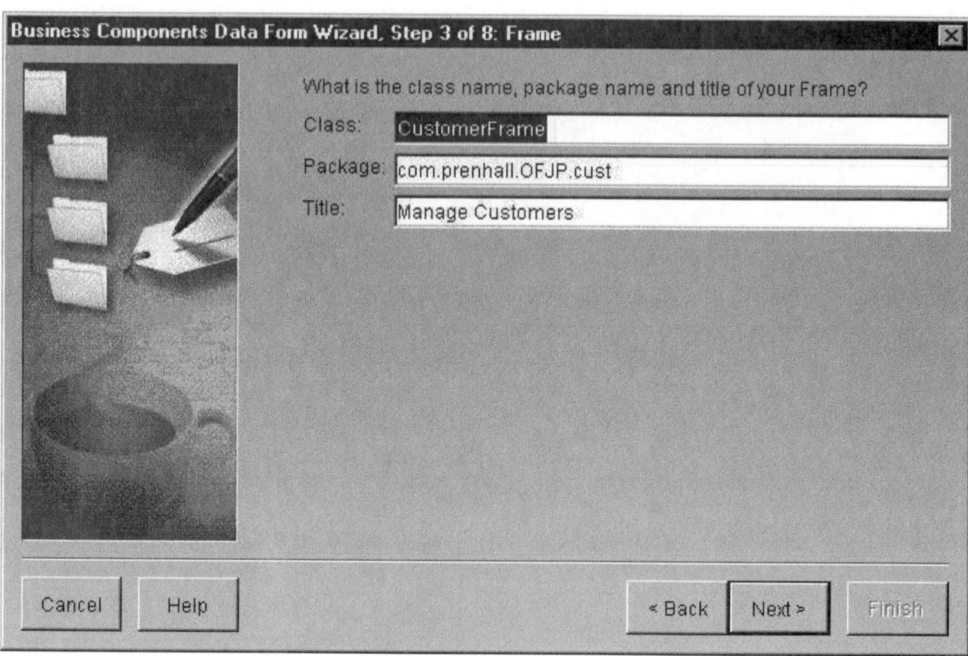

FIGURE 13.28 Enter the frame class name, package name, and title.

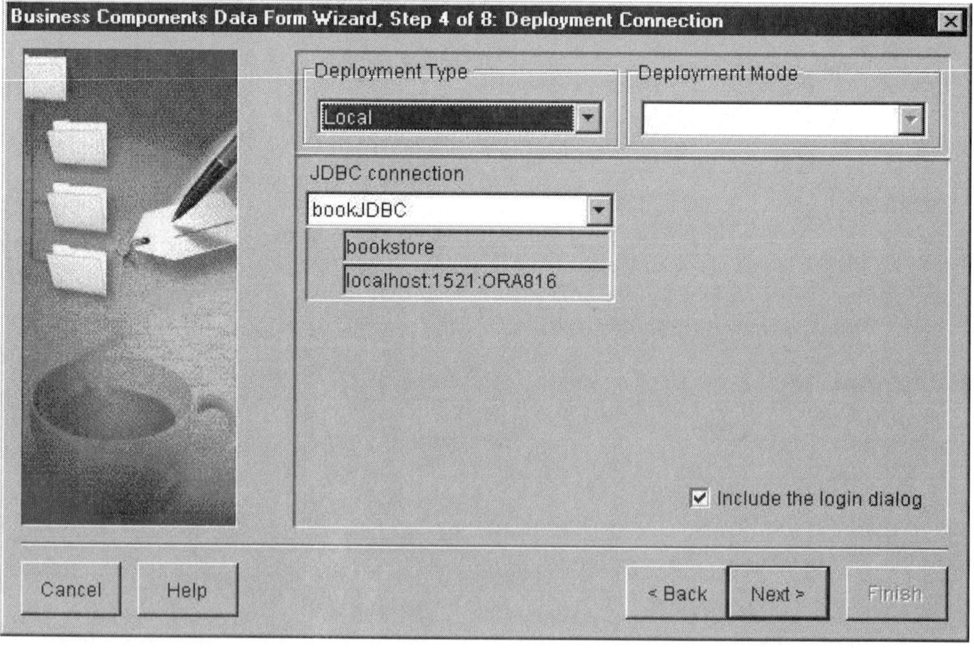

FIGURE 13.29 Select named connection and deployment mode.

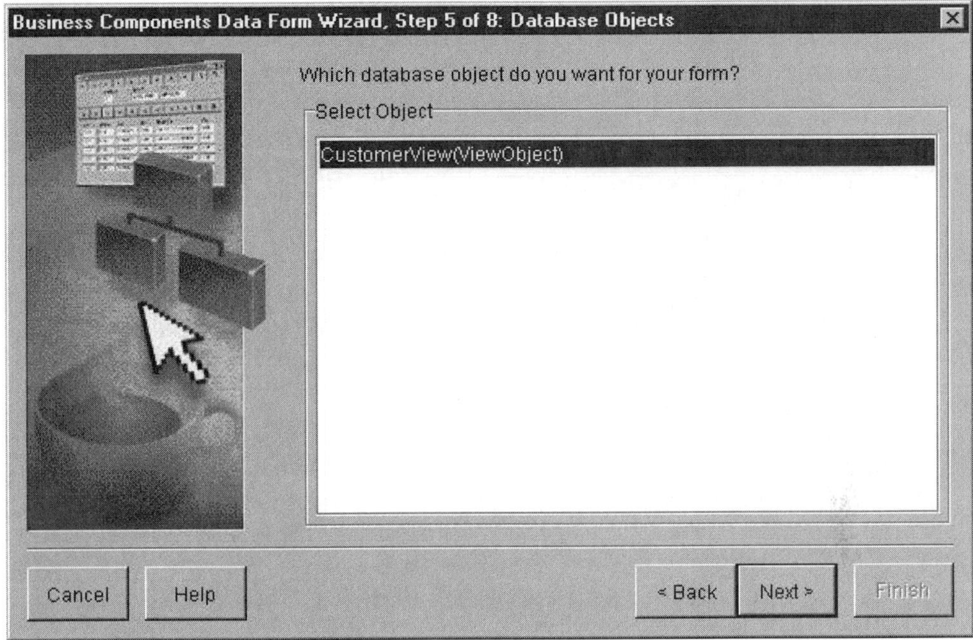

FIGURE 13.30 Selecting the view object for the frame.

This example demonstrates how to create a Frame that uses the business component module locally (i.e., in the same JVM). Selecting "`Include the login dialog`" checkbox makes the application present a dialog box for user name and password entries before displaying the database data.

The frame contains GUI text fields for each attribute moved to the selected list. The available attributes are derived from the view object's definition.

The default layout provides a navigation bar with icons and actions that resemble the test tool provided in JDeveloper. The default choices include:

- ❑ A frame with navigation bar.
- ❑ A frame with Find Dialog and logo.

In a GUI client/server application, the first option is aesthetically more pleasing than the second, because it is preferable to display search criteria only when needed rather than all the time. However, in a Web/HTML application, it may be preferable and friendlier to display search options in the window all the time. JDeveloper provides a Style Editor API that can be used to fully customize the look-and-feel of your application.

The finish page of the wizard, not shown in this chapter, allows you to select a checkbox to invoke the JDeveloper User Interface (UI) designer to display

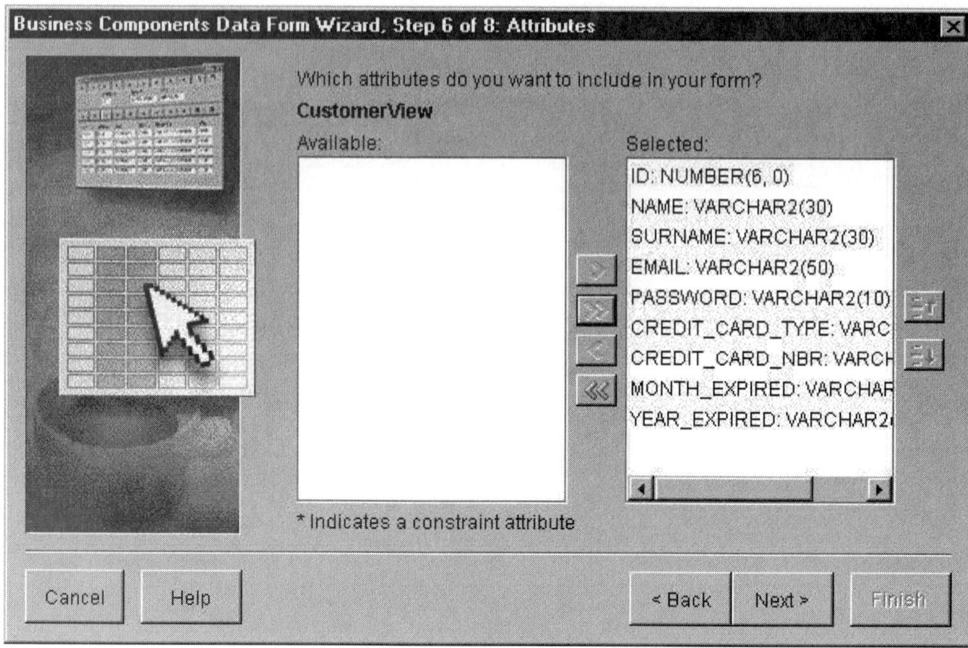

FIGURE 13.31 Select attributes to be displayed.

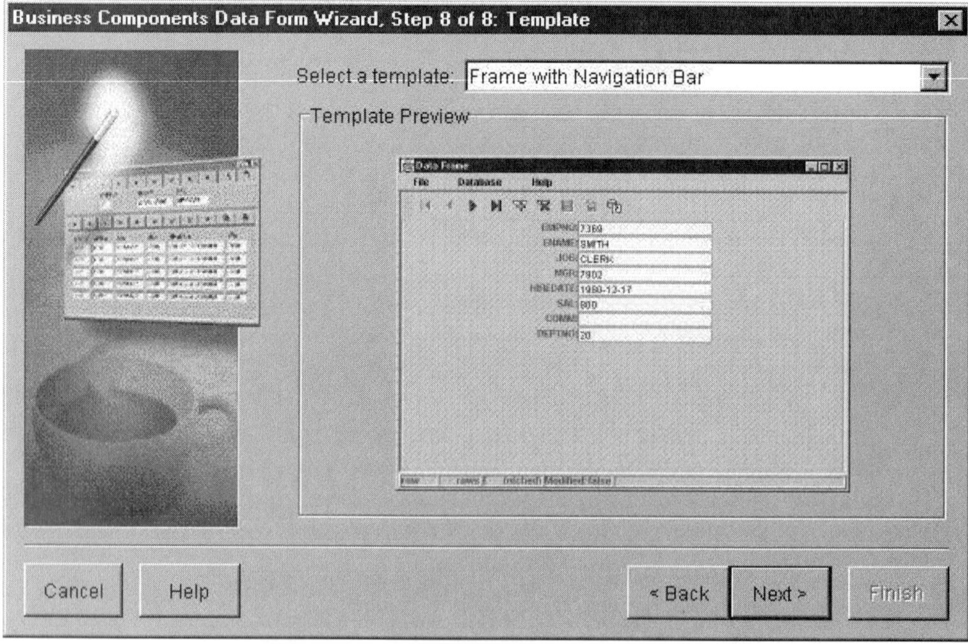

FIGURE 13.32 Select a default layout and presentation.

the generated form's visual structure. Note that you did not write any code during this process. All the code is generated by information provided through the wizards. This is a typical feature of Rapid Application Development tools.

Having created your frame, you can create a simple Java application to test and run it. This code can be built manually or can be generated by the JDeveloper application wizard. The application instantiates the frame and makes it visible. Listing 13.6 shows some simple application code to display the form.

```
package com.prenhall.OFJP.cust;
import java.awt.Frame;

public class CustomerApp {

  public static void main(String[] args) {
    Frame custFrame = new CustomerFrame();
    custFrame.setVisible(true);
  }
}
```

LISTING 13.6 Application to invoke business component data form.

After the application and frame are compiled, running the application in Listing 13.6 the login dialog built into the form is displayed as shown in Figure 13.33.

In the login dialog you can pick from a list of named connections. These are read from the `connection.properties` file discussed earlier in the chapter. After a successful login into the database, the application window is presented, showing the navigation toolbar to find, query, insert, update, and delete data. Figure 13.34 shows an image of the preliminary GUI application.

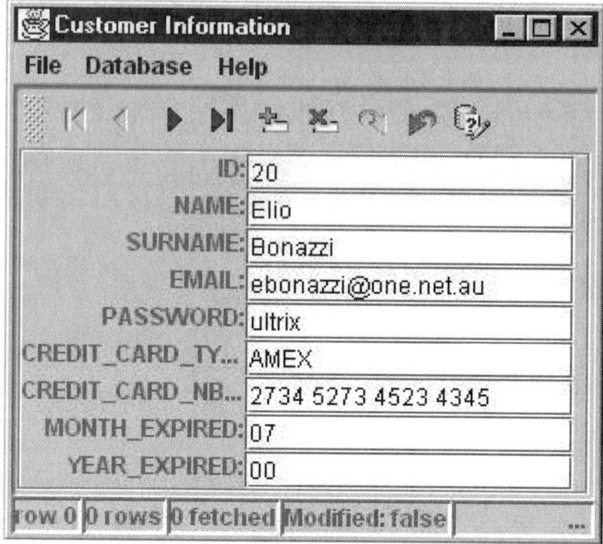

FIGURE 13.33 Database Login Dialog.

This is a preliminary application that would need more work with the user interface to be productionized. However, the business component layer of code handles all the data-access, data-modification, and data-validation rules. This is a simple example showing how you can separate the data logic, often called business logic, from the presentation layer.

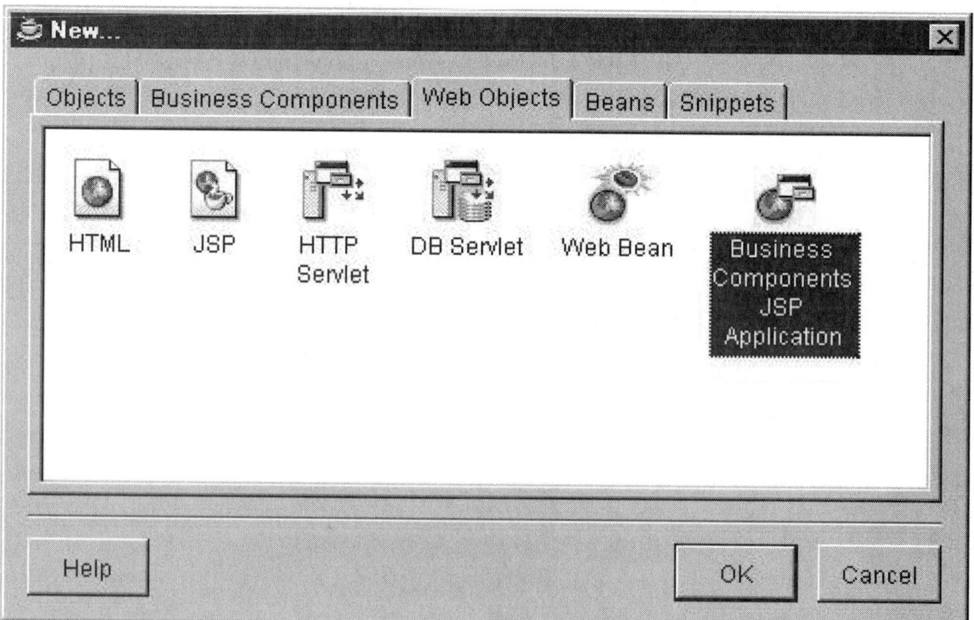

FIGURE 13.34 Manager customer BC4J/GUI application.

13.5.2 CREATING A JSP CLIENT

The business component application module invoked in the GUI client application can be used unchanged to build a JavaServer Page (JSP) client. You can generate an initial JSP client by selecting the `Business Components JSP Application` icon from the `Objects` tab in the JDeveloper Object Gallery shown in Figure 13.35.[15]

The wizard provides pages for you to enter the following information:

- Select a name for your Web, the Project HTML root directory, and the application directory (see Figure 13.36).
- Choose the business component application module for the JSP application (see Figure 13.37).
- Choose a template for the style control via style sheets (see Figure 13.38).
- Select the named database connection (see Figure 13.39).
- Select the BC4J view object (see Figure 13.40).

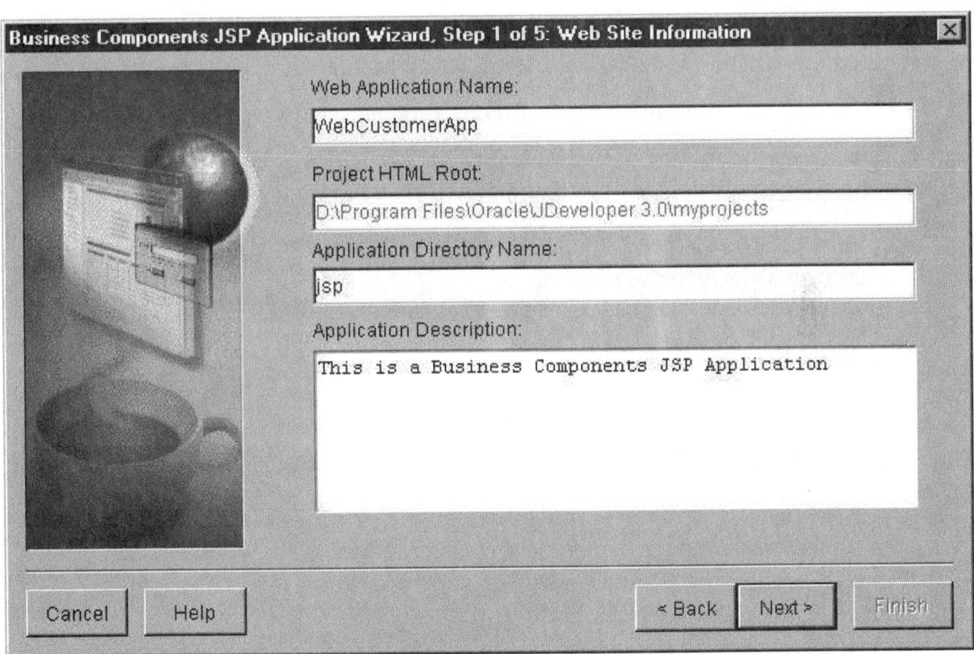

FIGURE 13.35 Business Component JSP Application Wizard Icon.

[15]Display the object gallery by selecting the `File->New...` menu option.

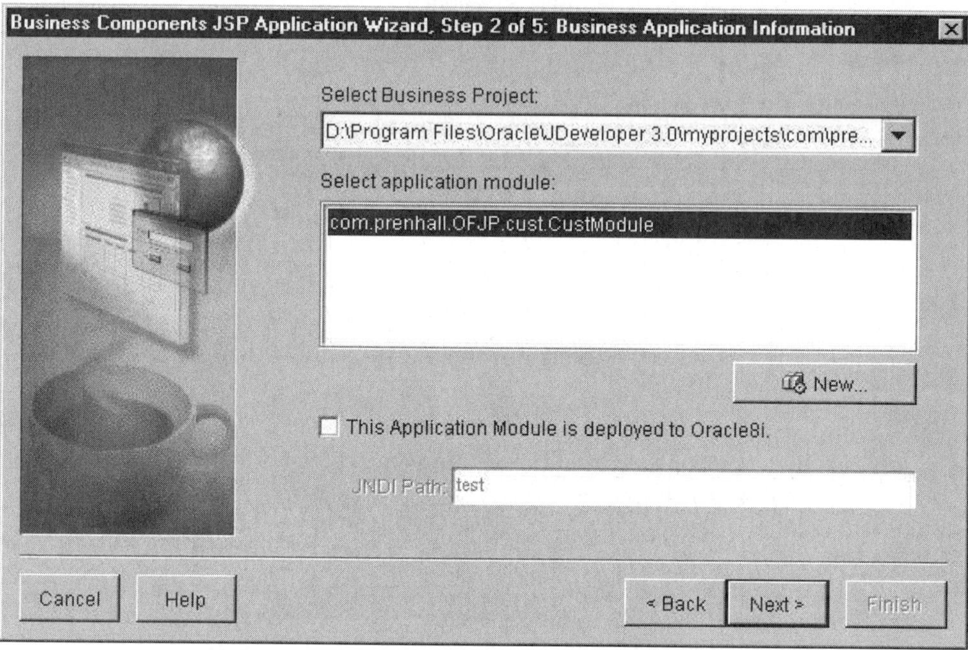

FIGURE 13.36 Enter JSP application Web site information.

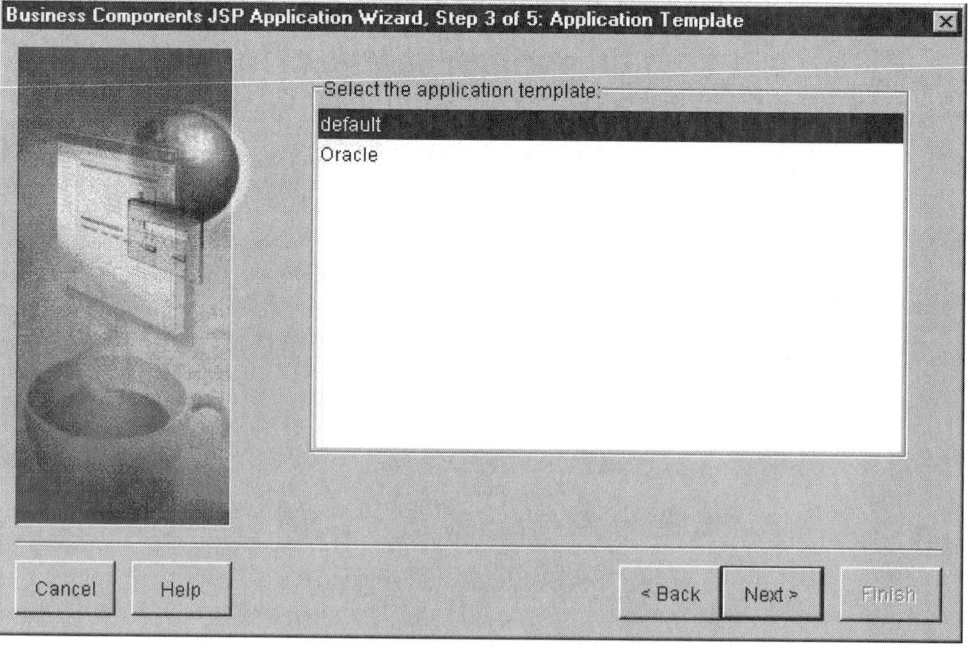

FIGURE 13.37 Select the business application module.

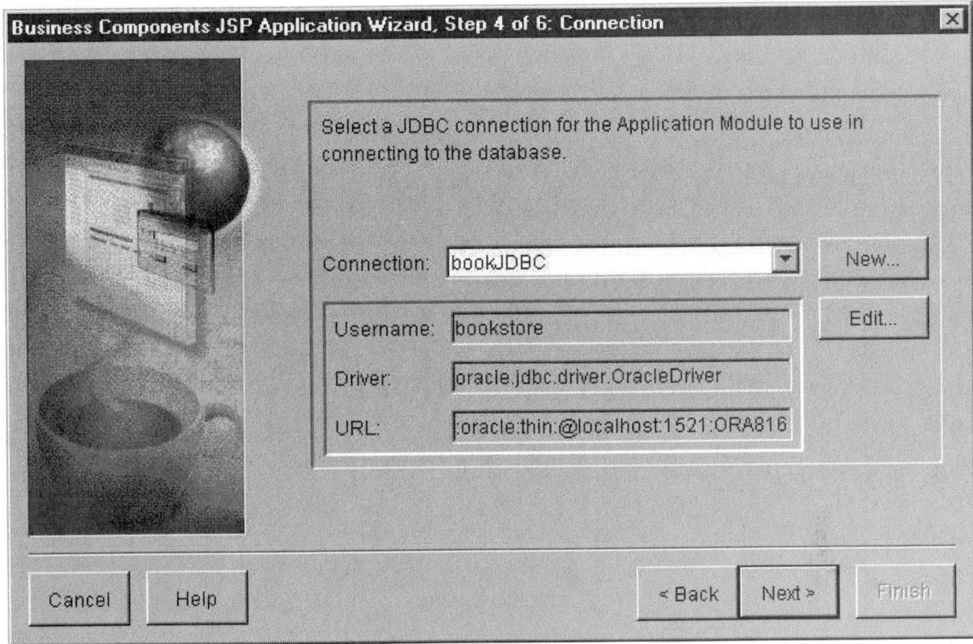

FIGURE 13.38 Select a template.

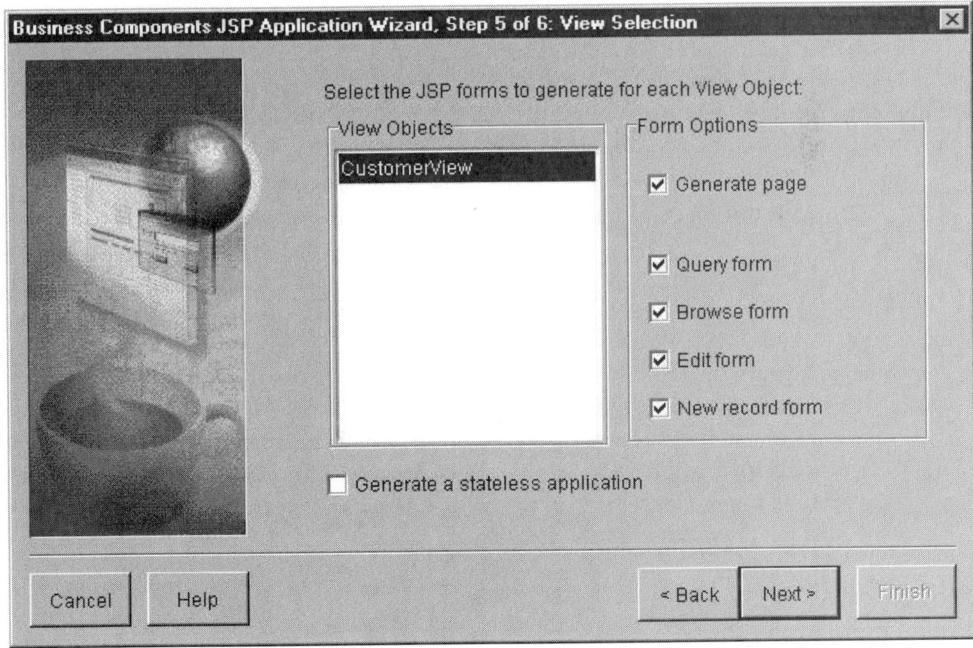

FIGURE 13.39 Choose the name JDBC connection.

The Web application name is displayed in the banner of the main JSP page. The `Project HTML Root` field is combined with the `Application Directory Name` to define the base location for JSP files generated by the wizard. The `Project HTML Root` cannot be changed in this page, but can be altered in the project properties.[16] You have to change the project properties before starting the wizard whose pages are modal.

The checkbox "`The Application is deployed to Oracle8i`" is not relevant for this example because it implies that you have stored the business component classes in an Oracle8i database for use as a remote module in the form of an Enterprise JavaBean (EJB) or a CORBA object (EJB's are discussed in Chapters 21 and 22; CORBA in Chapters 23, 24, and 25).

Note that the preceding three page titles showing "Step n of 5" (where n = 1, 2, 3) are minor display bugs, not a printing error in this book.

The view object provides access to the database data, and you can selectively generate one or four JSP forms for each view object included in the application. The JSP forms are:

- A *query form*, to enter search criteria to request a browse form containing data matching the query criteria.
- A *browse form*, to navigate through the queried data records.
- An *edit form*, to edit the current record displayed in the browse form.
- A *new record form*, to insert a new record into the database.

The new record form is launched via the browse form. Records can be deleted using an icon on the navigation bar displayed with the browse form. The JSP file names are generated with the name of the view object as a prefix. For example:

- <view-object-name>_Browse.jsp for the browse form
- <view-object-name>_Edit.jsp for the edit form

The `Generate a stateless application` checkbox, if selected, generates a JSP application that connects to and disconnects from the application module for each JSP page request. Since a stateless application does not save client session state between requests, each request represents a transaction that must be the subject of a commit or rollback operation before completion. A stateless application is best used for supporting more application users at the cost of the extra overhead forming a database connection for each request. A stateless JSP application does not guarantee that it will use the same business component application module across subsequent requests.

---

[16]To change project properties select the `Project->Project Properties` menu, or double-click the project folder name in the JDeveloper Navigator pane.

The wizard, by default, generates a stateful application to maintain the database connection across multiple HTTP requests, thereby improving the response time for specific HTTP sessions. The same application module is reused across requests from the same HTTP client. The downside of a stateful application is that it uses resources.

The last wizard page, not shown in of the figures, controls the look-and-feel, using the Oracle theme. You can add your own themes by providing the appropriate cascading style sheets and modifying a property file. The subject of adding a new theme is not covered in this book.

13.5.2.1 Files Generated by the JSP Wizard. The number of files generated by the JSP wizard varies depending on the number of view objects and JSP display forms selected (see Figure 13.40). Figure 13.41 shows the default set of files JSP generates when all JSP forms have been selected for the `CustomerView`

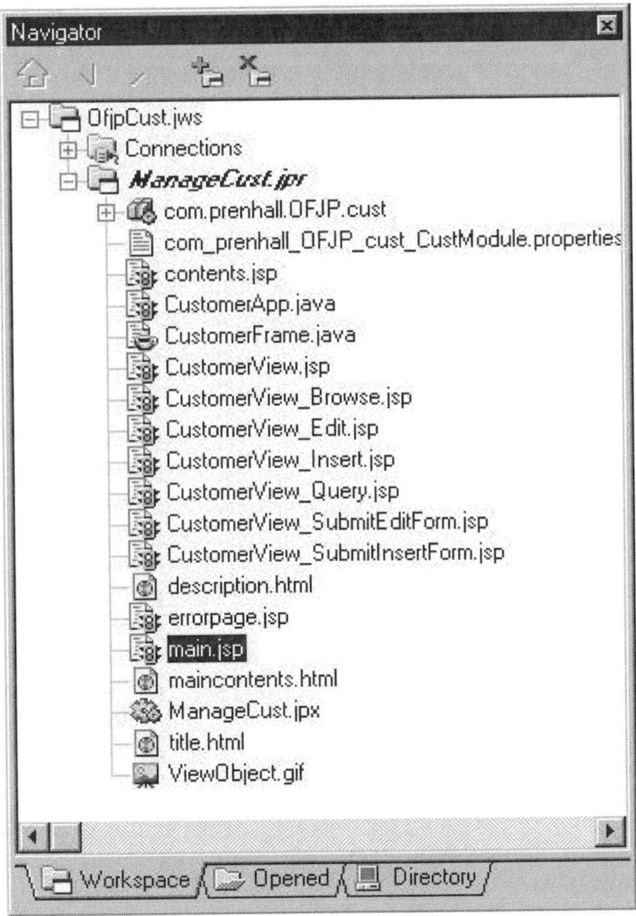

FIGURE 13.40 Select the BC4J view object and JSP pages.

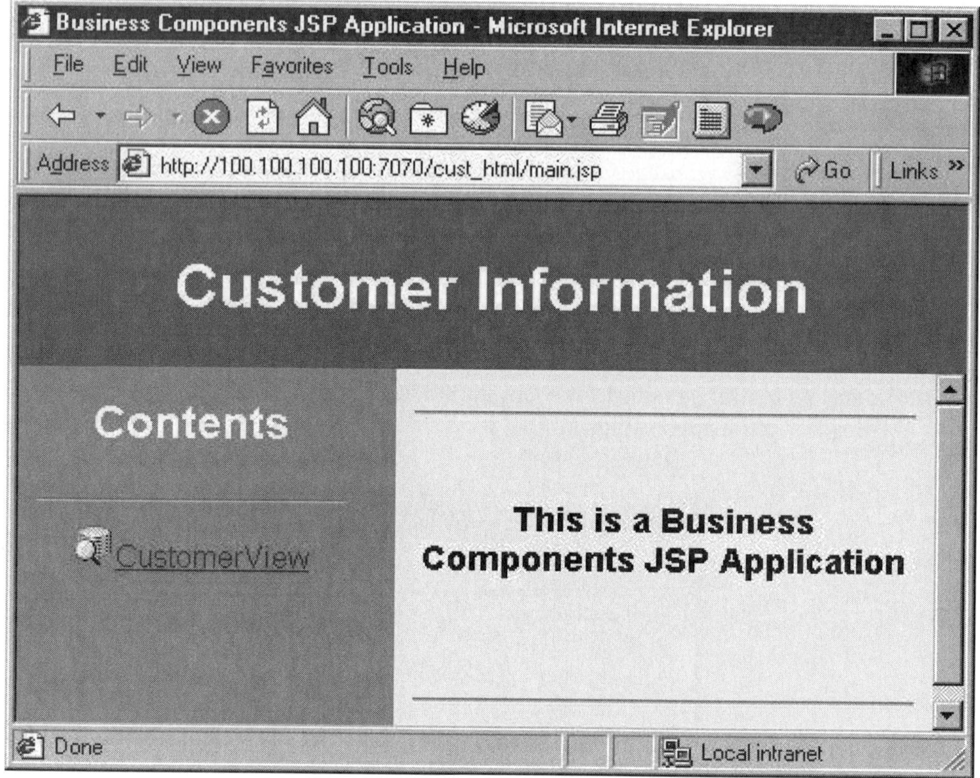

FIGURE 13.41 Generated JSP files for `CustomerView`.

`object`. The `main.jsp` file, highlighted in Figure 13.40, displays the first HTML page of the JSP application. Generated application pages are a preliminary design, and should be modified for production-quality presentation. The wizard is a great tool for Rapid Application Development, but some additional tweaking may be required for a finished product.

Note that two static HTML files are generated to provide the content for the HTML frames display formed by the `main.jsp` file.

- The `title.html` file displays the application title in the top frame.
- The `description.html` file displays the initial right-hand contents frame.

The desired look-and-feel of the JSP application requires additional directories and files containing cascading style sheets and icon images for presentation purposes. These directory settings are specified in a properties file named using the fully qualified name of the business component application module (i.e., the Java package name and the application module name). For example:

```
com_prenhall_OFJP_cust_CustModule.properties
```

The contents of the properties file are shown in Listing 13.7.

```
ApplicationModuleName=com.prenhall.OFJP.cust.CustModule

# can be 8i , EJB or local
ConnectMode=Local

#in 8i mode this is an IIOP connection name
ConnectionName=bookJDBC

# used only if password not provided by connection definition
Password=bookstore

#only used in 8i mode
JndiPath=test

#Defines if application is stateless or not
IsStateLessRuntime=false

#CSS File Name
CSSURL=/webapp/css/oracle.css

#Root Image Directory
ImageBase=/webapp/images
```

LISTING 13.7 JSP application properties file.

The bold text in Listing 13.7 highlights the properties used to specify the cascading style sheet file (`CSSURL`) and the directory for image files (`ImageBase`) used by the JSP application.

13.5.2.2 Testing the JSP Application. JDeveloper provides a lightweight built-in Web server that can be used to test JSP applications. However, the built-in Web server is only intended for developing, debugging, and testing JSP or servlet code. You can run the JSP application by selecting the `main.jsp` file in the JDeveloper navigator pane and clicking the Run icon. You can choose to run any of the JSP files to test the appearance and behavior of the page. The resulting Web page displayed for the `CustomerView` JSP example is presented in Figure 13.42.

The `main.jsp` file generates an HTML frame window with a line in the left-hand contents frame for each view object in the application. The example only has one view object: the `CustomerView`.

Clicking the `CustomerView` line in the JSP-generated HTML page requests a display of the CustomverView.jsp page, which appears in the right-hand content frame, as shown in Figure 13.42.

The `CustomerView.jsp` page displays one customer record at a time and provides an iconic Navigation toolbar. When an icon is clicked, an HTTP request to display the appropriate JSP is sent to the Web server. Most icons have the same meaning as their GUI client Navigation toolbar cousins. The JSP application provides the following additional toolbar icons:

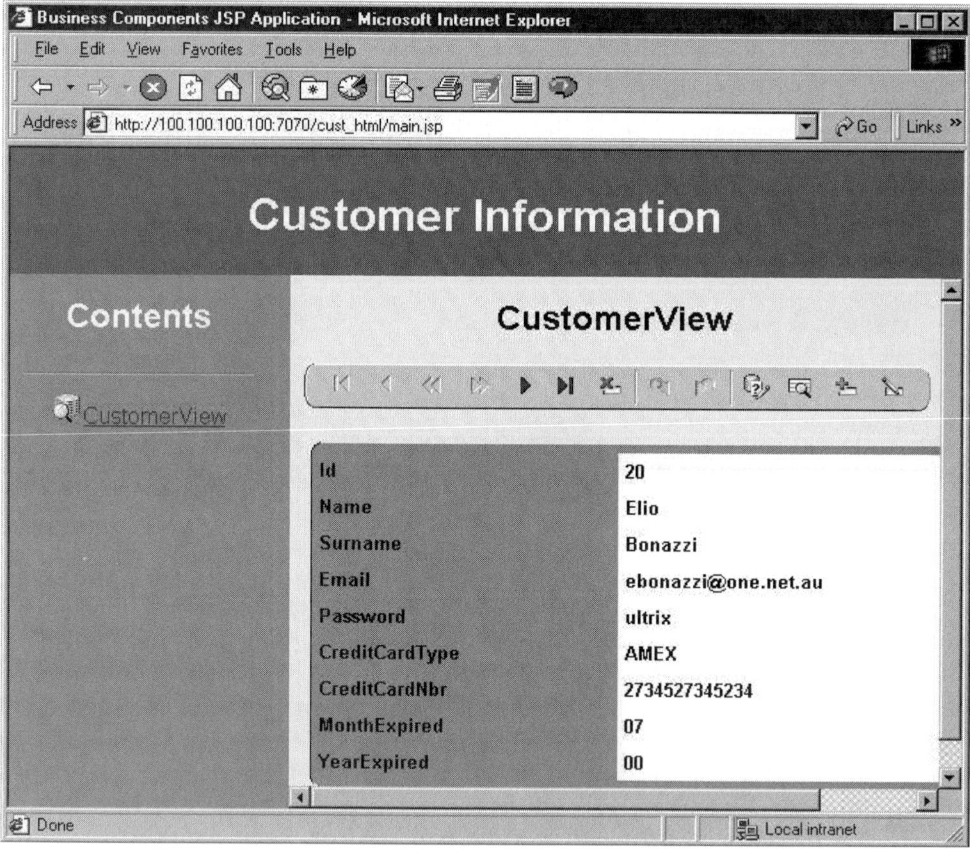

FIGURE 13.42 The main page for the `CustomerView` JSP application.

- Request the edit form for the current record.
- Launch the browse form for all records.

13.5.2.3 The Business Component JSP Application Architecture. The business component JSP application architecture generated by JDeveloper is represented in Figure 13.43.

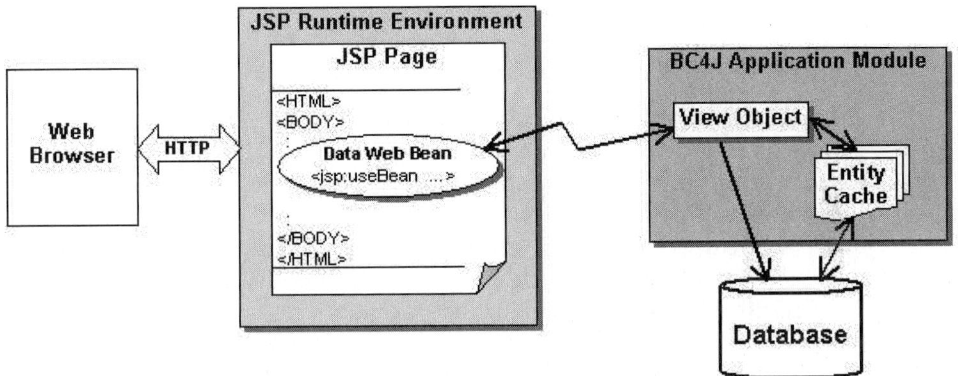

FIGURE 13.43 `CustomerView` JSP browse form.

The architecture depends on the use of JavaBean technology and the ability of the JavaServer page to create and invoke JavaBean methods. The JavaServer page application uses a `<jsp:useBean>` tag[17] to instantiate a JavaBean to create a business component application module and access the view object. This architecture has several advantages:

- The separation of business logic from user-presentation logic.
- The ability to build scalable Web applications by enabling the business logic to be distributed.

You can customize the HTML look-and-feel without affecting the Web bean logic, or you can modify the business logic with minimal impact on the look-and-feel interface. Basic JSP coding techniques are covered in detail in Chapter 15. In the JSP context, Java beans are called *Web beans*. Each Web bean has a `render()` method to print the HTML it encapsulates. JDeveloper provides two types of Web beans:

[17]The <jsp:useBean> tag is documented as part of the JSP specifications; it is covered in more detail in Chapter 15.

- HTML Web beans for visual controls (e.g., toolbar, table control, and edit forms). The data displayed by these beans must be programmatically provided.
- Data Web beans as data-aware alternatives to HTML Web beans. They obtain data directly from a business component view object (e.g., Navigator Bar, RowSet Browser, Edit Current Record).

The HTML Web beans in an HTML application are loosely analogous to the Swing controls in a GUI application. Data Web beans are Web-based data-aware controls in an HTML environment, analogous to the Oracle Swing-based data-aware controls used in a client/server GUI application.

13.5.3 MANUALLY CODING A BUSINESS COMPONENT CLIENT

The Business Components for Java classes and XML files are built on a set of classes that provide the infrastructure for the framework. The class library for business components is contained in several Java archive (`jar`) files shipped with JDeveloper. The `jar` files for the Business Components for Java framework usually start with the letters `jbo` and can be found in the `lib` subdirectory of the JDeveloper installation directory.

In this section, you will see how to use some of the classes and interfaces to query, update, and delete data through a business component view object.

The basic coding steps required of your hand-coded applications are:

1. Set your environment to load a local or a remote application module.
2. Load the application module.
3. Create a view object.
4. Use the view object to access or modify the data.
5. Use the application module database transaction object to save or discard changes made to data through the view object.
6. Disconnect from the application module and release resources.

13.5.3.1 Setting Your Environment. Initial environment variables are set in a `java.util.Hashtable.` For clarity the environment variable values are hard-coded. The environment variables specified are either for a local or a remote application module. Listing 13.8 uses environment settings for connecting to a local application module.

```
package com.prenhall.OFJP.cust;

import java.util.Hashtable;
import javax.naming.Context;
import oracle.jbo.JboContext;
```

LISTING 13.8 Environment for a local application module.

```
public class Bc4jClient {
   private static Hashtable  env = new Hashtable(10);

   public static void setLocalEnv() {
     env.put(Context.INITIAL_CONTEXT_FACTORY,
             JboContext.JBO_CONTEXT_FACTORY);
     env.put(JboContext.DEPLOY_PLATFORM,
           JboContext.PLATFORM_LOCAL);
   }
   :
}
```

LISTING 13.8 *Continued*

If the application module is a remote module, as in the Oracle8i CORBA server, set the environment values using code similar to Listing 13.9.

```
package com.prenhall.OFJP.bc4j;

import java.util.Hashtable;
import javax.naming.Context;
import javax.naming.InitialContext;
import oracle.jbo.JboContext;

public class Bc4jClient {
  private static Hashtable  env = new Hashtable(10);

  public static void setRemoteEnv() {
    env.put(Context.INITIAL_CONTEXT_FACTORY,
            JboContext.JBO_CONTEXT_FACTORY);
    env.put(JboContext.DEPLOY_PLATFORM,
            JboContext.PLATFORM_ORACLE8I);
    env.put(Context.SECURITY_PRINCIPAL, "bookstore");
    env.put(Context.SECURITY_CREDENTIALS, "bookstore");
    env.put(JboContext.HOST_NAME, "localhost");
    env.put(JboContext.CONNECTION_PORT, "2481"); //IIOP port
    env.put(JboContext.ORACLE_SID, "ORA816");
    env.put(JboContext.APPLICATION_PATH, "test");// JNDI init path
  }
  :
}
```

LISTING 13.9 Environment for a remote application module.

The environment variables for a remote application module require that you identify the name of a remote host, the IIOP listener port, login credentials, an Oracle8i database instance name, and a JNDI path name for the application module.[18] Subsequent examples use environment settings for the local application module.

13.5.3.2 Loading the Application Module. After setting the environment variables, you can load an application module using a JNDI connection sequence, with the following steps:

1. Establish an initial context to search for/lookup the application module by name.
2. Perform a lookup for the application module home interface. The home interface is an object factory for creating the application module.
3. Create an application module.
4. Get a transaction and connection context.

Listing 13.10 shows sample code to load the application module and create a connection and transaction context.

```
package com.prenhall.OFJP.cust;
import java.util.Hashtable;
import javax.naming.Context;
import javax.naming.InitialContext;
import oracle.jbo.JboContext;
import oracle.jbo.ApplicationModule;
import oracle.jbo.ApplicationModuleHome;

public class Bc4jClient {
  private static Hashtable  env = new Hashtable(10);
  private static ApplicationModule appMod = null;
  private static String url = "jdbc:oracle:thin:" +
          "bookstore/bookstore@localhost:1521:ORA816";

  public static void setLocalEnv() {
    env.put(Context.INITIAL_CONTEXT_FACTORY,
            JboContext.JBO_CONTEXT_FACTORY);
    env.put(JboContext.DEPLOY_PLATFORM,
```

LISTING 13.10 Loading the application module.

[18]See Chapter 10 for more information about JNDI (Java Naming and Directory Interface).

```
19:             JboContext.PLATFORM_LOCAL);
20:    }
21:
22:   public static void loadApplication() {
23:     String appModuleName="com.prenhall.OFJP.cust.CustModule";
24:
25:     // assume setLocalEnv() has been called
26:
27:     // Load the Application module
28:     try {
29:       Context ic = new InitialContext(env);
30:       ApplicationModuleHome home =
31:           (ApplicationModuleHome) ic.lookup(appModuleName);
32:       appMod = home.create();
33:       appMod.getTransaction().connect(url);
34:     }
35:     catch (Exception e) {
36:       e.printStackTrace();
37:     }
38:   }
39:   :
40: }
```

LISTING 13.10 *Continued*

Notes on Listing 13.10:

- Lines 6 and 7 import `ApplicationModuleHome` and `ApplicationModule` interfaces from the `oracle.jbo` package needed to locate and load an application module.
- Line 11 declares a static variable for the application module.
- Line 23 declares a local variable containing the name of the application module to be loaded.
- Line 29 sets the initial context for the JNDI lookup request. This line requires the `import javax.naming.Context;`
- Line 30 performs the JNDI lookup for an application module by name from the initial JNDI context set in line 29. If successful, a reference to an `ApplicationModuleHome` interface representing a factory class is returned.
- Line 32 creates and loads the named application module.
- Line 33 gets a transaction context from the application module and connects to the database using the JDBC URL string from line 12.

This `loadApplication()` method is quite generic. With minor modifications it can be used to load both local and remote application modules.

13.5.3.3 Creating and Using a View Object. After setting the environment and loading an application module, use the application module methods to create a view object, and use the view object methods to query and manipulate the data. Listing 13.11 uses the methods shown in Listing 13.10, and creates a view object to iterate through and display some of the attributes from customer rows, and modify the credit card expiry year.

```
package com.prenhall.OFJP.cust;
import java.util.Hashtable;
import javax.naming.Context;
import javax.naming.InitialContext;
import oracle.jbo.JboContext;
import oracle.jbo.ApplicationModule;
import oracle.jbo.ApplicationModuleHome;
import oracle.jbo.ViewObject;
import oracle.jbo.Row;
import oracle.jbo.domain.Number;

public class Bc4jClient {
  private static Hashtable  env = new Hashtable(10);
  private static ApplicationModule appMod = null;
  private static String url = "jdbc:oracle:thin:" +
         "bookstore/bookstore@localhost:1521:ORA816";

  public static void setLocalEnv() {
    env.put(Context.INITIAL_CONTEXT_FACTORY,
            JboContext.JBO_CONTEXT_FACTORY);
    env.put(JboContext.DEPLOY_PLATFORM,
            JboContext.PLATFORM_LOCAL);
  }

  public static void loadApplication() {
    String appModuleName =
        "com.prenhall.OFJP.cust.CustModule";
    try {
      Context ic = new InitialContext(env);
      ApplicationModuleHome home =
          (ApplicationModuleHome) ic.lookup(appModuleName);
      appMod = home.create();
```

LISTING 13.11 Creating a view object from an application module.

```
      appMod.getTransaction().connect(url);
    }
    catch (Exception e) {
      e.printStackTrace();
      System.exit(0);
    }
  }

  public static void main(String[] args) {
    ViewObject v = null;
    Row row = null;
    Number id = null;
    String name = null,
           surname = null,
           yearExpired = null,
           monthExpired = null;

    setLocalEnv();
    loadApplication();
    v = appMod.createViewObject("Customers",
           "com.prenhall.OFJP.cust.CustomerView");
    while (v.hasNext()) {
      row = v.next();
      id = (Number) row.getAttribute("Id");
      name = (String) row.getAttribute("Name");
      surname = (String) row.getAttribute("Surname");
      yearExpired = (String) row.getAttribute("YearExpired");
      monthExpired =(String) row.getAttribute("MonthExpired");
      System.out.println(id.toString() + " " +
          name + " " + surname + " " +
          yearExpired + "/" + monthExpired);
      if (Integer.parseInt(yearExpired) == 99) {
        row.setAttribute("YearExpired", "02");
        System.out.println("Year expiry updated to 02");
      }
    }
    appMod.getTransaction().commit();
    appMod.getTransaction().disconnect();
    v.remove();
    appMod.remove();
  }
}
```

LISTING 13.11 *Continued*

Notes on Listing 13.11:

- Lines 5 to 10 import interfaces from the `oracle.jbo` package. These interfaces are used to declare object references.
- Lines 13 to 16 create an instance variable for the application module and declare a JDBC URL for creating a database connection.
- Lines 18 to 23 set the environment properties used to locate and load the application module.
- Lines 25 to 39 locate and load the application module.
- Lines 52 and 53 create a view object where the first parameter is an internal name for the view object, and the second parameter is the fully qualified name for the view object name defined in a `<ViewUsage>` element in the application module XML file (i.e., `CustModule.xml`).
- Lines 54 to 68 iterate through the rows, satisfying the query defined in the view object.
  - Line 54 checks whether there is a row to be processed using the `hasNext()` method of the View object. If true, the row can be processed; otherwise the loop terminates because there are no more rows.
  - Line 55 fetches the next row instance by calling the `next()` method of the view object.
  - Line 56 uses the `oracle.jbo.domain.Number` class in the cast operation, which should not be confused with the `java.lang.Number` class.
  - Lines 56 to 60 show how to obtain attribute/column values for each row. The parameter to `Row.getAttribute()`method is the case-sensitive name of the attribute as defined in the view object XML file. The data type used to cast the return value of the `getAttribute()` method should correspond to the data type defined in the `<Attribute>` element of the entity object XML file associated with the view object.
  - Line 65 alters the year expiry date for any row whose current year expired value is 99. The code rule is shown to demonstrate how you can modify an attribute value with the `Row.setAttribute()` method. `Row.setAttribute()` requires the attribute name as the first argument, and the new value in the second argument. The change is made to the copy of the database row in memory (i.e., in the entity object instance for the row). In addition, the database row will be locked, but not modified, if the application module is using pessimistic locking.
- Line 60 uses the application module object to get a transaction context, which is used to issue a commit operation causing the framework to execute the SQL DML operations needed to modify the actual database rows, reflecting the changes made to their entity objects.
- Line 61 releases the database connection held by the application module.
- Line 71 destroys the view object, releasing resource used.
- Line 72 destroys the application module, releasing resource used.

The processing steps demonstrated in this example reflect the processing principle commonly applied when working with database data; namely, after getting a database connection, start a transaction, query the data, modify some data, and commit the changes before releasing the database connection.

13.5.3.4 Understanding the View Object and Row Methods. The `ViewObject` interface is part of a class hierarchy in the oracle.jbo package, as shown in Figure 13.44

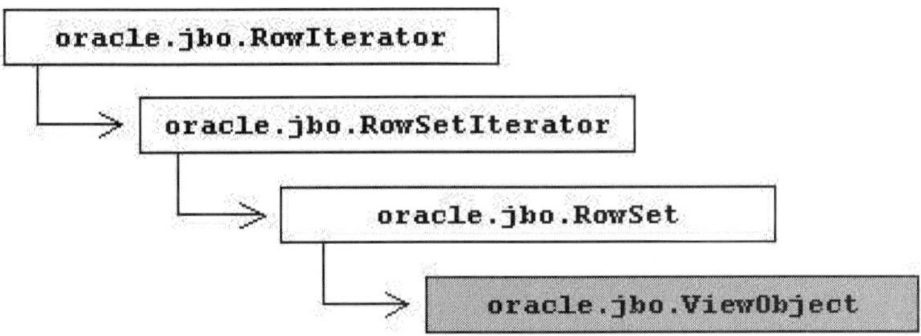

FIGURE 13.44 `ViewObject` inheritance hierarchy.

The view object inherits the following methods to interact with the database:

- `oracle.jbo.RowSet.executeQuery()` to execute the query defined by the view object XML metadata file and create the entities for each row.
- `oracle.jbo.RowSetIterator.hasNext()` and `oracle.jbo.RowSetIterator.hasPrevious()` to test, respectively, for the existence of a row after or before the current row.
- `oracle.jbo.RowSetIterator.first()`, `oracle.jbo.RowSetIterator.next()`, `oracle.jbo.RowSetIterator.previous()`, and `oracle.jbo.RowSetIterator.last()` to start at the first row, iterate forward, iterate backward, or start at the last row, respectively. These methods return a reference to an `oracle.jbo.Row` object held in the entity cache for the application module.
- oracle.jbo.RowSetIterator.removeCurrentRow() to mark a row for deletion.

The `oracle.jbo.Row` interface is used to access the data queried by the view object. The `oracle.jbo.Row` interface in Figure 13.45 is a superclass for the `Entity` interface, which is implemented by an entity object.

When you obtain a reference to an `oracle.jbo.Row` returned by calling the `next()` method of the view object, you effectively get a reference to an entity object. The row inherits the following methods to access the attribute data:

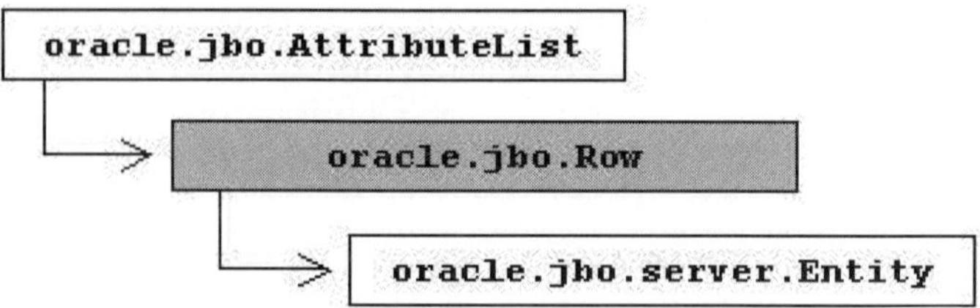

FIGURE 13.45 The entity and row interface hierarchy.

- Object getAttribute(String attrName).
- Object getAttribute(int attrIndex).
- void setAttribute(String attrName, Object value).
- void setAttribute(int attrIndex, Object value).

The `getAttribute()` and `setAttribute()` methods are overloaded to allow you to access an attribute by name or by an index of the attribute. Here are some additional methods inherited from the `oracle.jbo.AttributeList`:

- `getAttributeCount()` returns an integer indicating the number of attributes available in the row.
- `getAttributeIndexOf()` returns the index of the attribute name in the `String` argument. The indexes are zero based.

13.5.3.5 Saving or Discarding Changes. Each row queried by a view object is stored in memory as an entity object. The entity object is an object-oriented representation of a row and its data. Changes made to the attribute values in an entity object affect:

- The attribute values in memory not in the database
- The status of the entity object

Since your changes are buffered in memory (i.e., the entity object), the related data in the database row is not synchronized until the corresponding DML operation is performed. The process of executing DML operations on the database data to be synchronized with changes in memory is called *posting*. Since posting does not cause a database commit operation to occur, you can still roll back the posted data. Posting can be programmatically requested by calling the `postChanges()` method in the transaction context for the application module. The BC4J framework uses two states to track the status of each entity object

- The *post-state* indicates the type of DML operation required when posting is done. The post-state is reset to `STATUS_UNMODIFIED` (see the state values given below) after the DML operations are performed, thus preventing the same entity data from being posted again if there have been no more changes since the last posting.

- The *entity-state* indicates whether the database row for the entity has been modified by a DML operation. The entity-state is reset to `STATUS_UNMODIFIED` by a commit or a rollback operation.

The values for the post-state and entity-state can be:

- `STATUS_NEW` for a new row created in memory, causing a database insert operation to be executed in the posting phase.
- `STATUS_MODIFIED` for row whose attributes are modified, causing an update operation to be done in the posting phase.
- `STATUS_DELETED` for a deleted row, causing a delete operation in the posting phase.
- `STATUS_DEAD` for a new row that has been discarded. No database operation is required.
- `STATUS_UNMODIFIED` when a row is first queried, the post-state after the entity has been posted but not yet committed, and the entity-state after a commit or rollback operation has been performed.

You must execute a `postChanges()` or `commit()` operation to flush changes in the entity cache to the database. A commit request causes posting to occur prior to the real database commit operation. During the posting phase entity an attribute-level validation is performed. If validation fails for an entity, it is not posted to the database. To execute a `postChanges()`, `commit()` or `rollback()` operation, you must obtain the transaction context for the application module, as follows:

```
oracle.jbo.Transaction appModTx = appMod.getTransaction();
```

The `Transaction` interface has the following methods of interest:

- `postChanges()` executes insert, update, and delete operations for all entity rows marked with a changed status. A commit operation is not performed when you execute the `postChanges()` method. The changes are still subject to a rollback operation.
- `commit()` executes a commit operation.
- `rollback()` executes a rollback operation.
- `connect()` connects the application module to the database specified by the `String` argument.
- `disconnect()` disconnects the application module from the database.

- `setLockingMode()` changes the locking mode used by the application module. The valid locking values, defined as public static final variables in the `Transaction` interface, are:
  - `Transaction.LOCK_NONE` for row locking that is manual and not done automatically by the framework.
  - `Transaction.LOCK_OPTIMISTIC` for automatic locking that occurs post-cycle (i.e., locks occur due the DML operations).
  - `Transaction.LOCK_PESSIMISTIC` for automatic locking of rows when a row attribute is modified. Pessimistic locking is the default if the lock mode is not explicitly specified.
- `getLockingMode()` returns the current locking mode.
- `isDirty()` indicates whether application module data have been modified but not committed.
- `executeCommand()` allows you to execute any SQL statement against the database to which the application module is connected.

Some of these methods are shown in lines 33, 69, and 70 of Listing 13.11.

13.5.3.6 Releasing Resources. You can dynamically release resources such as the view object and the application module, by executing their `remove()` methods. Removing an application module implicitly disconnects from the database and removes all view objects from the application module. Changes to the entity cache are not saved unless you explicitly call the `Transaction.commit()` method before removing the application module. Take care when executing the `remove()` method on a `oracle.jbo.Row` object, since the row status is marked for deletion from the database.

13.5.3.7 Some Words on Using Business Components Manually. The manually coded examples in this section should provide you with an understanding and appreciation of how the business component framework operates. It is not that difficult, and your code can be used in a variety of contexts other than printing data to the console. For example, you can easily extend the examples in this chapter to work in:

- A Java GUI application
- A Java applet
- A Java servlet
- A JavaServer page
- A Java bean
- A distributed component (e.g., an Enterprise JavaBean)

The code in this section mostly uses the interfaces defined in the `oracle.jbo` package. It is highly recommended that you always work with these interfaces to minimize direct dependency on the `<interface>Impl` classes. The `<interface>Impl` is part of the `oracle.jbo.server` package; since this is designed for use in the application module itself, client use should be avoided. If you follow this recommendation, your client will be able to maintain a clean independence from the application module code, allowing you to deploy the application module locally or remotely without changing the client code and without any performance impact on the client application.

13.6 CUSTOMIZING THE COMPONENTS

The Java classes generated by the business component wizard can be modified to customize their structure and behavior. Some customizations, such as adding validation rules, or defining and applying domains, are performed by the business components editor wizard.

If you intend to modify the Java source directly, consider creating a subclass of the generated code, because the business components editor wizard always make modifications to either the XML file, the Java file, or both. Therefore, if you add code directly into the generated classes, you risk losing your changes.

By creating a subclass, you keep the intended default functionality, preserve your extensions in a separate class, and simply modify the rules and structure of the superclass, when required, using the standard business component wizard editors already discussed in this chapter.

In this section, you will examine various customization options, such as:

- Adding validation rules.
- Adding and applying domains.
- Overriding SQL statements in the entity object to perform a logical deletion.
- Creating a subclass of the Java or XML file to extend components.

13.6.1 DATA-VALIDATION RULES

You may want to add data-validation rules to your code if the database is not enforcing them via database constraints or triggers. Sometimes there are performance advantages to doing validation outside the database, at the risk of decentralizing your validation logic. Basic data-validation rules can be added using the entity object wizard; they can be added as entity-level or attribute-level validation rules.

The Business Components for Java framework provides default validation rules that are implemented as Java beans. The validation-rule classes are located in the `oracle.jbo.server.rules` package. Several types of validation rules are provided.

- `CompareValidator` performs a logical comparison between an attribute and a value. The compared value can be a literal, a query, or an attribute in a view object. The implementation class name is `oracle.jbo.server.rules.JboCompareValidator`.
- `ListValidator` compares an attribute against a list of values. The list of values can be static, based on a query, or based on an attribute from a view object. The implementation class name is `oracle.jbo.server.rules.JboListValidator`.
- `RangeValidator` tests attribute values within a range of specified minimum and maximum values. The implementation class name is `oracle.jbo.server.rules.JboRangeValidator`.
- `MethodValidator` invokes a customized, or user-defined, method that must be added to the Java file prior to its use for validation. The implementation class is `oracle.jbo.server.rules.JboMethodValidator`.

In addition to the above four options, you can create your own validation classes, but that is not covered in this section.

Figure 13.46 shows the `Validation` tab in the entity object wizard where you can apply validation rules to each attribute. The entity object wizard is

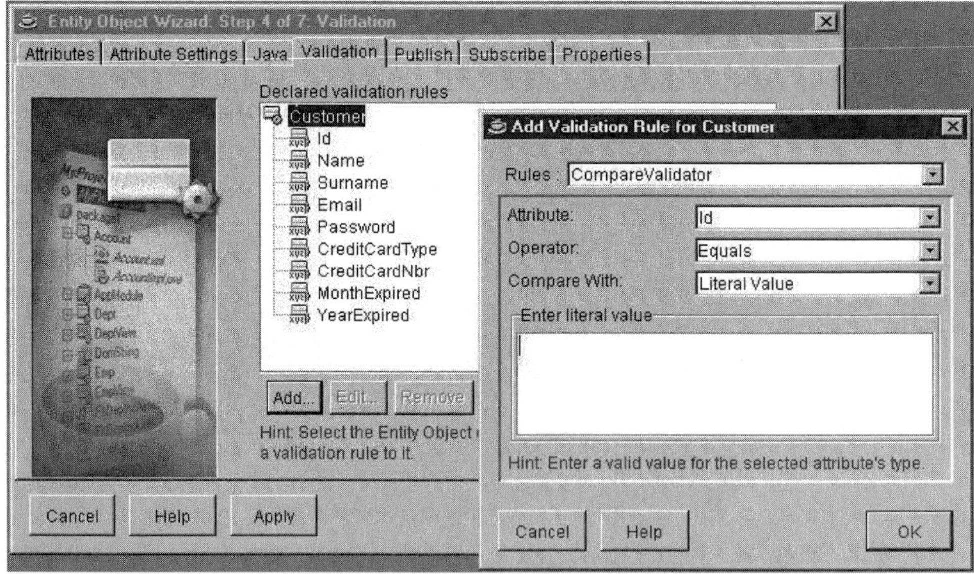

FIGURE 13.46 Adding/applying validation rules to entity attributes.

launched by selecting in the `Edit <entity>...` menu item from a menu displayed when you right-click on the name of the entity object folder in JDeveloper Navigator. In the `Validation` tab, select the attribute and then click on the `Add` button to display the validation rule dialog.

The Add Validation Rule dialog provides the following common settings:

- Rules—to choose the type of rule, such as `CompareValidator`.
- Attribute— to choose the attribute to which the rule is applied.

Additional settings are dependent on the type of rule chosen. If you choose the `CompareValidator`, additional options are:

- Operator—the choice is Equals, NotEquals, LessThan, GreaterThan, LessOrEqualTo, or GreaterOrEqualTo.
- Compare With—the choice is a literal value, query result, or view object attribute.

For the `ListValidator`, additional options are:

- Operator—the choice is `In` or `NotIn`.
- List—the choice is literal values, query result, or view object attribute.

For the `RangeValidator`, additional settings are:

- Operator—choose `Between` or `NotBetween`.
- Minimum value.
- Maximum value.

In the `Compare With/List` field, for the `CompareValidator` and `ListValidator` rules, if you choose:

- Literal value—you must provide the literal value.
- Query result—you must enter a SQL SELECT statement to obtain the value.
- View object attribute—you must select a view object attribute from a view object in the application module.

The result, after making a selection and applying the changes, is that JDeveloper appropriately modifies the XML file for the entity object. The Java source is not changed unless you use the MethodValidator option.

13.6.1.1 Creating an Entity- and Attribute-Level Validation Rule. We will now look at adding two ListValidator rules to the customer entity object. One validation rule will ensure that the `MonthExpired` attribute is a valid string of two digits (i.e., "01", "02", to "12") This is applied as an attribute-level rule. The second ListValidator rule, used as an entity-level rule, checks that the `CreditCardType` field contains a valid string (e.g., "VISA," "MASTERCARD," "AMEX").

An entity-level validation rule is suitable for checking values in related attributes of the same entity object to ensure that the overall state of related data is consistent. Here are two examples: A credit card type has a unique initial number sequence that can be used to validate the card type and number combination; in a customer order entity, you would check that the date ordered is earlier than the date shipped. A validation rule applied to an attribute level is appropriate if it is specific to that attribute alone.

The example validation rule for the credit card type should be added as an attribute-level rule, but it is used as an entity-level validation rule to demonstrate the runtime behavior of validation logic.

Adding the `MonthExpired` validation rule to the `MonthExpired` attribute is shown in Figure 13.47. You must select the attribute before clicking the `Add` button.

After the attribute-level rule is applied, changes are made to the entity XML file within the `<Attribute>` XML element for `MonthExpired`, as shown in bold in Listing 13.12.

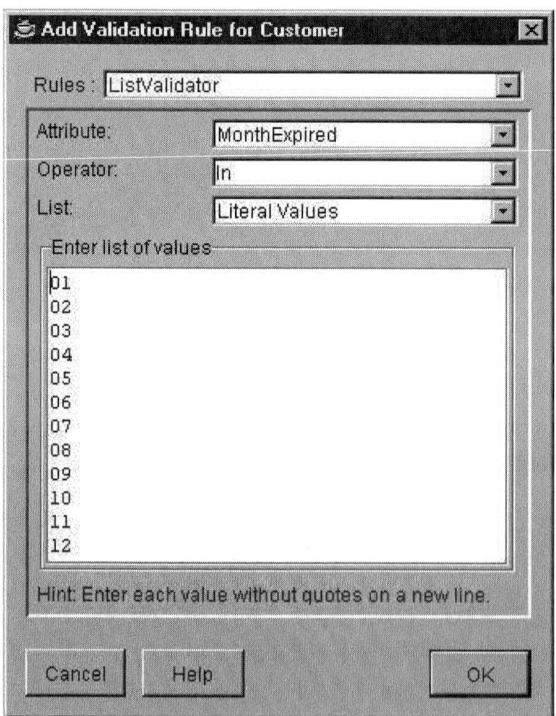

FIGURE 13.47 `MonthExpired` attribute-level ListValidator rule.

```
<Attribute
   Name="MonthExpired"
   Type="java.lang.String"
   ColumnName="MONTH_EXPIRED"
   ColumnType="VARCHAR2"
   SQLType="VARCHAR"
   IsNotNull="true"
   TableName="CUSTOMER"
   Precision="2" >
   <DesignTime>
      <Attr Name="_DisplaySize" Value="2" />
   </DesignTime>
   <ListValidationBean
      OnAttribute="MonthExpired"
      OperandType="LITERAL" >
      <AttrArray Name="List">
         <Item Value="01" />
         <Item Value="02" />
              :
         <Item Value="11" />
         <Item Value="12" />
      </AttrArray>
   </ListValidationBean>
</Attribute>
```

LISTING 13.12 Attribute-level `<ListValidationBean>` XML tag.

To add the credit card type validation rule as an entity-level rule (see Figure 13.48), select the entity name (i.e., `Customer)` before clicking the `Add` button.

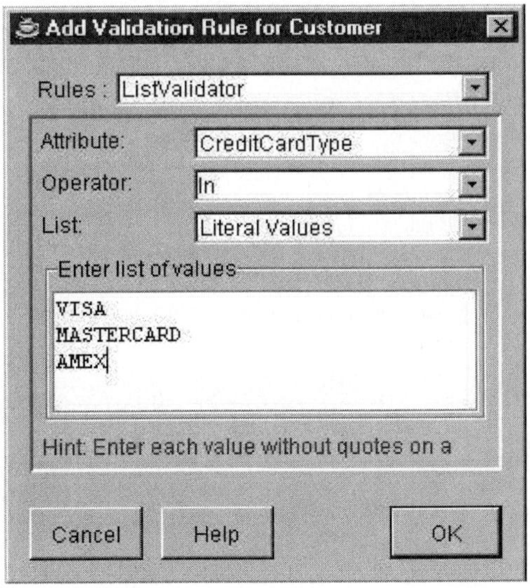

Add Validation Rule for Customer

Rules : ListValidator

Attribute: CreditCardType

Operator: In

List: Literal Values

Enter list of values

VISA
MASTERCARD
AMEX

Hint: Enter each value without quotes on a

Cancel | Help | OK

FIGURE 13.48 `CreditCardType` entity-level ListValidator rule.

The entity XML file is altered to include the <ListValidationBean> element within the <Entity> element, as shown in Listing 13.13.

```
<Entity>
    :
    :
   <ListValidationBean
      OnAttribute="CreditCardType"
      OperandType="LITERAL" >
      <AttrArray Name="List">
         <Item Value="VISA" />
         <Item Value="MASTERCARD" />
         <Item Value="AMEX" />
      </AttrArray>
   </ListValidationBean>
</Entity>
```

LISTING 13.13 Entity-level <ListValidationBean> XML tag.

After adding validation rules, the entity object wizard shows them in the Validation tab. The entity-level rules are shown below the entity name, and the attribute rules below the attribute to which it is assigned (see Figure 13.49).

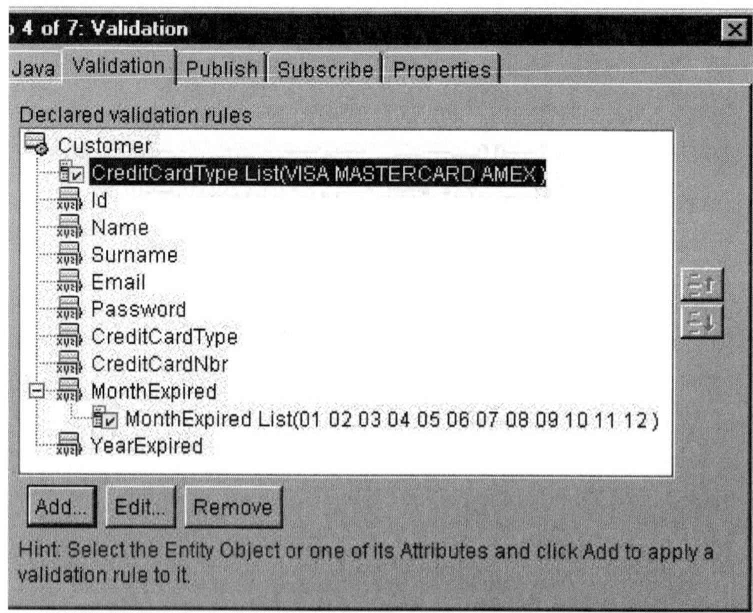

FIGURE 13.49 Validation rules in the entity object wizard.

There is an important advantage to implementing these rules declaratively as an XML tag: if you know the XML tags and formatting of the validation rules, you can modify the XML file in production without changing the Java code to change validation behavior.

Entity-level rules are automatically invoked by the framework when you navigate out of the entity object/row that has been modified. In a GUI application, this occurs when you modify a field in one row and click in an attribute of another displayed row. In the manual code examples, entity validation occurs when you fetch the next row.

Attribute-level rules are invoked when you modify the attribute value with the `setAttribute()` method. In a GUI application, the validation rule is invoked after you visually navigate out of the modified field, using a tab key or by clicking the mouse in another field. The code in Listing 13.14 demonstrates validation behavior.

```
package com.prenhall.OFJP.cust;

import java.util.Hashtable;
import javax.naming.Context;
import javax.naming.InitialContext;
import oracle.jbo.JboContext;
import oracle.jbo.ApplicationModule;
import oracle.jbo.ApplicationModuleHome;
import oracle.jbo.ViewObject;
import oracle.jbo.Row;
import oracle.jbo.domain.Number;
import oracle.jbo.AttrSetValException;

public class Bc4jValidateTest {
  private static Hashtable  env = new Hashtable(10);
  private static ApplicationModule appMod = null;
  private static String
      connStr = "bookstore/bookstore@localhost:1521:ORA816";
  private static String url = "jdbc:oracle:thin:" + connStr;

  public static void setLocalEnv() {
    env.put(Context.INITIAL_CONTEXT_FACTORY,
            JboContext.JBO_CONTEXT_FACTORY);
    env.put(JboContext.DEPLOY_PLATFORM,
            JboContext.PLATFORM_LOCAL);
  }

  public static void loadApplication() {
```

LISTING 13.14 Testing entity- and attribute-level validation rules.

```
    String appModuleName="com.prenhall.OFJP.cust.CustModule";
    try {
      Context ic = new InitialContext(env);
      ApplicationModuleHome home =
          (ApplicationModuleHome) ic.lookup(appModuleName);
      appMod = home.create();
      appMod.getTransaction().connect(url);
    }
    catch (Exception e) {
      e.printStackTrace(); System.exit(0);
    }
  }

  public static void main(String[] args) {
    Row row = v.next();
    Number id = null;
    String name = null;
    String surname = null;
    String cardType = null;
    String monthExp = null;

    setLocalEnv();  loadApplication();
    ViewObject v = appMod.findViewObject("CustomerView");
    v.setWhereClause("year_expired = '00'");
    v.executeQuery();
    try {
      while (v.hasNext()) {
        row = v.next();
        id =  (Number) row.getAttribute("Id");
        name = (String) row.getAttribute("Name");
        surname = (String) row.getAttribute("Surname");
        cardType =(String) row.getAttribute("CreditCardType");
        monthExp = (String) row.getAttribute("MonthExpired");
        System.out.println("BEFORE: "+id + " " + name + " " +
          surname+" card: "+cardType+" MonthExp: "+monthExp);
        if (cardType.equals("MASTERCARD")) {
          row.setAttribute("CreditCardType", "MC");
          try {
            row.setAttribute("MonthExpired", "13");
          }
          catch (AttrSetValException e) {
            System.out.println(
               "setAttribute() error: " + e.getMessage());
```

LISTING 13.14 *Continued*

```
          }
        }
        System.out.println("AFTER: " + id + " " + name + " " +
        surname+" card: "+row.getAttribute("CreditCardType") +
          " MonthExp: " + row.getAttribute("MonthExpired"));
        try {
          row.validate();
        }
        catch (AttrSetValException e) {
          System.out.println(
             "row.validate() error: " + e.getMessage());
        }
      }
    }
    catch (AttrSetValException e) {
      System.out.println("Entity level error: " +
         e.getMessage()); }
    try {
      appMod.getTransaction().commit();
    }
    catch (AttrSetValException e) {
      System.out.println("commit() error: " + e.getMessage());
    }
    appMod.getTransaction().disconnect();
    v.remove(); appMod.remove();
  }
}
```

LISTING 13.14 *Continued*

The code example attempts, erroneously, to abbreviate the MASTERCARD credit card type and set the month expired to thirteen. This code is designed to force the errors, as seen in the sample data and output results for Listing 13.14.

```
SQL Statement
select id, name, credit_card_type, month_expired
from customer
where year_expired = '00';
```

```
Sample Data
 ID NAME     CREDIT_CAR MO
--- -------- ---------- --
 20 Elio     AMEX       10
 50 Glenn    VISA       10
 30 Eivets   MASTERCARD 02
 31 Oej      MASTERCARD 07

Output results from Listing 13-22
BEFORE: 20 Elio Bonazzi card: AMEX MonthExp: 10
AFTER: 20 Elio Bonazzi card: AMEX MonthExp: 10

BEFORE: 50 Glenn Stokol card: VISA MonthExp: 10
AFTER: 50 Glenn Stokol card: VISA MonthExp: 10

BEFORE: 30 Eivets Rednow card: MASTERCARD MonthExp: 02
setAttribute() error: JBO-27011: Attribute set with
value 13 for MonthExpired in Customer failed
AFTER: 30 Eivets Rednow card: MC MonthExp: 02
row.validate() error: JBO-27011: Attribute set with
value MC for CreditCardType in Customer failed

BEFORE: 31 Oej Luniwaz card: MASTERCARD MonthExp: 07
setAttribute() error: JBO-27011: Attribute set with
value 13 for MonthExpired in Customer failed
AFTER: 31 Oej Luniwaz card: MC MonthExp: 07
row.validate() error: JBO-27011: Attribute set with
value MC for CreditCardType in Customer failed

commit() error: JBO-27011: Attribute set with value MC
for CreditCardType in Customer failed
```

Notes on Listing 13.14:

- Line 12 imports the `AttrSetValException` for catching exceptions thrown when a validation error occurs.
- Line 52 shows how to dynamically alter the view object search criteria to control the rows returned.
- Line 53 executes the view query to populate to apply the search condition added on line 52.
- Line 65 forces a validation rule to fail by setting the credit card type to an invalid value. The entity-level validation rule applied to credit card type is not applied until an attempt is made to navigate to another row, calling the `next()` method on line 56 again. The `next()` method changes the currency

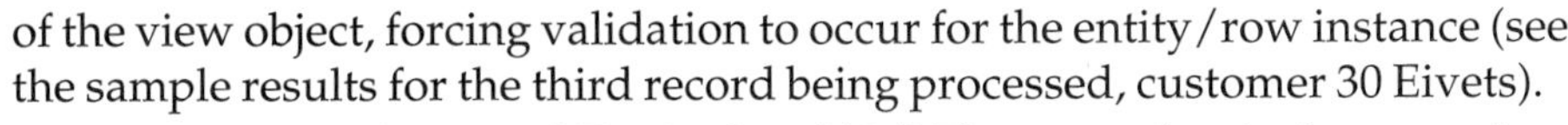

of the view object, forcing validation to occur for the entity/row instance (see the sample results for the third record being processed, customer 30 Eivets).

- ❑ Line 67 changes the MonthExpired to "13." The exception is thrown when the `setAttribute()` method is called, because the validation is applied at the attribute level (see the results for customer 30 Eivets where the `setAttribute()` error occurs before the credit card error).
- ❑ Lines 69 to 72 are the exception-handler code lines to catch a validation exception when changing the `MonthExpired` attribute.
- ❑ Line 78 manually forces/requests validation to occur, causing entity-level validation rules to be evaluated immediately, rather than waiting for a subsequent call to the view object `next()` method.
- ❑ Lines 86 and 88 are the exception handler for entity-level errors not previously handled. However, this exception handler is not invoked because the `try-catch` block used around the `row.validate()` statement in line 78 handles the exceptions. It will be invoked if you remove the `try-catch` block and the `row.validate()` statement.
- ❑ Line 79 attempts to commit the changes made, but since some of the modified attributes in the rows are still in an invalid state, the BC4J framework automatically invokes a validation request before the commit request. In this case, the commit fails because of validation-rule exceptions (see the last error message in the sample output).

In a book, it is easy to write code to demonstrate a validation, but remember that JDeveloper provides a built-in test tool with which you can check the validation rules in a GUI environment. The visual controls in a GUI environment prevent navigation until the validation is successful. In Listing 13.14, the validation throws an exception, but the data have been changed. This is not a problem, since you can undo the changes when you catch the exception. Moreover, a commit request does not succeed until the entity and all its attributes pass validation.

13.6.2 USING DOMAINS

A domain is like a named macrodefinition for a specific data type, and can be specified with a precision and scale. A domain name can be used for one or more attribute definitions to inherit the data type and other characteristics of the domain.

Naming a domain allows you to modify the domain characteristics in one place and have the change be effective wherever the domain is used. This is a time-saving way to manage business validation logic that is required for more than one attribute in an application system.

JDeveloper creates domain objects as additional separate components from other business components. As with other components, creating a domain generates a Java source file and an associated XML file.

13.6.2.1 Creating Domain Components. The two ways of creating a domain in JDeveloper are shown in Figure 13.50.

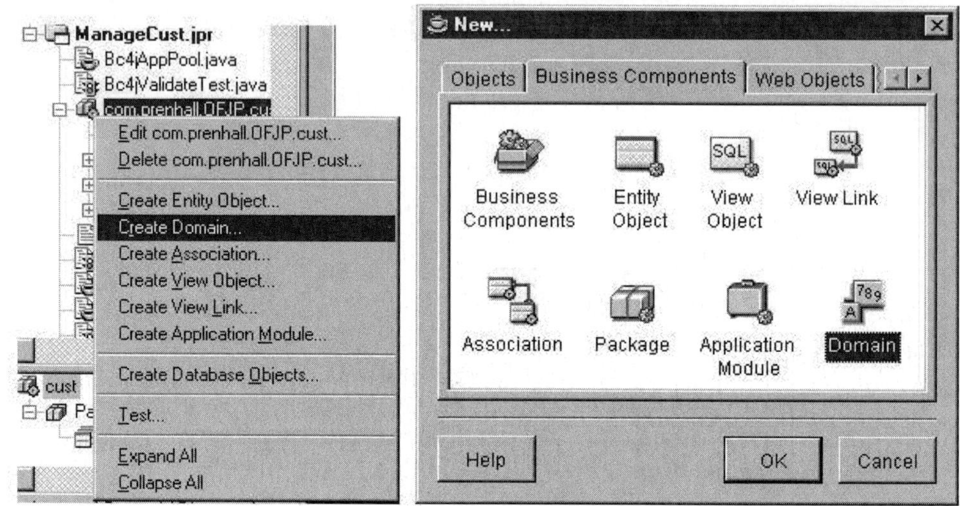

FIGURE 13.50 Choices for creating domains in JDeveloper.

The choices are:

1. Right-click on the business component package name in the navigator pane (the image on the left in Figure 13.51).
2. Select the `File->New` menu, and in the object gallery `Business Components` tab, select the `Domain` icon (the image on the right in Figure 13.51).

Regardless of your choice, you step-through the domain wizard, which requires two steps:

a. Choose the name of your domain class (see Figure 13.51).
b. Define the domain characteristics (see Figure 13.52).

The default package name for the domain class is derived from the business component package to which the domain is added.

The `Attribute Value` group of fields specifies the base Java data type for the domain, an optional default value assigned to the field when a row is created, an indicator to check the uniqueness of the value as a primary key, and a mandatory flag indicating that the attribute defined with the domain requires a value. The persistent flag indicates that the domain will be used with an attribute mapped to a database column. The persistent flag should be left unchecked if the

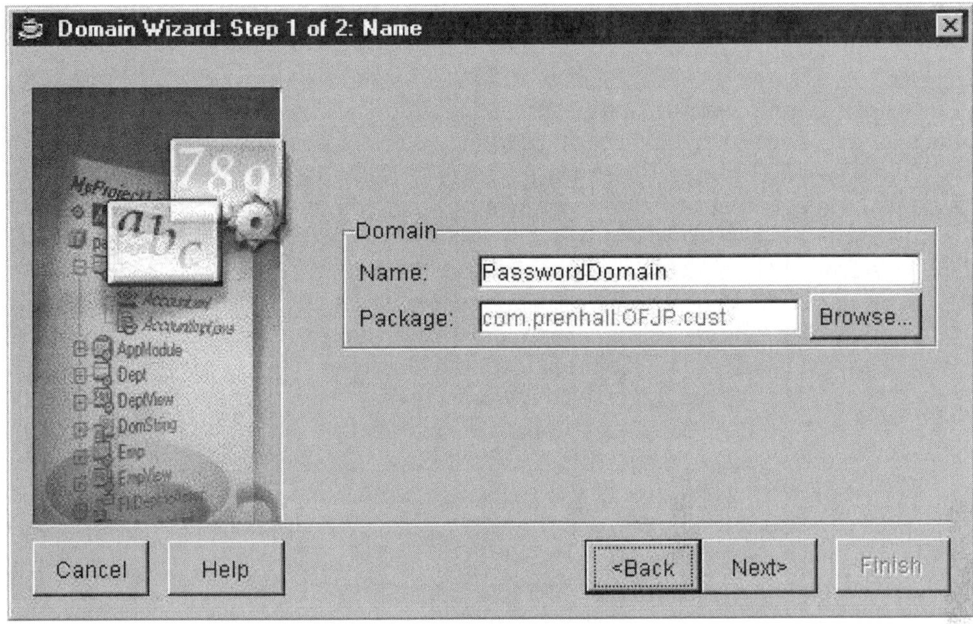

FIGURE 13.51 Selecting the domain name.

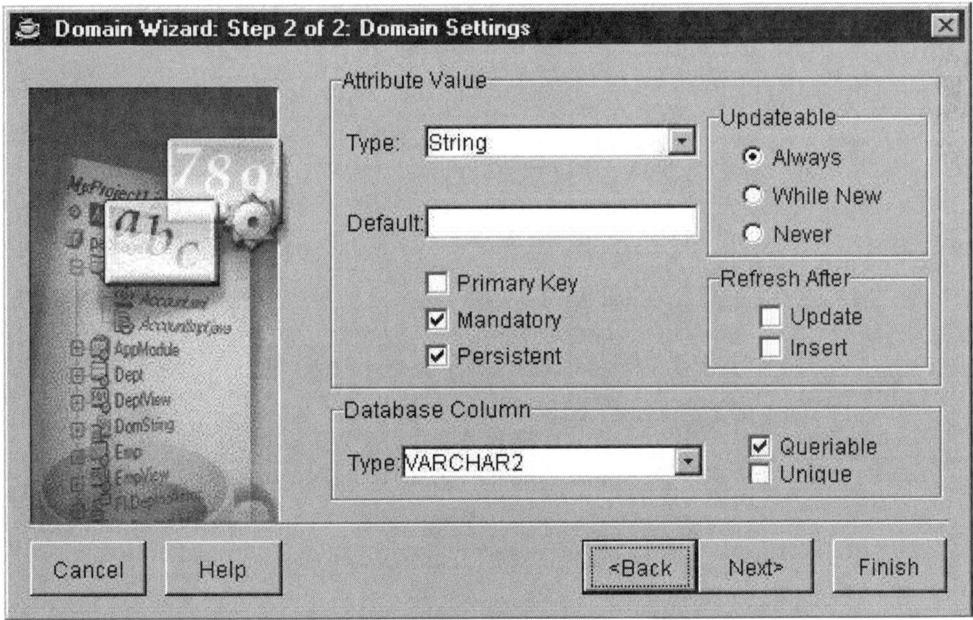

FIGURE 13.52 Setting the domain characteristics.

attribute using the domain is transient (i.e., the attribute not mapped to a column). For example, a derived attribute value is not always mapped to a column.

The `Updateable` section determines when and if the attribute defined with the domain can be modified.

The `Refresh After` options are selected if you want the BC4J entity cache to be synchronized with changes made to the data during the post-cycle or with changes made by activity external to the framework. For example, database triggers or procedures may modify the fields of a table, and the cached entity object may not show these changes unless refreshed.

The `Database Column` section is used for forward generation (i.e., the database objects are created from the business components). The database column settings are not required for this example.

13.6.2.2 Writing the Domain Validation Rules. The Java source file generated by the wizard can be given a validate() method to add validation rules to the domain definition. The `validate()` method for the `PasswordDomain.java` is shown in Listing 13.15.

```
package com.prenhall.OFJP.cust;

// -----------------------------------------------------------
// --- File generated by Oracle Business Components for Java.
// -----------------------------------------------------------


import oracle.jbo.server.*;
import oracle.jbo.domain.DomainInterface;
import oracle.jbo.JboException;

public class PasswordDomain implements
  oracle.jbo.domain.DomainInterface, java.io.Serializable {

  private String mData;
  /**
    * This is the default constructor (do not remove)
    */
  protected PasswordDomain() {
    mData = "";
  }

  public PasswordDomain(String val) {
    mData = new String(val);
```

LISTING 13.15 Domain `PasswordDomain` with validation code.

```
25:       validate();
26:     }
27:
28:     public Object getData() {
29:       return mData;
30:     }
31:     /**
32:       * Implements domain validation logic and
33:       * throws a JboException on error.
34:       */
35:     protected void validate() {
36:       // ### Implement custom domain validation logic here. ###
37:       if (mData == null || mData.length() < 6) {
38:         throw new JboException(
39:           "Password must be 6 or more characters");
40:       }
41:     }
42:
43:     public String toString() {
44:       if (mData != null) {
45:         return    mData.toString();
46:       }
47:       return "<null>";
48:     }
49:
50:     public boolean equals(Object obj) {
51:       if (obj instanceof DomainInterface) {
52:         if (mData != null) {
53:           return mData.equals(((DomainInterface)obj).getData());
54:         }
55:         return ((DomainInterface)obj).getData() == null;
56:       }
57:       return false;
58:     }
59: }
```

LISTING 13.15 *Continued*

The PasswordDomain enforces a password attribute to have a minimum of six characters. The domain can be more sophisticated; for example, it can check that the password also contains at least one digit.

Notes on Listing 13.15:

- Line 15 is an instance variable to hold the value assigned to the attribute defined with the domain. The variable data type corresponds to the base data type chosen for the domain.

- Line 25 shows that the domain `validate()` method is called when the domain is created to validate a value assigned to an attribute. *Note:* this code can be called when an attribute value is queried, and if your database data is invalid, an exception will be thrown for rows with invalid attribute values.
- Lines 35 to 41 represent the body of the `validate()` method implementing the validation rule. The password is checked for six characters, and if it is too short, a `JboException` is thrown. The `JboException` is the easiest exception to use for reporting an error application code. As an alternative, you can throw `AttrSetValException`, a subclass of `JboException`, but it requires more parameters than the error message.

13.6.2.3 Applying a Domain to an Attribute. After creating a domain, you assign it as a data type setting to an attribute in the entity object wizard, as shown in Figure 13.53.

After assigning a domain to an attribute, you work with the attribute, using the domain class name. The code in Listing 13.16 tests the domain functionality.

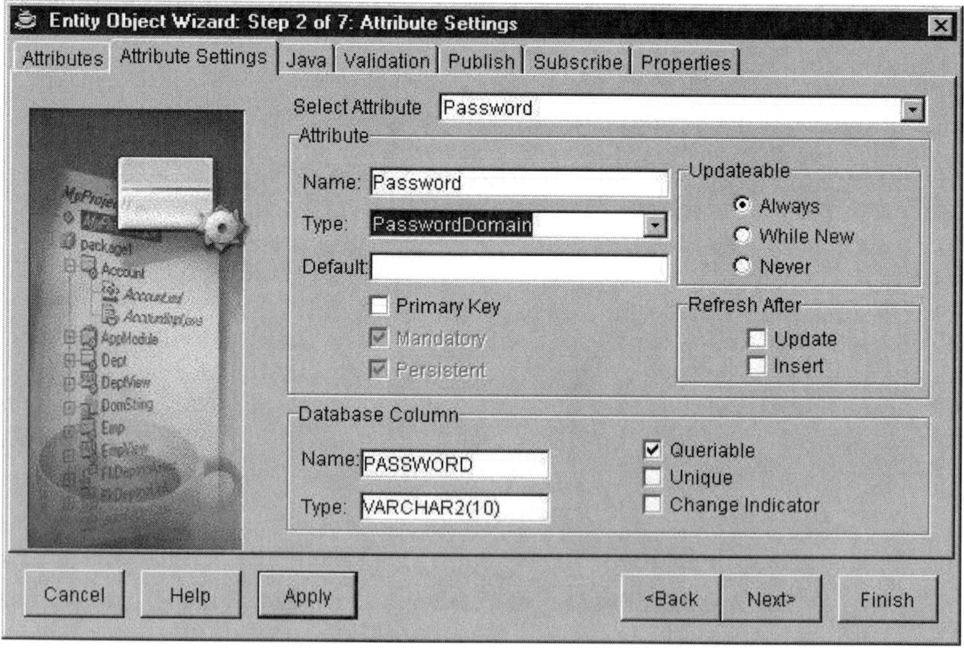

FIGURE 13.53 Applying a domain to an entity attribute.

```
package com.prenhall.OFJP.cust;

import java.util.Hashtable;
import javax.naming.Context;
import javax.naming.InitialContext;
import oracle.jbo.JboContext;
import oracle.jbo.ApplicationModule;
import oracle.jbo.ApplicationModuleHome;
import oracle.jbo.ViewObject;
import oracle.jbo.Row;
import oracle.jbo.domain.Number;
import oracle.jbo.JboException;

public class Bc4jDomainTest {
  private static Hashtable  env = new Hashtable(10);
  private static ApplicationModule appMod = null;
  private static String
     connStr = "bookstore/bookstore@localhost:1521:ORA816";
  private static String url = "jdbc:oracle:thin:";

  public static void setLocalEnv() {. . .}
  public static void loadApplication() {. . .}

  public static void main(String[] args) {
    PasswordDomain pwd = null;
    String name = null;
    Number id = null;

    if (args.length == 1) connStr = args[0];
    url += connStr;
    setLocalEnv();
    loadApplication();
    ViewObject v = appMod.findViewObject("CustomerView");
    v.executeQuery();
    try {
      while (v.hasNext()) {
        Row row = v.next();
        id = (Number) row.getAttribute("Id");
        name = (String) row.getAttribute("Name");
        pwd = (PasswordDomain) row.getAttribute("Password");
        System.out.println(id + "  " + name +
            " pwd=" + pwd + " (new pwd=" +
          name + " len=" + name.length() +")");
```

LISTING 13.16 Testing the `PasswordDomain` functionality.

```
44:         if (name.length() <= 6) {
45:           try {
46:             row.setAttribute("Password", name);
47:             System.out.println(" -> Password changed");
48:           }
49:           catch (JboException e) {
50:            System.out.println(
51:             "setAttribute() Password Error: "+e.getMessage());
52:           }
53:         }
54:       }
55:     }
56:     catch (Exception e) {
57:       System.out.println("Error: " + e.getMessage());
58:       appMod.getTransaction().rollback();
59:     }
60:     finally {
61:       v.remove();
62:       appMod.getTransaction().rollback();
63:     }
64:     appMod.getTransaction().disconnect();
65:     appMod.remove();
66:   }
67: }
```

LISTING 13.16 *Continued*

Notes on Listing 13.16:

- Lines 21 and 22 are the methods for setting environment and loading the application module. The code is not shown because it is identical to previous examples in this chapter.
- Line 25 declares a local variable using the `PasswordDomain` class, to read the customer `password` column value into the `Password` attribute.
- Line 40 reads the password value. Validation occurs when the attribute is read (check the public constructor in the `PasswordDomain` of Listing 13.15). If validation fails, an exception is thrown.
- Line 44 uses the name of the customer to test the password domain functionality. If the customer name is less than six characters, it is used to set the password for the customer to force the validation error.
- Lines 49 to 52 throw a `JboException` when the value used to set the password attribute fails the domain validation rule.

Here are the sample database data used to test the functionality of Listing 13.16:

```
SQL query on data
select id, name, length(name) nlen, password,
length(password) len
from customer;

Customer Data
 ID NAME        NLEN PASSWORD    LEN
--- ---------- ----- ---------- ----
 20 Elio           4 ultrix        6
 23 Ilaria         6 Ilaria        6
 22 Joe            3 user11        6
 41 George         6 elio11        6
 50 Glenn          5 orajav        6
 51 Mailliw        7 numberone     9
 60 Jack           4 Frostie       7
 30 Eivets         6 wonder        6
 31 Oej            3 mrgone        6
```

The resulting output for the sample data is:

```
Bc4jDomainTest results based on above data
20 Elio pwd=ultrix (new pwd=Elio len=4)
setAttribute() Password Error: Password must be 6 or
more characters
23 Ilaria pwd=Ilaria (new pwd=Ilaria len=6)
 -> Password changed
22 Joe pwd=user11 (new pwd=Joe len=3)
setAttribute() Password Error: Password must be 6 or
more characters
41 George pwd=elio11 (new pwd=George len=6)
 -> Password changed
50 Glenn pwd=orajav (new pwd=Glenn len=5)
setAttribute() Password Error: Password must be 6 or
more characters
51 Mailliw pwd=numberone (new pwd=Mailliw len=7)
60 Jack pwd=Frostie (new pwd=Jack len=4)
setAttribute() Password Error: Password must be 6 or
more characters
30 Eivets pwd=wonder (new pwd=Eivets len=6)
 -> Password changed
31 Oej pwd=mrgone (new pwd=Oej len=3)
setAttribute() Password Error: Password must be 6 or
more characters
```

13.6.3 LOGICAL DELETION OF RECORDS

In many applications, there is a need to perform logical deletions of data. Logically deleting a record in the database is usually implemented by updating a column used to track the state/status of the row. This means that queries on the data, via the view object, must use query condition to exclude rows where the status column indicates that the row has been logically deleted. A row is marked for deletion when one of two conditions occurs.

1. The `removeCurrentRow()` method in a view object is called.
2. The `remove()` method of a row object is invoked.

In either case, the post-state for entity is set to `STATUS_DELETED`. The default SQL delete operation that would be executed during the post-changes phase can be replaced by an update operation. The two ways t replace the default DML behavior are to modify the entity object's Java class to override:

1. The `postChanges()` method; or
2. The doDML() method.

The `postChanges()` method uses the post-state of the entity object to call the `doDML()` method with the appropriate DML operation. The actual DML operation is done by the `doDML()` method.

The logical delete examples given below assume that you have added a status column to the customer table, and have updated the entity object with a `Status` attribute and its `setStatus` and `getStatus` accessor methods to track active and inactive customers. Marking the customer inactive is considered a logical deletion, and the view object is be modified to exclude inactive customers.

13.6.3.1 Overriding the Entity Object postChanges() Method. Edit the Java implementation class for the entity object (i.e., `CustomerImpl.java`) and add a method with the following signature:

```
public void postChanges(TransactionEvent event)
```

This `postChanges()` method is called once for each entity object with a post-state of `STATUS_NEW`, `STATUS_DELETED`, or `STATUS_MODIFIED`. You can manually add the `postChanges()` method to your entity object code, or can use the JDeveloper `Wizards->Override Methods...` menu to generate the declaration and an empty body for the `postChanges()` method.

The `postChanges()` method in Listing 13.17 is added to the customer entity object to implement a logical delete operation.

```
01: public void postChanges(TransactionEvent p0) {
02:   if (super.getPostState() == STATUS_DELETED) {
03:     this.revert();
04:     this.setStatus("INACTIVE");
05:   }
06:   super.postChanges(p0);
07: }
```

LISTING 13.17 Logical delete with the postChanges() method.

Notes on Listing 13.17:

- Line 2 tests the post-state of the entity object to be posted. If the post-state indicates that the object has been marked for deletion, it is reverted before updating the status. The `STATUS_DELETED` value inherited from the `oracle.jbo.server.Entity` interface is implemented by `oracle.jbo.server.EntityImpl` superclass of the customer entity object.
- Line 3 executes the `revert()` method to reset the post-state to `STATUS_UNMODIFIED`. This is required to call the `setStatus()` method on line 4 because you cannot change attributes of an entity whose post-state is `STATUS_DELETED` or `STATUS_DEAD`.
- Line 6 executes the superclass `postChanges()` method that invokes the `doDML()` method to perform the SQL operation. The calls in lines 3 and 4 must occur before calling the superclass `postChanges()` method to ensure that the Entity object post-state set to `STATUS_MODIFIED` indicates that update operation is required.

13.6.3.2 Overriding the Entity Object doDML() Method. Using the JDeveloper entity object wizard you select the checkbox labeled "`Data Manipulation Methods`" in the `Java` tab to generate the `doDML()` method, as shown in Figure 13.54.

JDeveloper generates `doDML()` code shown in Listing 13.18.

```
package com.prenhall.OFJP.cust;

// ---------------------------------------------------------------------
// ---    File generated by Oracle Business Components for Java.
// ---------------------------------------------------------------------


import oracle.jbo.server.*;
import oracle.jbo.RowIterator;
```

LISTING 13.18 The `doDML()` method in the entity object.

```
import oracle.jbo.domain.Number;
import com.prenhall.OFJP.cust.PasswordDomain;

public class CustomerImpl extends oracle.jbo.server.EntityImpl {
  :
  // get and set Accessor methods …
  :
  /**
    * Add locking logic here.
    */

  public void lock() {
    super.lock();
  }
  /**
    * Custom DML update/insert/delete logic here.
    */

  public void doDML(int operation, TransactionEvent e) {
    super.doDML(operation, e);
  }
}
```

LISTING 13.18 *Continued*

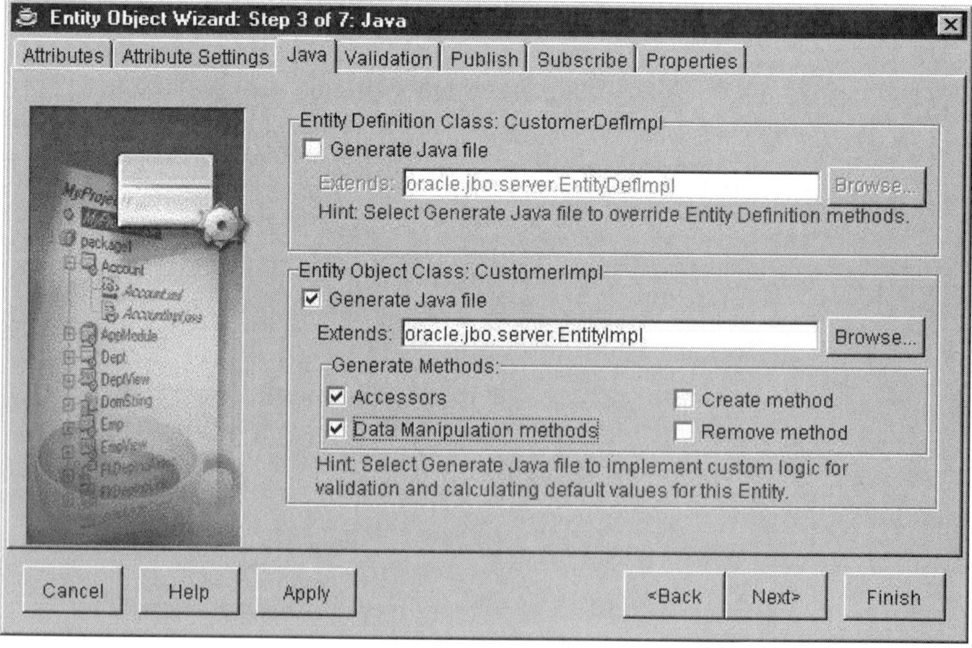

FIGURE 13.54 Add data-manipulation methods to an entity object.

When you override the doDML() method, you take complete control over the database operations performed using JDBC calls. For example, you can replace a delete with an update statement, or call a stored procedure to perform the required changes.

Listing 13.19 uses the doDML() method to replace the delete operation for the database row of the entity object with an update operation, using a JDBC PreparedStatement (see Chapter 9 for details on JDBC).

```
package com.prenhall.OFJP.cust;

// ---------------------------------------------------------
// --- File generated by Oracle Business Components for Java.
// ---------------------------------------------------------


import oracle.jbo.server.*;
import oracle.jbo.RowIterator;
import oracle.jbo.domain.Number;
import com.prenhall.OFJP.cust.PasswordDomain;

public class CustomerImpl extends oracle.jbo.server.EntityImpl {
    :
  public void doDML(int operation, TransactionEvent e) {
    if (operation != DML_DELETE) {
      super.doDML(operation, e);
    }
    else {
      java.sql.PreparedStatement p =
       e.getDBTransaction().createPreparedStatement(
        "update customer set status = 'INACTIVE' where id =?",
        1);
      try {
        p.setInt(1, ((Number) getAttribute("Id")).intValue());
        System.out.println("Set INACTIVE - Logical Delete");
        p.executeUpdate();
      }
      catch (Exception ex) {
        throw new oracle.jbo.JboException(
           "Logical Delete Error: " + ex.getMessage());
      }
      finally {
```

LISTING 13.19 Logical deletion with the doDML() method.

```
34:         try {p.close();} catch (Exception ex) {}
35:       }
36:     }
37:   }
38:   :
39: }
```

LISTING 13.19 *Continued*

Notes on Listing 13.19:

- Line 15 is the `doDML()` method declaration. The `operation` argument is set to a value corresponding to one of the following constant values: `DML_INSERT`, `DML_UPDATE`, or `DML_DELETE`. The second argument is a `TransactionEvent` object reference providing access to the database transaction context for executing JDBC requests.
- Lines 16 and 17 check whether the operation is a DELETE. If it is not, line 17 executes the superclass' doDML() method to perform the INSERT and UPDATE operations normally.
- Lines 20 through 27 execute the code to replace the DELETE operation.
  - Lines 20 to 23 create a JDBC `PreparedStatement` by getting the `DBTransaction` context from the `TransactionEvent` object. The prepared statement is an SQL UPDATE operation to change the value of the status column to the string 'INACTIVE', effectively performing a logical deletion. It is still up to the client application to exclude rows with the INACTIVE status value from its queries. In line 23, the second parameter to the `createPreparedStatement()` method is a JDBC driver row prefetch count of one.
  - Line 25 gets the primary key value of the current entity object and converts it to an integer to be used as the value for placeholder one in the JDBC update statement of line 22.
  - Line 26 prints a trace write indicating the logical delete operation. This is useful for seeing when the actual operation is processed (see the output generated from Listing 13.20).
  - Line 27 executes the JDBC statement to update rather than delete the row. The view object used to delete the rows will no longer be able to access them, unless the changes are first committed and the view query is refreshed to include the inactive records.

The example in Listing 13.19 shows how easy it is to perform low-level SQL operations through the `DBTransaction` object, which is also accessible to a client application through the `getDBTransaction()` method of the application module.

Listing 13.20 is an application used to test the logical-delete operation added to the `CustomerImpl.java` class by invoking a delete operation for customers with expired credit cards.

```
package com.prenhall.OFJP.cust;

import java.util.Hashtable;
import javax.naming.Context;
import javax.naming.InitialContext;
import oracle.jbo.JboContext;
import oracle.jbo.ApplicationModule;
import oracle.jbo.ApplicationModuleHome;
import oracle.jbo.ViewObject;
import oracle.jbo.Row;
import oracle.jbo.domain.Number;
import oracle.jbo.JboException;
import java.util.Calendar;

public class Bc4jLogicalDelete {
  private static Hashtable  env = new Hashtable(10);
  private static ApplicationModule appMod = null;
  private static String connStr =
    "bookstore/bookstore@localhost:1521:ORA815";
  private static String url = "jdbc:oracle:thin:";

  public static void setLocalEnv() { ... }
  public static void loadApplication() { ... }

  public static int toInt(String val) {
    try { return Integer.parseInt(val); }
    catch (NumberFormatException e) { return -1; }
  }

  public static void main(String[] args) {
    Calendar today = Calendar.getInstance();
    int theYear = today.get(Calendar.YEAR);
    int theMonth = today.get(Calendar.MONTH);
    int theCentury = theYear - (theYear % 100);
    System.out.println("Current Month/Year: " +
                          theMonth + "/" + theYear);
    Number id = null;
    String name, status;
    int monthExpired;
```

LISTING 13.20 Test application for logical deletion.

```
int yearExpired;

if (args.length == 1) connStr = args[0];
url += connStr;
setLocalEnv();
loadApplication();

ViewObject v1 = appMod.findViewObject("CustomerView");
v1.setWhereClause("status = 'ACTIVE'");
v1.executeQuery();
try {
  while (v1.hasNext()) {
    Row row = v1.next();
    id =  (Number) row.getAttribute("Id");
    name = (String) row.getAttribute("Name");
    status = (String) row.getAttribute("Status");
    monthExpired = toInt(
      (String) row.getAttribute("MonthExpired")) - 1;
    yearExpired = toInt(
      (String) row.getAttribute("YearExpired")) + theCentury;
    System.out.println(id + "\t" + name + "\t" + status +
     " Card Expiry: " + monthExpired + "/" + yearExpired);
    if ((yearExpired <= theYear)&(monthExpired < theMonth)) {
      System.out.println("Card expired - delete logically!");
      v1.removeCurrentRow();
    }
  }

  System.out.println("Execute commit()!");
  appMod.getTransaction().commit();
  ViewObject v2 = appMod.findViewObject("CustomerView");
  v2.setWhereClause("status = 'INACTIVE'");
  v2.executeQuery();
  while (v2.hasNext()) {
    Row rowV2 = v2.next();
    id =  (Number) rowV2.getAttribute("Id");
    name = (String) rowV2.getAttribute("Name");
    status = (String) rowV2.getAttribute("Status");
    System.out.println(id + "\t" + name + "\t" + status);
  }
}
catch (Exception e) {
  System.out.println("Error: " + e.getMessage());
```

LISTING 13.20 *Continued*

```
83:         appMod.getTransaction().rollback();
84:       }
85:       finally {
86:         v1.remove();
87:         appMod.getTransaction().commit();
88:       }
89:       appMod.getTransaction().disconnect();
90:       appMod.remove();
91:     }
92: }
```

LISTING 13.20 *Continued*

Notes on Listing 13.20:

- Line 13 imports the `java.util.Calendar` class, which is used to determine the current month, year, and century for comparison against the customer credit card expiry.
- Lines 16 through 24 show the code to initialize and load the application module for the client code.
- Lines 25 to 28 show a local static method to convert the input string into an integer, used to convert the `YearExpired` and `MonthExpired` string attributes into their integer values.
- Lines 31 to 36 set the current month and year, using a Calendar instance. The current century is calculated from the year.
- Line 48 sets the search criteria for the view object query to include active customer records and not show inactive records.
- Lines 56 and 57 convert the `MonthExpired` attribute to an integer value. One is subtracted from the month before being compared to the `java.util.Calendar` month, which is numbered from 0 to 11 for January to December, respectively.
- Lines 58 and 59 convert the `YearExpired` string attribute (containing the year without century) into its integer value, and then add the century, before the comparison is done with the year obtained from the `java.util.Calendar` instance.
- Line 62 compares the credit card expiry dates with the current month and year; if the credit cards have expired, it executes the body of the `if` statement.
- Line 63 prints a message to indicate that the card has expired and logically deleted (since the entity object implementation performs this action).
- Line 64 calls the view object `removeCurrentRow()` method to delete the row. This operation causes the post-state of the row's entity object to

marked as STATUS_DELETED, and the entity object becomes unavailable to the application, unless reverted or a rollback operation is requested. At this stage, the database row is still unaffected until the commit operation is executed (see commentary on the output results for this code).

- Line 68 prints a message to indicate that a commit will be performed.
- Line 69 executes the commit operation.
- Lines 71 to 79 create a new view object to read the inactive customers. This view only sees the changes to the underlying database table after a commit operation is done.

Listing 13.21 shows the output generated for the code in Listing 13.20, with sample data printed before the logical-delete operation and commit actions are performed. Note that the numbers listed before the customer name are the customer id. The bold lines indicate the results of interest.

```
Current Month/Year: 8/2000
Diagnostics: Silencing all diagnostic output (use -
Djbo.debugoutput=console to see it)
20 Elio   ACTIVE Card Expiry: 9/2000
23 Ilaria       ACTIVE Card Expiry: 1/2002
22 Joe    ACTIVE Card Expiry: 5/2001
41 George       ACTIVE Card Expiry: 2/2001
50 Glenn  ACTIVE Card Expiry: 9/2000
51 Mailliw      ACTIVE Card Expiry: 1/2001
60 Jack   ACTIVE Card Expiry: 0/2001
30 Eivets       ACTIVE Card Expiry: 1/2000
Card expired - delete logically!
31 Oej    ACTIVE Card Expiry: 6/2000
Card expired - delete logically!
Execute commit()!
Set INACTIVE - Logical Delete
Set INACTIVE - Logical Delete
30 Eivets      INACTIVE
31 Oej   INACTIVE
```

LISTING 13.21 Sample data and output results for logical deletion.

Notes on Listing 13.21:

- Customers 30 and 31 both have expired credit cards (see the first line of the results, indicating the current month and year used for this example; and remember that months are zero-based in the example). The output text "Card expired - delete logically!" is printed when the view object calls the `removeCurrentRow()` method. Internally, in the entity cache, these rows are marked to have a deleted status until a commit or a rollback operation is executed.

- The bold output text "`Execute commit()`" appears after the view object has deleted the rows, followed by the output "`Set INACTIVE - Logical Delete`" for each entity row processed. The "`Set INACTIVE - Logical Delete`" message is generated from the `doDML()` method in the `CustomerImpl` Entity object. This example clearly demonstrates the view object performing the query and data retrieval to create the entity object instances, and INSERT, UPDATE, and DELETE operations are orchestrated through a mechanism that checks the post-state of each entity at commit time.

Whether you are using a Web-based or GUI-based data-aware control application to invoke the DELETE operation, the business component will ensure that a logical deletion takes place.

13.7 DEPLOYING A BUSINESS COMPONENT

Deploying your business component application module and associated classes depends on the type of client application, and whether the application module is local or remote to the client. In this section, only local deployment is covered. The simplest approach is to use JDeveloper wizards to automate the deployment process to create a Java archive containing the business component classes and, optionally, the client code.

To execute the client application, make sure that your `CLASSPATH` includes the jar file generated by the deployment wizard, plus any other class libraries required.

13.7.1 CREATING A JAVA ARCHIVE WITH THE DEPLOYMENT WIZARD

JDeveloper provides a deployment wizard that generates a Java archive (`jar` file). The deployment wizard provides pages where you can choose the project classes to be included in the archive, and can selectively include/exclude additional libraries, archives, package trees, specific packages, or specific classes from the archive.

The JDeveloper `Project->Deploy->New Deployment Profile...` menu item starts the deployment wizard. Figure 13.55 shows the first page where you select the delivery option to create a simple archive.

The page shown in Figure 13.56 allows you to select the classes, or files, from the current project added to the Java archive file. Clicking the `Advanced...` button opens the advanced-deployment page shown in Figure 13.57. The `Preview...` button, which is best clicked after setting the advanced options, displays a list of classes that will be added to the archive.

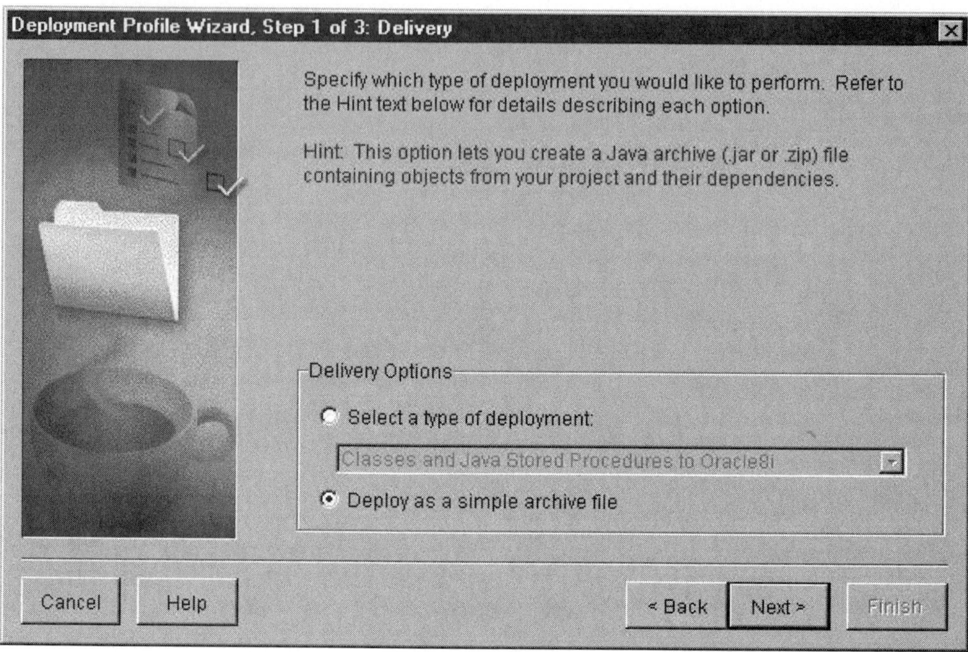

FIGURE 13.55 Selecting deployment to a simple archive.

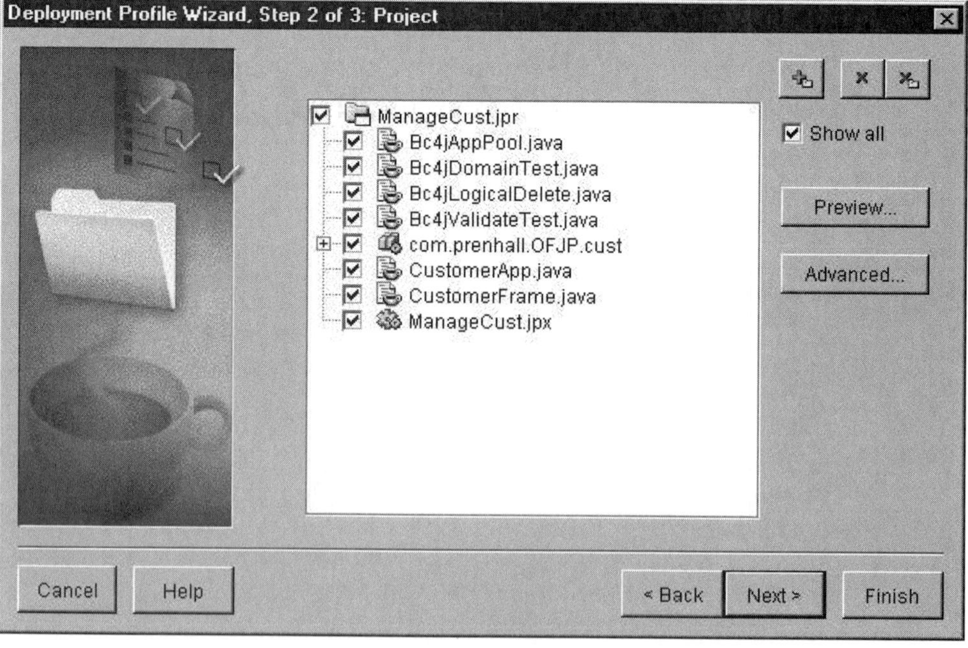

FIGURE 13.56 Choose the files to be added to the archive.

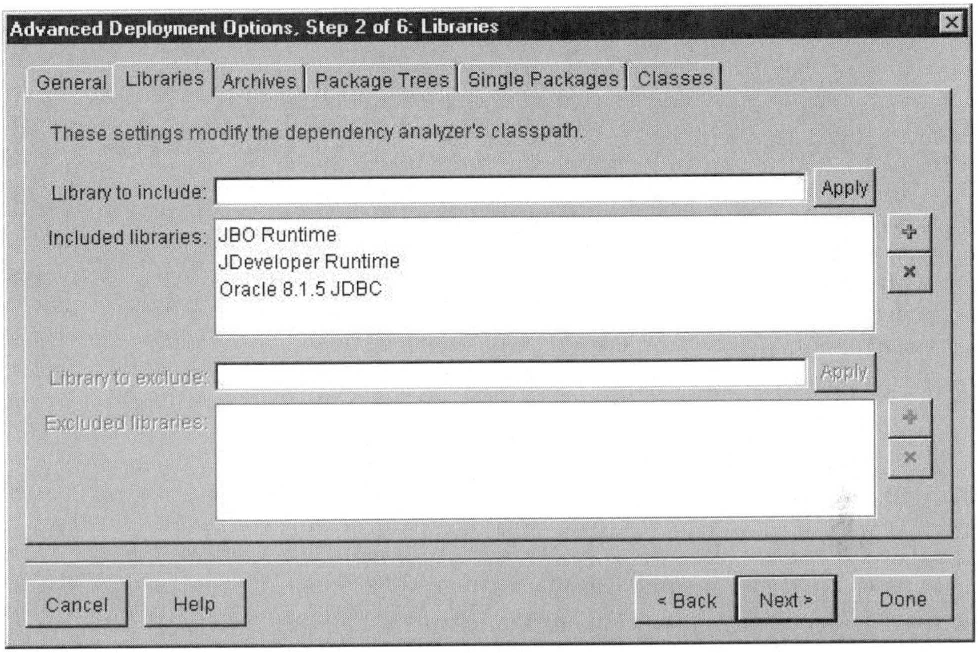

FIGURE 13.57 The deployment wizard's advanced-options page.

The advanced-deployment options allow you to include or exclude classes from other libraries, archives, package trees,[19] single package,[20] or classes. A library in JDeveloper is represented by a name associated with one or more Java archives. Classes included/excluded in the `Archives` tab override settings in the `Libraries` tab. Classes specified in the `Package Trees` tab override settings in the `Archives` and `Libraries` tab, and so on. This means, for example, that you can exclude all the classes in an entire library but selectively include a few classes in a specific package in the library.

Figure 13.58 provides you with the page to name your archive file.

On the final page of the deployment wizard (see Figure 13.59), you select a file name in which you save the choices made to create the archive file. The choices are saved to a file called a deployment profile file, which is added to your JDeveloper project under the `Deployment` folder. The profile file can be used to re-create the archive when changes are made to application code.

It is recommended that you only add the files from the project to the JAR/ZIP file. That will keep the archive file small, and any additional archives

[19]Selecting a package tree includes/excludes all the classes in the specified package and in package subdirectories below the specified package.

[20]Selecting a single package includes/exclude a set of classes in the specified package.

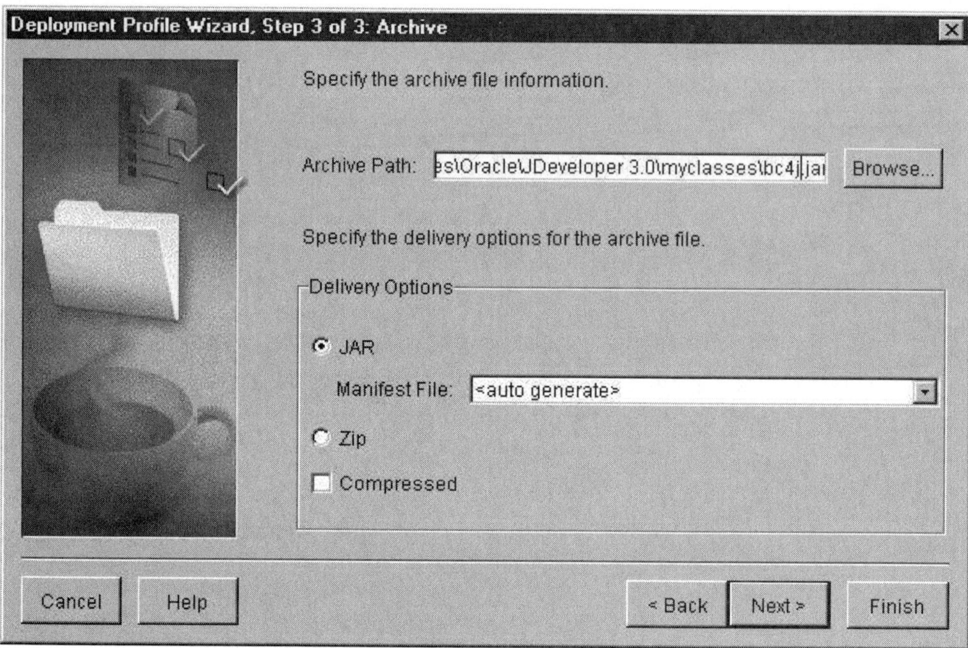

FIGURE 13.58 Choosing the name and format of the archive.

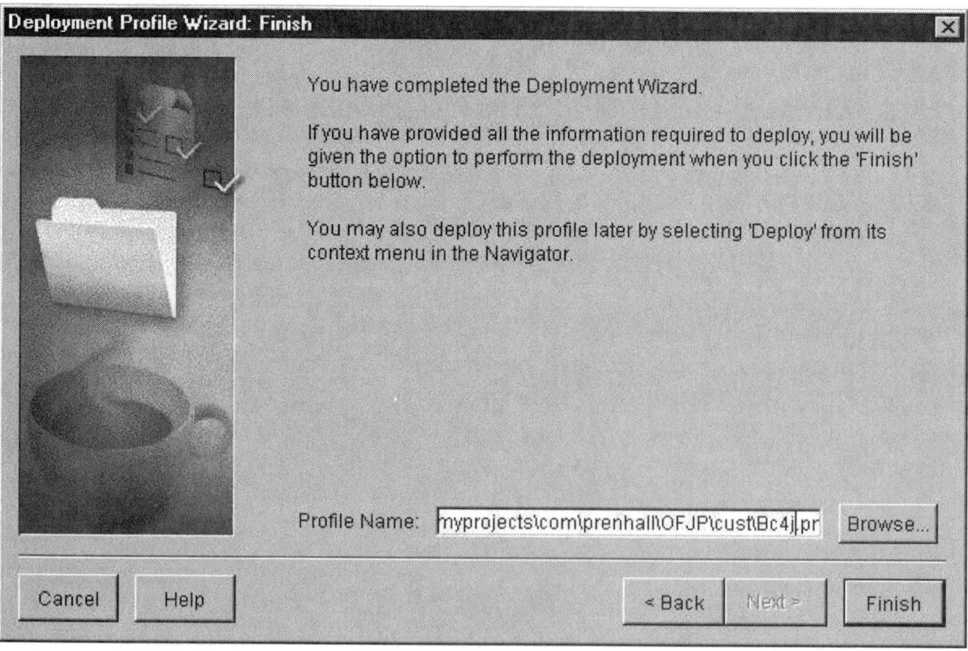

FIGURE 13.59 Saving choices in a deployment profile file.

needed can be added directly to your CLASSPATH. This is better than creating a very large archive file containing every required class.

13.7.2 SETTING THE CLASSPATH FOR A LOCAL CLIENT

You have several options for setting the correct CLASSPATH.

- Manually construct the CLASSPATH.
- Use the batch/script file generated by the deployment profile wizard.
- Use the `setobjenv.bat` command-line tool.

13.7.2.1 Setting the CLASSPATH Manually. When you set the CLASSPATH manually, ensure that all the classes, XML files, and the JPX file from your project are in their CLASSPATH. It is easier to create a Java archive containing files from your business components project, and possibly to keep these separate from the client application classes. You can add additional archives to the CLASSPATH as required by the type of client application you have created.

Assuming you have installed Oracle JDeveloper in `<D>:\Program Files\Oracle\JDeveloper 3.0\` (where <D> is the drive letter):

- Command-line clients require the following archives to be added to the CLASSPATH:
  - <D>:\Program Files\Oracle\JDeveloper 3.0\myclasses*your-bc4j-proj-file*.jar
  - <D>:\Program Files\Oracle\JDeveloper 3.0\lib\jdev-rt.zip
  - <D>:\Program Files\Oracle\JDeveloper 3.0\lib\xmlparserv2.jar
  - <D>:\Program Files\Oracle\JDeveloper 3.0\lib\connectionmanager.zip
  - <D>:\Program Files\Oracle\JDeveloper 3.0\lib\jndi.jar
  - <D>:\Program Files\Oracle\JDeveloper 3.0\lib\jbomt.zip
  - <D>:\Program Files\Oracle\JDeveloper 3.0\jdbc\lib\oracle8.1.5\classes111.zip
  - <D>:\Program Files\Oracle\JDeveloper 3.0\java\lib\classes.zip
- Archives for GUI clients:
  - <D>:\Program Files\Oracle\JDeveloper 3.0\lib\dacf.zip
  - <D>:\Program Files\Oracle\JDeveloper 3.0\infobus\lib\infobus.jar
  - <D>:\Program Files\Oracle\JDeveloper 3.0\jfc\lib\swingall.jar
- Archives required for JSP/servlet clients:
  - <D>:\Program Files\Oracle\JDeveloper 3.0\myprojects*your-jsp-files-path*
  - <D>:\Program Files\Oracle\JDeveloper 3.0\lib\jbohtml.zip
  - <D>:\Program Files\Oracle\JDeveloper 3.0\lib\ojsprun.jar
  - <D>:\Program Files\Oracle\JDeveloper 3.0\jswdk-1.0\lib\servlet.jar
- Additional archives are required for EJB or CORBA applications.

Here is a good tip to help you to manually construct the correct `CLASSPATH` for your client application: Copy the value of `-classpath` option from the `javaw.exe` command line in the JDeveloper `Message View` window.

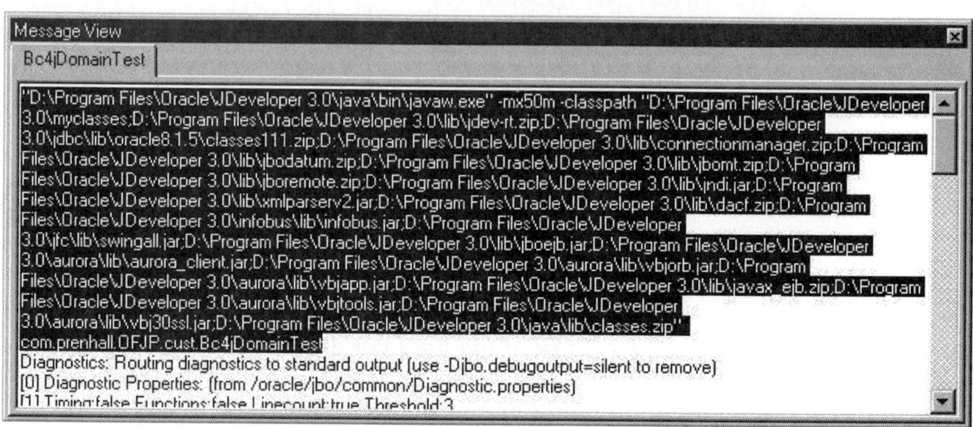

Right-click with your mouse in the `Message View` window and select the `Save To File...` menu item.

13.7.2.2 Using a Generated Batch/Script File. JDeveloper can generate an MS-DOS batch file and a Unix shell script to set the `CLASSPATH` for your applications. The deployment profile wizard generates these batch/script files when you select the checkbox labeled "`Generate scripts (.bat and .sh) for setting the classpath in a command shell`" in the `General` tab of the advanced options page, shown in Figure 13.60.

In the advanced options page, be sure to select the checkbox labeled "`Include the 'connections.properties' file in the generated archive`", because the `connections.properties` is used by the business component application to translate a connection name into its associated JDBC connect string.

13.7.2.3 Using the setjboenv.bat Script. The `setjboenv.bat` file is located in the `<drive>:\<jdeveloper>\bin` subdirectory of your JDeveloper installation. You can use this file to set environment variables for invoking your client from the command line. The syntax to use the `setjboenv.bat` script is shown below.

```
setjboenv <drive>:\<jdeveloper>\ LOCAL
```

Where `<drive>:\<jdeveloper>\` is the directory where JDeveloper is installed.

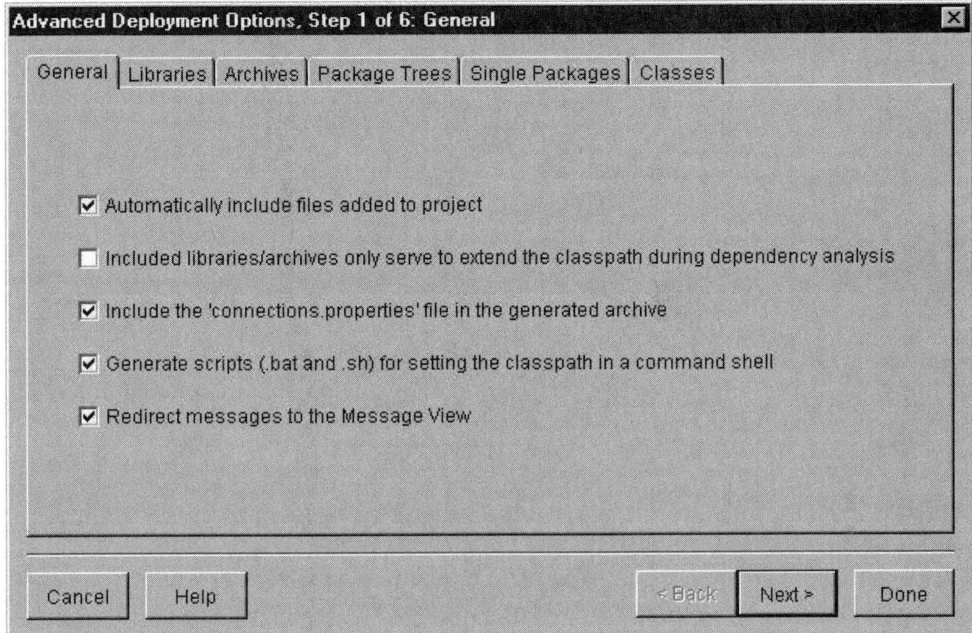

FIGURE 13.60 Batch/script files for setting the `CLASSPATH`.

13.7.3 RUNNING THE CLIENT APPLICATION

Assuming that you have set the correct `CLASSPATH`, and included the directory containing the `java` command line executable in your PATH, you can execute your Business Components for Java client application. For example:

```
$ java com.prenhall.OFJP.cust.CustomerApp
```

By default, the business component application module components generate a debug output message intermingled with your output, as follows:

```
Diagnostics: Routing diagnostics to standard output (use
Djbo.debugoutput=silent to remove)
[0] Diagnostic Properties: (from
/oracle/jbo/common/Diagnostic.properties)
[1] Timing:false Functions:false Linecount:true
Threshold:3
[2] ViewObjectImpl's default fetch mode = 0
[3] Reached getInterface
[4] Oracle SQL Builder Version 3.0.0.0.0
```

```
[5] OracleSQLBuilder: populating ORACLE TypeMap entries
[6] UtilMessageBundle (language base) being initialized
[7] CSMessageBundle (language base) being initialized
[8] Created root application module:
'com.prenhall.OFJP.cust.CustModule'
[9] Locale is: 'en_US'
[10] Connected to Oracle JBO Server - Version:
3.0.5.32.0
 :
 :
```

These debug output messages are a useful learning aid and a useful debugging aid. You can suppress these debug output messages with the following `-D` command-line option:

```
$ java -Djbo.debugoutput=silent com.prenhall.OFJP.cust.CustomerApp
```

SUMMARY

This chapter provided you with some of the basics needed to build applications using Business Components for Java technology. The benefit of using the business component framework is that you develop a shared code base used by variety of client applications with different presentation requirements, and you save time by building code that already provides sophisticated data-management functionality.

Much more than one chapter would be needed to cover the additional functionality supported by business components. The topics covered in a more advanced discussion would include:

- Creating and using associations
- Creating and using view links
- Deploying a remote business component
- Publishing and subscribing to events in entity objects
- And more about transactions and exception handling

All this, indeed, amounts to a topic worthy of a book in its own right. The business component class libraries are part of the JDeveloper product and, at the time of writing, are not available outside of JDeveloper unless you use the Business Component Editor for Linux. This is available for developers using a Linux-based Java development platform.

Chapter 14

DATA ACCESS USING JAVA SERVLETS AND CONNECTION POOLING

- Multiple Threads, Session State, and Security
- Connection Pooling
- A Servlet Example
- BookServlet: Pros and Cons
- Running BookServlet
- Summary

When Sun first released Java in 1995, most Web developers believed that it would rapidly become the language of choice for client/applet programming, but that traditional languages like C and C++, and script languages like Perl and REXX, would continue to dominate the back-end world. A few years after the beginning of the Java revolution, it is clear that the opposite is true. The shift in the focus of Java technology from client to server is largely due to the attitude of Microsoft toward Java and compatibility issues that affect developers who want to support the most popular browsers. After an initial tepid embracing of Java, Microsoft attempted to fragment the platform, releasing a virtual machine that was designed to extend the Java specifications in proprietary ways. Developers using the Microsoft extensions to Java would have not been able to port their codes to operating systems other than Windows. That attempt failed. After a fierce legal battle resulting from Sun's decision to sue Microsoft over the matter, the courts ordered Microsoft to comply with Sun's Java specifications. Microsoft appealed the decision, and the litigation between Sun and Microsoft is still far from resolved. This explains Microsoft's attitude toward Java, which can be described as "passive resistance." The firm can no longer pursue a fragmentation strategy, but is doing nothing to facilitate developers' access to the use of Java technologies under the Windows platform. For example, while a patch that implements the missing features originally left out of the illegal implementation of the Java Virtual Machine released by Microsoft is supposedly available from the firm's Web site, instructions on how to install it are not provided. Among the Java features not implemented in the Microsoft version of the JDK, Remote Method Invocation (RMI) is the most notable. The Redmond–based company is trying hard to impose its DCOM/Ole/ActiveX technology on the rest of the industry, and it cannot tolerate alternative technologies that facilitate distributed computing. Another example of the Microsoft sabotage strategy against Java is the decision to ship Internet Explorer 5 without Java. The Java component is downloaded only after the first Web page containing an applet tag is hit. The average end-user, connecting to the Internet with a slow link, say a 28.8K modem, is severely penalized in respect to use of Java. In addition, while Netscape will eventually support Java 2 and the Java Foundation Classes natively in the browser, it is not clear whether Internet Explorer will ever do so; most likely it won't.

Sun's solution to this problem is the Java plug-in, which enables applets or Java beans components to run using the official Java 2 Runtime Environment (JRE) instead of the browser's default Java runtime. It works very well in theory, but an occasional Internet user using a slow connection will have to download the plug-in the first time a Web page containing an <OBJECT> or <EMBED> tag is hit. This could take a quarter of an hour or more over a 28.8K modem connection. In addition, the tags that instruct the browser to use the plug-in instead of the default Java runtime are different from the traditional <APPLET> tag. A server that wants to serve both the Java plug-in and the native Java runtime must implement logic to understand what type of user configuration it is dealing with, and redirect the request to the page containing the appropriate tags.

The Java plug-in is meant to resolve, once and for all, the compatibility issues that affect developers who want to support both Internet Explorer and Netscape Navigator. Under many circumstances, the identical Java code produces different results when run in the two competing browser environments. Even worse, the same Java code can produce different results when run under different releases of the same browser. Supporting Java applets that must run under all the recent releases of both IE and Navigator has become a daunting task.

Security also plays a big role in limiting the effectiveness of Java applets. The Java native protocol for distributed computing, RMI, is not adequately supported by the popular browsers. Navigator supports RMI on most platforms, but not on MacOS. And, as stated above, Internet Explorer 4 and 5 do not support RMI. In addition, RMI requires a significant administrative overhead if deployed in environments where firewalls and proxy server are used to ensure security. Installing RMI-based communication in a secure environment usually requires the intervention of network/system administrators with the necessary privileges to alter the configuration of the network to allow RMI to operate.

The outcome of the Microsoft strategy toward Java, the issues pertaining to browser compatibility, and concerns about security is that HTML is the minimum common denominator in the client world, not Java. This means that large on-line retailers, such as amazon.com, must use plain-vanilla HTML tags if they want to reach the largest possible audience. They cannot afford to lose business because a customer who wants to buy their books must download the Java Virtual Machine if using Internet Explorer 5 or the plug-in.

The situation is different in corporate intranets, where the environment is under the control of administrators who can determine the minimal software/hardware requirements for corporate users.

While Java has definitely lost its popularity on the client, it has gained a lot of ground in the server arena. The CGI-BIN paradigm is being progressively replaced by Java servlets, which offer several distinct advantages.

14.1 MULTIPLE THREADS, SESSION STATE, AND SECURITY

The considerable commercial success obtained by the Java servlet API is mainly due to the three major advantages that this model offers over its CGI predecessor. First, and most important, servlets run as threads of a process that interacts with the Web server. With some Web-server configurations, the Web server and the servlet engine run in the same process context. In any case, the servlet architecture avoids the process-forking step required by the CGI architecture. This characteristic alone makes the servlet model more attractive, because it avoids both performance problems and uncontrolled proliferation of server processes. Second, the multi-threaded nature of servlets makes it possible to maintain state information between client requests, thereby overcoming the problems associated with the stateless nature of the CGI protocol. The servlet API provides the *getSession()* method, implemented in the HTTPServletRequest object, which returns a handle to the session object. The latter is assigned a session id, which can be queried using the *getId()* method. A servlet can store the ids of all the connected clients in the Java collection classes (e.g., vectors, lists, hash tables), making use of session tracking with little or no effort.

Finally, servlets provide the advantage of security. Memory-access violations and strong typing violations are the most likely cause of Web-server crashes provoked by faulty CGI scripts and integrity violations perpetrated by malicious attackers. Since servlets are implemented in Java, these cannot occur.

The Java servlet API also allows for security-policy support. A security manager can be used to relax the security limitations imposed upon servlets. By default, servlets are untrusted. This means that they cannot access network services or local files. Servlets can be digitally signed and selectively granted more permissions by the security manager. The improvement over CGI security is considerable, as the control over URLs sent from the client is much more precise.

14.2 CONNECTION POOLING

Since servlets (effectively) run in the context of the Web-server process, which services client requests by spawning threads, they are either preloaded when the Web server starts up or loaded on demand, when the first Web page containing a servlet reference is served. Servlets remain loaded while the Web server is active. This servlet characteristic makes it easy to implement connection pooling. Connection pooling is currently a buzzword in the database field, and all the major vendors have recently implemented this feature. Here is how connection pooling works: Since establishing a database connection consumes both resources and time, the system creates a configurable number of connections at startup time and places them in a pool. When a client requests an operation that involves a database access, a connection is taken from the pool, used to perform the database lookup, and then released back to the pool. This arrangement offers several benefits, including the ability to monitor connection usage, limit the maximum number of connections to the database, and establish timeouts that can be used to kill stale connections.

The Microsoft Data Access Components (MDAC) architecture offers two forms of pooling:

- Connection pooling through the ODBC drivers.
- Resource pooling as part of the OLE DB core components.

The release of Oracle 8 in June 1997 represented a major breakthrough with regard to scalability. The number of concurrent users supported by the server engine grew from a few hundred to a few thousand. In order to keep pace with the increased scalability of the Oracle server, Net8 has been enhanced to allow a greater number of user connections. In particular, three features have been implemented in the Oracle network architecture to increase the number of concurrent connections:

- Connection manager's connection concentration
- Connection pooling
- Listener load balancing

The Oracle connection manager, a software layer that must be configured and enabled on the server, makes use of multiplexing techniques to combine the network traffic from multiple clients onto a single physical network connection to the server.

Connection pooling allows a limited number of physical, transport-level connections to be shared among a greater number of logical network connections. This is implemented by temporarily releasing idle transport connections while maintaining their network sessions. A single transport connection can only be released if:

- It was idle long enough to reach a preconfigured time-out.
- All the transport connections in the pool are busy.
- An additional network session requests a transport connection.

The main difference between connection concentration operated by the connection manager and connection pooling is this: With connection pooling, an idle client that loses a transport connection may have to wait for a different transport connection to become available when it resumes its activity. With connection concentration, a client connection is maintained continuously.

Connection pooling is therefore adequate for applications where most of the user time is spent looking at the screen to analyze and interpret the output of a query that returns the expected results. Connection concentration is more suitable when the data flow between clients and the servers is continuous, as in the cases of process control and batch uploading.

Listener load balancing can happen either on the client side, where one listener is chosen randomly from a list of listeners that are all connected to the same data source, or on the server side, enabling active listeners to take their routing decisions based on the current load on each instance dispatcher.

The three features described above are only supported when the Multi-Threaded Server (MTS) option is enabled. In an MTS configuration, multiple client processes are connected to a limited number of dispatchers, which in turn talk to shared servers. If Oracle offers connection pooling to clients connecting to the database server, why should servlet developers bother implementing connection pooling programmatically? To answer this question, we must consider the different design goals of the two types of pooling. Connection pooling, as natively implemented by Net8, is designed for client/server applications where the clients keep a connection to the database open for the entire duration of their interaction with the back-end data source. Once established, a connection to Oracle could potentially be maintained for a very long time, including long periods of client inactivity. The pooling mechanism implemented through MTS simply makes better use of idle connections, temporarily using them to serve other active clients.

In a Web environment, things work very differently. Due to the stateless nature of the HTTP protocol, each client request, originated either by the click of the mouse over a URL or by the submission of an HTML form, is seen by the server as an atomic, self-contained, independent unit of work. Unlike the traditional client/server model, a user who interacts with an application through a Web browser is not physically connected to the back-end database. A socket connection is established each time the client submits a request and closed when the response is sent back to the client, which concludes the request/response lifecycle. The servlet serving the client requests, on the other hand, is not subjected to the stateless rule, and can keep its database connections open for the entire duration of its operations. A common arrangement for HTTP servlets is to override the *init()* method, opening several database connections and releasing them to the connection pool. Accordingly, the *destroy()* method is also overridden to close all the connections stored in the pool and release all the resources used by the servlet during its lifetime. These techniques are illustrated in the next section, where we build a servlet-based application.

14.3 A SERVLET EXAMPLE

In this section you will implement a rudimentary, yet complete and self-contained, e-commerce application in the amazon.com style. The users will interact with your application through a Web browser, which will send basic HTML tags over HTTP. The content of each Web page will be dynamically created by a few servlets that will encapsulate all the required business logic.

Your application, called *BookServlet*, will allow users to open an account with a virtual bookstore (which specializes in selling Oracle books), add the books they choose to a shopping basket, and place an order for the books stored in the shopping basket.

In order to keep the source code to a reasonable limit, we are going to simplify the business rules a little. For example, the shipper chosen determines the shipment price, but each shipper declares only one price, which applies nationwide to all items irrespective of the distance between the warehouse and the customer's household. A real-world application would have to deal with complex rules that determine a shipment price based on the number of items, their weight, the distance that separates the warehouse from the shipping address, and the urgency of the shipment.

Furthermore, real e-commerce applications thoroughly check customers' credit records when they open an account, making sure that the credit card details have been entered correctly and that the customer has a good credit record. Our simple BookServlet will completely trust the customers who want to open an account, bypassing all financial checks.

Since your application is definitely database-centric, you start by designing the database.

14.3.1 DATABASE DESIGN

The first step is the definition of a logical model that sketches how the data are to be organized, and how many and what relationships are to exist among the data that constitute the application.

Figure 14.1 shows the logical model for the database supporting the application. Data-modeling purists might question your decision to store information about customers together with their credit card details. A better design would create a separate entity to store credit card details, perhaps in a one-to-many relationship with the customer entity. In your logical model, each customer can have at most one credit card. If you had opted for a more complex model, and did indeed create a separate entity to store the credit card details, you would have to modify the cust_order entity, because each order must now store the payment method. You should therefore add to the order entity a foreign key that references the credit card entity.

This example shows, in a simplified manner, the entity-relationship data-modeling process in which application designers and data modelers shape entities and relationships, carefully evaluating the impact of each design decision on the entire system.

A few words to explain the logical model: The CUSTOMER entity stores the information you will need to keep about the customers, including their passwords and e-mail addresses, which the system will use as the user id. The SALES_ITEM entity stores information related to the books we are selling, including price and discount policy.

The CUST_ORDER entity stores information about the orders issued by the customers. ORDER_ITEM includes information about items that make up an order. There is a one-to-many relationship between CUST_ORDER and ORDER_ITEM, which implies a master-detail hierarchy, where every item is a child of a parent order. The COURIER entity stores information about the courier chosen by the customers to ship their books. Note, again, that choosing to store the foreign key that references the courier entity into cust_order implies that only

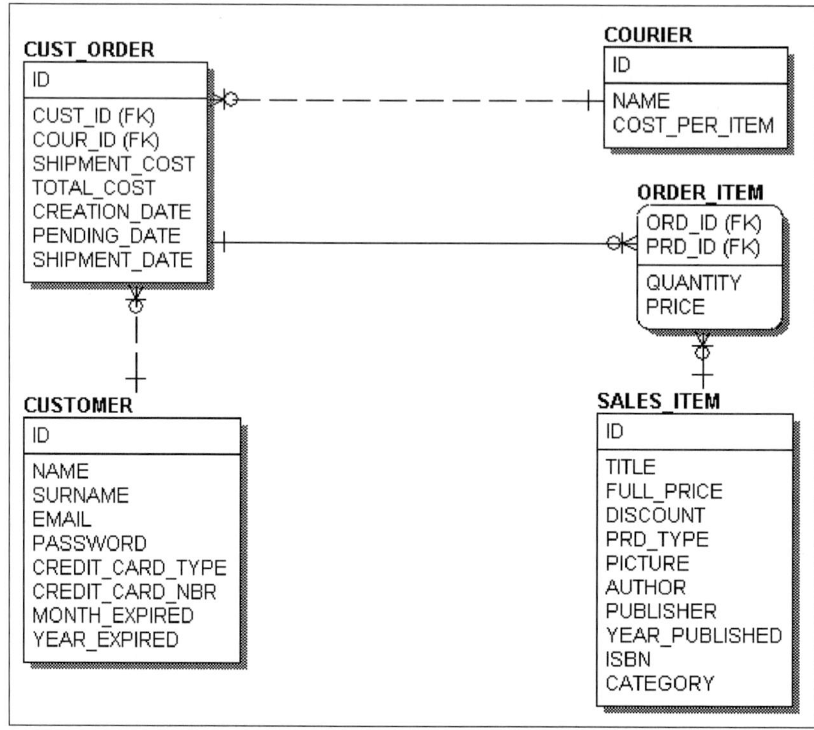

FIGURE 14.1 The logical data model for BookServlet.

one shipper will ship all the items contained in the order. If we wanted to make it possible for one or more items to be shipped by one courier, and other items belonging to the same order to be shipped by a different courier, the foreign key that references the courier entity would have to be moved from cust_order to order_item.

Figure 14.2 illustrates the physical data model generated from the logical model discussed above. The entity attributes, which in the logical model were vaguely specified in terms of string, number, date, and blob, are mapped into columns using Oracle-specific datatypes. For example, the *name* attribute in the customer entity becomes an Oracle VARCHAR2 that stores a string up to 30 characters in length, which belongs to the customer table.

Logical entities roughly correspond to physical tables, and logical attributes correspond to physical columns. One of the most serious mistakes commonly made by inexperienced application designers is to apply an automatic mapping between logical entities and physical tables. Most data-modeling CASE tools can automatically generate a physical data model out of a logical model. This is definitely a good feature, but it must be regarded only as a starting point. Switching

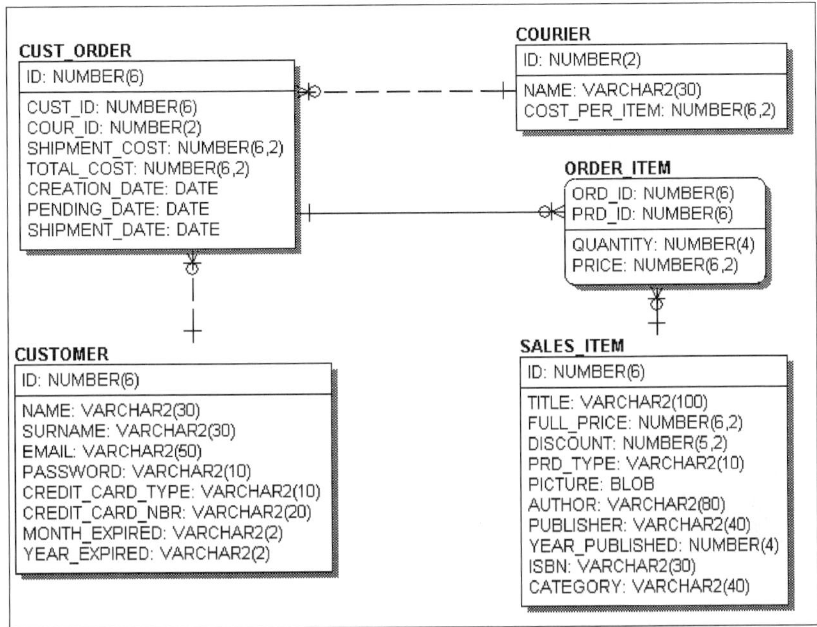

FIGURE 14.2 The physical data model for BookServlet.

from a logical data model to a physical data model is not merely a mapping between entities and tables. A good physical data model also implements denormalization and other performance-enhancing techniques. A physical model must be carefully analyzed, and its key aspects evaluated with an eye to performance.

In Figure 14.2 a table is represented by a rectangle in which key columns are separated from non-key columns by a horizontal line. Key columns uniquely identify rows in a table. In other words, each row in a table must contain a unique element that will be used to retrieve that specific row. Consider CUST_ORDER, which has one primary key, ID. Each order issued by a customer will have a unique number that will be used by the application to identify a specific order. Oracle enforces the uniqueness of a primary key. If you try to insert two rows with the same order number, Oracle will complain, issuing the following message:

```
ORA-00001: unique constraint (<Constraint Name>) violated
```

There are two types of keys, natural and artificial. A natural key is made of unique attributes that occur normally in the table, while an artificial key contains no meaningful column information and is included in the table solely to uniquely identify the rows.

A typical example is a table that contains information about people. Usually name and surname are not enough to uniquely identify a person; it is very likely, for instance, that a given name like "John" and a surname like "Smith" will identify more than one person. If you add the data of birth to the key elements in the table, the chance to uniquely identify a person increases considerably. The drawback associated with the use of natural keys is that you must concatenate two or more columns to identify without ambiguity each row stored in the table. Every time you want to select a specific person from the table, your WHERE clause will have to include three columns:

```
where name = 'John' and
surname = 'Smith' and
date_of_birth='07/29/1956'
```

If you arbitrarily assign a unique number to each person stored in the table, and include the person identifier in the table, you are creating an artificial key. The advantage provided by the artificial key is that you only need one column to uniquely identify one person. Furthermore, database lookups based on artificial keys, which are usually numbers, are more efficient than database lookups based on concatenated strings.

In your model, CUST_ORDER uses the artificial key ID to ensure that each order is uniquely identified. The order number is arbitrarily assigned by the application, to avoid identifying each order using the customer id and the creation date, which are the natural keys.

To simplify the use of artificial keys Oracle provides a facility called a *sequence generator* that provides an ever-increasing sequential series of numbers. The sequence generator is useful in multi-user environments, because it generates unique sequential numbers in a memory cache, without the overhead of disk I/O or transaction locking.

You are going to use the sequence generator in BookServlet. You want a mechanism that automatically increments the order number each time a new order is issued. Oracle SQL provides the CREATE SEQUENCE statement, which creates a sequence object and initializes it according to a few parameters specified in the statement. Sequence parameters specify the minimum and maximum values allowed for the sequence, the sequence increment, the number of sequence values kept in the Oracle cache, and so forth. The statement shown below creates the sequence that will be used by BookServlet.

```
create sequence order_seq
start with 1
increment by 1
nomaxvalue
cache 50;
```

You have created a sequence; now you have to fetch its sequential values. For this purpose, Oracle makes two pseudo-columns available to developers, sequence_name.CURRVAL and sequence_name.NEXTVAL. The order number column can be populated during an insert statement into the CUST_ORDER table using the following syntax:

```
insert into cust_order (id, cust_id, creation_date,
pending_date, cour_id, shipment_cost, total_cost)
values
(order_seq.NEXTVAL,56, SYSDATE, SYSDATE,3,56.95,12.95,69.89);
```

The NEXTVAL pseudo-column generates the next value in the sequence, while CURRVAL returns the "current" number of the sequence. This is useful when you want to create a new sequence number for a new order, but you want to use the same number to populate ORDER_ITEM in the same transaction, as in the next example.

```
insert into cust_order (id, cust_id, creation_date,
pending_date, courier_id, all_item_cost, shipment_cost, total_cost)
values
(order_seq.NEXTVAL,56, SYSDATE, SYSDATE,3,56.95,12.95,69.89);

insert into order_item (ord_id, prd_id, quantity,price)
values
(order_seq.CURRVAL, 23, 5, 32.95);
```

Embedding the pseudo-column NEXTVAL directly into the INSERT statement is not always a good idea, because your code does not have access to the generated number, which is the key to the newly inserted row. For example, BookServlet allows users to submit orders after they have checked the items added to the shopping basket. The application should create the new order and display the order number to the user. If you use the technique shown above, and embed the pseudo-column in the INSERT statement, you must reselect the row just inserted in order to determine the key generated by the sequence generator, and this is inefficient.

It would be better to fetch the next number in the sequence into a host variable and use the generated number to perform both operations. That is, to insert the row into the CUST_ORDER table and create an HTML page that displays the order number to the user. To fetch the next number produced by the sequence generator into a host variable, you must use a well-known Oracle feature, the DUAL table. DUAL is a publicly available dummy table that contains only one column, named DUMMY, and is guaranteed to contain only one row. You can use DUAL to select the pseudo-column NEXTVAL into a variable provided by the application:

```
Statement s = connection.createStatement();
ResultSet rs = s.executeQuery("select order_seq.NEXTVAL from DUAL");
rs.next();
long seq = rs.getLong(1);
```

The sequence-generated number is stored in the Java long variable seq. The number is now available to your application for future use.

Note that you can select a pseudo-column from any table, not just from DUAL. But DUAL guarantees that the pseudo-column will always return one value, because DUAL only contains one row.

The SQL script that creates the Oracle tables and sequence needed by BookServlet follows.

```
CREATE TABLE SALES_ITEM (
       ID                     NUMBER(6) NOT NULL,
       TITLE                  VARCHAR2(100) NOT NULL,
       FULL_PRICE             NUMBER(6,2) NOT NULL,
       DISCOUNT               NUMBER(5,2) NOT NULL,
       PRD_TYPE               VARCHAR2(10) NOT NULL,
       PICTURE                BLOB NULL,
       AUTHOR                 VARCHAR2(80) NULL,
       PUBLISHER              VARCHAR2(40) NULL,
       YEAR_PUBLISHED         NUMBER(4) NULL,
       ISBN                   VARCHAR2(30) NULL,
       CATEGORY               VARCHAR2(40) NULL,
       CHECK (PRD_TYPE IN ('BK', 'CD')));

ALTER TABLE SALES_ITEM
       ADD  ( PRIMARY KEY (ID) ) ;

CREATE TABLE CUSTOMER (
       ID                     NUMBER(6) NOT NULL,
       NAME                   VARCHAR2(30) NOT NULL,
       SURNAME                VARCHAR2(30) NOT NULL,
       EMAIL                  VARCHAR2(50) NOT NULL,
       PASSWORD               VARCHAR2(10) NOT NULL,
       CREDIT_CARD_TYPE       VARCHAR2(10) NOT NULL,
       CREDIT_CARD_NBR        VARCHAR2(20) NOT NULL,
       MONTH_EXPIRED          VARCHAR2(2) NOT NULL,
       YEAR_EXPIRED           VARCHAR2(2) NOT NULL);

ALTER TABLE CUSTOMER
       ADD  ( PRIMARY KEY (ID) ) ;
```

```
CREATE TABLE COURIER (
       ID                          NUMBER(2) NOT NULL,
       NAME                        VARCHAR2(30) NOT NULL,
       COST_PER_ITEM               NUMBER(6,2) NOT NULL);

ALTER TABLE COURIER
       ADD  ( PRIMARY KEY (ID) ) ;

CREATE TABLE CUST_ORDER (
       ID                          NUMBER(6) NOT NULL,
       CUST_ID                     NUMBER(6) NOT NULL,
       COUR_ID                     NUMBER(2) NOT NULL,
       SHIPMENT_COST               NUMBER(6,2) NOT NULL,
       TOTAL_COST                  NUMBER(6,2) NOT NULL,
       CREATION_DATE               DATE NOT NULL,
       PENDING_DATE                DATE NOT NULL,
       SHIPMENT_DATE               DATE NULL);

CREATE INDEX ORD_CUST_FK_I ON CUST_ORDER
       ( CUST_ID );

CREATE INDEX ORD_COUR_FK_I ON CUST_ORDER
       ( COUR_ID );

ALTER TABLE CUST_ORDER
       ADD  ( PRIMARY KEY (ID) ) ;

CREATE TABLE ORDER_ITEM (
       ORD_ID                      NUMBER(6) NOT NULL,
       PRD_ID                      NUMBER(6) NOT NULL,
       QUANTITY                    NUMBER(4) NOT NULL,
       PRICE                       NUMBER(6,2) NOT NULL);
CREATE INDEX ITEM_ORD_FK_I ON ORDER_ITEM
( ORD_ID );

CREATE INDEX ITEM_PRD_FK_I ON ORDER_ITEM
( PRD_ID );

ALTER TABLE ORDER_ITEM
       ADD  ( PRIMARY KEY (ORD_ID, PRD_ID) ) ;

ALTER TABLE CUST_ORDER
       ADD  ( FOREIGN KEY (CUST_ID)
              REFERENCES CUSTOMER ) ;
```

```
ALTER TABLE CUST_ORDER
       ADD  ( FOREIGN KEY (COUR_ID)
              REFERENCES COURIER ) ;

ALTER TABLE ORDER_ITEM
       ADD  ( FOREIGN KEY (PRD_ID)
              REFERENCES SALES_ITEM ) ;

ALTER TABLE ORDER_ITEM
       ADD  ( FOREIGN KEY (ORD_ID)
              REFERENCES CUST_ORDER ) ;

CREATE SEQUENCE ORDER_SEQ
START WITH 1
INCREMENT BY 1
NOMAXVALUE
CACHE 50;

CREATE SEQUENCE USER_SEQ
START WITH 1
INCREMENT BY 1
NOMAXVALUE
CACHE 50;
```

You are not quite finished yet. You still need to define indexes to improve the performance of Referential Integrity (RI) and to speed up commonly used retrieval paths to the data stored into the database. Oracle automatically creates an index on primary keys. When an index is a composite index (i.e., includes several columns), Oracle can use it to quickly select rows when the WHERE clause of the query contains either all the columns comprising the composite index or the first column of the composite index.

Consider the ORDER_ITEM table, which uses a composite primary key that includes the two columns ORD_ID and PRD_ID. The index created by Oracle to support the primary key will be used when the WHERE clause includes both ORD_ID and PRD_ID, but also when the WHERE clause only includes ORD_ID, because this column appears first in the primary key definition. You need to create an index on PRD_ID in order to speed up the lookup operations internally performed by Oracle. To ensure referential integrity, Oracle must be able to scan both parent and child tables. When a row is deleted from the parent table or a primary key is modified, Oracle scans the child table to delete all the children (if the ON DELETE CASCADE clause has been enabled) or verify that there are no orphans left. Conversely, when a record is inserted in the child table, Oracle scans the parent table to ensure that a parent exists. When an index supports referential integrity on the child table, only the child rows affected by the check or deletion are locked. If the foreign key is not indexed, Oracle places a share lock on the entire child table for the duration of the transaction. With a share lock, other sessions can access the rows in the tables in read-only mode, but they cannot update or insert. Since the transaction can last for many seconds, even minutes, locking becomes an issue for applications with hundreds of concurrent users.

The CUST_ORDER table needs a couple of extra indexes to support RI, specifically on ID and on COUR_ID. The index on ID is particularly useful, because it will be used not only internally by Oracle, but also by the BookServlet application. You want to give your customers the option of listing all thel orders they have submitted up to a certain date. The SQL statement used by the servlet to fetch the orders is:

```
select * from cust_order where id = ?
```

If your virtual bookstore becomes successful, as you hope, you could potentially have thousands of orders, and an index on CUST_ORDER.ID will speed up your query considerably.

Consider now the SALES_ITEM table. You would like to select all the books published by a specific publisher or written by a certain author. Before you start creating indexes indiscriminately, you should consider their *selectivity,* which measures the number of table entries identified by each key. The fewer rows that are matched by an index key, the more selective is the index. The selectivity of an index is a very important factor for application designers who are evaluating a physical model, looking for retrieval paths to the data used by the application. If an index is not highly selective, it becomes more efficient to scan the entire table sequentially. As a rule of thumb, several Oracle experts advise setting the threshold at about 15–20 percent. In other words, if a query is likely to select less than 20 percent of the rows in the table, an index should be used to support the query. Conversely, if the number of rows selected by a query is likely to exceed that percentage, a full table scan should be preferred. In your case, an index on the PUBLISHER column is not likely to be highly selective, given that a small number of publishers publish the majority of Oracle books. It makes much more sense to create an index on the AUTHOR column, because the most prolific author will probably have fewer than five books published.

The assertion that it is more efficient to perform a sequential scan of a table than to use an index seems rather counterintuitive. This is due to the strategy used by Oracle to retrieve the data blocks that contain the data selected by the query. Index traversal in Oracle begins with the index root node access, and reads the subsequent nodes via direct I/O to fetch exactly the wanted block. Each block read requires a single read call. When Oracle is requested to perform a full table scan, it uses a smart look-ahead algorithm that fetches multiple blocks at once, up to the number defined by the DB_FILE_MULTI_BLOCK_READ_COUNT parameter. This is a database parameter read by the engine at boot time. A single block usually contains multiple rows, which are all read in one I/O call. To understand why a full table scan can be more efficient than an index lookup, consider the following example. A table contains 1,000 rows, and each block contains, on average, 10 rows. If DB_FILE_MULTI_BLOCK_READ_COUNT is set to 8 (the default), in one read Oracle will fetch (10 * 8) = 80 rows from disk to memory. It would take Oracle approximately 13 I/O operations to fetch the entire table into memory. Now consider an index lookup that fetches 6 rows. It takes 12 I/O calls, one to read the index, and one to fetch the block, multiplied by the number of rows. If the query selects 7 rows, a full table scan becomes more efficient. This example is very hypothetical and oversimplifies the way Oracle works, since reality is more complex than the situation presented here. It is likely that the index lookup would not perform exactly 12 I/O calls, because the probability of finding the required block already in memory increases with the number of I/O calls. Nevertheless, it should be clear why the selectivity of an index must be considered before opting for index creation.

The last few paragraphs stressed the importance of supporting referential integrity with the creation of indexes on foreign keys. BookServlet is a very limited application—it only uses five tables—and the number of foreign keys per table is small, two or three at most. You can safely create one index per foreign key without incurring performance penalties. The situation changes, however, when large applications, built around a few core tables that include a large number of columns, have relationships with many referenced tables. It is not uncommon to see tables that potentially include 20 or 30 foreign keys. Creating one index per foreign key would be impractical, for at each row insertion Oracle would update all the indexes referenced by the table, with severe consequences for the overall response time of insertions.

Discussing the possible solutions to this issue is beyond the scope of this book. For present purposes, the point is that you should not indiscriminately create one index per foreign key, especially if there are more than five foreign keys per table.

14.3.2 JAVA CONNECTION POOLING

The database you have designed and implemented is "frozen," which is to say that no further modifications to its design are allowed. Before delving into GUI design issues, it is now necessary to focus on the next-most-important component of BookServlet: the data access layer. Servlets are persistent objects that are initialized once and destroyed either upon request or when the Web server shuts down. Their persistence is the essence of the advantage they have over conventional CGI. A servlet can maintain one or more connections to Oracle throughout its lifetime. Furthermore, a servlet can pre-open several connections to the database, cache them in memory, and temporarily allocate them to client requests for database lookups. This is precisely what you are going to build in this section, a connection pool object that will be used by BookServlet. Since you like the idea of software reuse, you want to keep the code for the connection pool object very generic, so that different servlets can use the connection pool component. In order to reuse the connection pool infrastructure, you must decouple the pooling mechanism from the connection object. The latter can be a complex object, carrying a variable number of prepared statements that are decidedly application-specific. But a generic connection pooling mechanism can easily be reused across different projects.

To be effective, a connection pool object must support the following features:

1. It should be highly configurable, meaning that user-defined parameters influence its behavior.
2. It should be able to provide database connections on demand, thereby relieving the application programmer of concurrency-related issues (i.e. locking should be taken care of).
3. It should be able to expand the pool of connections under heavy load and contract the pool during off-peak activity, in order to save precious database resources.
4. It should be easily accessible through a simple and consistent API.

Expanding on each of the above points:

1. You want your connection pool object to be able to connect to an Oracle database and to support, at the least, the thin and OCI-based JDBC drivers. Even better, you would also like to support the new JDBC 2.0 style of connection, based on data sources and easily integrated with Java Naming and Directory Interface (JNDI). Oracle usernames and passwords, used by the connection objects instantiated by the connection pool, should be passed as command-line parameters or stored, possibly in encrypted form, in a property file.
2. The various methods called by the *doGet()* servlet entry point should request connection objects that allow for direct database access. Preventing two methods that are concurrently executing in different threads from using the same connection object must be the responsibility of the connection pool object.
3. At application startup, a few connection objects should be pre-allocated in the pool. As soon as the application is heavily accessed, more connection objects should be created, up to a predefined limit. If more connection objects are needed, the connection pool object should allocate the connection objects already in the pool, queuing the requests using a first-in first-out type of algorithm. When the load on the servlet decreases, the connection pool object should destroy the connection objects that have been idle for the longest time, until it reaches the minimum number of connection objects that must be present in the pool.

4. The methods requesting connection objects need to have the business knowledge required to accomplish their tasks. Their interaction with the connection pool should be kept to a minimum, possibly two methods: "give me a connection object" and "take back the connection object, I am finished with it."

The connection pool object is created by the *init()* method of the servlet, which reads initialization parameters from a property file (see Table 14.1).

The property file is passed to the servlet by the servlet engine during the startup phase. The *init()* method, provided by the HttpServlet class, and guaranteed to run at least once at the moment of servlet activation, is the most appropriate method for reading property files and creating connection pools. The standard technique for preventing two threads from accessing the same connection object is to serialize each connection object request submitted by application methods using the Java *synchronized* method modifier.

A timer object, which runs in a separate thread, is also needed to allow for a periodic check of the connection pool. Each inactive connection object that has been idle for longer than the allowed time, can be destroyed by a "watchdog" method, implemented in the connection pool object. Finally, the connection pool class needs only to expose two methods, getConnection() and releaseConnection() to the rest of the application classes.

TABLE 14.1 Initialization parameters passed to the BookServlet *init()* method

PROPERTY	MEANING
OracleDriver	Oracle JDBC driver. Usually this string is `"oracle.jdbc.driver.OracleDriver"`
ConnectionString	Oracle connection string. Allows servlet to establish connections to Oracle database using either JDBC type 2 driver (OCI-based) or JDBC type 4 (100% pure Java).
Username	Oracle database username.
Password	Oracle database password.
MinConnections	Number of connection objects always available in pool.
MaxConnections	Maximum number of connection objects that can be created by connection pool.
MaxIdleTime	Maximum time, in seconds, that connection objects can remain active before being killed. Connection objects are only killed if there are more than the minimum number.
ServletString	String that should be returned by the *getRequestURL()* method provided by HttpServletRequest. Since several servlet engines mistakenly return the URL with the query string associated to the URL appended to the URL, that string is made accessible to servlet through property file, to avoid portability problems.

The source code for the connection pool class is shown below.[1]

```
package com.prenhall.OFJP.ConnectionPool;

import java.util.Enumeration;
import java.sql.*;

/** Connection Pool class.
**  @implement TimerListener
*/
public class ConnectionPool implements TimerListener
{
  /** The single instance of ConnectionPool.
  */
  private static ConnectionPool connPool;

  /** JDBC Driver
  */
  private String jdbcDriver;

  /** JDBC  URL
  */
  private String jdbcURL;

  /** Oracle username
  */
  private String username;

  /** Oracle password
  */
  private String password;

  /** Minimum number of connections in the pool
  */
  private int minConnection;

  /** Maximum number of connections in the pool
  */
  private int maxConnection;

  /** Maximum idle time for each connection (in minutes)
  */
```

[1]The connection pool mechanism shown in these pages is intended to be introductory and is only suitable for training purposes. A sophisticated, production-ready connection pool object requires far more demanding effort than what is attempted here. If you are interested in a serious alternative, consider PoolMan, developed by Code Studio and freely available from http://www.codestudio.com.

```
    private int connectionIdleTime;

    /** The Connection pool. A vector of Connections
    */
    private java.util.Vector connectionPool;

    /** The timer used to disconnect problematic sessions.
    */
    private Timer timer;

    /** Class constructor. It is defined as private, to implement
    **  the singleton pattern
    **  @param jdbcDriver String containing the required JDBC driver
    **  @param jdbcURL String containing the connection URL
    **  @param username String. Oracle account name.
    **  @param password String. Oracle password.
    **  @param minConnection Int that defines how many connection
    **         objects must be allocated in the pool at startup.
    **  @param maxConnection Int that defines the absolute maximum
    **         number of connection objects ever allocated by the
    **         connection pool object.
    **  @param connectionIdleTime Int. Number of seconds a connection
    **         object can remain idle before being destroyed.
    */
    private ConnectionPool(String jdbcDriver,
                           String jdbcURL,
                           String username,
                           String password,
                           int minConnection,
                           int maxConnection,
                           int connectionIdleTime)
            throws SQLException,
                   ClassNotFoundException
    {
       this.jdbcDriver          = jdbcDriver;
       this.jdbcURL             = jdbcURL;
       this.username            = username;
       this.password            = password;
       this.minConnection       = minConnection;
       this.maxConnection       = maxConnection;
       this.connectionIdleTime  = connectionIdleTime;
       Class.forName (jdbcDriver);
       this.connectionPool = new java.util.Vector();

       this.initializePool();
       this.timer = new Timer(this,60);
       timer.start();
    }

```

```
/** This method calls the private class constructor
**  to create an instance of this class, if an instance
**  doesn't exist already.
**  @param jdbcDriver String containing the required JDBC driver
**  @param jdbcURL String containing the connection URL
**  @param username String. Oracle account name.
**  @param password String. Oracle password.
**  @param minConnection Int that defines how many connection
**         objects must be allocated in the pool at startup.
**  @param maxConnection Int that defines the absolute maximum
**         number of connection objects ever allocated by the
**         connection pool object.
**  @param connectionIdleTime Int. Number of seconds a connection
**         object can remain idle before being destroyed.
**  @throws SQLException
**  @throws ClassNotFoundException
*/
public static ConnectionPool getInstance(String jdbcDriver,
                                         String jdbcURL,
                                         String username,
                                         String password,
                                         int minConnection,
                                         int maxConnection,
                                         int connectionIdleTime)
                                         throws SQLException,
                                         ClassNotFoundException
{
    if (connPool == null)
    {
       connPool = new ConnectionPool(jdbcDriver,
                                     jdbcURL,
                                     username,
                                     password,
                                     minConnection,
                                     maxConnection,
                                     connectionIdleTime);
    }
    return connPool;
}

/** The overloaded instance() method returns an instance of the
**  ConnectionPool class. It assumes that an instance has already
**  been initialized. If this is not true, an exception
**  is raised
**  @return ConnectionPool - An initialized ConnectionPool object
**  @throws Exception - If no connection pool object has been
**         allocated
*/
public static ConnectionPool instance() throws Exception
```

```
    {
        if (connPool == null)
           throw new Exception("Connection Pool not initialized!");
        return connPool;
    }

    /** This method implements the TimerListener interface. It is
    **  called by the timer when the sleep interval expires.
    */
    public synchronized void TimerEvent()
    {
        // If the connection pool is empty, simply return.
        if (this.connectionPool == null)
        {
          return;
        }

        // Get the current time in milliseconds
        long now = System.currentTimeMillis();

        // Look for any expired connection. If any one is found,
        // remove it.
        for (int ii = this.connectionPool.size() - 1; ii >= 0; ii--)
        {
          ConnectionObject co = (ConnectionObject)
            this.connectionPool.elementAt(ii);

          // If the connection is not in use and it has not been
          // used recently, close it
          if (!co.isUsed())
          {
            if ((this.connectionIdleTime > 0) &&
                (co.getUseTime() +
                 ( this.connectionIdleTime * 1000) < now))
            {
                co.close();
            }
          }
        }

        // Remove all connections no longer open
        for (int ii = this.connectionPool.size() - 1; ii >= 0; ii--)
        {
          ConnectionObject co = (ConnectionObject)
            this.connectionPool.elementAt(ii);
          try
          {
            // If the connection is closed, remove it from the pool
            if (co.isClosed())
```

```
          {
            removeConnection(ii);
          }
        }
        catch (Exception exc) {}
      }
  }

  /** This method empties the connection pool
  */
  public synchronized void destroy()
  {
      if (this.timer != null)
         this.timer = null;
      for (int ii = 0; ii<this.connectionPool.size(); ii++)
      {
         ConnectionObject co =
            (ConnectionObject) this.connectionPool.elementAt(ii);
         co.close();
         co.setUsed(true);
      }
      this.connectionPool.removeAllElements();

  }

  /** This method removes a given connection from the pool.
  **  @param index Int corresponding to the position of the
  **  connection in the vector that stores the connection pool.
  */
  private synchronized void removeConnection(int index)
  {
    if (this.connectionPool != null)
    {
      if (index < this.connectionPool.size())
      {
        // Remove the element from the pool
        this.connectionPool.removeElementAt(index);
      }
    }
  }

  /** This method initializes the pool, creating as many
  **  connection objects as specified by the minConnection
  **  parameter, which is user-defined
  **  @throws SQLException
  */
  public void initializePool() throws SQLException
  {
       for (int ii = 0; ii < this.minConnection; ii++)
```

```
      {
         ConnectionObject co = new ConnectionObject(this.jdbcDriver,
                                                    this.jdbcURL,
                                                    this.username,
                                                    this.password);
         this.connectionPool.addElement(co);
      }
  }

  /** Method that returns a connection objects obtained from
  **  the connection pool.
  **  @return co - Handle to a connection object
  public synchronized ConnectionObject getConnection()
  {
    java.sql.Connection connection = null;
    ConnectionObject connectionObject = null;
    int currentPoolSize = this.connectionPool.size();
    for (int ii=0; ii< currentPoolSize; ii++)
    {
      // Get the ConnectionObject from the pool
      ConnectionObject co = (ConnectionObject)
        this.connectionPool.elementAt(ii);

      // If this is a valid connection and it is not in use,
      // get it and pass it to the caller
      if (!co.isUsed())
      {
        connectionObject = co;
        break;
      }
    }
    // If no connection object was found, try to increase the pool
    if ( connectionObject == null )
    {
       if(this.maxConnection > this.connectionPool.size())
       {
         int connIndex = this.incrementConnection();
         if (connIndex > -1)
           connectionObject = (ConnectionObject)
             this.connectionPool.elementAt(connIndex);
       }
    }

    // If the pool could not be increased, return null to the caller
    if ( connectionObject == null )
       return null;
    else // Initialize the connection object
    {
         connectionObject.setUsed(true);
```

```
286:         connectionObject.setUseTime(System.currentTimeMillis());
287:     }
288:
289:     // Return the allocated connection object to the client
290:     return connectionObject;
291:   }
292:
293:   /** This method returns a connection object to the pool
294:   **  @param connection Handle to a ConnectionObject object
295:   */
296:   public synchronized void releaseConnection(
297:                     ConnectionObject connection)
298:   {
299:       connection.setUsed(false);
300:       connection.setUseTime(0);
301:   }
302:
303:   /** This method adds a connection object to the pool
304:   **  @return ConnectionPoolSize - Int. Returns -1 if the pool
305:   **  could allocate an additional connection object.
306:   */
307:   private synchronized int incrementConnection()
308:   {
309:     try
310:     {
311:         ConnectionObject co = new ConnectionObject(this.jdbcDriver,
312:                                                     this.jdbcURL,
313:                                                     this.username,
314:                                                     this.password);
315:         this.connectionPool.addElement(co);
316:         return this.connectionPool.size()-1;
317:     }
318:     catch (SQLException SQLExc)
319:     {
320:         return -1;
321:     }
322:   }
323: }
```

9 ConnectionPool class definition. It implements TimerListener, so that a timer object will be able to interact with the ConnectionPool object.

13–49 Class attribute definition. The class contains a private static reference to a single instance of itself, which allows for the creation of a single instance of the class. Most of the class attributes are the connection pool parameters read from the property file passed to the class by the servlet's *init()* method. A vector that will contain

JDBC connections is also defined, together with a handle to a timer object that will regularly check whether expired connections are living in the pool, killing them if necessary.

65–73 Class constructor. It is declared private to implement the Singleton design pattern. If the constructor is declared private, the only way to create an instance of the class is to call a public static method, which in turns calls the constructor. This is done by the *instance()* method (line 107). The parameters passed to the constructor are the JDBC driver type (thin or thick-OCI), the JDBC URL, the username to use to connect to the Oracle database, the password, the minimum number of connection objects to always be available in the pool, the maximum number of connection objects allowed to be instantiated by the pool, and the idle time for connections before they are destroyed, to bring the pool down to the minimum number of connections when the load on the database decreases.

82 The class implementing the Oracle JDBC driver is loaded.

83 The vector that will contain the connection object is initialized.

85 The pool is initialized, creating as many connection objects as specified by the minConnection parameter.

86–87 The timer object is instantiated and its thread started.

107–115 The public and static method that returns the single instance of this class is declared. It takes the same parameters as the class constructor.

117 If the private reference to a connection pool object is empty, it means that no instances of this class exist.

118–126 An instance of ConnectionPool is created, and a reference to it is stored in the private attribute of the same class.

127 A handle to a connection pool object is returned.

138–143 An overloaded *instance()* method that is called without parameters. This method can only work if an instance of the class has already been created. This method cannot create a new instance, so if it is called before an instance of the class exists, it will throw an exception.

148 The TimerEvent() method, which implements the TimerListener interface, is defined.

151–154 If the connection pool is empty (i.e., does not contain a connection object), the control is passed back to the method caller.

157 The current timestamp is obtained from the System object.

161–177 All connection objects are accessed and their status checked. If they have exceeded the allowed idle time, the JDBC connection is closed.

180–194 All connection objects are accessed again. If the JDBC connection was closed during the previous loop, the connection object is destroyed (i.e., removed from the pool).

198–211 This method empties the pool. It first closes the JDBC connection of all connection objects, and then removes all elements from the vector that stores the connection objects.

217–227 This method removes a single connection from the pool. The connection is identified by its vector index, which is passed as a parameter to the method.

234–244 This method initializes the pool. It creates as many connection objects as specified by the minConnection parameter, storing them into the vector that implements the pool.

249 The *getConnection()* method is defined. It returns the first available connection to the caller.

254–267 During this first loop, initiated at line 254, all connections stored in the pool are accessed, and each one checked for availability. The first available connection is stored in a connection handle previously defined, and the loop is terminated.

269–278 If the preceding step did not find any available connection (if the connection handle is still null), the method tries to expand the pool. If the number of connections currently stored in the pool does not exceed the maximum number of connections allowed, a new connection is created and stored in the pool.

281–287 If the pool could not be increased, a null object is returned to the caller; otherwise the connection object just created is initialized and returned to the caller.

307–323 This method increases the pool, adding one additional connection to the vector containing all the connection objects and returning the vector index to the caller.

ConnectionPool implements the TimerListener interface, which consists of one method, TimerEvent. The latter is executed each time by the timer object when the sleep interval expires. The timer is automatically reset after each timer expiration.

You have built the database and the means to efficiently access data stored in it. It is now time to focus on the look-and-feel of BookServlet from the client's perspective. Its user interface is somehow limited by HTML, which does not provide a highly interactive experience. The communication between the user of the application and the servlet occurs through HTML forms, dynamically built by Java code and sent to the user's browser. The trade-off is between a graphically appealing user interface that requires a sophisticated client environment, such as Java, Javascript, or Dynamic HTML, which introduce serious compatibility issues, and a Spartan user interface that supports a large variety of end-user environments, with no associated compatibility issues.

The purpose of Bookservlet is to teach you how to develop servlets, not how to develop sophisticated GUIs. Chapter 15 will shift the focus to presentation services, and in particular to the subject of decoupling the content from the presentation logic, using the Java Server Pages (JSP) mechanism.

What follows is a preview of BookServlet. Figure 14.3 shows the welcome page of the application, which prompts the user to open a new account or to enter account name and password if an account already exists.

If a new account is to be created for a user who is visiting the site for the first time, a form that collects personal as well as financial details is presented to the user. The form appears in Figure 14.4.

When personal and financial information has been entered into the system, or upon a successful login, users can access the virtual bookshop catalog of Oracle books (see Figure 14.5). In this oversimplified environment, the whole catalog is displayed in one bottomless Web page. Professionally deployed Web applications will display the catalog over more pages, possibly providing the user with a search engine to help narrow down the content to be displayed.

The book catalog form allows an interactive user to view the shopping basket, accessed by clicking on a button displayed in the top-right corner, and to dis-

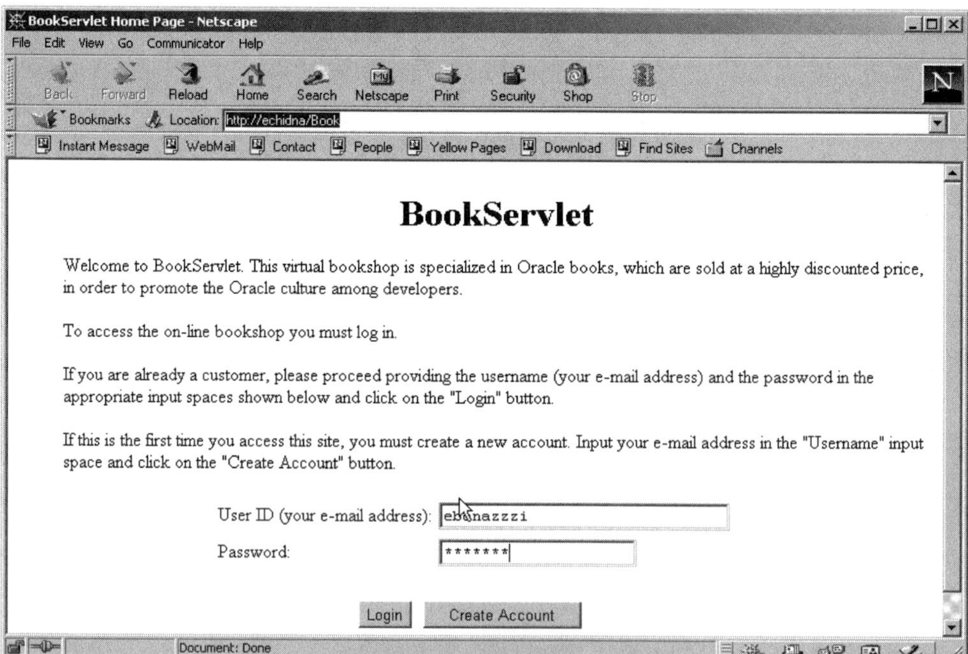

FIGURE 14.3 The BookServlet welcome page.

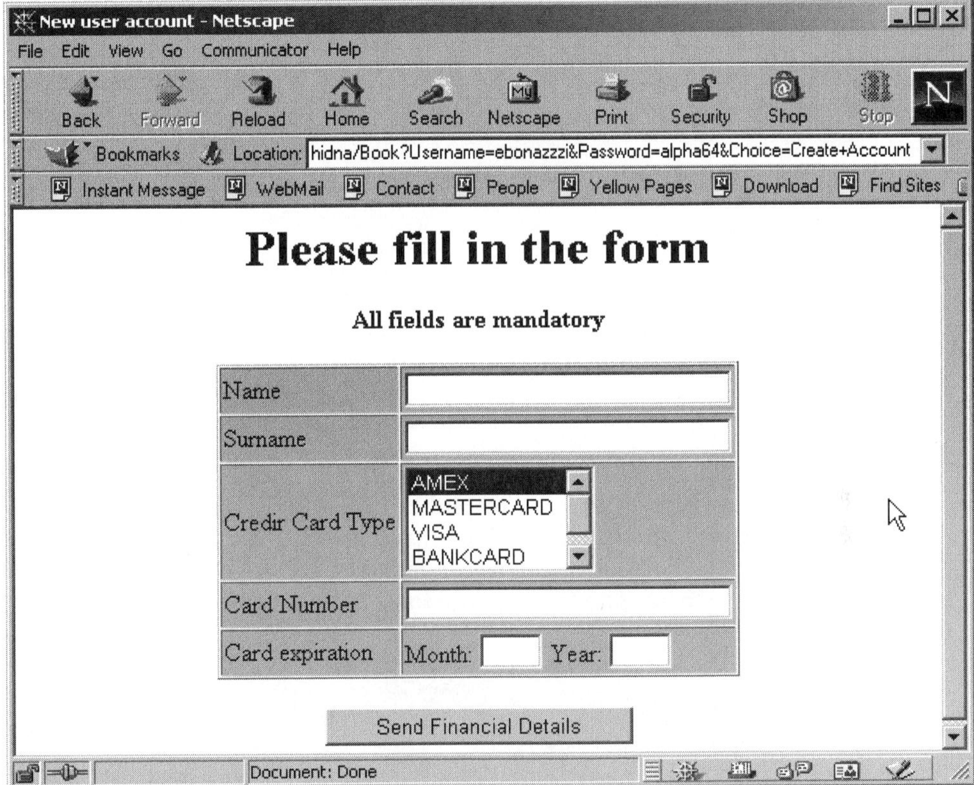

FIGURE 14.4 New users must fill in the form asking for credit details.

play the details of each book in the catalog. Each book entry in the HTML table displayed on the form provides a command button that allows interactive users to display the details of the required book.

By clicking on the "View Book Details," users can access a form that displays detailed information about a given book. For each book, users can see a picture of the book cover, the retail price, the discount offered by the virtual bookshop, the discounted price, and how much they would save by buying the book online instead of paying the recommended retail price.

The form also displays a command button that allows users to add the book to their shopping basket. The book details form is shown in Figure 14.6.

At any time, users can access their shopping basket to see how many and what items they have put into it. The shopping basket form must be accessed in order to submit the order at the end of the virtual shopping session.

The form displays all the books entered in the basket, one after the other, and two command buttons at the left-hand bottom of the form. The leftmost but-

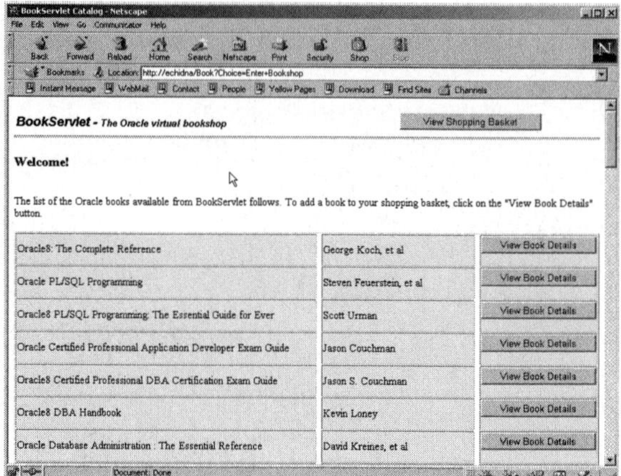

FIGURE 14.5 The virtual bookshop catalog.

ton submits the order, and the second button allows users to empty the basket. In order to submit an order, the user must indicate the courier of choice. This is done by picking one of the couriers displayed by the list box, located toward the top part of the form. The form is shown in Figure 14.7.

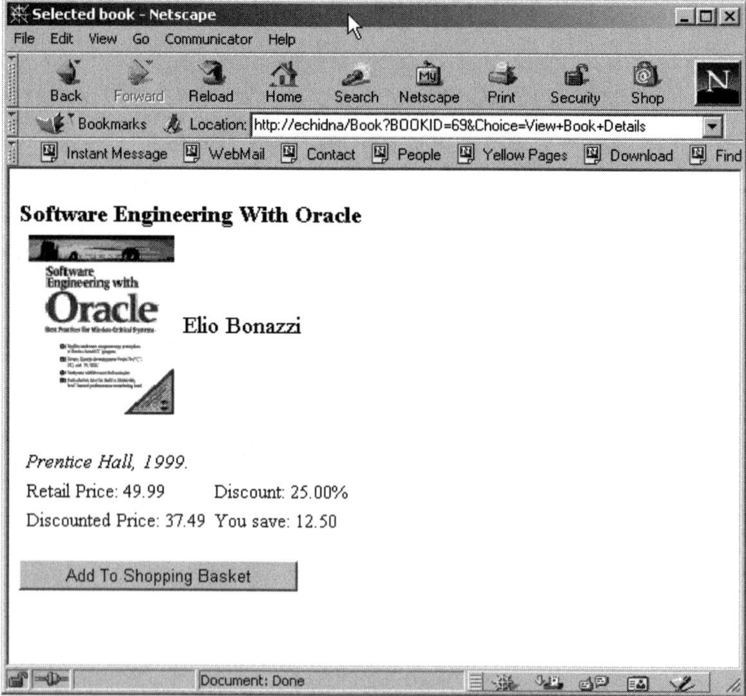

FIGURE 14.6 Users can access the details of every book in the catalog.

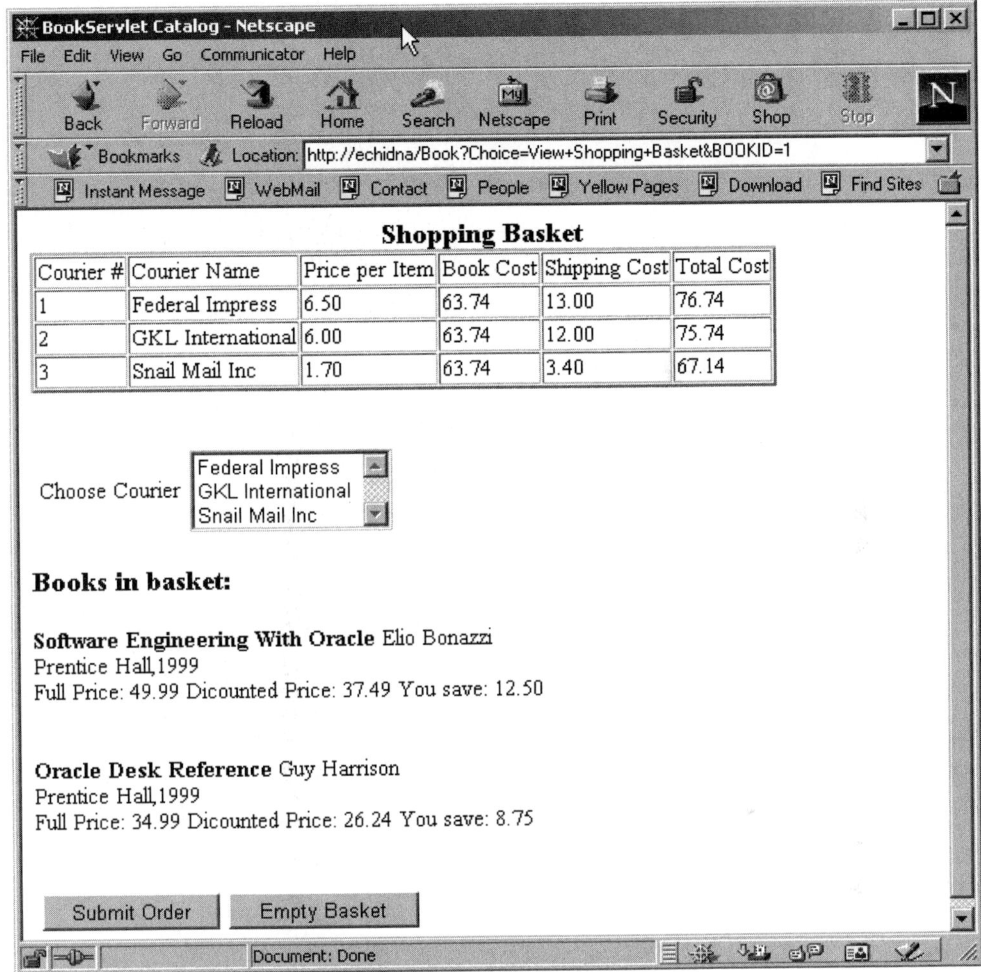

FIGURE 14.7 The shopping basket form.

When an order has been successfully submitted, the user receives a feedback form confirming that the system has accepted the order. The feedback form is shown in Figure 14.8.

Although BookServlet offers a rather Spartan user interface, it accurately simulates a real-life e-commerce application. All the basic operations usually performed by both the user and the system interacting with the user in a Web-based application are well represented.

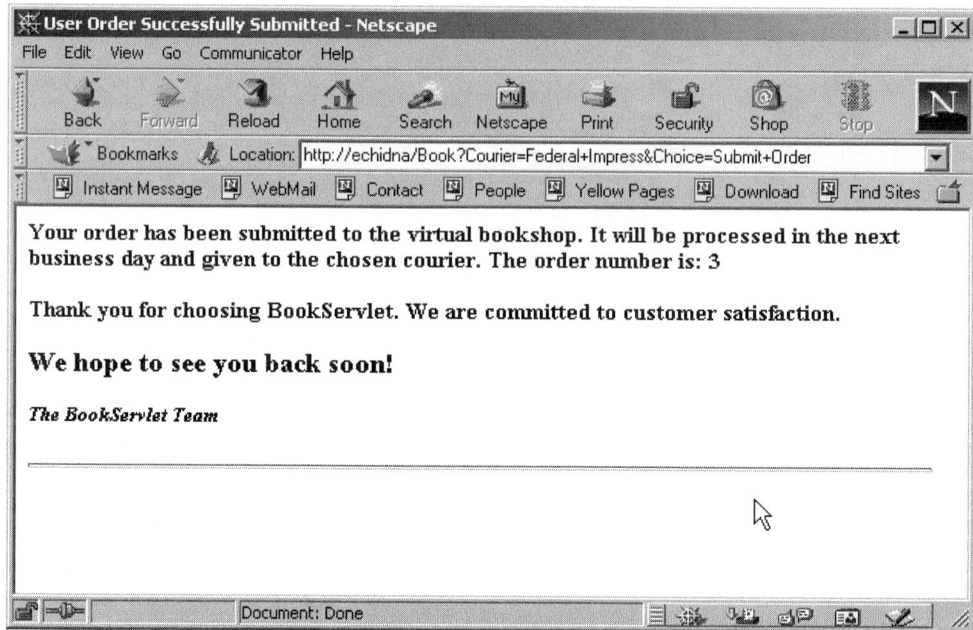

FIGURE 14.8 An order has been successfully submitted.

TABLE 14.2 BookServlet Java files

CONNECTION FILES	TYPE	COMMENT
TimerListener.java	Interface	Defines interface to be implemented by classes that wish to use timer.
Timer.java	Class	Implements timer. Used by connection pool object to periodically check on status of each connection object.
ConnectionObject.java	Class	Implements connection to Oracle. Also prepares SQL statements most often used by application.
ConnectionPool.java	Class	Implements connection pool that preloads set of connection objects to speed up database access.

SERVLET FILES	TYPE	IMPLEMENTS SERVLET SERVICE	COMMENT
ServletService.java	Interface	—	Defines interface that all classes providing servlet behavior must implement.
AddBasket.java	Class	Yes	Implements adding a book to user's shopping basket.

TABLE 14.2 *Continued*

SERVLET FILES	TYPE	IMPLEMENTS SERVLET SERVICE	COMMENT
BasketItem.java	Class	No	Defines attributes and methods for each item to be stored in shopping basket.
BookServlet.java	Class	No	Extends HttpServlet and implements servlet mainline. Overrides the *init()*, *destroy()*, *doGet()*, and *doPost()* methods.
Courier.java	Class	No	Defines attributes and methods for courier object.
CreateUser.java	Class	Yes	Implements application logic that creates new user in database.
Customer.java	Class	No	Defines attributes and methods for customer (read user) object.
DestroyBasket.java	Class	Yes	Implements application logic that resets shopping basket.
DisplayBooks.java	Class	Yes	Implements application logic that displays entire book catalog in user's browser.
Initialize.java	Class	No	Implements initialization tasks performed at servlet startup.
LoginUser.java	Class	Yes	Implements application logic that allows user login to virtual bookshop.
ProcessImage.java	Class	Yes	Implements application logic that displays e book-cover picture when user requests book details.
ShowBasket.java	Class	Yes	Implements application logic that displays content of shopping basket.
SubmitCredit.java	Class	Yes	Implements application logic that stores e user's financial details to BookServlet database.
SubmitOrder.java	Class	Yes	Implements application logic that submits order to BookServlet.
ViewBookDetails.java	Class	Yes	Implements application logic that displays details of required book.
WelcomeScreen.java	Class	Yes	Implements application logic that displays initial screen of BookServlet.

14.3.3 THE CORE SERVLET METHODS

By now, you have an idea of what the application is about. You have already built the connection pool component, and you have a complete database structure. It is time to delve into the source code of BookServlet. As usual, only a small percentage of the source code is shown in the following pages. Only those classes and methods that implement core servlet techniques will be presented here and discussed in detail. You should, however, edit all the files comprising the application and examine the source code. Even better, set up a Web server and a servlet engine in your own environment, compile all the classes, and try to run BookServlet. There is no substitute for hands-on experience. Table 14.2 lists all the Java files that constitute the application.

In order to compile the classes and interfaces listed in the table, you need to include the servlet and Oracle JDBC libraries. If you are using a Java IDE, include servlet.jar and classes111.zip if you want JDBC version 1, or classes12.zip if you want JDBC version 2, in IDE's CLASSPATH. If you are a command-line user, either add these files to your CLASSPATH environment variable or invoke java using the –classpath command-line option, providing the absolute pathname of the JDBC library you want to include.

The first component you are going to examine is the connection object. The source code of the ConnectionObject class is shown below. This component does not employ sophisticated techniques; the only difference, compared with most connection objects freely available from either the Web or other books, is the extensive use of prepared statements. If you examine the class constructor, you will see that the most commonly used SQL statements of BookServlet are "prepared," that is, pre-compiled, as soon as a connection to Oracle is established. Most of the methods implemented by the class are getter methods that simply return prepared statements.

Connection objects are instantiated by the ConnectionPool object, which dispatches connections to the various application components that request access to the database.

```
package com.prenhall.OFJP.ConnectionPool;

import java.sql.*;
import oracle.jdbc.driver.*;
import oracle.sql.*;

/** Class that implements the connection object
*/
public class ConnectionObject
{
  /** Oracle JDBC connection */
  private              Connection          connection;

  /** Flags that indicates if this connection is currently used */
  private              boolean             inUse;

  /** Flags that indicates if this connection has been closed */
  private              boolean             closed;

  /** Connection creation timestamp */
  private              long                creationTime;

  /** Timestamp set when a user gets the connection */
  private              long                useTime;
```

```
/** SQL statement that displays the image of the book front cover */
private             PreparedStatement  imageSQL;

/** SQL statement that fetches all orders belonging to a
**  given customer */
private             PreparedStatement  listOrders;

/** SQL statement that fetches the user password given the user
**  username (which corresponds to the e-mail address) */
private             PreparedStatement  userPasswd;

/** SQL statement that fetches the book details given the book id */
private             PreparedStatement  bookDetails;

/** SQL statement that inserts the details of a new user into the
**  customer table */
private             PreparedStatement  createUser;

/** SQL statement that inserts a new order into the cust_order
**  table  */
private             PreparedStatement  insertOrder;

/** SQL statement that inserts a new order item into the
**  order_item table */
private             PreparedStatement  insertOrderItem;

/** SQL statement that fetches the courier ID given the
**  courier name. */
private             PreparedStatement  getCourierId;

/** Class constructor.
**  @param jdbcURL String containing the database URL
**  @param username String containing the Oracle username
**  @param password String containing the Oracle password
**  @throws SQLException If a connection cannot be obtained from
**  the Oracle driver manager
*/
public ConnectionObject(String jdbcDriver, String jdbcURL, String username,
                        String password)
                        throws SQLException
{
    // Obtain a connection from the JDBC driver
    this.connection = DriverManager.getConnection(jdbcURL,
                                                  username,password);
    // Initialize instance variables
    this.inUse = false;
    this.closed = false;
    this.creationTime = System.currentTimeMillis();
    this.useTime = 0;
    // Turn auto commit off
    connection.setAutoCommit(false);
    // Initialize all prepared statements...
```

```
      imageSQL = connection.prepareStatement("select PICTURE from "+
                                        "SALES_ITEM WHERE ID = ?");
      listOrders = connection.prepareStatement("select A.ID, "+
                "A.CREATION_DATE,A.PENDING_DATE,A.SHIPMENT_DATE,"+
                "B.NAME,A.TOTAL_COST,A.SHIPMENT_COST,"+
                " A.TOTAL_COST FROM CUST_ORDER A, COURIER B WHERE "+
                "A.COUR_ID = B.ID AND A.CUST_ID = ? ");
      userPasswd = connection.prepareStatement("select id, "+
                                        "password from "+
                                        "CUSTOMER  WHERE EMAIL = ?");
      bookDetails = connection.prepareStatement("select title,author, "+
                  "publisher, year_published,full_price,discount FROM "+
                  "sales_item WHERE ID = ?");
      createUser =  connection.prepareStatement("insert into customer "+
                  "(ID,NAME,SURNAME,EMAIL,PASSWORD,CREDIT_CARD_TYPE,"+
                  "CREDIT_CARD_NBR,MONTH_EXPIRED,YEAR_EXPIRED)"+
                  "VALUES (?,?,?,?,?,?,?,?,?)");
      insertOrder = connection.prepareStatement("insert into cust_order "+
                  "(ID,CUST_ID,CREATION_DATE,PENDING_DATE,"+
                  "COUR_ID,SHIPMENT_DATE,SHIPMENT_COST,TOTAL_COST)"+
                  "VALUES (?,?,SYSDATE,SYSDATE,?,?,?,?)");
      insertOrderItem =
connection.prepareStatement("insert into order_item "+
                   "(ord_id,prd_id,quantity,price) VALUES (?,?,?,?)");
      getCourierId = connection.prepareStatement("select id, "+
                   "cost_per_item from courier where name = ?");

  }

  /** Method that returns the getCourierId prepared statement.
  **  @return getCourierId Prepared Statement.
  */
  public PreparedStatement getGetCourierId()
  {
      return this.getCourierId;
  }

  /** Method that returns the insertOrder prepared statement.
  **  @return insertOrder Prepared Statement.
  */
  public PreparedStatement getInsertOrder()
  {
      return this.insertOrder;
  }

  /** Method that returns the insertOrderItem prepared statement.
  **  @return insertOrderItem Prepared Statement.
  */
  public PreparedStatement getInsertOrderItem()
  {
      return this.insertOrderItem;
  }
```

```
/** Method that returns the createUser prepared statement.
**  @return createUser Prepared Statement.
*/
public PreparedStatement getCreateUser()
{
    return this.createUser;
}

/** Method that returns the bookDetails prepared statement.
**  @return bookDetails Prepared Statement.
*/
public PreparedStatement getBookDetails()
{
    return this.bookDetails;
}

/** Method that returns the imageSQL prepared statement.
**  @return imageSQL Prepared Statement.
*/
public PreparedStatement getImageSQL()
{
    return this.imageSQL;
}

/** Method that returns the listOrders prepared statement.
**  @return listOrders Prepared Statement.
*/
public PreparedStatement getListOrders()
{
    return this.listOrders;
}

/** Method that returns the userPasswd prepared statement.
**  @return userPasswd Prepared Statement.
*/
public PreparedStatement getUserPasswd()
{
    return this.userPasswd;
}

/** Method that closes the connection to Oracle. If an exception
**  occurs, it is not propagated back to the caller.
*/
public void close()
{
    try
    {
       this.connection.close();
    }
    catch ( SQLException SQLExc) {}

    this.closed = true;
}
```

```
/** Method that tests if this connection is closed.
**  @return boolean True if the connection is closed, false otherwise
*/
public boolean isClosed()
{
    return this.closed;
}

/** Method that returns the Oracle JDBC connection used by this
**  connection object.
**  @return JDBCConnection - A handle to a JDBC connection.
*/
public Connection getConnection()
{
    return this.connection;
}

/** Method that returns a boolean value indicating if this
**  connection object is used (true) or idle (false).
**  @return Boolean - True if this connection is in use, false
**          otherwise.
*/
public boolean isUsed()
{
    return inUse;
}

/** Method that returns the timestamp of connection object creation.
**  @return creationTime - long containing the creation timestamp.
*/
public long getCreationTime()
{
    return this.creationTime;
}

/** Method that returns the timestamp set at the moment this
**  connection was allocated to a requester.
**  @return useTime - long containing the timestamp
*/
public long getUseTime()
{
    return this.useTime;
}

/** Method that sets the timestamp of the moment this connection
**  was allocated to a connection requester.
**  @param useTime long containing the timestamp.
*/
public void setUseTime(long useTime)
{
    this.useTime = useTime;
}
```

```
    /** This method set the attribute flag that indicates if the
    **  connection is currently being used.
    **  @param used Boolean. True if the connection is used, false
    **         otherwise.
    */
    public void setUsed(boolean used)
    {
        this.inUse = used;
    }

    /** Method that makes the database changes permanent. */
    public void commit() throws java.sql.SQLException
    {
        this.connection.commit();
    }

    /** Method that rolls back the transaction changes. */
    public void rollback()
    {
        try
        {
           this.connection.rollback();
        }
        catch ( java.sql.SQLException exc) {}
    }

}
```

The next application component we will examine is the servlet mainline. You are going to subclass HttpServlet and override a few key methods, such as *init(), doGet(), doPost(),* and *destroy()*. Pay a particular attention to the *doGet()* method, which performs the application's basic functions. The *doPost()* method simply calls doGet(), but the HTML code produced by BookServlet never uses a POST command, so overriding *doPost(),* which is technically superfluous, can be seen as an example of defensive programming.

The *doGet()* method calls HttpServletRequest.getParameter() to find the option chosen by the user, who interacts with the application through HTML forms and URLs. An easy way to deal with the issue of interpreting the user request is to code a long series of *if* statements, each testing for all possible options available to the user. This technique is succinctly illustrated by the pseudo-code that follows.

```
    public void doGet(HttpServletRequest request,
                      HttpServletResponse response)
                   throws ServletException, IOException
// Get the action code
String actionCode = request.getParameter(ACTION_CODE);
if (actionCode.equals == <INITIAL LOGIN> )
```

```
{
      … perform login tasks
}
if (actionCode.equals(<DISPLAY BOOKS>))
{
      … perform book displaying tasks
}
etc, etc
```

The problem with this approach is that it works fine when the application consists of only a few options, say 10 or 15, but when the application grows and its complexity increases, offering hundreds of options to users, the cascading series of *if* statements becomes unmanageable.

A better solution is to create an interface to be implemented by all classes that provide specialized behavior for the servlet. The interface defines a method, and the servlet invokes it.

If you look at the source code of all the classes that implement specific behavior, such as *DisplayBooks* or *LoginUser*, you can see that each class implements the *ServletService* interface. *ServletService* defines a method, called *perform()*, which receives a BookServlet object, an HttpServletRequest, and an HttpServletResponse object. During servlet initialization, all application components that provide a service (e.g., handling user logins, displaying the book catalog, accepting user financial details) are instantiated and stored in a hash table. The hash key for each entry is the action code, or a constant that determines the option chosen by the user.

Whenever the *doGet()* method is called, it requests the ACTION_CODE parameter invoking HttpServletRequest.getParameter(). The value returned is used to retrieve the handle to the required service provider, using the hash table *get()* method. An example will illustrate the concept. Consider the ShowBasket class, which displays the shopping basket when a user clicks on the "View Shopping Basket" button shown in the top-right corner of the HTML page that displays the book catalog. The HTML code that implement the button is:

```
<table border=0 cellpadding=0 cellspacing=0>
<tr>
<td width=56 align=right><form method=GET
    action="http://wallaby/servlet/Book">
  <input type=submit name="Choice"
     value="View Shopping Basket">
</td>
```

When the button is clicked, the servlet engine calls the *doGet()* method in BookServlet, since the form tag specified GET as the delivery method. The *doGet()* method invokes getParameter, passing the string "Choice" as the name. The *getParameter()* method, implemented in the HttpServletRequest object, returns the string "View Shopping Basket" as the value specified in the HTML form code.

The servlet uses the "View Shopping Basket" string to retrieve a reference to the object that implements the displaying of the shopping basket. During initialization, all the objects implementing application behavior are instantiated and stored in a hash table. The hash key used to retrieve the objects is a string that describes the function performed by the object, in this case "View Shopping Basket." Thanks to the magic of polymorphism, the three lines of code shown below work with all objects that implement the ServletService interface.

```
String actionCode = request.getParameter("Choice");
ServletService servServ = this.getServiceProvider(actionCode);
servServ.perform(this,request,response);
```

The technique shown above allows developers to avoid large numbers of *if* statements, and provides an additional benefit. To add a new application component:

- The new class that implements the additional behavior must be added to the BookServlet jar file.
- The Initialize class must be modified to instantiate the new object and store it in the hash table,

However, the BookServlet class does not even need to be recompiled.

The source code of the BookServlet.class follows.

```
package com.prenhall.OFJP.ConnectionPool;

import javax.servlet.*;
import javax.servlet.http.*;
import java.sql.*;
import oracle.sql.*;
import oracle.jdbc.driver.*;
import java.io.*;
import java.util.*;
import java.text.DecimalFormat;

/** BookServlet class.
*/
public class BookServlet extends HttpServlet
{
  // The following are mnemonics identifying the Web pages used
  // by the application.
  public static final String ACTION_CODE          = "Choice";
  public static final String F_USERNAME           = "Username";
  public static final String F_PASSWORD           = "Password";
  public static final String F_NAME               = "Name";
```

```
public static final String F_SURNAME            = "Surname";
public static final String F_COURIER            = "Courier";
public static final String F_CREDIT_CARD        = "Credit Card Type";
public static final String F_CARD_NUMBER        = "Card Number";
public static final String F_EXPIRE_MONTH       = "MonthExpire";
public static final String F_EXPIRE_YEAR        = "YearExpire";
public static final String F_BOOKID             = "BOOKID";
public static final String A_INITIAL_SCREEN     = "Initial";
public static final String A_IMAGE              = "Image";
public static final String A_DISPLAY_BOOKS      = "Enter Bookshop";
public static final String A_LOGIN              = "Login";
public static final String A_CREATE_ACCOUNT     = "Create Account";
public static final String A_SUBMIT_CREDIT      = "Send Financial Details";
public static final String A_VIEW_BOOK_DETAILS  = "View Book Details";
public static final String A_SHOW_BASKET        = "View Shopping Basket";
public static final String A_ADD_BASKET         = "Add To Shopping Basket";
public static final String A_SUBMIT_ORDER       = "Submit Order";
public static final String A_DESTROY_BASKET     = "Empty Basket";

/** Instance handle to the connection pool object
*/
private ConnectionPool connectionPool;

/** Instance handle to the hash table containing all customer
**  sessions */
private Hashtable customers;

/** Instance handle to the hash table that stores all services
**  provided by the servlet. */
private Hashtable ServiceProviders;

/** String that contains the URL entry point for the servlet. */
private String servletInvoke = "";

/** Handle to an exception object that can be raised during
**  the initialization phase */
private Exception initException;

/** The initialization method runs in a separate thread. If
** an error occurs during initialization, the servlet class will
** store the exception in the instance attribute. The doGet method
** checks if an exception has been raised, alerting the user if the case.
** setInitException is called from Initialize when an exception
** occurs.
** @param initExc Handle to an Exception object
*/
public void setInitException(Exception initExc)
{
    this.initException = initExc;
}
```

```
/** This method stores a handle to a connection pool object
**  into the connection pool instance attribute
**  @param cp Handle to a connection pool object
*/
public void setConnPool(ConnectionPool cp)
{
    this.connectionPool = cp;
}

/** This method stores a customer object, together with its key,
**  into the customer hash table.
**  @param key String containing the customer key (which corresponds
**          to the session ID as returned by HttpSession.getId()
**  @param cust Handle to a customer object to be stored in to the
**          customer hash table
*/
public void storeCustomer(String key,Customer cust)
{
    this.customers.put(key,cust);
}

/** This method returns a handle to a customer object given
**  its hash key.
**  @param key String containing the customer's hash key
**  @return Customer - Handle to a customer object
*/
public Customer retrieveCustomer(String key)
{
    return (Customer) this.customers.get(key);
}

/** Method that stores the URL that invoke BookServlet in the
**  instance attribute.
**  @param si String containing the URL used to invoke the servlet
*/
public void setServletInvoke(String si)
{
    this.servletInvoke = si;
}

/** Method that returns the URL used to invoke the servlet.
**  @return URL - The basic URL that contains the servlet alias.
*/
public String getServletInvoke()
{
    return this.servletInvoke;
}

/** Method that overrides the parent's init method. It performs
**  initialization tasks local to this servlet.
**  @param config Handle to a servlet config object, passed by
```

```
**          the servlet engine.
**  @throws ServletException If something fails during initialization
*/
public void init(ServletConfig config) throws ServletException
{
  super.init(config);
  customers = new Hashtable();
  ServiceProviders = new Hashtable();
  Initialize.instance(this);
}

/** Method that cleans up the resources associated to the running of
**  of the servlet.
*/
public void destroy()
{
    // Empty the connection pool
    connectionPool.destroy();
    // Elects the connection pool to be garbage collected
    connectionPool = null;
    super.destroy();
}

/** This method store a service provider into the service provider
**  hash table.
**  @param id String containing the service provider ID
**  @param ss Handle to a ServletService object
*/
public void setServiceProvider(String id, ServletService ss)
{
    this.ServiceProviders.put(id,ss);
}

/** This method retrieves a service provider from the service
**  provider hash table given its id.
**  @param id String containing the service provider ID
**  @return ServletService A handle to a servlet service object
*/
public ServletService getServiceProvider(String id)
{
    return (ServletService) this.ServiceProviders.get(id);
}

/** This method retrieves the first available connection object.
**  If none is available, it sleeps and tries again, until a
**  connection object is finally fetched.
**  @return ConnectionObject A handle to a connection object.
*/
public ConnectionObject getConnection()
{
    ConnectionObject co = null;
```

```
    while (true)
    {
       co = this.connectionPool.getConnection();
       if (co == null)
       {
          try
          {
             Thread.sleep(250);
          }
          catch (Exception exc) {}
       }
       else
          break;
    }
    return co;
}

/** Method that processes the HTTP Get request
** @param request Handle to a HttpServletRequest object.
** @param response Handle to a HttpServletResponse object.
** @throws ServletException
** @throws IOException
*/
public void doGet(HttpServletRequest request, HttpServletResponse response)
                   throws ServletException, IOException
{

    if (this.initException != null)
    {
       java.io.PrintWriter out =
          new java.io.PrintWriter(response.getOutputStream());
       this.printError(out,"Initialization error: "+
          this.initException.getMessage()+
          "<p>Please contact the help desk. " +
          "This is an internal severe error that prevents you from" +
          " accessing the virtual bookshop.");
       return;
    }
    // Get the action code
    String actionCode = request.getParameter(ACTION_CODE);
    if (actionCode == null)
    {
       actionCode = this.A_INITIAL_SCREEN;
    }

    ServletService servServ = this.getServiceProvider(actionCode);
    if (servServ == null)
    {
       java.io.PrintWriter out =
          new java.io.PrintWriter(response.getOutputStream());
          this.printError(out,"Servlet Internal Error: "+
```

```
                "Unrecognized Servlet Service. Please contact the helpdesk.");
            return;
        }
        servServ.perform(this,request,response);
        return;
    }

    /** Method that processes the HTTP Post request
    ** @param request Handle to a HttpServletRequest object.
    ** @param response Handle to a HttpServletResponse object.
    ** @throws ServletException
    ** @throws IOException
    */
    public void doPost(HttpServletRequest request,
     HttpServletResponse response)
                        throws ServletException, IOException
    {
        this.doGet(request,response);
    }


     /**
     ** Displays an error message to the client's browser
     **
     ** @param out PrintWriter stream
     ** @param msg String containing the error message
     */
     public void printError(java.io.PrintWriter out,
                            String msg)
     {
        out.println("<html>");
        out.println("<head>");
        out.println("<title>Book Servlet Error</title>");
        out.println("</head>");
        out.println("<body>");
        out.println("<center>");
        out.println("<br>");
        out.println("<h1>Error:</h1><br>");
        out.println("<h3>"+msg + "</h3>");
        out.println("<br><hr>");
        out.println("Click the 'Back' icon and correct the error");
        out.println("</center>");
        out.println("</body>");
        out.println("</html>");
        out.flush();
        out.close();
     }

    /** This method releases a connection object back into the connection
    **  pool.
    **  @param co Handle to the ConnectionObject object to be released.
```

```
   */
   public void releaseConnection(ConnectionObject co)
   {
      this.connectionPool.releaseConnection(co);
   }

   /** This method retrieves a customer session object from the
   **  hash table storing all sessions, given the session id.
   **  @param sessionId String containing the session id of the required
   **         customer session
   **  @return Customer A handle to a customer object.
   public synchronized Customer getCustomer(String sessionId)
   {
      return (Customer) this.customers.get(sessionId);
   }
}
```

The *getConnection()* method implemented by BookServlet looks like a perfect replica of the *getConnection()* method implemented in ConnectionPool, and indeed the former method calls the latter. However, the *getConnection()* method implemented in BookServlet blocks, waiting until a connection can be obtained from pool. If the connection pool object finds all the connection objects busy, and the pool cannot be further extended, it returns a null to BookServlet. The latter tests the returned value; if the value is null, the *getConnection()* method will force the BookServlet thread to sleep until a connection can be obtained.

This arrangement only works for training and testing purposes. A production release of BookServlet should implement a more fair method for queuing the connection requests. If a connection is requested from the pool, and all available connections are already taken and the pool cannot be expanded, the thread requesting the connection is put to sleep for 250 milliseconds. What if a connection becomes available in the pool 100 milliseconds later? A separate thread could request a connection after the free connection becomes available but before the first thread can test for free connections, thus "stealing" the connection from the thread that should rightfully obtain it. In the next chapter we will implement a real queue that will avoid this issue.

BookServlet runs the servlet initialization logic in a separate thread. While this is not required by the servlet API, it is done to better support environments such as Apache/JServ. JServ is connected to Apache via sockets, and the connection is subject to TCP timeouts. If the servlet initialization method performs many tasks and lasts for a reasonably long time, say a few seconds, the socket connection incurs the timeout and the Apache server closes the channel, killing the Java Virtual Machine. The watchdog mechanism built into Apache realizes that JServ has died. It attempts to restart JServ, which in turns tries to boot the servlet that is causing the problem with its initialization method. This vicious cycle is continuously repeated, and you can only detect it by inspecting the JServ log file, which records every attempt to start the Java Virtual Machine.

Because the servlet initialization runs in a separate thread, the *servlet init()* method immediately returns, and the TCP timeout is avoided. The only problem with this approach is that the servlet is started anyway, irrespective of whether an exception occurs during initialization. For this reason, a reference to the BookServlet object is passed to the initialization class. If an error occurs during servlet initialization, the exception object is stored in an instance variable in BookServlet. The *doGet()* method's first action is to check the exception object stored in the instance variable. If the latter is not null, it means that an exception indeed occurred, an error message is displayed and *doGet()* returns. The *run()* method that starts the initialization thread checks that a valid configuration file has been passed by the servlet, then reads the required parameters from the configuration file. The parameters are used to create the connection pool, which connects to the Oracle database using the user-supplied username and password. The parameters contained in the configuration file also determine the minimum and maximum number of connection objects that can be available at any one time in the pool. As its last task before returning, the *run()* method instantiates all the servlet service providers and stores them in the hash table defined in BookServlet.

```
package com.prenhall.OFJP.ConnectionPool;

import java.sql.SQLException;
import java.io.*;
import java.util.Properties;

/** This class implements all tasks that must be performed during
**  the initialization of the servlet. Since initialization is
**  performed in a separate thread, the class implements the
**  Runnable interface.
**  Initialize doesn't raise an exception is an error occurs. Instead,
**  it stores a handle to the exception object into an appropriate
**  attribute of the calling object (BookServlet).
*/
public class Initialization implements Runnable
{

  /** The unique instance of the initialize class */
  private static Initialization initialize;

  /** Handle to a BookServlet object */
  BookServlet bs;

  /** Class constructor. Defined as private to implement the
  **  singleton design pattern. */
  private Initialization(BookServlet bs)
  {
      this.bs = bs;
```

```
}

/** Method that returns the instance of the initialization class.
**  The first time this method is called an Initialization object
**  is created. Subsequent calls to this method will return a
**  handle to the object already created.
**  @param bs Handle to a BookServlet object.
*/
public synchronized static void instance(BookServlet bs)
{
    if (initialize == null)
    {
          initialize = new Initialization(bs);
          new Thread(initialize).start();
    }
}

/** This method is the thread starter. */
public void run()
{
  // Check if a configuration file has been received
  String configFile = bs.getServletConfig().getInitParameter("ConfigFile");
  if (configFile == null)
  {
      Exception exc = new Exception( "Servlet did not receive "+
                                     "the config file parameter. A "+
                                     "configuration file is required. ");
      bs.setInitException(exc);
      return;
  }
  // Create a property object to read the properties stored in the
  // file into it.
  Properties props = new Properties();
  try
  {
     props.load(new BufferedInputStream(new FileInputStream(configFile)));
  }
  catch (IOException IOE)
  {
     Exception exc = new Exception("Configuration file error!");
     bs.setInitException(exc);
     return;
  }

  // Read the properties from the property object into strings
  String oracleDriver = props.getProperty("OracleDriver",
                              "oracle.jdbc.driver.OracleDriver");
  String connectionString = props.getProperty("ConnectionString");
```

```
String username = props.getProperty("Username");
String password = props.getProperty("Password");
String minConnections = props.getProperty("MinConnections");
String maxConnections = props.getProperty("MaxConnections");
String idleTime = props.getProperty("MaxIdleTime");

// Store the URL used to invoke the servlet into the appropriate
// BookServlet attribute
bs.setServletInvoke(props.getProperty("ServletString"));

// Create a connection pool object, storing a reference to it
// into the BookServlet object.
try
{
  bs.setConnPool(ConnectionPool.instance(oracleDriver,
                                          connectionString,
                                          username,password,
                                         Integer.parseInt(minConnections),
                                         Integer.parseInt(maxConnections),
                                         Integer.parseInt(idleTime)));
}
catch(ClassNotFoundException cnf)
{
  bs.setInitException(cnf);
  return;
}
catch (SQLException SQLExc)
{
  bs.setInitException(SQLExc);
  return;
}
// Initialize all servlet service providers and store
// them in the hash table defined in BookServlet
ServletService addBasket       = new AddBasket();
bs.setServiceProvider(BookServlet.A_ADD_BASKET,addBasket);
ServletService createUser      = new CreateUser();
bs.setServiceProvider(BookServlet.A_CREATE_ACCOUNT,createUser);
ServletService destroyBasket   = new DestroyBasket();
bs.setServiceProvider(BookServlet.A_DESTROY_BASKET,destroyBasket);
ServletService displayBooks    = new DisplayBooks();
bs.setServiceProvider(BookServlet.A_DISPLAY_BOOKS,displayBooks);
ServletService loginUser       = new LoginUser();
bs.setServiceProvider(BookServlet.A_LOGIN,loginUser);
ServletService processImage    = new ProcessImage();
bs.setServiceProvider(BookServlet.A_IMAGE,processImage);
ServletService showBasket      = new ShowBasket();
bs.setServiceProvider(BookServlet.A_SHOW_BASKET,showBasket);
ServletService submitCredit    = new SubmitCredit();
bs.setServiceProvider(BookServlet.A_SUBMIT_CREDIT,submitCredit);
ServletService submitOrder     = new SubmitOrder();
bs.setServiceProvider(BookServlet.A_SUBMIT_ORDER,submitOrder);
```

```
    ServletService viewBookDetails  = new ViewBookDetails();
    bs.setServiceProvider(BookServlet.A_VIEW_BOOK_DETAILS,viewBookDetails);
    ServletService welcomeScreen    = new WelcomeScreen();
    bs.setServiceProvider(BookServlet.A_INITIAL_SCREEN,welcomeScreen);
  }

}
```

14.4 BOOKSERVLET: PROS AND CONS

Building BookServlet gave you an understanding of server-side Web technology, such as the servlet API. BookServlet is very simple, even spartan, yet it provides a complete example that you can use as a starting point.

In order to promote BookServlet to a production-ready application, you will have to improve the features listed in Table 14.3.

The next chapter will address two of these four issues. In it you will improve the connection pool mechanism, and through the use of Java Server Pages (JSP) you will achieve separation between source code and formatting tags.

TABLE 14.3 BookServlet weaknesses

FEATURE	ISSUE
Connection Pool	Three major weaknesses affect the current version of the connection pool: 1) Only thin and thick JDBC 1.0 drivers are supported. 2) The mechanism that deals with concurrent requests for connection objects is too coarse-grained. A real queue should be implemented. 3) The JDBC syntax implemented in ConnectionObject is very generic, and does not use the powerful Oracle extensions that significantly improve SQL performance by minimizing network roundtrips.
GUI	The HTML interface is not sophisticated enough. The output requested by users should be nicely formatted across several HTML pages rather than one bottomless page. Perhaps a search engine should be implemented to help users filter the information requested from the database.
Session Recovery	User and shopping basket information is kept in the servlet volatile memory. If a session, or even the system, crashes, users must restart the entire session from scratch. It would be nice to make user information persistent, so that it can survive failures.
Content Separation from code	The HTML tags needed to display the Web pages requested by users are hard-coded in Java code. A much better approach would be to clearly separate the Java code from the page layout.

If you want to refine the application's GUI, you should consult some HTML references. This book only covers server-side Java and Oracle topics, and a discussion of GUI-related topics is beyond its scope.

14.5 RUNNING *BOOKSERVLET*

Compiling the Java code of BookServlet to create a JAR file is relatively easy. If you are using a Java IDE, such as Oracle JDeveloper or Borland JBuilder, the JAR file can be automatically created by the deployment wizard. You can copy all the Java files from the *Chapter14/BookServlet* directory of the companion CD into a directory of your hard disk and create a new project or workspace that includes all these Java files. Remember to include the JSDK servlet.jar and the Oracle JDBC zip files (classes111.zip or classes12.zip) as part of the project, and recompile all your sources. The same applies if you are using the *javac* compiler from the command line. Be sure to include servlet.jar (the jar file containing the servlet implementation) and classes111.zip or classes12.zip (Oracle JDBC implementation) in your CLASSPATH before performing the compilation. Add all the class files produced by the compilation to a .jar file, say bookstore.jar.

You are finished with the Java code; now comes the difficult part.

First, you must load the virtual bookshop data into your database.[2] You do this with the help of the Oracle import utility, which is invoked from the command line using the *imp* command. Make sure that your shell or Windows console window environment is properly configured to run Oracle executables. Issue the following command from a Windows NT/2000 command prompt or Unix shell:

```
sqlplus scott/tiger
```

If you are accessing a remote database, add its connection string at the end, as in:

```
sqlplus scott/tiger@my_remote_database
```

If you see the Sql*Plus prompt, it is likely that your environment is properly set up and you will not have any problem running imp.

Copy the bookstore.dmp file from the *Chapter14/BookServlet* directory of your CD into your default directory and type the following command:

```
imp scott/tiger file=bookstore.dmp fromuser=scott
touser=scott ignore=y log=bookstore.log
```

The scott account is created by default when the database is created. If you want to simplify the setting up of BookServlet, just use scott, as in the example above.

[2] In order to import bookstore.dmp, you must have access to an Oracle 8.1.5 or greater server.

Otherwise, if you feel confident about your Oracle skills and want to venture into database administration, give yourself DBA privileges and create a new Oracle database user. Then use the import utility, changing the command-line options slightly.

```
imp system/manager file=bookstore.dmp  fromuser=scott
touser=<user_you_created> ignore=y log=bookstore.log
```

After having successfully run the import utility you can check that the BookServlet tables have been loaded correctly. Issue the following query while connected to the user you chose for the import:

```
sqlplus scott/tiger
SQL*Plus: Release 8.1.5.0.0 - Production on Tue Feb 1
23:34:12 2000
(c) Copyright 1999 Oracle Corporation.  All rights
reserved.
Connected to:
Oracle8i Enterprise Edition Release 8.1.5.0.0 -
Production
With the Partitioning and Java options
PL/SQL Release 8.1.5.0.0 - Production
SQL> select table_name from user_tables;
```

Verify that the tables courier, sales_item, customer, order_item, cust_order, etc., are displayed by Sql*Plus.

TABLE 14.4 Supported platforms for BookServlet.

WEB SERVER	VERSION	OS	SERVLET ENGINE
Microsoft IIS	3, 4	Win32	Allaire JRun 2.3
Apache	1.3	Unix, Linux, Win32	Allaire JRun 2.3
Apache	1.3	Unix, Linux, Win32	JServ
Netscape Enterprise Server	3.51, 3.52, 3.6	Unix, Win32	Allaire JRun 2.3
Netscape iPlanet	4.0	Unix, Win32	Built-In servlet engine
Sun Java Web Server	1.1.3	Unix, Win32	Built-In servlet engine
Oracle Application Server	4.08	Unix, Win32	OAS 4.08 servlet cartridge
JSDK Servlet Runner	2.1	Unix, Win32	Built-In servlet engine

You are finished with the setup of the database. Now you have to configure your Web server and servlet engine. BookServlet has been successfully run and thoroughly tested in several environments that probably cover more than 90 percent of the servlet engine market. Table 14.4 shows the supported platforms for BookServlet. The steps required to configure each of the environments listed in the table will be discussed in the sections that follow.

14.5.1 CONFIGURING ALLAIRE JRUN

JRun stands out from all the other servlet engines because it shields the servlet environment from the Web server. If you want to enable a servlet in a JRun environment, you only have to access JRun admin applets. No changes are required for the configuration parameters of the hosting Web server that uses JRun as a servlet engine. JRun communicates with the Web server using "connectors" that intercept the traffic directed to the Web server only if specific URLs are detected; a common arrangement is to specify a servletdirectory in the URL, as in `www.wallaby/servlet/snoopservlet`. When the Web server "sees" a URL containing "servlet," it forwards the request to the servlet engine.

As long as the initial JRun configuration is successful, and one or more connectors are properly initialized, configuring an additional servlet is very simple. Furthermore, JRun is configured in the same way across all Jrun-supported Web servers. In other words, the instructions on how to configure BookServlet apply to any supported combination of JRun plus Web server (MS IIS, Apache, Nestcape Enterprise Server 3.5/3.6).

The JRun administrative front-end is a Java application that offers an intuitive user interface. Assuming that you have a working and tested Web server, plus the JRun engine on your system, you can configure BookServlet by simply launching JRun Administrator, shown in Figure 14.9.

Select the row showing the servlet engine (usually the top row) and click on "Service Config." When the JRun servlet engine (jse) configuration form displays on your screen, click on the "Aliases" tab and enter the servlet details, as shown in Figure 14.10.

Figure 14.10 assumes that you are configuring JRun in a Unix environment, and that the property file passed by the servlet engine to BookServlet resides on /usr/local/bookstore. It also assumes that you invoke BookServlet using its alias, which has been set to Book (note the capital "B"). Adapt these fields to reflect your environment and your directory structure.

To complete the JRun configuration, two more steps are required. The servlet jar file and the Oracle implementation of the JDBC driver, included in classes111.zip (or classes12.zip), must be copied into a directory, and the CLASSPATH variable passed by JRun to the JVM must include them. This is accomplished by editing the jsm.properties file, located under the <jrun_root>/jsm-default/properties directory tree. Under Windows just replace the forward slashes with backward slashes. In the file, the entry marked:

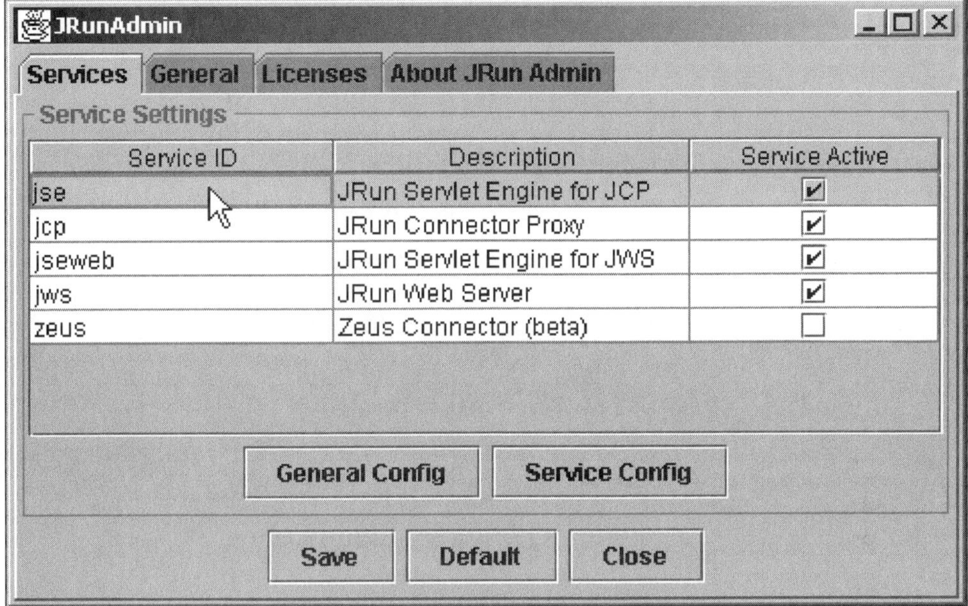

FIGURE 14.9 JRun administrator.

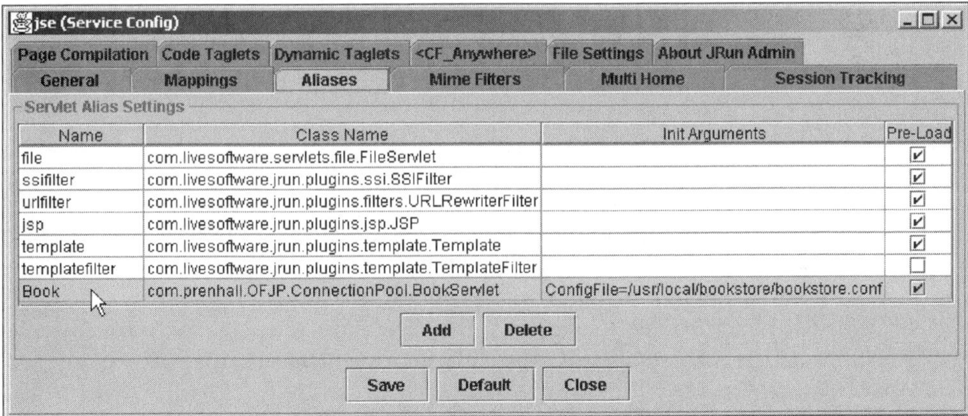

FIGURE 14.10 The jse configuration form.

```
java.classpath=
```

must be modified to include the absolute path to bookstore.jar and classes111.zip. Reboot JRun, and enter the BookServlet URL in your browser. Do not forget to modify the ServletString entry in bookstore.conf to match the servlet virtual path. With JRun, the default virtual directory for servlets is called servlet, so the entry will look like this:

```
ServletString=http://<hostname>/servlet/Book
```

Remember to modify the bookstore.conf file *before* rebooting JRun.

14.5.2 CONFIGURING NETSCAPE IPLANET

Long before the release of iPlanet, Netscape claimed it could support servlets natively, but the servlet engines previously implemented in Netscape Enterprise Server were not robust enough to support production environments. iPlanet finally provides a good servlet implementation, together with an easy-to-use administrative interface.

The entire configuration procedure can be performed through the iPlanet Web interface, using your browser of choice.

To begin with, access the iPlanet administration page, appending the port number specified during the installation procedure to the URL of your host. For example, if your host is named foobar, and when you installed iPlanet you specified TCP port 9080 for administration, point your browser to http://foobar:9080. You must provide a password for the admin username, the same password you specified while installing the product. When the initial page is displayed on your screen, click on the "Manage" button after selecting the required server name. Click on the "Servlets" tab, and access the page marked "Enable/Disable Servlets." Make sure that the servlet engine is active. This is shown in Figure 14.11.

The next step is to modify the CLASSPATH passed by the servlet engine to the JVM to include the BookServlet jar file, which is called, by convention, bookstore.jar, and the Oracle JDBC driver, called classes111.zip (or classes12.zip if you are using the Java 2 version). This step is shown in Figure 14.12.

You can now configure the servlet attributes or the servlet name, the class that contains the *main()* method, the classpath that points to the BookServlet jar file, and the servlet arguments. This is done by activating the "Configure Servlet Attributes" page, filling in the fields displayed by the form. An example is shown in Figure 14.13.

In the example presented here, BookServlet is configured to run from a Solaris server, the hostname of which is echidna. The iPLanet admin port is 9090, and the directory where the BookServlet jar file is located is /usr/local/bookstore. The directory also contains bookstore.conf, the property file passed by the servlet engine to BookServlet.

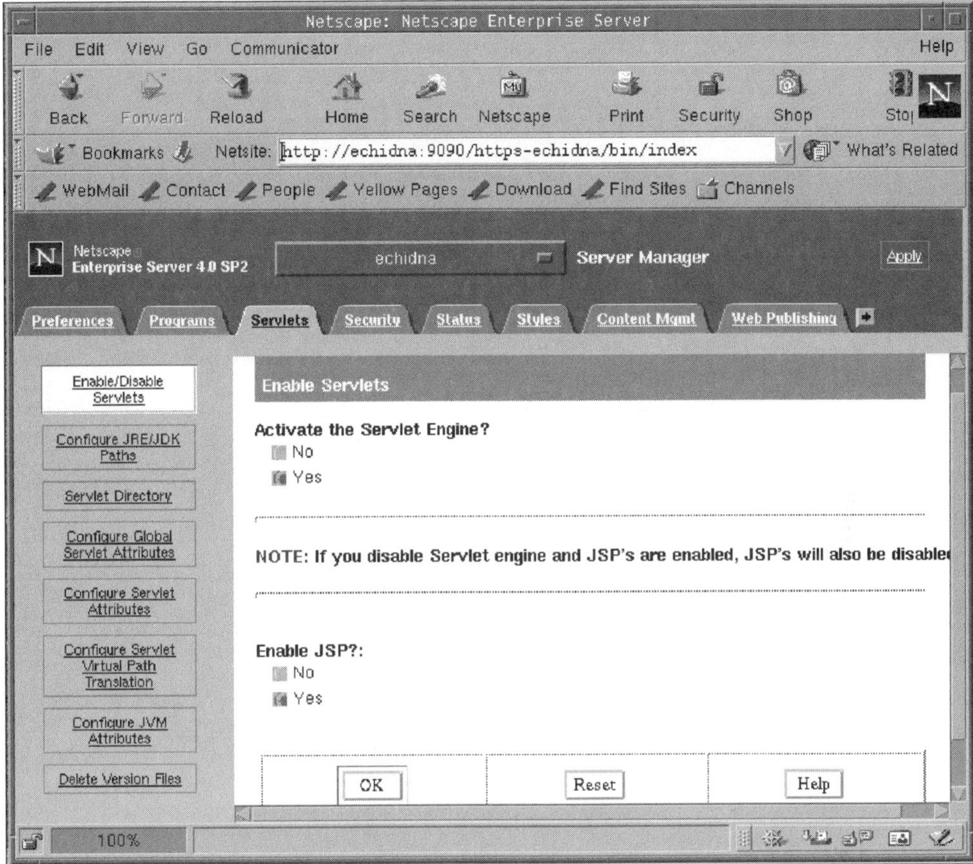

FIGURE 14.11 Make sure that the servlet engine is enabled.

Simply adapt the example to your environment, replacing the directory structure shown in the example with your directory tree. If you created a jar file with a different name, replace bookstore.jar with your BookServlet jar file name.

There are two steps left for a complete configuration of iPlanet. In the first, you set the virtual path that will activate the servlet engine that will run the servlet. Remember to adjust the ServletString entry in bookstore.conf to reflect the virtual path you defined in the form shown in Figure 14.14. In the last step, you add the servlet alias (*Book* in the example) to the "Startup Servlets" field, displayed by the "Configure Global Servlet Attributes" form, shown in Figure 14.15.

It is now time to try your configuration. Point your browser to the virtual path that triggers the servlet. If the configuration is correct, the initial BookServlet HTML form will be displayed.

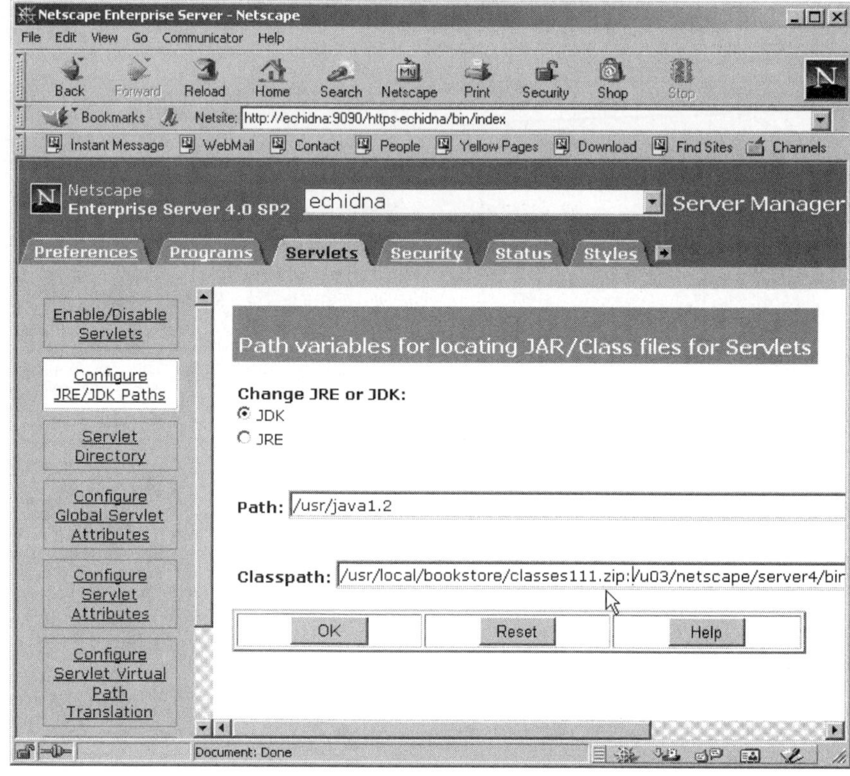

FIGURE 14.12 Configuring the iPlanet JDK paths.

14.5.3 CONFIGURING SUN JAVA WEB SERVER

In addition to iPlanet, Sun JWS also offers a complete GUI configuration in four easy steps.

First, connect to the JWS using the admin port. A Java applet started by JWS will guides you during the configuration task. Click on the "Manage" button, as shown in Figure 14.16.

The "Manage" button instructs the admin applet to display the "Web Service" form, characterized by four image buttons located in the top-left corner. Click on the "Setup" button and then on the "Servlet Aliases" node of the Setup tree control. This is shown in Figure 14.17. Click on the "Add" button, and add the servlet alias to the new row displayed by JWS. Click on the "Save" button to make your entry permanent. In the example, the alias /Book (notice the forward slash) points to the servlet called Bookstore.

Now, click on the "Servlets" image button and on the "Add" node of the Servlets tree control. Add the servlet name (Bookstore), and type the class name

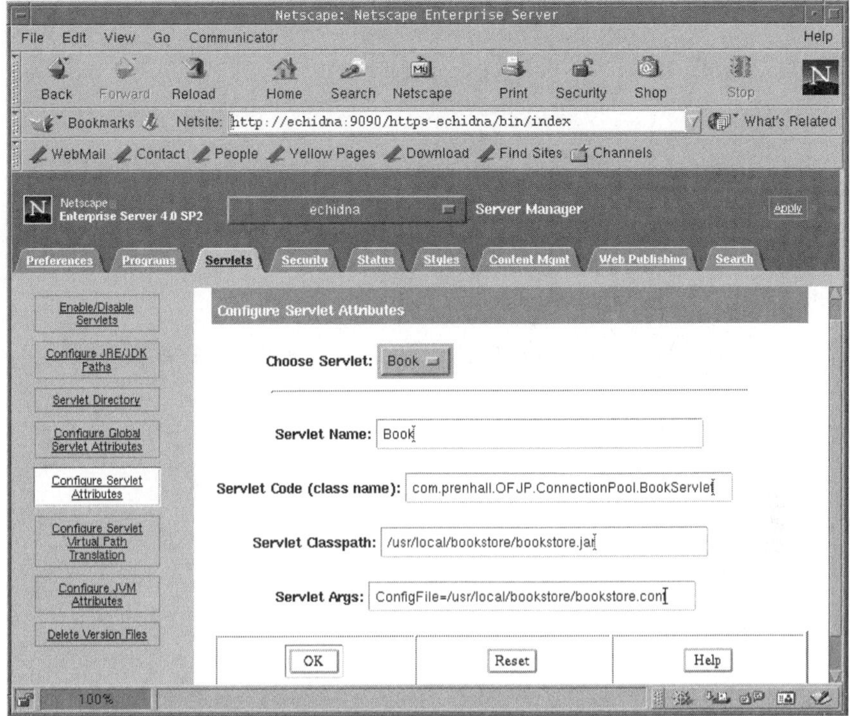

FIGURE 14.13 Servlet attributes are entered into the iPlanet admin applet.

for the servlet (in the example, *com.prenhall.OFJP.ConnectionPool.BookServlet*) Specify that you want the servlet loaded at startup by selecting the radio button. This is shown in Figure 14.18.

To have the servlet engine pass a parameter to the servlet, you must click on the "Properties" tab and specify the parameter, in your case the pathname to bookstore.conf. This is shown in Figure 14.19.

In the example shown here, you have set the virtual path for the servlet to be /Book. You must change the ServletString entry in bookstore.conf to reflect the virtual path. Now try the newly configured servlet by pointing your browser to the URL that triggers its execution.

14.5.4 CONFIGURING APACHE AND JSERV

When compared to iPlanet or JWS, Apache is at the opposite end of the spectrum. There is no GUI front-end to the Apache parameters; everything is accomplished by modifying configuration files.

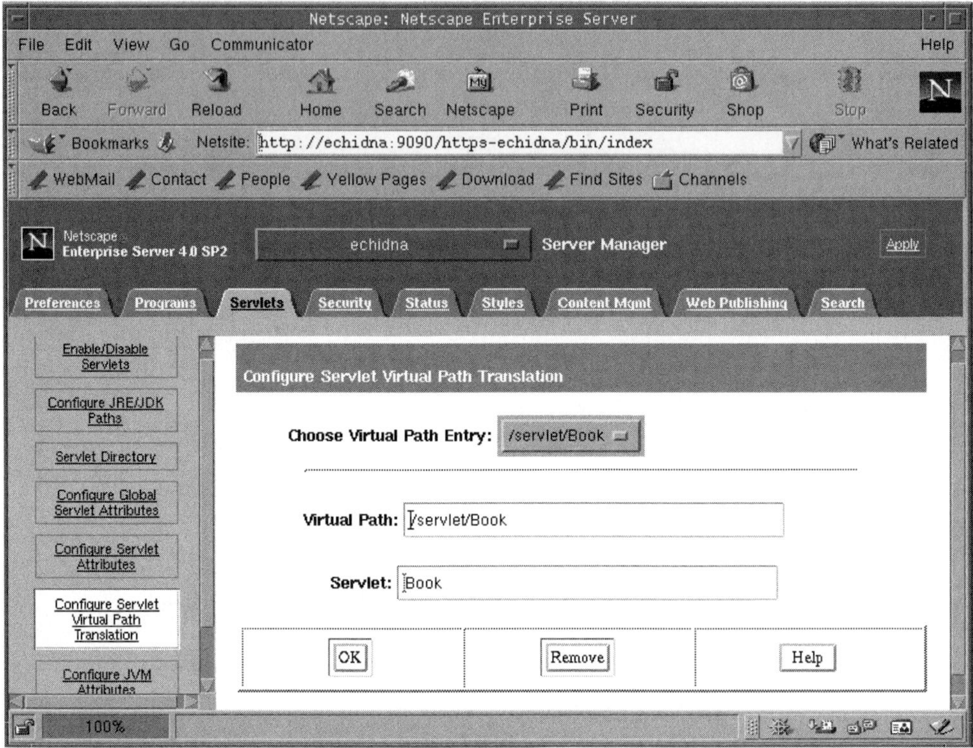

FIGURE 14.14 The virtual path to BookServlet must be defined in iPlanet.

Apache introduces the notion of servlet "zones," separate execution environments or areas that act as distinct servlet engines. The zones apply to servlets the same concept as virtual host.

The instructions given here on how to configure BookServlet in an Apache/JServ environment assume that you have already successfully set up and tested Apache and JServ. An easy way to test your Apache/JServ environment is to run the SnoopServlet servlet, which is installed by default when you extract all files from the JServ tarball.

You are going to create an additional servlet zone, called "bookstore," which will contain BookServlet. The configuration example assumes that you already have one servlet zone, called "root."

The first step is to edit httpd.conf, looking for the ApJServMount entry. This directive instructs JServ on how to mount the servlet zone t you are going to create. Add the following line to httpd.conf:

```
ApJServMount /servlets /bookstore
```

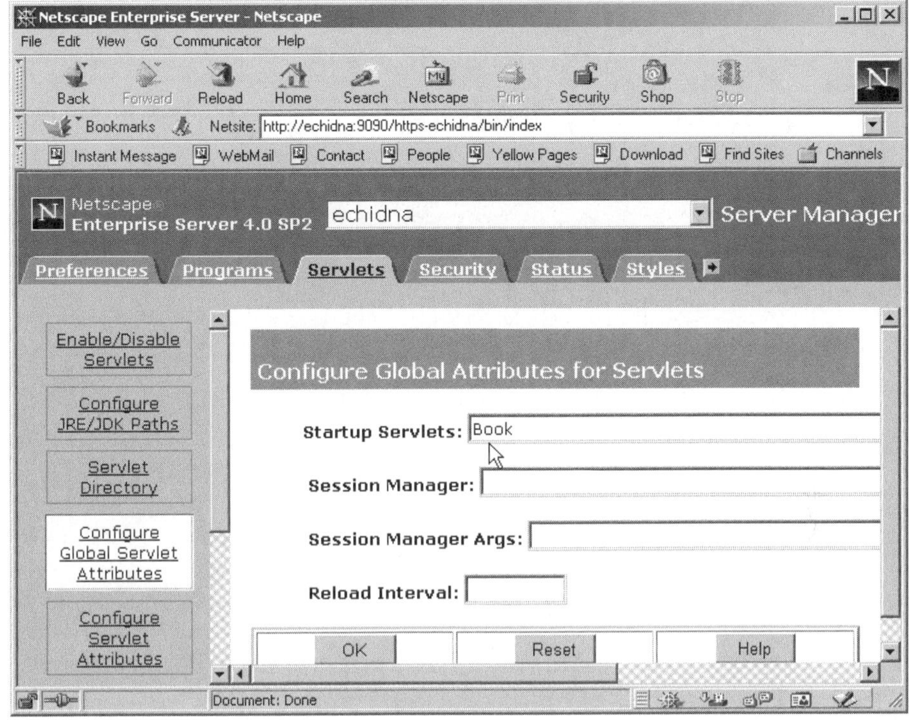

FIGURE 14.15 BookServlet will be started by iPlanet when it first boots.

Next, search for the ApJServProperties entry, and make sure that it points to the jserv.properties. This is the default file that instructs JServ on how to load its parameters during the bootstrap phase. Save httpd.conf and edit jserv.properties (or the file indicated by ApJServProperties). Look for the *zones* entry, and add bookstore to it. Assuming that the other servlet zone, which is already installed, is called root, the zones parameter will be:

```
zones=root,bookstore
```

Before saving and leaving the file you must add the bookstore.properties entry, which tells JServ where to find the property file containing the bookstore details. If you are operating in a Unix environment, and your Apache root directory is located in /usr/local/apache, the bookstore.properties parameter will look like this:

```
bookstore.properties=/usr/local/apache/conf/bookstore.properties
```

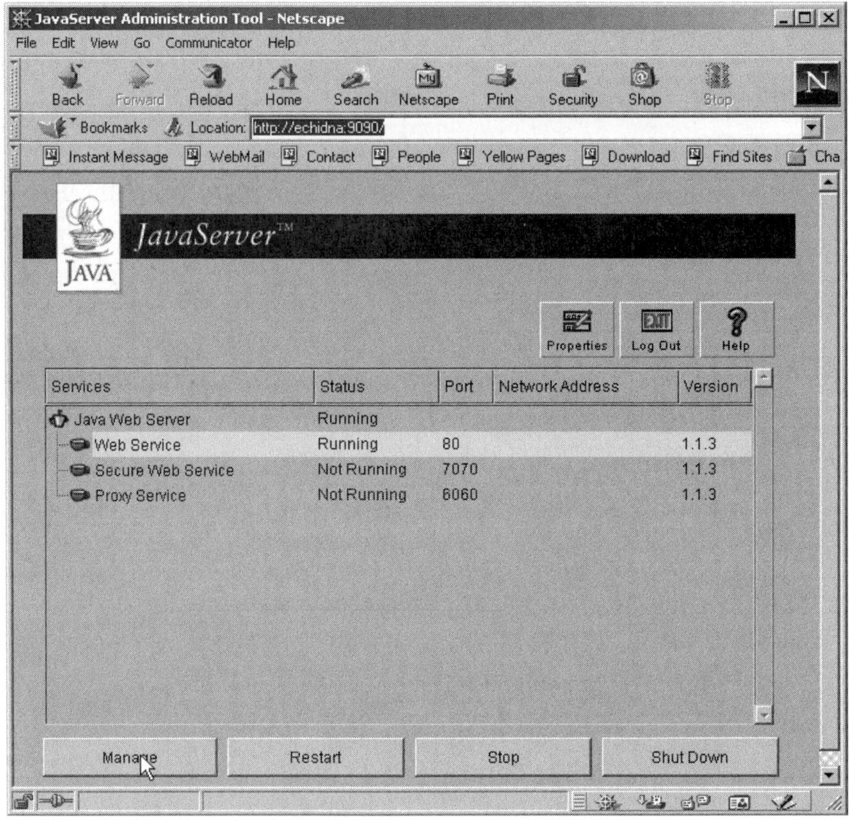

FIGURE 14.16 The initial page of the JWS admin applet.

It is now time to create the bookstore.properties file that will contain the servlet zone parameters. Copy the default file named zone.properties to bookstore.properties, edit the latter and adapt the entries to reflect your configuration. The main parameters are shown in Table 14.5.

Note the addition of classes111.zip to the repositories parameter, to make JServ aware of the Oracle JDBC driver. You can now restart Apache and access the URL that triggers the servlet. If something goes wrong, look in the /usr/local/apache/logs directory for jserv.log and mod_jserv.log; these two files contain useful clues that will help you to find the problem.

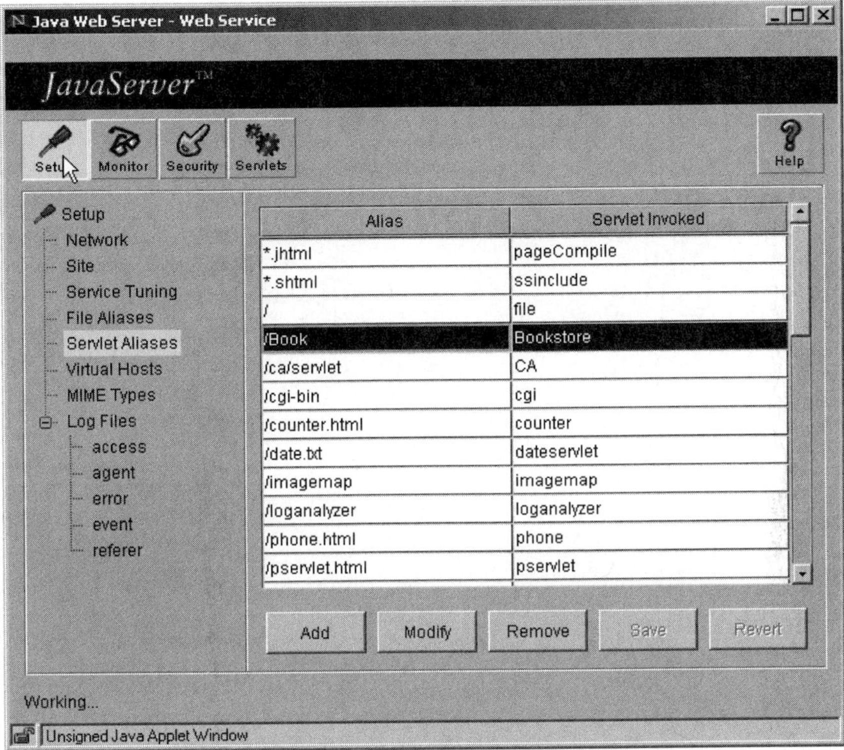

FIGURE 14.17 Assigning a servlet alias.

14.5.5 CONFIGURING THE JSDK SERVLETRUNNER OR THE JSWDK SERVER

If you do not have access to a full-fledged Web server and servlet engine, don't despair; technology will not leave you behind, you can still be part of the Java revolution. Simply download the Java Servlet Development Kit (JSDK) or the JavaServer Web Development Kit (JSWDK) directly from the Java Web site. They both offer a rudimentary Web server capable of serving simple HTML pages and, more important, servlets and Java Server Pages (JSP).

If you use JSDK, edit the default.cfg file, located in the JSDK root directory, and set the required parameters, such as the host name of your machine, its IP address, and the port number used by the Web server to listen to incoming connections. With JSWDK, you accomplish the same by editing the webserver.xml file.

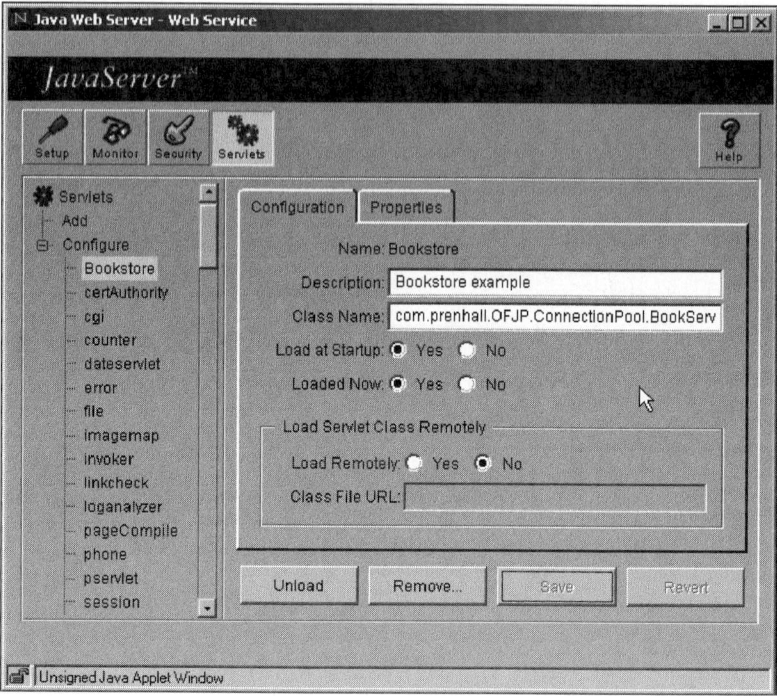

FIGURE 14.18 The Bookstore servlet is configured to load during the servlet engine boot.

Configuring BookServlet is very easy in both environments. You must edit the servlets.properties file, located in the <JS(W)DK root>/webpages/WEB-INF directory. Append the following lines to servlets.properties:

```
Book.code=com.prenhall.OFJP.ConnectionPool.BookServlet
Book.initparams=ConfigFile=<path to bookstore.conf>
```

In both environments the limited version of the Web server is started from the command line by typing *startserver*. The latter is a bat file under Windows, and a shell script under Unix. Startserver appends its own jar files to the content of the CLASSPATH environment variable and launches the Web server. Before invoking startserver, define CLASSPATH, including bookstore.jar and classes111.zip. In this way the Web server/servlet engine will find the required classes to run BookServlet.

Unfortunately, neither JSDK nor JSWDK is able to preload the servlet when the Web server boots up. The first time you invoke BookServlet you will have to live with a slight delay, due to the initialization tasks carried out by the servlet's *init()* method.

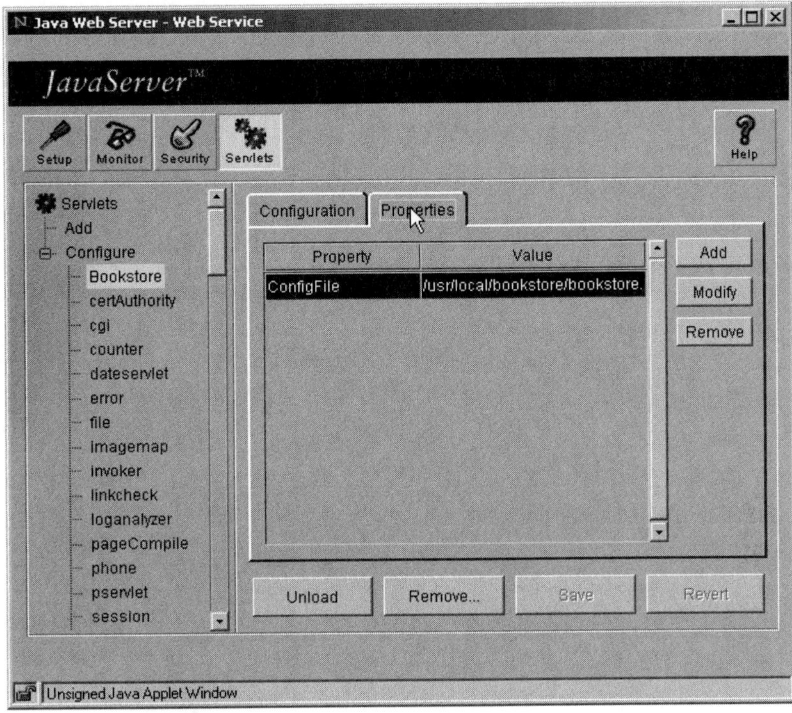

FIGURE 14.19 Servlet parameter definition in JWS.

TABLE 14.5 JServ configuration paramaters

PARAMETER	MEANING	SHOULD BE SET TO
Repositories	Jar files, zip files, and directories containing servlet-related supporting classes.	Repositories= /usr/local/apache/servlets,/usr/local/bookstore/bookstore.jar,/usr/local/bookstore/classes111.zip
Servlets.startup	Lists all servlets belonging to this servlet zone which should be launched at startup.	servlets.startup=Book
Servlet.Book.code	The class that extends HttpServlet.	servlet.Book.code= com.prenhall.OFJP.ConnectionPool.BookServlet
Servlet.Book. initArgs	Parameters to be passed by JServ	servlet.Book.initArgs= ConfigFile=/usr/local/bookstore/bookstore.conf

14.5.6 CONFIGURING THE ORACLE APPLICATION SERVER (OAS)

The Oracle Application Server relies on a server-side application called *cartridge server* to provide most of its functionality. A cartridge server is a process in which one or more cartridge instances run. A *cartridge instance* consists of code that executes application logic and configuration data that enable the cartridge to locate and control cartridge parameters.

OAS offers two administrative levels for user-written application configuration and deployment.

1. At the application level, the same configuration parameters are applied to a set of cartridges of the same type, thus simplifying the management of common parameters shared by multiple cartridges.
2. At the cartridge level, configuration settings and parameters only apply to specific instances of cartridges.

In order to configure BookServlet, you have to create an application first and then configure its cartridge.

Assuming that you have successfully installed OAS, point your browser to the node name of the server where OAS runs, suffixing the URL with the port where the OAS manager is listening. In this example the host name of the server is wallaby, and the port number is 7777 (see Figure 14.20).

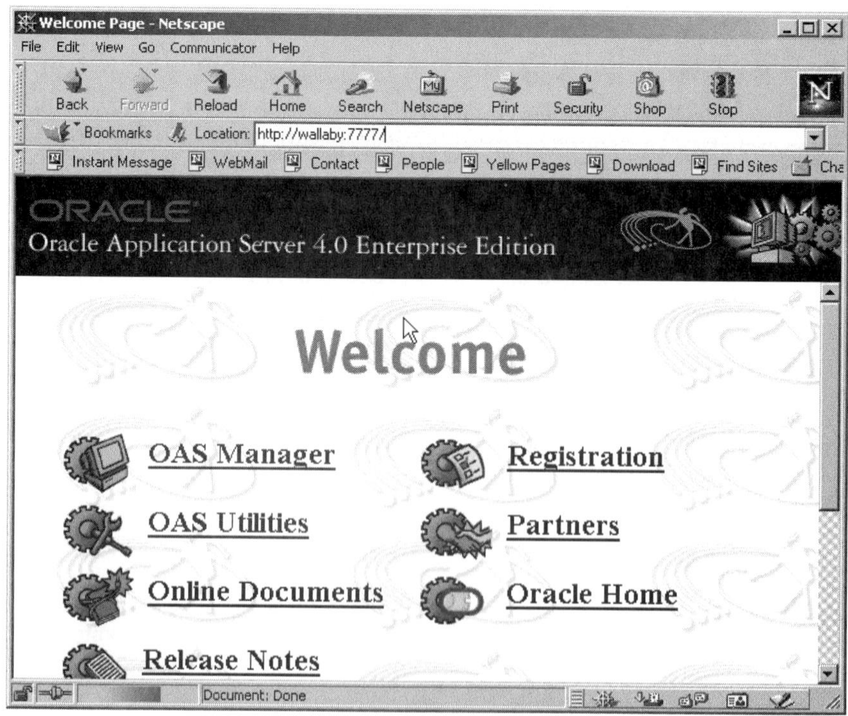

FIGURE 14.20 The OAS administration utility.

When the OAS administration applet appears in your browser, click on "OAS Manager." When the OAS Manager applet appears, expand the tree that starts with the node name (in this example wallaby), and highlight the "Applications" node. Click on the icon marked with a plus sign (+) to add a new application (see Figure 14.21).

When the "Add" window displays, choose JServlet as the application type (see Figure 14.22).

After you click on the "Apply" button, the first "Add Application" window disappears, and a second window is displayed in your browser. You have to fill in three fields: application name, display name, and application version. The display name is the name that will be displayed in the OAS manager tree. An example is shown in Figure 14.23.

If everything is OK, a "Success" message box will appear. Click on the button marked "Add Cartridge to this application," which will trigger the display of the first "Add Cartridge" window, shown in Figure 14.24.

Choose the radio button marked "Manually" and click on "Apply."

A second "Add Cartridge" window will appear. You must provide a few parameters, such as the cartridge name (which can be the same as the application

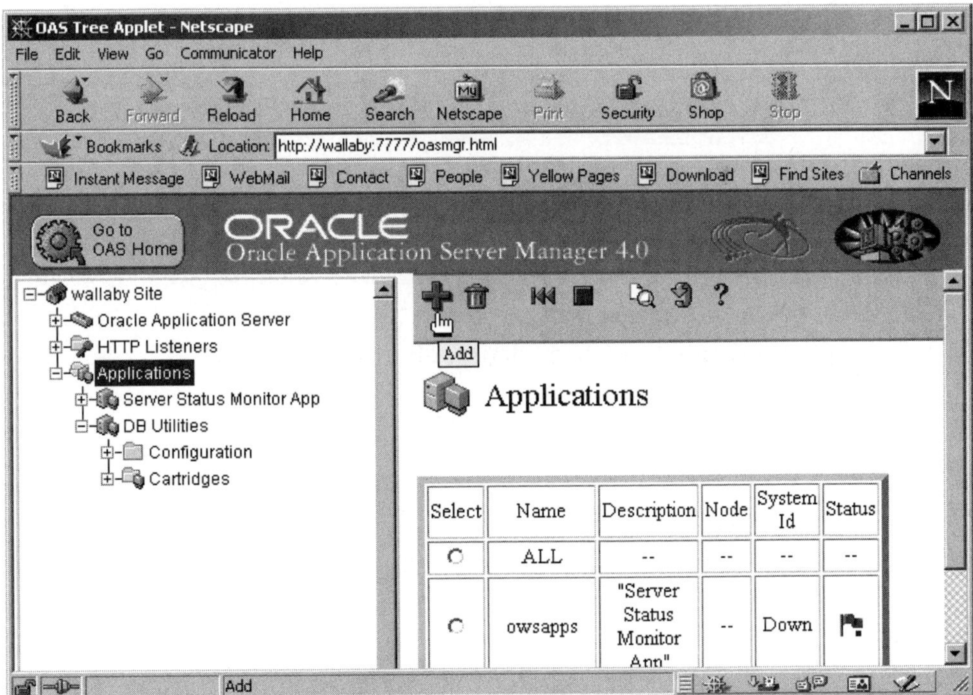

FIGURE 14.21 Adding a new application to the OAS.

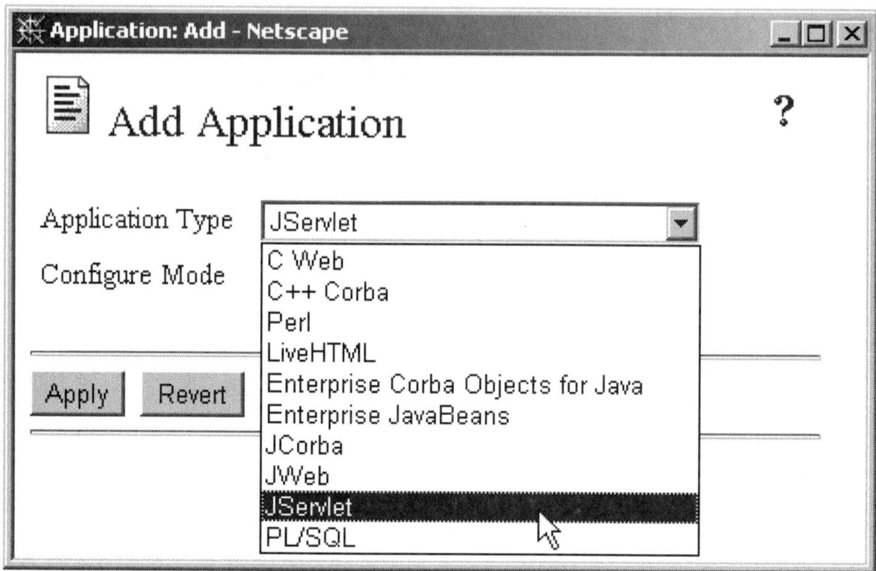

FIGURE 14.22 The "Add Application" window.

Application: Add - Netscape

Add Application

?

Application Name BookServlet

Display Name BookServlet

Application Version 0.99

Apply Revert Cancel Help

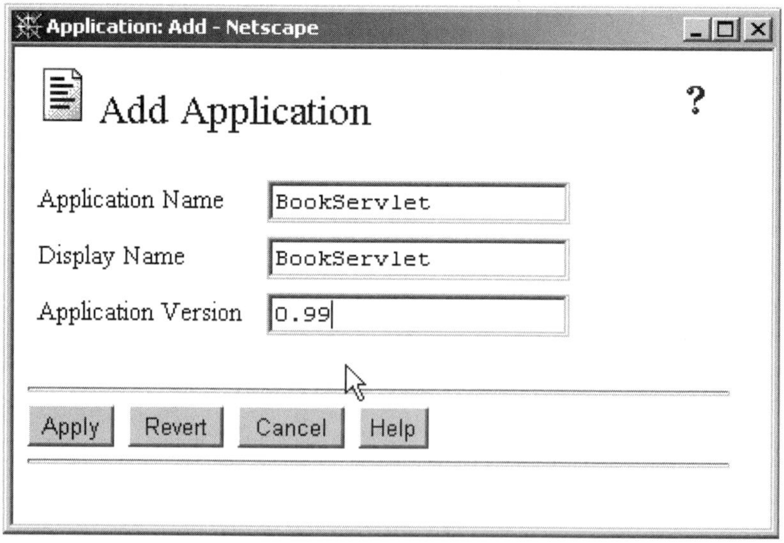

FIGURE 14.23 The second "Add Application" window.

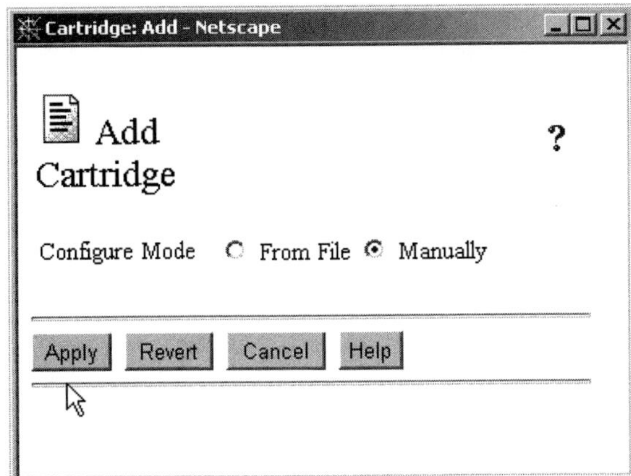

FIGURE 14.24 The first "Add Cartridge" window.

name), the display name (for the tree entry in the OAS manager), and the virtual path and physical path for the cartridge. The latter is the absolute pathname to either a directory containing the servlet classes or a corresponding jar (or zip) file that groups all the required classes together. The first is the URL suffix that identifies the servlet. An example is shown in Figure 14.25.

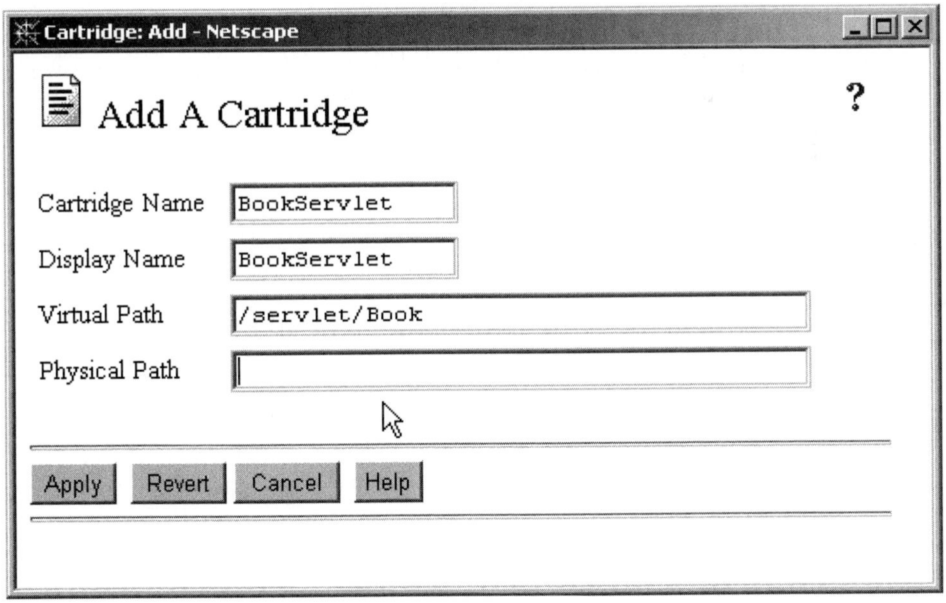

FIGURE 14.25 The second "Add Cartridge" window.

You are almost done, but you still have to tell OAS how to pass the configuration file to BookServlet. You do this in the "Java Environment" node of the application tree. The HTML page displays the two columns for a name-value pair to be entered in the blank fields. The name goes in the leftmost column, and its corresponding value goes in the rightmost column. An example is shown in Figure 14.26.

It is now time to test BookServlet in OAS. Point your browser to the virtual path you configured for BookServlet (in the example, /servlet/Book), and you should see the initial login window of the virtual shop. Again, remember to change the ServletString property in bookservlet.conf to reflect the virtual path you chose in the preceding steps.

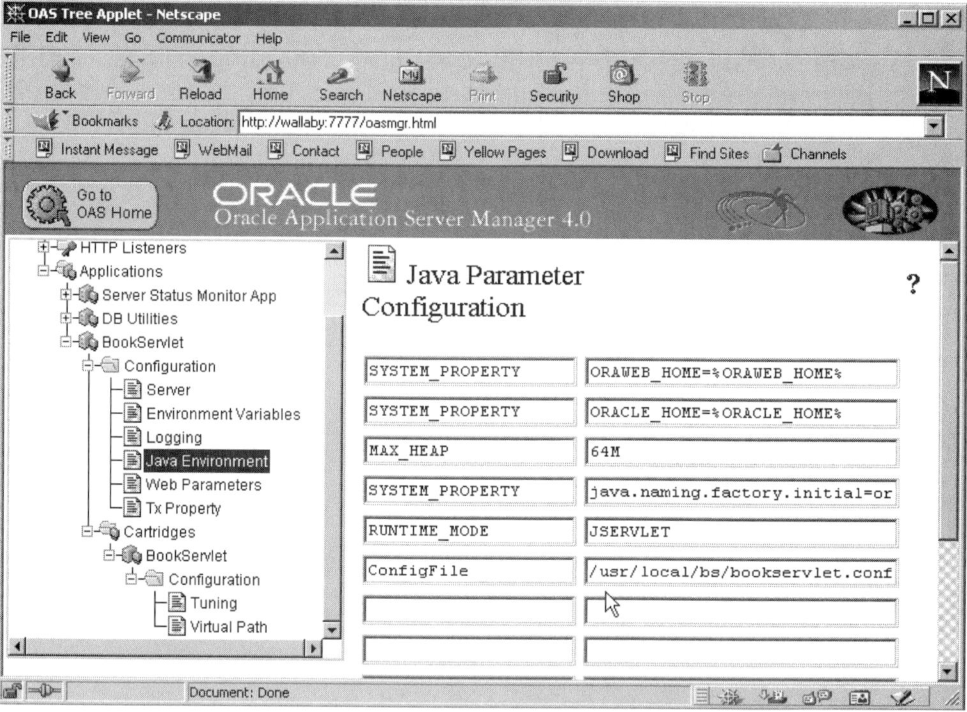

FIGURE 14.26 The Java configuration parameter page.

SUMMARY

This chapter has acquainted you with the server-side Java technologies that are becoming increasingly popular in the marketplace. After an initial historical background on older Web-development approaches, such as CGI, you were introduced to a development environment based on Java servlets. Servlets offer better performance and scalability, thanks to their multi-threaded nature, and better security. To reinforce the concepts explained in the chapter, you developed a servlet-based application, BookServlet., going through the entire lifecycle of Web software development. You designed the database, supporting the most likely data-retrieval path with indexes. You prevented data inconsistency by implementing referential integrity, and then you delved into Java coding, implementing the server-side classes needed to allow the HTML client to interact with the database. Special emphasis was given to the connection pooling mechanism, which allows for connection sharing and caching, significantly improving throughput and scalability.

While servlets represent a technological breakthrough over the previous, CGI-based Web application approach, they suffer from a major drawback in that they do not allow for a clear separation between content generation and presentation logic. The Java code you wrote to implement the servlet methods is intermixed with HTML tags. This is not very elegant, and in addition forces graphic designers to learn Java or Java programmers to become graphic designers, neither of which is a good idea. This is not to say that servlets are obsolete; quite the opposite, they still have their place in Web development—for instance, to support Java applets that communicate to the back-end using HTTP tunneling, as well as back-end support for JSPs. In fact JSPs are silently converted into servlets by the JSP engine. But for applications that must support HTML on the client, the JSP API, recently made available by Sun, represents a more appealing solution. That will be the topic of the next chapter.

Chapter 15

JAVA SERVER PAGES AND ACTIVE SERVER PAGES

- JSP: An Overview
- ASP: An Overview
- JSP and ASP Compared
- Reworking BookServlet Using JSP
- Summary

In this chapter, you will explore the Java Server Pages (JSP) technology recently introduced by Sun Microsystems and the competing technology offered by Microsoft Corporation, Active Server Pages (ASP). The basic syntax elements of both environments are presented, as well as a high-level comparison of the two technologies in terms of flexibility, scalability, and portability. A simple application is developed using JSP and then redeveloped using ASP, to give you a full appreciation of the similarities and differences between the two environments.

The chapter concludes with a reworking of the BookServlet application developed in the preceding chapter. BookJSP, the new application built using the old BookServlet framework, makes use of JSPs and Java beans, and implements a better connection-pooling mechanism.

15.1 JSP: AN OVERVIEW

Chapter 14 pointed out that while servlets are definitely an effective server-side technology that allows for scalability in serving Web requests, they suffer from the drawback of tightly coupling the user interface content with the dynamic, logic-driven content. If you looked at the source code of the example presented in Chapter 14, you saw a lot of HTML tags hard-coded into Java statements. The problem with this approach is that Java programmers are generally not very good at designing Web sites; they cannot replace graphic designers, who are, in general, very imaginative people, with a strong sense of aesthetics. Graphic designers are not supposed to be accomplished programmers; they simply want tools that facilitate their task. Clearly, a greater separation between application/data-gathering logic and presentation logic is necessary in order to allow graphic designers to work without interfering with Java programmers, and vice versa. Sun released the specifications for the JSP technology with precisely this goal in mind.

15.1.1 JSP ELEMENTS

JSP is a presentation-layer technology that sits on top of the Java servlet model. It presents itself as an addition to the HTML tags contained in a Web page. The JSP engine, running on the server, reads the JSP page, interprets the JSP tags, creates Java source code that accomplishes what is specified in the page, compiles it into servlets, and runs it. Subsequent calls to the same page are served immediately, avoiding the compilation, since the servlet generated by the JSP engine the first time the page was requested is kept in a memory cache.

The JSP engine works in conjunction with a Web server. JSP pages are text files with a jsp file type. When a client submits a request for a page with a .jsp file type, the Web server accepting the request forwards it to the JSP engine.

Sun Microsystems teamed up with the Apache group to release the JSP technology. The result is the Jakarta project, which delivers reference implementations of the Java servlet and Java Server pages specifications. Major contributions to the Jakarta project were made by Sun and IBM engineers, as well as independent Apache developers.

Jakarta's flagship product is Tomcat, freely available for download at *http://jakarta.apache.org/downloads/binindex.html*. Tomcat ships with an embedded Web Server that is ideal for development, but if you want to deploy your servlet/JSP-based application to a larger audience, you should use a "real" Web server, capable of serving hundreds or even thousands of pages per minute. The Tomcat's JSP and servlets engines can be used with the following Web servers:

- Apache
- Netscape Enterprise Server, releases 3.0 through 3.61, via an NSAPI connector[1]
- Microsoft Internet Information Server (IIS), via an ISAPI connector[2]

More recent releases of Netscape Enterprise Server, now renamed iPlanet Application Server, support Java servlets and JSP natively; so you don't need Jakarta/Tomcat if you are an iPlanet user.

15.1.2 JSP TAGS

JSP tags, directives, and objects appear intermixed with HTML tags in files. The JSP engine, when it parses the requested page, identifies and interprets the JSP syntax, producing the appropriate output. For example, the JSP engine expands the JSP syntax into Java servlets, then compiles the servlet into Java bytecodes the first time a JSP page is requested. Subsequent requests for the same page will not produce expansion and compilation, because the JSP will realize that the requested page is already cached. Files containing JSP syntax are recognizable from the JSP extension. JSP files can be referenced in lieu of HTML files. In other words, whenever it is syntactically legal to reference HTML files, it is also legal to use JSP files. A typical example is the action clause of an HTML form:

```
<FORM METHOD=POST ACTION="getData.html"">
```

JSP files are very frequently used to implement the actions submitted via HTML forms, as in the following example:

---

[1]NSAPI is the Netscape Server API, a mechanism for extending the functionality of Netscape servers.

[2]Internet Server Application Procedural Interface (ISAPI) is a mechanism for extending the functionality of Microsoft IIS.

```
<FORM METHOD=POST ACTION="perform_action.jsp">
```

As long as the JSP syntactical conventions are followed, JSP tags and directives can appear everywhere in an HTML/JSP file. Entire Java classes with their methods can be embedded into JSP files. While the freedom to do this is welcome, you will soon learn that it is better to exercise restraint, limiting the JSP syntax intermixed with HTML tags to a minimum. Remember, separating the presentation layer from the business logic is a major goal of this architecture; if your JSP pages mostly contain HTML tags, graphic designers will find it easy to modify them and to improve on their aesthetic appearance. Conversely, if a JSP page contains too much Java code, non-programmers will find it difficult to interpret the programmatic constructs and to understand the HTML syntax.

A typical JSP application comprises a set of JSP files that contain the presentation logic, and a set of Java classes (beans) that contain the business logic and provide the JSP files with high-level methods that implement the core functionality of the application.

JSP tags are available that "connect" the JSP page to the Java beans that provide application behavior. Once a JSP page has obtained a "handle" to a Java bean, it can use it to refer to the bean and invoke its methods. For example, a Java bean provides a method (*getDate()*) that returns the current date. The bean name is *DateBean*, and the class exists and is accessible to the JSP engine. A JSP page that wants to use the services provided by *DateBean* will use the following syntax to invoke the *getDate()* method:

```
<HTML>
<jsp:useBean id = "dtb" class = "DateBean" />
<HEAD>
<TITLE>
Using DateBean
</TITLE>
</HEAD>
```

The jsp:useBean tag "links" the *DateBean* class to the JSP page. From that point onwards, a JSP developer can refer to the *DateBean* class through the dtb identifier.

All JSP tags are enclosed in angle brackets (< … >). By using appropriate tags, it is possible to output the result of Java *expressions* directly to the HTML page seen by the users. The tag that accomplishes this is the expression tag <%= …%>. For example, if you want the return value of the *getDate()* method to be displayed "as is" in the HTML page generated by the JSP engine, you could use the following syntax:

```
<P> Current date: <%=dtb.getDate() %>
```

In this case the Java expression dtb.getDate() would be evaluated and the result put in the HTML file generated by the JSP engine.

Other tags allow developers to embed Java code in JSP pages. A *scriptlet* is a block of Java code executed when the HTTP request is processed. Scriptlets are enclosed between the tags <% and %>. *Declarations* are blocks of Java code used to define variables and methods that have classwide scope in the generated class file. All definitions are enclosed by the <%! And %> tags are available for the lifetime of the JSP to other declarations, expressions, and scriptlets.

Table 15.1 lists the JSP tags that appear intermixed with HTML in .jsp files.

JSP pages go through two conceptually distinct phases. The first, called the "translation phase," occurs when the JSP engine transforms the file into a servlet. The second, called the "request phase," occurs when the generated servlet actually runs to generate the HTML page that will be sent to the requesting client.

The include and page directives, the last two entries in Table 15.1, are handled by the JSP engine during the translation phase. The other tags affect the creation of the HTML page during the request phase.

In addition to the basic tags shown above, two important JSP objects complete the JSP specifications:

- ❑ Implicit objects
- ❑ Java beans

Implicit objects are predefined Java entities that are available by default, created by the JSP engine when the JSP page is translated into a servlet. They are shown in Table 15.2.

TABLE 15.1 JSP tags

TAG NAME	OPEN TAG	CLOSE TAG	PURPOSE
Output Comment	<! - -	- - >	Generates a comment that is sent to the requesting client in the viewable page source.
Hidden Comment	<% - -	- - %>	Documents the JSP, but the comment is not sent to the client requesting the JSP page.
Declaration	<%!	%>	Declares variables and method that are valid in the context of the JSP.
Expression	<%=	%>	Defines an expression valid in the context of the JSP.
Scriptlet	<%	%>	Contains a Java code fragment that is inserted into the automatically generated servlet.
Include Directive	<@	%>	Provokes the inclusion of a file or code fragment in the JSP source file.
Page Directive	<@	%>	Defines attributes that influence the entire JSP page.

TABLE 15.2 Implicit JSP objects

OBJECT	DESCRIPTION	SCOPE
request	The request that triggers the JSP service invocation.	request
response	The response to the request.	page
pageContext	The page context for this JSP page.	page
session	The session object created to satisfy the requesting client.	session
application	The servlet context obtained from the servlet configuration object through a call to `getServletConfig().getContext()`.	application
out	The writer object that populates the output stream.	page
config	The `ServletConfig` for this JSP page.	page
page	The instance of this page's implementation class processing the current request. Synonymous with `this` in Java.	page

Since the implicit objects are always available, JSP-page authors can use them at will while coding JSP pages. No definitions or declarations are required. Here is an example of a JSP page using the implicit request object:

```
<HTML>
<BODY>
Hello user!  The JSP engine is running on a computer called
<b><%= request.getServerName() %></b>, and you logged in from a
 computer called <b><%= request.getRemoteHost() %></b>!
</BODY>
</HTML>
```

The two expression tags delimited by `<%=` and `%>` refer to the request object, calling two of its methods. The result of the JSP page is shown in Figure 15.1.

The JSP tags introduced so far are essential ingredients for building interactive and dynamic Web pages. In theory, you could create a complete JSP application using only the JSP elements seen so far. Database access and business logic could be entirely coded using scriptlets, or portions of Java code enclosed within the <% and %>tags. The problem with this approach, however, is that you would end up with a few HTML tags intermixed with a lot of Java code in the JSP page. This is hardly desirable, for two reasons:

- The situation would be the converse of an application entirely coded using servlets, where Java statements are intermixed with calls to the write method of the standard output object containing HTML tags.
- The main goal of the JSP specifications, or the separation of user interface elements from the logic-driven content, is not achieved.

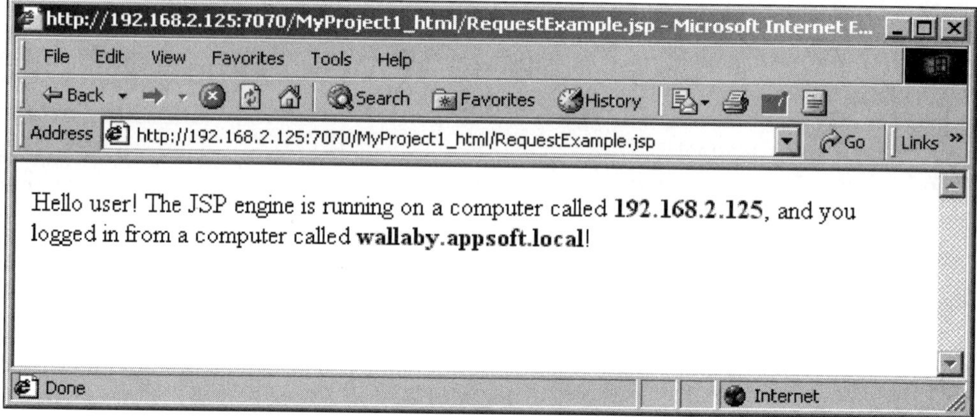

FIGURE 15.1 Output produced by the first JSP page.

If you want your site to become a major attraction on the Web, offload its graphical design to graphics professionals, who are only expected to know HTML. Since they are usually not accomplished programmers, they would find the large amount of Java code scattered in scriptlets distracting because it "pollutes" the HTML tags.

Luckily, the designers of JSP were far-sighted, and included direct support for Java beans in the JSP specifications. Java programmers can concentrate business logic and data retrieval in Java beans, exposing simple interfaces to the HTML designers, who are thus shielded from unnecessary complexity and from the need to know the details of data gathering and back-end processing logic. As shown in Table 15.3, three basic tags are available for working with beans.

TABLE 15.3 JSP tabs for working with Java beans

<table>
<tr><th>JSP TAG</th><th>PURPOSE</th></tr>
<tr><td><jsp:useBean id= "Bean Name" class= "java class" scope= "application | session | request | page" /></td><td>Makes the Java class implementing the bean available to the JSP page.</td></tr>
<tr><td><jsp:getProperty name = "bean name" property = "* | property name" /></td><td>Returns the value associated with the specified property implemented by the named bean.</td></tr>
<tr><td><jsp:setProperty name = "bean name property = "property name" value = "property value" /></td><td>Sets the property implemented by the named bean with the value indicated by the "value." tag.</td></tr>
</table>

In order to see the bean tags in action, you are going to develop a very simple example. The simplest bean is a Java class that only publishes a getter method. In your case, the method called *getDate()* returns a string containing the current date, formatted according to the default locale of your server. The Java class, DateBean.java, is shown below.

```
// Copyright (c) 2000 Prentice Hall
import java.text.DateFormat;
import java.util.Date;

public class DateBean extends Object
                          implements Serializable
{
  public String getDate()
  {
     Date d = new Date();
     DateFormat df = DateFormat.getDateTimeInstance();
     return df.format(d);
  }
}
```

Next, you need to develop a JSP page that makes use of the bean just developed. This simple page, called JSPDateFormat.jsp, declares the bean that wants to use through the <jsp:useBean> tag, and prints the date obtained from the bean by calling the <jsp:getProperty> tag while printing HTML strings on the standard output.

```
<HTML>
<jsp:useBean id = "DateBean" class = "DateBean" />
<HEAD>
<TITLE>
First Example
</TITLE>
</HEAD>
<BODY>
<H4>The following output is from JSP code:</H4>
<P><jsp:getProperty name="DateBean" property = "date"/></P>
</BODY>
</HTML>
```

Note the apparent discrepancy between the method name as defined in the bean, *getDate()*, and its invocation from the JSP, *date* with a lowercase *d*. This is, in fact, the convention used to map bean getter and setter methods to <jsp:getProperty> and <jsp:setProperty> tags. You take the getter method, discard the "get"

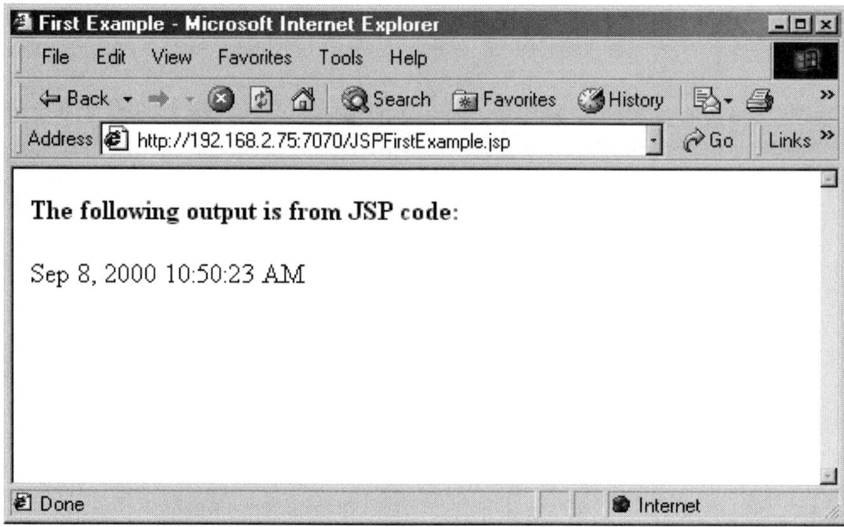

FIGURE 15.2 A JSP that uses Java beans.

prefix, convert to lowercase, and pass the resulting string to the <jsp:getProperty> tag. A similar convention applies to <jsp:setProperty> tags.

The result of this simple application is shown in Figure 15.2.

15.1.3 ADVANCED JSP: BEAN SCOPES, INCLUDES, REDIRECTION, AND TAG EXTENSIONS

The basic JSP tags introduced so far are enough to build simple applications to be used in getting acquainted with this promising technology. As soon as you attempt more complex tasks, however, you will realize that there is still something missing. For example, what if you want to maintain the state of a variable across page requests? Or, how would you implement a global counter, accessible to all clients of a specific application?

The solution is to use bean scopes. The <jsp:useBean> tag allows JSP developers to specify the scope of the bean, which can be of four types:

- Page
- Request
- Session
- Application

The list goes from the most local scope (page) to the most global scope (application). The simplest (and the default) scope for a bean is a page, which means that a bean instantiated from a JSP page will vanish as soon as the page is generated. Remember, JSP pages are not static pages, like their HTML counterparts, but generated each time they are loaded. The JSP engine instantiates the beans associated with the page in question, and they go out of scope when the page is displayed back to the requesting browser. The next scope up is the request scope; all beans created within the realm of the request persist for its duration, and are destroyed as soon as the request is satisfied. You may be wondering what the difference is between a page and a request. They are not the same, because a request can be satisfied by more than one page, thanks to the JSP forwarding mechanism. JSP developers can use a specific tag, <jsp:forward page="<<page name>>"/>, to "call" another JSP page, passing the flow control to it. A Java bean declared with a request scope is available to all pages interested in the request.

The data associated with a user interacting with a JSP application are kept in the session scope. There is no one-to-one correspondence between a user and a session. The latter identifies the specific interval of time the user in question spends interacting with the JSP application. Sessions usually have timeouts. Say you start using a Web application and are distracted by a long telephone call halfway through the compilation of an HTML form. When you click on the submit button after you terminate the call, the browser may return an error message, explaining that the session has timed out and inviting you to re-login.

A Java bean associated with a session persists for the entire duration of the session, spanning as many pages and requests as the user hits during the lifetime of the session.

The session scope is the ideal container for the shopping carts used in e-commerce applications. Users normally access several pages, looking for items to purchase, selecting some of them, and placing them in a shopping cart, sometimes called a "basket." The tension between the HTTP protocol, stateless by nature, and the need to store state between calls is solved by the session scope. A common arrangement is to store the items selected by purchasers into vectors or hash tables implemented by Java beans with session scope. More sophisticated applications provide persistence for the shopping cart in the database, to avoid frustration for the user who incurs a session timeout while filling the shopping basket.

When a Java bean is associated with the application scope, its methods and attributes are available to all users and all pages for the entire duration of the application. This scope is the more appropriate for storing global counters, set and incremented in real-time by the activity performed by the users. Since concurrent users share Java beans in the application scope, particular care must be taken to synchronize access to their methods and attributes so as to avoid inconsistent updates or even deadlocks.

If a scope is not specified in the <jsp:useBean> tag, the default scope for Java is the page that references them. Page scope is the most volatile scope assigned by the JSP engine.

Java beans are not the only objects to have a scope: variables created with the declaration tag have an instance scope, meaning that they live within an instance of the servlet built by the JSP engine. For example, the variable defined by the declaration tag:

```
<%! java.util.Date time_now = new  java.util.Date(); %>
```

Is defined as an instance attribute in the Java class produced by the JSP engine. This implies that *time_now* is initialized only once during the lifetime of the servlet. On the other hand, attributes defined and initialized in scriptlets are *local*, that is, reloaded each time the page is served by the JSP engine. In the next example, the attribute *time_now* is declared and initialized by a declaration tag (<%! %>), while the *current_timestamp* attribute is declared and initialized in a scriptlet tag (<% %>). If you try to run the JSP, you will notice that if you hit the reload button of your browser several times, only *current_timestamp* is continuously refreshed, while *time_now* reports the timestamp at the moment of the initial running of the servlet created by the JSP engine. There is rarely any need for instance attributes (i.e., attributes declared with declaration tags). They are, unfortunately, a source of problems if not handled properly. The persistent nature of these attributes requires synchronized access when multiple pages and concurrent clients use them. To avoid these types of problems, use scriptlet-based attributes, or, even better, Java beans, which provide better encapsulation.

```
<HTML>
<%! java.util.Date time_now = new  java.util.Date(); %>
<HEAD>
<TITLE>
First Example
</TITLE>
</HEAD>
<BODY>
<H4>The following output is from JSP code:</H4>
<P>Current time (Instance var) <%= time_now.toString() %> </P>
<% java.util.Date current_timestamp = new java.util.Date(); %>
<P>Current time (Local var) <%= current_timestamp.toString() %>
</BODY>
</HTML>
```

15.1.3.1 JSP Includes. In order to modularize your JSPs, and to avoid cutting and pasting JSP code from one page to the other, which leads to redundant replication of source code, you should consider using JSP includes. If you wish to maintain a consistent look-and-feel throughout your application, you can have a header, a footer, and a navigational menu for every page. These can be implemented as separate JSP pages and included in the pages that drive the application flow. Here is the JSP directive that allows for file inclusion:

```
<%@include file="<<file_name.jsp | file_name.html>>" %>
```

The included file can be either another JSP page or simply a file containing HTML tags. Graphic designers usually like to keep recurring items, such as logos, in separate files and include them in the relevant pages. This arrangement helps in maintaining a consistent look-and-feel across different pages. Java programmers can code scriptlets in specific JSP pages that can be included whenever the function provided by the scriptlet is needed. Note that the include directive is resolved at translation time, when the servlet is automatically created by the JSP engine. If you modify a page after the application begins running, the application won't reload it.

The JSP specifications also support a different type of file inclusion, the <jsp:include page> tag. Unlike the corresponding directive, this is resolved at request time. Each invocation of the JSP page will trigger an inclusion, "on the fly," of the file specified by the include tag. If the application is running when you change a page included through a tag, the next time a user hits the page in question, the new version of the included file will be displayed.

Another powerful mechanism provided in the JSP specifications allows JSP developers to redirect the application flow from one page to another, using the `<jsp:forward page="<<page_name.jsp>>" />` tag. The next example shows this technique in action.

```
<% String param = request.getParameter("Database"); %>
<% if (param.equals("Oracle")) { %>
  <jsp:forward page=db/Oracle.jsp" />
<% } else if (param.equals("Informix")) { %>
  <jsp:forward page="db/Informix.jsp" />
<% } else if (param.equals("Sybase")) { %>
  <jsp:forward page = "db/Sybase.jsp" />
<% } %>
<HTML>
<BODY>
<P><H2>You chose an unsupported database! Please re-submit
your choice… </H2></P>
</BODY>
</HTML>
```

Java beans allow JSP developers to concentrate most of the business logic and data processing in Java classes, offering simple interfaces to Web designers, who can focus on the aesthetic appearance of the application's front-end. In most cases, the standard JSP tags are sophisticated enough to get the job done. Sooner or later, however, you will reach the point where you want something that standard JSPs cannot offer. Starting with version 1.1, the JSP specifications allow for the creation of custom tags. Developers are free to extend and enhance the JSPs, defining new tags that can be freely included in their .jsp files. A custom tag is defined by an XML file that describes what the tag is, the correct syntax for its invocation, and the name and location of the Java classes that implement the tag behavior. Developers "inform" the JSP engine about the new tag using the taglib tag:

```
<%@ taglib uri="<<UniversalResourceIdentifier>>" prefix="<<prefix>>" %>
```

A detailed explanation of the steps required to implement custom tags is beyond the scope of this brief introduction to JSP. Nonetheless, you should know about this feature if you decide to embrace this technology to develop your Web applications. You can obtain more advanced material on the JSP technology, by downloading the JSP specifications from the Java Developer Connection site. For a more accessible treatment of the topic, see *Core Servlets and Java Server Pages (JSP)* by Marty Hall (Prentice-Hall, 2000).

15.1.4 A JSP EXAMPLE

In this section, you will develop a complete mini-application that makes extensive use of JSP. An initial login screen allows users to connect to their default Oracle schema. All the tables defined in the schema are displayed as an unordered list. The table name is a hyperlink that displays a table showing the columns and column attributes belonging to the table. The application consists of seven files: three Java classes and four jsp files (see Table 15.4). All seven files will be found on the companion CD, under the directory Chapter15/JSPExample.

TABLE 15.4 Java/JSP files used in the JSP example

FILE NAME	PURPOSE
LoginModule.java	Provides the Oracle connection and prepared statements used throughout the application.
UserTableData.java	Implements attributes and methods needed to fetch the name of the table created in the user schema and to display them in a list.
TableColumnData.java	Implements attributes and methods needed to retrieve all column attributes for a given table.
Error.jsp	Error page. If any exception is thrown by the application, the JSP engine will invoke this page, and the relevant exception messages will be displayed in the user's browser.
login.jsp	This page performs user login and displays the table defined in the user's schema in an unordered list.
shwocol.jsp	This page displays an HTML table that contains information on all the columns belonging to a given table.
welcome.jsp	This page implements the entry point in the application. Users input their username and password in the HTML form displayed in this page to attempt a connection to Oracle.

The initial screen is implemented in welcome.jsp. This is a pure HTML file that includes a FORM tag. Two input fields are defined, *username* and *password*. The source code of welcome.jsp is shown below.

```
<%@ page contentType="text/html;charset=WINDOWS-1252"%>
<HTML><HEAD><TITLE>JSP Example</TITLE></HEAD>
<BODY>
<H3>Oracle Login:</H3>
<form method=post action=login.jsp><P>
<center>
<table border="2">
<tr>
<td>Username</td>
<td><input type=text name="username" size=30></td>
</tr>
<tr>
<td>Password:</td>
<td><input type=password name="password" size=30></td>
</tr>
</table>
<input type=submit name=login value="Login">
</form>
</P>
</BODY>
</HTML>
```

The form is submitted via a POST method to another jsp page, login.jsp. The form displayed by welcome.jsp is shown in Figure 15.3.

The Java bean LoginModule implements methods for connecting to an Oracle database and submitting two prepared statements to it. The LoginModule bean also implements getter and setter methods for the username and password attributes. The setter methods are used to connect the input fields of the HTML form to the Java bean. The <jsp:setProperty> tag allows developers to specify an asterisk (*) as the property being set. The asterisk instructs the JSP engine to associate all input values appearing in the form with the corresponding setter methods in the bean. In login.jsp you find the following two lines:

```
<jsp:useBean id="login" class="LoginModule" scope="session"/>
  ...
<jsp:setProperty name="login" property="*"/>
```

If the form provides input values called username, password, and so on, and the bean has methods called *setUsername()*, *setPassword()*, and so on, everything matches up, and the JSP engine will make sure that each setter method is

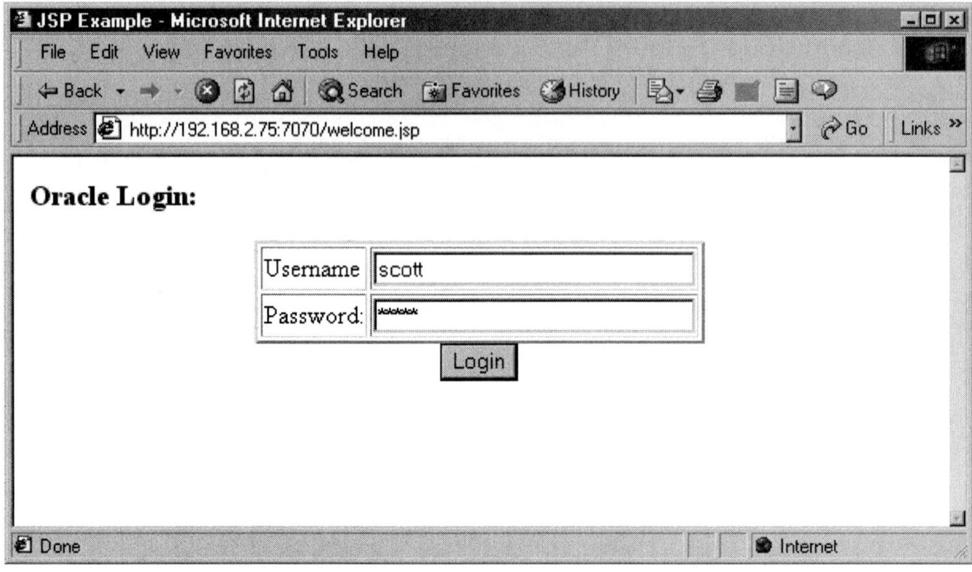

FIGURE 15.3 The HTML form displayed by welcome.jsp.

called to set each input value provided by the HTML form "connected" to the JSP page.

If the HTML form provides an input value for which there is no corresponding setter method, the value is ignored and no error or exception occurs. In your example, the form implemented in welcome.jsp has an input value called "login." Since the LoginModule bean does not implement a *setLogin()* method, the JSP page can safely ignore that value.

The source code for LoginModule.java is shown below.

```
// Copyright © 2000 Prentice Hall
import java.sql.*;
public class LoginModule
{
  private Connection conn;
  private String uname;
  private String pwd;
  private PreparedStatement userTables;
  private PreparedStatement tableColumns;

  public void connect() throws SQLException
  {
      this.connect(this.uname,this.pwd);
  }
  public void connect(String user, String passwd)
               throws SQLException
```

```
        {
           DriverManager.registerDriver (new
                  oracle.jdbc.driver.OracleDriver());
           this.conn = DriverManager.getConnection
           ("jdbc:oracle:thin:@koala:1521:W2K816",user, passwd);
           userTables = this.conn.prepareStatement("SELECT "+
            "table_name FROM user_tables");
           tableColumns =
            this.conn.prepareStatement("column_name, "+
            "substr(DATA_TYPE,1,15),data_length,data_precision,"+
            "nullable FROM user_tab_columns WHERE "+
            "table_name= ? ORDER BY column_id ");
        }
        public void disconnect() throws SQLException
        {
           this.conn.close();
        }
        public PreparedStatement getUserTables()
        {
            return this.userTables;
        }
        public PreparedStatement getTableColumns()
        {
            return this.tableColumns;
        }
        public void setUsername(String us)
        {
            this.uname = us;
        }
        public void setPassword(String pa)
        {
            this.pwd = pa;
        }
        public String getUsername()
        {
            return this.uname;
        }
        public String getPassword()
        {
            return this.pwd;
        }
        public static void main(String [] args)
        {
            LoginModule lm = new LoginModule();
            try
```

```
        {
          lm.connect("scott","tiger");
          PreparedStatement pstmt = lm.getUserTables();
          ResultSet rs = pstmt.executeQuery();
          while (rs.next())
          {
             System.out.println(rs.getString(1));
          }
          rs.close();
          PreparedStatement tblStmt = lm.getTableColumns();
          tblStmt.setString(1,"EMP");
          rs = tblStmt.executeQuery();
          while (rs.next())
          {
               System.out.print(rs.getString(1)+"\t");
               System.out.print(rs.getString(2)+"\t");
               System.out.print(rs.getString(3)+"\t");
               System.out.print(rs.getString(4)+"\t");
               System.out.println(rs.getString(5)+"\t");
          }
          rs.close();
        }catch (SQLException exc) {}
    }
}
```

The LoginModule bean implements several methods that are useful for the other components of the application, such as *getUserTables()* and *getUserColumns()*, which both return a prepared statement ready to be executed by the method caller. The *connect()* method should be modified to reflect your Oracle connection parameters. Simply replace the host name and the instance name in the string

```
"jdbc:oracle:thin:@koala:1521:W2K816"
```

with your specific host and instance names.

Note, too, that the bean implements a static *main()* method containing code that tests the correct functioning of the bean. It is a good practice to implement a *main()* method that allows for individual standalone testing of the Java components outside the JSP environment. You must be sure that your bean works before putting it into an environment that does not usually provide advanced debugging capabilities. The source code of login.jsp is shown below.

```
<%@ page errorPage="Error.jsp"
contentType="text/html"%>
<HTML>
```

```
<jsp:useBean id="login" class="LoginModule" scope="session"/>
<jsp:useBean id="utbl" class="UserTableData" scope="request" />
<jsp:setProperty name="login" property="*"/>
<HEAD>
<TITLE>Default Oracle Schema
</TITLE>
</HEAD>
<BODY>
<% login.connect(); %>
<% utbl.select(login); %>
<h3>Tables available in your login schema:</h3>
<P><UL>
<% while (utbl.next()) { %> <LI>
<A HREF="showcol.jsp?tableName=<jsp:getProperty name="utbl"
property="tableName"/>"</A>
<jsp:getProperty name="utbl" property="tableName"/></LI>
<% } %>
</UL>
</BODY>
</HTML>
```

The JSP code shown above is relatively straightforward, and you should be able to recognize the tags introduced in the preceding sections. The only exception is the redirection to an error page performed by the `<%@ page>` tag. This is a powerful feature provided by the JSP specifications. If a bean throws an exception, or if any error occurs during the processing of the page, the JSP engine will display the associated error page.

Three lines of code perform the hard work in this page:

```
<% login.connect(); %>
<% utbl.select(login); %>
<% while (utbl.next()) { %>
```

The first line forces a connection to the Oracle database, using the LoginModule bean. The second line uses the services provided by the UserTableData bean to fetch the table defined in the user's schema from the data dictionary. The third line initiates the loop that displays all the table names stored in the result set. Note that the LoginModule bean has been given session scope, whereas the UserTableData bean has been given request scope. This makes sense: the login bean "contains" the Oracle database connection, which you want to be active and accessible throughout the session. The UserTableData bean, on the other hand, should be instantiated for each request submitted by the user.

The HTML page produced by login.jsp is shown in Figure 15.4.

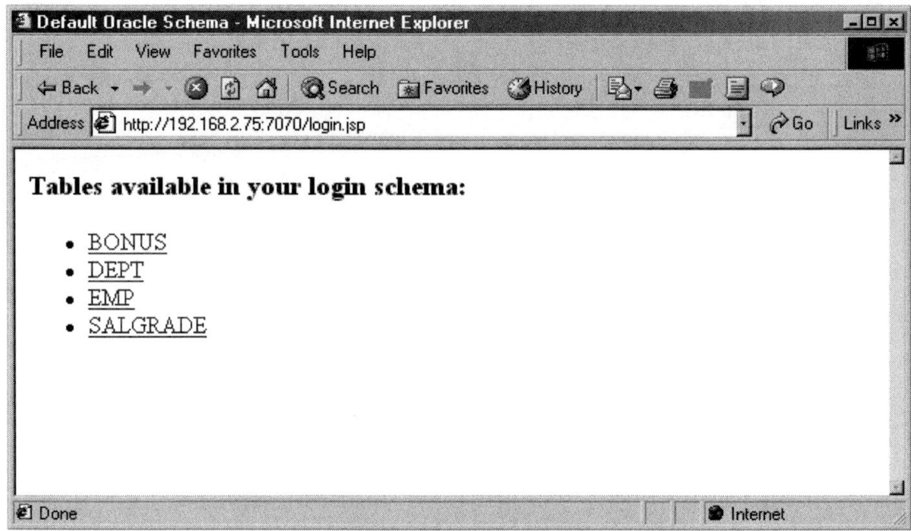

FIGURE 15.4 The output of login.jsp.

The source code of Error.jsp follows. Note that the element `isErrorPage=true` included in the initial line, started by the `<%@ page>` tag. This tells the JSP engine that the page in question is an error page.

```
<%@ page import="java.util.Enumeration" isErrorPage="true"
contentType="text/html;charset=WINDOWS-1252" %>
<html>
<head>
<title>Error Page for JSP Example</title>
</head><body>
<h2>The application produced an error</h2>
<p>The following is the exception thrown:<BR>
<%= exception %>
<p><table align = center border="2">  <tr>
<th colspan="2">Application Parameters</th></tr>
<% Enumeration enum = application.getAttributeNames();
   while (enum.hasMoreElements()) {
   String name = (String)enum.nextElement(); %>
<tr><th><%= name %> </th><td>
<%= application.getAttribute(name) %> </td></tr>
<% } %>
</table><p><table align=center border="1">
<tr><th colspan="2">Request Parameters</th></tr>
<% Enumeration enumAttr = request.getAttributeNames();
   while (enumAttr.hasMoreElements()) {
   String name = (String)enumAttr.nextElement(); %>
```

```
<tr><th><%= name %> </th><td>
<%= request.getAttribute(name) %> </td></tr>
<% } %>
</table><p><table align=center border="1"><tr>
<th colspan="2">Form Parameters</th></tr>
<% Enumeration enumPars = request.getParameterNames();
   while (enumPars.hasMoreElements()) {
   String name = (String)enumPars.nextElement(); %>
<tr><th><%= name %> </th><td>
<%= request.getParameter(name) %></td></tr> <% }%>
</table><p><a href="welcome.jsp">Start again!</a>
</body></html>
```

Error.jsp uses the implicit objects exception, application, and request to display detailed information about the page the caused the error. An example of an error page is shown in Figure 15.5. To display that page, simply enter a wrong password in the form displayed by welcome.jsp.

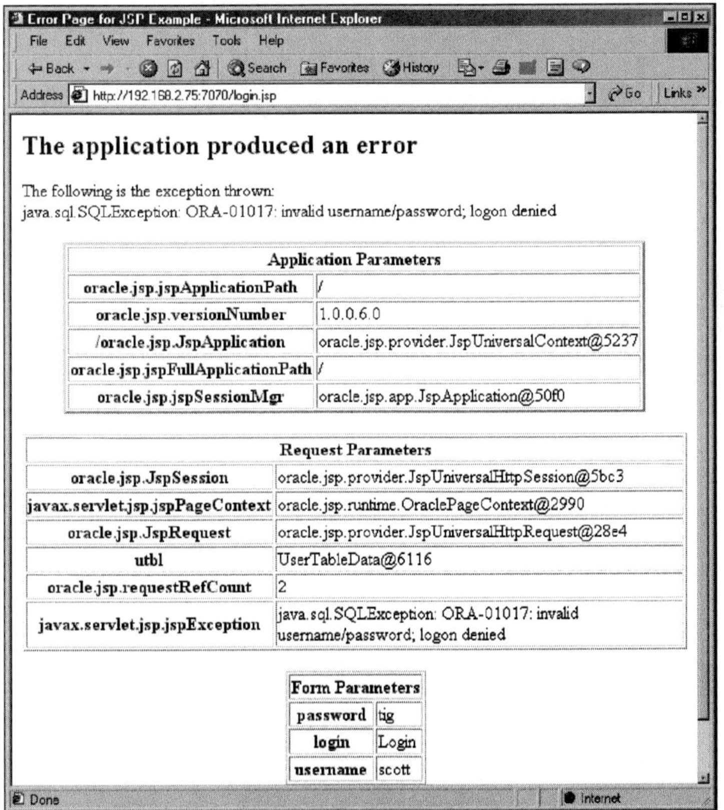

FIGURE 15.5 The error page displayed by the JSP engine.

The error page in Figure 15.5 is decidedly an error page that is only useful during the development phase. It would probably be too overwhelming for an end-user, who only needs a simple one-line sentence explaining clearly what happened. The verbose output can be redirected into a log file on the server that can be accessed later by application maintainers looking for error details, while keeping the error messages displayed by the user's browser simple and brief.

UserTableData is a bean that provides methods for retrieving and displaying the table names of the tables created in the Oracle schema to which the user has connected. The goal of this bean is to hide as much as possible of the data-gathering logic from the JSP page. Only two method calls are needed to retrieve the table names, *select()* and *next()*. This bean also implements a static *main()* method that allows for standalone testing.

```
// Copyright (c) 2000 Prentice Hall
import java.util.Vector;
import java.sql.*;

public class UserTableData implements Serializable
{

  private String tableName;
  private ResultSet rs;

  public void select(LoginModule lm)
                     throws SQLException
  {
       PreparedStatement pstmt =  lm.getUserTables();
       this.rs = pstmt.executeQuery();
  }

  public boolean next() throws SQLException
  {
      boolean status = rs.next();
      if (status)
      {
         this.tableName = rs.getString(1);
         return true;
      }
      else
      {
         this.rs.close();
         return false;
      }
  }
```

```
        public String getTableName()
        {
            return  this.tableName;
        }


        public static void  main(String [] args)
                            throws SQLException
        {
            LoginModule lm = new LoginModule();
            lm.connect("scott","tiger");
            UserTableData utd = new UserTableData();
            utd.select(lm);
            while(utd.next())
            {
               System.out.println(utd.getTableName());
            }
        }
    }
```

The TableColumnData bean is not printed here because of its great structural similarity to UserTableData. It provides the canonical *select()* and *next()* methods that allow JSP developers to access the column details for the given table. You can find it in your companion CD, together with all the files comprising this example.

Below you will see the source code for the showcol.jsp page. Again, note that the login bean is in the session scope, while the TableColumnData bean is in the request scope. An HTML table is created and populated with data fetched from the TableColumnData bean. The non-HTML tags included in the page are kept to a minimum, and their meaning is reasonably clear to graphic designers and other non-technical professionals.

```
<HTML>
<%@ page errorPage="Error.jsp"
contentType="text/html;charset=WINDOWS-1252"%>
<jsp:useBean id="tbd" class="TableColumnData" scope="request" />
<jsp:useBean id="login" class="LoginModule" scope="session" />
<jsp:setProperty name="tbd" property="*" />
<HEAD>
<TITLE>
Columns for table <jsp:getProperty name="tbd" property="tableName"/>
</TITLE>
</HEAD>
<BODY>
<H2>Columns belonging to <jsp:getProperty name="tbd"
property="tableName"/></H2>
<% tbd.select(login); %>
<P><table border="2" align=center><tr><td>
```

```
<b>Column Name</b></td>
<td><b>Data Type</b></td>
<td><b>Length</b></td>
<td><b>Precision</b></td>
<td><b>Nullable</b></td></tr>
<% while (tbd.next()) { %><tr>
<td><jsp:getProperty name="tbd" property="columnName" /></td>
<td><jsp:getProperty name="tbd" property="dataType" /></td>
<td><jsp:getProperty name="tbd" property="dataLength" /></td>
<td><jsp:getProperty name="tbd" property="dataPrecision" /></td>
<td><jsp:getProperty name="tbd" property="nullable" /></td>
</tr> <% } %>
</table>
</BODY>
</HTML>
```

The output produced by showcol.jsp is displayed in Figure 15.6.

15.1.5 USING JDEVELOPER SUPPORT FOR JSP

Oracle JDeveloper provides extensive support for JSP development. The JDeveloper's Business Components JSP application wizard can be used to generate a special set of JavaServer Pages (JSP) pages called a Business Components JSP Application. A JSP application uses middle-tier Oracle business components to browse and update an Oracle database. More specifically, a JSP application gen-

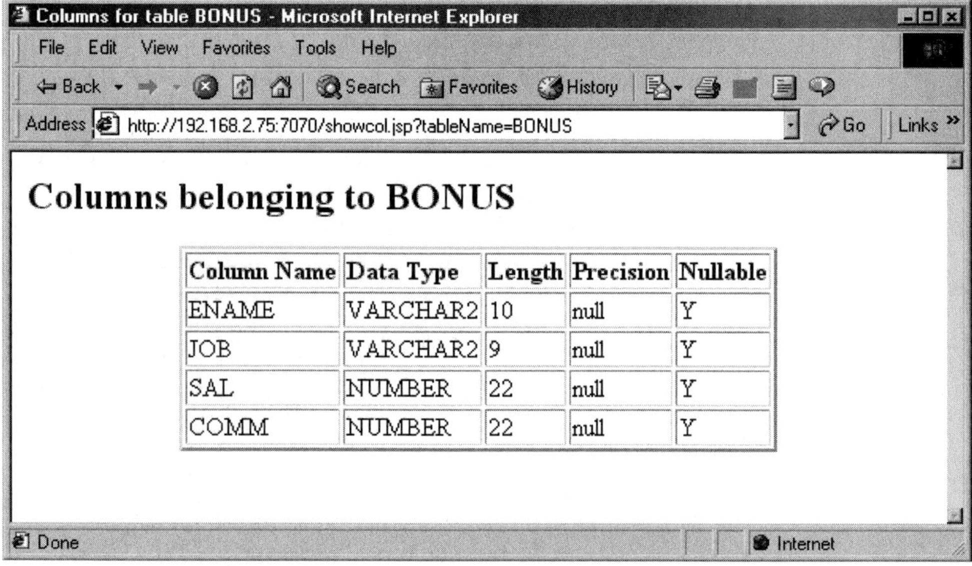

Column Name	Data Type	Length	Precision	Nullable
ENAME	VARCHAR2	10	null	Y
JOB	VARCHAR2	9	null	Y
SAL	NUMBER	22	null	Y
COMM	NUMBER	22	null	Y

FIGURE 15.6 The output produced by showcol.jsp.

erated using the wizard communicates with an application module and its associated view objects. The business components JSP application wizard generates a set of JSP forms for each of the application module's view objects. You choose which JSP forms to generate for each view object. These forms use a set of JDeveloper's predefined Web beans. You may wish to consult Chapter 13 for a more detailed treatment of the topic. Business components are tailored, using the JSP application wizard, to a JSP environment. JDeveloper provides two distinct sets of Web beans that can be used to design JSP forms:

- ❑ Standard Web beans for a standard user interface (UI).
- ❑ Javascript (JS) Web beans for a richer, more interactive user interface.

Beans of the first type are useful for rapid prototyping, but sacrifice sophistication in exchange for simplicity. For a better user experience, Javascript-based Web beans require more programming effort, but give production-quality results.

Even if you decide not to use the various wizards provided by JDeveloper to integrate Business Components for Java in your application, you can still use JDeveloper for its really advanced debugging capabilities. It allows you to step through JSP code, accessing the Java objects created by the underlying servlets generated by the JSP pages. Figure 15.7 shows JDeveloper during a debugging session.

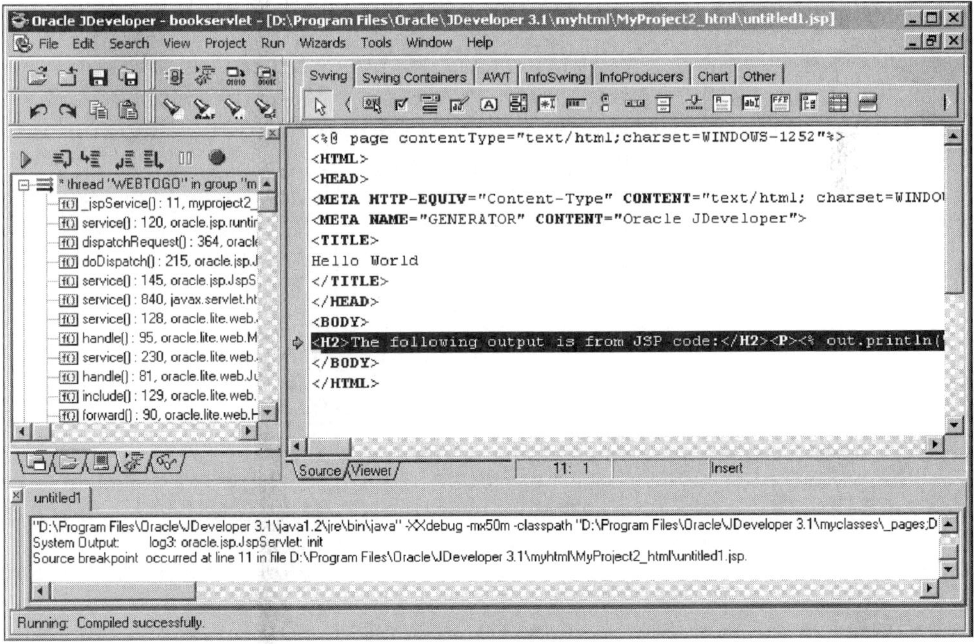

FIGURE 15.7 A debugging session in JDeveloper.

The breakpoint is set on a line of HTML code. The navigator pane, on the left-hand side of the IDE, displays the JSP implicit objects that can be accessed in the debug window, allowing developers to "see" inside the Java objects specified in the JSP pages and instantiated by the servlets automatically generated by the JSP engine.

15.2 ASP: AN OVERVIEW

Active Server Pages, or ASP, is the Microsoft environment used to deliver dynamic content to Web browsers. The Microsoft Web server, Internet Information Server (IIS), provides extensibility through the Internet Server Application Programmer's Interface (ISAPI). ISAPI programs can be either *extensions* or *filters*. ISAPI extensions are Windows DLLs, capable of responding to HTTP get or post requests, and are very similar to CGI programs. ISAPI filters are not invoked by HTTP requests, but intercept requests from Web browsers, shipping them to software components that are capable of dealing with them. Once a request has been processed, the resulting HTML page is returned to the Web browser, bypassing the normal action taken by the Web server.

ASP is a special type of ISAPI filter that acts as an interpreter for script code embedded inside HTML files. When a user requests a file with an .asp file type from IIS, IIS passes the request to the ISAPI filter, which invokes the ASP engine, passing the request data as parameters. The ASP engine parses the script code embedded in the asp file and builds the HTML file that will be sent to the requesting user.

ASP is built upon a Microsoft standard named *ActiveX scripting*. ASP is language-neutral as long as the scripting language complies with ActiveX scripting. In theory, many scripting languages are available to developers who want to use ASP to provide dynamic Web content. However, by default, ASP ships with two languages that can be readily used after a successful installation: VBScript and JScript. All the examples illustrating the ASP technology are in VBScript, which is the Microsoft-preferred environment for ASP scripting. This very fact means that most ASP scripts powering Microsoft-based Web servers are in VBScript.

ASP scripts are interpreted, not compiled. To counteract the inherent suboptimal speed of an interpreted environment, ASP relies heavily on COM objects to carry out its operation. The advanced integration with the Microsoft-distributed COM environment is probably the best feature of ASP. Since it is very easy to call COM components from ASP scripts, integrating advanced transaction management such as MTS/COM+[3] with an ASP-based application is within the reach of the average developer using Microsoft technologies, who can leverage the extreme simplicity provided by MTS/COM+ to produce robust and scalable transaction-based applications.

---

[3]In a Windows2000 environment, the Microsoft Transaction Server is integrated with COM+.

When the overall scalability of Microsoft technologies is a concern, a common arrangement is to integrate Windows-based front-ends with more powerful machines on the back-end. The back-end machines provide scalability and redundancy/fault-tolerance, perhaps by running an Oracle Parallel Server configuration in a clustered environment. The front-end computers run Microsoft Windows NT or Windows 2000 Advanced Server, with a combination of IIS and ASP. The ASP scripts access the Oracle database, using MTS/COM+ through Ole DB using the Ole Db provider. This architecture allows for expansion, simply by adding front-end computers, if the number of Web requests grows beyond initial expectations. In large e-commerce applications, where reliability is critical, a form of load-balancing devices, for example the very popular CISCO LocalDirector, completes the architecture described above.

LocalDirector is a sophisticated server-connection management system that enables administrators to direct TCP traffic to different servers based on service requested, distribution method, and server availability. The Session Distribution Algorithm (SDA) implemented by LocalDirector enables proportionate forwarding of traffic based on weight and maximum number of open connections, ensuring that servers do not fail from traffic overload. LocalDirector can also probe server applications to determine real-time availability. Figure 15.8 shows a possible configuration for an application that integrates Microsoft and Oracle/Unix technologies.

The architecture in Figure 15.8 combines the scalability and robustness of a Unix-based back-end with Microsoft technologies in the middle tier. Two CISCO

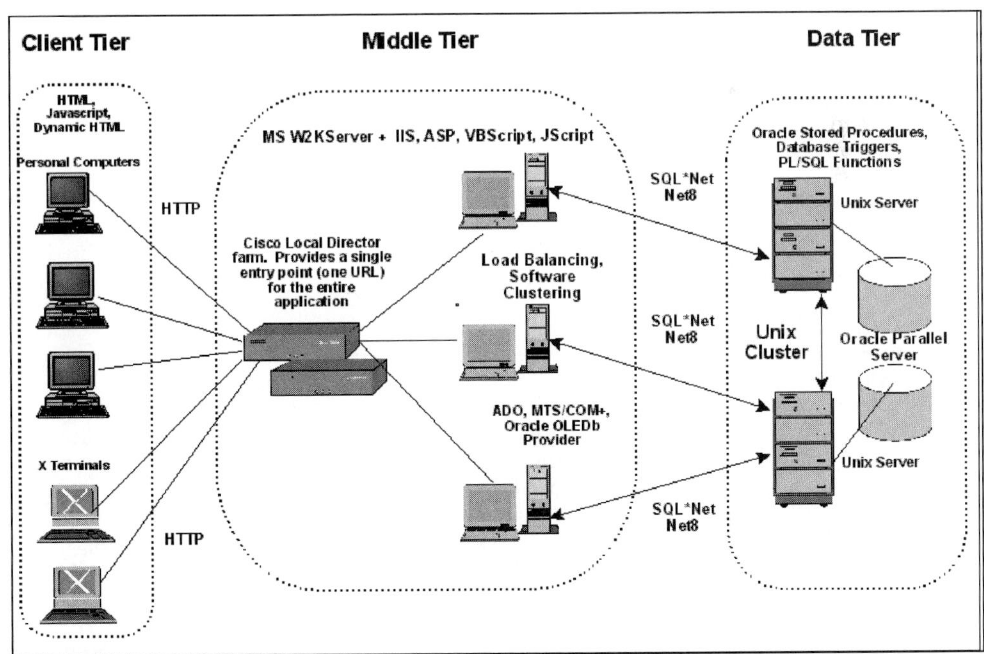

FIGURE 15.8 A mixed configuration integrating Unix and Microsoft technologies.

LocalDirector devices provide a high level of redundancy, load balancing, and a single, virtual URL for the application. Each request is forwarded to the most appropriate MS IIS server. ASP scripts and COM components apply business logic to data gathered from Oracle-performing MTS/COM+ transactions, which involve a few protocols and network layers, such as the Oracle OLE Db provider, SQL*Net/Net8, and Microsoft ADO. The data tier is represented by an Oracle Parallel Server configuration supported by a Unix cluster, which ensures redundancy and high availability.

15.2.1 ASP ELEMENTS

The preceding section introduced the high degree of integration of ASP with the COM environment. In fact, the basic objects that comprise the ASP architecture, or *intrinsic objects*, are COM components. Their JSP counterparts are the implicit objects. The six ASP intrinsic objects are shown in Table 15.5.

The COM component objects expose properties and methods. Although several properties are read-only, most can be changed using the familiar dot notation, as in this example:

```
Session.Timeout = 50
```

You can create variables and store them into intrinsic object from VBScript, using the following syntax:

```
IntrinsicObject("<variable name>") = <value>
<variable> = IntrinsicObject("<variable name>")
```

For example:

```
Session("username") = "scott"
Dim uname
```

TABLE 15.5 ASP intrinsic objects

INTRINSIC OBJECT	PURPOSE
Application	Provides management facilities for the entire ASP application; stores application-wide data that needs to persist and to be accessible by all clients across requests and sessions.
Session	Stores session-persistent data and allows ASP developers to keep track of the user's session, whose lifetime spans multiple requests.
Request	Stores all data received from a browser's request.
Response	Stores data sent back to the user's browser.
Server	Exposes server-wide properties and provides miscellaneous functions.
ObjectContext	Used in conjunction with MS MTS/Com+ to manage transactions.

```
uname = Session("username")
```

ASP files usually begin by specifying the scripting language in use. The IIS Web server must be made aware of the type of scripting engine it has to forward the request, so the following line is usually seen at the beginning of every ASP file:

```
<% Language = VBScript %>
```

The <%tag denotes the beginning of a code segment, and the %>tag denotes the end of a code segment.

You can retrieve input fields of HTML forms using the following syntax:

```
Request.Form("<input field>")
```

For example, if an HTML form specifies the "username" input field, as in:

```
<form method=post action=login.asp>
...
...
<input type=text name="username" size=30>
```

The VBScript code in login.asp, available from the companion CDROM, can access the content of the username input field using the following statement:

```
request.Form("username")
```

Variables that are sent to the ASP engine, not through forms, but through HTML queries (CGI GETs) like:

```
showcol.asp?tableName=EMP
```

can be retrieved by VBScript using the QueryString method provided by the Request object. To retrieve the value EMP stored in tableName, an ASP developer would use the following syntax:

```
request.QueryString("tableName")
```

The program flow-control statements implemented in VBScript adhere to the classical BASIC syntax found in all BASIC dialects, including MS Visual Basic. The constructs shown below are used to execute code conditionally, based on certain conditions.

```
If… Then… Else … End If
Select Case … Case… End Select
```

VBScript supports four types of loops, shown in Table 15.6.

TABLE 15.6 Loop types supported by VBScript

LOOP TYPE	DESCRIPTION
Do ... Loop	Executes statements inside the loop until a test expression is true. The test expression can be evaluated at the beginning or end of the loop. In the latter case, statements inside the loop are executed at least once, irrespective of the value of the testing condition.
For ... Next	Executes statements inside a loop for a specified number of times.
For Each ... Next	Special type of for loop used to traverse arrays and collection of objects.
While ... Wend	Executes statements inside the body of the loop as long as the test expression is true.

The ASP elements introduced so far will allow you to create the first ASP example.

15.2.2 AN ASP EXAMPLE

In this section, you will use ASP to develop the same example application that you developed a few pages back using the JSP syntax. Users login to an Oracle instance through a Web form; the tables created in the default schema are displayed as hyperlinks, allowing users to display the table structure by clicking on the hyperlink. Since the two examples perform identical operations, you can easily compare the source code to discover the peculiarities and unique features of the competing environments.

The ASP application's entry point is an HTML file that implements the form used to enter the username and password of an Oracle database account. Note the *action* clause of the *form* tag: it specifies the ASP file *login.asp*.

```
<HTML>
<HEAD><TITLE>ASP Example</TITLE></HEAD>
<BODY>
<H3>Oracle Login:</H3>
<form method=post action=login.asp><P>
<center><table border="2">
<tr><td>Username</td>
<td><input type=text name="username" size=30></td>
</tr><tr>
<td>Password:</td>
<td><input type=password name="password" size=30></td>
</tr>
</table>
<input type=submit name=login value="Login">
</form>
```

```
</P>
</BODY>
</HTML>
```

The ASP logic contained in *login.asp* takes care of connecting to Oracle using an ADO connection. Username and password are retrieved from the HTML input form using a request.FORM("<variable>") call. The ADO connection object is stored into the session intrinsic object, in order to be used by other requests submitted by the user in the same session. The OleDB provider in this example is the Microsoft OleDB provider for Oracle, referred to as MSDAORA. You can also use the Oracle alternative, the OleDB provider for the Oracle RDBMS by Oracle Corporation. In the latter case you would use the string "`Provider=OraOLEDB.Oracle;`".

The ADO connection object is created using the *createobject()* method provided by the server intrinsic object. If you want to run the example in your environment, make sure to change the Data Source clause, replacing *w2k816* with your TNS connection name. The source code of login.asp is shown below.

```
<%@ Language = VBScript %>
<HTML>
<HEAD>
<TITLE>Oracle Tables</TITLE>
</HEAD>
<BODY BGCOLOR="#FFFFF1" LINK="#0000FF" VLINK="#800080"
TEXT="#000000">
<%
set session("Connection") = server.createobject ("ADODB.connection")
session("Connection").open  "Provider=MSDAORA.1;Password=" &_
request.Form("password") &";User Id=" &_
 request.Form("username") & ";Data Source=W2K816"
set rsTbl = session("Connection").Execute(&_
"select table_name from user_tables")
%>
<P><UL>
<% do Until rsTbl.EOF %>
<LI>
<A HREF="showcol.asp?tableName=
<%response.write rsTbl("Table_name") %>"
</A>
<%response.write rsTbl("Table_name") %></LI>
<%
   rsTbl.MoveNext
   loop
%>
</BODY>
</HTML>
```

Login.asp does not implement any error-handling logic. If an error occurs while you are establishing a connection to Oracle, say because you entered an incorrect password in the HTML form, the browser will display a page similar to the one shown in Figure 15.9.

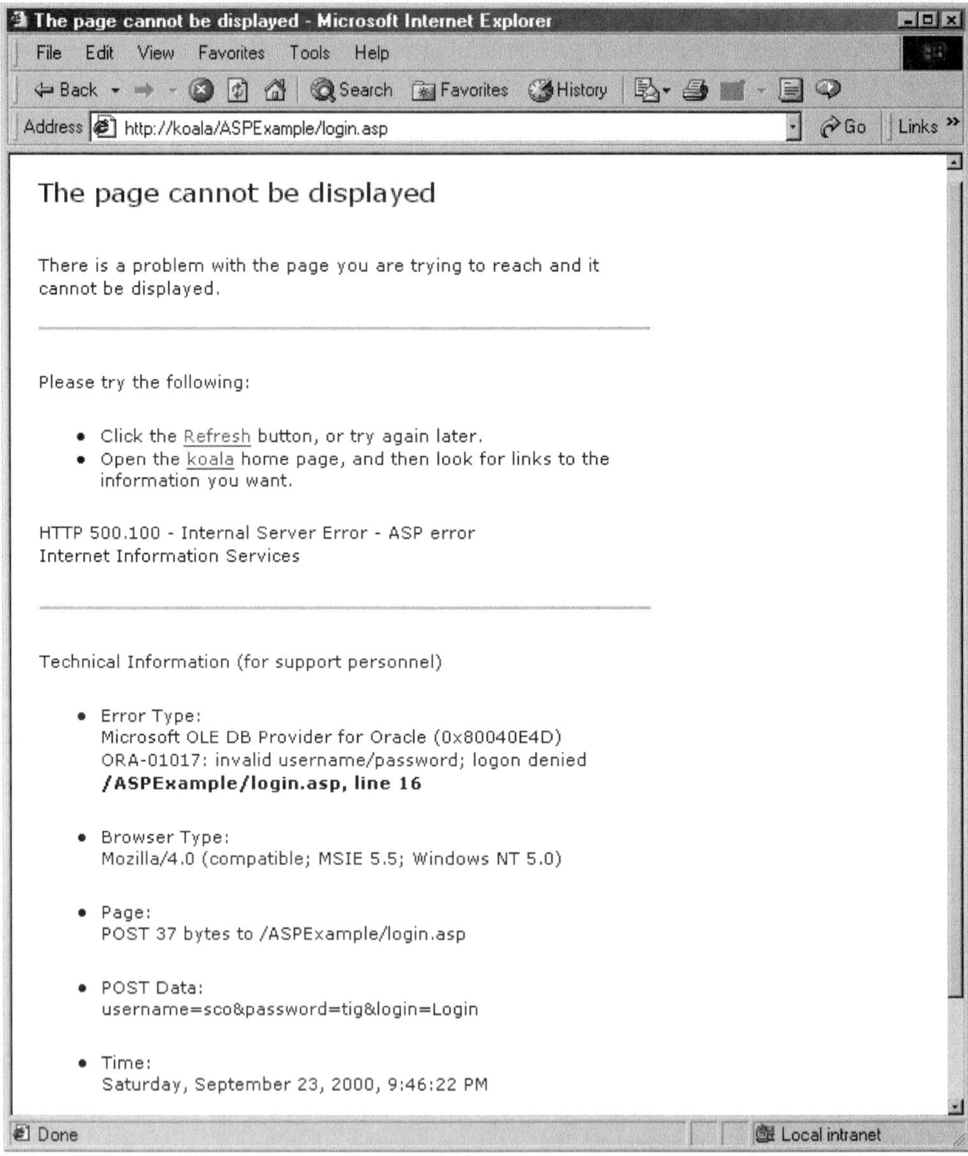

FIGURE 15.9 Standard ASP error handling.

The VBScript construct can be used to override the standard behavior of the ASP engine in case of error:

```
On Error Resume Next
```

If you opt to create your own specialized error handler, use the Err object to provide error-related information to the users. For example, using the code shown below, you can test whether the connection to the Oracle database has failed:

```
On Error Resume Next
set conn = server.createobject ("ADODB.connection")
conn.open  "Provider=MSDAORA.1;Password=" &_
request.Form("password") &";User Id=" &_
 request.Form("username") & ";Data Source=W2K816"
if Err.Number <> 0 Then
      For Each vErr In conn.Errors
         response.write "Error!: " & vErr.Description & "<BR>"
      Next
End If
```

The problem with this approach is that you must provide error-handling logic for every statement that can potentially generate an error, littering your ASP code with so many error handlers that the readability of your code will soon be obfuscated. That is the reason why you should accept the default error handler for this simple ASP application.

The hyperlinks displayed by login.asp use the HTML query mechanism to communicate to the server the Oracle database table name required by the user. This is equivalent to using a form with a GET method, where the parameters of the query are displayed in the address field of the browser, separated from the file name specified by the action clause by a question mark, as in the following example:

```
http://koala/ASPExample/showcol.asp?TableName=EMP
```

In ASP, you use the QueryString method provided by the request object to retrieve the parameters of the HTML query. This is performed by *showcol.asp*, which uses QueryString to retrieve the name of the table whose structure must be displayed. The table name is concatenated to the end of the string containing the query to be submitted to the RDBMS. The ADO connection is retrieved from the session object, and a result set is built by executing the SELECT string passed to the connection object. The result set is traversed with a Do..Until loop, and the column parameters are formatted in HTML tags defining a table. The listing is shown below.

```
<%@ Language = VBScript %>
<%
Dim tname
%>
<HTML>
<HEAD>
<TITLE>Oracle Tables</TITLE>
</HEAD>
<BODY BGCOLOR="#FFFFF1" LINK="#0000FF" VLINK="#800080"
TEXT="#000000">
<%
tname = request.QueryString("tableName")
selStat="select COLUMN_NAME, DATA_TYPE,DATA_LENGTH," &_
"DATA_PRECISION,NULLABLE from user_tab_columns where " &_
"TABLE_NAME= '" & tname &  "' order by COLUMN_ID "
set rsCol = session("Connection").execute(selStat)
%>
<H2>Columns belonging to <% response.write tname %></H2>
<P><table border="2" align=center><tr><td>
<b>Column Name</b></td>
<td><b>Data Type</b></td>
<td><b>Length</b></td>
<td><b>Precision</b></td>
<td><b>Nullable</b></td></tr>
<% Do Until rsCol.EOF %>
<TR>
<TD><% response.write rsCol(0).value %></TD>
<TD><% response.write rsCol(1).value %></TD>
<TD><% response.write rsCol(2).value %></TD>
<TD><% response.write rsCol(3).value %></TD>
<TD><% response.write rsCol(4).value %></TD>
</TR>
<% rsCol.movenext
      loop
%>
</TABLE>
</BODY>
</HTML>
```

This simple ASP application uses VBScript to perform its tasks. VBScript, an interpreted scripting environment, is inherently slower than Java bytecodes. The alternative approach of coding most of the business logic in compiled languages exposes subroutines and methods to the ASP environment through ActiveX DLLs. MS Visual Basic offers better speed than VBScript, but if you want to achieve true scalability use Visual C++, combined with the Active Template Library, which allows for the most sophisticated threading model offered by the Microsoft Windows platform (free threads). While Visual Basic is simpler and arguably more productive, it only offers apartment threads, which are not as efficient as free threads. If you concentrate most of your business logic in ActiveX DLLs and keep the VBScript lines of code to a minimum, you can achieve more performance and relative scalability.

The ASP files of Web applications are grouped together in virtual directories. The IIS Web server must know the location of the files it must serve to the requesting users. You make IIS aware of the files comprising your application by using "Internet Information Services," the IIS administration front-end. From the main window of this front-end, click on "Action"->"New"->"Virtual Directory" to create a directory that will store the files, images, and sounds of your application. This is shown in Figure 15.10.

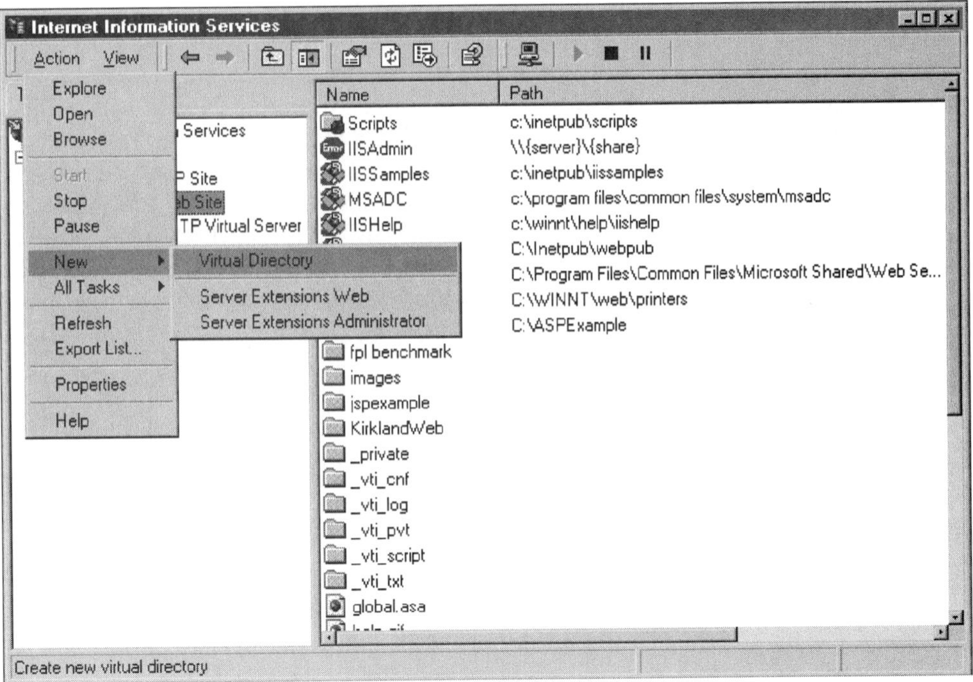

FIGURE 15.10 The IIS administrative applet allows you to create virtual directories.

15.3 JSP AND ASP COMPARED

ASP and JSP share common features and philosophical principles, such as separation of the content displayed to the users' browser from the data-gathering and -formatting logic. They make life simpler for graphic designers, who can focus on the aesthetic appearance of the Web site without being confronted with the complex programming syntax needed to retrieve data from the back-end.

ASP and JSP also make life simpler for programmers, since they cut development time and help produce cleaner code, where the execution flow is not intermixed with HTML tags. However, ASP and JSP are fundamentally different technologies. ASP is fully supported only under MS Windows. Third-party companies offer ASP-like environments under Unix, but the reliance of ASP on Windows-only components severely limits its portability to non-Microsoft platforms. Since JSP is Java-based, it is inherently portable to all platforms for which a JVM is available. While native Web servers, such as iPlanet or Allaire Jrun, provide efficient implementations of servlets and JSP, the Jakarta-Tomcat project, currently considered the standard implementation for JSP specifications, provides ISAPI and NSAPI connectors for Microsoft IIS and iPlanet, as well as an Apache module. JSP is therefore a much more portable environment. From the scalability perspective, environments like Jakarta-Tomcat offer flexible configuration options, whereby you can spawn more than one JVM to serve JSPs when the Web traffic exceeds the serving capabilities of a single JVM.

Both ASP and JSP are well equipped for transactionally intensive applications. The high-level ASP integration with MS MTS/Com+ simplifies the deployment of sophisticated applications relying on ACID messages. ASP developers need to know very little to exploit the powerful capabilities of Com+. The ObjectContext intrinsic object hides much of the complexity of transactions, offering a very simple API (the *setAbort()* and *setComplete()* methods implemented in ObjectContext).

JSP-based applications rely on Enterprise Java Beans (EJBs), which usually offer transaction handling through the Java Transaction API (JTA). JTA is a high-level interface that allows for transaction control through simple and powerful method calls.

Apart from portability and scalability, another area where the JSP environment has an edge over ASP is extensibility. In ASP, you can choose between VBScript and JScript, but if neither scripting language implements a particular tag needed in your application, you cannot extend the language by defining your own customized tags. This is possible with JSP, which allows for custom tag libraries.

From the standpoint of practicality, if you opt for ASP, you limit your application to run in a Windows-only environment. If you choose JSP, not only will your application run more efficiently than ASP under Windows, but with little effort it can be ported to more powerful and scalable architectures.

15.4 REWORKING BOOKSERVLET USING JSP

In Chapter 14, you developed BookServlet, an e-commerce-like application that allows customers to buy Oracle books over the Internet. In doing so you learned about servlets and servlet engines, but also became aware of the limitations of a servlet-only solution for Web applications. The HTML tags are buried in the Java servlet classes, so changing a small GUI detail means recompiling and re-deploying the project. The preceding sections of this chapter introduced the JSP paradigm, which solves the basic issue of separating the GUI presentation layer from the data-gathering layer. The optimal solution, however, is not a complete port of servlets to JSPs, but a combination of the two technologies in which they cooperate in providing a rich and powerful development and deployment environment.

For example, serving binary images is performed more efficiently and more easily from a servlet, whereas formatting a textual page is more suitable for JSP.

The BookServlet application developed in Chapter 14 now becomes, after a small face-lift, BookJSP. Two major were issues identified while developing BookServlet:

- The connection pool was less than optimal.
- The HTML tags were intermixed with Java code.

BookJSP attempts to overcome both issues. Connecting to an Oracle database is accomplished through the connection cache mechanism provided by the Oracle JDBC driver. HTML tags are extracted from the Java code and grouped into JSP pages. Each JSP page uses one or more Java beans, which provide the data-gathering logic. The principal design goal of the redevelopment of BookServlet is to avoid, as much as possible, Java statements and execution control logic in the JSP pages. This means minimizing the use of scriptlets, and concentrating most of the execution logic in Java beans.

15.4.1 CONNECTION CACHING

Connection caching is a means of keeping and using caches of physical database connections. In the Oracle-specific implementation provided with the JDBC 2.0 driver, each connection cache is represented by an instance of a *connection cache class,* which has an associated group of pooled connection instances. For a single connection cache instance, the associated pooled connection instances represent physical connections to the same database and schema. Pooled connection instances are created as needed, whenever a connection is requested and the connection cache does not have any free pooled connection instances. A "free" pooled connection instance is one that currently has no logical connection instance associated with it. In other words, it is a pooled connection instance whose physical connection is not being used.

As shown in Table 15.7, the Oracle-provided connection cache implementation allows users to choose between two *cache schemes* to cater for situations where a new connection has been requested, all existing pooled connections are in use, and the maximum number of connections in the cache has been reached. One of these is known as the *dynamic scheme*, and the other as the *fixed with no wait* scheme. The cache scheme you will implement for BookJSP is the dynamic scheme, because it is the default.

To use the Oracle connection cache mechanism you must:

- ❑ Import `oracle.jdbc.pool.*`
- ❑ Include the *jndi.jar* file in the CLASSPATH of your IDE.
- ❑ Create an instance of the *OracleConnectionCacheImpl* class.

OracleConnectionCacheImpl implements a *getConnection()* method that returns a logical connection to the database and schema associated with the cache.

The source code of ConnectionCache.java follows.

```
// Copyright (c) 2000 Prentice Hall

import java.util.Enumeration;
import java.sql.*;
import oracle.jdbc.driver.*;
import oracle.jdbc.pool.*;

/** Connection Cache class.
*/
public class ConnectionCache
{
  /** The single instance of ConnectionCache.
  */
  private static ConnectionCache cache;
```

TABLE 15.7 Oracle-provided connection cache schemes

Dynamic scheme	New connections can be created beyond the maximum limit upon request, but closed and freed when the logical connections are closed. When all the connections are active and busy, requests for new connections create new physical connections, but these are closed when the corresponding logical connections are closed. A typical grow-and-shrink mechanism.
Fixed with no wait	The maximum limit can never be exceeded. Requests for connections when the maximum has already been reached will return null.

```
/** The Oracle connection cache object.
*/
private OracleConnectionCacheImpl oraCache;

/** JDBC  URL
*/
private String jdbcURL;

/** Oracle username
*/
private String username;

/** Oracle password
*/
private String password;

/** Maximum number of pooled connections in the cache
*/
int maxConnection;

/** Class constructor. It is defined as private, to implement
**  the singleton pattern
**  @param jdbcURL String containing the connection URL
**  @param username String. Oracle account name.
**  @param password String. Oracle password.
**  @param maxConnection Int that defines the absolute
**    maximum number of pooled connections in the cache.
*/
private ConnectionCache(String jdbcURL,
                        String username,
                        String password,
                        int maxConnection)
                        throws SQLException
 {
   this.jdbcURL             = jdbcURL;
   this.username            = username;
   this.password            = password;
   this.maxConnection       = maxConnection;
   oraCache = new OracleConnectionCacheImpl();
   oraCache.setURL(jdbcURL);
   oraCache.setUser(username);
   oraCache.setPassword(password);
   oraCache.setMaxLimit(maxConnection);
 }
```

```
/** This method calls the private class constructor
**  to create an instance of this class, if an instance
**  doesn't exist already.
**  @param jdbcURL String containing the connection URL
**  @param username String. Oracle account name.
**  @param password String. Oracle password.
**  @param maxConnection Int that defines the absolute
**      maximum number of pooled connections in the cache.
**  @throws SQLException
**  @throws ClassNotFoundException
*/
public static ConnectionCache getInstance(String jdbcURL,
                                          String username,
                                          String password,
                                          int maxConnection)
                                          throws SQLException
{
    if (cache == null)
    {
       cache = new ConnectionCache(jdbcURL,
                                   username,
                                   password,
                                   maxConnection);
    }
    return cache;
}

/** The overloaded instance() method returns an instance of
**  the ConnectionCache class. It assumes that an instance has
**  already been initialized. If this is not true, an exception
**  is raised
**  @return ConnectionCache - An initialized ConnectionCache
**                            object
**  @throws Exception - If no connection cache object has been
**         instantiated
*/
public static ConnectionCache getInstance() throws Exception
{
    if (cache == null)
       throw new Exception("Connection Cache not initialized!");
    return cache;
}
```

```
    /**
    */
    public Connection getConnection() throws SQLException
    {
        Connection conn = this.oraCache.getConnection();
        conn.setAutoCommit(false);
        return conn;
    }
}
```

The connection cache is instantiated at the beginning of the application, as soon as the first JSP request is submitted to the JSP engine.

The connection-caching mechanism implemented in BookJSP is a considerable improvement over the simple connection-pooling component built for BookServlet. With the Oracle-provided connection cache, client requests for connections are always satisfied and do not have to wait because the connection pool has exhausted all connections. Whenever a logical connection is released, the connection cache realizes what has happened. If, in order to satisfy all concurrent requests, the connection cache engine temporarily allocates more connections than are specified in the MaxLimit parameter, it will automatically reduce the number of physical connections as soon as the number of client requests decreases.

15.4.2 JAVA BEANS AND JAVA SERVER PAGES

The complete source code of BookJSP can be found on the companion CD-ROM, under the Chapter15/BookJSP directory. A small subset of the source code of BookJSP is shown in this section to illustrate the techniques used to minimize the number of non-HTML tags coded in the JSPs. In terms of functionality, BookJSP is substantially identical to BookServlet. In Book JSP, as in BookServlet, the catalog of all the books available from the virtual bookshop is displayed after a user successfully logs in. Figure 15.11 shows the HTML page displayed by the JSP file *catalog.jsp*.

The JSP file that generates the catalog page is shown below. Note that only three scriptlet lines are needed to open a database cursor, fill the cursor with data, and loop through all the cursor rows, formatting the data in HTML tags. The scriptlet lines are shown in bold.

```
<%@ page errorPage = "error.jsp"
contentType="text/html;charset=WINDOWS-1252"%>
<jsp:useBean id="global" class="Global" scope="application" />
<jsp:useBean id="ctlg" class="CatalogModule" scope="request"/>
<HTML>
<HEAD>
<TITLE>BookJSP Catalog</TITLE>
```

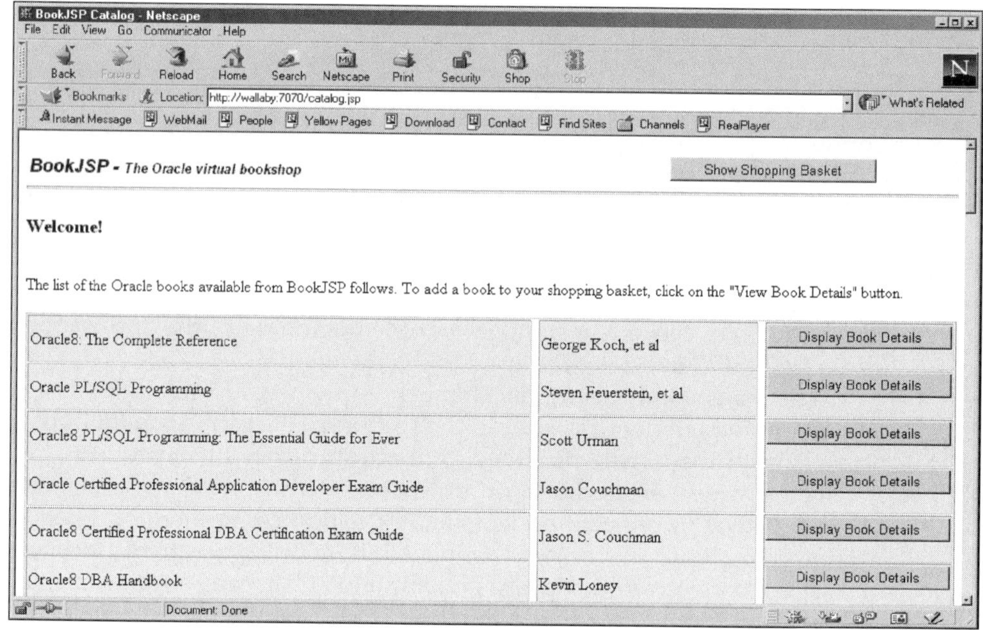

FIGURE 15.11 The book catalog displayed by catalog.jsp.

```
</HEAD>
<BODY>
<table border=0 cellpadding=2 cellspacing=0
width=100% height=39><tr valign=bottom>
<td align=left valign=bottom height=31>
<font size=+1 face="Arial,Helvetica" color=black>
<b><i>BookJSP - <font size=-1>The Oracle virtual
bookshop</b></i></td><td align=right valign=bottom height=31>
<table border=0 cellpadding=0 cellspacing=0><tr>
<td width=56 align=right><form method = POST
action="showbasket.jsp">
<input type=submit name="shbskt"
value="Show Shopping Basket"></td></form>
<td align=left valign=middle width=78></td></tr><tr>
<td colspan=2 nowrap></td></tr></table></td>
</tr></table>
<hr><p><h3>Welcome!</h3><br>
<p>The list of the Oracle books available from BookJSP
follows. To add a book to your shopping basket, click
on the "View Book Details" button.<br>
<P><TABLE BORDER="1" CELLSPACING="1"
```

```
CELLPADDING="1" BGCOLOR="#CCFFFF"
BORDERCOLORLIGHT="#33CCFF"
BORDERCOLORDARK="#0033FF">
<% ctlg.select(global); %>
<% while(ctlg.next()) { %>
<form method=POST action="bookdetails.jsp">
<input type=hidden name = "bookId" value=<jsp:getProperty
    name="ctlg" property = "id"/>
<TR><TD><jsp:getProperty name="ctlg" property="title"/><TD>
<TD><jsp:getProperty name="ctlg" property="author"/><TD>
<TD VALIGN="MIDDLE"><input type=submit name="button"
   value="Display Book Details"></form>
</td></tr>
<% } %>
</TABLE>
</BODY>
</HTML>
```

The catalog JSP uses two Java beans, Global, alias global, and CatalogModule, alias ctlg. The Global bean contains application-wide parameters, as well as the connection cache, so its scope is application. The CatalogModule bean implements the supporting methods used by catalog.jsp. It has to be instantiated by the JSP engine every time a user requests the catalog page, so its scope is request. The *select()* method implemented by CatalogModule receives a reference to the Global bean. The *next()* method advances the database cursor pointer, returning true if more rows are to be fetched from the cursor. When the last row has been fetched, *next()* closes the cursor, releases the connection, and returns false. The implementation of the CatalogModule class is shown below.

```
// Copyright © 2000 Prentice Hall
import java.sql.*;

public class CatalogModule extends Object
{
   private String id;
   private String title;
   private String author;
   private Global gbl;
   private Connection conn;
   private ResultSet rs;

   public void setId(String id)
   {
      this.id = id;
   }
```

```
public String getId()
{
   return this.id;
}
public void setTitle(String tl)
{
   this.title = tl;
}
public String getTitle()
{
   return this.title;
}
public void setAuthor(String auth)
{
   this.author = auth;
}
public String getAuthor()
{
   return this.author;
}
public void select(Global gbl) throws SQLException
{
   this.gbl = gbl;
   this.conn = this.gbl.getConnection();
   Statement stmt = this.conn.createStatement();
   this.rs = stmt.executeQuery("select id, title, author from "+
                               "sales_item order by id asc");
}
public boolean next()  throws SQLException
{
   boolean status = this.rs.next();
   if(status)
   {
       this.setId(this.rs.getString(1));
       this.setTitle(this.rs.getString(2));
       this.setAuthor(this.rs.getString(3));
       return true;
   }
   else
   {
      this.rs.close();
      this.gbl.releaseConnection(this.conn);
      return false;
   }
}
```

CatalogModule implements getter and setter methods for all the columns retrieved from the sales_item table (id,title,author). References to the Global bean, the logical Oracle database connection, and the result set used to fetch the sales_item data are defined as instance fields, so that they are accessible from all methods in CatalogModule. The *select()* method receives a reference to the Global bean, which is used to obtain a logical Oracle database connection from the connection cache. Note that the *select()* method, once the connection has been obtained, creates the statement and executes the query, pulling the data into the database cursor. The cursor, however, is not advanced. This is left for the *next()* method, which advances the cursor and stores the data in the corresponding instance fields using the setter methods. The JSP page, before calling the *next()* method again, can access the retrieved data by calling the getter methods. This technique is used extensively throughout the BookJSP application.

Table 15.8 lists all the JSP and Java beans used by BookJSP, so that you can more easily identify the files you may want to edit and examine.

TABLE 15.8 JSP and Java beans used by BookJSP

JSP	BEAN USED	PURPOSE
welcome.jsp	Global.java	Displays initial page inviting users to enter the virtual bookshop.
login.jsp	Global.java, LoginModule.java	Verifies user's credentials.
createuser.jsp	none	Creates a new user if this is the first time the application is used.
useradded.jsp	Global.java, UserModule.java	Displays a user-creation confirmation message. Allows newly created users to access book catalog.
catalog.jsp	Global.java, CatalogModule.java	Displays e catalog of all books on sale at the virtual bookshop.
addbasket.jsp	Global.java, ShoppingBasket.java AddBasketModule.java	Allows user to add an item to the shopping basket.
alreadyinbasket.jsp	none	Displays warning message if item has already been added to the shopping basket.
bookdetails.jsp	Global.java, BookDetailsModule.java	Displays details of specific book chosen by customer.
showbasket.jsp	Global.java, ShoppingBasket.java, ShowBasketModule.java	Shows all items currently stored in shopping basket.
emptyshoppingbasket.jsp	none	Allows user to completely wipe out the shopping basket.
orderdone.jsp	Global.java, OrderModule.java	Displays page confirming that the order has been submitted to the virtual bookshop.
error.jsp	none	This is the JSP error page shown whenever an unhandled exception is thrown.

15.4.3 THE SERVEIMAGE SERVLET

When BookJSP users request the page that lists the details of a particular book, a picture representing the book cover is displayed in the Web browser.

The picture is stored in GIF format in an Oracle table. JSP pages are not very good at handling binary images, so the job of fetching the GIF image from Oracle, sending the bytes back to the user's browser, is done by a specialized servlet. The ServeImage servlet shares with BookJSP the connection cache mechanism implemented by the ConnectionCache class. The connection cache is instantiated by the servlet *init()* method, which is overridden by ServeImage. The source code of the ServeImage servlet follows.

```
import javax.servlet.*;
import javax.servlet.http.*;
import java.io.*;
import java.util.*;
import java.sql.*;
import oracle.sql.*;
import oracle.jdbc.driver.*;

public class ServeImage extends HttpServlet
{
  private ConnectionCache cache;
  /**
   * Initialize global variables
   */
  public void init(ServletConfig config)
                throws ServletException
  {
    super.init(config);
    //
    String configFile =
       this.getServletConfig().getInitParameter("ConfigFile");
    if (configFile == null)
    {
        ServletException se =
         new ServletException("Servlet did not receive "+
                         "the config file parameter. A "+
                         "configuration file is required. ");
        throw se;
    }
    Properties props = new Properties();
    try
    {
       props.load(new
         BufferedInputStream(new FileInputStream(configFile)));
    }
```

```
    catch (IOException IOE)
    {
       ServletException se =
         new ServletException("Configuration file error!");
       throw se;
    }
    String connectionString =
props.getProperty("ConnectionString");
    String username = props.getProperty("Username");
    String password = props.getProperty("Password");
    String maxConnections = props.getProperty("MaxConnections");
    try
    {
       this.cache =
          ConnectionCache.instance(connectionString,
                                   username,password,
                                  Integer.parseInt(maxConnections));
    }

    catch (SQLException SQLExc)
    {
      String err = SQLExc.getMessage();
      int errnum = SQLExc.getErrorCode();
      ServletException se =
         new ServletException("Connection cache raised an " +
                 "SQLEexception: "+errnum+". "+err);
      throw se;
    }
  }


  /**
   * Process the HTTP Get request
   */
  public void doGet(HttpServletRequest request,
                    HttpServletResponse response)
            throws ServletException, IOException
  {
      oracle.sql.BLOB blob;
      response.setContentType("image/gif");
      ServletOutputStream out = response.getOutputStream();
      String bookId = request.getParameter("BOOKID");
      Connection conn = null;
      PreparedStatement imageSQL = null;
      try
      {
         conn = this.getConnection();
```

```
    }
    catch (SQLException exc)
    {
         String err = exc.getMessage();
         int errnum = exc.getErrorCode();
         ServletException se =
           new ServletException("Get picture raised an " +
                "SQLEexception: "+errnum+". "+err);
         throw se;
    }
    try
    {
       imageSQL = this.getImageSQL(conn);
       imageSQL.setInt(1, Integer.parseInt(bookId));

       ResultSet rset = imageSQL.executeQuery();

       if (rset.next())
       {
          // Get the blob data - cast to OracleResult set to
          // retrieve the data in oracle.sql format
          blob = ((OracleResultSet)rset).getBLOB(1);

          // get the length of the blob
          int  length = (int) blob.length();
          InputStream instream = blob.getBinaryStream();
          byte bytes[] = new byte[length];
          // read the blob into a byte array
          length = instream.read(bytes);
          System.out.println("Blob Length: "+blob.length());
          out.write(bytes,0,length);
          rset.close();
          out.flush();
          out.close();
        }
        else
          System.out.println("No data found");
    }
    catch (SQLException  sqlExc)
  {
sqlExc.printStackTrace();
  }
    catch (IOException ioe)
    {
         ioe.printStackTrace();
```

```
    }
      finally
      {
         this.releaseConnection(conn);
      }
  }

  /**
   * Process the HTTP Post request
   */
  public void doPost(HttpServletRequest request,
                     HttpServletResponse response)
          throws ServletException, IOException
  {
      this.doGet(request,response);
  }

  /**
   * Get Servlet information
   * @return java.lang.String
   */
  public String getServletInfo() {
    return "ServeImage Information";
  }

  private Connection getConnection() throws SQLException
  {
      return this.cache.getConnection();
  }

  private void releaseConnection(Connection conn)
  {
      try
      {
         conn.close();
      }catch (SQLException exc) {}
  }

  private PreparedStatement getImageSQL(Connection conn)
          throws SQLException
  {
      return conn.prepareStatement("select PICTURE from "+
                                    "sales_item WHERE id = ?");

  }
}
```

The "core" method of ServeImage is *doGet()*, which implements the fetching of the GIF image from the sales_item table. The image is obtained as a binary input stream and serialized through the standard output stream.

The ServeImage servlet must already be running when the BookJSP application is accessed by online users. In Jakarta/Tomcat, the best way to start the servlet is to set the environment to load ServeImage on startup. Edit the web.xml configuration file, located in the <path-to-tomcat>/conf directory. Add the following lines:

```
<servlet>
    <servlet-name>
        ServeImage
    </servlet-name>
    <servlet-class>
        ServeImage
    </servlet-class>
<init-param>
   configFile=/usr/local/tomcat/bookstore.properties
</init-param>
<load-on-startup>
        -2147483646
</load-on-startup>
</servlet>
<servlet-mapping>
<servlet-name>ServeImage</servlet-name>
<url-pattern>/servlet/ServeImage</url-pattern>
</servlet-mapping>
```

The next time you boot Tomcat, your servlet will be loaded and initialized, ready to serve requests for binary images from the BookJSP application.

SUMMARY

In this chapter, you were introduced to the two most popular technologies for displaying dynamic content to Web browsers: Java Server Pages by Sun Microsystems and Active Server Pages by Microsoft Corporation. You learned the basic syntax elements of the two technologies, and used each of them to develop a simple application. This exercise acquainted you with the JSP and ASP environments, and allowed you to decide which technology best satisfies your needs. At the end of the chapter, you reworked the BookServlet application developed in Chapter 14 to make use of JSPs instead of hard-coding HTML tags into Java methods.

Chapter 16

Using Java in Oracle Application Server

- Evolution of Oracle Application Server
- Oracle Application Server Architecture
- Configuring PL/SQL Applications
- Configuring Java Applications
- Introducing Oracle9i Application Server
- Summary

Oracle Application Server (OAS) is a middle-tier technology that enhances the traditional Web-server approach in a variety of ways to provide access to database data and thereby deliver dynamic content to Web clients. This chapter highlights the use of Oracle Application Server for Internet applications that exploit PL/SQL or Java. Although the main focus of the chapter is on Java in OAS, the use of PL/SQL is also covered. Specifically, the chapter covers:

- A brief history of the evolution of the Oracle Application Server architecture
- A configuration guide on setting up Java execution environments for:
  - PL/SQL applications
  - JServlet/JSP applications
- Installing and running a servlet, and a Java Server Page (JSP)

Oracle Application Server provides an execution environment for distributed application components, such as Enterprise JavaBeans and CORBA objects. Developing Enterprise JavaBeans is covered in Chapters 21 and 22, and CORBA objects are covered in Chapters 23, 24, and 25. Chapter 22 covers the deployment of Enterprise JavaBeans in an Oracle8i database and in the Oracle Application Server.

This chapter provides a brief introduction, together with examples of using the PL/SQL Web Toolkit in a PL/SQL application, and the JWeb Toolkit in a JServlet application. The Web toolkits help you to dynamically generate HTML without embedding the HTML tags in your code.

When the writing of this book began, Oracle Application Server appeared to have a long life ahead of it, but this changed when Oracle Corporation introduced Oracle9i Application Server (9iAS) as a natural successor to Oracle Application Server for building Oracle Internet applications. In consequence, the chapter concludes with a brief discussion of the 9iAS architecture and discusses, on a high level, migrating your code from OAS to 9iAS.

16.1 EVOLUTION OF ORACLE APPLICATION SERVER

Around 1995, when the World Wide Web began to gain acceptance in the business world, Oracle responded to the growing interest by bringing Oracle Web Server 1.0 into the marketplace.

16.1.1 ORACLE WEB SERVER 1.0

Oracle Web Server 1.0 was an HTTP server, called a Web listener, licensed from Spyglass, a third party. The Web listener provided support for the Hypertext Transport (HTTP) and the Common Gateway Interface (CGI) protocols.[1] Figure 16.1 represents the Oracle Web Server 1.0 architecture.

---

[1]The CGI protocol is a programmatic interface for Web servers.

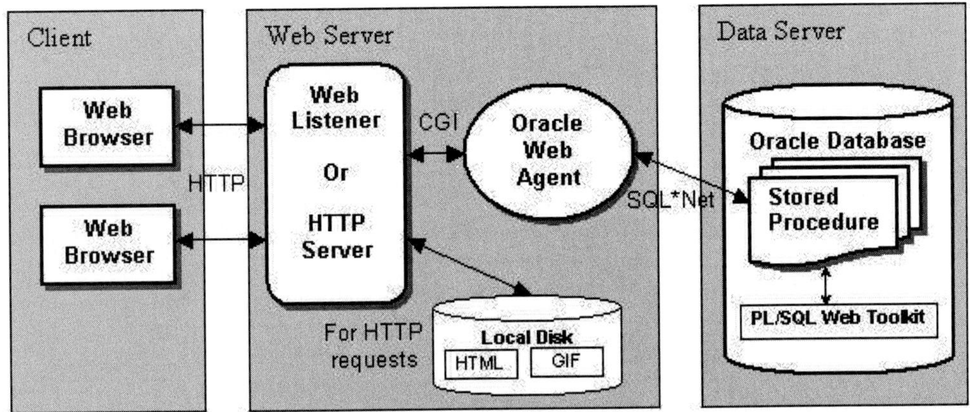

Figure 16.1 Architecture of Oracle Web Server 1.0.

Oracle Web Server 1.0 shipped with a CGI program called the Oracle Web Agent (OWA). The Oracle Web Agent CGI application was invoked by the Web listener to execute stored PL/SQL procedures that generated an HTML response for an HTTP request. The stored PL/SQL procedures used a PL/SQL Web Toolkit to generate an HTML response containing data retrieved from the database,[2] ensuring that the content delivered to the Web browser was dynamic and current.

Creating a CGI application process for each HTTP request represented a major obstacle toward achieving a scalable infrastructure, due to the cost of spawning a process for each request, particularly for large numbers of simultaneous client requests.

16.1.2 ORACLE WEB SERVER 2.0

To address the scalability issues inherent in CGI, Oracle released Web Server 2.x, with a redesigned architecture that provided plug-in services, as depicted in Figure 16.2.

A major design change with Oracle Web Server 2.0 saw the inclusion of a persistent process called the Web Request Broker (WRB). The Web Request Broker provided an application program interface (API) to build plug-in applications, and acted as a switch to direct each HTTP request to a specific plug-in application. The OWA CGI application that executed stored PL/SQL procedures in Oracle Web Server 1.0 was converted into a plug-in called the PL/SQL Agent.

Another significant addition to Oracle Web Server 2.0 was a Java plug-in to execute Java applications for dynamically generating HTML. The Java plug-in, based in JDK 1.1.2, was an integrated Java Virtual Machine (JVM) that effectively had the standard input and output streams rewired to communicate with the Web Request Broker. The Web Request Broker directed HTTP requests to the

---

[2]The PL/SQL Web Toolkit is a collection of stored PL/SQL packages used to produce HTML tags containing database data.

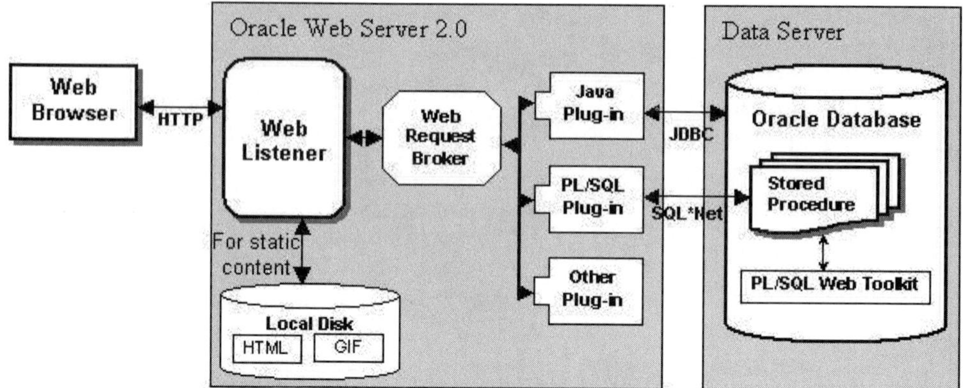

Figure 16.2 Oracle Web Server 2.x architecture.

PL/SQL Agent or Java plug-in, and returned HTTP responses to the client via the Web listener.

The LiveHTML plug-in for Server-Side Includes (SSI) was also provided;[3] and Oracle published the Web Request Broker API to allow anyone to build a plug-in application. All of this made Oracle Web Server 2.0 an extensible environment. A Web Request Broker process was assigned to each Web listener and was already executing before an HTTP request arrived. This eliminated the overhead of starting a new process for each request, as required by the older CGI implementation, thereby providing improved performance when processing requests.

Writing a Java application for Oracle Web Server 2.0 was easy because all you needed to do was to provide a standard public static `main()` method in your Java class, and write generated HTML to standard output using calls to `System.out.println()`.

Notably, the Sun Servlet API was a work-in-progress at the time Oracle Web Server 2.0 was released and had not yet been published. Oracle Web Server 2.0 was Oracle's first step into the Java world. To provide developers with a Java development tool, Oracle licensed Borland's JBuilder technology, and renamed it AppBuilder for Java, which has since evolved to become JDeveloper.

16.1.3 ORACLE WEB APPLICATION SERVER 3.0

In the quest for a more scalable architecture, Oracle Web Application Server (OWAS) 3.0 refined and extended the work started in Web Server 2.x, and laid the foundation for the later generation of the product known as Oracle Application Server (OAS) 4.0. Figure 16.3 depicts the architecture for OWAS 3.0.

The major change in OWAS version 3.0 was the introduction of a CORBA infrastructure through which other components communicated. The CORBA in-

---

[3]Server-Side Includes (SSI) is a standard way to mix static HTML with dynamic content through a basic set of commands. SSI can be thought of as the precursor to Active Server Pages or Java Server Pages.

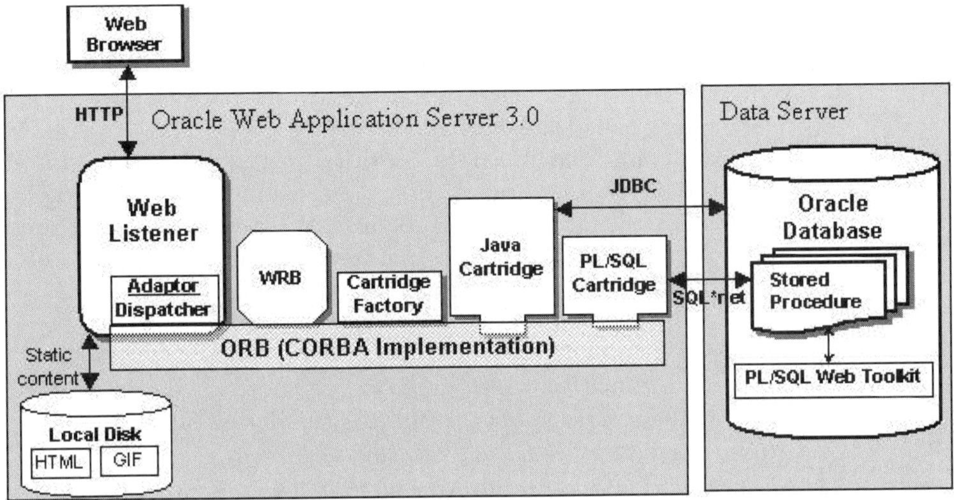

Figure 16.3 Oracle Web Application Server 3.0 architecture.

frastructure allowed OWAS 3.0 processes to be distributed across multiple server nodes and provided load balancing of requests over the nodes. This led to more scalability and provided redundancy when a remote node failed.

The term *node* refers to a single host machine running OAS software. The first OAS node installed is called the primary node, and subsequent ones are called remote nodes. Unlike Web Server 2.x, which started one Web Request Broker for each Web listener in the site, only one Web Request Broker is started for an Oracle Web Application Server 3.0 site, independent of the number of Web listeners running.

The OWAS 3.0 architecture added a cartridge factory process, whose role was to start, stop, and monitor cartridge-based applications, such as the Java cartridge or the PL/SQL cartridge.

The CORBA infrastructure and resulting multi-node architecture provided more scalability at the cost of some administrative complexity. Since administration of a multi-node site was still manual, each node had to be started in a controlled fashion, starting with the primary node. The plug-in services from Oracle Web Server 2.0 came to be known as cartridges. Additional preinstalled cartridges became available, such as Perl, and the Java/CORBA cartridge for Java clients using the Internet InterORB Protocol (IIOP) to connect to CORBA objects. The IIOP protocol allows a client to invoke a method in a remote server facilitating the development of distributed applications based on a CORBA infrastructure. The JVM used to execute the Java cartridge code in Oracle Web Application Server 3.0 was upgraded to support JDK 1.1.4.

OWAS 3.0 also provided a choice of the Web listener from Spyglass (Oracle Web Listener), the Microsoft Internet Information Server (IIS) Web listener, or the Netscape FastTrack or Enterprise Server.

16.1.4 ORACLE APPLICATION SERVER 4.0

Oracle Application Server 4.0 extended the technology again in order to provide even more scalability. The cartridge processes from OWAS 3.0 became a multi-threaded process called a cartridge server, or application, process. A cartridge server process could run multiple cartridge instances (or threads) of the same type; that is, a PL/SQL cartridge server could run multiple PL/SQL cartridges, each cartridge servicing one HTTP request. This was a great improvement over OWAS 3.0, where each cartridge handling an HTTP request was a separate process. Significant changes in the architecture included:

- The node manager now provided administration of a multi-node OAS installation from a single location.
- The JServlet cartridge now supported the Sun Servlet API and replaced the original Java cartridge, the JWeb cartridge.
- Support was added for the Apache Web listener on Unix systems.
- The Java VM was upgraded to support JDK 1.1.6.

The next section takes a closer look at the Oracle Application Server 4.0.x architecture, and the lifecycle of a HTTP request.

16.2 ORACLE APPLICATION SERVER ARCHITECTURE

The Oracle Application Server 4.0 architecture is shown in Figure 16.4

Oracle Application Server 4.0, like its predecessor, can be installed on a single node, or across multiple nodes if you are using the Enterprise Edition. The main components shown in Figure 16.4 are:

- A *Web listener* (HTTP server), typically on port 80, installed as the www listener and used for general HTTP access.[4]
- A Web listener on default port 8889, installed as the `admin` listener, which provides some of the functions performed via Web-based administration.[5]
- A Web listener on default port 8888, called the `node manager`, which is primarily used for Web-based site configuration and management by the administrator.[6] HTTP access via `node manager` and the `admin` listener is

---

[4]The name www is an internal name assigned to the listener for OAS management purposes, and is typically on port 80. The name and port are set at installation time.

[5]The port number listed is the default port, which can be changed at installation time. It is recommended you choose an unused port greater than 1024.

[6]The port number for the node manager can be changed at installation time.

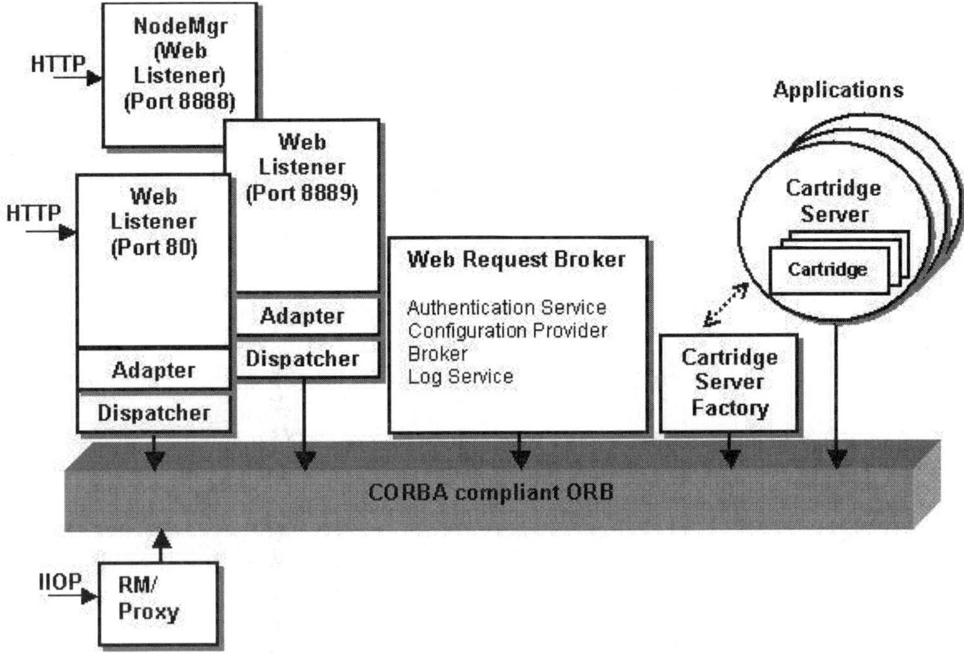

Figure 16.4 Oracle Application Server 4.0 architecture.

password-protected. The username and password, chosen at installation time, is used to authorize access to administration and configuration functions.

- Each Web listener added to an OAS site, except the `node manager`, uses a dispatcher to interact with cartridge-based services through the CORBA infrastructure, via an adapter library. The adaptor/dispatcher design allows the use of the following supported third-party HTTP servers:
  - Oracle Web listener (Spyglass listener), installed by default.
  - Microsoft Internet Information Server (IIS) 4.0 (on the Windows Platform).
  - Netscape FastTrack or Enterprise Server.
  - Apache (Unix only).
- The *Web Request Broker (WRB)* can be thought of as the heart of OAS, and acts as the registry for other components executing in the OAS environment. The WRB also provides the following services:
  - Authentication for protecting cartridge-based applications.
  - A configuration provider for managing WRB application and cartridge configuration.
  - Logging services to record a log of HTTP activity.

    - A broker service to register and monitor OAS components, and to direct requests from clients to an appropriate cartridge server in the OAS configuration.
- The *Cartridge Server Factory* is called by the WRB to create or delete cartridge server processes on demand.
- A *Cartridge Server,* called an Application Server, loads a cartridge to handle a client request. OAS can start one or more cartridge servers, which are implemented as operating system processes, represented as circles in Figure 16.4. The cartridge server process is a multithreaded application that can execute one or more cartridge instances. Each cartridge instance in a cartridge server can handle a single client request.
- A *cartridge* that plugs into a cartridge server, implemented as a dynamic link library (or shared library on UNIX) conforming to the OAS WRB API model. A cartridge executes application-specific code written in a particular programming language, such as PL/SQL, Java, or Perl.
- The CORBA server infrastructure is used by all OAS components except the `node manager`. The CORBA layer also provides services to IIOP-based clients. The Resource Manager/Proxy (RM/Proxy) receives connection requests from IIOP-based clients, and directs them to the Web Request Broker to start a CORBA-based application service, such as the Enterprise JavaBean (EJB) or Enterprise CORBA Objects for Java (ECO/Java) services provided by OAS. EJB and ECO/Java services are used for building distributed applications.

16.2.1 BASIC FLOW OF AN HTTP REQUEST

Before looking at how OAS handles a request, it would be helpful to understand the flow of an HTTP request through a Web Server, as depicted in Figure 16.5.

The HTTP protocol is called a stateless request-response protocol. The protocol is stateless because the Web server does not track client state between requests, and releases the connection to the client after the response is returned to the client. The flow involves the following steps:

- A client, typically a browser, sends an HTTP request to the Web server.
- The Web/HTTP listener translates the request into a target file by performing a lookup via a directory map. The directory map is used to translate the URL `path` in the HTTP request into a target, which may be a file, a script, or an application located in a directory on the server.
- If the target is a file, it is read by the Web listener and returned as the response to the client. If the target is a script or an application, it is executed using CGI principles. CGI applications write their data to standard output, which is redirected by the Web listener as the response to the client. If the target does not exist, the Web listener returns an error response to the client.
- The Web server sends the response containing the static or generated content to the client.

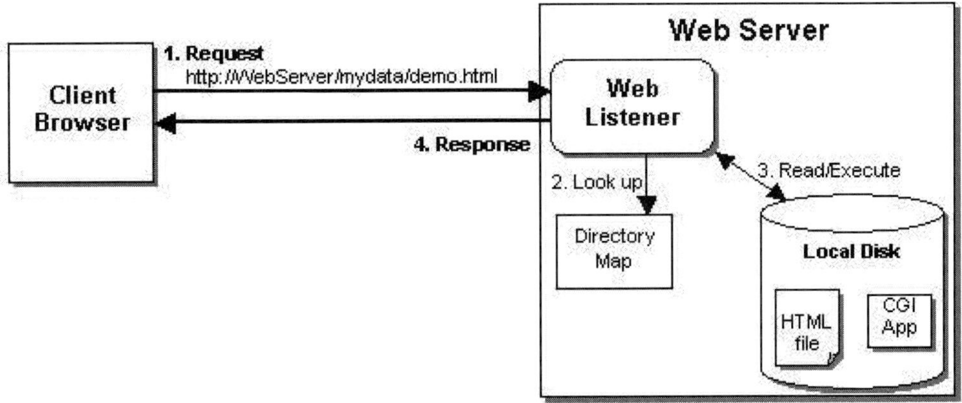

Figure 16.5 Basic flow of HTTP request through a Web server.

16.2.1.1 The HTTP Request. An HTTP request is made up of the following elements:[7]

- A *request line* identifying a method and a resource.
- An optional *request header* followed by a new line.[8]
- Two new line separators before the message body; for example:
  ```
  header<newline>
  <newline>
  body
  ```
- An optional m*essage body* containing posted data from a form.

A request line contains the method (or command) name, followed by a Uniform Resource Locator (URL), an HTTP version, and a carriage-return line feed sequence. For example:

```
GET http://WebServer/mydata/demo.html HTTP/1.1
```

Note: when using the `GET` method there is no request header and no message body. Method names, such as `GET` or `POST`, are the two commands most frequently used by a Web server.

- `GET` requests information specified by the URL. The response may be static or dynamically generated.

[7]Full details of the HTTP protocol can be found at http://www.w3c.org, which contains additional links and references to related Request For Comment (RFC) documents, such as MIME-type information.

[8]A new line is a combination of a U.S. ASCII carriage return and a linefeed character sequence.

- POST submits data from a form, and allows a larger quantity of data to be submitted to the server than is possible using the GET method. The response may be static or dynamically generated.

A fully formatted URL that uses the GET method is:

```
http://host:port/path?query
```

Where:

- http:// specifies the protocol.
- host is the domain name or IP address of the Web server.
- :port is the port number of the Web server. This is optional; if it is omitted, the default is port 80.
- path is a path relative to a server root directory. This is optional; if it is omitted, the Web server locates a default file typically named index.html. The last name in the path (e.g., demo.html) represents the target name.
- ?query is an optional parameter or query string data.

Using the GET method you can provide a query string made up of name=value pairs separated by an ampersand. For example:

```
http://WebServer/mycode/getprice?prodid=100&store=10
```

A Web browser uses the query string to send data to the Web-server application, which can read the name=value pairs and process them. This is one way the Web client submits information for query purposes or storage in a server environment. Since the query string is appended to the URL request, the amount of data that can be sent to the Web server is limited.

Another way the browser can send data to the Web server is to use the POST method, where the name=value pairs are sent to the Web server as part of the message body. Since the POST method sends the name=value pairs in the message body and not at the end of the URL, the query string is not visible in the URL in the browser window, and you send much more data to the Web server than is possible using the GET method.

16.2.1.2 The HTTP Response. An HTTP response is made up of the following parts:

- A *status line* containing a three-digit status code and a reason text message. The status line is not normally visible to the client application or browser. A status code of 1xx is an informational message in which xx are the other two digits of the status code, a code of 2xx is a success, and codes of 4xx and 5xx represent a client or server error, respectively.

- An optional *response header* that typically includes the format of the response body (actually, its content type, specified as a MIME type[9]) and the length of the information returned in the response body. The response header is terminated with a new line.
- An additional new line is required after the header new line, forming a blank line between the header and the body.
- The response body containing the information content in the specified MIME format.

Here is an example of a response returning an HTML file:

```
200 OK
Content-Type: text/html
Content-Length: 88

<HTML>
<HEAD><TITLE>Demo Page</TITLE></HEAD>
<BODY>
<H1>Demo</H1>
</BODY>
</HTML>
```

Notes on the example:

- `200 OK` is the success status line.
- The `Content-type:` is the part of the response header that indicates the format of the content—in this case a MIME type of `text/html`. A MIME type is made up of two parts, separated by a slash:
  - A type (e.g., `text`)
  - A subtype (e.g., `html`)

  The combination of the type and subtype is interpreted by the Web browser, which can either handle the context itself or launch a helper (or plug-in) application to display or act on the content.
- The `Content-Length` is the part of the response header that indicates the byte length of the content.
- A blank line follows the response header data.
- The rest of the example is the HTML content.

---

[9]MIME is an acronym for Multipurpose Internet Mail Extensions, which is used to describe the format of multimedia data transferred between client and server.

16.2.2 FLOW OF AN HTTP REQUEST IN OAS

The flow of an HTTP request, depicted in Figure 16.6, represents a client request for a cartridge-based service. The Web listener typically handles requests for all static content and Common Gateway Interface (CGI) applications via the directory map configuration file. Normally, an error response is generated if the Web server cannot translate a URL to a target. However, when using OAS, the Web listener passes unresolved URLs to the Web Request Broker for resolution before an error response is generated.

The numbered lines in Figure 16.6 represent the flow of an HTTP request. In sequence these are:

1. The HTTP client sends a URL request to the Web listener.
2. The Web listener attempts to resolve the request to a target. Because the request is for a cartridge-based service, the Web listener does not recognize the URL request, and so forwards part of the URL, known as the Uniform Resource Indicator (URI),[10] to the WRB to locate the service, if it is configured. The WRB also determines whether authentication is required. If authentication is required, the Web server sends a response requiring the client to enter a username and password that must returned to the server for valid authentication before the request can continue.
3. After authentication, the WRB translates the base of the URI, excluding the target name, into a suitable cartridge server type. If a cartridge server is not already executing, the WRB sends a request to the cartridge server factory to create a new cartridge server process to handle the request.
4. The cartridge server factory starts an application instance (an application is a process called a cartridge server).

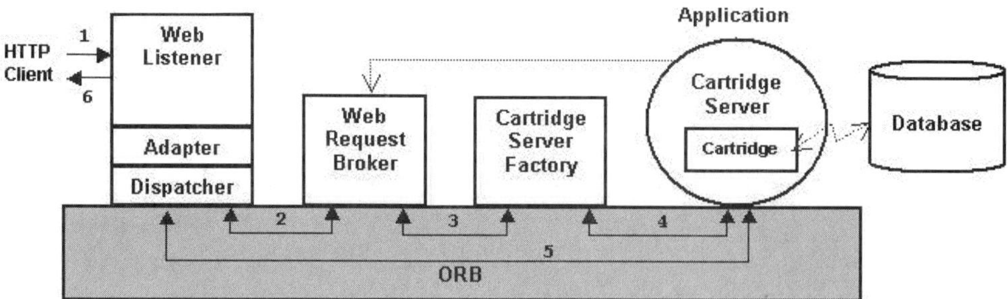

Figure 16.6 Flow of an HTTP request for an OAS cartridge.

---

[10]If the URL is `http://www.oas1.demo.com:2000/servlet/examples/DemoServlet`, the URI component is `/servlet/examples/DemoServlet`.

5. The cartridge server loads a cartridge to process the request. The code executed by the cartridge is written by the developer, and may optionally connect to an Oracle database, as depicted in Figure 16.6. The cartridge server then interacts directly with Web listener via its dispatcher to direct the response created by the cartridge code to the client.
6. The Web listener forwards the HTTP response to the client.

One of the HTTP-based cartridges provided with OAS is the PL/SQL cartridge, which executes PL/SQL procedures in the database. The PL/SQL cartridge requires a database access descriptor (DAD) to identify the database that contains the stored procedures to be executed (see subsection 16.3.2 for more information about DADs).

The JServlet cartridge is used to execute Java servlets or JavaServer pages. Java applications use JDBC to connect to the database.

Other HTTP-based cartridges include the Perl Cartridge for executing Perl applications, and the LiveHTML cartridge for support of Server-Side Includes (SSI) functionality.

16.2.3 FLOW OF AN IIOP REQUEST IN OAS

An IIOP CORBA or EJB client can make a connection request on the IIOP port to the Resource Manager/Proxy (RM/Proxy) agent in the OAS configuration. The RM/proxy provides an object lookup service for the IIOP client to locate the cartridge service. The flow of the request is shown in Figure 16.7.

The flow of an IIOP session after the client connects to the IIOP server is shown below.

1. The IIOP client requests a lookup for a registered object via the RM/Proxy.
2. The RM/Proxy acts as an agent for the client to locate and/or start up an object instance and return the IOR for the object. The RM/Proxy checks its registry for an available object instance. If one is present, the RM/Proxy will

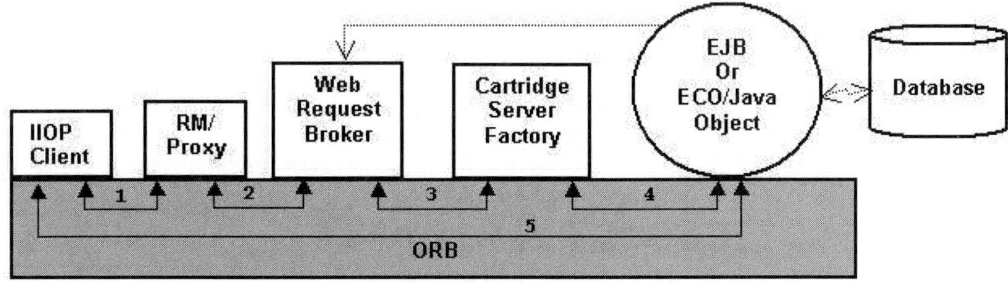

Figure 16.7 Lifecycle of an IIOP request for a cartridge service.

return the object instance's IOR to the client. The client will directly interact with the object instance (step 5).

3. If the RM/Proxy does not have a registered object instance, it passes the request to the WRB, which in turn asks the cartridge factory for a new object instance.
4. The cartridge server factory sends a request to the EJB container or to a Java component deployed as CORBA object (the ECO/Java service) to instantiate an object instance.
5. The object instance's IOR is registered with the WRB, which is sent to the RM/Proxy, which then forwards it to the IIOP client. The IIOP client and the object instance directly communicate via the IOR. The object instance may also interact with a database.

Object-based services using the IIOP protocol can be stateful, unlike HTTP requests, which are stateless. A stateful connection is maintained between the client and the server object as long as required. By contrast, an HTTP request is completed when the response has been delivered to the client.

The preceding discussion provides the foundation for understanding the OAS architecture. Now you can delve into examples of configuring cartridge-based services, and of sample code that executes PL/SQL and Java code for client requests.

16.2.4 UNDERSTANDING AN OAS CONFIGURATION

The directory structure and standard installation settings for an OAS installation are described in this section. They will then be used as a basis for subsequent examples that show how to configure P/SQL-based or Java-based services.

OAS installation manuals provide comprehensive documentation on the installation options. The examples in this book assume that OAS has been installed on a single node. You are strongly advised to consult the OAS installation guide and release notes prior to installation, to ensure that you are adequately informed about platform-specific details. OAS should be installed on a separate physical server; if installed on a host that is also executing other Oracle database software, it should be installed in a separate `ORACLE_HOME`.[11]

16.2.4.1 Default OAS Listener Port Configuration. By default, OAS has three Web listeners, each configured on its own port.

1. Default www listener on port 80, or a port of your choice, such as port 8080.
2. The `node` manager on port 8888, password-protected by a username and password choice at installation time.

[11]`ORACLE_HOME` here refers to the directory tree used to install the Oracle software.

3. The `admin` listener on port 8889, password-protected by the same username and password used for the node manager.

The ORB/IIOP services are configured on a port called the boot port, which by default is port 2649. A multicast IP address and port are selected at installation time for a multinode site.

You can display the configuration details using the `oasnetconfig` OAS command-line utility with the "lowercase L" option:

```
oasnetconfig -l
```

The option causes a `oasnetconfig` to list some of the configuration information held in WRB configuration files. You can use the `oasnetconfig` utility to change the IIOP port or the host and domain names stored in OAS configuration files. This may be required if you change your server host or domain name, since an OAS installation is tightly coupled with its host and domain name.

To list the status information of a Web listener, use the `owsctl` command-line utility. For example:

```
owsctl status -l www
```

This command displays the status, port number, and process id (if running) of a Web listener called www.

16.2.4.2 OAS Configuration Directories and Files This section describes the location of key OAS configuration files in the directory relative to your `ORACLE_HOME` for the installed OAS software.

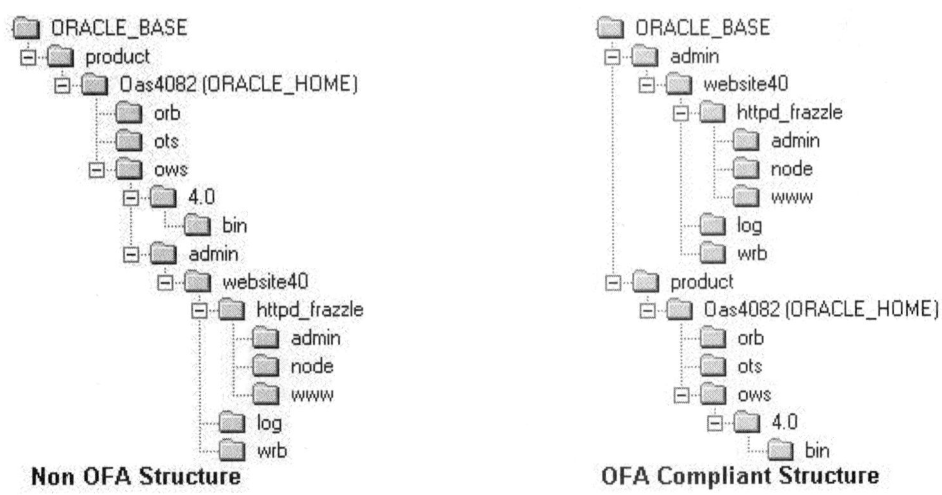

FIGURE 16.8 Directory tree diagram.

In the directory tree diagram shown in Figure 16.8, ORACLE_BASE is a representation of some of the directories forming part of the installed OAS software base. The ORACLE_HOME directory is shown in parentheses after the Oas4082 directory, indicating that it is the ORACLE_HOME directory for this example. The figure shows two directory structures that can be created, depending on your installation requirements:

- The Optimal Flexible Architecture (OFA) compliant structure (only valid for the Unix platform). The OFA structure is a prescribed way to set up the operating system, disk mount points, and directory structures for your Oracle database files and software. The OFA design addresses several installation issues. Here are the key points:
  - It provides an easily administered file system.
  - It distributes the I/O across disks.
  - It isolates the impact of disk failure.
- The ORACLE_BASE environment variable must be defined for an OFA compliant installation. The result is a different disk and directory structure for the Oracle software.
- The non-OFA compliant directory structure (valid for Unix and Windows NT). *Note:* The ORACLE_BASE environment variable should not be defined for a non-OFA compliant installation.

Environment Variables

The following environment variables are used to define parts of the tree structure:

- ORACLE_HOME is the Oracle home directory for the installed OAS software.
- ORAWEB_HOME is the home directory for the OAS binaries. It is always set to ORACLE_HOME/ows/4.0
- ORAWEB_ADMIN is the administration home for OAS configuration. It is set to ORACLE_HOME/ows/4.0/admin for a non-OFA installation, but to ORACLE_BASE/admin for an OFA compatible installation.
- ORAWEB_SITE defines the name of the installed OAS Web site, that is, website40 (by default). It allows you to identify other OAS Web sites installed on the same server but each in a different ORACLE_HOME.

HTTP Listener Configuration Files

The HTTP listener configuration files are located under the http_<hostname> directory, where <hostname> is the host name for the OAS server. The http_<hostname> directory has a file called owl.cfg[12] that lists all the registered HTTP listeners and the TCP/IP port numbers.

---

[12]The acronym *owl* stands for Oracle Web Listener.

Each HTTP listener has its own subdirectory (e.g., `node` for the node manager shown in the configuration directory tree). The listener directory contains two files:

- The `sv<listener>.cfg` file contains the Web listener configuration data (e.g., `svnode.cfg`).
- The `sv<listener>.err` file tracks listener errors.

Application Configuration Files

The applications and cartridge-based configuration files are located in the `ORAWEB_ADMIN/website40/wrb` directory, which includes the files listed below.

- `site.app` contains a list of applications, cartridges, and their configuration commands.
- `wrb.app` contains the configuration parameters for each OAS application and cartridge. This file is kept in synchronization with the `site.app` file.
- `.omnaddr` contains the OAS ORB boot port. (*Note:* This is a hidden file in the Unix environment.)

These files are modified by actions performed using the OAS tree management applet. They are text files and are readable, but you should avoid manually editing them, because of the danger of corrupting the OAS configuration. As you change the configuration, backup copies of the `site.app` and `wrb.app` files are kept.

The `ORACLE_HOME/orb` directory also contains the file called `resources.ora` that is used for the OAS ORB configuration.

16.2.4.3 Starting and Stopping OAS from the Command Line. You can use the `owsctl` command-line utility to start and stop your whole OAS site or components within the site. To start OAS, enter:

```
owsctl start
```

To stop OAS, enter:

```
owsctl stop
```

Note that the node manager listener is not started or stopped with the above two examples. The node manager must be started if you want to perform configuration and management tasks from the Web management interface. To start the node manager, manually type:

```
owsctl start -nodemgr
```

To stop the node manager, enter:

```
owsctl stop -nodemgr
```

16.2.4.4 Using the OAS Web Management Interface. Managing OAS with the Web management interface allows you to connect to the node manager URL from a Web browser. For example, assuming that the host name is `frazzle` and the node manager listener port is 8888, enter the following URL in your browser address line:

```
http://frazzle:8888
```

The browser will display a dialog box prompting you for the username and password chosen when OAS was installed. An example is shown in Figure 16.9.

After logging in as the administrator, the OAS welcome page is displayed, as shown in Figure 16.10. To manage the OAS configuration, click on the OAS Manager link.

After clicking the `OAS Manager` link, the OAS management tree applet is loaded into the browser window. Figure 16.11 shows the OAS management tree applet with its top-level nodes expanded.

The management tree applet provides most of the functions needed to manage most of the OAS configuration data. Clicking the tree applet folder or page icons causes HTTP requests to be sent to the node manager Web listener to execute CGI-based applications that populate the right-hand frame in the browser window with configuration forms and information.

The row of image icons above the right-hand pane provides actions that can be performed in the context of the configuration screen displayed. For example, in Figure 16.11, if you select a radio button in the right-hand window and then click the start icon ( ), you can start the entire OAS Web site or a node in the

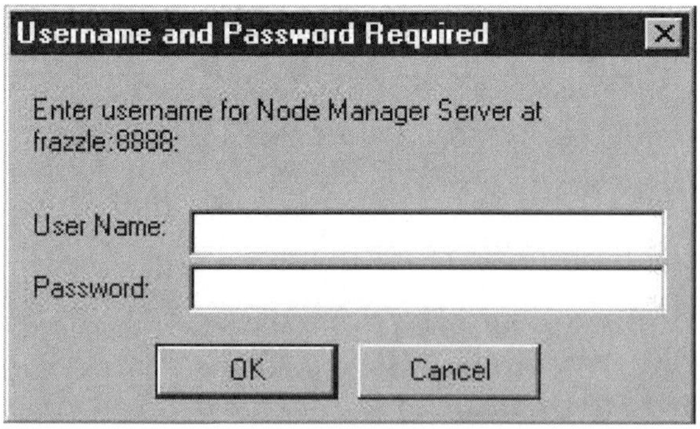

FIGURE 16.9 OAS dialog box after installation.

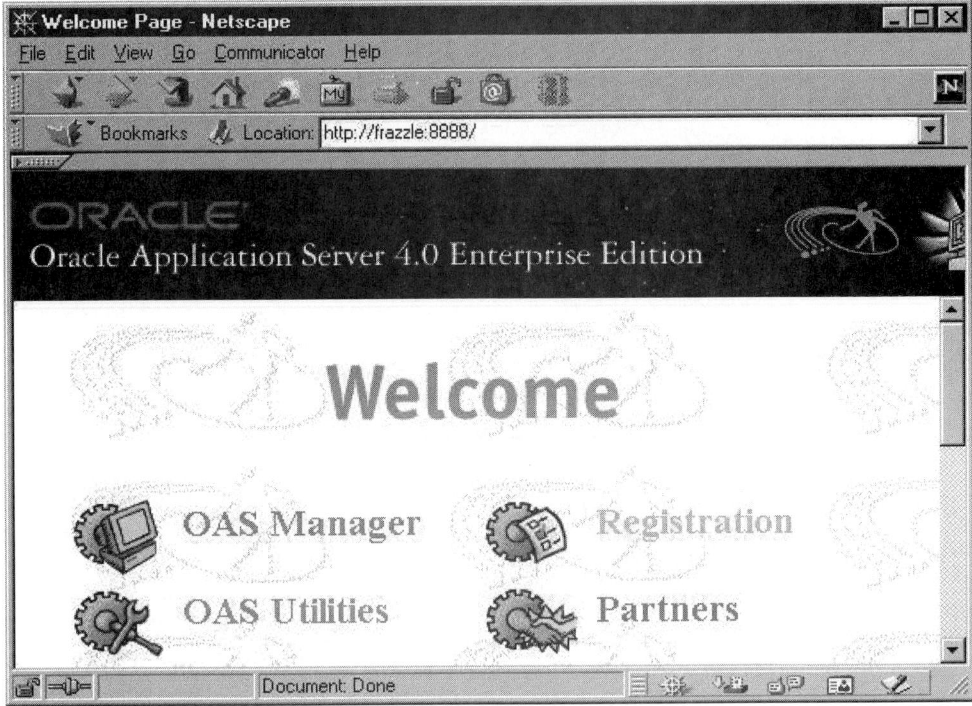

FIGURE 16.10 OAS administration welcome page.

OAS configuration. If you click the stop icon (■), you can shut down the entire OAS Web site.

By default, the tree applet is not expanded as shown in Figure 16.11. The major configuration sections shown in the expanded tree applet are listed below.

- `Oracle Application Server` contains nodes used to configure logging, security, database access descriptors, ORB configuration, failure recovery, and the OAS transaction service.
- `HTTP listeners` contains nodes for managing the Web listener configuration.
- `Applications` configures cartridge-based application services (e.g., to define and configure PL/SQL, Java servlet, JavaServer page application services). An *application* stores the configuration data for a cartridge server process and cartridge instance threads created within the cartridge server process. Several default application services, like the `JservletApp` for executing Java servlets, are pre-created by the OAS installation process. You can add, delete, or rename these services according to your requirements.

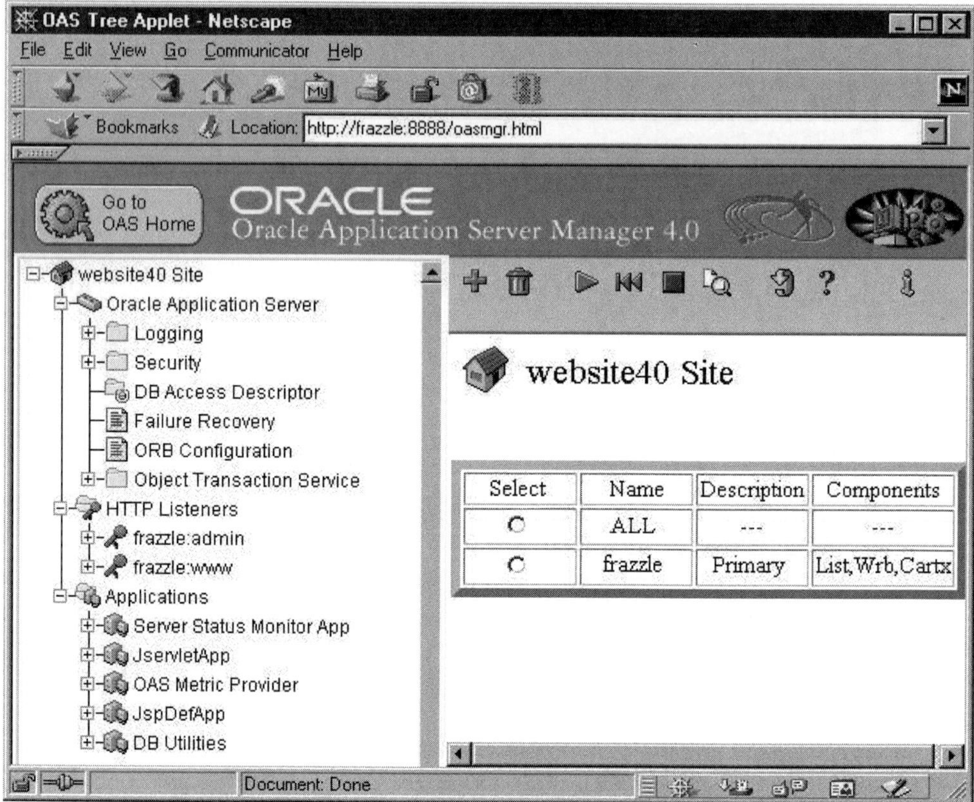

FIGURE 16.11 OAS management tree applet.

Note: You cannot manage the configuration of the OAS node manager via the Web interface.

Here are the key principles to understand when you use the Web management interface:

- Clicking on a node in the tree applet tells the applet to read configuration data and display it in the right-hand frame of the Web page.
- Modifying configuration data in the browser and applying the change modifies the OAS configuration files. OAS processes that are executing do not dynamically recognize changes made to the configuration files. Therefore, depending on the change made, you may have to stop some or all OAS components to apply the changes.

This explains why it is important to avoid clicking the browser back button when using the Web management interface, since you may be seeing configuration data cached by the Web browser that does not reflect the information written to the configuration files. The OAS tree applet and generated HTML forms provide ample links to navigate reliably from one management page to another, without having to resort to clicking the browser back button.

If you integrate a supported third-party Web listener into your OAS Web site, then you manage the configuration of that listener through its own management mechanism, and not through the OAS tree applet.

Subsequent sections of this chapter will guide you through the management tasks needed to configure OAS application services. There is minimal discussion of managing the Web listener configuration.

If you are not performing management tasks, you can shut down the node manager listener as a security precaution when it is not required. This will discourage others from hacking into your OAS administration management interface.

16.3 CONFIGURING PL/SQL APPLICATIONS

The most commonly used OAS application service is the PL/SQL cartridge, which allows you to execute server-side PL/SQL code that dynamically generates HTML data. Before you can use the PL/SQL cartridge services, you must perform the following configuration tasks:

- Install the PL/SQL Toolkit into the database that will be executing the PL/SQL procedures.
- Create one or more Database Access Descriptors (DADs) to configure an access path for the PL/SQL cartridge to locate and execute the stored procedures.[13]
- Create a PL/SQL Application containing a PL/SQL cartridge that uses the DAD to connect to a database.

In order for a new DAD to become available, you must shut down the entire OAS site and restart the OAS services. Installing the PL/SQL Toolkit does not require OAS to be restarted.

16.3.1 INSTALLING THE PL/SQL TOOLKIT

To install the PL/SQL Toolkit, you must know a username and password combination for a database user with DBA privileges. Installing the PL/SQL Toolkit creates two database schemas:

- The `OAS_PUBLIC` schema, which contains several PL/SQL packages that make up the PL/SQL Toolkit functionality used to generate HTML dynamically from a PL/SQL-stored procedure.

---

[13]See subsection 16.3.2 for more information about DADs.

- The `WEBSYS` schema, which contains database tables used for content-management services. The content-management service is accessible to PL/SQL cartridge application, which can use the `WEBSYS` tables as a document repository. A user can upload files into the database, and later download them when required, if enabled via PL/SQL cartridge applications.

The Oracle interMedia service provides much better content-management functionality than the WEBSYS schema, and is more accessible to Java applications via the Java API libraries provided with the Oracle interMedia product. A description of Oracle interMedia functionality is outside the scope of this book.

As the OAS administrator, you can install the PL/SQL Toolkit by clicking on the `OAS Utilities` link on the OAS welcome Web page (see Figure 16.9). In the Utilities Web page:

- Expand the tree applet to show the `Install` folder.
- Expand the Install folder and click on the `PL/SQL Toolkit` node.

The result after the preceding steps have been done is shown in Figure 16.12.

To install the PL/SQL Toolkit, enter the following information in the form in the browser's right-hand frame:

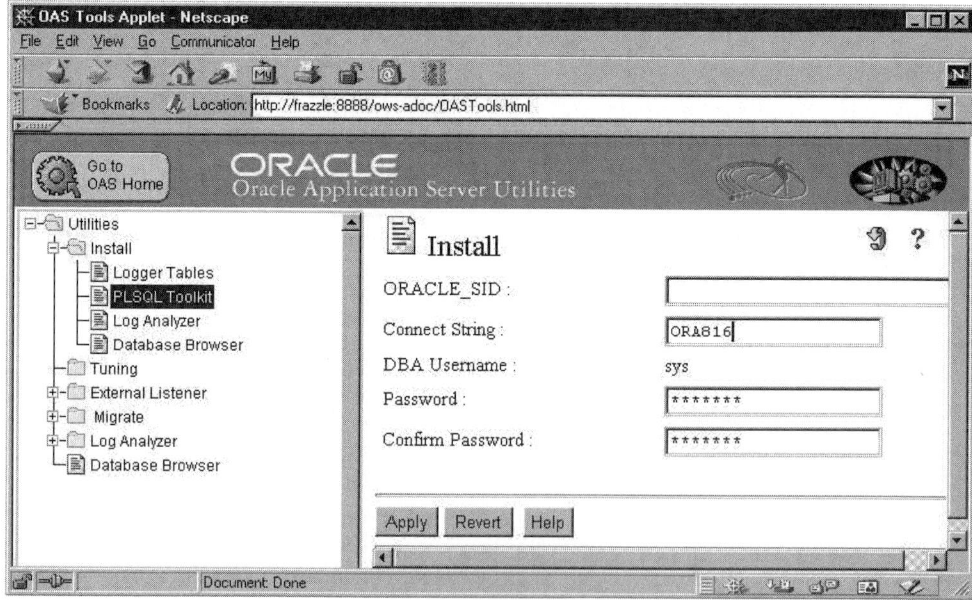

FIGURE 16.12 OAS utilities page for installing the PL/SQL toolkit.

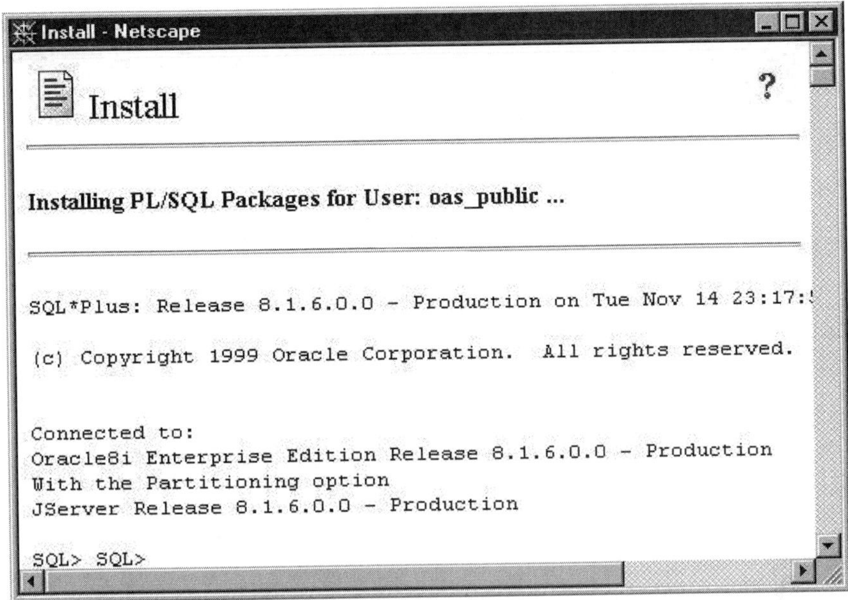

FIGURE 16.13 OAS PL/SQL toolkit installation log window.

- Enter either the ORACLE_SID for a local database, or the `Connect String` using an Oracle TNS name to identify a remote database.
- Enter the password for the `SYS` user of the database instance that will host the PL/SQL Toolkit.

Do not forget to click the `Apply` button. Most of the time, OAS will be installed on a separate node, or in a different `ORACLE_HOME`, from the database, so the `ORACLE_SID` text box will never be filled.

After you click on the `Apply` button, a new browser window pops up to display the execution log of the PL/SQL Toolkit installation script, as shown in Figure 16.13. This window should be closed, using the `Ok` button that appears after all the log text in the window. The `Ok` button is not visible in Figure 16.13.

16.3.1.1 The PL/SQL Toolkit Packages. Once installed, the PL/SQL Toolkit consists of several PL/SQL packages. The main PL/SQL Toolkit packages and a brief description of their functionality are listed in Table 16.1.

The `HTP`, `HTF` and `OWA_UTIL` packages are the most frequently used packages and provide most of the based HTML functionality you require. The `OWA_COOKIE` package is useful for maintaining client state via HTTP cookies. Subsection 16.3.4 shows some simple examples of using PL/SQL Toolkit packages.

TABLE 16.1 PL/SQL Web Toolkit packages

PACKAGE NAME	FUNCTIONALITY PROVIDED
HTP	Package of procedures used to generate most of the HTML tags. The output from these procedures is written to an internal system buffer whose contents are eventually sent to the client's browser. For example, the procedure `htp.htmlOpen;` generates the `<HTML>` tag, and `htp.htmlClose;` generates the `</HTML>` tag.
HTF	Package of PL/SQL functions for generating HTML returned as strings into your PL/SQL application. These strings will eventually be output to the browser by calling HTP procedures. For example, the function `htf.bold('hello world')` returns the string `<B>hello world</B>`.
OWA_UTIL	Package containing several utilities. For example, procedures that generate HTML page signatures, or HTML tables populated with SQL query data, and management of HTTP header contents.
OWA_COOKIE	For sending cookies and reading them in the HTTP headers exchanged by the Web server and the Web browser.
OWA_CONTENT	Provides access to the content-management services and table installed with the `WEBSYS` user.
OWA_IMAGE	Provides functions to programmatically handle HTTP requests from image maps and image buttons in HTML forms.
OWA_OPT_LOCK	Contains features to implement an optimistic locking scheme in your stored procedure for data concurrency management. For example, you should check whether a database row about to be updated has not already been changed by another user since you last retrieved the information.
OWA_SEC	Provides functionality to implement custom authentication schemes in your PL/SQL applications, instead of using the authentication schemes provided by OAS.
OWA_PATTERN	Provides functionality to implement pattern matching on string variables using regular expressions.
OWA_TEXT	Contains subprograms for manipulating text strings and large quantities of textual data.

16.3.2 CONFIGURING DATABASE ACCESS DESCRIPTORS

A PL/SQL cartridge cannot function without a database access descriptor. The DAD is required by the PL/SQL cartridge to identify a database that executes the PL/SQL code. The database used to execute PL/SQL code for an OAS PL/SQL cartridge must have access to the PL/SQL Toolkit packages.

You create a DAD by first clicking on the `DB Access Descriptor` tree node in the OAS tree applet, and then clicking on the add icon () in the `DB Access Descriptor` page shown in Figure 16.14.

Clicking the add icon displays the Web form window shown in Figure 16.15.

The database access descriptor can be used for two purposes:

1. Transparent database login to the schema specified in the Database User field. For transparent login to the specified schema, the "`Store username`

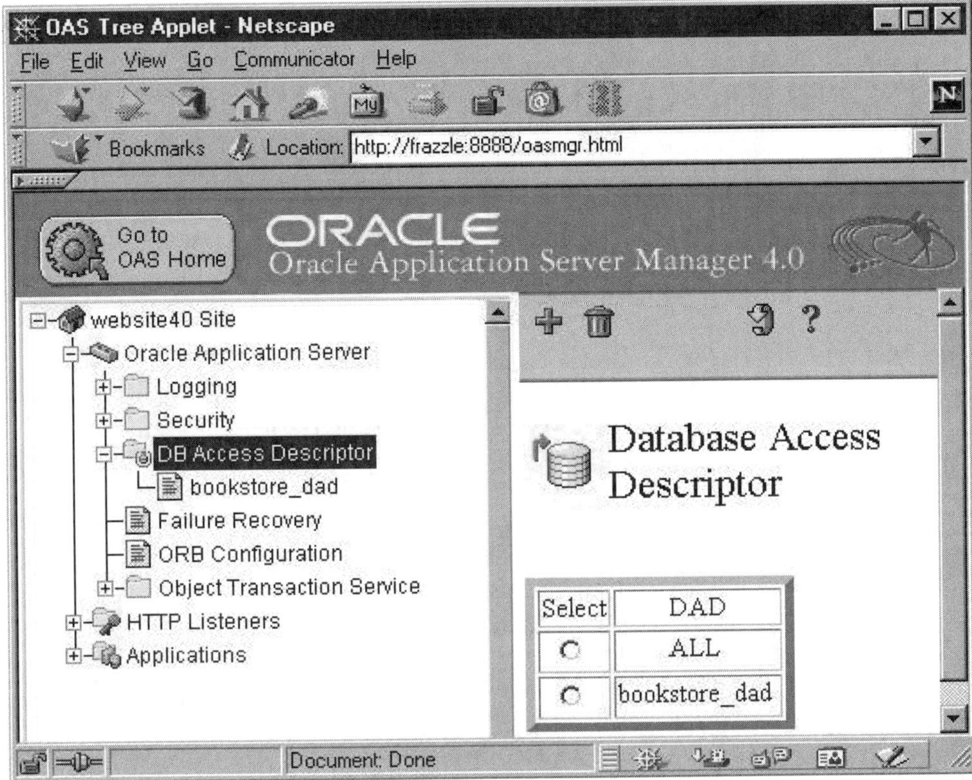

FIGURE 16.14 Adding a database access descriptor.

`and password in the DAD`" checkbox must be checked. In that case, the user calling the procedure is not prompted for a username and password.

2. Invoking the OAS database authentication scheme called Basic Oracle authentication. Invoking Basic Oracle authentication means that you wish to prompt the browser user for a valid database username and password the first time the user executes a PL/SQL application from the browser session. In this case, *uncheck* the checkbox labeled "`Store username and password in the DAD.`" Storing the username and password in the DAD means that the username and password are saved in the `wrb.app` configuration file. The database name specified in the DAD is used for authenticating the username and password supplied by the user. If an invalid username and password combination is entered, access to executing a stored procedure is denied. If the login is successful, the client must close all browser windows to perform an effective logout operation, because the Web browser caches authentication data for subsequent HTTP requests in the same session.

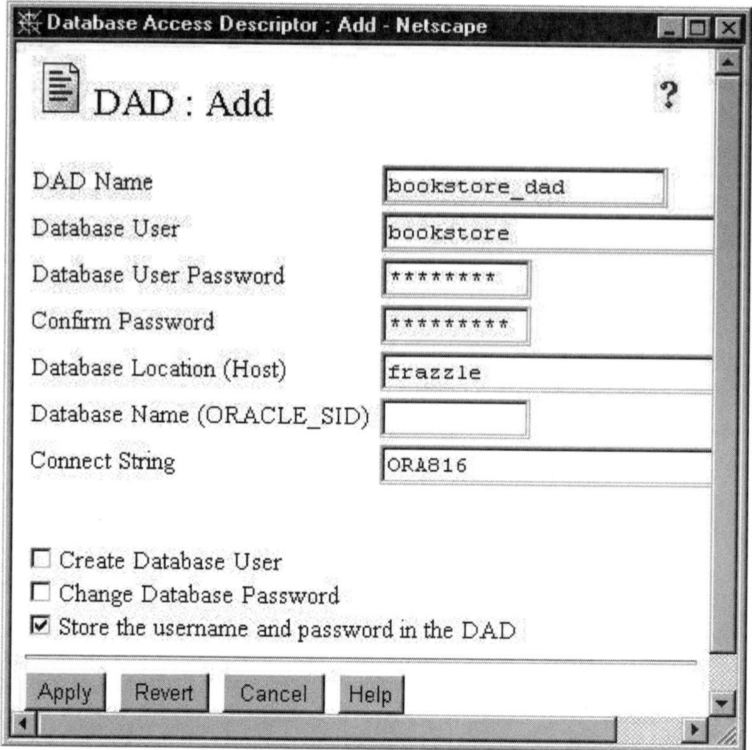

FIGURE 16.15 Database access descriptor configuration.

A DAD can also be used to protect access to other cartridge-based services, such as JServlet cartridge applications. If you use a DAD to protect access to other OAS applications, the username and password should not be stored in the DAD (i.e., in the `wrp.app` configuration file). The password is stored in an encrypted form in the `wrb.app` text file.

16.3.3 CREATING A PL/SQL APPLICATION AND CARTRIDGE SERVICE

To create a PL/SQL application containing a cartridge, select the application node in the OAS manager tree applet, and click the add icon in the right-hand pane toolbar. The application information is entered using the dialog windows in Figures 16.16 and 16.17.

After selecting the PL/SQL application type, click OK; you are required to enter application configuration data, as shown in Figure 16.15.

The `Application Name` should be entered as a single word. It can include underscore characters, but must not contain spaces or special characters, such as white space or punctuation, because the application name forms part of the URL used by the browser to access PL/SQL procedures from a HTTP request.

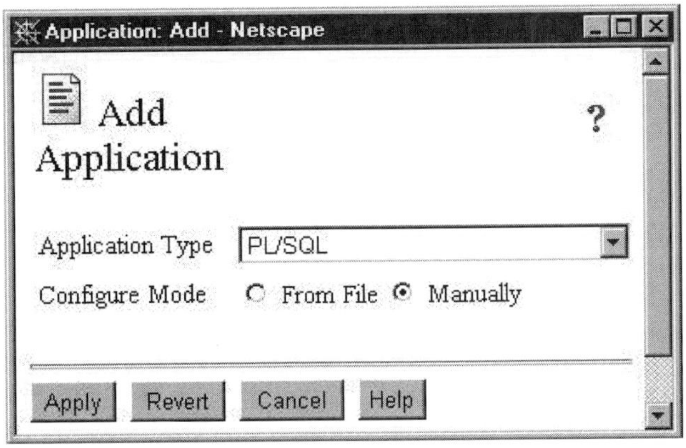

FIGURE 16.16 Creating a PL/SQL application.

The `Display Name` is descriptive text displayed next to the application node in the OAS management applet tree. It is a good idea to put the application type name, e.g. [PL/SQL], in the display name as an easy way to visually identify the application type.

The `Application Version` field is only used as documentation for the administrator to assign any meaning desired.

Once you apply these changes, the application is created. You can immediately add a cartridge to the application to complete the process of configuring OAS to execute PL/SQL code. This is done by clicking the "`Add Cartridge to this Application`" button in the success dialog displayed after adding the application, as shown in Figure 16.18.

You must create at least one cartridge in an application to execute PL/SQL procedures. The cartridge can be added at a later stage if you do not add it imme-

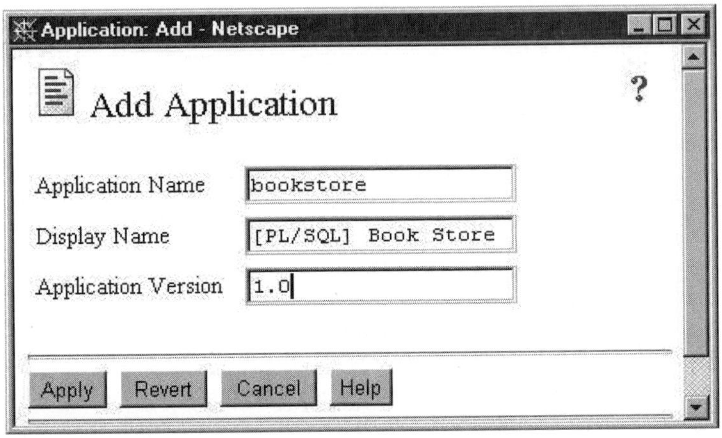

FIGURE 16.17 Naming the PL/SQL application.

FIGURE 16.18 Success dialog after adding the application.

diately when the application is created. An application can contain many cartridges of the same type, with each cartridge able to invoke PL/SQL code from schemas in the same or different databases. Figure 16.19 shows the dialog used to add and configure a PL/SQL cartridge.

The `Cartridge Name` is appended to the application name to form the URL used to access the PL/SQL code via this cartridge, and should be a valid

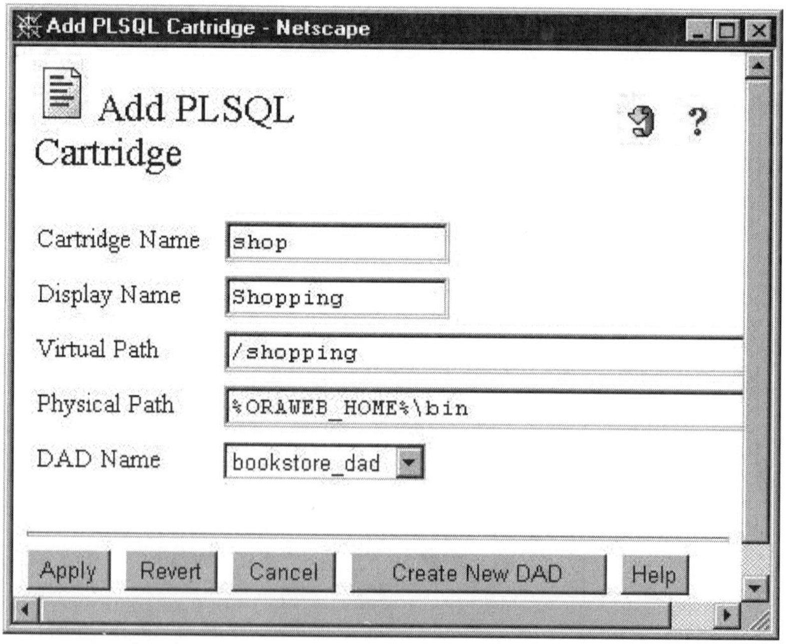

FIGURE 16.19 Adding a PL/SQL cartridge to an application.

name for use in a URL request. The display name is descriptive text used by the OAS management tree applet.

You are required to enter a `Virtual Path`, which can be the same as the application name and cartridge name (e.g., `/bookstore/shop`). Alternatively, it can be an entirely different path (e.g., `/shopping`), as shown in Figure 16.19. These virtual paths are used by the Web Request Broker to map and direct a client URL requests to a PL/SQL application cartridge instance to service the request.

The names used for these virtual paths must not appear in the directory map configuration of your Web listener. If they do, the Web listener will handle the URL request and not pass it on to the Web Request Broker as well as to an OAS application for handling.

The `Physical Path` must not be changed, because the application process loads the cartridge library code from this directory.

The `DAD Name` is set to the DAD that identifies the database and schema used by cartridge to execute PL/SQL procedures. If a DAD has been not created, you can create one at this point by clicking the `Create New DAD` button. If you do not select a DAD, then PL/SQL procedures cannot be invoked.

Now that you have created the application and cartridge, the URL you use to invoke a stored procedure has the following format for the example application and cartridge created:

```
http://frazzle/bookstore/shop/<plsql_procname>
```

or

```
http://frazzle/shopping/<plsql_procname>
```

The text `<plsql_procname>` should be replaced with the actual name of the stored procedure that uses the PL/SQL Toolkit to dynamically generate the HTML. A package PL/SQL procedure can also be invoked by prefixing the package name followed by a dot to the procedure name. For example:

```
http://frazzle/shopping/<package_name>.<plsql_procname>
```

After creating the application and cartridge, you can create a simple PL/SQL stored procedure to test whether the configuration works. The next section presents example procedures showing how to use some of the PL/SQL Toolkit packages to generate HTML from PL/SQL containing your database data.

16.3.3.1 A Word About the URL Structure. Given the following URL structure:

```
http://<host>/shopping/store.home
```

The entire string is called the Uniform Resource Locator (URL). It includes:

- The protocol (`http`)
- The host (`frazzle`)
- The path (`/shopping/`)
- The target (`store.home`), which is a procedure (`home`) in a PL/SQL package called `store`

The bold portion of the URL (`/shopping/`) is a relative path from a root directory defined by the Web-server configuration. This path should not be defined in the Web-listener directory mapping; otherwise, the Web listener will look for a file called `<package>.<proc>`. In an OAS environment, this path is sent to the Web Request Broker, which maps the path to a cartridge service for handling the request. The components of the URL, such as the path information, are available to the PL/SQL application invoked by the request.

Some documents refer to the combination of path name and packaged procedure as the Uniform Resource Identifier (URI).[14] The URI for the above example (excluding the http://frazzle portion) is:

```
/shopping/<package>.<proc>
```

Note, however, that the HTTP 1.1 specification refers to the URI as *a simple formatted string identifying a resource via name, location, or any other characteristic*. This is a rather broad statement and is left open to interpretation.[15]

16.3.4 PL/SQL EXAMPLES

The PL/SQL example presented here uses features provided by the `HTP` package in the PL/SQL Toolkit. The `HTP` procedures are extensive, and provide a one-to-one mapping to HTML tags. Table 16.2 shows a subset of procedures from the HTP package used in some of the examples. The naming convention for procedure arguments is that the name indicates the procedure's use, and the first character of the name indicates the data type of the parameter.

- C represents a varchar2 argument (e.g., ctitle).
- N represents a number argument.
- D represents a DATE argument.

The parameter names provided in the procedures are shown in italics in the generated tag column to indicate the position where the value will appear in the generated HTML tags.

---

[14]In Oracle documentation the acronym URI stands for Uniform Resource Indicator.

[15]The HTTP 1.1 specification (RFC 2616) can be found at http://www.w3c.org.

TABLE 16.2 HTP procedures and related HTML tags

HTP PROCEDURE AND ARGUMENT	GENERATED TAG
htp.htmlOpen;	<HTML>
htp.htmlClose;	</HTML>
htp.headOpen;	<HEAD>
htp.title(ctitle);	<TITLE>*ctitle*</TITLE>
htp.headClose;	</HEAD>
Htp.bodyOpen(cbgnd, cattrib);	<BODY BACKGROUND="cbgnd" cattrib>
Htp.bodyClose;	</BODY>
Htp.print(ctext);	Ctext

The `htp.print` procedure is the most basic procedure that you can use to generate any text or HTML. It does not generate HTML tags unless you explicitly include them in the parameter string. For example:

```
htp.print('<b>Hello</b>');
```

You can, of course, exclusively use the `htp.print` procedure to generate your entire HTML page. This technique will minimize the procedure call overhead, but mixes the logic with HTML presentation data.

All of the `HTP` procedures that generate HTML tags with attributes provide a `cattrib` parameter. The value assigned to the `cattrib` parameter is added as options to the generated HTML tag, which allows you to generate tags not provided via the supplied arguments.

For example, the `htp.bodyOpen` procedure does not provide a parameter to specify the background color for the Web page, since the first parameter is used to set the background image for the Web page. To set a background color, you need to set the `BGCOLOR` attribute in the `<BODY>` tag. For example:

```
htp.bodyOpen(null, 'BGCOLOR="cyan"');
```

The `htp.bodyOpen` call generates the following HTML tag:

```
<BODY BGCOLOR="cyan">
```

Notes:

- The first parameter is set to a PL/SQL NULL value to suppress the output of the `BACKGROUND="cbgnd"` attribute value pair in the `BODY` tag. The general rule is that a NULL parameter value prevents the attribute and value from appearing in the generated HTML tag.
- The `cattrib` parameter is used unmodified in the `BODY` tag.

Listing 16.1 is a simple procedure you can create to test your OAS PL/SQL cartridge. It can be used as a template for other procedures you may want to create.

```
CREATE OR REPLACE PROCEDURE home IS
BEGIN
  htp.htmlOpen;
  htp.headOpen;
  htp.title('Bookstore Home Page');
  htp.headClose;
  htp.bodyOpen;
  htp.header(1, 'Bookstore Home');
  htp.print('The bookstore is under construction');
  htp.bodyClose;
  htp.htmlClose;
END;
```

LISTING 16.1 Sample PL/SQL procedure to test PL/SQL cartridge.

You can test the HTML generated with Listing 16.1 by typing an appropriate URL in a Web browser to invoke the procedure using a PL/SQL cartridge. For example:

```
http://frazzle/bookstore/shop/home
```

The Web browser should display the result shown in Figure 16.20.

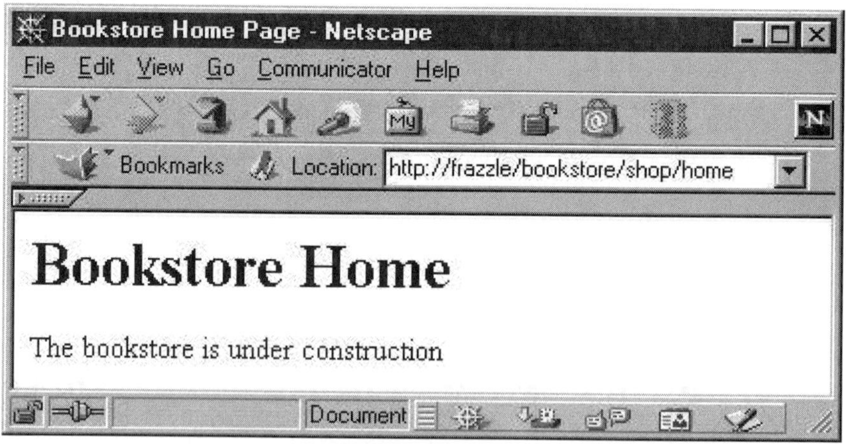

FIGURE 16.20

Alternatively, you can view the HTML generated by your PL/SQL code by using the following commands in Oracle SQL*Plus:

```
SQL> set serveroutput on
SQL> execute home

PL/SQL procedure successfully completed.

SQL> execute owa_util.showpage
Content-type: text/html
Content-length: 140
<HTML>
<HEAD>
<TITLE>Bookstore Home Page</TITLE>
</HEAD>
<BODY>
<H1>Bookstore Home</H1>
The bookstore is under construction
</BODY>
</HTML>

PL/SQL procedure successfully completed.
```

Executing PL/SQL procedures that use the PL/SQL Toolkit routines from SQL*plus will not produce output because the generated HTML is written to an internal database buffer and not to the screen. The `owa_util.showpage` procedure is designed to display the contents of the database buffer after executing a procedure using the PL/SQL Toolkit functionality.

The best approach is to build your PL/SQL Web applications as a PL/SQL package, because this will keep related functionality together while maintaining a high degree of modularity.

Listing 16.2 shows a skeleton PL/SQL package that can be used to give a consistent look-and-feel to your Web pages.

```
CREATE OR REPLACE PACKAGE store IS
  PROCEDURE home;
END;
/

CREATE OR REPLACE PACKAGE BODY store IS
  homePage varchar2(100) := owa_util.get_owa_service_path||
                            'store.home';
```

LISTING 16.2 PL/SQL Package structure for Web applications.

```

  PROCEDURE openPage(ctitle varchar2 := 'Bookstore',
                     clogo varchar2 := 'smiley.gif') is
    plogo varchar2(50);
  BEGIN
    htp.htmlOpen;
    htp.headOpen;
    htp.title(ctitle);
    htp.headClose;

    htp.bodyOpen;
    if clogo is not null then
      plogo := htf.img('/images/'||clogo)||' ';
    end if;
    htp.tableOpen(cattributes=>'WIDTH="100%" BGCOLOR="cyan"');
    htp.tableRowOpen;
    htp.tableData(
      plogo||htf.bold('<font size=+2>'||ctitle||'</font>'),
      calign=>'LEFT');
    htp.tableRowClose;
    htp.tableClose;
    htp.hr;
  END;

  PROCEDURE closePage is
  BEGIN
    htp.hr;
    htp.tableOpen(cattributes=>'WIDTH="100%" BGCOLOR="cyan"');
    htp.tableRowOpen;
    htp.tableData(
      htf.anchor(homePage, 'Home'), calign=>'CENTER');
    htp.tableRowClose;
    htp.tableClose;
    htp.bodyClose;
    htp.htmlClose;
  END;

  PROCEDURE home IS
  BEGIN
     openPage('Bookstore Online');
     htp.centerOpen;
     htp.print('Welcome to the Web Bookstore<BR>' ||
         'The Store will be opening soon<BR>'||
```

LISTING 16.2 *Continued*

```
52:          'Get ready to sign up for <b>great discounts</b> '||
53:          'for regular customers');
54:      htp.centerClose;
55:      closePage;
56:   END;
57: END;
58: /
```

LISTING 16.2 *Continued*

The PL/SQL in Listing 16.2 demonstrates the use of a PL/SQL package with reusable HTML page header and footer procedures. You may want to store the `openPage`, and `closePage` procedures in their own package, and declare them in the specification so that they can be called from other procedures or packages used to generate HTML. The URL: `http://frazzle/shopping/store.home` produces the HTML page displayed in Figure 16.21.

Notes on Listing 16.2:

- Lines 1 to 4 create the PL/SQL `store` package specification. There is only one public procedure called `home`. Assuming you created a PL/SQL application and a cartridge as shown in Figure 16.21, you can invoke the `store.home` packaged procedure with the following URL: `http://frazzle/shopping/store.home`.

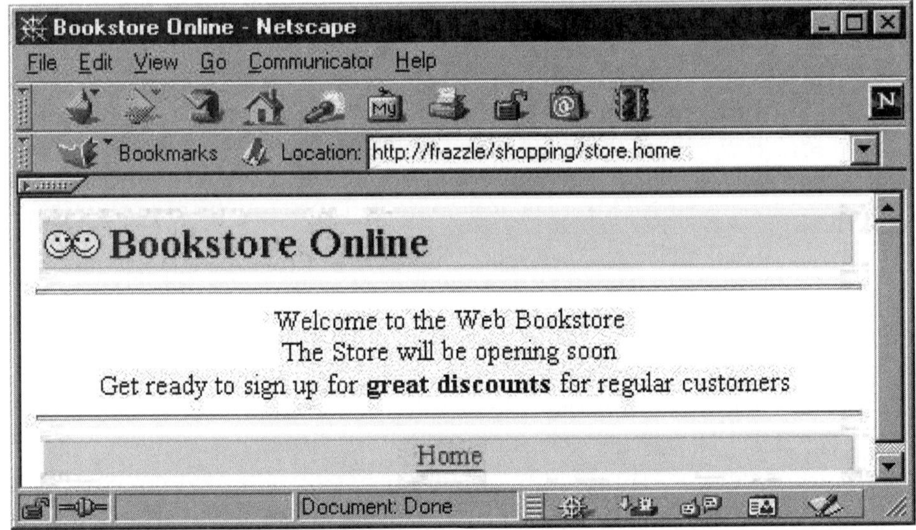

FIGURE 16.21 HTML page with a standard header and footer.

- Lines 7 and Line 8 in the package body define a private package variable to store the URL to the home page. The URL is constructed from two concatenated strings:
  - The path string for the current request returned by calling the `owa_util.get_owa_service_path` PL/SQL Toolkit function. The value returned for the example in Figure 16.21 is `/shopping/`.
    Using the `owa_util.get_owa_service_path` function avoids hard-coding a path, thus giving you the flexibility to execute the PL/SQL code in another cartridge with a different virtual path without changing your source code.
  - A literal string identifying the package procedure (i.e., "`store.home`").
- Lines 10 to 31 are the `openPage` procedure code used to produce the page header. This procedure opens the HTML page with `htp.htmlOpen` (<HTML> tag), generates the <HEAD>...</HEAD> section, and opens the page body with `htp.bodyOpen` (<BODY> tag). The input parameters have default values if none are provided. The first parameter is used for a window and page title. The second parameter is the image name for a logo prefixed to the page heading text. The code shows an example of creating an HTML table using the following HTP package procedures:
  - `htp.tableOpen` generates the <TABLE> tag to start a table.
  - `htp.tableRowOpen` generates the <TR> tag to start a row.
  - `htp.tableData` generates the <TD>*text*</TD> pattern to define a column with data, where *text* is the table cell contents provided by the input parameter string.
  - `htp.tableRowClose` generates the </TR> tag to end a row.
  - `htp.tableRowClose` generates the </TABLE> tag to end a table.
- Line 23 is an example of the use of the `cattributes` parameter of the HTP procedures to provide HTML tag attributes not available via the default parameters for `HTP` procedures. See the discussion of PL/SQL parameter passing in Chapter 8 to understand the syntax used.
- Lines 21 and 26 show the use of HTF functions, which return strings of the generated HTML tags and context. These functions are typically nested inside procedure parameters to generate nested tags.
- Lines 33 to 44 create the page footer and close the HTML body with the `htp.bodyClose` (</BODY> tag) and page with `htp.htmlClose` (</HTML> tag).
- Lines 46 to 57 generate the home page. Here the `openPage` procedure is called first, and the `closePage` procedure last. Between the `openPage` and `closePage` calls is the code to generate the contents of the page. Additional procedures added to the package would follow this coding pattern.

This section concludes the use of PL/SQL in Oracle Application Server. The rest of the chapter concentrates on executing Java code in OAS.

16.4 CONFIGURING JAVA APPLICATIONS

The Java servlet cartridge, called JServlet, provides an execution environment for Java code written with the Java Servlet API. The process of creating a JServlet application and its JServlet cartridge is similar to the steps in creating a PL/SQL application and cartridge. See Chapter 14 for an example of the OAS Web administration pages used to configure a JServlet application and cartridge.

The JServlet cartridge in OAS 4.0.8.2 is an implementation of a JVM that executes Java servlets written using JDK 1.2 and the Sun Servlet API version 2.1. The OAS architecture can create more than one JServlet cartridge, which can be distributed among multiple hosts in a multi-node OAS installation. This provides a great deal of scalability. OAS uses the Web Request Broker to perform the load balancing of HTTP requests for the JServlet cartridge. Figure 16.22 represents the architecture of a JServlet cartridge server and cartridge.

Figure 16.22 represents a single JServlet application or process. As can be seen, the cartridge instance is a JVM servlet runner capable of executing multiple simultaneous requests. An application/cartridge server can launch more than one JVM/cartridge instance.

Each URL request for the JServlet cartridge can be serviced by a separate servlet instance using the single-threaded model. You make your servlet single-threaded by implementing the javax.servlet.SingleThreaded interface. For example:

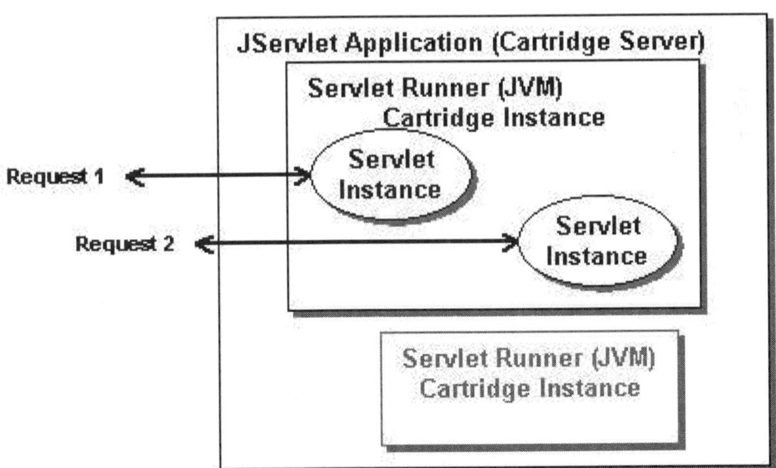

FIGURE 16.22 Architecture of the JServlet cartridge.

```
package com.prenhall.OFJP.servlet;
import javax.servlet.SingleThreadedModel;
import javax.servlet.http.HttpServlet;
import java.io.*;
import java.util.*;

public class BookStoreServlet extends HttpServlet
   implements SingleThreadedModel {
  :
}
```

If you do not implement the SingleThreadedModel interface, then the servlet is threaded by default and capable of handling multiple simultaneous requests. In the OAS environment, Oracle recommends that your servlet implement the `javax.servlet.SingleThreadModel` interface, allowing OAS to manage the scheduling of threads at the cartridge-instance level, thus gaining the benefits of the OAS distributed and threaded environment. OAS cannot monitor Java threads inside the Java servlet for effective load-balancing purposes.

You learned how to write Java servlets in Chapter 14. The discussion in the current chapter provides an introduction to the JWeb Toolkit, a class library created for use with JWeb or JServlet applications in Oracle Application Server.

16.4.1 DEVELOPING A SERVLET WITH THE JAVA WEB TOOLKIT

The Oracle Application Server product installation provides a `jar` file called `jweb.jar` that contains many classes you can use to dynamically generate HTML. The benefit of using the Java Web Toolkit is that the Java servlet code you write to generate HTML will not be cluttered with HTML tags, and thus will be more readable and easier to maintain.

The Java Web Toolkit classes encapsulate HTML tags in the same way that the PL/SQL Toolkit procedures encapsulate PL/SQL procedures. The Java Web Toolkit can be used on any Java servlet in any Java Web server, because the Java Web Toolkit is pure Java code.

Table 16.3 shows a small subset of the Java Web Toolkit classes you can use to build a HTML page dynamically using Java.

The `jweb.jar` file was originally created for use in the Java Web cartridge, and is located in the directory `ORACLE_HOME/ows/cartx/jweb/classes` of the Oracle application installation directory tree. Make sure to add the `jweb.jar` file to your `CLASSPATH`. The following section shows an example of a standard Java servlet for generating a skeleton bookstore home page, and an equivalent example using the Java Web Toolkit classes.

TABLE 16.3 Classes for generating HTML with the Java Web Toolkit

CLASS NAME	DESCRIPTION
Oracle.html.HtmlPage	Encapsulates an HTML page. The constructor creates an instance of an HTML page, with HtmlHead and HtmlBody as parameters.
oracle.html.HtmlHead	Encapsulates the <HEAD>...</HEAD> tags. Items added to the HtmlHead object using its *addItem()* method are placed between the head tags.
oracle.html.Title	Encapsulates the <TITLE>...</TITLE> tags.
oracle.html.HtmlBody	Encapsulates the <BODY>...</BODY> tags. Using the *addItem()* method, content is added to the body of the page.
oracle.html.SimpleItem	Adds items representing other HTML tags that appear in HTML page header or body (e.g., HTML tables, forms, and links).

16.4.2 EXAMPLE OF A JSERVLET WITH THE JAVA WEB TOOLKIT

The servlet code presented in Listing 16.3 handles the HTTP request and response and also performs the same work as the PL/SQL `store` package example presented earlier in the chapter.

```
package com.prenhall.OFJP.servlet;
import javax.servlet.*;
import javax.servlet.http.*;
import java.io.*;
import java.util.*;
import oracle.html.*;

public class StoreServlet extends HttpServlet
   implements SingleThreadModel {

  private String homeURI = null;
  private PrintWriter out = null;
  private HtmlHead htmlHead = null;
  private HtmlBody htmlBody = null;
  private HtmlPage htmlPage = null;
  private String title = "Bookstore";
  private String logo = "smiley.gif";

  public void doGet(HttpServletRequest request,
                    HttpServletResponse response)
    throws ServletException, IOException {
```

LISTING 16.3 Java `StoreServlet` using Java Web Toolkit class library.

```
    doPost(request, response);
  }

  public void doPost(HttpServletRequest request,
                     HttpServletResponse response)
    throws ServletException, IOException {
    homeURI = request.getRequestURI();
    response.setContentType("text/html");
    out = new PrintWriter (response.getOutputStream());
    createPage();
    out.print(htmlPage.toString());
    out.close();
  }

  public void createPage() {
    String bodyText = getContent();
    openPage(title, logo);
    htmlBody.addItem(new SimpleItem(bodyText));
    closePage();
  }

  public final void openPage(String title, String logo) {
    String banner = new SimpleItem(title)
                       .setBold().setFontBig().toHTML();
    if (logo != null) {
      Image logoImage = new Image("/images/" + logo);
      banner = logoImage.toHTML() + " " + banner;
    }
    DynamicTable headTable = new DynamicTable(1);
    headTable.setBorder(0);
    headTable.setWidth("100%");

    TableRow tableRow = new TableRow();
    tableRow.setIHAlign(IHAlign.LEFT);
    tableRow.setBackgroundColor(Color.cyan);
    headTable.addRow(tableRow);
    TableDataCell tableDataCell = new TableDataCell(banner);
    tableRow.addCell(tableDataCell);

    htmlHead = new HtmlHead();
    htmlHead.setTitle(title);
    htmlBody = new HtmlBody();
```

LISTING 16.3 *Continued*

```
64:     htmlBody.addItem(headTable)
65:       .addItem(new HorizontalRule("CENTER", true, 2, "100%"));
66:     htmlPage = new HtmlPage(htmlHead, htmlBody);
67:   }
68:
69:   public final void closePage() {
70:     DynamicTable footTable = new DynamicTable(1);
71:     footTable.setBorder(0);
72:     footTable.setWidth("100%");
73:     TableRow tableRow = new TableRow();
74:     tableRow.setIHAlign(IHAlign.CENTER);
75:     tableRow.setBackgroundColor(Color.cyan);
76:     footTable.addRow(tableRow);
77:
78:     Link homeLink = new Link(homeURI, "Home");
79:     TableDataCell tableDataCell = new TableDataCell(homeLink);
80:     tableRow.addCell(tableDataCell);
81:     htmlBody
82:       .addItem(new HorizontalRule("CENTER", true, 2, "100%"))
83:       .addItem(footTable);
84:   }
85:
86:   public String getContent() {
87:     CompoundItem bodyText = new CompoundItem();
88:     bodyText.setCenter();
89:     bodyText.addItem(
90:         "Welcome to the Web Bookstore" +
91:         SimpleItem.LineBreak +
92:         "The Store will be opening soon" +
93:         SimpleItem.LineBreak +
94:         "Get ready to sign up for " +
95:         new SimpleItem("great discounts").setBold().toHTML() +
96:       " for regular customers");
97:     return bodyText.toHTML();
98:   }
99: }
```

LISTING 16.3 *Continued*

Notes on Listing 16.3:

- Line 1 is the `StoreServlet` package name, which forms part of the URL used to invoke the servlet. For example, assuming the virtual path to the Servlet is `/servlet/`: http://frazzle/servlet/com.prenhall.OFJP.servlet

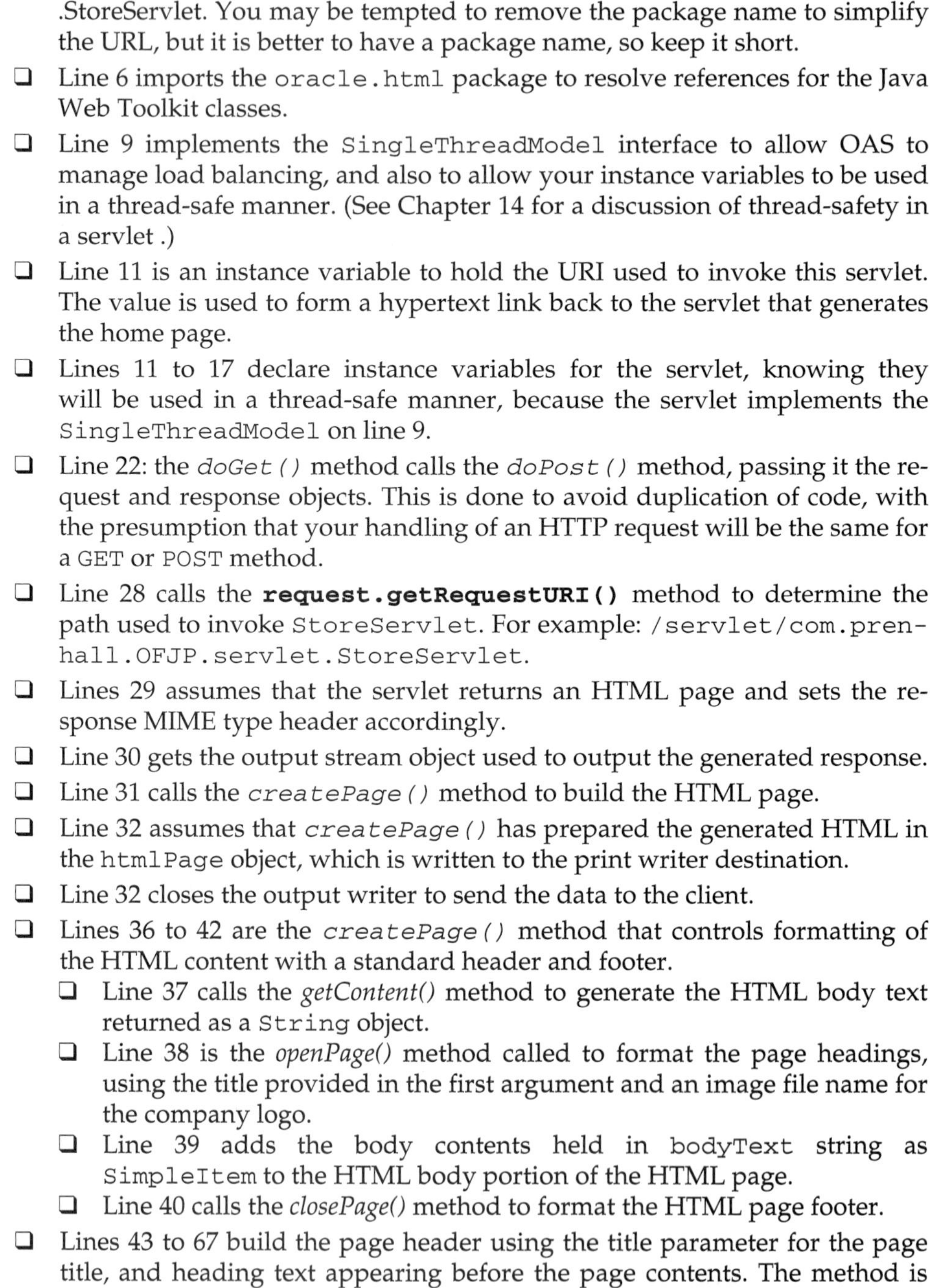

.StoreServlet. You may be tempted to remove the package name to simplify the URL, but it is better to have a package name, so keep it short.

- Line 6 imports the `oracle.html` package to resolve references for the Java Web Toolkit classes.
- Line 9 implements the `SingleThreadModel` interface to allow OAS to manage load balancing, and also to allow your instance variables to be used in a thread-safe manner. (See Chapter 14 for a discussion of thread-safety in a servlet .)
- Line 11 is an instance variable to hold the URI used to invoke this servlet. The value is used to form a hypertext link back to the servlet that generates the home page.
- Lines 11 to 17 declare instance variables for the servlet, knowing they will be used in a thread-safe manner, because the servlet implements the `SingleThreadModel` on line 9.
- Line 22: the *`doGet()`* method calls the *`doPost()`* method, passing it the request and response objects. This is done to avoid duplication of code, with the presumption that your handling of an HTTP request will be the same for a `GET` or `POST` method.
- Line 28 calls the **`request.getRequestURI()`** method to determine the path used to invoke `StoreServlet`. For example: `/servlet/com.prenhall.OFJP.servlet.StoreServlet`.
- Lines 29 assumes that the servlet returns an HTML page and sets the response MIME type header accordingly.
- Line 30 gets the output stream object used to output the generated response.
- Line 31 calls the *`createPage()`* method to build the HTML page.
- Line 32 assumes that *`createPage()`* has prepared the generated HTML in the `htmlPage` object, which is written to the print writer destination.
- Line 32 closes the output writer to send the data to the client.
- Lines 36 to 42 are the *`createPage()`* method that controls formatting of the HTML content with a standard header and footer.
    - Line 37 calls the *getContent()* method to generate the HTML body text returned as a `String` object.
    - Line 38 is the *openPage()* method called to format the page headings, using the title provided in the first argument and an image file name for the company logo.
    - Line 39 adds the body contents held in `bodyText` string as `SimpleItem` to the HTML body portion of the HTML page.
    - Line 40 calls the *closePage()* method to format the HTML page footer.
- Lines 43 to 67 build the page header using the title parameter for the page title, and heading text appearing before the page contents. The method is

marked `final` to prevent a subclass from overriding the method enforcing a consistent display format.

- Lines 44 and 45 format the title parameter in a banner for the page header.
- Lines 46 to 49 prefix the HTML for site logo image before the page title text. This code assumes that images can be located in the "/images/" virtual path on the Web server.
- Lines 50 to 59 build an HTML table with the Java Web Toolkit.
  - Line 50 creates a `DynamicTable` object.
  - Lines 51 and 52, respectively, set HTML table attributes to exclude a border and fill the browser window (100%).
- Line 54 to 56 create and set the options of a `TableRow` object .
- Line 57 adds the `TableRow` object to the dynamic table. To add additional rows, you would create and add additional `TableRow` objects.
- Line 58 creates the `TableDataCell` object with its content for the column/cell in the `TableRow`.[16] The Java Web Toolkit provides two `TableDataCell` constructors, one accepting a Java `String`, and the other accepting any `Item` object.
- Line 59 adds the `tableDataCell` object to the `tableRow` object to populate the table.
- This example of building the HTML table demonstrates the object-oriented approach to building page contents by calling several methods to alter the table or row properties/attributes.
- Line 61 creates the <HEAD>...</HEAD> section encapsulated in the `HtmlHead` object.
- Line 62 sets the `<TITLE>...</TITLE>` tag contents in the `HtmlHead` object.
- Line 63 creates the `HtmlBody` object, which encapsulates the `<BODY>...</BODY>` tags and all the contents in between. The `HtmlBody` class provides an *`addItem()`* method that makes it possible to add any Item object in between the `BODY` tags.
- Lines 64 and 65 add the `tableHead` object to the body, followed by a horizontal rule object. This example shows how to chain calls using the *`addItem()`* method, which returns a reference to the `htmlBody` object. The *`addItem()`* method accepts a `Container` object as a parameter. A `Container` object can hold one or more `Item` objects, but is not a kind of Item class.
- Line 66 creates an `HtmlPage` object that consists of the `HtmlHead` and `HtmlBody` objects.

---

[16]Use the `TableHeaderCell` class to create table headers.

- Lines 69 to 84 show the *`closePage()`* method designed to format the page footer details, which contain an HTML table with a hypertext link to the `StoreServlet` generating the same page.
- Line 78 uses the `Link` class to create the hypertext link, where the first parameter specifies the link URL, and the second argument is the highlighted link text on the HTML page.
- Line 75 uses the `oracle.html.Color` class, which should not be confused with the `java.awt.Color` class. The `oracle.html.Color` class is not related to the AWT version. There should be no conflict, because you are not likely to be using AWT classes in the context of a servlet.
- Lines 86 to 98 use the `oracle.html.CompoundItem` class to build the contents for the page. A `CompoundItem` comprises one or more `Item` objects. Objects added to a `CompoundItem` are printed in the order they are added. The `CompoundItem`[17] and `SimpleItem` classes are subclasses of the `Item` class.
- Line 97 returns the HTML contents of the compound item as a string object, which is returned calling the method in line 37 and added to the HTML body in line 39.

16.4.2.1 Reusing Your Servlet Look-and-Feel. You may want to simplify future servlet development work and reuse the look-and-feel presented by `StoreServlet`. This can be accomplished in the following way:

- Convert `StoreServlet` into an abstract class.
- Change the *`getContent()`* method in the abstract class to an abstract method forcing the servlet subclass to implement its behavior.
- Creating your servlet as a subclass of the abstract class releases you from having to format the HTML for page header and footer. You are free to focus on the code required to build the HTML page contents.

16.4.2.2 Converting the StoreServlet into `AbstractStoreServlet`.

```
package com.prenhall.OFJP.servlet;

// required imports here

public abstract class AbstractStoreServlet extends HttpServlet
    implements SingleThreadModel {
```

LISTING 16.4 The `AbstractStoreServlet` example.

---

[17]Think of a `CompoundItem` as an HTML equivalent of a Swing container like `javax.swing.JPanel`.

```
07:
08:   :
09:   private String title = "Bookstore";
10:   private String logo = "smiley.gif";
11:
12:   // doGet(), doPost() and other StoreServlet methods here
13:
14:   public final void createPage(String content) {
15:     String bodyText = getContent();
16:     openPage(title, logo);
17:     htmlBody.addItem(new SimpleItem(bodyText));
18:     closePage();
19:   }
20:
21:   public abstract String getContent();
22:
23:   public void setTitle(String newTitle) {
24:     title = newTitle;
25:   }
26:
27:   public void setLogo(String newLogo) {
28:     logo = newLogo;
29:   }
30: }
```

LISTING 16.4 *Continued*

The listing here is a copy of the `StoreServlet` in Listing 16.3, with common code excluded except the key pieces needed to understand the changes.

Notes on Listing 16.4:

- Line 5 declares the servlet class as an abstract class. The changes made in this line include the servlet name and add the abstract keyword.
- Lines 9 and 10 represent default title and logo strings. They can now be replaced by the addition of two new methods, on lines 23 and 27, to set the values of these instance variables.
- Line 14 declares the `createPage()` method as final so that the subclass cannot override this method and destroy the intended functionality.
- Line 15 is the one of the keys to this design where the *`getContent()`* method is called before the HTML page is generated. As a side effect of this design, the *`setTitle()`* method (line 23) and the *`setLogo()`* method (line 27) should be called in the subclass implementation of the *`getContent()`*

method to ensure that the page title and logo will differ from their default values in the AbstractStoreServlet.

- Line 21 is the other key to this design where the *getContent()* method is abstract, forcing the subclass to generate the HTML body contents.
- Lines 23 and 27 add the *setTitle()* and *setLogo()* methods to allow the writer of the subclass to alter predefined attributes of the page look-and-feel.

16.4.2.3 Creating a Subclass of the **AbstractStoreServlet**.

```
01: package com.prenhall.OFJP.servlet;
02:
03: import oracle.html.CompoundItem;
04: import oracle.html.SimpleItem;
05:
06: public class MyStoreServlet extends AbstractStoreServlet {
07:
08:   public String getContent() {
09:     setTitle("MyStore.com");
10:     setLogo("mystore.gif");
11:     CompoundItem bodyText = new CompoundItem();
12:     bodyText.setCenter();
13:     bodyText.addItem(
14:        "Welcome to the Web Bookstore" +
15:        SimpleItem.LineBreak +
16:        "The Store will be opening soon" +
17:        SimpleItem.LineBreak +
18:        "Get ready to sign up for " +
19:        new SimpleItem("great discounts").setBold().toHTML() +
20:       " for regular customers");
21:     return bodyText.toHTML();
22:   }
23:
24: }
```

LISTING 16.5 Example subclass of AbstractStoreServlet.

Notes on Listing 16.5:

- Line 6 declares MyStoreSerlvet as a subclass of AbstractStore-Servlet and makes MyStoreServlet single-threaded through inheritance.

- Lines 8 to 22 are an implementation of a *getContent()* method showing how your coding is dramatically reduced to one method. The `doGet()`, *doPost()*, and related functionality are all handled by the abstract superclass.
    - Lines 9 and 10 call the superclass *setTitle()* and *setLogo()* methods to respectively change the page title and logo values before the page is generated by the `AbstractStoreServlet` code.
    - Lines 11 to 20 build the dynamic HTML content in a Java Web Toolkit container object. Alternatively, you can replace this code to use a `StringBuffer` implementation and append HTML tags to the string buffer in the desired sequence.
    - Line 21 returns a string containing the generated HTML tags to the *createPage()* method in the `AbstractStoreServlet` class, which adds the content to the output returned to the client.

The preceding examples demonstrate a way for you to consistently generate the same look-and-feel for all your servlet applications, isolating subsequent changes to the look-and-feel to one class.

The details of the basic servlet class structure have not been explained here. These subjects are covered in Chapter 14, which provides examples and a discussion in greater depth on programming with Java servlets.

16.4.3 JAVASERVER PAGE APPLICATIONS

Oracle Application Server 4.0.8.2, the last OAS version to go into production, was the first version to provide an integrated JavaServer Pages engine. The earlier release, OAS 4.0.7.1, required a patch to implement the JavaServer Pages engine.

Oracle Application Server 4.0.8.2 installs with a preconfigured JavaServer Page application and cartridge. The virtual path (or URI) is set to `/jsp`, which maps to the physical directory identified by `ORACLE_HOME/ows/cartx/jsp`. To quickly test your JavaServer Page applications, place the JSP files in the `ORACLE_HOME/ows/cartx/jsp` directory.

The process of creating a JavaServer Page application (cartridge server) and cartridge resembles the process used to create a JServlet cartridge or a PL/SQL cartridge. The application and cartridge configuration parameters resemble the JServlet cartridge parameters, discussed in Chapter 14. The major configuration differences from the JServlet cartridge are the use of the following additions to the JavaServer Page `CLASSPATH`:

- ORACLE_HOME/ows/cartx/jsp/defapp/beans
- ORACLE_HOME/ows/cartx/jsp/lib/ojsp.jar
- ORACLE_HOME/ows/cartx/jsp/lib/jsdk.jar

In addition, the JDK bin directory is included in the PATH environment variable for the JSP cartridge to ensure that the JSP engine can create a Java source from the JSP file, and compile and run the Java class the first time it is requested.

Assuming that the `/jsp/` path maps to the physical directory `ORACLE_HOME/ows/cartx/jsp`, the Java source and class files for your converted JavaServer Page file are created in the `_pages/jsp` subdirectory below the directory where the JSP source file is located.

For example, if the URL to invoke the JSP file is

```
http://frazzle/jsp/BookStore.jsp
```

because the `BookStore.jsp` file is located in the `ORACLE_HOME/ows/cartx/jsp` directory, the Oracle JSP engine creates the Java source and class file in directory:

```
ORACLE_HOME/ows/cartx/jsp/_pages/jsp
```

A sample JavaServer Page code that mimics the `StoreServlet` page presented earlier is provided next. See Chapter 15 for the details of writing a JavaServer page.

16.4.4 A SIMPLE JAVASERVER PAGE

The `BookStore.jsp` file in Listing 16.6 replicates the work of the `StoreServlet` code provided earlier. The code is primarily made up of HTML text, with simple JSP scriptlets (i.e., Java code) enclosed within `<% ... %>` tags.

```
<HTML>
<HEAD>
<TITLE>Bookstore</TITLE>
</HEAD>
<BODY>
<TABLE BORDER=0 WIDTH=100%>
<TR ALIGN=LEFT BGCOLOR=#00FFFF>
 <TD><IMG SRC="/images/smiley.gif"> <B><BIG>Bookstore</BIG></B></TD>
</TABLE>
<HR>

<CENTER>Welcome to the Web Bookstore<BR>
The Store will be opening soon<BR>
Get ready to sign up for <B>great discounts</B> for regular customers</CENTER>
<HR>
```

LISTING 16.6 Simple JavaServer Page BookStore.jsp home page.

```
<TABLE BORDER=0 WIDTH=100%>
<TR ALIGN=CENTER BGCOLOR=#FFFF00>
 <TD><A HREF="<% request.getRequestURI(); %>BookStore.jsp">Home
     </A></TD>
</TABLE>
</BODY>
</HTML>
```

LISTING 16.6 *Continued*

Note on Listing 16.6:

- The bold text in the example shows the JSP scriptlet. Interestingly, under the OAS JSP engine, the call to `request.getRequestURI()` in the scriptlet only returns the virtual path information (e.g. `/jsp/`). Thus, the name of the JSP file has been appended to the output from the scriptlet.

The JSP code could be constructed from the JSP file by using a Java bean to encapsulate the code that performs the page title and footer formatting. The JSP file could instantiate the Java bean with a `<jsp:useBean>` tag and call methods from the bean instance to format the start and end of the page. In this way you could reuse your Java bean code in a servlet as well, to give a consistent look-and-feel across your JSP and servlet applications.

16.5 INTRODUCING ORACLE9i APPLICATION SERVER

Oracle9i Application Server (Oracle9i AS) is Oracle's new application server platform and follows on from OAS with far more performance and scalability than before. In a significant move, acknowledging a market favorite, Oracle9i AS uses the Apache Web server software for HTTP traffic, and the Apache Jserv module for Java servlets.[18] Oracle has written the PL/SQL cartridge as an Apache module (called a mod). For example: mod_plsql, which is called the PL/SQL Gateway.

In addition to the Apache modules, Oracle provides its own JavaServer Page engine,[19] and the Oracle8i JVM for executing Enterprise JavaBeans or CORBA components. In order to run the Oracle8i JVM with Oracle9i AS, you effectively install an Oracle database instance with the Apache software configured to direct requests to the Oracle JVM when required.

---

[18] At time of writing this chapter, the use of the Apache/Tomcat implementation was being considered.

[19] The Apache/Tomcat implementation is under consideration for a future release of Oracle9i Application Server.

16.5.1 MIGRATION FROM OAS TO ORACLE9i AS

Oracle has provided its OAS customers with a smooth, seamless migration of PL/SQL cartridge-based applications to Oracle9i AS. There should be minimal code changes, unless you are using OAS specific features. The same applies to JServlet applications, which should run unchanged under Oracle9i AS, provided that the Java servlets you developed conform to Sun Servlet API standards and do not use OAS JServlet extensions.

All Java code that uses the classes from the `oracle.html` package in the Java Web Toolkit should execute unchanged in Oracle9i AS, provided you add the Java Web Toolkit library to the CLASSPATH. However, you may want to consider replacing Java Web Toolkit with the Element Construction Set (ECS) API developed by the Apache Foundation.

SUMMARY

This chapter has given you a quick tour of the history of Oracle Application Server, and a brief introduction to the new Oracle9i Application Server architecture. The Oracle9i Application Server is not covered in detail because most of the chapter was written before it became available.

The code examples in this chapter have been kept simple in order to focus on the architectural and configuration aspects of the OAS PL/SQL cartridge, and primarily the Java application environments. Writing servlets and JavaServer pages is discussed more thoroughly in other chapters of the book.

There is a lesson to be learned from the gradual phasing out of OAS from Oracle's product line: if you follow the principle of writing your Java code based on the standard API classes and methods, your code will be highly portable, and less prone to the ramifications of product-platform changes.

Chapter 17

Web-Enabling Legacy Applications Using Network Sockets

- The Mediator Design Pattern
- Java Sockets
- Summary

This chapter and the next focus on the important role Java can play in rejuvenating legacy applications that were created before the advent of the World Wide Web.

Applications that are critical for the businesses they support usually require massive investments, which are repaid over a long time. Thus financial controllers and technical managers are confronted by a trade-off between the maturity of the chosen technology and its expected lifetime. No careful planner wants to venture into the unknown territory of a promising but immature technology. On the other hand, choosing a well-established and mature technology may appear less risky in the short term, but can become a problem in the long run if the chosen technology is progressively abandoned by the market before the natural end of the application. To be economically viable, a large mission-critical application must be in use for many years. Over such a long period, the IT landscape can radically change. Technologies that are state-of-the-art when a particular application is designed and implemented may well become obsolete before the natural end of the application's lifetime.

In light of all this, IT managers and financial controllers quite understandably welcome technologies, artifices, and tricks that can extend the lifetime of applications at little extra cost. Java is very effective in increasing the lifetime of aging applications, because it can easily be interfaced with older technologies.

Java puts two very powerful weapons into the hands of system integrators, designers, and developers charged with maintaining existing applications while gradually switching to Java:

- Java network sockets, analyzed in this chapter.
- Java Native Interface (JNI), examined in Chapter 18.

Before delving into the programming-specific issues related to the use of these technologies, it is appropriate to start from a perspective that focuses on design issues.

17.1 THE MEDIATOR DESIGN PATTERN

A Java program is made up of numerous classes. In theory, these classes should be self-sufficient and self-contained, specialized to provide one and only one type of service. To cooperate, however, the classes must communicate with one other. The more a single class must know about the methods and attributes of other classes in order to provide its services, the more tangled and convoluted the program structure becomes.

The solution is to extract knowledge of the methods and attributes of other classes into one class that mediates and "supervises" the interactions between multiple classes. This "mediator" class concentrates application knowledge and dispatches messages to all the classes registered with it. Basically, it is the only class that is aware of the other classes that comprise the subsystem. When the time comes to change the business logic, it is easy to add one more class and modify the mediator to become aware of the new class, its methods, and its role in the application framework.

While the mediator design pattern is useful in general, and is applicable to most Java application domains, it becomes even more useful when other technologies, such as C or C++, are intermixed with Java. It is a very poor practice to have each of your Java classes implement native methods to communicate with the legacy world.

A better solution is to encapsulate the legacy world within one large mediator that allows other Java classes to interact with the legacy world in Java terms. The mediator becomes a bridge that links the old with the new. It is the only class that implements either JNI methods or socket calls to retrieve data from the legacy application and to furnish data for it. The mediator provides the data required by the application, using well-established legacy procedures, and makes them available using Java data structures, such as vectors or hash tables, in a format readily accessible to Java methods.

Figure 17.1 illustrates a mediator that allows a Java application to access data and information related to customers, invoices, and orders through APIs and primitives made available by a legacy application layer written in C.

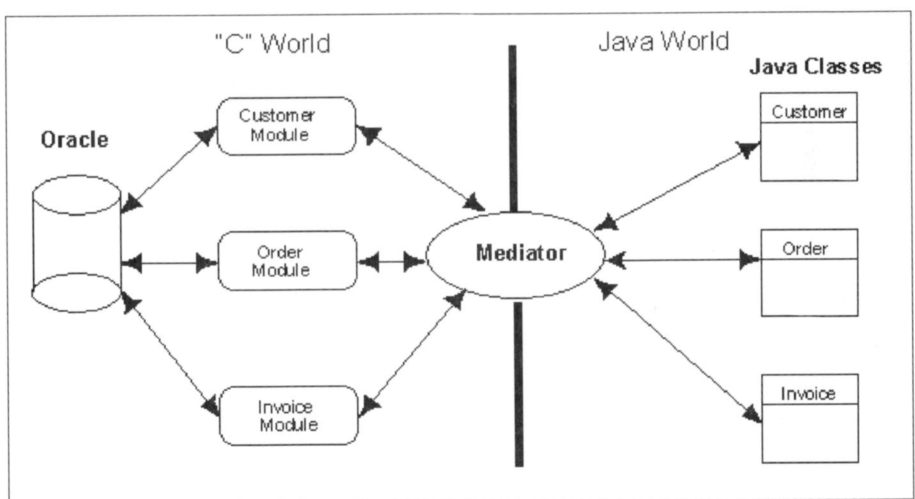

FIGURE 17.1 The mediator as a bridge between the Java and Legacy worlds.

The mediator completely hides the legacy calls to the rest of the Java application. If the C modules constituting the application are eventually going to be replaced by Java code, the Java classes already working in an intermixed environment do not need to be reworked when the C APIs are phased out.

Today, the mediator furnishes the Order class (written in Java) with data fetched from the Oracle legacy application using a C call. The mediator uses a native method to accomplish this, but the data obtained from the C call are stored in a vector local to the mediator. This data are in turn passed back to the Order class, which accesses all the Oracle rows stored in the vector. Tomorrow, the native method can easily be replaced by a pure Java method that uses JDBC to accomplish the same task. The Order class receives its data using the same mechanism used today by the mediator, and no modifications are required.

In addition to being shielded from any interference by the legacy application, the Java classes are loosely coupled in their relationships with one another. The Order class does not need to know how many methods are supported by the Invoice class or its method signatures, because the two classes never interact. The mediator concentrates all business logic in itself, having specific knowledge about attributes and methods supported by the cooperating classes.

A Web-enabling legacy application usually entails having to deal with two main kinds of interfaces, either calls to C language functions or sockets. The degree of indirection increases if, for example, the legacy application that you want to Web-enable is written in COBOL. Since Java native methods only support C or C++, you need a C wrapper which in turn calls the COBOL routines. This environment becomes inherently cumbersome and error-prone, to the point that in most cases it is more cost-effective to dump the COBOL application in favor of a Java-only solution. In computer science (almost) everything is possible; but it is usually the business aspect, together with its budget constraints, that determines the feasibility of solutions and architectures.

Many applications developed in the Unix and MS Windows environments, however, are written in C or C++, which considerably simplifies interfacing with Java applications.

Network-oriented applications, designed and developed before the widespread diffusion of distributed programming frameworks like CORBA, largely use sockets as the principal means of exchanging messages among distributed computers. Java supports sockets, although with a few considerable limitations (explained in the next section), so it is easy to intermix Java and C socket clients. Since the mediator acts as a bridge between the legacy application and the new Java-based application extension, it must have the logic to understand the packets exchanged by the application components. It has the ability to interpret the information contained in the packets, and performs the datatype conversion, transforming the basic, relational datatypes into objects easily accessible from the other Java components that comprise the extended application.

17.2 JAVA SOCKETS

The Java socket implementation follows the infamous 80/20 rule, meaning 80 percent of the functionality with 20 percent of the effort. The two main socket classes, Socket and ServerSocket, provide a highly abstracted interface that simplifies such tasks as connecting a client to a socket server written either in Java or in C. Unfortunately, the same cannot be said for more complex TCP tasks.

Creating a Java socket server is a question of one line of code:

```
ServerSocket ss = new ServerSocket(<portNumber>, <queuedConnections>);
```

The number of lines of C code to accomplish the same functionality varies from 15 to 20. Good old C is definitely more verbose, but allows for a much finer granularity. Not only are the most sophisticated TCP/IP features, such as out-of-band data transmission, not available to Java programmers, but much more mundane socket features are not supported through the Java interface.

For example, you want to implement a socket server that allows for one or more clients to connect and request information. Under certain circumstances, you want to be able to shut down your socket server abruptly and restart listening on the same port for new connections. If you try to close the socket from the server side, using ServerSocket.close(), and the client connections are still active, you cannot recreate a new socket server using the same well-known port. When you attempt to do so, you get a runtime exception associated with an error that reads:

```
Address already in use.
```

To avoid this error, the SO_REUSEADDR socket option can be used when sockets are implemented in C. SO_REUSEADDR allows a listening socket server to bind to a well-known socket port even if previously established connections are still active on the same port. The C call *bind()* call would not fail in this case.

In Java, the SO_REUSEADDR can be set for datagrams or UDP packets, but, inexplicably, cannot be set for sockets. The `SocketOption` interface provides a *`setOption()`* method, and defines a SO_REUSEADDR static int. But the documentation clearly states that setting SO_REUSEADDR is implemented for multicast sockets, which use UDP as the underlying protocol. If you have access to the JDK source code, take a look at the PlainSocketImpl.c file. The implementation of the *`Java_java_net_PlainSocketImpl_socketSetOption()`* function clearly indicates that the SO_REUSEADDR option is not implemented.

The socket methods exposed through the Java interface also prevent programmers from creating so-called *Raw Sockets*, which are needed when ICMP packets must be sent through the network.[1] This protocol is commonly used to implement the *ping* program, which finds out whether a particular host is reachable from the local host. Several versions of the ping program written in Java are available from introductory Java textbooks and through the Internet. They all mimic the real ping, using tricks that emulate its behavior; for instance, by opening a normal socket connection to a well-known port, usually port 23 (telnet) or port 13 (daytime). If the socket is successfully created, the program assumes that the remote host is alive. Implementing a real ping can only be accomplished using JNI and interfacing with the appropriate C code that implements the ICMP protocol.

In spite of the limitations discussed above, Java sockets can easily be used to write interfaces to legacy socket servers.

In the next few pages, to demonstrate how effectively Java sockets can be used in communicating with legacy network-based applications, you will build a socket server written in C that accepts concurrent connections from clients written either in C or in Java. The server, which in this example is a convenient emulation of a legacy application, maintains a connection to the Oracle database and provides the clients with read and write statistics computed against all the data files comprising the Oracle database. In order to understand this example, you will have to familiarize yourself with certain Oracle concepts and tools, such as Pro*C, the Oracle pre-compiler, which translates embedded SQL contained in C or C++ files into instructions that the C compiler can understand, and the Oracle Dynamic Performance Tables, or virtual tables, where the Oracle database stores engine-related statistics.

Pro*C is included in Oracle Programmer, a set of tools and interfaces, such as pre-compilers, networking services, and connection-oriented client software, that allows developers to write applications that connect to an Oracle database using traditional languages like C or Cobol. Oracle Programmer is licensed separately from the database server, so be sure to check the availability of the license in your site before you use the Pro*C pre-compiler.

To access Oracle Programmer you must install the software using the Universal Installer, as outlined in Figure 17.2.

If Microsoft Windows NT/2000 is your platform, Pro*C is shipped with an optional graphical front-end that allows developers to enter the various options interactively. On other platforms, Pro*C is a command-line tool.

The socket server you will build is multi-threaded and supports both Unix (using Posix threads) and Microsoft Windows NT/2000 (using NT/2000 threads). Under NT/2000 it runs as a console application. A production version of a socket server for the NT/2000 platform should probably run as an NT/2000 service; but you want to keep this example simple, and you do not want to spend much time coding in C, since this is a book about Java.

---

[1]ICMP stands for Internet Control Message Protocol.

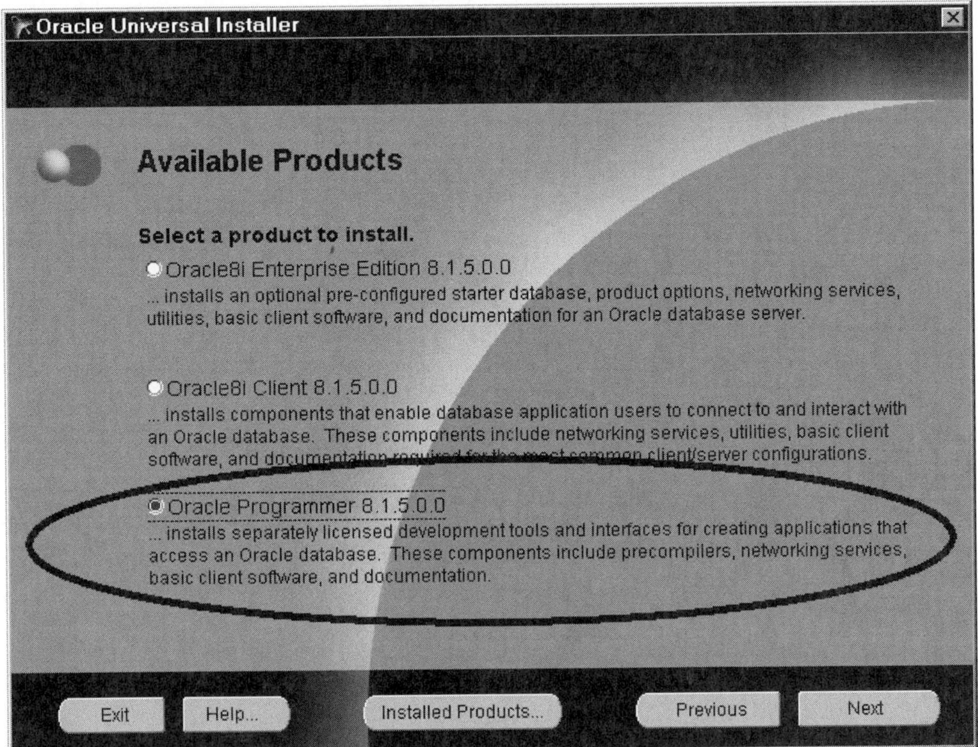

FIGURE 17.2 The Universal Installer about to install Oracle Programmer.

The socket server makes use of the pre-processor directives #ifdef … #endif for conditional compilation of Win32 (Microsoft Windows 32-bit) or Unix-specific code.

The socket implementation is straightforward. It is a simple re-elaboration of the multi-threaded socket server presented in *Unix Network Programming* by R. Stevens, enhanced to support MS Windows NT/2000. The Oracle-embedded SQL statements access two virtual tables, V$DATAFILE and V$FILESTAT. An Oracle database uses V$FILESTAT to store statistics on I/O operations performed against each data file comprising the database, and V$DATAFILE to store detailed information about each data file, such as the file name, the file's status and checkpoints, and the tablespace to which it belongs.

V$FILESTAT only contains a file reference (i.e., a file id), so if you want to retrieve and display a more descriptive file name, you must also access V$DATAFILE and join the two tables together, using the column FILE# as the common column for the join. The NAME column in the V$DATAFILE virtual table stores the data file path. The SQL statement that forms the join is shown below.

```
select substr(df.name,1,100), fs.phyrds, fs.phywrts
from
      v$datafile df, v$filestat fs
where
      df.file# = fs.file#
order by phyrds desc;
```

The SUBSTR function retrieves only the first 100 characters of the data file name. The SQL statement shown above gives the absolute values for physical reads and writes, but you need to provide the user with percentage values to make it clear which files are most accessed. To accomplish this, you select the sum of physical reads and physical writes from all the rows of V$FILESTAT.

```
select sum(phyrds),sum(phywrts)
from v$filestat;
```

You can now divide the physical read and write values for each data file by the sum of the physical reads and writes that occurred since the RDBMS engine started, obtaining the percentage values that summarize the access rate for each file.

The socket server is coded in one C file, which contains both C and embedded SQL statements. The default file type given to such files is .pc instead of .c, to clearly indicate that such files required a pre-compilation pass performed by Pro*C.

The syntax that supports embedded SQL into C constructs is slightly different from standard SQL. When single row selects are coded, the keyword INTO specifies the host variables that receive the corresponding values from the database. In this case, you fetch the sum of all the physical reads into the variables *SumPhysReads* and *SumPhysWrites* defined and initialized in the host language, C.

```
EXEC SQL select sum(phyrds),sum(phywrts) INTO
:SumPhysReads, :SumPhysWrites
from v$filestat;
```

Two things in the embedded SQL statement presented above are worthy of mention. One is the EXEC SQL prefix, which alerts the pre-compiler that what follows is an SQL statement that must be expanded into C calls to the SQLLIB library.[2] The other is the colon that prefixes each host variable reference, indicating the presence of bind variables to the pre-compiler. This notation differs from the one used by JDBC, which uses a question mark to flag parameterized queries. The colon is also used in SQLJ, which is closer than JDBC to the traditional Oracle syntax.

---

[2]Pro*C/C++ generates data structures and calls to its runtime library SQLLIB (*libsql.a* in UNIX).

When a query returns more than one row, a *cursor* must be defined and opened.

A cursor is an area of memory that temporarily stores multiple rows fetched by a query that returns more than one record. Here is the embedded SQL syntax required to declare a cursor:

```
EXEC SQL DECLARE FileCur CURSOR FOR
select substr(df.name,1,100), fs.phyrds, fs.phywrts
from  v$datafile df, v$filestat fs
where df.file# = fs.file# order by phyrds desc;
```

You need to invoke the Pro*C pre-compiler to resolve all the embedded SQL statements into calls to the SQLLIB, the low-level library used by Pro*C to interface to Oracle.

Under MS Windows NT/2000, you can use the graphical interface to Pro*C, which allows for point-and-click selection of the pre-compiler options. Figure 17.3 shows the main screen displayed by the tool.

A few parameters must be set in order to successfully compile your socket server. Since you are using threads, the appropriate Pro*C option must be set to instruct the pre-compiler to generate thread-safe code. This is done by selecting the "Threads" checkbox that appears in the Pro*C option form (see Figure 17.4). If you are using MS Visual C/C++, you should include two libraries in your workspace: WSOCK32.lib, found in the \Vc98\lib subdirectory under the Microsoft Visual Studio directory tree, and Orasql8.lib, found in the \Precomp\lib\Msvc subdirectory under the Oracle directory tree.

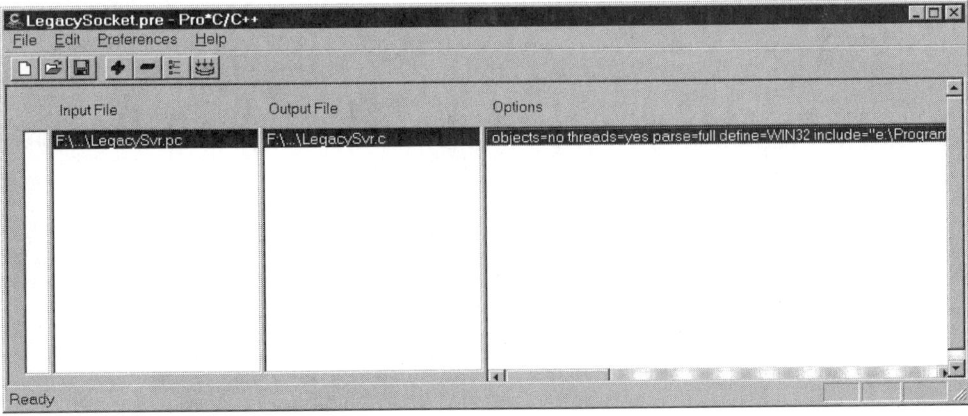

FIGURE 17.3 The graphical interface to Pro*C available in Windows.

If you are operating under Unix, use the make file demo_proc.mk, found in $ORACLE_HOME/precomp/demo/proc, as a pattern for your Pro*C make files. Copy it to your directory and rename it "makefile". Copy the legacy socket server example files from the CD directory/chapter17/LegacySocketServer into a subdirectory created from your home directory. You only need two files, LegacySvr.pc and LegacySvr.h, plus the renamed makefile. Edit makefile, and add the following lines:

```
legacy: $(LEGACY)
LEGACY=LegacySvr.o
```

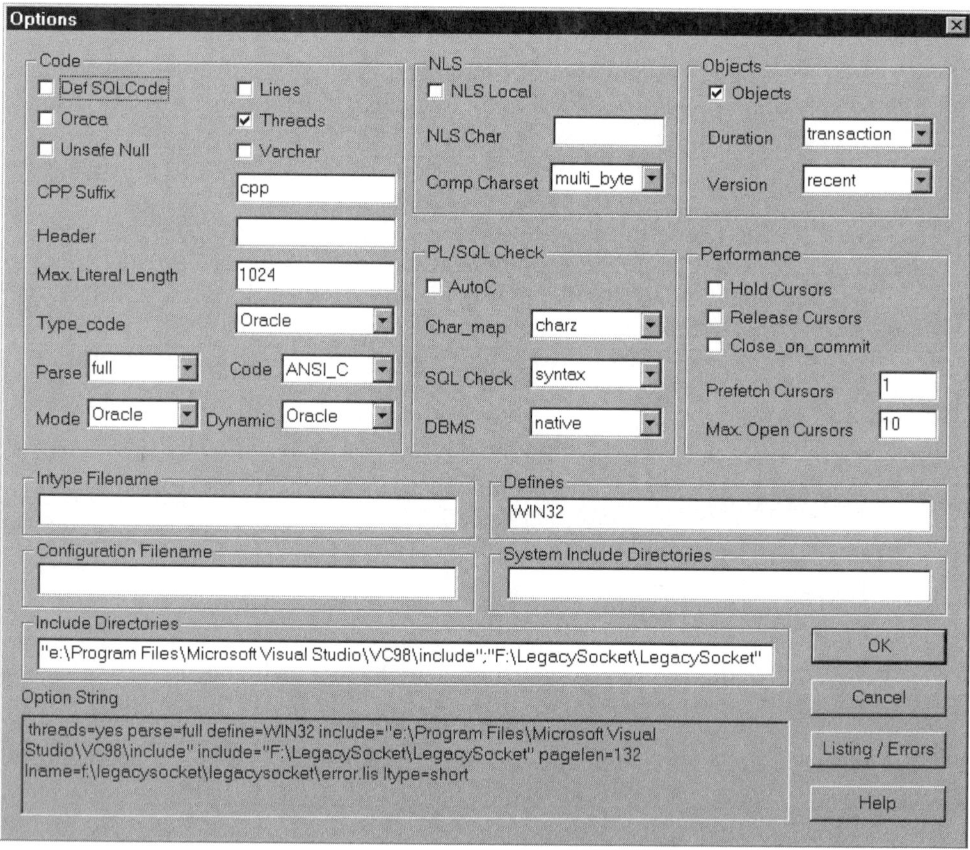

FIGURE 17.4 The Windows Pro*C option form showing the relevant parameters.

```
LegacySvr: $(LEGACY)
	$(ECHO) $(CC) -g $(LDFLAGS) $(DEBUG) $(LEGACY)  -L$(LIBHOME)\
$(STATICPROLDLIBS) -lpthread

LegacySvr.o: LegacySvr.pc LegacySvr.h
	$(PROC) $(PROCPLSFLAGS) THREADS=YES iname=$*
	$(CC) -g $(CFLAGS) $(DEBUG) -c $*.c
```

Save the file, leave the editor, and invoke make using the following command line:

```
make -f makefile build EXE=LegacySvr OBJS="LegacySvr.o"
```

If your environment is properly set up for Oracle development, and you have a valid ORACLE_HOME environment variable that points to a directory where the Oracle software has been installed, you should see Pro*C in action. If everything goes well, the make file will invoke CC and you will find the LegacySvr executable file in your directory. If not, fix the problems with the code or the environment, and try again.

If you are using Windows, you can trigger the pre-compilation from the Pro*C GUI. The C file can be created by Pro*C straight into the directory defined by the Visual C/C++ workspace for the LegacySocket project, so that by switching to Visual C/C++ you can perform a build.

Before focusing on the Java client that uses the services provided by the legacy socket server, a few words must be said about the protocol that enables client and server to communicate in a well-defined manner. Every packet exchanged between the two parts is prefixed by a packet header. The header contains key information about the trailing packet, such as its length, the packet creation timestamp, packet type, packet subtype, and whether the packet is compressed or uncompressed. The packet header definition appears in LegacySvr.h. An excerpt of that file is shown below.

```
typedef struct
{
	char compressed[1];      /* C - compressed, */
	                         /* U - uncompressed */
	char packet_length[4];   /* Packet length in hexadecimal */
	char originator[1];      /* C - client, S - server */
	char packet_type[1];
	char packet_subtype[1];
	char packet_date[8];     /* YYYYMMDD */
	char packet_time[8];     /* HH:MM:SS   HH is in the military */
	                         /* format (00 - 24) */
}PACKET_HEADER;
```

Only ASCII characters are used in the packet header. This simplifies communication between Java and C, since no conversion is required at either end to "understand" the information contained in the packet header. If numbers were used instead of characters, in their internal format (16- or 32-bit integers), the complexity of the application would have been greatly increased. This is the various computer architectures use different formats to store numeric entities. Most Unix servers use the so-called big-endian convention, where the most-significant byte of a two-byte integer is stored at the starting address. Systems based on the Intel architecture mostly use the little-endian convention, where the least-significant byte of a two-byte integer is stored at the starting address. In order to exchange messages containing numeric entities (e.g., integers), conversion processes must be provided, to cater for the different internal representation of numbers. In this example, you will concentrate on salvaging legacy applications rather than marshaling and unmarshaling techniques;[3] for this reason you will use an ASCII-only packet format.

The source code of the legacy socket server *main()* function follows. The key points are commented to facilitate the reading of the C code. The C functions called by the main line are omitted here, but are available on the companion CD-ROM, in the directory */chapter17/LegacySocket*.

```
/*
*****************************************************************************
**
** $Header: /LegacySocket/LegacySvr.pc 2     29-10-99 10:57p Ebonazzi $
** $Revision: 2 $
** $Workfile: LegacySvr.pc $
**
** PROJECT:      Oracle for Java Programmers - Legacy Socket Server
** DESCRIPTION: This C module implements a multi-threaded, multi-platform
**          socket server. It connects to Oracle and gathers Oracle
**          datafile statistics, which are sent to the connected clients.
**          The program is launched by typing:
**          LegacySvr <tcp port> <Oracle connection string>.
**          Example:
**          LegacySvr 3400 "system/manager@orcl"
**          The program needs access to the Oracle virtual tables
**          v$datafile and v$filestat.
**
*****************************************************************************
*/
EXEC SQL INCLUDE SQLCA;
#ifndef WIN32
```

[3]Marshaling is the process of converting numbers from a specific internal representation to a format comprehensible to both big-endian and little endian machines. Unmarshaling is the opposite process, whereby previously marshaled data is converted to an internal format comprehensible to the target machine.

```
#include <unistd.h>
#include <time.h>
#include <values.h>
#include <netinet/in.h>
#include <netdb.h>
#include <fcntl.h>
#include <sys/errno.h>
#include <sys/socket.h>
#include <sys/times.h>
#include <errno.h>
#include <pthread.h>
#define SOCKET int
#else
#include <winsock2.h>
#include <process.h>
#endif
#include <time.h>
#include <stdlib.h>
#include <stdio.h>
#include <string.h>
#include <sys/types.h>

#include "LegacySvr.h"

#define NO_DATA_FOUND 1403 /* Oracle SQL code that informs that no more */
                           /* rows are available in the cursor          */

#define ROW_DELIM       '\001'   /* We use char(1) to delimit each row   */
                                 /* returned by Oracle with datafile     */
                                 /* statistics                           */

int ProcessPackets(SOCKET); /* This function processes all packets   */
                            /* received from the socket channel      */

int FetchFileStatsData(SOCKET); /* This function fetches stats info from */
                                /* the Oracle virtual tables             */
struct timeval          tv;

/* InThreadProcess is the function run by each thread. We need two */
/* definitions of the same function, because it has to be platform       */
/* specific.                                                        */

#ifdef WIN32
DWORD WINAPI  InThreadProcess(LPVOID);
HANDLE            db_mutex;
#else
static void *InThreadProcess(void *);
pthread_mutex_t db_mutex = PTHREAD_MUTEX_INITIALIZER;
#endif
sql_context             main_ctx;
```

```
int main(int argc, char *argv[])
{

        struct sockaddr_in      serveraddr;
        struct sockaddr_in      clientaddr;
        int                     clientaddrlen = sizeof(clientaddr);
        short int               nPort=0;
        int                     nSts=0;
        char                    szPort[21];
        int                     reuse = 0;
        struct linger           l;
#ifdef WIN32
        WSADATA                 wsaData;
        HANDLE                  t_1;
        DWORD                   t_1Id;
#endif
        SOCKET                  sockfd;
        SOCKET                  *sock;

      memset(szPort,'\0',sizeof(szPort));
        if (argc < 3)
        {
                fprintf(stdout,
                "Usage: LegacySvr <TCP Port> "
                "<Oracle Connection String>\n");
                exit(1);
        }
        strcpy(szPort,argv[1]);
        nPort=atoi(szPort);

      /* This informs the sqllib interface to Oracle that our program */
      /* is multi-threaded                                             */
      EXEC SQL ENABLE THREADS;

      /* Allocating a context is mandatory in multi-threaded programs */
      EXEC SQL CONTEXT ALLOCATE :main_ctx;

      /* We inform the sqllib that we are using the context previously */
      /* allocated                                                      */
      EXEC SQL CONTEXT USE :main_ctx;

      /* Connection to Oracle using the connection string passed from  */
      /* the command line as the second argument                        */
      EXEC SQL CONNECT :argv[2];
      if (sqlca.sqlcode != 0)
      {
            fprintf(stderr,"Oracle Error: %d\n",sqlca.sqlcode);
            exit(1);
      }

      /* Win32-specific initialization routine */
#ifdef WIN32
      if (WSAStartup(0x202,&wsaData) == SOCKET_ERROR)
```

```
	{
		fprintf(stderr,"WSAStartup failed with error
			%d\n",WSAGetLastError());
		WSACleanup();
		exit(1);
	}
	/* In Win32 we allocate our mutex here */
	db_mutex = CreateMutex(NULL,FALSE,NULL);
#endif
	/* Socket creation */
	if ((sockfd = socket(AF_INET, SOCK_STREAM, 0)) < 0)
	{
		perror("socket_create");
		exit(1);
	}

	/* We set a few basic options for our socket server... */
	memset(&serveraddr,'\0',sizeof(struct sockaddr_in));
	serveraddr.sin_family      = AF_INET;
	serveraddr.sin_addr.s_addr = htonl(INADDR_ANY);
	serveraddr.sin_port        = htons(nPort);
	setsockopt(sockfd, SOL_SOCKET, SO_REUSEADDR, (void *) &reuse,
		sizeof(reuse));
	l.l_onoff = 1;
	l.l_linger = 0;
	setsockopt(sockfd, SOL_SOCKET, SO_LINGER, (void *) &l, sizeof(l));

	/* Socket is now bound */
	if ( bind(sockfd,
		(struct sockaddr *)&serveraddr,
		 sizeof(struct sockaddr_in)) < 0)
	{
		perror("socket_bind");
		exit(1);
	}
#ifdef _DEBUG
		fprintf(stdout,"Socket bound\n");
#endif
	/* The server now listens for incoming connections on the */
	/* socket port */

	listen(sockfd, 8);
	while(1)
	{
	 /* To understand the code below refer to "Unix Network Programming" */
	 /* by R. Stevens, page 610                                          */
	    sock = malloc(sizeof(SOCKET));
	    if ((*sock = accept(sockfd,
				(struct sockaddr *) &clientaddr,
				 &clientaddrlen)) < 0)
	    {
		    perror("socket_accept");
		    exit(1);
```

```
            }
#ifdef _DEBUG
            fprintf(stdout,"Accept on %d \n",*sock);
#endif
           /* Each connection originates a new thread that  */
           /* executes the InThreadProcess routine          */
#ifdef WIN32
           t_1 = CreateThread(NULL, 0, InThreadProcess, sock, 0, &t_1Id);
#else
           pthread_create(NULL, NULL, &InThreadProcess, sock);
#endif
      } /* end while */

    return 0;  // Standard return value for success.
} /* end function */
```

The LegacySvr.pc file, shown above, contains a few routines that have been omitted from the listing to save space. Table 17.1 gives their names and purposes. Again, edit the file directly from the companion CD in order to examine the file in its entirety.

You are done with the legacy stuff. Now you can focus on the Java client that displays the Oracle data file statistics, reading the packets sent by the socket server.

The client application/applet consists of the seven java classes listed in Table 17.2.

In order to save space, the entire Java code of the client application is not shown in the following pages. Only a few selected methods are illustrated, but the complete source code is available in the companion CD-ROM, under the directory */chapter17/LegacySocket/Java*.

TABLE 17.1 Routines implemented in LegacySvr.pc and omitted from the listing

FUNCTION	PURPOISE
void *InThreadProcess(void *arg)	Executed by each thread spawned by main(). Enters an endless loop that repeatedly calls the *ProcessPackets* routine until the latter returns a non-zero value. This happens either when the client decides to close the connection or when an error occurs.
int ProcessPackets(SOCKET s)	Performs a blocking read over the socket channel. The header of the incoming packets is read; according to the value contained in packet_type and packet_subtype, the appropriate routine to process the packet is called.
Int FetchFileStatsData(SOCKET s)	Performs a database lookup, formats a packet that contains the value fetched from the dynamic performance tables, and sends the packet over the socket channel received as a parameter.

TABLE 17.2 Java classes comprising the client application

CLASS FILE NAME	PURPOSE
Comms.java	Encapsulates all socket-related methods and attributes used to create a socket channel, reads packets from it, and writes packets to it.
ConnectionDialog.java	Dialog that allows user to connect to the socket server.
DatafileStats.java	Dialog that displays Oracle data file statistics, allowing user to periodically refresh the information displayed.
DataPacket.java	Encapsulates knowledge about data packets (i.e., how to format packets and packet headers, how to read packets coming from the socket server).
LegacySocketApplet.java	Application startup. It handles running as an application or as an applet.
MainFrame.java	Application frame that displays the main menu.
MessageBox.java	Dialog used by the application to display messages to user. Can be modal or non-modal.

Most modern Java IDEs, such as Borland JBuilder or Oracle JDeveloper, automatically generate most of the code needed to populate and display visual controls. You will therefore ignore the GUI-related code and focus attention on the *Comms* and *DataPacket* classes, which implement the socket connection and data communication between the Java client and the legacy server. You will also examine the method that responds to the click on the "Connect" button displayed by the connection dialog and the method that responds to the selection of the "File Statistics" menu option.

The *Comms* class represents the core of your example. It contains methods to create a socket and associate input and output streams to it, methods to write and read packets to or from the socket channel, and a method to close the socket.

Since the *Comms* class constructor is declared as private, the only way to create an instance of the class is by calling the static method *getInstance()*, which returns a reference to the *Comms* class. The first call to *getInstance()* actually creates the Comms object; all subsequent calls merely return a reference to it. This ensures that only one Comms object is ever instantiated by your application.[4]

The source code showing the class constructor, together with the attributes defined at a class level, follows.

```
package com.prenhall.OFJP.legacysocket;

import java.net.*;
import java.io.*;
```

[4]This represents the classical implementation of the Singleton pattern. See Gamma et al., *Design Patterns: Elements of Reusable Object-Oriented Software* (Addison–Wesley, 1995).

```
/** This class implements a TCP connection to a legacy socket server.
*   Since only one connection class may exist at any one point in time,
*   the singleton design pattern is applied.
*/
public class Comms extends Object
{
  /** The single copy of Comms
  */
  private static Comms comms;

  /** Handle to the main frame object.
  */
  private MainFrame frame;

  /** Total number of bytes received. Counter incremented at each
  *   Input operation.
  */
  private long totalBytesReceived;

  /** Total number of bytes sent. Counter incremented at each Output
  ** operation.
  */
  private long totalBytesSent;

  /** Flag that stores true if a TCP connection has been successfully
  **  established.
  */
  private boolean isConnected;

  /** Socket channel.
  */
  private Socket socket;

  /** Input stream from the socket channel.
  */
  private DataInputStream    inStream;

  /** Output stream to the socket channel.
  */
  private DataOutputStream    outStream;

  /** Host name for the connection to the legacy socket server.
  */
  private String remoteHost;
```

```
/** TCP/IP port number used by the legacy socket server.
*/
private int tcpPort;


/** Class constructor. It is implemented as a private constructor, so
*   a singleton object can be instantiated.
*/
private Comms(MainFrame frame)
{
  this.frame = frame;
  totalByteReceived = 0;
  totalByteSent = 0;
  this.boolConnected = false;
}

/** This method returns the single instance of the Comms class.
*   If no instance exists yet, this method creates one.
*   @param frame Reference to the MainFrame object.
*   @return ServerSideComms - Instance of the class ServerSideComms.
*/
public synchronized static Comms getInstance(MainFrame frame)
{
    if (comms == null)
    {
       comms = new Comms(frame);
    }
    return comms;
}
```

Note that you keep two counters to store the total number of bytes sent and received. You also define a flag that is set to true when a TCP connection is established, and to false when the socket disconnects.

The source code that implements the creation of the socket channel, and the association of input and output streams to it, is shown below.

```
/** Method to create a socket connection.
*/
public synchronized void createTCPConnection()  throws Exception
{
    try
    {
       this.socket = new Socket(remoteHost,tcpPort);
       this.boolConnected = true;
    }
```

```
      catch (UnknownHostException uhe)
      {
         System.out.println("Error occurred while trying to connect to "+
                            "the socket server - " + uhe.toString());
         throw uhe;
      }
      catch (IOException ioe)
      {
         System.out.println("I/O Error occurred while connecting to "+
                            "the socket server. "+ ioe.toString());
         throw ioe;
      }
      try
      {
         outStream = new DataOutputStream(socket.getOutputStream());
         inStream  = new DataInputStream(socket.getInputStream());
      }
      catch (IOException ioe)
      {
         System.out.println("I/O Error occurred while associating "+
                            "an input/output stream to the remote socket" +
                            ioe.toString());
         throw ioe;
      }
}
```

Exceptions caused by low-level socket calls are handled locally by printing an error message, and are thrown, so that the GUI can display an appropriate error message in a message box.

Once you have wrapped input and output streams around the socket, it is easy to exchange messages with the socket server. The source code that implements the methods for our application to write to the socket and to read from it is shown below.

```
/** Method to read a stream of bytes from the socket channel. This method
*   blocks until all requested bytes are received.
*   @param iLen The length of the stream of bytes to be read.
*   @return array of bytes - The bytes read from the socket channel.
*/
public synchronized byte[] read(int iLen)
{
   byte [] bytesToBeReceived = new byte[iLen];
   try
   {
         inStream.readFully(bToBeReceived);
         addByteReceived(iLen);
   }
```

```
        catch  (Exception exc)
        {
            System.out.println("Error! - " + exc.toString());
        }
        return( bToBeReceived);
    }

    /** Method to write an array of bytes to the socket channel.
    *   @param bOut Array of bytes containing the message to be written.
    */
    public synchronized void writeRemote(byte [] bOut)
    {
        try
        {
            outStream.write(bOut);
            addByteSent(bOut.length);
        }
        catch (Exception exc)
        {
            System.out.println("Error while writing! - " + exc.toString());
        }
    }

    /** This method increments the number of bytes received.
    *   @param nBytes Int containing the number of bytes received, to be added
    *   to the internal counter.
    */
    private void addBytesReceived(int nBytes)
    {
        totalBytesReceived += nBytes;
    }

    /** This method increments the number of bytes sent.
    *   @param nBytes Int containing the number of bytes sent, to be added
    *   to the internal counter.
    */
    private void addBytesSent(int nBytes)
    {
        totalBytesSent += nBytes;
    }
    /** Sends a packet to the socket server.
    *   @param packet Array of bytes containing the data to be sent to the
    *   socket server.
    */
    public void sendPacket(byte [] packet) throws IOException
    {
        this.writeRemote(packet);
    }
```

Now that you are finished with the communication infrastructure needed by the program, we will turn to application-specific messages, and how to send them to the socket server. The DataPacket class encapsulates the logic needed to format a packet header. The *formatClientPacket()* overloaded methods receive the message payload as either a string or an array of bytes, and two chars, which supply the message type and subtype. The method fills in the remaining fields of the header, and returns a complete packet, ready to be sent.

The DataPacket class defines certain constants (known as final static objects in Java parlance), including several packet types and subtypes, then implements a *readPacket()* method that performs a blocking read on the socket channel for a number of bytes equal to the length of the packet header. When the latter has been retrieved, the method computes the length of the message payload and performs a second blocking read, this time blocking until the entire message payload has been read from the socket. The method then returns the complete packet to the caller as an array of bytes.

The source code of the DataPacket class is shown below.

```
package com.prenhall.OFJP.legacysocket;

import java.text.*;
import java.util.*;
public class DataPacket extends Object
{

  public static final char OFJP_SERVER_PACKET       = 'S';
  public static final char OFJP_CLIENT_PACKET       = 'C';
  public static final char OFJP_TYPE_STATS          = 'S';
  public static final char OFJP_FILE_STATS          = 'F';
  public static final char OFJP_TYPE_CONTROL        = 'C';
  public static final char OFJP_EXIT_APP            = 'E';
  public static final char OFJP_COMPRESSED_PACKET   = 'C';
  public static final char OFJP_UNCOMPRESSED_PACKET = 'U';
  public static final char OFJP_ROW_DELIM           = '\001';

  /** Packet Header length in bytes.
  */
  public static final int  PACKET_LEN = 24;

  /** Position at which the Hex string containing the packet length
  *   begins in the packet header.
  */
  public static final int  PACKET_LENGTH_BEGIN = 1;

  /** Position at which the Hex string containing the packet length
  *   ends in the packet header.
  */
  public static final int  PACKET_LENGTH_END = 5;
```

```
/** Position of the header (0 based) that contains the packet type.
*/
public static final int PACKET_TYPE_POS = 6;

/** Position of the header (0 based) that contains the packet subtype.
*/
public static final int PACKET_SUBTYPE_POS = 7;

/** Method to assemble a packet sent from the client to
*   the legacy socket server.
*   @param msg Array of bytes containing the message to be formatted
*      into the packet.
*   @param packetType Char indicating the client packet type.
*   @param packetSubType Char indicating the client packet sub-type.
*   @return finalPacket - Array of bytes containing the assembled packet.
*/


/** Method to assemble a packet sent from the client to
*   the legacy socket server.
*   @param msg String containing the message to be formatted into the
*   packet.
*   @param packetType Char indicating the client packet type.
*   @param packetSubType Char indicating the client packet sub-type.
*   @return finalPacket - Array of bytes containing the assembled packet.
*/
public static byte[] formatClientPacket(byte[] msg, char packetType,
                                        char packetSubType)
{
    SimpleDateFormat formatter = new SimpleDateFormat ("yyyymmddHH:mm:ss");
    Date currentTime = new Date();
    String dateString = formatter.format(currentTime);
    int len = msg.length;
    byte [] finalPacket = new byte[24+len];
    String pcklen = new String(Integer.toHexString(len));
    int lenPckLen = pcklen.length();
    if (lenPckLen < 4)
    {
       int remaining = 4 - lenPckLen;
       StringBuffer sb = new StringBuffer();
       for(int ii =0; ii < remaining; ii++)
          sb.append("0");
       sb.append(pcklen);
       pcklen = sb.toString();
    }
    char [] pck = new char[8];
    pck[0] = OFJP_UNCOMPRESSED_PACKET;
    pck[1] = pcklen.charAt(0);
    pck[2] = pcklen.charAt(1);
    pck[3] = pcklen.charAt(2);
```

```
        pck[4] = pcklen.charAt(3);
        pck[5] = OFJP_CLIENT_PACKET;
        pck[6] = packetType;
        pck[7] = packetSubType;
        StringBuffer sb = new StringBuffer();
        sb.append(pck);
        sb.append(dateString);
        String ttt = sb.toString();
        byte[] header = ttt.getBytes();
        System.arraycopy(header,0,finalPacket,0,PACKET_LEN);
        System.arraycopy(msg,0,finalPacket,PACKET_LEN,len);
        return finalPacket;
    }

    public static byte[] formatClientPacket(String msg, char packetType,
                              char packetSubType)
    {
        byte[] bMsg = new byte[msg.length()];
        bMsg = msg.getBytes();
        byte[] finalPacket = formatClientPacket(bMsg,packetType,
                                          packetSubType);
        return finalPacket;
    }

    /** Reads an entire packet. It reads the header and blocks until all packet
    *   has been read.
    *   @param ServerSideComms Communication object.
    *   @return packet - Array of bytes containing the data packet.
    *   If the packet contains compressed data, decompression is not performed.
    *   @throws IOException If an I/O error occurs.
    */
    public synchronized byte[] readPacket(Comms comms)
                    throws java.io.IOException
    {
        byte [] remainingBytes;
        byte[] packet;
        String header = comms.readString(PACKET_LEN);
        String strPackLen = header.substring(PACKET_LENGTH_BEGIN,
                                        PACKET_LENGTH_END);
        Integer packLen = Integer.valueOf(strPackLen,16);
        int intLen = packLen.intValue();
        byte[] headerByte = new byte[PACKET_LEN];
        headerByte = header.getBytes();
        packet = new byte[PACKET_LEN + intLen];
        System.arraycopy(headerByte,0,packet,0,PACKET_LEN);
        if (intLen > 0)
        {
           remainingBytes =  new byte[intLen];
           remainingBytes = comms.read(intLen);
           System.arraycopy(remainingBytes,0,packet,PACKET_LEN,intLen);
```

```
      }
      return packet;
  }
}
```

When you start the client application/applet, you are presented with an empty window containing a menu displaying two main options, "File" and "Display Statistics" (see Figure 17.5).

If you start the client as an applet, the <APPLET> tag stored in the .html file that launches the applet specifies two parameters, Host and Port.[5] If you start the client as an application, you must provide the two parameters on the command line.

When you select the "Connect to Socket Server" menu option, a dialog box appears, displaying the host name and socket port passed as parameters (see Figure 17.6). By clicking on the "Connect" button, the client attempts to connect to the socket server. If the socket server is active and listening on the well-known port, a connection occurs.

The source code that displays the connection dialog follows. The method appears in the MainFrame class.

```
//Connect to Socket Server
void jMenuConnect_actionPerformed(ActionEvent e)
{
  //Connection dialog instantiation. It will be a modal dialog.
  ConnectionDialog cd = new ConnectionDialog(this,
                              "Connection to remote host",
                              true);
  // Host name and socket port are set.
  cd.setRemoteHost(this.host);
  cd.setRemotePort(this.port);

  // Code needed to center the dialog on the screen.
  Dimension parentSize = Toolkit.getDefaultToolkit().getScreenSize();
  Dimension localSize = cd.getPreferredSize();
  cd.setLocation((parentSize.width-localSize.width)/2,
            (parentSize.height-localSize.height)/2);
  // Modal dialog is shown.
  cd.show();
  // After the dialog has been dismissed, we can check if the user
  // clicked on "Connect"
  if(this.getDialogAction() == this.ACTION_TYPE_CONFIRM)
```

[5]At the moment of writing, there is no direct support for Java 1.2 in Microsoft IE5 or Netscape Navigator. In order to see your example application from a Web browser, you must use the Java plug-in. The HTML tag to enable the plug-in is <OBJECT> for Internet Explorer 4/5 and <EMBED> for Netscape Communicator.

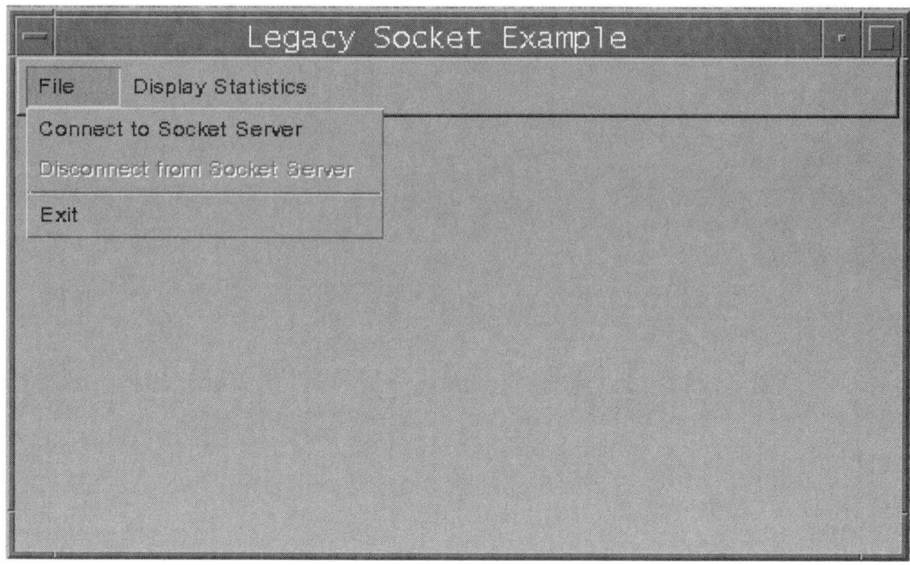

FIGURE 17.5 Client application main window.

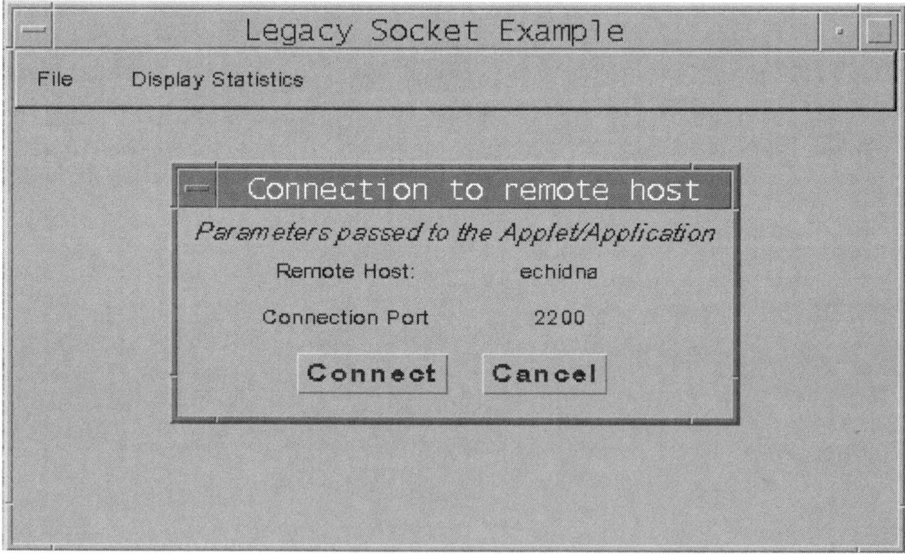

FIGURE 17.6 The dialog box that allows users to connect to the socket server.

```
{
  try
  {
     // Attempt a connection to the socket server
     comms.createTCPConnection();
     // Upon successful connection we inform the users.
     MessageBox mb = new MessageBox(this,"Connection Successful",true);
     mb.setMessageFirstRow("Message from remote host:");
     mb.setMessageSecondRow("Connected to the legacy socket server");
     mb.show();
     // The code below enables menu options that allow the user to
     // progress with the application.
     this.jMenuFileStats.setEnabled(true);
     this.jMenuConnect.setEnabled(false);
     this.jMenuDisconnect.setEnabled(true);
  }
  catch(Exception exc)
  {
     // If the connection attempt has been unsuccessful, we inform
     // the users.
     MessageBox mb = new MessageBox(this,"Connection Unsuccessful",
                                    true);
     mb.setMessageFirstRow("Message from remote host:");
     mb.setMessageSecondRow("Could not connect: "+
                              exc.getMessage());
     mb.show();
  }
}
```

If the connection attempt succeeds, the “File Statistics” menu option, accessible from the “Display Statistics” main menu, is enabled. A client who selects this option sends a request packet to the server, which gathers the requested statistics, formats them into a packet, and sends it back to the client. The latter uses StringTokenizer to extracts rows and fields from the packet, and displays the data file statistics using a JTable.

Each row is delimited by an ASCII character 1 (‘\0001’), and each field is delimited by a pipe character (‘|’).

The source code of the method that responds to the “File Statistics” menu option, contained in the MainFrame class, is shown below.

```
// File Statistics Menu Option
void jMenuFileStats_actionPerformed(ActionEvent e)
{
  DatafileStats ds = new DatafileStats(this,
                             "Oracle datafile statistics",true);
  Dimension parentSize = Toolkit.getDefaultToolkit().getScreenSize();
  Dimension localSize = ds.getSize();
```

```
    ds.setLocation((parentSize.width-localSize.width)/2,
              (parentSize.height-localSize.height)/2);
    // The refresh method collects the statistics from the server
    ds.refresh();
    this.jMenuDisconnect.setEnabled(false);
    ds.setSize(800,400);
    ds.show();
    this.jMenuDisconnect.setEnabled(true);
  }
```

When a user asks for data file statistics to be displayed, the dialog is created and the *refresh()* method invoked. The *refresh()* method performs the most important operation in the example, sending the request packet and receiving the server's response.

```
// Refresh
public void refresh()
{
  // Handle to the packet that contains the datafile stats.
  byte [] packet;

  // Request packet. This packet does not have any payload. Only the
  // header is meaningful in the context of this application.
  byte [] locPacket =
          DataPacket.formatClientPacket("", // empty payload
                          DataPacket.OFJP_TYPE_STATS,  // packet type
                          DataPacket.OFJP_FILE_STATS); // packet subtype
  try
  {
     // Display message box informing the user that we are gathering
     // the requested statistics.
     this.displayMessageBox();

     // Send the request packet.
     frame.comms.sendPacket(locPacket);

     // Blocking socket read. It returns the packet sent by the
     // socket server.
     packet = frame.dataPacket.readPacket(frame.comms);

     // We convert the message payload into a string, which can
     // processed using StringTokenizer.
     String packStr = new String(packet,24,packet.length-24);

     // The first tokenizer looks for row delimiters...
     StringTokenizer st =
```

```
            new StringTokenizer(packStr,
            new String(new char[] {DataPacket.OFJP_ROW_DELIM}));
    rows.removeAllElements();
    while(st.hasMoreTokens())
    {
      // The second tokenizer looks for field delimiters...
      String tok = st.nextToken();
      StringTokenizer st2 =
              new StringTokenizer(tok,
              new String(new char [] {'|'}));

      // Each row consists of 5 data items.
      String [] data  = new String[5];

      data[0]=(String)  st2.nextToken();
      data[1]=(String)  st2.nextToken();
      data[2]=(String)  st2.nextToken();
      data[3]=(String)  st2.nextToken();
      data[4]=(String)  st2.nextToken();
      // Each array of strings is added to the vector used by
      // the AbstractTableModel to feed the Jtable with data.
      rows.add(data);
    }
  }
  catch (Exception exc)
  {
  }
  // If after a refresh we have new or modified data,
  // we fire the event to updated the JTable.
  model.fireTableDataChanged();
  if (this.mb != null)
    this.mb.dispose();
}
```

Figure 17.7 shows the Oracle data file statistics dialog. Application users must click on the refresh button if they want to force a reread of the Oracle dynamic performance table. An alternative solution implements a Java thread that performs an automatic periodic refresh, but that is left as an exercise for you.

The infrastructure built to support the legacy socket server example is flexible enough to be reused in more complex applications. By modifying the switch statement that queries the packet type and subtype on the server, you can extend the range of messages recognized by the server. You can then extend the client, making it aware of the additional message types. Following the same scheme, you could implement several more dialogs, each showing relevant statistics gathered from the Oracle database that you wish to monitor.

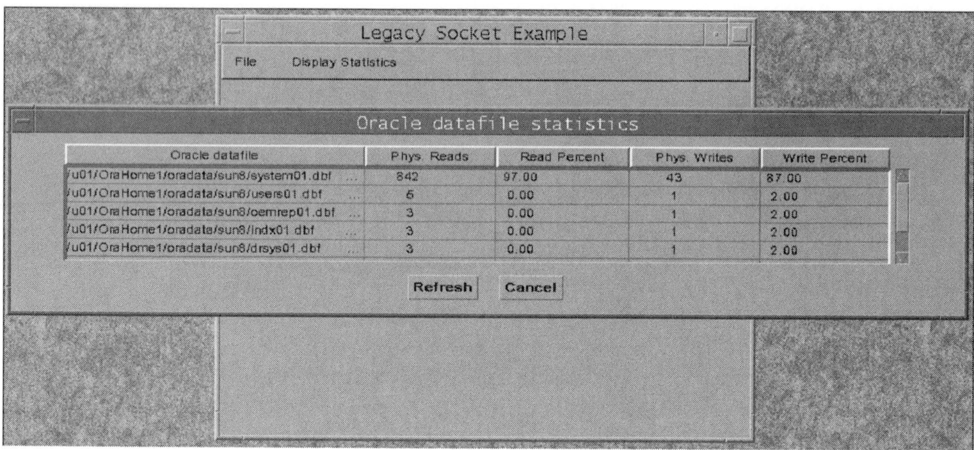

FIGURE 17.7 The Oracle datafile statistics dialog.

SUMMARY

This chapter focused on how to rejuvenate legacy applications using the Java networking primitives. You began by examining the important role played by the mediator design pattern in promoting loose coupling between legacy modules and Java-based objects. Applications designed according to the principles of the mediator pattern are easier to implement and maintain.

Most of the chapter was devoted to the implementation, using legacy technologies, of a socket server that would serve clients written in Java. The legacy application provides performance data gathered from an Oracle database. The Java clients display the data in a tabular format, using a Java2 JTable component.

A crucial element, allowing for seamless integration between C and Java, is the implementation of a communication protocol establishing the basic rules that all participants in the distributed application must follow in order to avoid chaos and deadlocks. In your example, all the messages exchanged by the server and its clients are formatted into packets, and each packet is prefixed by a packet header that carries crucial information about the message payload (e.g., packet length, whether the packet is compressed, the timestamp of the packet creation).

Many legacy applications, especially in the Unix world, use sockets or other communication mechanisms, such as datagrams, to ensure interprocess communication among remote nodes. Java can easily tap into this mature and robust application infrastructure, allowing designers and developers to rejuvenate aging applications.

In the next chapter you will learn about Java Native Interface (JNI), another powerful means to link Java to the legacy world of C, COBOL, and C++.

Chapter 18

Web-Enabling Legacy Applications Using JNI

This chapter focuses on the use of Java Native Interface (JNI) as a technology for deploying interim solutions during the transition phase that characterizes the migration path from traditional technologies to the new Web-centric environment.

At the beginning of the Java revolution, the performance of the virtual machine was a major concern of developers and designers willing to venture into the new technology. At the time of this writing, JVM performance is no longer an issue. Companies like Borland/Inprise have demonstrated that a carefully designed and implemented Java application can perform as well as a native application. On Microsoft Windows, JBuilder Foundation, an IDE written totally in Java, is as fast as JBuilder 3.0, written in C++. In a few areas, such as the help subsystem and the smart completion of Java constructs through the CodeInsight facility, JBuilder Foundation even outperforms the Win32 native version of JBuilder. The user-perceived performance of JBuilder Foundation is very good, and developers can switch to a Java-only IDE without sacrificing performance. With the improvement of Java performance, one of the most compelling reasons for the use of JNI has disappeared.

Using JNI should be regarded as a last resort, since it defeats the very purpose of Java: compatibility across different platforms.

In database-centric applications the performance bottlenecks are network bandwidth and raw data retrieval rather than the language used to access the engine. Furthermore, several industry benchmarks confirm that at an Oracle internals level, Java is faster than PL/SQL for computationally intensive tasks.

The major reason for using JNI nowadays is compatibility with a large code base of legacy C or COBOL functions that IT managers are not prepared to throw away simply because Java is "more fashionable." Being in fashion doesn't justify the cost associated with the porting effort.

JNI is neither an easy nor a small topic, and this chapter does not try to be a full JNI tutorial. The focus is on the interaction of Java with C code that accesses a database, making data stored in Oracle tables and/or objects available to Java methods. The assumption here is that data retrieval and business logic are implemented in libraries written in C with either embedded SQL or OCI calls, and a Java application only needs to interface to those libraries.

By reading and studying this chapter you will learn how to create C wrappers around your legacy code, reading parameters from and passing parameters to C functions. Your Java classes will fetch data from an Oracle database and write data into Oracle tables. You will also learn how to invoke the debugger in order to debug the C code called from your Java native methods.

18.1 ORACLE PRE-COMPILERS

Before the widespread popularity of Rapid Application Development (RAD) tools, such as Microsoft Visual Basic or Borland Delphi, most database-centric applications accessed Oracle database tables using embedded SQL. In embedded

SQL, SQL statements are intermixed with COBOL or C code, which is pre-compiled in order to translate the SQL syntax into language calls to APIs able to implement the SQL layer.

Even after the advent of the client/server model, where database front-ends are usually built using Client/Server RAD tools, the Oracle pre-compilers are still in widespread use, mainly for such back-end tasks as database housekeeping, old data purging, periodical reporting, and integration with legacy systems.

The two most popular Oracle pre-compilers are Pro*C and Pro*COBOL. This chapter focuses on Pro*C, but the same concepts can be easily applied to other pre-compilers.

In the next few paragraphs, you will integrate a library of C functions that use Pro*C to access an Oracle database through Java. The legacy functions provide primitives for connecting to an Oracle database, fetching the performance data stored in one dynamic performance view (V$SYSSTAT),[1] storing the performance data in a custom-defined table, committing or rolling back the transaction, and, finally, disconnecting from the database.

The example you will be working on in this chapter uses six C functions that use embedded SQL (see Table 18.1).

Table 18.2 lists all the files that constitute the example used in this chapter to illustrate the use of JNI.

Although only a few functions are included in your simulated legacy library, the example exercises the most common database operations. The purpose and meaning of most of the functions are self-explanatory and easily understood, but you should give special attention to the *FetchSystats()* function.

FetchSystats retrieves multiple rows from the V$SYSSTAT dynamic performance view, the structure of which is shown in Table 18.3.

The V$SYSSTAT dynamic performance view stores important database instance-wide statistics accumulated since the time the instance was started. Since statistical values are only available cumulatively, it makes sense to store them periodically in a user-defined table, thereby facilitating comparative analysis between different points in time. That is precisely the goal of the example used throughout this chapter.

If you look at the source code that implements FetchSystats, located in the */chapter18/JNIExample/legacy* directory of the companion CD, you will realize that multiple rows are fetched in one pass rather than one per database call. Oracle allows for fetching a set of rows in a *batch*, or *array*, which minimizes the number of database calls and thereby reduces network traffic. *Host arrays* can be used for both bulk insert and bulk retrieval of multiple rows. The network performance gain obtained by the use of host arrays is significant in any kind of Oracle archi-

[1]The Oracle RDBMS exposes performance counters kept by the engine through pseudo-views that reside in memory. Such views are called "dynamic performance views" and are characterized by the V$ prefix.

TABLE 18.1 C functions used by the JNI example developed throughout the chapter

C FUNCTION	PURPOSE
int OraConnect(char * , char *)	Connects to an Oracle instance, given database and password.
int OraDisconnect(void)	Disconnects from an Oracle instance.
int Commit(void)	Commits a pending transaction.
int Rollback(void)	Rolls back a pending transaction.
int FetchSystats(SYSTAT_DATA * , SYSTAT_PAR *)	Fetches performance data from the Oracle dynamic performance view V$SYSSTAT.
int StoreEvents(EVENT_DATA * , int)	Stores performance data fetched from V$SYSSTAT in a custom-defined table.

tecture, especially two-tier client/server. The efficient data retrieval on the server side is enhanced by an even more efficient use of network resources.

While this technique promotes the overall efficiency of Oracle-based applications, it raises the issue of correct array sizing and multiple calls to the routine that performs the database lookup. The problem results from the fact that you do not know in advance how many rows your SQL query will return. If you dimension your arrays too big, you risk wasting a lot of memory; if you dimension

TABLE 18.2 Files comprising JNI example

FILE NAME	PURPOSE	CD LOCATION
JNIExample.h	Contains definitions needed by legacy code to fetch data from Oracle.	Chapter18/JNIExample/legacy Chapter18/JNIExample/jni
JNIExample.pc	Implements connection, disconnection, and data retrieval from Oracle using embedded SQL.	Chapter18/JNIExample/legacy
JNIWrapper.h	Generated by javah.	Chapter18/JNIExample/jni
JNIShared.c	Implements JNI layer that interfaces to legacy code.	Chapter18/JNIExample/jni
JNIRunner.java	Java main line that uses functionality provided by JNI.	Chapter18/JNIExample/java
JNIWrapper.java	Wrapper class that defines all native methods.	Chapter18/JNIExample/java
OraStats.java	Class that encapsulates value pair statistic-value.	Chapter18/JNIExample/java
SysEvent.java	Class that defines attributes and methods to store and retrieve performance data.	Chapter18/JNIExample/java

TABLE 18.3 The structure of V$SYSSTAT

COLUMN NAME	NULL?	TYPE	DESCRIPTION
STATISTIC#	Yes	NUMBER	Statistic code. The dynamic performance view V$STATNAME lists the name corresponding to each number.
NAME	Yes	VARCHAR2	Statistic name.
CLASS	Yes	NUMBER	Statistic class: 1 (User); 2 (Redo); 4 (Enqueue); 8 (Cache); 16 (OS), 32 (Parallel Server); 64 (SQL); 128 (Debug).
VALUE	Yes	NUMBER	Statistic value.

them too small, you won't fully exploit the benefits offered by host arrays, because you will have to perform too many database calls to fetch all the required rows.

In order to make available to the program that interacts with the database the multiple rows fetched by a query with a WHERE clause that identifies more than one record, Oracle uses a *cursor*, or a memory area that temporarily stores the rows returned by the query. An user-written program will DECLARE a cursor, specifying its name and the types of columns associated with it. It will then OPEN the cursor and FETCH the cursor data into the provided structure. When all rows have been fetched from the Oracle table, the user-written program will CLOSE the cursor, releasing memory and other associated resources.

Oracle customers frequently separate the functions that use embedded SQL statements from the rest of the program. If a custom application is decomposed in several layers or modules, typically business logic, logical data access, and physical data access, embedded SQL will only "pollute" the physical data-access layer. All the other modules can be coded using plain C without SQL syntax.

Structuring the application code in layers enormously simplifies debugging by isolating the incomprehensible lines of code automatically generated by the pre-compiler in the physical data-access modules. Furthermore, decoupling the data-access logic from the business logic makes it easy to modify the physical structure of the database without reworking the business logic code.

The problem outlined above stems from not knowing in advance the number of rows that a given query will return. One elegant solution to this problem is to have the business logic pass to the logical data-access function in charge of populating the linked list with data fetched from the Oracle database, a pointer to the root node of a linked list. The logical data-access function repeatedly calls the physical data-access function, until no more rows are available. At each pass, it stores the retrieved rows in the linked list, which is returned to the business logic function. The business logic function has access to the data fetched from the Oracle database by traversing the linked list.

The mechanism just described requires the two data-access layers, the logical and the physical, to communicate with each other. The physical data-access layer must be informed whether the current call is an initial call, which implies declaring and opening a cursor, or a subsequent call, which implies one more fetch into a previously opened cursor. The physical data-access layer must inform the logical data-access layer whether the current query fetched all rows identified by the WHERE clause or whether more database calls are needed to complete the database lookup. This two-way communication is achieved by using a "protocol" structure, the fields of which are accessed and modified by both layers. If you look at the JNIExample.h include file, located in the */chapter18/JNIExample/legacy* directory, you will find a definition of the SYSTAT_PAR, which defines the query parameters for *FetchSystats()*. An excerpt from that file is shown below.

```
/* "Protocol" structure for SYSTAT_DATA. It allows the C mainline
to
** communicate with the physical data access function
*/
typedef struct
{
  int  nToBeFetched; /* IN - Size of the host array */
  int  nWhatToDo;     /* IN - 0 Open cursor - 1 Fetch and close */
  int  nCloseCursorNow; /* IN - terminates fetch abruptly */
  int  nMoreRowsToFetch; /* OUT - 0 No - 1 yes*/
  int  nTotalFetchedSoFar; /* OUT - cumulative counter of */
                           /* rows fetched               */
  int nBufferCardinality;  /* OUT - Number of rows in the */
                           /* host array                  */
}SYSTAT_PAR;
```

The SYSTAT_PAR structure contains six elements or fields. The first three are IN parameters, or parameters passed from the caller to the callee, and the last three parameters are OUT parameters, passed from the callee to the caller. The meaning of the six fields of the protocol structure is examined in Table 18.4.

The logical data-access layer calls the *FetchSystats()* function, which requires two parameters, a structure containing the fields that is filled with data fetched from Oracle, and the protocol structure. Before calling *FetchSystats()* for the first time, the logical data-access function sets `nToBeFetched` to the host array dimension (which in your example is 20) and `nWhatToDo` to 0. After the first call to *FetchSystats()* the logical data-access function checks the `nMoreRowsToFetch` field in the protocol structure to find out whether more calls are needed to fetch the rows identified by the query. If this field is set to 1, the logical data-access function sets `nWhatToDo` to 1 (fetch and possibly close the cursor) and calls *FetchSystats()* again, until the value in `nMoreRowsToFetch` becomes 0.

TABLE 18.4 SYSTAT_PAR protocol structure.<< title ok?>><<YES>>

STRUCTURE FIELD	PURPOSE
nToBeFetched	Specifies the size of the host arrays passed to the physical data-access function.
nWhatToDo	A value of 0 means that the physical data-access function must declare and open the cursor associated to the SQL query. A value of 1 means that the physical data-access function must perform a fetch and, if no more rows are to be returned by Oracle, close the cursor.
nCloseCursorNow	A value different from 0 in this field instructs the physical data-access function to close the cursor straightaway, even if not all the rows were fetched from Oracle.
nMoreRowsToFetch	A value of 0 means that all the rows have been fetched and the cursor has been closed. A value of 1 means that more rows are waiting to be fetched into the cursor.
nTotalFetchedSoFar	This field holds the cumulative total number of rows fetched by repeatedly calling the physical data-access function.
nBufferCardinality	This field holds the number of rows fetched in the current buffer. If the host array is dimensioned to 20 positions, but the query only returned 8 rows, this field will contain 8.

Figure 18.1 depicts a state transition diagram for a SQL query that returns 55 rows. The host array size is set to 20.

If you look at the contents of the JNIExample.h file, you will see the definition of the structure that contains the fields populated by *FetchSystats()*. The definition is replicated below.

```
#define ROWS  20
#define STATS_STR_SIZE  65

typedef struct
{
  char szStatistic[ROWS][STATS_STR_SIZE];
  long lValue[ROWS];
}SYSTAT_DATA;
```

The SQL query issued against V$SYSSTAT fetches two fields, NAME and VALUE. Each call fetches a batch of 20 rows. The source code of *FetchSystats()* follows.

```
/* This function performs a database fetch of performance data        */
/* gathered from the V$SYSSTAT dynamic performance view.               */
/* Parameters:
**      SYSTAT_DATA *     Empty structure that will be filled with
**                        data fetched from V$SYSSTAT
```

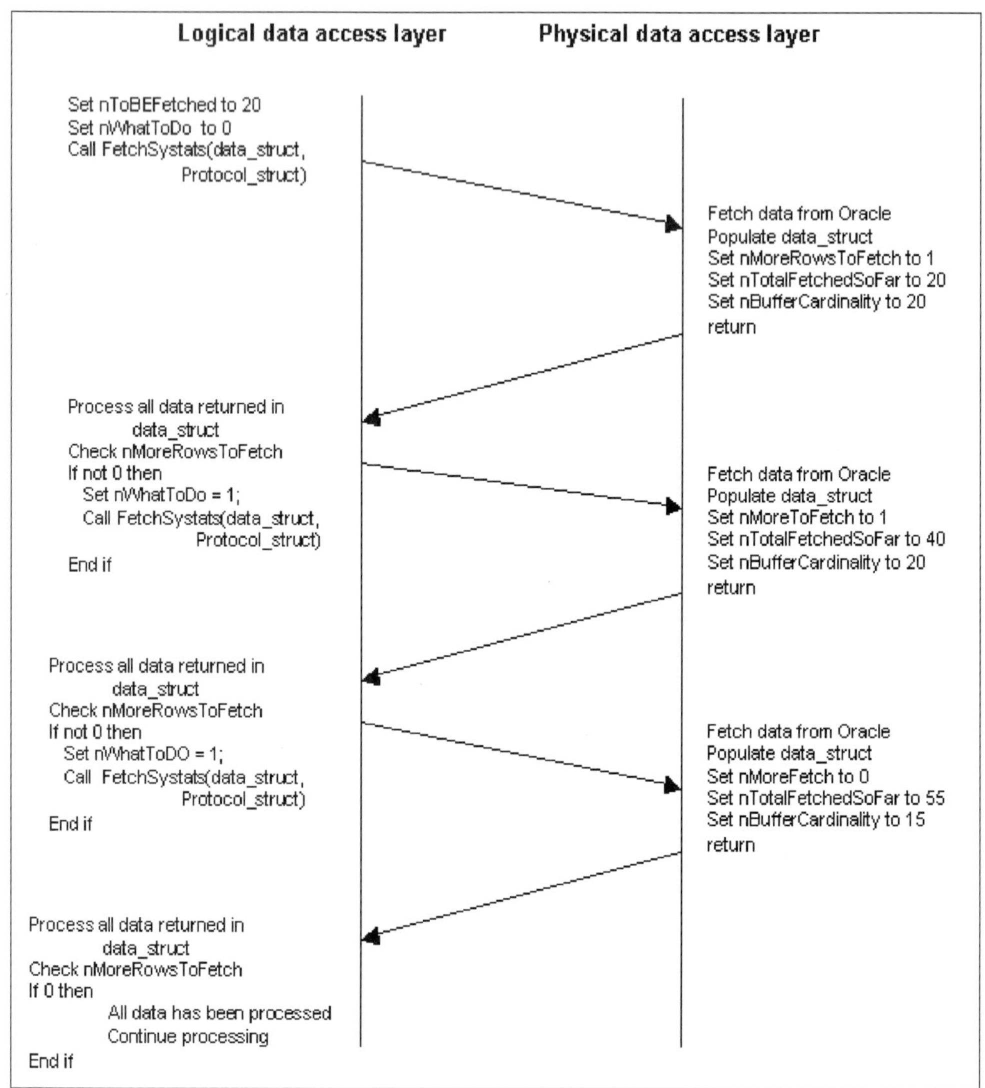

FIGURE 18.1 State transition diagram for an SQL query that returns 55 rows.

```
**      SYSTAT_PAR *      Protocol structure used to communicate
**                           information about the fetch operation
**                             between the caller and the
**                             callee (this function).           */
int FetchSystats( SYSTAT_DATA * systat_data, SYSTAT_PAR * parameters)
{
  int nOpenCursor = 0;
```

```
int nRowsDone = parameters->nTotalFetchedSoFar;
                                /* Keeps a line counter */
if ( parameters->nWhatToDo == 0)
                          /* If this is the first call, declare  */
                          /* and open the cursor...              */
{
      EXEC SQL DECLARE systats CURSOR FOR

      SELECT NAME, VALUE
      FROM V$SYSSTAT;

      EXEC SQL OPEN systats;
      if ( sqlca.sqlcode != 0)
      {
            int error = sqlca.sqlcode;
            EXEC SQL CLOSE systats;
            return(error);
      }
      else
            nOpenCursor = 1;
}
/* If the caller requested a cursor closure, perform it! */
if (parameters->nCloseCursorNow > 0 )
{
      int sts;
      if (nOpenCursor)
      {
            EXEC SQL CLOSE systats;
            sts = sqlca.sqlcode;
            nOpenCursor = 0;
      }
      return(sts);
}

EXEC SQL FOR :parameters->nToBeFetched FETCH systats
INTO  :systat_data;

parameters->nBufferCardinality = sqlca.sqlerrd[2] - nRowsDone;
parameters->nTotalFetchedSoFar = sqlca.sqlerrd[2];
if(sqlca.sqlcode == NO_MORE_ROWS)
{
      EXEC SQL CLOSE systats;
      nOpenCursor = 0;
      parameters->nMoreRowsToFetch = NO_MORE_TO_FETCH;
      return(0);
}
else if (sqlca.sqlcode == 0)
{
      parameters->nMoreRowsToFetch= MORE_TO_FETCH;
      return(0);
```

```
63:     }
64:     else
65:     {
66:             int error = sqlca.sqlcode;
67:             EXEC SQL CLOSE systats;
68:             nOpenCursor = 0;
69:             return(error);
70:     }
71: }
```

10 FetchSystats receives a pointer to a structure of the SYSTAT_DATA type, and a pointer to a structure of the SYSTAT_PAR type. It uses the former to store the data fetched from the Oracle database; the latter implements the protocol used to communicate with the caller information about the fetching process.

12–13 nOpenCursor is a boolean flag that is set to 1 upon a successful opening of the cursor. nRowsDone keeps a counter for the rows fetched so far from Oracle.

15–33 If the caller requests the cursor to be opened, FetchSysstats will declare it first, and then will open it. If an error occurs, the function will return the Oracle error code.

35–45 If the caller needs to abruptly terminate the fetch operation, FetchSystats closes the cursor and returns the Oracle code to the caller.

47–48 The rows fetched into the cursor from Oracle are copied into the structure passed as a parameter, which contains host arrays. The FOR clause limits the number of rows copied into the structure to the size of the array.

51–52 The "OUT" parameters of the protocol structure are set by FetchSystats. The number of rows copied into the host arrays (nBufferCardinality) is computed by subtracting the row counter from the total number of rows fetched so far, as returned by the SQLCA structure. The total number of rows fetched so far is set in the protocol structure, taking its value straight from SQLCA.

52–58 If, after the last fetch, the SQLCA structure reports that all the rows identified by the SQL query have been fetched, the cursor is closed and the nMoreRowsToFetch field of the protocol structure is set to NO_MORE_TO_FETCH. The control is then passed back to the caller.

59–63 If, after the last fetch, the SQLCA structure reports that more rows are waiting to be fetched into the cursor, the nMoreRowsToFetch field of the protocol structure is set to MORE_TO_FETCH and control is passed back to the caller.

64–70 If an error occurs during the last fetch, the cursor is closed and the error code is returned to the caller.

Note the syntax used at line 47, where the FOR clause is used to limit the number of rows retrieved to the size of the host arrays. The use of FOR is not strictly necessary in this context, since the Oracle pre-compiler is smart enough to work out the array dimension by itself. In fact, it goes even further, making sure that if the host variables in one SQL operation involving host arrays are dimensioned using different sizes, the pre-compiler automatically uses the smallest array received from the program as the global size for all variables.

The FOR keyword demonstrates its usefulness in the *StoreEvents()* function, which stores a batch of rows in one pass. In the example shown in this chapter, the default array size is set to 20 cells. If your program only partially populates the array, leaving a few positions inside the array empty, and then calls *StoreEvents()*, the net effect is that Oracle inserts 20 rows in the target table, including the empty rows that correspond to the unfilled array cells. Usually this "wild" insertion provokes an error, if referential integrity is enabled on the table in question. You cannot insert rows with nulls in the column(s) that constitute the primary key of a table.

To avoid this problem, the *StoreEvents()* function takes two parameters, the first a C structure containing the host arrays with data to be inserted, the second an integer that specifies how many rows must be inserted. *StoreEvents()* limits the number of rows to be inserted, using the FOR clause in the INSERT statement, as shown by the source code fragment below:

```
int StoreEvents(EVENT_DATA * sysevt, int how_many)
{
 EXEC SQL FOR :how_many
 INSERT INTO SYS_EVENT (statistic,when,value) values
        (:sysevt);
 if (sqlca.sqlcode == 0)
        return(0);
 else
        return(sqlca.sqlcode);
}
```

18.2 JAVA NATIVE METHODS

Java is a modern, object-oriented language that uses abstract data structures, such as vectors and hash tables, rather than structs/records or linked lists. Implementing a linked list in Java is easy, but vectors and hash tables are decidedly more in line with the spirit of the Java language. This means that you want to shield your Java methods from the details and bad habits of C. A clear separation between Java and C is easily accomplished in the JNI layer, which connects your legacy code to the Java application. A JNI method can instantiate Java objects and return them to the Java environment. This approach is explored in the next few paragraphs, where the JNI wrapper for the *FetchSystats()* function instantiates a Java object, populates its internal vector with the performance data fetched from Oracle, and returns the object to the Java layer.

The JNIWrapper.java file contains the class definition for JNIWrapper. This class defines six native methods, which map one-to-one the six legacy C functions coded in JNIExample.pc. The source code of JNIWrapper is shown below.

```
public class JNIWrapper  extends Object
{
   public static native boolean  connect(String user, String pwd)
                                 throws java.sql.SQLException;
   public static native void commit()
                             throws java.sql.SQLException;
   public static native void Rollback()
                             throws java.sql.SQLException;
   public static native void disconnect()
                             throws java.sql.SQLException;
   public static native SysEvent getSystemStats()
                        throws java.sql.SQLException;
   public static native void  setSystemEvents(SysEvent se)
                              throws java.sql.SQLException;
}
```

All native methods throw an SQLException, which must be instantiated by the JNI environment. The *getSystemStats()* native method returns a SysEvent object. Here is the class definition for SysEvent.

```
import java.util.Vector;

public class SysEvent
{
   // This Vector will contain the V$SYSSTAT statistics gathered
   // by the native methods
   private Vector statistic = new Vector();


   // Method that creates an OraStats object, populated with
   public void setStat(String st, long v)
   {
      OraStats os = new OraStats(st,v);
      this.statistic.addElement(os);
   }
```

```
   public OraStats getStats(int index)
   {
      return (OraStats) this.statistic.get(index);
   }

   // Method that returns a string containing the description
   // of the statistics contained at a given position of the Vector.
   public String getStatistic(int index)
   {
      OraStats os = this.getStats(index);
      return os.getStat();
   }

   // Method that returns the numerical value (long)
   // associated with an Oracle statistics, given its position
   // in the Vector.
   public long getStatisticValue(int index)
   {
      OraStats os = this.getStats(index);
      return os.getValue();
   }

   // This method returns the size of the Vector where the
   // V$SYSSTAT statistics are stored
   public int getStatSize()
   {
      return this.statistic.size();
   }

}
```

The SysEvent implementation is quite straightforward. A vector containing OraStats objects is defined and created by the class constructor. The other methods are getters and setters that access the vector, storing OraStats objects into it and retrieving OraStats objects from it, given their position in the vector.

The OraStats class definition is shown below.

```
public class OraStats extends Object
{
  private String statistic;
  private long   lValue;

  public OraStats(String st, long v)
  {
   this.statistic = st;
   this.lValue = v;
```

```
    }
    public String getStat()
    {
        return this.statistic;
    }
    public long getValue()
    {
        return this.lValue;
    }
}
```

The implementation of OraStats consists of a Java-revisited C structure that does not offer setter methods because the class constructor sets the value for the statistic and lValue attributes.

You can now examine the Java *main()* method, which uses the native methods to fetch performance data from Oracle, storing the collected data in a user-defined table. Take a close look at the source code shown below; it exhibits a true Java look-and-feel. Your Java layer has been completely shielded from the C ugliness, yet the data that materialize in the vector contained in the SysEvent object after the call to *getSystemStats()* are fetched by your library of legacy C functions.

```
public class JNIRunner
{
  static { System.loadLibrary("JNIShared");}
  public static void main(String[] args)
  {
    SysEvent se=null;
    JNIWrapper jw = new JNIWrapper();
    try
    {
      jw.connect(args[0],args[1]);
      se = jw.getSystemStats();
      jw.setSystemEvents(se);
      jw.commit();
    }
    catch (java.sql.SQLException exc)
    {
     System.out.println(exc.getMessage());
    }
    finally
    {
       jw.disconnect();
    }

  }
}
```

The lines in bold show the calls to the native methods. The reference to SysEvent, *se*, refers to an object that is created by the native method *getSystemStats()*. That function calls Java methods from C, populating the vector contained in SysEvent with performance data retrieved through calls to the C function FetchSystats, which contains embedded SQL (see above). The same reference to the SysEvent object (*se*) is passed to the *setSystemEvents()* method, which calls Java methods to retrieve the OraStats objects from the vector in SysEvent. The data extracted from the vector are stored in an Oracle table by calling the C function *StoreEvents()*, which contains embedded SQL.

18.2.1 CODING THE JNI LAYER

Before delving into the specifics of the JNI example used to illustrate the concepts covered in this chapter, we must revise the steps that link the procedures written in other languages to a Java environment.

Calling functions implemented in C from Java involves the six-step process shown in Table 18.5.

The Java source file JNIWrapper.java (see above) contains the Java wrappers for six native methods/functions (connect, disconnect, commit, rollback, get-

TABLE 18.5 Steps required to call functions implemented in C from Java

STEP	OPERATIONS PERFORMED
1	Code the Java wrappers for the native methods. In your example, this was done in the JNIWrapper class. The *native* keyword tells the Java compiler that the method is implemented in a “foreign” language. Methods declared as native resemble abstract methods, as they only declare method signatures, but do not implement any logic.
2	Compile the Java source file containing native methods into a .class file.
3	Run the *javah* utility, included in the Java JDK, against the .class file built in the preceding step. javah reads the Java bytecodes from the .class file and produces C include files that contain method signatures for the native methods declared in the Java source file. The method names declared in Java are mangled by javah (i.e., the original name is altered). Usually, the original name is prefixed with the Java keyword, followed by an underscore and the class name, an underscore, and finally the method name.
4	Code and compile the C functions, matching names and signatures specified by the include files generated by javah.
5	Generate a dynamic (or shared) library (or object). In Windows. This means creating a DLL with the C functions coded in the preceding step. Under Linux and Solaris they are called shared objects and have the *.so* extension. Under HP/UX they are called shared libraries and have the *.sl* extension.
6	Link the shared library built in the preceding step to the Java environment. This is accomplished by creating a static initializer for the class containing the native methods. Two methods, implemented in the System class, allow developers to link the external shared libraries to the JVM: *System.load()* and *System.loadLibrary()*.

SystemStats, setSystemEvents). It must be compiled into bytecodes before you can use javah to generate the include file (.h):

```
javac JNIWrapper.java
```

A successful compilation creates the file JNIWrapper.class. You can now run javah (step 3 in Table 18.5), which takes JNIWrapper.class as a parameter, to produce the C include file with the method signatures. Make sure that the current directory (indicated as a single dot) is part of the CLASSPATH environment variable. In Windows you can accomplish this with the following command:

```
set CLASSPATH=%CLASSPATH%;.;
```

If you use the Bourne, the bash, or the Korn shell under Unix, the corresponding command is:

```
CLASSPATH=$CLASSPATH:.:
export CLASSPATH
```

After you have added the current directory to the CLASSPATH environment variable, you can invoke javah:

```
javah -jni JNIWrapper
```

The file created by javah is JNIWrapper.h. Its content is shown below:

```
/* DO NOT EDIT THIS FILE - it is machine generated */
#include <jni.h>
/* Header for class JNIWrapper */

#ifndef _Included_JNIWrapper
#define _Included_JNIWrapper
#ifdef __cplusplus
extern "C" {
#endif
/*
 * Class:     JNIWrapper
 * Method:    Connect
 * Signature: (Ljava/lang/String;Ljava/lang/String;)Z
 */
JNIEXPORT jboolean JNICALL Java_JNIWrapper_connect
  (JNIEnv *, jclass, jstring, jstring);
```

```
/*
 * Class:     JNIWrapper
 * Method:    Commit
 * Signature: ()V
 */
JNIEXPORT void JNICALL Java_JNIWrapper_commit
  (JNIEnv *, jclass);

/*
 * Class:     JNIWrapper
 * Method:    Rollback
 * Signature: ()V
 */
JNIEXPORT void JNICALL Java_JNIWrapper_rollback
  (JNIEnv *, jclass);

/*
 * Class:     JNIWrapper
 * Method:    Disconnect
 * Signature: ()V
 */
JNIEXPORT void JNICALL Java_JNIWrapper_disconnect
  (JNIEnv *, jclass);

/*
 * Class:     JNIWrapper
 * Method:    getSystemStats
 * Signature: ()LSysEvent;
 */
JNIEXPORT jobject JNICALL Java_JNIWrapper_getSystemStats
  (JNIEnv *, jclass);

/*
 * Class:     JNIWrapper
 * Method:    setSystemEvents
 * Signature: (LSysEvent;)V
 */
JNIEXPORT void JNICALL Java_JNIWrapper_setSystemEvents
  (JNIEnv *, jclass, jobject);

#ifdef __cplusplus
}
#endif
#endif
```

So far the process has been easy. Now comes the difficult part. Step 4 is about writing the native functions in C, respecting the parameter-passing convention established by the pre-processing operated by javah. This means using the JNI API to map Java datatypes to C datatypes, and vice versa. Using JNI, complex objects, and not just simple datatypes, can be passed back and forth between Java and C. Furthermore, a native function can instantiate a complex Java object using C JNI calls. In your example, this feature is used by the native function *Java_JNIWrapper_getSystemStats()*. This function creates (i.e., instantiates) the Java object SysEvent and populates its vectors with performance data by repeatedly calling *FetchSystats()* until all the rows have been fetched. The *Java_JNIWrapper_getSystemStats()* function uses the same include file as its physical data-access counterpart, JNIExample.h, so that it can share the data and the protocol structures passed to *FetchSystats()*.

The C functions called directly from Java, or from the JNI layer, play the role of the logical data-access function in legacy applications. They interact with the physical data-access functions, the ones that contain embedded SQL, and they are responsible for the data flow from and to Oracle. The JNI layer has access both to the inner structures of the C legacy code and to the internal Java data structures, such as vectors and hash tables. The JNI layer is in a perfect position to "objectify" data that belong in a procedural environment. It gets data from the Oracle database by calling *functions* in a procedural environment, and stores them, using Java calling *methods*, in an object-oriented environment. In this process, a C variable or structure field is "promoted" to a Java attribute.

If you want to use the same approach to integrate your libraries of legacy code into Java, use your editor to examine all the Java and C files that constitute the example used throughout the chapter. For brevity's sake, you examine only one JNI function here. It is probably the most difficult and representative of the techniques illustrated in this chapter.

Table 18.6 lists the JNI APIs used by *Java_JNIWrapper_getSystemStats()*, together with a simple description of their purpose.

The source code of *Java_JNIWrapper_getSystemStats()* is shown below, followed by a detailed explanation of each statement.

```
JNIEXPORT jobject JNICALL Java_JNIWrapper_getSystemStats
(JNIEnv *env, jclass cl)
{
 jclass          SysEventClass;
 jmethodID       initMethod;
 jmethodID       setStat;
 jobject         SysEvent;
 jstring         SysStat;
 jlong           lValue;
 jclass          SQLExcClass;
 char            err_msg[80];
 SYSTAT_DATA     systat;
 SYSTAT_PAR      systat_par;
```

TABLE 18.6 JNI APIs used in the example

API NAME	SYNTAX	DESCRIPTION	ARGUMENTS
NewStringUTF	jstring NewStringUTF(JNIEnv *, const char *)	Constructs a new java.lang.String object from an array of UTF-8 characters.	(1) JNI interface pointer (2) Pointer to a UTF-8 string
GetMethodID	jmethodID GetMethodID (JNIEnv *, jclass, const char *, Const char *)	Returns the method ID for an instance method of a class or interface.	(1) JNI interface pointer (2) Java class object (3) Method name in a null-terminated UTF-8 string (4) Method signature in a null-terminated UTF-8 string
NewObject	Jobject NewObject(JNIEnv *, jclass, jmethod, ...)	Constructs a new Java object. The method ID indicates which constructor method to invoke.	(1) JNI interface pointer (2) Java class object (3) Method ID of the constructor (4) One or more arguments to the constructor
ThrowNew	jint ThrowNew(JNIEnv *, jclass, const char *)	Constructs a java.lang.Throwable object from the specified class.	(1) JNI interface pointer (2) Subclass of java.lang.Throwable (3) Exception message
FindClass	jclass FindClass(JNIEnv *, const char *)	Loads a locally defined class.	(1) JNI interface pointer (2) Fully qualified class name
CallVoidMethod	void CallVoidMethod (JNIEnv *, jobject, jmethod, ...)	Calls a Java instance method that returns void from a native function.	(1) JNI interface pointer (2) Java object (3) Method ID (4) One or more arguments to the method

```
int             status,ii;

SysEventClass = (*env)->FindClass(env,"SysEvent");
initMethod = (*env)->GetMethodID(env,SysEventClass,
                                     "<init>","()V");
setStat     = (*env)->GetMethodID(env,SysEventClass,"setStat",
                                 "(Ljava/lang/String;J)V");
```

```
21:  SysEvent = (*env)->NewObject(env,SysEventClass,initMethod);
22:  memset(&systat,'\0',sizeof(systat));
23:  memset(&systat_par,'\0',sizeof(systat_par));
24:  systat_par.nToBeFetched = 20;
25:  systat_par.nWhatToDo = OPEN_CURSOR;
26:  status = FetchSystats(&systat,&systat_par);
27:  if ( status != 0)
28:  {
29:    SQLExcClass = (*env)->FindClass(env,
30:                          "java/sql/SQLException");
31:    sprintf(err_msg,"Oracle reported error number: %d",
32:                                status);
33:          (*env)->ThrowNew(env,SQLExcClass,err_msg);
34:    return NULL;
35:  }
36:  while(1)
37:  {
38:    systat_par.nWhatToDo = FETCH_AND_CLOSE;
39:    for (ii = 0; ii < systat_par.nBufferCardinality; ii++)
40:    {
41:       SysStat = (*env)->NewStringUTF(env,systat.szStatistic[ii]);
42:       lValue  = (jlong) systat.lValue[ii];
43:       (*env)->CallVoidMethod(env,SysEvent,setStat,SysStat,lValue);
44:    }
45:    if(systat_par.nMoreRowsToFetch == NO_MORE_TO_FETCH)
46:                break;
47:    else
48:    {
49:          memset(&systat,'\0',sizeof(systat));
50:          if ( (status = FetchSystats(&systat,&systat_par)) != 0)
51:          {
52:             SQLExcClass = (*env)->FindClass(env,
53:                                         "java/sql/SQLException");
54:             sprintf(err_msg,"Oracle reported error number: %d",
55:                                 status);
56:             (*env)->ThrowNew(env,SQLExcClass,err_msg);
57:             return NULL;
58:          }
59:    }
60:  }
61:  return SysEvent;
62:}
```

1–2 Java_JNIWrapper_getSystemStats is declared as a function that returns a Java object (jobject), and receives a pointer to the JNI interface (*env) and a reference to a Java class (cl).

4–14 The variables needed by the function are declared here.

16 FindClass stores a reference to the SysEvent class in SysEventClass. A reference to such a class is needed by the GetMethodID call, which returns a handle to the SysEvent class constructor. The convention used to obtain a constructor method is to pass <init> as the method name, and void "()V" as the return type.

17–18 A handle to the SysEvent class constructor is stored in initMethod. It will be needed when the program creates a new object of SysEvent type.

19–20 A handle to the setStat method, implemented by the SysEvent class, is stored in setStat.

21 A new Java object is created. It is an object of type SysEvent, and its constructor method is initMethod.

22–23 The data and protocol structures are initialized to null.

24–25 The protocol structure fields nToBeFetched and nWhatToDo are set to 20 and OPEN_CURSOR.

26 FetchSystats is called, passing the data and the protocol structures to it. The result is stored in the status variable.

27–35 If the call to FetchSystats fails, a new exception object of the SQLException type is instantiated and thrown to the Java environment. The JNI function returns immediately after throwing the exception.

36 An endless loop is started at this line. It terminates when all the rows have been retrieved from Oracle.

38 The nWhatToDo field of the protocol structure is set to FETCH_AND_CLOSE, to signal to the physical data-access function that from this point on you want to fetch rows into the cursor, which has been already opened.

39–44 The host arrays returned by the call to FetchSystats are accessed, and one by one the statistics and the corresponding values are stored in the SysEvent object, calling the setStat method (line 43). The protocol structure systat_par provides the upper limit for the loop that iterates through the host arrays.

45–46 If the last call to FetchSystats retrieves all the rows identified by the SQL query, the nMoreRowsToFetch field of the protocol structure holds the NO_MORE_TO_FETCH mnemonic. If this is the case, then line 46 halts the endless loop started at line 36.

47–50 If more rows need to be fetched into the cursor, the FetchSytats function calls again (line 50). Before calling Systats, the structure that contains the host arrays is reinitialized to null (line 49).

51–57 If FetchStats signals that an error occurred while fetching rows from Oracle, a new exception object is created and thrown back to the Java environment. The Oracle error code is stored in the message attribute of the SQLException object.

62 When all the processing is finished, the SysEvent object is returned to the Java method that called Java_JNIWrapper_getSystemStats(). The Java caller finds the SysEvent object populated with performance data collected from Oracle.

Once all the native functions specified in JNIWrapper.h have been implemented, and the source code successfully compiles, it is time to progress through step 5, which involves creating a shared object (or dynamic link library) from the C object file. The next section goes through this process in detail, covering both Windows and Unix environments.

18.3 SETTING UP YOUR ENVIRONMENT TO RUN THE EXAMPLE

To have the three components that comprise the example up and running with minimal effort, follow the steps outlined in this paragraph. First, start with the Java files. Copy all files with a Java extension from the companion CD, under the directory Chapter18/JNIExample/java, into a directory of your choice on your hard disk.

If you are using a Java IDE, such as Oracle JDeveloper, Borland Jbuilder, or IBM VisualAge, create a new project and add the following four files:

- JNIRunner.java
- JNIWrapper.java
- OraStats.java
- SysEvent.java

Build the project, compiling all the Java files into classes. If you are not using an IDE, use the *javac* compiler to compile the java source files listed above. This step is the same for both Microsoft Windows and Solaris.

It is now the turn of the library of C functions that contain embedded SQL. Copy the files JNIExample.h and JNIExample.pc (the C includes files used by the legacy library of Oracle functions plus the C file containing embedded SQL implementing the data-gathering logic) from Chapter18/JNIExample/legacy into a directory on your hard disk called Jni.

18.3.1 MICROSOFT WINDOWS

If your environment is Microsoft Windows, make sure that the directory that contains the Oracle executables is in your PATH. To access the Oracle pre-compiler, simply open a "Command prompt" or MS-DOS window, and type `proc` . The pre-compiler should display a long list of options. If the system does not recognize the command, check to see whether Oracle is correctly installed, including the Oracle Programmer extension (see Chapter 19 for a detailed explanation of how to install Oracle Programmer), and whether that your PATH includes the Oracle *bin* directory, which is a subdirectory of ORACLE_HOME.

In the MS-DOS window, change your path to where you copied the JNIExample.pc, by switching to the appropriate disk drive and typing "cd <directory>". Type the following command:

```
proc iname=JNIExample.pc parse=full include="<X>:\Program Files\Microsoft
Visual Studio\VC98\Include" include=<Y>:\JNIExample pagelen=132
errtype=<Y>:\jniexample\err.log ltype=short
```

replacing the <X> and <Y> symbols with the drive letters where you installed MS Visual C/C++ and your C files, respectively. Check that no errors have occurred and make sure that the pre-compiler has created file jniexample.c.

Start Visual C/C++ and create a new workspace, which will contain two projects. The first, called JNIExample, will build a static library (.lib) containing the legacy code that accesses the Oracle database. The second project, called JNIShared, will build a DLL containing the code that uses JNI to exchange data between the JVM and Oracle.

To create the new workspace in Visual C/C++, click on File->New and choose the Workspaces tab (see Figure 18.2) Accept the default blank workspace,

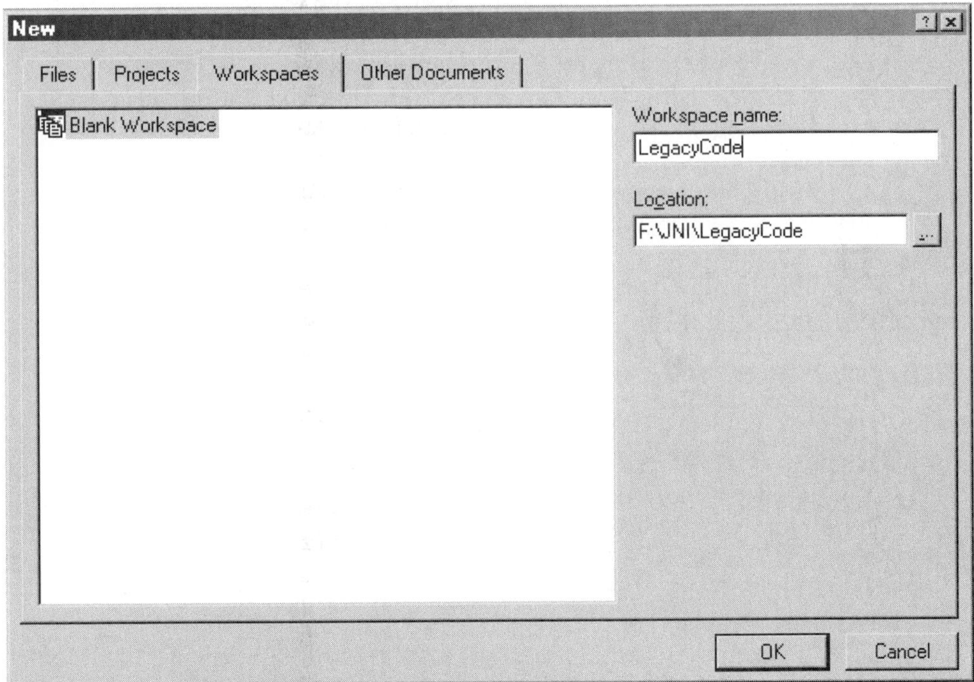

FIGURE 18.2 Creating a new workspace in Visual C/C++.

and select the Jni directory as the workspace location. Call the workspace "LegacyCode" and click on the Ok button to create it.

You can create the first project once the workspace becomes available. You do this through the project wizard, which is invoked by highlighting the LegacyCode workspace, right-clicking on its name, and choosing the option "Add new project to Workspace" from the drop-down menu. The project wizard appears, with its default tab set to "Projects". Choose a Win32 static library. When the project wizard asks if you want pre-compiled headers or support for MFC, leave the two checkboxes unchecked.

Add jniexample.c to the project. Build the project by creating a file with a .lib extension. Click on "File->Save All" to save source and project files, and then close the workspace. For the sake of the example, assume that the name of the project, and consequently of the library, is JNIExample.

Using Windows Explorer, create a new directory, naming it JNIShared. Access the companion CD and copy the following files into the JNIShared directory from */Chapter18/JNIExample/jni*:

- JNIExample.h
- JNIShared.c

Access Visual C/C++ again, and create a new project, choosing Win32 Dynamic Link Library. Name the project JNIShared. When the project wizard asks what kind of DLL you want to create, click on the radio button marked "An empty DLL project", then click on the "Finish" button.

Go back to the directory where you compiled the Java classes. Run the *javah* executable against the JNIWrapper class. It should create the JNIWrapper.h include file.

Copy the resulting JNIWrapper.h to the JNIShared directory. Reactivate the Visual C/C++ window and add the following files to the project:

- JNIShared.c
- JNIExample.lib
- oraSQX8.lib
- oraSQL8.lib

Since you copied the first three files in the previous steps, you should already have them in the JNIShared directory. JNIExample.lib should be in the debug subdirectory of the JNIExample directory if you built using the debug mode; otherwise it should be in the JNIExample directory. The last two files, oraSQX8.lib and oraSQL8.lib, are Oracle-provided files, found in the <ORACLE HOME>\Ora81\PRECOMP\LIB\MSVC directory.

If you try and build the project now, it will fail because the JNI include files are not found by Visual C/C++. In order to fix this problem, click on "Tools->Options…" and access the "Directories" tab. In the "Show directories for" combo box, choose "Include files" and add the include subdirectories of the Java JDK. For example, assuming that you have installed Sun JDK 1.2.2 in F:\Jdk1.2.2, you should include the following subdirectories:

- `F:\Jdk1.2.2\Include`
- `F:\Jdk1.2.2\Include\Win32`

You are now able to rebuild your project. One last thing: add the JNIShared/debug directory to your systemwide PATH; otherwise Java will not find the dll that contains the native methods.

18.3.2 UNIX/SOLARIS

To successfully compile and link the JNI example in a Solaris environment, you need to go through a few preparatory steps. This is because of the way the Oracle pre-compiler includes the several shared objects required by the linker to resolve all symbols.

The easiest approach is to use the default makefile provided by Oracle in the $ORACLE_HOME/precomp/demo/proc directory. The file is called demo_proc.mk, and should be copied into the directory you have chosen to hold the example files, which you assume is called *jni*, and renamed to *makefile*. Under Solaris, the directory is likely to be /export/home/users/<account name>/jni, where <account name> is your username. If you examine demo_proc.mk, you will see that the first line includes the file *env_precomp.mk*, located in $ORACLE_HOME/precomp/lib. The latter defines literally hundreds of macros, which are used by the Pro*C makefile to perform compilation and linking. You should also copy *env_precomp.mk* to the jni directory. Edit makefile and modify the first line to force the inclusion of your local copy of env_precomp.mk, instead of the Oracle-provided file located in $ORACLE_HOME/precomp/lib. Modify the line that reads:

```
include $ORACLE_HOME/precomp/lib/env_precomp.mk
```

and change it to:

```
include env_precomp.mk
```

Don't leave your editor; you haven't quite finished with makefile. Locate the following lines:

```
build: $(OBJS)
 $(CC) -o $(EXE) $(OBJS) -L$(LIBHOME) $(PROLDLIBS) -lpthread
```

Copy the two lines shown above to your clipboard (or *yank* them if you are using *vi*) and copy them twice, inserting them just below the original lines.

Modify the first copy as indicated below:

```
build_so: $(OBJS)
 $(CC) -g -G -o $(EXE) $(OBJS) -L$(LIBHOME) $(PROLDLIBS) -lpthread
```

Now modify the second copy:

```
build_jni: $(OBJS)
 $(CC) -g -G -o $(EXE) $(OBJS) -L. -R. -lJNIExample
```

Insert the following line anywhere in your makefile:

```
LOCCFLAGS= -g -DUNIX -I$(JDK_HOME)/include \
 -I$(JDK_HOME)/include/solaris $(CFLAGS)
```

And perform a global replace of `$(CFLAGS)` to `$(LOCCFLAGS)`.

The step indicated above allows you to insert debugging information into your object files, and the –DUNIX bit prevents JNIShared.c from including "windows.h", which under Solaris is meaningless. It also instructs the C compiler to look in the appropriate JDK include directories for the JNI include files. Make sure that the environment variable $JDK_HOME is set and correctly points to the directory where the JDK is installed. You can now save makefile.

Next comes env_precomp.mk. If you want to be able to debug your C code, you have to compile disabling all optimizations. Optimizations in env_precomp.mk are turned on by default. To disable them, comment out $(OPTIMIZE) from the definition of the CFLAGS macro, prefixing $(OPTIMIZE) with a hash sign (#) in the first position of the line. CFLAG is defined four times in env_precomp.mk, so you have to repeat this operation four times. Once you have finished your debugging session, remember to uncomment the $(OPTIMIZE) macro, so that you deploy efficient code to production! You can now save env_precomp.mk and leave your editor.

Copy all C, include, and Java files from the companion CD into the jni directory. You could create separate directories for each component, but this would involve a more complex setting of environment variables, such as LD_LIBRARY_PATH, so for the sake of simplicity, put up with the bad habit of mixing Java and C files in the same directory.

Compile your Java source code using the javac compiler. Alternatively, if you are using a Solaris Java IDE, such as Borland JBuilder, create a new project and include the four Java files. Create the include file "JNIWrapper.h" by running *javah* against the JNIWrapper class. You can now compile your C files, starting with the file that contains embedded SQL. The following command compiles and creates a shared object that encapsulates your library of legacy C code that accesses an Oracle database:

```
make -f makefile build_so EXE=libJNIExample.so OBJS=JNIExample.o
```

Make sure that the `libJNIExample.so` shared library contains all references to the Oracle-shared libraries. Issue the *ldd* command against libJNIExample.so; ldd displays the following lines on your screen:

```
$ ldd libJNIExample.so
        libclntsh.so.8.0 =>       /u01/OraHome1/lib/libclntsh.so.8.0
        libskgxp8.so =>   /u01/OraHome1/lib/libskgxp8.so
        libnsl.so.1 =>    /usr/lib/libnsl.so.1
        libsocket.so.1 =>         /usr/lib/libsocket.so.1
        libgen.so.1 =>    /usr/lib/libgen.so.1
        libdl.so.1 =>     /usr/lib/libdl.so.1
        libthread.so.1 =>         /usr/lib/libthread.so.1
        libpthread.so.1 =>        /usr/lib/libpthread.so.1
        libaio.so.1 =>    /usr/lib/libaio.so.1
        libm.so.1 =>      /usr/lib/libm.so.1
        libc.so.1 =>      /usr/lib/libc.so.1
        libmp.so.2 =>     /usr/lib/libmp.so.2
```

Now It is the turn of JNIShared. Make the shared library:

```
make -f makefile build_jni EXE=libJNIShared.so OBJS=JNIShared.o
```

Again, make sure that the shared library contains a reference to the required shared libraries, including libJNIExample.so. Use ldd, as shown below:

```
$ ldd libJNIShared.so
        libJNIExample.so =>       ./libJNIExample.so
        libclntsh.so.8.0 =>       /u01/OraHome1/lib/libclntsh.so.8.0
        libskgxp8.so =>   /u01/OraHome1/lib/libskgxp8.so
        libnsl.so.1 =>    /usr/lib/libnsl.so.1
        libsocket.so.1 =>         /usr/lib/libsocket.so.1
        libgen.so.1 =>    /usr/lib/libgen.so.1
        libdl.so.1 =>     /usr/lib/libdl.so.1
        libthread.so.1 =>         /usr/lib/libthread.so.1
        libpthread.so.1 =>        /usr/lib/libpthread.so.1
        libaio.so.1 =>    /usr/lib/libaio.so.1
        libm.so.1 =>      /usr/lib/libm.so.1
        libc.so.1 =>      /usr/lib/libc.so.1
        libmp.so.2 =>     /usr/lib/libmp.so.2
```

You have finished building the example. You can try it out, but first you have to include the jni directory in the LD_LIBRARY_PATH environment variable. This is necessary because you chose to link the library into the Java runtime system using the System.loadLibrary(<library name>) call (see JNIRunner.java). An alternative is to use System.load(<absolute pathname to shared object>). The latter call makes deploying the application more difficult, because loading the shared object becomes dependent on the directory structure of the target platform. The preferred option for deployment is to append the required shared objects implementing JNI calls to the LD_LIBRARY_PATH environment variable.

The next section explains how to debug your native methods.

Note

Before running the example, you should create the SYS_EVENT table in the Oracle schema used for the connection to your Oracle database. Connect to your Oracle database account using SQL*Plus and issue the following command:

```
SQL> create table sys_event
  (
  statistic varchar2(64),
  when number,
  value number
  );
```

Warning

Without modifications, the JNI example requires an Oracle instance running on the same computer where the Java executable is launched. If your database resides on a different node, you should modify the OraConnect C function, to include the “USING” clause in the EXEC SQL CONNECT statement. Consult the “Pro*C/C++ Precompiler Programmer’s Guide” for guidance on connecting to Oracle from embedded SQL.

Alternatively, if you are operating under Solaris, you can set up the TWO_TASK environment variable to point to the remote database. You can find out about the TWO_TASK environment variable on the “Net8 Administrator Guide.”

18.4 DEBUGGING JNI FUNCTIONS

You have learned how to reuse existing legacy code, and how to unleash the power of JNIEnv to instantiate Java objects from C, throwing exceptions back to the Java environment if something goes wrong with your C routines. If you are involved in serious development, though, the moment will inevitably arrive when the C code called from your Java methods does not perform as expected. Your initial instinct may be to sprinkle your C code with *printf* statements to output to standard output, or with *fprintf* statements to output to a log file. This might even work, if you made an easy-to-catch mistake. For fine-grained debugging, however, the *printf* or *fprintf* technique is not usually very effective. You definitely need the full power of a debugger, but have no fear: debugging native methods is quite easy, once you know a few tricks of the trade.

18.4.1 DEBUGGING IN MICROSOFT VISUAL C/C++

If MS Windows is your platform of choice, and Microsoft Visual C/C++ your development environment for legacy code, setting the debugging environment is as simple as accessing the "Project Settings". Click on Project->Settings, and the window shown in Figure 18.3 appears:

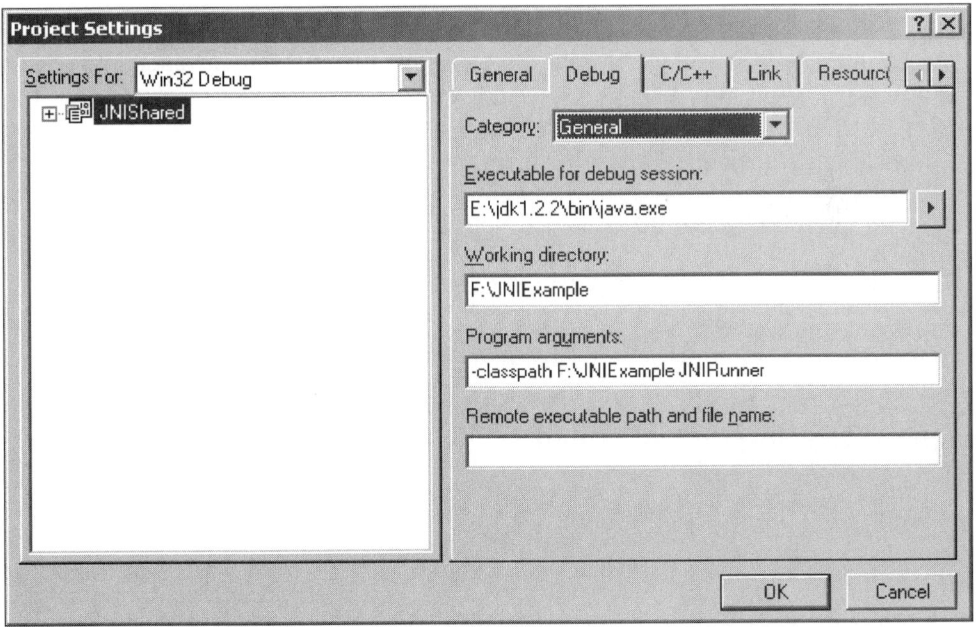

FIGURE 18.3 Project settings in Microsoft Visual C/C++.

Click on the "Debug" tab, then on the right arrow beside the first editable field, "Executable for debug session". A popup menu appears; choose the "Browse" option, which displays the usual file dialog box. Navigate the directories until you find the executable for the Java interpreter (java.exe). It is usually located under the directory where you installed the JDK, under the *bin* subdirectory (you have to specify the extension, as in <drive>\jdkx.x.x\bin\java.exe). Select the java.exe executable, then click on the OK button, and the file dialog disappears. Press the tab key, and move to the field marked "Working directory". Here, you must enter the directory where you saved the C files containing the native functions. In the example shown in Figure 18.3, the directory is called "F:\JNIShared". Press the tab key, positioning the cursor in the field marked "Program arguments", and enter the classpath option for the java executable, followed by the class that contains the main method. In the example, the option is:

```
-classpath F:\JNIShared JNIRunner
```

This completes the settings for Microsoft Visual C/C++, but you must also configure the system's PATH variable to include the directory where the DLL that contains the implementation for the native methods is located. If you are using Microsoft Windows NT/2000, click on the "Start" button, then Settings->Control Panel, and double-click the System icon. Add the F:\JNIShared\debug directory to the user's PATH, then confirm your choice. Go back to Visual C/C++, click on File->Save All, then close the IDE. Restart the IDE, which reads the modified PATH environment variable, and access the C file which contains the native methods. Set a breakpoint and start a debugging session. The message box shown in Figure 18.4 appears.

If you don't want to be annoyed by this message in the future, simply check the box marked "Do not prompt in the future" and click OK. If all your settings are correct, the program flow stops at the line where you set the breakpoint, as shown in Figure 18.5.

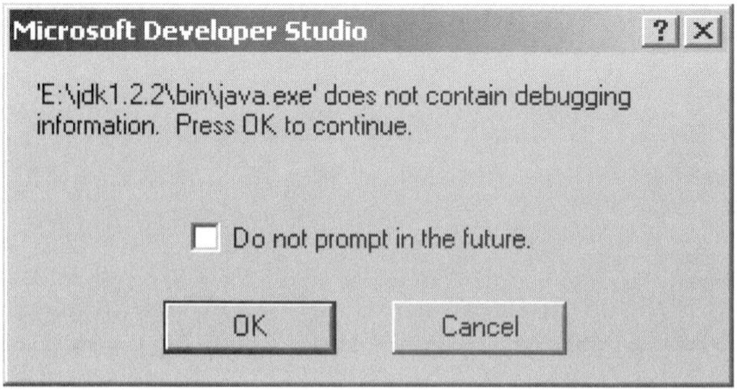

FIGURE 18.4 Message box that warns that the Java executable is not debuggable.

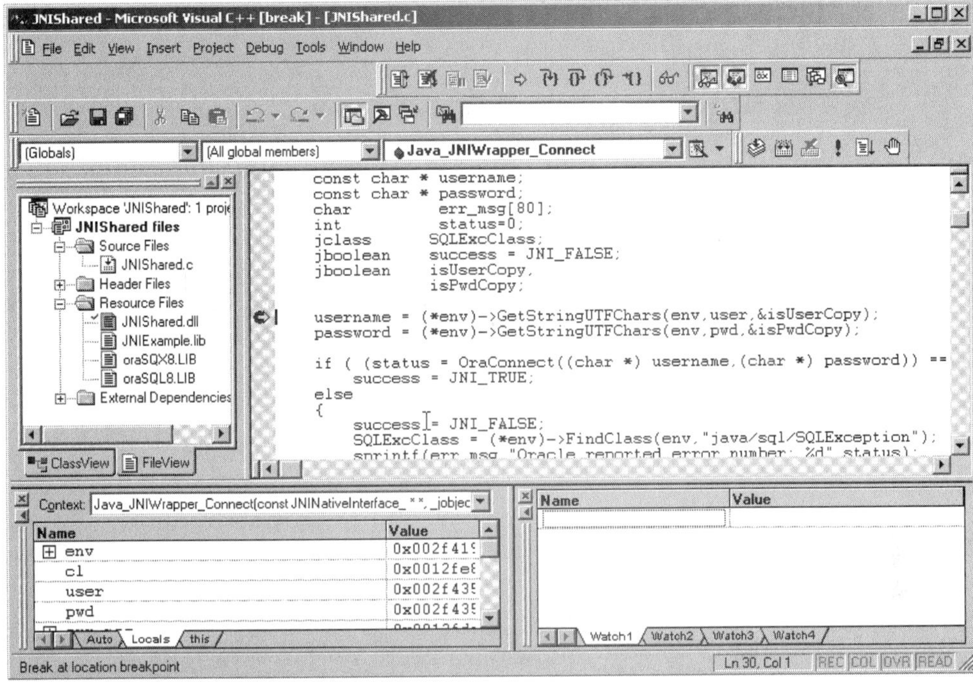

FIGURE 18.5 The program flow stops at the line with an associated breakpoint.

18.4.2 DEBUGGING IN A SOLARIS ENVIRONMENT

In order to debug your native methods under Solaris, a few more steps are required. To begin, examine the settings required to invoke a debugging session using the character-based version of the dbx debugger. Then you have to get acquainted with the steps that control the Sun Workshop debugger.

First, set your LD_LIBRARY_PATH environment variable, making sure that it includes the $ORACLE_HOME/lib directory, as well as the directory that contains the shared library for the native methods you developed. If your default directory is the one used to compile and link the native methods, you can set the LD_LIBRARY_PATH variable by issuing the following statements:

```
LD_LIBRARY_PATH=$ORACLE_HOME/lib:`pwd`:$LD_LIBRARY_PATH:
export LD_LIBRARY_PATH
```

The commands specified above work for the Korn, bash, and Bourne shells. If you are using different command shells, adapt the commands to your environment.

In addition, set the DEBUG_PROG variable, which forces the shell wrapper that launches the java interpreter to invoke the debugger:

```
DEBUG_PROG=dbx; export DEBUG_PROG
```

You now invoke the Java interpreter:

```
java
```

The dbx debugger displays the libraries loaded by the dynamic linker during the program startup phase:

```
..
..omitted lines
..
Reading java
Reading ld.so.1
Reading libthread.so.1
Reading libhpi.so
Reading libjvm.so
Reading libdl.so.1
Reading libc.so.1
Reading libX11.so.4
Reading libsocket.so.1
Reading libnsl.so.1
Reading libm.so.1
Reading libXext.so.0
Reading libmp.so.2
Reading libc_psr.so.1
detected a multithreaded program
(/opt/SUNWspro/bin/../WS5.0/bin/sparcv9/dbx)
```

When dbx stops executing, you may be tempted to use the file command to list your C code and set a breakpoint. Unfortunately, this does not work, because the dynamic linker has not yet loaded the library containing your native methods. You can force pre-loading of a shared library by issuing the *loadobjects* dbx command, with the -p option. An example follows:

```
(/opt/SUNWspro/bin/../WS5.0/bin/sparcv9/dbx) loadobjects -p
      /export/home/users/ebonazzi/jni/libJNIShared.so
(/opt/SUNWspro/bin/../WS5.0/bin/sparcv9/dbx) file JNIShared.c
(/opt/SUNWspro/bin/../WS5.0/bin/sparcv9/dbx) list
    1   #include "jni.h"
    2   #include "JNIWrapper.h"
    3   #include "JNIExample.h"
```

```
    4    #include <string.h>
    5    #include <stdio.h>
    6    #include <time.h>
    7    #ifndef UNIX
    8    #include <windows.h>
    9    #endif
   10
(/opt/SUNWspro/bin/../WS5.0/bin/sparcv9/dbx)
```

You can now set your breakpoints. Start the program by issuing the following command:

```
run JNIRunner
```

The program flow stops at the first breakpoint:

```
Running: java JNIRunner
(process id 3451)
Reading libjava.so
Reading libzip.so
Reading en_AU.so.2
Reading libsunwjit.so
Reading libJNIShared.so
Reading libJNIExample.so
Reading libpthread.so.1
Reading libclntsh.so.8.0
Reading libskgxp8.so
Reading libgen.so.1
Reading libaio.so.1
t@1 (l@1) stopped in Java_JNIWrapper_Connect at line 30 in file
      "JNIShared.c"
   30    username = (*env)->GetStringUTFChars(env,user,&isUserCopy);
(/opt/SUNWspro/bin/../WS5.0/bin/sparcv9/dbx)
```

You can examine your variables and step through your code looking for bugs.

If you are lucky enough to have access to the Sun Workshop visual environment, you have to set the environment variables yourself. When you set the DEBUG_PROG variable in a character-based environment, the shell wrapper to the Java interpreter does all the variable setting. In Sun Workshop, you have to include in the LD_LIBRARY_PATH environment variable all the JDK directories that contain shared objects, in addition to $ORACLE_HOME/lib and the default directory that contains the shared object with your native methods. To start setting your environment, click on the "Debug->New Program" option displayed in the main menu of Workshop (see Figure 18.6).

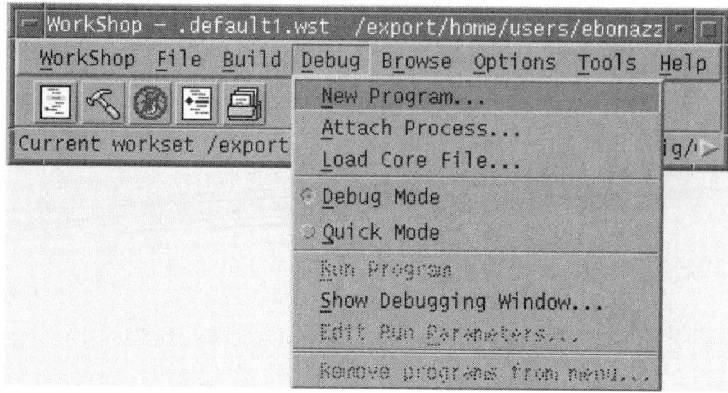

FIGURE 18.6 The Sun Workshop menu option that triggers the "New Program" window.

Workshop displays the "Debug New Program" window. A screenshot of the window is shown in Figure 18.7.

In the field marked by "Name" you must enter the absolute pathname that points to the Java interpreter executable, not the shell wrapper.[2] You must also fill in the remaining fields, as in the example shown in Figure 18.7.

Click on the "Environment Variables" button, and a new dialog box pops up (see Figure 18.8)

The dynamic linker invoked by Sun Workshop needs to load a few shared objects that are located in the following directories:

```
/usr/jdk1.2.2/jre/lib/sparc/native_threads:
/usr/jdk1.2.2/jre/lib/sparc/classic:
/usr/jdk1.2.2/jre/lib/sparc:
```

These directories must be included in the LD_LIBRARY_PATH variable, together with $ORACLE_HOME/lib and the default directory containing the shared object with the user-defined native methods.

When you are finished with the dialog box shown in Figure 18.8, click on the "Apply" button and then the "Ok" button.

Sun Workshop displays the debug window, which shows a few panels and controls. Identify the "Dbx Commands" panel, located toward the bottom of the

[2]Under Unix, the Java interpreter executable is usually invoked from a shell script. By default, when you install JDK on Solaris, a symbolic link is created as /usr/bin/java. The link points to the shell script, which determines the parameters to be passed to the Java executable (e.g., native or green threads, hot-spot or jit compiler, etc). The form in Figure 18.7 requires you to input the binary file that implements the Java Virtual Machine rather than the shell script that invokes it.

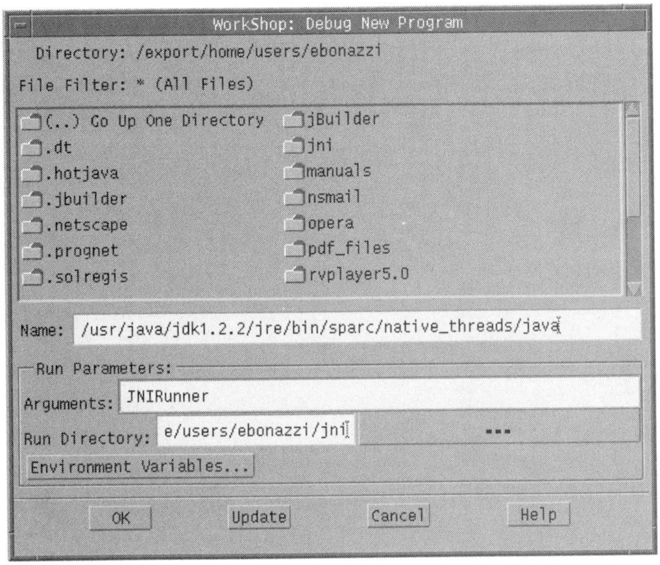

FIGURE 18.7 The "Debug New Program" window.

window, and enter the loadobjects –p command, in exactly the same way used for the character-based environment. When you issue the *file* command, Sun Workshop displays the file in the visual environment, where you can set breakpoints by pointing and clicking with your mouse, almost as in MS Visual C/C++. This is shown in Figure 18.9.

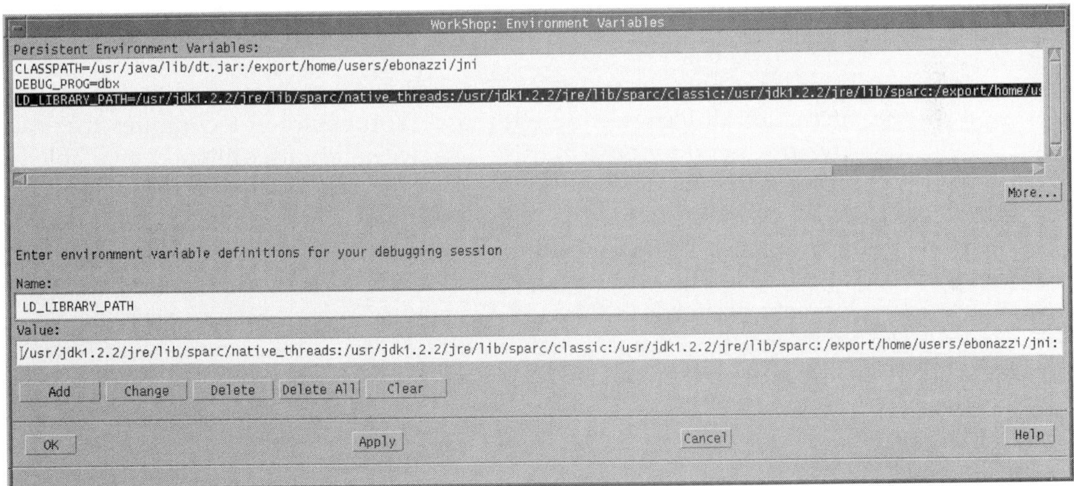

FIGURE 18.8 The dialog box that allows the setting of environment variables.

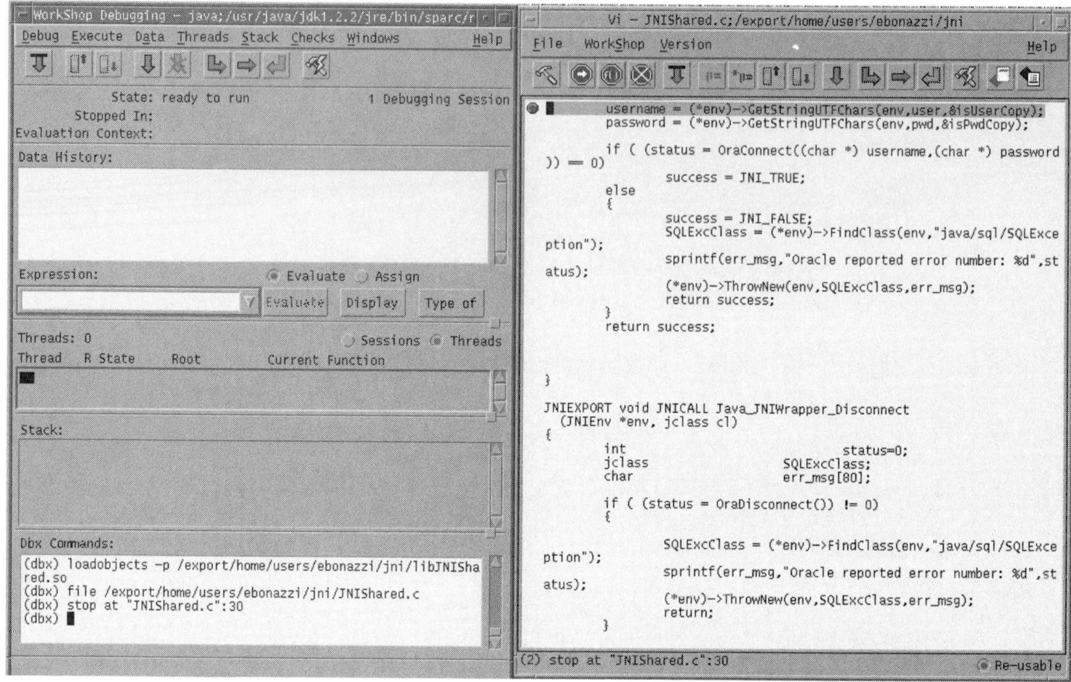

FIGURE 18.9 The debugging environment offered by Sun Workshop.

SUMMARY

In this chapter, you became familiar with problems and issues that often arise from the interaction of legacy code with Java. You explored techniques that can help your Java front-end to reuse mature data-access libraries already available in your organization. Throughout the chapter, you learned about the role of the Java Native Interface, which shields the object-oriented Java code from the world of legacy code, populated as that world is with structures, pointers, and procedural logic. You also learned how to debug JNI methods using two of the most widely used development platforms, Microsoft Visual C/C++ and Sun Workshop.

The next chapter explores the world of Message-Oriented Middleware (MOM), as implemented in Oracle.

Chapter 19

ACCESSING ORACLE ADVANCED QUEUING THROUGH JAVA

- Application Queues
- Oracle Advanced Queuing
- Examples of Advanced Queuing
- Summary

Before the Internet and Java became mainstream computing environments, client/server applications were designed according to a request/response model. This model is very effective for On-Line Transaction Processing (OLTP) environments, such as financial applications where debiting and crediting of money must occur in one atomic operation. However, there are situations where a different model, called disconnected/deferred data processing, is more suited to the way the business works. In recent years, an increasing number of development environments, including Oracle, have been providing primitives, APIs, and tools to support this new application paradigm. The following sections introduce the model and explore its implementation as provided by Oracle.

19.1 APPLICATION QUEUES

In traditional client/server applications, the client issues a request and blocks until the server satisfies the request. Users must wait until the requested data have been fetched from the database, formatted into packets, sent over the network, interpreted, and displayed by the client front-end. During this time, the client cannot use any other part of the application. In graphical environments, the mouse cursor becomes either an hourglass or a watch, indicating that a lengthy operation is taking place, and the user must wait.

While the classical request/response model is essentially synchronous, the queue-based model introduces an asynchronous communication flow between clients and servers. Many business practices follow a queue-based approach. Consider the processing of orders placed by a company's salespersons in the inbox of the order-processing department. A common arrangement is to have several employees check each order for completeness and consistency, then pass the validated orders to other employees in the same department for further processing. Every morning, the employees in the order-processing department find a pile of orders accumulated by the salespersons during the business hours of the preceding day. An inconsistent order is put in a specific box, along with other inconsistent orders, and is considered to be rejected. Other employees process the rejected orders, sometimes contacting the customers in order to sort out the discrepancies.

The important aspect of the workflow presented above is that a single order is not processed immediately, as soon as the customer's salesperson issues it. There is a delay between when the order is taken by the salesperson and when the appropriate department processes it. The order is created and queued, and its processing is postponed to a later time. Somewhere along the order-processing chain somebody "dequeues" the order for its assessment.

Application queues are the information technology equivalent of the plastic boxes where piles of order forms would be accumulated during manual processing. Adding a message to a queue takes merely a few milliseconds. The application that queues the message regains control of the processing flow almost immediately, and is then free to continue with other tasks. The processing of the message occurs later, and if one dequeuing process cannot keep up with the number of messages accumulated in the queue, other dequeuing processes can be added, to allow the dequeuing of messages to be performed in parallel.

Needless to say, this model offers excellent scalability. Furthermore, it satisfies the needs of the e-commerce business model. Consider the virtual shopping basket filled by a customer while browsing the Web pages that represent a shop's shelves. When a customer finishes virtual shopping, and all the items have been selected, the customer order is ready to be queued. Some e-commerce sites accept orders for out-of-stock items without informing the customer that they are not currently in stock. The order is processed anyway at a later stage, and the stock is reordered on the spot to satisfy the customer's request. Sometimes this is not possible, perhaps because the time the virtual shop needs to obtain the missing items from the distributor exceeds the delivery time it has committed to its customers. In this case, the customer is informed that the required item is out-of-stock and is presented with options, such as ordering everything in the virtual basket at once irrespective of the time required to collect individual items. Alternatively, the customer can drop the out-of-stock items from the basket and only order the ones currently available. The point is that no matter what arrangement is implemented, the customer's order is most likely queued, and not processed interactively. Many e-commerce sites ask customers to provide their e-mail addresses so that the virtual shop can send an order confirmation message. Only after the customer has confirmed the order via e-mail, will the virtual shop actually start processing it.

The disconnected/deferred data-processing model works quite well in the e-commerce world. Oracle8i supports message queuing through the its advanced queuing facility.

19.2 ORACLE ADVANCED QUEUING

Oracle8i Enterprise Edition offers message queuing, an advanced feature that used to be offered only by Message-Oriented Middleware (MOM) products, such as BEA Systems Message/Q or IBM MQ Series. While the request/response model is effective for many applications, a growing number of business domains require different handling of the interactions between systems and users of the systems. It is not only possible, but also useful, to decouple requests for services from the processing of the requested services. An application can queue messages that are read by the recipients at the application's convenience rather than immediately. The same application can read the answers to the messages at a later time, without making interactive users wait until the server has completed its processing cycle before they can regain control of their computers. Workflow management has traditionally been the preferred environment for message queuing, but other business areas, such as e-commerce, are now showing a strong interest in this relatively new model.

Oracle8i message queuing allows for the implementation of several variations of the message-based application model. The simplest form is represented by the "one producer/one consumer" model. In this model, one producer may enqueue different messages into a single queue. Each message is dequeued and processed once by each consumer. A message can be given an expiration time; if the message is not retrieved before the expiration time, Oracle can flag it as expired and therefore unavailable for retrieval by the consumer. Oracle Advanced Queuing also supports the "many producers/one consumer" and "many producers/many consumers" variations of the same model.

Message queuing provides the necessary infrastructure for the implementation of an even newer application model, called publish-and-subscribe. This paradigm, also known as push technology, is characterized by the decoupling of the producers and consumers of messages. Consumers subscribe to queues of interest and receive all the messages "published" by the producers. The two roles are interchangeable, and consumers can unsubscribe from queues at any time. The basic principle is that the producer does not need to know the recipients of its messages. The message-queuing system makes sure that each consumer receives the message only once.

Oracle8i supports the publish-and-subscribe model, which opens the door to a great variety of client-server application models. There are three native interfaces to Oracle Advanced Queuing:

- One for PL/SQL.
- One for the Oracle Call Interface (OCI), a very low-level interface accessible only from C or C++.
- One for Java.

The Oracle-specific Java interface to AQ was introduced with Oracle 8.1.5. Oracle 8.1.6 went one step further, offering the advanced queuing facility through Java Message Service (JMS) calls.[1] In situations where older versions of Oracle 8 must be supported, or where Abstract Data Type (ADT) message payloads must be supported,[2] Java programmers can use Java wrappers to enable the PL/SQL Advanced Queuing interface to use the facility from a Java environment.

The terminology used by Oracle AQ differs to some extent from the similar terminology used by other queuing environments, such as IBM MQ Series. Ora-

---

[1]JMS is a set of specifications that define the standard for implementing Message Oriented Middleware (MOM) products in Java.

[2]The Java interface to Oracle AQ, shipped with release 8.1.5 of the database server, only supports RAW type message payloads. If you want to support Abstract Data Types (ADT) message payloads, you must use Java wrappers for PL/SQL.

cle AQ offers features unique among message-oriented middleware systems, mainly because of its being based on a relational engine, which provides very advanced storage capabilities unmatched by other message-queuing systems.

Table 19.1 lists the basic terms used in an AQ environment.

The queuing model offered by AQ allows for great sophistication, giving designers many flexible options for the implementation of message-based applications. The very fact that messages are stored in Oracle tables opens the door to a many possibilities, such as using standard SQL commands and techniques. In addition, Oracle tools like import/export[3] can be used to access messages stored by applications that use queuing as a major means of communication. When messages are retained in a queue, and not discarded after consumption or expiration, message history and event journals can be built using standard SQL queries.

Apart from the intrinsic flexibility resulting from the way queuing is implemented in Oracle, AQ provides a rich set of advanced capabilities, some of which are not even found in MOM-specific products like BEA Systems Message/Q or IBM MQ Series. Table 19.2 summarizes the advanced features offered by Oracle AQ.

TABLE 19.1 Terms used in an AQ environment

QUEUING ENTITY	PURPOSE
Message	The smallest unit of information that AQ can manage. It has two parts, control information and payload, or user data.
Payload	The user data associated to a message or the part of the message that carries the message content. Contrast with control information.
Control Information	The administrative part of the message. It allows the queuing system to correctly route the message and contains all message-specific attributes (e.g., correlation identifier, expiry time).
Queue	Repository for messages. There are two types, normal queues and exception queues, which store messages that cannot be processed for some reason.
Queue Table	Physical location where logical queues store their messages. More queues can be stored in one queue table. Each queue table contains a default exception queue.
Agent	A queue user. Agents can be producers (i.e., they enqueue messages) or consumers (they dequeue messages). Agents are identified by name, address, and protocol.
Queue Monitor	Background process that provides mechanisms for time-based operations (e.g., message expiration, propagation, retry). A parameter in the init.ora file specifies queue monitor creation and characteristics.

[3]Import and export are utilities shipped together with the standard Oracle distribution kit. They allow DBAs to export Oracle data into a portable format. An entire database can be exported into a large file and reimported in a different database, even one running a different release of Oracle.

TABLE 19.2 Advanced features of Oracle AQ

AQ FEATURE	COMMENT
Correlation Identifier	Part of the control information stored with the message. It can be used to selectively dequeue specific messages.
Message Grouping	When multiple messages belong to one group, they must be stored and retrieved in one atomic transaction. Complex messages can thus be segmented into simple messages, which must be stored and retrieved in one block.
Message Priority and Ordering	Messages are assigned priority, sort orders, and sequence deviation to position them relative to other messages. Complex dequeuing policies can be implemented through this feature.
Propagation	Through standard Oracle database links, messages can be propagated to remote instances.
Time Specification	Messages can be made available only after a certain time, or can be defined such that they expire (i.e., are no longer available) if not consumed within a certain interval.
Subscriber and Recipient Lists	Single messages can be specified to be consumed by multiple recipients, whether agents or other queues. This feature allows for fan-out of messages.
Transaction Scope	Enqueuing or dequeuing requests can be bracketed in a transaction that includes multiple steps. Alternatively, a single enqueuing or dequeuing can be made a transaction in itself, which guarantees immediate visibility of the message queued to other transactions.
Blocked Dequeuing and Event-Based Dispatching	Polling can be avoided by specifying an interval of time that a dequeuing request is allowed to wait. Alternatively, dequeuing can be triggered by the arrival of a message in a queue.
Consumption and Retention	Applications can browse a queue to access messages that remain in it for further consumption. Messages can be retained in the queue even after having been consumed by consumer agents.
Exception Handling	Messages that cannot be consumed according to the specified constraints (e.g., expiration intervals) are automatically moved to exception queues.

An administrator can define default subscribers for a specific queue. The subscribers so defined are implicit recipients of the messages stored in the queue. But Oracle AQ goes even further in ensuring flexibility, making it possible to programmatically override the default subscriber list and store a message in a queue for a specific target not in the list of default subscribers.

By using the DBMS_AQADM PL/SQL package, an administrator can implement complex configurations, supporting fanning-out of messages, meaning that multiple queues are designated as recipients of the messages in one queue, or funneling-in of messages, meaning that multiple queues route their messages to a single queue. By using message propagation, fanning-out and funneling-in policies can be implemented across distributed databases, potentially propagating thousands of messages to hundreds of nodes with little administrative effort.

Basic queuing capabilities have been offered since Oracle release 8.0.x. Oracle 8.1.5 increases the features of AQ, allowing for publish-and-subscribe propagation of messages having LOB-based payloads,[4] rule-based subscribers, and listening capabilities, such as waiting for messages to arrive on multiple queues. Oracle 8.1.6 provides a Java Message Service (JMS) implementation. Basically, the Oracle AQ APIs become available through JMS, dramatically increasing the portability of your code, which no longer depends on the Oracle-specific AQ interface; in fact, it can be run in any environment that supports JMS (e.g., IBM and Sybase).

From an e-commerce perspective, the two most interesting aspects of Oracle AQ are the decoupling of requests for services from the supply of requested services, and the possibility of propagating messages across distributed databases.

19.3 EXAMPLES OF ADVANCED QUEUING

Three simple examples are provided below to illustrate the use of Oracle AQ,. To understand the techniques used in the examples, you will need:

- A general knowledge of SQL and PL/SQL (explained in Chapters 4 to 6).
- Familiarity with JDBC concepts and Java stored procedures (Chapter 11).
- Use of the Oracle JPublisher tool.
- Ability to use Oracle SQL*Plus.

In addition, it is assumed that you have access to an Oracle Server Enterprise Edition, release 8.0.x or higher, running under MS Windows NT or Unix (including Linux). The latter requirement applies if you plan to run the example that uses a Java wrapper to AQ calls made through PL/SQL. If you want to run the Java example that uses the Oracle Java interface to Advanced Queuing, you will need Oracle Enterprise Edition release 8.1.5 or higher. Finally, if you want to test the JMS example, you will need Oracle Enterprise Edition release 8.1.6 or higher.

Access to a DBA-privileged account is needed in order to set up a schema and start the application queue used by the example. The steps required to create and start the queue are explained in the next few paragraphs. If you are using your own release of Oracle on your personal workstation, this should not be an

[4] LOB means large object, an Oracle data type introduced with Oracle release 8. It is generally used to store graphic images or similar unstructured data.

issue, but if you are planning to use a shared instance in a broader development environment, coordinate your efforts with the Oracle DBA for your site.

Oracle AQ offers two types of interfaces, administrative and operational. The administrative interface is implemented through a PL/SQL package, DBMS_AQADM. It allows you to create, alter, and drop queue tables and queues, manage subscribers, grant and revoke system privileges, and schedule propagation policies.

Operational interfaces are provided through PL/SQL (DBMS_AQ) and Oracle OCI. This means that the Java wrappers for the PL/SQL interface must be created in order to use Oracle AQ from Java. A few advanced features are only available through the OCI operational interface, such as registering a callback function for notification when a message is available on a queue.

The first step is to create a queue. This entails defining a queue table, or an Oracle table that will be used as a queue by the Advanced Queuing subsystem. A queue table can be based on a user-defined type (i.e., an object created through the `CREATE TYPE <user defined type> AS OBJECT` syntax) or can be defined as RAW rather than object-based, and implemented as a LOB with a maximum size of 32 kilobytes.

The following script, run from SQL*Plus, creates an Oracle object that will be used in the example as the message payload, and a queue that will use an object-based queue table. You connect to the privileged account `system` to create a user, called `aq`, with the privileges required to run both the administrative and operational Advanced Queuing interfaces. You use an Oracle instance running on an MS Windows NT workstation, called nt8i.

The statements to be typed are shown in bold, the feedback given by SQL*Plus is shown in plain text. Comment lines start with a double hyphen (--).

```
$ sqlplus system/manager@nt8i
SQL*Plus: Release 8.1.5.0.0 - Production on Sun Sep 12 16:11:26 1999
© Copyright 1999 Oracle Corporation. All rights reserved.
Connected to:
Oracle8i Enterprise Edition Release 8.1.5.0.0 - Production
With the Partitioning and Java options
PL/SQL Release 8.1.5.0.0 - Production
SQL>
SQL> create user aq identified by aq
2 default tablespace users temporary tablespace temp
3 quota unlimited on users;
User created.
SQL> grant connect,resource to aq;
Grant succeeded.
SQL> grant execute on sys.dbms_aqadm to aq;
Grant succeeded.
SQL> grant execute on sys.dbms_aq to aq;
```

```
Grant succeeded.
SQL> -- The aq user has been created, receiving the execute
SQL> -- privilege for the administrative and operational
SQL> -- advanced queuing interfaces.
SQL> -- You now connect to the database as aq.
SQL> connect aq/aq@nt8i
Connected.
SQL> create type payload_t as object
2 (
3 item_id number (12),
4 description varchar2(80),
5 quantity number(5),
6 unit_price number(12,2),
7 total_price number(12,2));
8 /
Type created.
SQL> -- You just created the object-relational object that
SQL> -- becomes the payload of our messages. You can now create
SQL> -- the queue table:
SQL> begin
2 dbms_aqadm.create_queue_table (
3 queue_table => 'OFJP_1_TAB',
4 queue_payload_type => 'payload_t');
5 end;
6 /
PL/SQL procedure successfully completed.
SQL> -- You can finally create the queue that uses the queue
SQL> -- table OFJP_1_TAB.
SQL> begin
2 dbms_aqadm.create_queue (
3 queue_name => 'OFJP_1_QUEUE',
4 queue_table => 'OFJP_1_TAB');
5 end;
6 /
PL/SQL procedure successfully completed.
SQL> -- To really make the queue operational you have to start
SQL> -- it.
execute dbms_aqadm.start_queue('OFJP_1_QUEUE',TRUE,TRUE);
PL/SQL procedure successfully completed.
SQL>
```

The queue created by the steps explained above is now ready to receive and dispatch messages. You used the administrative AQ interface exposed through PL/SQL. While more recent releases of the Oracle server provide Java native administrative interfaces, you are not going to repeat the steps illustrated above using Java code. Instead you will create an additional RAW-payload queue, used to queue and dequeue messages with RAW payloads. using the Java native operational interface, shipped with Oracle 8.1.5, and the JMS-based operational interface, shipped with Oracle 8.1.6.

19.3.1 HANDLING MESSAGES THROUGH JAVA WRAPPERS TO PL/SQL

In an Oracle 8.0.x–8.1.5 environment, In order to be able to enqueue messages to the queue just created, you must write a PL/SQL wrapper that calls the DBMS_AQ package on your behalf. The wrapper is needed because DBMS_AQ is wrapped (i.e., made unreadable and inaccessible), and thus you cannot run JPublisher directly against it. To protect developers' PL/SQL code against exposure to potential competitors or other developers who could misuse the packages by relying on undocumented features, Oracle provides a utility, called *wrap,* that transforms the PL/SQL code contained in a clear text files into object code. In other words, after a package is wrapped, its definitions and procedures/functions can no longer be reverse-engineered from the database. Most of the PL/SQL packages provided by Oracle are wrapped. If you create a PL/SQL procedure that calls DBMS_AQ on your behalf and you leave its definition in clear (i.e., you don't wrap it), JPublisher can create a Java class that will allow you to queue messages directly from your Java code.

The PL/SQL convenience package definition follows.

```
create or replace package aq_submit as
procedure enqueue(p_item_id in number,
                  p_description in varchar2,
                  p_quantity in number,
                  p_unit_price in number,
                  p_total_price in number);
procedure dequeue(p_item_id out number,
                  p_description out varchar2,
                  p_quantity out number,
                  p_unit_price out number,
                  p_total_price out number);
end aq_submit;
/
create or replace package body aq_submit as
procedure enqueue(p_item_id in number,
                  p_description in varchar2,
                  p_quantity in number,
                  p_unit_price in number,
                  p_total_price in number) is
enqueue_options dbms_aq.enqueue_options_t;
message_properties dbms_aq.message_properties_t;
message_handle raw(16);
```

```
p_payload payload_t;
BEGIN
      p_payload := payload_t(p_item_id,p_description,
                  p_quantity,p_unit_price,p_total_price);
      dbms_aq.enqueue(
                  queue_name => 'OFJP_1_QUEUE',
                  enqueue_options=> enqueue_options,
                  message_properties=> message_properties,
                  payload=> p_payload,
                  msgid=> message_handle);
      COMMIT;
END;
procedure dequeue(p_item_id out number,
                  p_description out varchar2,
                  p_quantity out number,
                  p_unit_price out number,
                  p_total_price out number) is
dequeue_options dbms_aq.dequeue_options_t;
message_properties dbms_aq.message_properties_t;
message_handle raw(16);
p_payload payload_t;
BEGIN
      dbms_aq.dequeue(
                  queue_name => 'OFJP_1_QUEUE',
                  dequeue_options => dequeue_options,
                  message_properties => message_properties,
                  payload => p_payload,
                  msgid => message_handle);
      p_item_id := p_payload.item_id;
      p_description := p_payload.description;
      p_quantity := p_payload.quantity;
      p_unit_price := p_payload.unit_price;
      p_total_price := p_payload.total_price;
      COMMIT;
END;
END;
/
```

Using your customized package, you can now perform enqueuing and dequeuing indirectly. There are two options for interacting with a PL/SQL package from Java. You can use JDBC calls to the two stored procedures defined in the package, using the CallableStatement object. A more elegant solution is to use JPublisher to generate a Java class containing wrapper methods that act as interfaces between Java and PL/SQL.

In order to invoke *jpub*, the front-end to JPublisher, your CLASSPATH must include two archives, translator.zip, found in $ORACLE_HOME/sqlj/lib, and classes111.zip, found in $ORACLE_HOME/jdbc/lib.

You can now invoke jpub:

```
jpub -user=aq/aq -url= jdbc:oracle:thin:@wallaby:1521:nt8I -
sql=aq_submit -methods=true
```

Jpub creates an SQLJ file called aq_submit.sqlj in the current directory. The file, automatically generated by jpub, is shown below.

```
package com.prenhall.OFJP.aq;
import java.sql.SQLException;
import oracle.jdbc.driver.OracleConnection;
import oracle.jdbc.driver.OracleTypes;
import oracle.sql.CustomDatum;
import oracle.sql.CustomDatumFactory;
import oracle.sql.Datum;
import sqlj.runtime.ref.DefaultContext;
import sqlj.runtime.ConnectionContext;
import java.sql.Connection;
public class aq_submit
{
#sql static context _Ctx;
_Ctx _ctx;
      /* constructors */
      public aq_submit() throws SQLException
      {
            _ctx = new _Ctx(DefaultContext.getDefaultContext());
      }
      public aq_submit(ConnectionContext c) throws SQLException
      {
            _ctx = new _Ctx(c);
      }
      public aq_submit(Connection c) throws SQLException
      {
            _ctx = new _Ctx(c);
      }
      public void dequeue (
            java.math.BigDecimal pItemId[],
            String pDescription[],
            java.math.BigDecimal pQuantity[],
            java.math.BigDecimal pUnitPrice[],
            java.math.BigDecimal pTotalPrice[])
            throws SQLException
```

```
        {
        #sql [_ctx] { CALL AQ_SUBMIT.DEQUEUE(
                :OUT (pItemId[0]),
                :OUT (pDescription[0]),
                :OUT (pQuantity[0]),
                :OUT (pUnitPrice[0]),
                :OUT (pTotalPrice[0])) };
        }
        public void enqueue (
                java.math.BigDecimal pItemId,
                String pDescription,
                java.math.BigDecimal pQuantity,
                java.math.BigDecimal pUnitPrice,
                java.math.BigDecimal pTotalPrice)
        throws SQLException
        {
                #sql [_ctx] { CALL AQ_SUBMIT.ENQUEUE(
                :pItemId,
                :pDescription,
                :pQuantity,
                :pUnitPrice,
                :pTotalPrice) };
        }
}
```

If you use Oracle JDeveloper as your Java IDE, you merely need to include aq_submit.sqlj in your project; JDeveloper does the rest. If you are using some other commercial Java IDE, such as JBuilder or VisualCafe, you must compile aq_submit.sqlj manually, invoking the sqlj front-end application from the command line.

To test your PL/SQL package and the aq_submit class generated by JPublisher, you can code a Java class with a main method that connects to the Oracle database and enqueues a message, dequeuing it again after a little while. The source code follows:

```
package com.prenhall.OFJP.aq;
import java.sql.SQLException;
import oracle.sqlj.runtime.Oracle;
import java.math.BigDecimal;
public class AdvancedQueuingExample
{
    public AdvancedQueuingExample()
    {
    }
    public static void main(String[] args)
```

```
    {
        try
        {
            Oracle.connect("jdbc:oracle:thin:@wallaby:1521:nt8i",
                                  "aq", "aq");
            aq_submit adv_queuing = new aq_submit();
            adv_queuing.enqueue( new BigDecimal(67.00),
            new String("Example desc"),
            new BigDecimal(5.00),
            new BigDecimal(20.00),
            new BigDecimal(100.00));
            BigDecimal[] bgInputId=new BigDecimal[1];
            BigDecimal[] bgQuantity=new BigDecimal[1];
            BigDecimal[] bgUnitPrice=new BigDecimal[1];
            BigDecimal[] bgTotalPrice=new BigDecimal[1];
            String[] description = new String[1];
            java.lang.Thread.sleep(2000);
            adv_queuing.dequeue(bgInputId,description,bgQuantity,
                                  bgUnitPrice,bgTotalPrice);
        }
        catch (Exception exc) {}
    }
}
```

You must replace the Oracle connection string shown above (@wallaby:1521:nt8i) with your own connection string before compiling the example.

19.3.2 HANDLING MESSAGES THROUGH THE NATIVE JAVA INTERFACE

In the next example, you will use the AQ administrative interface to create a queue table that supports RAW-based message payloads. The Java interface to Oracle AQ, as implemented in the 8.1.5 release of the database server, only supports messages with RAW payloads. This limitation prevents you from reusing the queue table (and the queue) created to support the first example, called OFJP_1_QUEUE. You have to create a new queue table, called AQ_TRIAL, with a RAW message payload. The source code listed below instantiates an AQ session, creates a queue table and a queue, enqueues a message, and then immediately dequeues it. The administrative and operational AQ interfaces are both exercised by the example, which uses Java native calls.

In order to use the native Java interface to Oracle AQ, your project or workspace must include the aqapi.jar library, which Oracle installs by default into <ora_root>/rdbms/jlib. If you are using the javac compiler from the command line, include aqapi.jar in your CLASSPATH or set the command-line option –classpath to include aqapi.jar.

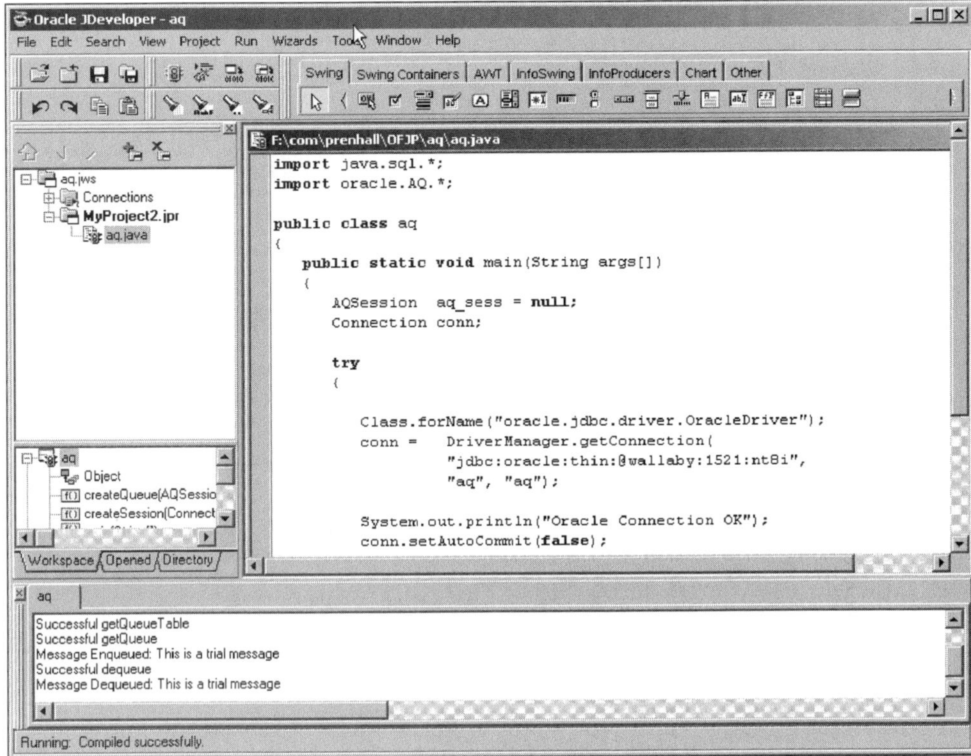

FIGURE 19.1 Oracle JDeveloper at work, editing your example.

Warning

Before running the example, you should grant the execute privilege on the SYS.DBMS_AQIN package to the AQ schema. If you forget to do it, the Java program will terminate with an SQL exception, generated by Oracle error 6550:

System Error: oracle.AQ.AQOracleSQLException: ORA-06550: line 1, column 7:

System Error: PLS-00201: identifier 'SYS.DBMS_AQIN' must be declared

The Java interface to AQ internally uses the DBMS_AQIN package. For this reason the execute privilege on that package must be granted to the schema owner of the queue.

The syntax used to grant the required privilege is:

```
connect system/manager@nt8i
grant execute on sys.dbms_aqin to aq;
```

```
import java.sql.*;
import oracle.AQ.*;

public class aq
{
   public static void main(String args[])
   {
      AQSession  sess = null;
      Connection conn;
      aq      AdvQue = new aq();
      try
      {
         Class.forName("oracle.jdbc.driver.OracleDriver");
         conn =   DriverManager.getConnection(
                  "jdbc:oracle:thin:@wallaby:1521:nt8i",
                  "aq", "aq");

         System.out.println("Oracle Connection OK");
         conn.setAutoCommit(false);

       // Create AQ session
         sess = AdvQue.createSession(conn);

         // Create queue table and queue
         AdvQue.createQueue(sess);

       // Queue and dequeue a message
         AdvQue.queue_dequeueMessage(aq_sess,conn);

      }
      catch (Exception exc)
      {
         System.out.println("Exception: " + exc);
         exc.printStackTrace();
      }
   }

  // Create an AQ session for the 'aq' user
  public AQSession createSession(Connection conn)
  {
      AQSession  sess = null;

      try
      {
```

```
            // Load the Oracle8i AQ driver
            Class.forName("oracle.AQ.AQOracleDriver");

            // Create an AQ Session
            sess = AQDriverManager.createAQSession(conn);
            System.out.println("AQSession created");
         }
         catch (Exception exc)
         {
            System.out.println("Exception: " + exc);
            exc.printStackTrace();
         }
         return sess;
      }

   public void queue_dequeueMessage(AQSession sess,
                                    Connection conn)
                                    throws AQException,
                                    java.sql.SQLException
   {
      AQQueueTable                 queue_table;
      AQQueue                      queue;
      AQMessage                    message;
      AQRawPayload                 payload;
      AQEnqueueOption              enqueue_option;
      String                       msg =
       "This is a trial message";
      AQDequeueOption              dequeue_option;
      byte[]                       msg_byte_array;

      // Obtain a handle to a queue table - aq_trial
      // in the aq schema
      queue_table = sess.getQueueTable ("aq", "aq_trial");
      System.out.println("getQueueTable OK");

      // Obtain a handle to a queue - aq_trial in aq schema
      queue = sess.getQueue ("aq", "aq_trial");
      System.out.println("Successful getQueue");

      // Create a message
      message = queue.createMessage();

      // Obtain a handle to a AQRawPayload object
      msg_byte_array = msg.getBytes();
```

```
        // Store RAW payload into the message
        payload = message.getRawPayload();
        payload.setStream(msg_byte_array,
         msg_byte_array.length);

        // Instantiate a AQEnqueueOption object with
        // default options
        enqueue_option = new AQEnqueueOption();

        // Enqueue the message
        queue.enqueue(enqueue_option, message);

        // Persistify the message in the queue
        conn.commit();
        System.out.println("Message Enqueued: "+msg);

        // Instantiate a AQDequeueOption object with
        // default options
        dequeue_option = new AQDequeueOption();

        // Dequeue the message previously queued
        message = queue.dequeue(dequeue_option);

        conn.commit();

        // Retrieve the raw payload from the message
        // just dequeued
        payload = message.getRawPayload();
        msg_byte_array = payload.getBytes();

        // Read the array of bytes containing the
        // message payload into a string
        String deq_msg = new String(msg_byte_array);

        System.out.println("Message Dequeued: "+deq_msg);
    }

    // Create a queue table and a queue in the 'aq' schema
    public void createQueue(AQSession sess)
        throws AQException
    {
      AQQueueTableProperty     queue_table_prop;
      AQQueueProperty          queue_prop;
      AQQueueTable             queue_table;
      AQQueue                  queue;
```

```
      // Create a AQQueueTableProperty object carrying
      // a RAW payload
      queue_table_prop = new AQQueueTableProperty("RAW");

      // Create a queue table called aq_trial in the
      // 'aq' schema
      queue_table =
         sess.createQueueTable ("aq", "aq_trial",
        queue_table_prop);
      System.out.println("Created aq_trial in aq schema");

      // Create a new AQQueueProperty object
      queue_prop = new AQQueueProperty();

      // Create a queue, called aq_trial, which uses
      // the aq_trial  queue table.
      queue = sess.createQueue (queue_table,
        "aq_trial", queue_prop);
      System.out.println("Created the aq_trial queue");
    }
}
```

The usual recommendation to replace the Oracle connection parameters shown in the example with your own specific parameters still applies.

The RAW message payload can be 32 Kbytes at most. This is not a very stringent limitation, if you keep your messages to a reasonable size. After all, application queues should be designed to exchange a large number of small messages rather than a few large messages. Since a RAW message payload is loaded into the message as a stream of bytes and extracted as a stream of bytes, the message payload could be a serialized Java object if queue producers and consumers are all coded in Java. If you keep the size of the Java class that must be serialized small enough, and you check the size of the serialized Java object before loading it into the message payload, to make sure it does not exceed 32 Kbytes, storing Java objects directly in messages can be an elegant solution for distributed communication between application producers and application consumers.

19.3.3 HANDLING MESSAGES THROUGH THE JMS INTERFACE

In the next example, you will use the JMS interface, supplied in Oracle release 8.1.6, to open a queue connection for JMS operations. As in the previous examples, you will enqueue a message to the target queue and then dequeue it. Since the JMS interface supports ADT-based payloads, you will reuse the OFJP_1_QUEUE and the object that defines the attributes for an e-commerce item (price, quantity, description, etc.). The message your code enqueues to the

OFJP_1_QUEUE using JMS is very similar to the message enqueued by the first example, which used the Java wrapper to the PL/SQL AQ interface.

In order to allow an Oracle Abstract Data Type (ADT) object to be included in a JMS payload, the message body must implement the CustomDatum and CustomDatumFactory interfaces. While these interfaces can be implemented manually, the process is tedious and error-prone. A better alternative is the use of JPublisher. The AQ schema should already define the object PAYLOAD_T, created with the first example. JPublisher can be directed to create a payload_t Java class that implements the required interfaces, using the `-sql` option. The following example shows how to use the syntax:

```
jpub -user=aq/aq -url=jdbc:oracle:thin:@echidna:1521:sun816
  sql=payload_t -usertypes=oracle
```

Simply replace the JDBC url with your own, and jpub should create two files:

- payload_t.sqlj
- payload_tRef.java

With this example, you only need to include payload_t in your Java environment. If you use JDeveloper, include the sqlj file in your project. If you use another Java IDE, you may have to pre-process the file, using the sqlj pre-processor, and include the .java file generated by sqlj in your project.

The sqlj file generated by JPublisher is shown below.

```
import java.sql.SQLException;
import oracle.jdbc.driver.OracleConnection;
import oracle.jdbc.driver.OracleTypes;
import oracle.sql.CustomDatum;
import oracle.sql.CustomDatumFactory;
import oracle.sql.Datum;
import oracle.sql.STRUCT;
import oracle.jpub.runtime.MutableStruct;
import sqlj.runtime.ref.DefaultContext;
import sqlj.runtime.ConnectionContext;
import java.sql.Connection;

public class payload_t implements CustomDatum,
                      CustomDatumFactory
{
  public static final String _SQL_NAME = "AQ.PAYLOAD_T";
  public static final int _SQL_TYPECODE = OracleTypes.STRUCT;
```

```
#sql static context _Ctx;
_Ctx _ctx;

MutableStruct _struct;

static int[] _sqlType =
{
  2, 12, 2, 2, 2
};

static CustomDatumFactory[] _factory =
    new CustomDatumFactory[5];
static final payload_t _payload_tFactory = new payload_t();
public static CustomDatumFactory getFactory()
{
  return _payload_tFactory;
}

/* constructors */
public payload_t()
{
  _struct = new MutableStruct(new Object[5],
_sqlType, _factory);
  try
  {
    _ctx = new _Ctx(DefaultContext.getDefaultContext());
  }
  catch (Exception e)
  {
    _ctx = null;
  }
}
public payload_t(ConnectionContext c) throws SQLException
{
  _struct = new MutableStruct(new Object[5],
    _sqlType, _factory);
  _ctx = new
  _Ctx(c == null ? DefaultContext.getDefaultContext(): c);
}
public payload_t(Connection c) throws SQLException
{
  _struct = new MutableStruct(new Object[5],
    _sqlType, _factory);
  _ctx = new _Ctx(c);
}
```

```
/* CustomDatum interface */
public Datum toDatum(OracleConnection c) throws
    SQLException
{
  _ctx = new _Ctx(c);
  return _struct.toDatum(c, _SQL_NAME);
}

/* CustomDatumFactory interface */
public CustomDatum create(Datum d, int sqlType) throws
    SQLException
{
  if (d == null) return null;
  payload_t o = new payload_t();
  o._struct = new MutableStruct((STRUCT) d,
    _sqlType, _factory);
  o._ctx = new _Ctx(((STRUCT) d).getConnection());
  return o;
}

/* accessor methods */
public java.math.BigDecimal getItemId() throws
    SQLException
{ return (java.math.BigDecimal) _struct.getAttribute(0); }

public void setItemId(java.math.BigDecimal itemId) throws
                      SQLException
{ _struct.setAttribute(0, itemId); }

public String getDescription() throws SQLException
{ return (String) _struct.getAttribute(1); }

public void setDescription(String description) throws
                           SQLException
{ _struct.setAttribute(1, description); }

public java.math.BigDecimal getQuantity() throws
                                          SQLException
{ return (java.math.BigDecimal) _struct.getAttribute(2); }

public void setQuantity(java.math.BigDecimal quantity) throws
                        SQLException
{ _struct.setAttribute(2, quantity); }
```

```
  public java.math.BigDecimal getUnitPrice() throws
      SQLException
  { return (java.math.BigDecimal) _struct.getAttribute(3); }

  public void setUnitPrice(java.math.BigDecimal unitPrice)
      throws SQLException
  { _struct.setAttribute(3, unitPrice); }

  public java.math.BigDecimal getTotalPrice() throws
                               SQLException
  { return (java.math.BigDecimal) _struct.getAttribute(4); }

  public void setTotalPrice(java.math.BigDecimal totalPrice)
      throws SQLException
  { _struct.setAttribute(4, totalPrice); }
}
```

After you create the necessary wrapper for your ADT message payload, you can concentrate on the program that uses the JMS infrastructure to enqueue/dequeue messages to/from the OFJP_1_QUEUE queue.

Oracle exposes its queuing system through a JMS interface. This means that messages are queued and dequeued according to the JMS specifications. For example, in order to send a message to a queue, you must create a QueueSender object and call its *send()* method to dispatch the message to the required destination. Accordingly, to read a message from a queue, you must create a QueueReceiver object and call its *receive()* method to fetch the required message.

The Oracle-JMS implementation provides two types of destinations, queues and topics. Queues are mapped to single-consumer AQ queues, and implement the JMS point-to-point model for message delivery. Topics are mapped to multi-consumer AQ queues and implement the JMS publish-and-subscribe model. Your example uses a point-to-point model. If you want to know more about JMS and its more powerful publish-and-subscribe model, start with the JMS specifications, freely available from the Java Web site (http://java.sun.com/products/jms/index.html).

To send a message to a queue according to the JMS model, you must follow the sequential steps summarized in Table 19.3.

After the six steps outlined in Table 19.3 have been performed, the JMS infrastructure is in place, and messages can be enqueued and dequeued.

The steps for enqueuing a message are shown in Table 19.4.

In step 3 you create a message that contains an ADT payload, using the *createAdtMessage()* method implemented in AQjmsSession. The AQjmsSession object can create several types of message, such as a StreamMessage, a BytesMessage, and a TextMessage. For a complete list of message types, see Chapter 12 of

TABLE 19.3

STEP #	DESCRIPTION	API CALL
1	Obtain a queue connection factory.	AQjmsFactory.getQueueConnectionFactory()
2	Create a queue connection.	AQjmsQueueConnectionFactory.CreateQueueConnection()
3	Create a queue session.	AQjmsConnection.createQueueSession()
4	Start the queue session.	AQjmsConnection.start()
5	Obtain a handle to a required queue.	AQjmsSession.getQueue()
6	Start the queue.	AQjmsDestination.start()

Application Developer's Guide: Advanced Queuing, a manual available in the standard Oracle documentation set.

Dequeuing a message is the opposite of enqueuing a message. A QueueReceiver object is required instead of a QueueSender object, but the steps are similar.

The correct sequence of steps in the source code of the example is shown below.

```
// Copyright © 2000 Prentice Hall
import java.sql.*;
import oracle.AQ.*;
import javax.jms.*;
import oracle.jms.*;
```

TABLE 19.4

STEP #	DESCRIPTION	API CALL
1	Obtain a handle to the required queue.	AQjmsSession.getQueue()
2	Create the sender object.	AQjmsSession.createSender()
3	Create the message.	AQjmsSession.createAdtMessage()
4	Send the message.	QueueSender.send()
5	Make the message persistent in the queue.	AQjmsSession.commit()

```
public class JmsSession
{

  private AQjmsConnection q_conn;
  public AQjmsSession createJmsSession(String ora_sid,
                     String host, int port,String driver)
  {
      AQjmsQueueConnectionFactory qc_fact = null;
      AQjmsSession q_sess = null;
      Queue queue = null;
      BytesMessage bytes_msg = null;
      AQQueueTableProperty qt_prop = null;
      AQQueueTable q_table = null;
      AQjmsDestinationProperty dest_prop = null;
      try
      {
         /* get queue connection factory */
         qc_fact = (AQjmsQueueConnectionFactory)
            AQjmsFactory.getQueueConnectionFactory(host,
               ora_sid,port, driver);
         /* create queue connection */
         q_conn = (AQjmsConnection)
            qc_fact.createQueueConnection("aq", "aq");
         /* create queue session */
         q_sess = (AQjmsSession)
            q_conn.createQueueSession(true,
                  Session.CLIENT_ACKNOWLEDGE);
         /* start the queue connection */
         q_conn.start();
         /* Obtain a handle to the required queue */
         queue = ((AQjmsSession)q_sess).getQueue("aq",
                                    "ofjp_1_queue");
         /* start the queue */
         ((AQjmsDestination)queue).start(q_sess, true, true);
      }
      catch (Exception exc)
      {
            System.out.println("Exception: " + exc);
      }
      return q_sess;
   }
   public static void main (String [] args)
   {
      AQjmsSession q = null;
```

```
      try
      {
         Class.forName("oracle.jdbc.driver.OracleDriver");
         JmsSession js = new JmsSession();
         q = js.createJmsSession("sun816","echidna",
                                 1521,"thin");
         payload_t pt = new payload_t();
         pt.setDescription("JMS Message example");
         pt.setItemId(new java.math.BigDecimal(56));
         pt.setQuantity(new java.math.BigDecimal(7));
         pt.setTotalPrice(new java.math.BigDecimal(2450));
         pt.setUnitPrice(new java.math.BigDecimal(350));
         js.enqueue_msg(q,pt);
         js.dequeue_msg(q);
         q.close();
         js.closeConnection();

      }
      catch (Exception exc) {exc.printStackTrace();}
   }

   public void enqueue_msg(AQjmsSession jms_session,
                           payload_t msg)
   {
      QueueSender sender;
      Queue queue;
      AQjmsAdtMessage adt_message;
      try
      {
         /* Obtain a queue handle to the required queue */
         queue = ((AQjmsSession)
            jms_session).getQueue("aq", "ofjp_1_queue");

         /* Create a sender object that is able to
            queue messages to the JMS queue */
         sender = jms_session.createSender(queue);

         /* Create a message whose payload is of ADT type */
         adt_message = jms_session.createAdtMessage(msg);

         /* Send the message using the sender object */
         sender.send(adt_message);

         /* Make the message persistent in the JMS queue */
         jms_session.commit();
```

```
      }
      catch (JMSException ex)
      {
         System.out.println("Exception: " + ex);
         ex.printStackTrace();
      }
   }

   public void dequeue_msg(AQjmsSession jms_session)
   {
      AQjmsQueueReceiver receiver;
      Queue queue;
      AQjmsAdtMessage adt_message;
      payload_t msg = new payload_t();
      try
      {
         /* get a handle to the OFJP_1_QUEUE */
         queue = ((AQjmsSession)
            jms_session).getQueue("aq", "ofjp_1_queue");

         /* Create a queue receiver. Since we browse a queue
         with  an ADT type of payload, we need to provide the
         CustomDatumFactory (payload_t) as the
         second parameter to the createReceiver call */
         receiver = (AQjmsQueueReceiver)
            jms_session.createReceiver(queue,msg);
         for(;;)
         {
            /* Fetch the pending message on the queue */
            adt_message = (AQjmsAdtMessage) receiver.receive(1);
            if(adt_message != null)
            {
               /* Get the payload form the message */
               msg = (payload_t) adt_message.getAdtPayload();

               /* Print the description field of the message,
                  to be sure that the message has been
                  actually retrieved */
               System.out.println(msg.getDescription());
               /* If we don't commit, the message is not
                 consumed from the queue */
               jms_session.commit();
            }
            else
```

```
                    break;
                }
            }
            catch (Exception exc) {exc.printStackTrace();}
        }

        private void closeConnection()
        {
            try
            {
                this.q_conn.close();
            }catch (Exception exc) {}
        }
    }
```

The preceding example has been kept simple, to help developers and designers who are approaching the disconnected/deferred paradigm and Oracle AQ for the first time.

The JMS interface, however, offers features that are much more sophisticated than simple point-to-point queuing and dequeuing of messages. The publish-and-subscribe paradigm supported by JMS may become the preferred option for message-oriented middleware modules that use Oracle AQ. You are encouraged to explore the more advanced features offered by Oracle AQ if the disconnected/deferred paradigm is suitable for your business domain.

SUMMARY

The AQ example presented in this chapter introduced the disconnected/deferred client/server paradigm. You performed all the preliminary tasks necessary to start a simple queue. You created an infrastructure in Java, using JPublisher and JDeveloper, which enabled you to enqueue and dequeue simple messages. Using the AQ facility through PL/SQL is significantly more labor-intensive than using the native Java interface, but it allows you to be compatible with older releases of Oracle.

You reworked the simple example presented above using the Oracle proprietary Java interface to AQ, available with Oracle 8.1.5. While this solution has a few advantages over a Java-PL/SQL bridge, it locks your code into Oracle-only technologies. A better solution, available with Oracle 8.1.6 and higher, allows you to access the AQ feature from JMS calls, which can be ported to other middleware environments, such as the IBM MQ Series.

The examples in this chapter only scratch the surface of the Oracle AQ world, which can offer much more than the features used in the code shown above. One of the most useful AQ features is the ability to define other queues, even if they reside on remote computers, as recipients for messages. This feature allows designers and developers of e-commerce applications to decentralize and distribute their application hosts, thus minimizing network latency and improving the overall usability of the client front-end. At the same time, messages queued from remote sites can be propagated, relying on Oracle mechanisms, to a central master site that supervises the activities of all the peripheral branches.

Message-oriented middleware (MOM) is becoming an increasingly important application infrastructure in the e-commerce field. Through advanced queuing, Oracle offers a credible alternative to MOM-specific third-party products, bundled with the Oracle Enterprise Server at no extra cost. It is strongly recommended that you further explore this interesting and challenging new application paradigm.

Chapter 20

USING ORACLE REPLICATION TO BUILD DISTRIBUTED SYSTEMS

Although it is relatively easy to Web-enable a corporation's central database, so that external customers can access it directly from their browsers, this arrangement makes MIS managers uneasy. As pointed out in Chapter 8, security is a crucial issue in the e-commerce game. Implementing a strict security policy, and incurring the increased administrative burden it entails, is a cost of doing business, no different from buying computers and paying to insure them. Knowing that the central repository of corporate data is exposed to electronic attack by hackers of all types, situated all over the world, alarms even the most adventurous and risk-taking MIS manager.

This is an area where data replication can play a primary role. Using a few advanced features offered by Oracle, it is possible to create a database that acts as a Web "front-end" freely accessed by external customers. This database is connected to the central database via a highly secure link that allows for strictly controlled uploading of information collected during interactions with customers. In other words, the information collected by the Web application and stored in the front-end database can be automatically replicated to the central database, and in the process data-integrity checks can be performed.

Data replication can also be used effectively to minimize network latency and implement load balancing. Consider a large corporation with many branches, several in key areas of the United States and a few worldwide, perhaps in Europe and Australia. Latency (the amount of time it takes for a single data packet to travel from one computer to another) is likely to become a significant issue if all the branches access a single centrally located machine. This is why many open-source projects are replicated in mirror sites. If a project originates, say, in the United States, and the number of downloads is significant, the entire directory containing source code and documentation for the project can be replicated in one or more locations on different continents. Conversely, if the open-source project originates, say, in Europe, one or more American hosts can become mirror sites for the open-source project. If network latency is minimized in this way, Web users located on different continents will not incur excessive delays and downloading problems because of the physical distance between the server hosting the data and the Web-browsing device downloading the data.

Data replication allows for the creation of mirror sites that are dynamic rather than static. Customers very dispersed geographically can each access the closest site where a database is available. Synchronization of all the copies of the database takes place later, using data-replication techniques and features, as implemented by Oracle. In order to use this technique effectively, you need to familiarize yourself with data-replication concepts and terminology.

20.1 DATA REPLICATION

Data replication is the copying of data in databases to multiple locations to support distributed applications. Replication provides users with their own local copies of data. These local, updatable data copies support increased local processing, reduced network traffic, easy scalability, and more cost-effective approaches for distributed, nonstop processing.

Given the intrinsic nature of data replication, the concept of data integrity actually refers to what might be called "deferred integrity," meaning that integrity is attained later on (i.e., when data across the various sites are reconciled). With Oracle data replication, you have much more than a mechanism that gives persistence to your Java objects. In fact, you have an e-commerce platform that can be tailored to fulfill disparate needs, ranging from data storage to data replication, from security to fault tolerance.

Several business markets have taken advantage of data replication. Order processing for e-commerce, as well as many other business functions, such as hotel and airline reservations, have been successfully implemented using data replication. Airlines and hotels often overbook intentionally, then solve the resulting problems at a later stage, when the relevant data have been stabilized and reconciled. In such cases, data replication is even more in line with the business model.

Data replication is a very young discipline, but there are already many different approaches to it, each aimed at solving a different class of problems. To begin with, Oracle supports two fundamental categories of replication: basic replication (the master/slave approach) and advanced replication (the peer-to-peer update-anywhere approach).

The master/slave approach eliminates transaction collisions, but is more rigid and less generic than the peer-to-peer update-anywhere approach. In the master/slave model, only one site (the master) can update a table, which is later replicated to the slave site (or sites). The latter sees the table in a read-only mode. In the peer-to-peer model, on the other hand, all the sites can update the same table, which is later reconciled against all sites.

A collision occurs when a record is physically replicated at two or more sites and then is updated during the asynchronous latency period. In other words, after a first update at one site, a second update occurs at another site before the first update has been propagated. So, although a peer-to-peer approach provides the most general solution for transaction distribution, it requires policies for collision resolution.

Data replication policies that avoid data collision are relatively easy to implement and administer. Unfortunately, there is a trade-off between simplicity and flexibility. The master/slave approach is not flexible enough for some specific needs. Organizations also require the ability to support updates at multiple sites working independently from one other. Every local branch can then function autonomously, irrespective of the availability of other systems or networks participating in the distributed environment. In a peer-to-peer environment it is not possible to avoid data collisions—one simply has to live with them. Nonetheless, the software provided by Oracle can help in detecting and resolving data collisions.

The peer-to-peer model supports disconnected environments. For example, the sales representative who records all sales made during the day on a laptop computer and then synchronizes it with the central company database at the end of the day, connecting from home or from a hotel. Another possible use of this technology is to provide a completely replicated *failover* site, in case the principal site is down because of a crash or for maintenance. Oracle supports both synchronous and asynchronous replication. In an environment replicated synchronously, data collisions do not occur because all transactions are propagated atomically. The synchronous replication model overlaps with the more traditional distributed model, which makes use of the two-phase commit protocol.[1] The drawback of such a model is that it requires all participating nodes to be up and running in order for a single transaction to succeed. Furthermore, performance can become an issue if many different nodes, geographically dispersed, participate in the same transaction.

Most replicated applications use the asynchronous mechanism for change propagation. Oracle offers different options, suitable for the implementation of heterogeneous replicated environments, where different replication models can coexist and cooperate in hybrid configurations. In a *multimaster* configuration, for instance, multiple sites are peers and manage groups of replicated database objects. This means that applications are able to update any replicated table in any participating site. A different configuration has the master site managing data propagation through the use of updatable snapshots. The two configurations can coexist in the same replicated environment.

The main difference between a multimaster configuration and a configuration based on updatable snapshots is that the first forces the replicated tables to be identical at all sites, while the second allows for an updatable snapshot to be a subset of the master site's tables. With updatable snapshots, propagation happens in both directions. A change made on a table in the master site is replicated in all snapshots, whereas conversely, a change made on a remote updatable snapshot is replicated to the master and to all other snapshots.

The Oracle replication option offers fine granularity, allowing for row-level propagation. To design and manage an Oracle replicated environment effectively, you should familiarize yourself with the terminology used in this context. Table 20.1 lists the key terms used in data replication.

---

[1]The two-phase commit (2PC) protocol is an algorithm used to ensure that transactions succeed in all their parts and all interested nodes, or in none. That is, the 2PC protocol guarantees the atomicity of distributed transactions.

TABLE 20.1 Terms used in data replication

Replication Object: A database object existing on multiple servers in a replicated database system.

Replication Group: A set of related replication objects grouped together to facilitate administration and management. A replication object can be a member of only one replication group.

Replication Site: A database node participating in a replicated database environment. There are two types of replication sites: a master site maintains a complete copy of all objects in a replication group, whereas a snapshot site supports read-only and updatable snapshots of the table data residing in an associated master site.

Replication Catalog: A set of data dictionary tables and views that maintains information about replicated objects and replicated groups at every site.

Oracle8i uses kernel-level triggers to support replicated tables. The triggers build remote procedure calls (RPCs) to propagate data changes made at the local site to all remote replication participating sites. The automatically generated RPCs are stored by Oracle in its deferred-transaction queue, which is implemented at every site. To manage propagation, Oracle uses its own job-queue mechanism, implemented as a table holding data about which PL/SQL procedures must be invoked to incur propagation, when to apply them, to what sites, and so on.

Designers may choose further options when determining the replication configuration of the application being built. They can decide to implement serial propagation, where Oracle replicates transactions one at a time, using the same order of commit observed at the originator site. If the nodes participating in a replicated environment are symmetrical multi-processor (SMP) machines, then Oracle offers parallel propagation, where multiple transit streams are open and used concurrently in a parallel environment.

Oracle replication allows designers to choose either a pull or a push model for data propagation. When a master site table is modified, the changes are asynchronously pulled from the table to the snapshots. When an updatable snapshot is changed at a remote site, the changes are pushed to the master site table.

The main issue when dealing with asynchronous replication is data collision. If a true peer-to-peer model is to be implemented, then a conflict-resolution policy must be designed.

There are three types of replication conflicts:

- Uniqueness conflicts
- Update conflicts
- Delete conflicts

A uniqueness conflict occurs when the replication of a row violates a referential integrity constraint. An update conflict occurs when an update to a row conflicts with another update to the same row that took place during the latency period.

A delete conflict occurs when a transaction that originated in one site deletes a row that was updated in another site during the latency period. Oracle organizes every column in a replicated table in column groups. The DBA assigns conflict-resolution methods to each column group.

Oracle has prebuilt mechanisms to detect and resolve update collisions, but does not offer a prebuilt mechanism to resolve delete collisions. The prebuilt methods for update resolution are:

1. Overwrite and discard value
2. Minimum and maximum value
3. Earliest and latest timestamp value
4. Additive and average value
5. Priority groups and site priority

To understand how these methods work, you need to understand the notion of data convergence. Data convergence is the goal of the replication process. It means that all sites ultimately have the same content for any given row. Every conflict-resolution strategy or policy must guarantee data convergence. If an administrator does not assign conflict-resolution methods to the columns of replicated tables, Oracle simply logs conflict data at the sites where they happen. This forces the DBA to resolve all conflicts manually, a task that can soon become overwhelming. A better solution is to use the Oracle prebuilt methods or to create customized methods if the basic ones are insufficient. Note that customized methods must be used to resolve delete collisions. Multiple conflict-resolution methods can be applied to the same column. Oracle tries to resolve the conflict by applying each specified method in succession, until either the conflict is resolved or an error is logged, and later manual resolution is required to ensure data convergence.

An exhaustive treatment of peer-to-peer update-anywhere advanced data-replication strategies is beyond the scope of this book. An experienced database administrator is needed to implement them. As a Java developer/designer approaching Oracle technologies for the first time, you should familiarize yourself with this important feature offered by the database server. Even if you do not master its details, at least you are in a position, as a designer of an Oracle/Java application, to consider its adoption should the need arise.

20.2 BASIC REPLICATION IN ORACLE

A simpler approach to data replication is the one offered by the master/slave model, based on the concept of the table snapshot. The table snapshot mechanism allows the replication of a master table by an unlimited number of snapshots on other connected nodes of a distributed database.

Data can only be changed on the master table, and the replicates are read-only. The slave nodes can query the snapshots but cannot modify or add data to them. Snapshots are periodically refreshed, either automatically or manually. The database administrator determines the refresh interval, but it can be modified at any time. Users with appropriate privileges can force a snapshot refresh on demand. A snapshot refresh can be either complete or partial. A complete refresh empties the snapshot on the target node and creates a new set of rows each time a refresh occurs. This arrangement can lead to performance issues if the replicated table becomes too large. For this reason, Oracle provides partial refreshes, whereby only newly inserted rows are propagated with each refresh. To partially refresh replicated snapshots, Oracle requires the creation of snapshot logs (tables residing in the master database) associated with the master tables.

Oracle uses the snapshot logs to track the table rows updated in the master table. When a remote snapshot based on a master table is refreshed, only the rows inserted during the latency period need to be applied to the snapshot to refresh it. Oracle refers to the information stored in the snapshot log to select the rows inserted into the master table during the latency period.

There are at least three different types of data replication based on the master/slave model:

1. Data dissemination
2. Data consolidation
3. Workload partitioning

The data-dissemination approach defines only one master site empowered to access the tables to be replicated in read/write mode. All the other sites participating in the replicated database are prevented from updating the replicated tables, which are refreshed periodically from the master to the slaves. This is the simplest form of data replication, and it is implemented by all the major database vendors. The tables in common between the master and the slaves are called snapshots.

An example of applied data dissemination, illustrated in Figure 20.1 is a computer store chain whose headquarters sends updated price lists of available computer components overnight. The stores have read-only access to the prices, while headquarters can modify them.

The data-consolidation model implements the opposite philosophy: the peripheral sites update either a separate table or non-overlapping records within one table, and then the central server receives the consolidated data from all the sites. The central server cannot update the snapshots, but simply queries the replicated tables to produce reconciled reports from all sites.

An example of data consolidation, illustrated in Figure 20.2, is a retail store chain that gathers point-of-sale information throughout the day. Each store must supply a copy of this information to headquarters on a daily basis. When this in-

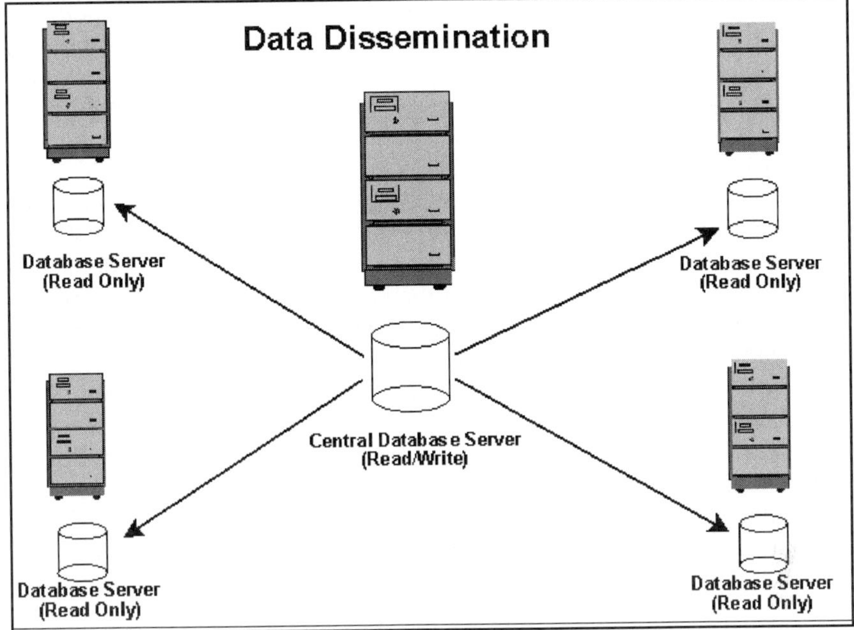

FIGURE 20.1 Example of applied data dissemination.

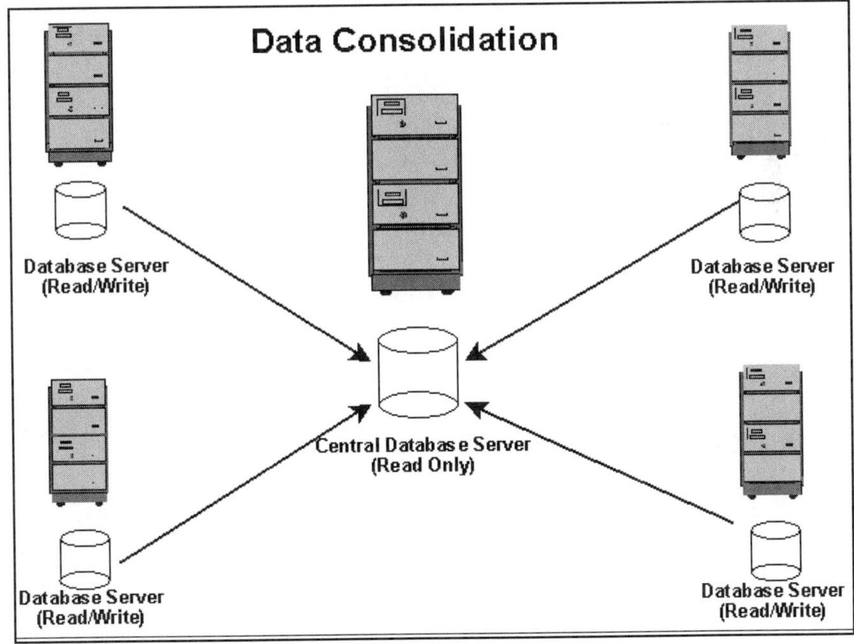

FIGURE 20.2 Example of data consolidation.

formation is transmitted to headquarters at the end of each day, it is consolidated into the central data warehouse, which management can use to perform a trend analysis on its business.

The workload partitioning model introduces yet another important concept widely used in data replication: ownership of data. An example of workload partitioning is given in Figure 20.3.

The replication schema matches the partitioning schema for the order-entry tables. The Australia-based server has ownership of its partition and therefore can update, insert, and delete order-entry records for orders in its region. The changes are then propagated to the United States and New Zealand regions. Australia can query or read the other partitions locally, but is not able to update them. This strategy applies to other regions as well.

The three techniques described above can be combined to provide flexible and articulate solutions to e-commerce issues. For example, consider a geographically dispersed virtual shop that implements basic data replication. The master site, using data dissemination, can propagate information about item price and availability to peripheral sites. At the same time, the peripheral sites, using data consolidation, can propagate customer-order information to the central site.

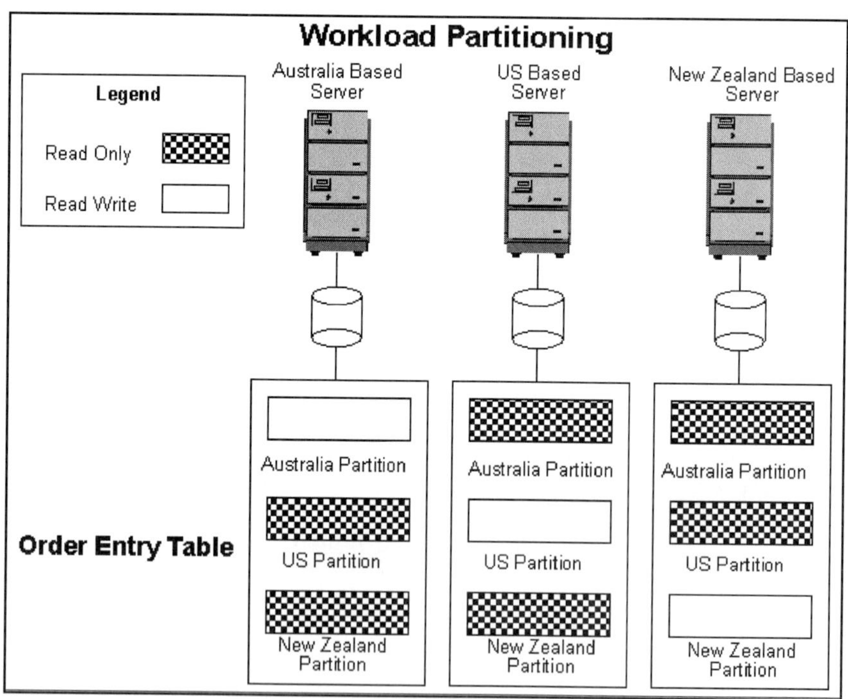

FIGURE 20.3 Example of workload partitioning.

Data replication provides several benefits.

- Peripheral sites can work in isolation. If the master site or any other site is down, customers can connect and do business with the sites that are still working.
- Security is enhanced because customers connecting worldwide do not access the corporate database directly. Information is propagated from peripheral sites to the master site in a strictly controlled manner.
- Performance is improved because queries are performed against local tables or snapshots and not across the remote nodes constituting the distributed database.

20.3 AN EXAMPLE OF DATA REPLICATION

Mastering and properly implementing the peer-to-peer update-anywhere data-replication model requires advanced skills. However, a snapshot-based, basic replication model is definitely within the reach of developers approaching Oracle technologies for the first time. You will now be shown how to develop a simple replicated application that implements data-dissemination and data-consolidation techniques. To understand the example, you must have:

- General knowledge of SQL and PL/SQL, as explained in Chapters 2 to 4 and 7 to 8.
- Familiarity with JDBC concepts (Chapter 9).
- Ability to use SQL*Plus.

Concurrent access to at least two Oracle instances is also required. The two instances can run on different operating systems, for instance Solaris and MS Windows NT/2000, and need not be of the same Oracle release. For example, a snapshot created on an instance running Oracle release 8.1.5 can be refreshed from a master table created on an instance running Oracle 8.0.5.

The two instances must be reachable through SQL*Net; that is, database links must be created to support basic data replication.

In the example in this chapter, you will use an Oracle instance called sun8i, running on a Sun Ultra 5 workstation, and an Oracle instance called nt8i, running on a PC equipped with MS Windows NT 4.0. You will test the example using two PCs both running NT, where one assumes the role of master and the other the role of peripheral site.

It is assumed for the purposes of the example that the Oracle instances and the SQL*Net listeners are properly configured and running. This is usually the case after a successful installation has created the seed database, a small database created automatically by the installation program. The seed database allows the user to run the demonstration and example programs shipped with the Oracle release bundle.

In the example, you will use data replication to facilitate the transfer of price-related data from a central site running Oracle on a Sun Solaris system to a peripheral site running Oracle on MS Windows NT. An e-commerce application allows customers to buy the items sold by the company. The orders entered by the customers, who interact with the Web application running at the peripheral site, are propagated to the central database via a snapshot.

Figure 20.4 is a pictorial representation of the central and peripheral sites, and the access that each site has to each table: either read/write or read only.

To set up a replicated configuration, the steps listed below are mandatory:

1. Set up the master site.
2. Set up the snapshot site.
3. Create a master group.
4. Create a snapshot group.

It is important to perform the configuration operations in the order shown above.

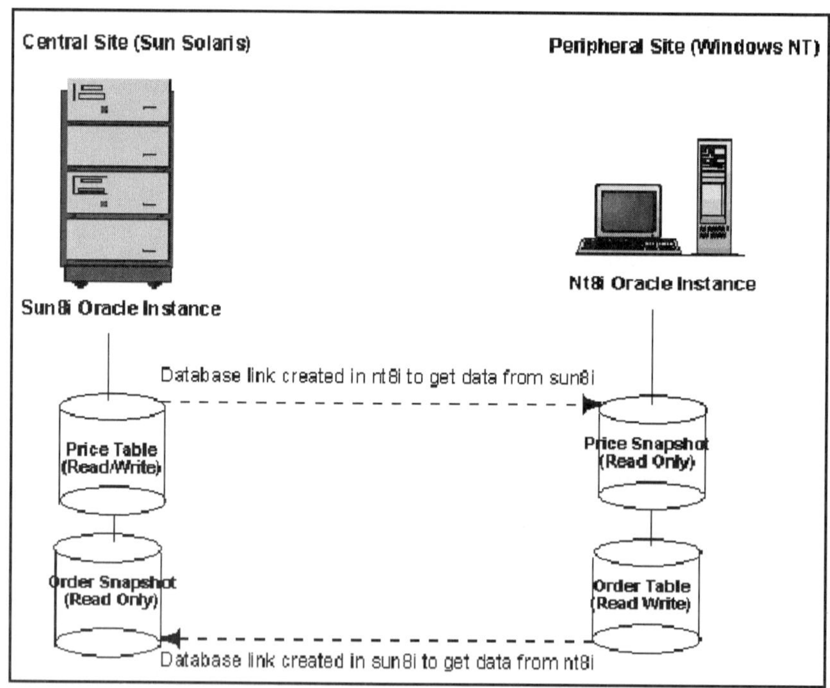

FIGURE 20.4 Replication setup used in the example.

First, set up the replication environment for the price table, replicated from the master site (sun8i) to the peripheral site (nt8i). The application schema name is `web_sales`.

The task of creating a replicated environment in Oracle8i is long and complex. For this reason Oracle provides a visual front-end called Replication Manager, which ships with Oracle Enterprise Manager (OEM), a tool offered by Oracle to manage all databases deployed in the enterprise from a single console. A powerful replication manager wizard completely automates the process, allowing DBAs to create complex replicated environments visually.

For the purpose of the example, you will instead create all the database objects, including application schema, tables, snapshots, and snapshot logs, by calling PL/SQL procedures directly from SQL*Plus.

You start by creating the master site:

```
/*****************************************************************
STEP 1 @ SUN8I:
CONNECT AS SYSTEM AT MASTER SITE
*****************************************************************/
--You need to connect as SYSTEM to the database that you want to
--setup for replication.
CONNECT SYSTEM/MANAGER@SUN8I
/*******************************************************************
STEP 2 @ SUN8I:
CREATE REPLICATION ADMINISTRATOR
*******************************************************************/
--The replication administrator must be granted the necessary
--privileges to create and manage a replicated environment.
--The replication administrator needs to be created at each database
--that participates in the replicated environment.
CREATE USER repadmin IDENTIFIED BY repadmin;
/*******************************************************************
STEP 3 @ SUN8I:
GRANT PRIVILEGES TO REPLICATION ADMINISTRATOR
*******************************************************************/
--Executing the GRANT_ADMIN_ANY_SCHEMA API grants the replication
--administrator powerful privileges to create and manage a replicated
--environment.
BEGIN
DBMS_REPCAT_ADMIN.GRANT_ADMIN_ANY_SCHEMA
(
      USERNAME => 'repadmin'
);
END;
/
```

```
/*****************************************************************
STEP 4 @ SUN8I:
REGISTER PROPAGATOR
*****************************************************************/
--The propagator is responsible for propagating the deferred
--transaction queue to other master sites.
BEGIN
DBMS_DEFER_SYS.REGISTER_PROPAGATOR
(
      USERNAME => 'repadmin'
);
END;
/
/*****************************************************************
STEP 5 @ SUN8I:
REGISTER RECEIVER
*****************************************************************/
--The receiver receives the propagated deferred transactions sent
--by the propagator from other master sites.
BEGIN
DBMS_REPCAT_ADMIN.REGISTER_USER_REPGROUP
(
      USERNAME => 'repadmin',
      privilege_type => 'receiver',
      list_of_gnames => NULL
);
END;
/
/*****************************************************************
STEP 6 @ SUN8I:
SCHEDULE PURGE AT MASTER SITE
*****************************************************************/
--In order to keep the size of the deferred transaction queue under
--control, you should purge successfully completed deferred
--transactions. The SCHEDULE_PURGE API automates the purge
--process for you. You must execute this procedure as the replication
--administrator. The expression sysdate + 1/24 forces the job to run
--every hour. Sysdate returns the current timestamp. 1/24th of a day
--is added to the current timestamp. Every time the job is run, the
--expression is re-evaluated, and the next new time of run is
--computed
CONNECT repadmin/repadmin@sun8I
BEGIN
DBMS_DEFER_SYS.SCHEDULE_PURGE
(
      next_date => SYSDATE,
      interval => 'sysdate + 1/24',
```

```
      delay_seconds => 0,
      rollback_segment => ''
);
END;
/
/*******************************************************************
STEP 7:
CREATE MASTER SITE USERS
*******************************************************************/
--STEP 7a: CREATE PROXY SNAPSHOT ADMINISTRATOR
--The proxy snapshot administrator performs tasks at the target
--master site on behalf of the snapshot administrator at the snapshot
--site.
CONNECT system/manager@sun8i
CREATE USER proxy_snapadmin IDENTIFIED BY proxy_snapadmin;
BEGIN
DBMS_REPCAT_ADMIN.REGISTER_USER_REPGROUP
(
      username => 'PROXY_SNAPADMIN',
      privilege_type => 'PROXY_SNAPADMIN',
      list_of_gnames => NULL
);
END;
/
--STEP 7b: CREATE PROXY REFRESHER
--The proxy refresher performs tasks at the master site on behalf of
--the refresher at the snapshot site.
CREATE USER proxy_refresher IDENTIFIED BY proxy_refresher;
GRANT CREATE SESSION TO proxy_refresher;
GRANT SELECT ANY TABLE TO proxy_refresher;
```

After successfully creating the master site, you focus on the snapshot site.

```
/*******************************************************************
STEP 1:
CONNECT AS SYSTEM AT SNAPSHOT SITE
*******************************************************************/
--You need to connect as SYSTEM to the database that you want to
--setup as a snapshot site.
CONNECT system/manager@nt8i
/*******************************************************************
STEP 2:
CREATE SNAPSHOT SITE USERS
*******************************************************************/
--There are several users that need to be created at the snapshot
```

```
--site.
--These users are:
-- SNAPSHOT ADMINISTRATOR
-- PROPAGATOR
-- REFRESHER
--STEP 2a: CREATE SNAPSHOT ADMINISTRATOR
--The snapshot administrator is responsible for creating and managing
--the snapshot site. Execute the GRANT_ADMIN_ANY_SCHEMA
--procedure to grant the snapshot administrator the appropriate
--privileges.
create user SNAPADMIN identified by SNAPADMIN;
BEGIN
DBMS_REPCAT_ADMIN.GRANT_ADMIN_ANY_SCHEMA
(
      username => 'SNAPADMIN'
);
END;
/
--STEP 2b: CREATE PROPAGATOR
--The propagator is responsible for propagating the deferred
--transaction queue to the target master site.
CREATE USER propagator IDENTIFIED BY propagator;
BEGIN
DBMS_DEFER_SYS.REGISTER_PROPAGATOR
(
      username => 'propagator'
);
END;
/
--STEP 2c: CREATE REFRESHER
--The refresher is responsible for "pulling" changes made to the
-- replicated tables at the target master site to the snapshot site.
create user REFRESHER identified by REFRESHER;
GRANT CREATE SESSION TO refresher;
GRANT ALTER ANY SNAPSHOT TO refresher;
/*******************************************************************
STEP 3:
CREATE DATABASE LINKS TO MASTER SITE
*******************************************************************/
--STEP 3A: CREATE PUBLIC DATABASE LINK
CONNECT system/manager@nt8I
CREATE PUBLIC DATABASE LINK sun8i USING 'sun8i';
--STEP 3b: CREATE SNAPSHOT ADMINISTRATOR DATABASE LINK
--You need to create a database link from the snapshot administrator
--at the snapshot site to the proxy snapshot administrator at
--the master site.
```

```
CONNECT snapadmin/snapadmin@nt8i;
CREATE DATABASE LINK sun8i
CONNECT TO proxy_snapadmin IDENTIFIED BY proxy_snapadmin;
--STEP 3c: CREATE PROPAGATOR/RECEIVER DATABASE LINK
--You need to create a database link from the propagator at the
--snapshot site to the receiver at the master site (the receiver was
--defined when you created the master group)
CONNECT propagator/propagator@nt8i
CREATE DATABASE LINK sun8i
CONNECT TO repadmin IDENTIFIED BY repadmin;
/*******************************************************************
STEP 4:
SCHEDULE PURGE AT SNAPSHOT SITE
*******************************************************************/
--In order to keep the size of the deferred transaction queue in
--check, you should purge successfully completed deferred
--transactions. The SCHEDULE_PURGE API automates the purge
--process for you. If your snapshot site only contains "read-
--only" snapshots, then you not need to execute this procedure. The
--expression sysdate + 1/(60*24) means every minute.

CONNECT snapadmin/snapadmin@nt8i
BEGIN
DBMS_DEFER_SYS.SCHEDULE_PURGE
(
       next_date => SYSDATE,
       interval => 'sysdate + 1/(60*24)',
       delay_seconds => 0,
       rollback_segment => ''
);
END;
/
/*******************************************************************
STEP 5:
SCHEDULE PUSH AT SNAPSHOT SITE
*******************************************************************/
--The SCHEDULE_PUSH API schedules when the deferred transaction queue
--should be propagated to the target master site.
CONNECT snapadmin/snapadmin@nt8i
BEGIN
DBMS_DEFER_SYS.SCHEDULE_PUSH
(
       destination => 'SUN8I',
       interval => 'sysdate + 1/(60*24)',
       next_date => SYSDATE,
       stop_on_error => FALSE,
```

```
        delay_seconds => 0,
        parallelism => 0
);
END;
/
```

Setting up the master and snapshot sites is a preliminary operation that must be done to support any replicated object. Before creating the master and snapshot groups, however, you need to create the objects that you want to replicate across the instances. In the case of this example, you must create the price table at your master site, sun8i.

```
CONNECT web_sales/supersecret@sun8i
create table price
(
        item_id number constraint price_pk PRIMARY KEY,
        net_price number (10,2),
        sales_tax_perc number(5,2),
        gross_price number(10,2)
);
```

You can now proceed with the creation of the master group.

```
/*********************************************************************
STEP 1:
CREATE MASTER GROUP
*********************************************************************/
--Use the CREATE_MASTER_REPGROUP API to define a new master group.
--When you add an object to your master group or perform other
--replication administrative tasks, you reference the master
--group name defined during this step. The following must be executed
--by the replication administrator.
CONNECT repadmin/repadmin@sun8i
BEGIN
DBMS_REPCAT.CREATE_MASTER_REPGROUP
(
        gname => 'WEB_SALES_MG'
);
END;
/
/*********************************************************************
STEP 2:
ADD OBJECTS TO MASTER GROUP
*********************************************************************/
--Use the CREATE_MASTER_REPOBJECT API to an object to your master
```

```
--group. In most cases, you will probably be adding tables to your
--master group, but you can also add indexes, procedures, views,
--synonyms, etc.
BEGIN
DBMS_REPCAT.CREATE_MASTER_REPOBJECT
(
      gname => 'WEB_SALES_MG',
      type => 'TABLE',
      oname => 'PRICE',
      sname => 'WEB_SALES',
      use_existing_object => TRUE,
      copy_rows => TRUE
);
END;
/
/*******************************************************************
STEP 3:
GENERATE REPLICATION SUPPORT
*******************************************************************/
BEGIN
DBMS_REPCAT.GENERATE_REPLICATION_SUPPORT
(
      sname => 'WEB_SALES',
      oname => 'PRICE',
      type => 'TABLE',
      min_communication => TRUE
);
END;
/
/*******************************************************************
STEP 4:
RESUME REPLICATION
*******************************************************************/
--After you have completed creating your master group, adding
--replication objects, generating replication support, and adding
--additional master databases, you need to resume replication
--activity. The RESUME_MASTER_ACTIVITY procedure API will "turn on"
--replication for the specified master group.
BEGIN
DBMS_REPCAT.RESUME_MASTER_ACTIVITY
(
      gname => 'WEB_SALES_MG'
);
END;
/
```

Finally, you create the snapshot group. After creating a snapshot log in the master site, you must create a snapshot group and a refresh group. To create the refresh group, call the PL/SQL procedure DBMS_REFRESH.MAKE, which requires several parameters, including "next_date" and "interval." These parameters allow you to specify the refresh interval: how often the master table is replicated into the snapshot. This is an important design decision and should be carefully considered, since it will affect the overall performance of the application you are going to develop. If you are replicating a table that is mainly static, it makes sense to set a long refresh interval, say every 24 hours, and let your application perform a "manual" refresh when the table is updated. This is achieved by calling the DBMS_REFRESH.REFRESH procedure, which takes only one parameter, the name of the snapshot group to be refreshed. If you are replicating a table that is heavily accessed in read/write mode, perform a few benchmarks to determine the optimal refresh interval. If you choose an interval that is too short, you risk overburdening your database with a lot of background activity to support data replication. If you choose an interval that is too long, the backlog accumulated during the latency period could be significant; that is, too much time may be required to replicate the data into the snapshots. Beyond technical considerations, business logic should also be considered. For example, even in a replicated environment where data integrity across all nodes is not reached immediately, but is deferred and eventually achieved, time constraints may play an important role in your design decisions. Say that an application requirement specifies that the maximum lag time for the orders collected by the peripheral branches to reach the master site is one hour. Set your refresh interval accordingly, taking into account that when a data-consolidation strategy is implemented, multiple master sites may try to refresh at the same time.

In this example, you set a refresh interval of one minute, so that you won't have to wait too long when you test your application. Insert a row in the master table, and after a few tens of seconds access the remote site to make sure that the snapshot has been refreshed.

```
/******************************************************************
STEP 1:
CREATE SNAPSHOT LOGS AT MASTER SITE
******************************************************************/
--If you want one of your master sites to support a snapshot site,
--then you need to create snapshot logs for each master table that
--is replicated to a snapshot.
CONNECT web_sales/supersecret@sun8i
CREATE SNAPSHOT LOG ON web_sales.price;
/******************************************************************
STEP 2:
CREATE REPLICATED SCHEMA AND LINKS
******************************************************************/
```

```
--Before you begin building your snapshot group, you must make sure
--that the replicated schema exists at the remote snapshot site and
--that the necessary database links have been created.
CONNECT system/manager@nt8i
CREATE USER web_sales IDENTIFIED BY supersecret;
GRANT connect, resource TO web_sales;
CONNECT web_sales/supersecret@nt8i
--The owner of the snapshots needs a database link pointing to
--the proxy_refresher that was created when the snapshot site was
--setup.
CREATE DATABASE LINK sun8i
CONNECT TO proxy_refresher IDENTIFIED BY proxy_refresher;
/*********************************************************************
STEP 3:
CREATE SNAPSHOT GROUP
*********************************************************************/
--The following procedures must be executed by the snapshot
--administrator at the remote snapshot site.
CONNECT snapadmin/snapadmin@nt8i
--The master group that you specify in the GNAME parameter must match
--the name of the master group that you are replicating at the target
--master site.
BEGIN
DBMS_REPCAT.CREATE_SNAPSHOT_REPGROUP
(
      gname => 'WEB_SALES_MG',
      master => 'sun8i',
      propagation_mode => 'ASYNCHRONOUS'
);
END;
/
/*********************************************************************
STEP 4:
CREATE REFRESH GROUP
*********************************************************************/
--All snapshots that are added to a particular refresh group is
--refreshed at the same time. This ensures transactional consistency
--between the related snapshots in the refresh group.
BEGIN
DBMS_REFRESH.MAKE
(
      name => 'SNAPADMIN.WEB_SALES_RG',
      list => '',
      next_date => SYSDATE,
      interval => 'sysdate + 1/(60*24)',
      implicit_destroy => FALSE,
```

```
        rollback_seg => '',
        push_deferred_rpc => TRUE,
        refresh_after_errors => FALSE
);
END;
/
/*****************************************************************
STEP 5:
ADD OBJECTS TO SNAPSHOT GROUP
*****************************************************************/
BEGIN
DBMS_REPCAT.CREATE_SNAPSHOT_REPOBJECT
(
        gname => 'WEB_SALES_MG',
        sname => 'WEB_SALES',
        oname => 'PRICE',
        type => 'SNAPSHOT',
        ddl_text => 'create snapshot WEB_SALES.PRICE refresh fast with
        primary key for update as select * from
        WEB_SALES.PRICE@sun8i',
        min_communication => TRUE
);
END;
/
/*****************************************************************
STEP 6:
ADD OBJECTS TO REFRESH GROUP
*****************************************************************/
--Each of the snapshot group objects that you add to the refresh
--group is refreshed at the same time to preserve referential
--integrity between related snapshots.
BEGIN
DBMS_REFRESH.ADD
(
        name => 'SNAPADMIN.WEB_SALES_RG',
        list => 'WEB_SALES.PRICE',
        lax => TRUE
);
END;
/
```

You now have a replicated environment. All of the operations done so far must be repeated for the `order` table, where the nt8i instance becomes the master site and the sun8i instance becomes the remote snapshot site. The files containing the SQL statements that will accomplish this are on the companion CD-ROM. To test data replication in your environment, you must edit all the files and replace the instance names specific to the example environment, sun8i and nt8I, to match the Oracle instance names of your environment. You can then launch SQL*Plus and execute the scripts one after the other. It is important to execute them in the correct sequence, as shown in Table 20.2.

You can now test your replicated environment. Write a small Java program that connects to the sun8i instance, storing a new entry in the price table. Then connect to the nt8i instance, using SQL*Plus.

You should find the newly inserted record in the price snapshot. The Java test program follows.

```
package com.appsoft.ofjp;
import java.sql.*;
import oracle.jdbc.driver.*;
import java.util.*;
import java.math.*;

public class TestProgram
{
   public static void main(String[] args)
   {
      try
      {
```

TABLE 20.2 Steps required to successfully run the example

STEP	SCRIPT	COMMENT
1	master_site_price.sql	Creates the master site that enables the price table to be replicated into the remote snapshot.
2	snapshot_site_price.sql	Creates the snapshot site for the price table.
3	price.sql	Price table definition.
4	master_group_price.sql	Creates the master group at the master site for the price table.
5	snapshot_group_price.sql	Creates the snapshot group and adds the snapshot object to it. The price table is now replicated.
6	master_site_order.sql	Creates the master site that enables the order table to be replicated into the remote snapshot.
7	snapshot_site_order.sql	Creates the snapshot site for the order table.
8	order.sql	Order table definition.
9	master_group_order.sql	Creates the master group at the master site for the order table.
10	snapshot_group_order.sql	Creates the snapshot group and adds the snapshot object to it. The order table is now replicated.

```
            DriverManager.registerDriver(
                new oracle.jdbc.driver.OracleDriver());
            Connection conn =
                DriverManager.getConnection(
                      "jdbc:oracle:thin:@echidna:1521:sun8i",
                                       "web_sales", "supersecret");
            PreparedStatement ps = conn.prepareStatement(
                 "insert into price (item_id, net_price,"+
                 "sales_tax_perc,gross_price) "+
         "values( ?,?,?,?) ");
            conn.setAutoCommit(false);
            ps.setBigDecimal(1,new BigDecimal(23.0));
            ps.setBigDecimal(2,new BigDecimal(45.50));
            ps.setBigDecimal(3,new BigDecimal(21.50));
            ps.setBigDecimal(4,new BigDecimal(55.28));
            ps.executeUpdate();
            conn.commit();
            conn.close();
          }
          catch(Exception exc) {System.exit(1);}
      }
}
```

Before executing the Java test program shown above, access the sun8I instance using SQL*Plus. Make sure that there are no rows stored in the price table. Then connect to the nt8i instance to repeat the same check.

```
$ sqlplus web_sales/supersecret@sun8i
SQL*Plus: Release 8.1.5.0.0 - Production on Mon Sep 20 00:23:37
1999
(c) Copyright 1999 Oracle Corporation. All rights reserved.
Connected to:
Oracle8i Enterprise Edition Release 8.1.5.0.0 - Production
With the Partitioning and Java options
PL/SQL Release 8.1.5.0.0 - Production
SQL> select * from price;
no rows selected
SQL> connect web_sales/supersecret@nt8i
Connected.
SQL> select * from price;
no rows selected
```

You can now run the Java test program, which stores one row into the price table at the sun8i instance, either from your Java IDE or from the command line. When

TestProgram terminates, launch SQL*Plus again, connecting to the nt8i Oracle instance. If you are fast enough, you won't see the row in the price snapshot the first time you issue the SQL request. After a little while, however, the replication group refreshes, and the row is "pulled" from the price table residing in the sun8i instance.

```
SQL> connect web_sales/supersecret@nt8i
Connected.
SQL> select * from price;
no rows selected
SQL> /
no rows selected
SQL> /
ITEM_ID   NET_PRICE SALES_TAX_PERC GROSS_PRICE
--------- --------- -------------- -----------
23        45.5      21.5           55.28
```

In the SQL*Plus session presented above, you issued the SQL select twice before getting the data on the third attempt. You can now be sure that your replication setup is correct. You stored the row connecting to sun8I, and you were able to "see" the row in nt8i, thanks to the magic of data replication.

SUMMARY

The example presented in the preceding section introduced you to the world of data replication. The concept of data replication is quite important. It is very useful in the e-commerce environment because it can provide improved security and better use of distributed computing resources.

If you are deploying a Web-based application that will be used by a geographically dispersed user population, and you want to minimize network latency, data replication is definitely an option to consider. If one of the sites participating in the replicated environment is temporarily down, its outage will not affect the other sites, and they will continue to work normally.

The most advanced form of data replication, peer-to-peer update-anywhere, introduces complex data-collision issues. Oracle offers powerful mechanisms to help DBAs and designers cope with data collision, including the replication manager, an interactive tool that allows for visual definition of collision-resolution policies.

The example shown in this chapter focused instead on a simpler form of data replication, based on read-only remote snapshots that are periodically refreshed from master tables. While not as flexible as its peer-to-peer counterpart, basic replication is much simpler to implement and manage.

Chapter 21

THE ENTERPRISE JAVABEAN: AN INTRODUCTION

- EJB Environment and Structure
- Creating an Enterprise JavaBean
- Creating EJB Client Application
- Creating an EJB and Client with JDeveloper
- Running the Enterprise JavaBean
- Summary

The Enterprise JavaBean specification defines a component-based architecture that executes components in a server-side environment. The server-side environment provides for transactions, security, and a distributed object system. Unlike a Java Bean, an Enterprise JavaBean is a not a GUI component.

Enterprise bean technology provides you with the means to rapidly build server-side applications by connecting reusable bean components via their published interfaces. For example, you are provided with a shopping cart bean, a credit card validation bean, and a purchase order bean. The shopping cart bean uses the credit card bean to validate a customer credit card when the items in the cart are purchased. If the credit card is valid, the application sends the items in the cart along with the credit card to a purchase order bean to process the order. In this way, you are assembling a complex set of interactions through well-defined interfaces provided by code designed around reusable components. The benefit of this approach is that you do not have to be an expert in all areas, and may, for example, be able to purchase the credit card validation bean that performs the work for you. This chapter will guide you through the basic architecture and structure of the Enterprise JavaBean (EJB).

The design of the EJB specification resulted in a set of interfaces whose goals are portability and a common platform for development. The enterprise bean specification defines two types of enterprise beans:

- The *session bean* represents a transient bean instance (i.e., non-persistent, containing business logic associated with one session at a time). Session beans can perform database operations using the JDBC API. A session bean is either stateless or stateful. A stateless bean does not maintain its state across method invocations, whereas a stateful bean does. A session bean is assigned to only one client at a time, and not to multiple clients at the same time.
- The *entity bean* represents a persistent bean containing data held in a data source. The EJB container[1] must guarantee to preserve the state of an entity bean. Many clients can access the same entity bean.

The EJB 1.x specification defines both session and entity beans, but implementation of the entity bean feature is optional. The implementation of entity beans is mandatory in the EJB 2.x specification. At the time of writing, the JServer engine in the Oracle8i database only supports the EJB 1.0 standard, with no distinction between stateless and stateful session beans, and no support for entity beans. Therefore, this chapter covers:

- The EJB execution environment
- Developing a stateful session bean manually

[1] An EJB container provides the execution environment for an Enterprise JavaBean.

- ❑ Developing an EJB client application manually
- ❑ Developing an EJB and its client with Oracle JDeveloper

This chapter is not intended to be a comprehensive text on all aspects of Enterprise JavaBeans (entire books have been written on that subject!), but covers enough of the basics to help you start building an Enterprise JavaBean for use in an Oracle8i database.

The task of deploying an Enterprise JavaBean into the Oracle8i environment, together with the associated runtime security and transaction issues, is covered in Chapter 22.

21.1 EJB ENVIRONMENT AND STRUCTURE

An Enterprise JavaBean executes in an environment called an EJB container. The EJB container manages the creation, execution, and removal of the enterprise bean.

21.1.1 THE ENTERPRISE JAVABEAN ENVIRONMENT

Figure 21.1 depicts an EJB container in relationship to a client application.

The EJB client makes requests of the enterprise bean that resides inside an EJB container. The client does not directly interact with the bean, but uses the infrastructure provided by a layer of code called the stub in the client, and the skeleton in the server. The stub acts as a proxy for method calls to the enterprise bean. The skeleton code manages the client requests on the server side, delegates the calls to the bean instance, and directs the responses back to the client. The stub and skeleton cooperate to provide the communication infrastructure between the client and the bean, and to deal with passing data between them.

The EJB container is responsible for managing enterprise beans at runtime. This includes:

- ❑ Handling client requests to create, call, and remove a bean
- ❑ Security
- ❑ Transaction context
- ❑ Concurrency
- ❑ Pooling of bean resources
- ❑ Persistence

As seen in Figure 21.1, the EJB container isolates the enterprise bean from direct access by the client application. The skeleton component residing in the EJB container delegates client calls to the bean, and uses the EJB container to impose security, demarcate transactions, apply persistence on behalf of the bean.

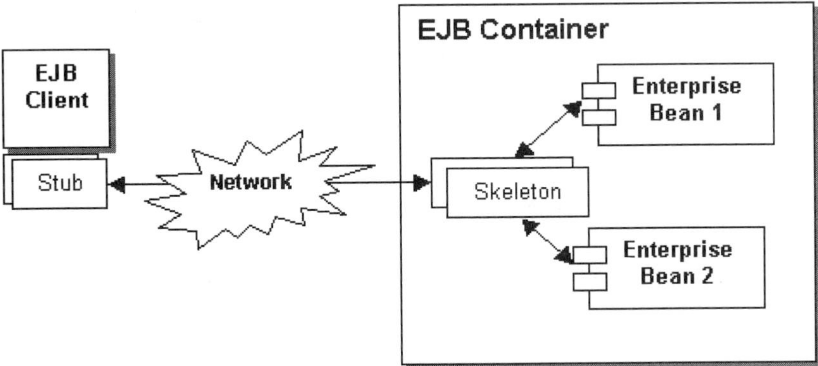

FIGURE 21.1 Enterprise bean container.

Since the container can manage security, transactions, and persistence automatically, you do not have to write the code for these services. Your task is to develop the functionality provided by the enterprise bean.

Many implementations of an EJB container are built on top of a Common Object Request Broker (CORBA) infrastructure,[2] such as the Oracle8i EJB container implementation that uses the Oracle8i CORBA infrastructure to perform container-managed services. Chapters 23, 24, and 25 cover various aspects of the Oracle8i CORBA services in some detail.

21.1.2 STRUCTURE OF THE ENTERPRISE JAVABEAN

An Enterprise JavaBean consists of the following key components:

- The *bean class* is the enterprise bean that implements the desired functionality.
- The *Home interface* contains methods used by a client application to create and delete bean instances (see Figure 21.3 and subsection 21.2.5),
- The *Remote interface* defines the enterprise bean methods that can be invoked by a client application.
- The *deployment descriptor* defines a set of properties that describe the bean components and bean usage of the EJB container runtime services, such as security and transactional services.[3]

Figure 21.2 depicts the relationship between a client and the EJB components.

---

[2]The CORBA technology is a standard, developed by the Object Management Group (OMG), to provide a programming-language-neutral architecture for executing distributed code.

[3]The EJB 1.1 specification requires the deployment descriptor to be written in XML format. Oracle8i supports the EJB 1.0 specification and provides the deployment descriptor in a non-XML format that loosely resembles the structure of a Java class.

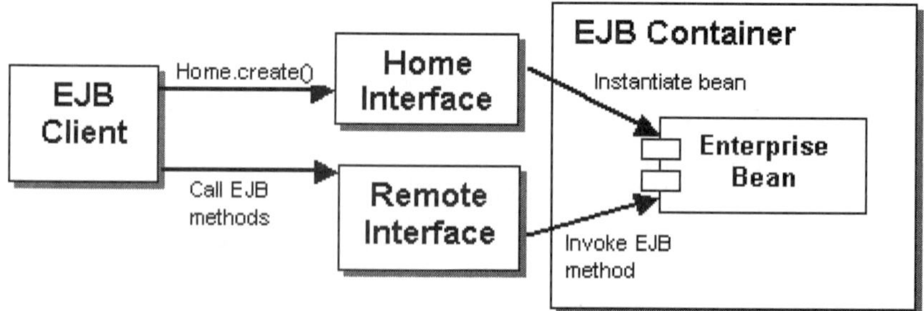

FIGURE 21.2 Relationship between EJB client and EJB components.

After creating the Home and Remote interfaces and the bean class, you can begin to write the client code. Only the definitions of the Home and Remote interfaces are needed for successful compilation of the client code, but to execute the client application, the Enterprise Java bean must be deployed to its runtime container. Briefly, deployment consists of the following steps:

- Create an *Ejb-jar* file containing files required by the bean in the EJB container, including:
  - The Home and Remote interfaces
  - The enterprise bean class
  - The deployment descriptor
- Generate an *Ejb-client* Jar file containing additional classes required by the client to communicate over the network with the EJB in the server, containing the stub and the skeleton code with other supporting classes.
  - Store the EJB in the execution environment, using the Ejb-jar file and the generated jar.
  - Publish a JNDI name for the bean home object that implements the Home interface (the bean name is specified in the deployment descriptor).

At the end of the chapter you will learn how to use Oracle JDeveloper to deploy your bean and the steps in running the client that invokes the bean. Chapter 22 discusses the deployment of an Enterprise JavaBean into an Oracle8i EJB server in more detail.

21.2 CREATING AN ENTERPRISE JAVABEAN

We will now go through the steps in creating a bean class, and the Home and Remote interfaces. In the next section, you will learn how to manually code a client for your enterprise bean.

21.2.1 THE BEAN CLASS

The bean class is a Java class representing the enterprise bean and all its functionality. The bean class must be a subclass of one of the following interfaces:

- `javax.ejb.SessionBean` (for session beans)
- `javax.ejb.EntityBean` (for entity beans)

The `SessionBean` and `EntityBean` interfaces extend the `javax.ejb.EnterpriseBean` interface. The class in Listing 21.1 represents the basic structure of a session bean called `CustomerEJB`, showing the EJB callback methods, and additional methods providing the bean with some functionality. Each `CustomerEJB` instance represents a single customer and the associated functionality for managing the customer object.

The EJB container uses the EJB callback methods to manage the bean instance and provide a way for the bean to obtain information from the EJB container in order to interact with the container.

```
package com.prenhall.OFJP.ejb;
import java.rmi.RemoteException;
import javax.ejb.*;
import com.prenhall.OFJP.ejb.*;

public class CustomerEJB implements SessionBean{
  private int id;
  private String name;
  private String surname;
  private String email;
  private String password;
  private CreditCard creditCard;

  public CustomerEJB() {}

  // EJB Container Callback Methods
  public void ejbCreate() throws RemoteException, CreateException {}
  public void ejbActivate() throws RemoteException {}
  public void ejbPassivate() throws RemoteException {}
  public void ejbRemove() throws RemoteException {}
  public void setSessionContext(SessionContext ctx)
     throws RemoteException {}

  // Business Logic
```

LISTING 21.1 A `CustomerEJB` Session bean.

```
  public int getId() throws RemoteException { return id; }
  public void setId(int newId) throws RemoteException { id = newId; }

  public String getName() throws RemoteException { return name; }
  public void setName(String newName) throws RemoteException {
    name = newName;
  }

  public String getSurname() throws RemoteException {return surname;}
  public void setSurname(String newSurname) throws RemoteException {
    surname = newSurname;
  }

  public String getEmail() throws RemoteException { return email; }
  public void setEmail(String newEmail) throws RemoteException {
    email = newEmail;
  }

  public String getPassword() throws RemoteException {
    return password;
  }
  public void setPassword(String newPassword) throws RemoteException{
    password = newPassword;
  }

  public CreditCard getCreditCard() throws RemoteException {
    return creditCard;
  }
  public void setCreditCard(CreditCard newCreditCard)
   throws RemoteException {
    creditCard = newCreditCard;
  }

  public String toText() throws RemoteException {
   return id + " " + name + " " + surname + " mailto:" + email;
  }
}
```

LISTING 21.1 *Continued*

Notes on Listing 21.1:

- The variables are usually declared as instance variables. Static variables are shared among all EJB instances, which are threads in the EJB container. For this reason, you need to synchronize changes to the static variables.

- The EJB contains several callback methods, which are called by the EJB container and never directly by the client. The callback methods are:
  - `ejbCreate()` performs initialization of the bean instance. For each `ejbCreate()` method in the bean, a corresponding `create()` method should be defined in the bean's Home interface. See subsection 21.2.5 for details on when the `ejbCreate()` and other callback methods are invoked.
  - `ejbActivate()` is used to restore the bean state from temporary storage.
  - `ejbPassivate()` is used to save the bean state to temporary storage.
  - `ejbRemove()` is called before the bean instance is removed from the container; this allows you to release resources allocated by the bean.
  - `setSessionContext()` provides access to a `SessionContext` object through which you can interact with the EJB container.
- The remaining set-and-get methods implement the functional behavior of the bean to manage its state and the business rules needed to maintain the state of a customer. Here is an example of a business rule: "All e-mail addresses must contain a name followed by an at-sign and then the domain name. The absence of an at-sign should be treated as an e-mail format error."
- To call an EJB method from a client application, such as `getId()` in the `CustomerEJB` class, the method signature must:
  - Be declared `public`.
  - Declare that it could throw `java.rmi.RemoteException`.
  - Be added to the Remote interface.
- The `com.prenhall.OFJP.ejb.CreditCard` class is provided for the client to pass a credit card object by parameter to the `CustomerEJB`, via the `setCreditCard()` method. The EJB can return a credit card object to the client when the `getCreditCard()` method is called. The EJB specification requires an object to be serializable if it is to be exchanged between the EJB client application and EJB object in the server. Thus, the `CreditCard` class implements the `java.io.Serializable` interface.

21.2.2 THE HOME INTERFACE

The Home interface defines methods that can be called by client applications to create and initialize an enterprise bean. The Home interface declares a `create()` method for each `ejbCreate()` method found in the definition of the bean class. The Home interface `create()` methods are used to request that the Home object in the EJB container instantiates a bean. The Home object can be thought of as the bean factory in the EJB container. Listing 21.2 is the Home interface for the `CustomerEJB` class.

```
package com.prenhall.OFJP.ejb;
import java.rmi.*;
import javax.ejb.*;

public interface CustomerHome extends EJBHome {
  CustomerRemote create()
      throws java.rmi.RemoteException, javax.ejb.CreateException;
}
```

LISTING 21.2 Home Interface for `CustomerEJB`.

Notes for Listing 21.2:

- The Home interface must extend `javax.ejb.EJBHome`.
- The `create()` methods must declare that they can throw either a `javax.ejb.CreateException` or a `java.rmi.RemoteException`.
- The create() method must return a Remote interface object (e.g., `Customer-Remote`).
- The `create()` method signature, except for its name, must correspond with the `ejbCreate()` method in the bean class of Listing 21.1.

See subsection 21.2.5 for a description of the client usage of the Home Interface and interaction with the Home object.

21.2.3 THE REMOTE INTERFACE

The Remote interface contains the signatures of the bean methods you wish to invoke from the EJB client. Listing 21.3 is the Remote interface for the `CustomerEJB` bean.

```
package com.prenhall.OFJP.ejb;
import java.rmi.*;
import javax.ejb.*;
com.prenhall.OFJP.ejb.CreditCard;

public interface CustomerRemote extends EJBObject {

  public int getId() throws java.rmi.RemoteException;
  public void setId(int newId) throws java.rmi.RemoteException;

  public String getName() throws java.rmi.RemoteException;
  public void setName(String newName)
    throws java.rmi.RemoteException;
```

LISTING 21.3 Remote interface for `CustomerEJB`.

```
  public String getSurname() throws java.rmi.RemoteException;
  public void setSurname(String newSurname)
    throws java.rmi.RemoteException;

  public String getPassword() throws java.rmi.RemoteException;
  public void setPassword(String newPassword)
    throws java.rmi.RemoteException;

  public String getEmail() throws java.rmi.RemoteException;
  public void setEmail(String newEmail)
    throws java.rmi.RemoteException;

  public CreditCard getCreditCard() throws java.rmi.RemoteException;
  public void setCreditCard(CreditCard newCreditCard)
    throws java.rmi.RemoteException;

  public String toText() throws java.rmi.RemoteException;
}
```

LISTING 21.3 *Continued*

Notes on Listing 21.3:

- The Remote interface must extend `javax.ejb.EJBObject`.
- Methods must be public and declare they throw a `java.rmi.RemoteException`. These signatures have been copied directly from the bean class.

21.2.4 ADDITIONAL CLASSES

In the `CustomerEJB` example, the additional `CreditCard` class is required for passing credit card details between the client application and the bean. For completeness, Listing 21.4 shows the definition of the `CreditCard` class.

```
package com.prenhall.OFJP.ejb;
import java.util.Calendar;
import java.text.DecimalFormat;

public class CreditCard implements java.io.Serializable {
  private String cardType;
  private String cardNumber;
  private String monthExpired;
  private String yearExpired;
```

LISTING 21.4 CreditCard class used by CustomerEJB.

```
  public CreditCard() {
    Calendar c = Calendar.getInstance();
    DecimalFormat df = new DecimalFormat("00");
    int year = c.get(Calendar.YEAR);
    int month = c.get(Calendar.MONTH);
    monthExpired = df.format(month + 1);
    yearExpired = df.format((year + 2) % 100);
  }

  public CreditCard(String newCardType, String newCardNumber) {
    this();
    cardType = newCardType;
    cardNumber = newCardNumber;
  }

  public String getCardNumber() { return cardNumber; }
  public void setCardNumber(String newCardNumber) {
    cardNumber = newCardNumber;
  }

  public String getCardType() { return cardType; }
  public void setCardType(String newCardType) {
    cardType = newCardType;
  }

  public String getMonthExpired() { return monthExpired; }
  public void setMonthExpired(String newMonthExpired) {
    monthExpired = newMonthExpired;
  }

  public String getYearExpired() { return yearExpired; }
  public void setYearExpired(String newYearExpired) {
    yearExpired = newYearExpired;
  }

  public String toString() {
    return cardType + " Nbr: " + cardNumber +
           " Expires:" + monthExpired + "/" + yearExpired;
  }
}
```

LISTING 21.4 *Continued*

Notes on Listing 21.4:

The `CreditCard` class implements `java.io.Serializable`, because it is passed as a parameter to the `setCreditCard()` EJB method, and returned from the `getCreditCard()` EJB method. The EJB specification requires that the Java class for an object exchanged between an EJB client and the bean must be serializable; otherwise an exception is thrown, indicating that the object cannot be transmitted across the network between the client and the bean. Just watch out for an exception beginning with the message text:

```
org.omg.CORBA.MARSHAL: minor code: 0  completed: No
```

The rest of the exception text is a too cryptic to be of value here.

Now that the environment and structure of an Enterprise JavaBean have been discussed, you will be able to appreciate how a bean instance is created when the lifecycle of a session bean is examined in the next section.

21.2.5 THE LIFECYCLE OF A SESSION BEAN

The lifecycle of a session bean is shown in Figure 21.3. The numbered arrows indicate the main parts of the bean lifecycle, starting from the first client request to create a bean and concluding with the invocation of a bean method call. The unnumbered arrows inside the EJB container between the Home object, the EJB, and the storage media represent the bean passivation and activation process that is part of the bean's lifecycle. However, the EJB container, and not the EJB client application, manages bean passivation and activation.

The bean creation and execution cycle will be discussed first, followed by the bean passivation and activation process.

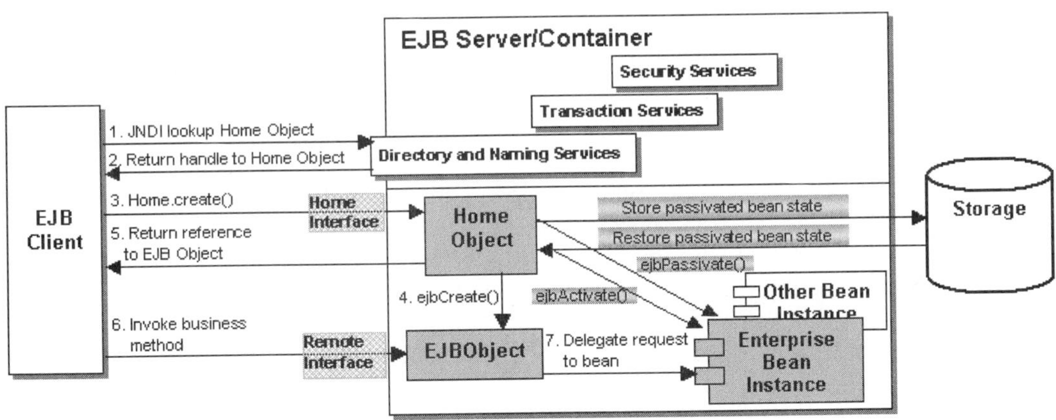

FIGURE 21.3 Session enterprise bean lifecycle.

21.2.5.1 The Bean Creation and Execution Cycle

1. The client issues a request to a directory service to locate the Home object of an enterprise bean. The Home object is looked up using the Java Naming and Directory Interface (JNDI) API. The directory and naming service may be implemented by the EJB container, or can be provided by another server, such as an LDAP server (see chapter 10 for more information on JNDI, or http://www.javasoft.com/jndi).
2. The directory service returns an object reference to the Home object.
3. The client calls a `create()` method defined in the Home interface to request the creation of a bean instance.
4. The Home object acts on the client `create()` request to instantiate the bean, and calls the `ejbCreate()` callback method matching the signature of the `create()` method to initialize the bean instance.
5. The `create()` method returns a remote reference to the `EJBObject`, which acts as a proxy for EJB methods defined in the Remote interface.
6. Using the remote reference to the `EJBObject`, the client invokes any bean method defined in the Remote interface.
7. The `EJBObject` receives the client bean method invocations, and delegates them to the bean class for execution. Remember: the client does not interact directly with the bean.

Bean methods may require parameters or return values to the client. Since data are passed across the network between the client and the bean, all parameters and return values must follow the Java serialization rules (i.e., any classes and subcomponents, such as the `CreditCard` class, must be serializable). The stub and skeleton code manages serialization of Java primitives and objects passed between the client and bean.

21.2.5.2 The Bean Passivation and Activation Cycle. *Passivation* is a when the EJB container saves the state of a bean instance to temporary storage. The storage for a passivated session bean is temporary because it is no longer required when the bean is activated or destroyed; and the passivated state does not survive failure or a shutdown of the bean container. Passivation may occur if the container needs to free container resources, such as memory, for new bean instances added to the pool. The container usually passivates the least recently used bean and performs the following steps:

1. It invokes the `ejbPassivate()` callback method in your EJB object.
2. It serializes and saves the state of the bean to some storage media.
3. It removes the bean instance from the container.

Activation, the reverse process of passivation, begins when the client calls a method for a bean instance that is in the passivated state. The container then performs the following steps to reactivate the bean:

1. It retrieves the enterprise bean state from the storage media.
2. It deserializes and reconstructs the bean instance.
3. It invokes the `ejbActivate()` callback method in the EJB Object.
4. It invokes the bean method called by the client.

The passivation/activation cycle is the responsibility of the EJB container; the algorithm used is up to the vendor who implements the EJB container. Passivation and activation are only applied to stateful session beans or entity beans. The state of these beans must be preserved across calls from the client, in case the container needs to swap them out of the bean pool. Since stateless session beans do not maintain state across client invocations, they do not need to be passivated and reactivated.

21.3 CREATING EJB CLIENT APPLICATION

You will now be taken through the steps required to write the EJB client code, using an enterprise bean deployed in an Oracle8i EJB server. To develop and compile the client code, you only need the definitions of the Home and Remote interfaces created with the bean class. However, to run or debug the client code, you must first deploy the Enterprise JavaBean into its target environment (see Chapter 22).

21.3.1 DEVELOPING THE CLIENT CODE

An Enterprise JavaBean client uses the Java Naming and Directory Service (JNDI) API to lookup the EJB Home object, which is identified by a published name in the directory of a naming service (for information about JNDI, see Chapter 10). The client code developed in this section is a command-line Java application used to show the key steps in creating an Enterprise JavaBean and invoking its methods. The code samples can be used in any Java client, including another Enterprise Bean.

1. Set the environment and initial context for the JNDI lookup request.
2. Look up the Home object using its published name. An example of a published name is: `test/CustomerBean`.
3. Call a `create()` method defined in the Home Interface, and obtain a remote reference to the Enterprise JavaBean.

4. Use the remote reference to the bean to invoke the bean methods defined in the Remote interface.
5. Remove the bean and disconnect.

21.3.2 STEPS 1 AND 2: LOCATING THE HOME OBJECT

21.3.2.1 Set the JNDI Initial Context. To set the JNDI initial context, you first create a hashtable containing the property names and their values, known as the JNDI environment. Then you pass the environment properties to the `javax.naming.InitialContext` constructor. The JNDI environment property values depend on the directory service you are using. Listing 21.5 shows the code that sets the property values used for an Oracle8i database as the JNDI service provider.

```
java.util.Hashtable env = new java.util.Hashtable();
env.put(javax.naming.Context.URL_PKG_PREFIXES, "oracle.aurora.jndi");
env.put(javax.naming.Context.SECURITY_PRINCIPAL, username);
env.put(javax.naming.Context.SECURITY_CREDENTIALS, password);
env.put(javax.naming.Context.SECURITY_AUTHENTICATION,
        oracle.aurora.jndi.sess_iiop.ServiceCtx.NON_SSL_LOGIN);
javax.naming.Context env = new javax.naming.InitialContext(env);
```

LISTING 21.5 Setting the JNDI environment and initial context.

Notes on Listing 21.5:

- `javax.naming.Context.URL_PKG_PREFIXES` informs JNDI to use the Oracle JServer Session-IIOP protocol. Session-IIOP (`sess_iiop:`) protocol is a session-based extension to the basic IIOP, which does not support the concept of a session.
- `javax.naming.Context.SECURITY_PRINCIPAL` is an Oracle8i user name used to create a JNDI session with the Session-IIOP protocol.
- `javax.naming.Context.SECURITY_CREDENTIALS` is the user password required to establish the session-IIOP connection.
- `javax.naming.Context.SECURITY_AUTHENTICATION` indicates that a non-SSL (non-Secure Sockets Layer, or unencrypted session) should be established with the directory service. The value used here is a class specified to the Oracle8i JServer environment.

To avoid hard-coding property values into your application, pass in the properties and values through the command line, or read them from a properties file. To do this, you need to know the text strings for the property constant names and values used to establish the environment for the JNDI initial context. The strings values for the `javax.naming.Context` class constants are as follows:

```
URL_PKG_PREFIXES=java.naming.factory.url.pkgs
SECURITY_PRINCIPLE=java.naming.security.principal
SECURITY_CREDENTIALS=java.naming.security.credentials
SECURITY_AUTHENTICATION=java.naming.security.authentication
```

The string value for oracle.aurora.jndi.sess_iiop.ServiceCtx constant is:

```
NON_SSL_LOGIN=Login
```

You pass these properties on the command line with the `-D` option, as shown below:

```
java -Djava.naming.factory.url.pkgs=oracle.aurora.jndi
     -Djava.naming.security.principal=bookstore
     -Djava.naming.security.credentials=bookstore
     -Djava.naming.security.authentication=Login ClientApp
```

(The command line has been split over more than one line, for clarity). In this way, you can replace the code in Listing 21.5 to set the JNDI environment and initial context, using the following code:

```
java.util.Properties env = System.getProperties();
javax.naming.Context env = new javax.naming.InitialContext(env);
```

These lines of code make the code vendor-independent by setting the property values in the property files where they should reside.

21.3.2.2 Look Up Home Object via Published JNDI Name. The code to look up the EJB Home object is shown in bold text in Listing 21.6.

```
package com.prenhall.OFJP.ejb;
import java.sql.*;
import java.util.*;
import javax.naming.*;
import oracle.aurora.jndi.sess_iiop.*;
import com.prenhall.OFJP.ejb.CustomerHome;

public class CustomerEJBClient {
  public static void main(String[] args) {
    Hashtable env = new Hashtable();
```

LISTING 21.6 Look up the Home object via published JNDI name.

```
11:     env.put(javax.naming.Context.URL_PKG_PREFIXES,
12:             "oracle.aurora.jndi");
13:     env.put(Context.SECURITY_PRINCIPAL, "bookstore");
14:     env.put(Context.SECURITY_CREDENTIALS, "bookstore");
15:     env.put(Context.SECURITY_AUTHENTICATION,
16:             ServiceCtx.NON_SSL_LOGIN);
17:
18:     // Lookup the URL
19:     CustomerHome homeInterface = null;
20:     try {
21:       Context ic = new InitialContext(env);
22:       homeInterface = (CustomerHome) ic.lookup(
23:         "sess_iiop://localhost:2481:ORA816/test/CustomerEJB");
24:     }
25:     /*
26:     ** Other runtime exceptions that should be caught include:
27:     **  oracle.aurora.jndi.sess_iiop.ActivationException
28:     **  javax.naming.CommunicationException
29:     */
30:     catch (NamingException e) {
31:       e.printStackTrace();
32:       System.exit(1);
33:     }
34:     // Ready to create and use an EJB instance here
35:   }
36: }
```

LISTING 21.6 *Continued*

Notes on Listing 21.6:

- Line 6 imports the class name, `CustomerHome`, which is the Home interface for the bean.
- Lines 10 to 16 set up the JNDI environment, with hard-coded values for clarity.
- Line 19 declares and initializes the `homeInterface` variable that will reference the Home object that implements the Home interface `CustomerHome`.
- Line 21 sets the JNDI initial context.
- Line 22 performs the JNDI look-up request to locate the Home object. The return value of the look-up request is assigned to the `homeInterface` variable by casting it to `(CustomerHome)`. This must be done because the JNDI `lookup()` method has no knowledge of this specific interface, and so returns a `java.lang.Object` type.

- In line 22, the URL parameter in the `lookup()` method has two parts:
  - `sess_iiop://localhost:2481:ORA816/` connects to the naming service for the JNDI look-up request:
    - The server name, in this case, `localhost`
    - IIOP port, here, `2481`
    - Oracle SID, here, `ORA816`
  - `test/CustomerBean` is the published JNDI name of the EJB Home object.
- Lines 26 to 30 catch runtime exceptions that can be thrown by the `lookup()` method, like the `javax.naming.NamingException`, which is a runtime exception and is not declared in the `lookup()` method signature.

If you have successfully obtained the reference to the Home object, you can create the enterprise bean.

21.3.3 STEP 3: CREATE A BEAN INSTANCE USING THE HOME OBJECT

Using the reference to the Home object, you instantiate a bean instance by calling a `create()` method defined in the Home interface. Listing 21.7 highlights the code changes in bold text, this time using system properties to set the JNDI environment and initial context.

```
package com.prenhall.OFJP.ejb;
import java.sql.*;
import java.util.*;
import javax.naming.*;
import oracle.aurora.jndi.sess_iiop.*;
import com.prenhall.OFJP.ejb.CustomerHome;
import com.prenhall.OFJP.ejb.CustomerRemote;

public class CustomerEJBClient {
  public static void main(String[] args) {

    Properties env = System.getProperties();
    CustomerHome homeInterface = null;
    try {
      Context ic = new InitialContext(env);
      homeInterface = (CustomerHome) ic.lookup(
        "sess_iiop://localhost:2481:ORA816/test/CustomerEJB");
    }
```

LISTING 21.7 Creating a bean instance via the Home interface.

```
19:     catch (Exception e) {
20:       e.printStackTrace();
21:       System.exit(1);
22:     }
23:
24:     try {
25:       System.out.println("Create a new EJB instance");
26:       CustomerRemote remoteInterface = homeInterface.create();
27:
28:       // Start calling EJB methods ...
29:     }
30:     catch (Exception e) {
31:       System.out.println(e.getMessage());
32:       e.printStackTrace();
33:     }
34:
35:   }
36: }
```

LISTING 21.7 *Continued*

Notes on Listing 21.7:

- Line 7 imports the Remote interface `CustomerRemote` to declare a variable for the `EJBObject` that implements the Remote interface.
- Line 12 uses the `System.getProperties()` method to set the JNDI environment values from definitions passed from the command line.
- Line 19 generically catches all the exceptions listed in lines 27, 28, and 30 of Listing 21.6. This is done for brevity of presentation.
- Lines 24 to 33 create the bean instance and will eventually contain the code to invoke bean methods.
- Line 26 is responsible for initiating the creation of the bean instance. The `homeInterface.create()` method returns a reference to an object that implements the `CustomerRemote` interface.

The bean is created if there are no exceptions from the call to the `create()` method, and you can commence calling the enterprise bean methods.

21.3.4 STEP 4: INVOKE BEAN METHODS

The client application calls the enterprise bean method using the standard Java calling convention. Listing 21.8 completes the preceding examples by adding the code, in bold text, to call bean methods. The method calls set details for the new customer bean instance, and return a text string that indicates the state of the bean.

```
package com.prenhall.OFJP.ejb;
import java.sql.*;
import java.util.*;
import javax.naming.*;
import oracle.aurora.jndi.sess_iiop.*;
import com.prenhall.OFJP.ejb.CustomerHome;
import com.prenhall.OFJP.ejb.CustomerRemote;

public class CustomerEJBClient {
  public static void main(String[] args) {

    Properties env = System.getProperties();
    CustomerHome homeInterface = null;
    try {
      Context ic = new InitialContext(env);
      homeInterface = (CustomerHome) ic.lookup(
        "sess_iiop://localhost:2481:ORA816/test/CustomerEJB");
    }
    catch (Exception e) {
      e.printStackTrace();
      System.exit(1);
    }

    try {
      System.out.println("Create a new EJB instance");
      CustomerRemote remoteInterface = homeInterface.create();

      remoteInterface.setId(1);
      remoteInterface.setName("Jeromy");
      remoteInterface.setSurname("Cricket");
      remoteInterface.setPassword("crikcrik");
      remoteInterface.setEmail("jcricket@cartoon.com");
      remoteInterface.setCreditCard(
         new CreditCard("AMEX", "1234987645662222"));
      System.out.println(remoteInterface.toText());
    }
    catch (Exception e) {
      System.out.println(e.getMessage());
      e.printStackTrace();
    }
  }
}
```

LISTING 21.8 Invoking bean methods defined in the Remote interface.

Notes on Listing 21.8:

- Lines 28 to 36 show examples of calling the remote bean methods. Note that there is no visible difference in syntax compared to the calling methods on local objects.
- In Line 34, a new `CreditCard` object is created and passed as a parameter to the `setCreditCard()` bean method. The `CreditCard` object is serialized and passed to the remote bean.

21.3.5 STEP 5: EJB REMOVAL AND RELEASING RESOURCES

When you finish working with the bean instance, you can call the `remove()` method via the Remote interface object. The EJB container removes the bean and returns it to the pool, if appropriate.

```
remoteInterface.remove();
```

You can release resources allocated to the JNDI initial context by calling the `close()` method of the initial context object.

21.4 CREATING AN EJB AND CLIENT WITH JDEVELOPER

In this section, you will be guided through the steps in creating your enterprise bean components and a client application, using JDeveloper wizards.

21.4.1 CREATING THE ENTERPRISE JAVABEAN CLASSES

Before you start creating the EJB in Oracle JDeveloper, create a project for your Enterprise JavaBean by selecting the `File->New Project` menu, and fill in the details required, such as the package name (see Chapter 13 for the sequence of the project wizard). After creating a project, display the Object gallery by selecting the `File->New` menu. In the Objects tab of the Object gallery dialog, double-click on the Enterprise JavaBean icon to launch the Enterprise JavaBean wizard.

The Enterprise JavaBean wizard has a welcome page and three steps, as shown in Figures 21.4, 21.5, 21.7, and 21.8.

In step 1, you choose your bean name and select whether it is to be a `SessionBean` or an `EntityBean` bean. If you select the `EntityBean` radio-button, Oracle JDeveloper will issue the following warning message shown Figure 21.6.

The "`Wrap (delegate to) existing class`" checkbox allows you to place an EJB wrapper around an existing Java class. This wrapper feature makes it possible to quickly convert an existing Java class into an Enterprise JavaBean. The enterprise bean wrapping the existing class creates an instance of the existing class, and provides methods that call the wrapped class functionality.

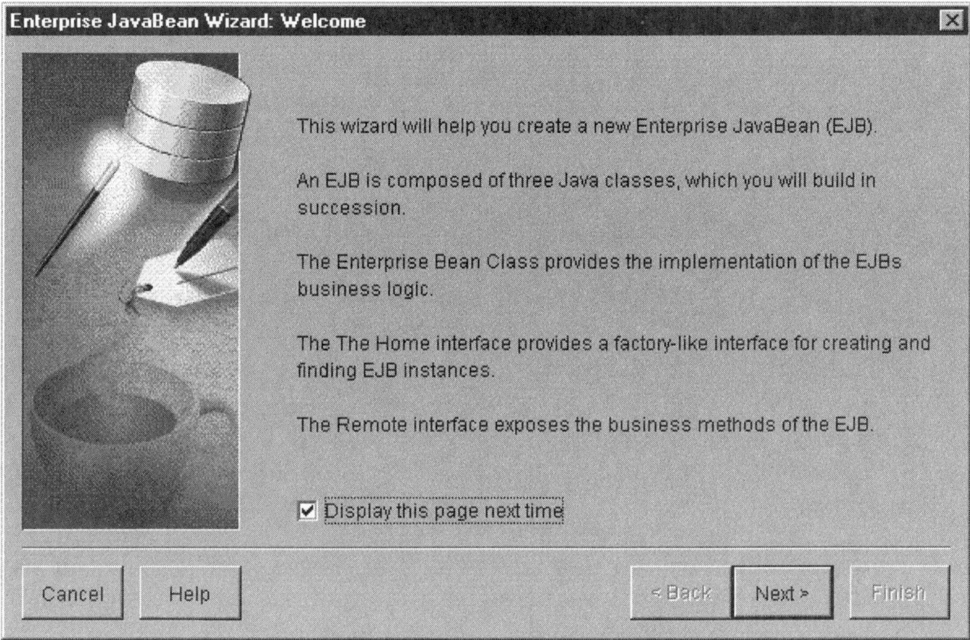

FIGURE 21.4 EJB wizard: Welcome.

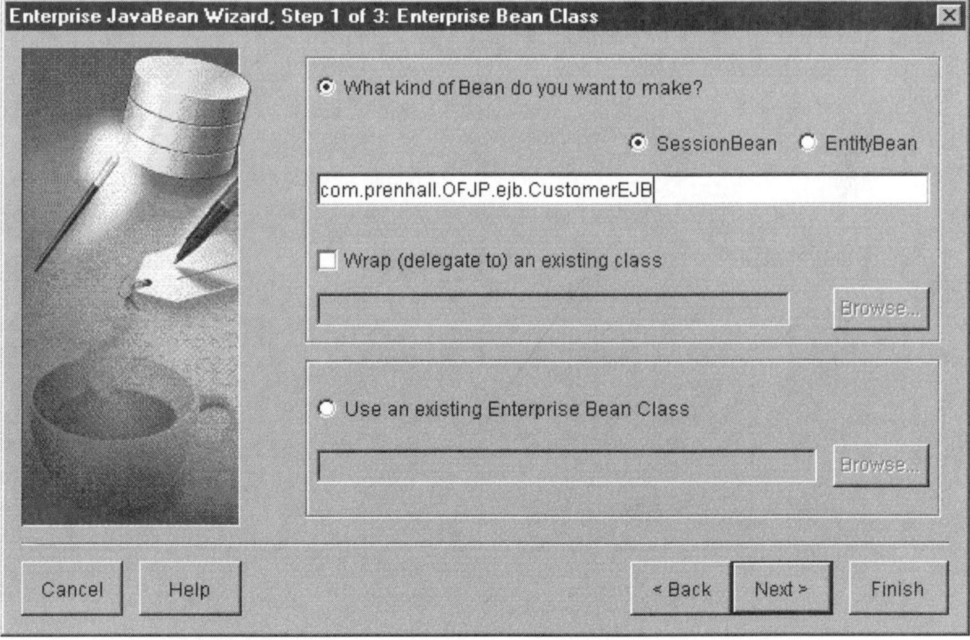

FIGURE 21.5 EJB wizard, step 1 of 3: Enterprise bean class.

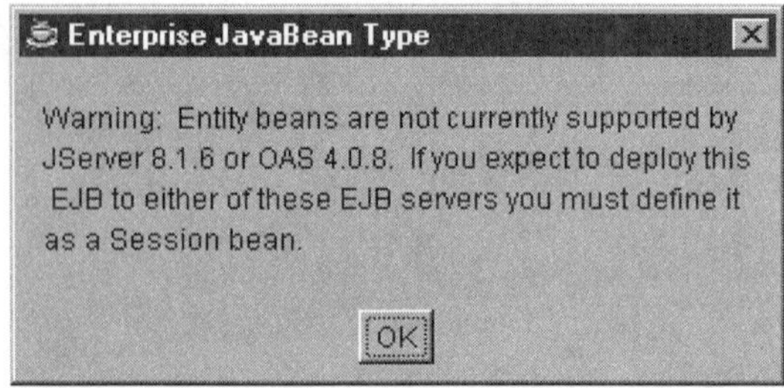

FIGURE 21.6 Oracle JDeveloper warning message.

At this stage, the method list is empty for Remote interface because the methods do not yet exist in the bean class. After completing these wizard steps to generate the base Home interface, Remote interface, and bean class, you can add methods to your bean class. You then select the methods to add to the Remote interface using the enterprise bean wizard shown in Figure 21.11.

The deployment profile referred to in the finish step (see Figure 21.9) should not be confused with the deployment descriptor. The deployment profile is a JDeveloper file with a `.prf` extension, which saves the steps chosen to deploy classes from a project with their supporting libraries into a target runtime environment. The rules for deployment are often used to create a JAR file. At this stage, it is better to select "`Do not create a deployment profile`" be-

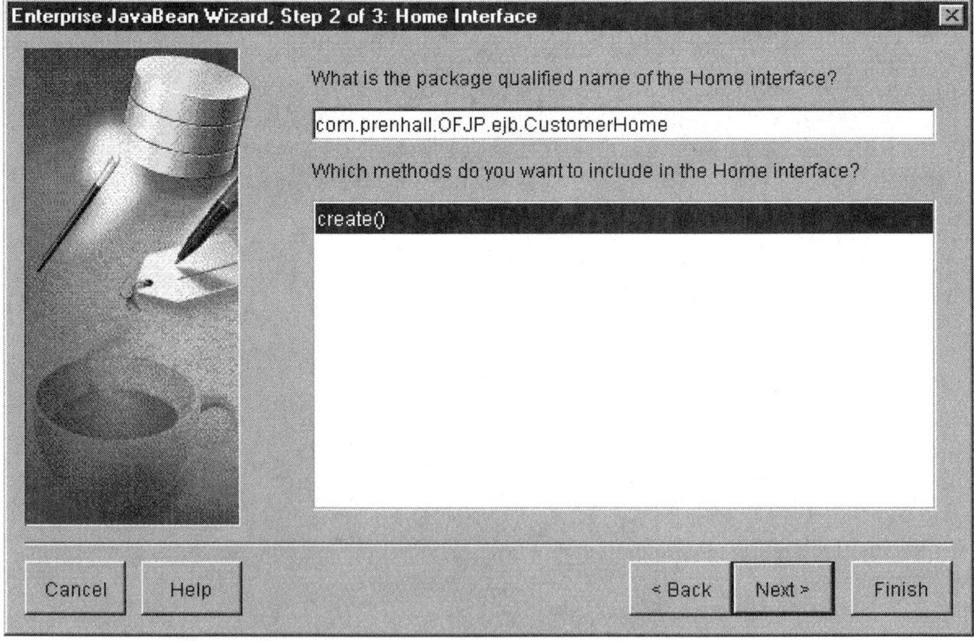

FIGURE 21.7 EJB wizard, step 2 of 3: Home interface.

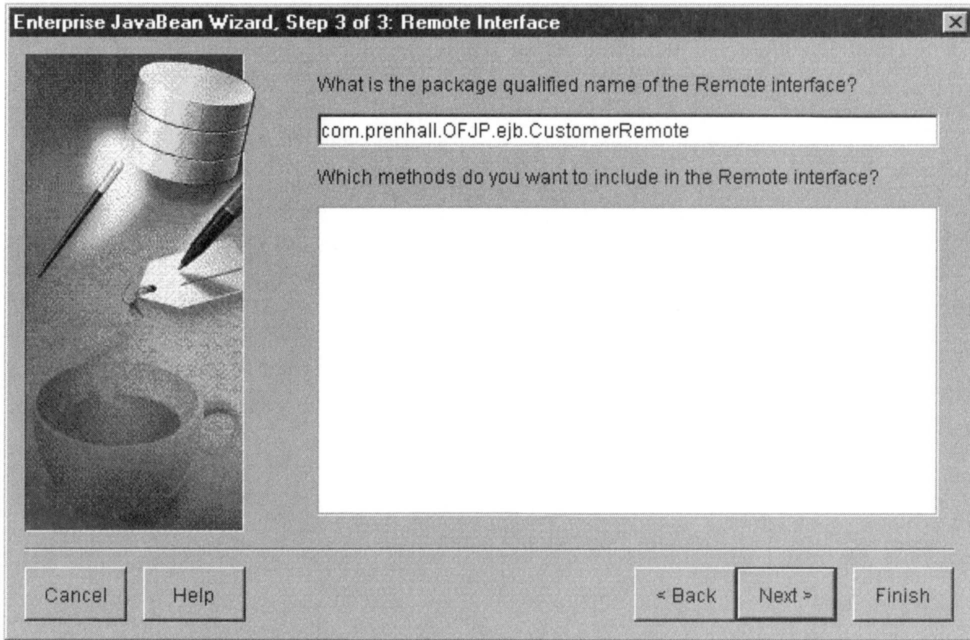

FIGURE 21.8 EJB wizard, step 3 of 3: Remote interface.

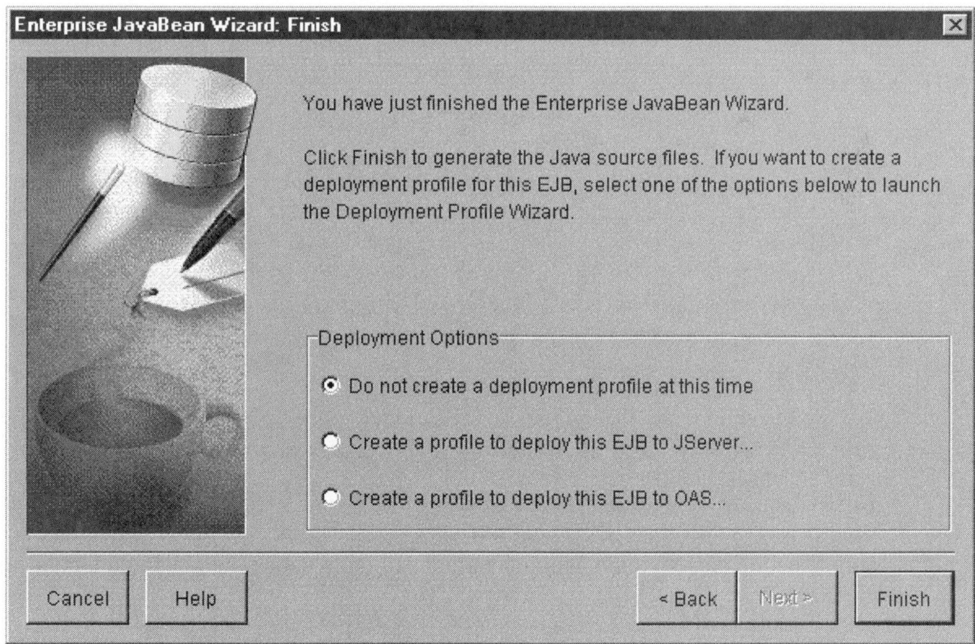

FIGURE 21.9 EJB wizard: Finish.

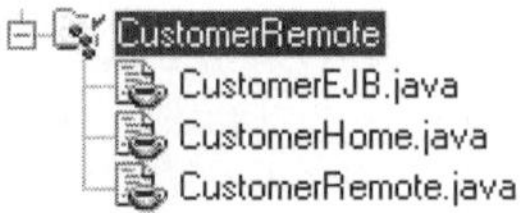

FIGURE 21.10 Enterprise JavaBean files created by JDeveloper.

cause you still have to add your methods to the enterprise bean class. Figure 21.10 shows the JDeveloper folder and files created by the wizard.

After creation the `CustomerEJB` file only contains the EJB callback methods required to implement the `javax.ejb.SessionBean` interface. You must add methods to initialize your bean and provide its functionality. After adding your methods to the bean, you can select the methods to be added to the Remote interface by right-clicking on the folder containing your EJB Java files to display the menu shown in Figure 21.11.

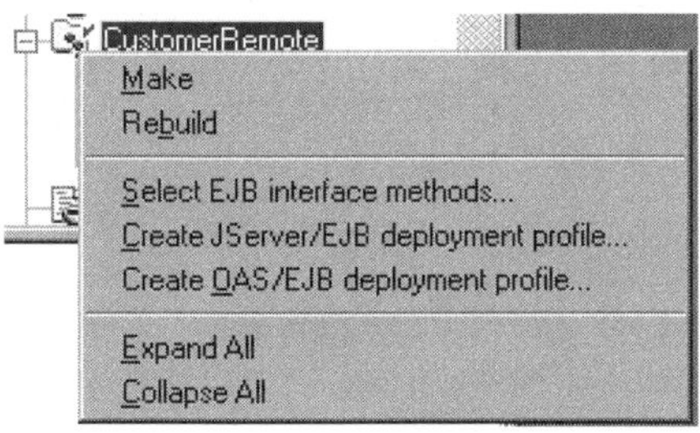

FIGURE 21.11 JDeveloper EJB menu options.

Choose the "`Select EJB interface methods...`" menu item and select the Remote interface tab, shown in Figure 21.12.

Click the `Done` button after selecting the methods to be included in the Remote interface. Based on your selection, the wizard updates the Remote interface and Home interface Java files in the project.

Now that the Home interface, Remote interface, and bean class are completed, you can generate the basic EJB client code using a JDeveloper snippet. You can create additional classes for your Enterprise JavaBean manually or use other JDeveloper wizards.

21.4.2 CREATING THE CLIENT WITH JDEVELOPER

After creating the Enterprise JavaBean interfaces and class, you can generate the starting EJB client code by selecting the `File->New` menu, then the `Snippets` tab, and double-click on the "`Example Jserver/EJB Client`" icon to launch the code snippet, shown in Figure 21.13.

Click on the parameters button to set the names of the Home interface, Remote interface, and IIOP connection details for the JNDI lookup request, including the published name for the EJB. The published name must match the name used in the EJB deployment descriptor.

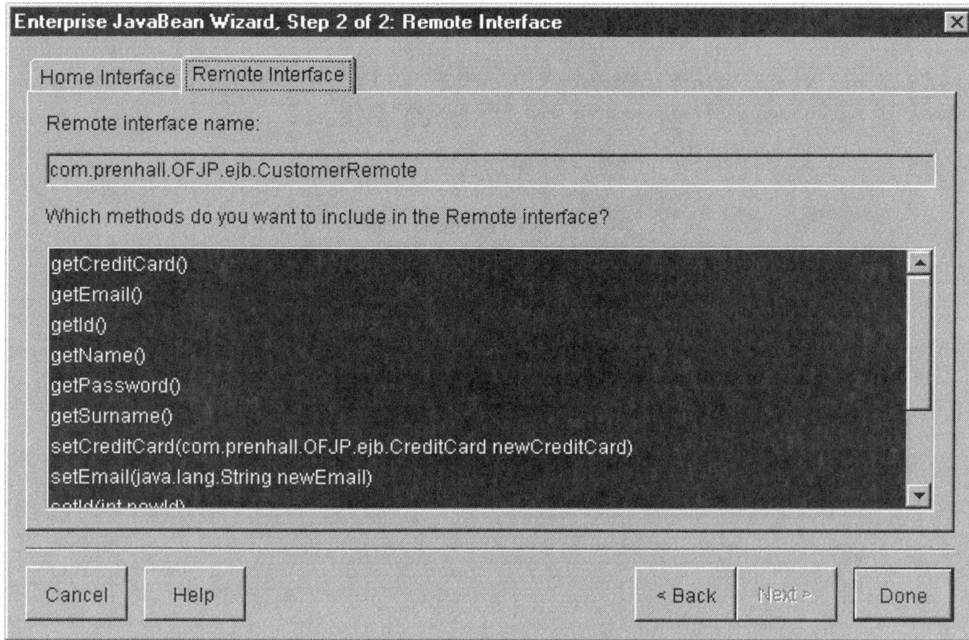

FIGURE 21.12 Selecting the EJB Remote interface methods.

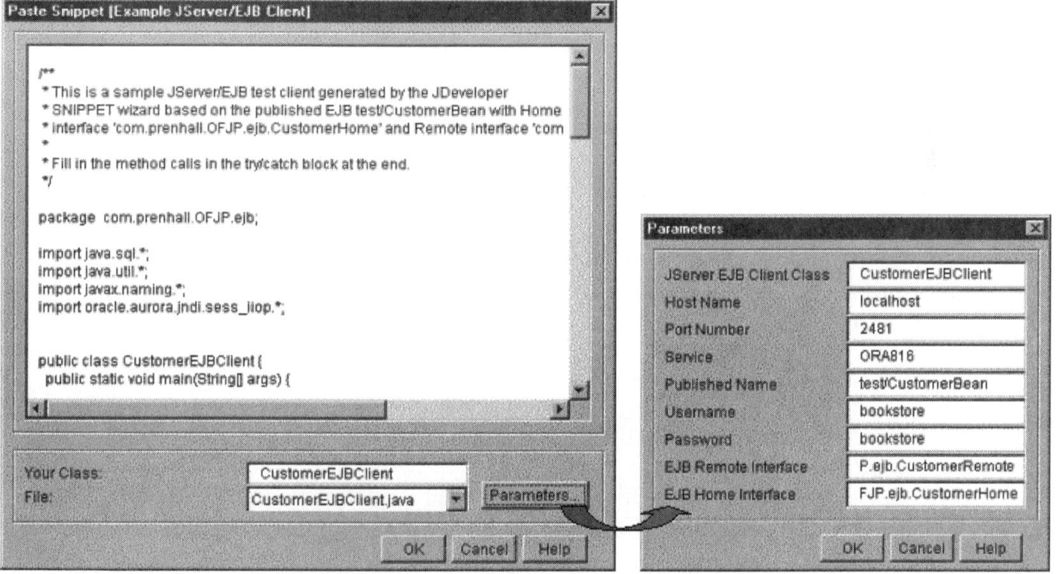

FIGURE 21.13 Paste snippet [Example/EJB Client] and parameters.

The paste wizard creates the named client class containing the Java code for:

- ❑ The JNDI environment for an Oracle8i EJB server.
- ❑ The JNDI lookup for the EJB Home interface.
- ❑ The code to create the EJB via the Home interface.
- ❑ Comments that indicate where you can add calls to the EJB methods.

The code generated by the paste snippet wizard resembles the code examples presented in the previous listings of EJB client code. The generated code uses hard-coded values for the environment properties, based on the paste snippet parameter values you entered. You now modify the generated code to call the appropriate method from the EJB.

21.5 RUNNING THE ENTERPRISE JAVABEAN

In this section, you are shown how to deploy and run your Enterprise JavaBean. The Enterprise JavaBean and related classes must be installed (deployed) in the server-side execution environment before you can run the EJB client.

The task of deployment can be simplified by creating a JDeveloper deployment profile that automates deploying your Enterprise JavaBean into its target environment, such as the Oracle8i JServer. The JDeveloper deployment profile wizard creates a deployment profile file that stores the rules used to:

- ❑ Build the Jar files containing the EJB classes
- ❑ Select additional Java libraries required by your EJB component
- ❑ Generate or select a deployment descriptor file
- ❑ Select a database connection name identifying the execution environment for the enterprise bean

In JDeveloper, you can create a deployment profile file with a mouse right-click on the EJB folder name in the navigator window to display the menu shown in Figure 21.14.

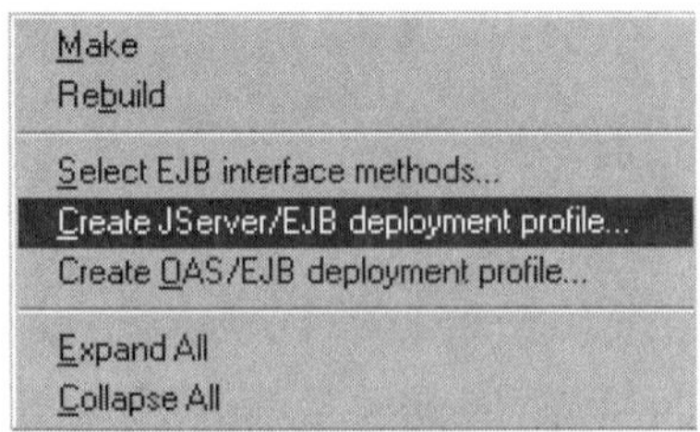

FIGURE 21.14 Menu to create JDeveloper EJB deployment profile.

Select the "Create JServer/EJB Deployment profile..." to start the EJB deployment profile wizard. The EJB deployment profile wizard tab pages are shown in Figures 21.15, 21.16, and 21.17.

In the first page of the wizard, the Project tab, select all the Java classes in the project that are required by your EJB. At a minimum, these will be the Home interface, Remote interface, and bean class. For example, selecting the CustomerRemote folder selects all the items it contains, which includes the Home interface, Remote interface, and bean class. Clicking the Advanced... button lets you select additional Java libraries, packages, or classes required by your EJB. You typically will select libraries that are not part of your EJB package and are also not provided in the target execution environment for your EJB. For example, since the Oracle8i JServer already has the JDBC drivers and SQLJ class libraries installed in the database, you would not select the JDBC or SQLJ libraries to be part of the deployment profile for your EJB.

In the second page of the deployment wizard, the EJB tab, you select the name of the EJB deployment descriptor file. The deployment descriptor file can be generated or selected from an existing descriptor file. The deployment descriptor identifies the classes for the Remote interface, the Home interface, the bean class, and the published name for the EJB Home object. Initially, it is easier to generate the deployment descriptor and then edit the generated descriptor file to

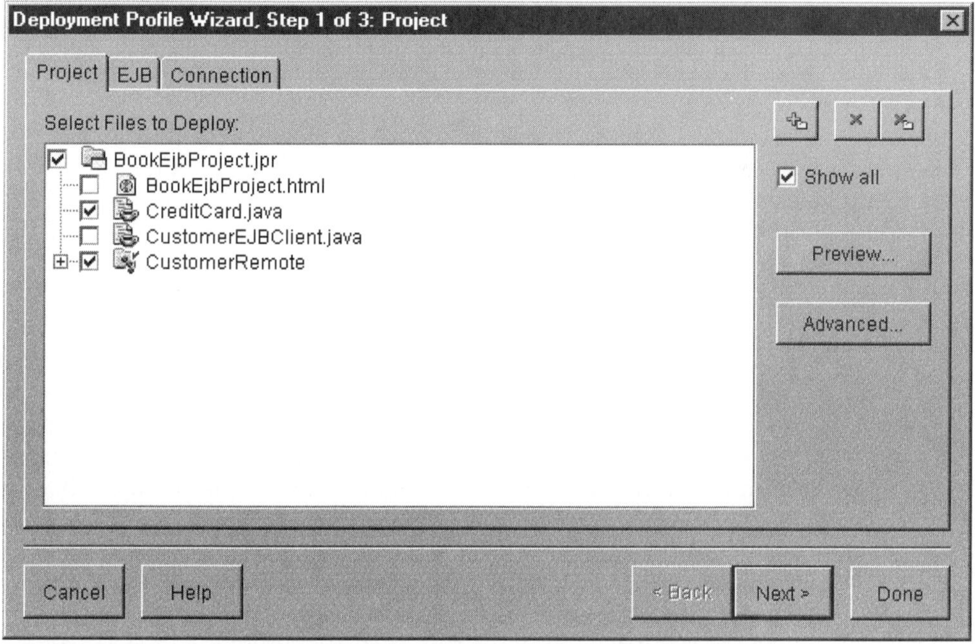

FIGURE 21.15 Deployment profile Project tab.

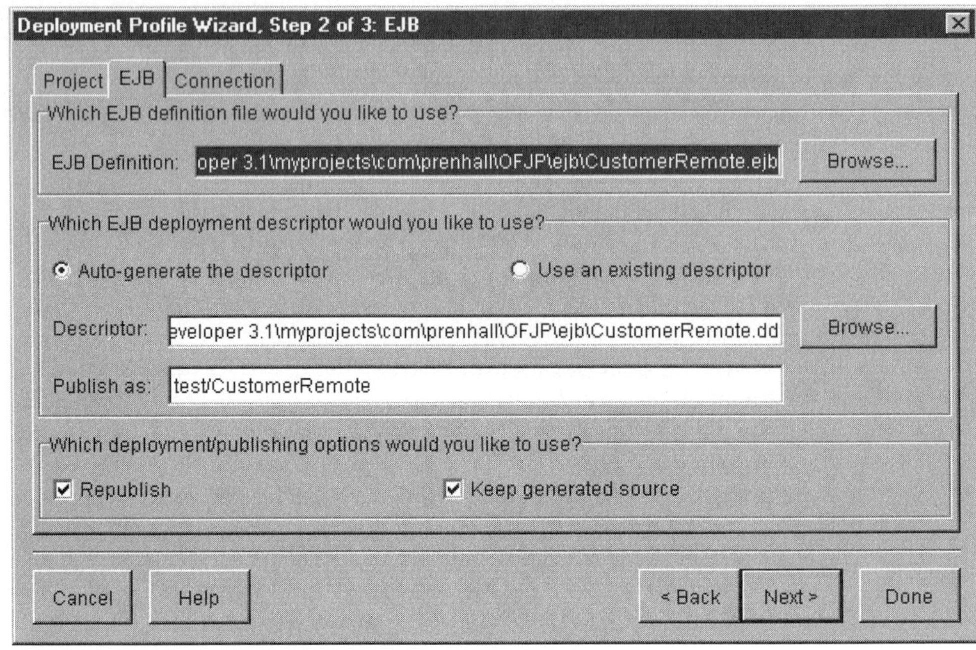

FIGURE 21.16 Deployment profile EJB tab.

customize its contents. The contents of the deployment descriptor are covered in Chapter 22.

You also chose the published name for your EJB Home object. Make sure you select the same name used by the EJB client application. JDeveloper always suggests a published JNDI name starting with the path `test/`, because the `test/` path is created with public read/write access when you install the JServer software. An administrator can create alternative path names for use in production environment.

In the third page of the deployment wizard, the `Connection` tab, you chose the names of the `Source Jar` (Ejb-jar file) and `Generated Jar` files. The `Source Jar` file contains the Home interface, Remote interface, and enterprise bean classes. The `Generated Jar` file contains classes that implement the EJB interfaces, such as the Home object, the stub, the skeleton, and classes that facilitate communication between EJB client and server components. It is crucial to add both the `Source Jar` and the `Generated Jar` file to the EJB client application's CLASSPATH.

In the third page you also select or create a connection name to identify the target database into which the EJB will be deployed. The details of the deployment process using Oracle8i command-line tools, the contents of the deployment descriptor file, and the contents of the generated Jar file are covered in Chapter 22.

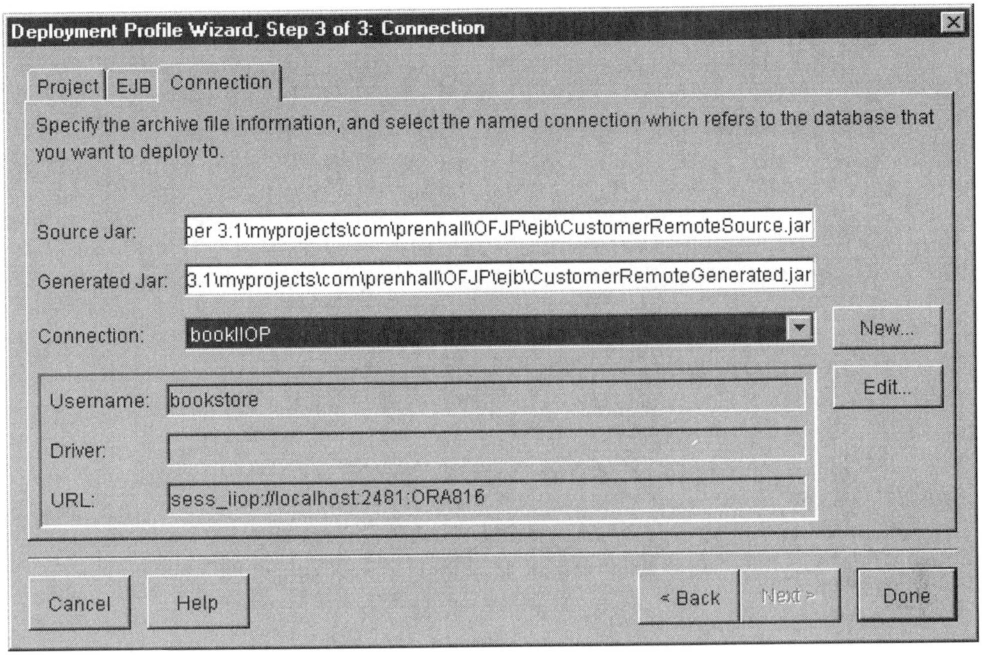

FIGURE 21.17 Deployment profile EJB tab.

The wizard finish page (not shown) asks you for the name of a file with a `.prf` extension in which to save the rules defined in the deployment profile wizard. The `.prf` file is added to a `Deployment` folder in the JDeveloper project.

21.5.1 DEPLOYING THE ENTERPRISE JAVABEAN TO ORACLE8I

To physically deploy the EJB to an Oracle8i database from JDeveloper, right click on the name of the Deployment Profile (`.prf`) file in the JDeveloper navigator window, and select the `Deploy` menu option provided. This action causes JDeveloper to deploy the EJB classes into its target environment. The deployment request performs the following tasks:

- It creates a `Source Jar` file (the Ejb-jar file) and a `Generated Jar` file.
- It generates or reads the deployment descriptor settings to determine the EJB container and bean runtime properties.
- It loads the EJB classes in the Oracle8i database, using the details defined in the deployment descriptor,
- It publishes the name of the EJB Home object, as specified in the deployment descriptor, in the Oracle8i naming service.

After successful deployment, the enterprise bean is ready for use by a client application.

21.5.2 RUNNING THE ENTERPRISE JAVABEAN CLIENT

As stated above, the last thing to do before you run the EJB client is to add the `Source Jar` file (Ejb-jar file) and the `Generated Jar` file to the client's CLASSPATH.[4] This can be done in JDeveloper by double-clicking on the EJB client project folder to display the project properties window. The `Source Jar` file and the `Generated Jar` file can be added to the project CLASSPATH in a new library, via the `Libraries` tab of the `Project properties` window. Using the command line shown below, the client application can now be executed on a Windows NT platform.

```
set JDEV=D:\Program Files\Oracle\JDeveloper 3.1
java -classpath "%JDEV%\myclasses;
 %JDEV%\lib\javax_ejb.zip;
 %JDEV%\aurora\lib\aurora_client.jar;
 %JDEV%\aurora\lib\vbjorb.jar;
 %JDEV%\aurora\lib\vbjapp.jar;
 %JDEV%\myprojects\com\prenhall\OFJP\ejb\CustomerRemoteSource.jar;
 %JDEV%\myprojects\com\prenhall\OFJP\ejb\CustomerRemoteGenerated.jar;
 %JDEV%\java1.2\jre\lib\rt.jar"
  com.prenhall.OFJP.ejb.CustomerEJBClient
```

> **NOTES**
>
> The `set` command assigns the JDeveloper installation root directory to the `JDEV` environment variable. This simplifies typing in the value for the `-classpath` option in the `java` command. The `-classpath` option has been split over more than one line in these notes for clarity; there should be no spaces or new lines separating the lines between the double quotes.

The directory `%JDEV%/myclasses` represents the root directory for classes in the `com.prenhall.OFJP.ejb` package. The Jar files created by the deployment process, the `CustomerRemoteSource.jar`, and the `CustomerRemoteGenerated.jar` are located in the project directory `%JDEV%\myprojects\com\prenhall\OFJP\ejb\`.

Executing the EJB client application in Listing 21.8 produces the following results:

[4]Invoking the project deployment profile creates the generated Jar file.

```
Creating an initial context
Looking for the EJB published as 'test/CustomerEJB'
Creating a new EJB instance
Calling com.prenhall.OFJP.ejb.CustomerRemote methods...
1 Jerome Cricket mailto:jcricket@cartoon.com
```

Running the EJB client requires the addition of certain class libraries to the CLASSPATH when the EJB is deployed to an Oracle8i server. The additional class libraries required, other the basic Java runtime environment, include:

- <JDEV_HOME>\lib\javax_ejb.zip is the EJB class library.
- <JDEV_HOME>\aurora\lib\aurora_client.jar is the Oracle8i client classes.
- <JDEV_HOME>\aurora\lib\vbjorb.jar is the Visigenics ORB classes library.
- <JDEV_HOME>\aurora\lib\vbjapp.jar is the Visigenics ORB classes library.
- <JDEV_HOME> represents the root installation directory for Oracle JDeveloper.

All of these class libraries are provided with the Oracle8i server software. Optional libraries could include JDBC libraries and the SQLJ Translator, depending on the code executed in the EJB client.

SUMMARY

This chapter has introduced the basic process of creating an Enterprise JavaBean and its associated EJB client application. The Enterprise JavaBean approach will help you to partition your application processing from the user presentation layer. With your application logic encapsulated in an Enterprise JavaBean, any client can reuse the EJB functionality from its container and provide the end-user with a variety of interfaces. The EJB code can be changed with minimal impact on the client presentation, and the client interface can be changed with minimal impact on the EJB code.

You should now have a good understanding of the structure and environment of session Enterprise JavaBeans, the steps required to deploy a session bean into an Oracle8i server, and the creation and execution of an EJB client application. Using Oracle JDeveloper will greatly reduce the time needed to develop and deploy an Enterprise JavaBean, but the command-line tools provided with Oracle8i software can achieve the same result. The EJB deployment command-line tools, with additional details about the EJB deployment process and advanced topics like EJB transactions and security, are covered in Chapter 22.

Chapter 22

Deploying and Using an Enterprise JavaBean

- Preparing to Run Oracle8i EJB Services
- Deploying an EJB with Command-Line Utilities
- Running the Client Application after Deployment
- Transaction-Enabling an Enterprise JavaBean
- Restrictions and Limitations with Oracle8i EJBs
- EJB Security in Oracle8i
- Removing an EJB from Oracle8i Server
- Deploying an Enterprise JavaBean to Oracle Application Server
- Summary

This chapter assumes that you have received or developed a complete Enterprise JavaBean ready to be installed for use in a runtime context. An Enterprise JavaBean is a component similar in principle to a JavaBean, but it can be distributed and is not GUI-based. An Enterprise bean should be constructed in a way that is free of platform dependencies so that it can be used in a variety of containers. The idea is that you assemble an application by connecting completed components together, as required, to provide the application functionality. Each Enterprise JavaBean (EJB) provides a piece of the functionality, allowing you to build plug-and-play applications ranging from simple to complex.

As the application assembler, you need to know how to locate the EJB at runtime via its published name, how to create a bean instance, and how to call its methods, as discussed in Chapter 21. However, before you can use an Enterprise JavaBean, it must be installed into its container. This is called deployment. This chapter covers the deployment of Enterprise JavaBeans, and especially how to specify and use transaction and security features when executing EJBs in an Oracle8i server environment.

Deploying an Enterprise JavaBean is the role of the EJB deployer, who must be conversant with the platform and execution environment into which the EJB will be placed.[1] These subjects will be discussed below in the following sequence:

- Required administrative tasks before deploying and executing an Enterprise JavaBean.
- Command-line utilities used to deploy the bean.
- Using JDBC or SQLJ code and transaction enabling a session bean.
- Using the deployment descriptor properties to specify how the bean or container manages transactions and security.

The deployment descriptor is a file that can either be generated by EJB container provider tools or manually constructed by the EJB deployer. The deployment descriptor contains several properties that identify the deployed enterprise bean classes, and how the bean and its EJB container interact. For example, you can set properties to let the EJB container control transaction boundaries (i.e., the start and end of a transaction). This is known as *demarcating the transaction.* You can also specify how the EJB container applies security when executing the enterprise bean.

As the EJB deployer, you should become conversant with the contents of the deployment descriptor and know how to specify the appropriate value supported by the EJB container you are using. The last section of this chapter has a brief discussion on deploying an EJB to an Oracle application server.

---

[1]The EJB specification defines specific roles. The *EJB Deployer* is responsible for deploying the Ejb-jar file and generated client-jar file using deployment tools supplied by the *EJB Container Provider.* The Ejb-jar file contains EJB classes developed and supplied by the *Bean provider.*

22.1 PREPARING TO RUN ORACLE8i EJB SERVICES

The major tasks required to run an Enterprise JavaBean in the Oracle8i server are:

- Install Oracle JServer in order to install the database Java Virtual Machine.
- Set up Internet Inter-ORB Protocol (IIOP) network services so that EJB clients can communicate with EJB components in a server using the IIOP protocol.
- Manage database server memory to provide sufficient space for Java application code in the database at runtime.

22.1.1 INSTALLING ORACLE JSERVER

If you create the default database during an installation of the Oracle8i database software, the JServer (Oracle JVM) environment is automatically included, and the settings for accepting an IIOP connection are configured.

If you set up your database instance manually but Oracle JServer has not been installed, you can use either of the following techniques to install the database JVM:

- Use the Oracle `dbassist` utility, covered in Chapter 23.
- Log into the database instance as user SYS, and execute the SQL*Plus script called `initjvm.sql`.

For the latter case, you will find the `initjvm.sql` script in the `ORACLE_HOME/javavm/install` directory of your Oracle8i database software installation.[2]

22.1.2 SETTING UP THE IIOP SERVICES

In the Oracle8i environment, a client application must use the Internet Inter-ORB Protocol (IIOP) to connect with an EJB in the server. You will find a bit more detail about IIOP in Chapter 23. The Oracle database provides two communication paths to the Oracle8i server and EJB service using the IIOP protocol:

- Indirect access to a dispatcher process through the database listener, known as the TNS listener.
- Direct access to a dispatcher process.

---

[2]ORACLE_HOME represents the home directory chosen for your database software when you install Oracle8i. Replace the forward slashes with backward slashes under the Windows platform.

Using the indirect access method, the client application can specify any database accessible to the listener that can service a request for one or more database instance. With direct access, the client application chooses a specific database, because the dispatcher process belongs to a specific database instance.

Figure 22.1 is a high-level diagram of the Oracle8i communication services, showing sample port numbers, that a client application can use to interact with database server components. As can be seen, an Enterprise JavaBean client (in this case, client2 or client3) uses the Session-IIOP protocol to interact with an Enterprise JavaBean component in the server.[3]

To use Oracle8i EJB and CORBA services,[4] the database instance must be configured to run in multi-threaded server (MTS) mode.

To configure indirect IIOP access via a listener, you must:

- Modify the database initialization file (`init.ora`) and set the `mts_dispatchers` parameter,
- Add an address for the IIOP port to the database listener file (`listener.ora`)

The `mts_dispatchers` parameter and value added to the database initialization file are:

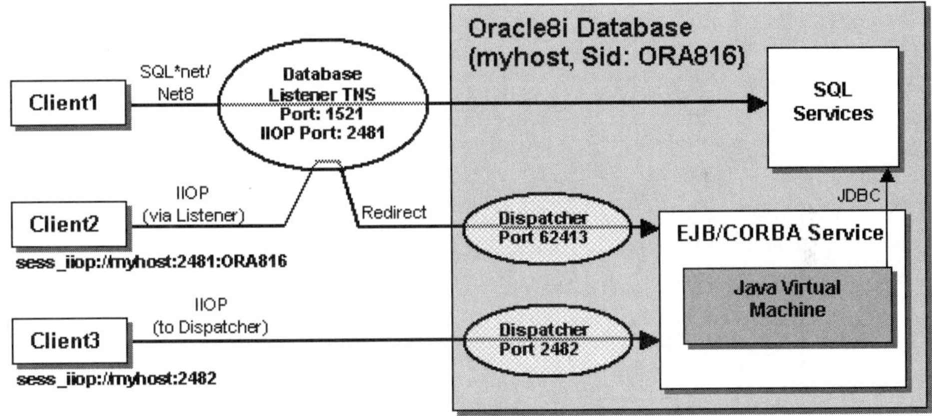

FIGURE 22.1 Oracle8i SQL*Net/Net8 and IIOP communication services.

---

[3]Session IIOP protocol is an extension of the basic IIOP protocol. The standard IIOP protocol does not know about sessions. Session IIOP protocol adds a unique identifier that identifies sessions.

[4]CORBA is an acronym for Common Object Request Broker Architecture. Oracle8i CORBA services are covered in detail in Chapter 23.

```
mts_dispatchers=
  "(PROTOCOL=TCP)(PRE=oracle.aurora.server.SGiopServer)"
```

This mts_dispatchers setting in the database initialization file allows the database listener process to handle a client IIOP connection request (typically on the default IIOP port of 2481), and redirects it to a dispatcher process that manages the connection for the user session invoking IIOP-based services. The Oracle database listener configuration file listener.ora should include the following entry in its address list:

```
(DESCRIPTION =
 (PROTOCOL_STACK =
   (PRESENTATION = GIOP)
    (SESSION = RAW)
   )
   (ADDRESS = (PROTOCOL = TCP)(HOST = <your-host-name>)
    (PORT = 2481))
   )
 )
```

Chapter 23 discusses how the Oracle Net8 Assistant tool can be used to add the default IIOP port on port 2481. The database listener should be started prior to starting the database with this configuration with the Oracle8i lsnrctl command-line utility, assuming the default listener is called LISTENER:[5]

```
lsnrctl start LISTENER
```

Alternatively, you can configure direct IIOP access for the client using the following initialization parameter syntax, where the case for the value of the PRESENTATION option must be preserved:

```
mts_dispatchers="
  (ADDRESS=(PROTOCOL=TCP)(PORT=2482))
  (DISPATCHERS=1)
  (PRESENTATION=oracle.aurora.server.SGiopServer)"
```

In this case, choose the IIOP port number (such as 2482, above) and make sure that the DISPATCHERS option is set to a value of 1 to minimize port contention.

---

[5]If you are using the default listener called LISTENER, the listener name is optional in the lsnrctl command line, otherwise it must be present.

See Chapter 5 for a more detailed discussion of the listener and dispatcher server processes when using a multithreaded server configuration. An EJB client connecting to the database using indirect IIOP access, via the listener, will specify the following URL base for a JNDI based connection:

```
sess_iiop://localhost:2481:ORA816
```

Where:

- `sess_iiop` is the protocol.
- `localhost` should be the name of the host running a listener servicing IIOP requests on port 2481.
- `2481` is the listener port for IIOP connections.
- `ORA816` is the database identity or service name.

An EJB client using the direct-to-dispatcher service specifies the same connect string without the database identifier, and the port number specified must be the appropriate dispatcher port. For example:

```
sess_iiop://localhost:2482
```

In either case, you will be connecting to a session-based IIOP service to interact with an Enterprise JavaBean on the same host (localhost) as the client application.

To check your listener and dispatcher configuration after starting the listener and then the database, you can use the Oracle8i `lsnrctl` command-line utility:

```
lsnrctl services LISTENER
```

The sample output returned should resemble the following output:

```
LSNRCTL for 32-bit Windows: Version 8.1.6.0.0 - Production on 22-OCT-2000 21:52:53

(c) Copyright 1998, 1999, Oracle Corporation.  All rights reserved.

Connecting to (DESCRIPTION=(ADDRESS=(PROTOCOL=IPC)(KEY=EXTPROC0)))
Services Summary...
  PLSExtProc          has 1 service handler(s)
    DEDICATED SERVER established:0 refused:0
      LOCAL SERVER
  ora816              has 1 service handler(s)
    DEDICATED SERVER established:0 refused:0
      LOCAL SERVER
  ora816              has 3 service handler(s)
```

```
      DEDICATED SERVER established:0 refused:0
        LOCAL SERVER
      DISPATCHER established:2 refused:0 current:0 max:1022 state:ready
        D001 <machine: FRAZZLE, pid: 349>
        (DESCRIPTION=(ADDRESS=(PROTOCOL=tcp)
        (HOST=frazzle.au.oracle.com)(PORT=2482))
        (PRESENTATION=oracle.aurora.server.SGiopServer)
        (SESSION=RAW))
        Presentation: oracle.aurora.server.SGiopServer
      DISPATCHER established:0 refused:0 current:0 max:1022 state:ready
        D000 <machine: FRAZZLE, pid: 352>
         (DESCRIPTION=(ADDRESS=(PROTOCOL=tcp)
         (HOST=frazzle.au.oracle.com)(PORT=2115))
         (PRESENTATION=oracle.aurora.server.SGiopServer)
         (SESSION=RAW))
         Presentation: oracle.aurora.server.SGiopServer
The command completed successfully
```

The bold text in the example output for the `lsnrctl` command line shows that two dispatchers have been created, D000 and D001. This output is appropriate if you configured both a listener for indirect IIOP access and a dispatcher for direct access. In this case, the listener redirects IIOP requests on default port 2481[6] to the dispatcher `D000` on an arbitrary[7] port number; and dispatcher `D001` handles direct IIOP connection requests on port 2482.

You can also test your IIOP configuration settings with the `sess_sh` command-line tool (a Java application), as follows:

```
$ sess_sh -user bookstore -password bookstore \
  -service sess_iiop://localhost:2481:ORA816
--Aurora/ORB Session Shell--
--type "help" at the command line for help message
$
```

To test the direct access configuration, change the `-service` option value in the `sess_sh` command as follows:

```
-service sess_iiop://localhost:2482
```

The `sess_sh` utility can be used to test the IIOP connection with any user name registered to access the database. The `sess_sh` command-line utility is discussed in more detail in Chapter 24, "Advanced CORBA Topics."

---

[6]The default port number 2481 is not obvious in the visible output from the `lsnrctl` command.

[7]The port number is arbitrary from the client application point of view, because it does not need to know the dispatcher port. The client makes a connection request to the listener on port 2481, which handles the redirection to the dispatcher port. The dispatcher identifies its port number to the listener when it starts.

22.1.3 MANAGE DATABASE SERVER MEMORY

The Oracle database initialization file has several parameters that control memory allocation and utilization. This section provides a brief description and some guidelines for certain database initialization parameters that can affect the execution environment of an Enterprise JavaBean. The parameters are listed below.

- `SHARED_POOL_SIZE` controls the size in bytes of the shared pool portion. The shared pool is part of the System Global Area (SGA).
- `LARGE_POOL_SIZE` provides large memory allocations for session memory for the multi-threaded server, Oracle-distributed transaction services implemented by the XA interface,[8] I/O server processes, and backup and restore operations.
- `JAVA_POOL_SIZE`sets the size of the Java pool, which is a part of SGA.[9]

The Java pool is used when loading Java sources and/or classes into the server, and for all session-specific Java code and state during runtime execution in the JVM.

To install the JServer software in the database set:

- `SHARED_POOL_SIZE` = 52428800 # must >= 50Mb, and
- `JAVA_POOL_SIZE` = 20971520 # must be >= 20Mb.

To execute the Java code under the EJB or CORBA services, it is best to maintain these settings. If you are only executing Java Stored Procedures, set the `JAVA_POOL_SIZE` to about 10Mb, and reduce the `SHARED_POOL_SIZE` accordingly, depending on the work being done.

Under the multi-threaded server, the area allocated by the `LARGE_POOL_SIZE` is used for some of the Java object states and should be set to a size appropriate for the number and size of classes actively loaded or used. On average, loading a Java class consumes 8Kb.

Under EJB and CORBA services, using MTS, the Java pool contains:

- The shared part of each Java class, which on average runs about 4 to 8 Kb.
- Some parts of the user process area used for per-session state data.

Since the Java pool memory size is fixed, it is necessary to estimate the total requirement for your applications and multiply the number of concurrent sessions

---

[8]XA is an acronym meaning *X/Open Architecture* that defines a standard way of managing distributed transactions. The Oracle7 (from 7.3), Oracle8, and Oracle8i databases all provide an implementation of the XA interfaces via the XA libraries installed with the database software.

[9]The Oracle System Global Area (SGA) is discussed in Chapter 5.

expected by the average size of Java classes. The parts of the user process area memory stored in the Java pool must all be able to fit within the fixed Java pool space for all sessions.

Two other parameters you may wish to control are:

- JAVA_SOFT_SESSIONSPACE_LIMIT to specify a soft limit on Java memory usage in a session. The default value is 1Mb, and the database issues a warning in the database log file if the value is exceeded.
- JAVA_MAX_SESSIONSPACE_SIZE sets a hard limit on the Java memory usage per session. You may want to limit this size, because the default value is set to 4G. The value of 4Gb is set to a large value to minimize the number and frequency of error messages that the Oracle database server generates when the limit is reached. If the JAVA_MAX_SESSIONSPACE_SIZE is exceeded, the session is killed with an out-of-memory failure with the following error message: `ORA-29554: unhandled Java out of memory condition`.

Managing and changing these settings for optimal database and application performance is a tuning exercise that is beyond the scope of this book, and Chapter 5 contains a limited discussion of Oracle database performance. In addition to the *Oracle8i Administrator Guide* and *Oracle8i Tuning* reference manuals,[10] several books are devoted to the subject, including *Oracle 8i and UNIX Performance Tuning*, by Ahmed Alomari (Prentice-Hall).[11]

22.2 DEPLOYING AN EJB WITH COMMAND-LINE UTILITIES

Having installed the JServer engine, configured your database listener services, and written your Enterprise JavaBean code (see Chapter 21 for information on developing an EJB), you are ready to deploy and run your EJB. To do this, you have to create the Ejb-jar file and deployment descriptor to deploy the EJB to the server. If you are the deployer of the enterprise bean,[12] and not the bean developer, you may receive an Ejb-jar file from the developer. The command-line tools covered in this section will help you to deploy an EJB, whether developed by you

---

[10]Oracle reference manuals are available online to registered members of Oracle Technology Network at http://technet.oracle.com.

[11]*Oracle Performance Tuning* by Mark Gurry and Peter Corrigan (O'Reilly and Associates), *Oracle8 Advanced Tuning and Administration* by Kevin Loney (Oracle Press).

[12]The EJB Specification defines five different roles in the context of building and deploying an EJB. One is the *EJB developer*, who develops the EJB code, and another is the *EJB deployer*, who installs the code into its execution environment. Different people or the same person can carry out these two roles.

or by a third party. The discussion that follows assumes that you are a bean developer who both compiles the code and creates the Ejb-jar file.

First, ensure that you have the correct JDK classes in your CLASSPATH for the deployment environment. Use JDK 1.1.8 for Oracle 8.1.5, and JDK 1.2.2 for Oracle 8.1.6. The steps required to deploy the code are:

- Compile the EJB Code and combine into a JAR file.
- Create a deployment descriptor.
- Run the `deployejb` command-line utility and generate the client JAR file.
- Add the client Jar file to the CLASSPATH of the client environment.
- Run the client application.

22.2.1 COMPILING THE EJB CODE AND CREATING AN EJB-JAR FILE

Set your CLASSPATH to contain the appropriate Oracle8i class libraries and the EJB class library in addition to the JDK classes. The following example is for Windows NT, but is split over several lines for clarity. Be sure to use syntax appropriate for your operating system.

```
set CLASSPATH=%JAVA_DIR%\myclasses;
              %ORACLE_HOME%\lib\aurora_client.jar;
              %ORACLE_HOME%\lib\vbjorb.jar;
              %ORACLE_HOME%\lib\vbjapp.jar;
```

Notes:

- The `aurora_client.jar` contains classes in the `javax.ejb` package.
- The directory `%JAVA_DIR%\myclasses` is also in the `CLASSPATH` to resolve references to your EJB classes.
- The core JDK class library (`classes.zip` for JDK 1.1.x, or `rt.jar` for JDK 1.2.x) is not added to the `CLASSPATH` because it is automatically located by the `javac` command -line utility, as documented in the JDK command-line tool java documentation (`javadocs`).
- You may need to add other class libraries in addition to the core JDK classes, depending on the type of code in the bean class. For example, if you use JDBC, add the appropriate Oracle JDBC 1.0 driver (`classes111.zip`) or the JDBC 2.0 driver (`classes12.zip`) class library to the `CLASSPATH`.

In this section, you are deploying the `CustomerEJB` (discussed in Chapter 21) and its related classes. The EJB classes involved are:

- CreditCard.java — an additional serializable class used in the parameter and return values in some bean methods.
- CustomerEJB.java — the EJB bean class.
- CustomerRemote.java — the Remote interface.
- CustomerHome.java —The Home interface.

Compile the components required for your EJB in the following order:

- Additional supporting classes, such as CreditCard.java.
- The EJB bean class.
- The Remote Interface.
- The Home Interface.

The additional supporting classes are compiled first, because they are used by the bean and are likely to appear in methods signatures found in the Remote and Home interfaces. You can compile the bean before or after the Remote and Home interfaces. However, compile the Remote Interface before compiling the Home interface, because the `create()` methods in the Home interface return a reference to the Remote interface. The following commands are used to compile the EJB classes:

```
javac -d %JAVA_DIR%\myclasses CreditCard.java
javac -d %JAVA_DIR%\myclasses CustomerEJB.java
javac -d %JAVA_DIR%\myclasses CustomerRemote.java
javac -d %JAVA_DIR%\myclasses CustomerHome.java
```

The `-d` option on the `javac` command line causes the generated class files to be created in the subdirectory relative to the directory name specified after the `-d` option; for example: `%JAVA_DIR%\myclasses`. This is necessary to ensure that your Ejb-jar file is constructed with the Java package name qualifying the name of the class file. For example, if your class files are defined with the Java package name `com.prenhall.OFJP.ejb`, the compiled class files will be created in the directory called `%JAVA_DIR%\myclasses\com\prenhall\OFJP\ejb`.

Using the JDK `jar` utility, you can then create the Ejb-jar file to contain your compiled EJB classes and supporting files, each with the correct Java path names derived from its Java package name, as follows:

```
cd %JAVA_DIR%\myclasses
jar cf0 CustomerBean.jar com\prenhall\OFJP\ejb\*.class
```

The parameters supplied to the `jar` command are:

- `cf0`
  - c creates new archive.
  - `f` indicates the second argument is the archive name (CustomerBean.jar),
  - `0` means do not compress the file.
- `CustomerBean.jar`—the name of the archive file to create.
- `com\prenhall\OFJP\ejb\*.class`— list of files to be included in the archive.

The `jar` utility will automatically create a manifest file named `META-INF/MANIFEST.MF` that lists the archive contents. For example, here is part of the contents of the manifest file created by the `jar` tool for the `CustomerBean.jar` file:

```
Manifest-Version: 1.0

Name: com/prenhall/OFJP/ejb/CreditCard.class
Digest-Algorithms: SHA MD5
SHA-Digest: oPNlIyKDWSEPNjz63xivv7cbgm4=
MD5-Digest: O1/kHWsTqYmfSb3g6HTprw==

Name: com/prenhall/OFJP/ejb/CustomerHome.class
Digest-Algorithms: SHA MD5
SHA-Digest: ad4anPe7CKFdgjDWYFiKNZqdCIY=
MD5-Digest: s01nv6ezmVFkJUarJ/h5Ow==
```

Briefly, the first line in the manifest file indicates the manifest version, followed by one or more sections separated by blank lines. Each section has several lines consisting of `<tag>:<value>` pairs. At a minimum, the tags are:

- The `Name` tag, whose value is the relative path and name of file in the archive.
- A `Digest-Algorithm` tag, show value is a space-separated list of digest algorithm acronyms; for example, MD5 for Message Digest 5.[13]

The detailed format of the manifest file is beyond the scope of this book, but is covered by the HTML version of the Java JDK documentation by following links to `Tools Documentation` on the `jar` command utility. The notes about the `jar` command utility provide links to information about the manifest file format.

[13]A discussion of security implementations, such as Message Digest, is beyond the scope of this chapter and book.

The EJB 1.0 specification requires that the manifest file include a section naming a serialized deployment descriptor file in the archive. This deployment descriptor is used to identify the Enterprise JavaBean classes. For example:

```
Name: CustomerRemote.ser
Enterprise-Bean: True
```

The `jar` utility does not automatically identify the deployment descriptor file with the `Enterprise-Bean:` name and `True` value pair. You would have to manually edit the manifest file and add the `Enterprise-Bean` tag and value into the appropriate section for the deployment descriptor file. *However, you do not need to create your own manifest file when deploying the EJB to the Oracle8i server, because the deployment tools use a deployment descriptor combined with the Ejb-jar files to accomplish this task.*

Other EJB containers may require you to manually edit the manifest file, which can be done as follows:

- ❑ Use the `jar` tool to create the Java archive containing a manifest file.
- ❑ Extract the manifest file from the archive file.
- ❑ Edit the file with a standard text editor, adding the two lines mentioned above.
- ❑ Re-create the Ejb-jar file using the `jar` tool with the `m` option to make the utility use the name of your manifest file name as specified on the first command-line parameter, thereby suppressing the `jar` tool from generating its own manifest file.

When deploying to the Oracle8i environment, the deployment descriptor is not added to the Ejb-jar file even though the EJB specification indicates that the deployment descriptor should be part of the Ejb-jar file.

The Ejb-jar file (e.g., the `CustomerBean.jar` created with the `jar` command containing the required manifest file from the preceding example in this section) is used in conjunction with a deployment descriptor, generated by Oracle8i deployment tools, to install the EJB and its associated classes into the Oracle8i server.

22.2.2 CREATING A DEPLOYMENT DESCRIPTOR

To deploy an Enterprise JavaBean, you must create a deployment descriptor to accompany the Ejb-jar file. The deployment descriptor is used to identify the Home interface, Remote interface, bean class, security, and transaction properties of the EJB. In the Oracle8i environment, the deployment descriptor is a text file that is not added to the Ejb-jar file. The EJB implementations of other vendors may require that the deployment descriptor be included in the Ejb-jar file, and their content is likely to be different. Here is the basic syntax of a deployment descriptor for an Oracle8i EJB server:

```
SessionBean <bean-class-name> {
  <attribute>=<value>
  ...
}
```

The <bean-class-name> is replaced with the fully qualified name of the class representing the bean implementation, which is always preceded by the keyword SessionBean.[14] The descriptor file contains lines of <attribute>=<value> pairs. The syntax structure of the deployment descriptor resembles a Java class. Listing 22.1 provides a brief example of the deployment descriptor for the CustomerEJB bean.

```
SessionBean com.prenhall.OFJP.ejb.CustomerEJB
{
  BeanHomeName = "test/CustomerEJB";
  HomeInterfaceClassName = com.prenhall.OFJP.ejb.CustomerHome;
  RemoteInterfaceClassName = com.prenhall.OFJP.ejb.CustomerRemote;

  SessionTimeout = 0;
  StateManagementType = STATEFUL_SESSION;

  TransactionAttribute = TX_REQUIRED;
  RunAsMode = CLIENT_IDENTITY;
  AllowedIdentities = { bookstore };
}
```

LISTING 22.1 Example deployment descriptor.

Notes on Listing 22.1:

- Required components are shown in bold text. They include:
  - The name of the bean class in the first line.
  - BeanHomeName—the published name of the bean, used in JNDI lookup requests.
  - HomeInterfaceClassName—the fully qualified name of the bean Home interface.

[14]Oracle8i up to version 8.1.6 only supports session beans.

    - RemoteInterfaceClassName—the fully qualified name of the bean remote interface.
- Attributes that apply to the whole bean are:
    - The SessionTimeOut has a value of zero to indicate that the bean terminates when the client has terminated the last connection with the bean.
    - The StateManagementType is always STATEFUL_SESSION in an Oracle8i environment, because all session beans in Oracle8i are treated as stateful session beans. Therefore, a value of STATELESS_SESSION has no meaning in the Oracle8i context, and is treated as if it were a stateful session bean.
- The attributes in Listing 22.1 apply to the bean as a whole, unless overridden for a bean method (see Listing 22.2). Attributes that relate to transaction and security services are shown in Table 22.1.
- A semicolon terminates lines inside the braces of the deployment descriptor.

Table 22.1 explains the additional properties in the deployment descriptor from Listing 22.1 that can be applied to the bean or individual methods.

The ability, through these properties, to separate control of how to use transaction and security services from the bean code is one of the major advantages of the EJB approach. Listing 22.2 shows how to specify attributes for the bean and some methods.

```
SessionBean com.prenhall.OFJP.ejb.CustomerEJB
{
  BeanHomeName = "test/CustomerEJB";
  HomeInterfaceClassName = com.prenhall.OFJP.ejb.CustomerHome;
  RemoteInterfaceClassName = com.prenhall.OFJP.ejb.CustomerRemote;

  SessionTimeout = 0;
  StateManagementType = STATEFUL_SESSION;
```

LISTING 22.2 Transaction and security attributes for a bean method.

TABLE 22.1 Deployment descriptor properties

PROPERTY	DESCRIPTION
TransactionAttribute	Specifies whether the EJB is container-managed or bean-managed (see section 22.4 for more detail).
RunAsMode	Specifies whether the EJB container uses the security credentials provided by the client application when set to CLIENT_IDENTITY, or a descriptor- specified user when set to SPECIFIED_IDENTITY, or the EJB system container running the bean when set to SYSTEM_IDENTITY.
AllowedIdentities	List of usernames or roles in the database that are allowed to execute the bean.

```
  TransactionAttribute = TX_REQUIRED;
  RunAsMode = CLIENT_IDENTITY;
  AllowedIdentities = { bookstore };

  java.lang.String toText ()
  {
    TransactionAttribute = TX_REQUIRED;
    RunAsMode = CLIENT_IDENTITY;
    AllowedIdentities = { bookstore };
  }
  :
  void setPassword (java.lang.String)
  {
    TransactionAttribute = TX_REQUIRED;
    RunAsMode = CLIENT_IDENTITY;
    AllowedIdentities = { bookstore };
  }
  :
}
```

LISTING 22.2 *Continued*

Notes on Listing 22.2:

- Attributes can be specified for the bean applying to all of its methods, or an attribute can be specified for bean methods to override the setting for the bean as a whole. The example includes attribute values specified for the method, which have the same values as specified for the bean as a whole, only to show the syntax of where and how attributes can be specified for the bean and each method. In this example, including the methods with the same values as set for the bean is redundant.
- Method names appear in the deployment descriptor with their Java signature, including parameter types, but not parameter names.
- The attributes that apply to the method are entered between braces and terminated with a semicolon.
  The transaction and security attributes are discussed later in this chapter.

22.2.3 RUNNING THE `deployejb` UTILITY

After creating the Ejb-jar file and the deployment descriptor, you execute the `deployejb` command-line utility to store the EJB classes in the Oracle8i EJB environment and publish its JNDI name. The general syntax for the deployejb command-line tool is:

```
deployejb [options] Ejb-jar
```

Each option entered before the name of the Ejb-jar file is prefixed with a dash and typically followed by white space and a value. Listing 22.3 is an example of the `deployejb` command line using some of its options. The example is split over several lines for clarity.

```
deployejb -user bookstore -password bookstore
          -service sess_iiop://localhost:2481:ORA816
          -descriptor CustomerRemote.dd
          -temp tmp
          -generated CustomerBeanClient.jar
          CustomerBean.jar
```

LISTING 22.3 Deploying an EJB into an Oracle8i server.

The meaning and use of the command-line options in Listing 22.3 are discussed in Table 22.2. The sample output for the `deployejb` command line in Listing 22.3 is:

```
Reading Deployment Descriptor...done
Verifying Deployment Descriptor...done
Gathering users...done
Generating Comm Stubs.......................................done
Compiling Stubs...done
Generating Jar File...done
Loading EJB Jar file and Comm Stubs Jar file...done
Generating EJBHome and EJBObject on the server...done
Publishing EJBHome...done
```

Notes on the output of `deployejb`:

```
Generating Jar File...done
```

- Indicates that the client-jar file (i.e., `CustomerBeanClient.jar`) is generated. The name client-jar file is a little misleading because it contains the stub classes for the client code to interact with the EJB in the server, as well as the skeleton classes required used by the EJB server components to interact with the client. Therefore, the generated client-jar file must also be loaded into the database along with the Ejb-jar file, which contains the enterprise bean classes. Both jar files must be present in the client `CLASSPATH` at runtime.

```
Loading EJB Jar file and Comm Stubs Jar file...done
```

TABLE 22.2 Some `deployejb` command-line options

OPTION	DESCRIPTION
-user *<username>*	The database schema/user name into which the EJB classes are loaded. Abbreviated as -u.
-password *<password>*	The password for the database schema/user. Abbreviated as -p.
-service *<url>*	A URL identifying database session namespace into which the EJB name is published. The URL uses the sess_iiop protocol. Abbreviated as -s.
-descriptor *<file>*	Specifies the name of the text version of the deployment descriptor.
-generated *<jarfile>*	Specifies the name of the generated client-jar file (e.g., CustomerBeanClient.jar). If this option is not specified, the client-jar file is created with the Ejb-jar file name prefixed to _generated.jar.
-temp *<dir>*	Specifies the name of the directory used to create the classes for the generated client-jar file. This is automatically removed unless you specify the -keep option.[15]
-keep	Keeps the Java source and class files generated for the stub and skeleton code in the temporary directory.
-republish	Overwrites the published name for the EJB when the name already exists; otherwise an error is generated.

- The `loadjava` utility is invoked to store classes contained in the Ejb-jar (e.g., `CustomerBean.jar`) and the client-jar file (e.g., `CustomerBeanClient.jar`) in the database.

```
Publishing EJBHome...done
```

- Publishes the JNDI name of the bean in the Oracle8i naming service.

To summarize, the `deployejb` command performs the following tasks:

- Read and validate the deployment descriptor.
- Generate the client-jar file containing stub and skeleton classes.
- Load the classes in the Ejb-jar and the generated client-jar file into the Oracle8i database.
- Create EJBHome and EJBObject on the server.
- Publish the name for bean Home object interface.

Table 22.2 describes some of the `deployejb` command-line options and their arguments where required.

---

[15]It is interesting to specify the `-keep` option because you can view the Java source code generated by the `deployejb` tool. Oracle JDeveloper keeps these generated source files. The names and types of files generated are covered in Chapter 23.

The client-jar generated by the `deployejb` tool and the Ejb-jar must be added into the `CLASSPATH` for the EJB client application.

22.2.3.1 Notes on Running the deployejb Tool. To run the deploy EJB tool you must include the JDK `bin` directory in your `PATH` environment variable,[16] because the `deployejb` tool is a script that executes the `java` command.

On Windows NT, if you are using the `deployejb` tool from Oracle8i 8.1.6, and the JDK 1.1.x `bin` directory in your `PATH`, you should explicitly add the JDK 1.1.x `classes.zip` file to the `CLASSPATH`; otherwise, you will get the following error message:

```
Unable to initialize threads: cannot find class java/lang/Thread
```

If you are using a JDK 1.2 environment, the `rt.jar` file does not have to be explicitly added into the `CLASSPATH`.

Also on the Windows NT platform, avoid spaces in directory or `jar` file names that are added to `CLASSPATH`, because they will cause the `deployejb` script to terminate with an error. The error is caused when the `deployejb` script sets the `-classpath` option for the `java` command line used to execute a Java class that performs the deployment tasks.

22.3 RUNNING THE CLIENT APPLICATION AFTER DEPLOYMENT

The steps to run the client code are: **<<renumber list from 1>>**

- ❑ Set the `PATH` to include the bin directory of the Java runtime environment.[17]
- ❑ Add to the `CLASSPATH` the Ejb-jar and client-jar files generated by the `deployejb` utility.
- ❑ Compile and execute the client application.

For example, on Windows NT (with text split over more than one line for clarity), type:

```
path %PATH%;%JAVA_HOME%\bin
set CLASSPATH=%ORACLE_HOME%\lib\aurora_client.jar;
              %ORACLE_HOME%\lib\vbjorb.jar;
              %ORACLE_HOME%\lib\vbjapp.jar;
```

---

[16]If you are using Oracle8i 8.1.5, use the JDK 1.1 bin directory. If using Oracle8i 8.1.6, use the JDK 1.2 bin directory.

[17]In Oracle8i 8.1.5, use the Java 1.1 runtime environment. With Oracle8i 8.1.6, you can use Java 1.1 or the 1.2 runtime environment.

```
              .\CustomerBeanClient.jar;
              .\CustomerBean.jar
```

The equivalent Unix *Bourne* shell commands are listed below (note that the separator for CLASSPATH on Unix is colon (:), and not semicolon (;)).[18]

```
set PATH=$PATH:$JAVA_HOME/bin
set CLASSPATH=$ORACLE_HOME/lib/aurora_client.jar: \
              $ORACLE_HOME/lib/vbjorb.jar: \
              $ORACLE_HOME/lib/vbjapp.jar: \
              ./CustomerBeanClient.jar: \
              ./CustomerBean.jar
```

The commands for setting the PATH and CLASSPATH make the following assumptions:

- The JAVA_HOME environment variable contains the root directory of the JDK software.
- The ORACLE_HOME environment variable is set to the directory where the Oracle database software is installed.
- The Ejb-jar and client-jar files are in the current directory.

Compile the EJB client:

```
javac -d .  CustomerEJBClient.java
```

Run the EJB client:

```
java com.prenhall.OFJP.ejb.CustomerEJBClient
```

Here is the output from the EJB client application:

```
ejbUrl: sess_iiop://localhost:2481:ORA816/test/CustomerEJB
Creating an initial context
Looking for the EJB published as 'test/CustomerEJB'
Creating a new EJB instance
Calling com.prenhall.OFJP.ejb.CustomerRemote methods...

1 Jerome Cricket mailto:jcricket@cartoon.com
```

See Chapter 21 for the source code of the CustomerEJBClient.java application that produces these results.

---

[18]If you are using the C shell Unix command-line interpreter, the Javasoft recommendation is to use the setenv command to set the environment variables.

22.4 TRANSACTION-ENABLING AN ENTERPRISE JAVABEAN

Transaction-enabling an EJB requires that you add code to make one or more changes to the database, and that you demarcate the transaction; that is, manage its start and end points. In an Enterprise JavaBean environment, transaction-enabled applications must meet the following requirements:

- A transaction service must be used to create a context for the transaction. The transaction context is used to track the start and end of the transaction and related transactional operations. The Oracle8i database provides the transaction service using the CORBA infrastructure.
- The value for the `TransactionAttribute` of the bean, and for the bean methods, must be set in the deployment descriptor. The `TransactionAttribute` value specifies whether the bean is subject to container-managed persistence (CMP) or bean-managed persistence (BMP) and control if, and how, a bean method participates in the context of the transaction. Container-managed and bean-managed persistence are described in later sections of this chapter.
- The bean method code performing transactional operations must be written in accordance with the value of the `TransactionAttribute`.

In an EJB environment, the following ACID properties for transactions must still be observed:

- *Atomic*—all changes are saved as a logical unit or are rolled back if any change fails.
- *Consistent*—the data after completing a transaction are left in consistent state.
- *Isolated*—changes during the transaction are not visible to other users until completed.
- *Durable*—on completion (commit or rollback), the transactional changes are persistent.

Transactional operations can be performed using JDBC or SQLJ or both in your Enterprise JavaBean methods. The EJB 1.x specifications only specify support for flat transactions. A flat transaction is a logical unit of work comprising of a series of changes to data in a database between the start and end of a transaction.

22.4.1 USING JDBC IN EJB METHODS

When you use JDBC code in an Oracle8i EJB server, the JDBC driver is already loaded implicitly. Thus, the first step for your bean method is to create a JDBC connection before you execute SQL statements. The EJB can use the Oracle8i internal server-side driver to create a JDBC connection. For example:

```
Connection conn = null;
conn = DriverManager.getConnection("jdbc:oracle:kprb:");
```

The `DriverManager.getConnection()` method is passed a JDBC URL that specifies the internal server-side JDBC driver to access the data in the same Oracle8i database. The internal driver always uses the connection context created by the EJB client to interact with the EJB. Therefore, user name and password credentials are not required in the JDBC connection request because the client has already been authenticated.

Standard JDBC calls are used inside the bean methods to perform DML operations (see Chapters 9 and 10 for details on using JDBC functionality).

When using the internal server-side JDBC driver, do not close the JDBC connection, because closing it can impact other code using the same connection. The JDBC connection is released when the client IIOP session terminates by closing the IIOP connection.

In addition, the JDBC auto-commit mode is automatically set to false inside the server.[19]

Since Oracle8i 8.1.6, a server-side thin JDBC driver can also be used to create a database connection. The code to form a connection with the server-side thin JDBC driver uses the same URL syntax used by the client thin JDBC driver (see Chapter 9 for details of the client thin JDBC driver). For example:

```
Connection conn = null;
conn = DriverManager.getConnection(
        "jdbc:oracle:thin:@host:port:SID","user","pass");
```

The server-side thin JDBC driver can be used to connect to a remote database from inside the Oracle8i EJB container, subject to being granted appropriate security permissions (see section 22.6 for a discussion of EJB security). Using the server-side thin JDBC driver creates a new connection, even when connecting to the local database and the client connection context is not shared. Therefore, you must call the `Connection.close()` method to release the connection resources, and the scope and lifetime of the connection should be carefully considered.

NOTE: EJB methods should never explicitly call the JDBC `Connection.commit()` or `Connection.rollback()` method. The EJB container performs these operations for container-managed beans, and a bean-managed EJB calls the EJB container commit or rollback methods, not the JDBC commit and rollback methods. Container- and bean-managed transactions in an Enterprise JavaBean will be treated later in this chapter.

---

[19]The Oracle JDBC documentation indicates that JDBC auto commit is off when using server-side Java, but tests done with JDBC in an Oracle8i EJB environment calling the `getAutoCommit()` method returned a `true` value indicating that it is on. To be safe, you can always call the `setAutoCommit(false)` just to be sure the JDBC driver does not do the wrong thing.

22.4.2 USING SQLJ IN EJB METHODS

If you write the Bean class as an SQLJ source, you do not have to load the JDBC driver or create the default SQLJ connection context (see Chapter 11 for more detail about using and compiling SQLJ, SQLJ profile files, and SQLJ connection contexts). When you use SQLJ in your bean, the source is saved in a file with a `.sqlj` extension, and you simply write the SQLJ statement in the body of your methods. For example:

```
package com.prenhall.OFJP.ejb;
import sqlj.runtime.*;
import sqlj.runtime.ref.*;

public class CustomerEJB extends SessionBean {
  :
  public String getCustomerName(int custId)
        throws java.rmi.RemoteException, java.sql.SQLException
  {
    String custName = null;
    #sql { select name into :custName
           from customer
           where id = :custId };
    return custName;
  }
  :
}
```

If you use an SQLJ source for your EJB bean class, you must perform the following tasks before you deploy the EJB into the Oracle8i container:

- Translate the SQLJ source and compile it into a Java class, ensuring that the SQLJ profile files are created as standard Java classes and not serialized Java classes.
- Add the EJB class and associated SQLJ profile classes to the Ejb-jar file.

To compile the SQLJ file, use the following command:

```
sqlj -ser2class  CustomerEJB.sqlj
```

Using the `-ser2class` option ensures that the SQLJ profile files are compiled into normal Java classes. The following files created by the SQLJ command line must be included in the Ejb-jar file:

```
CustomerEJB.class                   // bean class
CustomerEJB_SJProfile0.class        // SQLJ profile file
CustomerEJB_SJProfileKeys.class     // SQLJ profile file
```

Note: SQLJ profile files are covered in Chapter 11.

If you use SQLJ in your Enterprise JavaBean, you must perform these tasks using the command-line techniques described in this chapter, because Oracle JDeveloper 3.1 and earlier versions do not directly support the use of SQLJ source files in your EJB bean class. Alternatively, use SQLJ code indirectly in your EJB application by loading the SQLJ classes into the database together with your EJB classes, and then the EJB can use the SQLJ classes and invoke their methods like any other Java class.

As with regular JDBC execution in an EJB environment, an SQLJ commit or rollback statement should not be used in your EJB methods.

22.4.3 THE TRANSACTION SERVICE AND DISTRIBUTED TRANSACTIONS

A distributed transaction is one in which changes are made to more than one data source, typically on a number of remote systems. The classic example is an electronic funds transfer. The funds transfer application must credit one account and debit the other, and both changes must be successful or else both will be rolled back. Performing transaction management tasks when multiple data sources are involved is time-consuming, and it is difficult to ensure that the ACID properties are maintained. However, using a transaction manager provided by a transaction service to control the tracking of changes made in a distributed transaction saves you a great deal of development effort. In particular, you typically do not get access to the necessary hooks needed to implement distributed transactions; only vendors can do this. Therefore, it is not practical for you to support distributed transactions; a more appropriate way is to use a transaction manager that does it for you.

One of the powerful features of the EJB specification is the ability to perform distributed transactions, with the aid of a transaction service usually provided by the EJB container. The application connects to a transaction service, requests the start of a transaction, and receives a transaction context from the service for transactional operations. The transaction service manages and propagates the transaction context to all the data sources, called *resources,* involved in the transaction.

22.4.3.1 Understanding a Transaction Context. The application starting a transaction uses a transaction service to initialize and create a transaction context. A *transaction context* is an object passed from the transaction service to client and server resources involved in the transaction. The transaction context is propagated with method calls to all the resources that participate in the transaction. Methods called by the EJB client can make use of the transaction context, depending on the transaction settings in the EJB deployment descriptor. The runtime behavior of a container-managed EJB depends on:

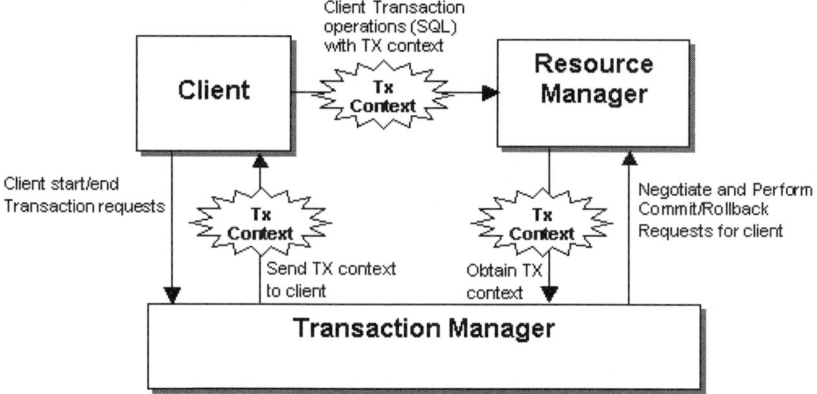

FIGURE 22.2 X/Open distributed transaction model.

- the presence, or absence, of a transaction context provided by the client application, and
- the value assigned to `TransactionAttribute` for the method in the deployment descriptor.

Figure 22.2 depicts the interaction between a client, a transaction service, and a resource manager (database) based on the X/Open distributed transaction model implemented by the Oracle8i database XA library code. The refinements, extensions, and complexity that have been added to the X/Open model are beyond the scope of this book.

The transaction context is created after a client initializes the transaction service and requests a start transaction from the transaction service (the transaction manager in Figure 22.2). The transaction service creates and maintains the transaction context. The transaction context has an associated unique transaction ID number propagated to the client and to each resource in the transaction.[20] The resources involved in the transaction include every EJB object that the client calls, including the database.

22.4.3.2 Creating a Transaction Context from a Java Client. The client application executing outside of an EJB container can use the Java Transaction Service API (JTS) directly. The JTS API provides a Java binding to the OMG Object Transaction Service (OTS) for transaction management in a CORBA server environment, such as the Oracle8i implementation. The JTS API is used by an application that wants to use client-side demarcated transactions.

---

[20]Propagation of the transaction context is transparent to the client program.

The `oracle.aurora.jts.client.AuroraTransactionService` is used by a client application to initialize the transaction service and obtain a transaction context. Listing 22.4 shows the key statements to initialize, begin, and end the transaction using this service.

```
package com.prenhall.OFJP.ejb;

import java.util.Hashtable;
import javax.naming.Context;
import javax.naming.InitialContext;
import oracle.aurora.jts.client.AuroraTransactionService;
import oracle.aurora.jts.util.TS;

public class CustomerClient {
  public static void main(String[] args) {
    Hashtable env = System.getProperties();
    try {
      Context ctx = new InitialContext (env);

      // initialize the transaction service

      AuroraTransactionService.initialize(
          ctx, "sess_iiop://localhost:2481:ORA816");

      // Lookup and create bean instance . . .

      TS.getTS().getCurrent().begin();

      // invoke bean transactional methods . . .

      TS.getTS().getCurrent().commit(true);
    }
    catch (Exception e) {
      if (TS.getTS().getCurrent().get_status() ==
          org.omg.CosTransactions.Status.StatusActive) {
        TS.getTS().getCurrent().rollback();
      }
      e.printStackTrace();
    }
  }
}
```

LISTING 22.4 Using `AuroraTransactionService` for client-side transaction demarcation.

Notes on Listing 22.4:

- Lines 5 and 6 show the imports required to use the `AuroraTransactionService`.
- Lines 16 and 17 initialize the transaction service. The initial context object is used to locate the transaction service. The context object is also used to create the EJB objects, in code omitted from this example but implied by the comment on line 19. The `initialize()` method accepts the JNDI initial context, and the `sess_iiop` URL to identify the transaction service. The `initialize()` method can throw the following exception: `oracle.aurora.jts.util.NoTransactionServiceException`.
- Line 21 uses the `oracle.aurora.jts.util.TS` class methods `getTS()` to get a reference to the transaction service. The `oracle.aurora.jts.util.TransactionService` provides the `getCurrent()` method to return a transaction context object. The transaction context object is obtained by the chained method calls on the `TS` class using the following call sequence: `TS.getTS().getCurrent()`, which in turn provides the methods to control the transaction boundaries, i.e., the `begin()` method to start the transaction.
- Line 25 performs a commit operation to complete the transaction, via the transaction context object. The `true` parameter in the `commit()` method is for reporting extra information on two-phase commit operations. However, Oracle8i 8.1.6 and earlier versions do not support the two-phase commit protocol for distributed objects. Thus, using a true value for the report heuristics parameter is not meaningful until future releases.
- Line 30 performs the rollback operations, after first checking whether the transaction is active. Line 28 uses the transaction context to check the status of the transaction. The status values, as defined in the `org.omg.CosTransactions.Status` class, can be:
  - `StatusActive`
  - `StatusMarkedRollback`
  - `StatusNoTransaction`

The Enterprise JavaBean transactional methods are called between the `begin()` and `commit()` or `rollback()` requests. Subsection 22.4.6 gives an example of calling a transactional method after the client has initialized the transaction service and started a transaction. When the EJB method is called, the state of the transaction depends on the value assigned to `TransactionAttribute` in the deployment descriptor.

22.4.3.3 Creating a Transaction Context within an Enterprise JavaBean. An Enterprise JavaBean using bean-managed transactions uses the server-side JTS API via the `javax.jts.UserTransaction` interface. A `User-`

Transaction object is obtained from the EJB container via the javax.ejv.SessionContext object. The SessionContext object is passed as a parameter when the setSessionContext() method is called during the creation phase of an Enterprise JavaBean. Listing 22.5 shows a code fragment that you can use to get the UserTransaction object, and then begin and end a transaction.

```
package com.prenhall.OFJP.ejb;

import java.rmi.RemoteException;
import javax.ejb.*;
import java.sql.*;
import javax.jts.UserTransaction;

public class CreditCardEJB implements SessionBean {

  SessionContext sessCtx = null;

  public void setSessionContext(SessionContext ctx)
    throws RemoteException {
    sessCtx = ctx;
  }
  :
  public void insertInvalidCard() throws RemoteException {
    Connection conn = null;
    PreparedStatement ps = null;
    UserTransaction userTx = sessCtx.getTransaction();

    try {
      userTx.begin();
      :
      // do some JDBC or SQLJ work
      :
      userTx.commit();
    }
    catch (Exception e) {
      if (userTx.getStatus() == userTx.STATUS_ACTIVE) {
        userTx.rollback();
      }
    }
  }
  :
}
```

LISTING 22.5 Using UserTransaction for server-side transaction demarcation.

Notes on Listing 22.5:

- Line 6 imports the `UserTransaction` interface to use methods for managing the server-side bean-managed transaction context.
- Line 10 declares an instance variable to hold the session context object, which is used to get a reference to the `UserTransaction` object.
- Line 14 saves the session context provided by the EJB container. The `setSessionContext()` method is called during the bean initialization phase. You must retain the session context to allow the bean to manage transactions.
- Line 20 obtains the `UserTransaction` transaction context object from the session context.
- Line 24 starts the transaction by executing the `begin()` method.
- Line 27 executes the `UserTransaction.commit()` method to save changes made after transactional operations are performed with JDBC or SQLJ.
- Line 31 executes a `rollback()` operation if the transaction status is still active. `UserTransaction.getStatus()` returns the status of the transaction.

In the server for bean-managed transactions, the transaction service does not need to be initialized; the Oracle8i server implicitly does it. The request to begin the transaction (`UserTransaction.begin()`) can be called in a different method from the one that ends the transaction (`UserTransaction.commit()` or `UserTransaction.rollback()`). If the bean is not under bean-managed control, then an exception occurs when you attempt to use the `UserTransaction` interface methods.

Before we look at some detailed code examples, we will examine the values that can be assigned to the `TransactionAttribute` property in the deployment descriptor.

22.4.4 SETTING THE TRANSACTIONATTRIBUTE VALUE

The deployment descriptor specifies whether the bean uses container-managed or bean-managed transactions by setting the `TransactionAttribute` value. The `TransactionAttribute` value and description for a container-managed bean and its methods are:

- `TX_NOT_SUPPORTED`—The EJB method executes independent of the client transaction state without a transaction context. The client transaction, if any, is suspended, and DML performed by the EJB method is effectively rolled back. In Oracle8i, DML operations performed using SQLJ throw an excep-

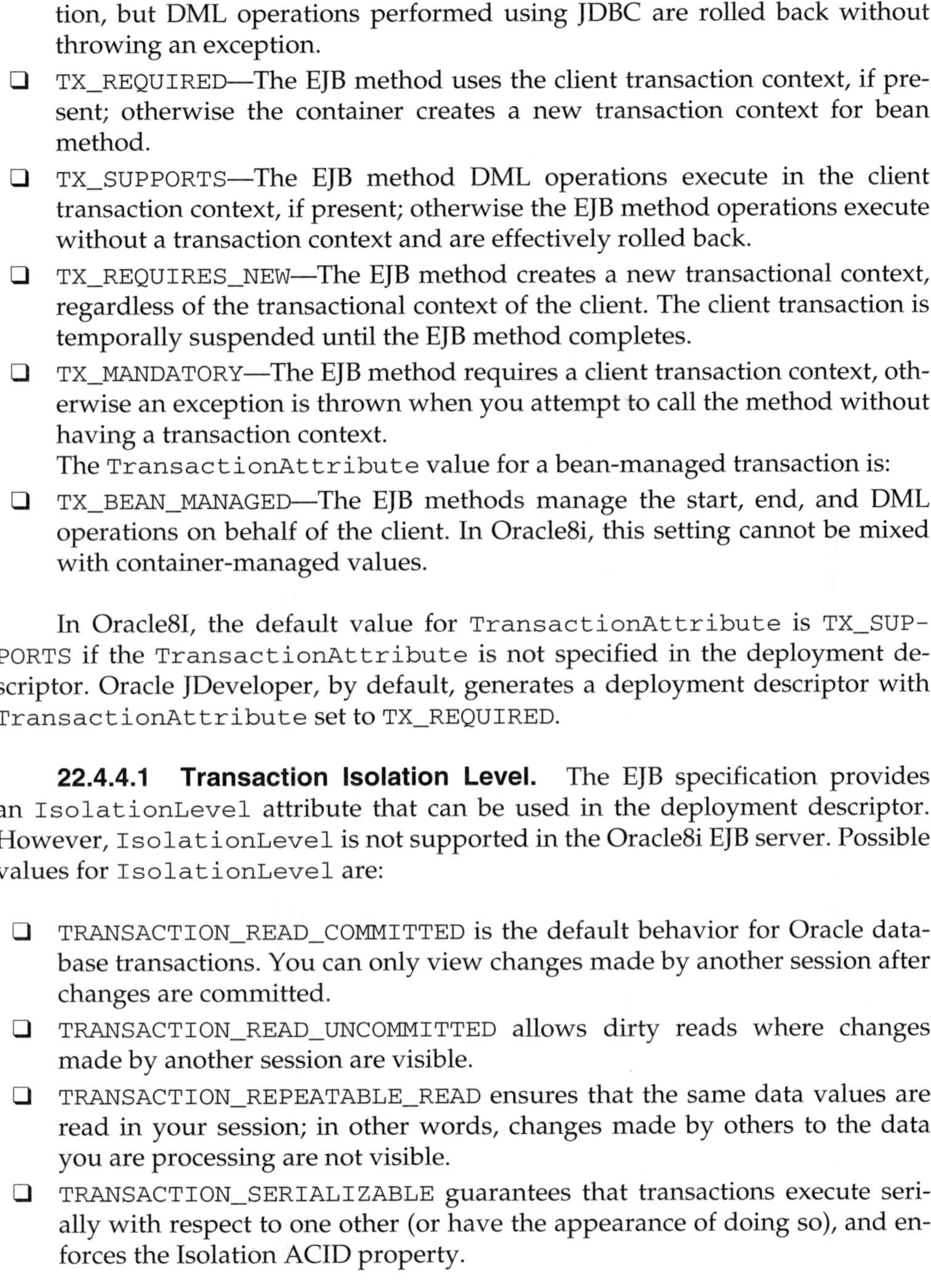

tion, but DML operations performed using JDBC are rolled back without throwing an exception.

- ❑ `TX_REQUIRED`—The EJB method uses the client transaction context, if present; otherwise the container creates a new transaction context for bean method.
- ❑ `TX_SUPPORTS`—The EJB method DML operations execute in the client transaction context, if present; otherwise the EJB method operations execute without a transaction context and are effectively rolled back.
- ❑ `TX_REQUIRES_NEW`—The EJB method creates a new transactional context, regardless of the transactional context of the client. The client transaction is temporally suspended until the EJB method completes.
- ❑ `TX_MANDATORY`—The EJB method requires a client transaction context, otherwise an exception is thrown when you attempt to call the method without having a transaction context.

The `TransactionAttribute` value for a bean-managed transaction is:

- ❑ `TX_BEAN_MANAGED`—The EJB methods manage the start, end, and DML operations on behalf of the client. In Oracle8i, this setting cannot be mixed with container-managed values.

In Oracle8I, the default value for `TransactionAttribute` is `TX_SUPPORTS` if the `TransactionAttribute` is not specified in the deployment descriptor. Oracle JDeveloper, by default, generates a deployment descriptor with `TransactionAttribute` set to `TX_REQUIRED`.

22.4.4.1 Transaction Isolation Level. The EJB specification provides an `IsolationLevel` attribute that can be used in the deployment descriptor. However, `IsolationLevel` is not supported in the Oracle8i EJB server. Possible values for `IsolationLevel` are:

- ❑ `TRANSACTION_READ_COMMITTED` is the default behavior for Oracle database transactions. You can only view changes made by another session after changes are committed.
- ❑ `TRANSACTION_READ_UNCOMMITTED` allows dirty reads where changes made by another session are visible.
- ❑ `TRANSACTION_REPEATABLE_READ` ensures that the same data values are read in your session; in other words, changes made by others to the data you are processing are not visible.
- ❑ `TRANSACTION_SERIALIZABLE` guarantees that transactions execute serially with respect to one other (or have the appearance of doing so), and enforces the Isolation ACID property.

22.4.5 APPLICATION SCENARIOS WITH EJB TRANSACTIONS

There are a variety of application designs that can be created for managing transactions with an EJB. Client-demarcated transactions involve a client application that starts the transaction, calls *transactional EJB methods* (i.e., methods that perform DML operations),[21] and ends the transaction. Transactional EJB methods are subject to container-managed persistence, and may also be invoked in a non-transactional context. Methods invoked without a transaction context usually have the `TransactionAttribute=TX_NOT_SUPPORTED` and cause an existing transaction to be suspended.

If you write a bean-managed transactional application, the client does not initiate or terminate the transaction but relies on calling the EJB methods in an appropriate sequence to allow the EJB to control the transaction boundaries and operations.

The example in this chapter is based around a client application that invokes an EJB, which in turn becomes the client to another EJB component, as depicted in Figure 22.3. The client can be any Java application (e.g., a servlet) that processes an HTTP request and uses an EJB to register a customer and record the customer's credit card details. The customer EJB processes the customer details and passes the credit card information to a credit card EJB for validation. The credit card EJB records invalid or expired credit card data in a database table during the transaction.

Figure 22.3 shows the interaction between the client application and the `CustomerEJB`, the `CustomerEJB`, and the `CreditCardEJB`. The `CustomerEJB` writes information for a newly registered customer into the `customer` table, and the `CreditCardEJB` writes information about invalid or expired cards to the `invalid_card` table.

The EJB specification provides for the possibility of the CustomerEJB and CreditCardEJB being in different EJB containers/servers; and the data tables being in different databases, for implementing a distributed transaction. In this case, the transaction context would need to be propagated to all components across connections and sessions, as an EJB in a different server would require a different session to be established. However, since not all containers can propagate the transaction context across sessions, EJB transactions cannot be supplemented across EJB containers. Thus, a true distributed transaction is not possible when calling EJB methods across different EJB containers.

In Figure 22.3, the client establishes a session with the `CustomerEJB`, and the `CustomerEJB` creates the `CreditCardEJB` instance in the same session as the `CustomerEJB`. Although the Oracle8i EJB environment supports the creation of multiple sessions either from the client or within an EJB, an Oracle8i transac-

---

[21]Transactional methods perform DML operations and should not directly call commit or rollback operations.

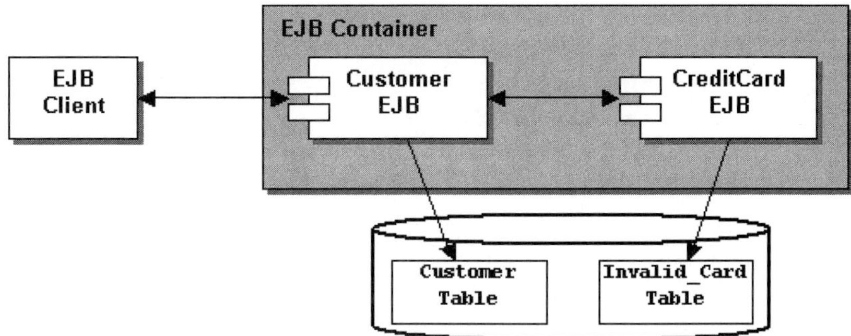

FIGURE 22.3 Customer registration and credit card validation.

tion context cannot span multiple sessions within the Oracle8i EJB server. This limitation applies to Oracle8i versions up to and including 8.1.6 (see below, section 22.5).

The following sections discuss client-managed transaction code coupled with container-managed enterprise beans (i.e., `CustomerEJB` and `CreditCardEJB`). An example of bean-managed code follows the container-managed examples.

22.4.6 CLIENT-MANAGED EJB TRANSACTIONS

A client application (e.g., a servlet) external to the EJB can create the transaction context using a transaction service. The client application manages the transaction boundaries by using the Oracle8i server as the transaction manager via the underlying CORBA COSTransaction services. The steps required to use client-managed transactions are:

- ❑ Initialize the transaction service to create a transaction context.
- ❑ Start the transaction.
- ❑ Call EJB methods to perform DML operations.
- ❑ End the transaction.

Listing 22.6 shows template code for a client-demarcated application using Oracle8i transaction services. The code demonstrates how to initialize the transaction service, start the transaction, look up an EJB bean to execute its methods within the transaction context, and end the transaction. The client example in Listing 22.6 invokes the EJB code shown in Listing 22.7 running as a container-managed bean.

```
package com.prenhall.OFJP.ejb;

import java.util.Hashtable;
import javax.naming.Context;
import javax.naming.InitialContext;
import oracle.aurora.jndi.sess_iiop.ServiceCtx;
import oracle.aurora.jts.client.AuroraTransactionService;
import oracle.aurora.jts.util.TS;
import com.prenhall.OFJP.ejb.Input;
import com.prenhall.OFJP.ejb.CustomerHome;
import com.prenhall.OFJP.ejb.CustomerRemote;

public class TxEJBClient {

  public static void setCustomerDetails(CustomerRemote r)
                           throws java.rmi.RemoteException {
    r.setId(Integer.parseInt(Input.readLine("Id: ")));
    r.setName(Input.readLine("Name: "));
    r.setSurname(Input.readLine("Surname: "));
    r.setPassword(Input.readLine("Password: "));
    r.setEmail(Input.readLine("Email: "));
    r.setCreditCard(new CreditCard(Input.readLine(
      "Card Type:"), Input.readLine("Card Number:")));
  }

  public static void main(String[] args) {
    CustomerHome homeInterface = null;
    Hashtable env = new Hashtable ();
    env.put (Context.URL_PKG_PREFIXES, "oracle.aurora.jndi");
    env.put (Context.SECURITY_PRINCIPAL,
             System.getProperty("user"));
    env.put (Context.SECURITY_CREDENTIALS,
             System.getProperty("password"));
    env.put (Context.SECURITY_AUTHENTICATION,
             ServiceCtx.NON_SSL_LOGIN);
    try {
      System.out.println("Set Initial Context");
      Context ic = new InitialContext (env);

      // initialize the transaction service
      System.out.println("Initialize Transaction Service");
      AuroraTransactionService.initialize (ic,
```

LISTING 22.6 Code example for client-managed transactions.

```
        "sess_iiop://localhost:2481:ORA816");
      homeInterface = (CustomerHome) ic.lookup(
        "sess_iiop://localhost:2481:ORA816/test/CustomerEJB");
    }
    catch (Exception e) {
    /* Possible Exceptions include:
       javax.naming.NamingException
       oracle.aurora.jndi.sess_iiop.ActivationException
       javax.naming.CommunicationException
       oracle.aurora.jts.util.NoTransactionServiceException
    */
    }

    CustomerRemote customerBean = null;
    try {
      System.out.println("Start TX");
      TS.getTS().getCurrent().begin();
      System.out.println("Transaction Name: " +
        TS.getTS().getCurrent().get_transaction_name());

      customerBean = homeInterface.create();
      setCustomerDetails(customerBean);
      System.out.println(customerBean.toText());
      customerBean.writeCustomer();

      System.out.println("Commit TX");
      TS.getTS().getCurrent().commit(false);
    }
    catch (Exception e) {
      System.out.println("Exception: " + e.getMessage());
      try {
         if (TS.getTS().getCurrent().get_status() ==
             org.omg.CosTransactions.Status.StatusActive) {
           System.out.println("Rollback TX");
           TS.getTS().getCurrent().rollback();
         }
      }
      catch (Exception ie) {}
    }
    finally {
      try { if (customerBean != null) customerBean.remove(); }
      catch (Exception e) {
```

LISTING 22.6 *Continued*

```
85:          /* Either: javax.ejb.RemoveException
86:             Or:     java.rmi.RemoteException */
87:        }
88:      }
89:    }
90: }
```

LISTING 22.6 *Continued*

Notes on Listing 22.6:

- The client code uses the public static method `readLine()` from a class called `Input` that prompts the user for some input and returns a string of user entered data. The code for Input class is listed at the end of this section.
- The exception handling is incomplete to focus on the main logic of the application.
- Lines 15 to 24 are a local method that receives the handle to the remote interface of the EJB object. The calls made to methods in setCustomerDetails() invoke EJB bean instance methods providing user-entered input for each value.
- Line 22 invokes the `CustomerEJB.setCreditCard()` method, which checks the validity and expiration date of the credit card. It is here that the `CustomerEJB` invokes a `CreditCardEJB` instance to perform the validation work (see Listing 22.7).
- Lines 29 to 35 set the environment to look up the CustomerEJB. Note that in lines 31 and 33 the user name and password are supplied via system properties (e.g., using the `-Duser=name -Dpassword=pswd` options on the `java` command line).
- Lines 42 and 43 initialize the transaction service after setting the initial context. The transaction service is identified by the `sess_iiop` URL provided in the second argument, using the initial context of the first argument in the `AuroraTransactionService.initialize()` method.
- Lines 44 and 45 look up the `CustomerEJB` home interface.
- Lines 49 to 53 list some of the exceptions that should be handled for the preceding `try` block.
- Line 59 requests a start transaction from the transaction service.
- Line 61 prints out a line to show the representation of the unique transaction name assigned to the transaction context. An example of an Oracle8i transaction name is: `ORACLE AURORA9735871233941ORACLE AURORA9735871233941`

- Line 63 creates the CustomerEJB instance.
- Line 64 calls the method to initialize the state of the CustomerEJB instance. If an exception occurs, the customer details are not permanently stored in the database table. If the credit card is invalid, the exception thrown can prevent the customer from being added to the database, depending on the value used in the `TransactionAttribute` for the credit card validation method (see the deployment descriptor settings for the CustomerEJB example in subsection 22.4.8).
- Line 65 calls the bean toText() method to return a string representation of the EJB state. This is a simple technique you can use to debug your EJB state from a client application. The toText() method may not be required In the final version of the bean if testing confirms that the EJB logic maintains the integrity of your bean state.
- Line 66 invokes the `writeCustomer()` method, which inserts the customer data into the customer table. The `writeCustomer()` method executes in the context of the client transaction (i.e., it joins the client transaction if the `TransactionAttribute` value for the method is set to `TX_REQUIRED`, or `TX_SUPPORTS` in the deployment descriptor. `TX_REQUIRED` is used in the deployment descriptor and the EJB container joins the client transaction).
- Line 69 performs the commit operation from the client via the transaction service.
- Line 77 requests a rollback operation from the transaction service if an exception has been thrown in the body of the try block, and if the transaction status is active.

The code executes by default with the EJB settings shown in Figure 22.4.

The default scenario has `TX_REQUIRED` set for all methods in the `CustomerEJB` and `CreditCardEJB`. As a result, if the `CreditCardEJB` throws an exception for an invalid card, the customer record and the invalid card data are not saved to the database because of the way the exception-handling code is written. If the `TransactionAttribute` is set to `TX_REQUIRES_NEW` for the method saving invalid card data in the `CreditCardEJB`, then the invalid credit card row will be inserted, but the customer record will not be saved. Changing `TransactionAttribute=TX_REQUIRES_NEW` would result in a more desirable behavior for the transaction of this example. The `TX_REQUIRES_NEW` setting causes the `CreditCardEJB` method to execute with its own transaction context, suspending the transaction started by the EJB client while the `CreditCardEJB` transaction is active.

See Listing 22.7 for the `CustomerEJB` implementation, and the `CreditCardEJB`. The `Input` class code is:

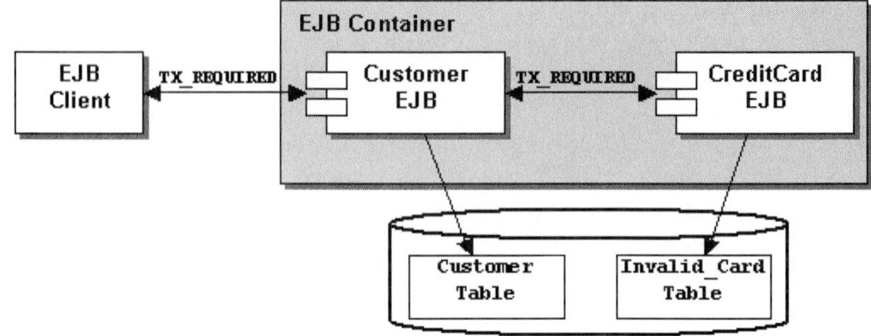

FIGURE 22.4 TransactionAttribute for `CustomerEJB` and `CreditCardEJB`.

```
package com.prenhall.OFJP.ejb;

public class Input {
  private static java.io.BufferedReader in =
     new java.io.BufferedReader(
       new java.io.InputStreamReader(System.in));

  public static String readLine(String prompt) {
    System.out.print(prompt);
    try {
       return in.readLine();
    }
    catch (Exception e) {
      return null;
    }
  }
}
```

The Input class creates a private static instance of a `BufferedReader` that wraps the standard input (`System.in`) as the source of input.

22.4.7 CONTAINER-MANAGED PERSISTENCE

Container-Managed Persistence is where the EJB container demarcates the transaction boundaries, meaning that the EJB container implicitly starts and ends (commits or rolls back) the transaction.

Figure 22.5 illustrates the flow of a container-managed transaction, assuming that the client has not started the transaction.

For the container-managed bean in Figure 22.5, the EJB container (EJB Object) starts a transaction at the beginning of a method call depending on the value

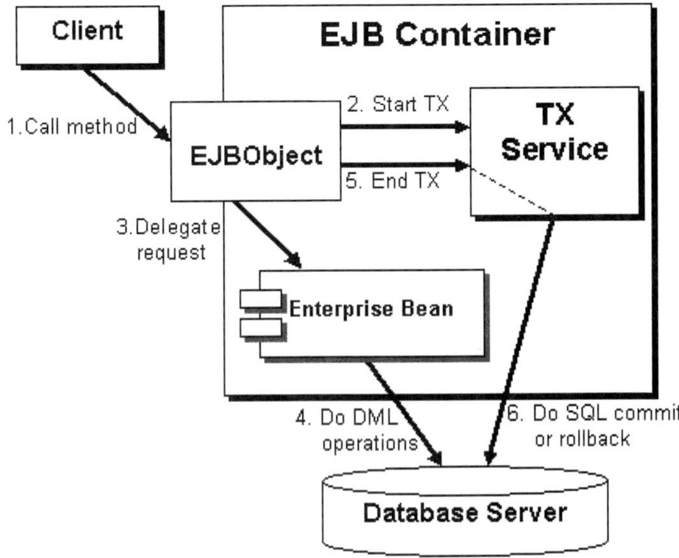

FIGURE 22.5 Container-managed transactions.

of `TransactionAttribute`. The EJB container ends the transaction when the method terminates by performing either a commit or a rollback operation. If the bean method terminates with an exception, the container performs a rollback operation. The steps shown in Figure 22.5 are:

- The client invokes an EJB method.
- The `EJBObject` starts a transaction with the EJB container transaction service, depending on the value set for `TransactionAttribute` in the deployment descriptor.
- The `EJBObject` delegates the method call to the enterprise bean.
- The enterprise bean performs one or more DML operations and returns.
- The `EJBObject` knows the method is finished and initiates an end transaction (commit or rollback) via the transaction service.
- The transaction service performs the SQL commit or rollback operation on the database to complete the transaction.

22.4.8 USING CONTAINER-MANAGED TRANSACTIONS

This section discusses the case when an EJB client initiates a transaction and calls bean methods in a container-managed environment. At the start of the method call, the EJB container controls transactional behavior such that the method can:

- Join the client transaction using the transaction context created by a client (for TX_REQUIRED or TX_SUPPORTS or TX_MANDATORY).
- Start a new transaction and suspend the client transaction (for TX_REQUIRES_NEW).
- Start a new transaction if the client has not already done so (for TX_REQUIRED or TX_REQUIRES_NEW).
- Run without a transaction context suspending the client transaction, if present (for TX_NOT_SUPPORTED).
- Terminate with an exception if a client-initiated transaction is not started (for TX_MANDATORY).

At the end of the called method, the EJB container can commit or rollback the transaction. As discussed in previous sections of this chapter, these behavioral characteristics depend on the TransactionAttribute value set in the EJB deployment descriptor.

Listing 22.7 shows the CustomerEJB code called by a client application using the following snippet of its deployment descriptor.

```
SessionBean com.prenhall.OFJP.ejb.CustomerEJB
{
  BeanHomeName = "test/CustomerEJB";
  HomeInterfaceClassName = com.prenhall.OFJP.ejb.CustomerHome;
  RemoteInterfaceClassName = com.prenhall.OFJP.ejb.CustomerRemote;

  SessionTimeout = 0;
  StateManagementType = STATEFUL_SESSION;

  TransactionAttribute = TX_REQUIRED;
  RunAsMode = CLIENT_IDENTITY;
  AllowedIdentities = { bookstore };
}
```

The CustomerEJB deployment descriptor specifies that all methods will be subject to behavior required with TransactionAttribute=TX_REQUIRED (i.e., all methods join the client transaction if present or start a new one_. The CustomerRemote interface code is:

```
package com.prenhall.OFJP.ejb;
import .*;
import javax.ejb.*;
import com.prenhall.OFJP.ejb.*;

public interface CustomerRemote extends EJBObject {
```

```
  public CreditCard getCreditCard() throws RemoteException;
  public String getEmail() throws RemoteException;
  public int getId() throws RemoteException;
  public String getName() throws RemoteException;
  public String getPassword() throws RemoteException;
  public String getSurname() throws RemoteException;
  public void readCustomer(int id) throws RemoteException;
  public void setCreditCard(CreditCard newCreditCard)
    throws RemoteException;
  public void setEmail(String newEmail) throws RemoteException;
  public void setId(int newId) throws RemoteException;
  public void setName(String newName) throws RemoteException;
  public void setPassword(String newPassword)
    throws RemoteException;
  public void setSurname(String newSurname)
    throws RemoteException;
  public String toText() throws RemoteException;
  public int writeCustomer() throws RemoteException;
}
```

The `CustomerHome` interface code is:

```
package com.prenhall.OFJP.ejb;
import java.rmi.*;
import javax.ejb.*;

public interface CustomerHome extends EJBHome {
  public CustomerRemote create()
     throws RemoteException, CreateException;
}
```

The `CustomerEJB` code is:

```
package com.prenhall.OFJP.ejb;
import java.rmi.RemoteException;
import javax.ejb.*;
import javax.naming.*;
import com.prenhall.OFJP.ejb.*;
import java.sql.*;
import java.util.Hashtable;
import com.prenhall.OFJP.ejb.CreditCardHome;
import com.prenhall.OFJP.ejb.CreditCardRemote;

```

LISTING 22.7 Example of a `CustomerEJB` container-managed bean.

```
public class CustomerEJB implements SessionBean{
  private int id;
  private String name;
  private String surname;
  private String email;
  private String password;
  private CreditCard creditCard;

  public CustomerEJB() {}

  public void ejbCreate()
    throws RemoteException, CreateException {}

  public void ejbActivate() throws RemoteException {}
  public void ejbPassivate() throws RemoteException {}
  public void ejbRemove() throws RemoteException {}

  public void setSessionContext(SessionContext ctx)
    throws RemoteException {}

  public int getId() throws RemoteException { return id; }
  public void setId(int newId) throws RemoteException {
    id = newId;
  }

  public String getName() throws RemoteException {
    return name;
  }
  public void setName(String newName)
    throws RemoteException {
    name = newName;
  }

  public String getSurname() throws RemoteException {
    return surname;
  }
  public void setSurname(String newSurname)
    throws RemoteException {
    surname = newSurname;
  }

  public String getEmail() throws RemoteException {
    return email;
  }
```

LISTING 22.7 *Continued*

```
  public void setEmail(String newEmail)
    throws RemoteException {
    email = newEmail;
  }

  public String getPassword() throws RemoteException {
    return password;
  }
  public void setPassword(String newPassword)
    throws RemoteException {
    password = newPassword;
  }

  public CreditCard getCreditCard() throws RemoteException {
    return creditCard;
  }

  public void setCreditCard(CreditCard newCreditCard)
    throws RemoteException {
    creditCard = newCreditCard;
    checkCard();
  }

  private void checkCard() throws RemoteException {
    String ejbUrl =
     "sess_iiop://thisServer/:thisSession/test/CreditCardEJB";
    Hashtable env = new Hashtable();
    env.put(Context.URL_PKG_PREFIXES, "oracle.aurora.jndi");
    CreditCardHome homeInterface = null;
    CreditCardRemote remoteInterface = null;
    try {
      Context ic = new InitialContext(env);
      homeInterface = (CreditCardHome) ic.lookup(ejbUrl);
      remoteInterface =
         (CreditCardRemote)homeInterface.create(creditCard);
      try {
        remoteInterface.validateCard();
      }
      catch (RemoteException e) {
        remoteInterface.insertInvalidCard();
        throw new RemoteException(
          "Invalid CreditCard: " + e.getMessage());
      }
    }
```

LISTING 22.7 *Continued*

```
   catch (Exception e) {
      throw new RemoteException(
        "Unable to activate : " + e.getMessage());
    }
  }

  public int writeCustomer() throws RemoteException {
    int rowCnt = 0;
    Connection conn = null;
    PreparedStatement ps = null;
    try {
      conn=DriverManager.getConnection("jdbc:oracle:kprb:");

      ps = conn.prepareStatement(
         "insert into customer (id, name, surname, " +
         "email,password,credit_card_type,credit_card_nbr, "+
         "month_expired, year_expired) " +
         "values (?,?,?,?,?,?,?,?,?)");
      ps.setInt(1, id);
      ps.setString(2, name);
      ps.setString(3, surname);
      ps.setString(4, email);
      ps.setString(5, password);
      ps.setString(6, creditCard.getCardType());
      ps.setString(7, creditCard.getCardNumber());
      ps.setString(8, creditCard.getMonthExpired());
      ps.setString(9, creditCard.getYearExpired());
      rowCnt = ps.executeUpdate();
    }
    catch (SQLException e) {
      throw new RemoteException(e.getMessage()); }
    finally {
      if (ps != null)
        try { ps.close(); } catch (SQLException e) {}
    }
    return rowCnt;
  }

  public void readCustomer(int id) throws RemoteException {
    Connection conn = null;
    PreparedStatement ps = null;
    ResultSet rset = null;
    try {
```

LISTING 22.7 *Continued*

```
      conn=DriverManager.getConnection("jdbc:oracle:kprb:");

      ps = conn.prepareStatement(
         "select id, name, surname, email, password, " +
             "credit_card_type, credit_card_nbr, " +
             "month_expired, year_expired " +
         "from customer where id = ?");
      ps.setInt(1, id);
      rset = ps.executeQuery();
      if (rset.next()) {
        name = rset.getString(2);
        surname = rset.getString(3);
        email = rset.getString(4);
        password = rset.getString(5);
        creditCard = new CreditCard();
        creditCard.setCardType(rset.getString(6));
        creditCard.setCardNumber(rset.getString(7));
        creditCard.setMonthExpired(rset.getString(8));
        creditCard.setYearExpired(rset.getString(9));
      }
      else {
        throw new RemoteException(
          "Customer: " + id + " not found");
      }
    }
    catch (SQLException e) {
      throw new RemoteException(
        "SQLException: " + e.getMessage());
    }
    finally {
      if (rset != null)
        try { rset.close(); } catch (SQLException e) {}
      if (ps != null)
        try { ps.close(); } catch (SQLException e) {}
    }
  }

  public String toText() throws RemoteException {
   return id + " " + name + " " + surname +
          " mailto:" + email + " " + creditCard;
  }
}
```

LISTING 22.7 *Continued*

Notes on Listing 22.7:

- Since the bulk of the method calls in this example are self-documenting, subsequent notes cover the `setCreditCard()`, `checkCard()`, `writeCustomer()`, and `readCustomer()` methods.
- Line 75 calls the `checkCard()` method to validate the credit card details in the customer bean instance, when the `setCreditCard()` method is invoked from a client.
- Lines 78 to 103 show the checkCard() method that creates a CreditCardEJB instance in the same session as the CustomerEJB. The CreditCardEJB instance is used for validation purposes.
- Line 80 forms a URL string for the sess_iiop request to lookup the EJB instance. The main difference from a Java client external to the EJB is the use of the string `//thisServer/:thisSession` in the URL. Using `//thisServer/:thisSession` in the URL indicates to the EJB server that you want to create a connection in the same session as the client request for this `CustomerEJB`. In release Oracle8i 8.1.7 and later, you can omit the text `//thisServer/:thisSession` from the URL, and only provide the JNDI name for another bean if you want to invoke the other EJB in the same session. If you use a host name and IIOP port, as in the code in the EJB client, then you establish a new session. Remember that the transaction context cannot be propagated to another session because of limitations in the Oracle8i EJB server implementation.
- Lines 81 and 82 set the environment for the JNDI initial context. Note that you do not have to provide security credentials, since you are already authenticated in the server if executing this code in the `CustomerEJB`.
- Lines 87 to 89 create the CreditCardEJB instance in the same way you would create an EJB from any other client, by looking up the home interface, creating an EJB object implementing the remote interface, and invoking the methods.
- Line 91 calls the `CreditCardEJB validateCard()` method (see Listing 22.8) that throws an exception if there is an error. The catch block traps the exception and allows the `insertInvalidCard()` method to be called to execute the SQL INSERT operation to save the invalid card details. If the `insertInvalidCard()` method executes with `TransactionAttribute=TX_REQUIRED` or `TX_SUPPORTS`, unhandled exceptions will cause the EJB container to roll back the operation. If the `insertInvalidCard()` method executes with `TransactionAttribute=TX_REQUIRES_NEW`, then the INSERT operation will have been committed and saved before the exceptions are thrown.
- Lines 105 to 135 write the customer data to the `customer` database table. The code contains classic JDBC calls using a `PreparedStatement`. The only step not required is that of loading the JDBC driver, and the JDBC con-

nection uses the Oracle server-side internal driver with URL "`jdbc:oracle:kprb`" to form an internal connection (see Chapter 9 for more on Oracle JDBC drivers). From Oracle8i 8.1.6, you can use a server-side Oracle JDB-Thin driver to create a new session that connects to a remote database, subject to having the appropriate Java2 security rights granted to the user executing the JDBC code.

- Lines 137 to 177 show a convenient method of allowing the client to find an existing customer record in the database by populating the `CustomerEJB` instance state with values from the columns.

The `writeCustomer()` method could be rewritten using SQLJ as follows:

```
public int writeCustomer() throws RemoteException {
  int rowCnt = 0;
  try {
    #sql { insert into customer (id, name, surname,
           email, password, credit_card_type, credit_card_nbr,
           month_expired, year_expired)
           values (:id, :name, :surname,
                   :email, :password, :(creditCard.getCardType()),
                   :(creditCard.getCardNumber()),
                   :(creditCard.getMonthExpired()),
                   :(creditCard.getYearExpired())) };
    rowCnt=DefaultContext.getExecutionContext().getUpdateCount();
  }
  catch (SQLException e) {
    throw new RemoteException(e.getMessage());
  }
  return rowCnt;
}
```

22.4.8.1 A Note on SQLJ vs. JDBC in a Container-Managed EJB.

Test done with Oracle8i 8.1.6 have revealed that the server-side SQLJ runtime engine throws the following exception if an EJB method using the `TX_SUPPORTS` value for `TransactionAttribute` is invoked from a client without a transaction context:

```
java.sql.SQLException: Not in a transaction
```

A method executing JDBC code using `TX_SUPPORTS` without client transaction context does not throw an exception, and the SQL operations are rolled back.

The rest of the code to view is the `CreditCardJEJB` code, whose client is the `CustomerEJB`, via its `checkCard()` method. The code for the `CreditCardRemote` interface is:

```
package com.prenhall.OFJP.ejb;
import java.rmi.*;
import javax.ejb.*;
import com.prenhall.OFJP.ejb.CreditCard;

public interface CreditCardRemote extends EJBObject {

  public String getCardDetails() throws java.rmi.RemoteException;
  public void insertInvalidCard() throws RemoteException;
  public void setCardNumber(String newNumber)
    throws RemoteException;
  public void setCreditCard(CreditCard newCard)
    throws RemoteException;
  public void validateCard() throws RemoteException;
}
```

The code for `CreditCardHome` interface is:

```
package com.prenhall.OFJP.ejb;
import java.rmi.*;
import javax.ejb.*;
import com.prenhall.OFJP.ejb.CreditCard;

public interface CreditCardHome extends EJBHome {

  public CreditCardRemote create()
    throws RemoteException, CreateException;

  public CreditCardRemote create(CreditCard c)
    throws RemoteException, CreateException;
}
```

The Home interface has an overridden `create()` method to allow a client application to instantiate the `CreditCardEJB` with or without a `CreditCard` instance. The code for `CreditCardEJB` is:

```
package com.prenhall.OFJP.ejb;
import java.rmi.RemoteException;
import javax.ejb.*;
import java.sql.*;
import java.util.Calendar;
import javax.jts.UserTransaction;

```

LISTING 22.8 Example of `CreditCardEJB` credit card validation code.

```
public class CreditCardEJB implements SessionBean {

  SessionContext sessCtx = null;
  CreditCard cardInfo = null;

  public void ejbCreate()
    throws RemoteException, CreateException {}

  public void ejbCreate(CreditCard c)
    throws RemoteException, CreateException {
    cardInfo = c;
  }

  public void ejbActivate() throws RemoteException {}
  public void ejbPassivate() throws RemoteException {}
  public void ejbRemove() throws RemoteException {}

  public void setSessionContext(SessionContext ctx)
    throws RemoteException {
    sessCtx = ctx;
  }

  public void setCreditCard(CreditCard newCard)
    throws RemoteException {
     cardInfo = newCard;
  }

  public String getCardDetails() throws RemoteException {
    if (cardInfo == null) {
      throw new RemoteException(
        "Exception: create or set the card first");
    }
    return cardInfo.toString();
  }

  public void setCardNumber(String newNumber)
    throws RemoteException {
     if (cardInfo != null) {
       cardInfo.setCardNumber(newNumber);
     }
     else {
       throw new RemoteException(
```

LISTING 22.8 *Continued*

```
         "Exception: create or set the card first");
    }
  }

  public void insertInvalidCard() throws RemoteException {
    Connection conn = null;
    PreparedStatement ps = null;
    if (cardInfo != null) {
      try {
        conn = DriverManager.getConnection(
                 "jdbc:oracle:kprb:");
        ps = conn.prepareStatement(
          "insert into invalid_card " +
          "(nbr, card_type, month_exp, year_exp) " +
          "values (?,?,?,?)");
        ps.setString(1, cardInfo.getCardNumber());
        ps.setString(2, cardInfo.getCardType());
        ps.setString(3, cardInfo.getMonthExpired());
        ps.setString(4, cardInfo.getYearExpired());
        ps.executeUpdate();
      }
      catch (SQLException e) {
        throw new RemoteException(
          "SQLException: " + e.getMessage());
      }
      finally {
        if (ps != null) try { ps.close(); }
        catch (SQLException e) {}
      }
    }
    else {
      throw new RemoteException(
       "CreditCardEJB: CardInfo has null fields " +
       "and does not represent a valid card");
    }
  }

  public void validateCard() throws RemoteException {
    Connection conn = null;
    PreparedStatement ps = null;
    ResultSet rset = null;
    int currYear = Calendar.getInstance().get(Calendar.YEAR);
```

LISTING 22.8 *Continued*

```
    int currYearNoCentury =
      Calendar.getInstance().get(Calendar.YEAR) % 100;
    int currMonth = Calendar.getInstance()
                     .get(Calendar.MONTH) + 1;
    int currCentury = currYear - currYearNoCentury;

    if (cardInfo != null) {
       // Check if card is in the invalid card database
       try {
         conn = DriverManager.getConnection(
                           "jdbc:oracle:kprb:");
         ps = conn.prepareStatement(
                "select 1 from invalid_card where nbr = ?");
         ps.setString(1, cardInfo.getCardNumber());
         rset = ps.executeQuery();
         if (rset.next()) {
           throw new RemoteException(
            "Exception: card #" +
            cardInfo.getCardNumber() + " is not valid");
         }
       }
       catch (SQLException e) {
         throw new RemoteException(e.getMessage());
       }
       finally {
         if (rset != null)
           try { rset.close(); } catch (SQLException e) {}
         if (ps != null)
           try { ps.close(); } catch (SQLException e) {}
       }
       // Check card number length
       if (cardInfo.getCardNumber().length() != 16) {
         throw new RemoteException(
           "Exception: Card number must contain 16 digits");
       }
       // Check Card Expiry details
       int yearExpired = Integer.parseInt(
                            cardInfo.getYearExpired());
       if (yearExpired < 50) {
         yearExpired += currCentury;
       }
       else {
```

LISTING 22.8 *Continued*

```
134:         yearExpired += (currCentury-100);
135:       }
136:
137:       if (yearExpired < currYear) {
138:         throw new RemoteException(
139:           "Exception: Card Expired");
140:       }
141:       else {
142:         if ((yearExpired == currYear) && (currMonth >
143:             Integer.parseInt(cardInfo.getMonthExpired()))) {
144:           throw new RemoteException("Card Expired");
145:         }
146:       }
147:     }
148:     else {
129:       throw new RemoteException(
150:        "CardInfo null and is not a valid card");
151:     }
152:   }
153: }
```

LISTING 22.8 *Continued*

Notes on Listing 22.8:

- Line 11 stores an instance of a CreditCard object. The technique of creating an EJB instance variable for an object and providing wrapper methods that invoke methods of the object in the EJB instance variable is a useful way to create an EJB out of an existing class. The EJB does not provide many wrapper methods for the credit card instance variable.
- Line 18 saves the credit card instance in the EJB `cardInfo` variable if the client creates the `CreditCardEJB` with a `CreditCard` object in the first parameter. The `cardInfo` instance must not be `null` if the validation logic is invoked.
- Lines 25 to 28 show how you can save the SessionContext object provided by the EJB container when the EJB instance is created. You can use the session context object for bean-managed transactions (see subsection 22.4.10 for an example).
- Lines 35 to 41 represent an example wrapper function for the `CreditCard` instance held in the `cardInfo` variable. The `getCardDetails()` method returns the string form of the credit card instance.
- Lines 54 to 85 contain the code for inserting the details of a credit card into the `invalid_card` database table. This method is called by the client when

it catches an exception from a call to the `validateCard()` method. Once again, the code is standard JDBC using the Oracle8i server-side internal JDBC driver.

- Lines 86 to 153 represent the business logic for validating a credit card. The logic first searches a database table for the card by number and then checks the length of the card number. An exception is thrown if the card number is not 16 digits long. If the length check is valid, the expiration date is checked.
- Lines 91 to 96 initialize local variables for comparing card expiration dates with the current date and century.
- Lines 99 to 121 perform a check for invalid cards stored in the `invalid_card` table to provide a predefined list of invalid cards. If a card number is found in the table, no additional checks are done.
- Lines 122 to 126 check the length of the credit card number to see whether it contains 16 digits; if not, an exception is thrown.
- Lines 127 to 147 check the card expiry dates to the current date based on the month and year. Because the year is stored in the database with two digits, the century value is used in calculations to assist with date validation. To keep your code simple, dates should always be stored as four digits; however, the example provides a suitable example of validation. The previous century is used if the year of the card year expired is in the range 50 to 99, and the current century is used if the card year expired is in the range 00 to 49. This is a similar algorithm to the Oracle RR date format.

The deployment descriptor for the CreditCardEJB was created with the following entries:

```
SessionBean com.prenhall.OFJP.ejb.CreditCardEJB
{
  BeanHomeName="test/CreditCardEJB";
  HomeInterfaceClassName=com.prenhall.OFJP.ejb.CreditCardHome;
  RemoteInterfaceClassName=com.prenhall.OFJP.ejb.CreditCardRemote;

  SessionTimeout = 0;
  StateManagementType = STATEFUL_SESSION;

  TransactionAttribute = TX_REQUIRED;
  RunAsMode = CLIENT_IDENTITY;
  AllowedIdentities = { bookstore };

  void insertInvalidCard ()
  {
    TransactionAttribute = TX_REQUIRES_NEW;
```

```
    RunAsMode = CLIENT_IDENTITY;
    AllowedIdentities = { bookstore };
  }
}
```

The `TransactionAttribute` value for the `insertInvalidCard()` method has changed to `TX_REQUIRES_NEW`, allowing the method to override the bean setting of `TX_REQUIRED`. The `TX_REQUIRES_NEW` value ensures that an invalid card is stored in the `invalid_card` table, and not rolled back with an exception raised by subsequent code.

22.4.9 BEAN-MANAGED PERSISTENCE

Bean-Managed Persistence is where the bean developer writes the code to demarcate transaction boundaries (i.e., the bean code explicitly starts and ends the transaction).

Figure 22.6 represents the flow of the transaction when a non-transactional client calls an EJB method that is subject to bean-managed persistence.

An EJB method in a bean-managed transaction must explicitly start the transaction, perform the DML operations, and end the transaction. The bean method uses the transaction service of the EJB container to start and end the transaction through well-defined interfaces provided by the container. Unlike container-managed transactions, a bean-managed transaction does not have to

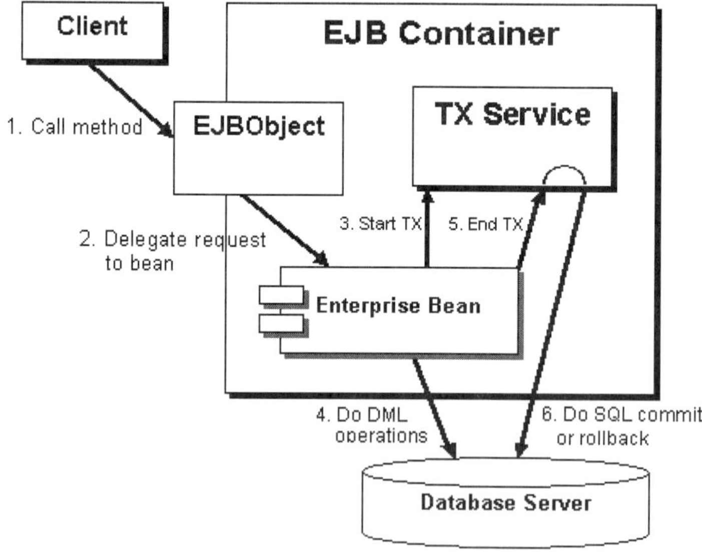

FIGURE 22.6 Bean-managed transactions.

start at the beginning of a method or terminate at the end of the same method call (i.e., bean-managed transactions can span method calls). Assuming that the transaction is managed in a single method call, the steps shown in Figure 22.6 are:

1. The client invokes an EJB method.
2. The `EJBObject` delegates the method call to the enterprise bean.
3. The enterprise bean method requests a start transaction from the EJB container providing the transaction service. The value of `TransactionAttribute` must be `TX_BEAN_MANAGED`.
4. The enterprise bean method performs one or more DML operations and optional returns.
5. The same or another enterprise bean method requests an end to the transaction, a commit or rollback operation, via the transaction service.
6. The transaction service performs the commit or rollback operation in the database.

Note that methods in a session EJB bean class, whether container-managed or bean-managed, must still perform the actual database DML operations. By contrast, an EJB container supporting container-managed entity beans must also provide the means to perform the DML operations.

22.4.10 USING BEAN-MANAGED TRANSACTIONS

A client application that calls EJB methods subject to bean-managed persistence does not need to start a transaction. The bean does the transaction management via the `javax.ejb.UserTransaction` interface. The client application controls the sequence in which the methods are called, but the EJB methods control when the transaction starts and ends. This section rewrites the `CreditCardEJB` to use a bean-managed transaction management. The key steps in bean-managed transactions are:

- ❑ The EJB instance must save the `SessionContext` object passed to the `setSessionContext()` method.
- ❑ To start the transaction use a `SessionContext` object to get an object implementing the `javax.ejb.UserTransaction` interface, and call the `begin()` method from `UserTransaction`.
- ❑ Perform one or more DML statements.
- ❑ To end the transaction, call the `commit()` or `rollback()` method in the `UserTransaction` interface.

Listing 22.9 shows the `CreditCardEJB insertInvalidCard()` method as modified to use bean-managed transaction control and methods that support writing bean-managed code. `CreditCardEJB` methods that have not been changed are not shown in the code.

```
package com.prenhall.OFJP.ejb;
import java.rmi.RemoteException;
import javax.ejb.*;
import java.sql.*;
import java.util.Calendar;
import javax.jts.UserTransaction;

public class CreditCardEJB implements SessionBean {

  SessionContext sessCtx = null;

  CreditCard cardInfo = null;
  public void ejbCreate()
    throws RemoteException, CreateException {}

  public void ejbCreate(CreditCard c)
    throws RemoteException, CreateException {
    cardInfo = c;
  }

  public void setSessionContext(SessionContext ctx)
    throws RemoteException {
    sessCtx = ctx;
  }

  :
  public void insertInvalidCard() throws RemoteException {
    Connection conn = null;
    PreparedStatement ps = null;
    if (cardInfo != null) {
      UserTransaction userTx = sessCtx.getUserTransaction();
      try {
        userTx.begin();
        conn = DriverManager.getConnection(
                                "jdbc:oracle:kprb:");
        ps = conn.prepareStatement(
          "insert into invalid_card " +
          "(nbr, card_type, month_exp, year_exp) " +
          "values (?,?,?,?)");
```

LISTING 22.9 Using a bean-managed transaction in `CreditCardEJB`.

```
40:           ps.setString(1, cardInfo.getCardNumber());
41:           ps.setString(2, cardInfo.getCardType());
42:           ps.setString(3, cardInfo.getMonthExpired());
43:           ps.setString(4, cardInfo.getYearExpired());
44:           ps.executeUpdate();
45:           userTx.commit();
46:         }
47:         catch (SQLException e) {
48:           userTx.rollback();
49:           throw new RemoteException(
50:             "SQLException: " + e.getMessage());
51:         }
52:         finally {
53:           if (ps != null)
54:             try { ps.close(); } catch (SQLException e) {}
55:         }
56:       }
57:       else {
58:         throw new RemoteException(
59:            "CreditCardEJB: Null cardInfo is invalid");
60:       }
61:     }
62:     :
63: }
```

LISTING 22.9 *Continued*

Notes on Listing 22.9:

- Line 6 imports the `UserTransaction` interface, providing the gateway to the transaction services of the EJB container.
- Line 10 creates the `SessionContext` instance variable that provides the means to obtain the object implementing the `UserTransaction` interface.
- Line 23 saves the session context object in the `sessCtx` variable. The `set-SessionContext()` method is called by the EJB container during bean initialization.
- Line 31 gets the `UserTransaction` object via a method call from the session context instance variable.
- Line 33 asks the EJB container to start the transaction and creates a transaction context.
- Lines 34 5o 44 perform the transactional operation (i.e., inserting the invalid credit card).

- Line 45 ends the transaction with a commit request if the insert operation is successful.
- Line 48 calls the rollback operation via the `UserTransaction` interface for unsuccessful operations.

Although the bean methods control the transaction boundaries, the bean issues the start and end transaction requests to the EJB container. The deployment descriptor used for the bean-managed `CreditCardEJB` is:

```
SessionBean com.prenhall.OFJP.ejb.CreditCardEJB
{
  BeanHomeName="test/CreditCardEJB";
  HomeInterfaceClassName=com.prenhall.OFJP.ejb.CreditCardHome;
  RemoteInterfaceClassName=com.prenhall.OFJP.ejb.CreditCardRemote;

  SessionTimeout = 0;
  StateManagementType = STATEFUL_SESSION;

  TransactionAttribute = TX_BEAN_MANAGED;
  RunAsMode = CLIENT_IDENTITY;
  AllowedIdentities = { bookstore };

  void insertInvalidCard ()
  {
    TransactionAttribute = TX_BEAN_MANAGED;
    RunAsMode = CLIENT_IDENTITY;
    AllowedIdentities = { bookstore };
  }
}
```

Instead of the container-managed bean calling the `insertInvalidCard()` method with `TransactionAttribute=TX_REQUIRES_NEW`, an alternative solution is to make the `insertInvalidCard()` method manage the transaction with `TransactionArribute=TX_BEAN_MANAGED`.

22.5 RESTRICTIONS AND LIMITATIONS WITH ORACLE8i EJBS

Container-managed and bean-managed transactions are limited by the fact that a transaction context cannot span multiple sessions. Each new session connection requires a new transaction context. The JTS transaction API supplied with Oracle8i JServer manages only one resource: an Oracle8i database session. A container-managed or bean-managed transaction in Oracle8i cannot span multiple servers or multiple database sessions in a single service.[22] Therefore, a transaction context is never propagated to another session or outside the server. However, one or more objects can be involved in a transaction within the same session, and can encompass calls to one or more methods among the objects.

The limitation means that you cannot have distributed transactions within the server, and thus an EJB starting a transaction cannot propagate the transaction to another EJB object within the same server. Distributed transactions among multiple database servers, supporting the required two-phase commit protocol, will become available in releases after Oracle8i 8.1.6 JServer.

The EJB 1.0 specification identifies the following programming restrictions that must be followed by the methods in your EJB class:

- An EJB should not start new threads or attempt to terminate the running thread. In Oracle8i release 8.1.6 or earlier, no exception is thrown if an EJB starts a new thread, but application behavior becomes unpredictable due to interactions with local thread objects in the ORB.
- A method is not allowed to use thread synchronization primitives (e.g., synchronized blocks or methods) and calls to thread wait() or notify() methods.
- A method is not allowed to call the transaction manager directly unless the EJB is deployed with the TX_BEAN_MANAGED transaction attribute.
- The EJB is not allowed to change its `java.security.Identity`. If this is attempted, then a `java.security.SecurityException` is thrown.
- An EJB should not issue direct SQL commit or rollback commands using SQLJ or JDBC.

22.6 EJB SECURITY IN ORACLE8i

The examples presented in this chapter have been developed by a single database user who owns all the EJB classes in the server and all the database tables accessed by the EJB. This section examines the tasks to be performed to allow a user to invoke your EJB from a client application using the user's name and password, which differ from those of the owner of the EJB classes. To share access to an EJB, consider the layers of security applied to an EJB deployed in an Oracle8i EJB server. Figure 22.7 portrays the layers of access control in the Oracle8i database.

As seen in Figure 22.7, the EJB security model in Oracle8i involves multiple layers of access control. In order of access from the client, these layers are:

---

[22]A client application can start a transaction that spans multiple database sessions using the implementation of JTS API supplied with Oracle8i 8.1.6 or earlier releases. The JTS API is intended for the client to initiate and terminate a transaction outside the server via a transaction service.

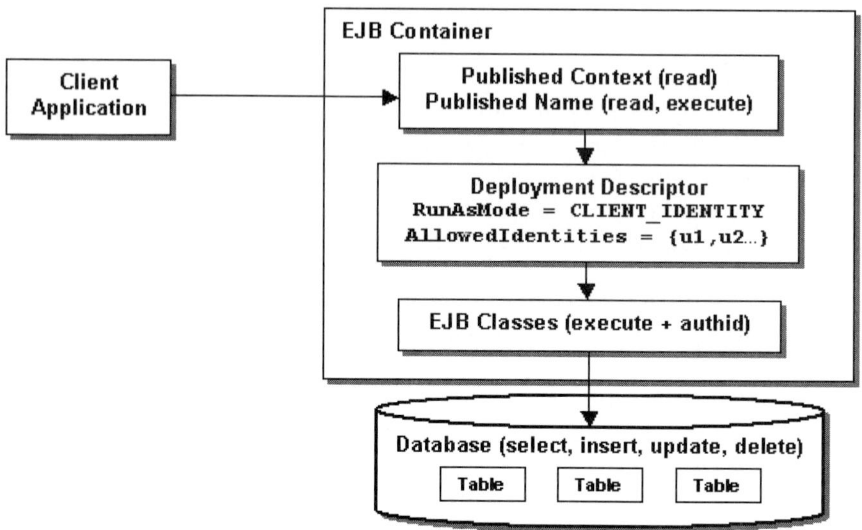

FIGURE 22.7 Access control to execute an EJB in Oracle8i.

- ❑ Permission to look up and access the published name of the EJB. Managed by security settings in the deployment descriptor, or commands entered in the `sess_sh` or `publish` command-line tool.[23]
- ❑ Permission to execute EJB methods. Managed through deployment descriptor settings for `RunAsMode` and `AllowedIdentities` attributes.
- ❑ Execute access to the EJB Java classes in the database. Managed by the deployment process, based on settings in the deployment descriptor or through the SQL `GRANT` statement.
- ❑ Access privileges to perform the desired SQL operations on the database objects used by the EJB code. Managed with the SQL `GRANT` statement or the `AUTHID` mode of the Java class.

Exceptions occur if the database tables cannot be accessed with the proper privileges. In addition to the above three layers, you can enable the Secure Sockets Layer (SSL) for authentication and encryption on the IIOP communication path between the client application and the EJB. The process of enabling SSL access to an EJB is not covered in this book.

22.6.1 CONTROLLING ACCESS TO THE PUBLISHED NAME

The published name for the EJB home object, specified in the deployment descriptor, is automatically created when you run the `deployejb` command-line tool or the deployment wizard in Oracle JDeveloper.

---

[23]The `sess_sh` tool is covered in detail in Chapter 24.

In the Oracle8i object namespace, a published name is called a *published object*. Published objects are created in a *published context*. A simple analogy is a file system where:

- A published context is like a directory name.
- A published object is like a file name in a directory. A file name in a directory is associated to data held in the file. Similarly, a published name is associated with the EJB home object..

Using the `sess_sh` or `publish` command-line tool provided with your Oracle8i software, you can manually create a published context that contains one or more published objects in the Oracle8i object namespace. Both tools also provide a way to set the security access rights to a published name for client applications.

The following list of commands shows how to start the `sess_sh` tool and manually list the access rights to a published context and published object; and then grant read execute access to a published object. For a more detailed description of the `sess_sh` tool, see Chapter 24.

```
os_prompt>sess_sh -u bookstore -p bookstore
                  -s sess_iiop://localhost:2481:ORA816
--Aurora/ORB Session Shell--
--type "help" at the command line for help message
$
```

The preceding command starts the `sess_sh` as the user `bookstore`. The command-line options are:

- `-u` for the user name
- `-p` for the password
- `-s` for the Oracle8i Object name service

```
$ ls
bin/    etc/    test/
```

The ls command displays published contexts and objects. Published context names (represented as the directory path) are displayed with a trailing forward-slash character. The trailing forward slash is not displayed for published object names. The published context `test/` is predefined when you create the Oracle8i database. The next `ls -l` command shows that all registered users (PUBLIC) in the database have read, write, and execute access to the published context `test/`.

```
$ ls -l
 Read      Write     Exec      Owner     Date Time     Name        Schema
Class
Helper
PUBLIC    SYS       PUBLIC    SYS       Feb 27 12:46 bin/
PUBLIC    SYS       PUBLIC    SYS       Feb 27 12:46 etc/
PUBLIC    PUBLIC    PUBLIC    SYS       Feb 27 12:46 test/

$ cd test
$ ls
CreditCardEJB    CustomerEJB
```

The last two commands change to the published context test/ and list its contents, showing two published object names: `CreditCardEJB` and `CustomerEJB`. The following command displays the full listing of the contents. Performing a full listing reveals security settings on the object.

```
$ ls -l
Read      Write     Exec      Owner     Date    Time   Name
Schema    Class Helper
BOOKSTORE BOOKSTORE BOOKSTORE BOOKSTORE Nov 02 01:01 CreditCardEJB
SYS
oracle.aurora.ejb.gen.test_CreditCardEJB.EjbHome_CreditCardHome
com.prenhall.OFJP.ejb.CreditCardHomeHelper
BOOKSTORE BOOKSTORE BOOKSTORE BOOKSTORE Nov 02 00:53 CustomerEJB
SYS
oracle.aurora.ejb.gen.test_CustomerEJB.EjbHome_CustomerHome
com.prenhall.OFJP.ejb.CustomerHomeHelper
```

Here the `bookstore` user is the owner of the published objects and has full read, write, and execute access to them. Use the `chmod` command to grant the user `scott` read and execute permission to `CreditCardEJB`. The *read* access right allows the user of the client application to look up the published object name. The *execute* right allows the client to obtain a reference to the home object associated with the published object name.

```
$ chmod +re scott CreditCardEJB

$ ls -l
Read      Write     Exec      Owner     Date    Time   Name
Schema   Class   Helper
BOOKSTORE BOOKSTORE BOOKSTORE BOOKSTORE Nov 02 01:01 CreditCardEJB
SYS
oracle.aurora.ejb.gen.test_CreditCardEJB.EjbHome_CreditCardHome
com.prenhall.OFJP.ejb.CreditCardHomeHelper
```

```
SCOTT                    SCOTT
BOOKSTORE BOOKSTORE BOOKSTORE BOOKSTORE Nov 02 00:53 CustomerEJB
SYS
oracle.aurora.ejb.gen.test_CustomerEJB.EjbHome_CustomerHome
com.prenhall.OFJP.ejb.CustomerHomeHelper

$ exit
```

The `ls -l` command confirms that user `scott` has the required access rights. The `exit` command terminates the sess_sh command-line tool. Note that `sess_sh` commands resemble the corresponding Unix shell commands. An example of using the `publish` tool with CORBA components is shown in Chapter 24.

The next task is to ensure that the user `scott` has access to the EJB methods invoked by the client application.

22.6.2 CONTROLLING ACCESS TO THE EJB METHODS

The deployment descriptor is used to control the list of users that can execute the EJB class and each of its methods. This is accomplished by specifying a combination of the three deployment descriptor attributes listed below.

- `RunAsMode` can have one of the following values:
  - `CLIENT_IDENTITY` indicates that the AllowedIdentities attribute specifies the list of user names or roles.
  - `SPECIFIED_IDENTITY` indicates that the RunAsIdentity attribute specifies the user name.
  - `SYSTEM_IDENTITY` indicates that code executes as the SYS user in the database. Use with caution.
- `AllowedIdentities` specifies a comma-separated list of Oracle8i database usernames or roles, and depends on the value used for `RunAsMode`.
- `RunAsIdentity` specifies a single database username (roles are not allowed) and is only required if `RunAsMode` is set to `SPECIFIED_IDENTITY`.

The following text is a sample part of the `CreditCardEJB` deployment descriptor, with the security settings shown in bold.

```
SessionBean com.prenhall.OFJP.ejb.CreditCardEJB
{
  BeanHomeName="test/CreditCardEJB";
  HomeInterfaceClassName=com.prenhall.OFJP.ejb.CreditCardHome;
  RemoteInterfaceClassName=com.prenhall.OFJP.ejb.CreditCardRemote;
```

```
  SessionTimeout = 0;
  StateManagementType = STATEFUL_SESSION;

  TransactionAttribute = TX_BEAN_MANAGED;
  RunAsMode = CLIENT_IDENTITY;
  AllowedIdentities = { gs, scott, bookstore };

  void insertInvalidCard ()
  {
    TransactionAttribute = TX_BEAN_MANAGED;
    RunAsMode = CLIENT_IDENTITY;
    AllowedIdentities = { gs, scott, bookstore };
  }

  java.lang.String getCardDetails ()
  {
    TransactionAttribute = TX_BEAN_MANAGED;
    RunAsMode = CLIENT_IDENTITY;
    AllowedIdentities = { bookstore };
  }

  void validateCard ()
  {
    TransactionAttribute = TX_BEAN_MANAGED;
    RunAsMode = CLIENT_IDENTITY;
    AllowedIdentities = { gs, scott, bookstore };
  }
        :
}
```

The sample `CreditCardEJB` deployment descriptor allows users `gs`, `scott`, and `bookstore` execute access to the EJB, `insertInvalidCard()`, and validateCard() methods. Only the `bookstore` user can execute all other methods. If user `gs` had not been granted access to the published object name for the EJB, the EJB instance could not be created without access to the published name for the EJB home object.

In your EJB code, you can obtain security information programmatically using methods in the `java.security.Principle` class. A `java.security.Principle` object can be obtained from the `getCallerPrinciple()` method inherited by the `SessionContext` object from the `javax.ejb.EJBContext` class. The security principle information will give you the user name of the client application. You can then apply special security rules based on the information derived from the security principle object.

Now that the `scott` user has access to the published name, and execute rights on the bean and methods, you are almost ready to run the client.

NOTE: The `deployejb` tool automatically grants the users listed in the `AllowedIdentities` list access to the published object name, and the database `EXECUTE` right to all Java classes in the Ejb-jar and client-jar file. The next section describes how you can manually grant `EXECUTE` rights to the EJB classes, if required.

22.6.3 GRANTING EXECUTE PERMISSION TO THE EJB CLASSES

As mentioned, users listed in the deployment descriptor are automatically granted `EXECUTE` access to all EJB classes. If you want to grant additional users access without modifying the deployment descriptor and redeploying the EJB classes, you can execute the following Oracle SQL statement in SQL*Plus:

```
GRANT EXECUTE ON "class-name" TO user, …;
```

The *`class-name`* value must be enclosed in double quotes and specified as the fully qualified Java class name. The users can be a comma-separated list of Oracle users and/or database roles. The forward slash is used as the separator between package and class name components. For example:

```
GRANT EXECUTE ON "com/prenhall/OFJP/ejb/CreditCardEJB" TO scott;
```

Alternatively, you could use the `loadjava` utility to store the Ejb-jar file and the generated client-jar file in the database, using the `-grant` option. For example:

```
loadjava -u bookstore/bookstore@localhost:1521:ORA816 -thin
  -grant scott CreditCardRemoteGenerated.jar
  CreditCardRemoteSource.jar
```

If you redeploy the EJB jar files using the `deployejb` command line, you can add the `-role` option followed by the user name.

22.6.4 GRANTING ACCESS TO DATABASE OBJECTS USED BY THE EJB

The final security task is to ensure that the user executing the EJB has access to the database tables or objects used by the EJB code. The EJB code executes as the client user in the database when `RunAsMode = CLIENT_IDENTITY`, and, by default, the EJB classes execute with the privileges assigned to the user invoking the EJB classes. For example, if user `scott` executes an EJB owned by user `bookstore`, the EJB executes with the privileges of `scott`. Therefore, if the JDBC or

SQLJ code references unqualified database tables or object names, then the database objects must be owned by scott.

If the tables are actually owned by the bookstore user, then you have two ways to resolve access to the database tables and objects required by the EJB code.

- Grant scott access to bookstore database objects. This requires two steps:
  - Grant the appropriate combination of SELECT, INSERT, UPDATE, and DELETE privileges on the bookstore database objects to scott.
  - Create private synonyms for scott, referencing the appropriate bookstore database objects, for all database objects used by the EJB class.
- Use definer execution rights on the bookstore Java classes—Alter the AUTHID value to DEFINER for all Java classes accessing unqualified database object names owned by bookstore.

22.6.4.1 Example of Granting Access to the Database Objects. The insertInvalidCard() and validateCard() methods in the CreditCardEJB class access the bookstore user invalid_card table. Using SQL*Plus, login as the bookstore user and grant scott access to the invalid_card table with the following SQL statement:

```
GRANT select, insert ON invalid_card TO scott;
```

Then, login as the user scott and create a synonym using the Oracle SQL command:

```
CREATE SYNONYM invalid_card FOR bookstore.invalid_card;
```

These two statements allow the methods in the CreditCardEJB class to run with CURRENT_USER execution rights (i.e., in the context of the invoker—the user scott).[24]

If the GRANT and CREATE SYNONYM commands have not been executed, then the insertInvalidCard() and validateCard() methods fail with SQL exceptions related to insufficient privileges when they attempt to access the invalid_card table.

22.6.4.2 Example of Using Definer Execution Rights on the Class. The alternative option for granting database object privileges to other users is to change the AUTHID mode for the EJB classes, using unqualified references to database objects in the JDBC or SQLJ code.[25] You can use the ALTER JAVA

[24]The AUTHID mode for Java classes in the database is CURRENT_USER by default. This means that the code executes with the privileges of the user invoking the methods.

[25]An unqualified reference means that the SQL statements identify the table name, without the owner prefixed to the table name.

CLASS command to change the AUTHID mode for a Java class in the database. For example, to change the AUTHID execution mode to use DEFINER rights, type the following SQL command in SQL*Plus:

```
ALTER JAVA CLASS "com/prenhall/OFJP/ejb/CreditCardEJB"
  AUTHID DEFINER;
```

To change the AUTHID mode back to invoker rights, use the following command:

```
ALTER JAVA CLASS "com/prenhall/OFJP/ejb/CreditCardEJB"
  AUTHID CURRENT_USER;
```

The bottom line is: if you cannot access the database objects, the code will fail with an exception.

22.7 REMOVING AN EJB FROM ORACLE8i SERVER

You can remove or drop an EJB from the database by using the following steps:

- Run the dropjava tool to delete the classes from the database. To simplify this task, supply to the dropjava command the name of the Ejb-jar file containing the bean classes and the generated client-jar file.
- Use the session shell tool i.e. sess_sh to remove the bean home interface name from the published object name space. The Oracle8i software provides a remove command-line tool that performs the same task.

Here is an example of the commands used to drop the CustomerEJB and its associated components:

```
dropjava -u bookstore/bookstore@localhost:1521:ORA816 -thin
  CreditCardRemoteGenerated.jar
  CreditCardRemoteSource.jar
```

Using the sess_sh tool to remove the published name.

```
os_prompt>sess_sh -u bookstore -p bookstore
                  -s sess_iiop://localhost:2481:ORA816
--Aurora/ORB Session Shell--
--type "help" at the command line for help message
$ cd test
$ ls
```

```
CreditCardEJB CustomerEJB
$ rm CreditCardEJB
$ exit
```

The `rm` command deletes the published object name.

22.8 DEPLOYING AN ENTERPRISE JAVABEAN TO ORACLE APPLICATION SERVER

The section discusses setting up an EJB to run under OAS; that is, deploying the Enterprise JavaBean into an OAS EJB container. In this case, it is assumed that you have been supplied an Ejb-jar file containing the EJB classes from the EJB provider/developer. Chapter 16 discusses the basic features of Oracle Application server.

You take on the role of the EJB deployer to create a deployment profile file that identifies the names of the enterprise bean classes. Oracle Application Server will use a deployment descriptor file with an `.APP` extension if you have the following EJB classes:

- The Bean class: ShoppingBasketEJB.java
- The Remote interface: ShoppingBasketEJBRemote.java
- The Home interface: ShoppingBasketEJBHome.java

For example, the file may be called `ShoppingBasketEJB.APP` and contain the following details:

```
[APPLICATION]
name=ShoppingBasket

[ShoppingBasketEJB]
className=com.prenhall.OFJP.oasejb.ShoppingBasketEJB;
remoteInterface=com.prenhall.OFJP.oasejb.ShoppingBasketEJBRemote;
homeInterface=com.prenhall.OFJP.oasejb.ShoppingBasketEJBHome;

[ShoppingBasketEJB.ENV]
initBasketSize=1
```

The `[APPLICATION]` section describes the OAS application name assigned to the EJB. The name becomes part of the URL used by the client to locate the bean.

The `[ShoppingBasketEJB]` section is used to identify the fully qualified `className` of the bean, `remoteInterface`, and `homeInterface`.

The `[ShoppingBasketEJB.ENV]` section contains property name-value pairs for the EJB to read when instantiated.

Next, use the `eco2ejb` command-line utility, provided with OAS software, to translate the deployment descriptor (`.APP`) file into three files:

- A MANIFEST.MF file.
- Two serialized Java files. For example:
  - `ShoppingBasketDeployement.ser` used by the process of registering the EJB application in OAS.
  - `ShoppingBasketEJBDeployment.ser` used for installing the EJB component classes.

These three generated files are added to the EJB-jar file with the compiled EJB classes. To compile the EJB classes and then create the EJB-jar file, for example, use the following commands:

```
javac -d . ShoppingBasket*.java
eco2ejb ShoppingBasketEJB.APP
jar cmf MANIFEST.MF ShoppingBasketEJB.jar *.ser
    com/prenhall/OFJP/oasejb/*.class
```

You can now use the OAS tree management applet to navigate to the pages that allow you to create the EJB application and install the components contained in the EJB-Jar file. Alternatively, you can execute the `oasdeploy` command-line utility to create and install the EJB application. Here is an example of the `oasdeploy` command line:

```
oasdeploy -u admin/manager@frazzle:8888
     -j ShoppingBasketEJB.jar -t EJB -a ShoppingBasket -force
```

There are several options on the command line:

- The `-u` option specifies the administrator user name and password for the OAS node manager, the host name, and the port number running the node manager process.
- The `-j` option identifies the EJB-jar file.
- The `-t EJB` option indicates that you are deploying an EJB application.
- The `-a` option gives an OAS application name to the EJB component.
- The `-force` option is used to update a set of existing EJB classes. If you do not use the `-force` option, you would first need to remove the existing EJB classes before you add new ones with the same name.

After deployment has occurred, a client-jar file containing additional client-side classes is generated and saved in the OAS directory structure. The client-jar file must be obtained from the OAS server and added to the CLASSPATH of the EJB client. From a client environment, you can use the oasdeploy tool to download the client-jar file by specifying the -c option on the command line. The directory name entered after the -c option identifies the location for the downloaded client-jar file. For example:

```
oasdeploy -a ShoppingBasket
   -u admin/manager@frazzle:8888 -c /client/jar
```

Using a JNDI lookup request,[26] the client application locates the bean home interface, creates the bean instance, and calls the EJB methods with the support of classes found in the client-jar. The EJB client application uses a URL similar to the one shown below to look up the EJB object from the OAS EJB container:

```
oas://frazzle:8080/ShoppingBasket/ShoppingBasketEJBRemote
```

The URL forming the JNDI name used by the client application to locate an EJB object in OAS is made up of:

- The keyword oas followed by :// specifying the service to be used
- The OAS host (frazzle) and OAS HTTP listener port number (8080)
- The OAS application name (ShoppingBasket)
- The EJB remote interface name (ShoppingBasketEJBRemote)

Although the discussion of writing the EJB classes and an EJB client in Chapter 21 focuses primarily on using the EJB server in an Oracle8i database, the coding principles for EJB classes developed for OAS and for developing an EJB for an Oracle8i server are the same As this section highlights, the task of deployment requires very different steps for each EJB server to install and register an EJB application.

SUMMARY

The world of Enterprise JavaBeans is a vast and expanding area of Java technology, and two chapters are woefully insufficient to cover all of its many features. The bulk of this chapter has been devoted to deploying an Enterprise JavaBean into an Oracle8i server using the manual approach of command-line utilities. Or-

[26]The basics of Java Naming and Directory Service (JNDI) are discussed in Chapter 10.

acle JDeveloper has wizards that automate all the manual command-line steps covered in this chapter.

You also were given a glimpse at some more advanced features of Enterprise JavaBeans by learning about transaction management for a client-managed, container-managed, or bean-managed Enterprise JavaBean.

The remaining chapters on Oracle8i CORBA services fill in the details of the infrastructure used to provide EJB services to Java client applications.

Chapter 23

CORBA and Its Implementation in Oracle8i: An Overview

- Distributed Computing: Historical Background
- The Common Object Broker Architecture
- Putting It All Together: The First CORBA Program
- The Java Transaction Service (JTS)
- Summary

This chapter will introduce you to CORBA. Since so many books, articles, and training material about CORBA are freely available on the Internet, the focus of the chapter will be on the specifics of the CORBA implementation offered by Oracle Corporation.

Many database-centric applications are based on transactions. You briefly encountered this topic in Chapter 6 when you were introduced to the transaction verbs of Oracle SQL (SET TRANSACTION, COMMIT, and ROLLBACK). The CORBA engine bundled with the Oracle 8i kernel includes an implementation of the CORBA Transaction Service that shows great potential, despite its current lack of important features, because Oracle Corporation is committed to fill the gaps in the next release of the database server. This chapter will discuss transaction concepts and how to implement transaction-enabled applications using Java and CORBA.

The aim of this chapter is to gently introduce you to the Oracle implementation of CORBA, which provides tools and facilities that simplify distributed programming. Compared to other CORBA environments, the Oracle flavor of CORBA is easier to work with. Later in the chapter, you will become famiiar with Oracle- and Inprise-specific tools. These tools simplify the automatic generation of classes that support remote method invocation and object location and discovery.

23.1 DISTRIBUTED COMPUTING: HISTORICAL BACKGROUND

The idea of running programs across multiple computers, each cooperating with its processing power in order to reach a common goal, is not new. The natural evolution of the minicomputer, which occurred in the 1970s and the 1980s, ultimately made it possible to implement distributed architectures. These architectures in many respects represented the antithesis of mainframe architectures. The push to create and promote minicomputers was prompted by the desire to avoid the long backlog typical of time-sharing systems. A programmer in the 1960s would have submitted a collection (called a "deck") of punch cards with the source code of a program in the evening, and would have not have received the results until the next day. Fixing a simple mistake in the source code, such as the omission of a comma or a semicolon, would mean having to resubmit the card deck for the next run. Thus a simple mistake often resulted in a 24-hour delay in obtaining the results of a program. The turnaround time for compilation and linking of the program was measured in days. The advent of the minicomputer began the decentralization of computing. Small departmental machines like the Digital Equipment Corporation (DEC) PDP line allowed programmers to be in closer proximity to the machine's console, and therefore to react on the spot to errors signaled by the compiler.

The next evolution after decentralization was the integration of minicomputers into networks that formed the foundation for distributed computing. Imagine walking into a university laboratory full of inter-networked workstations, some being used, some idle. Struggling for computational power, you try to solve the complex equations that constitute your assignment. It is intolerable to see so many other workstations underutilized or even idle while the time required to compute your equations on only one computer is measured in hours. The idea of running your equation-solver program across many computers, to better utilize network resources and significantly improve computing power, almost spontaneously thrives in your mind. The answer to this need was the Remote Procedure Call (RPC) paradigm. Sun Microsystems pioneered the field, releasing the Open Network Connectivity (ONC) RPC. A different and more widely followed standard, the Distributed Computing Environment (DCE) soon began competing with ONC RPC for supremacy in the distributed computing market. In its initial implementation, the RPC model was rigidly synchronous, meaning that a client calling a remote procedure would be blocked until the remote call returned. More sophisticated RPC implementations later allowed for asynchronous remote calls, and RPC became the infrastructure for complex distributed systems, including middleware solutions. An example of a successful middleware product, based on the DCE RPC model, was Transarc Encina (today an IBM product), a set of components that included, among others, a TP monitor and a message-queuing system.

The RPC model of distributed computing has a serious inherent limitation. As its very name indicates, it is *procedural*, or sequential. In other words, it is not object-oriented. When you use RPC, your client program calls a specific function provided by a server, which not only does not encapsulate data, but is also static; that is, its behavior is rigidly predefined and cannot dynamically vary at runtime. All functions identified by the same name will be implemented in the same way. Their behavior cannot change between calls. In contrast, a truly object-oriented system allows for method calling within specific objects. The important consequence is that the same method call can invoke different method implementations through polymorphism. In other words, the same method, exposed by objects derived from the same ancestor but at different levels of the inheritance tree, would produce different results.

The Common Object Broker Architecture (CORBA) is a standard framework that promotes distributed computing in an object-oriented way.[1] CORBA provides a platform- and language-independent architecture and infrastructure for developing and deploying distributed and object-oriented applications.

23.2 THE COMMON OBJECT BROKER ARCHITECTURE

The fundamental model that forms the basis for CORBA is that objects provide services requested by distributed clients. Services are defined and advertised through their *interfaces*, formally described by the Interface Definition Language

---

[1]CORBA is a standard specified by the Object Management Group (OMG). For more details, see http://www.omg.org, and http://www.corba.org.

(IDL). Distributed objects are identified by object references, typed by their IDL interfaces.

23.2.1 THE OBJECT REQUEST BROKER

The Object Request Broker (ORB) is the essential CORBA component that locates remote objects advertised on the network, communicates a request to them, and delivers the results of the interaction with them back to the clients that requested the service. Figure 23.1 shows the role of the ORB.

The ORB is responsible for most of the activities necessary for object management; the mechanisms for object invocation, request routing, and object discovery are abstracted and completely decoupled from the object implementation. This high level of abstraction and decoupling greatly simplifies the implementation of distributed objects. Figure 23.1 shows the essence of a CORBA environment:

1. A client submits a request, calling a stub method.
2. The request is forwarded to the ORB, which locates the server that provides the implementation of the objects affected by the request.

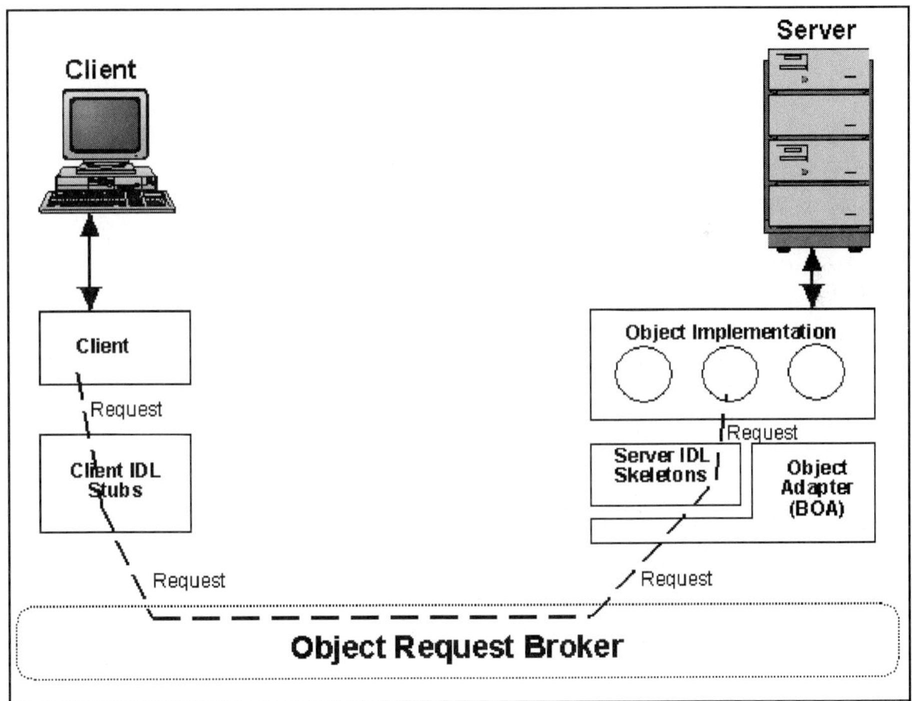

FIGURE 23.1 Objects communicate through the ORB.

3. If the ORB successfully locates the required objects, the request can be satisfied. Usually a client requests a reference to a remote object, so that the methods implemented by the object can be invoked locally.

The methods actually run remotely, on the server side, and only parameters and result values are transferred across the network. However, this occurs transparently: the client program does not have to deal with network complexities, because they are all hidden by the CORBA infrastructure.

23.2.2 THE OBJECT ADAPTER

The Object Adapter (OA) is another important component of the CORBA architecture. It can be defined as a set of facilities that extend the functionality of the ORB and provide the means for the ORB and the object implementation to communicate with each other. Typically, an OA provides the following services:

- Registration of servers
- Object activation and deactivation
- Instantiation of objects from their classes at runtime
- Mapping of object references to the instantiated objects that provide services

The OA is a layer that resides on top of the ORB core implementation and provides an interface between the ORB and the implementation of the objects. The CORBA 2.0 specification requires vendors to provide a Basic Object Adapter (BOA), leaving most of the details of the interface between the ORB and the objects to the CORBA vendors. In consequence of this lack of specifications, the BOA implementations provided by the various vendors are not compatible. As a result, the BOA has recently been deprecated in favor of a Portable Object Adapter (POA), a new and stricter set of specifications that should improve interoperability among different CORBA implementations.

The CORBA implementation shipped with Oracle 8i is based on Inprise (formerly Borland) Visibroker for Java, release 3.4, which only provides a BOA implementation. More recent releases of Visibroker for Java implement the new POA, but since you are learning the Oracle implementation of CORBA, the focus in the rest of the chapter will be on the BOA.

23.2.3 THE INTERFACE DEFINITION LANGUAGE

The Interface Definition Language (IDL) is a standard-specification metalanguage that defines the interfaces an object presents to the outside world. Through IDL, CORBA achieves the goal of language-independence. An object can be implemented, say, in Java and can request services provided by another object written, say, in C++. The IDL syntax only allows for interface definitions, such as methods, data, and exceptions. You cannot write procedural code in IDL; that is left to the implementation of object methods and data structures. The CORBA infrastructure strives to abstract everything it can so as to simplify your life as a distributed application designer/developer. When operating in heterogeneous environments, one of the most tedious tasks is the need to make sure that an integer stored with the least significant byte first (little-endian) will be correctly converted into an integer with the least significant byte last in those architectures that support big-endian formats for storing numbers. Intel-based and Compaq Alpha machines use the little-endian convention, whereas most other architectures use the big-endian convention.

The process of packing the stream of bytes representing characters, integers, and floating point numbers is called *marshaling*; the unpacking of a stream of bytes back to strings and numbers is called *de-marshaling*. The information provided through the IDL syntax helps CORBA perform marshaling and de-marshaling of user-defined data and method attributes.

In Chapter 17, you implemented a socket server in C that was accessed by Java clients. To avoid implementing marshaling and de-marshaling routines, all information was sent in pure ASCII. This is fine if the supported architectures are Windows and Unix, which universally use ASCII as their character-representation standard. A very few other architectures, such as IBM MVS/ESA, use EBCDIC instead of ASCII, so the program you built in Chapter 17 does not support EBCDIC machines. Furthermore, in Chapter 17, you implemented a very simple protocol to allow client and server to understand each other. You built a packet and a packet header that contained information about the packet, such as its length and its type. Although the application built in Chapter 17 was very simple, it illustrates how the complexity of defining and maintaining hundreds or even thousands of different packet types can rapidly become unmanageable.

When a CORBA infrastructure is available, you are relieved from the hard work and complexity of protocol definition. If you want to call a remote method to pass an integer and a floating-point number, you do not have to worry about most- and least-significant bytes for integers or exponent and mantissa format for floating-point numbers. The CORBA IDL takes care of all of this, leaving you free to concentrate on your business problem rather than on network-related technicalities.

The IDL provides Java/CORBA mappings not only for basic data types, such as boolean and string, but also for structures, unions, and enumerations. The IDL example shown below illustrates the definition of an interface named *lookup*, an exception, *SQLError*, and a method, *exist()*, which receives two strings as parameters and returns a boolean. The exist() method performs a database lookup to verify whether a specific employee, given his/her first name and surname, exists in the database. The method returns true if the employee is found, false otherwise. The source code of the IDL example is located in the Chapter 23/CORBAExample directory on the CD_ROM.

```
module com
{
   module prenhall
   {
        module OFJP
        {
           module CORBAExample
           {
               exception SQLError
               {
                   wstring explain;
               };
               interface lookup
               {
                   boolean exist(in string name,
                                 in string surname)
                                 raises (SQLError);
               };
           };
        };
   };
};
```

If you run the Visibroker *idl2java* utility against the idl file shown above, you will see that several java files are automatically produced by idl2java. The files are located by default in the same directory as the idl file. If the idl syntax specifies nested modules, as in the example, idl2java will create the required subdirectories. Table 23.1 describes the purpose of each generated file.

You must be familiar with the IDL and its function in the CORBA environment in order to build CORBA-based applications. Inprise Visibroker, the CORBA implementation that Oracle Corporation bundles with the Oracle server, provides the *Caffeine* compiler, which enables development of pure Java distributed applications that follow the CORBA conventions. It is possible to write interface specifications in Java and use the *java2iiop* tool to generate CORBA-compatible Java stubs and skeletons. In other words, if you use the Caffeine compiler, your development lifecycle will not start with IDL, but with Java interfaces from which CORBA stubs and skeletons are generated. In the rest of the chapter you will use the Caffeine compiler, so you can avoid learning yet another language. If you must still provide IDL definitions (e.g., because your implementation must be available to CORBA servers that do notsupport Java), you can use the *java2idl* tool, which generates IDL code from Java interface specifications.

TABLE 23.1 Files generated by idl2java

GENERATED FILE	COMMENT
lookup.java	Specifies the interface to a Lookup object.
lookupHelper.java	The helper classes contain methods that read and write the object to a stream, and cast the object to and from the type of the base class.
lookupHolder.java	A holder class is needed when the interface specifies OUT or INOUT parameters. The ORB passes Java parameters by value, so specific holder classes must be available to store the parameter objects.
lookupOperations.java	When delegation, rather than inheritance, is used to associate the class implementation with the generated skeleton, the server needs the class identified by the Operations suffix to tie the object to the skeleton.
_tie_lookup.java	When delegation, rather than inheritance, is used to associate the class implementation with the generated skeleton, the server needs the class identified by the _tie prefix to tie the object to the skeleton.
_st_lookup.java	Stub file. When a client calls a method on the remote object, it is in reality calling a mirror method in the stub, which performs all the operations required to activate a remote call.
_lookupImplBase.java	Skeleton file. A skeleton file is installed on the server and communicates with the stub file on the client, in that it receives the message on the ORB from the client and upcalls to the server. The skeleton file also returns parameters and return values to the client.
_example_lookup.java	This file provides an empty implementation of the methods defined by the interface. You should edit this file and add the source code that implements the server methods.
SQLError.java	Specifies the interface to an exception of type SQLError.
SQLErrorHelper.java	The helper classes contain methods that read and write the object to a stream, and cast the object to and from the type of the base class.
SQLErrorHolder.java	A holder class is needed when the interface specifies OUT or INOUT parameters. The ORB passes Java parameters by value, so specific holder classes must be available to store the parameter objects.

23.2.4 THE INTERNET INTER-ORB PROTOCOL (IIOP)

The initial CORBA specification did not address ORB interoperability. As a result, you could not invoke a method available through, say, an ORBIX ORB from a Visibroker ORB. Proprietary semantics and calls prevented a seamless integration between ORBs from different vendors. CORBA release 2.0 addressed the issue of ORB interoperability. A new CORBA mandatory component, the General Inter-ORB Protocol (GIOP), was defined. While GIOP is a wider standard and covers different network-level protocols, a more specific standard, the Internet Inter-ORB Protocol (IIOP), was created to address the immediate and specific needs of interoperability over TCP/IP. To be CORBA 2.0–compliant, an ORB must support IIOP.

The IIOP protocol is particularly relevant for developers who want to use the Oracle CORBA implementation. Clients access CORBA applications in the database through an IIOP connection. All IIOP connections for CORBA clients that communicate with the database must have IIOP configured in the database and within the Net8 listener. If you connect to a database installed on a large server, contact the DBA to make sure that both the database and the SQL*Net/Net8 parameters are properly set.

If you are using a local workstation equipped with your own Oracle instance, you must choose the JServer option if you want to enable the Multi-Threaded Server (MTS) configuration needed by the database configuration assistant tool to properly configure your server to accept IIOP connections. Figure 23.2 shows the page displayed by the Database Configuration Assistant (*dbassist*), the tool used to create or modify databases. It allows for selection of the JServer option. dbassist, located in the $ORACLE_HOME/bin in Unix environments. On Windows NT, choose Start > Programs > Oracle - *HOME_NAME* >Database Administration >Database Configuration Assistant.

Choosing the JServer option causes the Database Configuration Assistant to configure MTS by default, and also stores the following line in the init<ORACLE_SID>.ora paramater file:

```
mts_dispatchers=
      "(protocol=tcp)(presentation=oracle.aurora.server.SGiopServer)"
```

The default configuration does not install a Secure Socket Layer (SSL) environment. If you purchased the Advanced Security Option and want to enable SSL, edit the init.ora file and change the protocol from `(protocol=tcp)` to `(protocol=tcps)`.

For the rest of the chapter, it is assumed that you are operating in a nonsecure environment (i.e., that you do not use SSL).

Enabling MTS and configuring it to accept IIOP connections is not enough to allow your CORBA clients to connect to the ORACLE ORB. One more step is required: configuring the Net8 listener. To start the Net8 Assistant configuration tool, invoke $ORACLE_HOME/bin/netasst in a Unix environment; under Windows NT choose Start>Programs>Oracle-*HOME_NAME*>Network Administration>Net8 Assistant.

To enable listening on the TCP/IP port, make sure that the checkbox marked "Dedicate this endpoint to IIOP connections" is checked.

To verify that the Net8 Assistant tool correctly configured the listener, look at the contents of the file listener.ora, located in the $ORACLE_HOME/network/admin directory. You should see an entry similar to the following:

```
(DESCRIPTION =
 (PROTOCOL_STACK =
   (PRESENTATION = GIOP)
    (SESSION = RAW)
```

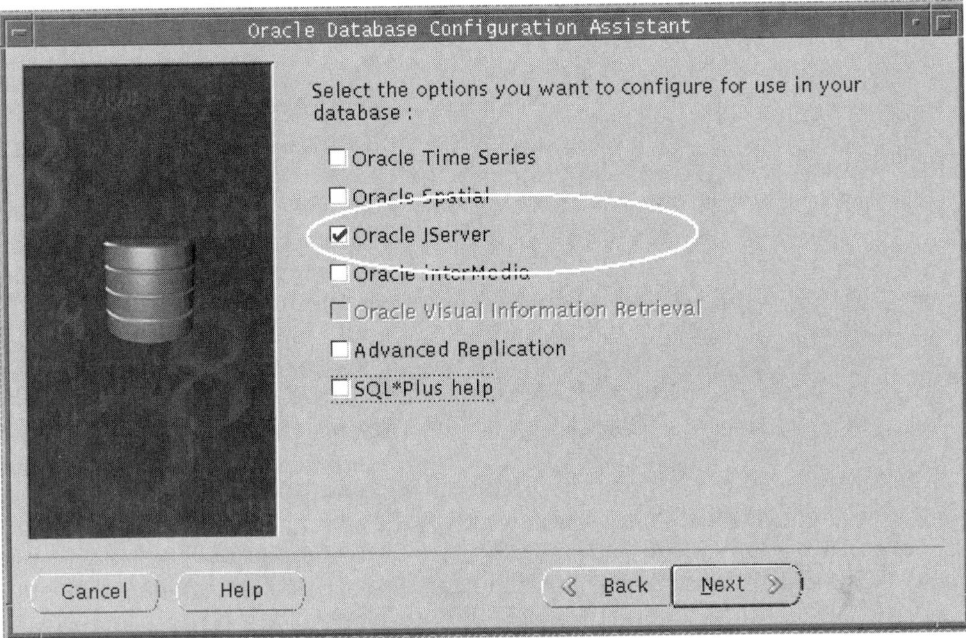

FIGURE 23.2 The JServer option is checked in dbassist.

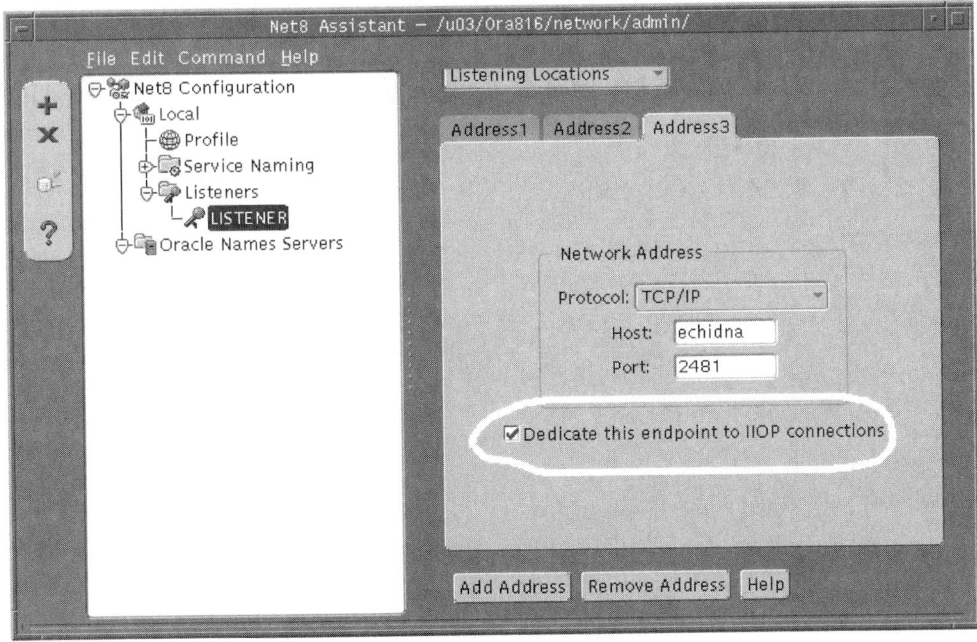

FIGURE 23.3 Enabling IIOP in Net8 Assistant.

```
 )
(ADDRESS = (PROTOCOL = TCP)(HOST = <your host name>)(PORT = 2481))
)
```

If you want to use CORBA in an Oracle environment, check that the database has been configured to accept IIOP connections as a preliminary step, before delving into coding issues. You will likely save yourself some frustration and a lot of wasted time.

23.2.5 CORBA SERVICES

CORBA not only specifies the components seen so far (ORB, OA, IDL, and IIOP), but also a set of 15 CORBA services (COS). These collections of system-level facilities, accessible through IDL-specified interfaces, increase and complement the functionality of the ORB.

Of the 15 services specified by the Object Management Group (OMG),[2] such as the transaction management service, the object persistence service, and the object security service, the leading CORBA vendors (Inprise and Iona) offer only a few. To proficiently use the Oracle implementation of CORBA effectively, you only need to know about a couple of services: the naming service and the transaction service.

- The naming service (COSNaming) allows CORBA components that communicate through the ORB bus to locate other components or objects using a name. COSNaming integrates existing network directories, such as LDAP or Novel NDS, with CORBA.
- The transaction service (COSTransactions) provides two-phase commit coordination among recoverable components participating in a CORBA network.

Oracle offers an alternative simpler than the naming service. The Java Naming and Directory Interface (JNDI) can locate objects by name and to use directory services. You first encountered the JNDI when you learned about JDBC version 2, and also when you were introduced to Enterprise Java Beans (EJB). The COSNaming service is actually used internally by Oracle, but only the simpler JNDI interface is exposed Developers interact with JNDI to establish an IIOP connection to Oracle and to locate objects available through the ORB bus. Of course, it is still possible for experienced developers to use COSNaming directly, bypassing the JNDI interface.

Java Transaction Service (JTS) methods are available to CORBA developers who want to use the mapping provided by JTS to a subset of the object transaction service (OTS). The object transaction service defines a complex framework for managing distributed transactions, while the JTS only supports a small subset of functions. The JTS implementation shipped in Oracle 8i Release 2 is even more

[2]The OMG is the consortium of more than 700 companies that supervises CORBA.

limited; for example, neither distributed transactions nor nested transactions are supported. In addition, the Oracle JTS implementation does not offer interoperability with other OTS implementations, nor does it support transaction timeouts. If you need the missing functionality, you have to resort to different means to support transactions in your application. But if the current functionality fits your bill, it is worth considering the use of JTS instead of the Oracle proprietary transaction handling, given the huge portability advantage offered by JTS.

23.2.6 CONNECTION AND AUTHENTICATION

The CORBA implementation offered by the Oracle server runs inside JServer. The major implication of having the ORB run inside the database is that CORBA clients must connect to the database in order to look up published objects. A client must establish an Oracle session to be able to obtain references to objects that will be instantiated by JServer. This arrangement deviates a little from standard CORBA, which does not include the concept of sessions. The simpler way to connect to Oracle via IIOP and obtain a session is to create an environment for a JNDI context, populate it with connection information, and create the JNDI context passing the environment to it. When the client calls the lookup method of the context object, in order to obtain a reference to an object published through the ORB, a session IIOP connection is made to the Oracle instance of the host database specified in the environment context. The server establishes a database session, and the client is authenticated, using the user name and password specified in the environment context. _Using the COSNaming service, the client locates the published object, specified as a parameter to the lookup method, in the session name space. When a method belonging to an object whose reference was obtained through the lookup method is called, the server activates the object and registers it with the BOA. The client-side ORB uses the *narrow()* method to cast the remote object to the correct type, using the helper class, automatically generated by either idl2java or java2iiop.

JNDI is not the only way to obtain a reference to a remote object. Clients can also use the COSNaming service directly, as you will see in the next chapter. For now, the JNDI interface is a simpler way to obtain a reference to a remote object made available by a server through the CORBA ORB.

23.3 PUTTING IT ALL TOGETHER: THE FIRST CORBA PROGRAM

Writing a CORBA application is a multistep process that involves:

- ❑ Creating the Java interface
- ❑ Generating the necessary stubs and skeletons

- Populating the skeleton methods with code that implements the required functionality, etc.

In this chapter, you will use the Caffeine compiler, which avoids the need to create IDL files. You will learn more about IDL in Chapter 24. Table 23.2 lists the steps required to build a simple CORBA application that consists of a single remote method called by a Java client.

The application you build here is really quite simple: a single method, named *exist()*, which requires two parameters and returns a boolean value indicating whether the required customer exists in the database,. The two parameters required are the name and surname of the required customer, passed as strings.

The customer table, defined in the SCOTT schema, contains the following fields:

TABLE 23.2 Steps in building a simple CORBA application

STEP #	ACTION	COMMENT
1	Create an interface that exposes the required methods.	The methods exposed by the interface will be made available to the client through the ORB.
2	Compile the interface using javac.	This is required because java2iiop requires bytecodes as its input.
3	Run java2iiop against the class produced by step 2.	java2iiop produces the ancillary java classes listed in Table 23.1.
4	Edit the _example_<Interface_name>.java file produced by java2iiop and implement the required methods.	java2iiop automatically generates a source file that can be used as the basis for the interface implementation. You can change file and class names at will.
5	Compile all classes produced by java2iiop and the class customized in step 4.	All classes must be compiled before loading into the Oracle8i database.
6	Load all classes into the database.	The loadjava utility is used to physically load the Java bytecodes into the Oracle database.
7	Publish the name of the CORBA server object implementation in the Oracle8i database.	The class that implements the interface, together with its helper class, must be published in the Oracle name space. The object name is thus registered with the database name server and made available to JNDI and COSNaming.
8	Implement the CORBA client class that uses the services provided by the server.	The client class must implement the methods required to obtain a remote reference to the object that provides the requested services.
9	Compile the Java source code produced in step 8.	The class produced in step 8 must be compiled. The client application consists of that class plus the helper and the holder classes generated by java2iiop.

```
Name                                      Null?    Type
----------------------------------------- -------- ----------------------------
NAME                                               VARCHAR2(30)
SURNAME                                            VARCHAR2(50)
AGE                                                NUMBER(3)
```

To create the table, execute the following SQL statement from SQL*Plus:

```
CREATE TABLE customer
(
 NAME          VARCHAR2(30),
 SURNAME       VARCHAR2(50),
 AGE           NUMBER(3)
)
/
```

While it is not only possible but indeed recommended to use a Java IDE to produce CORBA applications visually, in this example the application is developed using command-line tools. When you develop the advanced CORBA examples in the next chapter using Oracle JDeveloper, you will no doubt appreciate its powerful features and source code generation capabilities. But at this stage, in order for you to understand what happens behind the scenes, it is better to manually enter each command. When you use a visual environment whose very purpose is to hide the details of building a CORBA application, it is harder to grasp what is happening.

Step 1: You need an interface that exposes the exist() method.

```
public interface CustomerVerify extends org.omg.CORBA.Object
{
   public boolean exist(java.lang.String name,
java.lang.String surname);
}
```

Note that the interface extends a CORBA Object. This is necessary for the java2iiop compiler to correctly produce stubs and skeletons.

Step 2: Compile the interface into Java bytecodes using javac.

```
javac CustomerVerify.java
```

Step 3: Use java2iiop to generate stubs and skeletons.

Before you use the java2iiop tool, you need to know about the two mechanisms supported by Visibroker for associating an implementation class with the skeleton class generated by the IDL compiler or the Caffeine compiler. Both methods are variations of the Adapter design pattern. The first approach, the class adapter, relies on inheritance to associate the class implementation with the generated skeleton. The second approach relies on delegation to achieve the same goal. Rather than a class adapter, the second method uses an instance adapter to forward requests to the implementation object. Since developers use a generated Java class to *tie* together the implementation class with the skeleton, the latter method is commonly referred to as the "tie approach."

In this example, for the sake of simplicity, you use the inheritance approach (the first method). You invoke the java2iip compiler specifying the –no_tie option on the command line. The net effect of this option is that two fewer classes are generated. The next chapter will discuss more about the use of inheritance versus delegation. Here is the java2iiop command:

```
java2iiop -no_tie -no_comments CustomerVerify.class
```

java2iiop prints a few dots on the screen to inform the user that the generation of Java classes is progressing. Note that you invoked the tool specifying that the classes supporting the tie approach are not to be generated, and that the generated code will be comment-free. When the java2iiop tool completes its work, your directory will contain several classes in addition to CustomerVerify.java:

```
_CustomerVerifyImplBase.java
_example_CustomerVerify.java
_st_CustomerVerify.java
CustomerVerify.java
CustomerVerifyHelper.java
CustomerVerifyHolder.java
```

You only need to edit and modify `_example_CustomerVerify.java`, which provides the source code that correctly calls the remote method defined in CustomerVerify. You decide not to accept the generated name for the class, so you perform a fourth step:

Step 4: Change the class name to CustomerVerifyServer.class, then edit the class, using the search-and-replace feature to substitute each occurrence of *_example_CustomerVerify* with CustomerVerifyServer.

Toward the end of the file, you find a comment that reads:

```
// IMPLEMENT: Operation
```

This is the marker that signals where your implementation code should begin. The Java source given below shows the content of CustomerVerifyServer; the custom code that implements the behavior for the exist() method is in bold.

```
public class CustomerVerifyServer extends
 _CustomerVerifyImplBase
{
  public CustomerVerifyServer(java.lang.String name)
  {
    super(name);
  }
  public CustomerVerifyServer()
  {
    super();
  }
  public boolean exist(
    java.lang.String arg0,
    java.lang.String arg1)
  {
    // IMPLEMENT: Operation
    int cnt = dbLookup.lookupCustomer(arg0,arg1);
    if (cnt > 0)
      return true;
    else
      return false;
  }
}
```

You can save your modifications and leave the editor. Note that the class has been generated with two default constructors, one parameterless and one that receives a single String parameter. This is done in order to support both *persistent* and *transient* object references. Persistent objects are of global scope, constantly available to the naming service or other CORBA smart agents. Persistent objects are created once and persist for the lifetime of the CORBA infrastructure. Transient objects, on the other hand, only have meaning during the execution of the server process. When the server object terminates, transient objects are destroyed. Transient objects are created by the parameterless constructor, whereas persistent objects are created by the constructor that takes a string containing the object name as parameter.

You now have to implement the class that provides the LookupCustomer() method, dbLookup. LookupCustomer() accesses the database to check whether the required customer, identified by name and surname, has been recorded in the customer table. You use SQLJ to perform the database lookup.

```
import sqlj.runtime.*;
import sqlj.runtime.ref.*;
import java.sql.*;

public class dbLookup
{
   public static int lookupCustomer(String locName,
                                    String locSurname)
   {
      int cnt=0;
      try
      {
         #sql { select count(*) into :cnt from customer
              where name = :locName and surname = :locSurname };
         return cnt;
      }
      catch (SQLException se)
      {
         return -1;
      }
   }
}
```

You must invoke the SQLJ precompiler to generate two Java files from dbLookup.sqlj.

```
sqlj -J-classpath .:$ORACLE_HOME/jdbc/lib/classes111.zip:\
> $ORACLE_HOME/sqlj/lib/translator.zip:\
> -ser2class  dbLookup.sqlj
```

The SQLJ compiler generates one .java file (dbLookup.java) and three .class files (dbLookup.class, dbLookup_SJProfile0.class, and dbLookup_ SJProfileKeys.class). Remember to load all of these classes into the database later on.

You have completed the fourth step.

Step 5: You can now compile all the classes generated so far:

```
javac _CustomerVerifyImplBase.java
javac _example_CustomerVerify.java
javac _st_CustomerVerify.java
javac CustomerVerify.java
javac CustomerVerifyHelper.java
javac CustomerVerifyHolder.java
javac CustomerVerifyServer.java
javac dbLookup.java
```

You now have all the class files you need for your application.

Step 6: Load into JServer the classes that constitute the server-side application. To accomplish this, use the loadjava utility.

```
$ loadjava -verbose -oracleresolver -resolve -oci8 -u \
> scott/tiger  CustomerVerify.class CustomerVerifyHolder.class \
> CustomerVerifyHelper.class _st_CustomerVerify.class \
> _CustomerVerifyImplBase.class dbLookup.class \
> dbLookup_SJProfile0.class dbLookup_SJProfileKeys.class
```

All the required classes are now available to the CORBA environment inside the Oracle database.

Step 7: Associate the classes that will be called remotely by the clients with a name used to identify the required object. The name is used by the naming service (COSNaming), often through the JNDI interface, to locate the objects advertised on the ORB bus. Oracle offers the *publish* utility to register the name with the Oracle Name Space, the directory service that looks like a file system. Using the `sess_sh` utility, developers can access the Name Space, to list the objects contained in it, and to grant and revoke privileges to users who need to access published objects.

Step 7 uses the `publish` utility. It is not sufficient to only publish the class that implements the method that will be invoked remotely. Its helper class must be associated with the name that will be used to obtain a reference to the required object. In your case, the two classes to publish are CustomerVerifyServer and CustomerVerifyHelper. The following example shows the use of the `publish` utility:

```
$ publish -republish -u scott -p tiger -schema SCOTT -s \
> sess_iiop://localhost:2481:$ORACLE_SID \
> /test/trial CustomerVerifyServer CustomerVerifyHelper
```

Note that the `publish` utility accesses the database through the IIOP protocol rather than through SQL*Net, as loadjava does. After a successful Oracle installation, the Oracle Name Space contains three directories: /etc, /bin, and /test. You should not mess with /etc and /bin, so in this example, for the sake of simplicity, store your published objects in /test. Of course, nothing stops you from creating your own name space subdirectory. This will be done in the next chapter.

Publishing the name that helps the ORB locate the object which provides the required services concludes your server-side work. It is now time to work on the client-side implementation:

Step 8: Write the class that remotely calls the method offered by CustomerVerifyServer.

In subsection 23.2.6, you learned to use JNDI to establish a connection to the CORBA ORB running in JServer. In Oracle8i, JNDI internally relies on the COSNaming service to locate the required object. To use JNDI:

- Set up a context environment. This means instantiating a hash table that contains a set of name-value pairs, each pair specifying a JNDI property.
- Instantiate an InitialContext. You pass the environment hash table to the InitialContext constructor.
- Define an object from the class implemented remotely (in your case CustomerVerify), and use the lookup() method implemented in InitialContext to bind the remote object to the local object handle.

The Lookup.java source follows. Now you will see how the context environment is initialized and how the initial context is instantiated.

```
/**
 * This class implements a remote call to a CORBA method
 * published on the Oracle JServer.
 *
 */

import java.util.*;
import javax.naming.*;
import java.rmi.RemoteException;
import oracle.aurora.jndi.sess_iiop.*;


public class Lookup
{
  public static void main(String[] args)
  {
    // args[0] = Customer name
    // args[1] = Customer Surname
    String corbaUrl =
       "sess_iiop://echidna:2481:sun816/test/trial";
    String username = "scott";
    String password = "tiger";

    // Setup the environment
    Hashtable environment = new Hashtable();
```

```
// Tell JNDI to speak sess_iiop
environment.put(
   Context.URL_PKG_PREFIXES,
   "oracle.aurora.jndi");
// Tell sess_iiop who the user is
environment.put(Context.SECURITY_PRINCIPAL, username);
// Tell sess_iiop what the password is
environment.put(Context.SECURITY_CREDENTIALS, password);
// Tell sess_iiop to use credential authentication
environment.put(Context.SECURITY_AUTHENTICATION,
          ServiceCtx.NON_SSL_LOGIN);

// Lookup the URL
CustomerVerify corbaInterface = null;
try
{
  System.out.println("Creating an initial context");
  Context ic = new InitialContext(environment);
  System.out.println(
    "Looking for the CORBA server object "+
    "published as 'test/trial'");
  corbaInterface = (CustomerVerify) ic.lookup(corbaUrl);
}
catch (ActivationException e)
{
  System.out.println("Unable to activate : " +
    e.getMessage());
  e.printStackTrace();
  System.exit(1);
}
catch (CommunicationException e)
{
  System.out.println("Unable to connect: " + corbaUrl);
  e.printStackTrace();
  System.exit(1);
}
catch (NamingException e)
{
  System.out.println("Exception occurred!");
  System.out.println("Cause:  This may be an "+
         "unknown URL, or some classes required "+
  "by the CORBA object are missing from "+
         "your classpath.");
  e.printStackTrace();
```

```
      System.exit(1);
    }

    // Try invoking the remote method...
    try
    {
      System.out.println("Calling CustomerVerify methods...\n");
      boolean exst = corbaInterface.exist(args[0],args[1]);
      System.out.println("Customer "+args[0]+" "+args[1]+"...");
      if(exst)
              System.out.println("Exists!");
      else
              System.out.println("Does not exist!");
      System.out.println("...done!");
    }
    catch (Exception e)
    {
      System.out.println(e.getMessage());
      e.printStackTrace();
    }
  }
}
```

The most significant lines of code are shown in bold. JNDI requires at least four properties to be set, in order to successfully connect to the database and look up remote objects (see Table 23.3).

The other important aspect of a client class that invokes remote methods through an ORB is the parameter passed to the lookup() method. In the listing above, lookup() is called passing the corbaURL string, which contains the service name and the object name concatenated together. The service name is a URL that consists of four parts, as shown in Table 23.4.

TABLE 23.3 JNDI properties that must be set to obtain a connection

PROPERTIES	MEANING
Context.URL_PKG_PREFIXES	Always set to “oracle.aurora.jndi.”
Context.SECURITY_PRINCIPAL	Username used to connect to the database.
Context.SECURITY_CREDENTIALS	The clear-text password.
Context.SECURITY_AUTHENTICATION	The type of authentication to be used. Since you are not using secure SSL connections, you specify ServiceCtx.NON_SSL_LOGIN.

TABLE 23.4 The four components that constitute a CORBA URL string

SERVICE NAME COMPONENT	EXPLANATION
Protocol	sess_iiop means using the session IIOP protocol.
Host name	The host name of the computer where the Oracle database is located.
Listener port number	The TCP port where the IIOP listener runs. By default this is port 2481.
Oracle SID	The Oracle SID (database system identifier) served by the IIOP listener.

In the example shown above, the Oracle instance `sun816` runs on the host `echidna`, where the IIOP listener listens for incoming connections to port 2481. Thus, the service name becomes:

```
sess_iiop://  + echidna: + 2481: + sun816 = sess_iiop://echidna:2481:sun816
```

You associated CustomerVerify and CustomerVerifyHelper with the name /test/trial on the server. To allow JNDI to locate the CustomerVerify object running on the server, you must concatenate /test/trial to the service name.

The final result, stored in corbURL, is:

```
sess_iiop://echidna:2481:sun816/test/trial
```

The InitialContext class, which implements the JNDI Context interface, provides the lookup() method, which obtains a reference to the remote object. Note that the object returned by lookup() must be cast into a reference of the same type as the expected remote object. In your case, you expect the lookup method to return a CustomerVerify object. You define an object handle of the CustomerVerify type:

```
CustomerVerify corbaInterface = null;
```

and you invoke InitialContext.lookup(), casting the returned object into a CustomerVerify object:

```
corbaInterface = (CustomerVerify) ic.lookup(corbaUrl);
```

Several things can go wrong when a client requests a reference to a remote object. For this reason, the instantiation of the InitialContext class and the invocation of the lookup() method are enclosed within a try…catch block. Three different exceptions are caught: ActivationException, CommunicationException, and NamingException. These represent the most common sources of errors during an exchange between client and server using a CORBA ORB.

NamingException is the superclass of all exceptions thrown by operations in the Context and DirContext interfaces. The exception object extending from NamingException reports detailed messages that help in diagnosing the cause of a failure of name resolution.

CommunicationException is thrown when the client is unable to communicate with the directory or naming service. The inability to communicate with the service may be caused by many factors, such as network partitioning, hardware or interface problems, or generic failures on either the client or server side.

ActivationException is a subclass of NamingException, and is defined in Aurora, the Oracle implementation of the JVM. It is thrown when an object inside the Aurora JVM fails to activate.

You can now test your first CORBA application. Using SQL*Plus, insert one record into the customer table.

```
SQL> insert into customer (name, surname, age) values
    2> ('John','Harris',29);
Row inserted.
SQL> commit;
```

Invoke the CORBA client, Lookup, passing the Java virtual machine a CLASSPATH that includes the JAR files required by the CORBA infrastructure.

```
$ java -classpath .:$ORACLE_HOME/lib/aurora_client.jar:\
> $ORACLE_HOME/lib/vbjorb.jar:$ORACLE_HOME/lib/vbjapp.jar: \
> Lookup John Harris
Creating an initial context
Looking for the CORBA server object published as 'test/trial'
Calling CustomerVerify methods...

Customer John Harris...
Exists!
...done!
```

Et voilà! You have successfully run the example. A word of caution: Don't think that you have mastered CORBA yet. There is much more to CORBA than what you have seen so far. The next chapter focuses on more advanced CORBA topics, such as mastering the IDL syntax, persistent object references, and using the COSNaming service directly. Before facing these challenges, however, you should get acquainted with the Java Transaction Service (JTS), as implemented by Oracle in JServer.

23.4 THE JAVA TRANSACTION SERVICE (JTS)

JServer supports a limited implementation of the Java Transaction Server (JTS). While Oracle Corporation is committed to provide a full implementation of JTS in upcoming releases of Oracle8i, the current JTS lacks a few important features, such as support for distributed transactions, support for nested transactions, and support for interoperability with other OMG-compliant Object Transaction Services (OTSs).

Furthermore, a transaction cannot currently span multiple database sessions, and transaction timeouts are not supported (the default timeout, which is not modifiable, is 60 seconds).

In spite of the limitations outlined above, JTS can be used effectively for single-session, single-database transactions.

23.4.1 CLIENT-SIDE AND SERVER-SIDE TRANSACTION DEMARCATION

You already know the four properties of a transaction, summarized by the acronym ACID (atomic, consistent, isolated, durable). A transaction must have, by definition, a definite starting point and a definite end. If you are using SQL*Plus, every DML statement implicitly starts a new transaction if it is not already part of a previously started transaction. The end of a transaction occurs when either the SQL COMMIT or ROLLBACK command is executed. You can also explicitly start a transaction by issuing the SET TRANSACTION command.

The act of marking the beginning and end of a transaction is known as *demarcating* a transaction. Another name for the same operation, *bracketing* a transaction, is popular among users of BEA Systems TUXEDO.

In a distributed environment, a transaction can be demarcated from the client side. The client encloses one or more method invocations on a server object with methods that explicitly begin and end a transaction. Thus, the client controls the transactional behavior of the application. An alternative approach has the server maintaining the transactional integrity of an application. All such transactions are server-side demarcated, and the connected clients are not responsible for starting transactions or ending them. The distinction between client-side and server-side transaction demarcation is particularly relevant in an Oracle/JTS environment, because the steps required for dealing with transactionally enabled objects are different.

In the case of client-side demarcated transactions, the client must use the AuroraTransactionService object to initialize a transaction context. This step is not required when the transaction is server-side demarcated.

An important component of the JTS architecture is the Transaction Context, a pseudo-object used to carry information about the state of the current transaction. The transaction context is passed from one object to another, usually from a client object to a server object that participates in the transaction, so that the server object can be informed of the status of the transaction initiated by the client. A transaction context is implicitly created by the transaction service after the latter is initialized and the `begin` transaction method is invoked. The transaction service then propagates the transaction context to every object that participates in the transaction.

The JTS provides methods for suspending and resuming transactions, and a method to force a rollback as the only outcome of a transaction. Table 23.5 lists the methods provided by the Oracle implementation of JTS.

23.4.2 CLIENT-SIDE TRANSACTIONS

If you want your transactions to be controlled by the client, follow the steps outlined below:

1. Import the following packages in your code:
   - ❑ oracle.aurora.jts.client.AuroraTransactionService

TABLE 23.5 Methods provided in the Oracle JTS implementation

JTS METHOD	PURPOSE
public void begin()	Starts a transaction.
public void commit(boolean report_heuristics)	Commits the current transaction. The report_heuristics boolean is not yet implemented, so it should be set to false.
public void rollback()	Rolls back the effects of the current transaction.
public Control suspend()	Suspends the current transaction. Control is a handle to a transaction context. It must be known by the method that will resume() to resume the transaction.
public void resume(Control ctrl)	Resumes a transaction that was suspended. Control is a handle to a transaction context.
public void rollback_only()	After a call to rollback_only() the only possible outcome of the current transaction is a rollback.
public Status get_status()	Retrieves the status of the current transaction. Possible values are: StatusActive StatusMarkedRollback StatusNoTransaction
public String get_transaction_name()	Retrieves the transaction ID as a string. If this method is called outside of a transaction context, the returned string is null.
public void set_timeout(int seconds)	Sets the transaction timeout. Currently not implemented. The default timeout is 60 seconds.

- oracle.aurora.jts.util.TS
- org.omg.CosTransactions

2. Invoke the initialize() method of the AuroraTransactionService class. You must pass two parameters to it:
   - the JNDI context, and
   - the URL of the application, of the form sess_iiop://<hostname>:<port>:<OracleSID>.
3. Begin a transaction by invoking the following method:

   ```
   oracle.aurora.jts.util.TS.getTS().getCurrent().begin()
   ```

4. End a transaction, by invoking either

   ```
   oracle.aurora.jts.util.TS.getTS().getCurrent().commit(false);
   ```

   or

   ```
   oracle.aurora.jts.util.TS.getTS().getCurrent().rollback();
   ```

The following code snippet illustrates the steps you have to take to drive the Aurora transaction service from a CORBA client. Customer is a remote object that exposes a few methods, such as getCustomer(), which returns an object of type CustomerInfo, and updateCustomer(), which updates the database with data taken from the CustomerInfo object. The code snippet increases the discount policy for the customer by 5 percent. Since the updated information is checkpointed to the database, the change occurs under transaction control.

```
Hashtable env = new Hashtable ();
env.put (Context.URL_PKG_PREFIXES,
"oracle.aurora.jndi");
env.put (Context.SECURITY_PRINCIPAL, "SCOTT");
env.put (Context.SECURITY_CREDENTIALS, "TIGER");
env.put (Context.SECURITY_AUTHENTICATION,
ServiceCtx.NON_SSL_LOGIN);
Context ic = new InitialContext (env);

AuroraTransactionService.initialize (ic, serviceURL);

Customer customer =
(Customer)ic.lookup (serviceURL + objectName);
CustomerInfo info;

TS.getTS ().getCurrent ().begin ();

info = customer.getCustomer ("SCOTT");
System.out.println (info.name + " " + " " + info.discount);
System.out.println ("Increase discount by 5%");
info.discount += (info.discount * 5) / 100;
```

```
customer.updateCustomer (info);
info = customer.getCustomer ("SCOTT");
System.out.println (info.name + " " + " " + info.discount);

TS.getTS ().getCurrent ().commit (true);
```

23.4.3 SERVER-SIDE TRANSACTIONS

If you want your server to drive the transactional behavior of the application, you don't need to import the transaction service definitions with

```
oracle.aurora.jts.client.AuroraTransactionService
```

because the server initializes a transaction context automatically. The two import statements

```
import oracle.aurora.jts.util.TS;
import org.omg.CosTransactions;
```

however, must be included in your server-side code. Note that the client can still control the flow of a transactionally enabled application, even if a transaction context is not created on the client side. The object remotely accessed by the client provides methods that use the JTS on the server. The only difference between true client-side demarcation and this technique is that the transaction context is never transferred over the network.

SUMMARY

This chapter introduced the world of CORBA. It began by familiarizing you with the fundamental elements of the CORBA architecture, such as the IDL, the ORB, the BOA, IIOP, and CORBA services like COSNaming and COSTransaction. Subsequently, you delved into code, crafting your first CORBA application. The chapter ended with a discussion of JTS as implemented by the Oracle JServer.

Chapter 24

ADVANCED CORBA TOPICS

- More on Interface Definition Language
- Managing the Oracle Name Space
- Using the CORBA Tie Mechanism
- Further References
- Summary

In this chapter, you will deepen your knowledge of the CORBA elements provided by Oracle8i. The discussion begins with a more thorough coverage of Interface Definition Language, an essential component of the CORBA architecture that must be mastered by all developers aspiring to create CORBA applications. The focus then moves to the Oracle Name Space, a fundamental component upon which the Oracle JNDI and COSNaming implementations are based. The ability to manage the Oracle Name Space will give you more control of the security aspects of the deployment of CORBA applications that run within the Oracle environment.

The next topic is the implementation of a CORBA server using delegation rather than inheritance. Implementing this component will give you a chance to familiarize yourself with the advanced features of Oracle JDeveloper, the Oracle standard tool for developing Java applications.

A section that shows how to use CORBA Interoperable Object References (IORs) concludes the chapter.

24.1 MORE ON INTERFACE DEFINITION LANGUAGE

In Chapter 23, you were briefly introduced to the CORBA Interface Definition Language. To facilitate introducing the entire CORBA architecture, including the ORB, the Object Adapter, the IIOP protocol, and so on, we did not provide a detailed treatment of IDL. This section provides more information about IDL.

In order to become an accomplished CORBA developer, you should be familiar with the IDL datatypes and their Java counterparts. CORBA is all about platform- and language-independence, which means that in the course of your professional career as a Java developer you will probably be confronted with the task of integrating C or C++ with Java through a CORBA ORB. Procedural languages like C and Pascal organize related information in *structures* (C) or *records* (Pascal). Java does not have either structures or records, but the `idl2java` compiler automatically generates a mapping between IDL structures and Java classes. The same is true for IDL collections and enumerations.

You need to understand how the mapping between IDL data structures and Java occurs. Before we discuss complex data types, though, you will first have to be acquainted with the basic IDL to Java datatype mapping.

24.1.1 IDL TO JAVA BASIC DATATYPE MAPPING

Table 24.1 summarizes the most commonly used IDL datatypes, together with their mappings to Java datatypes. It lists the minimum and maximum values that can be stored in a given numeric datatype.

The mapping is straightforward because both IDL and Java have adopted the IEEE 754-1985 standard for binary floating-point representation. The map-

TABLE 24.1 IDL to Java datatype mapping

IDL DATATYPE	JAVA DATATYPE	MINIMUM VALUE	MAXIMUM VALUE
boolean	boolean	–	–
char	char	–	–
wchar	char	–	–
octet	byte	–128	+127
string	String	–	–
wstring	String	–	–
short	short	-2^{15}	$+2^{15}-1$
long	int	-2^{31}	$+2^{31}-1$
long long	long	-2^{63}	$+2^{63}-1$
float	float	–3.4028237E+38F	+3.4028237E+38F
double	double	–1.79769313486231570E+308	+1.79769313486231570E+308

pings between IDL signed integers and Java integers are also direct. Unfortunately, Java does not support *unsigned* integers, and the high-order bit of the IDL range cannot be represented in Java as a positive value. This leads to an inelegant workaround: unsigned integers that exceed the storage capacity of the Java signed integers are represented as negative numbers, according to the following formula:

$$\text{original unsigned large value} - 2^{x}$$

where x is the number of bits in the Java mapped type. Table 24.2 illustrates the concept.

A Java short is a 16-bit type. Applying the formula introduced above, you subtract 2 to the power of 16 to the value of the corresponding IDL number:

$$65{,}392 - 2^{16} = 65{,}392 - 65{,}536 = -144$$

TABLE 24.2 IDL to Java datatype mapping for unsigned integers

IDL DATATYPE	JAVA TYPE	MINIMUM VALUE	MAXIMUM VALUE	
			IDL MAXIMUM	JAVA MAXIMUM
unsigned short	short	0	65,392	–144
unsigned long	int	0	4,037,130,942	–257,836,354
unsigned long long	long	0	17,870,556,004,450,629,632	–576,188,069,258,921,984

A Java int is a 32-bit integer. Applying the same formula, you obtain:

$$4{,}037{,}130{,}942 - 2^{32} = 4{,}037{,}130{,}942 - 4294967296 = -257836354$$

It is up to the developer to deal with large unsigned IDL numbers transformed according to the representation described above. If you encounter an unexpected negative number where an unsigned number was expected, you must perform the conversion yourself.

To see how idl2java performs the mapping between IDL and Java types, you will generate Java classes from the following IDL file:

```
module explain_datatypes
{
   interface dtypes
   {
        attribute boolean      myBoolean;
        attribute char         myChar;
        attribute wchar        myWchar;
        attribute octet        myOctet;
        attribute string       myString;
        attribute wstring      myWstring;
        attribute short        myShort;
        attribute long         myLong;
        attribute long long    myLongLong;
        attribute float        myFloat;
        attribute double       myDouble;
    };
};
```

If you invoke the idl2java pre-processor using the following syntax:

```
idl2java -no_tie -no_comments dtypes.idl
```

and look at the generated dtypes.java file, you can see how the IDL types have been translated by the IDL pre-processor.

```
package explain_datatypes;

public interface dtypes extends
com.inprise.vbroker.CORBA.Object
{
  public void myBoolean( boolean myBoolean);
  public boolean myBoolean();
  public void myChar( char myChar);
  public char myChar();
```

```
      public void myWchar( char myWchar);
      public char myWchar();
      public void myOctet( byte myOctet);
      public byte myOctet();
      public void myString( java.lang.String myString);
      public java.lang.String myString();
      public void myWstring( java.lang.String myWstring);
      public java.lang.String myWstring();
      public void myShort( short myShort);
      public short myShort();
      public void myLong( int myLong);
      public int myLong();
      public void myLongLong( long myLongLong);
      public long myLongLong();
      public void myFloat( float myFloat);
      public float myFloat();
      public void myDouble( double myDouble);
      public double myDouble();
    }
```

The attributes defined in the IDL file have been translated into getter and setter methods. The translation of the IDL types into Java types follows the convention illustrated in Table 24.1.

Now that you know how to map the basic IDL datatypes, you can take on the more challenging task of mapping complex data structures, such as CORBA structs and collections, to their Java counterparts.

24.1.2 MAPPING RECORDS, ENUMS, UNIONS, SEQUENCES, AND ARRAYS

CORBA is all about interoperability and language/platform independence. When you use IDL, as opposed to the Caffeine compiler, you can generate not only Java, but also C/C++ stubs and skeletons, as well as stubs and skeletons for all CORBA-supported languages. The discussion in this section mainly concerns interoperability with C/C++, so it will focus on elements commonly used in C/C++, such as structs, unions, and enums. In addition, IDL provides two types of ordered collections, sequence and array. Since these are commonly used in CORBA applications, you must understand their mapping to Java entities.

24.1.2.1 IDL Structs. An IDL struct is mapped to a final Java class that implements one instance variable for each field defined in the struct. The name of the class corresponds to the struct name, and two constructors are generated. One takes the values of all the fields comprising the struct, which are used to initialize the instance variables. The other is a zero-argument constructor that initializes all instance variables to 0 for primitive types or null for reference types. The holder and helper classes are also generated by the idl2java compiler.

The following IDL struct:

```
struct Customer
{
        string name;
        string surname;
        long   age;
        string companyName;
        string address;
};
```

generates the Java class shown below:

```
final public class Customer
{
  public java.lang.String name;
  public java.lang.String surname;
  public int age;
  public java.lang.String companyName;
  public java.lang.String address;
  public Customer() { }
  public Customer(java.lang.String name,
                  java.lang.String surname,
                  int age,
                  java.lang.String companyName,
                  java.lang.String address)
  {
    this.name = name;
    this.surname = surname;
    this.age = age;
    this.companyName = companyName;
    this.address = address;
  }
  public java.lang.String toString()
  {
    org.omg.CORBA.Any any =
        org.omg.CORBA.ORB.init().create_any();
    CustomerHelper.insert(any, this);
    return any.toString();
  }
}
```

Note that all the elements of the IDL struct become public instance variables. Developers can use the dot notation to access and modify each variable, as in:

```
Customer cust = new Customer();
cust.name = "John";
cust.surname = "Smith";
...
etc, etc.
```

24.1.2.2 IDL Enums. IDL Enumerations are mapped to public final Java classes. Each mapped element of the IDL enumeration produces two static constants. The first constant, which is of type `int`, replicates the name of the element identifier, prefixed with an underscore. The second constant is a reference to an instance of the mapped final class; it has the same name as the element that represents the element's value. An example will make this clear. Given the following IDL enumeration:

```
enum sex {female,male,unknown};
```

the generated Java class is:

```
public class sex
{
  final public static int _female = 0;
  final public static int _male = 1;
  final public static int _unknown = 2;
  final public static sex female = new sex(_female);
  final public static sex male = new sex(_male);
  final public static sex unknown = new sex(_unknown);
  private int __value;
  protected sex(int value)
  {
    this.__value = value;
  }
  public int value() { return __value; }
  public static sex from_int(int $value)
  {
    switch($value)
    {
    case _female:
      return female;
    case _male:
      return male;
```

```
        case _unknown:
          return unknown;
        default:
          throw new org.omg.CORBA.BAD_PARAM("Enum out of
range: "+
                    "[0.." + (3 - 1) + "]: " + $value);
        }
      }
      public java.lang.String toString()
      {
        org.omg.CORBA.Any any =
          org.omg.CORBA.ORB.init().create_any();
        sexHelper.insert(any, this);
        return any.toString();
      }
    }
```

Once your enumeration is implemented in Java, you can use the following expressions:

```
sex._male
sex._female
```

Alternatively, you can instantiate an object, as in:

```
sex gender = new sex(sex._male);
System.out.println(gender.value());
```

24.1.2.3 IDL Unions. An IDL union is a little different from a C/C++ union. In both cases, the amount of storage required corresponds to the storage of the largest element in the union. In IDL, a union must be discriminated, that is, the union header specifies a tag field indicating which element of the union is used by the current instance of the call. All expressions following the case keyword must be compatible with the tag type. The type specified after the switch keyword can be an integer, a char, a boolean, or an enum. A default case can appear in the union declaration only if the declaration does not include every possible value specified by the discriminator. Here is an example of an IDL union declaration:

```
enum Season {Spring,Summer,Autumn,Winter};

union currentSeason switch (Season)
{
        case Spring:
                long Temperature;
```

```
                case Winter:
                        long Rigid;
                case Autumn:
                        long lessRigid;
                case Summer:
                        long hotTemperature;
        };
```

When you process the IDL file by running `idl2java`, the generated Java class contains:

- A default (no-argument) constructor.
- An accessor method, called discriminator(), which implements the union's discriminant.
- An accessor method for each union variant.
- A mutator method for each union variant.

The generated Java class follows:

```
final public class currentSeason
{
  private java.lang.Object _object;
  private Season _disc;
  public currentSeason() { }
  public Season discriminator() { return _disc; }
  public int Temperature()
  {
    if(_disc.value() != (int) Season.Spring.value() &&
      true)
    {
      throw new org.omg.CORBA.BAD_OPERATION("Temperature");
    }
    return ((java.lang.Integer) _object).intValue();
  }
  public int Rigid()
  {
    if(_disc.value() != (int) Season.Winter.value() &&
      true)
    {
      throw new org.omg.CORBA.BAD_OPERATION("Rigid");
    }
    return ((java.lang.Integer) _object).intValue();
  }
  public int lessRigid()
```

```
  {
    if(_disc.value() != (int) Season.Autumn.value() &&
      true)
    {
      throw new org.omg.CORBA.BAD_OPERATION("lessRigid");
    }
    return ((java.lang.Integer) _object).intValue();
  }
  public int hotTemperature()
  {
    if(_disc.value() != (int) Season.Summer.value() &&
      true)
    {
      throw new org.omg.CORBA.BAD_OPERATION("hotTemperature");
    }
    return ((java.lang.Integer) _object).intValue();
  }
  public void Temperature(int value)
  {
    _disc = (Season) Season.Spring;
    _object = new java.lang.Integer(value);
  }
  public void Rigid(int value)
  {
    _disc = (Season) Season.Winter;
    _object = new java.lang.Integer(value);
  }
  public void lessRigid(int value)
  {
    _disc = (Season) Season.Autumn;
    _object = new java.lang.Integer(value);
  }
  public void hotTemperature(int value)
  {
    _disc = (Season) Season.Summer;
    _object = new java.lang.Integer(value);
  }
  public java.lang.String toString()
  {
    org.omg.CORBA.Any any = org.omg.CORBA.ORB.init().create_any();
    currentSeasonHelper.insert(any, this);
    return any.toString();
  }
}
```

The accessor and mutator methods for all variants are overloaded. The names of each of them match the corresponding variant's name. The accessor method takes no parameters, and simply returns the value associated with the union's variant. The mutator method takes a single parameter of the same type as the union's variant. When you access the union in your Java code, call the discriminator method before calling a union accessor method, to make sure that the union is in the expected mode.

24.1.2.4 IDL Arrays. IDL provides multi-dimensional fixed-size arrays that are used to store sets of elements of the same type. The size of each array dimension must be specified when the array is defined (i.e., it must be known at compile time).

An example of IDL array follows:

```
typedef short cells [200] [200];
typedef long skirtSize[6];
```

The idl2java compiler only creates the helper and holder classes for cells and skirtSize, but no array class is generated. You must define and use the cells and skirtSize arrays in your Java code, as in:

```
public short cells[][];
public int skirtSize[];
...
cells = new short[200][200];
skirtSize = new int [6];
```

The array size specified in the IDL definition is used by the helper class, so if your code mistakenly exceeds the array boundary, a CORBA:MARSHAL exception is raised.

24.1.2.5 IDL Sequences. An IDL sequence is a one-dimensional array characterized by a maximum size and a maximum length. Sequences can be bounded or unbounded. They are bounded if a maximum size is specified during sequence definition. An unbounded sequence can be of unlimited length. This feature makes sequences very attractive to developers, who usually prefer IDL sequences to IDL arrays. An example of IDL sequence definition follows:

```
typedef sequence <short,100> CustomerAge; // Bounded sequence
typedef sequence <float> LabMeasurement;  // Unbounded sequence
```

As is true for arrays, the idl2java compiler only generates helper and holder classes, but not a sequence class. You must define and use the IDL sequence in your Java code:

```
public short CustomerAge[];
public float LabMeasurement[];
...
CustomerAge = new short [100];
LabMeasurement = new float [1324];
```

If the sequence is bounded and you exceed the sequence boundary, a CORBA:MARSHAL exception is raised.

24.2 MANAGING THE ORACLE NAME SPACE

CORBA applications perform the crucial step of obtaining, through the ORB, references to objects published by the server. Oracle publishes nontransient objects in a database instance, using an implementation of the CORBA COSNaming service; it provides a URL-based JNDI interface to COSNaming to make it easy for clients written in Java to locate and activate published objects.

Published objects are stored in the Oracle Name Space, whose structure resembles that of a file system. A file system *directory* in the Oracle Name Space corresponds to a *publishing context*. By default, a newly created Oracle instance provides three publishing contexts: /bin, /etc, and /test. In order to manage an Oracle Name Space, you must use the `sess_sh` utility. Under both Unix and Windows NT/2000, `sess_sh` is a wrapper that sets the appropriate environment variables (e.g., JAVA_HOME and CLASSPATH) and invokes the Aurora/JServer shell.

`Sess_sh` takes a few parameters, such as username, password, and IIOP service name. If you want to create a new publishing context directly under root, you must connect to the Oracle instance as SYS. Here is how `sess_sh` is used:

```
$ sess_sh -user sys -password change_on_install \
  -service sess_iiop://localhost:2481:sun816
--Aurora/ORB Session Shell--
--type "help" at the command line for help message
$ ls
bin/    etc/    test/
$
```

You connected as SYS. At database creation, the SYS account is given the default password of `change_on_install`. If you are using your own personal Oracle instance, chances are that you did not change the default password. If you are using an Oracle instance managed by a DBA, the password is likely to have been changed, and you must negotiate the creation of a publishing context with that DBA.

Assuming that you can connect as SYS, this is how to create a new publishing context:

```
$ mkdir trial
$ ls
bin/    etc/    test/    trial/
```

The *mkdir* command creates publishing contexts. Most of the commands used to manage the Oracle Name Space closely resemble the Unix commands used to interact with file systems. You can modify the access level and ownership of publishing contexts and published objects using *chmod* and *chown*, respectively.

In order to change the ownership of contexts or objects, you must log in as SYS. For example, using the chown command in sess_sh, you can change the ownership of the /trial publishing context to user jtaylor.

```
$ chown jtaylor  /trial
$ ls -l
Read      Write     Exec      Owner     Date Time     Name       Schema
Class      Helper
PUBLIC    SYS       PUBLIC    SYS       Feb 28   2000 bin/
PUBLIC    SYS       PUBLIC    SYS       Feb 28   2000 etc/
PUBLIC    PUBLIC    PUBLIC    SYS       Feb 28   2000 test/
SYS       SYS       SYS       JTAYLOR   Apr 24   2000 trial/
```

If you wanted to give execute access to the /trial directory to PUBLIC, you could use the chmod command, as shown below.

```
$ chmod +e public /trial
$ ls -l
 Read      Write     Exec      Owner     Date Time     Name       Schema
Class      Helper
PUBLIC    SYS       PUBLIC    SYS       Feb 28   2000 bin/
PUBLIC    SYS       PUBLIC    SYS       Feb 28   2000 etc/
PUBLIC    PUBLIC    PUBLIC    SYS       Feb 28   2000 test/
SYS       SYS       PUBLIC    JTAYLOR   Apr 24   2000 trial/
                    SYS
```

A very useful command implemented in sess_sh is the *java* command, which is analogous to the JDK java command: it invokes a class-static main method. The class must have been loaded in JServer using loadjava. The real advantage of running a Java class from sess_sh is that the standard output and all exceptions are captured and displayed on the terminal associated with sess_sh. The usual destination of exceptions and output messages is one or more database trace files, which require tools like tkprof to be read, formatted, and interpreted.[1]

[1]Tkprof is a formatting utility that produces a human-readable output from a database trace file.

TABLE 24.3 Commands and syntax implemented by `sess_sh`

<table>
<tr><th>COMMAND</th><th>SYNTAX</th><th>PURPOSE</th></tr>
<tr><td>exit</td><td>Exit</td><td>Leaves sess_sh.</td></tr>
<tr><td>pwd</td><td>Pwd</td><td>Prints the current publishing context.</td></tr>
<tr><td>cd</td><td>cd [path]</td><td>Changes the current publishing context to the new publishing context specified in [path].</td></tr>
<tr><td>ls</td><td>ls {-l|-R|-ldir}</td><td>Shows the content of publishing objects. The –l option causes a long listing, the –R option lists recursively, the –ldir option lists publishing contexts in the long format ignoring published objects.</td></tr>
<tr><td>chmod</td><td>chmod {+|-} {r|w|e} {<user>|<role>}[,{<user>| <role>}…] <objectname></td><td>Changes user or role rights over publishing contexts or published objects. The + signs grants the privilege, while the – sign revokes the privilege. Privileges are in the form wre, or write, read, and execute.</td></tr>
<tr><td>chown</td><td>chown {<user>|<role>} <objectname></td><td>Changes the ownership of publishing contexts and published objects.</td></tr>
<tr><td>mkdir</td><td>mkdir [-path] <name></td><td>Creates a publishing context. When issued with the –path option, intermediate publishing contexts are created if they don't already exist.</td></tr>
<tr><td>mv</td><td>mv <old> <new></td><td>Moves or renames published objects.</td></tr>
<tr><td>rm</td><td>rm [-r] <object> … <object></td><td>Removes publishing contexts and published objects. The –r option removes recursively.</td></tr>
<tr><td>publish</td><td>publish <name> <class> <helper> [{-e| -g| -h}] [-republish] [-schema <schema>]</td><td>Creates or replaces (republishes) a published object in a publishing context.</td></tr>
<tr><td>java</td><td>java class [arg1 ... argn] {-schema|-version}</td><td>Invokes a class-static main()method. The class must have been loaded with loadjava.</td></tr>
</table>

For this reason, running a Java class through `sess_sh` can prove to be an invaluable debugging tool.

When you are finished with `sess_sh`, you return to the operating system shell by typing `exit`. Table 24.3 summarizes the most-used commands and syntax implemented by `sess_sh`.

24.3 USING THE CORBA TIE MECHANISM

Chapter 23 introduced the two main mechanisms for associating an implementation class with the skeleton class generated by the IDL (or Caffeine) compiler. Both are variations of the Adapter design pattern; the class adapter uses inheritance, while the instance adapter uses delegation to accomplish the same goal. The example provided in Chapter 23 made use of the inheritance mechanism. The alternative approach, known as the *tie* mechanism, is based on delegation.

In this section you will use Oracle JDeveloper to produce the code required to develop the example application, which implements a tie approach to associate the implementation class with the IDL-generated skeleton. While it is possible to apply Oracle CORBA technologies by using an editor, and by launching the required compilers from the shell prompt or from an editing environment such as `emacs`, a visual tool like JDeveloper enormously simplifies the production of CORBA code. From the JDeveloper IDE, it is even possible to deploy the finished application to a remote Oracle database simply by answering a few questions in the deployment wizard. JDeveloper can only execute under Microsoft Windows, however, so Unix and Linux cannot be used as development environments if you decide to give JDeveloper a go (although, with some effort, the resulting applications can be deployed to those platforms).

After installing JDeveloper, you should see a menu entry under Start->Programs->Oracle JDeveloper that permits you to launch the IDE. Once you are in the IDE environment, you can create a new workspace, as shown in Figure 24.1.

When you have created a new workspace, you can then create a new project by clicking on the "New Project" option on the File menu. This starts the new project wizard, which allows you to specify several options related to the type of project you want to create. In the present case, you choose "CORBA Server Object," as shown in Figure 24.2.

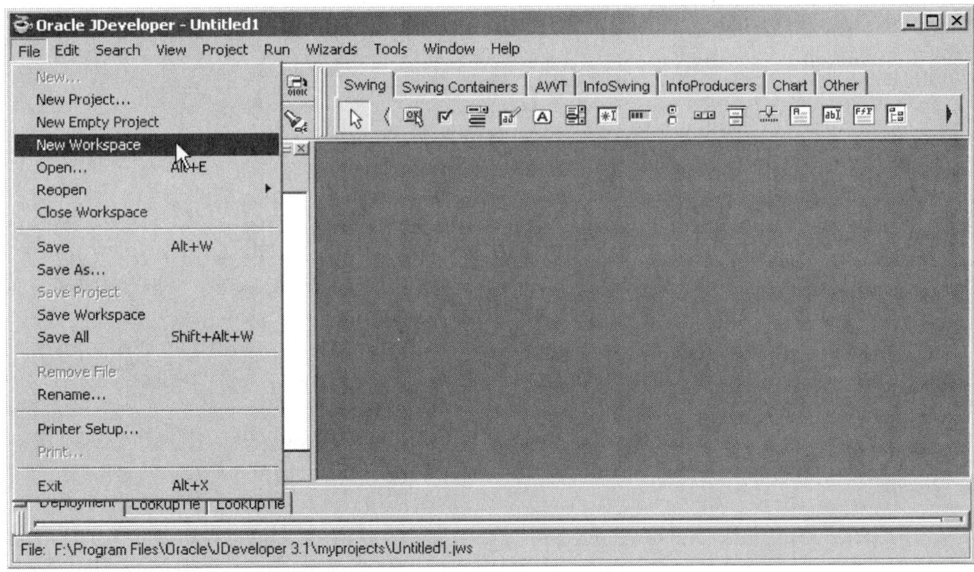

FIGURE 24.1 Creating a new workspace in JDeveloper.

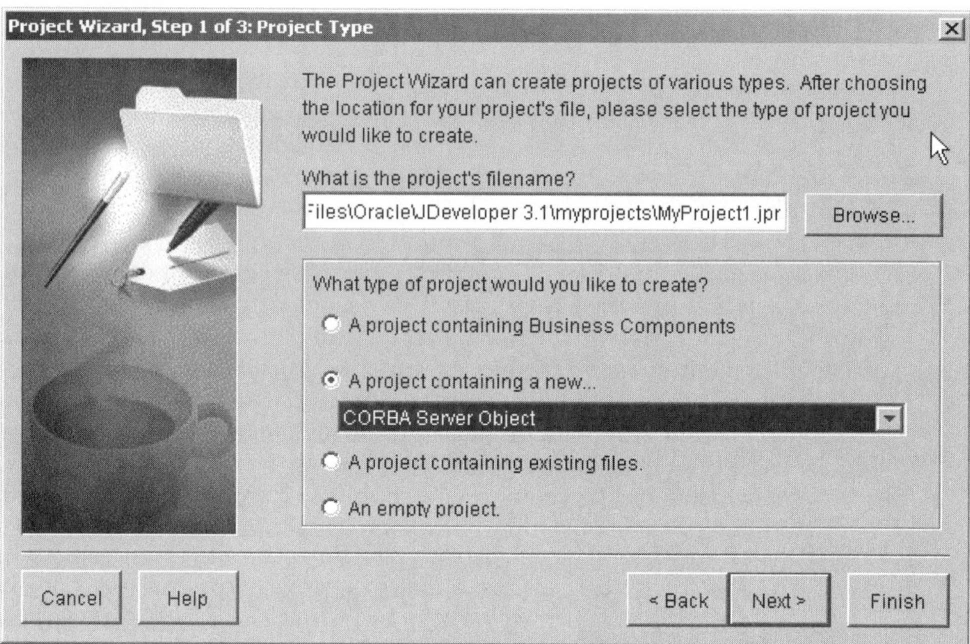

FIGURE 24.2 Using the new project wizard to create a CORBA server object.

After answering all the questions asked by the wizard, you return to the IDE, and a new wizard, the CORBA server wizard, is automatically started. For the sake of this exercise, click on cancel to dismiss the wizard. In the JDeveloper navigator pane, you should find a root node named Untitled1.jws and two child nodes named Connections and MyProject1.jpr. Click on Untitled1.jws to make it current, and then click on File->Rename. Give the workspace a meaningful name and close the message box by clicking on the save button. Click on MyProject1.jpr and do the same, renaming the project with a meaningful name. Now click on Connections and create the required connections to Oracle. You need a JDBC and an IIOP connection. The JDBC connection is used by JDeveloper to deploy the Java objects to the database, and the IIOP connection is used to publish the CORBA objects. You create the connections by using the connection manager, which can be launched by double-clicking on the Connections node displayed in the navigator pane tree. As an alternative, you can use the "Connections..." option from the Tools menu. The connection manager window displays an empty listbox the first time you access it. Click on the "New..." button to have JDeveloper display the connection window. Create a JDBC connection to the Oracle database where you wish to deploy your CORBA application by filling in the relevant fields. An example is shown in Figure 24.3.

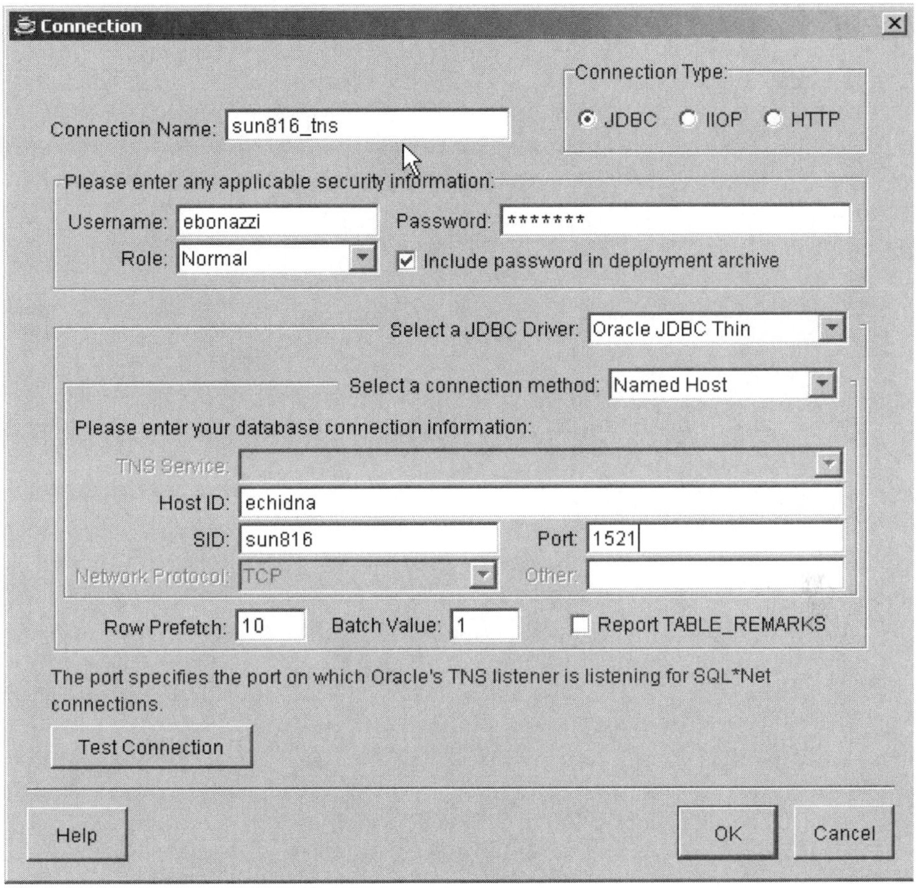

FIGURE 24.3 Creating a JDBC connection from the connection manager.

In this example, the host id named `echidna` identifies a Sun Solaris server running Oracle 8.1.6. Click OK to create the JDBC connection.

You must also create an IIOP connection, as illustrated in Figure 24.4.

Before leaving the connection dialog, test the connection to ensure that the parameters are correct. Simply click on the "Test Connection" button after you have filled in the form.

You can now start coding your application. First, create the IDL file that contains the IDL interfaces to the remote objects. You do this by clicking on the "New…" option of the File menu. When the dialog is displayed, select "IDL File," as shown in Figure 24.5.

Click OK to return to the IDE, which now displays a new element in the project navigator pane, called Untitled1.idl. Select Untitled1.idl and use the re-

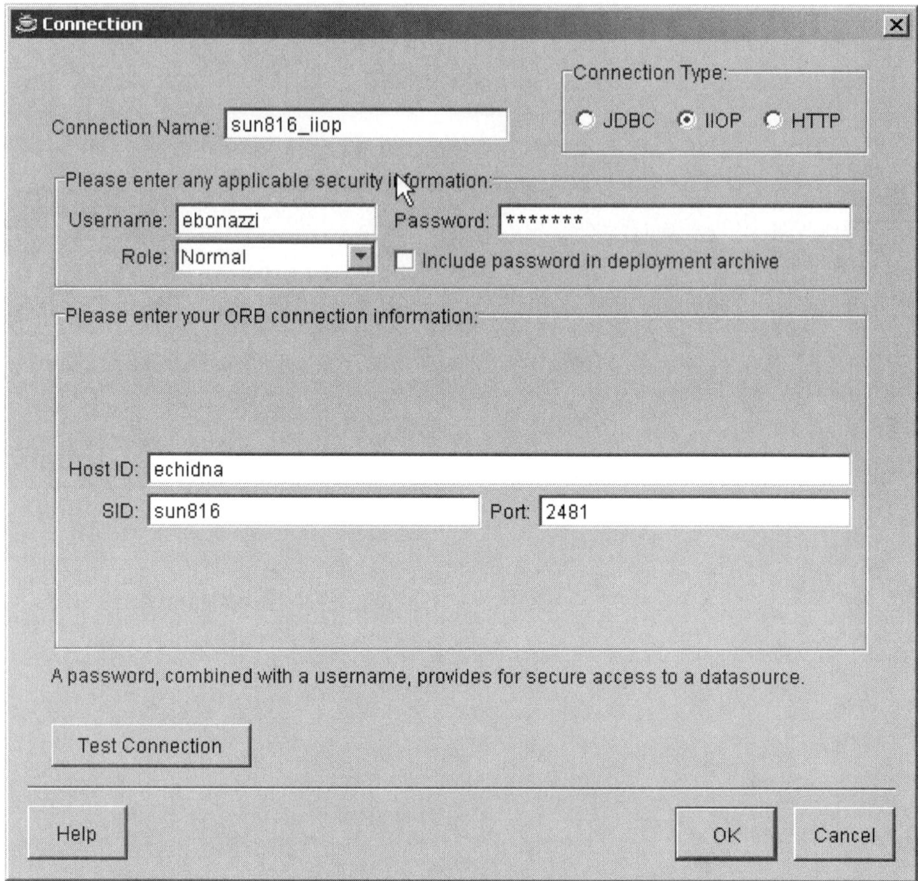

FIGURE 24.4 Creating an IIOP connection from the connection manager.

name option of the File menu to give the IDL file a more meaningful name, such as tie.idl. If you double-click the IDL object, the viewer source pane displays the empty IDL file. Enter the IDL syntax to define the interface used by your example, which is a variation of the CustomerVerify program introduced in Chapter 23, modified to use the delegation mechanism instead of the inheritance mechanism. The IDL contents follow:

```
exception SQLError
{
   wstring explain;
};
interface lookup
{
```

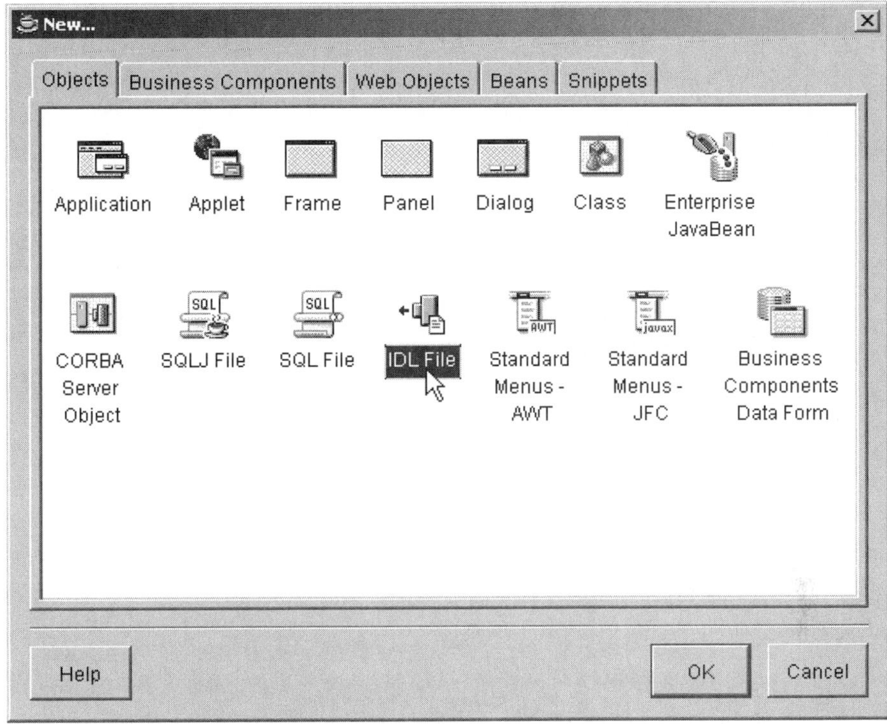

FIGURE 24.5 Creating an IDL file.

```
        boolean exist(in string name,
                      in string surname)
                      raises (SQLError);
    };
```

After you complete the IDL file, invoke the `idl2java` compiler to produce CORBA stubs and skeletons. In JDeveloper, you do this visually, highlighting the IDL node and clicking on the right-hand mouse button, which displays a pop-up menu, as shown in Figure 24.6.

The idl2java compiler creates a folder called "Generated CORBA Files," which contains all the generated stub and skeleton files. If you double-click on this folder's icon, the project navigator displays the generated files, as shown in Figure 24.7.

It is now time to customize the file _example_lookup.java, produced by `idl2java`, to provide the services included in the lookup interface. By default, the Visigenic `idl2java` generates a set of source files that use an inheritance-based mechanism. You should therefore erase all automatically produced source

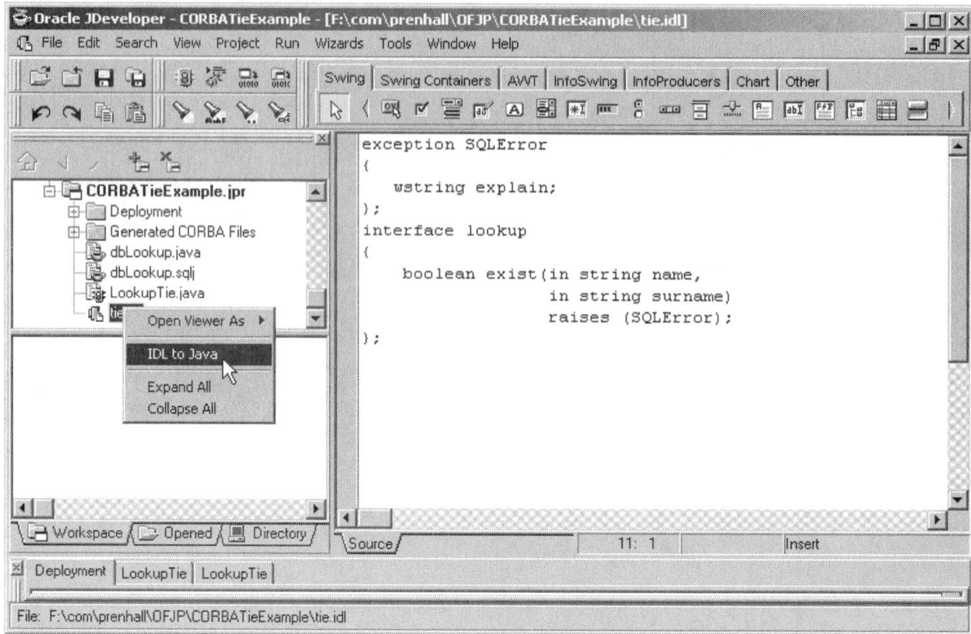

FIGURE 24.6 Generating stubs and skeletons from the IDL file.

code contained in _example_lookup.java. Rename the file LookupInvoke.java and enter the following code:

```
import oracle.aurora.AuroraServices.ActivatableObject;

public class LookupInvoke implements lookupOperations,
ActivatableObject
{

  public boolean exist(
    java.lang.String name,
    java.lang.String surname
  ) throws
    SQLError
  {
    int cnt = dbLookup.lookupCustomer(name,surname);
    if (cnt > 0)
      return true;
    else
      return false;
```

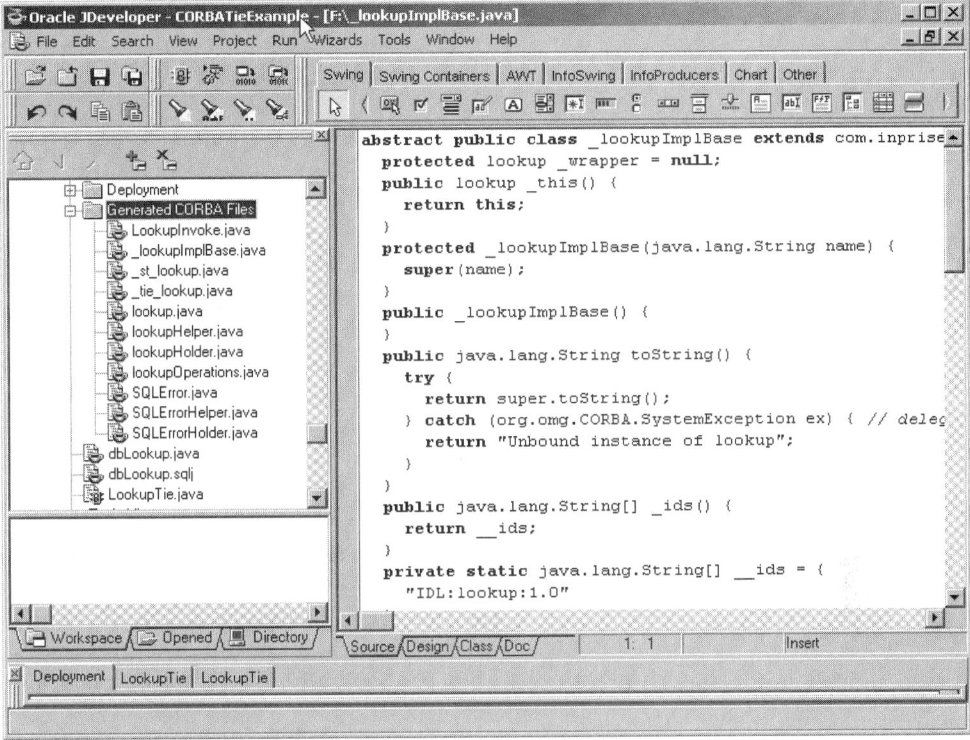

FIGURE 24.7 Stub and skeleton files generated by the idl2java compiler.

```
    }
    public org.omg.CORBA.Object _initializeAuroraObject ()
    {
      return new _tie_lookup (this);
    }
}
```

The first line imports the definition for the ActivatableObject, which is required when you want to use the tie mechanism in Aurora/JServer.[2] ActivatableObject is an interface specific to the Oracle implementation of CORBA, defining a method called *_initializeAuroraObject()* that all classes implementing the tie mechanism must implement. Your class, LookupInvoke, implements lookupOperations, the interface automatically generated by idl2java that defines the *exist()* method, and ActivatableObject, required by Aurora/JServer.

[2]Aurora is the name of the Java Virtual Machine implemented in the Oracle kernel in Oracle 8i release 1. The kernal-bundled JVM has been subsequently renamed JServer."

The exist() method calls the lookupCustomer() method implemented in the dbLookup class. Since this class is the same as the one used in the CustomerVerify example presented in Chapter 23, it will not be discussed any further here. Instead, focus your attention on the way the LookupInvoke class is built, to understand the difference between the inheritance and the delegation approaches. To use the inheritance mechanism, you would have LookupInvoke extend _lookupImplBase, and you would implement two constructor methods, one parameterless and one receiving a string. They would both call the superclass' constructor. For the details of such an inheritance implementation, see the discussion of the CustomerVerifyServer class included in the CustomerVerify example in Chapter 23. By using the tie approach, you avoid inheriting from the _*<inteface-name>*ImplBase class, but you need one more instance per object reference and one more method invocation per client request. If you are striving to achieve maximum performance, the approach based on inheritance is probably better, especially if your CORBA server instantiates thousands of objects in a very short time.

On the other hand, Java does not support multiple inheritance, and in large projects the CORBA-server implementation class is often required to inherit from a higher-level, application-specific class. If you want your server implementation class to inherit from a parent class, you must use the tie approach.

Note that the CORBA client that uses the services provided by the CORBA server (or, more accurately, the CORBA *servant*) does not change. It still invokes the lookup method implemented in the InitialContext class to obtain a reference to the remote CORBA object.

Once you have provided an implementation for the exist() method, you are finished with the CORBA server. You can now compile all the classes and deploy them to the target Oracle database. In JDeveloper, click on Project->Rebuild Project to recompile all the Java classes in your project, and then start the deployment wizard by clicking on Project->Deploy->New Deployment Profile. The wizard page shown in Figure 24.8 is displayed by JDeveloper.

Select "CORBA object to Oracle8i" as delivery option and click on the Next button. The next page displayed by the wizard allows you to specify all the Java objects to be deployed (see Figure 24.9).

When you have selected all the necessary files and clicked on the Next button, JDeveloper presents a page that allows you to choose the publishing parameters (see Figure 24.10).

In the field named "Object Name," specify the absolute pathname of the CORBA object you are deploying. In this case you are using the "test" Name Space, one of the default name spaces provided by Oracle8i (see above, section 24.2). The server class is the one that contains your tie implementation of the CORBA server, LookupServer. The helper class, lookupHelper, was automatically produced by `idl2java`. You also select the Republish, Create Public Synonyms, and Resolve checkboxes. Finally, click on the Next button. JDeveloper displays the JDBC connection page (see Figure 24.11), where you can enter the connection previously created and named `sun816_tns`.

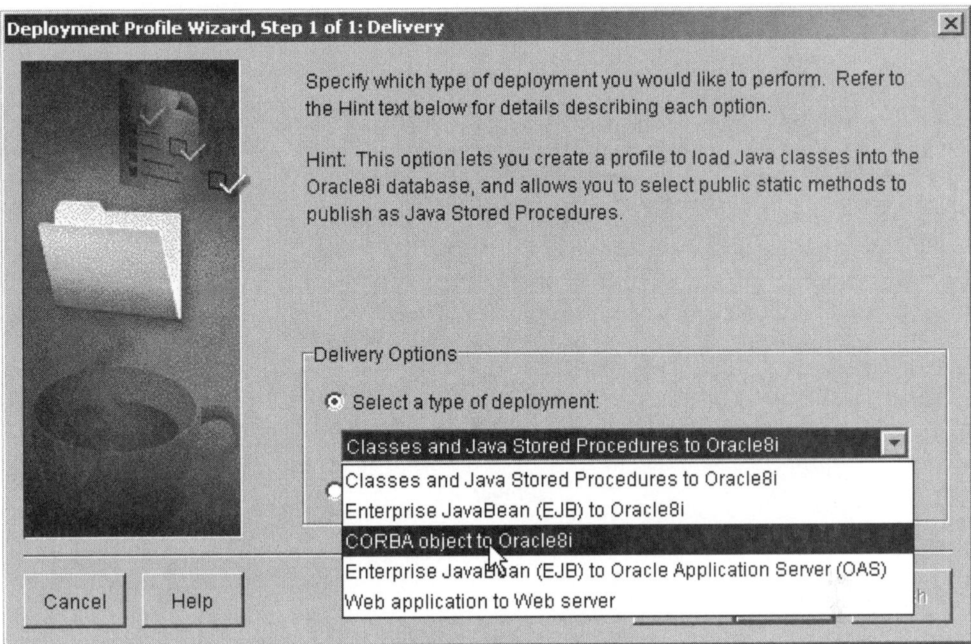

FIGURE 24.8 The initial step performed by the deployment wizard.

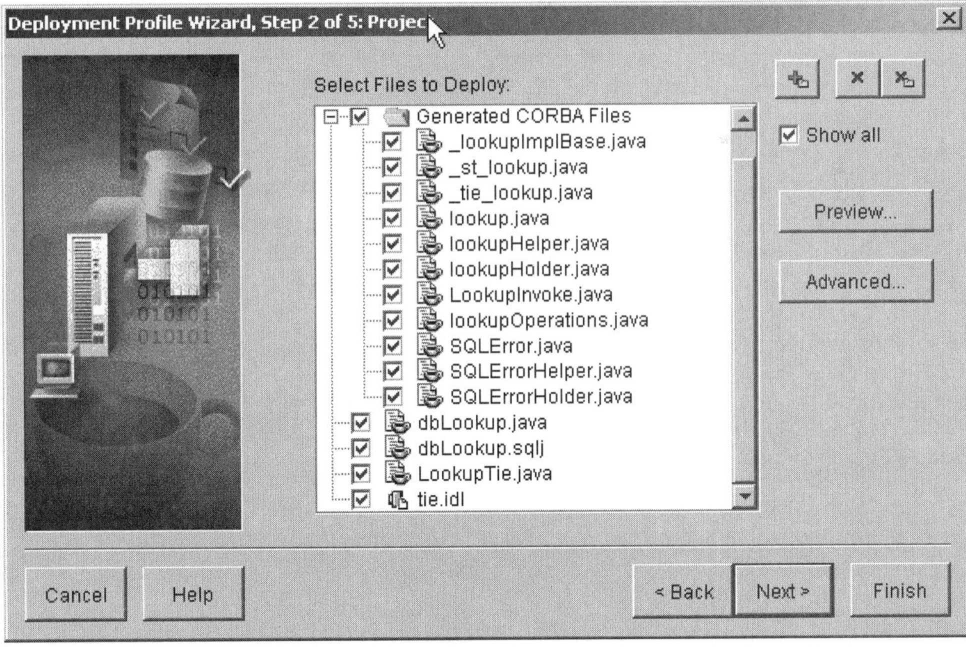

FIGURE 24.9 The Java objects to be deployed are selected.

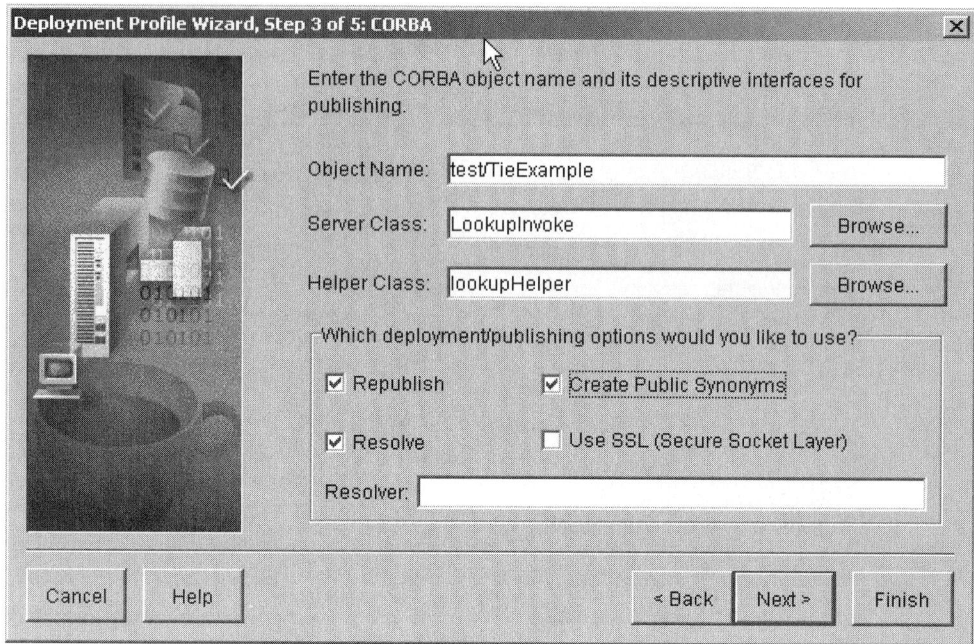

FIGURE 24.10 Providing the publishing parameters to the deployment wizard.

Select the connection `sun816_tns` from the list box and click on Next. The form displayed by the deployment wizard asks you to provide an IIOP connection (see Figure 24.12).

In the list box marked "Connection," choose the IIOP connection previously defined and named Sun816_iiop. Click on the Next button to move to the last wizard page, where you specify the jar file that contains the Java objects to be deployed (see Figure 24.13).

After you click on the Finish button, JDeveloper starts deploying the application onto the target Oracle database instance. In this example, the target database instance resides on a different machine, a Sun server running Solaris.

JDeveloper displays all the steps performed during deployment in a pane shown at the bottom of the IDE (see Figure 24.14). If an error occurs during deployment, you can look at the pane to evaluate any diagnostic messages that may be helpful in troubleshooting the problem. If you place the mouse pointer on the IDE pane that displays the deployment log and then click on the right-hand mouse button, a popup menu appears. One of the options allows you to save the content of the log window into a file, a very useful option when troubleshooting a faulty deployment.

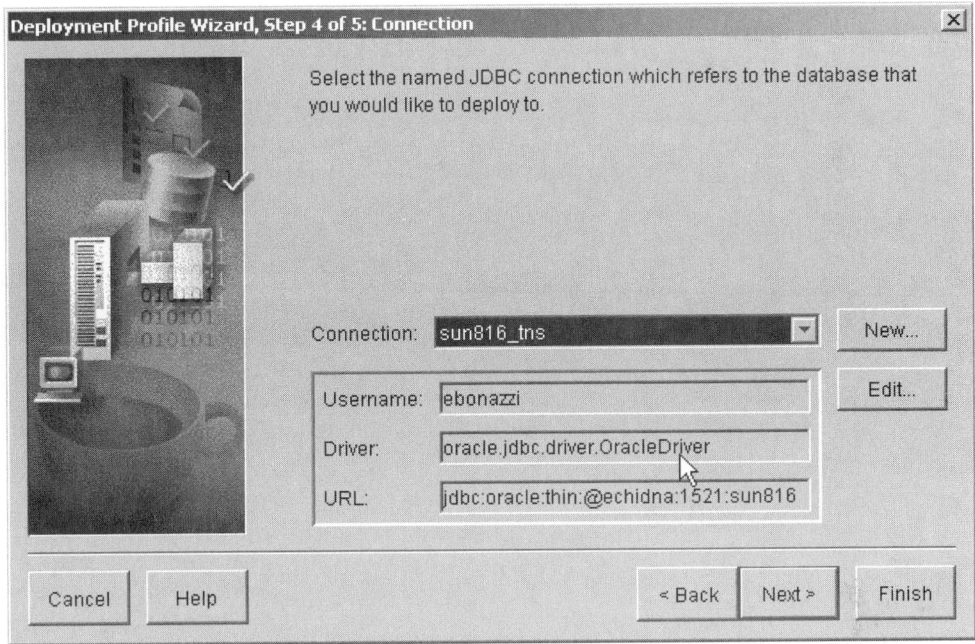

FIGURE 24.11 The JDBC connection page displayed by the deployment wizard.

You are finished with the server implementation. It is now time to implement the CORBA client, but you already did this in Chapter 23. Remember, whether you use an inheritance-based or delegation-based mechanism is something that only affects the server implementation, not the client. You can reuse the client developed for the CustomerVerify example. The only thing that must be changed is the IIOP URL that identifies /test/TieExample, so that you can access the remote object implemented using the tie mechanism. Change the corbaUrl string in Lookup.java, and rename Lookup.java to LookupTie.java. Compile the file in JDeveloper, set a breakpoint, and debug your program. Note that you have created a complete server-side and client-side application, deploying your objects onto a remote host, without leaving the visual environment provided by JDeveloper. This is quite remarkable!

24.5 FURTHER REFERENCES

What you have learned in Chapter 23 and in this chapter should be enough to get you started in the Oracle/CORBA world. However, since this book does not focus specifically on CORBA, its coverage of the topic is not exhaustive. Many as-

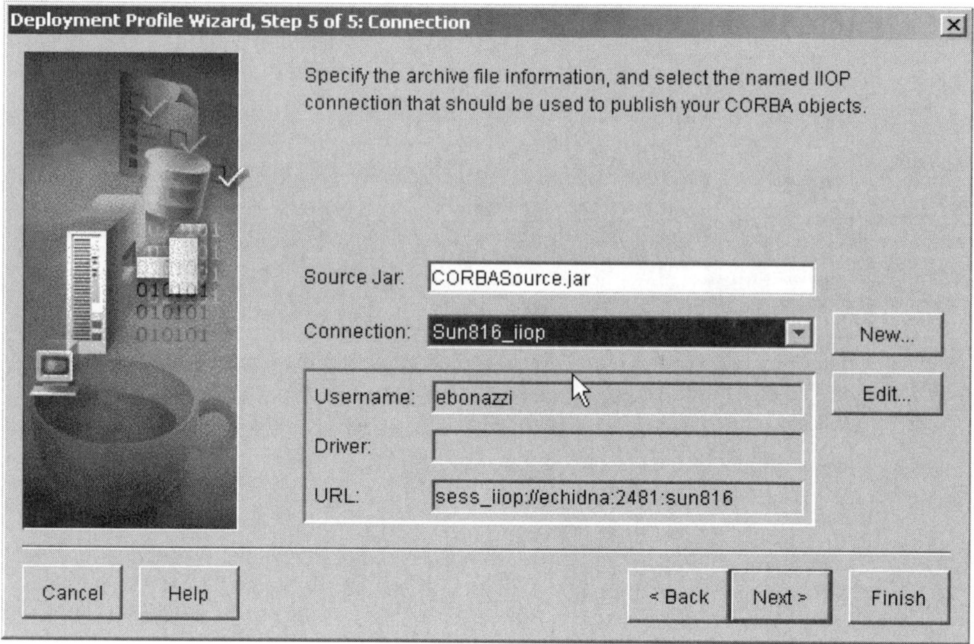

FIGURE 24.12 The IIOP connection page shown by the wizard.

pects of the CORBA environment, of necessity, have been left out. Visibroker, the CORBA implementation provided by Oracle, offers a set of nice features. These include client callbacks (methods implemented by CORBA clients that can be asynchronously called by CORBA servants) and CORBA interceptors, which provide mechanisms that specify additional methods to be executed before or after the code of an operation. Interceptors are low-level hooks into the Visibroker ORB, which make it possible to implement sophisticated add-on functionality to applications without modifying the application code. For example, using an interceptor, application architects can add sophisticated data-dependent routing and load balancing even if they do not have access to the application source code. In other words, a third-party application could be significantly extended even if no source code is available.

In order to exploit this advanced CORBA functionality, you must reach a higher level of proficiency that exceeds the scope of this book.

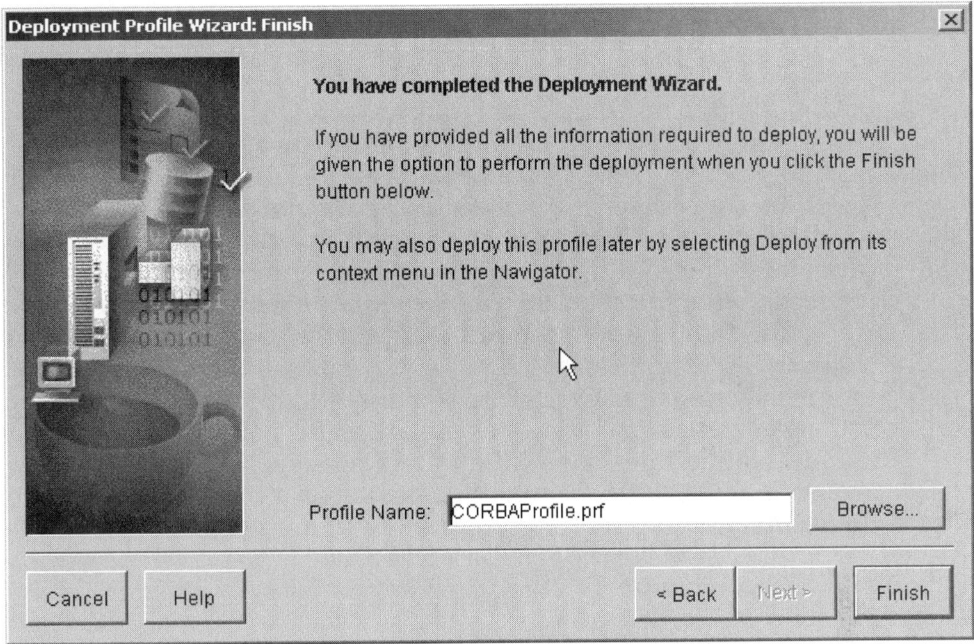

FIGURE 24.13 The final page displayed by the deployment wizard.

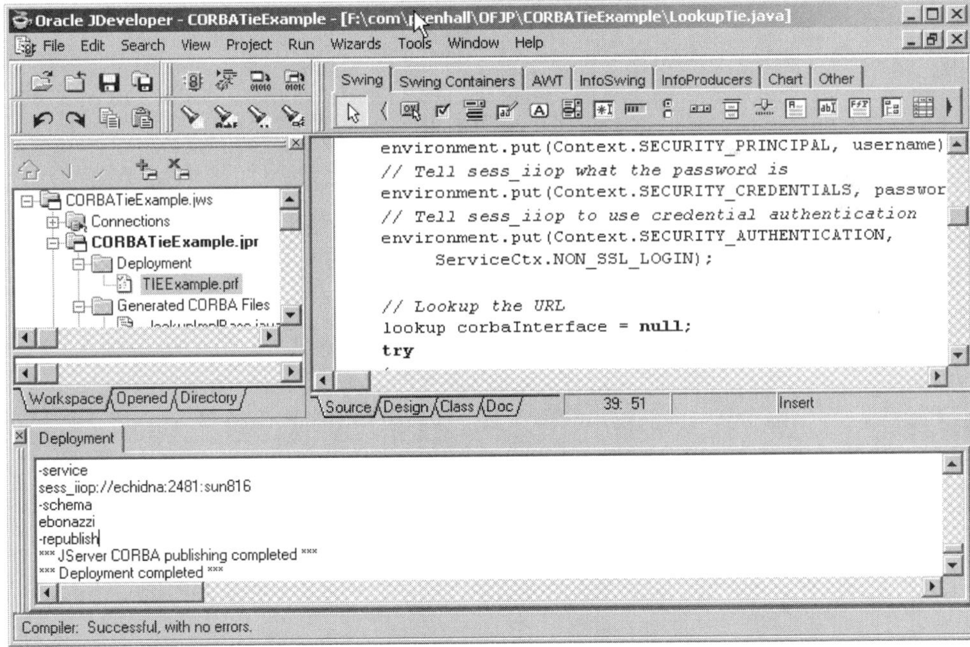

FIGURE 24.14 JDeveloper shows the deployment pane in the IDE's lower part.

SUMMARY

In this chapter you learned more about the CORBA Interface Definition Language (IDL). You mapped the most commonly used IDL datatypes to the corresponding Java datatypes. You also learned how to deal with more complex data structures, such as unions, enumerations, and structures.

The focus then shifted to the Oracle Name Space, a crucial element upon which the Oracle JNDI and COSNaming services are based. You used this knowledge to locate and instantiate remote objects published in an Oracle8i database. You learned how to manage objects and their security levels using the `sess_sh` utility.

Finally, you used Oracle JDeveloper to reimplement an example developed in Chapter 23, this time using the delegation mechanism. You learned how to use the advanced features provided by JDeveloper, including its ability to remotely deploy Java/CORBA applications developed on a client computer, such as a PC running Windows.

INDEX

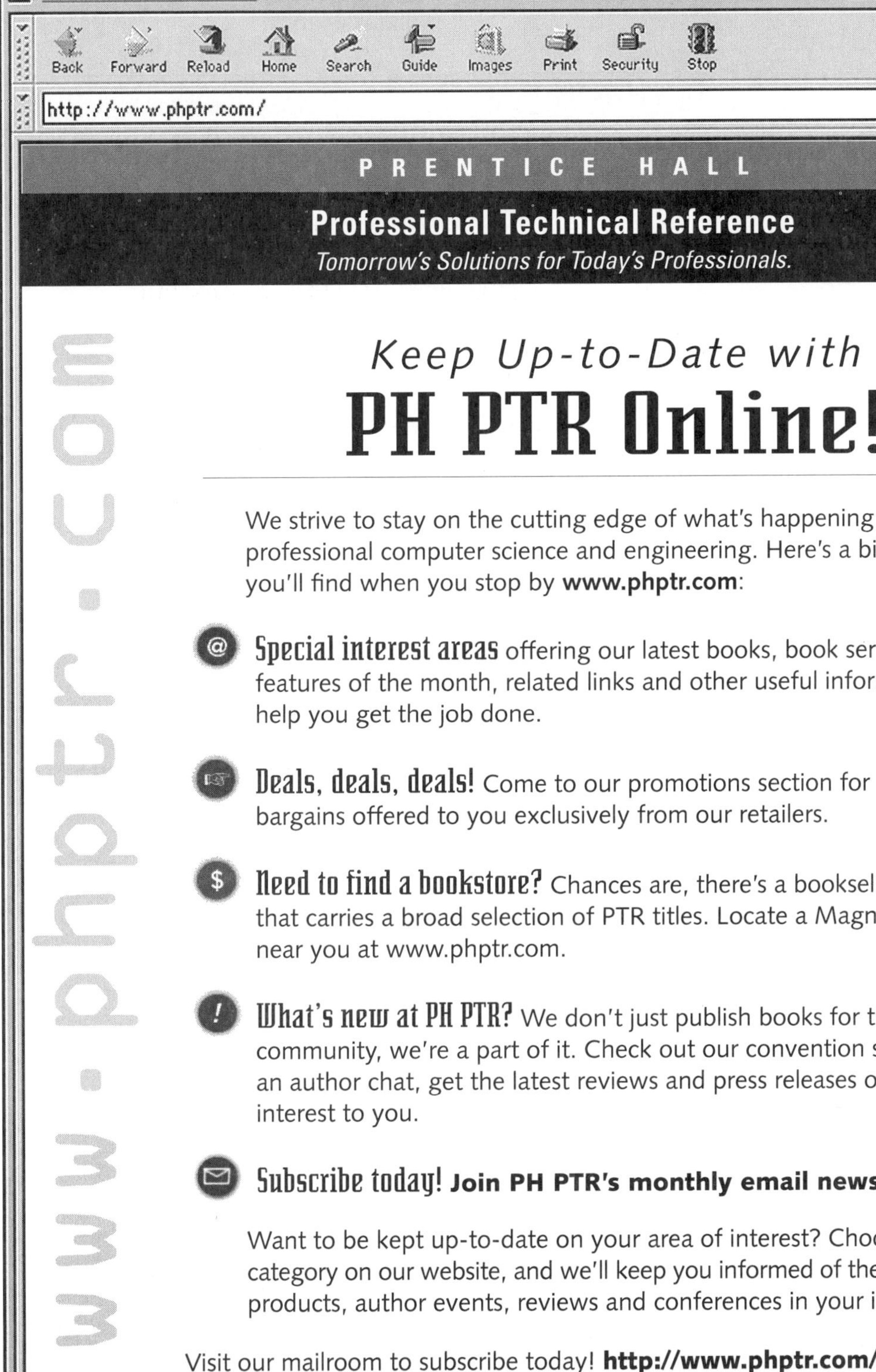

LICENSE AGREEMENT AND LIMITED WARRANTY

READ THE FOLLOWING TERMS AND CONDITIONS CAREFULLY BEFORE OPENING THIS DISK PACKAGE. THIS LEGAL DOCUMENT IS AN AGREEMENT BETWEEN YOU AND PRENTICE-HALL, INC. (THE "COMPANY"). BY OPENING THIS SEALED DISK PACKAGE, YOU ARE AGREEING TO BE BOUND BY THESE TERMS AND CONDITIONS. IF YOU DO NOT AGREE WITH THESE TERMS AND CONDITIONS, DO NOT OPEN THE DISK PACKAGE. PROMPTLY RETURN THE UNOPENED DISK PACKAGE AND ALL ACCOMPANYING ITEMS TO THE PLACE YOU OBTAINED THEM FOR A FULL REFUND OF ANY SUMS YOU HAVE PAID.

1. **GRANT OF LICENSE:** In consideration of your payment of the license fee, which is part of the price you paid for this product, and your agreement to abide by the terms and conditions of this Agreement, the Company grants to you a nonexclusive right to use and display the copy of the enclosed software program (hereinafter the "SOFTWARE") on a single computer (i.e., with a single CPU) at a single location so long as you comply with the terms of this Agreement. The Company reserves all rights not expressly granted to you under this Agreement.

2. **OWNERSHIP OF SOFTWARE:** You own only the magnetic or physical media (the enclosed disks) on which the SOFTWARE is recorded or fixed, but the Company retains all the rights, title, and ownership to the SOFTWARE recorded on the original disk copy(ies) and all subsequent copies of the SOFTWARE, regardless of the form or media on which the original or other copies may exist. This license is not a sale of the original SOFTWARE or any copy to you.

3. **COPY RESTRICTIONS:** This SOFTWARE and the accompanying printed materials and user manual (the "Documentation") are the subject of copyright. You may not copy the Documentation or the SOFTWARE, except that you may make a single copy of the SOFTWARE for backup or archival purposes only. You may be held legally responsible for any copying or copyright infringement which is caused or encouraged by your failure to abide by the terms of this restriction.

4. **USE RESTRICTIONS:** You may not network the SOFTWARE or otherwise use it on more than one computer or computer terminal at the same time. You may physically transfer the SOFTWARE from one computer to another provided that the SOFTWARE is used on only one computer at a time. You may not distribute copies of the SOFTWARE or Documentation to others. You may not reverse engineer, disassemble, decompile, modify, adapt, translate, or create derivative works based on the SOFTWARE or the Documentation without the prior written consent of the Company.

5. **TRANSFER RESTRICTIONS:** The enclosed SOFTWARE is licensed only to you and may not be transferred to any one else without the prior written consent of the Company. Any unauthorized transfer of the SOFTWARE shall result in the immediate termination of this Agreement.

6. **TERMINATION:** This license is effective until terminated. This license will terminate automatically without notice from the Company and become null and void if you fail to comply with any provisions or limitations of this license. Upon termination, you shall destroy the Documentation and all copies of the SOFTWARE. All provisions of this Agreement as to warranties, limitation of liability, remedies or damages, and our ownership rights shall survive termination.

7. **MISCELLANEOUS:** This Agreement shall be construed in accordance with the laws of the United States of America and the State of New York and shall benefit the Company, its affiliates, and assignees.

8. **LIMITED WARRANTY AND DISCLAIMER OF WARRANTY:** The Company warrants that the SOFTWARE, when properly used in accordance with the Documentation, will operate in substantial conformity with the description of the SOFTWARE set forth in the Documentation. The Company does not warrant that the SOFTWARE will meet your requirements or that the operation of the SOFTWARE will be uninterrupted or error-free. The Company warrants that the media on which the SOFTWARE is delivered shall be free from defects in materials and workmanship under normal use for a period of thirty (30) days from the date of your pur-

chase. Your only remedy and the Company's only obligation under these limited warranties is, at the Company's option, return of the warranted item for a refund of any amounts paid by you or replacement of the item. Any replacement of SOFTWARE or media under the warranties shall not extend the original warranty period. The limited warranty set forth above shall not apply to any SOFTWARE which the Company determines in good faith has been subject to misuse, neglect, improper installation, repair, alteration, or damage by you. EXCEPT FOR THE EXPRESSED WARRANTIES SET FORTH ABOVE, THE COMPANY DISCLAIMS ALL WARRANTIES, EXPRESS OR IMPLIED, INCLUDING WITHOUT LIMITATION, THE IMPLIED WARRANTIES OF MERCHANTABILITY AND FITNESS FOR A PARTICULAR PURPOSE. EXCEPT FOR THE EXPRESS WARRANTY SET FORTH ABOVE, THE COMPANY DOES NOT WARRANT, GUARANTEE, OR MAKE ANY REPRESENTATION REGARDING THE USE OR THE RESULTS OF THE USE OF THE SOFTWARE IN TERMS OF ITS CORRECTNESS, ACCURACY, RELIABILITY, CURRENTNESS, OR OTHERWISE.

IN NO EVENT, SHALL THE COMPANY OR ITS EMPLOYEES, AGENTS, SUPPLIERS, OR CONTRACTORS BE LIABLE FOR ANY INCIDENTAL, INDIRECT, SPECIAL, OR CONSEQUENTIAL DAMAGES ARISING OUT OF OR IN CONNECTION WITH THE LICENSE GRANTED UNDER THIS AGREEMENT, OR FOR LOSS OF USE, LOSS OF DATA, LOSS OF INCOME OR PROFIT, OR OTHER LOSSES, SUSTAINED AS A RESULT OF INJURY TO ANY PERSON, OR LOSS OF OR DAMAGE TO PROPERTY, OR CLAIMS OF THIRD PARTIES, EVEN IF THE COMPANY OR AN AUTHORIZED REPRESENTATIVE OF THE COMPANY HAS BEEN ADVISED OF THE POSSIBILITY OF SUCH DAMAGES. IN NO EVENT SHALL LIABILITY OF THE COMPANY FOR DAMAGES WITH RESPECT TO THE SOFTWARE EXCEED THE AMOUNTS ACTUALLY PAID BY YOU, IF ANY, FOR THE SOFTWARE.

SOME JURISDICTIONS DO NOT ALLOW THE LIMITATION OF IMPLIED WARRANTIES OR LIABILITY FOR INCIDENTAL, INDIRECT, SPECIAL, OR CONSEQUENTIAL DAMAGES, SO THE ABOVE LIMITATIONS MAY NOT ALWAYS APPLY. THE WARRANTIES IN THIS AGREEMENT GIVE YOU SPECIFIC LEGAL RIGHTS AND YOU MAY ALSO HAVE OTHER RIGHTS WHICH VARY IN ACCORDANCE WITH LOCAL LAW.

ACKNOWLEDGMENT

YOU ACKNOWLEDGE THAT YOU HAVE READ THIS AGREEMENT, UNDERSTAND IT, AND AGREE TO BE BOUND BY ITS TERMS AND CONDITIONS. YOU ALSO AGREE THAT THIS AGREEMENT IS THE COMPLETE AND EXCLUSIVE STATEMENT OF THE AGREEMENT BETWEEN YOU AND THE COMPANY AND SUPERSEDES ALL PROPOSALS OR PRIOR AGREEMENTS, ORAL, OR WRITTEN, AND ANY OTHER COMMUNICATIONS BETWEEN YOU AND THE COMPANY OR ANY REPRESENTATIVE OF THE COMPANY RELATING TO THE SUBJECT MATTER OF THIS AGREEMENT.

Should you have any questions concerning this Agreement or if you wish to contact the Company for any reason, please contact in writing at the address below or call the at the telephone number provided.

PTR Customer Service
Prentice Hall PTR
One Lake Street
Upper Saddle River, New Jersey 07458

Telephone: 201-236-7105

About the CD-ROM

The CD-ROM included with *Oracle® 8i and Java™: From Client/Server to E-Commerce* contains source code files from the text. If you want to install the examples on your hard disk, open the Installer folder and select the appropriate installer.

The supported environments are Linux®/UNIX®, Windows®, and MacOS®. If you use an unsupported OS, open the Other folder (found inside the Installer folder), where you can find a ZIP file containing all folders/files.

II. GETTING STARTED

To install the examples to your hard disk, open the Installer folder and select the appropriate installer. If you use an unsupported OS (one not listed above), open the Other folder (found inside the Installer folder), where you can find a ZIP file containing all the folders/files. In the event you do not have a ZIP program to unzip the files, you can obtain one at: http://www.WinZip.com

The CD-ROM uses the InstallAnywhere utility to install the code examples on your disk. InstallAnywhere requires a Java Virtual Machine (JVM) to be previously installed on your system, and visible in the execution path. If you do not have a JVM installed then you can simply copy the required files from their respective directories on the CD-ROM.

III. LICENSE AGREEMENT

Use of the software accompanying *Oracle® 8i and Java™: From Client/Server to E-Commerce* is subject to the terms of the License Agreement and Limited Warranty, found on the previous two pages.

IV. TECHNICAL SUPPORT

Prentice Hall does not offer technical support for any of the content on the CD-ROM. However, if the CD-ROM is damaged, you may obtain a replacement copy by sending an email message that describes the problem to: disc_exchange@prenhall.com.